- **Writing Resource Center** provides an online writing center that supplies links to online directories, thesauruses, writing tutors, style and grammar guides, and additional tools.

- **Career Center** helps students access career information, view sample résumés, and even apply for jobs online.

- **Study Tips** provides an area where students can learn to develop better study skills.

- **Downloadable Resources** may include software, spreadsheets, PowerPoints, and much more.

FREE Online Courses –
Available in BlackBoard & CourseCompass!

CourseCompass

Are you teaching an online course now? Or would you like to teach a Web-enhanced course? Here's how Prentice Hall can help you to optimize your class!

- **Online Quizzes** with results that automatically feed into the Gradebook.
- **Bulletin Boards** let you and your students post critical messages.
- An **Online Syllabus** keeps students aware of deadlines and updates.
- **Discussion Groups** enable you to hold synchronous or asynchronous meetings with classes, speakers, or groups of students.
- **Link** your students (via the syllabus) to key Internet sites.

Most importantly, you can post any of your own materials—create and post your own lectures, assignment options, and class projects!

New Supplements for Auditing

Dear Auditing Professor:

Before you place your auditing textbook order, we would like to introduce you to exciting options that will most definitely enhance your auditing course. In addition to the complete list of ancillaries found within the text preface or *on the web site at www.prenhall.com/arens*, we are proud to offer two new case books:

Beasley/Buckless/Glover/Prawitt *Auditing Cases: An Interactive Learning Approach,* 2e contains 34 cases appropriate for graduate or undergraduate auditing courses. The cases address most major activities performed during the conduct of an audit, from client acceptance to issuance of an audit report. A sample case is enclosed for your reference. To see the solution to this case go to *www.prenhall.com/arens* and click on the Auditing Cases, 2e site. To assist you with your teaching, an Instructor's Manual is available with complete case notes and teaching suggestions.

Cullinan/ Wright *Cases from the SEC Files: Topics in Auditing* Available for the first time, Charlie Cullinan and Gail Wright from Bryant College have compiled a collection of the best SEC cases. Take a look at the enclosed sample case. To access instructor's notes and solutions, go to *www.prenhall.com/cullinan*.

Create your own custom case book! Want to mix and match cases from either or both case books? The solution is easy. For details go to *www.pearsoncustom.com*.

We hope you will consider enhancing your auditing course with the inclusion of one or both of these casebooks. For more information, please contact your Prentice Hall Representative or go to *www.prenhall.com/accounting*.

Your business is important to us and we appreciate your careful consideration of Prentice Hall texts and technology products.

Regards,

Thomas Sigel
Acquisitions Editor

Beth Toland
Executive Marketing Manager

Comptronix Corporation
Identifying Inherent Risk and Control Risk Factors
From: Beasley/Buckless/Glover/Prawitt
Auditing Cases: An Interactive Learning Approach, 2e

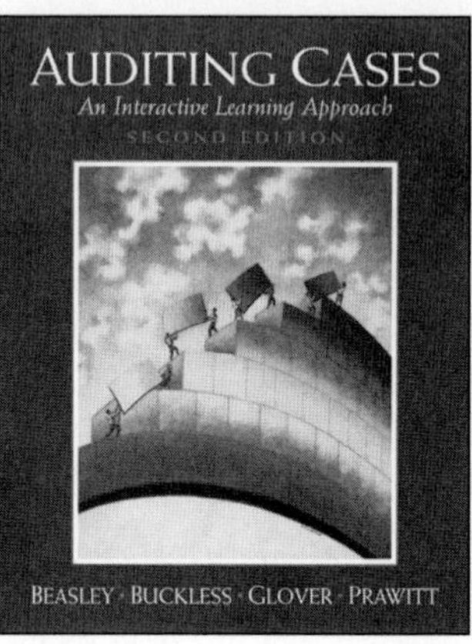

LEARNING OBJECTIVES

After completing and discussing this case you should be able to

- Understand how managers can fraudulently manipulate financial statements.
- Recognize key inherent risk factors that increase the potential for financial reporting fraud.
- Recognize key control risk factors that increase the potential for financial reporting fraud.
- Understand the importance of effective corporate governance for overseeing the actions of top executives.

INTRODUCTION

All appeared well at Comptronix Corporation, a Guntersville, Alabama based electronics company, until word hit the streets November 25, 1992 that there had been a fraud. When reports surfaced that three of the company's top executives inflated company earnings for the past three years, the company's stock price plummeted 72 percent in one day, closing at $61/8 a share down from the previous day's closing at $22 a share.[1]

The Securities and Exchange Commission's (SEC) subsequent investigation determined that Comptronix's chief executive officer (CEO), chief operating officer (COO), and the controller/treasurer all colluded to overstate assets and profits by recording fictitious transactions. The three executives overrode existing internal controls so that others at Comptronix would not discover the scheme. All this unraveled when the executives surprisingly confessed to the company's board that they had improperly valued assets, overstated sales, and understated expenses. The three were immediately suspended from their duties.

Within days, class action lawsuits were filed against the company and the three executives. Immediately, the company's board of directors formed a special committee to investigate the alleged financial reporting fraud, an interim executive team stepped in to take charge, and Arthur Andersen, LLP was hired to conduct a detailed fraud investigation.

Residents of the small Alabama town were stunned. How could a fraud occur so close to home? Were there any signs of trouble that were ignored?

BACKGROUND ABOUT COMPTRONIX CORPORATION

Comptronix based its principal operations in Guntersville, Alabama, a town of approximately 7,000 residents located about 35 miles southeast of Huntsville, Alabama. The company provided contract manufacturing services to original equipment manufacturers in the electronics industry. Their primary product was circuit boards for personal computers and medical equipment. Neighboring Huntsville's heavy presence in the electronics industry provided Comptronix a local base of customers for its circuit boards. In addition to the Alabama facility, the company also maintained manufacturing facilities in San Jose, California and Colorado Springs, Colorado. In total, Comptronix employed about 1800 people at the three locations, and was one of the largest employers in Guntersville.

The company was formed in the early 1980s by individuals who met while working in the electronics industry in nearby Huntsville. Three of those founders became senior officers of the company. William J. Hebding became Comptronix's chairman and chief executive officer (CEO), Allen L. Shifflet became Comptronix's president and chief operating officer (COO), and J. Paul Medlin served as the controller and treasurer. Prior to creating Comptronix, all three men worked at SCI Systems, a booming electronics maker. Mr. Hebding joined SCI Systems in the mid-1970s to assist the chief financial officer. While in that role, he met Mr. Shifflet, the SCI Systems operations manager. Later when Mr. Hebding become SCI Systems' CFO, he hired Mr. Medlin to assist him. Along with a few other individuals working at SCI Systems, these three men together formed Comptronix in late 1983 and early 1984.[2]

The local townspeople in Guntersville were excited to attract the startup company to its local area. The city enticed Comptronix to the area by providing it with an empty knitting mill in town. As additional incentive, a local bank offered Comptronix an attractive credit arrangement. Comptronix in turn appointed the local banker to its board of directors. Town business leaders were excited to have new local employment opportunities and looked forward to a boost to the local economy.

---

1 Source: "Company's profit data were false," The New York Times, November 26, 1992, D:I

2 Source: "Comptronix fall from grace: Clues were there Alabama locals saw lavish spending, feud," *The Atlanta Journal and Constitution,* December 5, 1992, D:1.

The early years were difficult with Comptronix suffering losses through 1986. Local enthusiasm for the company attracted investments from venture capitalists. One of those investors included a partner in the Massey Burch Investment Group, a venture capital firm located in Nashville, Tennessee, just over a 100 miles to the north. The infusion of venture capital allowed Comptronix to generate strong sales and profit growth during 1987 and 1988. Based on this strong performance, senior management took the company's stock public in 1989, initially selling Comptronix stock at $5 a share in the over-the-counter markets.[3]

THE ACCOUNTING SCHEME[4]

According to the SEC's investigation, the fraud began soon after the company went public in 1989 and was directed by top company executives. Mr. Hebding as chairman and CEO, Mr. Shifflett as president and COO, and Mr. Medlin as controller and treasurer used their positions of power and influence to manipulate the financial statements issued from early 1989 through November 1992.

They began their fraud scheme by first manipulating the quarterly statements filed with the SEC during 1989. They misstated those statements by inappropriately transferring certain costs from cost of goods sold into inventory accounts. This technique allowed them to overstate inventory and understate quarterly costs of goods sold, which in turn overstated gross margin and net income for the period. The three executives made monthly manual journal entries, with the largest adjustments occurring just at quarter's end. Some allege that the fraud was motivated by the loss of a key customer in 1989 to the three executives' former employer, SCI.

The executives were successful in manipulating quarterly financial statements partially because their quarterly filings were unaudited. However, as fiscal year 1989 came to a close, the executives grew wary that the company's external auditors might discover the fraud when auditing the December 31, 1989 year-end financial statements. To hide the manipulations from their auditors, they devised a plan to cover up the inappropriate transfer of costs. They decided to remove the transferred costs from the inventory account just before year-end, because they feared the auditors would closely examine the inventory account as of December 31, 1989 as part of their year-end testing. Thus, they transferred the costs back to cost of goods sold. However, for each transfer back to cost of goods sold, the fraud team booked a fictitious sale of products and a related fictitious accounts receivable. That, in turn, overstated revenues and receivables.

The net effect of these activities was that interim financial statements included understated cost of goods sold and overstated inventories, while the annual financial statements contained overstated sales and receivables. Once they had tasted success in their manipulations of year-end sales and receivables, they later began recording fictitious quarterly sales in a similar fashion.

So that the auditors would believe the fictitious sales and receivables were legitimate, the three company executives recorded cash payments on the bogus customer accounts due Comptronix. In order to do this, they developed a relatively complex fraud scheme. First, they recorded fictitious purchases of equipment on account. That, in turn, overstated equipment and accounts payable. Then, Hebding, the chairman and CEO, and Medlin, the controller and treasurer, cut checks to the bogus accounts payable vendors associated with the fake purchases of equipment. But they didn't mail the checks. Rather, they deposited them in Comptronix's disbursement checking account and recorded the phony payments as debits against the bogus accounts payable and credits against the bogus receivables. This accounting scheme allowed the company to eliminate the bogus payables and receivables, while still retaining the fictitious sales and equipment on the income statement and balance sheet, respectively.

This scheme continued over four years, stretching from the beginning of 1989 to November 1992, when the three executives confessed to their manipulations. The SEC investigation noted that the Form 10-K filings for the years ended December 31, 1989, 1990, and 1991 were materially misstated as shown in the table on the next page.

THE COMPANY'S INTERNAL CONTROLS[5]

The three executives were able to perpetrate the fraud by bypassing the existing accounting system. They avoided making the standard entries in the sales and purchases journals as required by the existing internal control, and recorded the fictitious entries manually. Other employees were excluded from the manipulations to minimize the likelihood of the fraud being discovered.

According to the SEC's summary of the investigation, Comptronix employees normally created a fairly extensive paper trail for equipment purchases, including purchase orders and receiving reports. However, none of these documents were created for the bogus purchases. Approval for cash disbursements was typically granted once the related purchase order, receiving report, and vendor invoice were matched. Unfortunately, Mr. Shifflett or Mr. Medlin could approve payments based

---

3 Source: See footnote 2.

4 Source: Accounting and Auditing Enforcement Release No. 543, Commerce Clearing House, Inc., Chicago.

5 Source: See footnote 4.

solely on an invoice. As a result, the fraud team was able to bypass internal controls over cash disbursements. They simply showed a fictitious vendor invoice to an accounts payable clerk, who in turn prepared a check for the amount indicated on the invoice.

Internal controls were also insufficient to detect the manipulation of sales and accounts receivable. Typically, a shipping department clerk would enter the customer order number and the quantity to be shipped to the customer into the computerized accounting system. The accounting system then automatically produced a shipping document and a sales invoice. The merchandise was shipped to the customer, along with the invoice and shipping document. Once again, Mr. Medlin, as controller and treasurer, had the ability to access the shipping department system. This allowed him to enter bogus sales into the accounting system. He then made sure to destroy all shipping documents and sales invoices generated by the accounting system to keep them from being mailed to the related customers. The subsequent posting of bogus payments on the customers' accounts were posted personally by Mr. Medlin to the cash receipts journal and accounts receivable subsidiary ledger.

The fraud scheme was obviously directed from the top ranks of the organization. Like most companies, the senior executives at Comptronix directed company operations on a day-to-day basis, with only periodic oversight from the company's board of directors.

The March 1992 proxy statement to shareholders noted that the Comptronix board of directors consisted of seven individuals, including Mr. Hebding who served as board chairman. Of those seven individuals serving on the board, two individuals, Mr. Hebding, chairman and CEO and Mr. Shifflett, president and COO, represented management on the board. Thus,

	1989	1990	1991
Sales (in 000's)			
Reported Sales	$42, 420	$70,229	$102, 026
Restated Sales	37, 275	63,444	88,754
Overstatement of Sales	5,145	6,785	13,272
Percentage Overstatement	13.8%	10.7%	14.9%
Net Income (in 000's)			
Reported Net Income	$1, 470	$3,028	$5,071
Restated Net Income	(3,524)	(3,647)	(3,225)
Overstatement of Net Income	4,994	6,675	8,296
Earnings Per Share (EPS)			
Reported EPS	$.19	$.35	$.51
Restated EPS (loss)	(.47)	(.43)	(.34)
Overstatement of EPS	.66	.78	.85
Property, Plant, & Equipment (in 000's)			
Reported PP&E	$18,804	$26,627	$38,720
Restated Sales	13,856	15,846	20,303
Overstatement of PP&E	4,948	10,781	18,417
Percentage Overstatement	35.7%	68.0%	90.7%
Stockholders' Equity (in 000's)			
Reported Stockholders' Equity	$19,145	$22,237	$39,676
Restated Stockholders' Equity	14,151	10,568	18,778
Overstatement of Stockholders' Equity	4,994	11,669	20,898
Percentage Overstatement	35.3%	110.4%	111.3%

The executives' fraud scheme helped the company avoid reporting net losses in each of the three years, with the amount of the fraud increasing in each of the three years affected.[6] The fraud scheme also inflated the balance sheet by overstating property, plant, and equipment and stockholders' equity. By the end of 1991, property, plant, and equipment was overstated by over 90%, with stockholders' equity overstated by 111%.

6 Information about fiscal year 1994 was not reported because the fraud was disclosed before that fiscal year ended.

28.6% of the board consisted of inside directors. The remaining five directors were not employed by Comptronix. However, two of those five directors had close affiliations with management. One served as the company's outside general legal counsel and the other served as vice president of manufacturing for a significant customer of Comptronix. Directors with these kinds of close affiliations with company management are frequently referred to as "grey" directors due to their perceived lack of objectivity. The three remaining "outside" directors had no apparent affiliations with company management. One of the remaining outside directors was a partner in the venture capital firm that owned 574,978 shares (5.3%) of Comptronix's common stock. That director was previously a partner in a Nashville law firm and was currently serving on two other corporate boards. A second outside director was the vice chairman and CEO of the local bank originally loaning money to the company. He also served as chairman of the board of another local bank in a nearby town. The third outside director was president of an international components supplier based in Taiwan. All of the board members had served on the Comptronix board since 1984, except for the venture capital partner who joined the board in 1988 and the president of the key customer who joined the board in 1990.

Each director received an annual retainer of $3,000 plus a fee of $750 for each meeting attended. The company also granted each director an option to purchase 5,000 shares of common stock at an exercise price that equaled the market price of the stock on the date that the option was granted.

The board met four times during 1991. The board had an audit committee that was charged with recommending outside auditors, reviewing the scope of the audit engagement, consulting with the external auditors, reviewing the results of the audit examination, and acting as a liaison between the board and the internal auditors. The audit committee was also charged with reviewing various company policies, including those related to accounting and internal control matters. Two outside directors and one grey director made up the three-member audit committee. One of those members was an attorney, and the other two served as president and CEO of the companies where they were employed. There was no indication of whether any of these individuals had accounting or financial reporting backgrounds. The audit committee met two times during 1991.

MANAGEMENT BACKGROUND

The March 1992 proxy statement provided the following background information about the three executives allegedly committing the fraud: Mr. Hedding, Mr. Shifflett, and Mr. Medlin.

William J. Hebding served as the Comptronix Chairman and CEO. He was responsible for sales and marketing, finance and general management of the company. He also served as a director from 1984 until 1992 when the fraud was disclosed. He was the single largest shareholder of Comptronix common stock by beneficially owning 6.7% (720,438 shares) of Comptronix common stock as of March 2, 1992. Before joining Comptronix, Mr. Hebding worked for SCI Systems Inc., from 1974 until October 1983. He held the title of Treasurer and CFO at SCI from December 1976 to October 1983. In October 1983, Mr. Hebding left SCI to form Comptronix. He graduated from the University of North Alabama with a degree in accounting, and was a certified public accountant. Mr. Hebding's 1991 cash compensation totaled $187,996.

Allen L. Shifflett served as the Comptronix's president and chief operating officer (COO) where he was responsible for manufacturing, engineering, and programs operations. He also served as a board of director from 1984 until 1992 when the fraud unfolded. He owned 4.0% (433,496 shares) of Comptronix common stock as of March 2, 1992. Like Mr. Hebding, he joined the company after previously being employed at SCI as a plant manager and manufacturing manager from October 1981 until April 1984 when he left to help form Comptronix. Mr. Shifflett obtained his B.S. degree in industrial engineering from Virginia Polytechnic Institute. Mr. Shifflett's 1991 cash compensation totaled $162,996

Paul Medlin served as Comptronix controller and treasurer. He also previously worked at SCI as Mr. Hebding's assistant after graduating from the University of Alabama. Mr. Medlin did not serve on the Comptronix board. The 1992 proxy noted that the board of directors approved a company loan to him for $79,250 on November 1, 1989 to provide funds for him to repurchase certain shares of common stock. The loan, which was repaid on May 7, 1991, bore interest at an annual rate equal to one percentage point in excess of the interest rate designated by the company's bank as that bank's "Index Rate." The 1992 proxy did not disclose Mr. Medlin's 1991 cash compensation.

The company had employment agreements with Mr. Hebding and Mr. Shifflett, which expired April 1992. Those agreements provided that if the company terminated employment with them prior to the expiration of the agreement for any reason other than cause or disability, they would each receive their base salary for the remaining term of the agreement. If terminated for cause or disability, each would receive their base salary for one year following the date of such termination.

The company had both an Employee Stock Incentive Plan and an Employee Stock Option Plan that the compensation committee of the board of directors administered. The committee made awards to key employees at its discretion. The compensation committee consisted of three non-employee directors. One of these directors was an attorney who served as Comptronix's outside counsel on certain legal matters. Another served as an officer of a significant customer of Comptronix. The third member of the committee was a partner in the venture capital firm providing capital for Comptronix.

The SEC's investigation noted that during the period of the fraud, the three men each sold thousands of shares of Comptronix common stock. Their knowledge of material non-public information about Comptronix's actual financial position allowed them to avoid trading losses in excess of $500,000 for Mr. Hebding and Mr. Shifflett, and over $90,000 for Mr. Medlin. Each also received bonuses: $198,000 for Mr. Hebding, $148,000 for Mr. Shifflett, and $46,075 for Mr. Medlin. These bonuses were granted during the fraud years as a reward for the supposed strong financial performance.

After the fraud was revealed, newspaper accounts reported that red flags had been present. The New York Times reported that Mr. Hebding and Mr. Shifflett created reputations in the local community that contrasted with their conservative professional reputations. Mr. Hebding purchased a home worth over $1 million, often described as a mansion with two boathouses, a pool, a wrought-iron fence with electric gate, and a red Jaguar in the driveway. The Atlanta Journal and Constitution reported that Mr. Hebding's marriage had failed, and that he had led an active bachelor's life that led to some problems in town. He also had a major dispute with another company founder who was serving as executive vice president. That individual was suddenly fired from Comptronix in 1989. Later it was revealed that he was allegedly demoted and fired for trying to investigate possible wrongdoing at Comptronix.[7]

Mr. Shifflett, too, had divorced and remarried. He and his second wife purchased an expensive scenic lot in an exclusive country club community in a neighboring town. Mr. Shifflett reportedly had acquired extensive real estate holdings in recent years.[8]

Others were shocked, noting that they were the last to be suspected of any kind of fraud. In the end, it was unclear why the three stunned the board with news of the fraud. There was some speculation that an on-going IRS tax audit triggered their disclosure of the shenanigans.

EPILOGUE

After the fraud was revealed, all three men were suspended and the board appointed an interim CEO and an interim president to take over the reins. The SEC's investigation led to charges being filed against all three men for violating the antifraud provisions of the Securities Act of 1933 and the Securities and Exchange Act of 1934, in addition to other violations of those securities acts. None of the men admitted or denied the allegations against them. However, all three men agreed to avoid any future violations of the securities acts. They also consented to being permanently prohibited from serving as officers or directors of any public company. The SEC ordered them to pay back trading losses avoided and bonuses paid to them by Comptronix during the fraud period, and directed Mr. Hebding and Mr. Shifflett to pay civil penalties of $100,000 and $50,000, respectively. The SEC did not impose civil penalties against Mr. Medlin due to his inability to pay.

The company struggled financially. They sold their San Jose operations in 1994 and eventually filed for Chapter 11 bankruptcy protection in August 1996. Chapter 11 allowed the company to continue operating while developing a restructuring plan. In September 1996, the company announced that it sold substantially all of its assets to a California-based leading electronics manufacturer. As a result of the sale, the secured creditors of Comptronix were fully repaid; however, the unsecured creditors received less than 10 cents on the dollar.

REQUIREMENTS

1. Professional auditing standards present the audit risk model, which is used to determine thenature, timing, and extent of audit procedures. Describe the components of the model and discuss how changes in each component affect the auditor's need for evidence.

2. One of the components of the audit risk model is inherent risk. Describe typical factors that auditors evaluate when assessing inherent risk. With the benefit of hindsight, what inherent risk factors were present during the audits of the 1989 through 1992 Comptronix financial statements?

3 Another component of the audit risk model is control risk. Describe the five components of internal control. What characteristics of Comptronix's internal control increased control risk for the audits of the 1989 – 1992 year-end financial statements?

4. The board of directors, and its audit committee, can be an effective corporate governance mechanism. Discuss the pros and cons of allowing inside directors to serve on the board. Describe typical responsibilities of audit committees. What strengths or weaknesses were presentrelated to Comptronix's board of directors and audit committee?

5. Public companies must file quarterly financial statements in Form 10-Qs. Professional standards allow CPAs to perform timely reviews of those statements. Briefly describe the key requirements of SAS No. 71, Interim Financial Statements. Why wouldn't all companies engage their auditors to perform SAS No. 71 reviews?

6. Do you think Comptronix's executive team was inherently dishonest from the beginning? How is it possible for otherwise honest people to become involved in frauds like the one at Comptronix?

---

7 Source: "A Comptronix founder, in 1989 suit, says he flagged misdeeds," The Wall Street Journal, December 7, 1992, A:3.

8 Sources: See footnote 2 and "In town, neighbors saw it coming," The New York Times, December 4, 1992, D:1.

RICHARD VALADE, CPA
(PERRY DRUG)
From: Cullinan/Wright *Cases from the SEC Files: Topics in Auditing*

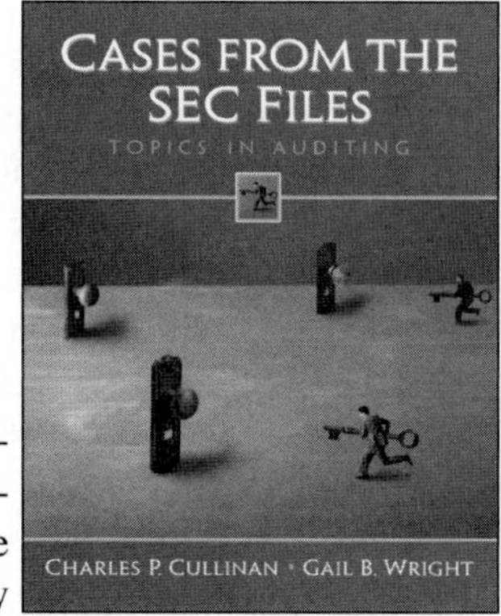

SYNOPSIS:

Perry Drug, while conducting periodic rolling inventories, discovered a material ($20 million) discrepancy between its inventory records and the physical inventory. The inventory records overstated the inventory balance, and therefore, overstated net income. Perry personnel disclosed the issue to Richard Valade, a partner at Arthur Andersen. Valade sought to investigate the issue by performing analytical review, and by physically observing the inventory at a sample of stores. The analytical review disclosed no material changes in the cost of goods sold percentage (despite Perry having changed inventory reporting method twice). The physical observation supported the client's counts which showed a material overstatement. Valade issued an unqualified audit opinion on Perry financial statements, which were not adjusted for the inventory discrepancy.

SEC FINDINGS:

On the basis of this Order and Valade's Offer of Settlement, the Commission finds that[1]

A. RESPONDENT AND OTHER RELATED PARTIES

1. Respondent

Richard Valade (Valade), age 48, is a partner with Arthur Andersen, LLP (AA) based in its Detroit, Michigan Office. Valade was the engagement partner at AA for the 1991, 1992 and 1993 audits of Perry Drug Stores, Inc. (Perry). Valade also served as an engagement manager on the 1984 through 1987 Perry audits. He has been a Certified Public Accountant (CPA) licensed in the state of Michigan since 1979.

2. Other Related Party

Perry Drug Stores, Inc. (Perry) was a Michigan corporation which operated a chain of drugstores located primarily in Michigan. Perry was a publicly traded company whose common stock was registered pursuant to Section 12(b) of the Securities Exchange Act of 1934 (Exchange Act). As of October 31, 1992, the end of Perry's fiscal year, Perry operated 205 retail drugstores. In January 1993, Perry filed a Form 10-K with the Commission pursuant to Section 13(a) of the Exchange Act. Perry attached a copy of AA's Report of Independent Public Accountants which contained an unqualified opinion signed by Richard Valade dated December 15, 1992, and which accompanied Perry's October 31, 1992 financial statements.

B. SUMMARY

Valade, the engagement partner on the Perry audit for the year ended October 31, 1992, issued an unqualified audit report on Perry's financial statements without obtaining sufficient competent evidential matter. Valade knew that Perry's valuation of physical inventory counts during the year generated results that were approximately $20 million less than the inventory carried on Perry's books and records and reflected in its financial statements. Nevertheless, Valade, relying on the results of other audit procedures and analytic data, agreed with Perry's decision to include the $20 million in inventory as an asset and signed the unqualified audit report. Perry later determined that this inventory did not exist.

C. BACKGROUND

In fiscal year 1990, Perry began using a base cost method to value inventory at its stores. Perry employed an outside service to conduct physical inventory counts of its stores on a cyclical basis during each fiscal year. Perry conducted a physical inventory of a percentage of its stores each month from February through September until it had completed an inventory of all stores. Beginning in late 1991 and throughout fiscal year 1992 Perry changed to a last received cost method.[2]

In order to value inventory and calculate cost of goods sold in the books and records, between each physical count, Perry used the gross profit method typical to retail merchants. Using this method, Perry would add to the amount of the beginning

---

1 The findings herein are made pursuant to Valade's Offer of Settlement and are not binding on any other person or entity in this or any other proceeding.

2 Pursuant to the last received cost method, inventory is valued by multiplying the number of units of a particular product by the cost of the most recently purchased unit of that product.

inventory the actual cost of its goods purchased through its accounts payable system (cost of goods acquired for sale). Perry would then reduce the inventory by an estimate of the cost of goods sold calculated using the estimated gross profit margin[3] Perry included the estimated inventory balance on its general ledger, until the actual inventory was verified through a new physical count. Perry would then adjust this inventory figure to reflect the results of the physical inventory.

Perry reconciled the recorded inventory at each store with the results of the physical inventory for that store when it conducted the next cyclical count. If the recorded inventory was greater than the value of the physical inventory, Perry increased the cost of goods sold and decreased the recorded inventory to reflect the results of the physical inventory. If the physical count revealed that a store had more inventory than was recorded in the books and records, Perry adjusted the general ledger to reflect the additional inventory.

D. DISCUSSION

1. Perry's Inventory Discrepancies in Fiscal 1992 Totaled over $20 Million

During the second quarter of fiscal year 1992 (February through April), Perry conducted cycle counts of its inventory at approximately 48% of its stores. The valuations of these inventory counts were available in May and June 1992 and reflected store inventory in the general merchandise categories substantially less than those reflected in the recorded estimates of inventory on Perry's books. By the end of the second quarter of fiscal year 1992, Perry identified a discrepancy of approximately $8.5 million between the value of the physical inventory and the recorded inventory. Perry identified an additional discrepancy of approximately $7.6 million at the end of the third quarter and another approximately $4 million at the end of the year. Combined, these discrepancies, or "shrinks," totaled over $20 million for fiscal year 1992. The amount of these discrepancies was far in excess of discrepancies identified in prior fiscal years.

As described above, Perry had historically adjusted the inventory balances recorded in its books and records by writing off the amount of the discrepancy as a part of its cost of sales. However, in fiscal year 1992, because it did not believe that the unusually large store inventory discrepancies were reasonable, Perry's management did not follow its usual course of conduct. Instead of writing off the discrepancy to cost of sales, Perry recorded it in a suspense account, which was called the "Store 100" inventory account, while it investigated the source of the discrepancy. Perry then reflected the balance of the Store 100 account in its overall store inventory in its second and third quarter and year end fiscal 1992 financial statements.

In order to determine the cause of the unusually large discrepancy, Perry conducted numerous tests on its inventory systems and processes during and after fiscal year 1992. Perry also hired AA's computer risk management group to analyze the inventory related systems to determine whether systems problems were the cause of the discrepancy. Perry also hired private investigators and internal auditors to discover whether any large-scale theft had occurred. Perry also tried to determine whether the change, in fiscal year 1990, from the retail method of valuing inventory to a base cost method caused the discrepancy. Perry also conducted a more detailed internal audit of one its stores which used a point of sale ("POS") system.[4] Despite all of these procedures, Perry was unable to explain, nor was it able to determine, the cause of the physical inventory discrepancies during fiscal year 1992.

2. The Fiscal Year 1992 Audit Conducted by Valade Failed to Verify Perry's Inventory

Before the audit of Perry's 1992 financial statements began, Perry notified Valade of the inventory discrepancies described above. Perry also informed Valade of the status and results of its on-going investigation. Accordingly, as part of its fieldwork, the audit team expanded its audit work in this area and conducted numerous tests to verify the value of Perry's inventory.

Under Valade's direction, the audit team conducted various analytical tests including tests to assess the validity of the gross profit margins as well as tests which examined warehouse and store data. Among other things, the team also examined margin and quantity data from warehouse shipments, available POS data, comparable industry wide margin data and Perry's historical margin data, all of which was inconsistent with the size of the shrink indicated by the physical inventory results. The audit team also investigated the possibility that thefts at the warehouse or changes in Perry's merchandising and business plans were the cause of the inventory discrepancies.

The audit team also observed and tested the physical count at five Perry stores which confirmed that the value of the physical inventory at those stores was much smaller than the estimated value reflected in Perry's general ledger. However, the audit team did not recommend that Perry record the shrink at the five stores as a cost of goods sold. Instead, Perry recorded the book-to-physical differences from these five stores as an asset in the Store 100 account, along with the results of the other physical counts.

---

3 The estimated gross profit margin was based upon factors such as merchandising plans and physical inventory results and generally was reviewed and adjusted more than once a year.

4 The "POS" system was new to Perry's stores in 1992 and had only been installed in about one-third of its stores by fiscal 1992 year end. The POS system permitted a more accurate accounting of actual products sold and related gross margins on those sales than was possible using Perry's former "department key" method. Traditionally, Perry accumulated sales information by classifying merchandise into six register keys. Key 1, the largest category, encompassed general non-pharmacy items.

None of the tests or analyses conducted by Valade and the audit team explained the cause of the inventory discrepancies. Nevertheless, Valade relied upon the results of the testing and analyses summarized above instead of the physical inventory results.

3. Valade was Aware of the Inventory Discrepancies Prior to Issuing the Audit Report

In September 1992, Valade and the Senior Accountant on the Perry engagement drafted a General Risk Analysis Memorandum (GRA) for the fiscal year 1992 Perry audit. Valade noted in the GRA the significant inventory discrepancies and the need to evaluate the problem during the audit. The GRA concluded that the risk of the overall audit would be "moderate" with emphasis placed on auditing inventory and payables. A "moderate" risk assessment reflects that the auditor expects errors but has reason to believe they are not likely to be material in relation to the financial statements. In the GRA, the audit team also set a materiality standard of $700,000. At the time Valade drafted the GRA with a "moderate" risk rating, he was aware that: (1) Perry had discovered at least $17 million in inventory discrepancies, (2) Perry had not recorded, as cost of sales, any of the inventory discrepancies; and (3) neither Perry nor anyone on the audit team could explain the cause of the inventory discrepancies.

In addition, Valade was aware of the study conducted by his firm's computer risk management group. The group concluded that while the inventory systems were operating as designed, the systems might not provide an accurate estimate of the value of the inventory in all circumstances.

Finally, Valade was aware of extensive month-long testing done on one of Perry's stores identified as "Store 152." In this testing Perry audited all shipments and followed all deliveries to the store to ensure that shipments were delivered. The company also did an extensive analysis regarding inventory reconciliations. Valade felt that these results verified the accuracy of the gross profit margin. However, this testing also showed the existence of an unusually large inventory discrepancy which was consistent with the physical counts done at other stores. Valade relied on the results of the analytic work rather than the data which showed the existence of the shrink in inventory.

4. Despite Uncertainties as to the Inventories' Existence, Valade Caused an Unqualified Audit Opinion to be Issued on the 1992 Financial Statements

In December 1992, Perry's management recommended to its board of directors and its audit committee that the company continue to include the $20 million in Store 100 inventory as an asset on its October 31, 1992 balance sheet. During the audit, Valade consulted with a number of his partners concerning the inventory issue, including the Regional Practice Director. After further audit tests and additional discussions with his partners, Valade and two of his partners, attended Perry's Audit Committee meeting on this issue, which was also attended by Perry's outside counsel. At that meeting, Valade reported that he did not object to including the Store 100 inventory as an asset on Perry's balance sheet and that he would sign an unqualified opinion.

Valade acknowledged the possibility that the unexplained inventory discrepancy could have resulted from several changes in costing procedures over the previous three years. The minutes of the December 1992 Board Meeting reflect "uncertainties" as to the reasons for the inventory discrepancy. The minutes also reflect that Valade recommended that Perry conduct additional tests, including a simultaneous chain-wide inventory, as soon as possible to discover the reasons for the discrepancy.

Pursuant to the discussions at the Board Meeting, including a separate discussion by the outside directors with outside counsel, Perry's Board approved the filing of financial statements filed with Perry's 1992 Form 10-K which included the $20 million of inventory in the Store 100 account as an asset. This represented over fourteen percent of the approximately $140 million in inventory that Perry carried on its books and reported in its balance sheet and over seven percent of its assets of approximately $270 million. Had Perry followed its normal procedure of expensing inventory shrinks to cost of sales, Perry would have reported a net loss of close to $6 million for fiscal year 1992 instead of the net income of $8.3 million it originally reported.

Indeed, despite uncertainties as to the Store 100 inventory's existence that led to Valade's recommendations for further testing, Valade signed an unqualified audit opinion on Perry's 1992 financial statements, which included the $20 million of Store 100 inventory as an asset. As previously stated, Valade recommended that Perry conduct additional inventory counts and value the physical inventory using both the cost and retail methods at 20 stores. Valade also recommended that Perry conduct a simultaneous inventory of all its stores to reduce the number of variables that could have skewed the results of the inventories taken at the stores. Perry accepted Valade's recommendation for a simultaneous chain-wide physical store inventory, and scheduled it to be taken early in calendar 1993, shortly after the Christmas sales season. Valade also recommended that Perry reduce the gross profit margin being used in fiscal year 1993.

5. Perry Continued to Improperly Account for the Inventory Shrinkage in Fiscal Year 1993

In January 1993, pursuant to Valade's recommendation, Perry took sample physical inventories at cost and retail at 19 stores to determine whether its change in accounting methodology contributed to the shrinkages. Pursuant to Valade's suggestion, Perry began the full chain-wide physical inventory in February 1993. Reconciliation of book-to-physical results from the full chain inventory were completed in May 1993. These results confirmed the inventory shrink.

As a result of full chain inventories, Perry concluded that it could not verify the existence of the inventory in the Store 100 account. Near the end of fiscal year 1993, Perry disclosed a non cash charge of $33.4 million relating to, among other things, an adjustment of store inventory. Approximately two-thirds of the charge taken in 1993 had been discovered by Perry during fiscal year 1992. Nevertheless, Perry, without objection from Valade, inappropriately categorized the adjustment as a "change in estimate" and did not restate the 1992 financial statements at that time. However, on July 27, 1994, upon the insistence of the Commission's Division of Corporation Finance, Perry restated its 1992 and 1993 financial statements. The 1992 and 1993 financial statements were restated to reflect a portion of this adjustment as a "correction of error" resulting in an additional $20 million cost of sales for fiscal year 1992.

E. ACCOUNTING PRINCIPLES AND AUDITING STANDARDS

The auditor's role is to express an opinion about whether the audited financial statements fairly present the required information in conformity with Generally Accepted Accounting Principles (GAAP). The audit must be conducted in accordance with Generally Accepted Auditing Standards (GAAS). In reaching an opinion, auditors are required to obtain sufficient competent evidential matter. The third standard of field work of GAAS, states that sufficient competent evidential matter is to be obtained through inspection, observation, inquiries and confirmations to afford a reasonable basis for an opinion regarding the financial statements under audit. Auditing Standards, AU326.01. The auditing standards specifically require those auditing inventory "to make, or observe, some physical counts of the inventory . . ." unless certain conditions, which are not applicable to the Perry Audit, are present. Auditing Standards, AU331.12. Section 326.19 of the Auditing Standards states that evidence obtained through physical examinations is more persuasive than information obtained indirectly, such as analytical results.

To the extent that the auditor remains in substantial doubt about any assertion of material significance, he or she must refrain from forming an opinion until such time as the auditor has obtained sufficient competent evidential matter to remove such substantial doubt, or he must express a qualified opinion or a disclaimer of opinion. Auditing Standards, AU326.23.

F. CONCLUSION

Valade understood the significance of the discrepancy between the value of the physical inventory and the recorded inventory and accordingly, using various audit procedures, sought to determine whether there was any flaw in the valuations of either the physical inventory or the recorded inventory. Valade was unable to verify the accuracy of the recorded inventory through physical observations. In fact, the results of the physical inventories which the audit team observed confirmed the existence of inventory shrinks at those locations.

Valade failed to identify an appropriate basis for selecting the recorded inventory over thephysical inventory. He could not point to any error generated by either system of computing the inventory. Despite Valade's consultations with his partners and the additional audit procedures he performed, he nevertheless failed to obtain sufficient competent evidential matter to resolve the inventory discrepancy issue. Valade failed to either: (a) require Perry to reconcile the recorded inventory and the physical inventory and record the proper adjustment to the books and records; (b) discredit either the recorded inventory or the physical inventory and require Perry to adjust the books and records accordingly; (c) issue a qualified opinion; or (d) refrain from issuing an audit opinion until the matter was resolved.

Accordingly, for the reasons set forth above, Valade failed to comply with GAAS and failed to require Perry to comply with GAAP when he signed an unqualified audit report despite the fact that he had not obtained sufficient competent evidential matter to verify the existence of the store inventory. Thus, Valade engaged in improper professional conduct within the meaning of Rule 102(e)(1)(ii) of the Commission's Rules of Practice.

DISCUSSION QUESTIONS

1. Demonstrate, using a journal entry format (numbers not necessary), a) the gross profit estimation method for valing inventory and b) the adjustment that should have resulted from the physical count. Did Perry Drug make the adjustment in b? If not what entry did they make?

2. Does Perry's write-off of differences between recorded and physical inventory to CGS prior to1992 obscure possible theft? Why/why not? What other problems might the write-off of differences obscure?

3. What do you believe might be another name for "last received cost method?" What is the likely effect of Perry's change to this method on net income in 1990 from the "base cost" method (what ever that is) when prices are rising and inventory is stable or rising?
4. Identify how the inclusion of "Store 100" in ending inventory affects net income.
5. Given the $17 million discrepancy at the point of the GRA memorandum in 1992 and assuming the "quick and dirty" 5% of income rule for determining materiality, what would income have to be for this discrepancy to fall below the materiality threshold? If the discrepancy falls below the 5% of income level, would the misstatement necessarily be immaterial?
6. In the Perry Drug Case, what factors may prevent the auditor from forming clear expectations for the relevant account balances and linking them to the results of analytical tests?
7. Evaluate the relative competence of the analytical review evidence Valade gathered and the physical observation evidence obtained with regard to the inventory balance. Which evidence type is stronger? Why?
8. If financial statements knowingly contained the inventory error, what audit report(s) might be appropriate and why? What if the auditor was unable to satisfy him or herself as to whether the inventory discrepancy represented a material misstatement?
9. Does soliciting and obtaining the advice from his colleagues in the firm relieve Valade of professional responsibility for his audit opinion?
10. Explain thoroughly how Valade violated GAAS. In addition to violating GAAS, do you believe Valade may have violated the Code of Professional Conduct?
11. Do you believe the client applied undo pressure to the auditor to permit filing of misstated financial statements for 1992? For 1993? Do you believe there was a threat of losing this client if Valade had reacted differently? Why or why not?

ESSENTIALS OF AUDITING AND ASSURANCE SERVICES

An Integrated Approach

ESSENTIALS OF AUDITING AND ASSURANCE SERVICES

An Integrated Approach

Alvin A. Arens
PricewaterhouseCoopers
Auditing Professor
Michigan State University

Randal J. Elder
Syracuse University

Mark S. Beasley
North Carolina State University

with Web Content provided by
Gregory J. Jenkins
North Carolina State University

Prentice Hall, Upper Saddle River, New Jersey 07458

Library of Congress Cataloging-in-Publication Data

Arens, Alvin A.
Essentials of auditing and assurance services/Alvin A. Arens, Randal J. Elder, Mark S. Beasley; with Web content provided by Gregory J. Jenkins.
p. cm.
Brief version of: Auditing, an integrated approach.
Includes index.
ISBN 0-13-046303-5
1. Auditing I. Elder, Randal J. II. Beasley, Mark S. III. Jenkins, Gregory J. IV. Arens, Alvin A. Auditing, an integrated approach. V. Title.

HF5667 .A692 2002
657'.45–dc21

2002072730

Acquisitions Editor: Thomas Sigel
Editor-in-Chief: P. J. Boardman
Assistant Editor: Beth Romph
Senior Media Project Manager: Nancy Welcher
Executive Marketing Manager: Beth Toland
Accounting & CIS Program Consultant: Walter Mendez
Managing Editor (Production): Cynthia Regan
Production Editor: Michael Reynolds
Production Assistant: Dianne Falcone
Permissions Supervisor: Suzanne Grappi
Associate Director, Manufacturing: Vinnie Scelta
Production Manager: Arnold Vila
Interior/Cover Design: Steven Frim
Cover Illustration: Steven Frim
Manager, Print Production: Christy Mahon
Print production Liaison: Ashley Scattergood
Composition: Progressive Information Technologies
Full-Service Project Management: Progressive Publishing Alternatives
Printer/Binder: R. R. Donnelley/Willard

Credits and acknowledgements borrowed from other sources and reproduced, with permission, in this textbook appear on appropriate page within text.

Pearson Education LTD.
Pearson Education Australia PTY, Limited
Pearson Education Singapore, Pte. Ltd
Pearson Education North Asia Ltd
Pearson Education, Canada, Ltd
Pearson Educación de Mexico, S.A. de C.V.
Pearson Education–Japan
Pearson Education Malaysia, Pte. Ltd

10 9 8 7 6 5 4 3 2
ISBN 0-13-046303-5

CONTENTS

PART 2 The Audit Process

6

7

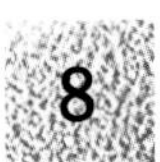
8

PREFACE

OBJECTIVE

Essentials of Auditing and Assurance Services: An Integrated Approach is designed to provide all the essential concepts for an integrated understanding of the audit process for courses that require a briefer text.

The book is an introduction to auditing and other assurance services for students who have not had significant experience in providing such services. It is intended for either a one-quarter or one-semester course at the undergraduate or graduate level. This book is also appropriate for introductory professional development courses for CPA firms, internal auditors, and government auditors.

The primary emphasis in this text is on the auditor's decision-making process. We believe that the most fundamental concepts in auditing relate to determining the nature and amount of evidence the auditor should accumulate after considering the unique circumstances of each engagement. If a student of auditing understands the objectives to be accomplished in a given audit area, the circumstances of the engagement, and the decisions to be made, he or she should be able to determine the appropriate evidence to gather and how to evaluate the evidence obtained.

Thus, as the title of this book reflects, our purpose is to integrate the most important concepts of auditing and other assurance services as well as certain practical aspects in a logical manner to assist students in understanding audit decision making and evidence accumulation. For example, internal control is integrated into each of the chapters dealing with a particular functional area and is related to tests of controls and substantive tests of transactions; tests of controls and substantive tests of transactions are, in turn, related to the tests of details of financial statement balances for the area; and audit sampling is applied to the accumulation of audit evidence rather than treated as a separate topic. Technology and e-commerce issues are integrated throughout all chapters.

MOST IMPORTANT ASPECTS OF THE FIRST EDITION

Author Team

Leading auditing textbook author Al Arens is joined by Randy Elder (Syracuse University) and Mark Beasley (North Carolina State University) for this first edition. The new authors have joined the team to enhance current coverage of all aspects of this book, but especially technology and e-commerce. Randy and Mark have significant auditing and other assurance professional experience, regularly teach auditing courses at the undergraduate and graduate levels, actively conduct research on relevant audit related practice issues, and serve on national committees and task forces for organizations such as the American Accounting Association, the AICPA Auditing Standards Board, and the Committee of Sponsoring Organizations of the Treadway Committee (COSO).

Client Business Risk and E-Commerce

Two concepts emphasized in this edition are (1) the importance of obtaining an understanding of the client's business and environment to effectively identify client business risks and (2) the effects of information technology and e-commerce on the audit process. Chapter 7 on audit planning highlights the importance of understanding the client's business and industry to identify client business risks that may ultimately lead to increased likelihood of material misstatements in financial statements. The process of obtaining an understanding of key client business objectives and strategies to identify related client business risks is also integrated throughout the remaining chapters that address specific transaction cycle audit issues. The effects of information technology and e-commerce on the audit process have been integrated throughout the book, including specific chapter sections and homework problems. These problems are highlighted by an e-commerce symbol.

Hillsburg Hardware Integration

Hillsburg Hardware, a medium size publicly-traded hardware wholesaler, is used as a case example throughout the text. The examples are integrated with the chapter material to better illustrate chapter concepts.

Internet Problems and Margin Links

All chapters include an Internet-based case/homework assignment that requires students to use the Internet to research relevant auditing issues. Internet-based margin links appear in every chapter, providing information on current events, companies, and professional standards.

Chapter 3 on Professional Ethics

Chapter 3 incorporates major changes affecting auditor independence recently implemented by the SEC and the AICPA. The chapter also includes a section that provides a broader conceptual framework of factors affecting auditor independence before examining specific independence rules.

ORGANIZATION

The text is divided into five parts.

Part 1, The Auditing Profession (Chapters 1–4) This book begins with a study of the demand for audit and other assurance services. Chapter 1 emphasizes new assurance services being offered by CPA firms such as *WebTrust* and *CPA ElderCare Services* and the CPA profession, including organization of CPA firms, the AICPA, and the SEC. In Chapter 2, there is a detailed discussion of audit reports. It emphasizes the conditions affecting the type of report the auditor must issue and the type of audit report applicable to each condition under varying levels of materiality. Chapter 3 explains ethical dilemmas, professional ethics, and the AICPA *Code of Professional Conduct.* Chapter 4 ends this part with an investigation of auditors' legal liability.

Part 2, The Audit Process (Chapters 5–10) The first two of these chapters deal with auditors' and managements' responsibilities, audit objectives, general concepts of evidence accumulation, and audit documentation. Chapter 7 deals with planning the engagement and using analytical procedures as an audit tool. Chapter 8 introduces materiality and risk and shows their effect on the audit. The study of internal control and assessment of control risk are discussed in Chapter 9, which emphasizes a proper methodology for obtaining an understanding of the five components of internal control. Chapter 10 summarizes Chapters 5 through 9 and integrates them with the remainder of the text.

Part 3, Application of the Audit Process to the Sales and Collection Cycle (Chapters 11–13) These chapters apply the concepts from Part 2 to the audit of sales, cash receipts, and the related income statement and balance sheet accounts. The appropriate audit procedures for accounts in the sales and collection cycle are related to internal control and audit objectives for tests of controls, substantive tests of transactions, and tests of details of balances. Students learn to apply audit sampling to the audit of sales, cash receipts, and accounts receivable.

Part 4, Application of the Audit Process to Other Cycles (Chapters 14–17) Each of these chapters deals with a specific transaction cycle or part of a transaction cycle in much the same manner as Chapters 11 through 13 cover the sales and collection cycle. Each chapter in Part 4 is meant to demonstrate the relationship of internal controls, tests of controls, and substantive tests of transactions for each broad category of transactions to the related balance sheet and income statement accounts. Cash in the bank is studied late in the text to demonstrate how the audit of cash balances is related to most other audit areas.

Part 5, Completing the Audit (Chapter 18) This part includes only one chapter, which deals with summarizing all audit tests, reviewing audit documentation, and all other aspects of completing an audit.

SUPPLEMENTS

Supplements for the Instructor

The Prentice Hall Accounting and Taxation Hotline 1-800-227-1816 Prentice Hall's unique Accounting and Taxation Hotline is your direct link to satisfying all your adoption needs! By calling our toll-free telephone number, you can receive information on Prentice Hall's Accounting and Tax texts and supplements. The Hotline will also process your orders and keep you up-to-date on the upcoming Prentice Hall Accounting Seminars for Educators (PHASE) in your area.

Instructor's Resource Manual This integrated source assists the instructor in teaching the course. The features include instructions for assignments, as well as helpful suggestions provided by the text authors on how to effectively teach each chapter. To enhance and simplify course planning, chapter Learning Objectives are integrated throughout the problem material. Also available on the Companion Website.

Solutions Manual This comprehensive resource provides detailed solutions to all the end-of-chapter review questions, multiple choice questions, and cases. Also available on the Companion Website.

Test Item File—prepared by Greg Jenkins of North Carolina State University The Test Item File contains more than 1,500 test items, including true/false, multiple-choice, exercises/problems, critical thinking/essay, questions adapted from CPA examinations, and questions on the chapter opening vignettes. Each test item in this effective testing tool includes a difficulty level and has been content-reviewed for clarity and checked for accuracy. Available in print.

Prentice Hall Custom Test Generator Available on Windows platform and Macintosh on request, this easy-to-use computerized testing program is available on CD-ROM. This user-friendly program allows you to create an exam, as well as evaluate and track student results. The PH Custom Test also provides on-line testing capabilities. Test material is adapted from the Test Item File.

Companion Website at **www.prenhall.com/arens** includes our ***new*** bi-annual newsletter of recent professional developments, ***new*** streaming videos featuring Al Arens, online study guide, PowerPoints, and more. Also includes a quick and easy conversion guide from the Essentials Table of Contents to the comprehensive book.

Supplements for the Student

Updated! Auditing Cases: An Active Learning Approach, 2e—by Mark S. Beasley, Frank A. Buckless, Steven M. Glover, and Douglas F. Prawitt This collection of 34 auditing cases addresses most major activities performed during the conduct of an audit, from client acceptance to issuance of an audit report. Many of the cases are based on actual companies, some of which were engaged in financial reporting fraud. Several cases involve students working with realistic audit evidence and preparing and evaluating audit documentation. Some cases expose students to assurance and other value-added services. This collection of cases provides an easy opportunity for instructors to promote an active learning environment by giving students an effective basis for in-class discussion of relevant professional issues. The cases are available as a collection or as part of the Pearson Custom Publishing Resources Program. For details, go to www.pearsoncustom.com.

***NEW!* Cases from the SEC Files: Topics in Auditing—prepared by Gail B. Wright and Charles P. Cullinan (both of Bryant College)** Available for the first time! Wright and Cullinan have compiled a collection of the best SEC cases. Now you have two choices: 1) select this paperback collection of cases or 2) **create your own** custom version of cases from www.pearsoncustom.com. Best of all? The collection of online SEC cases will continue to evolve so that your collection will always contain the most current cases that reflect SEC actions!

The Auditor: An Instructional Novella—by James K. Loebbecke The purpose of this 120-page paperback is to teach students about various aspects of a typical career in public accounting that students will most likely encounter during their own careers. The novella forms a single, on-going, fictional case study of 14 situations that trace the professional life of Jack Butler, CPA.

Updated! The Lakeside Company: Case Studies in the Life-Cycle of an Audit, Ninth Edition, prepared by John Trussel, Pennsylvania State University, Harrisburg, and Joe Ben Hoyle, University of Richmond An efficient and effective Practice Set that guides the student through the life cycle of an audit from beginning to end. The cases are designed to create a realistic view of how an auditor organizes and carries out an audit. An Instructor's Solutions Manual is also available on the Web. The Web component will also include additional *NEW* exercises that further probe the student's auditing knowledge. These exercises will be in the form of a second-partner review. Students can view auditing memos while simultaneously listening to audio clips in which the author provides additional insight and/or directions.

***NEW!* Comprehensive Assurance and Systems Tool—by Frank A. Buckless, Laura R. Ingraham, and Greg Jenkins, all of North Carolina State University** This **integrated** practice set enables students to complete accounting transactions based on the day-to-day operations of a real winery. Five modules with transactions are provided: assurance services, manual accounting information systems, spreadsheet applications, general ledger software, and database design and development. Includes a student CD-ROM. Appropriate for use in auditing, AIS, or intermediate accounting courses.

***NEW!* Microsoft Excel for Accounting: Auditing and AIS—by Katherine T. Smith, L. Murphy Smith, and Lawrence C. Smith, Jr.** Using this book, your students will learn how to complete their assignments in Excel—enabling them to work more efficiently while enhancing their understanding of accounting concepts. In addition, students will become more computer savvy with one of the most widely available and often used software products, Microsoft Excel. This knowledge will be beneficial both in college and future careers. *May be packaged with any Prentice Hall Accounting text for only $5.00 net—or sold stand-alone!*

ACKNOWLEDGMENTS

We acknowledge the American Institute of Certified Public Accountants for permission to quote extensively from statements on auditing standards, *the Code of Professional Conduct*, Financial Accounting Standards Board, Uniform CPA Examinations, and other publications. The willingness of this major accounting organization to permit the use of its materials is a significant contribution to the book.

The continuing generous support of the PricewaterhouseCoopers Foundation is acknowledged, particularly in regard to the word processing, editing, and moral support of this text.

We gratefully acknowledge the contributions of the following reviewers for their suggestions and support: Sherri Anderson, Sonoma State University; Stephen K. Asare, University of Florida; David Baglia, Elizabethtown College; Brian Ballou, Auburn University; William E. Bealing, Jr., Bloomsburg University; Stanley F. Biggs, University of Connecticut; Frank Buckless, North Carolina State University; Joseph V. Calmie, Thomas Nelson Community College; Eric Carlsen, Kean College of New Jersey; Freddie Choo, San

Francisco State University; Frank Daroca, Loyola Marymount University; Barb Esteves, University of Michigan at Flint; William L. Felix, University of Arizona; David S. Gelb, Seton Hall University; Charles L. Holley, Virginia Commonwealth University; Gary L. Holstrum, University of South Florida; C. Randy Howard, Montana State University at Billings; Rita P. Hull, Virginia Commonwealth University; Steve Hunt, Western Illinois University; Greg Jenkins, North Carolina State University; James Jiambalvo, University of Washington; David S. Kerr, Texas A & M University; Dennis Lee Kimmell, University of Akron; William R. Kinney, Jr., University of Texas at Austin; W. Robert Knechel, University of Florida; Heidi H. Meier, Cleveland State University; Alfred R. Michenzi, Loyola College in Maryland; Charles R. (Tad) Miller, California Polytechnic State University; Lawrence C. Mohrweis, Northern Arizona University; Patricia M. Myers, East Carolina University; Frederick L. Neumann, University of Illinois; Kristine N. Palmer, Longwood College; Vicki S. Peden, Cal Poly—Pomona; Philip H. Siegel, Long Island University—CW Post; Robert R. Tucker, Fordham University; D. Dewey Ward, Michigan State University; Robert J. Warth, Rochester Institute of Technology; Jeanne H. Yamamura, University of Nevada, Reno; and Doug Ziegenfuss, Old Dominion University.

A special recognition goes to Carol Borsum for her editorial, production, and moral support throughout the last four editions. Her concern for quality is beyond the ordinary. Thanks also to Mary Jo Mercer for excellence in word processing and final review and to Elizabeth Johnston for proofreading.

We especially thank the Prentice Hall book team for their hard work and dedication, including P. J. Boardman, Editor-in-Chief; Thomas Sigel, Acquisitions Editor; Beth Ann Romph, Assistant Editor; Fran Toepfer, Editorial Assistant; Cindy Regan, Managing Editor; Nancy Welcher, Senior Media Product Manager; Beth Toland, Executive Marketing Manager; Mike Reynolds, Production Editor; Pat Smythe, Design Manager; Steve Frim, Cover Design; and Arnold Vila, Senior Manufacturing Supervisor.

A. A. A.
R. J. E.
M. S. B.

ABOUT THE AUTHORS

Al Arens is PricewaterhouseCoopers Auditing Professor of Accounting at Michigan State University. His primary teaching and research area is auditing and he teaches undergraduate auditing at least one term annually. Al is a past president of the American Accounting Association and a former member of the AICPA Auditing Standards Board. He practiced public accounting with both a local CPA firm and the predecessor firm to Ernst & Young. He has received many awards including the AAA Auditing Section Outstanding Educator award, the AICPA Outstanding Educator award, the national Beta Alpha Psi Professor of the Year award and many teaching and other awards at Michigan State.

Randy Elder is an Associate Professor of Accounting at Syracuse University. He teaches undergraduate and graduate auditing courses, and has received several teaching awards. His research focuses on audit quality and current audit firm practices. He has extensive public accounting experience with a large regional CPA firm, and is a Certified Fraud Examiner and member of the AICPA and Michigan Association of CPAs.

Mark S. Beasley is an Associate Professor of Accounting at North Carolina State University. He teaches undergraduate and graduate auditing courses, and has received several teaching awards including membership in NC State's Academy of Outstanding Teachers. His research, which focuses primarily on financial statement fraud, audit quality, and corporate governance, received both the American Accounting Association's Competitive Manuscript Award and the Notable Contributions to the Auditing Literature Award. He has extensive professional audit experience with the predecessor firm to Ernst & Young and has extensive standards-setting experience working with the Auditing Standards Board as a Technical Manager in the Audit and Assurance Division of the AICPA. Currently he serves on the ASB's Fraud Standard Task Force and the Advisory Council overseeing COSO's Enterprise Risk Management Framework project.

PART 1 CHAPTERS 1-4

THE AUDITING PROFESSION

These first four chapters provide background for performing financial audits, which is our primary focus. This background will help you understand why auditors perform audits the way they do.

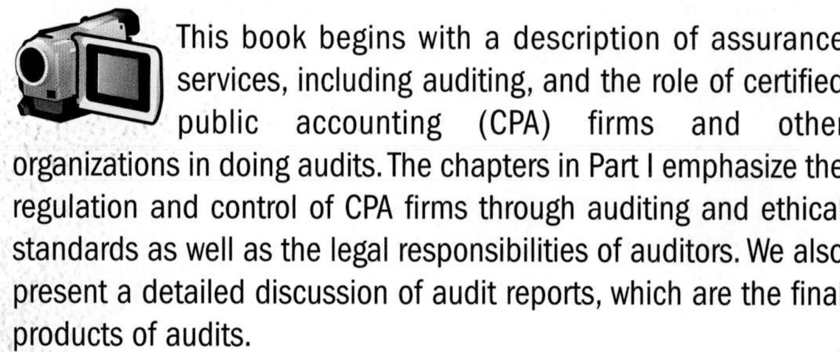

This book begins with a description of assurance services, including auditing, and the role of certified public accounting (CPA) firms and other organizations in doing audits. The chapters in Part I emphasize the regulation and control of CPA firms through auditing and ethical standards as well as the legal responsibilities of auditors. We also present a detailed discussion of audit reports, which are the final products of audits.

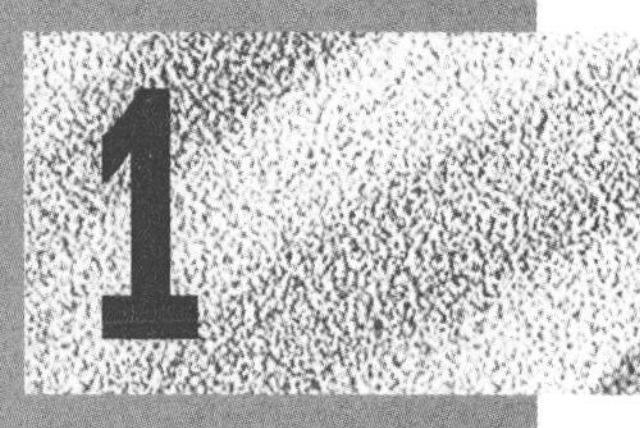

CHAPTER 1

ASSURANCE SERVICES AND THE CPA PROFESSION

LEARNING OBJECTIVES

After studying this chapter, you should be able to

1-1 Describe assurance services and distinguish audit services from other assurance and nonassurance services provided by CPAs.

1-2 Explain the causes of information risk and the importance of auditing in reducing this risk.

1-3 Describe auditing and distinguish between auditing and accounting.

1-4 Differentiate the three main types of audits.

1-5 Identify the primary types of auditors.

1-6 Discuss how e-commerce and the Internet affect CPA firm operations.

1-7 Describe the requirements for becoming a CPA.

1-8 Describe the AICPA and its role in setting standards.

1-9 Use generally accepted auditing standards as a basis for further study.

1-10 Identify quality control standards and practices within the accounting profession.

1-11 Summarize the role of the Securities and Exchange Commission in accounting and auditing.

THE AUDITOR IS A STRATEGIC BUSINESS PARTNER

Joe Anthony, a partner in Berger & Anthony, CPAs stares nervously at his computer screen. He breathes a sigh of relief as he watches the ticker symbol for his client, Hillsburg Hardware, as it begins initial trading as a public company. Five years ago, he would never have guessed that his client would go public, and he is proud of the role that his firm played in the process.

Two years ago, Berger & Anthony performed a strategic analysis of Hillsburg's wholesale distribution business. Based on the analysis, Berger & Anthony recommended that Hillsburg restructure its customer relations and invest heavily in information technology to allow Hillsburg to partner with its customers in inventory management. These investments greatly expanded Hillsburg's revenues and customer base, creating a need for expansion and further capital that was raised in the public offering.

Berger & Anthony had audited the financial statements of Hillsburg Hardware for many years as required by Hillsburg's bank loan agreement. Now, many other investors will rely on the Hillsburg Hardware financial statements audited by Berger & Anthony. Joe Anthony recognizes the responsibility that he has to those investors, and is also excited about future opportunities to help Hillsburg Hardware grow and expand as a public company.

Each chapter's opening vignette illustrates important auditing principles based on realistic situations. Some vignettes are based on public information about the audits of real companies, whereas others are fictitious. Any resemblance in the latter vignettes to real firms, companies, or individuals is unintended and purely coincidental.

As the Hillsburg Hardware example illustrates, certified public accountants (CPAs) provide assurances on financial statements and also help businesses be more successful. As businesses become more complex and need more reliable information, CPAs play a vital role, both in providing assurance on information other than financial statements and providing consulting and tax services. For example, businesses and consumers who use information technology and electronic communication networks such as the Internet to conduct business and make decisions need independent assurances about the reliability and security of that electronic information. Auditors are valued because of their technical knowledge and independence in providing assurances, as well as their competence and experience in assisting companies to improve operations. Auditors often make and help implement recommendations that improve profitability by enhancing revenue or reducing costs, including the reduction of errors and fraud, and by improving operational controls.

ASSURANCE SERVICES

OBJECTIVE 1-1

Describe assurance services and distinguish audit services from other assurance and nonassurance services provided by CPAs.

Assurance services are independent professional services that improve the quality of information for decision makers. Individuals who are responsible for making business decisions seek assurance services to help improve the reliability and relevance of the information used as the basis for their decisions. Assurance services are valued because the assurance provider is independent and perceived as being unbiased with respect to the information examined.

Assurance services can be performed by CPAs or by a variety of other professionals. For example, Consumers Union is a nonprofit organization that tests a wide variety of products used by consumers and reports their evaluations of the quality of the products tested in *Consumer Reports.* The information provided in *Consumer Reports* is intended to help consumers make intelligent decisions about the products they buy. The information provided in *Consumer Reports* is considered more reliable by many consumers than information provided by the product manufacturers because Consumers Union is independent of the product manufacturers. Similarly, the Better Business Bureau (BBB) online privacy program, BBB*OnLine* Reliability, allows qualifying companies to post the BBB*OnLine* Reliability seal on their Web site. The seal allows Web shoppers to check BBB information about a company and be assured the company will stand behind its service. Other examples of assurances provided by firms other than CPAs include the Nielsen television ratings and Arbitron radio ratings.

BBB*OnLine*[1]

The need for assurance is not new. CPAs have provided many assurance services for years, particularly assurances about historical financial statement information. CPA firms have also performed assurance services related to lotteries and contests to provide assurance that winners were determined in an unbiased fashion in accordance with contest rules. More recently, CPAs have been expanding the types of assurance services they perform to include engagements that provide assurance about other types of information, such as assurance about company financial forecasts and assurance about Web site controls. The demand for assurance services is expected to grow as the demand for forward-looking information increases and as more real-time information becomes available through the Internet.

Attestation Services

One category of assurance services provided by CPAs is attestation services. An **attestation service** is a type of assurance service in which the CPA firm issues a report about the reliability of an assertion that is the responsibility of another party. There are three categories of attestation services: audit of historical financial statements, review of historical financial statements, and other attestation services that may be applied to a broad range of subject matter.

[1]To illustrate or emphasize text material, the authors have identified interesting company or organization Web sites on the Internet. Internet links are noted by icons in the margins, and a brief description and hot link for each site can be found at Prentice Hall's Companion Web Site (CW site), www.prenhall.com/arens.

Audit of Historical Financial Statements An **audit of historical financial statements** is a form of attestation service in which the auditor issues a written report expressing an opinion about whether the financial statements are in material conformity with generally accepted accounting principles. Audits represent the predominant form of assurance performed by CPA firms.

When presenting information in the form of financial statements, the client makes various assertions about its financial condition and results of operations. External users who rely on those financial statements to make business decisions look to the auditor's report as an indication of the statements' reliability. They value the auditor's assurance because of the auditor's independence from the client and knowledge of financial statement reporting matters.

Publicly traded companies in the United States are required to have audits under the federal securities acts. Auditor reports can be found in any public company's annual financial report, and most companies' audited financial statements can be accessed over the Internet from the Securities and Exchange Commission's (SEC's) EDGAR database or directly from the company's Web site. Even before enactment of the federal securities acts, many public companies voluntarily contracted for audits to provide assurance to investors and to facilitate access to capital. Many privately held companies also have annual financial statement audits to obtain financing from banks and other financial institutions. Government and not-for-profit entities often have audits to meet the requirements of lenders or funding sources.

Report Gallery

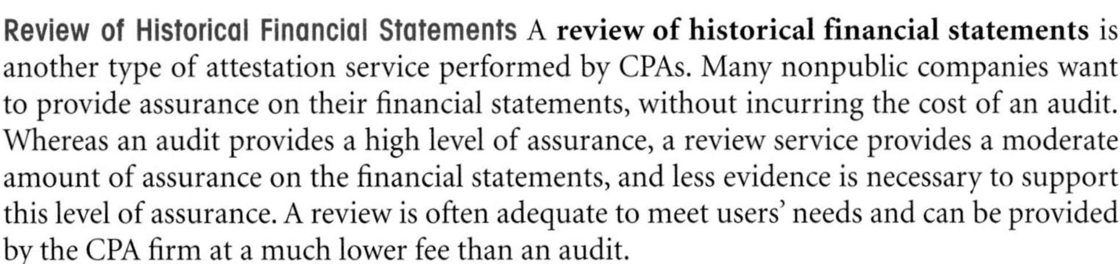

Review of Historical Financial Statements A **review of historical financial statements** is another type of attestation service performed by CPAs. Many nonpublic companies want to provide assurance on their financial statements, without incurring the cost of an audit. Whereas an audit provides a high level of assurance, a review service provides a moderate amount of assurance on the financial statements, and less evidence is necessary to support this level of assurance. A review is often adequate to meet users' needs and can be provided by the CPA firm at a much lower fee than an audit.

Other Attestation Services CPAs provide numerous other attestation services. Many of these services are a natural extension of the audit of historical financial statements, as users seek independent assurances about other types of information. For example, banks often require debtors to engage CPAs to provide assurance about the debtor's compliance with certain financial covenant provisions stated in the loan agreement. CPAs also provide assurance about the effectiveness of a client's internal controls over financial reporting. The information about internal controls is closely related to the financial statements, but it is also forward-looking because effective internal controls reduce the likelihood of future misstatements in the financial statements. CPAs also can attest to the information in a client's forecasted financial statements, which are often used to obtain financing.

Other Assurance Services

AICPA Assurance Services

Most of the other assurance services that CPAs provide do not meet the formal definition of attestation services. They are similar to attestation services in that the CPA must be independent and must provide assurance about information used by decision makers. They differ in that the CPA is not required to issue a written report, and the assurance does not have to be about the reliability of another party's written assertion about compliance with specified criteria. Rather, in these other assurance services engagements, the assurance is about the reliability and relevance of information, which may or may not have been asserted by another party. The common feature of all assurance services, including audits and attestation services, is the focus on improving the quality of information used by decision makers.

The demand for assurance on other types of information is expected to grow substantially with new types of risks faced by businesses and increases in the amount of available information sources. However, one important difference between attestation services and other assurance services is the potential competition faced by CPA firms

**"AND THE OSCAR GOES TO . . ."
"THERE SHE IS, MISS AMERICA . . ."
"WELCOME TO THE NEW YORK STATE LOTTERY . . ."**

You probably recognize these statements from the Academy Awards, the Miss America Pageant, and the New York State Lottery drawing. What you may not recognize is what these well-known events have to do with assurance services. Each event is observed by CPAs from a major accounting firm to assure viewers that the contests were fairly conducted. So when you become a member of a CPA firm, you might not win an Oscar—but you could be on the Oscars!

when performing other assurance services. Audits and many types of attestation services are limited by regulation to licensed CPAs, but the market for other forms of assurance is open to non-CPA competitors. For example, assisting clients in the preparation of customer surveys and evaluation of the reliability and relevance of information developed from those surveys is one potential assurance service that can be provided by CPAs. In the market for those services, CPAs will likely face competition from market research firms. One competitive advantage that CPA firms have in the market for assurance services is their reputation for competence and independence.

Assurance Services on Information Technology One of the major factors affecting the demand for other assurance services is the growth of the Internet and electronic commerce. Concern over privacy and security of information on the Internet has slowed the potential growth of electronic commerce. In addition, the volume of real-time information available on the Internet is shifting the need for assurance from historical information at a point in time, such as financial statements, to assurances about the reliability of processes generating information in a real-time format. For example, many business functions, such as ordering and making payments, are conducted over the Internet and directly between computers using electronic data interchange (EDI). As transactions and information are shared online and in real time, there is even greater demand for assurances about computer controls surrounding information transacted electronically and the security of the information related to the transactions. CPAs can help provide assurance about these functions. Two examples of assurance services related to information technology are assurances over Web site controls and assurances about information system reliability.

WebTrust

- *WebTrust services.* To respond to the growing need for assurance resulting from the explosion of business transacted over the Internet, the American Institute of Certified Public Accountants (AICPA) and the Canadian Institute of Chartered Accountants (CICA) jointly created the *WebTrust* assurance service. CPA firms that are licensed by the AICPA to perform this service provide assurance to users of Web sites through the CPA's electronic *WebTrust* seal affixed to the Web site. This seal assures the user that the Web site owner has met established criteria related to business practices, transaction integrity, and information processes. *WebTrust* is an attestation service, and the *WebTrust* seal is a symbolic representation of the CPA's report on management's assertions about its disclosure of electronic commerce practices. The *WebTrust* family of services includes best practices and e-business solutions for business-to-consumer and business-to-business electronic commerce, for service providers, and for certification authorities. A description of several *WebTrust* assurance services is included in Table 1-1.
- *SysTrust services.* The AICPA and CICA jointly created the *SysTrust* service to provide assurance on information system reliability. *SysTrust* is an attest-type engagement to evaluate and test system reliability in areas such as security and data integrity. Whereas the *WebTrust* assurance service is primarily designed to provide assurance to third-party users of a Web site, *SysTrust* services might be performed by CPAs to provide assurance to management, the board of directors, or third parties about the reliability of information systems used to generate real-time information.

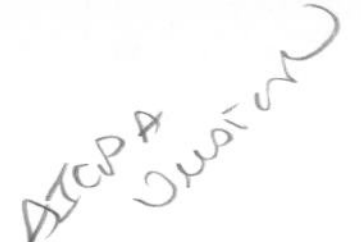

TABLE 1-1 Examples of *WebTrust* Services

WebTrust Program	Description of Assurance
Online privacy	Provides assurance that a Web site protects the privacy of personal information provided by individuals, such as social security numbers
Security	Provides assurance that access to a Web site's system and data is restricted to authorized individuals
Business practices/transaction integrity	Provides assurance that electronic commerce transactions are processed completely and accurately
Availability	Provides assurance that e-commerce systems and data will be available to users when they need it
Certification authorities	Provides assurance on the adequacy and effectiveness of controls used by certification authorities, who have the responsibility of verifying electronic transactions

Assurance Services on Other Types of Information The following is a brief description of three other services developed by the AICPA Special Committee on Assurance Services:

- *CPA Performance View.* Businesses need success factors other than financial information to manage their business. Examples include customer satisfaction and product quality. CPAs can help management identify and measure critical success factors.
- *CPA ElderCare Services.* As the U.S. population ages, elderly individuals increasingly require institutional care. CPAs can provide assurance to family members that care goals are being achieved and that the needs of the elderly person are being met.
- *CPA Risk Advisory Services.* To succeed in the New Economy, businesses must be successful in taking and managing risk. For example, a company expanding globally may face risks from changes in exchange rates or political upheaval in other countries. CPAs providing this service help their clients identify and manage risks.

There are almost no limits to the types of services that CPAs can provide. A survey of large CPA firms performed by the AICPA Special Committee on Assurance Services identified more than 200 assurance services that are currently being provided.

Nonassurance Services Provided by CPAs

CPA firms perform numerous other services that generally fall outside the scope of assurance services. Three specific examples of nonassurance services CPAs often provide include accounting and bookkeeping services, tax services, and management consulting services.

Some overlap exists between management consulting and assurance services. The primary purpose of a management consulting engagement is to generate a recommendation to management, whereas the primary purpose of an assurance services engagement is to improve the quality of information. Although the quality of information is often an important criterion in a consulting engagement, this goal is normally not the primary purpose. For example, a CPA may be engaged to design and install a new information technology

COMPETITION IN NEWSPAPER CIRCULATION AUDITS

One competitive battleground for assurance services is the market for newspaper circulation audits. Newspaper circulation audits are used to determine advertising rates and for promotional purposes. The Audit Bureau of Circulations is the official number counter for the publishing industry, but some newspapers have commissioned audits from other sources, including the largest CPA firms. At issue are the rules for counting paid circulation, since certain complimentary and discounted copies are excluded under rules used by the Audit Bureau of Circulations.

Source: Adapted from an article by Matthew Rose, "Circulation Counting Stirs Debate," *Wall Street Journal* (December 13, 1999), p. B-25.

FIGURE 1-1 Relationships Among Assurance Services, Attestation Services, and Nonassurance Services

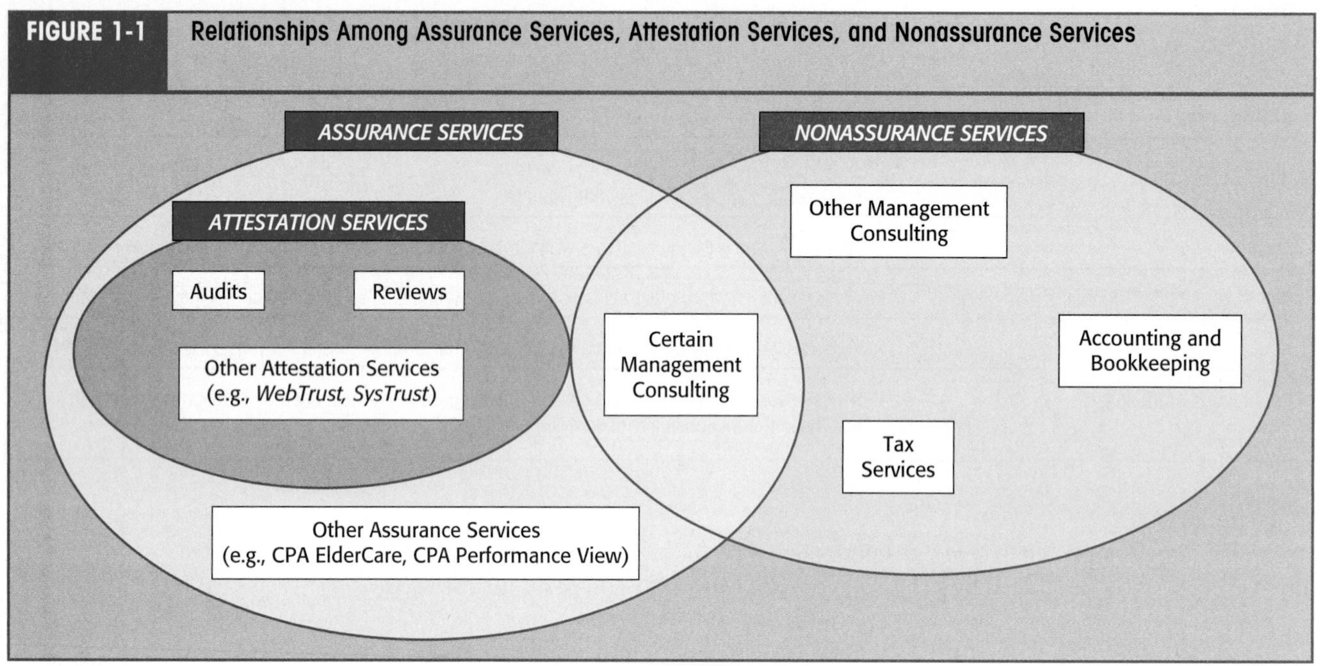

system for a client as a consulting engagement. The purpose of that engagement is to install the new system, with the goal of improved information being a by-product of that engagement. Occasionally, consulting engagements and assurance services overlap when improving the quality of information for decision makers is a primary goal.

CPA firm revenues from management consulting services have increased significantly in recent years. Many large CPA firms have departments involved exclusively in performing management consulting services, which are often called management advisory services (MAS). As these consulting services have expanded, some CPA firms have sold their consulting business to other firms, spun off their consulting practice as a separate entity, or offered shares in the consulting business in a public offering of stock.

Figure 1-1 reflects the relationship between assurance and nonassurance services. Audits, reviews, and other attestation services are all examples of attestation services, which fall under the scope of assurance services. Some of the new assurance services identified by the AICPA, such as *WebTrust* and *SysTrust,* are also attestation services. In contrast, most management consulting services, accounting and bookkeeping services, and tax services fall outside the scope of assurance services, although there is some common area of overlap between consulting and assurance services.

ECONOMIC DEMAND FOR AUDITING

OBJECTIVE 1-2

Explain the causes of information risk and the importance of auditing in reducing this risk.

This book emphasizes the audit of historical financial statements by CPA firms. Because of the need for reliance on the financial statements by external users, there is a well-defined set of standards for the audit of historical financial statements. Also, the ability to issue opinions on financial statements is restricted to licensed CPAs. Many of the skills and concepts necessary to perform an audit of historical financial statements are useful in the performance of other assurance services.

To illustrate the need for auditing, consider the decision of a bank manager in making a loan to a business. This decision will be based on such factors as previous financial relationships with the business and the financial condition of the business as reflected by its financial statements. If the bank makes the loan, it will charge a rate of interest determined primarily by three factors:

1. *Risk-free interest rate.* This is approximately the rate the bank could earn by investing in U.S. treasury notes for the same length of time as the business loan.

2. *Business risk for the customer.* This risk reflects the possibility that the business will not be able to repay its loan because of economic or business conditions such as a recession, poor management decisions, or unexpected competition in the industry.
3. *Information risk.* **Information risk** reflects the possibility that the information upon which the business risk decision was made was inaccurate. A likely cause of the information risk is the possibility of inaccurate financial statements.

Auditing has no effect on either the risk-free interest rate or business risk, but it can have a significant effect on information risk. If the bank manager is satisfied that there is minimal information risk because a borrower's financial statements are audited, the risk is substantially reduced and the overall interest rate to the borrower can be reduced. The reduction of information risk can have a significant effect on the borrower's ability to obtain capital at a reasonable cost. For example, assume a large company has total interest-bearing debt of approximately $10 billion. If the interest rate on that debt is reduced by only 1 percent, the annual savings in interest is $100 million.

Causes of Information Risk

As society becomes more complex, decision makers are more likely to receive unreliable information. There are several reasons for this: remoteness of information, biases and motives of the provider, voluminous data, and the existence of complex exchange transactions.

Remoteness of Information In the modern world, it is virtually impossible for a decision maker to have much firsthand knowledge about the organization with which he or she does business. Information provided by others must be relied upon. When information is obtained from others, the likelihood of it being intentionally or unintentionally misstated increases.

Biases and Motives of the Provider If information is provided by someone whose goals are inconsistent with those of the decision maker, the information may be biased in favor of the provider. The reason could be an honest optimism about future events or an intentional emphasis designed to influence users in a certain manner. In either case, the result is a misstatement of information. For example, in a lending decision in which the borrower provides financial statements to the lender, there is considerable likelihood that the borrower will bias the statements to increase the chance of obtaining a loan. The misstatement could be in the form of outright incorrect dollar amounts or inadequate or incomplete disclosures of information.

Voluminous Data As organizations become larger, so does the volume of their exchange transactions. This increases the likelihood that improperly recorded information will be included in the records—perhaps buried in a large amount of other information. For example, if a large government agency overpays a vendor's invoice by $2,000, there is a fairly good chance that it will not be uncovered unless the agency has instituted reasonably complex procedures to find this type of misstatement. If many minor misstatements remain undiscovered, the combined total could be significant.

Complex Exchange Transactions In the past few decades, exchange transactions between organizations have become increasingly complex and therefore more difficult to record properly. For example, the correct accounting treatment of the acquisition of one entity by another poses relatively difficult and important accounting problems. Other examples include properly combining and disclosing the results of operations of subsidiaries in different industries and properly disclosing derivative financial instruments under Financial Accounting Standards Board Statement No. 133 (SFAS 133).

Reducing Information Risk

Business managers and financial statement users may conclude that the best way to deal with information risk is simply to have it remain reasonably high. A small company may find it less expensive to pay higher interest costs than to increase the costs of reducing information risk.

For larger businesses, it is usually practical to incur costs to reduce information risk. There are three main ways to do so.

CAPITAL COSTS TO SHRINK

According to an article in *Accounting Today,* corporate America is paying too much for new capital and independent auditors are part of the solution. Robert Elliott, a senior partner with KPMG, believes the cost of capital could shrink significantly as a result of advances in technology, streamlined regulations, and broader audit coverage.

Elliott uses a hypothetical example to illustrate his prediction. Assuming a cost of capital of 13%, he estimates this rate is composed of the following:

- 5.5% risk-free interest rate
- 3.5% economic risk premium *(business risk)*
- 4% information cost *(information risk)*

According to Elliott's example, information risk comprises approximately 30% of the cost of capital. Elliott believes the following factors will drastically reduce information risk:

- Technological advances will drastically decrease the cost of providing relevant and timely information to investors.
- As more companies go "online," the risk of investors obtaining outdated information decreases.
- New accounting and auditing standards already require better disclosures about segment operations, risks, and uncertainties. New rules may require data on nonfinancial performance and forward-looking information.
- Auditors will find more efficient ways to audit, such as continuous auditing of computerized control systems, which may provide new levels of assurance.

Elliott predicts that if and when all of the preceding factors materialize, the cost of capital in his hypothetical example could be reduced from 13% to 11.5%. The entire reduction would result from reduced information risk.

Source: Adapted from *Accounting Today* (December 11, 1995), p. 16.

User Verifies Information The user may go to the business premises to examine records and obtain information about the reliability of the statements. Normally, this is impractical because of costs. In addition, it would be economically inefficient for all users to verify the information individually. Nevertheless, some users perform their own verification. For example, the Internal Revenue Service (IRS) does considerable verification of businesses and individuals to determine whether tax returns filed reflect the actual tax due the federal government. Similarly, if a business intends to purchase another business, it is common for the purchaser to use a special audit team to independently verify and evaluate key information of the prospective business.

User Shares Information Risk with Management There is considerable legal precedent indicating that management is responsible for providing reliable information to users. If users rely on inaccurate financial statements and as a result incur a financial loss, there is a basis for a lawsuit against management. A difficulty with sharing information risk with management is that users may not be able to collect on losses. If a company is unable to repay a loan because of bankruptcy, it is unlikely that management will have sufficient funds to repay users.

Audited Financial Statements Are Provided The most common way for users to obtain reliable information is to have an independent audit performed. The audited information is then used in the decision-making process on the assumption that it is reasonably complete, accurate, and unbiased.

Typically, management engages the auditor to provide assurances to users that the financial statements are reliable. If the financial statements are ultimately determined to be incorrect, the auditor can be sued by both the users and management. Auditors obviously have considerable legal responsibility for their work.

NATURE OF AUDITING

OBJECTIVE 1-3

Describe auditing and distinguish between auditing and accounting.

So far, we have discussed the importance of audits of financial statements and their relation to other attestation and assurance services offered by CPA firms. We now examine auditing more specifically using the following definition:

Auditing is the accumulation and evaluation of evidence about information to determine and report on the degree of correspondence between the information and established criteria. Auditing should be done by a competent, independent person.

This definition of the auditing process is considerably broader than the definition of an audit of historical financial statements and encompasses many attestation and assurance service activities. The definition also includes several key words and phrases. For ease of understanding, the terms are discussed in a different order than they occur in the description.

Information and Established Criteria

To do an audit, there must be information in a *verifiable form* and some standards (*criteria*) by which the auditor can evaluate the information. Information can and does take many forms. Auditors routinely perform audits of quantifiable information, including companies' financial statements and individuals' federal income tax returns. Auditors also perform audits of more subjective information, such as the effectiveness of computer systems and the efficiency of manufacturing operations.

The criteria for evaluating information also vary depending on the information being audited. For example, in the audit of historical financial statements by CPA firms, the criteria are usually generally accepted accounting principles. To illustrate, this means that in the audit of Boeing's financial statements, the CPA firm determines whether Boeing's financial statements have been prepared in accordance with generally accepted accounting principles. For the audit of tax returns by the IRS, the criteria are found in the Internal Revenue Code. In the audit of Boeing's corporate tax return by the IRS, the internal revenue agent would use the Internal Revenue Code as the criteria for correctness, not generally accepted accounting principles.

For more subjective information, such as auditing the effectiveness of specific aspects of computer operations, it is more difficult to establish criteria. Typically, auditors and the entities being audited agree on the criteria well before the audit starts. For a computer application, for example, the criteria might include the absence of input or output errors.

Accumulating and Evaluating Evidence

Evidence is any information used by the auditor to determine whether the information being audited is stated in accordance with the established criteria. Evidence takes many different forms, including oral testimony of the auditee (client), written communication with outsiders, observations by the auditor, and electronic data about transactions. It is important to obtain a sufficient quality and volume of evidence to satisfy the purpose of the audit. Determining the types and amount of evidence necessary and evaluating whether the information corresponds to the established criteria is a critical part of every audit. It is the primary subject of this book.

Competent, Independent Person

The auditor must be qualified to understand the criteria used and must be *competent* to know the types and amount of evidence to accumulate to reach the proper conclusion after the evidence has been examined. The auditor must also have an *independent mental attitude.* The competence of the individual performing the audit is of little value if he or she is biased in the accumulation and evaluation of evidence.

Auditors reporting on company financial statements are often called **independent auditors.** Even though an auditor of published financial statements is paid a fee by a company, he or she is normally sufficiently independent to conduct audits that can be relied on by users. Although absolute independence is impossible, auditors strive to maintain a high level of independence to keep the confidence of users relying on their reports. Although internal auditors work for the company, they usually report directly to top management to help maintain independence from the operating units being audited.

Reporting

The final stage in the auditing process is preparing the **audit report,** which is the communication of the auditor's findings to users. Reports differ in nature, but all must inform readers of the degree of correspondence between information and established criteria. Reports also differ in form and can vary from the highly technical type usually associated with financial statement audits to a simple oral report in the case of an operational audit of a small department's effectiveness.

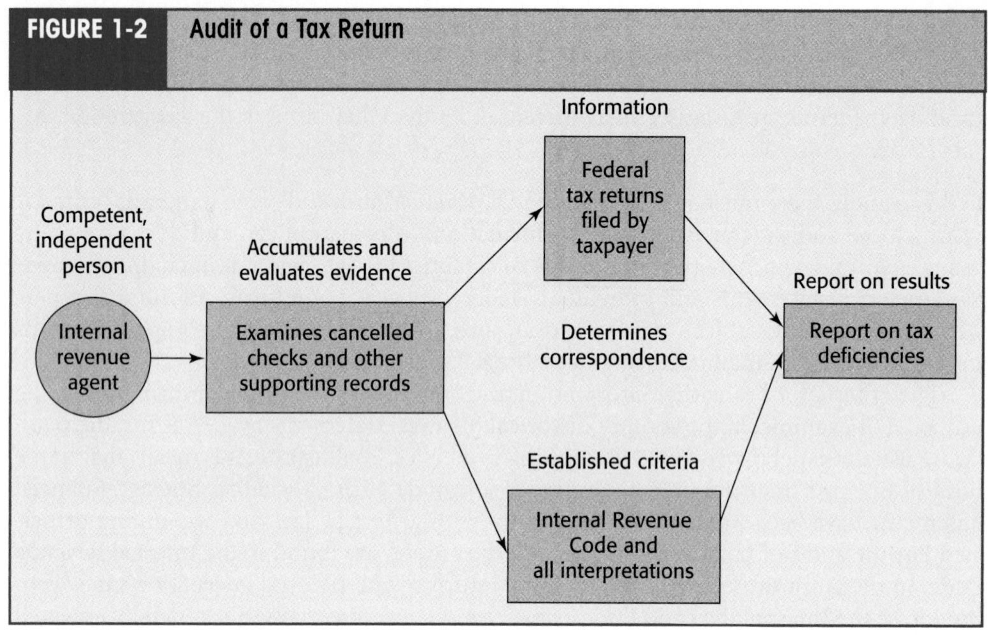

Figure 1-2 summarizes the important ideas in the description of auditing by illustrating an audit of an individual's tax return by an internal revenue agent. The objective is to determine whether the tax return was prepared in a manner consistent with the requirements of the federal Internal Revenue Code. To accomplish the objective, the agent examines supporting records provided by the taxpayer and from other sources, such as the taxpayer's employer. After completing the audit, the internal revenue agent will issue a report to the taxpayer assessing additional taxes, advising that a refund is due, or stating that there is no change in the status of the tax return.

Distinction Between Auditing and Accounting

Many financial statement users and members of the general public confuse auditing with accounting. The confusion results because most auditing is usually concerned with accounting information, and many auditors have considerable expertise in accounting matters. The confusion is increased by giving the title "certified public accountant" to many individuals who perform audits.

Accounting is the recording, classifying, and summarizing of economic events in a logical manner for the purpose of providing financial information for decision making. The function of accounting is to provide certain types of quantitative information that management and others can use to make decisions. To provide relevant information, accountants must have a thorough understanding of the principles and rules that provide the basis for preparing the accounting information. In addition, accountants must develop a system to make sure that the entity's economic events are properly recorded on a timely basis and at a reasonable cost.

In auditing accounting data, the concern is with determining whether recorded information properly reflects the economic events that occurred during the accounting period. Because accounting rules are the criteria for evaluating whether the accounting information is properly recorded, any auditor involved with these data must also thoroughly understand those rules. In the context of the audit of financial statements, the rules are generally accepted accounting principles. Throughout this text, the assumption is made that the reader has already studied generally accepted accounting principles.

In addition to understanding accounting, the auditor must possess expertise in the accumulation and interpretation of audit evidence. It is this expertise that distinguishes auditors from accountants. Determining the proper audit procedures, deciding the number and types of items to test, and evaluating the results are problems unique to the auditor.

TYPES OF AUDITS

OBJECTIVE 1-4

Differentiate the three main types of audits.

CPAs perform three primary types of audits: operational audits, compliance audits, and financial statement audits. The first two services are often called audit activities, even though they are most similar to assurance and attestation services. We now examine each of the three types of audits in more detail.

Operational Audits

An **operational audit** is a review of any part of an organization's operating procedures and methods for the purpose of evaluating *efficiency* and *effectiveness.* At the completion of an operational audit, management normally expects recommendations for improving operations. An example of an operational audit is evaluating the efficiency and accuracy of processing payroll transactions in a newly installed computer system. Another example, where most accountants would feel less qualified, is evaluating the efficiency, accuracy, and customer satisfaction in processing the distribution of letters and packages by a company such as Federal Express.

Because of the many different areas in which operational effectiveness can be evaluated, it is impossible to characterize the conduct of a typical operational audit. In one organization, the auditor might evaluate the relevancy and sufficiency of the information used by management in making decisions to acquire new fixed assets, whereas in a different organization, the auditor might evaluate the efficiency of the information flow in processing sales. In operational auditing, the reviews are not limited to accounting. They can include the evaluation of organization structure, computer operations, production methods, marketing, and any other area in which the auditor is qualified.

The conduct of an operational audit and the reported results are less easily defined than for either of the other two types of audits. Efficiency and effectiveness of operations are far more difficult to evaluate objectively than compliance or the presentation of financial statements in accordance with generally accepted accounting principles. In addition, establishing criteria for evaluating the information in an operational audit is an extremely subjective matter. In this sense, operational auditing is more like management consulting than what is generally regarded as auditing.

Compliance Audits

The purpose of a **compliance audit** is to determine whether the auditee is following specific procedures, rules, or regulations set by some higher authority. A compliance audit for a private business could include determining whether accounting personnel are following the procedures prescribed by the company controller, reviewing wage rates for compliance with minimum wage laws, or examining contractual agreements with bankers and other lenders to be sure the company is complying with legal requirements. In the audit of governmental units such as school districts, there is considerable compliance auditing because of the extensive regulation by higher government authorities. In virtually every private and not-for-profit organization, there are prescribed policies, contractual agreements, and legal requirements that may call for compliance auditing.

Financial Statement Audits

A **financial statement audit** is conducted to determine whether the overall financial statements (the information being verified) are stated in accordance with specified criteria. Normally, the criteria are generally accepted accounting principles (GAAP), although it is also common to conduct audits of financial statements prepared using the cash basis or some other basis of accounting appropriate for the organization. The financial statements most often included are the statement of financial position, income statement, and statement of cash flows, including accompanying footnotes.

In determining whether financial statements are fairly stated in accordance with GAAP, the auditor performs appropriate tests to determine whether the statements contain material errors or other misstatements. An integrated approach to auditing considers both the risk of errors and operating controls intended to prevent errors. Increasingly, this integrated approach incorporates a strategic perspective of the business entity.

As businesses increase in complexity, it is no longer sufficient for auditors to focus narrowly on accounting transactions. In a **strategic systems audit** approach, the auditor must have a thorough understanding of the entity and its environment. This holistic, top-level

TABLE 1-2	Examples of the Three Types of Audits			
Type of Audit	**Example**	**Information**	**Established Criteria**	**Available Evidence**
Operational audit	Evaluate whether the computerized payroll processing for subsidiary H is operating efficiently and effectively	Number of payroll records processed in a month, costs of the department, and number of errors made	Company standards for efficiency and effectiveness in payroll department	Error reports, payroll records, and payroll processing costs
Compliance audit	Determine whether bank requirements for loan continuation have been met	Company records	Loan agreement provisions	Financial statements and calculations by the auditor
Financial statement audit	Annual audit of Boeing's financial statements	Boeing's financial statements	Generally accepted accounting principles	Documents, records, and outside sources of evidence

understanding includes knowledge of the client's industry and its regulatory and operating environment, including external relationships, such as suppliers, customers, and creditors. In addition, the auditor considers the client's business strategies and processes and measurement indicators for critical success factors related to those strategies. This analysis helps the auditor identify risks associated with the client's strategies that may affect whether the financial statements are fairly stated. Many of the skills necessary for the strategic systems audit approach are similar to those needed to provide other types of assurance services that can provide added value to the audit function.

Table 1-2 summarizes the three types of audits and includes an example of each type and an illustration of three of the key parts of the definition of auditing applied to each type of audit.

TYPES OF AUDITORS

OBJECTIVE 1-5

Identify the primary types of auditors.

Several types of auditors are in practice today. The most common are certified public accounting firms, general accounting office auditors, internal revenue agents, and internal auditors.

Certified Public Accounting Firms

Certified public accounting firms are responsible for auditing the published historical financial statements of all publicly traded companies, most other reasonably large companies, and many smaller companies and noncommercial organizations. Because of the widespread use of audited financial statements in the U.S. economy, as well as businesspersons' and other users' familiarity with these statements, it is common to use the terms *auditor* and *CPA firm* synonymously, even though several different types of auditors exist. The title *certified public accounting firm* reflects the fact that auditors who express audit opinions on financial statements must be licensed as CPAs. CPA firms are often called *external auditors* or *independent auditors* to distinguish them from internal auditors.

More than 40,000 CPA firms exist in the United States, ranging in size from 1 person to more than 30,000 partners and staff. Four size categories are used to describe CPA firms: Big Five international firms, national firms, regional and large local firms, and small local firms.

- *Big Five international firms.* The five largest CPA firms in the United States are called the "Big Five" international CPA firms. These five firms have offices in cities throughout the United States and in many cities throughout the world. The Big Five firms audit nearly all of the largest companies both in the United States and worldwide and many smaller companies as well.

- *National firms.* Three CPA firms in the United States are called national firms because they have offices in most major cities. The national firms perform the same services as the Big Five firms and compete directly with them for clients. Each national firm is affiliated with firms in other countries and therefore has an international capability.
- *Regional and large local firms.* There are only approximately 100 CPA firms with professional staffs of more than 50 people. Some have only one office and serve clients primarily within commuting distance. Others have several offices in a state or region and serve a larger radius of clients. Regional and large local firms compete for clients with other CPA firms, including national and Big Five firms.
- *Small local firms.* More than 95 percent of all CPA firms have fewer than 25 professionals in a single-office firm. They perform audits and related services primarily for smaller businesses and not-for-profit entities, although some have one or two clients with public ownership. Many small local firms do not perform audits and primarily provide accounting and tax services to their clients.

Big Five, National, and Regional Firms

As discussed earlier, CPA firms provide audit services and have expanded their scope of services to provide additional attestation and assurance services. Additional services commonly provided by CPA firms include accounting and bookkeeping services, tax services, and management consulting services. CPA firms continue to develop new products and services, including financial planning, business valuation, forensic accounting, internal audit outsourcing, and information technology advisory services.

General Accounting Office Auditors

The United States General Accounting Office (GAO) is a nonpartisan agency in the legislative branch of the federal government. A **general accounting office auditor** is an auditor working for the GAO. The GAO, which is headed by the Comptroller General, reports to and is responsible solely to Congress. The audit staff's primary responsibility is to perform the audit function for Congress.

Many of the GAO's audit responsibilities are the same as those of a CPA firm. Much of the financial information prepared by various government agencies is audited by the GAO before it is submitted to Congress. Because the authority for expenditures and receipts of governmental agencies is defined by law, there is considerable emphasis on compliance in these audits.

Auditing Careers

An increasing portion of the GAO's audit efforts has been devoted to evaluating the *operational efficiency and effectiveness* of various federal programs. An example is the evaluation of the computer operations of a governmental unit. The auditor can review and evaluate any aspect of the computer system but is likely to emphasize the adequacy of the equipment, the efficiency of the operations, the adequacy and usefulness of the output, and similar matters, with the objective of identifying means of providing the same services at a lower cost.

Internal Revenue Agents

The IRS, under the direction of the Commissioner of Internal Revenue, is responsible for enforcing the *federal tax laws* as they have been defined by Congress and interpreted by the courts. A major responsibility of the IRS is to audit the taxpayers' returns to determine whether they have complied with the tax laws. The auditors who perform these examinations are called **internal revenue agents.** These audits are solely compliance audits.

It might seem that the audit of returns for compliance with the federal tax laws would be a simple and straightforward problem, but nothing could be farther from the truth. The tax laws are highly complicated, and there are hundreds of volumes of interpretations. The tax returns being audited vary from the simple returns of individuals who work for only one employer and take the standard tax deduction to the highly complex returns of multinational corporations. Taxation problems involve individual taxpayers, gift taxes, estate taxes, corporate taxes, trusts, and so on. An auditor involved in any of these areas must have considerable tax knowledge and auditing skills to conduct an effective audit.

Internal Auditors

Internal auditors are employed by individual companies to audit for management much as the GAO does for Congress. The internal audit group in some large firms can include more than 100 people and typically reports directly to the president, another high executive officer, or the audit committee of the board of directors.

Internal auditors' responsibilities vary considerably, depending on the employer. Some internal audit staffs consist of only one or two employees who may spend most of their time doing routine compliance auditing. Other internal audit staffs consist of numerous employees who have diverse responsibilities, including many outside the accounting area. Many internal auditors are involved in operational auditing or have expertise in evaluating computer systems.

To operate effectively, an internal auditor must be independent of the line functions in an organization, but he or she cannot be independent of the entity as long as an employer-employee relationship exists. Internal auditors provide management with valuable information for making decisions concerning effective operation of its business. Users from outside the entity are unlikely to want to rely on information verified solely by internal auditors because of their lack of independence. This lack of independence is the major difference between internal auditors and CPA firms.

E-COMMERCE AND CPA FIRM OPERATIONS

OBJECTIVE 1-6

Discuss how e-commerce and the Internet affect CPA firm operations.

Almost all businesses rely on information technology to assist in accounting for business transactions. Advances in information technologies and the explosion of the Internet continue to introduce new ways for conducting business electronically, often referred to as **e-commerce.** As these developments continue, businesses will expand their reliance on those technologies.

Like all industries, CPA firms are using the Internet to market their services. Firms of all sizes use the Internet to highlight such things as office locations or affiliations, service lines, and industry specializations and provide reference tools and materials to existing and potential clients. Firm Web sites feature news and insights about business issues, such as updates on changes in tax laws and calculators to determine which type of retirement account to choose. Firm Web sites also feature online software tools and databases to subscribers who pay a fee. For example, Ernst and Young sells its *Accounting and Auditing Tool Kit* to subscribers through its Ernst and Young *Online* Web site. PricewaterhouseCoopers LLP, through an alliance with Watchfire^{sm}, offers a privacy management software tool, *WatchfireWebCPO*, that provides protection to online information.

CPA firms also use the Internet to connect their global professional staff. Firm personnel from around the world can contribute services to a client on a timely basis without having to be physically present at the client's location. Communicating electronically among firm personnel is especially advantageous for firms that serve multinational clients with operations around the globe. For example, personnel in New York, Tokyo, and London who have expertise in local regulations and business cultures can serve local clients and branches of international clients with operations in those cities, and can also communicate with engagement team personnel serving those clients in other locations.

CPA firms are also taking advantage of online resources and databases that can be accessed through the Internet. These resources are useful to CPAs for staying current on emerging business and standards-setting issues. Databases, such as *Standard and Poor's Net Advantage Database* and *Goldman Sachs Research Database*, provide extensive industry-specific information and coverage of companies that CPAs use on a subscription basis to stay current on industry developments and to obtain industry data useful for auditing and consulting.

CERTIFIED PUBLIC ACCOUNTANT

OBJECTIVE 1-7

Describe the requirements for becoming a CPA.

Use of the title **certified public accountant** (CPA) is regulated by state law through the licensing departments of each state. Within any state, the regulations usually differ for becoming a CPA and retaining a license to practice after the designation has been initially achieved. To become a CPA, three requirements must be met. These are: educational, passing the CPA exam, and experience.

For a person planning to become a CPA, it is essential to know the requirements in the state where he or she plans to obtain and maintain the CPA designation. The best source of that information is the State Board of Accountancy for the state in which the person plans to be certified. It is possible to transfer the CPA designation from one state to another, but additional requirements often must be met for formal education, practice experience, or continuing education.

Most young professionals who want to become CPAs start their careers working for a CPA firm. After they become CPAs, many leave the firm to work in industry, government, or education. These people may continue to be CPAs but often give up their right to practice as independent auditors. CPAs who practice as independent auditors must meet defined continuing education and licensing requirements to maintain their right to practice in most states. Therefore, it is common for accountants to be CPAs who do not practice as independent auditors.

CPA Information and Requirements

Additional information about the CPA examination can be found in the *Uniform CPA Examination Brochure* and the *Uniform CPA Examination Content Specification Outline*, both which can be downloaded from the AICPA Web site (www.aicpa.org). The AICPA also publishes selected examination questions with unofficial answers that are indexed to the content specification outlines of the examination. Ordering information, as well as other information for CPA candidates, can be found at the AICPA Web site.

Some of the questions and problems at the end of the chapters in this book have been taken from past CPA examinations. They are designated "AICPA" or "AICPA adapted."

AMERICAN INSTITUTE OF CERTIFIED PUBLIC ACCOUNTANTS (AICPA)

OBJECTIVE 1-8

Describe the AICPA and its role in setting standards.

CPA firms provide oversight of individual firm members, but more formal regulatory bodies also exist. Although CPAs are licensed by the state in which they practice, the most important influence on CPAs is exerted by their national professional organization, the American Institute of Certified Public Accountants (**AICPA**). Membership in the AICPA is restricted to CPAs and currently exceeds 330,000, but not all members are practicing as independent auditors. Many members formerly worked for CPA firms but are currently working in government, industry, and education. AICPA membership is not required of CPAs. Because it is a voluntary organization, not all CPAs are members of the AICPA. However, the AICPA estimates that three out of every four CPAs in the United States are members of the AICPA.

The AICPA sets professional requirements for CPAs, conducts research, and publishes materials on many different subjects related to accounting, auditing, attestation and assurance services, management consulting services, and taxes. The AICPA is also an advocate for the accounting profession. Initiatives undertaken by the AICPA to promote CPA services include national advertising campaigns, development of specialist certifications, and the efforts of the Special Committee on Assurance Services to develop and promote new assurance services.

VISION FOR THE FUTURE

CPA Vision Project

The AICPA has established the CPA Vision Project to provide a core purpose and vision for the CPA profession in the year 2011 and beyond. The core purpose of the CPA Vision Project is "CPAs . . . making sense of a changing and complex world."

The CPA Vision Project has identified five core values, core competencies, core services, and issues for the future. The top five highest rated issues for the future are as follows:

- The future success of the CPA profession relies a great deal on public perceptions of CPAs' abilities and roles.
- CPAs must become market driven and not dependent on regulations to keep them in business.
- The market demands less audit and accounting and more value-adding consulting services.
- Specialization is critical for the future of the CPA profession.
- The market demands that CPAs be conversant in global business practices and strategies.

Establishing Standards and Rules

The AICPA is empowered to set standards (guidelines) and rules that all members and other practicing CPAs must follow. The requirements are set by committees made up of AICPA members. There are three major areas relevant to assurance services and CPAs in which the AICPA has authority to set standards and make rules.

1. *Auditing standards.* The Auditing Standards Board (ASB) is responsible for issuing pronouncements on auditing matters. They are called **Statements on Auditing Standards (SASs).** The ASB and its predecessor organizations have been responsible for a considerable portion of the existing auditing literature. The SASs are examined later in this chapter and discussed throughout the text.
2. *Other attestation standards.* Statement on Standards for Attestation Engagements was first issued in 1986 to provide a framework for attest engagements performed by practitioners and for the development of standards for those engagements. As the demand for attestation engagements increased, detailed standards were developed for specific types of attestation services. In 2001, the Auditing Standards Board issued SSAE 10, which supercedes the previously issued standards and recodifies standards for performing attestation engagements. The purpose of the standard is to improve the usefulness of the attestation standards and provide greater flexibility to practitioners in providing assurance services. Reports on prospective financial information in forecasts and projections is an example of an attestation service for which specific requirements have been developed.
3. *Code of Professional Conduct.* The AICPA Committee on Professional Ethics sets rules of conduct that CPAs are required to meet. These rules apply to all services performed by CPAs and provide a framework for the technical standards. The rules and their relationships to ethical conduct are the subject of Chapter 3.

GENERALLY ACCEPTED AUDITING STANDARDS

OBJECTIVE 1-9

Use generally accepted auditing standards as a basis for further study.

As noted in the previous section, setting auditing standards is one of the functions of the AICPA. Auditing standards are general guidelines to aid auditors in fulfilling their professional responsibilities in the audit of historical financial statements. They include consideration of professional qualities such as competence and independence, reporting requirements, and evidence.

The broadest guidelines available are the 10 **generally accepted auditing standards (GAAS).** Developed by the AICPA in 1947, they have, with minimal changes, remained the same. These standards are not sufficiently specific to provide any meaningful guide to practitioners, but they do represent a framework upon which the AICPA can provide interpretations. These 10 standards are stated in their entirety in Table 1-3.

There are three categories for the 10 generally accepted auditing standards: general standards, standards of field work, and reporting standards. The standards for each category are discussed next and are summarized in Figure 1-3 (p. 20).

General Standards

The general standards stress the important personal qualities that the auditor should possess.

Adequate Technical Training and Proficiency The first general standard is normally interpreted as requiring the auditor to have formal education in auditing and accounting, adequate practical experience for the work being performed, and continuing professional education. Recent court cases clearly demonstrate that auditors must be technically qualified and experienced in those industries in which their audit clients are engaged.

In any case in which the CPA or the CPA's assistants are not qualified to perform the work, a professional obligation exists to acquire the requisite knowledge and skills, suggest someone else who is qualified to perform the work, or decline the engagement.

Independence in Mental Attitude The importance of independence was stressed earlier in the chapter under the definition of auditing. The *Code of Professional Conduct* and SASs stress the need for independence. CPA firms are required to follow several practices to increase

TABLE 1-3 Generally Accepted Auditing Standards

General Standards

1. The audit is to be performed by a person or persons having adequate technical training and proficiency as an auditor.
2. In all matters relating to the assignment, an independence in mental attitude is to be maintained by the auditor or auditors.
3. Due professional care is to be exercised in the planning and performance of the audit and the preparation of the report.

Standards of Field Work

1. The work is to be adequately planned and assistants, if any, are to be properly supervised.
2. A sufficient understanding of internal control is to be obtained to plan the audit and to determine the nature, timing, and extent of tests to be performed.
3. Sufficient competent evidential matter is to be obtained through inspection, observation, inquiries, and confirmations to afford a reasonable basis for an opinion regarding the financial statements under audit.

Standards of Reporting

1. The report shall state whether the financial statements are presented in accordance with generally accepted accounting principles.
2. The report shall identify those circumstances in which such principles have not been consistently observed in the current period in relation to the preceding period.
3. Informative disclosures in the financial statements are to be regarded as reasonably adequate unless otherwise stated in the report.
4. The report shall either contain an expression of opinion regarding the financial statements, taken as a whole, or an assertion to the effect that an opinion cannot be expressed. When an overall opinion cannot be expressed, the reasons therefor should be stated. In all cases where an auditor's name is associated with financial statements, the report should contain a clear-cut indication of the character of the auditor's work, if any, and the degree of responsibility the auditor is taking.

the likelihood of independence of all personnel. For example, there are established procedures on larger audits when there is a dispute between management and the auditors. Specific methods to ensure that auditors maintain their independence are studied in Chapter 3.

Due Professional Care The third general standard involves due care in the performance of all aspects of auditing. Simply stated, this means that auditors are professionals responsible for fulfilling their duties diligently and carefully. As an illustration, due care includes consideration of the completeness of the audit documentation, the sufficiency of the audit evidence, and the appropriateness of the audit report. As a professional, the auditor must avoid negligence and bad faith, but the auditor is not expected to make perfect judgments in every instance.

Standards of Field Work

The standards of field work concern evidence accumulation and other activities during the actual conduct of the audit.

Adequate Planning and Supervision The first standard deals with ascertaining that the engagement is sufficiently planned to ensure an adequate audit and proper supervision of assistants. Supervision is essential in auditing because a considerable portion of the field work is done by less experienced staff members.

Understand the Client's Internal Control One of the most widely accepted concepts in the theory and practice of auditing is the importance of the client's system of internal control to generate reliable financial information. If the auditor is convinced that the client has an excellent system of internal control, one that includes adequate internal controls for providing reliable data and for safeguarding assets and records, the amount of audit evidence to be accumulated can be significantly less than when controls are not adequate. In some instances, internal control may be so inadequate as to preclude conducting an effective audit.

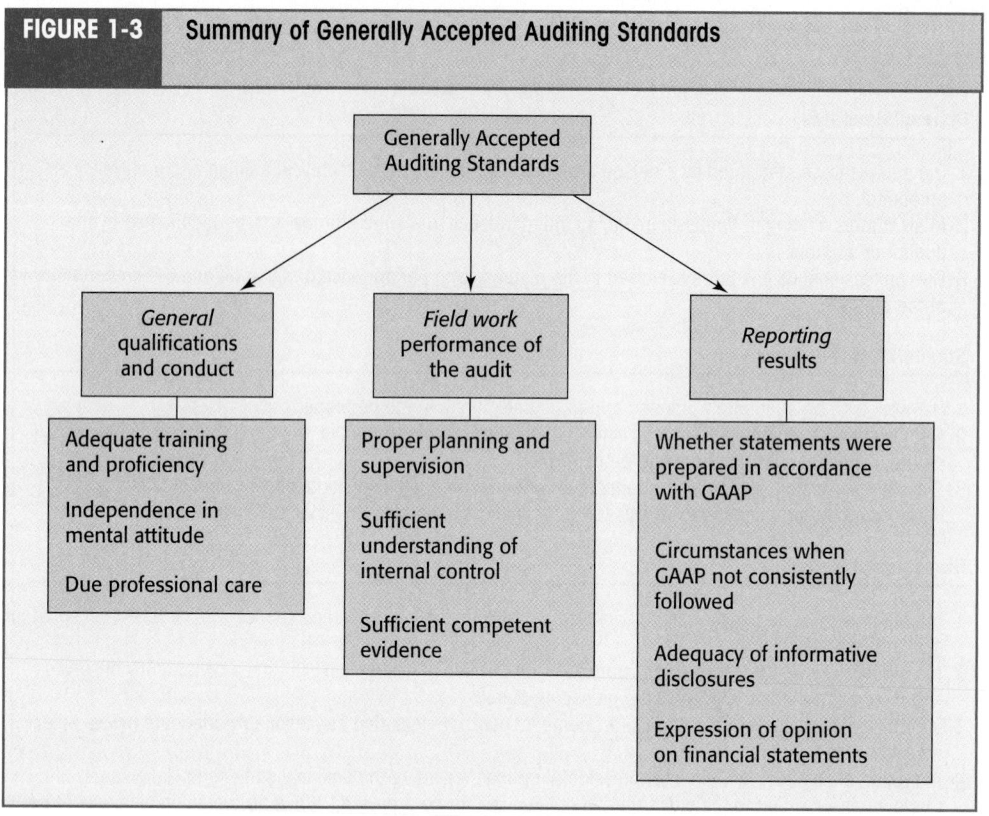

Sufficient Competent Evidence The decisions about how much and what types of evidence to accumulate for a given set of circumstances are ones requiring professional judgment. A major portion of this book is concerned with the study of evidence accumulation and the circumstances affecting the amount and types needed.

Standards of Reporting

The four reporting standards require the auditor to prepare a report on the financial statements taken as a whole, including informative disclosures. The reporting standards require that the report state whether the statements are presented in accordance with generally accepted accounting principles and also identify any circumstances in which generally accepted accounting principles have not been consistently applied in the current year compared with the previous one.

STATEMENTS ON AUDITING STANDARDS

The 10 generally accepted auditing standards are too general to provide meaningful guidance to auditors. More specific guidance is found in the SASs issued by the Auditing Standards Board of the AICPA. SASs interpret the 10 generally accepted auditing standards and are the most authoritative references available to auditors. These statements have the status of GAAS and are often referred to as auditing standards or GAAS, even though they are not part of the 10 generally accepted auditing standards. This book follows common practice and refers to these interpretations as auditing standards or SASs. Generally accepted auditing standards and SASs are regarded as *authoritative* literature, and every member who performs audits of historical financial statements is required to follow them under the AICPA *Code of Professional Conduct.* New statements are issued when an auditing problem arises of sufficient importance to warrant an official interpretation by the AICPA. At this writing, SAS 94 was the last one issued and incorporated into the text materials. Readers should be alert to subsequent standards that influence auditing requirements.

All SASs are given two classification numbers: an SAS and an AU number. For example, the Statement on Auditing Standards, *The Relationship of Generally Accepted Auditing Standards to Quality Control Standards,* is SAS 25 and AU 161. The SAS number identifies the order in which it was issued in relation to other SASs; the AU number identifies its location in the AICPA codification of all SASs. For example, AUs beginning with a "2" are always interpretations of the general standards. Those beginning with a "3" are related to field work standards, and those beginning with a "4," "5," or "6" deal with reporting standards. Both classification systems are used in practice.

Although GAAS and the SASs are the authoritative auditing guidelines for members of the profession, they provide less direction to auditors than might be assumed. There are almost no specific audit procedures required by the standards, and there are no specific requirements for auditors' decisions, such as determining sample size, selecting sample items from the population for testing, or evaluating results. Many practitioners believe that the standards should provide more clearly defined guidelines for determining the extent of evidence to be accumulated. Such specificity would eliminate some difficult audit decisions and provide a line of defense for a CPA firm charged with conducting an inadequate audit. However, highly specific requirements could turn auditing into mechanistic evidence gathering, devoid of professional judgment. From the point of view of both the profession and the users of auditing services, there is probably greater harm in defining authoritative guidelines too specifically than too broadly.

GAAS and the SASs should be looked on by practitioners as *minimum standards* of performance rather than as maximum standards or ideals. Any professional auditor who seeks means of reducing the scope of the audit by relying only on the standards, rather than evaluating the substance of the situation, fails to satisfy the spirit of the standards. At the same time, the existence of auditing standards does not mean the auditor must always follow them blindly. If an auditor believes that the requirement of a standard is impractical or impossible to perform, the auditor is justified in following an alternative course of action. Similarly, if the issue in question is immaterial in amount, it is also unnecessary to follow the standard. However, the burden of justifying departures from the standards falls on the auditor.

When auditors desire more specific guidelines, they must turn to less authoritative sources, including textbooks, journals, and technical publications. Materials published by the AICPA, mentioned earlier in this chapter, such as the *Journal of Accountancy* and industry audit guides, are useful in furnishing assistance on specific questions. There is further study of the standards and frequent reference to the SASs throughout the text.

QUALITY CONTROL

OBJECTIVE 1-10

Identify quality control standards and practices within the accounting profession.

In 1978, the AICPA established the Quality Control Standards Committee and gave it responsibility to help CPA firms develop and implement quality control standards. For a CPA firm, **quality control** comprises the methods used to ensure that the firm meets its professional responsibilities to clients and others. These methods include the organizational structure of the CPA firm and the procedures the firm establishes. For example, a CPA firm might have an organizational structure that ensures the technical review of every engagement by a partner who has expertise in the client's industry.

Quality control is closely related to but distinct from GAAS. A CPA firm must ensure that generally accepted auditing standards are followed on every audit. Quality controls are the procedures used by the CPA firm that help it meet those standards consistently on every engagement. Quality controls are therefore established for the entire CPA firm, whereas GAAS are applicable to individual engagements.

SAS 25 (AU 161) requires a CPA firm to establish quality control policies and procedures. The standard recognizes that a quality control system can provide only reasonable assurance, not a guarantee, that GAAS are followed.

Elements of Quality Control

The AICPA has not set specific quality control procedures for CPA firms. Procedures should depend on such things as the size of the firm, the number of practice offices, and the nature of the practice. For example, the quality control procedures of a 150-office international firm with many complex multinational clients should differ considerably from those of a 5-person firm specializing in small audits in one or two industries.

The Quality Control Standards Committee has identified five elements of quality control that firms should consider in setting up their own policies and procedures. The five elements of quality control deal with the following areas:

- Independence, integrity, and objectivity
- Personnel management
- Acceptance and continuation of clients and engagements
- Engagement performance
- Monitoring

Division of CPA Firms

The AICPA has established a **division of CPA firms** and created two sections: the SEC Practice Section and the Private Companies Practice Section (The AICPA Alliance for CPA Firms). The intent is to improve the quality of practice by CPA firms consistent with AICPA quality control standards. Each practice section has membership requirements and the authority to impose sanctions for noncompliance by members. A firm can choose to belong to one section, both sections, or neither. However, if a member CPA firm audits one or more publicly held companies, it is required to belong to the SEC Practice Section.

The following are requirements for belonging to the SEC Practice Section:

- *Adherence to quality control standards.* The CPA firm must agree to and adhere to the quality control standards set forth in the preceding section.
- *Mandatory peer review.* Each firm must have a periodic review of its quality controls and auditing and accounting practices by another qualified CPA firm.
- *Continuing education.* Every professional in the firm is required to have 120 hours of continuing professional education in every 3-year period.
- *Partner rotation.* The assignment of a new audit partner to be in charge of each SEC engagement is required if another audit partner has been in charge of the engagement for a period of 7 consecutive years. The incumbent partner is prohibited from returning to partner-in-charge status on the engagement for a minimum of 2 years. Very small firms may be exempted from this requirement.
- *Concurring partner review.* All audits of publicly held companies must have a review by a partner other than the engagement partner, who must concur with the audit report before it can be issued.
- *Proscription of certain services.* The CPA firm must refrain from performing certain types of management consulting services for audit clients that are publicly held. These services include psychological testing, public opinion polls, merger and acquisition assistance for a finder's fee, executive recruitment, and actuarial services to insurance companies.
- *Reporting on disagreements.* An auditor is required to report to the audit committee or board of directors of each SEC audit client on the nature of major disagreements with management about accounting, disclosure, or auditing matters.
- *Reporting on management consulting services performed.* An auditor is required to report to the audit committee or board of directors of each SEC audit client the types of management consulting services performed for the client during the audit year and the total fees received for such services.

Peer Review

Peer review is the review, by CPAs, of a CPA firm's compliance with its quality control system. The purpose of a peer review is to determine and report whether the CPA firm being reviewed has developed adequate policies and procedures for the five elements of quality control and follows them in practice. Unless a firm has a peer review, all members of the CPA firm lose their eligibility for AICPA membership.

CPA firms that are members of the SEC Practice Section (SECPS) or Private Companies Practice Section (PCPS) must be reviewed at least once every 3 years. Peer reviews of PCPS member firms are administered through the state CPA societies under the overall direction of the AICPA peer review board. Typically, the review is done by a CPA firm selected by the firm being reviewed. Another option is to request the AICPA or state society to send a review team. After the review is completed, the reviewers issue a report stating their conclusions and recommendations. Only firms satisfactorily passing an SECPS

FIGURE 1-4 Relationships Among GAAS, Quality Control, Division of CPA Firms, and Peer Review

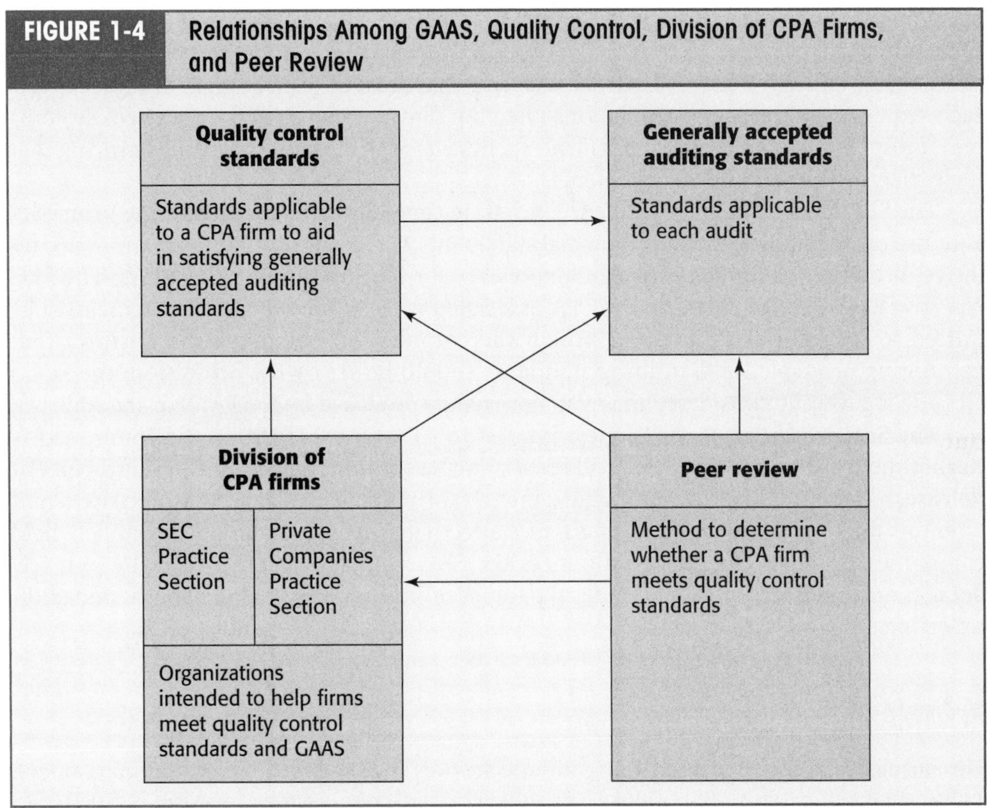

or PCPS peer review can be members of the two practice sections. Approximately 1,300 firms are enrolled in the SECPS peer review program, whereas more than 7,200 PCPS member firms participate in the AICPA peer review program.

AICPA member firms who are not members of the SECPS or PCPS are also required to have peer reviews every 3 years. This type of peer review has the same objective as a peer review of an SECPS or PCPS member, but it is typically less extensive in the review of the implementation of the firm's quality control system. These peer reviews are also administered through the state CPA societies under the overall direction of the AICPA peer review board. Currently, approximately 34,000 firms are enrolled in this part of the AICPA peer review program.

Peer reviews can be beneficial to the profession and individual firms. By helping firms meet quality control standards, the profession gains from improved practitioner performance and higher-quality audits. A firm having a peer review can also gain if it improves the firm's practice and thereby enhances its reputation and effectiveness and reduces the likelihood of lawsuits. Of course, these reviews are costly. There is always a trade-off between cost and benefit. Figure 1-4 summarizes the relationships among GAAS, quality control, division of CPA firms, and peer review.

SECURITIES AND EXCHANGE COMMISSION

OBJECTIVE 1-11

Summarize the role of the Securities and Exchange Commission in accounting and auditing.

The overall purpose of the **Securities and Exchange Commission (SEC)**, an agency of the federal government, is to assist in providing investors with reliable information upon which to make investment decisions. To this end, the Securities Act of 1933 requires most companies planning to issue *new securities* to the public to submit a registration statement to the SEC for approval. The Securities Exchange Act of 1934 provides additional protection by requiring the same companies and others to file detailed annual reports with the commission. The commission examines these statements for completeness and adequacy before permitting the company to sell its securities through the securities exchanges.

Although the SEC requires considerable information that is not of direct interest to CPAs, the securities acts of 1933 and 1934 require financial statements, accompanied by the

SEC

opinion of an independent public accountant, as part of a registration statement and subsequent reports.

Because large CPA firms usually have clients that must file one or more of these reports each year, and the rules and regulations affecting filings with the SEC are extremely complex, most CPA firms have specialists who spend a large portion of their time ensuring that their clients satisfy all SEC requirements.

The SEC has considerable influence in setting generally accepted accounting principles and disclosure requirements for financial statements as a result of its authority for specifying reporting requirements considered necessary for fair disclosure to investors. The SEC has power to establish rules for any CPA associated with audited financial statements submitted to the commission. Even though the commission has taken the position that accounting principles and auditing standards should be set by the profession, the SEC's attitude is generally considered in any major change proposed by the FASB or the ASB.

The SEC requirements of greatest interest to CPAs are set forth in the commission's Regulation S-X, Accounting Series Releases, and Accounting and Auditing Enforcement Releases. These publications constitute important regulations, as well as decisions and opinions on accounting and auditing issues affecting any CPA dealing with publicly held companies. Some of the major influences the SEC has had on auditors in the past few decades are discussed in the text under the topics of independence, legal liability, and audit reporting.

SUMMARY

This chapter first discussed audit and assurance services and described the relationships among audits, attestation services, and assurance services. The market for assurance services is expected to grow with increases in technology and information. Audits are valuable because they reduce information risk, which lowers the cost of obtaining capital. This chapter also defined auditing and described different types of audits and auditors.

The chapter also discussed the nature of the CPA profession and the activities of CPA firms. Because CPA firms play an important social role, the AICPA and other organizations provide mechanisms to increase the likelihood of appropriate audit quality and professional conduct. These are summarized in Figure 1-5. Shaded circles in the figure indicate items discussed in this chapter. The AICPA *Code of Professional Conduct* provides a standard of conduct for practitioners and is discussed in Chapter 3. The potential for legal liability is also a significant influence on auditor conduct and is discussed in Chapter 4.

FIGURE 1-5 Ways the Profession and Society Encourage CPAs to Conduct Themselves at a High Level

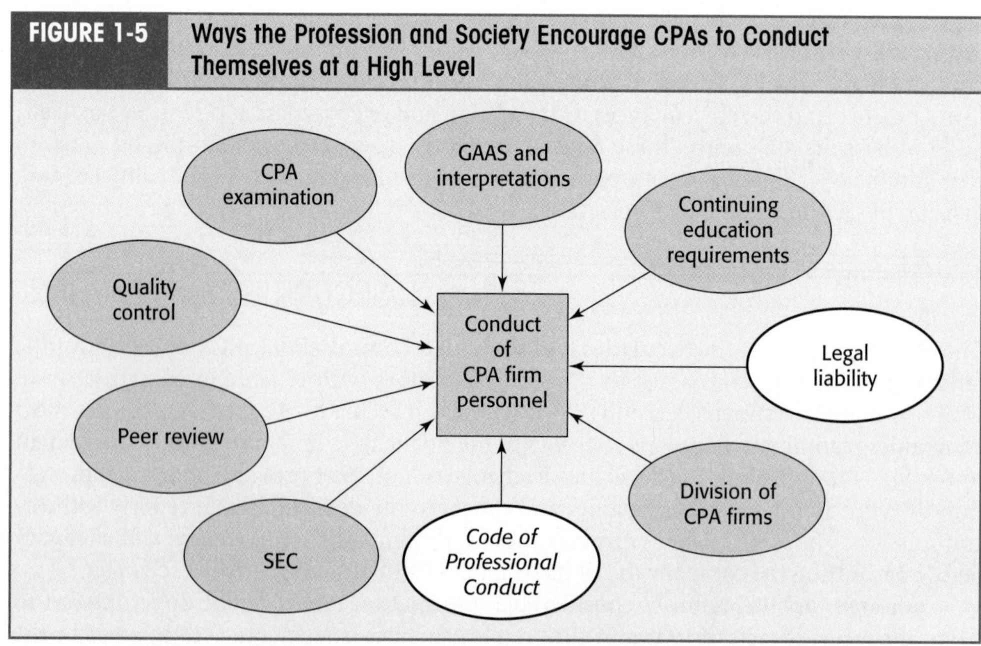

ESSENTIAL TERMS

Accounting—the recording, classifying, and summarizing of economic events in a logical manner for the purpose of providing financial information for decision making

AICPA—American Institute of Certified Public Accountants, a voluntary organization of CPAs that sets professional requirements, conducts research, and publishes materials relevant to accounting, auditing, management consulting services, and taxes

Assurance services—independent professional services that improve the quality of information for decision makers

Attestation service—a type of assurance service in which the CPA firm issues a report about the reliability of an assertion that is the responsibility of another party

Audit of historical financial statements—a form of attestation service in which the auditor issues a written report stating whether the financial statements are in material conformity with generally accepted accounting principles

Auditing—the accumulation and evaluation of evidence about information to determine and report on the degree of correspondence between the information and established criteria

Audit report—the communication of audit findings to users

Certified public accountant—a person who has met state regulatory requirements, including passing the Uniform CPA Examination, and has thus been certified; a CPA may have as his or her primary responsibility the performance of the audit function on published historical financial statements of commercial and noncommercial financial entities

Compliance audit—(1) a review of an organization's financial records performed to determine whether the organization is following specific procedures, rules, or regulations set by some higher authority; (2) an audit performed to determine whether an entity that receives financial assistance from the federal government has complied with specific laws and regulations

Division of CPA firms—a division of the AICPA established for CPA firms and consisting of two sections: the SEC Practice Section and the Private Companies Practice Section; the division was established to improve the quality of practice by CPA firms consistent with AICPA quality control standards

E-commerce—the use of information technology and electronic communication networks to exchange information and conduct transactions in electronic form

Evidence—any information used by the auditor to determine whether the information being audited is stated in accordance with established criteria

Financial statement audit—an audit conducted to determine whether the overall financial statements of an entity are stated in accordance with specified criteria (usually generally accepted accounting principles)

General accounting office auditor—an auditor working for the United States General Accounting Office (GAO); the GAO reports to and is responsible solely to Congress

Generally accepted auditing standards (GAAS)—10 auditing standards, developed by the AICPA, consisting of general standards, standards of field work, and standards of reporting, along with interpretations; often called *auditing standards*

Independent auditors—certified public accountants or accounting firms that perform audits of commercial and noncommercial financial entities

Information risk—the risk that information upon which a business decision is made is inaccurate

Internal auditors—auditors employed by a company to audit for the company's board of directors and management

Internal revenue agents—auditors who work for the Internal Revenue Service (IRS) and conduct examinations of taxpayers' returns

Operational audit—a review of any part of an organization's operating procedures and methods for the purpose of evaluating efficiency and effectiveness

Peer review—the review by CPAs of a CPA firm's compliance with its quality control system

Quality control—methods used by a CPA firm to ensure that the firm meets its professional responsibilities to clients and others

Review of historical financial statements—a form of attestation in which a CPA firm issues a written report that provides less assurance than an audit as to whether the financial statements are in material conformity with generally accepted accounting principles

Securities and Exchange Commission (SEC)—a federal agency that oversees the orderly conduct of the securities markets; the SEC assists in providing investors in public corporations with reliable information upon which to make investment decisions

Statements on Auditing Standards (SASs)—pronouncements issued by the AICPA to interpret generally accepted auditing standards

Strategic systems audit—audit approach based on understanding the client's business strategies and processes and external relations and factors that impact those strategies

REVIEW QUESTIONS

1-1 **(Objective 1-1)** Explain the relationships among audit services, attestation services, and assurance services, and give examples of each.

1-2 **(Objective 1-2)** Distinguish among the following three risks: risk-free interest rate, business risk, and information risk. Which one or ones does the auditor reduce by performing an audit?

1-3 **(Objective 1-3)** Explain what is meant by determining the degree of correspondence between information and established criteria. What are the information and established criteria for the audit of Jones Company's tax return by an internal revenue agent? What are they for the audit of Jones Company's financial statements by a CPA firm?

1-4 **(Objectives 1-3, 1-5)** Describe the nature of the evidence the internal revenue agent will use in the audit of Jones Company's tax return.

1-5 **(Objective 1-3)** In the conduct of audits of financial statements, it would be a serious breach of responsibility if the auditor did not thoroughly understand accounting. However, many competent accountants do not have an understanding of the auditing process. What causes this difference?

1-6 **(Objective 1-4)** What are the differences and similarities in audits of financial statements, compliance audits, and operational audits?

1-7 **(Objective 1-5)** What are the major differences in the scope of the audit responsibilities for CPAs, GAO auditors, IRS agents, and internal auditors?

1-8 **(Objective 1-6)** Explain how the Internet and online resources can be used by audit firms to improve auditing and other services.

1-9 **(Objective 1-7)** What is the best source of information to determine the requirements to be a CPA?

1-10 **(Objective 1-8)** What roles are played by the American Institute of Certified Public Accountants for its members?

1-11 **(Objective 1-9)** Distinguish between generally accepted auditing standards and generally accepted accounting principles, and give two examples of each.

1-12 **(Objective 1-9)** The first standard of field work requires the performance of the audit by a person or persons having adequate technical training and proficiency as an auditor. What are the various ways in which auditors can fulfill the requirement of the standard?

1-13 **(Objective 1-10)** What is meant by the term *quality control* as it relates to a CPA firm?

1-14 **(Objective 1-10)** State what is meant by the term *peer review*. What are the implications of peer review for the profession?

1-15 **(Objective 1-11)** Describe the role of the SEC in society and discuss its relationship with and influence on the practice of auditing.

MULTIPLE CHOICE QUESTIONS FROM CPA EXAMINATIONS

1-16 **(Objectives 1-1, 1-2, 1-3)** The following questions deal with audits by CPA firms. Choose the best response.

a. Independent auditing can best be described as
   (1) a branch of accounting.
   (2) a discipline that attests to the results of accounting and other functional operations and data.
   (3) a professional activity that measures and communicates financial and business data.
   (4) a regulatory function that prevents the issuance of improper financial information.

b. Which of the following professional services would be considered an attestation engagement?
   (1) A consulting service engagement to provide computer processing advice to a client.
   (2) An engagement to report on statutory requirements.
   (3) An income tax engagement to prepare federal and state tax returns.
   (4) The compilation of financial statements from a client's financial records.

c. In performing an attestation engagement, a CPA typically
   (1) supplies litigation support services.
   (2) assesses control risk at a low level.
   (3) expresses a conclusion about an assertion.
   (4) provides management consulting advice.

1-17 (Objectives 1-4, 1-5) The following questions deal with types of audits and auditors. Choose the best response.

a. Operational audits generally have been conducted by internal auditors and governmental audit agencies but may be performed by certified public accountants. A primary purpose of an operational audit is to provide
   (1) a means of assurance that internal accounting controls are functioning as planned.
   (2) a measure of management performance in meeting organizational goals.
   (3) the results of internal examinations of financial and accounting matters to a company's top-level management.
   (4) aid to the independent auditor, who is conducting the audit of the financial statements.

b. In comparison to the external auditor, an internal auditor is more likely to be concerned with
   (1) internal administrative control.
   (2) cost accounting procedures.
   (3) operational auditing.
   (4) internal control.

c. Which of the following best describes the operational audit?
   (1) It requires the constant review by internal auditors of the administrative controls as they relate to the operations of the company.
   (2) It concentrates on implementing financial and accounting control in a newly organized company.
   (3) It attempts and is designed to verify the fair presentation of a company's results of operations.
   (4) It concentrates on seeking aspects of operations in which waste could be reduced by the introduction of controls.

d. Compliance auditing often extends beyond audits leading to the expression of opinions on the fairness of financial presentation and includes audits of efficiency, economy, effectiveness, as well as
   (1) accuracy.
   (2) evaluation.
   (3) adherence to specific rules or procedures.
   (4) internal control.

1-18 (Objective 1-9) The following questions deal with generally accepted auditing standards. Choose the best response.

a. The first general standard, which states in part that the audit is to be performed by a person or persons having adequate technical training, requires that an auditor have
   (1) education and experience in the field of auditing.
   (2) ability in the planning and supervision of the audit work.
   (3) proficiency in business and financial matters.
   (4) knowledge in the areas of financial accounting.

b. Which of the following best describes what is meant by generally accepted auditing standards?
   (1) Acts to be performed by the auditor.
   (2) Measures of the quality of the auditor's performance.
   (3) Procedures to be used to gather evidence to support financial statements.
   (4) Audit objectives generally determined on audit engagements.

c. What is the general character of the three generally accepted auditing standards classified as standards of field work?
   (1) The competence, independence, and professional care of persons performing the audit.
   (2) Criteria for the content of the auditor's report on financial statements and related footnote disclosures.
   (3) The criteria of audit planning and evidence gathering.
   (4) The need to maintain an independence in mental attitude in all matters pertaining to the audit.

DISCUSSION QUESTIONS AND PROBLEMS

1-19 (Objective 1-1) The list below indicates various audit, attestation, and assurance engagements involving auditors.

1. An auditor's report on whether the financial statements are fairly presented in accordance with GAAP.
2. An electronic seal indicating that an electronic seller observes certain practices.
3. A report indicating whether a governmental entity has complied with certain government regulations.
4. A report on the examination of a financial forecast.
5. An evaluation of risk for investment securities.
6. A review report that provides moderate assurance about whether financial statements are fairly stated in accordance with GAAP.
7. A report on compliance with a royalty agreement.
8. A report about management's assertion on the effectiveness of controls over the availability, reliability, integrity, and maintainability of its accounting information system.
9. An evaluation of the effectiveness of key measures used to assess an entity's success in achieving specific targets linked to an entity's strategic plan and vision.

Required

a. Explain or use a diagram to indicate the relationships among audit services, attestation services, and assurance services.

b. For each of the services listed above, indicate the type of service from the list that follows.
   (1) An audit of historical financial statements.
   (2) An attestation service other than an audit service.
   (3) An assurance service that is not an attestation service.

1-20 (Objective 1-2) Vial-tek has an existing loan in the amount of $1.5 million with an annual interest rate of 9.5%. The company provides an internal company-prepared financial statement to the bank under the loan agreement. Two competing banks have offered to replace Vial-tek's existing loan agreement with a new one. First National Bank has offered to loan Vial-tek $1.5 million at a rate of 8.5% but would require Vial-tek to provide financial statements that have been reviewed by a CPA firm. City First Bank has offered to loan Vial-tek $1.5 million at a rate of 7.5% but would require Vial-tek to provide financial statements that have been audited by a CPA firm. The controller of Vial-tek approached a CPA firm and was given an estimated cost of $12,000 to perform a review and $20,000 to perform an audit.

Required

a. Explain why the interest rate for the loan that requires a review report is lower than that for the loan that did not require a review. Explain why the interest rate for the loan that requires an audit report is lower than the interest rate for the other two loans.

b. Calculate Vial-tek's annual costs under each loan agreement, including interest and costs for the CPA firm's services. Indicate whether Vial-tek should keep its existing loan, accept the offer from First National Bank, or accept the offer from City First Bank.

c. Discuss why Vial-tek may desire to have an audit performed, ignoring the potential reduction in interest costs.

d. Explain how knowledge of e-commerce technologies and use of a strategic systems audit approach may increase the value of the audit service.

1-21 (Objectives 1-1, 1-2) Consumers Union is a nonprofit organization that provides information and counsel on consumer goods and services. A major part of its function is the testing of different brands of consumer products that are purchased on the open market and then reporting the results of the tests in *Consumer Reports,* a monthly publication. Examples of the types of products it tests are middle-sized automobiles, residential dehumidifiers, canned tuna, and boys' jeans.

Required

a. In what ways are the services provided by Consumers Union similar to assurance services provided by CPA firms?

b. Compare the concept of information risk introduced in this chapter with the information risk problem faced by a buyer of an automobile.

c. Compare the four causes of information risk faced by users of financial statements as discussed in this chapter with those faced by a buyer of an automobile.

d. Compare the three ways users of financial statements can reduce information risk with those available to a buyer of an automobile.

1-22 (Objective 1-3) Fred Oatly is the loan officer of the National Bank of Dallas. National has a loan of $260,000 outstanding to Regional Delivery Service, a company specializing in delivering products of all types on behalf of smaller companies. National's collateral on the loan consists of 35 small delivery trucks with an average original cost of $17,000.

Oatly is concerned about the collectibility of the outstanding loan and whether the trucks still exist. He therefore engages Susan Virms, CPA, to count the trucks, using registration information held by Oatly. She was engaged because she spends most of her time auditing used automobile and truck dealerships and has extensive specialized knowledge about used trucks. Oatly requests that Virms issue a report stating the following:

1. Which of the 35 trucks is parked in Regional's parking lot on the night of June 30, 2002.
2. Whether all of the trucks are owned by Regional Delivery Service.
3. The condition of each truck, using the guidelines of poor, good, and excellent.
4. The fair market value of each truck, using the current "blue book" for trucks, which states the approximate wholesale prices of all used truck models, and also using the poor, good, and excellent condition guidelines.

Required

a. For each of the following parts of the definition of auditing, state which part of the preceding narrative fits the definition:
   (1) Information
   (2) Established criteria
   (3) Accumulating and evaluating evidence
   (4) Competent, independent person
   (5) Reporting results

b. Identify the greatest difficulties Virms is likely to have doing this audit.

1-23 (Objectives 1-4, 1-5) In the normal course of performing their responsibilities, auditors often conduct audits or reviews of the following:

1. Federal income tax returns of an officer of the corporation to determine whether he or she has included all taxable income in his/her return.
2. Disbursements of a branch of the federal government for a special research project to determine whether it would have been possible to accomplish the same research results at a lower cost to the taxpayers.
3. Computer operations of a corporation to evaluate whether the computer center is being operated as efficiently as possible.
4. Annual statements for the use of management.
5. Operations of the IRS to determine whether the internal revenue agents are using their time efficiently in conducting audits.
6. Statements for bankers and other creditors when the client is too small to have an audit staff.
7. Financial statements of a branch of the federal government to make sure that the statements present fairly the actual disbursements made during a period of time.
8. Federal income tax returns of a corporation to determine whether the tax laws have been followed.
9. Financial statements for use by stockholders when there is an internal audit staff.
10. A bond indenture agreement to make sure a company is following all requirements of the contract.
11. The computer operations of a large corporation to evaluate whether the internal controls are likely to prevent misstatements in accounting and operating data.
12. Disbursements of a branch of the federal government for a special research project to determine whether the expenditures were consistent with the legislative bill that authorized the project.

Required

a. For these 12 examples, state the most likely type of auditor (CPA, GAO, IRS, or internal) to perform each.

b. In each example, state the type of audit (financial statement audit, operational audit, or compliance audit).

1-24 (Objective 1-1) A small, but expanding, specialty home-products retailer recently implemented an Internet portal that allows customers to order merchandise online. In the first few months of operation, their Internet site attracted a large number of visitors; however, very few placed orders online. The retailer conducted several focus-group sessions with potential shoppers to identify reasons why shoppers were visiting the Web site without placing orders. Shoppers in the focus groups made these comments:

1. "I am nervous about doing business with this retailer because it is relatively unknown in the marketplace. How do I know the product descriptions on the Web site are accurate, and that the stated return policies are followed?"
2. "I am reluctant to provide my credit card information online. How do I know the transmission of my personal credit card information to the retailer's Web site is protected?"

3. "Retailers are notorious for selling information about customers to others. The last thing I want to do is enter personal information online, such as my name, address, telephone number, and e-mail address. I am afraid this retailer will sell that information to third parties and then I'll be bombarded with a bunch of junk e-mail messages!"
4. "Web sites go down all the time due to system failures. How do I know the retailer's Web site will be operating when I need it?"

Required

a. Discuss whether this situation provides an opportunity for CPAs to address these customer concerns.

b. For each customer comment, identify the appropriate *WebTrust* program that a *WebTrust* licensed CPA could perform for the retailer to address the concerns noted. Choose from the following:
   (1) *WebTrust* On-line Privacy
   (2) *WebTrust* Security
   (3) *WebTrust* Business Practices/Transaction Integrity
   (4) *WebTrust* Availability
   (5) *WebTrust* Certification Authorities

1-25 (Objective 1-10) The following comments summarize the beliefs of some practitioners about quality control and peer review.

> Quality control and peer review are quasi-governmental methods of regulating the profession. There are two effects of such regulation. First, it gives a competitive advantage to national CPA firms because they already need formal structures to administer their complex organizations. Quality control requirements do not significantly affect their structure. Smaller firms now need a more costly organizational structure, which has proven unnecessary because of existing partner involvement on engagements. The major advantage smaller CPA firms have traditionally had is a simple and efficient organizational structure. Now that advantage has been eliminated because of quality control requirements. Second, quality control and peer review are not needed to regulate the profession. The first four elements of quality control have always existed, at least informally, for quality firms. Three things already provide sufficient assurance that informal quality control elements are followed without peer review. They are competitive pressures to do quality work, legal liability for inadequate performance, and a code of professional conduct requiring that CPA firms follow generally accepted auditing standards.

Required

a. State the pros and cons of those comments.

b. Evaluate whether quality control requirements and peer reviews are worth their cost.

1-26 (Objective 1-9) Ray, the owner of a small company, asked Holmes, a CPA, to conduct an audit of the company's records. Ray told Holmes that an audit was to be completed in time to submit audited financial statements to a bank as part of a loan application. Holmes immediately accepted the engagement and agreed to provide an auditor's report within 3 weeks. Ray agreed to pay Holmes a fixed fee plus a bonus if the loan was granted.

Holmes hired two accounting students to conduct the audit and spent several hours telling them exactly what to do. Holmes told the students not to spend time reviewing the controls but instead to concentrate on proving the mathematical accuracy of the ledger accounts and summarizing the data in the accounting records that support Ray's financial statements. The students followed Holmes's instructions and after 2 weeks gave Holmes the financial statements, which did not include footnotes. Holmes reviewed the statements and prepared an unqualified auditor's report. The report did not refer to generally accepted accounting principles nor to the consistent application of such principles.

Required

Briefly describe each of the 10 generally accepted auditing standards and indicate how the action(s) of Holmes resulted in a failure to comply with each standard.

Organize your answer as follows:*

Brief Description of GAAS	Holmes' Actions Resulting in Failure to Comply with GAAS

1-27 (Objective 1-6) A local CPA, who has been in practice for several years, recently met with representatives of an Internet service provider that is interested in developing a Web site for the CPA's practice. The CPA has been reluctant to develop an Internet site but is willing to learn more about the types of information and resources that CPAs often provide through their Internet sites before making a final decision.

*AICPA adapted.

a. Describe the types of resources and Web links that CPAs often provide on their Internet Web sites.

b. State reasons why CPA firms invest resources in creating sophisticated Internet sites.

c. Discuss how the Internet can be a useful tool for a CPA firm's accounting and auditing practice.

Required

INTERNET PROBLEM 1-1: ASSURANCE SERVICES

Reference Prentice Hall's Companion Web Site (CW site).[2] Businesses must have access to more decision-relevant information than ever before. Furthermore, businesses and individuals need independent assurance that the information on which their decisions are based is reliable. By virtue of their training, experience, and reputation for integrity, CPAs are the logical choice to provide this assurance. To assist the profession's move forward, the AICPA formed the Special Committee on Assurance Services. This problem requires students to use the Internet to (1) research assurance services recommended by the committee, (2) examine components of assurance service business plans, and (3) identify and describe competencies needed by assurance providers in the upcoming decade.

INTERNET PROBLEM 1-2: CPA VISION PROJECT

Reference the CW site. The CPA Vision Project is all about helping the "CPA profession stay on top of the change curve." With input from CPAs across the nation, the CPA Vision Project has created a comprehensive and integrated vision of the profession's future. This problem requires students to use the Internet (1) to research the CPA Vision Statement, (2) to research the eight forces impacting the profession, and (3) to answer the question, "What is meant by moving up the economic value chain and how are CPAs going to accomplish this?"

[2] Internet problems can be found at Prentice Hall's Companion Web Site (CW site), www. prenhall.com/arens.

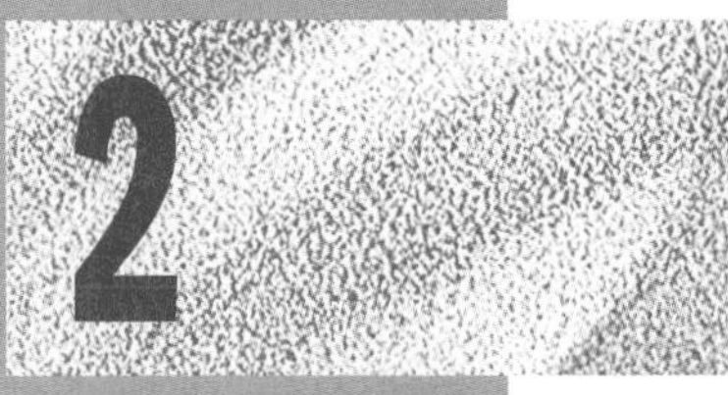

CHAPTER 2

AUDIT REPORTS

THE AUDIT REPORT WAS TIMELY, BUT AT WHAT COST?

Halvorson & Co., CPAs was hired as the auditor for Machinetron, Inc., a company that manufactured high-precision, computer-operated lathes. The owner, Al Trent, thought that Machinetron was ready to become a public company, and he hired Halvorson to conduct the upcoming audit and assist in the preparation of the registration statement for a securities offering.

Because Machinetron's machines were large and complex, they were expensive. Each sale was negotiated individually by Trent, and the sales often transpired over several months. As a result, improper recording of one or two machines could represent a material misstatement of the financial statements.

The engagement partner in charge of the Machinetron audit was Bob Lehman, who had significant experience auditing manufacturing companies. He recognized the risk for improper recording of sales, and he insisted that his staff confirm all receivables at year-end directly with customers. Lehman conducted his review of the Machinetron working papers the same day that Trent wanted to make the company's registration statement for the initial public stock offering effective. Lehman saw that a receivable for a major sale at year-end was supported by a fax, rather than the usual written confirmation reply. Apparently, relations with this customer were "touchy," and Trent had discouraged the audit staff from communicating with the customer.

At the end of the day, there was a meeting in Machinetron's office. It was attended by Lehman, Trent, the underwriter of the stock offering, and the company's attorney. Lehman indicated that a better form of confirmation would be required to support the receivable. After hearing this, Trent blew his stack. Machinetron's attorney stepped in and calmed Trent down. He offered to write a letter to Halvorson & Co. stating that in his opinion, a fax had legal substance as a valid confirmation reply. Lehman, feeling tremendous pressure, accepted this proposal and signed off on an unqualified audit opinion.

Six months after the stock offering, Machinetron issued a statement indicating that its revenues for the prior year had been overstated as a result of improperly recorded sales, including the sale supported by the fax confirmation. The subsequent SEC investigation uncovered that the fax had been sent by Trent, not the customer. Halvorson & Co. recalled their unqualified audit report, but this was too late to prevent the harm done to investors. Halvorson & Co. was forced to pay substantial damages, and Bob Lehman was forbidden to practice before the SEC. He subsequently left public accounting.

LEARNING OBJECTIVES

After studying this chapter, you should be able to

2-1 Describe the parts of the standard unqualified audit report.

2-2 Specify the conditions required to issue the standard unqualified audit report.

2-3 Describe the five circumstances when an unqualified report with an explanatory paragraph or modified wording is appropriate.

2-4 Identify the types of audit reports that can be issued when an unqualified opinion is not justified.

2-5 Explain how materiality affects audit reporting decisions.

2-6 Draft appropriately modified audit reports under a variety of circumstances.

2-7 Determine the appropriate audit report for a given audit situation.

2-8 Discuss the impact of e-commerce on audit reporting.

Reports are essential to audit and assurance engagements because they communicate the auditor's findings. Users of financial statements rely on the auditor's report to provide assurance on the company's financial statements. As the vignette at the beginning of this chapter illustrates, the auditor is likely to be held responsible if an incorrect audit report is issued.

The audit report is the final step in the entire audit process. The reason for studying it now is to permit reference to different audit reports as evidence accumulation is studied throughout this text. These evidence concepts are more meaningful after you understand the form and content of the final product of the audit. We begin by describing the content of the standard auditor's report.

STANDARD UNQUALIFIED AUDIT REPORT

The fourth standard of reporting requires that the audit report should contain a clear-cut indication of the character of the auditor's work and the degree of responsibility taken for the financial statements. To enable users to understand the audit report, professional standards provide uniform wording for the auditor's report.

An example of the auditor's **standard unqualified audit report** is included in Figure 2-1. Different auditors may vary the wording or presentation slightly, but the meaning will be the same. The seven parts of the audit report are described next.

Parts of Standard Unqualified Audit Report

OBJECTIVE 2-1

Describe the parts of the standard unqualified audit report.

The seven parts of the standard unqualified audit report are labeled in bold letters in the margin beside Figure 2-1.

1. *Report title.* Auditing standards require that the report be titled and that the title include the word *independent*. For example, appropriate titles would be "independent auditor's report," "report of independent auditor," or "independent accountant's opinion." The requirement that the title include the word *independent* is intended to convey to users that the audit was unbiased in all aspects.

2. *Audit report address.* The report is usually addressed to the company, its stockholders, or the board of directors. In recent years, it has become customary to address the report to the stockholders to indicate that the auditor is independent of the company and the board of directors.

3. *Introductory paragraph.* The first paragraph of the report does three things: First, it makes the simple statement that the CPA firm has done an *audit*. This is intended to distinguish the report from a compilation or review report. The scope paragraph (see part 4) clarifies what is meant by an audit.

Second, it lists the financial statements that were audited, including the balance sheet dates and the accounting periods for the income statement and statement of cash flows. The wording of the financial statements in the report should be identical to those used by management on the financial statements. Notice that the report in Figure 2-1 is on comparative financial statements. Therefore, a report on both years' statements is needed.

Third, the introductory paragraph states that the statements are the responsibility of management and that the auditor's responsibility is to express an opinion on the statements based on an audit. The purpose of these statements is to communicate that management is responsible for selecting the appropriate generally accepted accounting principles and making the measurement decisions and disclosures in applying those principles and to clarify the respective roles of management and the auditor.

4. *Scope paragraph.* The scope paragraph is a factual statement about what the auditor did in the audit. This paragraph first states that the auditor followed U.S. generally accepted auditing standards. Financial statements prepared in accordance with U.S. accounting principles and audited in accordance with U.S. auditing standards are increasingly available throughout the world on the Internet. Accordingly, SAS 93 requires that the country of origin of the accounting principles used in preparing the financial statements and auditing standards followed by the auditor be identified in the audit report.

FIGURE 2-1 Standard Unqualified Report on Comparative Statements

ANDERSON and ZINDER, P.C.
Certified Public Accountants
Suite 100
Park Plaza East
Denver, Colorado 80110
303/359-0800

Independent Auditor's Report — **Report Title**

To the Stockholders
General Ring Corporation — **Audit Report Address**

We have audited the accompanying balance sheets of General Ring Corporation as of December 31, 2002 and 2001, and the related statements of income, retained earnings, and cash flows for the years then ended. These financial statements are the responsibility of the Company's management. Our responsibility is to express an opinion on these financial statements based on our audits. — **Introductory Paragraph (Factual Statement)**

We conducted our audits in accordance with auditing standards generally accepted in the United States of America. Those standards require that we plan and perform the audit to obtain reasonable assurance about whether the financial statements are free of material misstatement. An audit includes examining, on a test basis, evidence supporting the amounts and disclosures in the financial statements. An audit also includes assessing the accounting principles used and significant estimates made by management, as well as evaluating the overall financial statement presentation. We believe that our audits provide a reasonable basis for our opinion. — **Scope Paragraph (Factual Statement)**

In our opinion, the financial statements referred to above present fairly, in all material respects, the financial position of General Ring Corporation as of December 31, 2002 and 2001, and the results of its operations and its cash flows for the years then ended in conformity with accounting principles generally accepted in the United States of America. — **Opinion Paragraph (Conclusions)**

ANDERSON AND ZINDER, P.C., CPAs — **Name of CPA Firm**

February 15, 2003 — **Audit Report Date (Date Audit Field Work Is Completed)**

The scope paragraph states that the audit is designed to obtain *reasonable assurance* about whether the statements are free of **material misstatement.** The inclusion of the word *material* conveys that auditors are responsible only to search for significant misstatements, not minor misstatements that do not affect users' decisions. The use of the term *reasonable assurance* is intended to indicate that an audit cannot be expected to completely eliminate the possibility that a material misstatement will exist in the financial statements. In other words, an audit provides a high level of assurance, but it is not a guarantee.

Audit Report Search

The remainder of the scope paragraph discusses the audit evidence accumulated and states that the auditor believes that the evidence accumulated was appropriate for the circumstances to express the opinion presented. The words *test basis* indicate that sampling was used rather than an audit of every transaction and amount on the statements. Whereas the introductory paragraph of the report states that management is responsible for the preparation and content of the financial statements, the scope paragraph states that the auditor evaluates the appropriateness of those accounting principles, estimates, and financial statement disclosures and presentations given.

5. *Opinion paragraph.* The final paragraph in the standard report states the auditor's conclusions based on the results of the audit. This part of the report is so important that often the entire audit report is referred to simply as the *auditor's opinion.* The opinion paragraph is stated as an opinion rather than as a statement of absolute fact or a guarantee. The intent is to indicate that the conclusions are based on professional judgment. The phrase *in*

our opinion indicates that there may be some information risk associated with the financial statements, even though the statements have been audited.

The opinion paragraph is directly related to the first and fourth generally accepted auditing reporting standards listed on page 19. The auditor is required to state an opinion about the financial statements taken as a whole, including a conclusion about whether the company followed U.S. generally accepted accounting principles.

One of the controversial parts of the auditor's report is the meaning of the term *present fairly*. Does this mean that if generally accepted accounting principles are followed, the financial statements are presented fairly, or something more? Occasionally, the courts have concluded that auditors are responsible for looking beyond generally accepted accounting principles to determine whether users might be misled, even if those principles are followed. Most auditors believe that financial statements are "presented fairly" when the statements are in accordance with generally accepted accounting principles but that it is also necessary to examine the substance of transactions and balances for possible misinformation.

6. *Name of CPA firm.* The name identifies the CPA firm or practitioner who performed the audit. Typically, the firm's name is used because the entire CPA firm has the legal and professional responsibility to ensure that the quality of the audit meets professional standards.

7. *Audit report date.* The appropriate date for the report is the one on which the auditor has completed the most important auditing procedures in the field. This date is important to users because it indicates the last day of the auditor's responsibility for the review of significant events that occurred after the date of the financial statements. In the audit report in Figure 2-1, the balance sheet is dated December 31, 2002, and the audit report is dated February 15, 2003. This indicates that the auditor has searched for material unrecorded transactions and events that occurred up to February 15, 2003.

Conditions for Standard Unqualified Audit Report

OBJECTIVE **2-2**

Specify the conditions required to issue the standard unqualified audit report.

The standard unqualified audit report is issued when the following conditions have been met:

1. All statements—balance sheet, income statement, statement of retained earnings, and statement of cash flows—are included in the financial statements.
2. The three general standards have been followed in all respects on the engagement.
3. Sufficient evidence has been accumulated, and the auditor has conducted the engagement in a manner that enables him or her to conclude that the three standards of field work have been met.
4. The financial statements are presented in accordance with U.S. generally accepted accounting principles. This also means that adequate disclosures have been included in the footnotes and other parts of the financial statements.
5. There are no circumstances requiring the addition of an explanatory paragraph or modification of the wording of the report.

When these conditions are met, the standard unqualified audit report, as shown in Figure 2-1, is issued. The standard unqualified audit report is sometimes called a clean opinion because there are no circumstances requiring a qualification or modification of the auditor's opinion. The standard unqualified report is the most common audit opinion. Sometimes circumstances beyond the client's or auditor's control prevent the issuance of a clean opinion. However, in most cases, companies make the appropriate changes to their accounting records to avoid a qualification or modification by the auditor.

If any of the five requirements for the standard unqualified audit report are not met, the standard unqualified report cannot be issued. Figure 2-2 indicates the categories of audit reports that can be issued by the auditor. The departures from a standard unqualified report are considered increasingly severe as one moves down the figure. Financial statement users would normally be much more concerned about a disclaimer or adverse opinion than an unqualified report with an explanatory paragraph. These other categories of audit reports are discussed in the following sections.

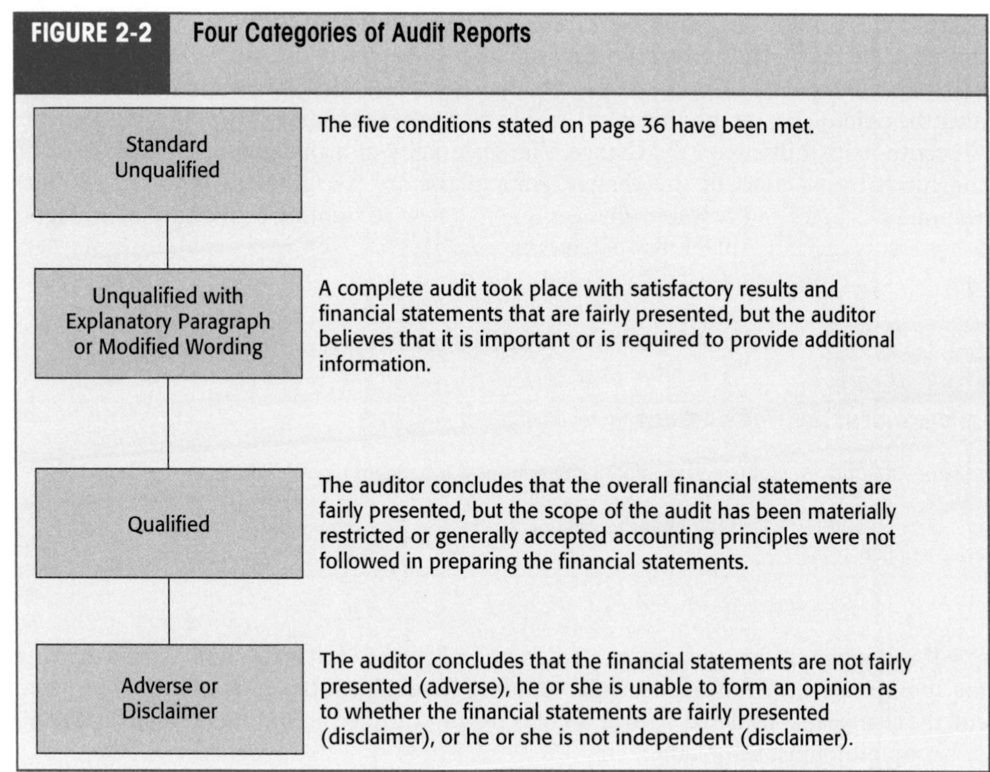

Standard Unqualified
The five conditions stated on page 36 have been met.
Unqualified with Explanatory Paragraph or Modified Wording
A complete audit took place with satisfactory results and financial statements that are fairly presented, but the auditor believes that it is important or is required to provide additional information.
Qualified
The auditor concludes that the overall financial statements are fairly presented, but the scope of the audit has been materially restricted or generally accepted accounting principles were not followed in preparing the financial statements.
Adverse or Disclaimer
The auditor concludes that the financial statements are not fairly presented (adverse), he or she is unable to form an opinion as to whether the financial statements are fairly presented (disclaimer), or he or she is not independent (disclaimer).

FIGURE 2-2 Four Categories of Audit Reports

UNQUALIFIED AUDIT REPORT WITH EXPLANATORY PARAGRAPH OR MODIFIED WORDING

OBJECTIVE 2-3

Describe the five circumstances when an unqualified report with an explanatory paragraph or modified wording is appropriate.

In certain situations, an unqualified audit report is issued, but the wording deviates from the standard unqualified report. The **unqualified audit report with explanatory paragraph or modified wording** meets the criteria of a complete audit with satisfactory results and financial statements that are fairly presented, but the auditor believes it is important or is required to provide additional information. In a qualified, adverse, or disclaimer report, the auditor either has not performed a satisfactory audit, is not satisfied that the financial statements are fairly presented, or is not independent.

The following are the most important causes of the addition of an explanatory paragraph or a modification in the wording of the standard unqualified report:

- Lack of consistent application of generally accepted accounting principles
- Substantial doubt about going concern
- Auditor agrees with a departure from promulgated accounting principles
- Emphasis of a matter
- Reports involving other auditors

The first four reports all require an explanatory paragraph. In each case, the three standard report paragraphs are included without modification and a separate explanatory paragraph follows the opinion paragraph.

Only reports involving the use of other auditors use a modified wording report. This report contains three paragraphs and all three paragraphs are modified.

Lack of Consistent Application of GAAP

The second reporting standard requires the auditor to call attention to circumstances in which accounting principles have not been consistently observed in the current period in relation to the preceding period. Generally accepted accounting principles require that changes in accounting principles or their method of application be to a preferable principle and that the nature and impact of the change be adequately disclosed. When a material change occurs, the auditor should modify the report by adding an explanatory paragraph after the opinion paragraph that discusses the nature of the change and points the reader to the footnote that discusses the change. The materiality of a change is evaluated based on the current year effect of the change. An explanatory paragraph is required for both voluntary changes and required changes due to a new accounting pronouncement. Figure 2-3 presents such an explanatory paragraph.

FIGURE 2-3 **Explanatory Paragraph Because of Change in Accounting Principle**

INDEPENDENT AUDITOR'S REPORT

(Same introductory, scope, and opinion paragraphs as the standard report)

Fourth Paragraph—Explanatory Paragraph

As discussed in Note 8 to the financial statements, the Company changed its method of computing depreciation in 2002.

It is implicit in the explanatory paragraph in Figure 2-3 that the auditor concurs with the appropriateness of the change in accounting principles. If the auditor does not so concur, the change is considered a violation of generally accepted accounting principles and his or her opinion must be qualified.

Consistency Versus Comparability The auditor must be able to distinguish between changes that affect consistency and those that may affect comparability but do not affect consistency. The following are examples of changes that affect consistency and therefore require an explanatory paragraph if they are material:

1. Changes in accounting principles, such as a change from FIFO to LIFO inventory valuation
2. Changes in reporting entities, such as the inclusion of an additional company in combined financial statements
3. Corrections of errors involving principles, by changing from an accounting principle that is not generally acceptable to one that is generally acceptable, including correction of the resulting error

Changes that affect comparability but not consistency and therefore need not be included in the audit report include the following:

1. Changes in an estimate, such as a decrease in the life of an asset for depreciation purposes
2. Error corrections not involving principles, such as a previous year's mathematical error
3. Variations in format and presentation of financial information
4. Changes because of substantially different transactions or events, such as new endeavors in research and development or the sale of a subsidiary

Items that materially affect the comparability of financial statements generally require disclosure in the footnotes. A qualified audit report for inadequate disclosure may be required if the client refuses to properly disclose the items.

Substantial Doubt About Going Concern

Even though the purpose of an audit is not to evaluate the financial health of the business, the auditor has a responsibility to evaluate whether the company is likely to continue as a going concern. SAS 59 (AU 341) addresses this problem under the heading *The Auditor's Consideration of an Entity's Ability to Continue as a Going Concern*. For example, the existence of one or more of the following factors causes uncertainty about the ability of a company to continue as a going concern:

1. Significant recurring operating losses or working capital deficiencies
2. Inability of the company to pay its obligations as they come due
3. Loss of major customers, the occurrence of uninsured catastrophes such as an earthquake or flood, or unusual labor difficulties
4. Legal proceedings, legislation, or similar matters that have occurred that might jeopardize the entity's ability to operate

The auditor's concern in such situations is the possibility that the client may not be able to continue its operations or meet its obligations for a reasonable period. For this purpose, a reasonable period is considered not to exceed 1 year from the date of the financial statements being audited.

When the auditor concludes that there is substantial doubt about the entity's ability to continue as a going concern, an unqualified opinion with an explanatory paragraph is required, regardless of the disclosures in the financial statements. Figure 2-4 provides an example in which there is substantial doubt about going concern.

FIGURE 2-4 Explanatory Paragraph Because of Substantial Doubt About Going Concern

INDEPENDENT AUDITOR'S REPORT

(Same introductory, scope, and opinion paragraphs as the standard report)

Fourth Paragraph–Explanatory Paragraph

The accompanying financial statements have been prepared assuming that Fairfax Company will continue as a going concern. As discussed in Note 11 to the financial statements, Fairfax Company has suffered recurring losses from operations and has a net capital deficiency that raise substantial doubt about the company's ability to continue as a going concern. Management's plans in regard to these matters are also described in Note 11. The financial statements do not include any adjustments that might result from the outcome of this uncertainty.

SAS 59 permits but does not require a disclaimer of opinion when there is substantial doubt about going concern. The criteria for issuing a disclaimer of opinion instead of adding an explanatory paragraph are not stated in the standards, and this type of opinion is rarely issued in practice. An example for which a disclaimer might be issued is when a regulatory agency, such as the Environmental Protection Agency, is considering a severe sanction against a company and, if the proceedings result in an unfavorable outcome, the company will be forced to liquidate.

Auditor Agrees with a Departure from a Promulgated Principle

Rule 203 of the AICPA *Code of Professional Conduct* states that in unusual situations, a departure from an accounting principle promulgated by a body designated by the AICPA to establish accounting principles may not require a qualified or adverse opinion. However, to justify an unqualified opinion, the auditor must be satisfied and must state and explain, in a separate paragraph or paragraphs in the audit report, that adhering to the principle would have produced a misleading result in that situation.

Emphasis of a Matter

Under certain circumstances, the CPA may want to emphasize specific matters regarding the financial statements, even though he or she intends to express an unqualified opinion. Normally, such explanatory information should be included in a separate paragraph in the report. The following are examples of explanatory information the auditor may think should be expressed: the existence of significant related party transactions, important events occurring subsequent to the balance sheet date, the description of accounting matters affecting the comparability of the financial statements with those of the preceding year, and material uncertainties disclosed in the footnotes.

Reports Involving Other Auditors

When the CPA relies on a different CPA firm to perform part of the audit, which is common when the client has several widespread branches or subdivisions, the principal CPA firm has three alternatives. Only the second is an unqualified report with modified wording.

1. Make No Reference in the Audit Report When no reference is made to the other auditor, a standard unqualified opinion is given unless other circumstances require a departure. This approach is typically followed when the other auditor audited an immaterial portion of the statements, the other auditor is well known or closely supervised by the principal auditor, or the principal auditor has thoroughly reviewed the other auditor's work. The other auditor is still responsible for his or her own report and work in the event of a lawsuit or SEC action.

2. Make Reference in the Report (Modified Wording Report) This type of report is called a shared opinion or report. A shared unqualified report is appropriate when it is impractical to review the work of the other auditor or when the portion of the financial statements audited by the other CPA is material in relation to the whole. An example of a shared report that should not be interpreted as a qualification is shown in Figure 2-5. Notice that the report does *not* include a separate paragraph that discusses the shared responsibility, but does so in the introductory paragraph and refers to the other auditor in the scope and opinion paragraphs. The portions of the financial statements audited by the other auditor can be stated as percentages or absolute amounts.

FIGURE 2-5 Unqualified Shared Report

INDEPENDENT AUDITOR'S REPORT

Stockholders and Board of Directors
Washington Felp
Midland, Texas

Introductory Paragraph—Modified Wording

We have audited the accompanying consolidated balance sheets of Washington Felp as of July 31, 2002 and 2001, and the related consolidated statements of income, retained earnings, and cash flows for the years then ended. These financial statements are the responsibility of the Company's management. Our responsibility is to express an opinion on these financial statements based on our audits. We did not audit the financial statements of Stewart Pane and Lighting, a consolidated subsidiary in which the Company had an equity interest of 84% as of July 31, 2002, which statements reflect total assets of $2,420,000 and $2,237,000 as of July 31, 2002 and 2001, respectively, and total revenues of $3,458,000 and $3,121,000 for the years then ended. Those statements were audited by other auditors whose report has been furnished to us, and our opinion, insofar as it relates to the amounts included for Stewart Pane and Lighting, is based solely on the report of the other auditors.

Scope Paragraph—Modified Wording

We conducted our audits in accordance with auditing standards generally accepted in the United States of America. Those standards require that we plan and perform the audit to obtain reasonable assurance about whether the financial statements are free of material misstatement. An audit includes examining, on a test basis, evidence supporting the amounts and disclosures in the financial statements. An audit also includes assessing the accounting principles used and significant estimates made by management, as well as evaluating the overall financial statement presentation. We believe that our audits and the report of other auditors provide a reasonable basis for our opinion.

Opinion Paragraph—Modified Wording

In our opinion, based on our audits and the report of other auditors, the consolidated financial statements referred to above present fairly, in all material respects, the financial position of Washington Felp as of July 31, 2002 and 2001, and the results of its operations and its cash flows for the years then ended in conformity with accounting principles generally accepted in the United States of America.

September 16, 2002
Farn, Ross, & Co.
Certified Public Accountants
Dallas, Texas

3. Qualify the Opinion The principal auditor may conclude that a qualified opinion is required. A qualified opinion or disclaimer, depending on materiality, is required if the principal auditor is not willing to assume any responsibility for the work of the other auditor. The principal auditor may also decide that a qualification is required in the overall report if the other auditor qualified his or her portion of the audit. Qualified opinions and disclaimers are discussed in a later section.

DEPARTURES FROM AN UNQUALIFIED AUDIT REPORT

OBJECTIVE 2-4

Identify the types of audit reports that can be issued when an unqualified opinion is not justified.

It is essential that auditors and readers of audit reports understand the circumstances when an unqualified report is inappropriate and the type of audit report issued in each circumstance. In the study of audit reports that depart from an unqualified report, there are three closely related topics: the conditions requiring a departure from an unqualified opinion, the types of opinions other than unqualified, and materiality.

First, the three conditions requiring a departure are briefly summarized. Each is discussed in greater depth later in the chapter.

1. The Scope of the Audit Has Been Restricted (Scope Limitation) When the auditor has not accumulated sufficient evidence to conclude whether financial statements are stated in accordance with GAAP, a scope restriction exists. There are two major causes of scope restrictions: restrictions imposed by the client and those caused by circumstances beyond either the client's or auditor's control. An example of a client restriction is management's refusal to permit the auditor to confirm material receivables or to physically examine inventory. An example of a restriction caused by circumstances is when the engagement is not agreed on until after the client's year-end. It may not be possible to physically observe inventories, confirm receivables, or perform other important procedures after the balance sheet date.

2. The Financial Statements Have Not Been Prepared in Accordance with Generally Accepted Accounting Principles (GAAP Departure) For example, if the client insists on using replacement costs for fixed assets or values inventory at selling price rather than historical cost, a departure from the unqualified report is required. When generally accepted accounting principles are referred to in this context, consideration of the adequacy of all informative disclosures, including footnotes, is especially important.

3. The Auditor Is Not Independent Independence ordinarily is determined by Rule 101 of the rules of the *Code of Professional Conduct.*

When any of the three conditions requiring a departure from an unqualified report exists and is material, a report other than an unqualified report must be issued. Three main types of audit reports are issued under these conditions: qualified opinion, adverse opinion, and disclaimer of opinion.

Qualified Opinion

A **qualified opinion** report can result from a limitation on the scope of the audit or failure to follow generally accepted accounting principles. A qualified opinion report can be used *only when the auditor concludes that the overall financial statements are fairly stated.* A disclaimer or an adverse report must be used if the auditor believes that the condition being reported on is highly material. Therefore, the qualified opinion is considered the least severe type of departure from an unqualified report.

A qualified report can take the form of a *qualification of both the scope and the opinion* or of the *opinion alone.* A scope and opinion qualification can be issued only when the auditor has been unable to accumulate all of the evidence required by generally accepted auditing standards. Therefore, this type of qualification is used when the auditor's scope has been restricted by the client or when circumstances exist that prevent the auditor from conducting a complete audit. The use of a qualification of the opinion alone is restricted to situations in which the financial statements are not stated in accordance with GAAP.

When an auditor issues a qualified report, he or she must use the term *except for* in the opinion paragraph. The implication is that the auditor is satisfied that the overall financial statements are correctly stated "except for" a specific aspect of them. Examples of this qualification are given later in this chapter. It is unacceptable to use the phrase *except for* with any other type of audit opinion.

Adverse Opinion

An **adverse opinion** is used only when the auditor believes that the overall financial statements are so *materially misstated or misleading* that they do not present fairly the financial position or results of operations and cash flows in conformity with GAAP. The adverse opinion report can arise only when the auditor has knowledge, after an adequate investigation, of the absence of conformity. This is uncommon and thus the adverse opinion is rarely used.

Disclaimer of Opinion

A **disclaimer of opinion** is issued when the auditor has been *unable to satisfy himself or herself* that the overall financial statements are fairly presented. The necessity for disclaiming an opinion may arise because of a *severe limitation on the scope* of the audit or a *nonindependent relationship* under the *Code of Professional Conduct* between the auditor and the client. Either of these situations prevents the auditor from expressing an opinion on the financial statements as a whole. The auditor also has the option to issue a disclaimer of opinion for a going concern problem.

The disclaimer is distinguished from an adverse opinion in that it can arise only from a *lack of knowledge* by the auditor, whereas to express an adverse opinion, the auditor must have knowledge that the financial statements are not fairly stated. Both disclaimers and adverse opinions are used only when the condition is highly material.

MATERIALITY

OBJECTIVE 2-5

Explain how materiality affects audit reporting decisions.

Materiality is an essential consideration in determining the appropriate type of report for a given set of circumstances. For example, if a misstatement is immaterial relative to the financial statements of the entity for the current period, it is appropriate to issue an unqualified report. A common instance is the immediate expensing of office supplies rather than carrying the unused portion in inventory because the amount is insignificant.

The situation is totally different when the amounts are of such significance that the financial statements are materially affected as a whole. In these circumstances, it is necessary to issue a disclaimer of opinion or an adverse opinion, depending on the nature of the misstatement. In situations of lesser materiality, a qualified opinion is appropriate.

Levels of Materiality

The common definition of materiality as it applies to accounting and therefore to audit reporting is as follows:

> A misstatement in the financial statements can be considered material if knowledge of the misstatement would affect a decision of a reasonable user of the statements.

In applying this definition, three levels of materiality are used for determining the type of opinion to issue.

Amounts Are Immaterial When a misstatement in the financial statements exists but is unlikely to affect the decisions of a reasonable user, it is considered to be immaterial. An unqualified opinion is therefore appropriate. For example, assume that management recorded prepaid insurance as an asset in the previous year and decides to expense it in the current year to reduce record-keeping costs. Management has failed to follow GAAP, but if the amounts are small, the misstatement would be immaterial and a standard unqualified audit report would be appropriate.

Audit Materiality Task Force

Amounts Are Material but Do Not Overshadow the Financial Statements as a Whole The second level of materiality exists when a misstatement in the financial statements would affect a user's decision, but the overall statements are still fairly stated and therefore useful. For example, knowledge of a large misstatement in fixed assets might affect a user's willingness to loan money to a company if the assets were the collateral. A misstatement of inventory does not mean that cash, accounts receivable, and other elements of the financial statements, or the financial statements as a whole, are materially incorrect.

To make materiality decisions when a condition requiring a departure from an unqualified report exists, the auditor must evaluate all effects on the financial statements. Assume that the auditor is unable to satisfy himself or herself whether inventory is fairly stated in deciding on the appropriate type of opinion. Because of the effect of a misstatement in inventory on other accounts and on totals in the statements, the auditor needs to consider the materiality of the combined effect on inventory, total current assets, total working capital, total assets, income taxes, income taxes payable, total current liabilities, cost of goods sold, net income before taxes, and net income after taxes.

When the auditor concludes that a misstatement is material but does not overshadow the financial statements as a whole, a qualified opinion (using "except for") is appropriate.

Amounts Are So Material or So Pervasive That Overall Fairness of the Statements Is in Question The highest level of materiality exists when users are likely to make incorrect decisions if they rely on the overall financial statements. To return to the previous example, if inventory is the largest balance on the financial statements, a large misstatement would probably be so material that the auditor's report should indicate the financial statements taken as a whole cannot be considered fairly stated. When the highest level of materiality exists, the auditor must issue either a disclaimer of opinion or an adverse opinion, depending on which conditions exist.

When determining whether an exception is highly material, the extent to which the exception affects different parts of the financial statements must be considered. This is called pervasiveness. A misclassification between cash and accounts receivable affects only those two accounts and is therefore not pervasive. On the other hand, failure to record a material sale is highly pervasive because it affects sales, accounts receivable, income tax expense, accrued income taxes, and retained earnings, which in turn affect current assets, total assets, current liabilities, total liabilities, owners' equity, gross margin, and operating income.

As misstatements become more pervasive, the likelihood of issuing an adverse opinion rather than a qualified opinion increases. For example, suppose the auditor decides a misclassification between cash and accounts receivable should result in a qualified opinion because it is material; the failure to record a sale of the same dollar amount may result in an adverse opinion because of pervasiveness.

Regardless of the amount involved, a disclaimer of opinion must be issued if the auditor is determined to lack independence under the rules of the *Code of Professional Conduct*. This harsh requirement reflects the importance of independence to auditors. Any deviation from the independence rule is therefore considered highly material. Table 2-1 summarizes the relationship between materiality and the type of opinion to be issued.

Materiality Decisions

In concept, the effect of materiality on the type of opinion to issue is straightforward. In application, deciding on actual materiality in a given situation is a difficult judgment.

TABLE 2-1 Relationship of Materiality to Type of Opinion

Materiality Level	Significance in Terms of Reasonable Users' Decisions	Type of Opinion
Immaterial	Users' decisions are unlikely to be affected.	Unqualified
Material	Users' decisions are likely to be affected only if the information in question is important to the specific decisions being made. The overall financial statements are presented fairly.	Qualified
Highly material	Most or all users' decisions based on the financial statements are likely to be significantly affected.	Disclaimer or Adverse

Note: Lack of independence requires a disclaimer regardless of materiality.

There are no simple, well-defined guidelines that enable auditors to decide when something is immaterial, material, or highly material. The evaluation of materiality also depends on whether the situation involves a failure to follow GAAP or a scope limitation.

Materiality Decisions—Non-GAAP Condition When a client has failed to follow GAAP, the audit report will be unqualified, qualified opinion only, or adverse, depending on the materiality of the departure. Several aspects of materiality must be considered.

Dollar Amounts Compared with a Base The primary concern in measuring materiality when a client has failed to follow GAAP is usually the total dollar misstatement in the accounts involved, compared with some base. A $10,000 misstatement might be material for a small company, but not for a larger one. Therefore, misstatements must be compared with some measurement base before a decision can be made about the materiality of the failure to follow GAAP. Common bases include net income, total assets, current assets, and working capital.

For example, assume that the auditor believes there is a $100,000 overstatement of inventory because of the client's failure to follow GAAP. Also assume recorded inventory of $1 million, current assets of $3 million, and net income before taxes of $2 million. In this case, the auditor must evaluate the materiality of a misstatement of inventory of 10 percent, current assets of 3.3 percent, and net income before taxes of 5 percent.

To evaluate overall materiality, the auditor must also combine all unadjusted misstatements and judge whether there may be individually immaterial misstatements that, when combined, significantly affect the statements. In the inventory example just given, assume the auditor believes there is also an overstatement of $150,000 in accounts receivable. The total effect on current assets is now 8.3 percent ($250,000 divided by $3,000,000) and 12.5 percent on net income before taxes ($250,000 divided by $2,000,000).

When comparing potential misstatements with a base, the auditor must carefully consider all accounts affected by a misstatement (pervasiveness). For example, it is important not to overlook the effect of an understatement of inventory on cost of goods sold, income before taxes, income tax expense, and accrued income taxes payable.

Measurability The dollar amount of some misstatements cannot be accurately measured. For example, a client's unwillingness to disclose an existing lawsuit or the acquisition of a new company subsequent to the balance sheet date is difficult if not impossible to measure in terms of dollar amounts. The materiality question the auditor must evaluate in such situations is the effect on statement users of the failure to make the disclosure.

Nature of the Item The decision of a user may also be affected by the kind of misstatement in the statement. The following may affect the user's decision and therefore the auditor's opinion in a different way than most misstatements:

1. Transactions are illegal or fraudulent.
2. An item may materially affect some future period even though it is immaterial when only the current period is considered.
3. An item has a "psychic" effect (for example, the item changes a small loss to a small profit, maintains a trend of increasing earnings, or allows earnings to exceed analysts' expectations).
4. An item may be important in terms of possible consequences arising from contractual obligations (for example, the effect of failure to comply with a debt restriction may result in a material loan being called).

Materiality Decisions—Scope Limitations Condition When there is a scope limitation in an audit, the audit report will be unqualified, qualified scope and opinion, or disclaimer, depending on the materiality of the scope limitation. The auditor will consider the same three factors included in the previous discussion about materiality decisions for failure to follow GAAP, but they will be considered differently. The size of *potential* misstatements, rather than known misstatements, is important in determining whether an unqualified report, a qualified report, or a disclaimer of opinion is appropriate for a scope limitation. For example, if recorded accounts payable of $400,000 was not audited, the auditor must evaluate the potential misstatement in accounts payable and decide how materially the financial statements could be affected. The pervasiveness of these potential misstatements must also be considered.

It is typically more difficult to evaluate the materiality of potential misstatements resulting from a scope limitation than for failure to follow GAAP. Misstatements resulting from failure to follow GAAP are known. Those resulting from scope limitations must usually be subjectively measured in terms of potential or likely misstatements. For example, a recorded accounts payable of $400,000 might be understated by more than $1 million, which may affect several totals, including gross margin, net earnings, and total assets.

DISCUSSION OF CONDITIONS REQUIRING A DEPARTURE

You should now understand the relationships among the conditions requiring a departure from an unqualified report, the major types of reports other than unqualified, and the three levels of materiality. This part of the chapter examines the conditions requiring a departure from an unqualified report in greater detail and shows examples of reports.

OBJECTIVE 2-6

Draft appropriately modified audit reports under a variety of circumstances.

Auditor's Scope Has Been Restricted

Two major categories of scope restrictions exist: those caused by a client and those caused by conditions beyond the control of either the client or the auditor. The effect on the auditor's report is the same for either, but the interpretation of materiality is likely to be different. When there is a scope restriction, the appropriate response is to issue an unqualified report, a qualification of scope and opinion, or a disclaimer of opinion, depending on materiality.

For client-imposed restrictions, the auditor should be concerned about the possibility that management is trying to prevent discovery of misstated information. In such cases, the AICPA has encouraged a disclaimer of opinion when materiality is in question. When restrictions result from conditions beyond the client's control, a qualification of scope and opinion is more likely.

Two restrictions occasionally imposed by clients on the auditor's scope relate to the observation of physical inventory and the confirmation of accounts receivable, but other restrictions may also occur. Reasons for client-imposed scope restrictions may be a desire to save audit fees and, in the case of confirming receivables, to prevent possible conflicts between the client and customer when amounts differ.

The most common case in which conditions beyond the client's and auditor's control cause a scope restriction is an engagement agreed on after the client's balance sheet date. The confirmation of accounts receivable, physical examination of inventory, and other important procedures may be impossible under those circumstances. When the auditor cannot perform procedures he or she considers desirable but can be satisfied with alternative procedures that the information being verified is fairly stated, an unqualified report is appropriate. If alternative procedures cannot be performed, a qualified scope and opinion or disclaimer of opinion is necessary, depending on materiality.

A restriction on the scope of the auditor's examination requires a qualifying paragraph preceding the opinion to describe the restriction. In the case of a disclaimer, the entire scope paragraph is excluded from the report.

For example, the report in Figure 2-6 (p. 46) would be appropriate for an audit in which the amounts were material but not pervasive and the auditor could not obtain audited financial statements supporting an investment in a foreign affiliate and could not satisfy himself or herself by alternate procedures. The entire introductory paragraph and most of the second paragraph are omitted because they use standard wording.

When the amounts are so material that a disclaimer of opinion rather than a qualified opinion is required, the auditor uses only three paragraphs. The first (introductory) paragraph is modified slightly to say "We were engaged to audit. . . ." The second paragraph is the same as the third paragraph in Figure 2-6. The scope paragraph is deleted and the final (opinion) paragraph is changed to a disclaimer. The reason for deleting the scope paragraph is to avoid stating anything that might lead readers to believe that other parts of the financial statements were audited and therefore might be fairly stated. Figure 2-7 (p. 46) shows the audit report assuming the auditor had concluded that the facts in Figure 2-6 required a disclaimer rather than a qualified opinion.

FIGURE 2-6 Qualified Scope and Opinion Report Due to Scope Restriction

INDEPENDENT AUDITOR'S REPORT

(Same introductory paragraph as standard report)

Scope Paragraph–Qualified

Except as discussed in the following paragraph, we conducted our audit . . . (remainder is the same as the scope paragraph in the standard report)

Third Paragraph–Added

We were unable to obtain audited financial statements supporting the Company's investment in a foreign affiliate stated at $475,000 or its equity in earnings of that affiliate of $365,000, which is included in net income, as described in Note X to the financial statements. Because of the nature of the Company's records, we were unable to satisfy ourselves as to the carrying value of the investment or the equity in its earnings by means of other auditing procedures.

Opinion Paragraph–Qualified

In our opinion, except for the effects of such adjustments, if any, as might have been determined to be necessary had we been able to examine evidence regarding the foreign affiliate investment and earnings, the financial statements referred to above present fairly, in all material respects, the financial position of Laughlin Corporation as of December 31, 2002, and the results of its operations and its cash flows for the year then ended in conformity with accounting principles generally accepted in the United States of America.

FIGURE 2-7 Disclaimer of Opinion Due to Scope Restriction

INDEPENDENT AUDITOR'S REPORT

Introductory Paragraph–Modification of Standard Report

We were engaged to audit . . . (remainder is the same as the introductory paragraph in the standard report)

Second Paragraph–Added

(Same wording as that used for the third paragraph in Figure 2-6)

Opinion Paragraph–Disclaimer

Because we were unable to obtain audited financial statements supporting the Company's investment in a foreign affiliate and we were unable to satisfy ourselves as to the carrying value of the investment or the equity in its earnings by means of other auditing procedures, the scope of our work was not sufficient to enable us to express, and we do not express, an opinion on these financial statements.

Note: In a disclaimer due to a scope restriction, the scope paragraph is omitted entirely.

Statements Are Not in Conformity with GAAP

When the auditor knows that the financial statements may be misleading because they were not prepared in conformity with GAAP, and the client is unable or unwilling to correct the misstatement, he or she must issue a qualified or an adverse opinion, depending on the materiality of the item in question. The opinion must clearly state the nature of the deviation from accepted principles and the amount of the misstatement, if it is known. Figure 2-8 shows an example of a qualified opinion when a client did not capitalize leases as required by GAAP. The first and second paragraphs are omitted because they include standard wording.

When the amounts are so material or pervasive that an adverse opinion is required, the scope would still be unqualified and the qualifying paragraph could remain the same, but the opinion paragraph might be as shown in Figure 2-9.

When the client fails to include information that is necessary for the fair presentation of financial statements in the body of the statements or in the related footnotes, it is the auditor's responsibility to present the information in the audit report and to issue a qualified or an adverse opinion. It is common to put this type of qualification in an added paragraph preceding the opinion (the scope paragraph will remain unqualified) and to refer to the added paragraph in the opinion paragraph. Figure 2-10 shows an example of an audit report in which the auditor considered the financial statement disclosure inadequate.

Rule 203 Reports Determining whether statements are in accordance with GAAP can be difficult. Rule 203 in the *Code of Professional Conduct* permits a departure from generally accepted accounting principles when the auditor believes that adherence to these would result in misleading statements.

FIGURE 2-8 Qualified Opinion Report Due to Non-GAAP

INDEPENDENT AUDITOR'S REPORT

(Same introductory and scope paragraphs as the standard report)

The Company has excluded from property and debt in the accompanying balance sheet certain lease obligations that, in our opinion, should be capitalized to conform with U.S. generally accepted accounting principles. If these lease obligations were capitalized, property would be increased by $4,600,000, long-term debt by $4,200,000, and retained earnings by $400,000 as of December 31, 2002, and net income and earnings per share would be increased by $400,000 and $1.75, respectively, for the year then ended.

Third Paragraph–Added

In our opinion, except for the effects of not capitalizing lease obligations, as discussed in the preceding paragraph, the financial statements referred to above present fairly, in all material respects, the financial position of Ajax Company as of December 31, 2002, and the results of its operations and its cash flows for the year then ended in conformity with accounting principles generally accepted in the United States of America.

Opinion Paragraph–Qualified

FIGURE 2-9 Adverse Opinion Due to Non-GAAP

INDEPENDENT AUDITOR'S REPORT

(Same introductory and scope paragraphs as the standard report)

(Same third paragraph as that used for the third paragraph in Figure 2-8)

Third Paragraph–Added

In our opinion, because of the effects of the matters discussed in the preceding paragraph, the financial statements referred to above do not present fairly, in conformity with accounting principles generally accepted in the United States of America, the financial position of Ajax Company as of December 31, 2002, or the results of its operations and its cash flows for the year then ended.

Opinion Paragraph–Adverse

FIGURE 2-10 Qualified Opinion Due to Inadequate Disclosure

INDEPENDENT AUDITOR'S REPORT

(Same introductory and scope paragraphs as the standard report)

On January 15, 2002, the company issued debentures in the amount of $3,600,000 for the purpose of financing plant expansion. The debenture agreement restricts the payment of future cash dividends to earnings after December 31, 2002. In our opinion, disclosure of this information is required to conform with accounting principles generally accepted in the United States of America.

Third Paragraph–Added

In our opinion, except for the omission of the information discussed in the preceding paragraph, the financial statements referred to above present fairly . . . (remainder is the same as the opinion in the standard report)

Opinion Paragraph–Qualified

When the auditor decides that adherence to GAAP would result in misleading statements, there should be a complete explanation in a third paragraph. The paragraph should fully explain the departure and why GAAP would have resulted in misleading statements. The opinion paragraph should then be unqualified except for the reference to the third paragraph. As discussed earlier in the chapter, this is called an unqualified audit report with an explanatory paragraph.

Lack of Statement of Cash Flows The client's unwillingness to include a statement of cash flows is specifically addressed in SAS 58 (AU 508). When the statement is omitted, there must be a third paragraph stating the omission and an "except for" opinion qualification.

Auditor Is Not Independent

If the auditor has not fulfilled the independence requirements specified by the *Code of Professional Conduct,* a disclaimer of opinion is required even though all the audit procedures considered necessary in the circumstances were performed. The wording in Figure 2-11 (p. 48) is recommended when the auditor is not independent.

FIGURE 2-11 Disclaimer Due to Lack of Independence

We are not independent with respect to Home Decors.com, Inc., and the accompanying balance sheet as of December 31, 2002, and the related statements of income, retained earnings, and cash flows for the year then ended were not audited by us. Accordingly, we do not express an opinion on them.

Note: When the auditor lacks independence, no report title is included.

The lack of independence overrides any other scope limitations. Therefore, no other reason for disclaiming an opinion should be cited. There should be no mention in the report of the performance of any audit procedures. It is an example of a one-paragraph audit report.

AUDITOR'S DECISION PROCESS FOR AUDIT REPORTS

OBJECTIVE 2-7

Determine the appropriate audit report for a given audit situation.

Auditors use a well-defined process for deciding the appropriate audit report in a given set of circumstances. The auditor must first assess whether any conditions exist requiring a departure from a standard unqualified report. If any conditions exist, the auditor must then assess the materiality of the condition and determine the appropriate type of report.

Determine Whether Any Condition Exists Requiring a Departure from a Standard Unqualified Report The most important of these conditions are identified in Table 2-2. Auditors identify these conditions as they perform the audit and include information about any condition in the working papers as discussion items for audit reporting. If none of these conditions exist, which is the case in most audits, the auditor issues a standard unqualified audit report.

TABLE 2-2 Audit Report for Each Condition Requiring a Departure from a Standard Unqualified Report at Different Levels of Materiality

Condition Requiring an Unqualified Report with Modified Wording or Explanatory Paragraph	Level of Materiality: Immaterial	Level of Materiality: Material
Accounting principles not consistently applied*	Unqualified	Unqualified report, explanatory paragraph
Substantial doubt about going concern†	Unqualified	Unqualified report, explanatory paragraph
Justified departure from GAAP or other accounting principle	Unqualified	Unqualified report, explanatory paragraph
Emphasis of a matter	Unqualified	Unqualified report, explanatory paragraph
Use of another auditor	Unqualified	Unqualified report, modified wording

Condition Requiring a Departure from Unqualified Report	Level of Materiality: Immaterial	Material, But Does Not Overshadow Financial Statements as a Whole	So Material That Overall Fairness Is in Question
Scope restricted by client or other conditions	Unqualified	Qualified scope, additional paragraph, and qualified opinion (except for)	Disclaimer
Financial statements not prepared in accordance with GAAP‡	Unqualified	Additional paragraph and qualified opinion (except for)	Adverse
The auditor is not independent		Disclaimer, regardless of materiality	

* If the auditor does not concur with the appropriateness of the change, the condition is considered a violation of GAAP.

† The auditor has the option of issuing a disclaimer of opinion.

‡ If the auditor can demonstrate that GAAP would be misleading, an unqualified report with an explanatory paragraph would be appropriate.

Decide the Materiality for Each Condition When a condition requiring a departure from a standard unqualified opinion exists, the auditor evaluates the potential effect on the financial statements. For departures from GAAP or scope restrictions, the auditor must decide among immaterial, material, and highly material. All other conditions, except for lack of auditor independence, require only a distinction between immaterial and material. The materiality decision is a difficult one, requiring considerable judgment. For example, assume that there is a scope limitation in auditing inventory. It is difficult to assess the potential misstatement of an account that the auditor does not audit.

Decide the Appropriate Type of Report for the Condition, Given the Materiality Level After making the first two decisions, it is easy to decide the appropriate type of opinion by using a decision aid. An example of such an aid is Table 2-2. For example, assume that the auditor concludes that there is a departure from GAAP and it is material, but not highly material. Table 2-2 shows that the appropriate audit report is a qualified opinion with an additional paragraph discussing the departure. The introductory and scope paragraphs will be included using standard wording.

Write the Audit Report Most CPA firms have computer templates that include precise wording for different circumstances to help the auditor write the audit report. Also, one or more partners in most CPA firms have special expertise in writing audit reports. These partners typically write or review all audit reports before they are issued.

More Than One Condition Requiring a Departure or Modification

Auditors often encounter situations involving more than one of the conditions requiring a departure from an unqualified report or modification of the standard unqualified report. In these circumstances, the auditor should modify his or her opinion for each condition unless one has the effect of neutralizing the others. For example, if there is a scope limitation and a situation in which the auditor is not independent, the scope limitation should not be revealed. The following situations are examples when more than one modification should be included in the report:

- The auditor is not independent and the auditor knows that the company has not followed generally accepted accounting principles.
- There is a scope limitation and there is substantial doubt about the company's ability to continue as a going concern.
- There is a substantial doubt about the company's ability to continue as a going concern and information about the causes of the uncertainties is not adequately disclosed in a footnote.
- There is a deviation in the statements' preparation in accordance with GAAP and another accounting principle was applied on a basis that was not consistent with that of the preceding year.

Number of Paragraphs in the Report

Many readers interpret the number of paragraphs in the report as an important "signal" as to whether the financial statements are correct. A three-paragraph report ordinarily indicates that there are no exceptions in the audit. However, three-paragraph reports are also issued when a disclaimer of opinion is issued due to a scope limitation or for an unqualified shared report involving other auditors. The presence of more than three paragraphs indicates some type of qualification or required explanation.

An additional paragraph is added before the opinion for a qualified opinion, an adverse opinion, and a disclaimer of opinion for a scope limitation. This results in a four-paragraph report, except for the disclaimer of opinion for a scope limitation. A disclaimer due to a scope limitation results in a three-paragraph report because the scope paragraph is omitted. A disclaimer due to a lack of independence is a one-paragraph report.

When an unqualified opinion with explanatory paragraph is issued, an explanatory paragraph usually follows the opinion. No explanatory paragraph is required for an unqualified shared report involving other auditors, but the wording in all three paragraphs is modified.

Table 2-3 (p. 50) summarizes the types of reports issued for the audit of financial statements, the number of paragraphs for each type, the standard wording paragraphs modified, and the location of the additional paragraph. The table excludes a disclaimer for a lack of independence, which is a special, one-paragraph report.

TABLE 2-3 Number of Paragraphs, Standard Wording Paragraphs Modified, and Location of Additional Paragraph for Audit Reports

Type of Report	Number of Paragraphs	Standard Wording Paragraphs Modified	Location of Additional Paragraph
Standard unqualified	3	None	None
Unqualified with explanatory paragraph	4	None	After opinion
Unqualified shared report with other auditors	3	All three paragraphs	None
Qualified–opinion only	4	Opinion only	Before opinion
Qualified–scope and opinion	4	Scope and opinion	Before opinion
Disclaimer–scope limitation	3	Introductory and opinion paragraphs modified; scope paragraph eliminated	Before opinion
Adverse	4	Opinion only	Before opinion

IMPACT OF E-COMMERCE ON AUDIT REPORTING

OBJECTIVE 2-8

Discuss the impact of e-commerce on audit reporting.

Most public companies provide access to financial information through their home Web page. Visitors to a company's Web site can view the company's most recent audited financial statements, including the auditor's report. In addition, it is common for the company to also include such information as unaudited quarterly financial statements, other selected financial information, and press releases often labeled as "About the Company" or "Investor Relations" on its Web site.

Even before the widespread use of the Internet, companies often published documents that contained information in addition to audited financial statements and the independent auditor's report. The most common example was and still is the company's annual report. Under generally accepted auditing standards, the auditor has no obligation to perform any procedures to corroborate the other information. The auditor is, however, responsible for reading the other information to determine whether it is materially inconsistent with information in the audited financial statements.

However, under current auditing standards, auditors are not required to read information contained in electronic sites, such as the company's Web site, that also contain the company's audited financial statements and the auditor's report. Auditing standards note that electronic sites are a means of distributing information and are not considered "documents," as that term is used in GAAS.

SUMMARY

This chapter described the four categories of audit reports and the auditor's decision process in choosing the appropriate audit report to issue. The conditions necessary to issue the auditor's standard unqualified audit report and the content of that report were discussed. In some circumstances, an explanatory paragraph or modification of the unqualified report is required. When there is a material departure from GAAP or a material limitation on the scope of the audit, an unqualified report cannot be issued. The appropriate report to issue in these circumstances depends on whether the situation involves a GAAP departure or a scope limitation, as well as the level of materiality.

ESSENTIAL TERMS

Adverse opinion—a report issued when the auditor believes the financial statements are so materially misstated or misleading as a whole that they do not present fairly the entity's financial position or the results of its operations and cash flows in conformity with GAAP

Disclaimer of opinion—a report issued when the auditor has not been able to become satisfied that the overall financial statements are fairly presented or the auditor is not independent

Material misstatement—a misstatement in the financial statements, knowledge of which would affect a decision of a reasonable user of the statements

Qualified opinion—a report issued when the auditor believes that the overall financial statements are fairly stated but that either the scope of the audit was limited or the financial data indicated a failure to follow GAAP

Standard unqualified audit report—the report a CPA issues when all auditing conditions have been met, no significant misstatements have been discovered and left uncorrected, and it is the auditor's opinion that the financial statements are fairly stated in accordance with GAAP

Unqualified audit report with explanatory paragraph or modified wording—an unqualified report in which the financial statements are fairly presented, but the auditor believes it is important, or is required, to provide additional information

REVIEW QUESTIONS

2-1 **(Objective 2-1)** Explain why auditors' reports are important to users of financial statements and why it is desirable to have standard wording.

2-2 **(Objective 2-1)** List the seven parts of a standard unqualified audit report and explain the meaning of each part. How do the parts compare with those found in a qualified report?

2-3 **(Objective 2-1)** What are the purposes of the scope paragraph in the auditor's report? Identify the most important information included in the scope paragraph.

2-4 **(Objective 2-1)** What are the purposes of the opinion paragraph in the auditor's report? Identify the most important information included in the opinion paragraph.

2-5 **(Objective 2-1)** On February 17, 2003, a CPA completed the field work on the financial statements for the Buckheizer Technology Corporation for the year ended December 31, 2002. The audit is satisfactory in all respects except for the existence of a change in accounting principles from FIFO to LIFO inventory valuation, which results in an explanatory paragraph to consistency. On February 26, the auditor completed the tax return and the draft of the financial statements. The final audit report was completed, attached to the financial statements, and delivered to the client on March 7. What is the appropriate date on the auditor's report?

2-6 **(Objective 2-2)** What five circumstances are required for a standard unqualified report to be issued?

2-7 **(Objectives 2-3, 2-6)** What type of opinion should an auditor issue when the financial statements are not in accordance with GAAP because such adherence would result in misleading statements?

2-8 **(Objectives 2-3, 2-4)** Distinguish between an unqualified report with an explanatory paragraph or modified wording and a qualified report. Give examples when an explanatory paragraph or modified wording should be used in an unqualified opinion.

2-9 **(Objective 2-3)** Describe what is meant by reports involving the use of other auditors. What are the three options available to the principal auditor and when should each be used?

2-10 **(Objective 2-3)** The client has restated the prior-year statements because of a change from LIFO to FIFO. How should this be reflected in the auditor's report?

2-11 **(Objective 2-3)** Distinguish between changes that affect consistency and those that may affect comparability but not consistency. Give an example of each.

2-12 **(Objective 2-4)** List the three conditions that require a departure from an unqualified opinion and give one specific example of each of those conditions.

2-13 **(Objective 2-4)** Distinguish between a qualified opinion, an adverse opinion, and a disclaimer of opinion, and explain the circumstances under which each is appropriate.

2-14 **(Objective 2-5)** Define *materiality* as it is used in audit reporting. What conditions will affect the auditor's determination of materiality?

2-15 **(Objective 2-5)** Explain how materiality differs for failure to follow GAAP and for lack of independence.

2-16 **(Objective 2-6)** How does the auditor's opinion differ between scope limitations caused by client restrictions and limitations resulting from conditions beyond the client's control? Under which of these two would the auditor be most likely to issue a disclaimer of opinion? Explain.

2-17 (Objective 2-4) Distinguish between a report qualified as to opinion only and one with both a scope and opinion qualification.

2-18 (Objectives 2-5, 2-6) Identify the three alternative opinions that may be appropriate when the client's financial statements are not in accordance with GAAP. Under what circumstance is each appropriate?

2-19 (Objectives 2-4, 2-6) Discuss why the AICPA has such strict requirements on audit opinions when the auditor is not independent.

2-20 (Objective 2-7) When an auditor discovers more than one condition that requires departure from or modification of the standard unqualified report, what should the auditor's report include?

2-21 (Objective 2-8) What responsibility does the auditor have for information on the company's Web site that may be linked to electronic versions of the company's annual financial statements and auditor's report? How does this differ from the auditor's responsibility for other information in the company's annual report that includes the financial statements and auditor's report?

MULTIPLE CHOICE QUESTIONS FROM CPA EXAMINATIONS

2-22 (Objectives 2-1, 2-2, 2-3) The following questions concern unqualified audit reports. Choose the best response.

a. An auditor's unqualified report
   (1) implies only that items disclosed in the financial statements and footnotes are properly presented and takes no position on the adequacy of disclosure.
   (2) implies that disclosure is adequate in the financial statements and footnotes.
   (3) explicitly states that disclosure is adequate in the financial statements and footnotes.
   (4) explicitly states that all material items have been disclosed in conformity with accounting principles generally accepted in the United States of America.

b. The date of the CPA's opinion on the financial statements of the client should be the date of the
   (1) closing of the client's books.
   (2) receipt of the client's letter of representation.
   (3) completion of all important audit procedures.
   (4) submission of the report to the client.

c. If a principal auditor decides to refer in his or her report to the audit of another auditor, he or she is required to disclose the
   (1) name of the other auditor.
   (2) nature of the inquiry into the other auditor's professional standing and extent of the review of the other auditor's work.
   (3) portion of the financial statements audited by the other auditor.
   (4) reasons for being unwilling to assume responsibility for the other auditor's work.

d. An entity changed from the straight-line method to the declining-balance method of depreciation for all newly acquired assets. This change has no material effect on the current year's financial statements but is reasonably certain to have a substantial effect in later years. If the change is disclosed in the notes to the financial statements, the auditor should issue a report with a(n)
   (1) qualified opinion.
   (2) unqualified opinion with explanatory paragraph.
   (3) unqualified opinion.
   (4) qualified opinion with explanatory paragraph regarding consistency.

2-23 (Objectives 2-4, 2-5, 2-6) The following questions concern audit reports other than unqualified audit reports with standard wording. Choose the best response.

a. A CPA will issue an adverse auditor's opinion if
   (1) the scope of the audit is limited by the client.
   (2) the exception to the fairness of presentation is so material that an "except for" opinion is not justified.
   (3) the auditor did not perform sufficient auditing procedures to form an opinion on the financial statements taken as a whole.
   (4) major uncertainties exist concerning the company's future.

b. An auditor would most likely disclaim an opinion because of
   (1) the client's failure to present supplementary information required by the Financial Accounting Standards Board (FASB).
   (2) inadequate disclosure of material information.

(3) a client-imposed scope limitation.
(4) the qualification of an opinion by the other auditor of a subsidiary when responsibility has been divided.

c. Under which of the following sets of circumstances should an auditor issue a qualified opinion?
(1) The financial statements contain a departure from generally accepted accounting principles, the effect of which is material.
(2) The principal auditor decides to make reference to the report of another auditor who audited a subsidiary.
(3) There has been a material change between periods in the method of the application of accounting principles.
(4) There are significant uncertainties affecting the financial statements.

DISCUSSION QUESTIONS AND PROBLEMS

2-24 (Objective 2-1) A careful reading of an unqualified report indicates several important phrases. Explain why each of the following phrases or clauses is used rather than the alternative provided:

a. "In our opinion, the financial statements present fairly" rather than "The financial statements present fairly."
b. "We conducted our audit in accordance with auditing standards generally accepted in the United States of America" rather than "Our audit was performed to detect material misstatements in the financial statements."
c. "The financial statements referred to above present fairly in all material respects the financial position" rather than "The financial statements mentioned above are correctly stated."
d. "In conformity with accounting principles generally accepted in the United States of America" rather than "are properly stated to represent the true economic conditions."
e. "Brown & Phillips, CPAs (firm name)," rather than "James E. Brown, CPA (individual partner's name)."

2-25 (Objectives 2-1, 2-2, 2-3, 2-5, 2-6) Roscoe, CPA, has completed the audit of the financial statements of Excelsior Corporation as of and for the year ended December 31, 2002. Roscoe also audited and reported on the Excelsior financial statements for the prior year. Roscoe drafted the following report for 2002.

We have audited the balance sheet and statements of income and retained earnings of Excelsior Corporation as of December 31, 2002. We conducted our audit in accordance with generally accepted accounting standards. Those standards require that we plan and perform the audit to obtain reasonable assurance about whether the financial statements are free of misstatement.

We believe that our audits provide a reasonable basis for our opinion.

In our opinion, the financial statements referred to above present fairly the financial position of Excelsior Corporation as of December 31, 2002, and the results of its operations for the year then ended in conformity with generally accepted auditing standards, applied on a basis consistent with those of the preceding year.

Roscoe, CPA
(Signed)

Other Information

- Excelsior is presenting comparative financial statements.
- Excelsior does not wish to present a statement of cash flows for either year.
- During 2002, Excelsior changed its method of accounting for long-term construction contracts and properly reflected the effect of the change in the current year's financial statements and restated the prior year's statements. Roscoe is satisfied with Excelsior's justification for making the change. The change is discussed in footnote 12.
- Roscoe was unable to perform normal accounts receivable confirmation procedures, but alternative procedures were used to satisfy Roscoe as to the existence of the receivables.
- Excelsior Corporation is the defendant in a litigation, the outcome of which is highly uncertain. If the case is settled in favor of the plaintiff, Excelsior will be required to pay a substantial amount of cash, which might require the sale of certain fixed assets. The litigation and the possible effects have been properly disclosed in footnote 11.
- Excelsior issued debentures on January 31, 2001, in the amount of $10 million. The funds obtained from the issuance were used to finance the expansion of plant facilities. The debenture agreement restricts the payment of future cash dividends to earnings after December 31, 2006. Excelsior declined to disclose this essential data in the footnotes to the financial statements.

Required

a. Identify and explain any items included in "Other Information" that need not be part of the auditor's report.

b. Explain the deficiencies in Roscoe's report as drafted.*

2-26 (**Objectives 2-3, 2-4, 2-5, 2-6, 2-7**) For the following independent situations, assume that you are the audit partner on the engagement:

1. During your audit of Debold.com, Inc., you conclude that there is a possibility that inventory is materially overstated. The client refuses to allow you to expand the scope of your audit sufficiently to verify whether the balance is actually misstated.
2. You are auditing Woodcolt Linen Services for the first time. Woodcolt has been in business for several years but has never had an audit before. After the audit is completed, you conclude that the current year balance sheet is stated correctly in accordance with GAAP. The client did not authorize you to do test work for any of the previous years.
3. You were engaged to audit the Cutter Steel Company's financial statements after the close of the corporation's fiscal year. Because you were not engaged until after the balance sheet date, you were not able to physically observe inventory, which is highly material. On the completion of your audit, you are satisfied that Cutter's financial statements are presented fairly, including inventory about which you were able to satisfy yourself by the use of alternative audit procedures.
4. Four weeks after the year-end date, a major customer of Prince Construction Co. declared bankruptcy. Because the customer had confirmed the balance due to Prince at the balance sheet date, management refuses to charge off the account or otherwise disclose the information. The receivable represents approximately 10% of accounts receivable and 20% of net earnings before taxes.
5. You complete the audit of Johnson Department Store, and in your opinion, the financial statements are fairly presented. On the last day of the field work, you discover that one of your supervisors assigned to the audit had a material investment in Johnson.
6. Auto Delivery Company has a fleet of several delivery trucks. In the past, Auto Delivery had followed the policy of purchasing all equipment. In the current year, they decided to lease the trucks. The method of accounting for the trucks is therefore changed to lease capitalization. This change in policy is fully disclosed in footnotes.

Required

For each situation, do the following:

a. Identify which of the conditions requiring a modification of or a deviation from an unqualified standard report is applicable.

b. State the level of materiality as immaterial, material, or highly material. If you cannot decide the level of materiality, state the additional information needed to make a decision.

c. Given your answers in parts a and b, state the type of audit report that should be issued. If you have not decided on one level of materiality in part b, state the appropriate report for each alternative materiality level.

2-27 (**Objectives 2-3, 2-4, 2-5, 2-6, 2-7**) For the following independent situations, assume that you are the audit partner on the engagement:

1. Kieko Technology Corporation has prepared financial statements but has decided to exclude the statement of cash flows. Management explains to you that the users of their financial statements find this statement confusing and prefer not to have it included.

2. HardwareFromHome.com is an Internet-based start-up company created to sell home hardware supplies online. Although the company had a promising start, a downturn in e-commerce retailing has negatively affected the company. The company's sales and cash position have deteriorated significantly, and you have reservations about the ability of the company to continue in operation for the next year.
3. Approximately 20% of the audit of Fur Farms, Inc. was performed by a different CPA firm, selected by you. You have reviewed their working papers and believe they did an excellent job on their portion of the audit. Nevertheless, you are unwilling to take complete responsibility for their work.
4. The controller of Fair City Hotels Co. will not allow you to confirm the receivable balance from two of its major customers. The amounts of the receivables are material in relation to Fair City's financial statements. You are unable to satisfy yourself as to the receivable balances by alternative procedures.

* AICPA adapted.

5. In the last 3 months of the current year, Oil Refining Company decided to change direction and go significantly into the oil drilling business. Management recognizes that this business is exceptionally risky and could jeopardize the success of its existing refining business, but there are significant potential rewards. During the short period of operation in drilling, the company has had three dry wells and no successes. The facts are adequately disclosed in footnotes.
6. Your client, Auto Rental Company, has changed from straight-line to sum-of-the-years' digits depreciation. The effect on this year's income is immaterial, but the effect in future years is likely to be material. The facts are adequately disclosed in footnotes.

Required

For each situation, do the following:

a. Identify which of the conditions requiring a modification of or a deviation from an unqualified standard report is applicable.

b. State the level of materiality as immaterial, material, or highly material. If you cannot decide the level of materiality, state the additional information needed to make a decision.

c. Given your answers in parts a and b, state the appropriate audit report from the following alternatives (if you have not decided on one level of materiality in part b, state the appropriate report for each alternative materiality level):
(1) Unqualified—standard wording
(2) Unqualified—explanatory paragraph
(3) Unqualified—modified wording
(4) Qualified opinion only—except for
(5) Qualified scope and opinion
(6) Disclaimer
(7) Adverse

d. Based on your answer to part c, indicate which paragraphs, if any, should be modified in the standard audit report. Also indicate whether an additional paragraph is necessary and its location in the report.

2-28 **(Objectives 2-3, 2-4, 2-5, 2-6, 2-7)** The following are independent situations for which you will recommend an appropriate audit report:

1. Subsequent to the date of the financial statements as part of his post–balance sheet date audit procedures, a CPA learned that a recent fire caused heavy damage to one of a client's two plants; the loss will not be reimbursed by insurance. The newspapers described the event in detail. The financial statements and appended notes as prepared by the client did not disclose the loss caused by the fire.
2. A CPA is engaged in the audit of the financial statements of a large manufacturing company with branch offices in many widely separated cities. The CPA was not able to count the substantial undeposited cash receipts at the close of business on the last day of the fiscal year at all branch offices.

   As an alternative to this auditing procedure used to verify the accurate cutoff of cash receipts, the CPA observed that deposits in transit as shown on the year-end bank reconciliation appeared as credits on the bank statement on the first business day of the new year. He was satisfied as to the cutoff of cash receipts by the use of the alternative procedure.
3. On January 2, 2003, the Retail Auto Parts Company received a notice from its primary supplier that effective immediately, all wholesale prices would be increased 10%. On the basis of the notice, Retail Auto Parts revalued its December 31, 2002, inventory to reflect the higher costs. The inventory constituted a material proportion of total assets; however, the effect of the revaluation was material to current assets but not to total assets or net income. The increase in valuation is adequately disclosed in the footnotes.
4. E-Lotions.com, Inc. is an online retailer of body lotions and other bath and body supplies. The company records revenues at the time customer orders are placed on the Web site, rather than when the goods are shipped, which is usually two days after the order is placed. The auditor determined that the amount of orders placed but not shipped as of the balance sheet date is not material.
5. For the past 5 years a CPA has audited the financial statements of a manufacturing company. During this period, the audit scope was limited by the client as to the observation of the annual physical inventory. Because the CPA considered the inventories to be material and he was not able to satisfy himself by other auditing procedures, he was unable to express an unqualified opinion on the financial statements in each of the 5 years.

The CPA was allowed to observe physical inventories for the current year ended December 31, 2002, because the client's banker would no longer accept the audit reports. In the interest of economy, the client requested the CPA to not extend his audit procedures to the inventory as of January 1, 2002.

6. During the course of his audit of the financial statements of a corporation for the purpose of expressing an opinion on the statements, a CPA is refused permission to inspect the minute books containing the significant decisions from the board of directors meetings. The corporation secretary instead offers to give the CPA a certified copy of all resolutions and actions involving accounting matters.
7. A CPA has completed her audit of the financial statements of a bus company for the year ended December 31, 2002. Prior to 2002, the company had been depreciating its buses over a 10-year period. During 2002, the company determined that a more realistic estimated life for its buses was 12 years and computed the 2002 depreciation on the basis of the revised estimate. The CPA has satisfied herself that the 12-year life is reasonable.

   The company has adequately disclosed the change in estimated useful lives of its buses and the effect of the change on 2002 income in a note to the financial statements.

Required For each situation, do the following:

a. Identify which of the conditions requiring a deviation from or modification of an unqualified standard report is applicable.
b. State the level of materiality as immaterial, material, or highly material. If you cannot decide the level of materiality, state the additional information needed to make a decision.
c. Given your answers in parts a and b, state the appropriate audit report from the following alternatives (if you have not decided on one level of materiality in part b, state the appropriate report for each alternative materiality level):
   (1) Unqualified—standard wording
   (2) Unqualified—explanatory paragraph
   (3) Unqualified—modified wording
   (4) Qualified opinion only—except for
   (5) Qualified scope and opinion
   (6) Disclaimer
   (7) Adverse*

2-29 **(Objectives 2-1, 2-2, 2-3)** The following tentative auditor's report was drafted by a staff accountant and submitted to a partner in the accounting firm of Better & Best, CPAs:

AUDIT REPORT

To the Audit Committee of American Broadband, Inc.

We have examined the consolidated balance sheets of American Broadband, Inc. and subsidiaries as of December 31, 2002 and 2001, and the related consolidated statements of income, retained earnings, and cash flows for the years then ended. These financial statements are the responsibility of the Company's management. Our responsibility is to express an opinion on these financial statements based on our audits.

Our audits were made in accordance with auditing standards generally accepted in the United States of America as we considered necessary in the circumstances. Other auditors audited the financial statements of certain subsidiaries and have furnished us with reports thereon containing no exceptions. Our opinion expressed herein, insofar as it relates to the amounts included for those subsidiaries, is based solely upon the reports of the other auditors.

As fully discussed in Note 7 to the financial statements, in 2002, the company extended the use of the last-in, first-out (LIFO) method of accounting to include all inventories. In examining inventories, we engaged Dr. Irwin Same (Nobel Prize winner 2000) to test check the technical requirements and specifications of certain items of equipment manufactured by the company.

In our opinion, the financial statements referred to above present fairly the financial position of American Broadband, Inc. as of December 31, 2002, and the results of operations for the years then ended, in conformity with accounting principles generally accepted in the United States of America.

To be signed by
Better & Best, CPAs

March 1, 2003

*AICPA adapted.

Identify deficiencies in the staff accountant's tentative report that constitute departures from the generally accepted standards of reporting.*

Required

2-30 (Objectives 2-1, 2-8) After the completion of the audit of the December 31, 2000, financial statements, IBM Corporation posted on its Web site (www.ibm.com) the following audit report as part of its online 2000 Annual Report:

REPORT OF INDEPENDENT ACCOUNTANTS

To the Stockholders and Board of Directors of
International Business Machines Corporation

In our opinion, the accompanying consolidated financial statements† present fairly, in all material respects, the financial position of International Business Machines Corporation and subsidiary companies at December 31, 2000 and 1999, and the results of their operations and their cash flows for each of the three years in the period ended December 31, 2000, in conformity with accounting principles generally accepted in the United States of America. These financial statements are the responsibility of the company's management; our responsibility is to express an opinion on these financial statements based on our audits. We conducted our audits of these statements in accordance with auditing standards generally accepted in the United States of America, which require that we plan and perform the audit to obtain reasonable assurance about whether the financial statements are free of material misstatement. An audit includes examining, on a test basis, evidence supporting the amounts and disclosures in the financial statements, assessing the accounting principles used and significant estimates made by management, and evaluating the overall financial statement presentation. We believe that our audits provide a reasonable basis for our opinion.

PricewaterhouseCoopers LLP
New York, New York
January 17, 2001

† For purposes of online presentation, audited financial information is identified as "Audited."

Required

a. List the seven parts of the standard unqualified report.
b. Identify the location of each of the seven parts of a standard unqualified report in the preceding audit report.
c. Read the note at the bottom of the report labeled with the "†" and describe why it is important for PricewaterhouseCoopers to include that note in its audit report available on IBM's Web site.
d. The PricewaterhouseCoopers audit report on IBM's Web site can be copied into other electronic files, such as a word processing software package. However, the signature on the report from PricewaterhouseCoopers LLP cannot be easily copied. Why would an audit firm place a copy restriction on its signature?

2-31 (Objectives 2-1, 2-2, 2-4, 2-6) Following are the auditor's report and the complete financial statements of the Young Manufacturing Corporation for the year ended January 31, 2003. The audit was conducted by John Smith, an individual practitioner who has audited the corporation's financial statements and has reported on them for many years.

List and discuss the deficiencies of the auditor's report prepared by John Smith. Your discussion should include justifications that the matters you cited are deficiencies. (Do not check the additions in the statements. Assume that the additions are correct.)*

Required

To: Mr. Paul Young, President
Young Manufacturing Corporation

January 31, 2003

I have audited the balance sheet of the Young Manufacturing Corporation and the related statements of income and retained earnings.

These statements present fairly the financial position and results of operations in conformity with generally accepted principles of accounting applied on a consistent basis. My audit was made in accordance with generally accepted auditing standards and, accordingly, included such tests of the accounting records and such other auditing procedures as I considered necessary in the circumstances.

(Signed) John Smith

* AICPA adapted.

YOUNG MANUFACTURING CORPORATION
Statements of Condition January 31, 2003 and 2002

	2003	2002
Assets		
Current assets:		
Cash	$ 43,822	$ 51,862
Accounts receivable, pledged—less allowances for doubtful accounts of $3,800 in 2003 and $3,000 in 2002 (see note)	65,298	46,922
Inventories, pledged—at average cost, not in excess of replacement cost	148,910	118,264
Other current assets	6,280	5,192
Total current assets	264,310	222,240
Fixed assets:		
Land—at cost	38,900	62,300
Buildings—at cost, less accumulated depreciation of $50,800 in 2003 and $53,400 in 2002	174,400	150,200
Machinery and equipment—at cost, less accumulated depreciation of $30,500 in 2003 and $25,640 in 2002	98,540	78,560
Total fixed assets	311,840	291,060
Total assets	$576,150	$513,300
Liabilities and Stockholders' Equity		
Current liabilities:		
Accounts payable	$ 27,926	$ 48,161
Other liabilities	68,743	64,513
Current portion of long-term mortgage payable	3,600	3,600
Income taxes payable	46,840	30,866
Total current liabilities	147,109	147,140
Long-term liabilities:		
Mortgage payable	90,400	94,000
Total liabilities	237,509	241,140
Stockholders' equity:		
Capital stock, par value $100, 1,000 shares authorized, issued and outstanding	100,000	100,000
Retained earnings	238,641	172,160
Total stockholders' equity	338,641	272,160
Total liabilities and stockholders' equity	$576,150	$513,300

YOUNG MANUFACTURING CORPORATION
Income Statements for the Years Ended January 31, 2003 and 2002

	2003	2002
Income:		
Sales	$884,932	$682,131
Other income	3,872	2,851
Total	888,804	684,982
Costs and expenses:		
Costs of goods sold	463,570	353,842
Selling expenses	241,698	201,986
Administrative expenses	72,154	66,582
Provision for income taxes	45,876	19,940
Other expenses	12,582	13,649
Total	835,880	655,999
Net income	$ 52,924	$ 28,983

INTERNET PROBLEM 2-1: RESEARCH ANNUAL REPORTS

Reference the CW site. The U.S. Securities and Exchange Commission (SEC) is an independent, nonpartisan, quasi-judicial regulatory agency with responsibility for administering the federal securities laws. Publicly traded companies must file electronically a variety of forms or reports with the SEC (for example, annual financial statements). The SEC makes most of these electronic documents available on the Internet via EDGAR. EDGAR stands for Electronic Data Gathering, Analysis, and Retrieval system. The primary purpose for EDGAR is to increase the efficiency and fairness of the securities market for the benefit of investors, corporations, and the economy by accelerating the receipt, acceptance, dissemination, and analysis of time-sensitive corporate information filed with the agency. This problem requires students to use the EDGAR site (1) to research the definitions of SEC filings (for example, 10-K, 8-K) and (2) to use several companies' 10-K reports to classify types of audit opinions issued.

CHAPTER 3

PROFESSIONAL ETHICS

THE VALUE OF THE AUDIT DEPENDS ON AUDITOR INDEPENDENCE

Bruce Smith has watched the stock of his audit client, Ultimate Networks, soar for the past 6 months. Ultimate Networks is gaining market share, and he knows that their sales will continue to soar with the new technology they have in the pipeline. Finally, he can't resist any longer. He calls his stockbroker, John Rizzo, and places an order for 200 shares of Ultimate Networks' stock. "Are you sure this is okay?" asked Rizzo. "I thought Ultimate Networks was your client." Rizzo knows about professional responsibilities because he worked with Bruce at the CPA firm before becoming a stockbroker, and they remained friends. "Why don't you check it out and get back to me?" Rizzo added.

The next morning, Bruce is glad that he has John Rizzo for a stockbroker. The SEC just announced that they had uncovered numerous independence violations at another CPA firm. The firm had to recall several audit reports, and a few partners and audit staff were terminated for making stock investments similar to the investment that Bruce contemplated the day before. As he thinks about the requirement that he not own stock in an audit client, he concludes, "There must be other good investments out there."

LEARNING OBJECTIVES

After studying this chapter, you should be able to

- 3-1 Distinguish ethical from unethical behavior in personal and professional contexts.
- 3-2 Resolve ethical dilemmas using an ethical framework.
- 3-3 Explain the importance of ethical conduct for the accounting profession.
- 3-4 Describe the purpose and content of the AICPA *Code of Professional Conduct.*
- 3-5 Describe factors that influence auditor independence.
- 3-6 Apply the AICPA *Code* rules and interpretations on independence and explain their importance.
- 3-7 Understand the requirements of other rules under the AICPA *Code.*
- 3-8 Describe the enforcement mechanisms for the rules of conduct.

In preceding chapters, audit reports and the demand for audit and other assurance services were discussed. The value of the audit report and the demand for audit services depend on public confidence in the independence and integrity of CPAs. This chapter discusses ethics and the independence and other ethical requirements for CPAs under the AICPA *Code of Professional Conduct.* We begin the chapter with a discussion of general ethical principles and their application to the CPA profession.

WHAT ARE ETHICS?

OBJECTIVE 3-1

Distinguish ethical from unethical behavior in personal and professional contexts.

Ethics can be defined broadly as a set of moral principles or values. Each of us has such a set of values, although we may or may not have considered them explicitly. Philosophers, religious organizations, and other groups have defined in various ways ideal sets of moral principles or values. Examples of prescribed sets of moral principles or values at the implementation level include laws and regulations, church doctrine, codes of business ethics for professional groups such as CPAs, and codes of conduct within individual organizations.

An example of a prescribed set of principles is included in Figure 3-1. These principles were developed by the Josephson Institute of Ethics, a nonprofit membership organization for the improvement of the ethical quality of society.

It is common for people to differ in their moral principles and values and the relative importance they attach to these principles. These differences reflect life experiences, successes and failures, as well as the influences of parents, teachers, and friends.

Need for Ethics

Ethical behavior is necessary for a society to function in an orderly manner. It can be argued that ethics is the glue that holds a society together. Imagine, for example, what would happen if we couldn't depend on the people we deal with to be honest. If parents, teachers, employers, siblings, co-workers, and friends all consistently lied, it would be almost impossible for effective communication to occur.

The need for ethics in society is sufficiently important that many commonly held ethical values are incorporated into laws. However, many of the ethical values found in Figure 3-1 cannot be incorporated into laws because of the judgmental nature of certain values. That does not imply, however, that the principles are less important for an orderly society.

Why People Act Unethically

Most people define *unethical behavior* as conduct that differs from what they believe is appropriate given the circumstances. Each of us decides for ourselves what we consider unethical behavior, both for ourselves and others. It is important to understand what causes people to act in a manner that we decide is unethical.

Josephson Institute

FIGURE 3-1 Illustrative Prescribed Ethical Principles

The following are the six core ethical values that the Josephson Institute associates with ethical behavior:

Trustworthiness includes honesty, integrity, reliability, and loyalty. Honesty requires a good faith intent to convey the truth. Integrity means that the person acts according to conscience, regardless of the situation. Reliability means making all reasonable efforts to fulfill commitments. Loyalty is a responsibility to promote and protect the interests of certain people and organizations.

Respect includes notions such as civility, courtesy, dignity, tolerance, and acceptance. A respectful person treats others with consideration and accepts individual differences and beliefs without prejudice.

Responsibility means being accountable for one's actions and exercising restraint. Responsibility also means pursuing excellence and leading by example, including perseverance and engaging in continuous improvement.

Fairness and justice include issues of equality, impartiality, proportionality, openness, and due process. Fair treatment means that similar situations are handled consistently.

Caring means being genuinely concerned for the welfare of others and includes acting altruistically and showing benevolence.

Citizenship includes obeying laws and performing one's fair share to make society work, including such activities as voting, serving on juries, and conserving resources.

There are two primary reasons why people act unethically: The person's ethical standards are different from those of society as a whole, or the person chooses to act selfishly. In many instances, both reasons exist.

Person's Ethical Standards Differ from General Society Extreme examples of people whose behavior violates almost everyone's ethical standards are drug dealers, bank robbers, and larcenists. Most people who commit such acts feel no remorse when they are apprehended because their ethical standards differ from those of society as a whole.

There are also many far less extreme examples when others violate our ethical values. When people cheat on their tax returns, treat other people with hostility, lie on employment applications, or perform below their competence level as employees, most of us regard that as unethical behavior. If the other person has decided that this behavior is ethical and acceptable, there is a conflict of ethical values that is unlikely to be resolved.

The Person Chooses to Act Selfishly The following example illustrates the difference between ethical standards that differ from general society's and acting selfishly. Person A finds a briefcase in an airport containing important papers and $1,000. He tosses the briefcase and keeps the money. He brags to his family and friends about his good fortune. Person A's values probably differ from most of society's. Person B faces the same situation but responds differently. He keeps the money but leaves the briefcase in a conspicuous place. He tells nobody and spends the money on a new wardrobe. It is likely that Person B has violated his own ethical standards, but he decided that the money was too important to pass up. He has chosen to act selfishly.

A considerable portion of unethical behavior results from selfish behavior. Political scandals result from the desire for political power; cheating on tax returns and expense reports is motivated by financial greed; performing below one's competence and cheating on tests typically arise from laziness. In each case, the person knows that the behavior is inappropriate but chooses to do it anyway because of the personal sacrifice needed to act ethically.

ETHICAL DILEMMAS

OBJECTIVE 3-2

Resolve ethical dilemmas using an ethical framework.

An **ethical dilemma** is a situation a person faces in which a decision must be made about the appropriate behavior. A simple example of an ethical dilemma is finding a diamond ring, which necessitates deciding whether to attempt to find the owner or to keep it. A far more difficult ethical dilemma to resolve is the following one, taken from *Easier Said Than Done*, a publication dealing with ethical issues. It is the type of case that might be used in an ethics course.

- In Europe, a woman was near death from a special kind of cancer. There was one drug that the doctors thought might save her. It was a form of radium that a druggist in the same town had recently discovered. The drug was expensive to make, but the druggist was charging ten times what the drug cost him to make. He paid $200 for the radium and charged $2,000 for a small dose of the drug. The sick woman's husband, Heinz, went to everyone he knew to borrow the money, but he could only get together about $1,000, which is half of what it cost. He told the druggist that his wife was dying and asked him to sell it cheaper or let him pay later. But the druggist said: "No, I discovered the drug and I'm going to make money from it." So Heinz got desperate and broke into the man's store to steal the drug for his wife. Should the husband have done that?[1]

Auditors, accountants, and other businesspeople face many ethical dilemmas in their business careers. Dealing with a client who threatens to seek a new auditor unless an unqualified opinion is issued presents a serious ethical dilemma if an unqualified opinion is inappropriate. Deciding whether to confront a supervisor who has materially overstated

[1]Norman Sprinthall and Richard C. Sprinthall, "Value and Moral Development," *Easier Said Than Done* (Vol. 1, No. 1, Winter 1988); p. 17.

departmental revenues as a means of receiving a larger bonus is a difficult ethical dilemma. Continuing to be a part of the management of a company that harasses and mistreats employees or treats customers dishonestly is a moral dilemma, especially if the person has a family to support and the job market is tight.

Rationalizing Unethical Behavior

There are alternative ways to resolve ethical dilemmas, but care must be taken to avoid methods that are rationalizations of unethical behavior. The following are rationalization methods commonly employed that can easily result in unethical conduct.

Everybody Does It The argument that it is acceptable behavior to falsify tax returns, cheat on exams, or sell defective products is commonly based on the rationalization that everyone else is doing it and therefore it is acceptable.

If It's Legal, It's Ethical Using the argument that all legal behavior is ethical relies heavily on the perfection of laws. Under this philosophy, one would have no obligation to return a lost object unless the other person could prove that it was his or hers.

Likelihood of Discovery and Consequences This philosophy relies on evaluating the likelihood that someone else will discover the behavior. Typically, the person also assesses the severity of the penalty (consequences) if there is a discovery. An example is deciding whether to correct an unintentional overbilling to a customer when the customer has already paid the full billing. If the seller believes that the customer will detect the error and respond by not buying in the future, the seller will inform the customer now; otherwise, the seller will wait to see if the customer complains.

Resolving Ethical Dilemmas

In recent years, formal frameworks have been developed to help people resolve ethical dilemmas. The purpose of such a framework is in identifying the ethical issues and deciding on an appropriate course of action using the person's own values. The six-step approach that follows is intended to be a relatively simple approach to resolving ethical dilemmas:

1. Obtain the relevant facts.
2. Identify the ethical issues from the facts.
3. Determine who is affected by the outcome of the dilemma and how each person or group is affected.
4. Identify the alternatives available to the person who must resolve the dilemma.
5. Identify the likely consequence of each alternative.
6. Decide the appropriate action.

An illustration is used to demonstrate how a person might use this six-step approach to resolve an ethical dilemma.

Ethical Dilemma

Bryan Longview has been working 6 months as a staff assistant for Barton & Barton CPAs. Currently he is assigned to the audit of Reyon Manufacturing Company under the supervision of Charles Dickerson, an experienced audit senior. There are three auditors assigned to the audit, including Bryan, Charles, and a more experienced assistant, Martha Mills. During lunch on the first day, Charles says, "It will be necessary for us to work a few extra hours on our own time to make sure we come in on budget. This audit isn't very profitable anyway, and we don't want to hurt our firm by going over budget. We can accomplish this easily by coming in a half hour early, taking a short lunch break, and working an hour or so after normal quitting time. We just won't enter that time on our time report." Bryan recalls reading in the firm's policy manual that working hours and not charging for them on the time report is a violation of Barton & Barton's employment policy. He also knows that seniors are paid bonuses, instead of overtime, whereas staff are paid for overtime but get no bonuses. Later, when discussing the issue with Martha, she says, "Charles does this on all of his jobs. He is likely to be our firm's next audit manager. The partners think he's great because his jobs always come in under budget. He rewards us by giving us good engagement evaluations, especially under the cooperative attitude category. Several of the other audit seniors follow the same practice."

Resolving the Ethical Dilemma Using the Six-Step Approach

Relevant Facts There are three key facts in this situation that deal with the ethical issue and how the issue will likely be resolved:

1. The staff person has been informed that he will work hours without recording them as hours worked.
2. Firm policy prohibits this practice.
3. Another staff person has stated that this is common practice in the firm.

Ethical Issue The ethical issue in this situation is not difficult to identify.

- Is it ethical for Bryan to work hours and not record them as hours worked in this situation?

Who Is Affected and How Is Each Affected? There are typically more people affected in situations in which ethical dilemmas occur than might be expected. The following are the key persons involved in this situation:

Who	*How Affected*
Bryan	Being asked to violate firm policy. Hours of work will be affected. Pay will be affected. Performance evaluations may be affected. Attitude about firm may be affected.
Martha	Same as Bryan.
Charles	Success on engagement and in firm may be affected. Hours of work will be affected.
Barton & Barton	Stated firm policy is being violated. May result in underbilling clients in the current and future engagements. May affect firm's ability to realistically budget engagements and bill clients. May affect the firm's ability to motivate and retain employees.
Staff assigned to Reyon Manufacturing in the future	May result in unrealistic time budgets. May result in unfavorable time performance evaluations. May result in pressures to continue practice of not charging for hours worked.
Other staff in firm	Following the practice on this engagement may motivate others to follow the same practice on other engagements.

Bryan's Available Alternatives

- Refuse to work the additional hours.
- Perform in the manner requested.
- Inform Charles that he will not work the additional hours or will charge the additional hours to the engagement.
- Talk to a manager or partner about Charles's request.
- Refuse to work on the engagement.
- Quit working for the firm.

Each of these options includes a potential consequence, the worst likely one being termination by the firm.

Consequences of Each Alternative In deciding the consequences of each alternative, it is essential to evaluate both the short- and long-term effects. There is a natural tendency to emphasize the short term because those consequences will occur quickly, even when the long-term consequences may be more important. For example, consider the potential consequences if Bryan decides to work the additional hours and not report them. In the short

SOME ETHICAL VIOLATIONS ARE MORE SEVERE THAN OTHERS

Bryan Longview's ethical dilemma involves a situation in which he is asked to work without recording the time, which is sometimes called kitchen-tabling. One of the concerns with kitchen-tabling is that it can lead to a more severe problem known as premature signoff, in which a staff person signs off as having completed work without performing the necessary procedures.

Tom Holton has far too busy a social life to work overtime. To make certain that work does not interfere with his social life, he tests only part of the assigned sample. For example, if he is asked to test 25 cash disbursement transactions, he tests the first 15 but indicates that he has tested all 25. A supervisor, curious about Tom's amazing ability to beat the time budget, decides to carefully review Tom's work. When the firm discovers that Tom is signing off procedures without completing them, he is dismissed *that day*—no counseling out, no 2 weeks' notice.

term, he will likely get good evaluations for cooperation and perhaps a salary increase. In the longer term, what will be the effect of not reporting the hours this time when other ethical conflicts arise? Consider the following similar ethical dilemmas Bryan might face in his career as he advances:

- A supervisor asks Bryan to work 3 unreported hours daily and 15 unreported hours each weekend.
- A supervisor asks Bryan to initial certain audit procedures as having been performed when they were not.
- Bryan concludes that he cannot be promoted to manager unless he persuades assistants to work hours that they do not record.
- Management informs Bryan, who is now a partner, that either the company gets an unqualified opinion for a $40,000 audit fee or the company will change auditors.
- Management informs Bryan that the audit fee will be increased $25,000 if Bryan can find a plausible way to increase earnings by $1 million.

Appropriate Action Only Bryan can decide the appropriate option to select in the circumstances after considering his ethical values and the likely consequences of each option. At one extreme, Bryan can decide that the only relevant consequence is the potential impact on his career. Most of us believe that Bryan is an unethical person if he follows that course. At the other extreme, Bryan can decide to refuse to work for a firm that permits even one supervisor to violate firm policies. Many people consider such an extreme reaction naive.

SPECIAL NEED FOR ETHICAL CONDUCT IN PROFESSIONS

OBJECTIVE 3-3

Explain the importance of ethical conduct for the accounting profession.

Our society has attached a special meaning to the term *professional*. Professionals are expected to conduct themselves at a higher level than most other members of society. For example, when the press reports that a physician, clergyperson, U.S. senator, or CPA has been indicted for a crime, most people feel more disappointment than when the same thing happens to people who are not labeled as professionals.

The term *professional* means a responsibility for conduct that extends beyond satisfying individual responsibilities and beyond the requirements of our society's laws and regulations. A CPA, as a professional, recognizes a responsibility to the public, to the client, and to fellow practitioners, including honorable behavior, even if that means personal sacrifice.

The underlying reason for a high level of professional conduct by any profession is the need for *public confidence* in the quality of service by the profession, regardless of the individual providing it. For the CPA, it is essential that the client and external financial statement users have confidence in the quality of audits and other services. If users of services do not have confidence in physicians, judges, or CPAs, the ability of those professionals to serve clients and the public effectively is diminished.

It is not practical for users to evaluate the quality of the performance of most professional services because of their *complexity*. A patient cannot be expected to evaluate whether an operation was properly performed. A financial statement user cannot be expected to evaluate audit performance. Most users have neither the competence nor the time for such an evaluation. Public confidence in the quality of professional services is enhanced when the profession encourages high standards of performance and conduct on the part of all practitioners.

In recent years, increased competition has made it more difficult for CPAs and many other professionals to conduct themselves in a professional manner. Increased competition sometimes has the effect of making CPA firms more concerned about keeping clients and maintaining a reasonable profit than with providing high-quality audits for users. Because of the increased competition, many CPA firms have implemented philosophies and practices that are often called improved business practices. These include such things as improved recruiting and personnel practices, better office management, and more effective advertising and other promotional methods. CPA firms are also attempting to provide more efficient audits through the use of engagement management software and more effective audit planning. These changes are desirable, as long as they do not interfere with the conduct of CPAs as professionals.

Difference Between CPA Firms and Other Professionals

CPA firms have a different relationship with users of financial statements than most other professionals have with the users of their services. Attorneys, for example, are typically engaged and paid by a client and have primary responsibility to be an advocate for that client. CPA firms are engaged and paid by the company issuing the financial statements, but the primary beneficiaries of the audit are statement users. Often, the auditor does not know or have contact with the statement users but has frequent meetings and ongoing relationships with client personnel.

It is essential that users regard CPA firms as competent and unbiased. If users believe that CPA firms do not perform a valuable service (reduce information risk), the value of CPA firms' audit and other attestation reports is reduced and the demand for audits will thereby also be reduced. Therefore, there is considerable incentive for CPA firms to conduct themselves at a high professional level.

Ways CPAs Are Encouraged to Conduct Themselves Professionally

As first discussed in Chapter 1, there are several ways in which the CPA profession and society encourage CPAs to conduct themselves appropriately and to do high-quality audits and related services. Figure 3-2 shows the most important ways. Several items already discussed include GAAS and their interpretations, the CPA examination, quality control, peer review requirements, SEC, division of CPA firms, and continuing education. The ability of individuals separately or together to sue CPA firms also exerts considerable influence on the way in which practitioners conduct themselves and audits. Legal liability is studied in Chapter 4. The AICPA *Code of Professional Conduct* also has a significant influence on

FIGURE 3-2 Ways the Profession and Society Encourage CPAs to Conduct Themselves at a High Level

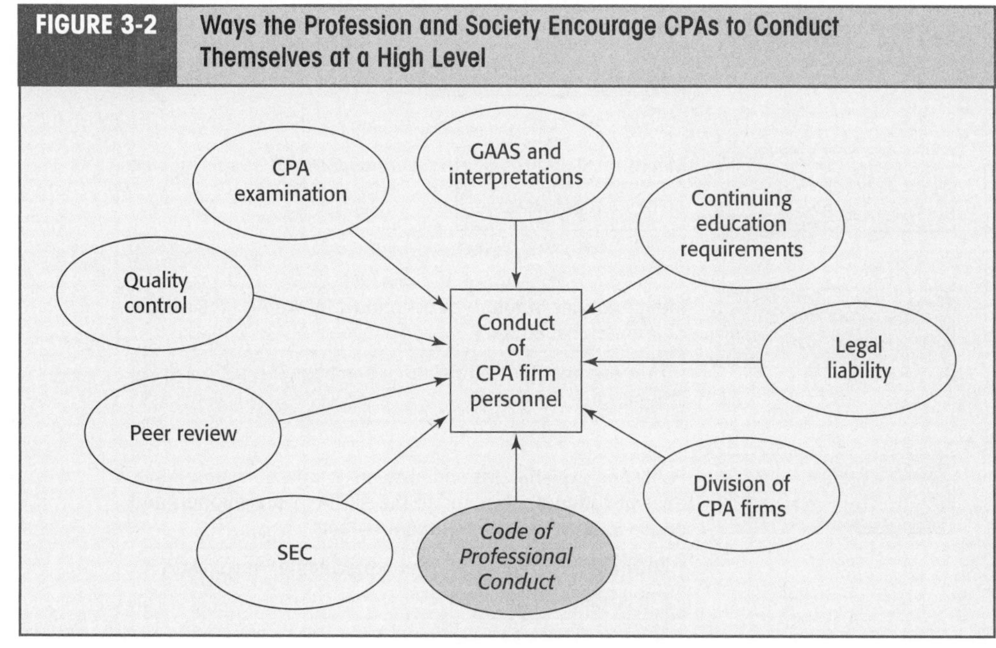

practitioners. It is meant to provide a standard of conduct for CPAs. The AICPA *Code* and related issues of professional conduct are the content of the remainder of this chapter. For this reason, the *Code of Professional Conduct* oval is shaded in Figure 3-2.

CODE OF PROFESSIONAL CONDUCT

OBJECTIVE **3-4**

Describe the purpose and content of the AICPA *Code of Professional Conduct.*

The AICPA *Code of Professional Conduct* provides both general standards of ideal conduct and specific enforceable rules of conduct. There are four parts to the code: principles, rules of conduct, interpretations of the rules of conduct, and ethical rulings. The parts are listed in order of increasing specificity; the principles provide ideal standards of conduct, whereas ethical rulings are highly specific. The four parts are summarized in Figure 3-3 and discussed on pages 69–71.

A few definitions, taken from the AICPA *Code of Professional Conduct,* must be understood to minimize misinterpretation of the rules.

AICPA *Code*

- *Client.* Any person or entity, other than the member's employer, that engages a member or a member's firm to perform professional services.
- *Firm.* A form of organization permitted by law or regulation whose characteristics conform to resolutions of the Council of the American Institute of Certified Public Accountants that is engaged in the practice of public accounting. Except for the purposes of applying Rule 101, Independence, the firm includes the individual partners thereof.
- *Institute.* The American Institute of Certified Public Accountants.
- *Member.* A member, associate member, or international associate of the American Institute of Certified Public Accountants.
- *Practice of public accounting.* The practice of public accounting consists of the performance for a client, by a member or a member's firm, while holding out as CPA(s), of the professional services of accounting, tax, personal financial planning, litigation support services, and those professional services for which standards are promulgated by bodies designated by Council.

FIGURE 3-3 **Code of Professional Conduct**

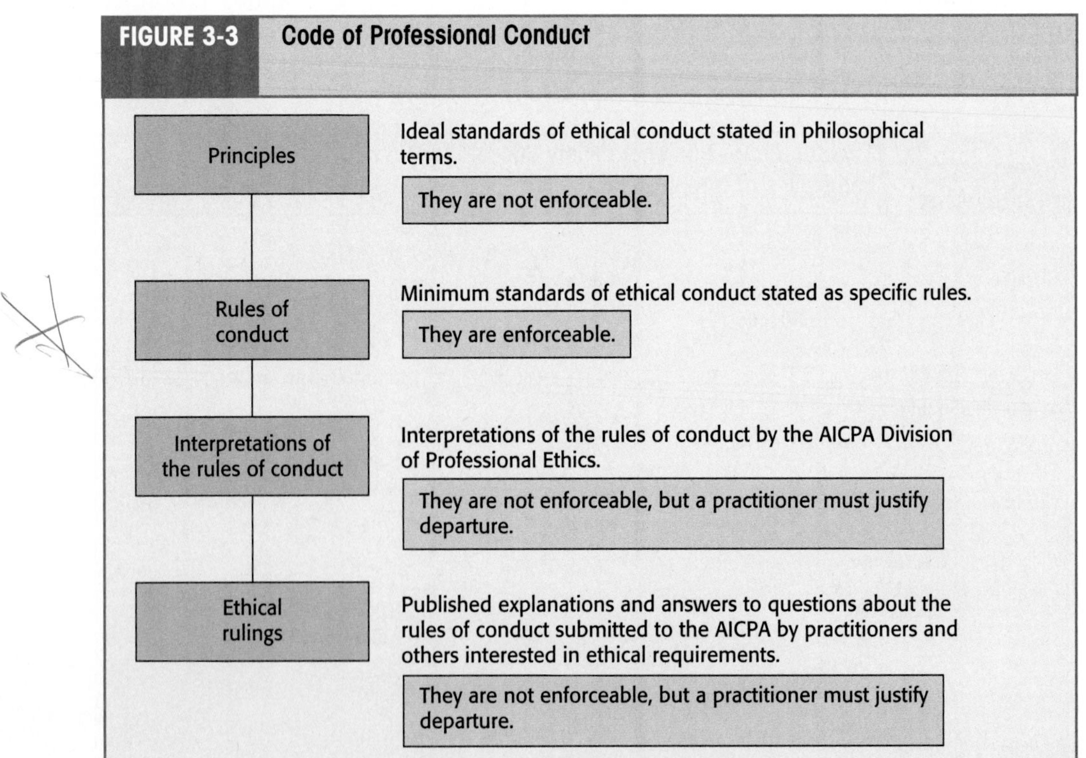

Principles
Ideal standards of ethical conduct stated in philosophical terms.
They are not enforceable.
Rules of conduct
Minimum standards of ethical conduct stated as specific rules.
They are enforceable.
Interpretations of the rules of conduct
Interpretations of the rules of conduct by the AICPA Division of Professional Ethics.
They are not enforceable, but a practitioner must justify departure.
Ethical rulings
Published explanations and answers to questions about the rules of conduct submitted to the AICPA by practitioners and others interested in ethical requirements.
They are not enforceable, but a practitioner must justify departure.

The section of the AICPA *Code* dealing with principles of professional conduct contains a general discussion of certain characteristics required of a CPA. The principles section consists of two main parts: six ethical principles and a discussion of those principles. The ethical principles are listed as follows. Discussions throughout this chapter include ideas taken from the principles section.

Principles of Professional Conduct

Ethical Principles

1. **Responsibilities** In carrying out their responsibilities as professionals, members should exercise sensitive professional and moral judgments in all their activities.
2. **The Public Interest** Members should accept the obligation to act in a way that will serve the public interest, honor the public trust, and demonstrate commitment to professionalism.
3. **Integrity** To maintain and broaden public confidence, members should perform all professional responsibilities with the highest sense of integrity.
4. **Objectivity and Independence** A member should maintain objectivity and be free of conflicts of interest in discharging professional responsibilities. A member in public practice should be independent in fact and appearance when providing auditing and other attestation services.
5. **Due Care** A member should observe the profession's technical and ethical standards, strive continually to improve competence and quality of services, and discharge professional responsibility to the best of the member's ability.
6. **Scope and Nature of Services** A member in public practice should observe the principles of the *Code of Professional Conduct* in determining the scope and nature of services to be provided.

The first five of these principles are equally applicable to all members of the AICPA, regardless of whether they practice in a CPA firm, work as accountants in business or government, are involved in some other aspect of business, or are in education. One exception is the last sentence of objectivity and independence. It applies only to members in public practice, and then only when they are providing attestation services such as audits. The sixth principle, scope and nature of services, applies only to members in public practice. That principle addresses whether a practitioner should provide a certain service, such as providing personnel consulting when an audit client is hiring a Chief Information Officer (CIO) for the client's IT function. Providing such a service can create a loss of independence if the CPA firm recommends a CIO who is hired and performs incompetently.

A careful examination of these six principles is likely to lead us to conclude that they are applicable to any professional, not just CPAs. For example, physicians should exercise sensitive professional and moral judgment, act in the public interest, act with integrity, be objective and avoid conflicts of interest, follow due care, and evaluate the appropriateness of the nature of medical services provided. One difference between auditors and other professionals, as discussed earlier, is that most professionals need not be concerned about remaining independent.

Rules of Conduct

This part of the *Code* includes the explicit rules that must be followed by every CPA in the practice of public accounting.[2] Those individuals holding the CPA certificate but not actually practicing public accounting must follow most, but not all, of the requirements. Because the section on rules of conduct is the only enforceable part of the code, it is stated in more precise language than the section on principles. Because of their enforceability, many practitioners refer to the rules as the AICPA *Code of Professional Conduct.*

The difference between the standards of conduct set by the *principles* and those set by the *rules of conduct* is shown in Figure 3-4 (p. 70). When practitioners conduct themselves at the minimum level in Figure 3-4, that does not imply unsatisfactory conduct. The profession has presumably set the standards sufficiently high to make the minimum conduct satisfactory.

[2]The AICPA *Code of Professional Conduct* is applicable to every CPA who is a member of the AICPA. Each state also has rules of conduct that are required for licensing by the state. Many states follow the AICPA rules, but some have somewhat different requirements.

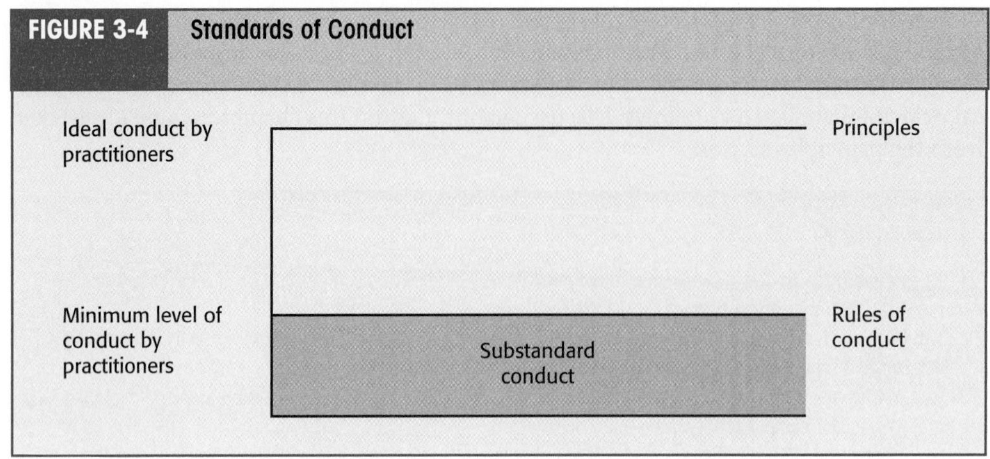

At what level do practitioners conduct themselves in practice? As in any profession, the level varies among practitioners. Most practitioners conduct themselves at a high level. Unfortunately, a few conduct themselves below the minimum level set by the profession. The activities designed to encourage CPAs to conduct themselves at a high level described in Figure 3-2 (p. 67) help minimize the extent of any substandard practice.

Interpretation of Rules of Conduct

The need for published interpretations of the rules of conduct arises when there are frequent questions from practitioners about a specific rule. The Division of Professional Ethics of the AICPA prepares each interpretation based on a consensus of a committee made up principally of public accounting practitioners. Before interpretations are finalized, they are sent to a large number of key people in the profession for comment. Interpretations are not officially enforceable, but a departure from the interpretations is difficult if not impossible for a practitioner to justify in a disciplinary hearing. The most important interpretations are discussed as a part of each section of the rules.

Ethical Rulings

Rulings are explanations by the executive committee of the professional ethics division of *specific factual circumstances.* A large number of ethical rulings are published in the expanded version of the AICPA *Code of Professional Conduct.* The following is an example (Rule 101—Independence; Ruling No. 16):

- *Question*—A member serves on the board of directors of a nonprofit social club. Is the independence of the member considered to be impaired with respect to the club?
- *Answer*—Independence of the member is considered to be impaired because the board of directors has the ultimate responsibility for the affairs of the club.

Applicability of the Rules of Conduct

The rules of conduct contained in the AICPA *Code of Professional Conduct* apply to all AICPA members for all services provided whether or not the member is in the practice of public accounting, unless it is specifically stated otherwise in the code. Table 3-1 (p. 85) indicates whether the rule applies to all members or only to members in public practice.

Each of the rules applies to attestation services, and *unless stated otherwise,* each rule also applies to all services provided by CPA firms such as taxes and management services. There are only two rules that exempt certain nonattestation services:

1. Rule 101—Independence. This rule requires independence only when the AICPA has established independence requirements through its rule-setting bodies, such as the Auditing Standards Board. The AICPA requires independence only for attestation engagements. For example, a CPA firm can perform management services for a company in which the partners own stock. Of course, if the CPA firm also does an audit, that violates the independence requirements for attestation services.
2. Rule 203—Accounting Principles. This rule applies only to issuing an audit opinion or review service report on financial statements.

It is a violation of the rules if someone does something on behalf of a member that is a violation if the member does it. An example is a banker who puts in a newsletter that Johnson and Able CPA firm has the best tax department in the state and consistently gets large refunds for its tax clients. That is likely to create false or unjustified expectations and is a violation of Rule 502 on advertising. A member is also responsible for compliance with the rules by employees, partners, and shareholders.

Because of its importance, independence is the first rule of conduct. Before discussing the specific independence requirements in the rules of conduct, the meaning of independence and factors other than the rules of conduct that influence auditor independence are discussed.

INDEPENDENCE

OBJECTIVE **3-5**

Describe factors that influence auditor independence.

The value of auditing depends heavily on the public's perception of the independence of auditors. Independence in auditing means taking an *unbiased viewpoint* in performing audit tests, evaluating the results, and issuing the audit report. If the auditor is an advocate for the client, a banker, or anyone else, the auditor cannot be considered independent. Independence is regarded as the auditor's most critical characteristic. The reason that many diverse users are willing to rely on the CPA's reports as to the fairness of financial statements is their expectation of an unbiased viewpoint. It is not surprising that independence is included as a generally accepted auditing standard and a rule of conduct.

Not only is it essential for auditors to maintain an independent attitude in fulfilling their responsibilities but it is also important that the users of financial statements have confidence in that independence. These two objectives are often identified as **independence in fact** and **independence in appearance.** Independence in fact exists when the auditor is actually able to maintain an unbiased attitude throughout the audit, whereas independence in appearance is the result of others' interpretations of this independence. If auditors are independent in fact but users believe them to be advocates for the client, most of the value of the audit function is lost.

The following sections discuss various organizations and standards other than the AICPA *Code of Professional Conduct* that influence auditor independence. Recent changes in the SEC's auditor independence requirements are discussed first.

Revision of SEC Auditor Independence Requirements

Changes in the audit environment have resulted in the need for significant changes in independence requirements. For example, increased stock ownership by individuals has created greater potential for unintentional violations of independence requirements due to stock ownership by family members and audit firm members not involved with the audit engagement. The organization and range of services offered by CPA firms has also changed significantly, and firms often enter into complex business and financial relationships with clients.

In response to these changes, the SEC issued revisions to its auditor independence requirements in November 2000 that apply to auditors for clients subject to SEC reporting requirements. These new independence rules adopted by the SEC address several issues related to an accounting firm's interaction with its SEC audit clients, especially financial and business relationships, and the disclosure of nonaudit services.

Ownership Interests Previous rules on ownership interests viewed independence from a firmwide perspective. The new rules on financial relationships take an engagement perspective and narrow the restrictions on ownership in clients to those persons who can influence the audit. For example, under the previous rules, all partners and their immediate family were prohibited from having any ownership in the client, regardless of materiality. The new rules restrict ownership to covered persons and their immediate family, including (a) members of the audit engagement team, (b) those in a position to influence the audit engagement in the firm chain of command, (c) partners and managers who provide more than 10 hours of nonaudit services to the client, and (d) partners in the office of the partner primarily responsible for the audit engagement. These changes were designed to make the independence rules more workable and still safeguard independence.

IT and Other Nonaudit Services The SEC is concerned that the growth of nonaudit services can jeopardize independence, and even considered prohibiting providing nonaudit services to audit clients. The new rules identify nonaudit services that impair independence unless certain specified conditions are met, in addition to codifying previous restrictions, such as restrictions on providing bookkeeping services for a client. The intent of the restrictions is to prevent the auditor from serving in a management function or being in a position where the audit firm is auditing its own work.

For example, the SEC's new rules state that independence is impaired if an accountant directly or indirectly operates or supervises the operation of an audit client's information system or manages a local area network on behalf of the client. The SEC rule also states that an auditor's independence is impaired by performing more than 40 percent of the audit client's internal audit work related to financial statements and internal controls, unless the audit client has $200 million or less in total assets.

In addition, SEC clients must disclose in their proxy statements the total fee paid for the annual audit and amounts paid for nonaudit services if the total exceeds the lesser of $50,000 or 10 percent of the audit fees. The nonaudit services should be separately reported for financial information systems design and implementation and all other services. These disclosures allow investors to assess the significance of nonaudit services provided by the auditor.

Audit Committee

An **audit committee** is a selected number of members of a company's board of directors whose responsibilities include helping auditors remain independent of management. Most audit committees are made up of three to five or sometimes as many as seven directors who are not a part of company management.

A typical audit committee decides such things as which CPA firm to retain and the scope of services the CPA firm is to perform. It meets periodically with the CPA firm to discuss audit progress and findings and helps resolve conflicts between the CPA firm and management. Audit committees for larger companies are looked upon with favor by most auditors, users, and management.

The requirement of an audit committee would be costly for smaller companies. An audit committee is required for all companies listed on the New York Stock Exchange. The SEC does not require audit committees, but does require proxy statement disclosure about audit committee activities for SEC clients that have audit committees. These disclosures provide additional information to help stockholders evaluate the audit committee's effectiveness in overseeing the financial reporting process.

Shopping for Accounting Principles

Both management and representatives of management, such as investment bankers, often consult with other accountants on the application of accounting principles. Although consultation with other accountants is an appropriate practice, it can lead to a loss of independence in certain circumstances. For example, suppose one CPA firm replaces the existing auditors on the strength of accounting advice offered but later finds facts and circumstances that require the CPA firm to change its stance. It may be difficult for the new CPA firm to remain independent in such a situation. SAS 50 (AU 625) sets forth requirements that must be followed when a CPA firm is requested to provide a written or oral opinion on the application of accounting principles or the type of audit opinion that would be issued for a specific or hypothetical transaction of an audit client of another CPA firm. The purpose of the requirement is to minimize the likelihood of management following the practice commonly called opinion shopping and the potential threat to independence of the kind described previously. Primary among the requirements is that the consulted CPA firm should communicate with the entity's existing auditors to ascertain all the available facts relevant to forming a professional judgment on the matters the firm has been requested to report on.

Approval of Auditor by Stockholders

Although not required by the AICPA or SEC, an increasing number of companies require stockholders to approve the selection of a new CPA firm or continuation of the existing one. Stockholders are usually a more objective group than management. However, it is questionable whether they are in a position to evaluate the performance of previous or potential auditors.

Engagement and Payment of Audit Fees by Management

Can an auditor be truly independent in fact and appearance if the payment of fees is dependent upon the management of the audited entity? There is probably no satisfactory answer to this question, but it does demonstrate the difficulty of obtaining an atmosphere of complete independence of auditors. The alternative to engagement of the CPA and payment of audit fees by management is probably the use of either government or quasi-government auditors. All things considered, it is questionable whether the audit function would be performed better or more cheaply by the public sector.

INDEPENDENCE RULE OF CONDUCT AND INTERPRETATIONS

OBJECTIVE 3-6

Apply the AICPA *Code* rules and interpretations on independence and explain their importance.

The previous section discussed the importance of auditor independence. It is not surprising that independence is the first subject addressed in the rules of conduct.

Rule 101—Independence A member in public practice shall be independent in the performance of professional services as required by standards promulgated by bodies designated by Council.

CPA firms are required to be independent for certain services that they provide, but not for others. The last phrase in Rule 101, "as required by standards promulgated by bodies designated by Council" is a convenient way for the AICPA to include or exclude independence requirements for different types of services. For example, the Auditing Standards Board requires that auditors of historical financial statements be independent. Rule 101 therefore applies to audits. Independence is also required for other types of attestations, such as review services and audits of prospective financial statements. However, a CPA firm can do tax returns and provide management services without being independent. Rule 101 does not apply to those types of services.

There are more interpretations for independence than for any of the other rules of conduct. Many of the interpretations have been revised to have an "engagement-team" focus and to be consistent with the revised SEC rules on independence. Some of the more significant issues and interpretations involving independence are discussed in the following sections.

Financial Interests

Interpretations of Rule 101 prohibit covered members from owning *any stock or other direct investment* in audit clients because it is potentially damaging to actual audit independence, and it certainly is likely to affect the users' perceptions of the auditors' independence. *Indirect investments,* such as ownership of stock in a client's company by an auditor's grandparent, are also prohibited, but *only if the amount is material* to the auditor. The ownership of stock rule is more complex than it appears at first glance. A more detailed examination of that requirement is included to aid in understanding and to show the complexity of one of the rules. There are three important distinctions in the rules as they relate to independence and stock ownership.

Covered Members Rule 101 applies to covered members in a position to influence an attest engagement. Covered members include the following:

1. Individuals on the attest engagement team
2. An individual in a position to influence the attest engagement, such as individuals who supervise or evaluate the engagement partner
3. A partner or manager who provides nonattest services to the client
4. A partner in the office of the partner responsible for the attest engagement
5. The firm and its employee benefit plans
6. An entity that can be controlled by any of the covered members listed above or by two or more of the covered individuals or entities operating together

For example, a staff member in a national CPA firm could own stock in a client corporation and not violate Rule 101 if the staff member is not involved in the engagement. However, if the staff member is assigned to the engagement or becomes a partner in the office of the partner responsible for the attest engagement, he or she would have to dispose of the stock or the CPA firm would no longer be independent with respect to that client.

These independence rules also generally apply to the covered member's immediate family. The interpretations of Rule 101 define immediate family as a spouse, spousal equivalent, or dependent.

Some CPA firms do not permit any ownership by staff of a client's stock regardless of which office serves the client. These firms have decided to have higher requirements than the minimums set by the rules of conduct.

Direct Versus Indirect Financial Interest The ownership of stock or other equity shares by members or their immediate family is called a **direct financial interest.** For example, if either a partner in the office in which an audit is conducted or the partner's spouse has a partnership interest in a company, the CPA firm is prohibited by Rule 101 from expressing an opinion on the financial statements of that company.

An **indirect financial interest** exists when there is a close, but not a direct, ownership relationship between the auditor and the client. An example of an indirect ownership interest is the covered member's ownership of a mutual fund that has an investment in a client.

Material or Immaterial *Materiality* affects whether ownership is a violation of Rule 101 only for *indirect* ownership. Materiality must be considered in relation to the member person's wealth and income. For example, if a covered member has a significant amount of his or her personal wealth invested in a mutual fund and that fund has a large ownership position in a client company, a violation of the *Code* is likely to exist.

Related Financial Interest Issues

Several interpretations of Rule 101 deal with specific aspects of financial relationships between CPA firm personnel and clients. These are summarized in this section.

Former Practitioners In most situations, the interpretations permit former partners or shareholders who left the firm due to such things as retirement or the sale of their ownership interest to have relationships with clients of the firm of the type that are normally a violation of Rule 101, without affecting a firm's independence. A violation by the firm would occur if the former partner was held out as an associate of the firm or took part in activities that are likely to cause other parties to believe the person was still active in the firm.

Normal Lending Procedures Generally, loans between a CPA firm or its members and an audit client are prohibited because it is a financial relationship. There are several exceptions to the rule, however, including automobile loans, loans fully collateralized by cash deposits at the same financial institution, and unpaid credit card balances not exceeding $5,000 in total. It is also acceptable to accept a financial institution as a client even if members of the CPA firm have existing home mortgages, other fully collateralized secured loans, and immaterial loans with the institution. No new loans are permitted, however. Both the restrictions and exceptions are reasonable ones, considering the trade-off between independence and the need to permit CPAs to function as businesspeople and individuals.

Financial Interests and Employment of Immediate and Close Family Members The financial interests of immediate family members, defined as a spouse, spousal equivalent, or dependent, are ordinarily treated as if they were the financial interest of the covered member. For example, if the spouse of a professional on the audit engagement team owns any stock in the client, Rule 101 is violated. Independence is also impaired if an immediate family member holds a key position such as financial officer or chief executive officer with the client that allows them to influence accounting functions, preparation of financial statements, or the contents of the financial statements.

Ownership interests of close family members, defined as a parent, sibling, or nondependent child, do not normally impair independence unless the ownership interest is material to the close relative. Imagine the potential difficulty in maintaining independence and objectivity if the firm is asked to audit a client where the parent of the audit partner is chief executive officer and has a significant ownership interest in the client. For individuals on the engagement team, independence is impaired if a close relative has a key position with the client or has a financial interest that is material to the close relative or enables the relative to exercise significant influence over the client. Similar rules apply for other individuals in a position to influence the attest engagement or partners in the attest-engagement office, except the ownership interest must be material to the close relative and allow the close relative to exercise significant influence over the audit client. Independence is not considered impaired if the covered individual is not aware of the close relative's ownership interest.

Joint Investor or Investee Relationship with Client Assume, for example, that a CPA owns stock in a nonaudit client, Jackson Company. Frank Company, which is an audit client, also owns stock in Jackson Company. This may be a violation of Rule 101. Interpretation 101-8 addresses situations where the client is either an investor or investee for a nonclient in which the CPA has an ownership interest.

1. *Client investor.* If the client's investment in the nonclient is material, any direct or material indirect investment by the CPA in the nonclient investee impairs independence. If the client's investment is not material, independence is impaired only if the CPA's investment is material.
2. *Client investee.* If investment in a client is material to a nonclient investor, any direct or material indirect investment by the CPA in the nonclient impairs independence. If the nonclient's investment in the client is not material, independence is not impaired unless the CPA's investment in the nonclient allows the CPA to exercise significant influence over the nonclient.

Director, Officer, Management, or Employee of a Company If a CPA is a member of the board of directors or an officer of a client company, his or her ability to make independent evaluations of the fair presentation of financial statements is affected. Even if holding one of these positions did not actually affect the auditor's independence, the frequent involvement with management and the decisions it makes is likely to affect how statement users perceive the CPA's independence. To eliminate this possibility, interpretations prohibit covered members, partners, and professional staff in the office of the partner responsible for the attest engagement from being a director or officer of an audit client company. Similarly, the auditor cannot be an underwriter, voting trustee, promoter, or trustee of a client's pension fund, or act in any other capacity of management, or be an employee of the company.

Interpretations permit CPAs to do audits and be *honorary* directors or trustees for not-for-profit organizations, such as charitable and religious organizations, as long as the position is purely honorary. To illustrate, it is common for a partner of the CPA firm doing the audit of a city's United Fund drive to also be an honorary director, along with many other civic leaders. The CPA cannot vote or participate in any management functions.

Litigation Between CPA Firm and Client

When there is a lawsuit or intent to start a lawsuit between a CPA firm and its client, the ability of the CPA firm and client to remain objective is questionable. The interpretations regard such litigation as a violation of Rule 101 for the current audit. For example, if management sues a CPA firm claiming a deficiency in the previous audit, the CPA firm is not considered independent for the current year's audit. Similarly, if the CPA firm sues management for fraudulent financial reporting or deceit, independence is lost. The CPA firm and client company or management may be defendants in a suit brought by a third party, such as in a securities class action. This litigation in itself does not affect independence. However, independence may be affected if cross-claims between the auditor and client are filed that have a significant risk of a material loss to the CPA firm or client.

Litigation by the client related to tax or other nonaudit services, or litigation against both the client and the CPA firm by another party, does not usually impair independence. The key consideration in all such suits is the likely effect on the ability of client, management, and CPA firm personnel to remain objective and comment freely.

Bookkeeping and Other Services

If a CPA records transactions in the journals for the client, posts monthly totals to the general ledger, makes adjusting entries, and subsequently does an audit, there is some question as to whether the CPA can be independent in the audit role. The interpretations *permit a CPA firm to do both bookkeeping and auditing for the same client.* The AICPA's conclusion is presumably based on a comparison of the effect on independence of having both bookkeeping and auditing services performed by the same CPA firm with the additional cost of having a different CPA firm do the audit. There are three important requirements that the auditor must satisfy before it is acceptable to do bookkeeping and auditing for the client:

1. The client must accept full responsibility for the financial statements. The client must be sufficiently knowledgeable about the enterprise's activities and financial condition and the applicable accounting principles so that the client can reasonably accept such responsibility, including the fairness of valuation and presentation and the adequacy of disclosure. When necessary, the CPA must discuss accounting matters with the client to be sure that the client has the required degree of understanding.
2. The CPA must not assume the role of employee or of management conducting the operations of an enterprise. For example, the CPA cannot consummate transactions, have custody of assets, or exercise authority on behalf of the client. The client must prepare the source documents on all transactions in sufficient detail to identify clearly the nature and amount of such transactions and maintain accounting control over data processed by the CPA, such as control totals and document counts.
3. The CPA, in making an audit of financial statements prepared from books and records that the CPA has maintained completely or in part, must conform to GAAS. The fact that the CPA has processed or maintained certain records does not eliminate the need to make sufficient audit tests.

The first two requirements are often difficult to satisfy for a smaller company whose owner may have little knowledge of or interest in accounting or processing transactions. For SEC clients, *the SEC prohibits performing bookkeeping services and auditing by the same CPA firm*. Most SEC clients are larger and are more likely to have an accounting staff. Therefore, this prohibition causes few difficulties.

In addition to bookkeeping, CPA firms offer many other services to attest clients that may potentially impair independence. Such activities are permissible as long as the member does not perform management functions or make management decisions. For example, a CPA firm may assist in the design or installation of a client's information system as long as the client makes necessary management decisions about the system. The CPA may also provide initial training and instruction to client employees on the new system. However, the CPA firm may not supervise client personnel in the daily operation of the information system.

Internal Auditing and Extended Audit Services

In recent years, many CPA firms have begun providing internal auditing and other extended auditing services to their clients. For example, a manufacturing client may engage its CPA firm to perform an operational review of the company's production processes to determine whether products are being produced efficiently. Such services do not impair independence as long as the CPA or his or her firm does not act or appear to act in a capacity equivalent to a member of client management or as an employee. The client must remain responsible for the internal audit function. This includes determining the scope of internal audit activities, evaluating the adequacy of procedures, and evaluating the findings and results arising from internal audit activities, including those performed by the AICPA member.

Unpaid Fees

Under Rule 101 and its rulings and interpretations, independence is considered impaired if billed or unbilled fees remain unpaid for professional services provided more than 1 year before the date of the report. Such unpaid fees are deemed to be a loan from the auditor to the client and are therefore a violation of Rule 101. Unpaid fees from a client in bankruptcy do not violate Rule 101.

ETHICS IN PLAIN ENGLISH

Many factors have contributed to increased complexity in the rules of conduct and interpretations, including the engagement-team approach to independence, new practice structures for CPA firms, and new services. In addition, SEC independence rules may differ from the AICPA rules. In response, the AICPA has published the AICPA *Plain English Guide to Independence*, available online on the AICPA Web site. The guide provides answers to ethics questions in straightforward language and also highlights areas where SEC rules differ from those issued by the AICPA.

Source: www.aicpa.org/members/div/ethics/plaineng.htm

OTHER RULES OF CONDUCT

Although independence is critical to public confidence in CPAs, it is also important that auditors adhere to the other rules of conduct listed in Table 3-1 (p. 85). We begin by discussing the rules for integrity and objectivity.

Integrity and Objectivity

OBJECTIVE 3-7

Understand the requirements of other rules under the AICPA *Code*.

Integrity means impartiality in performing all services. Rule 102 on integrity and objectivity is presented below:

Rule 102—Integrity and Objectivity In the performance of any professional service, a member shall maintain objectivity and integrity, shall be free of conflicts of interest, and shall not knowingly misrepresent facts or subordinate his or her judgment to others.

To illustrate the meaning of integrity and objectivity, assume that an auditor believes that accounts receivable may not be collectible but accepts management's opinion without an independent evaluation of collectibility. The auditor has subordinated his or her judgment and thereby lacks objectivity. Now assume that a CPA is preparing the tax return for a client and, as a client advocate, encourages the client to take a deduction on the returns that the CPA believes is valid, but for which there is some but not complete support. This is not a violation of either objectivity or integrity because it is acceptable for the CPA to be a client advocate in tax and management services. If the CPA encourages the client to take a deduction for which there is no support but has little chance of discovery by the IRS, a violation has occurred. That is a misrepresentation of the facts; therefore, the integrity of the CPA has been impaired.

Audit staff members should not subordinate their judgment to supervisors on the audit engagement. Staff auditors are responsible for their own judgments documented in the audit files and should not change those conclusions at the request of supervisors on the engagement unless the staff auditor agrees with the supervisor's conclusion. In rare instances where staff members do not agree with a conclusion involving a significant matter, they should document the reasons for the disagreement as a way of disassociating themselves from the resolution of the matter.

Freedom from conflicts of interest means the absence of relationships that might interfere with objectivity or integrity. For example, it would be inappropriate for an auditor who is also an attorney to represent a client in legal matters. The attorney is an advocate for the client, whereas the auditor must be impartial.

An interpretation of Rule 102 states that apparent conflicts of interest may not be a violation of the rules of conduct if the information is disclosed to the member's client or employer. For example, if a partner of a CPA firm recommends that a client have the security of its Internet Web site evaluated by a technology consulting firm that is owned by the partner's spouse, a conflict of interest may appear to exist. No violation of Rule 102 occurs if the partner informs the client's management of the relationship and management proceeded with the evaluation with that knowledge. The interpretation makes it clear that the independence requirements under Rule 101 cannot be eliminated by these disclosures.

Technical Standards

The next three standards of the *Code* relate to the auditor's adherence with the requirements of technical standards. The following are the requirements of the technical standards:

Rule 201—General Standards A member shall comply with the following standards and with any interpretations thereof by bodies designated by Council.

A. *Professional competence.* Undertake only those professional services that the member or the member's firm can reasonably expect to be completed with professional competence.
B. *Due professional care.* Exercise due professional care in the performance of professional services.
C. *Planning and supervision.* Adequately plan and supervise the performance of professional services.
D. *Sufficient relevant data.* Obtain sufficient, relevant data to afford a reasonable basis for conclusions or recommendations in relation to any professional services performed.

Rule 202—Compliance with Standards A member who performs auditing, review, compilation, management consulting, tax, or other professional services shall comply with standards promulgated by bodies designated by Council.

Rule 203—Accounting Principles A member shall not (1) express an opinion or state affirmatively that the financial statements or other financial data of any entity are presented in conformity with generally accepted accounting principles or (2) state that he or she is not aware of any material modifications that should be made to such statements or data in order for them to be in conformity with generally accepted accounting principles if such statements or data contain any departure from an accounting principle promulgated by bodies designated by Council to establish such principles that has a material effect on the statements or data taken as a whole. If, however, the statements or data contain such a departure and the member can demonstrate that due to unusual circumstances the financial statements or data would otherwise have been misleading, the member can comply with the rule by describing the departure, its approximate effects, if practicable, and the reasons why compliance with the principle would result in a misleading statement.

The primary purpose of the requirements of Rules 201 to 203 is to provide support for the ASB and FASB and other technical standard-setting bodies. For example, notice that requirements A and B of Rule 201 are the same in substance as general auditing standards 1 and 3, and C and D of Rule 201 have the same intent as field work standards 1 and 3. The only difference is that Rule 201 is stated in terms that apply to all types of services, whereas auditing standards apply only to audits. Rule 202 makes it clear that when a practitioner violates an auditing standard, the rules of conduct are also automatically violated.

Confidentiality

It is essential that practitioners not disclose confidential information obtained in any type of engagement without the consent of the client. The following are the specific requirements of Rule 301 related to **confidential client information:**

Rule 301 – Confidential Client Information A member in public practice shall not disclose any confidential client information without the specific consent of the client.

This rule shall not be construed (1) to relieve a member of his or her professional obligations under Rules 202 and 203, (2) to affect in any way the member's obligation to comply with a validly issued and enforceable subpoena or summons, or to prohibit a member's compliance with applicable laws and government regulations, (3) to prohibit review of a member's professional practice under AICPA or state CPA society or Board of Accountancy authorization, or (4) to preclude a member from initiating a complaint with, or responding to any inquiry made by, the professional ethics division or trial board of the Institute or a duly constituted investigative or disciplinary body of a state CPA society or Board of Accountancy.

Members of any of the bodies identified in (4) above and members involved with professional practice reviews identified in (3) above shall not use to their own advantage or disclose any member's confidential client information that comes to their attention in carrying out those activities. This prohibition shall not restrict members' exchange of information in connection with the investigative or disciplinary proceedings described in (4) above or the professional practice reviews described in (3) above.

Need for Confidentiality During an audit or other type of engagement, practitioners obtain a considerable amount of information of a confidential nature, including officers' salaries, product pricing and advertising plans, and product cost data. If auditors divulge this information to outsiders or to client employees who have been denied access to the information, their relationship with management can be seriously strained, and in extreme cases, the client can be harmed. The confidentiality requirement applies to all services provided by CPA firms, including tax and management services.

Ordinarily, the CPA's working papers can be provided to someone else only with the express permission of the client. This is the case even if a CPA sells the practice to another CPA firm or is willing to permit a successor auditor to examine the audit documentation prepared for a former client. Permission is not required from the client, however, if the audit documentation is subpoenaed by a court or are used as part of an authorized peer review program with other CPA firms. If the audit documentation is subpoenaed, the client should be informed immediately. The client and its legal counsel may wish to challenge the subpoena.

Exceptions to Confidentiality As stated in the second paragraph of Rule 301, there are four exceptions to the confidentiality requirements. All four exceptions concern responsibilities that are more important than maintaining confidential relations with the client.

1. *Obligations related to technical standards.* Suppose that 3 months after an unqualified audit report was issued, the auditor discovers that the financial statements were materially misstated. When the chief executive officer is confronted, he responds that even though he agrees that the financial statements are misstated, confidentiality prevents the CPA from informing anyone. This example is similar to an actual legal case, *Yale Express*. Disagreements during the *Yale Express* case resulted in AU 561, which deals with auditors' responsibilities when subsequent facts show that an inappropriate audit report has been issued. (AU 561 is discussed in Chapter 18.) Exception (1) in Rule 301 makes it clear that the auditor's responsibility to discharge professional standards is greater than that for confidentiality. In such a case, a revised, correct audit report must be issued. Note, however, that the conflict seldom occurs.
2. *Subpoena or summons.* Legally, information is called **privileged information** if legal proceedings cannot require a person to provide the information, even if there is a subpoena. Information communicated by a client to an attorney or by a patient to a physician is privileged. *Information obtained by a CPA from a client generally is not privileged.* Exception (2) of Rule 301 is therefore needed to put CPA firms in compliance with the law.

   There have been considerable discussions and disagreements among CPAs, attorneys, and legislators about the need for privileged communication between CPAs and clients. Most CPAs and businesspeople dealing with CPAs support legislation protecting privileged communications. In fact, a number of states have statutes that provide some level of privilege to accountant–client communication. Of course, these statutes would apply only to litigation in state courts and would have no bearing on federal court suits.

3. *Peer review.* When a CPA or CPA firm conducts a peer review of the quality controls of another CPA firm, it is normal practice to examine several sets of audit files. If the peer review is authorized by the AICPA, state CPA society, or state Board of Accountancy, client permission to examine the audit documentation is not needed. Requiring permission from each client may restrict access of the peer reviewers and would be a time burden on all concerned. Naturally, the peer reviewers must keep the information obtained confidential and cannot use the information for other purposes.
4. *Response to ethics division.* If a practitioner is charged with inadequate technical performance by the AICPA Ethics Division trial board under any of Rules 201 to 203, the board members are likely to want to examine audit documentation. Exception (4) in Rule 301 prevents a CPA firm from denying the inquirers access to audit documentation by saying that it is confidential information. Similarly, a CPA firm that observes substandard audit documentation of another CPA firm cannot use confidentiality as the reason for not initiating a complaint of substandard performance against the firm.

Contingent Fees

To help CPAs maintain objectivity in conducting audits or other attestation services, basing fees on the outcome of the engagement is prohibited. The requirements of Rule 302 related to contingent fees are shown below.

To illustrate the need for a rule on contingent fees, suppose a CPA firm was permitted to charge a fee of $50,000 if an unqualified opinion was provided but only $25,000 if the opinion was qualified. Such an agreement may tempt a practitioner to issue the wrong opinion and is a violation of Rule 302. It is also a violation of Rule 302 for members to prepare an original or amended tax return or a claim for tax refunds for a contingent fee.

An agreement between the AICPA and the Federal Trade Commission eliminated the restrictions on contingent fees *for nonattestation services, unless the CPA firm is also performing attestation services* for the same client. The agreement also permits the AICPA to prohibit tax return preparation on a contingent fee basis. Under the agreement, for example, it is *not* a violation for a CPA to charge fees as an expert witness determined by the

Rule 302—Contingent Fees A member in public practice shall not

(1) Perform for a contingent fee any professional services for, or receive such a fee from, a client for whom the member or member's firm performs:
   (a) an audit or review of a financial statement; or
   (b) a compilation of a financial statement when the member expects, or reasonably might expect, that a third party will use the financial statement and the member's compilation report does not disclose a lack of independence; or
   (c) an examination of prospective financial information;

or

(2) Prepare an original or amended tax return or claim for a tax refund for a contingent fee for any client.

The prohibition in (1) above applies during the period in which the member or the member's firm is engaged to perform any of the services listed above and the period covered by any historical financial statements involved in any such listed services.

Except as stated in the next sentence, a contingent fee is a fee established for the performance of any service pursuant to an arrangement in which no fee will be charged unless a specified finding or result is attained, or in which the amount of the fee is otherwise dependent upon the finding or result of such service. Solely for purposes of this rule, fees are not regarded as being contingent if fixed by courts or other public authorities, or, in tax matters, if determined based on the results of judicial proceedings or the findings of governmental agencies.

A member's fees may vary depending, for example, on the complexity of services rendered.

amount awarded to the plaintiff or to base consulting fees on a percentage of a bond issue *if the CPA firm does not also do an audit or other attestation for the same client.*

The reason for the agreement was a contention by the Federal Trade Commission that contingent fee restrictions reduce competition and therefore are not in the public interest. After considerable negotiation, the AICPA agreed to restrict the contingent fee prohibition only to attestation services clients and for tax return preparation. The Federal Trade Commission agreed to allow the AICPA to prohibit contingent fees for attestation services and tax return preparation because of the importance of independence and objectivity.

Discreditable Acts

Because of the special need for CPAs to conduct themselves in a professional manner, the *Code* has a specific rule prohibiting acts discreditable to the profession.

Rule 501—Acts Discreditable A member shall not commit an act discreditable to the profession.

A discreditable act is not well defined in the rules or interpretations. The following are some of the requirements contained in the interpretations:

1. *Retention of client records.* It is an act discreditable to retain a client's records after a demand is made for them. Assume, for example, that a client did not pay an audit fee and the partners of the CPA firm therefore refused to return client-owned records. The partners have violated Rule 501.
2. *Discrimination and harassment in employment practices.* A member is presumed to have committed an act discreditable whenever the member is found to have violated any federal, state, or local antidiscrimination laws.
3. *Standards on government audits and requirements of government bodies and agencies.* Audits of government units and federal grant recipients must be done in compliance with government auditing standards, in addition to GAAS. Both the government auditing standards and GAAS must be followed unless the audit report discloses the reasons for not following such requirements. When a member accepts an engagement that involves reporting to a regulatory agency such as the SEC, the member must follow the additional requirements of the regulatory agency, in addition to GAAS. If the additional requirements are not followed, the reasons should be noted in the report.
4. *Negligence in the preparation of financial statements or records.* A member is considered to have committed an act discreditable if by his or her negligence others are made or permitted or directed to make materially false and misleading entries in the financial statements and records of an entity, the member fails to correct financial statements that are materially false and misleading, or the member signs or permits or directs another to sign a document containing materially false and misleading information.
5. *Failure to follow requirements of governmental bodies, commissions, or other regulatory agencies.* If a member prepares financial statements or related information for reporting to governmental bodies, commissions, or regulatory agencies, the member should follow the requirements of such organizations in addition to GAAP. A material departure from such requirements is an act discreditable to the profession, unless the member discloses in the financial statements or the report, as applicable, that such requirements were not followed and the reasons therefor.
6. *Solicitation or disclosure of CPA examination questions and answers.* The Uniform CPA Examination became nondisclosed effective with the May 1996 examination. It is an act discreditable to solicit or disclose questions from the May 1996 or later examinations without the permission of the AICPA.
7. *Failure to file tax return or pay tax liability.* A member who fails to comply with federal, state, or local laws regarding the timely filing of personal tax returns or tax

returns of the member's firm or the timely remittance of all payroll and other taxes collected on behalf of others may be considered to have committed an act discreditable.

Do excessive drinking, rowdy behavior, or other acts that many people consider unprofessional constitute a discreditable act? Probably not. Determining what constitutes professional behavior continues to be the responsibility of each professional.

For guidance as to what constitutes a discreditable act, the AICPA bylaws provide clearer guidelines than the AICPA *Code of Professional Conduct.* The bylaws state that membership in the AICPA can be terminated without a hearing for judgment of conviction for any of the following four crimes: (1) a crime punishable by imprisonment for more than 1 year; (2) the willful failure to file any income tax return that the CPA, as an individual taxpayer, is required by law to file; (3) the filing of a false or fraudulent income tax return on the CPA's or client's behalf; or (4) the willful aiding in the preparation and presentation of a false and fraudulent income tax return of a client. Observe that three of these deal with income tax matters of the member or a client.

Advertising and Solicitation

To encourage CPAs to conduct themselves professionally, the rules also prohibit advertising or solicitation that is false, misleading, or deceptive.

Rule 502—Advertising and Other Forms of Solicitation A member in public practice shall not seek to obtain clients by advertising or other forms of solicitation in a manner that is false, misleading, or deceptive. Solicitation by the use of coercion, overreaching, or harassing conduct is prohibited.

Solicitation consists of the various means that CPA firms use to engage new clients other than accepting new clients who approach the firm. Examples include taking prospective clients to lunch to explain the CPA's services, offering seminars on current tax law changes to potential clients, and advertisements in the Yellow Pages of a phone book. The last example is advertising, which is only one form of solicitation. Advertising is the use of various media, such as magazines and radio, to communicate favorable information about the CPA firm's services.

Until 1978, advertising in any form was prohibited. As a result of the agreement with the Federal Trade Commission discussed earlier, solicitation or advertising that is not *false or deceptive* is acceptable. This change in the rules of conduct is similar to that for other professions. Advertising is now acceptable within most professions.

The effect of these changes has been an increased emphasis on marketing and more competitive pricing of services. Many CPA firms have developed sophisticated advertising for national journals read by businesspeople and for local newspapers. It is common for CPA firms to identify potential clients being serviced by other CPA firms and make formal and informal presentations to convince management to change CPA firms. Price bidding for audits and other services is now common and often highly competitive. As a result of these changes, some companies now change auditors more often than previously to reduce audit cost. Most practitioners believe audits are less profitable than previously.

Has the quality of audits become endangered by these changes? The existing legal exposure of CPAs, peer review requirements, and the potential for interference by the SEC and government has kept audit quality high. In the opinion of the authors, the changes in the rules have caused greater competition in the profession, but not so much that high-quality, efficiently run CPA firms have been significantly harmed. However, for this to continue to be so, CPA firms need to be on guard so that increasing competitive pressures do not cause auditors to reduce quality below an acceptable level.

Commissions and Referral Fees

Commissions are compensation paid for recommending or referring a third party's product or service to a client or recommending or referring a client's product or service to a third party. Restrictions on commissions are similar to the rules on contingent fees. CPAs are generally prohibited from receiving commissions for a client who is receiving attestation services from the CPA firm. Commissions are permissible for other clients, but they must be disclosed. Referral fees related to recommending or referring the services of a CPA are not considered commissions and are not restricted. However, any referral fees for CPA services must also be disclosed.

Rule 503—Commissions and Referral Fees

A. *Prohibited commissions.* A member in public practice shall not for a commission recommend or refer to a client any product or service, or for a commission recommend or refer any product or service to be supplied by a client, or receive a commission, when the member or the member's firm also performs for that client:
   (a) an audit or review of a financial statement; or
   (b) a compilation of a financial statement when the member expects, or reasonably might expect, that a third party will use the financial statement and the member's compilation report does not disclose a lack of independence; or
   (c) an examination of prospective financial information.

This prohibition applies during the period in which the member is engaged to perform any of the services listed above and the period covered by any historical financial statements involved in such listed services.

B. *Disclosure of permitted commissions.* A member in public practice who is not prohibited by this rule from performing services for or receiving a commission and who is paid or expects to be paid a commission shall disclose that fact to any person or entity to whom the member recommends or refers a product or service to which the commission relates.

C. *Referral fees.* Any member who accepts a referral fee for recommending or referring any service of a CPA to any person or entity or who pays a referral fee to obtain a client shall disclose such acceptance or payment to the client.

The rule for commissions and referral fees means that a CPA firm does not violate AICPA rules of conduct if it sells such things as real estate, securities, and entire firms on a commission basis *if the transaction does not involve a client who is receiving attestation services from the same CPA firm*. This rule enables CPA firms to profit by providing many services to nonattestation services clients that were previously prohibited.

The reason for the AICPA continuing to prohibit commissions for any attestation service client is the need to ensure that the CPA firm is independent. This requirement and the reasons for it are the same as those discussed under contingent fees.

The rationale for the AICPA's less restrictive enforcement of Rule 503 than before is the same as that discussed for contingent fees. The Federal Trade Commission contends that restrictions reduce competition and therefore are not in the public interest.

It is essential to understand that the Board of Accountancy in the state in which the firm is licensed may have more restrictive rules than the AICPA's. The CPA firm must follow the more restrictive requirements if different rules exist.

Form of Organization and Name

The rules of conduct restrict the permissible forms of organization for CPA firms and prohibit a member from practicing under a firm name that is misleading.

Rule 505—Form of Organization and Name A member may practice public accounting only in a form of organization permitted by state law or regulation whose characteristics conform to resolutions of Council.

A member shall not practice public accounting under a firm name that is misleading. Names of one or more past owners may be included in the firm name of a successor organization.

A firm may not designate itself as "Members of the American Institute of Certified Public Accountants" unless all of its CPA owners are members of the Institute.

Rule 505 permits practitioners to organize in any of six forms, as long as they are permitted by state law: proprietorship, general partnership, general corporation, professional corporation (PC), limited liability company (LLC), or limited liability partnership (LLP).

Prior to April 1994, all owners of a CPA firm had to be CPAs who were qualified to practice. Ownership of CPA firms by non-CPAs is now allowed under the following conditions:

- The CPAs must own a majority of the firm's financial interests and voting rights.
- A CPA must have ultimate responsibility for all financial statement attest, compilation, and other services provided by the firm that are governed by Statements on Auditing Standards or Statements on Standards for Accounting and Review Services.

- Owners must at all times own their equity in their own right.
- The following rules apply to all non-CPA owners:

  1. They must actively provide services to the firm's clients as their principal occupation.
  2. They cannot hold themselves out as CPAs but may use any title permitted by state law such as principal, owner, officer, member, or shareholder.
  3. They cannot assume ultimate responsibility for any financial statement attest or compilation engagement.
  4. They are not eligible for AICPA membership but must abide by the AICPA *Code of Professional Conduct.*
  5. New non-CPA owners must have a bachelor's degree. Beginning in 2010, they must also meet the AICPA 150-hour education requirement.
  6. They must meet the same continuing professional education requirements as AICPA members.

A recent development has been the acquisition of CPA firms by corporate entities such as American Express. In such instances, the CPA firm may form a subsidiary to provide attest services to clients. These alternative practice structures are permissible, but an AICPA Council resolution makes it clear that to protect the public interest, CPAs have the same responsibility for the conduct of their attest work as they have for traditional practice structures.

A CPA firm may use any name as long as it is not misleading. Most firms use the name of one or more of the owners. It is not unusual for a firm name to include the names of five or more owners. A CPA firm can use a trade name, although this is unusual in practice. Names such as Marshall Audit Co. or Chicago Tax Specialists are permissible if they are not misleading.

A summary of the rules of conduct is included in Table 3-1.

ENFORCEMENT

OBJECTIVE 3-8

Describe the enforcement mechanisms for the rules of conduct.

Failure to follow the rules of conduct can result in *expulsion* from the AICPA. This by itself does not prevent a CPA from practicing public accounting, but it certainly is a weighty social sanction. All expulsions from the AICPA for a violation of the rules are published in the *CPA Newsletter*, a publication that is sent to all AICPA members.

In addition to the rules of conduct, the AICPA bylaws provide for automatic suspension or expulsion from the AICPA for conviction of a crime punishable by imprisonment for more than 1 year and for various tax-related crimes.

Action by AICPA Professional Ethics Division

The AICPA Professional Ethics Division is responsible for investigating other violations of the *Code* and deciding disciplinary action. The division's investigations result from information obtained primarily from complaints of practitioners or other individuals, state societies of CPAs, or governmental agencies.

There are two primary levels of disciplinary action. For less serious, and probably unintentional violations, the division limits the discipline to a requirement of remedial or corrective action. An example is the unintentional failure to make sure that a small audit client included all disclosures in its financial statements, which violates Rule 203 of the rules of conduct. The division is likely to require the member to attend a specified number of hours of continuing education courses to improve technical competence. The second level of disciplinary action is action before the Joint Trial Board. This board has authority to *suspend or expel members from the AICPA* for various violations of professional ethics. Typically, action by the board also results in publication in the *CPA Newsletter* of the name and address of the person suspended or expelled and reasons for the action.

Action by a State Board of Accountancy

Even more important than expulsion from the AICPA is the existence of rules of conduct, similar to the AICPA's, that have been enacted by the Board of Accountancy of each of the 50 states. Because each state grants the individual practitioner a license to practice as a CPA, a significant breach of a state Board of Accountancy's code of conduct can result in the *loss*

TABLE 3-1 Summary of Rules of Conduct

Rules of Conduct		Applicability		Summary of Rules
Number	Topic	All Members	Members in Public Practice	
101	Independence		x	A member in public practice shall be independent in the performance of professional services as required by standards promulgated by bodies designated by Council.
102	Integrity and objectivity	x		In performing any professional service, a member shall maintain objectivity and integrity, shall be free of conflicts of interest, and shall not knowingly misrepresent facts or subordinate his or her judgment to others.
201	General standards	x		For all services, a member shall comply with the following professional standards and interpretations thereof by bodies designated by Council: (1) undertake only those professional services that the member can reasonably expect to complete with professional competence, (2) exercise due professional care, (3) adequately plan and supervise all engagements, and (4) obtain sufficient relevant data to afford a reasonable basis for all conclusions or recommendations.
202	Compliance with standards	x		A member who performs auditing, review, compilation, management consulting, tax, or other professional services shall comply with standards promulgated by bodies designated by Council.
203	Accounting principles	x		A member shall follow the professional audit reporting standards promulgated by bodies designated by Council in issuing reports about entities' compliance with generally accepted accounting principles.
301	Confidential client information		x	A member in public practice shall not disclose any confidential client information without the specific consent of the client, except for the four specific situations included in Rule 301.
302	Contingent fees		x	A member in public practice shall not perform for a contingent fee any professional service if the member also performs for the client an audit, review, or certain compilations of financial statements, or an examination of prospective financial statements. A member in public practice should also not prepare an original or amended tax return or claim for a tax refund for a contingent fee for any client.
501	Acts discreditable	x		A member shall not commit an act discreditable to the profession.
502	Advertising and other forms of solicitation		x	A member in public practice shall not seek to obtain clients by advertising or other forms of solicitation in a manner that is false, misleading, or deceptive. Solicitation by the use of coercion, overreaching, or harassing conduct is prohibited.
503	Commissions and referral fees		x	A member in public practice shall not receive or pay a commission or referral fee for any client if the member also performs for the client an audit, review, or certain compilations of financial statements, or an examination of prospective financial statements. For nonprohibited commissions or referral fees, a member must disclose the existence of such fees to the client.
505	Form of organization and name		x	A member may practice public accounting only in a form of organization permitted by state law or regulation whose characteristics conform to resolutions of Council and shall not practice public accounting under a firm name that is misleading.

of the CPA certificate and the license to practice. Although it rarely happens, the loss removes the practitioner from public accounting. Most states adopt the AICPA rules of conduct, but several have more restrictive codes. For example, some states have retained restrictions on advertising and other forms of solicitation. In recent years, an increasing number of states have adopted codes of conduct more restrictive than the AICPA's.

SUMMARY

The demand for audit and other assurance services provided by CPA firms depends on public confidence in the profession. This chapter discussed the role of ethics in society and the unique ethical responsibilities of CPAs.

The professional activities of CPAs are governed by the AICPA *Code of Professional Conduct.* Foremost of all ethical responsibilities of CPAs is the need for independence. The rules of conduct and interpretations provide guidance on permissible financial and other interests to help CPAs maintain independence. Other rules of conduct are also designed to maintain public confidence in the profession. The ethical responsibilities of CPAs are enforced by the AICPA for members and by state boards of accountancy for licensed CPAs.

ESSENTIAL TERMS

Audit committee—selected members of a client's board of directors, whose responsibilities include helping auditors to remain independent of management

Confidential client information—client information that may not be disclosed without the specific consent of the client except under authoritative professional or legal investigation

Direct financial interest—the ownership of stock or other equity shares by members or their immediate family

Ethical dilemma—a situation in which a decision must be made about the appropriate behavior

Ethics—a set of moral principles or values

Independence in appearance—the auditor's ability to maintain an unbiased viewpoint *in the eyes of others*

Independence in fact—the auditor's ability to take an unbiased viewpoint in the performance of professional services

Indirect financial interest—a close, but not direct, ownership relationship between the auditor and the client; an example is the ownership of stock by a member's grandparent

Privileged information—client information that the professional cannot be legally required to provide; information that an accountant obtains from a client is confidential but not privileged

REVIEW QUESTIONS

3-1 **(Objective 3-1)** What are the six core ethical values described by the Josephson Institute? What are some other sources of ethical values?

3-2 **(Objective 3-2)** Describe an ethical dilemma. How does a person resolve an ethical dilemma?

3-3 **(Objective 3-3)** Why is there a special need for ethical behavior by professionals? Why do the ethical requirements of the CPA profession differ from those of other professions?

3-4 **(Objective 3-4)** List the four parts of the *Code of Professional Conduct*, and state the purpose of each.

3-5 **(Objective 3-5)** Distinguish between independence in fact and independence in appearance. State three activities that may not affect independence in fact but are likely to affect independence in appearance.

3-6 **(Objective 3-5)** Why is an auditor's independence so essential?

3-7 **(Objective 3-6)** Explain how the rules concerning stock ownership apply to partners and professional staff. Give an example of when stock ownership would be prohibited for each.

3-8 **(Objectives 3-5, 3-6, 3-7)** What is the profession's position regarding providing management advisory services for an audit client?

3-9 **(Objective 3-5)** Many people believe that a CPA cannot be truly independent when payment of fees is dependent on the management of the client. Explain two approaches that could reduce this appearance of lack of independence.

3-10 **(Objective 3-7)** After accepting an engagement, a CPA discovers that the client's industry is more technical than he realized and that he is not competent in certain areas of the operation. What are the CPA's options?

3-11 **(Objective 3-7)** Assume that an auditor makes an agreement with a client that the audit fee will be contingent upon the number of days required to complete the engagement. Is this a violation of the *Code of Professional Conduct*? What is the essence of the rule of professional ethics dealing with contingent fees, and what are the reasons for the rule?

3-12 **(Objective 3-7)** The auditor's working papers usually can be provided to someone else only with the permission of the client. Give three exceptions to this general rule.

3-13 **(Objective 3-7)** Identify and explain factors that should keep the quality of audits high even though advertising and competitive bidding are allowed.

3-14 **(Objective 3-7)** Summarize the restrictions on advertising by CPA firms in the rules of conduct and interpretations.

3-15 **(Objective 3-7)** What is the purpose of the AICPA's *Code of Professional Conduct* restriction on commissions as stated in Rule 503?

3-16 **(Objective 3-7)** State the allowable forms of organization a CPA firm may assume.

3-17 **(Objective 3-8)** Distinguish between the effect on a CPA firm's practice of enforcing the rules of conduct by the AICPA versus a state Board of Accountancy.

MULTIPLE CHOICE QUESTIONS FROM CPA EXAMINATIONS

3-18 **(Objective 3-6)** The following questions concern independence and the *Code of Professional Conduct* or GAAS. Choose the best response.

a. What is the meaning of the generally accepted auditing standard that requires the auditor be independent?
   (1) The auditor must be without bias with respect to the client under audit.
   (2) The auditor must adopt a critical attitude during the audit.
   (3) The auditor's sole obligation is to third parties.
   (4) The auditor may have a direct ownership interest in the client's business if it is not material.

b. The independent audit is important to readers of financial statements because it
   (1) determines the future stewardship of the management of the company whose financial statements are audited.
   (2) measures and communicates financial and business data included in financial statements.
   (3) involves the objective examination of and reporting on management-prepared statements.
   (4) reports on the accuracy of all information in the financial statements.

c. An auditor strives to achieve independence in appearance to
   (1) maintain public confidence in the profession.
   (2) become independent in fact.
   (3) comply with the generally accepted auditing standards of field work.
   (4) maintain an unbiased mental attitude.

3-19 **(Objective 3-7)** The following questions concern possible violations of the AICPA *Code of Professional Conduct*. Choose the best response.

a. In which one of the following situations would a CPA be in violation of the AICPA *Code of Professional Conduct* in determining the audit fee?
   (1) A fee based on whether the CPA's report on the client's financial statements results in the approval of a bank loan.
   (2) A fee based on the outcome of a bankruptcy proceeding.
   (3) A fee based on the nature of the service rendered and the CPA's expertise instead of the actual time spent on the engagement.
   (4) A fee based on the fee charged by the prior auditor.

b. The AICPA *Code of Professional Conduct* states that a CPA shall not disclose any confidential information obtained in the course of a professional engagement except with the consent of the client. In which one of the following situations would disclosure by a CPA be in violation of the code?
   (1) Disclosing confidential information in order to properly discharge the CPA's responsibilities in accordance with the profession's standards.
   (2) Disclosing confidential information in compliance with a subpoena issued by a court.

(3) Disclosing confidential information to another accountant interested in purchasing the CPA's practice.
(4) Disclosing confidential information during an AICPA authorized peer review.

c. A CPA's retention of client records as a means of enforcing payment of an overdue audit fee is an action that is
(1) not addressed by the AICPA *Code of Professional Conduct.*
(2) acceptable if sanctioned by the state laws.
(3) prohibited under the AICPA rules of conduct.
(4) a violation of generally accepted auditing standards.

DISCUSSION QUESTIONS AND PROBLEMS

3-20 (**Objectives 3-6, 3-7**) Each of the following situations involves a possible violation of the AICPA's *Code of Professional Conduct*. For each situation, state the applicable section of the rules of conduct and whether it is a violation.

a. John Brown is a CPA, but not a partner, with 3 years of professional experience with Lyle and Lyle, CPAs. He owns 25 shares of stock in an audit client of the firm, but he does not take part in the audit of the client and the amount of stock is not material in relation to his total wealth.

b. In preparing the personal tax returns for a client, Phyllis Allen, CPA, observed that the deductions for contributions and interest were unusually large. When she asked the client for backup information to support the deductions, she was told, "Ask me no questions, and I will tell you no lies." Allen completed the return on the basis of the information acquired from the client.

c. A client requests assistance of J. Bacon, CPA, in the installation of a local area network. Bacon had no experience in this type of work and no knowledge of the client's computer system, so he obtained assistance from a computer consultant. The consultant is not in the practice of public accounting, but Bacon is confident of his professional skills. Because of the highly technical nature of the work, Bacon is not able to review the consultant's work.

d. Five small Chicago CPA firms have become involved in an information project by taking part in an interfirm working paper review program. Under the program, each firm designates two partners to review the working papers, including the tax returns and the financial statements of another CPA firm taking part in the program. At the end of each review, the auditors who prepared the working papers and the reviewers have a conference to discuss the strengths and weaknesses of the audit. They do not obtain authorization from the audit client before the review takes place.

e. James Thurgood, CPA, stayed longer than he should have at the annual Christmas party of Thurgood and Thurgood, CPAs. On his way home he drove through a red light and was stopped by a policeman, who observed that he was intoxicated. In a jury trial, Thurgood was found guilty of driving under the influence of alcohol. Because this was not his first offense, he was sentenced to 30 days in jail and his driver's license was revoked for 1 year.

f. Bill Wendal, CPA, set up a casualty and fire insurance agency to complement his auditing and tax services. He does not use his own name on anything pertaining to the insurance agency and has a highly competent manager, Frank Jones, who runs it. Wendal often requests Jones to review the adequacy of a client's insurance with management if it seems underinsured. He believes that he provides a valuable service to clients by informing them when they are underinsured.

g. Rankin, CPA, provides tax services, management advisory services, and bookkeeping services and conducts audits for the same client. Because the firm is small, the same person often provides all the services.

3-21 (**Objectives 3-6, 3-7**) Each of the following situations involves possible violations of the AICPA's *Code of Professional Conduct*. For each situation, state whether it is a violation of the *Code*. In those cases in which it is a violation, explain the nature of the violation and the rationale for the existing rule.

a. Ralph Williams is the partner on the audit of a nonprofit charitable organization. He is also a member of the board of directors, but this position is honorary and does not involve performing a management function.

b. Pickens and Perkins, CPAs, are incorporated to practice public accounting. The only shareholders in the corporation are existing employees of the organization, including partners, staff members who are CPAs, staff members who are not CPAs, and administrative personnel.

c. Fenn and Company, CPAs, has a sophisticated network-based computer server that supports the firm's technology systems and databases. Because of excess capacity available on the server, Fenn and Company agreed to maintain on its server accounting records for one of Fenn's audit clients, Delta Equipment Company.

d. Godette, CPA, has a law practice. Godette has recommended one of his clients to Doyle, CPA. Doyle has agreed to pay Godette 10% of the fee for services rendered by Doyle to Godette's client.

e. Theresa Barnes, CPA, has an audit client, Smith, Inc., which uses another CPA for management services work. Barnes sends her firm's literature covering its management services capabilities to Smith on a monthly basis, unsolicited.

f. A bank issued a notice to its depositors that it was being audited and requested them to comply with the CPA's effort to obtain a confirmation on the deposit balances. The bank printed the name and address of the CPA in the notice. The CPA has knowledge of the notice.

g. Myron Jones, CPA, is a member of a national CPA firm. His business card includes his name, the firm's name, address, and telephone number, and the title *IT consultant.*

h. Gutowski, a practicing CPA, has written an e-commerce-related article that is being published in a professional publication. The publication wishes to inform its readers about Gutowski's background. The information, which Gutowski has approved, includes his academic degrees, other articles he has had published in professional journals, and a statement that he is an e-commerce expert.

i. Poust, CPA, has sold his public accounting practice, which includes bookkeeping, tax services, and auditing, to Lyons, CPA. Poust obtained permission from all audit clients for audit-related working papers before making them available to Lyons. He did not get permission before releasing tax- and management services-related working papers.

j. Murphy and Company, CPAs, is the principal auditor of the consolidated financial statements of Lowe, Inc. and subsidiaries. Lowe accounts for approximately 98% of consolidated assets and consolidated net income. The two subsidiaries are audited by Trotman and Company, CPAs, a firm with an excellent professional reputation. Murphy insists on auditing the two subsidiaries because he deems this necessary to warrant the expression of an opinion.*

3-22 (**Objective 3-5**) The New York Stock Exchange now requires all its member firms to have audit committees.

Required

a. Describe an audit committee.

b. What are the typical functions performed by an audit committee?

c. Explain how an audit committee can help an auditor be more independent.

d. Some critics of audit committees believe that they bias companies in favor of larger and perhaps more expensive CPA firms. These critics contend that a primary concern of audit committee members is to reduce their exposure to legal liability. The committees will therefore recommend larger, more prestigious CPA firms, even if the cost is somewhat higher, to minimize the potential criticism of selecting an unqualified firm. Evaluate these comments.

3-23 (**Objectives 3-5, 3-6**) The following relate to auditors' independence:

Required

a. Why is independence so essential for auditors?

b. Compare the importance of independence of CPAs with that of other professionals, such as attorneys.

c. Explain the difference between independence in appearance and in fact.

d. Assume that a partner of a CPA firm owns two shares of stock of a large audit client on which he serves as the engagement partner. The ownership is an insignificant part of his total wealth.
   (1) Has he violated the *Code of Professional Conduct*?
   (2) Explain whether the ownership is likely to affect the partner's independence in fact.
   (3) Explain the reason for the strict requirements about stock ownership in the rules of conduct.

e. Discuss how each of the following could affect independence in fact and independence in appearance, and evaluate the social consequence of prohibiting auditors from doing each one:
   (1) Ownership of stock in a client company
   (2) Having bookkeeping services for an audit client performed by the same person who does the audit

* AICPA adapted.

(3) Recommending adjusting entries to the client's financial statements and preparing financial statements, including footnotes, for the client
(4) Having management services for an audit client performed by individuals in a department that is separate from the audit department
(5) Having the annual audit performed by the same audit team, except for assistants, for 5 years in a row
(6) Having the annual audit performed by the same CPA firm for 10 years in a row
(7) Having management select the CPA firm

f. Which of (1) through (7) are prohibited by the AICPA *Code of Professional Conduct*? Which are prohibited by the SEC?

3-24 **(Objective 3-6)** Marie Janes encounters the following situations in doing the audit of a large auto dealership. Janes is not a partner.

1. The sales manager tells her that there is a sale (at a substantial discount) on new cars that is limited to long-established customers of the dealership. Because her firm has been doing the audit for several years, the sales manager has decided that Janes should also be eligible for the discount.
2. The auto dealership has an executive lunchroom that is available free to employees above a certain level. The controller informs Janes that she can also eat there any time.
3. Janes is invited to and attends the company's annual Christmas party. When presents are handed out, she is surprised to find her name included. The present has a value of approximately $200.

Required

a. Assuming Janes accepts the offer or gift in each situation, has she violated the rules of conduct?
b. Discuss what Janes should do in each situation.

3-25 **(Objective 3-6)** Ann Archer serves on the audit committee of JKB Communications, Inc., a telecommunications start-up company. One of the audit committee's responsibilities is to evaluate the external auditor's independence in performing the audit of the company's financial statements. In conducting this year's evaluation, Ann learned that JKB Communications' external auditor also performed the following IT and e-commerce services for the company:

1. Installed JKB Communications' information system hardware and software selected by JKB management
2. Supervised JKB Communications personnel in the daily operation of the newly installed information system
3. Customized a prepackaged payroll software application, based on options and specifications selected by management
4. Trained JKB Communications employees on the use of the newly installed information system
5. Determined which JKB Communications products would be offered for sale on the company's Internet Web site
6. Operated JKB Communications' local area network for several months while the company searched for a replacement after the previous network manager left the company.

Required Consider each of the preceding services separately. Evaluate whether the performance of each service violates the AICPA's *Code of Professional Conduct.*

CASES

3-26 **(Objectives 3-2, 3-7)** Barbara Whitley had great expectations about her future as she sat in her graduation ceremony in May 2002. She was about to receive her Master of Accountancy degree, and next week she would begin her career on the audit staff of Green, Thresher & Co., CPAs.

Things looked a little different to Barbara in February 2003. She was working on the audit of Delancey Fabrics, a textile manufacturer with a calendar year-end. The pressure was enormous. Everyone on the audit team was putting in 70-hour weeks and it still looked as if the audit wouldn't be done on time. Barbara was doing work in the property area, vouching additions for the year. The audit program indicated that a sample of all items over $10,000 should be selected, plus a judgmental sample of smaller items. When Barbara went to take the sample, Jack Bean, the senior, had left the client's office and couldn't answer her questions about the appropriate size of the judgmental sample. Barbara forged ahead with her own judgment and selected 50 smaller items. Her basis for doing this was that there were about 250 such items, so 50 was a reasonably good proportion of such additions.

Barbara audited the additions with the following results: The items over $10,000 contained no misstatements; however, the 50 small items contained a large number of misstatements. In fact, when Barbara projected them to all such additions, the amount seemed quite significant.

A couple of days later, Jack Bean returned to the client's office. Barbara brought her work to Jack in order to apprise him of the problems she found and got the following response:

> My God, Barbara, why did you do this? You were only supposed to look at the items over $10,000 plus 5 or 10 little ones. You've wasted a whole day on that work, and we can't afford to spend any more time on it. I want you to throw away the schedules where you tested the last 40 small items and forget you ever did them.

When Barbara asked about the possible audit adjustment regarding the small items, none of which arose from the first 10 items, Jack responded, "Don't worry, it's not material anyway. You just forget it; it's my concern, not yours."

Required

a. In what way is this an ethical dilemma for Barbara?

b. Use the six-step approach discussed in the book to resolve the ethical dilemma.

3-27 (**Objective 3-2**) Frank Dorrance, a senior audit manager for Bright and Lorren, CPAs, has recently been informed that the firm plans to promote him to partner within the next year or two if he continues to perform at the same high-quality level as in the past. Frank excels at dealing effectively with all people, including client personnel, professional staff, partners, and potential clients. He has recently built a bigger home for entertaining and has joined the city's most prestigious golf and tennis club. He is excited about his future with the firm.

Frank has recently been assigned to the audit of Machine International, a large wholesale company that ships goods throughout the world. It is one of Bright and Lorren's most prestigious clients. During the audit, Frank determines that Machine International uses a method of revenue recognition called "bill and hold" that has recently been questioned by the SEC. After considerable research, Frank concludes that the method of revenue recognition is not appropriate for Machine International. He discusses the matter with the engagement partner, who concludes that the accounting method has been used for more than 10 years by the client and is appropriate, especially considering that the client does not file with the SEC. The partner is certain the firm would lose the client if the revenue recognition method is found inappropriate. Frank argues that the revenue recognition method was appropriate in prior years, but the SEC ruling makes it inappropriate in the current year. Frank recognizes the partner's responsibility to make the final decision, but he feels strongly enough to state that he plans to follow the requirements of SAS 22 (AU 311) and include a statement in the working papers that he disagrees with the partner's decision. The partner informs Frank that she is unwilling to permit such a statement because of the potential legal implications. However, she is willing to write a letter to Frank stating that she takes full responsibility for making the final decision if a legal dispute ever arises. She concludes by saying, "Frank, partners must act like partners, not like loose cannons trying to make life difficult for their partners. You have some growing up to do before I would feel comfortable with you as a partner."

Required

Use the six-step approach discussed in the book to resolve the ethical dilemma.

INTERNET PROBLEM 3-1: AICPA *CODE OF PROFESSIONAL CONDUCT*—ETHICS RULINGS AND CASE

Reference the CW site. Imagine a CPA has provided extensive advisory services for a client. In that connection, the member has attended board meetings; interpreted financial statements, forecasts, and other analyses; counseled on potential expansion plans; and counseled on banking relationships. Would the independence of the member be considered to be impaired under these circumstances? The answer to many such questions can be found in Ethics Rulings associated with the AICPA *Code of Professional Conduct.* This problem requires students to use the Internet to (1) research ethics rulings in the *Code* and (2) answer questions and cases associated with another CPA ethics site.

CHAPTER 4

LEGAL LIABILITY

IT TAKES THE NET PROFIT FROM MANY AUDITS TO OFFSET THE COST OF ONE LAWSUIT

Orange & Rankle, a CPA firm in San Jose, audited a small high-tech client that developed software. A significant portion of the client's capital was provided by a syndicate of 40 limited partners. The owners of these interests were knowledgeable business and professional people, including several lawyers.

Orange & Rankle audited the company for 4 consecutive years, from its inception, for an average annual fee of approximately $13,000. The audits were well done by competent auditors. It was clear to the firm and to others who subsequently reviewed the audits that they complied with generally accepted auditing standards in every way.

In the middle of the fifth year of the company's existence, it became apparent that the marketing plan it had developed was overly optimistic and the company was going to require additional capital or a significant strategy change. The limited partners were polled and refused to provide the capital. The company folded its tent and filed bankruptcy. The limited partners lost their investment in the company. They subsequently filed a lawsuit against all parties involved in the enterprise, including the auditors.

Over the next several years, the auditors proceeded through the process of preparing to defend themselves in the lawsuit. They went through complete discovery, hired an expert witness on auditing-related issues, filed motions, and so forth. They attempted a settlement at various times, but the plaintiffs would not agree to a reasonable amount. Finally, during the second day of trial, the plaintiffs settled for a nominal amount.

It was clear that the plaintiffs knew the auditors bore no fault but kept them in the suit anyway. The total *out-of-pocket* cost to the audit firm was $1 million, not to mention personnel time, possible damage to their reputation, and general stress and strain. Thus, the cost of this suit, in which the auditors were completely innocent, was more than 75 times the average annual audit fee earned from this client.

LEARNING OBJECTIVES

After studying this chapter, you should be able to

4-1 Understand the litigious environment in which CPAs practice.

4-2 Explain why the failure of financial statement users to differentiate among business failure, audit failure, and audit risk has resulted in lawsuits.

4-3 Use the primary legal concepts and terms concerning accountants' liability as a basis for studying legal liability of auditors.

4-4 Describe accountants' liability to clients and related defenses.

4-5 Describe accountants' liability to third parties under common law and related defenses.

4-6 Describe accountants' civil liability under the federal securities laws and related defenses.

4-7 Specify what constitutes criminal liability for accountants.

4-8 Describe what the profession and the individual CPA can do and what is being done to reduce the threat of litigation.

This chapter on legal liability and the preceding chapter on professional ethics highlight the environment in which CPAs operate. We focus on these chapters now to provide an overview of the importance of protecting the profession's reputation as being one that is viewed as highly ethical and to highlight consequences accountants face when others believe they have failed to live up to that ethical standard. Legal liability and its consequences for the profession are serious. This chapter highlights ways CPAs can be held liable for the professional services they provide.

As the auditors at Orange & Rankle in the opening vignette learned the hard way, legal liability and its consequences are significant for CPAs. It is estimated that the profession's aggregate liability exposure exceeds $40 billion. Although firms have insurance to help alleviate the impact of assessed damages, the premiums are high and the policies available to the firms have large deductible amounts. The deductibles are such that the large firms are essentially self-insured for losses of many millions of dollars.

This chapter focuses on legal liability for CPAs both on a conceptual level and in terms of specific legal suits that have been filed against CPAs. It also highlights actions available to the profession and individual practitioners to minimize liability while still meeting society's needs.

CHANGED LEGAL ENVIRONMENT

OBJECTIVE 4-1

Understand the litigious environment in which CPAs practice.

Professionals have always had a duty to provide a reasonable level of care while performing work for those they serve. Audit professionals have a responsibility under common law to fulfill implied or expressed contracts with clients. They are liable to their clients for negligence and/or breach of contract should they fail to provide the services or not exercise due care in their performance. Auditors may also be held liable under common law in certain circumstances to parties other than their clients. Although the criteria for legal actions against auditors by third parties vary by state, the most common view is that the auditor owes a duty of care to third parties who are part of a limited group of persons whose reliance is "foreseen" by the auditor. In addition to common law, auditors may be held liable to third parties under statutory law. Both the Securities Act of 1933 and the Securities Exchange Act of 1934 contain sections that serve as a basis for actions against auditors. Finally, in rare cases auditors have also been held liable for criminal acts. A criminal conviction against an auditor can result when it is demonstrated that the auditor intended to deceive or harm others.

Despite efforts to address legal liability of CPAs, both the number of lawsuits and size of awards to plaintiffs remain high, including suits involving third parties under both common law and the federal securities acts. There are no simple reasons for this trend, but the following are major factors:

Stanford's Securities Class Action Clearinghouse

- There is growing awareness of the responsibilities of public accountants by users of financial statements.
- There is an increased consciousness on the part of the Securities and Exchange Commission (SEC) regarding its responsibility for protecting investors' interests.
- Auditing and accounting are more complex because of factors such as the increasing size of business, the globalization of business, and the intricacies of business operations.
- Society accepts lawsuits by injured parties against anyone who might be able to provide compensation, regardless of who was at fault, coupled with the joint and several liability doctrine. This is often called the deep-pocket concept of liability.
- Large civil court judgments against CPA firms have been awarded in a few cases, which has encouraged attorneys to provide legal services on a contingent-fee basis. This arrangement offers the injured party a potential gain when the suit is successful, but minimal loss when it is unsuccessful.
- Many CPA firms are willing to settle their legal problems out of court in an attempt to avoid costly legal fees and adverse publicity rather than resolving them through the judicial process.

- Courts have difficulty in understanding and interpreting technical accounting and auditing matters.

Litigation costs for accountants and others caused great concern in Congress and in society in general during the last several years. It was recognized that all members of society bear these costs. As a result, legislation was introduced to attempt to control litigation costs, both by discouraging nonmeritorious lawsuits and by bringing damages more in line with relative fault. The Private Securities Litigation Reform Act of 1995 was passed to provide relief to accountants in the area of federal securities litigation. Nevertheless, accountants' liability is still onerous and a major consideration in the conduct of a CPA firm's professional practice.

DISTINCTION AMONG BUSINESS FAILURE, AUDIT FAILURE, AND AUDIT RISK

OBJECTIVE 4-2

Explain why the failure of financial statement users to differentiate among business failure, audit failure, and audit risk has resulted in lawsuits.

Many accounting and legal professionals believe that a major cause of lawsuits against CPA firms is the lack of understanding by financial statement users of the difference between a business failure and an audit failure and between an audit failure and audit risk. We will now examine these terms and the ways in which not understanding them can lead to lawsuits against auditors.

A **business failure** occurs when a business is unable to repay its lenders or meet the expectations of its investors because of economic or business conditions, such as a recession, poor management decisions, or unexpected competition in the industry. The extreme case of business failure is filing for bankruptcy. **Audit failure** occurs when the auditor issues an erroneous audit opinion as the result of an underlying failure to comply with the requirements of generally accepted auditing standards (GAAS). An example is assigning unqualified assistants to perform audit tasks who then fail to find material misstatements that qualified auditors would discover. **Audit risk** represents the risk that the auditor will conclude that the financial statements are fairly stated and an unqualified opinion can be issued when, in fact, they are materially misstated. Because auditors are able to gather evidence only on a test basis and detecting well-concealed frauds can be extremely difficult, there is always some risk that the auditor will not uncover a material misstatement due to fraud even though the auditor complied with GAAS.

Most accounting professionals agree that in most cases when an audit has failed to uncover material misstatements and the wrong type of audit opinion is issued, a legitimate question may be raised whether the auditor exercised due care. If the auditor failed to use due care in the conduct of the audit, there is an audit failure. In such cases, the law often allows parties who suffered losses as a result of the auditor's breach of a duty of care owed to them to recover some or all of the losses proximately caused by the audit failure. It is difficult in practice to determine when the auditor has failed to use due care because of the complexity of auditing. It is also difficult to determine who has a right to expect the benefits of an audit because of legal traditions. Nevertheless, an auditor's failure to follow due care often may be expected to result in liability and, when appropriate, damages against the CPA firm.

As highlighted by the lawsuit against Orange & Rankle in the opening vignette, the difficulty arises when there has been a business failure, but not an audit failure. For example, when a company goes bankrupt or cannot pay its debts, it is common for statement users to claim that there was an audit failure, especially when the most recently issued auditor's opinion indicates that the financial statements were fairly stated. Even worse, if there is a business failure and the financial statements are later determined to have been misstated, users may claim that the auditor was negligent even if the audit was conducted in accordance with GAAS. This conflict between statement users and auditors often arises because of what is called the expectation gap between users and auditors. Most auditors believe that the conduct of the audit in accordance with GAAS is all that can be expected of auditors. Many users believe that auditors guarantee the accuracy of financial statements, and some users even believe that the auditor guarantees the financial viability of the business. Fortunately for the profession, courts continue to support the auditor's view. Unfortunately, the expectation gap often results in unwarranted lawsuits. Perhaps the profession has a responsibility to educate statement users about the role of auditors and the difference among business failure, audit failure, and audit risk. Realistically, however, auditors must recognize that, in part, the claims of audit failure may also result from the hope of those who suffer a business loss to recover from any source, regardless of who is at fault.

LEGAL CONCEPTS AFFECTING LIABILITY

OBJECTIVE **4-3**

Use the primary legal concepts and terms concerning accountants' liability as a basis for studying legal liability of auditors.

The CPA is responsible for every aspect of his or her public accounting work, including auditing, taxes, management advisory services, and accounting and bookkeeping services. For example, if a CPA negligently failed to properly prepare and file a client's tax return, the CPA can be held liable for any penalties and interest that the client was required to pay plus the tax preparation fee charged. In some states, the court can also assess punitive damages.

Most of the major lawsuits against CPA firms have dealt with audited or unaudited financial statements. The discussion in this chapter is restricted primarily to those two aspects of public accounting. Several legal concepts apply to lawsuits against CPAs. These are the prudent person concept, liability for the acts of others, and the lack of privileged communication.

Prudent Person Concept

There is agreement within the profession and the courts that the auditor is not a guarantor or insurer of financial statements. The auditor is expected only to conduct the audit with due care. Even then, the auditor cannot be expected to be perfect.

The standard of due care to which the auditor is expected to be held is often called the **prudent person concept.** It is expressed in *Cooley on Torts* as follows:

- Every man who offers his service to another and is employed assumes the duty to exercise in the employment such skill as he possesses with reasonable care and diligence. In all these employments where peculiar skill is prerequisite, if one offers his service, he is understood as holding himself out to the public as possessing the degree of skill commonly possessed by others in the same employment, and, if his pretentions are unfounded, he commits a species of fraud upon every man who employs him in reliance on his public profession. But no man, whether skilled or unskilled, undertakes that the task he assumes shall be performed successfully, and without fault or error. *He undertakes for good faith and integrity, but not for infallibility,* and he is liable to his employer for negligence, bad faith, or dishonesty, but not for losses consequent upon pure errors of judgment.

Liability for the Acts of Others

Generally, the partners, or shareholders in the case of a professional corporation, are jointly liable for the civil actions against any owner. However, if the firm operates as a limited liability partnership (LLP), a limited liability company (LLC), a general corporation, or a professional corporation with limited liability, the liability for one owner's actions does not extend to another owner's *personal assets,* unless the other owner was directly involved in the actions of the owner causing the liability. Of course, the firm's assets are all subject to the damages that arise.

The partners may also be liable for the work of others on whom they rely under the laws of agency. The three groups an auditor is most likely to rely on are *employees, other CPA firms* engaged to do part of the work, and *specialists* called upon to provide technical information. For example, if an employee performs improperly in doing an audit, the partners can be held liable for the employee's performance.

Lack of Privileged Communication

CPAs do not have the right under common law to withhold information from the courts on the grounds that the information is privileged. As stated in Chapter 3, information in an auditor's documentation can be subpoenaed by a court. Confidential discussions between the client and auditor cannot be withheld from the courts.

A number of states have statutes that permit privileged communication between the client and auditor. Even then, the intent at the time of the communication must have been for the communication to remain confidential. A CPA can refuse to testify in a state with privileged communications statutes. The privilege does not extend to federal courts.

TABLE 4-1 Legal Terms Affecting CPAs' Liability

Legal Term	Description
Terms Related to Negligence and Fraud	
Ordinary negligence	Absence of reasonable care that can be expected of a person in a set of circumstances. For auditors, it is in terms of what other competent auditors would have done in the same situation.
Gross negligence	Lack of even slight care, tantamount to reckless behavior, that can be expected of a person. Some states do not distinguish between ordinary and gross negligence.
Constructive fraud	Existence of extreme or unusual negligence even though there was no intent to deceive or do harm. Constructive fraud is also termed *recklessness*. Recklessness in the case of an audit would be present if the auditor knew an adequate audit was not done but still issued an opinion, even though there was no intention of deceiving statement users.
Fraud	Occurs when a misstatement is made and there is both the knowledge of its falsity and the intent to deceive.
Terms Related to Contract Law	
Breach of contract	Failure of one or both parties in a contract to fulfill the requirements of the contract. An example is the failure of a CPA firm to deliver a tax return on the agreed-upon date. Parties who have a relationship that is established by a contract are said to have *privity of contract*.
Third-party beneficiary	A third party who does not have privity of contract but is known to the contracting parties and is intended to have certain rights and benefits under the contract. A common example is a bank that has a large loan outstanding at the balance sheet date and requires an audit as a part of its loan agreement.
Other Terms	
Common law	Laws that have been developed through court decisions rather than through government statutes.
Statutory law	Laws that have been passed by the U.S. Congress and other governmental units. The Securities Acts of 1933 and 1934 are important statutory laws affecting auditors.
Joint and several liability	The assessment against a defendant of the full loss suffered by a plaintiff, regardless of the extent to which other parties shared in the wrongdoing. For example, if management intentionally misstates financial statements, an auditor can be assessed the entire loss to shareholders if the company is bankrupt and management is unable to pay.
Separate and proportionate liability	The assessment against a defendant of that portion of the damage caused by the defendant's negligence. For example, if the courts determine that an auditor's negligence in conducting an audit was the cause of 30% of a loss to a defendant, only 30% of the aggregate damage would be assessed to the CPA firm.

Legal Terms Affecting CPAs' Liability

The material in the rest of the chapter can be covered more effectively if the most common legal terms affecting CPAs' liability are understood. Table 4-1 defines many of the terms that will be used throughout the remainder of this chapter.

The distinction between joint and several liability and separate and proportionate liability, which are both defined in Table 4-1, is an extremely significant one, as the amounts will vary greatly between these two bases for assessing damages. Generally, these damage approaches apply in cases of liability to third parties under common law and under the federal securities laws. When lawsuits are filed in state court, the state laws will determine which approach to damages applies. When lawsuits are brought under the federal securities laws, the separate and proportionate approach will apply except where it can be shown that the CPA defendant has actual knowledge of fraud or has participated in fraud, in which case joint and several liability would apply. It should be noted that under the federal statutes, the amount of damages under separate and proportionate liability can be increased to 150 percent of the amount determined to be proportionate to the CPA's degree of fault, where the main defendant is insolvent.

FIGURE 4-1 Four Major Sources of Auditors' Legal Liability

Source of Liability	Example of Potential Claim
Client—liability to client under common law	Client sues auditor for not discovering a material fraud during the audit.
Third party—liability to third parties under common law	Bank sues auditor for not discovering that a borrower's financial statements are materially misstated.
Liability under federal securities laws	Combined group of stockholders sues auditor for not discovering materially misstated financial statements.
Criminal liability	Federal government prosecutes auditor for knowingly issuing an incorrect audit report.

Sources of Legal Liability

The main focus of this chapter is on the four sources of auditor's **legal liability.** These four areas of liability are classified as (1) liability to clients, (2) liability to third parties under common law, (3) liability to third parties under the federal securities laws, and (4) criminal liability. Figure 4-1 provides examples of each of these classifications of liability. Next, each of these liability classifications is examined in more detail.

LIABILITY TO CLIENTS

OBJECTIVE 4-4

Describe accountants' liability to clients and related defenses.

The most common source of lawsuits against CPAs is from clients. The suits vary widely, including such claims as failure to complete a nonaudit engagement on the agreed-upon date, inappropriate withdrawal from an audit, failure to discover a defalcation (theft of assets), and breaching the confidentiality requirements of CPAs. Typically, the amount of these lawsuits is relatively small, and they do not receive the publicity often given to other types of suits. The *Fund of Funds* case, in which the court awarded the company $80 million in a suit against a CPA firm for breach of confidentiality requirements, is a notable exception.

A typical lawsuit involves a claim that the auditor did not discover an employee defalcation as a result of negligence in the conduct of the audit. The lawsuit can be for breach of contract, a tort action for negligence, or both. Tort actions can be based on ordinary negligence, gross negligence, or fraud. Tort actions are common because the amounts recoverable under them are normally larger than under breach of contract.

The principal issue in cases involving alleged negligence is usually the level of care required. Although it is generally agreed that nobody is perfect, not even a professional, in most instances, any significant error or mistake in judgment will create at least a presumption of negligence that the professional will have to rebut. In the auditing environment, failure to meet GAAS is often conclusive evidence of negligence. A typical example of an audit case raising the question of negligent performance by a CPA firm is the case of *Cenco Incorporated* v. *Seidman & Seidman.* The case involved alleged negligence by the auditor in failing to find a fraud. In the legal suit by Cenco's new management, the auditor was able to successfully argue that it was not negligent and that the deceitful actions on the part of the old management team prevented the auditor from uncovering the fraud. The reader should remember from the study of GAAS in Chapter 1 that determining whether there is a violation is highly subjective.

The question of level of care becomes more difficult in the environment of an unaudited review or compilation of financial statements in which there are fewer accepted standards to evaluate performance. A widely known example of a lawsuit dealing with the failure to uncover fraud in unaudited financial statements is the *1136 Tenants* case. Although the CPA was never engaged to conduct an audit for the 1136 Tenants Corporation, the CPA was found liable for failing to detect an embezzlement scheme conducted by one of the client's managers. One of the reasons for this outcome was the lack of a clear understanding between the client and the CPA as to the exact nature of the services to be performed by the CPA. As a result of this case, *engagement letters* between the client and the CPA firm developed. Now, CPA firms and clients typically sign engagement letters to formalize their agreements about the services to be provided, fees, and timing. There can be *privity of contract* (recall that was defined in Table 4-1) without a written agreement, but an engagement letter defines the contract more clearly.

Auditor's Defenses Against Client Suits

The CPA firm normally uses one or a combination of four defenses when there are legal claims by clients: lack of duty to perform the service, nonnegligent performance, contributory negligence, and absence of causal connection.

Lack of Duty The **lack of duty to perform** the service means that the CPA firm claims that there was no implied or expressed contract. For example, the CPA firm might claim that misstatements were not uncovered because the firm did a review service, not an audit. A common way for a CPA firm to demonstrate a lack of duty to perform is by use of an engagement letter. Many litigation experts believe that a well-written engagement letter is one of the most important ways in which CPA firms can reduce the likelihood of adverse legal actions.

Nonnegligent Performance For **nonnegligent performance** in an audit, the CPA firm claims that the audit was performed in accordance with GAAS. Even if there were undiscovered misstatements, the auditor is not responsible if the audit was conducted properly. The prudent person concept discussed earlier establishes in law that the CPA firm is not expected to be infallible. Similarly, SAS 47 (AU 312) and SAS 82 (AU 316) make it clear that an audit in accordance with GAAS is subject to limitations and cannot be relied on for complete assurance that all misstatements will be found. Requiring auditors to discover all material misstatements would, in essence, make them insurers or guarantors of the accuracy of the financial statements. The courts do not require that.

Contributory Negligence A defense of **contributory negligence** exists when the client's own actions either resulted in the loss that is the basis for damages or interfered with the conduct of the audit in such a way that prevented the auditor from discovering the cause of the loss. As an example of the first circumstance, suppose a client claims that a CPA firm was negligent in not uncovering an employee's theft of cash. If the CPA firm had notified the client (preferably in writing) of a weakness in internal control that would have prevented the theft but management did not correct it, the CPA firm would have a defense of contributory negligence. As an example of the second circumstance, suppose a CPA firm failed to determine that certain accounts receivable were uncollectible and, in reviewing collectibility, were lied to and given false documents by the credit manager. In this circumstance, assuming the audit of accounts receivable was done in accordance with GAAS, a defense of contributory negligence would exist.

Absence of Causal Connection To succeed in an action against the auditor, the client must be able to show that there is a close causal connection between the auditor's breach of the standard of due care and the damages suffered by the client. For example, assume that an auditor failed to complete an audit on the agreed-upon date. The client alleges that this caused a bank not to renew an outstanding loan, which caused damages. A potential auditor defense is that the bank refused to renew the loan for other reasons, such as the weakening financial condition of the client. This defense is called an **absence of causal connection.**

LIABILITY TO THIRD PARTIES UNDER COMMON LAW

OBJECTIVE **4-5**

Describe accountants' liability to third parties under common law and related defenses.

In addition to being sued by clients under common law, CPAs may be liable to third parties under common law. Third parties include actual and potential stockholders, vendors, bankers and other creditors, employees, and customers. A CPA firm may be liable to third parties if a loss was incurred by the claimant due to reliance on misleading financial statements. A typical suit might occur when a bank is unable to collect a major loan from an insolvent customer. The bank can claim that misleading audited financial statements were relied on in making the loan and that the CPA firm should be held responsible because it failed to perform the audit with due care.

Ultramares Doctrine

The leading precedent-setting auditing case in third-party liability is a 1931 case, *Ultramares Corporation* v. *Touche*. It established the traditional common-law approach known as the ***Ultramares* doctrine.** Take a look at the case, which is summarized in Figure 4-2.

FIGURE 4-2 ***Ultramares Corporation* v. *Touche* (1931)–Liability to Third Parties**

The creditors of an insolvent corporation (Ultramares) relied on the audited financials and subsequently sued the accountants, alleging that they were guilty of negligence and fraudulent misrepresentation. The accounts receivable had been falsified by adding to approximately $650,000 in accounts receivable another item of over $700,000. The creditors alleged that careful investigation would have shown the $700,000 to be fraudulent. The accounts payable contained similar discrepancies.

The court held that the accountants had been negligent but ruled that accountants would not be liable to third parties for honest blunders beyond the bounds of the original contract unless they were primary beneficiaries. The court held that only one who enters into a contract with an accountant for services can sue if those services are rendered negligently.

In this case, the court held that although the accountants were negligent, they were not liable to the creditors because the creditors were not deemed to be *primary beneficiaries*. In this context, a primary beneficiary is one about whom the auditor was informed before conducting the audit (a *known third party*). The key aspect of the *Ultramares* case was that the creditors lacked *privity of contract* with the auditor. This case established a precedent, commonly called the *Ultramares* doctrine, that ordinary negligence is insufficient for liability to third parties because of the lack of *privity of contract* between the third party and the auditor, unless the third party is a *primary beneficiary*. However, in a subsequent trial of the *Ultramares* case, the court pointed out that had there been fraud or gross negligence on the part of the auditor, the auditor could be held liable to more general third parties.

Foreseen Users

In recent years, many courts have broadened the *Ultramares* doctrine to allow recovery by third parties in more circumstances than previously by introducing the concept of foreseen users. Generally, a **foreseen user** is a member of a limited class of users whom the auditor is aware will rely on the financial statements. For example, a bank that has loans outstanding to a client at the balance sheet date may be a foreseen user. Under this concept, a foreseen user would be treated the same as a known third party.

Although the concept of foreseen users may seem straightforward, its application is not and has developed differently in different jurisdictions. At present, three approaches have emerged: the *Credit Alliance* approach, the *Restatement of Torts* approach, and the *Foreseeable User* approach.

Credit Alliance *Credit Alliance* v. *Arthur Andersen & Co.* (1986) was a case in New York in which a lender brought suit against the auditor of one of its borrowers, alleging that it relied on the financial statements of the borrower, who was in default, in granting the loan. The New York State Court of Appeals reversed a lower court's decision that prevented the defendant auditor from using absence of privity as a defense. In so doing, the appellate court upheld the basic concept of privity established by *Ultramares* and stated that to be liable (1) an auditor must know and intend that the work product would be used by the plaintiff third party for a specific purpose, and (2) the knowledge and intent must be evidenced by the auditor's conduct. Approximately 15 states follow some variation of this approach.

Restatement of Torts The approach followed by most states is to apply the rule cited in the *Restatement of Torts*, an authoritative compendium of legal principles. The *Restatement Rule* is that foreseen users must be members of a *reasonably limited and identifiable group of users* that have relied on the CPA's work, such as creditors, even though those persons were not specifically known to the CPA at the time the work was done.

Foreseeable User The broadest interpretation of the rights of third-party beneficiaries is to use the concept of **foreseeable users.** Under this concept, any users that the auditor should have reasonably been able to foresee as being likely users of financial statements have the same rights as those with privity of contract. These users are often called an unlimited class. Although a significant number of states have followed this approach in the past, there are now only two that use it, Mississippi and Wisconsin.

There has been confusion caused by differing views of liability to third parties under common law, but the movement is clearly away from the foreseeable user approach, and thus from three approaches to two. And there may be some movement from the *Restatement of Torts* approach toward *Credit Alliance.* For example, in New Jersey, where the foreseeable user approach had been followed by the courts, the legislature recently adopted a strict privity standard. And in *Bily* v. *Arthur Young* (1992), the California Supreme Court reversed a lower court decision against Arthur Young, clearly upholding the *Restatement* doctrine. In its decision, the court stated that "an auditor owes no general duty of care regarding the conduct of an audit to persons other than the client" and reasoned that the potential liability to auditors under the foreseeable user doctrine would be distinctly out of proportion to fault.

Auditor Defenses Against Third-Party Suits

Three of the four defenses available to auditors in suits by clients are also available in third-party lawsuits. Contributory negligence is ordinarily not available because a third party is not in a position to contribute to misstated financial statements.

The preferred defense in third-party suits is nonnegligent performance. If the auditor conducted the audit in accordance with GAAS, the other defenses are unnecessary. On the other hand, nonnegligent performance is difficult to demonstrate to a court, especially if it is a jury trial and the jury is made up of laypeople.

A lack of duty defense in third-party suits contends lack of privity of contract. The extent to which privity of contract is an appropriate defense and the nature of their defense depends heavily on the judicial jurisdiction. As has been shown there would, for example, be significant differences among New York, Florida, and Wisconsin in the nature of this defense.

Absence of causal connection in third-party suits often means nonreliance on the financial statements by the user. For example, assume that the auditor can demonstrate that a lender relied on an ongoing banking relationship with a customer, rather than the financial statements, in making a loan. The fact that the auditor was negligent in the conduct of the audit would not be relevant in that situation. Of course, it is difficult to prove nonreliance on the financial statements. And, losses can be caused by other factors, such as market behavior.

CIVIL LIABILITY UNDER THE FEDERAL SECURITIES LAWS

OBJECTIVE 4-6

Describe accountants' civil liability under the federal securities laws and related defenses.

Although there has been some growth in actions brought against accountants by their clients and third parties under common law, the greatest growth in CPA liability litigation has been under the federal securities laws.

The emphasis on federal remedies has resulted primarily from the availability of class-action litigation and the relative ease of obtaining massive recovery from defendants. In addition, several sections of the securities laws impose rather strict liability standards on CPAs. Federal courts are often likely to favor plaintiffs in lawsuits in which there are strict standards. However, this may change in light of recent tort reform legislation.

Securities Act of 1933

The **Securities Act of 1933** deals with the information in registration statements and prospectuses. It concerns only the reporting requirements for companies issuing new securities. The only parties who can recover from auditors under the 1933 act are original purchasers of securities. The amount of the potential recovery is the original purchase price less the value of the securities at the time of the suit. If the securities have been sold, users can recover the amount of the loss incurred.

1933 and 1934 Acts

The Securities Act of 1933 imposes an unusual burden on the auditor. Section 11 of the 1933 act defines the rights of third parties and auditors. These are summarized as follows:

- Any third party who purchased securities described in the registration statement may sue the auditor for material misrepresentations or omissions in audited financial statements included in the registration statement.
- Third-party users do not have the burden of proof that they relied on the financial statements or that the auditor was negligent or fraudulent in doing the audit. Users must only prove that the audited financial statements contained a material misrepresentation or omission.
- The auditor has the burden of demonstrating as a defense that (1) an adequate audit (that is, a "reasonable investigation") was conducted in the circumstances or (2) all or a portion of the plaintiff's loss was caused by factors other than the misleading financial statements. The 1933 act is the only common or statutory law where the burden of proof is on the defendant.

Furthermore, the auditor has responsibility for making sure that the financial statements were fairly stated beyond the date of issuance, up to the date the registration statement became effective, which could be several months later. For example, assume that the audit report date for December 31, 2002, financial statements is February 10, 2003, but the registration statement is dated November 1, 2003. In a typical audit, the auditor must review transactions through the audit report date, February 10, 2003. In statements filed under the 1933 act, the auditor is responsible for reviewing transactions through the registration statement date, November 1, 2003.

Although the burden may appear harsh to auditors, there have been few cases tried under the 1933 act. The most significant one is *Escott et al.* v. *BarChris Construction Corporation* (1968). In this case, the CPA firm was held liable for a lack of due diligence required under the 1933 act when performing its review of events occurring subsequent to the balance sheet date. Two significant results occurred directly because of this case:

1. Statements on Auditing Standards were changed to require greater emphasis on procedures that the auditor must perform regarding subsequent events, SAS 1 (AU 560). This change is a good example of the effect that the SEC has on the audits of all companies.
2. A greater emphasis began to be placed on the importance of the audit staff understanding the client's business and industry.

Securities Exchange Act of 1934

The liability of auditors under the **Securities Exchange Act of 1934** often centers on the audited financial statements issued to the public in annual reports or submitted to the SEC as a part of annual Form 10-K reports.

Every company with securities traded on national and over-the-counter exchanges is required to submit audited statements annually. Obviously, a much larger number of statements fall under the 1934 act than under the 1933 act.

In addition to annual audited financial statements, there is potential legal exposure to auditors for quarterly information (Form 10-Q) or other reporting information filed with the SEC, such as an unusual event filed in a Form 8-K. The auditor is required to perform a timely review of the Form 10-Q before filing with the SEC, and the auditor is frequently involved in reviewing the information in other reports; therefore, there may be legal responsibility. However, few cases have involved auditors for reports other than annual reports.

Rule 10b-5 of the Securities Exchange Act of 1934

The principal focus on CPA liability litigation under the 1934 act has been Rule 10b-5, a section of the federal Securities Exchange Act of 1934, which appears in the rules and regulations of the Securities and Exchange Commission. Rule 10b-5 states the following:

- It shall be unlawful for any person directly or indirectly, by the use of any means or instrumentality of interstate commerce, or of the mails or of any facility of any national securities exchange, (a) to employ any device, scheme, or artifice to defraud, (b) to make any untrue statement of a material fact or omit to state a material fact necessary in order to make the statements made, in the light of the circumstances under which they were made, not misleading, or (c) to engage in any act, practice, or course of business which operates or would operate as a fraud or deceit upon any person in connection with the purchase or sale of any security.

Section 10 and Rule 10b-5 are often called the antifraud provisions of the 1934 act because they were designed primarily to thwart the commission of fraud by persons selling securities. Numerous federal court decisions have clarified that Rule 10b-5 applies not only to direct sellers but also to accountants, underwriters, and others. Generally, accountants can be held liable under Section 10 and Rule 10b-5 if they intentionally or recklessly misrepresent information intended for third-party use.

In 1976, in *Hochfelder* v. *Ernst & Ernst,* a leading securities law case as well as CPA liabilities case, the U.S. Supreme Court ruled that knowledge and intent to deceive are required before CPAs could be held liable for violation of Rule 10b-5.

Many auditors believed the *Hochfelder* case would significantly reduce auditors' exposure to liability. However, suits have subsequently been brought under Rule 10b-5. In earlier suits, the knowledge and deceit standard was more easily met by plaintiffs in cases in which the auditor knew all the relevant facts but made poor judgments. In such a situation, the courts emphasized that the CPAs had requisite knowledge. The *Solitron Devices* case is an example of that reasoning. In that case, the court of appeals ruled that reckless behavior on the part of the auditor was sufficient to hold the auditor liable for violation of Rule 10b-5. However, in two more recent suits, *Worlds of Wonder* and *Software Toolworks,* two key Ninth Circuit decisions stated that poor judgment isn't proof of fraud. This view appears now to be winning in the courts. In a third case, *McLean* v. *Alexander,* the appellate court ruled that the auditors—who were at most guilty of negligence, but not of bad-faith recklessness—were not liable under Rule 10b-5.

It is clear from the previous discussion that Rule 10b-5 continues to be a basis for lawsuits against auditors, even though *Hochfelder* has limited the liability somewhat.

Auditor Defenses—1934 Act

The same three defenses available to auditors in common-law suits by third parties are also available for suits under the 1934 act. These are nonnegligent performance, lack of duty, and absence of causal connection.

As discussed in this section, the use of the lack of duty defense in response to actions under Rule 10b-5 has had varying degrees of success, depending on the jurisdiction. In the *Hochfelder* case, that defense was successful. In other cases, negligent or reckless behavior resulted in liability. Continued court interpretations are likely to clarify this unresolved issue.

SEC Sanctions

Closely related to auditors' liability is the SEC's authority to sanction. The SEC has the power in certain circumstances to sanction or suspend practitioners from doing audits for SEC companies. Rule 2(e) of the SEC's *Rules of Practice* says:

- The commission may deny, temporarily or permanently, the privilege of appearing or practicing before it in any way to any person who is found by the commission . . . (1) not to possess the requisite qualifications to represent others, or (2) to be lacking in character or integrity or to have engaged in unethical or improper professional conduct.

The SEC has temporarily suspended a number of individual CPAs from doing any audits of SEC clients in recent years. It has similarly prohibited a number of CPA firms from accepting any new SEC clients for a period, such as 6 months. At times, the SEC has required an extensive review of a major CPA firm's practices by another CPA firm. In some cases, individual CPAs and their firms have been required to participate in continuing education programs and to make changes in their practice. Sanctions such as these are published by the SEC and are often reported in the business press, making them a significant embarrassment to those involved.

CRIMINAL LIABILITY

OBJECTIVE **4-7**

Specify what constitutes criminal liability for accountants.

A fourth way CPAs can be held liable is under **criminal liability for accountants.** CPAs can be found guilty for criminal action under both federal and state laws. The most likely statutes to be used under state law are the Uniform Securities Acts, which are similar to parts of the SEC rules. The 1933 and 1934 securities acts, as well as the Federal Mail Fraud Statute and the Federal False Statements Statute, are the most relevant federal laws affecting auditors. All make it a criminal offense to defraud another person through *knowingly being involved* with false financial statements.

Unfortunately, there have been several criminal cases of notoriety involving CPAs. Although these are not great in absolute number, they have the effect of damaging the integrity of the profession and reducing the profession's ability to attract and retain outstanding people. On the positive side, criminal actions encourage practitioners to use extreme care and exercise good faith in their activities.

The leading case of criminal action against CPAs is *United States* v. *Simon,* which occurred in 1969. In this case, three auditors were prosecuted for filing false financial statements of a client with the government and held to be criminally liable. The consequences for these three men were significant. Simon has been followed by three additional major criminal cases. In *United States* v. *Natelli* (1975), two auditors were convicted of criminal liability under the 1934 act for certifying financial statements of National Student Marketing Corporation that contained inadequate disclosures pertaining to accounts receivable.

In *United States* v. *Weiner* (1975), three auditors were convicted of securities fraud in connection with their audit of Equity Funding Corporation of America. Equity Funding was a financial conglomerate whose financial statements had been overstated through a massive fraud by management. The fraud was so extensive and the audit work so poor that the court concluded that the auditors must have been aware of the fraud and were therefore guilty of knowing complicity.

In *ESM Government Securities* v. *Alexander Grant & Co.* (1986), it was revealed by management to the partner in charge of the audit of ESM that the previous year's audited financial statements contained a material misstatement. Rather than complying with professional and firm standards in such circumstances, the partner agreed to say nothing in the hope that management would work its way out of the problem during the current year. Instead, the situation worsened, eventually to the point where losses exceeded $300 million. The partner was convicted of criminal charges for his role in sustaining the fraud and was sentenced to a 12-year prison term.

Several critical lessons can be learned from these four cases:

- An investigation of the integrity of management is an important part of deciding on the acceptability of clients and the extent of work to perform. SAS 84 (AU 315) gives guidance to auditors in investigating new clients, which will be discussed in a subsequent chapter.
- The auditor can be found criminally guilty in the conduct of an audit even if the person's background indicates integrity in personal and professional life. The criminal liability can extend to partners and staff.
- Independence in appearance and fact by all individuals on the engagement is essential, especially in a defense involving criminal actions. SAS 1 (AU 200) requires a firm to implement policies to help ensure independence in fact and in appearance.
- Transactions with related parties require special scrutiny because of the potential for misstatement. SAS 45 (AU 334) gives guidance in auditing related-party transactions.
- Generally accepted accounting principles cannot be relied on exclusively in deciding whether financial statements are fairly presented. The substance of the statements, considering all facts, is required. The SEC preferability requirement provides guidelines in selecting accounting principles.
- Good documentation may be just as important in the auditor's defense of criminal charges as in a civil suit.
- The potential consequences of the auditor knowingly committing a wrongful act are so severe that it is unlikely that the potential benefits could ever justify the actions.

THE PROFESSION'S RESPONSE TO LEGAL LIABILITY

The AICPA and the profession as a whole can do a number of things to reduce practitioners' exposure to lawsuits: by seeking protection from nonmeritorious litigation, improving auditing to better meet users' needs, and educating users about the limits of auditing. Some specific activities are discussed briefly.

OBJECTIVE **4-8**

Describe what the profession and the individual CPA can do and what is being done to reduce the threat of litigation.

- *Research in auditing.* Continued research is important in finding better ways to do such things as uncover unintentional material misstatements or fraud, communicate audit results to statement users, and make sure that auditors are independent. Significant research already takes place through the AICPA, CPA firms, and universities.
- *Standard and rule setting.* The AICPA must constantly set standards and revise them to meet the changing needs of auditing. For example, changes in auditing standards on the auditor's responsibility to detect fraud and revisions to the auditor independence requirements in the interpretations of the rules of conduct have been issued in recent years to address users' needs and expectations as to auditor performance.
- *Set requirements to protect auditors.* The AICPA can help protect its members by setting certain requirements that better practitioners already follow. Naturally, these requirements should not be in conflict with meeting users' needs. An example of an auditor-set standard is the SAS 85 (AU 333) requirement of a written letter of representation from management in all audits.
- *Establish peer review requirements.* The periodic examination of a firm's practices and procedures is a way to educate practitioners and identify firms not meeting the standards of the profession.
- *Oppose lawsuits.* CPA firms must continue to oppose unwarranted lawsuits even if, in the short run, the costs of winning are greater than the costs of settling. The AICPA has aided practitioners in fighting an unwarranted expansion of legal liability for accountants by filing briefs as "a friend of the court" known as *amicus curiae* briefs.
- *Education of users.* Investors and others who read financial statements must be educated as to the meaning of the auditor's opinion and the extent and nature of the auditor's work. Users must be educated to understand that auditors do not test 100 percent of all records and do not guarantee the accuracy of the financial records or the future prosperity of the company. It is also important to educate users to understand that accounting and auditing are arts, not sciences, and that perfection and precision are not achievable.
- *Sanction members for improper conduct and performance.* One characteristic of a profession is its responsibility for policing its own membership. The AICPA has made progress toward dealing with the problems of inadequate CPA performance, but more rigorous review of alleged failures is still needed.
- *Lobby for changes in laws.* In recent years, several changes in state and federal laws have favorably impacted the legal environment for the profession. Most states have revised their laws to allow accounting firms to practice in different organizational forms, including limited liability organizations that provide some protection from litigation. The passage of the **Private Securities Litigation Reform Act of 1995** (the Reform Act) significantly reduced potential damages in securities-related litigation by providing for proportionate liability in most instances. However, the Reform Act applied only to federal courts, and lawyers began taking their cases to state courts, which the Reform Act did not cover. This loophole was closed by the Securities Litigation Uniform Standards Act of 1998, which requires that class actions involving covered securities be addressed in federal district court. The profession continues to pursue litigation reform at the state level, including application of a strict privity standard for liability to nonclients and proportionate liability in all cases not involving fraud.

1998 Litigation Reform Act

LESSONS LEARNED FROM AUDITOR LITIGATION

In considering the advisability of the laws being considered in reform of accountants' liability, it is useful to consider actual experiences with past accountants' litigation. Accordingly, a review was conducted of 23 cases of alleged audit failure with which I have been involved as a litigation consultant and expert witness. Of these 23 cases, 6 were clearly without merit and should not have been brought on equitable grounds. Of the 17 that were with merit, 13 did, in fact, represent a real audit failure. In considering the nature of the failure in each case, it was observed that the evidence that would lead the auditor to identify the misstatement that existed was usually there. In other words, the problem was not any inadequacy in the audit process as presented by professional standards; it was a *lack of professional skepticism* on the part of the auditor. The auditor had evidence in his or her possession that indicated the problem, but did not see it as such.

Source: Presentation by James K. Loebbecke at the Forum on Responsibilities and Liabilities of Accountants and Auditors, United Nations Conference on Trade and Development, March 16, 1995.

PROTECTING INDIVIDUAL CPAs FROM LEGAL LIABILITY

Practicing auditors may also take specific action to minimize their liability. Some of the more common actions are:

- *Deal only with clients possessing integrity.* There is an increased likelihood of having legal problems when a client lacks integrity in dealing with customers, employees, units of government, and others. A CPA firm needs procedures to evaluate the integrity of clients and should dissociate itself from clients found lacking.
- *Hire qualified personnel and train and supervise them properly.* A considerable portion of most audits is done by young professionals with relatively little experience. Given the high degree of risk CPA firms have in doing audits, it is important that these young professionals be qualified and well trained. Supervision of their work by experienced and qualified professionals is also essential.
- *Follow the standards of the profession.* A firm must implement procedures to ensure that all firm members understand and follow the SASs, FASB opinions, rules of conduct, and other professional guidelines.
- *Maintain independence.* Independence is more than merely financial. Independence in fact requires an attitude of responsibility separate from the client's interest. Much litigation has arisen from a too willing acceptance by an auditor of a client's representation or of a client's pressures. The auditor must maintain an attitude of *healthy skepticism.*
- *Understand the client's business.* The lack of knowledge of industry practices and client operations has been a major factor in auditors failing to uncover misstatements in several cases. It is important that the audit team be educated in these areas.
- *Perform quality audits.* Quality audits require that auditors obtain appropriate evidence and make appropriate judgments about the evidence. It is essential, for example, that the auditor understand a client's internal controls and modify the evidence to reflect the findings. Improved auditing reduces the likelihood of misstatements and the likelihood of lawsuits.
- *Document the work properly.* The preparation of good audit documentation helps the auditor organize and perform quality audits. Quality audit documentation is essential if an auditor has to defend an audit in court.
- *Obtain an engagement letter and a representation letter.* These two letters are essential in defining the respective obligations of the client and the auditor. They are helpful especially in lawsuits between the client and auditor, but also in third-party lawsuits.
- *Maintain confidential relations.* Auditors are under an ethical and sometimes legal obligation not to disclose client matters to outsiders.
- *Carry adequate insurance.* It is essential for a CPA firm to have adequate insurance protection in the event of a lawsuit. Although insurance rates have risen considerably as a result of increasing litigation, professional liability insurance is still available for all CPAs.

- *Seek legal counsel.* When serious problems occur during an audit, a CPA would be wise to consult experienced counsel. In the event of a potential or actual lawsuit, the auditor should immediately seek an experienced attorney.
- *Choose a form of organization with limited liability.* Many CPA firms now operate as professional corporations, limited liability companies, or limited liability partnerships in order to provide some personal liability protection to owners.
- *Exercise professional skepticism.* Auditors are often liable when they are presented with information indicating a problem that they fail to recognize. Auditors need to strive to maintain a healthy level of skepticism, one that keeps them alert to potential misstatements, so that they can recognize misstatements when they exist.

ASSURANCE SERVICES BRING LIABILITY EXPOSURE

Companies that rely on information systems can suffer significant losses due to system failures. For example, hackers shut down Yahoo! and eBay with denial-of-service attacks, and E-Trade lost $2.5 billion in market value when its system crashed. As a result, CPAs providing *SysTrust* assurance services on information systems may face significant legal liability exposure from clients and third parties.

The *SysTrust* service is new, and no legal case has yet directly addressed accountants' liability for this service. However, CPAs can protect themselves by taking many of the same actions used to protect against legal liability for audit services. For example, CPAs should carefully evaluate the client and risks involved before accepting a *SysTrust* engagement. A carefully written engagement letter should also be used that describes the limitations of the *SysTrust* engagement. In some cases, the engagement letter may include loss-limiting clauses and hold-harmless provisions to limit the amount for which the CPA can be sued.

Source: Leslie Higgins, William Hillison, Stephen E. Ludwig, Carl Pacini, and David Sinason, "*SysTrust* and Third Party Risk," *Journal of Accountancy* (August 2000), pp. 73-78.

SUMMARY

This chapter provides insight into the environment in which CPAs operate by highlighting the significance of the legal liability facing the CPA profession. No reasonable CPA would want to eliminate the profession's legal responsibility for fraudulent or incompetent performance. It is certainly in the profession's best interest to maintain public trust in the competent performance of the auditing profession, while avoiding liability for cases involving strictly business failure and not audit failure. To more effectively avoid legal liability, CPAs need to have an adequate understanding of how they can be held liable to their clients or third parties. Knowledge about how CPAs are liable to clients under common law, to third parties under common law, to third parties under federal securities laws, and for criminal liability provides auditors an awareness of issues that may subject them to greater liability. CPAs can protect themselves from legal liability in numerous ways, and the profession has worked diligently to identify ways to help CPAs reduce the profession's potential exposure. Fortunately, recent litigation reform efforts have been successful that are designed to limit abusive securities class-action suits against CPAs. It is necessary for the profession and society to determine a reasonable trade-off between the degree of responsibility the auditor should take for fair presentation and the audit cost to society. CPAs, Congress, the SEC, and the courts will all continue to have a major influence in shaping the final solution.

ESSENTIAL TERMS

Absence of causal connection—an auditor's legal defense under which the auditor contends that the damages claimed by the client were not brought about by any act of the auditor

Audit failure—a situation in which the auditor issues an erroneous audit opinion as the result of an underlying failure to comply with the requirements of generally accepted auditing standards

Audit risk—the risk that the auditor will conclude that the financial statements are fairly stated and an unqualified opinion can therefore be issued when, in fact, they are materially misstated

Business failure—the situation when a business is unable to repay its lenders or meet the expectations of its investors because of economic or business conditions

Contributory negligence—an auditor's legal defense under which the auditor claims that the client failed to perform certain obligations and that it is the client's failure to perform those obligations that brought about the claimed damages

Criminal liability for accountants—defrauding a person through knowing involvement with false financial statements

Foreseeable users—an unlimited class of users that the auditor should have reasonably been able to foresee as being likely users of financial statements

Foreseen user—a member of a limited class of users whom the auditor is aware will rely on the financial statements

Lack of duty to perform—an auditor's legal defense under which the auditor claims that no contract existed with the client; therefore, no duty existed to perform the disputed service

Legal liability—the professional's obligation under the law to provide a reasonable level of care while performing work for those served

Nonnegligent performance—an auditor's legal defense under which the auditor claims that the audit was performed in accordance with generally accepted auditing standards

Private Securities Litigation Reform Act of 1995—a federal law passed in 1995 that significantly reduced potential damages in securities-related litigation

Prudent person concept—the legal concept that a person has a duty to exercise reasonable care and diligence in the performance of obligations to another

Securities Act of 1933—a federal statute dealing with companies that register and sell securities to the public; under the statute, third parties who are original purchasers of securities may recover damages from the auditor if the financial statements are misstated unless the auditor proves that the audit was adequate or that the third party's loss was caused by factors other than misleading financial statements

Securities Exchange Act of 1934—a federal statute dealing with companies that trade securities on national and over-the-counter exchanges; auditors are involved because the annual reporting requirements include audited financial statements

Ultramares doctrine—a common-law approach to third-party liability, established in 1931 in the case of *Ultramares Corporation* v. *Touche,* in which ordinary negligence is insufficient for liability to third parties because of the lack of *privity of contract* between the third party and the auditor, unless the third party is a *primary beneficiary*

REVIEW QUESTIONS

4-1 (**Objective 4-1**) State several factors that have affected the incidence of lawsuits against CPAs in recent years.

4-2 (**Objective 4-1**) Lawsuits against CPA firms have increased dramatically in the past decade. State your opinion of the positive and negative effects of the increased litigation on CPAs and on society as a whole.

4-3 (**Objective 4-2**) Distinguish between business failure and audit risk. Why is business failure a concern to auditors?

4-4 (**Objective 4-3**) How does the prudent person concept affect the liability of the auditor?

4-5 (**Objective 4-3**) Distinguish between "fraud" and "constructive fraud."

4-6 (**Objectives 4-1, 4-8**) Discuss why many CPA firms have willingly settled lawsuits out of court. What are the implications to the profession?

4-7 (**Objective 4-4**) A common type of lawsuit against CPAs is for the failure to detect a fraud. State the auditor's responsibility for such discovery. Give authoritative support for your answer.

4-8 (**Objectives 4-3, 4-4**) What is meant by contributory negligence? Under what conditions will this likely be a successful defense?

4-9 (**Objective 4-4**) Explain how an engagement letter might affect an auditor's liability to clients under common law.

4-10 (**Objectives 4-4, 4-5**) Compare and contrast traditional auditors' legal responsibilities to clients and third-party users under common law. How has that law changed in recent years?

4-11 (**Objective 4-5**) Is the auditor's liability affected if the third party was unknown rather than known? Explain.

4-12 **(Objective 4-6)** Contrast the auditor's liability under the Securities Act of 1933 with that under the Securities Exchange Act of 1934.

4-13 **(Objectives 4-4, 4-5, 4-6, 4-7)** Distinguish between the auditor's potential liability to the client, liability to third parties under common law, civil liability under the securities laws, and criminal liability. Describe one situation for each type of liability in which the auditor could be held legally responsible.

4-14 **(Objective 4-6)** What sanctions does the SEC have against a CPA firm?

4-15 **(Objective 4-8)** In what ways can the profession positively respond and reduce liability in auditing?

MULTIPLE CHOICE QUESTIONS FROM CPA EXAMINATIONS

4-16 **(Objectives 4-4, 4-5)** The following questions concern CPA firms' liability under common law. Choose the best response.

a. Sharp, CPA, was engaged by Peters & Sons, a partnership, to give an opinion on the financial statements that were to be submitted to several prospective partners as part of a planned expansion of the firm. Sharp's fee was fixed on a per diem basis. After a period of intensive work, Sharp completed about half of the necessary field work. Then, because of unanticipated demands on his time by other clients, Sharp was forced to abandon the work. The planned expansion of the firm failed to materialize because the prospective partners lost interest when the audit report was not promptly available. Sharp offered to complete the task at a later date. This offer was refused. Peters & Sons suffered damages of $40,000 as a result. Under the circumstances, what is the probable outcome of a lawsuit between Sharp and Peters & Sons?
   (1) Sharp will be compensated for the reasonable value of the services actually performed.
   (2) Peters & Sons will recover damages for breach of contract.
   (3) Peters & Sons will recover both punitive damages and damages for breach of contract.
   (4) Neither Sharp nor Peters & Sons will recover against the other.

b. Magnus Enterprises engaged a CPA firm to perform the annual audit of its financial statements. Which of the following is a correct statement with respect to the CPA firm's liability to Magnus for negligence?
   (1) Such liability cannot be varied by agreement of the parties.
   (2) The CPA firm will be liable for any fraudulent scheme it does not detect.
   (3) The CPA firm will not be liable if it can show that it exercised the ordinary care and skill of a reasonable person in the conduct of its own affairs.
   (4) The CPA firm not only must exercise reasonable care in what it does but also must possess at least that degree of accounting knowledge and skill expected of a CPA.

c. Martin Corporation orally engaged Humm & Dawson to audit its year-end financial statements. The engagement was to be completed within 2 months after the close of Martin's fiscal year for a fixed fee of $75,000. Under these circumstances, what obligation is assumed by Humm & Dawson?
   (1) None. The contract is unenforceable because it is not in writing.
   (2) An implied promise to exercise reasonable standards of competence and care.
   (3) An implied obligation to take extraordinary steps to discover all defalcations.
   (4) The obligation of an insurer of its work, which is liable without fault.

d. If a CPA firm is being sued for common-law fraud by a third party based on materially false financial statements, which of the following is the best defense the accountants could assert?
   (1) Lack of privity.
   (2) Nonnegligent performance.
   (3) A disclaimer contained in the engagement letter.
   (4) Contributory negligence on the part of the client.

4-17 **(Objectives 4-5, 4-6, 4-7)** The following questions deal with important cases in accountants' liability. Choose the best response.

a. The most significant aspect of the *Continental Vending (United States* v. *Simon)* case was that it
   (1) created a more general awareness of the auditor's exposure to criminal prosecution.
   (2) extended the auditor's responsibility for financial statements of subsidiaries.
   (3) extended the auditor's responsibility for events after the end of the audit period.
   (4) defined the auditor's common-law responsibilities to third parties.

b. The *1136 Tenants* case was important chiefly because of its emphasis on the legal liability of the CPA when associated with
   (1) an SEC engagement.
   (2) unaudited financial statements.
   (3) an audit resulting in a disclaimer of opinion.
   (4) letters for underwriters.

4-18 **(Objective 4-6)** The following questions deal with liability under the 1933 and 1934 securities acts. Choose the best response.

a. Major, Major, & Sharpe, CPAs, are the auditors of MacLain Technologies. In connection with the public offering of $10 million of MacLain securities, Major expressed an unqualified opinion as to the financial statements. Subsequent to the offering, certain misstatements were revealed. Major has been sued by the purchasers of the stock offered pursuant to the registration statement that included the financial statements audited by Major. In the ensuing lawsuit by the MacLain investors, Major will be able to avoid liability if
   (1) the misstatements were caused primarily by MacLain.
   (2) it can be shown that at least some of the investors did *not* actually read the audited financial statements.
   (3) it can prove due diligence in the audit of the financial statements of MacLain.
   (4) MacLain had expressly assumed any liability in connection with the public offering.

b. Donalds & Company, CPAs, audited the financial statements included in the annual report submitted by Markum Securities, Inc. to the SEC. The audit was improper in several respects. Markum is now insolvent and unable to satisfy the claims of its customers. The customers have instituted legal action against Donalds based on Section 10b and Rule 10b-5 of the Securities Exchange Act of 1934. Which of the following is likely to be Donalds's best defense?
   (1) They did *not* intentionally certify false financial statements.
   (2) Section 10b does *not* apply to them.
   (3) They were *not* in privity of contract with the creditors.
   (4) Their engagement letter specifically disclaimed any liability to any party that resulted from Markum's fraudulent conduct.

c. Josephs & Paul is a growing, medium-sized partnership of CPAs. One of the firm's major clients is considering offering its stock to the public. This will be the firm's first client to go public. Which of the following is true with respect to this engagement?
   (1) If the client is a service corporation, the Securities Act of 1933 will not apply.
   (2) If the client is not going to be listed on an organized exchange, the Securities Exchange Act of 1934 will not apply.
   (3) The Securities Act of 1933 imposes important additional potential liability on Josephs & Paul.
   (4) As long as Josephs & Paul engages exclusively in intrastate business, the federal securities laws will not apply.

DISCUSSION QUESTIONS AND PROBLEMS

4-19 **(Objectives 4-4, 4-5)** Verna Cosden & Co., a medium-sized CPA firm, was engaged to audit Joslin Supply Company. Several staff were involved in the audit, all of whom had attended the firm's in-house training program on effective auditing methods. Throughout the audit, Cosden spent most of her time in the field planning the audit, supervising the staff, and reviewing their work.

A significant part of the audit entailed verifying the physical count, cost, and summarization of inventory. Inventory was highly significant to the financial statements and Cosden knew the inventory was pledged as collateral for a large loan to East City National Bank. In reviewing Joslin's inventory count procedures, Cosden told the president she believed the method of counting inventory at different locations on different days was highly undesirable. The president stated that it was impractical to count all inventory on the same day because of personnel shortages and customer preference. After considerable discussion, Cosden agreed to permit the practice if the president would sign a statement that no other method was practical. The CPA firm had at least one person at each site to audit the inventory count procedures and actual count. There were more than 40 locations.

Eighteen months later, Cosden found out that the worst had happened. Management below the president's level had conspired to materially overstate inventory as a means of covering up obsolete inventory and inventory losses resulting from mismanagement. The misstatement occurred by physically transporting inventory at night to other locations after it had been counted in a given location. The accounting records were inadequate to uncover these illegal transfers.

Both Joslin Supply Company and East City National Bank sued Verna Cosden & Co.

Answer the following questions, setting forth reasons for any conclusions stated: **Required**

a. What defense should Cosden & Co. use in the suit by Joslin?

b. What defense should Cosden & Co. use in the suit by East City National Bank?

c. Is Cosden likely to be successful in her defenses?

d. Would the issues or outcome be significantly different if the suit was brought under the Securities Exchange Act of 1934?

4-20 (Objective 4-5) The CPA firm of Bigelow, Barton, and Brown was expanding rapidly. Consequently, it hired several junior accountants, including a man named Small. The partners of the firm eventually became dissatisfied with Small's production and warned him they would be forced to discharge him unless his output increased significantly.

At that time, Small was engaged in audits of several clients. He decided that to avoid being fired, he would reduce or omit some of the standard auditing procedures listed in audit programs prepared by the partners. One of the CPA firm's clients, Newell Corporation, was in serious financial difficulty and had adjusted several of the accounts being audited by Small to appear financially sound. Small prepared fictitious audit documentation in his home at night to support purported completion of auditing procedures assigned to him, although he in fact did not examine the adjusting entries. The CPA firm rendered an unqualified opinion on Newell's financial statements, which were grossly misstated. Several creditors, relying on the audited financial statements, subsequently extended large sums of money to Newell Corporation.

Would the CPA firm be liable to the creditors who extended the money because of their reliance on the erroneous financial statements if Newell Corporation should fail to pay them? Explain.* **Required**

4-21 (Objectives 4-3, 4-5) Watts and Williams, a firm of CPAs, audited the accounts of Sampson Skins, Inc., a corporation that imports and deals in fine furs. Upon completion of the audit, the auditors supplied Sampson Skins with 20 copies of the audited financial statements. The firm knew in a general way that Sampson Skins wanted that number of copies of the auditor's report to furnish to banks and other potential lenders.

The balance sheet in question was misstated by approximately $800,000. Instead of having a $600,000 net worth, the corporation was insolvent. The management of Sampson Skins had doctored the books to avoid bankruptcy. The assets had been overstated by $500,000 of fictitious and nonexisting accounts receivable and $300,000 of nonexisting skins listed as inventory when in fact Sampson Skins had only empty boxes. The audit failed to detect these fraudulent entries. Martinson, relying on the audited financial statements, loaned Sampson Skins $200,000. He seeks to recover his loss from Watts and Williams.

State whether each of the following is true or false and give your reasons: **Required**

a. If Martinson alleges and proves negligence on the part of Watts and Williams, he will be able to recover his loss.

b. If Martinson alleges and proves constructive fraud (that is, gross negligence on the part of Watts and Williams), he will be able to recover his loss.

c. Martinson does not have a contract with Watts and Williams.

d. Unless actual fraud on the part of Watts and Williams could be shown, Martinson could not recover.

e. Martinson is a third-party beneficiary of the contract Watts and Williams made with Sampson Skins.*

4-22 (Objectives 4-4, 4-5, 4-7) Donald Sharpe recently joined the CPA firm of Spark, Watts, and Wilcox. He quickly established a reputation for thoroughness and a steadfast dedication to following prescribed auditing procedures to the letter. On his third audit for the firm, Sharpe examined the underlying documentation of 200 disbursements as a test of acquisitions, receiving, vouchers payable, and cash disbursement procedures. In the process, he found 12 disbursements for the acquisition of materials with no receiving reports in the documentation. He noted the exceptions in his working papers and called them to the attention of the in-charge accountant. Relying on prior experience with the client, the in-charge accountant disregarded Sharpe's comments, and nothing further was done about the exceptions.

Subsequently, it was learned that one of the client's purchasing agents and a member of its accounting department were engaged in a fraudulent scheme whereby they diverted the receipt of materials to a public warehouse while sending the invoices to the client. When the client discovered

* AICPA adapted.

the fraud, the conspirators had obtained approximately $70,000, $50,000 of which was recovered after the completion of the audit.

Required Discuss the legal implications and liabilities to Spark, Watts, and Wilcox as a result of the facts just described.*

4-23 (Objectives 4-4, 4-5, 4-7) Smith, CPA, is the auditor for Juniper Manufacturing Corporation, a privately owned company that has a June 30 fiscal year. Juniper arranged for a substantial bank loan that was dependent on the bank's receiving, by September 30, audited financial statements that showed a current ratio of at least 2 to 1. On September 25, just before the audit report was to be issued, Smith received an anonymous letter on Juniper's stationery indicating that a 5-year lease by Juniper, as lessee, of a factory building accounted for in the financial statements as an operating lease was, in fact, a capital lease. The letter stated that there was a secret written agreement with the lessor modifying the lease and creating a capital lease.

Smith confronted the president of Juniper, who admitted that a secret agreement existed but said it was necessary to treat the lease as an operating lease to meet the current ratio requirement of the pending loan and that nobody would ever discover the secret agreement with the lessor. The president said that if Smith did not issue his report by September 30, Juniper would sue Smith for substantial damages that would result from not getting the loan. Under this pressure and because the audit files contained a copy of the 5-year lease agreement that supported the operating lease treatment, Smith issued his report with an unqualified opinion on September 29.

Despite the fact that the loan was received, Juniper went bankrupt within 2 years. The bank is suing Smith to recover its losses on the loan and the lessor is suing Smith to recover uncollected rents.

Required Answer the following questions, setting forth reasons for any conclusions stated:

a. Is Smith liable to the bank?

b. Is Smith liable to the lessor?

c. Is there potential for criminal action against Smith?*

4-24 (Objective 4-4) Ward & East, CPAs, were the auditors of Southern Development, Inc., a real estate company that owned several shopping centers. It was Southern's practice to let each shopping center manager negotiate that center's leases; they thought that such an arrangement resulted in much better leases because a local person did the negotiating.

Two of the center managers were killed in a plane accident returning home from a company meeting at the head office in Phoenix. In both cases, the new managers appointed to take their places discovered kickback schemes in operation; the managers had negotiated lower rents than normal in return for kickbacks from the tenants.

Southern brought in a new CPA firm, Jasper & Co., to investigate the extent of the fraud at those two locations and the possibility of similar frauds at other centers. Jasper & Co. completed their investigation and found that four locations were involved quite independently of each other and that the total loss over 5 years was more than $1 million. Southern sued Ward & East for negligence for $1 million plus interest.

Required What defense would Ward & East use? What would they have to prove?

4-25 (Objective 4-6) Gordon & Groton, CPAs, were the auditors of Bank & Company, a brokerage firm and member of a national stock exchange. Gordon & Groton audited and reported on the financial statements of Bank, which were filed with the Securities and Exchange Commission.

Several of Bank's customers were swindled by a fraudulent scheme perpetrated by Bank's president, who owned 90% of the voting stock of the company. The facts establish that Gordon & Groton were negligent but not reckless or grossly negligent in the conduct of the audit, and neither participated in the fraudulent scheme or knew of its existence.

The customers are suing Gordon & Groton under the antifraud provisions of Section 10b and Rule 10b-5 of the Securities Exchange Act of 1934 for aiding and abetting the fraudulent scheme of the president. The customers' suit for fraud is predicated exclusively on the nonfeasance of the auditors in failing to conduct a proper audit, thereby failing to discover the fraudulent scheme.

Required Answer the following questions, setting forth reasons for any conclusions stated:

a. What is the probable outcome of the lawsuit?

b. What other theory of liability might the customers have asserted?*

* AICPA adapted.

CASE

4-26 **(Objectives 4-5, 4-6)** *Part 1.* Whitlow & Company is a brokerage firm registered under the Securities Exchange Act of 1934. The act requires such a brokerage firm to file audited financial statements with the SEC annually. Mitchell & Moss, Whitlow's CPAs, performed the annual audit for the year ended December 31, 2002, and rendered an unqualified opinion, which was filed with the SEC along with Whitlow's financial statements. During 2002, Charles, the president of Whitlow & Company, engaged in a huge embezzlement scheme that eventually bankrupted the firm. As a result, substantial losses were suffered by customers and shareholders of Whitlow & Company, including Thaxton, who had recently purchased several shares of stock of Whitlow & Company after reviewing the company's 2002 audit report. Mitchell & Moss's audit was deficient; if they had complied with GAAS, the embezzlement would have been discovered. However, Mitchell & Moss had no knowledge of the embezzlement, nor could their conduct be categorized as reckless.

Required

Answer the following questions, setting forth reasons for any conclusions stated:

a. What liability to Thaxton, if any, does Mitchell & Moss have under the Securities Exchange Act of 1934?

b. What theory or theories of liability, if any, are available to Whitlow & Company's customers and shareholders under common law?

Part 2. Jackson is a sophisticated investor. As such, she was initially a member of a small group that was going to participate in a private placement of $1 million of common stock of Clarion Corporation. Numerous meetings were held between management and the investor group. Detailed financial and other information was supplied to the participants. Upon the eve of completion of the placement, it was aborted when one major investor withdrew. Clarion then decided to offer $2.5 million of Clarion common stock to the public pursuant to the registration requirements of the Securities Act of 1933. Jackson subscribed to $300,000 of the Clarion public stock offering. Nine months later, Clarion's earnings dropped significantly and as a result the stock dropped 20% beneath the offering price. In addition, the Dow Jones Industrial Average was down 10% from the time of the offering.

Jackson has sold her shares at a loss of $60,000 and seeks to hold all parties liable who participated in the public offering, including Clarion's CPA firm of Allen, Dunn, and Rose. Although the audit was performed in conformity with GAAS, there were some relatively minor misstatements. The financial statements of Clarion Corporation, which were part of the registration statement, contained minor misleading facts. It is believed by Clarion and Allen, Dunn, and Rose that Jackson's asserted claim is without merit.

Required

Answer the following questions, setting forth reasons for any conclusions stated:

a. If Jackson sues under the Securities Act of 1933, what will be the basis of her claim?

b. What are the probable defenses that might be asserted by Allen, Dunn, and Rose in light of these facts?*

INTERNET PROBLEM 4-1: SEC ENFORCEMENT

Reference the CW site. The SEC's Enforcement Division posts Litigation Releases, which are descriptions of SEC civil and selected criminal suits in the federal courts proceedings. This problem requires students to use the Internet to look up and answer questions associated with litigation releases.

* AICPA adapted.

PART 2 CHAPTERS 5–10

THE AUDIT PROCESS

Part 2 presents the audit process in a manner that will enable you to apply the concepts developed in these chapters to any audit area. It is essential to understand the material in these chapters because the information will be used extensively in almost all chapters throughout the rest of the book. We also highlight the importance of audit planning.

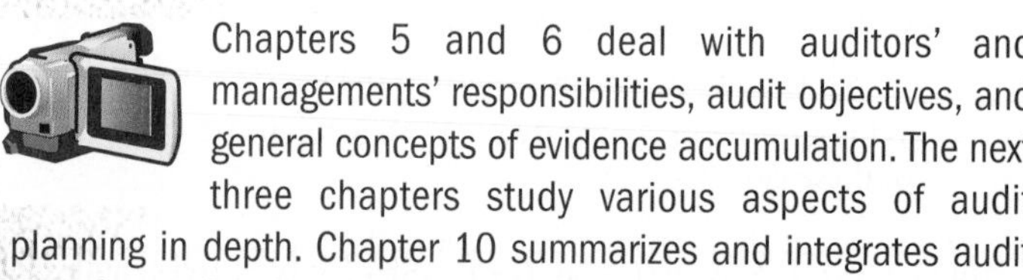

Chapters 5 and 6 deal with auditors' and managements' responsibilities, audit objectives, and general concepts of evidence accumulation. The next three chapters study various aspects of audit planning in depth. Chapter 10 summarizes and integrates audit planning and audit evidence. You will use these planning concepts throughout the rest of the book.

CHAPTER

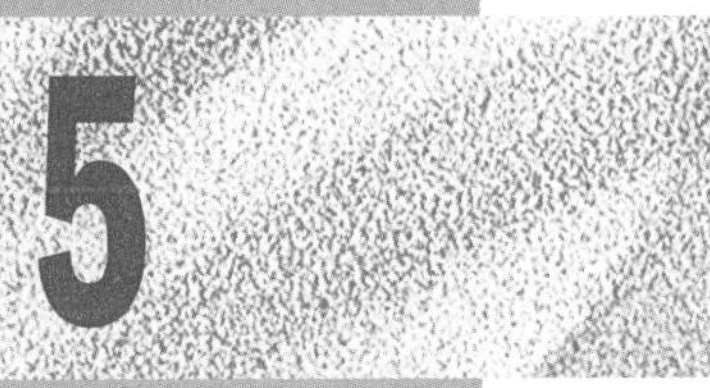

AUDIT RESPONSIBILITIES AND OBJECTIVES

WHERE WERE THE AUDITORS?

Barry Minkow was a true "whiz kid." He started ZZZZ Best Company, a high-flying carpet cleaning company specializing in insurance restoration contracts, at the age of 16. In 1982, when Minkow started the business, it was run out of his garage, but a mere 5 years later he had taken the company public and it had sales of $50 million and earnings of more than $5 million. The market value of Minkow's stock in ZZZZ Best exceeded $100 million.

As it turned out, Minkow's genius lay not in business, but in deception. Instead of being a solid operation company, ZZZZ Best was an illusion. There were no large restoration jobs and no real revenues and profits. They were only on paper and supported by an effective network of methods to deceive shareholders, the SEC, and the reputable professionals who served the company, including its auditors. Many, including members of Congress, asked, "How could this happen? Where were the auditors?"

When ZZZZ Best first started to grow, Minkow ran into the common problem of needing credit. He devised a scheme with an insurance adjuster to validate nonexistent jobs to potential creditors. Minkow could then get large sums of cash or credit despite not doing any real work. The scam was broadened when ZZZZ Best started needing audits. To fool the auditors, the coconspirator insurance adjuster was kept busy running a company that generated false contracts for ZZZZ Best. When the auditors tried to check on those contracts, the adjuster confirmed them. Minkow even went so far as taking auditors to real work sites, sites that weren't actually his. He even leased a partially completed building and hired subcontractors to perform work on the site, all for the sake of a visit by the auditors.

As incredible as the ZZZZ Best story may seem, when asked about it, most knowledgeable observers would answer: "It's not the first time, and it won't be the last." It is also not the last time people will ask, "Where were the auditors?"

LEARNING OBJECTIVES

After studying this chapter, you should be able to

5-1 Explain the objective of conducting an audit of financial statements.

5-2 Distinguish management's responsibilities for preparing financial statements from the auditor's responsibilities for verifying those financial statements.

5-3 Explain the auditor's responsibility for discovering material misstatements.

5-4 Classify transactions and account balances into financial statement cycles and identify benefits of a cycle approach to segmenting the audit.

5-5 Describe why the auditor obtains a combination of assurance by auditing classes of transactions and ending balances in accounts.

5-6 Distinguish among the five categories of management assertions about financial information.

5-7 Link the six general transaction-related audit objectives to the five management assertions.

5-8 Link the nine general balance-related audit objectives to the five management assertions.

5-9 Explain the relationship between audit objectives and the accumulation of audit evidence.

Before beginning the study of how to conduct an audit, it is necessary to understand the overall objectives of the audit, the auditor's responsibilities in conducting the audit, and the specific objectives the auditor tries to accomplish. Without an understanding of these topics, planning and accumulating audit evidence during the audit has no relevance. Figure 5-1 (bottom of this page) summarizes the five topics that provide keys to understanding evidence accumulation. These are the steps used to develop specific audit objectives.

OBJECTIVE OF CONDUCTING AN AUDIT OF FINANCIAL STATEMENTS

OBJECTIVE 5-1

Explain the objective of conducting an audit of financial statements.

SAS 1 (AU 110) states

> The objective of the ordinary audit of financial statements by the independent auditor is the expression of an opinion on the fairness with which they present fairly, in all material respects, financial position, results of operations, and its cash flows in conformity with generally accepted accounting principles.

Understand objectives and responsibilities for the audit
Divide financial statements into cycles
Know management assertions about accounts
Know general audit objectives for classes of transactions and accounts
Know specific audit objectives for classes of transactions and accounts

That section of the SAS appropriately emphasizes issuing an opinion on *financial statements.* The only reason auditors accumulate evidence is to enable them to reach conclusions about whether financial statements are fairly stated in all material respects and to issue an appropriate audit report.

When, on the basis of adequate evidence, the auditor concludes that the financial statements are unlikely to mislead a prudent user, the auditor gives an audit opinion on their fair presentation and associates his or her name with the statements. If facts subsequent to their issuance indicate that the statements were actually not fairly presented, the auditor is likely to have to demonstrate to the courts or regulatory agencies that he or she conducted the audit in a proper manner and drew reasonable conclusions. Although not an insurer or a guarantor of the fairness of the presentations in the statements, the auditor has considerable responsibility for notifying users whether the

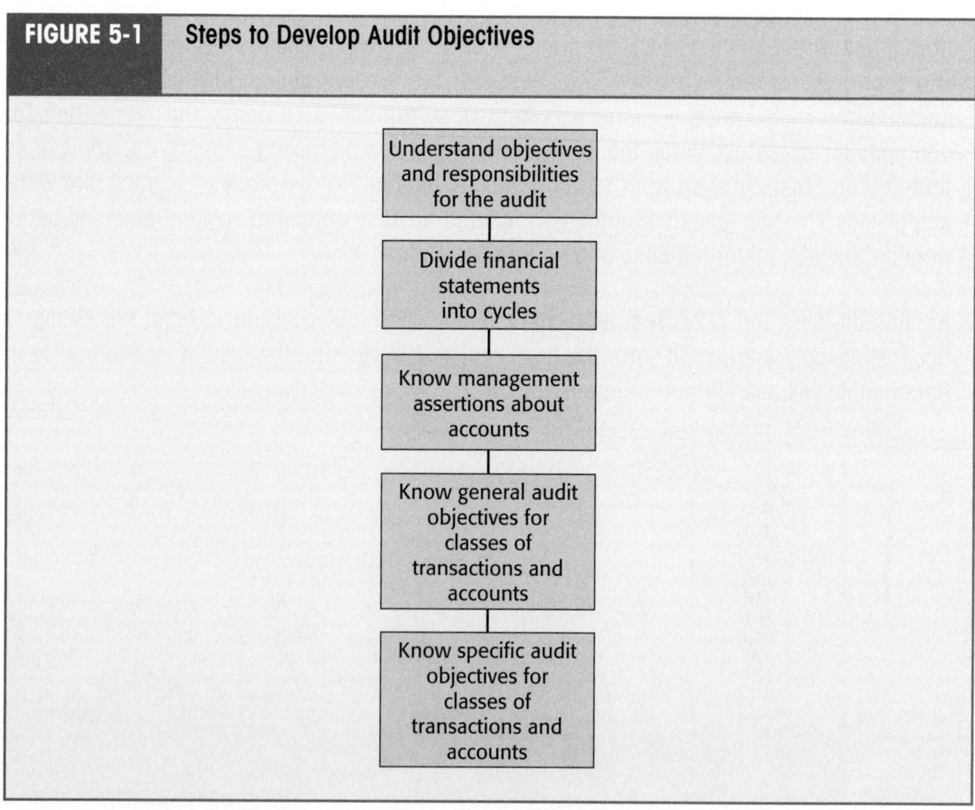

FIGURE 5-1 Steps to Develop Audit Objectives

statements are properly stated. If the auditor believes that the statements are not fairly presented or is unable to reach a conclusion because of insufficient evidence or prevailing conditions, the auditor has the responsibility for notifying the users through the auditor's report.

MANAGEMENT'S RESPONSIBILITIES

OBJECTIVE 5-2

Distinguish management's responsibilities for preparing financial statements from the auditor's responsibilities for verifying those financial statements.

The responsibility for adopting sound accounting policies, maintaining adequate internal control, and making fair representations in the financial statements *rests with management* rather than with the auditor. Because they operate the business daily, a company's management knows more about the company's transactions and related assets, liabilities, and equity than the auditor does. In contrast, the auditor's knowledge of these matters and internal control is limited to that acquired during the audit.

In recent years, the annual reports of many public companies have included a statement about management's responsibilities and relationship with the CPA firm. Figure 5-2

FIGURE 5-2 The Boeing Company's Report of Management

2000 ANNUAL REPORT

REPORT OF MANAGEMENT

To the Shareholders of The Boeing Company:

The accompanying consolidated financial statements of The Boeing Company and subsidiaries have been prepared by management who are responsible for their integrity and objectivity. The statements have been prepared in conformity with generally accepted accounting principles and include amounts based on management's best estimates and judgments. Financial information elsewhere in this Annual Report is consistent with that in the financial statements.

Management has established and maintains a system of internal control designed to provide reasonable assurance that errors or fraud that could be material to the financial statements are prevented or would be detected within a timely period. The system of internal control includes widely communicated statements of policies and business practices which are designed to require all employees to maintain high ethical standards in the conduct of Company affairs. The internal controls are augmented by organizational arrangements that provide for appropriate delegation of authority and division of responsibility and by a program of internal audit with management follow-up.

The financial statements have been audited by Deloitte & Touche LLP, independent certified public accountants. Their audit was conducted in accordance with generally accepted auditing standards and included a review of internal controls and selective tests of transactions. The Independent Auditors' Report appears above.

The Audit Committee of the Board of Directors, composed entirely of outside directors, meets periodically with the independent certified public accountants, management and internal auditors to review accounting, auditing, internal accounting controls, litigation and financial reporting matters. The independent certified public accountants and the internal auditors have free access to this committee without management present.

Philip M. Condit	Michael M. Sears	James A. Bell
Chairman of the Board and Chief Executive Officer	Senior Vice President and Chief Financial Officer	Vice President Finance and Corporate Controller

presents a report of management for the Boeing Company as a part of its annual report. Read the report carefully to determine what management states about its responsibilities.

Management's responsibility for the fairness of the representations (assertions) in the financial statements carries with it the privilege of determining which disclosures it considers necessary. Although management has the responsibility for the preparation of the financial statements and the accompanying footnotes, it is acceptable for an auditor to draft the financial statements for the client or to offer suggestions for clarification. In the event that management insists on financial statement disclosure that the auditor finds unacceptable, the auditor can either issue an adverse or qualified opinion or withdraw from the engagement.

AUDITOR'S RESPONSIBILITIES

OBJECTIVE 5-3

Explain the auditor's responsibility for discovering material misstatements.

SAS 1 (AU 110) states

> The auditor has a responsibility to plan and perform the audit to obtain reasonable assurance about whether the financial statements are free of material misstatement, whether caused by error or fraud. Because of the nature of audit evidence and the characteristics of fraud, the auditor is able to obtain reasonable, but not absolute, assurance that material misstatements are detected. The auditor has no responsibility to plan and perform the audit to obtain reasonable assurance that misstatements, whether caused by errors or fraud, that are not material to the financial statements are detected.

This paragraph and the related discussion in the standards include several important terms and phrases.

Material Versus Immaterial Misstatements Misstatements are usually considered material if the combined uncorrected errors and fraud in the financial statements would likely have changed or influenced the decisions of a reasonable person using the statements. Although it is extremely difficult to quantify a measure of materiality, auditors are responsible for obtaining reasonable assurance that this materiality threshold has been satisfied. It would be extremely costly (and probably impossible) for auditors to have responsibility for finding all immaterial errors and fraud.

Objectives of Financial Statement Audits

Reasonable Assurance Assurance is a measure of the level of certainty that the auditor has obtained at the completion of the audit. Reasonable assurance is not defined in the literature, but it is presumably less than certainty or absolute assurance and more than a low level of assurance. The concept of reasonable, but not absolute, assurance indicates that the auditor is not an insurer or guarantor of the correctness of the financial statements.

There are several reasons why the auditor is responsible for reasonable but not absolute assurance. First, most audit evidence results from testing a sample of a population such as accounts receivable or inventory. Sampling inevitably includes some risk of not uncovering a material misstatement. Also, the areas to be tested; the type, extent, and timing of those tests; and the evaluation of test results require significant auditor judgment. Even with good faith and integrity, auditors can make mistakes and errors in judgment. Second, accounting presentations contain complex estimates, which inherently involve uncertainty and can be affected by future events. As a result, the auditor has to rely on evidence that is persuasive, but not convincing. Third, fraudulently prepared financial statements are often extremely difficult, if not impossible, for the auditor to detect, especially when there is collusion among management.

If the auditor were responsible for making certain that all the assertions in the statements were correct, evidence requirements and the resulting cost of the audit function would increase to such an extent that audits would not be economically practical. Even then, auditors would be unlikely to uncover all material misstatements in every audit. The auditor's best defense when material misstatements are not uncovered in the audit is that the audit was conducted in accordance with generally accepted auditing standards.

Errors Versus Fraud SAS 82 (AU 316) distinguishes between two types of misstatements: errors and fraud. Either type of misstatement can be material or immaterial. An **error** is an *unintentional* misstatement of the financial statements, whereas **fraud** is *intentional.* Two examples of errors are a mistake in extending prices times quantity on a sales invoice and overlooking older raw materials in determining the lower of cost or market for inventory.

For fraud, there is a distinction between **misappropriation of assets,** often called defalcation or employee fraud, and **fraudulent financial reporting,** often called management fraud. An example of misappropriation of assets is a clerk taking cash at the time a sale is made and not entering the sale in the cash register. An example of fraudulent financial reporting is the intentional overstatement of sales near the balance sheet date to increase reported earnings.

Professional Skepticism SAS 1 (AU 230) requires that an audit be designed to provide reasonable assurance of detecting *both* material errors and fraud in the financial statements. To accomplish this, the audit must be planned and performed with an *attitude of professional skepticism* in all aspects of the engagement. Professional skepticism is an attitude that includes a questioning mind and a critical assessment of audit evidence. The auditor should not assume that management is dishonest, but the possibility of dishonesty must be considered. The auditor also should not assume that management is unquestionably honest.

Auditor's Responsibilities for Detecting Material Errors

Auditors spend a great portion of their time planning and performing audits to detect the unintentional mistakes made by management and employees. Auditors find a variety of errors resulting from such things as mistakes in calculation, omissions, misunderstanding and misapplication of accounting standards, and incorrect summarizations and descriptions. Most of the remainder of this book deals with how the auditor plans and performs audits for detecting both errors and fraud.

Auditor's Responsibilities for Detecting Material Fraud

Auditing standards make no distinction between the auditor's responsibilities for searching for errors and fraud, whether from fraudulent financial reporting or misappropriation of assets. For both errors and fraud, the auditor must obtain reasonable assurance about whether the statements are free of material misstatements.

The standards also recognize that it is often more difficult to detect fraud than errors because management or the employees perpetrating the fraud *attempt to conceal the fraud.* The difficulty of detection does not change the auditor's responsibility to properly plan and perform the audit.

Fraud Related Web Sites

Fraud Resulting from Fraudulent Financial Reporting Versus Misappropriation of Assets There is an important difference between fraudulent financial reporting and misappropriation of assets. Fraudulent financial reporting harms users by providing incorrect financial statement information for their decision making. When assets are misappropriated, stockholders, creditors, and others are harmed because assets are no longer available to their rightful owners. Both types of fraud are potentially harmful to users.

Typically, fraudulent financial reporting is committed by management, sometimes without the knowledge of employees. Management is in a position to make accounting and reporting decisions without employees' knowledge. An example is the decision to omit an important footnote about pending litigation.

Usually, but not always, theft of assets is perpetrated by employees and not by management, and the amounts are often immaterial. However, there are well-known examples of extremely material misappropriation of assets by employees and management.

An important concept for misappropriation of assets is the distinction between the theft of assets and misstatements arising from the theft of assets. To illustrate, following are three situations involving the theft of assets:

1. Assets were taken and the theft was covered by overstating assets. For example, cash collected from a customer was stolen, and the account receivable for the customer's account was not credited. The misstatement has not been discovered.

2. Assets were taken and the theft was covered by understating revenues or overstating expenses. For example, cash from a cash sale was stolen, and the transaction was not recorded. The misstatement has not been discovered.

3. Assets were taken, but the misappropriation was discovered. The income statement and related footnotes clearly describe the misappropriation.

In all three situations, there has been a misappropriation of assets, but the financial statements are misstated only in situations 1 and 2. In situation 1, the balance sheet is misstated, whereas in situation 2, revenues or expenses are misstated.

FRAUD STATISTICS

The two most common techniques used by management to misstate financial statement information involve improper revenue recognition and overstatements of assets. According to a study commissioned by the Committee of Sponsoring Organizations of the Treadway Commission (COSO), 50 percent of U.S. companies committing financial statement fraud between 1987 and 1997 recorded revenues prematurely or created fictitious revenue transactions. In addition to these revenue and receivable overstatements, 50 percent of the fraud companies overstated assets by overvaluing existing assets, recording fictitious assets or assets not owned, or capitalizing items that should have been expensed. Assets typically overstated included inventory, net accounts receivable due to understated allowances for doubtful accounts, and property, plant, and equipment. Only 18 percent of the fraud companies understated expenses or liabilities. Most of the financial statement fraud instances involved intentionally misstating financial information, with only 12 percent of the fraud cases involving misappropriation of company assets.

The median fraud was $4.1 million, which is relatively large given that the median company had total assets of $15.7 million. Eighty-three percent of the fraud cases were perpetrated by the chief executive officer (CEO) and/or the chief financial officer (CFO). These individuals allegedly engaged in the fraud to avoid reporting a pretax loss, to maintain requirements to continue trading company stock on one of the national stock exchanges, or to increase stock prices. The motivation to commit the fraud was high because, on average, company officers and members of the board of directors owned 32 percent of the company stock.

Consequences of the fraud were significant. More than 50 percent of the companies filed for bankruptcy or were under a substantially different form of ownership following the fraud period. Many of the individuals involved were forced to resign or were terminated as a result of the fraud. In some cases, those involved were jailed. Additionally, both the companies and individuals faced lawsuits filed by shareholders and the SEC.

Source: Adapted from *Fraudulent Financial Reporting: 1987–1997, An Analysis of U.S. Public Companies*, Committee of Sponsoring Organizations of the Treadway Commission, New York, 1999.

Auditor's Responsibilities for Discovering Illegal Acts

Illegal acts are defined in SAS 54 (AU 317) as violations of laws or government regulations *other than fraud.* Two examples of illegal acts are a violation of federal tax laws and a violation of the federal environmental protection laws.

Direct-Effect Illegal Acts Certain violations of laws and regulations have a direct financial effect on specific account balances in the financial statements. For example, a violation of federal tax laws directly affects income tax expense and income taxes payable. The auditor's responsibilities under SAS 54 for these direct-effect illegal acts is the same as for errors and fraud. On each audit, therefore, the auditor will normally evaluate whether or not there is evidence available to indicate material violations of federal or state tax laws. This might be done by discussions with client personnel and examination of reports issued by the Internal Revenue Service after they have completed an examination of the client's tax return.

Indirect-Effect Illegal Acts Most illegal acts affect the financial statements only indirectly. For example, if the company violates environmental protection laws, there is an effect on the financial statements only if there is a fine or sanction. Potential material fines and sanctions indirectly affect financial statements by creating the need to disclose a contingent liability for the potential amount that might ultimately be paid. This is called an indirect-effect illegal act. Other examples of illegal acts that are likely to have only an indirect effect

are violations of insider securities trading regulations, civil rights laws, and federal employee safety requirements.

Auditing standards clearly state that the auditor provides *no assurance* that indirect-effect illegal acts will be detected. Auditors lack legal expertise, and the frequent indirect relationship between illegal acts and the financial statements makes it impractical for auditors to assume responsibility for discovering those illegal acts.

There are three levels of responsibility that the auditor has for finding and reporting illegal acts.

Evidence Accumulation When There Is No Reason to Believe Indirect-Effect Illegal Acts Exist Many audit procedures normally performed on audits to search for errors and fraud may also uncover illegal acts. Examples include reading the minutes of the board of directors and inquiring of the client's attorneys about litigation. The auditor should also inquire of management about policies they have established to prevent illegal acts and whether management knows of any laws or regulations that the company has violated. Other than these procedures, the auditor should not search for indirect-effect illegal acts unless there is reason to believe they may exist.

Evidence Accumulation and Other Actions When There Is Reason to Believe Direct- or Indirect-Effect Illegal Acts May Exist The auditor may find indications of possible illegal acts in a variety of ways. For example, the minutes may indicate that an investigation by a government agency is in process or the auditor may have identified unusually large payments to consultants or government officials.

When the auditor believes that an illegal act may have occurred, it is necessary to take several actions: First, the auditor should inquire of management at a level above those likely to be involved in the potential illegal act. Second, the auditor should consult with the client's legal counsel or other specialist who is knowledgeable about the potential illegal act. Third, the auditor should consider accumulating additional evidence to determine whether there actually is an illegal act. All three of these actions are intended to provide the auditor with information about whether the suspected illegal act actually exists.

Actions When the Auditor Knows of an Illegal Act The first course of action when an illegal act has been identified is to consider the effects on the financial statements, including the adequacy of disclosures. These effects may be complex and difficult to resolve. For example, a violation of civil rights laws could involve significant fines, but it could also result in the loss of customers or key employees, which could materially affect future revenues and expenses. If the auditor concludes that the disclosures relative to an illegal act are inadequate, the auditor should modify the audit report accordingly.

The auditor should also consider the effect of such illegal acts on its relationship with management. If management knew of the illegal act and failed to inform the auditor, it is questionable whether management can be believed in other discussions.

The auditor should communicate with the audit committee or others of equivalent authority to make sure that they know of the illegal act. The communication can be oral or written. If it is oral, the nature of the communication and discussion should be documented in the audit files. If the client either refuses to accept the auditor's modified report or fails to take appropriate remedial action concerning the illegal act, the auditor may find it necessary to withdraw from the engagement. If the client is publicly held, the auditor must also report the matter directly to the SEC. Such decisions are complex and normally involve consultation by the auditor with the auditor's legal counsel.

FINANCIAL STATEMENT CYCLES

OBJECTIVE 5-4

Classify transactions and account balances into financial statement cycles and identify benefits of a cycle approach to segmenting the audit.

Audits are performed by dividing the financial statements into smaller segments or components. The division makes the audit more manageable and aids in the assignment of tasks to different members of the audit team. For example, most auditors treat fixed assets and notes payable as different segments. Each segment is audited separately but not on a completely independent basis. (For example, the audit of fixed assets may reveal an unrecorded note payable.) After the audit of each segment is completed, including interrelationships with other segments, the results are combined. A conclusion can then be reached about the financial statements taken as a whole.

There are different ways of segmenting an audit. One approach would be to treat every account balance on the statements as a separate segment. Segmenting that way is usually inefficient. It would result in the independent audit of such closely related accounts as inventory and cost of goods sold.

Cycle Approach to Segmenting an Audit

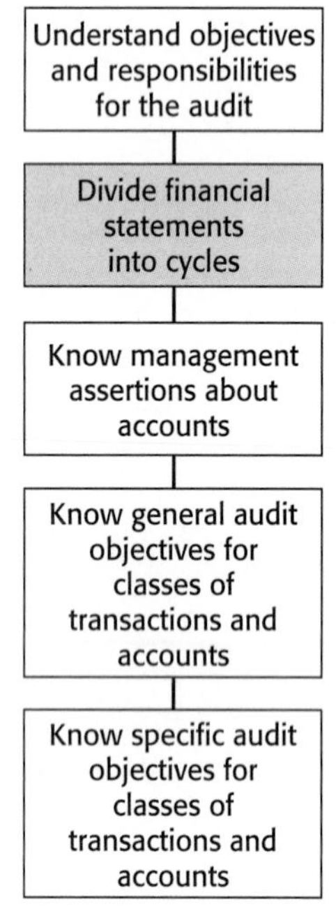

A more common way to divide an audit is to keep closely related types (or classes) of transactions and account balances in the same segment. This is called the **cycle approach.** For example, sales, sales returns, cash receipts, and charge-offs of uncollectible accounts are the four classes of transactions that cause accounts receivable to increase and decrease. Therefore, they are all part of the sales and collection cycle. Similarly, payroll transactions and accrued payroll are a part of the payroll and personnel cycle.

The logic of using the cycle approach can be seen by thinking about the way transactions are recorded in journals and summarized in the general ledger and financial statements. Figure 5-3 shows that flow. To the extent that it is practical, the cycle approach combines transactions recorded in different journals with the general ledger balances that result from those transactions.

The cycles used in this text follow and are then explained.

- Sales and collection cycle
- Acquisition and payment cycle
- Payroll and personnel cycle
- Inventory and warehousing cycle
- Capital acquisition and repayment cycle

To illustrate the application of cycles to audits, Figure 5-4 presents the December 31, 2002, trial balance for Hillsburg Hardware Company. A trial balance is used to prepare financial statements and is a primary focus of every audit. The letter representing a cycle is shown for each account in the left column beside the account name. Observe that each

FIGURE 5-3 Transaction Flow from Journals to Financial Statements

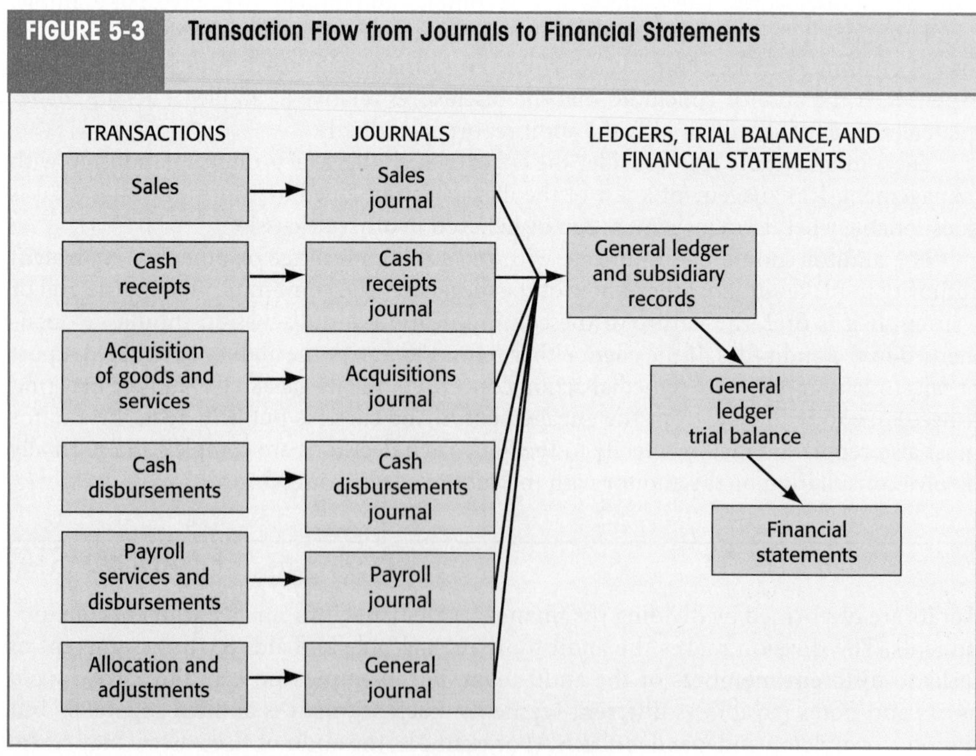

FIGURE 5-4 Hillsburg Hardware Co. Adjusted Trial Balance

HILLSBURG HARDWARE CO.
TRIAL BALANCE
December 31, 2002

		Debit	Credit
S,A,P,C	Cash in bank	$ 827,568	
S	Trade accounts receivable	20,196,800	
S	Allowance for uncollectible accounts		$ 1,240,000
S	Other accounts receivable	945,020	
A,I	Inventories	29,864,621	
A	Prepaid expenses	431,558	
A	Land	3,456,420	
A	Buildings	32,500,000	
A	Computer and other equipment	3,758,347	
A	Furniture and fixtures	2,546,421	
A	Accumulated depreciation		31,920,126
A	Trade accounts payable		4,719,989
C	Notes payable		4,179,620
P	Accrued payroll		1,349,800
P	Accrued payroll taxes		119,663
C	Accrued interest		149,560
C	Dividends payable		1,900,000
A	Accrued income tax		795,442
C	Long-term notes payable		24,120,000
A	Deferred tax		738,240
A	Other accrued payables		829,989
C	Capital stock		5,000,000
C	Capital in excess of par value		3,500,000
C	Retained earnings		11,929,075
S	Sales		144,327,789
S	Sales returns and allowances	1,241,663	
I	Cost of goods sold	103,240,768	
P	Salaries and commissions	7,738,900	
P	Sales payroll taxes	1,422,100	
A	Travel and entertainment–selling	1,110,347	
A	Advertising	2,611,263	
A	Sales and promotional literature	321,620	
A	Sales meetings and training	924,480	
A	Miscellaneous sales expense	681,041	
P	Executive and office salaries	5,523,960	
P	Administrative payroll taxes	682,315	
A	Travel and entertainment–administrative	561,680	
A	Computer maintenance and supplies	860,260	
A	Stationery and supplies	762,568	
A	Postage	244,420	
A	Telephone and fax	722,315	
A	Rent	312,140	
A	Legal fees and retainers	383,060	
A	Auditing and related services	302,840	
A	Depreciation	1,452,080	
S	Bad debt expense	3,323,084	
A	Insurance	722,684	
A	Office repairs and maintenance	843,926	
A	Miscellaneous office expense	643,680	
A	Miscellaneous general expense	323,842	
A	Gain on sale of assets		719,740
A	Income taxes	1,746,600	
C	Interest expense	2,408,642	
C	Dividends	1,900,000	
		$237,539,033	$237,539,033

Note: Letters in the left-hand column refer to the following transaction cycles:

S = Sales and collection
I = Inventory and warehousing
A = Acquisition and payment
C = Capital acquisition and repayment
P = Payroll and personnel

account has at least one cycle associated with it and only cash and inventory are a part of two or more cycles.

The cycles used in this text are shown again in Table 5-1. The accounts for Hillsburg Hardware Co. are summarized in Table 5-1, by cycle, and include the related journals and financial statements in which the accounts appear. The following observations expand the information contained in Table 5-1.

- All general ledger accounts and journals for Hillsburg Hardware Co. are included at least once. For a different company, the number and titles of journals and general ledger accounts would differ, but all would be included.

TABLE 5-1 Cycles Applied to Hillsburg Hardware Co.

Cycle	Journals Included in the Cycle (See Figure 5-3)	General Ledger Accounts Included in the Cycle (See Figure 5-4)	
		Balance Sheet	Income Statement
Sales and collection	Sales journal Cash receipts journal General journal	Cash in bank Trade accounts receivable Other accounts receivable Allowance for uncollectible accounts	Sales Sales returns and allowances Bad debt expense
Acquisition and payment	Acquisitions journal Cash disbursements journal General journal	Cash in bank Inventories Prepaid expenses Land Buildings Computer and other equipment Furniture and fixtures Accumulated depreciation Trade accounts payable Other accrued payables Accrued income tax Deferred tax	Advertising[S] Travel and entertainment[S] Sales meetings and training[S] Sales and promotional literature[S] Miscellaneous sales expense[S] Travel and entertainment[A] Stationery and supplies[A] Postage[A] Telephone and fax[A] Computer maintenance and supplies[A] Depreciation[A] Rent[A] Legal fees and retainers[A] Auditing and related services[A] Insurance[A] Office repairs and maintenance expense[A] Miscellaneous office expense[A] Miscellaneous general expense[A] Gain on sale of assets Income taxes
Payroll and personnel	Payroll journal General journal	Cash in bank Accrued payroll Accrued payroll taxes	Salaries and commissions[S] Sales payroll taxes[S] Executive and office salaries[A] Administrative payroll taxes[A]
Inventory and warehousing	Acquisitions journal Sales journal General journal	Inventories	Cost of goods sold
Capital acquisition and repayment	Acquisitions journal Cash disbursements journal General journal	Cash in bank Notes payable Long-term notes payable Accrued interest Capital stock Capital in excess of par value Retained earnings Dividends Dividends payable	Interest expense

S = Selling expense; *A* = general and administrative expense.

- Some journals and general ledger accounts are included in more than one cycle. When that occurs, it means that the journal is used to record transactions from more than one cycle and indicates a tie-in between the cycles. The most important general ledger account included in and affecting several cycles is general cash (cash in bank). General cash connects most cycles.
- The capital acquisition and repayment cycle is closely related to the acquisition and payment cycle. The acquisition of goods and services includes the purchase of inventory, supplies, and general services in performing the main business operations. Transactions in the capital acquisition and repayment cycle are related to financing the business, such as issuing stock or debt, paying dividends, and repayment of debt. The same three journals are used to record transactions for both cycles, and the transactions are similar. There are two reasons for treating capital acquisition and repayment separately from the acquisition of goods and services. First, the transactions are related to financing a company rather than to its operations. Second, most capital acquisition and repayment cycle accounts involve few transactions, but each is often highly material and therefore should be audited extensively. Considering both reasons, it is more convenient to separate the two cycles.
- The inventory and warehousing cycle is closely related to all other cycles, especially for a manufacturing company. The cost of inventory includes raw materials (acquisition and payment cycle), direct labor (payroll and personnel cycle), and manufacturing overhead (acquisition and payment and payroll and personnel cycles). The sale of finished goods involves the sales and collection cycle. Because inventory is material for most manufacturing companies, it is common to borrow money using inventory as security. In those cases, the capital acquisition and repayment cycle is also related to inventory and warehousing.

Relationships Among Cycles

Figure 5-5 illustrates the relationships of the cycles. In addition to the five cycles, general cash is also shown. Each cycle is studied in detail in later chapters. Figure 5-5 shows that cycles have no beginning or end except at the origin and final disposition of a company. A company begins by obtaining capital, usually in the form of cash. In a manufacturing company, cash is used to acquire raw materials, fixed assets, and related goods and services to produce inventory (acquisition and payment cycle). Cash is also used to acquire labor for the same reason (payroll and personnel cycle). Acquisition and payment and payroll and personnel are similar in nature, but the functions are sufficiently different to justify separate cycles. The combined result of these two cycles is inventory (inventory and warehousing cycle). At a subsequent point, the inventory is sold and billings and collections result (sales and collection cycle). The cash generated is used to pay dividends and interest

FIGURE 5-5 Relationships Among Transaction Cycles

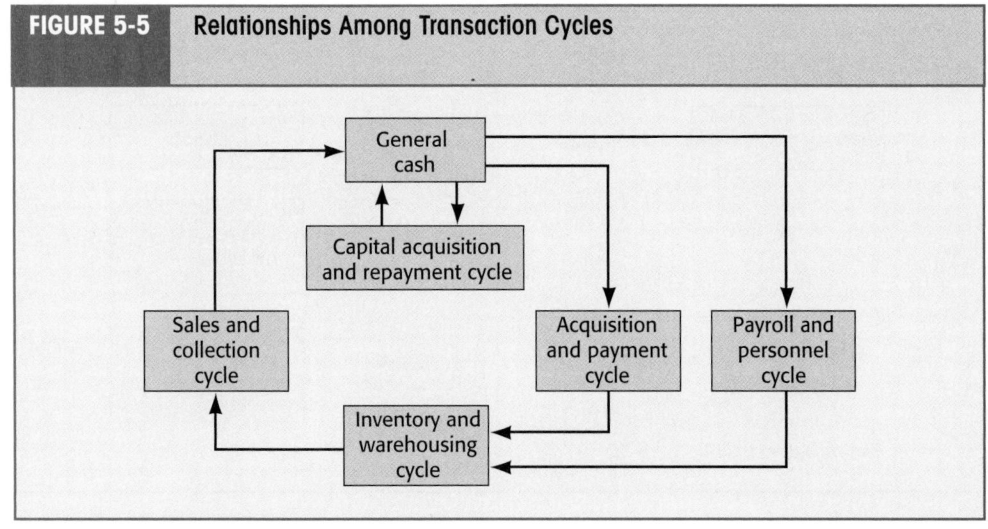

or finance capital expansion and to start the cycles again. The cycles interrelate in much the same way in a service company, where there will be no inventory, but there may be unbilled receivables.

Transaction cycles are of major importance in the conduct of the audit. For the most part, auditors treat each cycle separately during the audit. Although care should be taken to interrelate different cycles at different times, the auditor must treat the cycles somewhat independently to manage complex audits effectively.

SETTING AUDIT OBJECTIVES

OBJECTIVE 5-5

Describe why the auditor obtains a combination of assurance by auditing classes of transactions and ending balances in accounts.

Auditors conduct audits using the cycle approach by performing audit tests of the transactions making up ending balances and also by performing audit tests of the account balances themselves. Figure 5-6 illustrates this important concept by showing the four classes of transactions that determine the ending balance in accounts receivable for Hillsburg Hardware Co. Assume that the beginning balance of $18,827 was audited in the prior year and is therefore considered reliable. If the auditor could be completely sure that each of the four classes of transactions was correctly stated, the auditor could also be sure that the ending balance of $20,197 was correctly stated. But it may be impractical for the auditor to obtain complete assurance about the correctness of each class of transactions resulting in less than complete assurance about the ending balance in accounts receivable. In such a case, overall assurance can be increased by auditing the ending balance of accounts receivable. Auditors have found that, generally, the most efficient way to conduct audits is to *obtain some combination of assurance for each class of transactions and for the ending balance in the related account.*

For any given class of transactions, there are several audit objectives that must be met before the auditor can conclude that the transactions are properly recorded. They are called

transaction-related audit objectives in the remainder of this book. For example, there are specific sales transaction-related audit objectives and specific sales returns and allowances transaction-related audit objectives.

Similarly, there are several audit objectives that must be met for each account balance. They are called **balance-related audit objectives.** For example, there are specific accounts receivable balance-related audit objectives and specific accounts payable balance-related

FIGURE 5-6 Balances and Transactions Affecting Those Balances for Accounts Receivable

Accounts Receivable (in thousands)

Beginning balance	$ 18,827		
Sales	$144,328	$138,393	Cash receipts
		$ 1,242	Sales returns and allowances
		$ 3,323	Charge-off of uncollectible accounts
Ending balance	$ 20,197		

audit objectives. It will be shown later that the transaction-related and balance-related audit objectives are somewhat different but closely related. Throughout the remainder of this text, the term *audit objectives* refers to both transaction-related and balance-related audit objectives.

Before examining audit objectives in more detail, it is necessary to understand management assertions. These are studied next.

Management Assertions

OBJECTIVE 5-6

Distinguish among the five categories of management assertions about financial information.

Management assertions are implied or expressed representations by management about classes of transactions and the related accounts in the financial statements. As an illustration, the management of Hillsburg Hardware Co. asserts that cash of $827,568 (see Figure 5-4) was present in the company's bank accounts as of the balance sheet date. Unless otherwise disclosed in the financial statements, management also asserts that the cash was unrestricted and available for normal use. Similar assertions exist for each asset, liability, owners' equity, revenue, and expense item in the financial statements. These assertions apply to both classes of transactions and account balances.

Management assertions are directly related to generally accepted accounting principles (GAAP). These assertions are part of the *criteria that management uses to record and disclose accounting information in financial statements.* Return to the definition of auditing in Chapter 1. It states, in part, that auditing is a comparison of information (financial statements) to established criteria (assertions established according to GAAP). Auditors must therefore understand the assertions to do adequate audits.

Understand objectives and responsibilities for the audit → Divide financial statements into cycles → **Know management assertions about accounts** → Know general audit objectives for classes of transactions and accounts → Know specific audit objectives for classes of transactions and accounts

SAS 31 (AU 326) classifies assertions into five broad categories:

1. Existence or occurrence
2. Completeness
3. Valuation or allocation
4. Rights and obligations
5. Presentation and disclosure

Assertions About Existence or Occurrence Assertions about existence deal with whether assets, obligations, and equities included in the balance sheet actually existed on the balance sheet date. Assertions about occurrence concern whether recorded transactions included in the financial statements actually occurred during the accounting period. For example, management asserts that merchandise inventory included in the balance sheet exists and is available for sale at the balance sheet date. Similarly, management asserts that recorded sales transactions represent exchanges of goods or services that actually took place.

Assertions About Completeness These management assertions state that all transactions and accounts that should be presented in the financial statements are included. For example, management asserts that all sales of goods and services are recorded and included in the financial statements. Similarly, management asserts that notes payable in the balance sheet include all such obligations of the entity.

The completeness assertion deals with matters opposite from those of the existence or occurrence assertion. The completeness assertion is concerned with the possibility of omitting items from the financial statements that should have been included, whereas the existence or occurrence assertion is concerned with inclusion of amounts that should not have been included. Thus, violations of the existence assertion relate to account overstatements, whereas violations of the completeness assertion relate to account understatements.

The recording of a sale that did not take place would be a violation of the occurrence assertion, whereas the failure to record a sale that did occur would be a violation of the completeness assertion.

Assertions About Valuation or Allocation These assertions deal with whether asset, liability, equity, revenue, and expense accounts have been included in the financial statements at appropriate amounts. For example, management asserts that property is recorded at historical cost and that such cost is systematically allocated to appropriate accounting periods through depreciation. Similarly, management asserts that trade accounts receivable included in the balance sheet are stated at net realizable value.

Assertions About Rights and Obligations These management assertions deal with whether assets are the rights of the entity and liabilities are the obligations of the entity at a given date. For example, management asserts that assets are owned by the company or that amounts capitalized for leases in the balance sheet represent the cost of the entity's rights to leased property and that the corresponding lease liability represents an obligation of the entity.

Assertions About Presentation and Disclosure These assertions deal with whether components of the financial statements are properly combined or separated, described, and disclosed. For example, management asserts that obligations classified as long-term liabilities in the balance sheet will not mature within 1 year. Similarly, management asserts that amounts presented as extraordinary items in the income statement are properly classified and described.

TRANSACTION-RELATED AUDIT OBJECTIVES

OBJECTIVE 5-7

Link the six general transaction-related audit objectives to the five management assertions.

The auditor's transaction-related audit objectives follow and are closely related to management assertions. That is not surprising because the auditor's primary responsibility is to determine whether management assertions about financial statements are justified.

These transaction-related audit objectives are intended to provide a *framework* to help the auditor accumulate sufficient competent evidence required by the third standard of field work and decide the proper evidence to accumulate for classes of transactions given the circumstances of the engagement. The objectives remain the same from audit to audit, but the evidence varies, depending on the circumstances.

A distinction must be made between general transaction-related audit objectives and specific transaction-related audit objectives for each class of transactions. The general transaction-related audit objectives discussed here are applicable to every class of transactions but are stated in broad terms. Specific transaction-related audit objectives are also applied to each class of transactions but are stated in terms tailored to a class of transactions such as sales transactions. Once you know the general transaction-related audit objectives, they can be used to develop specific transaction-related audit objectives for each class of transactions being audited. The six general transaction-related audit objectives are discussed next.

General Transaction-Related Audit Objectives

Existence—Recorded Transactions Exist This objective deals with whether recorded transactions have actually occurred. Inclusion of a sale in the sales journal when no sale occurred violates the existence objective. This objective is the auditor's counterpart to the management assertion of existence or occurrence.

Completeness—Existing Transactions Are Recorded This objective deals with whether all transactions that should be included in the journals have actually been included. Failure to include a sale in the sales journal and general ledger when a sale occurred violates the completeness objective. The objective is the counterpart to the management assertion of completeness.

The existence and completeness objectives emphasize opposite audit concerns; existence deals with potential overstatement and completeness with unrecorded transactions (understatement).

Accuracy—Recorded Transactions Are Stated at the Correct Amounts This objective deals with the accuracy of information for accounting transactions. For sales transactions, there would be a violation of the accuracy objective if the quantity of goods shipped was different from the quantity billed, the wrong selling price was used for billing, extension or adding errors occurred in billing, or the wrong amount was included in the sales journal. Accuracy is one part of the valuation or allocation assertion.

It is important to distinguish between accuracy and existence or completeness. For example, if a recorded sales transaction should not have been recorded because the shipment was on consignment, the existence objective has been violated, even if the amount of the invoice was accurately calculated. If the recorded sale was for a valid shipment but the amount was calculated incorrectly, there is a violation of the accuracy objective but not of existence. The same relationship exists between completeness and accuracy.

Classification—Transactions Included in the Client's Journals Are Properly Classified Examples of misclassifications for sales are including cash sales as credit sales, recording a sale of operating fixed assets as revenue, and misclassifying commercial sales as residential sales. Classification is also a part of the valuation or allocation assertion.

Timing—Transactions Are Recorded on the Correct Dates A timing error occurs if transactions are not recorded on the dates the transactions took place. A sales transaction, for example, should be recorded on the date of shipment. Timing is also a part of the valuation or allocation assertion.

Posting and Summarization—Recorded Transactions Are Properly Included in the Master Files and Are Correctly Summarized This objective deals with the accuracy of the transfer of information from recorded transactions in journals to subsidiary records and the general ledger. For example, if a sales transaction is recorded in the wrong customer's record or at the wrong amount in the master file, it is a violation of this objective. Posting and summarization is also a part of the valuation or allocation assertion.

Because the posting of transactions from journals to subsidiary records, the general ledger, and other related master files is typically accomplished automatically by computerized accounting systems, the risk of random human error in posting is minimal. Once the auditor can establish that the computer is functioning properly, there is a reduced concern about posting process errors.

Understand objectives and responsibilities for the audit

Divide financial statements into cycles

Know management assertions about accounts

Know general audit objectives for classes of transactions and accounts

Know specific audit objectives for classes of transactions and accounts

Specific Transaction-Related Audit Objectives

The general transaction-related audit objectives must be applied to each material type (class) of transaction in the audit. Such transactions typically include sales, cash receipts, acquisitions of goods and services, payroll, and so on. Table 5-2 summarizes the six transaction-related audit objectives. It includes the general form of the objectives, the application of the objectives to sales transactions, and the assertions. Notice that only three assertions are associated with transaction-related audit objectives. This shows that two of the assertions are not satisfied by performing transaction-related audit tests.

TABLE 5-2 Transaction-Related Audit Objectives and Management Assertions for Sales Transactions

Management Assertions	General Transaction-Related Audit Objectives	Specific Sales Transaction-Related Audit Objectives
Existence or occurrence	Existence	Recorded sales are for shipments made to nonfictitious customers.
Completeness	Completeness	Existing sales transactions are recorded.
Valuation or allocation	Accuracy	Recorded sales are for the amount of goods shipped and are correctly billed and recorded.
	Classification	Sales transactions are properly classified.
	Timing	Sales are recorded on the correct dates.
	Posting and summarization	Sales transactions are properly included in the master file and are correctly summarized.
Rights and obligations	N/A	N/A
Presentation and disclosure	N/A	N/A

BALANCE-RELATED AUDIT OBJECTIVES

OBJECTIVE 5-8

Link the nine general balance-related audit objectives to the five management assertions.

Balance-related audit objectives are similar to the transaction-related audit objectives just discussed. They also follow from management assertions and they provide a framework to help the auditor accumulate sufficient competent evidence. There are also both general and specific balance-related audit objectives.

There are two differences between balance-related and transaction-related audit objectives. First, as the terms imply, balance-related audit objectives are applied to account balances, whereas transaction-related audit objectives are applied to classes of transactions such as sales transactions and cash disbursements transactions. Second, there are more audit objectives for account balances than for classes of transactions. There are nine balance-related audit objectives compared to six transaction-related audit objectives.

Because of the way audits are done, balance-related audit objectives are almost *always* applied to the ending balance in balance sheet accounts, such as accounts receivable, inventory, and notes payable. However, some balance-related objectives are applied to certain income statement accounts. These usually involve nonroutine transactions and unpredictable expenses, such as legal expense or repairs and maintenance. Other income statement accounts are closely related to balance sheet accounts and are tested simultaneously, such as depreciation expense with accumulated depreciation and interest expense with notes payable.

When using the balance-related audit objectives as a framework for auditing account balances, the auditor accumulates evidence to verify detail that supports the account balance, rather than verifying the account balance itself. For example, in auditing accounts receivable, the auditor obtains a listing of the accounts receivable master file from the client that agrees to the general ledger balance (see page 345 for an illustration). The accounts receivable balance-related audit objectives are applied to the customer accounts in that listing.

Following is a brief discussion of the nine general balance-related audit objectives. Throughout the discussion, there is reference to a supporting schedule, which refers to a client-provided schedule or electronic file such as the accounts receivable listing just described.

General Balance-Related Audit Objectives

Existence—Amounts Included Exist This objective deals with whether the amounts included in the financial statements should actually be included. For example, inclusion of an account receivable from a customer in the accounts receivable trial balance when there is no receivable from that customer violates the existence objective. This objective is the auditor's counterpart to the management assertion of existence or occurrence.

Completeness—Existing Amounts Are Included This objective deals with whether all amounts that should be included have actually been included. Failure to include an account receivable from a customer in the accounts receivable trial balance when a receivable exists violates the completeness objective. This objective is the counterpart to the management assertion of completeness.

The existence and completeness objectives emphasize opposite audit concerns; existence deals with potential overstatement and completeness with unrecorded transactions and amounts (understatement).

Accuracy—Amounts Included Are Stated at the Correct Amounts The accuracy objective refers to amounts being included at the correct arithmetic amount. An inventory item on a client's inventory listing could be wrong because the number of units of inventory on hand was misstated, the unit price was wrong, or the total was incorrectly extended. Each of these violates the accuracy objective. Accuracy is one part of the valuation or allocation assertion.

Classification—Amounts Included in the Client's Listing Are Properly Classified Classification involves determining whether items on a client's listing are included in the correct accounts. For example, on the accounts receivable listing, receivables must be separated into short-term and long-term, and amounts due from affiliates, officers, and directors must be classified separately from amounts due from customers. Classification is also a part of the valuation or allocation assertion.

Cutoff—Transactions Near the Balance Sheet Date Are Recorded in the Proper Period In testing for cutoff, the objective is to determine whether transactions are recorded in the proper period. The transactions that are most likely to be misstated are those recorded near the end of the accounting period. It is proper to think of cutoff tests as a part of verifying either the balance sheet accounts or the related transactions, but for convenience auditors usually perform them as a part of auditing balance sheet accounts. Cutoff is also a part of the valuation or allocation assertion.

Detail Tie-In—Details in the Account Balance Agree with Related Master File Amounts, Foot to the Total in the Account Balance, and Agree with the Total in the General Ledger Account balances on financial statements are supported by details in master files and schedules prepared by clients. The detail tie-in objective is concerned that the details on lists are accurately prepared, correctly added, and agree with the general ledger. For example, individual accounts receivable on a listing of accounts receivable should be the same in the accounts receivable master file and the total should equal the general ledger control account. Detail tie-in is also a part of the valuation or allocation assertion.

Realizable Value—Assets Are Included at the Amounts Estimated to Be Realized This objective concerns whether an account balance has been reduced for declines from historical cost to net realizable value. Examples when the objective applies are considering the adequacy of the allowance for uncollectible accounts receivable and write-downs of inventory for obsolescence. The objective applies only to asset accounts and is also a part of the valuation or allocation assertion.

Rights and Obligations In addition to existing, most assets must be owned before it is acceptable to include them in the financial statements. Similarly, liabilities must belong to the entity. Rights are always associated with assets and obligations with liabilities. This objective is the auditor's counterpart to the management assertion of rights and obligations.

Presentation and Disclosure—Account Balances and Related Disclosure Requirements Are Properly Presented in the Financial Statements In fulfilling the presentation and disclosure objective, the auditor tests to make certain that all balance sheet and income statement accounts and related information are correctly set forth in the financial statements and properly described in the body and footnotes of the statements. This objective has its counterpart in the management assertion of presentation and disclosure.

Presentation and disclosure is closely related to, but distinct from, classification. Accounting information for balance-related audit objectives is correctly classified if all information on a detailed schedule supporting an account balance is summarized in the appropriate accounts. The information is correctly disclosed if those account balances and related footnote information are properly combined, described, and presented in the financial statements. For example, if a long-term note receivable is included on an accounts receivable listing, there is a violation of the classification objective. If the long-term note receivable is correctly classified but combined with accounts receivable on the financial statements, there is a violation of the presentation and disclosure objective.

Specific Balance-Related Audit Objectives

After the general balance-related audit objectives are understood, specific balance-related audit objectives for each account balance on the financial statements can be developed. There should be at least one specific balance-related audit objective for each general balance-related audit objective unless the auditor believes that the general balance-related audit objective is not relevant or is unimportant in the circumstances. There may be more than one specific balance-related audit objective for a general balance-related audit objective. For example, specific balance-related audit objectives for rights and obligations of the inventory of Hillsburg Hardware Co. could include (1) the company

TABLE 5-3 **Hillsburg Hardware Co.: Management Assertions and Balance-Related Audit Objectives Applied to Inventory**

Management Assertions	General Balance-Related Audit Objectives	Specific Balance-Related Audit Objectives Applied to Inventory
Existence or occurrence	Existence	All recorded inventory exists at the balance sheet date.
Completeness	Completeness	All existing inventory has been counted and included in the inventory summary.
Valuation or allocation	Accuracy	Inventory quantities on the client's perpetual records agree with items physically on hand. Prices used to value inventories are materially correct. Extensions of price times quantity are correct and details are correctly added.
	Classification	Inventory items are properly classified as to raw materials, work in process, and finished goods.
	Cutoff	Purchase cutoff at year-end is proper. Sales cutoff at year-end is proper.
	Detail tie-in	Total of inventory items agrees with general ledger.
	Realizable value	Inventories have been written down where net realizable value is impaired.
Rights and obligations	Rights and obligations	The company has title to all inventory items listed. Inventories are not pledged as collateral.
Presentation and disclosure	Presentation and disclosure	Major categories of inventories and their bases of valuation are disclosed. The pledge or assignment of any inventories is disclosed.

has title to all inventory items listed and (2) inventory is not pledged as collateral unless it is disclosed.

Relationships Among Management Assertions and Balance-Related Audit Objectives

The reason there are more general balance-related audit objectives than management assertions is to provide additional guidance to auditors in deciding what evidence to accumulate. Table 5-3 illustrates this by showing the relationships among management assertions, the general balance-related audit objectives, and specific balance-related audit objectives as applied to inventory for Hillsburg Hardware Co. Notice that there is a one-to-one relationship between assertions and objectives, except for the valuation or allocation assertion. The valuation or allocation assertion has multiple objectives because of the complexity of valuation issues and the need to provide auditors with additional guidance.

HOW AUDIT OBJECTIVES ARE MET

OBJECTIVE 5-9

Explain the relationship between audit objectives and the accumulation of audit evidence.

The auditor must obtain sufficient competent audit evidence to support all management assertions in the financial statements. As stated earlier, this is done by accumulating evidence in support of some appropriate combination of transaction-related audit objectives and balance-related audit objectives. A comparison of Tables 5-2 and 5-3 shows a significant overlap between the two types of audit objectives. The only assertions that must be addressed through balance-related audit objectives, rather than some combination of balance- and transaction-related audit objectives, are rights and obligations and presentation and disclosure.

FIGURE 5-7 Four Phases of an Audit

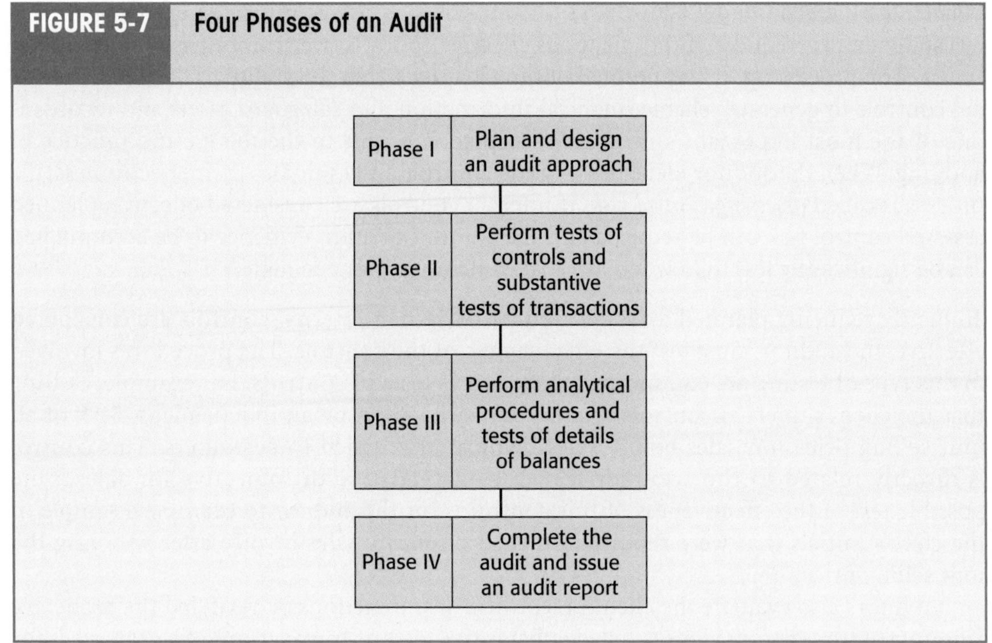

The auditor plans the appropriate combination of audit objectives and the evidence that must be accumulated to meet them by following an audit process. An audit process is a well-defined methodology for organizing an audit to ensure that the evidence gathered is both sufficient and competent and that all appropriate audit objectives are both specified and met. The audit process described in this text has four specific phases. These are shown in Figure 5-7. The remainder of this chapter provides a brief introduction to each of the four **phases of the audit process.**

Plan and Design an Audit Approach (Phase I)

For any given audit, there are many ways in which an auditor can accumulate evidence to meet the overall audit objectives. Two overriding considerations affect the approach the auditor selects: *sufficient competent evidence must be accumulated to meet the auditor's professional responsibility*, and *the cost of accumulating the evidence should be minimized.* The first consideration is the most important, but cost minimization is necessary if CPA firms are to be competitive and profitable. If there were no concern for controlling costs, evidence decision making would be easy. Auditors would keep adding evidence, without concern for efficiency, until they were sufficiently certain that there were no material misstatements.

Concern for sufficient competent evidence and cost control necessitates planning the engagement. The plan should result in an effective audit approach at a reasonable cost. Planning and designing an audit approach can be broken down into several parts. Two key aspects of audit planning are briefly introduced here and are discussed in subsequent chapters.

Obtain Knowledge of the Client's Business Strategies and Processes and Assess Risks To adequately assess the risk of misstatements in the financial statements and interpret information obtained throughout the audit, an understanding of the client's business strategies and processes is essential. For example, the auditor should study the client's business model and perform analytical procedures and other comparisons to competitors. In addition, the auditor must understand any unique accounting requirements of the client's industry. For example, when auditing an insurance company, an auditor must understand how loss reserves are calculated.

Once the auditor has an understanding of the client's industry and business strategies, he or she assesses the risk of misstatements in the financial statements. For example, the client may be expanding sales by taking on new customers with poor credit ratings. The auditor would assess a higher risk of misstatement for net realizable value of accounts receivable and plan to expand testing in this area.

Understand Internal Control and Assess Control Risk The risk of misstatement in the financial statements is reduced if the client has effective controls over computer operations and transaction processing. It was pointed out in Chapter 1 that the ability of the client's internal controls to generate reliable financial information and safeguard assets and records is one of the most important and widely accepted concepts in the theory and practice of auditing. When the auditor identifies internal controls and evaluates their effectiveness, the process is called *assessing control risk.* If internal controls are considered effective, planned assessed control risk can be reduced and the amount of audit evidence to be accumulated can be significantly less than when internal controls are not adequate.

Perform Tests of Controls and Substantive Tests of Transactions (Phase II)

To justify reducing planned assessed control risk when internal controls are considered effective, the auditor must test the effectiveness of the controls. The procedures involved in this type of testing are commonly referred to as **tests of controls.** For example, assume that the client's internal controls require the verification by an independent clerk of all unit selling prices on sales before sales invoices are mailed to customers. This control is directly related to the accuracy transaction-related audit objective for sales. One possible test of the effectiveness of this control is for the auditor to examine a sample of the clerk's initials that were required on each duplicate sales invoice after verifying the unit selling price.

Auditors also evaluate the client's recording of transactions by verifying the monetary amounts of transactions. This is called **substantive tests of transactions.** An example is for the auditor to compare the unit selling price on a duplicate sales invoice with the approved price list as a test of the accuracy objective for sales transactions. Like the test of control in the previous paragraph, this test satisfies the accuracy transaction-related audit objective for sales. Often, auditors perform tests of controls and substantive tests of transactions at the same time.

Perform Analytical Procedures and Tests of Details of Balances (Phase III)

There are two general categories of phase III procedures: analytical procedures and tests of details of balances. **Analytical procedures** use comparisons and relationships to assess whether account balances or other data appear reasonable. An example of an analytical procedure that would provide some assurance for the accuracy objective for both sales transactions (transaction-related audit objective) and accounts receivable (balance-related audit objective) is to examine sales transactions in the sales journal for unusually large amounts and to compare total monthly sales with prior years. If a company is consistently using incorrect sales prices, significant differences are likely.

Tests of details of balances are specific procedures intended to test for monetary misstatements in the balances in the financial statements. An example related to the accuracy objective for accounts receivable (balance-related audit objective) is direct written communication with the client's customers. Tests of details of ending balances are essential to the conduct of the audit because most of the evidence is obtained from a source independent of the client and therefore considered to be of high quality.

Complete the Audit and Issue an Audit Report (Phase IV)

After the auditor has completed all procedures for each audit objective and for each financial statement account, it is necessary to combine the information obtained to reach an *overall conclusion* as to whether the financial statements are fairly presented. This is a highly subjective process that relies heavily on the auditor's professional judgment. When the audit is completed, the CPA must issue an audit report to accompany the client's published financial statements. These reports have already been studied in Chapter 2.

SUMMARY

This chapter discussed the objectives of the audit and the way the auditor subdivides an audit to result in specific audit objectives. The auditor then accumulates evidence to obtain assurance that each audit objective has been satisfied. The illustration on meeting the accuracy objectives for sales transactions and accounts receivable shows that the auditor can obtain assurance by accumulating evidence using tests of controls, substantive tests of transactions, analytical procedures, and tests of details of balances. In some audits, there is more emphasis on certain of these tests such as analytical procedures and tests of controls, whereas in others, there is emphasis on substantive tests of transactions and tests of details of balances.

ESSENTIAL TERMS

Analytical procedures—use of comparisons and relationships to assess whether account balances or other data appear reasonable

Balance-related audit objectives—nine audit objectives that must be met before the auditor can conclude that any given account balance is fairly stated; the general balance-related audit objectives are existence, completeness, accuracy, classification, cutoff, detail tie-in, realizable value, rights and obligations, and presentation and disclosure

Cycle approach—a method of dividing an audit by keeping closely related types of transactions and account balances in the same segment

Error—an unintentional misstatement of the financial statements

Fraud—an intentional misstatement of the financial statements

Fraudulent financial reporting—intentional misstatements or omissions of amounts or disclosures in financial statements to deceive users

Illegal acts—violations of laws or government regulations other than fraud

Management assertions—implied or expressed representations by management about classes of transactions and related accounts in the financial statements

Misappropriation of assets—a fraud involving the theft of an entity's assets

Phases of the audit process—the four aspects of a complete audit: (1) plan and design an audit approach, (2) perform tests of controls and substantive tests of transactions, (3) perform analytical procedures and tests of details of balances, and (4) complete the audit and issue the audit report

Substantive tests of transactions—audit procedures testing for monetary misstatements to determine whether the six transaction-related audit objectives have been satisfied for each class of transactions

Tests of controls—audit procedures to test the effectiveness of controls in support of a reduced assessed control risk

Tests of details of balances—audit procedures testing for monetary misstatements to determine whether the nine balance-related audit objectives have been satisfied for each significant account balance

Transaction-related audit objectives—six audit objectives that must be met before the auditor can conclude that the total for any given class of transactions is fairly stated; the general transaction-related audit objectives are existence, completeness, accuracy, classification, timing, and posting and summarization

REVIEW QUESTIONS

5-1 **(Objective 5-1)** State the objective of the ordinary audit of financial statements. In general terms, how do auditors meet that objective?

5-2 **(Objectives 5-2, 5-3)** Distinguish between management's and the auditor's responsibility for the financial statements being audited.

5-3 **(Objective 5-3)** Distinguish between the terms *errors* and *fraud*. What is the auditor's responsibility for finding each?

5-4 **(Objective 5-3)** Distinguish between fraudulent financial reporting and misappropriation of assets. Discuss the likely difference between these two types of fraud on the fair presentation of financial statements.

5-5 **(Objective 5-3)** "It is well accepted in auditing that throughout the conduct of the ordinary audit, it is essential to obtain large amounts of information from management and to rely heavily on management's judgments. After all, the financial statements are management's representations, and the primary responsibility for their fair presentation rests with management, not the auditor. For example, it is extremely difficult, if not impossible, for the auditor to evaluate the obsolescence of inventory as well as management can in a highly complex business. Similarly, the collectibility of accounts receivable and the continued usefulness of machinery and equipment are heavily dependent on management's willingness to provide truthful responses to questions." Reconcile the auditor's responsibility for discovering material misrepresentations by management with these comments.

5-6 **(Objective 5-3)** List two major characteristics that are useful in predicting the likelihood of fraudulent financial reporting in an audit. For each of the characteristics, state two things that the auditor can do to evaluate its significance in the engagement.

5-7 **(Objective 5-4)** Describe what is meant by the cycle approach to auditing. What are the advantages of dividing the audit into different cycles?

5-8 **(Objective 5-4)** Identify the cycle to which each of the following general ledger accounts would ordinarily be assigned: sales, accounts payable, retained earnings, accounts receivable, inventory, and repairs and maintenance.

5-9 **(Objectives 5-4, 5-5)** Why are sales, sales returns and allowances, bad debts, cash discounts, accounts receivable, and allowance for uncollectible accounts all included in the same cycle?

5-10 **(Objective 5-6)** Define what is meant by a management assertion about financial statements. Identify the five broad categories of management assertions.

5-11 **(Objectives 5-6, 5-7)** Distinguish between the general audit objectives and management assertions. Why are the general audit objectives more useful to auditors?

5-12 **(Objective 5-7)** An acquisition of a fixed-asset repair by a construction company is recorded on the wrong date. Which transaction-related audit objective has been violated? Which transaction-related audit objective has been violated if the acquisition had been capitalized as a fixed asset rather than expensed?

5-13 **(Objective 5-8)** Distinguish between the existence and completeness balance-related audit objectives. State the effect on the financial statements (overstatement or understatement) of a violation of each in the audit of accounts receivable.

5-14 **(Objectives 5-7, 5-8)** What are specific audit objectives? Explain their relationship to the general audit objectives.

5-15 **(Objectives 5-6, 5-8)** Identify the management assertion and general balance-related audit objective for the specific balance-related audit objective: All recorded fixed assets exist at the balance sheet date.

5-16 **(Objectives 5-6, 5-8)** Explain how management assertions, general balance-related audit objectives, and specific balance-related audit objectives are developed for an account balance such as accounts receivable.

5-17 **(Objective 5-9)** Identify the four phases of the audit. What is the relationship of the four phases to the objective of the audit of financial statements?

MULTIPLE CHOICE QUESTIONS FROM CPA EXAMINATIONS

5-18 **(Objective 5-1)** The following questions concern the reasons auditors do audits. Choose the best response.

a. Which of the following *best* describes the reason why an independent auditor reports on financial statements?
   (1) A misappropriation of assets may exist, and it is more likely to be detected by independent auditors.
   (2) Different interests may exist between the company preparing the statements and the persons using the statements.
   (3) A misstatement of account balances may exist and is generally corrected as the result of the independent auditor's work.
   (4) Poorly designed internal controls may be in existence.

b. An independent audit aids in the communication of economic data because the audit
   (1) confirms the accuracy of management's financial representations.
   (2) lends credibility to the financial statements.
   (3) guarantees that financial data are fairly presented.
   (4) assures the readers of financial statements that any fraudulent activity has been corrected.

c. The major reason an independent auditor gathers audit evidence is to
   (1) form an opinion on the financial statements.
   (2) detect fraud.
   (3) evaluate management.
   (4) assess control risk.

5-19 **(Objective 5-3)** The following questions deal with errors and fraud. Choose the best response.

a. An independent auditor has the responsibility to design the audit to provide reasonable assurance of detecting errors and fraud that might have a material effect on the financial statements. Which of the following, if material, would be a fraud as defined in *Codification of Statements on Auditing Standards*?
   (1) Misappropriation of an asset or groups of assets.
   (2) Clerical mistakes in the accounting data underlying the financial statements.

(3) Mistakes in the application of accounting principles.
(4) Misinterpretation of facts that existed when the financial statements were prepared.

b. What assurance does the auditor provide that errors, fraud, and direct-effect illegal acts that are material to the financial statements will be detected?

Errors	Fraud	Direct-Effect Illegal Acts
(1) Limited	Negative	Limited
(2) Reasonable	Reasonable	Reasonable
(3) Limited	Limited	Reasonable
(4) Reasonable	Limited	Limited

5-20 (Objectives 5-2, 5-3, 5-6) The following are miscellaneous questions from this chapter. Choose the best response.

a. An auditor most likely would analyze inventory turnover rates to obtain evidence concerning management's assertions about
(1) existence or occurrence.
(2) rights and obligations.
(3) valuation or allocation.
(4) presentation and disclosure.

b. The audit client's board of directors and audit committee refused to take any action with respect to an immaterial illegal act that was brought to their attention by the auditor. Because of their failure to act, the auditor withdrew from the engagement. The auditor's decision to withdraw was primarily because of doubts concerning
(1) inadequate financial statement disclosures.
(2) compliance with the Foreign Corrupt Practices Act of 1977.
(3) scope limitations resulting from their inaction.
(4) reliance on management's representations.

c. The primary responsibility for the adequacy of disclosure in the financial statements and footnotes rests with the
(1) partner assigned to the engagement.
(2) auditor in charge of field work.
(3) staff member who drafts the statements and footnotes.
(4) client.

DISCUSSION QUESTIONS AND PROBLEMS

5-21 (Objectives 5-2, 5-3) The following two reports are taken from the same page of a published annual report. (The first two paragraphs of a standard unqualified report have been omitted.)

REPORT OF MANAGEMENT

The management of American Express Company (the company) is responsible for the preparation and fair presentation of its Consolidated Financial Statements, which have been prepared in conformity with accounting principles generally accepted in the United States, and include amounts based on the best judgment of management. The company's management is also responsible for the accuracy and consistency of other financial information included in this annual report.

In recognition of its responsibility for the integrity and objectivity of data in the financial statements, the company maintains a system of internal control over financial reporting which is designed to provide reasonable, but not absolute, assurance with respect to the reliability of the company's financial statements. The concept of reasonable assurance is based on the notion that the cost of the internal control system should not exceed the benefits derived.

The internal control system is founded on an ethical climate and includes: (i) an organizational structure with clearly defined lines of responsibility, policies and procedures; (ii) a Code of Conduct; and (iii) the careful selection and training of employees. Internal auditors monitor and assess the effectiveness of the internal control system and report their findings to management and the Board of Directors throughout the year. The company's independent auditors are engaged to express an opinion on the year-end financial statements and, with the coordinated support of the internal auditors, review the financial records and related data and test the internal control system over financial reporting.

The Audit Committee of the Board of Directors, which has only outside directors, meets regularly with the internal auditors, management and independent auditors to review their work and discuss the company's financial controls and audit and reporting practices. The independent auditors and the internal auditors independently have full and free access to the Committee, without the presence of management, to discuss any matters which they feel require attention.

REPORT OF ERNST & YOUNG LLP INDEPENDENT AUDITORS
The Shareholders and Board of Directors of American Express Company

(First two paragraphs of standard unqualified report have been omitted.)

In our opinion, the financial statements referred to above present fairly, in all material respects, the consolidated financial position of American Express Company at December 31, 2000 and 1999, and the consolidated results of its operations and its cash flows for each of the three years in the period ended December 31, 2000, in conformity with accounting principles generally accepted in the United States.

Ernst & Young LLP
New York, New York
February 8, 2001

Required

a. What are the purposes of the two reports and who was responsible for writing each?
b. What information does the report of management provide to users of financial statements?
c. Explain the purpose of the audit committee as described in the fourth paragraph of management's report. What is the relevance of the phrase "which has only outside directors"?
d. Is the audit report a standard wording unqualified, qualified—except for, or something else? Explain your answer.
e. How long after the balance sheet date did the CPA firm complete the audit field work?

5-22 **(Objectives 5-1, 5-3)** Often, questions have been raised "regarding the responsibility of the independent auditor for the discovery of fraud (including misappropriation of assets and fraudulent financial reporting), and concerning the proper course of conduct of the independent auditor when his or her audit discloses specific circumstances that arouse suspicion as to the existence of fraud."

Required

a. What are (1) the function and (2) the responsibilities of the independent auditor in the audit of financial statements? Discuss fully, but in this part do not include fraud in the discussion.
b. What are the responsibilities of the independent auditor for the detection of fraud? Discuss fully.
c. What is the independent auditor's proper course of conduct when the audit discloses specific circumstances that arouse suspicion as to the existence of fraud?*

5-23 **(Objectives 5-2, 5-3)** A competent auditor has done a conscientious job of conducting an audit, but because of a clever fraud by management, a material fraud is included in the financial statements. The fraud, which is an overstatement of inventory, took place over several years, and it covered up the fact that the company's financial position was rapidly declining. The fraud was accidentally discovered in the latest audit by an unusually capable audit senior, and the SEC was immediately informed. Subsequent investigation indicated that the company was actually near bankruptcy, and the value of the stock dropped from $26 per share to $1 in less than 1 month. Among the losing stockholders were pension funds, university endowment funds, retired couples, and widows. The individuals responsible for perpetrating the fraud were also bankrupt.

After making an extensive investigation of the audit performance in previous years, the SEC was satisfied that the auditor had done a high-quality audit and had followed generally accepted auditing standards in every respect. The commission concluded that it would be unreasonable to expect auditors to uncover this type of fraud.

Required

State your opinion as to who should bear the loss of the fraudulent financial reporting. Include in your discussion a list of potential bearers of the loss, and state why you believe they should or should not bear the loss.

5-24 **(Objective 5-4)** The following general ledger accounts are included in the trial balance for an audit client, Jones Wholesale Stationery Store.

Income tax expense
Income tax payable
Accounts receivable
Advertising expense
Travel expense
Accounts payable
Bonds payable
Common stock
Allowance for doubtful accounts
Inventory
Property tax expense
Interest expense
Depreciation expense—furniture and equipment
Retained earnings
Sales

*AICPA adapted.

Unexpired insurance	Salaries, office and general
Furniture and equipment	Telephone and fax expense
Cash	Bad debt expense
Notes receivable—trade	Insurance expense
Purchases	Interest receivable
Sales salaries expense	Interest income
Accumulated depreciation of furniture and equipment	Accrued sales salaries
	Rent expense
Notes payable	Prepaid interest expense
	Property tax payable

Required

a. Identify the accounts in the trial balance that are likely to be included in each transaction cycle. Some accounts will be included in more than one cycle. Use the format that follows.

Cycle	Balance Sheet Accounts	Income Statement Accounts
Sales and collection		
Acquisition and payment		
Payroll and personnel		
Inventory and warehousing		
Capital acquisition and repayment		

b. How would the general ledger accounts in the trial balance most likely differ if the company were a retail store rather than a wholesale company? How would they differ for a hospital or a government unit?

5-25 (Objectives 5-6, 5-8) The following are specific balance-related audit objectives applied to the audit of accounts receivable (a through h) and management assertions (1 through 5). The list referred to in the specific balance-related audit objectives is the list of the accounts receivable from each customer at the balance sheet date.

Specific Balance-Related Audit Objective

a. There are no unrecorded receivables.

b. Receivables have not been sold or discounted.

c. Uncollectible accounts have been provided for.

d. Receivables that have become uncollectible have been written off.

e. All accounts on the list are expected to be collected within 1 year.

f. Any agreement or condition that restricts the nature of trade receivables is known and disclosed.

g. All accounts on the list arose from the normal course of business and are not due from related parties.

h. Sales cutoff at year-end is proper.

Management Assertion

1. Existence or occurrence
2. Completeness
3. Valuation or allocation
4. Rights and obligations
5. Presentation and disclosure

Required

For each specific balance-related audit objective, identify the appropriate management assertion. (*Hint:* See Table 5-3.)

5-26 (Objectives 5-6, 5-7) The following are specific transaction-related audit objectives applied to the audit of cash disbursement transactions (a through f), management assertions (1 through 5), and general transaction-related audit objectives (6 through 11).

Specific Transaction-Related Audit Objective

a. Recorded cash disbursement transactions are for the amount of goods or services received and are correctly recorded.

b. Cash disbursement transactions are properly included in the accounts payable master file and are correctly summarized.

c. Recorded cash disbursements are for goods and services actually received.

d. Cash disbursement transactions are properly classified.

e. Existing cash disbursement transactions are recorded.

f. Cash disbursement transactions are recorded on the correct dates.

Management Assertion

1. Existence or occurrence
2. Completeness
3. Valuation or allocation
4. Rights and obligations
5. Presentation and disclosure

General Transaction-Related Audit Objective

6. Existence
7. Completeness
8. Accuracy
9. Classification
10. Timing
11. Posting and summarization

Required

a. Explain the differences among management assertions, general transaction-related audit objectives, and specific transaction-related audit objectives and their relationships to each other.

b. For each specific transaction-related audit objective, identify the appropriate management assertion.

c. For each specific transaction-related audit objective, identify the appropriate general transaction-related audit objective.

5-27 (Objective 5-8) The following are two specific balance-related audit objectives in the audit of accounts payable. The list referred to is the list of accounts payable taken from the accounts payable master file. The total of the list equals the accounts payable balance on the general ledger.

1. All accounts payable included on the list represent amounts due to valid vendors.
2. There are no unrecorded accounts payable.

Required

a. Explain the difference between these two specific balance-related audit objectives.

b. Which of these two specific balance-related audit objectives applies to the general balance-related audit objective of existence, and which one applies to completeness?

c. For the audit of accounts payable, which of these two specific balance-related audit objectives would usually be more important? Explain.

5-28 (Objective 5-8) The following are 9 general balance-related audit objectives for the audit of any balance sheet account (1 through 9) and 11 specific balance-related audit objectives for the audit of property, plant, and equipment (a through k).

General Balance-Related Audit Objective

1. Existence
2. Completeness
3. Accuracy
4. Classification
5. Cutoff
6. Detail tie-in
7. Realizable value
8. Rights and obligations
9. Presentation and disclosure

Specific Balance-Related Audit Objective

a. There are no unrecorded fixed assets in use.

b. The company has valid title to the assets owned.

c. Details of property, plant, and equipment agree with the general ledger.

d. Fixed assets physically exist and are being used for the purpose intended.

e. Property, plant, and equipment are recorded at the correct amount.

f. The company has a contractual right for use of assets leased.

g. Liens or other encumbrances on property, plant, and equipment items are known and disclosed.

h. Cash disbursements and/or accrual cutoff for property, plant, and equipment items are proper.
i. Expense accounts do not contain amounts that should have been capitalized.
j. Depreciation is determined in accordance with an acceptable method and is materially correct as computed.
k. Fixed asset accounts have been properly adjusted for declines in historical cost.

Required

a. What are the purposes of the general balance-related audit objectives and the specific balance-related audit objectives? Explain the relationship between these two sets of objectives.
b. For each general balance-related audit objective, identify one or more specific balance-related audit objectives. No letter can be used for more than one general balance-related audit objective.

INTERNET PROBLEM 5-1: ASSERTIONS AND EVIDENCE ASSOCIATED WITH NEW ASSURANCE SERVICES

Reference the CW site. Chapter 1 of the text includes a brief description of the new assurance service known as CPA ElderCare. The AICPA has developed a business plan for CPA ElderCare. This problem requires students to use the Internet to (1) identify possible performance criteria associated with a client living in a long-term care facility, (2) determine in what form and to whom CPAs would report findings, and (3) identify what assertions would be tested and how.

CHAPTER 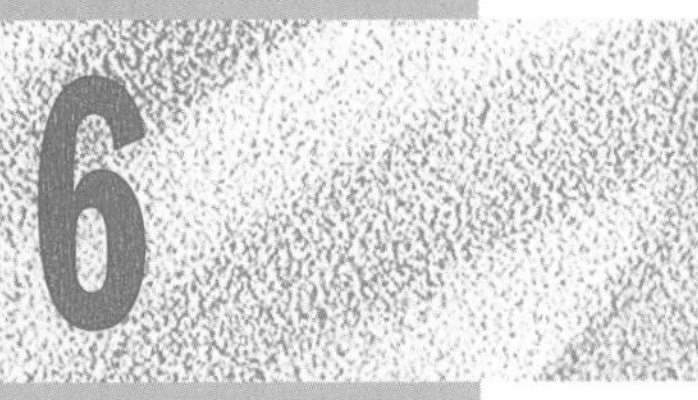

AUDIT EVIDENCE

LEARNING OBJECTIVES

After studying this chapter, you should be able to

- 6-1 Contrast audit evidence with evidence used by other professions.
- 6-2 Identify the four audit evidence decisions that are needed to create an audit program.
- 6-3 Specify the characteristics that determine the persuasiveness of evidence.
- 6-4 Identify and apply the seven types of evidence used in auditing.
- 6-5 Understand the purposes of audit documentation.
- 6-6 Prepare organized audit documentation.
- 6-7 Describe how e-commerce affects audit evidence and audit documentation.

SOMETIMES THE MOST IMPORTANT EVIDENCE IS NOT FOUND IN THE ACCOUNTING RECORDS

Crenshaw Properties was a real estate developer that specialized in self-storage facilities that it sold to limited partner investors. Crenshaw's role was to identify projects, serve as general partner with a small investment, and raise capital from pension funds. Crenshaw had an extensive network of people who marketed these investments on a commission basis. As general partner, Crenshaw earned significant fees for related activities, including promotional fees, investment management fees, and real estate commissions.

As long as the investments were successful, Crenshaw prospered. Because the investments were reasonably long-term, the underlying investors did not pay careful attention to them. However, in the mid-1980s, the market for self-storage units in many parts of the country became oversaturated. Occupancy rates, rental rates, and market values declined.

Ralph Smalley, of Hambusch, Robinson & Co., did the annual audit of Crenshaw. As part of the audit, Smalley obtained financial statements for all of the partnerships in which Crenshaw was the general partner. He traced amounts back to the original partnership documents and determined that amounts agreed with partnership records. Smalley also determined that they were mathematically accurate. The purpose of doing these tests was to determine that the partnership assets, at original cost, exceeded liabilities, including the mortgage on the property and loans from investors. Under the law, Crenshaw, as general partner, was liable for any deficiency.

Every year, Smalley concluded that there were no significant deficiencies in partnership net assets for which Crenshaw would be liable. What Smalley failed to recognize in the late 1980s, however, was that current market prices had declined significantly because cash flows were lower than those projected in the original partnership offering documents. In fact, Crenshaw went bankrupt in 1989, and Hambusch, Robinson & Co. was named in a suit to recover damages filed by the bankruptcy trustee.

The foundation of any audit is the evidence gathered and evaluated by the auditor. The auditor must have the knowledge and skill to accumulate sufficient competent evidence on every audit to meet the standards of the profession. As described in the opening vignette, Ralph Smalley learned the effect of not accumulating the appropriate evidence after being sued over his audit of Crenshaw Properties. This chapter deals with the types of evidence decisions auditors make, the evidence available to auditors, and the use of that evidence in performing audits.

NATURE OF EVIDENCE

OBJECTIVE 6-1

Contrast audit evidence with evidence used by other professions.

Evidence was defined in Chapter 1 as any *information used by the auditor* to determine whether the information being audited is stated in accordance with the established criteria. The information varies greatly in the extent to which it persuades the auditor whether financial statements are stated in accordance with generally accepted accounting principles. Evidence includes information that is highly persuasive, such as the auditor's count of marketable securities, and less persuasive information, such as responses to questions of client employees.

Audit Evidence Contrasted with Legal and Scientific Evidence

The use of evidence is not unique to auditors. Evidence is also used extensively by scientists, lawyers, and historians.

Through television, most people are familiar with the use of evidence in legal cases dealing with the guilt or innocence of a party charged with a crime such as robbery. In legal cases, there are well-defined rules of evidence enforced by a judge for the protection of the innocent. It is common, for example, for legal evidence to be judged inadmissible on the grounds that it is irrelevant, prejudicial, or based on hearsay.

Similarly, in scientific experiments, the scientist obtains evidence to draw conclusions about a theory. Assume, for example, that a medical scientist is evaluating a new medicine that may provide relief for asthma sufferers. The scientist will gather evidence from a large number of controlled experiments over an extended period to determine the effectiveness of the medicine.

The auditor also gathers evidence to draw conclusions. Different evidence is used by auditors than by scientists and in cases of law, and it is used in different ways, but in all

TABLE 6-1 Characteristics of Evidence for a Scientific Experiment, Legal Case, and Audit of Financial Statements

Basis of Comparison	Scientific Experiment Involving Testing a Medicine	Legal Case Involving an Accused Thief	Audit of Financial Statements
Use of the evidence	Determine effects of using the medicine	Decide guilt or innocence of accused	Determine whether statements are fairly presented
Nature of evidence used	Results of repeated experiments	Direct evidence and testimony by witnesses and parties involved	Various types of audit evidence generated by the auditor, third parties, and the client
Party or parties evaluating evidence	Scientist	Jury and judge	Auditor
Certainty of conclusions from evidence	Vary from uncertain to near certainty	Requires guilt beyond a reasonable doubt	High level of assurance
Nature of conclusions	Recommend or not recommend use of medicine	Innocence or guilt of party	Issue one of several alternative types of audit reports
Typical consequences of incorrect conclusions from evidence	Society uses ineffective or harmful medicine	Guilty party is not penalized or innocent party found guilty	Statement users make incorrect decisions and auditor may be sued

three cases, evidence is used to reach conclusions. Table 6-1 illustrates key characteristics of evidence from the perspective of a scientist doing an experiment, an attorney prosecuting an accused thief, and an auditor of financial statements. There are six bases of comparison. Note the similarities and differences among the three professions.

AUDIT EVIDENCE DECISIONS

OBJECTIVE 6-2

Identify the four audit evidence decisions that are needed to create an audit program.

A major decision facing every auditor is determining the *appropriate types and amounts* of evidence to accumulate to be satisfied that the components of the client's financial statements and the overall statements are fairly stated. This judgment is important because of the prohibitive cost of examining and evaluating all available evidence. For example, in an audit of financial statements of most organizations, it is impossible for the CPA to examine the contents of all computer files or available evidence such as cancelled checks, vendors' invoices, customer orders, payroll time cards, and the many other types of documents and records.

The auditor's *decisions* on evidence accumulation can be broken down into the following four subdecisions:

1. Which audit procedures to use
2. What sample size to select for a given procedure
3. Which items to select from the population
4. When to perform the procedures

Audit Procedures

An **audit procedure** is the detailed instruction for the collection of a type of audit evidence that is to be obtained at some time during the audit. In designing audit procedures, it is common to spell them out in sufficiently specific terms to permit their use as instructions during the audit. For example, the following is an audit procedure for the verification of cash disbursements:

- Obtain the cash disbursements journal and compare the payee name, amount, and date on the cancelled check with the cash disbursements journal.

Sample Size

Once an audit procedure is selected, it is possible to vary the sample size from one to all the items in the population being tested. In the preceding audit procedure, suppose 6,600 checks are recorded in the cash disbursements journal. The auditor might select a sample size of 50 checks for comparison with the cash disbursements journal. The decision of how many items to test must be made by the auditor for each audit procedure. The sample size for any given procedure is likely to vary from audit to audit.

Items to Select

After the sample size has been determined for an audit procedure, it is still necessary to decide which items in the population to test. If the auditor decides, for example, to select 50 cancelled checks from a population of 6,600 for comparison with the cash disbursements journal, several different methods can be used to select the specific checks to be examined. The auditor could (1) select a week and examine the first 50 checks, (2) select the 50 checks with the largest amounts, (3) select the checks randomly, or (4) select those checks that the auditor thinks are most likely to be in error. Or a combination of these methods could be used.

Timing

An audit of financial statements usually covers a period such as a year, and an audit is usually not completed until several weeks or months after the end of the period. The timing of audit procedures can therefore vary from early in the accounting period to long after it has ended. In part, the timing decision is affected by when the client needs the audit to be completed. In the audit of financial statements, the client normally wants the audit completed 1 to 3 months after year-end. The SEC requires that all public companies file audited financial statements with the SEC within 3 months of the companies' fiscal year-end. However, timing is also influenced by when the auditor believes the audit evidence will be most effective and when audit staff is available. For example, auditors often prefer to do counts of inventory as close to the balance sheet date as possible.

Audit procedures often incorporate sample size, items to select, and timing into the procedure. The following is a modification of the audit procedure previously used to include all four audit evidence decisions. (Italics identify the timing, items to select, and sample size decisions).

- Obtain the *October* cash disbursements journal and compare the payee name, amount, and date on the cancelled check with the cash disbursements journal for a *randomly selected sample of 40* check numbers.

Audit Program

Audit Programs Resource

The list of audit procedures for an audit area or an entire audit is called an **audit program.** The audit program always includes a list of the audit procedures. It usually also includes sample sizes, items to select, and the timing of the tests. Normally, there is an audit program, including several audit procedures, for each component of the audit. Therefore, there will be an audit program for accounts receivable, for sales, and so on. An example of an audit program that includes audit procedures, sample size, items to select, and timing is given on page 293 in Table 10-4. The right side of the audit program also includes the balance-related audit objectives for each procedure, as studied in Chapter 5.

Most auditors use computers to facilitate the preparation of audit programs. The simplest computer application involves typing the audit program on a word processor and saving it from one year to the next to facilitate changes and updating. A more sophisticated application involves the use of a specialized program designed to help the auditor think through the planning considerations of the audit and select appropriate procedures using audit program generator software.

PERSUASIVENESS OF EVIDENCE

OBJECTIVE 6-3

Specify the characteristics that determine the persuasiveness of evidence.

The third standard of field work that was introduced in Chapter 1 requires the auditor to accumulate *sufficient competent evidence to support the opinion issued.* Because of the nature of audit evidence and the cost considerations of doing an audit, it is unlikely that the auditor will be completely convinced that the opinion is correct. However, the auditor must be persuaded that the opinion is correct with a high level of assurance. By combining all evidence from the entire audit, the auditor is able to decide when he or she is persuaded to issue an audit report.

The two determinants of the **persuasiveness of evidence** are *competence* and *sufficiency,* which are taken directly from the third standard of field work.

Competence

Competence of evidence refers to the degree to which evidence can be considered believable or worthy of trust. If evidence is considered highly competent, it is a great help in persuading the auditor that financial statements are fairly stated. For example, if an auditor counted the inventory, that evidence would be more competent than if management gave the auditor its own figures. Most auditors, as well as the authors of this text, use the term **reliability of evidence** as being synonymous with competence.

Competence of evidence deals only with the audit procedures selected. Competence cannot be improved by selecting a larger sample size or different population items. It can be improved only by selecting audit procedures that contain a higher quality of one or more of the following seven characteristics of competent evidence.

Relevance Evidence must *pertain to or be relevant to the audit objective* that the auditor is testing before it can be reliable. For example, assume that the auditor is concerned that a client is failing to bill customers for shipments (completeness objective). If the auditor selected a sample of duplicate sales invoices and traced each to related shipping documents, the evidence would *not be relevant* for the completeness objective and therefore would not be considered reliable evidence for that objective. A relevant procedure would be to trace a sample of shipping documents to related duplicate sales invoices to determine whether each had been billed. The second audit procedure is relevant and the first is not because the shipment of goods is the normal criterion used for determining whether a sale has occurred and should have been billed. By tracing from shipping documents to duplicate sales invoices, the auditor can determine whether shipments have been billed to customers. When the auditor traces from duplicate sales invoices to shipping documents, it is impossible to find unbilled shipments.

Relevance can be considered only in terms of specific audit objectives. Evidence may be relevant to one audit objective but not to a different one. In the previous example, when the auditor traced from the duplicate sales invoices to related shipping documents, the evidence was relevant to the existence objective. Most evidence is relevant to more than one, but not all, audit objectives.

Independence of Provider Evidence obtained from a source outside the entity is more reliable than that obtained from within. For example, external evidence such as communications from banks, attorneys, or customers is generally considered more reliable than answers obtained from inquiries of the client. Similarly, documents that originate from outside the client's organization are considered more reliable than are those that originate within the company and have never left the client's organization. An example of the former is an insurance policy and of the latter a purchase requisition.

Effectiveness of Client's Internal Controls When a client's internal controls are effective, evidence obtained is more reliable than when they are weak. For example, if internal controls over sales and billing are effective, the auditor could obtain more competent evidence from sales invoices and shipping documents than if the controls were inadequate.

Auditor's Direct Knowledge Evidence obtained directly by the auditor through physical examination, observation, computation, and inspection is more competent than information obtained indirectly. For example, if the auditor calculates the gross margin as a percentage of sales and compares it with previous periods, the evidence would be more reliable than if the auditor relied on the calculations of the controller.

Qualifications of Individuals Providing the Information Although the source of information is independent, the evidence will not be reliable unless the individual providing it is qualified to do so. Therefore, communications from attorneys and bank confirmations are typically more highly regarded than accounts receivable confirmations from persons not familiar with the business world. Also, evidence obtained directly by the auditor may not be reliable if the auditor lacks the qualifications to evaluate the evidence. For example, examination of an inventory of diamonds by an auditor not trained to distinguish between diamonds and glass would not provide reliable evidence of the existence of diamonds.

Degree of Objectivity Objective evidence is more reliable than evidence that requires considerable judgment to determine whether it is correct. Examples of objective evidence include confirmation of accounts receivable and bank balances, the physical count of securities and cash, and adding (footing) a list of accounts payable to determine whether it agrees with the balance in the general ledger. Examples of subjective evidence include a letter written by a client's attorney discussing the likely outcome of outstanding lawsuits against the client, observation of obsolescence of inventory during physical examination, and inquiries of the credit manager about the collectibility of noncurrent accounts receivable. When the reliability of subjective evidence is being evaluated, the qualifications of the person providing the evidence are important.

Timeliness The timeliness of audit evidence can refer either to when it is accumulated or to the period covered by the audit. Evidence is usually more reliable for balance sheet accounts when it is obtained as close to the balance sheet date as possible. For example, the auditor's count of marketable securities on the balance sheet date would be more reliable than a count 2 months earlier. For income statement accounts, evidence is more reliable if there is a sample from the entire period under audit rather than from only a part of the period. For example, a random sample of sales transactions for the entire year would be more reliable than a sample from only the first 6 months.

Sufficiency

The *quantity* of evidence obtained determines its sufficiency. **Sufficiency of evidence** is measured primarily by the sample size the auditor selects. For a given audit procedure, the evidence obtained from a sample of 100 would ordinarily be more sufficient than from a sample of 50.

Several factors determine the appropriate sample size in audits. The two most important ones are the auditor's expectation of misstatements and the effectiveness of the client's internal controls. To illustrate, assume in the audit of Jones Computer Parts Co. that the auditor concludes that there is a high likelihood of obsolete inventory because of the nature of the client's industry. The auditor would sample more inventory items for obsolescence in an audit such as this than one where the likelihood of obsolescence was low. Similarly, if the auditor concludes that a client has effective rather than ineffective internal controls over recording fixed assets, a smaller sample size in the audit of acquisitions of fixed assets is warranted.

In addition to sample size, the individual items tested affect the sufficiency of evidence. Samples containing population items with large dollar values, items with a high likelihood of misstatement, and items that are representative of the population are usually considered sufficient. In contrast, most auditors would usually consider samples insufficient that contain only the largest dollar items from the population unless these items make up a large portion of the total population amount.

Combined Effect

The persuasiveness of evidence can be evaluated only after considering the combination of competence and sufficiency, including the effects of the factors influencing competence and sufficiency. A large sample of evidence provided by an independent party is not persuasive unless it is relevant to the audit objective being tested. A large sample of evidence that is relevant but not objective is also not persuasive. Similarly, a small sample of only one or two pieces of highly competent evidence also typically lacks persuasiveness. The auditor must evaluate the degree to which both competence and sufficiency, including all factors influencing them, have been met when determining the persuasiveness of evidence.

There are direct relationships among the four evidence decisions and the two qualities that determine the persuasiveness of evidence. Table 6-2 shows those relationships.

To illustrate the relationships shown in Table 6-2, assume an auditor is verifying inventory that is a major item in the financial statements. Generally accepted auditing standards require that the auditor be reasonably persuaded that inventory is not materially misstated. The auditor must therefore obtain a sufficient amount of competent evidence about inventory. This means deciding which procedures to use for auditing inventory to satisfy the competency requirements, as well as determining the appropriate sample size and items to select from the population to satisfy the sufficiency requirement. The combination of these four evidence decisions must result in sufficiently persuasive evidence to satisfy the auditor that inventory is materially correct. The audit program section for inventory will reflect these decisions. In practice, the auditor applies the four evidence decisions to specific audit objectives in deciding sufficient competent evidence.

Persuasiveness and Cost

In making decisions about evidence for a given audit, both persuasiveness and cost must be considered. It is rare when only one type of evidence is available for verifying information. The persuasiveness and cost of all alternatives should be considered before selecting the best type or types. The auditor's goal is to obtain a sufficient amount of competent evidence at the lowest possible total cost. However, cost is never an adequate justification for omitting a necessary procedure or not gathering an adequate sample size.

TABLE 6-2 Relationships Among Evidence Decisions and Persuasiveness

Audit Evidence Decisions	Qualities Affecting Persuasiveness of Evidence
Audit procedures and timing	Competence Relevance Independence of provider Effectiveness of internal controls Auditor's direct knowledge Qualifications of provider Objectivity of evidence Timeliness When procedures are performed Portion of period audited
Sample size and items to select	Sufficiency Adequate sample size Selecting appropriate population items

TYPES OF AUDIT EVIDENCE

OBJECTIVE 6-4

Identify and apply the seven types of evidence used in auditing.

In deciding which audit procedures to use, the auditor can choose from seven broad categories of evidence. These categories, called types of evidence, are listed below and defined and discussed in this section.

1. Physical examination
2. Confirmation
3. Documentation
4. Analytical procedures
5. Inquiries of the client
6. Reperformance
7. Observation

Before beginning the study of types of evidence, it is useful to show the relationships among auditing standards, which were studied in Chapter 1, types of evidence, and the four evidence decisions discussed earlier in this chapter. These relationships are shown in Figure 6-1.

Notice that the standards are general, whereas audit procedures are specific. Types of evidence are broader than procedures and narrower than the standards. Every audit procedure obtains one or more types of evidence.

Physical Examination

Physical examination is the inspection or count by the auditor of a *tangible asset.* This type of evidence is most often associated with inventory and cash, but it is also applicable to the verification of securities, notes receivable, and tangible fixed assets. The distinction between the physical examination of assets, such as marketable securities and cash, and the

FIGURE 6-1 Relationships Among Auditing Standards, Types of Evidence, and the Four Audit Evidence Decisions

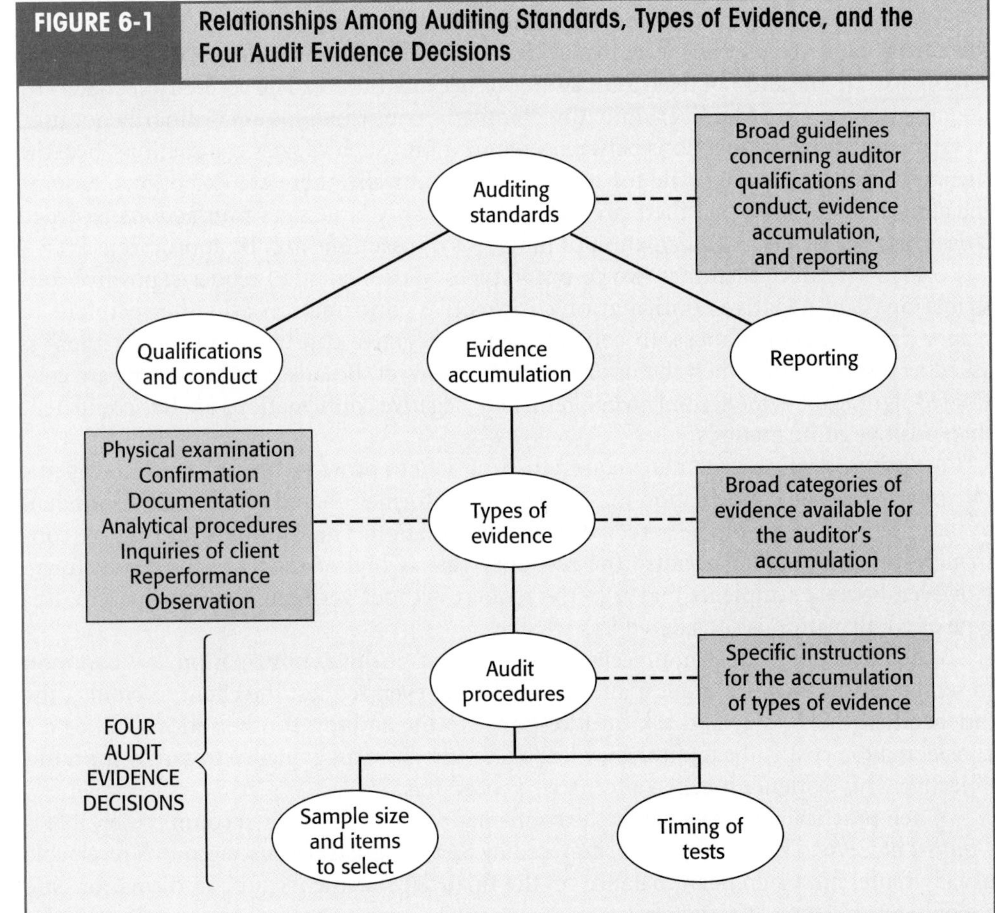

examination of documents, such as cancelled checks and sales documents, is important for auditing purposes. If the object being examined, such as a sales invoice, has no inherent value, the evidence is called documentation. For example, before a check is signed, it is a document; after it is signed, it becomes an asset; and when it is cancelled, it becomes a document again. Technically, physical examination of the check can occur only while the check is an asset.

Physical examination, which is a direct means of verifying that an asset actually exists (existence objective), is regarded as one of the most reliable and useful types of audit evidence. Generally, physical examination is an objective means of ascertaining both the quantity and the description of the asset. In some cases, it is also a useful method for evaluating an asset's condition or quality. However, physical examination is not sufficient evidence to verify that existing assets are owned by the client (rights and obligations objective), and in many cases the auditor is not qualified to judge qualitative factors such as obsolescence or authenticity (net realizable value objective). Also, proper valuation for financial statement purposes usually cannot be determined by physical examination (accuracy objective).

Confirmation

Confirmation describes the *receipt* of a *written or oral response* from an *independent third party* verifying the accuracy of information that was *requested by the auditor*. The request is made to the client, and the client asks the independent third party to respond directly to the auditor. Because confirmations come from sources independent of the client, they are a highly regarded and often-used type of evidence. However, confirmations are relatively costly to obtain and may cause some inconvenience to those asked to supply them. Therefore, they are not used in every instance in which they are applicable. Because of the high reliability of confirmations, auditors typically obtain written responses rather than oral ones when it is practical. Written confirmations are easier for supervisors to review, and they provide better support if it is necessary to demonstrate that a confirmation was received.

Whether or not confirmations should be used depends on the reliability needs of the situation as well as the alternative evidence available. Traditionally, confirmations are seldom used in the audit of fixed asset additions because these can be verified adequately by documentation and physical examination. Similarly, confirmations are ordinarily not used to verify individual transactions between organizations, such as sales transactions, because the auditor can use documents for that purpose. Naturally, there are exceptions. Assume the auditor determines that there are two extraordinarily large sales transactions recorded 3 days before year-end. Confirmation of these two transactions may be appropriate.

SAS 67 (AU 330) identifies two common types of confirmation requests: positive confirmations and negative confirmations. A positive confirmation asks the recipient to respond in all circumstances. In contrast, with a negative confirmation the recipient is asked to respond only when the information is incorrect. Because confirmations are considered significant evidence only when returned, negative confirmations are less competent than positive confirmations.

A positive confirmation may request the recipient to provide the information (called a blank form), or the confirmation may include the information and request the respondent to indicate whether he or she agrees with the information. The latter type of positive confirmation is often used because the response rate is higher than for the blank form. However, because recipients may sign the request without verifying the information, this type of confirmation is considered less reliable.

When the auditor does not receive a response to a positive confirmation, it is common to send a second or third request and in some cases even request the client to contact the independent third party and ask for a response to the auditor. If other efforts fail or are considered too costly, the auditor may be able to use different evidence to satisfy the audit objective. This evidence is called alternative procedures.

When practical and reasonable, the confirmation of a sample of accounts receivable is *required* of CPAs. This requirement, imposed by SAS 67, exists because accounts receivable usually represent a significant balance on the financial statements, and confirmations are a highly reliable type of evidence.

TABLE 6-3	Information Often Confirmed
INFORMATION	**SOURCE**
Assets	
Cash in bank	Bank
Accounts receivable	Customer
Notes receivable	Maker
Owned inventory out on consignment	Consignee
Inventory held in public warehouses	Public warehouse
Cash surrender value of life insurance	Insurance company
Liabilities	
Accounts payable	Creditor
Notes payable	Lender
Advances from customers	Customer
Mortgages payable	Mortgagor
Bonds payable	Bondholder
Owners' Equity	
Shares outstanding	Registrar and transfer agent
Other Information	
Insurance coverage	Insurance company
Contingent liabilities	Bank, lender, and client's legal counsel
Bond indenture agreements	Bondholder
Collateral held by creditors	Creditor

Although confirmation is not required for any account other than accounts receivable, this type of evidence is useful in verifying many types of information. The major types of information that are often confirmed, along with the source of the confirmation, are indicated in Table 6-3.

To be considered reliable evidence, confirmations must be controlled by the auditor from the time they are prepared until they are returned. If the client controls the preparation of the confirmation, does the mailing, or receives the responses, the auditor has lost control and with it independence; thus, the reliability of the evidence is reduced.

Documentation

Documentation is the auditor's examination of the *client's documents and records* to substantiate the information that is or should be included in the financial statements. The documents examined by the auditor are the records used by the client to provide information for conducting its business in an organized manner. Because each transaction in the client's organization is normally supported by at least one document, there is a large volume of this type of evidence available. For example, the client often retains a customer order, a shipping document, and a duplicate sales invoice for each sales transaction. These same documents are useful evidence for verification by the auditor of the accuracy of the client's records for sales transactions. Documentation is a form of evidence widely used in every audit because it is usually readily available to the auditor at a relatively low cost. Sometimes it is the only reasonable type of evidence available.

Documents can be conveniently classified as internal and external. An **internal document** is one that has been prepared and used within the client's organization and is retained without ever going to an outside party such as a customer or a vendor. Examples of internal documents include duplicate sales invoices, employees' time reports, and inventory receiving reports. An **external document** is one that has been in the hands of someone outside the client's organization who is a party to the transaction being documented, but which is either currently in the hands of the client or readily accessible. In some cases, external documents originate outside the client's organization and end up in the hands of the client. Examples of this type of external document are vendors' invoices, cancelled notes payable, and insurance policies. Other documents, such as cancelled checks, originate with the client, go to an outsider, and are finally returned to the client.

The primary determinant of the auditor's willingness to accept a document as reliable evidence is whether it is internal or external and, when internal, whether it was created and processed under conditions of good internal control. Internal documents created and processed under conditions of weak internal control may not constitute reliable evidence.

Because external documents have been in the hands of both the client and another party to the transaction, there is some indication that both members are in agreement about the information and the conditions stated on the document. Therefore, external documents are considered more reliable evidence than internal ones. Some external documents have exceptional reliability because they are prepared with considerable care and often have been reviewed by attorneys or other qualified experts. Examples include title papers to property such as land, insurance policies, indenture agreements, and contracts.

When auditors use documentation to support recorded transactions or amounts, it is often called **vouching.** To vouch recorded acquisition transactions, the auditor might, for example, trace from the acquisitions journal to supporting vendors' invoices and receiving reports and thereby satisfy the existence objective. If the auditor traces from receiving reports to the acquisitions journal to satisfy the completeness objective, it would not be appropriate to call it vouching.

Electronic Evidence

It is common in many companies for a considerable portion of clients' documentation to be available only in electronic form. For example, some companies use Electronic Data Interchange (EDI) to transact business electronically and complete purchase, shipping, billing, cash receipt, and cash disbursement transactions entirely by the exchange of electronic messages. Companies also use image processing systems to convert traditional documents into electronic images to facilitate storage and reference. Typically, the traditional documents are not retained.

Both written and electronic information, such as records of electronic transfers, are valid and useful. SAS 80 recognizes these changes in the nature of documentary audit evidence.

Analytical Procedures

Analytical procedures use comparisons and relationships to assess whether account balances or other data appear reasonable. An example is comparing the gross margin percent in the current year with the preceding year's. Analytical procedures are used extensively in practice and their use has increased with the availability of computers to perform the calculations. The Auditing Standards Board has concluded that analytical procedures are so important that they are *required during the planning and completion phases on all audits.* Analytical procedures are used for different purposes on an audit. The purposes are discussed next.

Understand the Client's Industry and Business Auditors must obtain knowledge about a client's industry and business as a part of planning an audit. By conducting analytical procedures in which the current year's unaudited information is compared with prior years' audited information or industry data, changes are highlighted. These changes can represent important trends or specific events, all of which will influence audit planning. For example, a decline in gross margin percentages over time may indicate increasing competition in the company's market area and the need to consider inventory pricing more carefully during the audit. Similarly, an increase in the balance in fixed assets may indicate a significant acquisition that must be reviewed.

Industry Information

Assess the Entity's Ability to Continue as a Going Concern Analytical procedures are often useful as an indication that the client company has financial problems. Certain analytical procedures can be helpful to the auditor in assessing the likelihood of failure. For example, if a higher-than-normal ratio of long-term debt to net worth is combined with a lower-than-average ratio of profits to total assets, a relatively high risk of financial failure may be indicated. Not only would such conditions affect the audit plan, they may indicate that substantial doubt exists about the entity's ability to continue as a going concern, which, as discussed in Chapter 2, would require a report modification.

Indicate the Presence of Possible Misstatements in the Financial Statements Significant unexpected differences between the current year's unaudited financial data and other data used in comparisons are commonly called **unusual fluctuations.** Unusual fluctuations occur when significant differences are not expected but do exist or when significant differences are expected but do not exist. In either case, one of the possible reasons for an unusual fluctuation is the presence of an accounting misstatement. Thus, if the unusual fluctuation is large, the auditor must determine the reason and be satisfied that the cause is a valid economic event and not a misstatement. For example, in comparing the ratio of the allowance for uncollectible accounts receivable to gross accounts receivable with that of the previous year, suppose that the ratio had decreased while, at the same time, accounts receivable turnover also decreased. The combination of these two pieces of information would indicate a possible understatement of the allowance. This aspect of analytical procedures is often called attention directing because it results in more detailed procedures in the specific audit areas where misstatements might be found.

Reduce Detailed Audit Tests When an analytical procedure reveals no unusual fluctuations, the implication is that the possibility of a material misstatement is minimized. In that case, the analytical procedure constitutes substantive evidence in support of the fair statement of the related account balances, and it is possible to perform fewer detailed tests in connection with those accounts. For example, if analytical procedures results of a small account balance such as prepaid insurance are favorable, no detailed tests may be necessary. In other cases, certain audit procedures can be eliminated, sample sizes can be reduced, or the timing of the procedures can be moved farther away from the balance sheet date.

Inquiries of the Client

Inquiry is the obtaining of *written* or *oral* information from the client in response to questions from the auditor. Although considerable evidence is obtained from the client through inquiry, it usually cannot be regarded as conclusive because it is not from an independent source and may be biased in the client's favor. Therefore, when the auditor obtains evidence through inquiry, it is normally necessary to obtain further corroborating evidence through other procedures. As an illustration, when the auditor wants to obtain information about the client's method of recording and controlling accounting transactions, the auditor usually begins by asking the client how the internal controls operate. Later, the auditor performs audit tests using documentation and observation to determine whether the transactions are recorded (completeness objective) and authorized (existence objective) in the manner stated.

Reperformance

As the word implies, **reperformance** involves rechecking a sample of the computations and transfers of information made by the client during the period under audit. Rechecking of computations consists of testing the client's arithmetical accuracy. It includes such procedures as extending sales invoices and inventory, adding journals and subsidiary records, and checking the calculation of depreciation expense and prepaid expenses. Rechecking of transfers of information consists of tracing amounts to be confident that when the same information is included in more than one place, it is recorded at the same amount each time. For example, the auditor normally makes limited tests to ascertain that the information in the sales journal has been included for the proper customer and at the correct amount in the subsidiary accounts receivable records and is accurately summarized in the general ledger. A considerable portion of auditors' reperformance is done by computer-assisted audit software.

Observation

Observation is the use of the senses to assess certain activities. Throughout the audit, there are many opportunities to exercise sight, hearing, touch, and smell to evaluate a wide range of items. For example, the auditor may tour the plant to obtain a general impression of the client's facilities, observe whether equipment is rusty to evaluate whether it is obsolete, and watch individuals perform accounting tasks to determine whether the person assigned a responsibility is performing it. Observation is rarely sufficient by itself because there is a risk that the client personnel involved in those activities are aware of the auditor's presence. Therefore, they may perform their responsibilities in accordance with company policy but resume normal activities once the auditor is not in sight. It is necessary to follow up initial impressions with other kinds of corroborative evidence. Nevertheless, observation is useful in most parts of the audit.

Competence of Types of Evidence

The characteristics discussed earlier in the chapter for determining the competence of evidence are related to the seven types of evidence in Table 6-4. Note that two of the characteristics that determine the competency of evidence—relevance and timeliness—are not included in Table 6-4. Each of the seven types of evidence included in the table has the potential to be both relevant and timely, depending on its source and when the evidence is obtained. Several other observations are apparent from a study of Table 6-4.

First, the effectiveness of the client's internal controls has a significant impact on the competence of most types of evidence. For example, internal documentation from a company with effective internal control is more reliable because the documents are more likely to be accurate. Similarly, analytical procedures will not be competent evidence if the controls that produced the data provide inaccurate information.

Second, both physical examination and reperformance are likely to be highly reliable if the internal controls are effective, but their use differs considerably. These two types of evidence effectively illustrate that equally reliable evidence may be completely different.

Third, a specific type of evidence is rarely sufficient by itself to provide competent evidence to satisfy any audit objective. It is apparent from examining Table 6-4 that observation, inquiries of the client, and analytical procedures are examples of this.

Cost of Types of Evidence

The two most expensive types of evidence are physical examination and confirmation. Physical examination is costly because it normally requires the auditor's presence when the client is counting the asset, often on the balance sheet date. For example, physical examination of inventory can result in several auditors traveling to widely separated geographical locations. Confirmation is costly because the auditor must follow careful procedures in the confirmation preparation, mailing, and receipt, and in the follow-up of nonresponses and exceptions.

Documentation and analytical procedures are moderately costly. If client personnel locate documents for the auditor and organize them for convenient use, documentation

TABLE 6-4 Competence of Types of Evidence

	Criteria to Determine Competence				
Type of Evidence	**Independence of Provider**	**Effectiveness of Client's Internal Controls**	**Auditor's Direct Knowledge**	**Qualifications of Provider**	**Objectivity of Evidence**
Physical examination	High (auditor does)	Varies	High	Normally high (auditor does)	High
Confirmation	High	Not applicable	Low	Varies—usually high	High
Documentation	Varies—external more independent than internal	Varies	Low	Varies	High
Analytical procedures	High/low (auditor does/ client responds)	Varies	Low	Normally high (auditor does/ client responds)	Varies—usually low
Inquiries of client	Low (client provides)	Not applicable	Low	Varies	Varies—low to high
Reperformance	High (auditor does)	Varies	High	High (auditor does)	High
Observation	High (auditor does)	Varies	High	Normally high (auditor does)	Medium

usually has a fairly low cost. When auditors must find those documents themselves, documentation can be extremely costly. Even under ideal circumstances, information and data on documents are sometimes complex and require interpretation and analysis. For example, it is usually time-consuming to read and evaluate a client's contracts, lease agreements, and minutes of the board of directors meetings. Analytical procedures are considerably less expensive than confirmations and physical examination. Therefore, most auditors prefer to replace tests of details with analytical procedures when possible. To illustrate, it may be far less expensive to calculate and review sales and accounts receivable ratios than to confirm accounts receivable. If it is possible to reduce or replace confirmation by performing analytical procedures, considerable cost savings can occur. But analytical procedures require the auditor to decide which analytical procedures to use, make the calculations, and evaluate the results. Doing so often takes considerable time.

The three least-expensive types of evidence are observation, inquiries of the client, and reperformance. Observation is normally done concurrently with other audit procedures. An auditor can easily observe whether client personnel are following appropriate inventory counting procedures at the same time he or she counts a sample of inventory (physical examination). Inquiries of clients are done extensively on every audit and normally have a low cost. Certain inquiries may be costly, such as obtaining written statements from the client documenting discussions throughout the audit. Reperformance is usually low cost because it involves simple calculations and tracing that can be done at the auditor's convenience. Often, the auditor's computer software is used to perform many of these tests.

Application of Types of Evidence to the Four Evidence Decisions

An application of three types of evidence to the four evidence decisions for one balance-related audit objective—inventory quantities on the client's perpetual records agree with items physically on hand—is shown in Table 6-5. First, examine column 3 in Table 5-3 on page 132. These are the balance-related audit objectives for the audit of inventory for Hillsburg Hardware Co. The overall objective is to obtain persuasive evidence at minimum cost that inventory is materially correct. The auditor must therefore decide which audit procedures to use to satisfy each balance-related audit objective, what the sample size should be for each procedure, which items from the population to include in the sample, and when to perform each procedure.

For the objective "inventory quantities on the client's perpetual records agree with items physically on hand," the auditor selected the three types of evidence included in Table 6-5. The auditor decided that the other four types of evidence studied in this chapter were not relevant or necessary for this objective. Only one audit procedure is included for each type of

TABLE 6-5 Types of Evidence and Four Evidence Decisions for a Balance-Related Audit Objective for Inventory*

		Evidence Decisions		
Type of Evidence	**Audit Procedure**	**Sample Size**	**Items to Select**	**Timing**
Observation	Observe client's personnel counting inventory to determine whether they are properly following instructions	All count teams	Not applicable	Balance sheet date
Physical examination	Count a sample of inventory and compare quantity and description to client's counts	120 items	40 items with large dollar value, plus 80 randomly selected	Balance sheet date
Documentation	Compare quantity on client's perpetual records to quantity on client's counts	70 items	30 items with large dollar value, plus 40 randomly selected	Balance sheet date

* Balance-related audit objective: Inventory quantities on the client's perpetual records agree with items physically on hand.

evidence, and illustrative decisions for sample size, items to select, and timing are shown for each procedure.

Terms Used in Audit Procedures

As stated earlier, audit procedures are the detailed steps, usually written in the form of instructions, for the accumulation of the seven types of audit evidence. They should be sufficiently clear to enable members of the audit team to understand what is to be done.

Several different terms are commonly used to describe audit procedures. These are presented and defined in Table 6-6. To help you understand each term, an illustrative audit procedure and the type of evidence that it is associated with are shown.

TABLE 6-6 Terms, Audit Procedures, and Types of Evidence

Term and Definition	Illustrative Audit Procedure	Type of Evidence
Examine—A reasonably detailed study of a document or record to determine specific facts about it.	*Examine* a sample of vendors' invoices to determine whether the goods or services received are reasonable and of the type normally used by the client's business.	Documentation
Scan—A less-detailed examination of a document or record to determine whether there is something unusual warranting further investigation.	*Scan* the sales journal, looking for large and unusual transactions.	Analytical procedures
Read—An examination of written information to determine facts pertinent to the audit.	*Read* the minutes of a board of directors meeting and summarize all information that is pertinent to the financial statements in a working paper.	Documentation
Compute—A calculation done by the auditor independent of the client.	*Compute* the inventory turnover ratios and compare with those of previous years as a test of inventory obsolescence.	Analytical procedures
Recompute—A calculation done to determine whether a client's calculation is correct.	*Recompute* the unit sales price times the number of units for a sample of duplicate sales invoices and compare the totals with the calculations.	Reperformance
Foot—Addition of a column of numbers to determine whether the total is the same as the client's.	*Foot* the sales journal for a 1-month period and compare all totals with the general ledger.	Reperformance
Trace—An instruction normally associated with documentation or reperformance. The instruction should state what the auditor is tracing and where it is being traced from and to. Often, an audit procedure that includes the term *trace* will also include a second instruction, such as *compare* or *recalculate.*	*Trace* a sample of sales transactions from the sales journal to sales invoices, and *compare* customer name, date, and the total dollar value of the sale. *Trace* postings from the sales journal to the general ledger accounts.	Documentation Reperformance
Compare—A comparison of information in two different locations. The instruction should state which information is being compared in as much detail as practical.	Select a sample of sales invoices and *compare* the unit selling price as stated on the invoice to the list of unit selling prices authorized by management.	Documentation
Count—A determination of assets on hand at a given time. This term should be associated only with the type of evidence defined as physical examination.	*Count* a sample of 100 inventory items and compare quantity and description to client's counts.	Physical examination
Observe—The act of observation should be associated with the type of evidence defined as observation.	*Observe* whether the two inventory count teams independently count and record inventory costs.	Observation
Inquire—The act of inquiry should be associated with the type of evidence defined as inquiry.	*Inquire* of management whether there is any obsolete inventory on hand at the balance sheet date.	Inquiries of client
Vouch—The use of documents to verify recorded transactions or amounts.	*Vouch* a sample of recorded acquisition transactions to vendors' invoices and receiving reports.	Documentation

AUDIT DOCUMENTATION

OBJECTIVE 6-5

Understand the purposes of audit documentation.

According to auditing standards, **audit documentation** is the *records kept by the auditor of the procedures applied, the tests performed, the information obtained, and the pertinent conclusions reached in the engagement.* Audit documentation should include all the information the auditor considers necessary to conduct the audit adequately and to provide support for the audit report. Audit documentation may also be referred to as working papers. Increasingly, audit documentation is maintained in computerized files.

Purposes of Audit Documentation

The overall objective of audit documentation is to aid the auditor in providing reasonable assurance that an adequate audit was conducted in accordance with generally accepted auditing standards (GAAS). More specifically, audit documentation, as it pertains to the current year's audit, provides a basis for planning the audit, a record of the evidence accumulated and the results of the tests, data for determining the proper type of audit report, and a basis for review by supervisors and partners.

If the auditor is to plan the current year's audit adequately, the necessary reference information must be available in the audit files. The files include such diverse planning information as descriptive information about internal control, a time budget for individual audit areas, the audit program, and the results of the preceding year's audit.

Audit documentation is the primary means of documenting that an adequate audit was conducted in accordance with GAAS. If the need arises, the auditor must be able to demonstrate to regulatory agencies and courts that the audit was well planned and adequately supervised; the evidence accumulated was competent, sufficient, and timely; and the audit report was proper, considering the results of the audit.

Audit documentation provides an important source of information to assist the auditor in deciding the appropriate audit report to issue in a given set of circumstances. The data in the files are useful for evaluating the adequacy of audit scope and the fairness of the financial statements. In addition, the audit files contain information needed to assist the client in the preparation of the financial statements.

The audit files are the primary frame of reference used by supervisory personnel to evaluate whether sufficient competent evidence was accumulated to justify the audit report. When audit procedures involve inspection of documents or confirmation of balances, the audit documentation should include an identification of the items tested. The audit files should also include documentation about significant audit findings or issues, actions taken to address them, and the basis for the conclusions reached. For example, the auditor may test several transactions at year-end to determine whether transactions were recorded in the proper period. The auditor should document the specific transactions tested. If misstatements are uncovered during these cutoff tests, the auditor should document additional procedures performed to determine the extent of cutoff misstatements, the conclusion as to whether the account balances affected are fairly stated, and whether any audit adjustments should be proposed.

In addition to the purposes directly related to the audit report, the audit files have other uses. They often serve as the basis for preparing tax returns, filings with the SEC, and other reports. They are a source of information for issuing communications to the audit committee and management concerning various matters such as internal control weaknesses or operations recommendations. Audit files are also a useful frame of reference for training personnel and as an aid in planning and coordinating subsequent audits.

Ownership of Audit Files

Audit documentation prepared during the engagement, including schedules prepared by the client for the auditor, is the *property of the auditor.* The only time anyone else, including the client, has a legal right to examine the files is when they are subpoenaed by a court as legal evidence. At the completion of the engagement, audit files are retained on the CPA's premises for future reference.

Confidentiality of Audit Files

The need to maintain a confidential relationship with the client is expressed in Rule 301 of the *Code of Professional Conduct,* which states

- A member shall not disclose any confidential information obtained in the course of a professional engagement except with the consent of the client.

During the course of the audit, auditors obtain a considerable amount of information of a confidential nature, including officers' salaries, product pricing and advertising plans, and product cost data. If auditors divulged this information to outsiders or to client employees who have been denied access, their relationship with management would be seriously strained. Furthermore, having access to the audit files would give employees an opportunity to alter information on them. For these reasons, care must be taken to protect the audit files at all times.

Ordinarily, audit documentation can be provided to someone else only with the express permission of the client. This is the case even if a CPA sells the practice to another CPA firm. Permission is not required from the client, however, if the audit documentation is subpoenaed by a court or is used as part of an AICPA or state society approved peer review program with other CPA firms.

THE BURDEN OF PROOF

Jury studies conducted by a professional liability insurance company in California show that jurors consider CPAs experts in documentation. Therefore, when practitioners are faced with a liability suit and have fallen short of that expectation, they are likely to be judged negligent. On the other hand, even an informal note documenting a brief telephone conversation can sway a jury in the CPA's favor. Legally, the burden of proof rests with the plaintiff, but as a practical matter, the burden to document falls on the CPA.

Source: Excerpted from an article by Ric Rosario, "Making Documentation Pay Off," *Journal of Accountancy* (February 1995), p. 70.

Contents and Organization

OBJECTIVE 6-6

Prepare organized audit documentation.

Each CPA firm establishes its own approach to preparing and organizing audit files, and the beginning auditor must adopt the firm's approach. The emphasis in this text is on the general concepts common to all audit documentation.

Figure 6-2 illustrates the contents and organization of a typical set of audit files. They contain virtually everything involved in the audit. There is a definite logic to the type of audit documentation prepared for an audit and the way it is arranged in the files, even though different firms may follow somewhat different approaches. In the figure, the audit files start with more general information, such as corporate data in the permanent files, and end with the financial statements and audit report. In between are the audit files supporting the auditor's tests.

Permanent Files

Permanent files are intended to contain data of a *historical or continuing nature* pertinent to the current audit. These files provide a convenient source of information about the audit that is of continuing interest from year to year. The permanent files typically include the following:

- Extracts or copies of such company documents of continuing importance as the articles of incorporation, bylaws, bond indentures, and contracts.
- Analyses, from previous years, of accounts that have continuing importance to the auditor.
- Information related to the understanding of internal control and assessment of control risk.
- The results of analytical procedures from previous years' audits.

Analytical procedures and the understanding of internal control and assessment of control risk are included in the current period audit files rather than in the permanent file by many CPA firms.

Current Files

The **current files** include all audit documentation applicable to the year under audit. There is one set of permanent files for the client and a set of current files for each year's audit. The types of information included in the current file are briefly discussed in the sections that follow.

Audit Program Auditing standards require a written audit program for every audit. The audit program is ordinarily maintained in a separate file to improve the coordination and integration of all parts of the audit, although some firms also include a copy of the audit program for each audit section with that section's audit documentation.

FIGURE 6-2 Audit File Contents and Organization

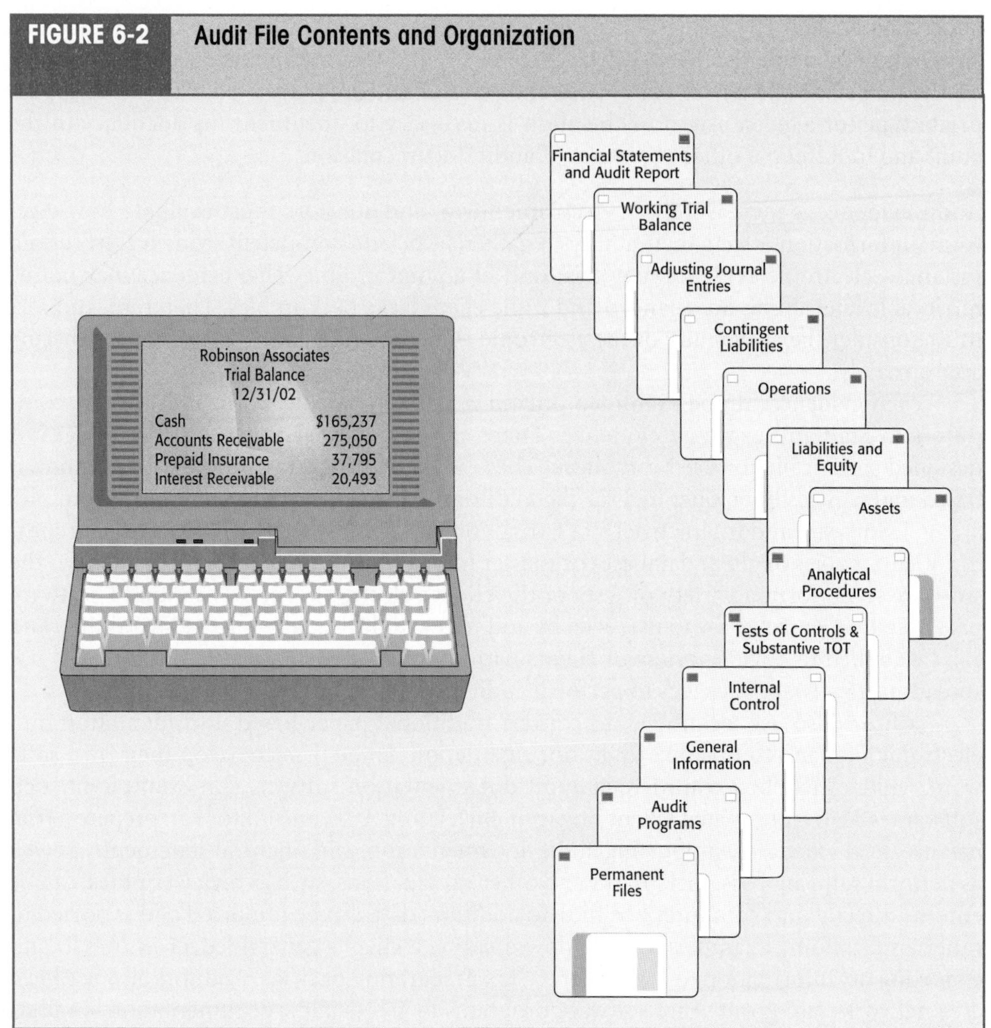

General Information This includes such items as audit planning memos, abstracts or copies of minutes of the board of directors meetings, abstracts of contracts or agreements not included in the permanent files, notes on discussions with the client, supervisors' review comments, and general conclusions.

Working Trial Balance Because the basis for preparing the financial statements is the general ledger, the amounts included in that record are the focal point of the audit. The technique used by many firms is to have the auditor's working trial balance in the same format as the financial statements. Each line item on the trial balance is supported by a **lead schedule,** containing the detailed accounts from the general ledger making up the line item total. Each detailed account on the lead schedule is, in turn, supported by appropriate schedules supporting the audit work performed and the conclusions reached.

Adjusting and Reclassification Entries When the auditor discovers material misstatements in the accounting records, the financial statements must be corrected. For example, if the client failed to properly reduce inventory for obsolete raw materials, an adjusting entry can be made by the auditor to reflect the realizable value of the inventory. Even though adjusting entries discovered in the audit are typically prepared by the auditor, they must be approved by the client because management has primary responsibility for the fair presentation of the statements.

Reclassification entries are frequently made in the statements to present accounting information properly, even when the general ledger balances are correct. A common example is the reclassification for financial statement purposes of material credit balances in accounts receivable to accounts payable.

Supporting Schedules The largest portion of audit documentation includes the detailed **supporting schedules** prepared by the client or the auditors in support of specific amounts on the financial statements. Many different types of schedules are used. Use of the appropriate type for a given aspect of the audit is necessary to document the adequacy of the audit and to fulfill the other objectives of audit documentation.

Effect of E-Commerce on Audit Evidence and Audit Documentation

OBJECTIVE 6-7

Describe how e-commerce affects audit evidence and audit documentation.

Audit evidence is increasingly in electronic form, and auditors must evaluate how electronic information affects their ability to gather sufficient, competent evidence. In certain instances, electronic evidence may exist only at a point in time. That evidence may not be retrievable later if files are changed and if the client lacks backup files. Therefore, auditors must consider the availability of the electronic evidence and plan their evidence gathering appropriately.

When evidence can be examined only in machine-readable form, auditors use computers to read and examine evidence. There are commercial audit software programs designed specifically for use by auditors. These software programs are typically Windows-based and can easily be operated on the auditor's desktop or laptop computer. Examples are ACL Software and Interactive Data Extraction and Analysis (IDEA) software. The auditor obtains copies of client databases or master files in machine-readable form and uses the software to perform a variety of tests of the client's electronic data. These audit software packages are relatively easy to use, even by auditors with little audit-related IT training, and can be applied to a wide variety of clients with minimal customization. Auditors also use spreadsheet software packages to perform audit tests.

ACL
IDEA

Auditors also use technology to convert traditional paper-based documentation into electronic files and to organize audit documentation. Some firms develop their own software, while others buy commercial audit documentation software. An example of such software is ACE (Automated Client Engagement). Using ACE, an auditor can prepare a trial balance, lead schedules, supporting audit documentation, and financial statements, as well as perform ratio analysis. Tick marks and other explanations, such as reviewer notes, can be entered directly into computerized files. In addition, data can be imported and exported to other applications. Examples include downloading a client's general ledger into ACE and exporting tax information to a commercial tax preparation package. Auditors also use local area networks and groupshare software programs to access audit documentation simultaneously from remote locations.

SUMMARY OF AUDIT DOCUMENTATION

Audit documentation is an essential part of every audit for effectively planning the audit, providing a record of the evidence accumulated and the results of the tests, deciding the proper type of audit report, and reviewing the work of assistants. CPA firms establish their own policies and approaches to audit documentation to make sure that these objectives are met. High-quality CPA firms make sure that audit documentation is properly prepared and is appropriate for the circumstances in the audit.

ESSENTIAL TERMS

Analytical procedures—use of comparisons and relationships to assess whether account balances or other data appear reasonable

Audit documentation—the records kept by the auditor of the procedures applied, the tests performed, the information obtained, and the pertinent conclusions reached in the engagement

Audit procedure—detailed instruction for the collection of a type of audit evidence

Audit program—list of audit procedures for an audit area or an entire audit; the audit program always includes audit procedures and may also include sample sizes, items to select, and timing of the tests

Competence of evidence—the degree to which evidence can be considered believable or worthy of trust; evidence is competent when it is obtained (1) from a relevant source, (2) from an independent provider, (3) from a client with effective internal controls, (4) from the auditor's direct knowledge, (5) from qualified providers such as law firms and banks, (6) from objective sources, and (7) in a timely manner

Confirmation—the auditor's receipt of a written or oral response from an independent third party verifying the accuracy of information requested

Current files—all audit files applicable to the year under audit

Documentation—the auditor's examination of the client's documents and records to substantiate the information that is or should be included in the financial statements

External document—a document, such as a vendor's invoice, that has been used by an outside party to the transaction being documented and that the client now has or can easily obtain

Inquiry—the obtaining of written or oral information from the client in response to specific questions during the audit

Internal document—a document, such as an employee time report, that is prepared and used within the client's organization

Lead schedule—an audit schedule that contains the detailed accounts from the general ledger making up a line item total in the working trial balance

Observation—the use of the senses to assess certain activities

Permanent files—auditors' files that contain data of a *historical or continuing nature* pertinent to the current audit such as copies of articles of incorporation, bylaws, bond indentures, and contracts

Persuasiveness of evidence—the degree to which the auditor is convinced that the evidence supports the audit opinion; the two determinants of persuasiveness are the competence and sufficiency of the evidence

Physical examination—the auditor's inspection or count of a tangible asset

Reliability of evidence—see *competence of evidence*

Reperformance—the rechecking of a sample of the computations and transfers of information made by the client during the period under audit

Sufficiency of evidence—the quantity of evidence; appropriate sample size

Supporting schedules—detailed schedules prepared by the client or the auditor in support of specific amounts on the financial statements

Unusual fluctuations—significant unexpected differences indicated by analytical procedures between the current year's unaudited financial data and other data used in comparisons

Vouching—the use of documentation to support recorded transactions or amounts

REVIEW QUESTIONS

6-1 (Objective 6-1) Discuss the similarities and differences between evidence in a legal case and evidence in an audit of financial statements.

6-2 (Objective 6-2) List the four major evidence decisions that must be made on every audit.

6-3 (Objective 6-2) Describe what is meant by an audit procedure. Why is it important for audit procedures to be carefully worded?

6-4 (Objective 6-2) Describe what is meant by an audit program for accounts receivable. What four things should be included in an audit program?

6-5 (Objective 6-3) State the third standard of field work. Explain the meaning of each of the major phrases of the standard.

6-6 (Objective 6-3) Explain why the auditor can be persuaded only with a reasonable level of assurance, rather than convinced, that the financial statements are correct.

6-7 (Objective 6-3) Identify the two factors that determine the persuasiveness of evidence. How are these two factors related to audit procedures, sample size, items to select, and timing?

6-8 (Objective 6-3) Identify the seven characteristics that determine the competence of evidence. For each characteristic, provide one example of a type of evidence that is likely to be competent.

6-9 (Objective 6-4) List the seven types of audit evidence included in this chapter and give two examples of each.

6-10 (Objective 6-4) What are the four characteristics of the definition of a confirmation? Distinguish between a confirmation and external documentation.

6-11 (Objective 6-4) Distinguish between internal documentation and external documentation as audit evidence and give three examples of each.

6-12 (Objective 6-4) Explain the importance of analytical procedures as evidence in determining the fair presentation of the financial statements.

6-13 **(Objective 6-4)** Identify the most important reasons for performing analytical procedures.

6-14 **(Objective 6-4)** Your client, Harper Company, has a contractual commitment as a part of a bond indenture to maintain a current ratio of 2.0. If the ratio falls below that level on the balance sheet date, the entire bond becomes payable immediately. In the current year, the client's financial statements show that the ratio has dropped from 2.6 to 2.05 over the past year. How should this situation affect your audit plan?

6-15 **(Objective 6-4)** Distinguish between attention-directing analytical procedures and those intended to eliminate or reduce detailed substantive procedures.

6-16 **(Objective 6-4)** Explain why the statement "Analytical procedures are essential in every part of an audit, but these tests are rarely sufficient by themselves for any audit area" is correct or incorrect.

6-17 **(Objective 6-5)** List the purposes of audit documentation and explain why each purpose is important.

6-18 **(Objective 6-6)** Define what is meant by a permanent file, and list several types of information typically included. Why does the auditor not include the contents of the permanent file with the current year's audit file?

6-19 **(Objective 6-6)** Why is it essential that the auditor not leave questions or exceptions in the audit documentation without an adequate explanation?

6-20 **(Objective 6-5)** Who owns the audit files? Under what circumstances can they be used by other people?

6-21 **(Objective 6-5)** A CPA sells his auditing practice to another CPA firm and includes all audit files as a part of the purchase price. Under what circumstances is this a violation of the *Code of Professional Conduct*?

6-22 **(Objective 6-7)** How does the auditor read and evaluate information that is available only in machine-readable form?

6-23 **(Objective 6-7)** Explain the purposes and benefits of audit documentation software.

MULTIPLE CHOICE QUESTIONS FROM CPA EXAMINATIONS

6-24 **(Objectives 6-3, 6-4)** The following questions concern persuasiveness of evidence. Choose the best response.

a. Which of the following types of documentary evidence should the auditor consider to be the most reliable?
   (1) A sales invoice issued by the client and supported by a delivery receipt from an outside trucker.
   (2) Confirmation of an account payable balance mailed by and returned directly to the auditor.
   (3) A check, issued by the company and bearing the payee's endorsement, that is included with the bank statements mailed directly to the auditor.
   (4) An audit schedule prepared by the client's controller and reviewed by the client's treasurer.

b. The most reliable type of audit evidence that an auditor can obtain is
   (1) physical examination by the auditor.
   (2) calculations by the auditor from company records.
   (3) confirmations received directly from third parties.
   (4) external documents.

c. Audit evidence can come in different forms with different degrees of persuasiveness. Which of the following is the *least* persuasive type of evidence?
   (1) Vendor's invoice.
   (2) Bank statement obtained from the client.
   (3) Computations made by the auditor.
   (4) Prenumbered sales invoices.

d. Which of the following is the *least* persuasive documentation in support of an auditor's opinion?
   (1) Schedules of details of physical inventory counts conducted by the client.
   (2) Notation of inferences drawn from ratios and trends.
   (3) Notation of appraisers' conclusions documented in the auditor's files.
   (4) Lists of negative confirmation requests for which *no* response was received by the auditor.

6-25 **(Objectives 6-5, 6-6)** The following questions concern audit documentation. Choose the best response.

a. Which of the following is *not* a primary purpose of audit documentation?
   (1) To coordinate the audit.
   (2) To assist in preparation of the audit report.

(3) To support the financial statements.
(4) To provide evidence of the audit work performed.

b. During an audit engagement, pertinent data are compiled and included in the audit files. The audit files primarily are considered to be
(1) a client-owned record of conclusions reached by the auditors who performed the engagement.
(2) evidence supporting financial statements.
(3) support for the auditor's representations as to compliance with generally accepted auditing standards.
(4) a record to be used as a basis for the following year's engagement.

c. Although the quantity, type, and content of audit documentation will vary with the circumstances, audit documentation generally would include the
(1) copies of those client records examined by the auditor during the course of the engagement.
(2) evaluation of the efficiency and competence of the audit staff assistants by the partner responsible for the audit.
(3) auditor's comments concerning the efficiency and competence of client management personnel.
(4) auditing procedures followed and the testing performed in obtaining evidential matter.

DISCUSSION QUESTIONS AND PROBLEMS

6-26 **(Objective 6-4)** The following are examples of documentation typically obtained by auditors:

1. Vendors' invoices
2. General ledgers
3. Bank statements
4. Cancelled payroll checks
5. Payroll time cards
6. Purchase requisitions
7. Receiving reports (documents prepared when merchandise is received)
8. Minutes of the board of directors
9. Remittance advices
10. Signed W-4s (Employees' Withholding Exemption Certificates)
11. Signed lease agreements
12. Duplicate copies of bills of lading
13. Subsidiary accounts receivable records
14. Cancelled notes payable
15. Duplicate sales invoices
16. Articles of incorporation
17. Title insurance policies for real estate
18. Notes receivable

Required

a. Classify each of the preceding items according to type of documentation: (1) internal or (2) external.

b. Explain why external evidence is more reliable than internal evidence.

6-27 **(Objective 6-4)** The following are examples of audit procedures:

1. Review the accounts receivable with the credit manager to evaluate their collectibility.
2. Stand by the payroll time clock to determine whether any employee "punches in" more than one time.
3. Count inventory items and record the amount in the audit files.
4. Obtain a letter from the client's attorney addressed to the CPA firm stating that the attorney is not aware of any existing lawsuits.
5. Extend the cost of inventory times the quantity on an inventory listing to test whether it is accurate.
6. Obtain a letter from an insurance company to the CPA firm stating the amount of the fire insurance coverage on buildings and equipment.
7. Examine an insurance policy stating the amount of the fire insurance coverage on buildings and equipment.
8. Calculate the ratio of cost of goods sold to sales as a test of overall reasonableness of gross margin relative to the preceding year.
9. Obtain information about internal control by requesting the client to fill out a questionnaire.

10. Trace the total on the cash disbursements journal to the general ledger.
11. Watch employees count inventory to determine whether company procedures are being followed.
12. Examine a piece of equipment to make sure that a major acquisition was actually received and is in operation.
13. Calculate the ratio of sales commissions expense to sales as a test of sales commissions.
14. Examine corporate minutes to determine the authorization of the issue of bonds.
15. Obtain a letter from management stating that there are no unrecorded liabilities.
16. Review the total of repairs and maintenance for each month to determine whether any month's total was unusually large.
17. Compare a duplicate sales invoice with the sales journal for customer name and amount.
18. Add the sales journal entries to determine whether they were correctly totaled.
19. Make a petty cash count to make sure that the amount of the petty cash fund is intact.
20. Obtain a written statement from a bank stating that the client has $15,671 on deposit and liabilities of $500,000 on a demand note.

Required Classify each of the preceding items according to the seven types of audit evidence: (1) physical examination, (2) confirmation, (3) documentation, (4) analytical procedures, (5) inquiries of the client, (6) reperformance, and (7) observation.

6-28 **(Objective 6-4)** List two examples of audit evidence the auditor can use in support of each of the following:

a. Recorded amount of entries in the acquisitions journal

b. Physical existence of inventory

c. Accuracy of accounts receivable

d. Ownership of fixed assets

e. Liability for accounts payable

f. Obsolescence of inventory

g. Existence of petty cash

6-29 **(Objective 6-4)** Seven different types of evidence were discussed. The following questions concern the reliability (competence) of that evidence:

a. Explain why confirmations are normally more reliable evidence than inquiries of the client.

b. Describe a situation in which confirmation would be considered highly reliable and another in which it would not be reliable.

c. Under what circumstances is the physical observation of inventory considered relatively unreliable evidence?

d. Explain why reperformance tests are highly reliable but of relatively limited use.

e. Give three examples of relatively reliable documentation and three examples of less reliable documentation. What characteristics distinguish the two?

f. Give several examples in which the qualifications of the respondent or the qualifications of the auditor affect the reliability of the evidence.

g. Explain why analytical procedures are important evidence even though they are relatively unreliable by themselves.

6-30 **(Objective 6-4)** The following audit procedures were performed in the audit of inventory to satisfy specific balance-related audit objectives as discussed in Chapter 5. The audit procedures assume that the auditor has obtained the inventory count sheets that list the client's inventory. The general balance-related audit objectives from Chapter 5 are also included.

Audit Procedures

1. Test extend unit prices times quantity on the inventory list, test foot the list, and compare the total to the general ledger.
2. Trace selected quantities from the inventory list to the physical inventory to make sure that it exists and the quantities are the same.
3. Question operating personnel about the possibility of obsolete or slow-moving inventory.
4. Select a sample of quantities of inventory in the factory warehouse and trace each item to the inventory count sheets to determine if it has been included and if the quantity and description are correct.
5. Compare the quantities on hand and unit prices on this year's inventory count sheets with those in the preceding year as a test for large differences.

6. Examine sales invoices and contracts with customers to determine whether any goods are out on consignment with customers. Similarly, examine vendors' invoices and contracts with vendors to determine whether any goods on the inventory listing are owned by vendors.
7. Send letters directly to third parties who hold the client's inventory and request that they respond directly to the auditors.

General Balance-Related Audit Objectives

Existence
Completeness
Accuracy
Classification
Cutoff
Detail tie-in
Realizable value
Rights and obligations
Presentation and disclosure

Required

a. Identify the type of audit evidence used for each audit procedure.

b. Identify the general balance-related audit objective or objectives satisfied by each audit procedure.

6-31 (Objectives 6-3, 6-4) The following are nine situations, each containing two means of accumulating evidence:

1. Confirm receivables with consumers versus confirming accounts receivable with business organizations.
2. Physically examine 3-inch steel plates versus examining electronic parts.
3. Examine duplicate sales invoices when several competent people are checking each other's work versus examining documents prepared by a competent person on a one-person staff.
4. Physically examine inventory of parts for the number of units on hand versus examining them for the likelihood of inventory being obsolete.
5. Discuss the likelihood and amount of loss in a lawsuit against the client with client's in-house legal counsel versus discussion with the CPA firm's own legal counsel.
6. Confirm the oil and gas reserves with a geologist specializing in oil and gas versus confirming a bank balance.
7. Confirm a bank balance versus examining the client's bank statements.
8. Physically count the client's inventory held by an independent party versus confirming the count with an independent party.
9. Obtain a physical inventory count from the company president versus physically counting the client's inventory.

Required

a. Identify the seven factors that determine the competence of evidence.

b. For each of the nine situations, state whether the first or second type of evidence is more reliable.

c. For each situation, state which of the seven factors affected the competence of the evidence.

6-32 (Objective 6-4) Following are 10 audit procedures with words missing and a list of several terms commonly used in audit procedures.

Audit Procedures

1. _____ whether the accounts receivable bookkeeper is prohibited from handling cash.
2. _____ the ratio of cost of goods sold to sales and compare the ratio to previous years.
3. _____ the sales journal and _____ the total to the general ledger.
4. _____ the sales journal, looking for large and unusual transactions requiring investigation.
5. _____ of management whether all accounting employees are required to take annual vacations.
6. _____ the balance in the bank account directly with the East State Bank.
7. _____ all marketable securities as of the balance sheet date to determine whether they equal the total on the client's list.
8. _____ a sample of duplicate sales invoices to determine if the controller's approval is included and _____ each duplicate sales invoice to the sales journal for agreement of name and amount.
9. _____ the unit selling price times quantity on the duplicate sales invoice and compare the total to the amount on the duplicate sales invoice.
10. _____ the agreement between Johnson Wholesale Company and the client to determine whether the shipment is a sale or a consignment.

Terms

a. Examine	g. Trace
b. Scan	h. Compare
c. Read	i. Count
d. Compute	j. Observe
e. Recompute	k. Inquire
f. Foot	l. Confirm

Required

a. For each of the 12 blanks in procedures 1 through 10, identify the most appropriate term. No term can be used more than once.

b. For each of the procedures 1 through 10, identify the type of evidence that is being used.

6-33 (Objectives 6-5, 6-6) The preparation of audit documentation is an integral part of a CPA's audit of financial statements. On a recurring engagement, a CPA reviews audit programs and audit documentation from the prior audit while planning the current audit to determine their usefulness for the current engagement.

Required

a. What are the purposes or functions of audit documentation?

b. What records may be included in audit files?

c. What factors affect the CPA's judgment of the type and content of the audit files for an engagement?*

CASE

6-34 (Objective 6-4) Grande Stores is a large discount catalog department store chain. The company has recently expanded from 6 to 43 stores by borrowing from several large financial institutions and from a public offering of common stock. A recent investigation has disclosed that Grande materially overstated net income. This was accomplished by understating accounts payable and recording fictitious supplier credits that further reduced accounts payable. An SEC investigation was critical of the evidence gathered by Grande's audit firm, Montgomery & Ross, in testing accounts payable and the supplier credits.

The following is a description of some of the fictitious supplier credits and unrecorded amounts in accounts payable, as well as the audit procedures.

1. McClure Advertising Credits—Grande had arrangements with some vendors to share the cost of advertising the vendor's product. The arrangements were usually agreed to in advance by the vendor and supported by evidence of the placing of the ad. Grande created a 114-page list of approximately 1,100 vendors, supporting advertising credits of $300,000. Grande's auditors selected a sample of 4 of the 1,100 items for direct confirmation. One item was confirmed by telephone, one traced to cash receipts, one to a vendor credit memo for part of the amount and cash receipts for the rest, and one to a vendor credit memo. Two of the amounts confirmed differed from the amount on the list, but the auditors did not seek an explanation for the differences because the amounts were not material.

   The rest of the credits were tested by selecting 20 items (1 or 2 from each page of the list). Twelve of the items were supported by examining the ads placed, and 8 were supported by Grande debit memos charging the vendors for the promotional allowances.
2. Springbrook Credits—Grande created 28 fictitious credit memos totaling $257,000 from Springbrook Distributors, the main supplier of health and beauty aids to Grande. Grande's controller initially told the auditor that the credits were for returned goods, then said they were a volume discount, and finally stated they were a payment so that Grande would continue to use Springbrook as a supplier. One of the Montgomery & Ross staff auditors concluded that a $257,000 payment to retain Grande's business was too large to make economic sense.

   The credit memos indicated that the credits were for damaged merchandise, volume rebates, and advertising allowances. The audit firm requested a confirmation of the credits. In response, Jon Steiner, the president of Grande Stores, placed a call to Mort Seagal, the president of Springbrook, and handed the phone to the staff auditor. In fact, the call had been placed to an officer of Grande. The Grande officer, posing as Seagal, orally confirmed the credits. Grande refused to allow Montgomery & Ross to obtain written confirmations supporting the credits. Although the staff auditor doubted the validity of the credits, the audit partner, Mark Franklin, accepted the credits based on the credit memoranda, telephone confirmation of the credits, and oral representations of Grande officers.

* AICPA adapted.

3. Ridolfi Credits—$130,000 in credits based on 35 credit memoranda from Ridolfi, Inc., were purportedly for the return of overstocked goods from several Grande stores. A Montgomery & Ross staff auditor noted the size of the credit and that the credit memos were dated subsequent to year-end. He further noticed that a sentence on the credit memos from Ridolfi had been obliterated by a felt-tip marker. When held to the light, the accountant could read that the marked-out sentence read, "Do not post until merchandise received." The staff auditor thereafter called Harold Ridolfi, treasurer of Ridolfi, Inc., and was informed that the $130,000 in goods had not been returned and the money was not owed to Grande by Ridolfi. Steiner advised Franklin, the audit partner, that he had talked to Harold Ridolfi, who claimed he had been misunderstood by the staff auditor. Steiner told Franklin not to have anyone call Ridolfi to verify the amount because of pending litigation between Grande and Ridolfi, Inc.
4. Accounts Payable Accrual—Montgomery & Ross assigned a senior with experience in the retail area to audit accounts payable. Although Grande had poor internal control, Montgomery & Ross selected a sample of 50 for confirmation of the several thousand vendors who did business with Grande. Twenty-seven responses were received, and 21 were reconciled to Grande's records. These tests indicated an unrecorded liability of approximately $290,000 when projected to the population of accounts payable. However, the investigation disclosed that Grande's president made telephone calls to some suppliers who had received confirmation requests from Montgomery & Ross and told them how to respond to the request.

   Montgomery & Ross also performed a purchases cutoff test by vouching accounts payable invoices received for nine weeks after year-end. The purpose of this test was to identify invoices received after year-end that should have been recorded in accounts payable. Thirty percent of the sample ($160,000) was found to relate to the prior year, indicating a potential unrecorded liability of approximately $500,000. The audit firm and Grande eventually agreed on an adjustment to increase accounts payable by $260,000.

Required

Identify deficiencies in the sufficiency and competency of the evidence gathered in the audit of accounts payable of Grande Stores.

INTERNET PROBLEM 6-1: ELECTRONIC EVIDENCE

WWW

Reference the CW site. This problem requires students to use the Internet to research and consider how electronic evidence affects the audit process.

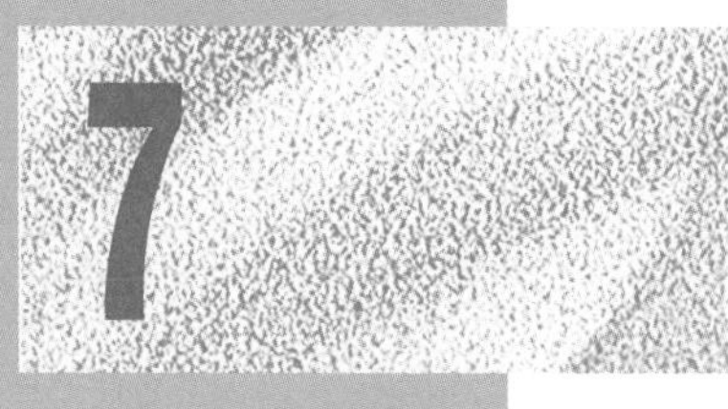

CHAPTER 7

AUDIT PLANNING AND ANALYTICAL PROCEDURES

THE FALL OF ENRON: DID ANYONE UNDERSTAND THEIR BUSINESS?

The bankruptcy of Enron Corporation, the nation's largest energy wholesaling company, represents the biggest corporate collapse in American history. Despite recently being listed as No. 7 on the Fortune 500 list with a market capitalization of $75 billion, the meltdown of Enron was rapid. The fall began in October 2001 when Enron officials reported a shocking $618 million quarterly loss related to allegedly mysterious and hidden related party partnerships with company insiders. Then, in early November 2001, company officials were forced to admit that they had falsely claimed almost $600 million in earnings dating back to 1997, requiring the restatement of four years of audited financial statements. By the end of 2001, the company was in bankruptcy.

Enron, which was created in 1985 out of a merger of two gas pipelines, was a pioneer in trading natural gas and electricity in the newly- deregulated utilities markets. In its earlier years, Enron made its money from hard assets like pipelines. However, by the end of the 1990s 80% of Enron's earnings were coming from a more vague business known as "wholesale energy operations and services." Enron had built new markets, such as trading of weather securities, and believed that it could handle trades for almost anything, including electrons and advertising space.

In early 2001, speculation about Enron's business dealings began to surface. One highly regarded investment banker publicly stated that no one could explain how Enron actually made money. Additionally, he pointed to an odd and opaque mention in Enron documents about transactions that Enron and other "Entities" had done with a "Related Party" that was run by a "senior officer of Enron." However, the disclosure was difficult to understand.

Now in the wake of the collapse, many are wondering how such problems could go undetected for so long. Many point to the incredibly complicated business structure at Enron and their related vague and confusing financial statements. "What we are looking at here is an example of superbly complex financial reports. They didn't have to lie. All they had to do was to obfuscate it with sheer complexity," noted John Dingell, U.S. Congressman from Michigan. Others even allege that the men running the company never even understood their business concept because it was too complicated.

Apparently the complexity and uncertainty surrounding Enron's business and financial statements fooled their auditors, too. Enron's auditor is facing a flurry of attacks and class action lawsuits accusing the firm of negligence. In December 2001 congressional testimony, the audit firm's CEO admitted that the firm's professional judgment "turned out to be wrong" and that they mistakenly let Enron keep the related entities separate when they should be consolidated.

Several lessons will likely come out of the Enron disaster. One to be underscored for auditors is the paramount importance of understanding the company's business and industry. Without that understanding, it's almost impossible to identify significant business risks impacting financial statements.

Source: Adapted from Bethany McLean, "Why Enron Went Bust," *Fortune* (December 24, 2001), pp. 58–68.

LEARNING OBJECTIVES

After studying this chapter, you should be able to

- 7-1 Discuss why adequate audit planning is essential.
- 7-2 Make client acceptance decisions and perform initial audit planning.
- 7-3 Gain an understanding of the client's business and industry.
- 7-4 Assess client business risk.
- 7-5 Perform preliminary analytical procedures.
- 7-6 State the purposes of analytical procedures and the timing of each purpose.
- 7-7 Select the most appropriate analytical procedure from among the five major types.
- 7-8 Compute common financial ratios.

As the chapter vignette illustrates, Enron's complex and confusing business structure helped disguise material misstatements in Enron financial statements for several years. Gaining an understanding of the client's business and industry is one of the most important steps in audit planning. This chapter explains audit planning in detail, including gaining an understanding of the client's business and industry, assessing client business risk, and performing preliminary analytical procedures.

PLANNING

OBJECTIVE 7-1

Discuss why adequate audit planning is essential.

The first generally accepted auditing standard of field work requires adequate planning.

> The work is to be adequately planned, and assistants, if any, are to be properly supervised.

There are three main reasons why the auditor should properly plan engagements: to enable the auditor to obtain sufficient competent evidence for the circumstances, to help keep audit costs reasonable, and to avoid misunderstandings with the client. Obtaining sufficient competent evidence is essential if the CPA firm is to minimize legal liability and maintain a good reputation in the business community. Keeping costs reasonable helps the firm remain competitive and thereby retain or expand its client base, assuming the firm has a reputation for doing high-quality work. Avoiding misunderstandings with the client is important for good client relations and for facilitating high-quality work at reasonable cost. For example, suppose that the auditor informs the client that the audit will be completed before June 30 but is unable to finish it until August because of inadequate scheduling of staff. The client is likely to be upset with the CPA firm and may even sue for breach of contract.

Figure 7-1 presents the seven major parts of audit planning. Each of the first six parts is intended to help the auditor develop the last part, an effective and efficient overall audit plan and audit program. The first four parts of the planning phase of an audit are studied in this chapter. The last three are studied separately in later chapters.

Before beginning the discussion of the first four parts of the planning phase, it is useful to briefly introduce two risk terms: *acceptable audit risk* and *inherent risk.* These two risks have a significant effect on the conduct and cost of audits. Much of the early planning on audits deals with obtaining information to help auditors assess these risks.

Acceptable audit risk is a measure of how willing the auditor is to accept that the financial statements may be materially misstated after the audit is completed and an unqualified opinion has been issued. When the auditor decides on a lower acceptable audit risk, it means that the auditor wants to be more certain that the financial statements are *not* materially misstated. Zero risk would be certainty, and a 100 percent risk would be complete uncertainty.

Inherent risk is a measure of the auditor's assessment of the likelihood that there are material misstatements in an account balance before considering the effectiveness of internal control. If, for example, the auditor concludes that there is a high likelihood of material misstatement in an account such as accounts receivable, the auditor would conclude that inherent risk for accounts receivable is high.

Assessments of acceptable audit risk and inherent risk are an important part of audit planning, because they affect the amount of evidence to be accumulated and staff to be assigned to the engagement. For example, if inherent risk for inventory is high because of complex valuation issues, more evidence will be accumulated in the audit of inventory and more experienced staff will be assigned to perform testing in this area.

ACCEPT CLIENT AND PERFORM INITIAL AUDIT PLANNING

OBJECTIVE 7-2

Make client acceptance decisions and perform initial audit planning.

Initial audit planning involves four things, all of which should be done early in the audit. First, the auditor decides whether to accept a new client or continue serving an existing one. This is typically done by an experienced auditor who is in a position to make important decisions. The auditor wants to make that decision early, before incurring any significant

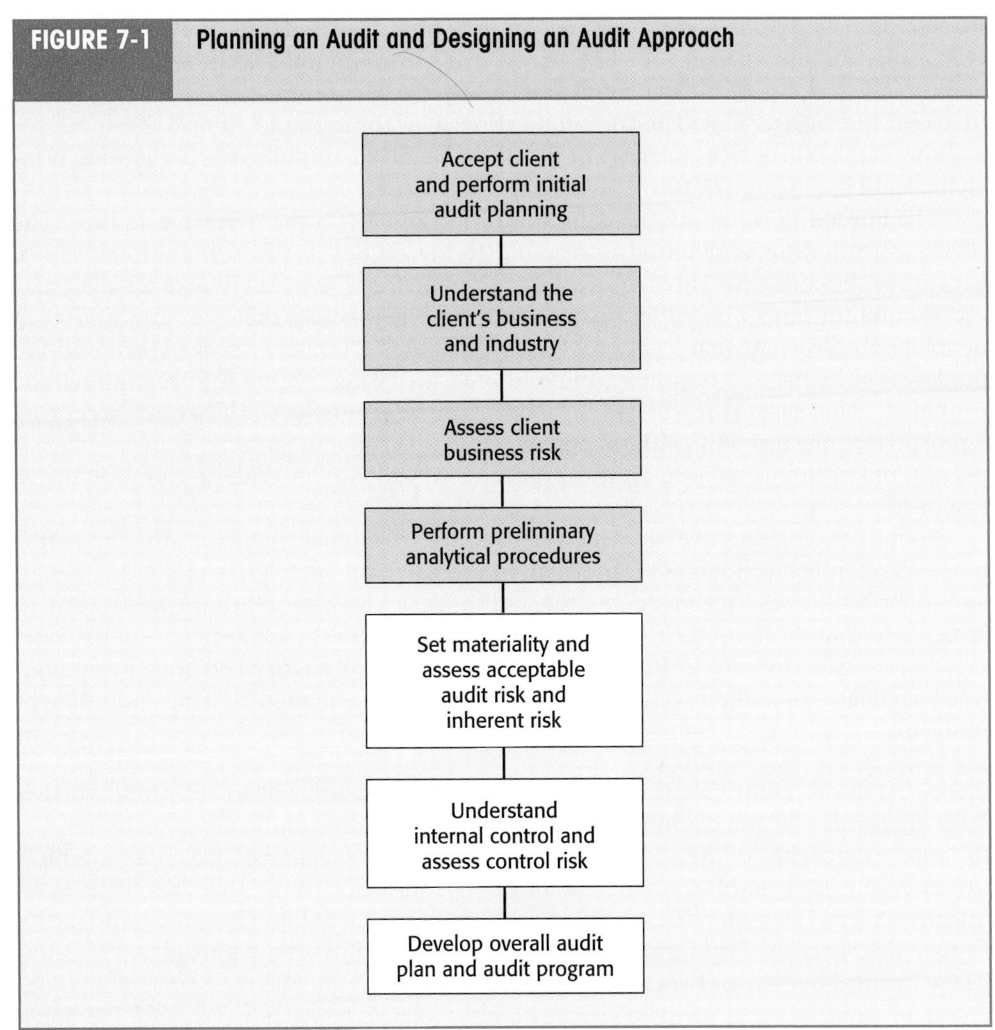

FIGURE 7-1 Planning an Audit and Designing an Audit Approach

costs that cannot be recovered. Second, the auditor identifies why the client wants or needs an audit. This information is likely to affect the remaining parts of the planning process. Third, the auditor obtains an understanding with the client about the terms of the engagement to avoid misunderstandings. Finally, the staff for the engagement is selected, including any required audit specialists.

Client Acceptance and Continuance

Even though obtaining and retaining clients is not easy in a competitive profession such as public accounting, a CPA firm must use care in deciding which clients are acceptable. The firm's legal and professional responsibilities are such that clients who lack integrity or argue constantly about the proper conduct of the audit and fees can cause more problems than they are worth. Some CPA firms now refuse any clients in certain high-risk industries, such as savings and loans, health, and casualty insurance companies, and may even discontinue auditing existing clients in those industries. Some smaller CPA firms will not do audits of publicly held clients because of the risk of litigation. Stated in terms of audit risk, an auditor is unlikely to accept a new client or continue serving an existing client if acceptable audit risk is lower than the CPA firm's threshold.

New Client Investigation Before accepting a new client, most CPA firms investigate the company to determine its acceptability. To the extent possible, the prospective client's standing in the business community, financial stability, and relations with its previous CPA firm should be evaluated. For example, many CPA firms use considerable caution in accepting new clients in newly formed, rapidly growing businesses. Many of these businesses fail financially and expose the CPA firm to significant potential liability.

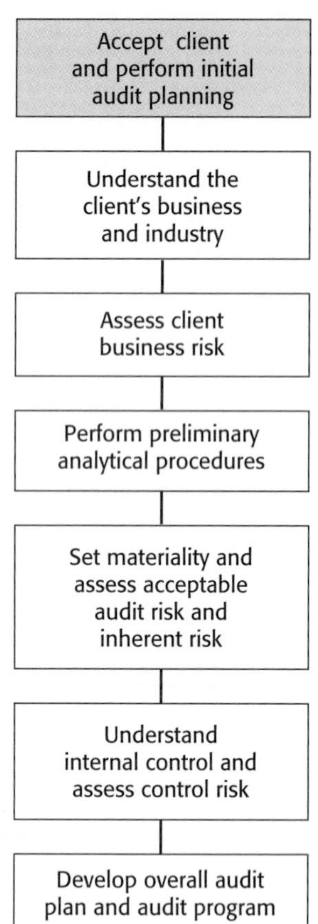

For prospective clients that have previously been audited by another CPA firm, the new (successor) auditor is *required* by SAS 84 (AU 315) to communicate with the predecessor auditor. The purpose of the requirement is to help the successor auditor evaluate whether to accept the engagement. The communication may, for example, inform the successor auditor that the client lacks integrity or that there have been disputes over accounting principles, audit procedures, or fees.

The burden of initiating the communication rests with the successor auditor. The predecessor auditor is required to respond to the request for information. However, because of the confidentiality requirement in the *Code of Professional Conduct,* the predecessor auditor must obtain permission from the client before the communication can be made. In the event that legal problems or disputes arise between the client and the predecessor, the latter's response can be limited to stating that no information will be provided. The successor should seriously consider the desirability of accepting a prospective engagement, without considerable other investigation, if a client will not permit the communication or the predecessor will not provide a comprehensive response.

Even when a prospective client has been audited by another CPA firm, other investigations are often made. Sources of information include local attorneys, other CPAs, banks, and other businesses. In some cases, the auditor may hire a professional investigator to obtain information about the reputation and background of the key members of management. More extensive investigation is appropriate when there has been no previous auditor, when a predecessor auditor will not provide the desired information, or if any indication of problems arises from the communication.

Continuing Clients Many CPA firms evaluate existing clients annually to determine whether there are reasons for not continuing to do the audit. Previous conflicts over such things as the appropriate scope of the audit, the type of opinion to issue, or fees may cause the auditor to discontinue association. The auditor may also determine that the client lacks integrity and therefore should no longer be a client. If the client files a lawsuit against a CPA firm or vice versa, the firm cannot do the audit. Similarly, if there are unpaid fees for services performed more than 1 year previously, the CPA firm cannot do the current year audit. To do an audit in either of these circumstances violates the AICPA *Code of Professional Conduct* rules on independence.

Even if none of the previously discussed conditions exist, the CPA firm may decide not to continue doing audits for a client because of excessive risk when acceptable audit risk is below the CPA firm's threshold. For example, a CPA firm might decide that there is considerable risk of a regulatory conflict between a governmental agency and a client, which could result in financial failure of the client and ultimately lawsuits against the CPA firm. Even if the engagement is profitable, the risk may exceed the short-term benefits of doing the audit.

Investigation of new clients and reevaluation of existing ones is an essential part of deciding acceptable audit risk. Assume a potential client in a reasonably risky industry, where management has a reputation of integrity but is also known to take aggressive financial risks. If the CPA firm decides that acceptable audit risk is extremely low, it may choose not to accept the engagement. If the CPA firm concludes that acceptable audit risk is low but the client is still acceptable, that is likely to affect the fee proposed to the client. Audits with a low acceptable audit risk will normally result in higher audit costs, which should be reflected in higher audit fees.

Identify Client's Reasons for Audit

Two major factors affecting acceptable audit risk are the likely statement users and their intended uses of the statements. The auditor is likely to accumulate more evidence when the statements are to be used extensively. This is often the case for publicly held companies, those with extensive indebtedness, and companies that are to be sold in the near future.

The most likely uses of the statements can be determined from previous experience with the client and discussion with management. Throughout the engagement, the auditor may get additional information about why the client is having an audit and the likely uses of the financial statements. This information may affect the auditor's assessment of acceptable audit risk.

Obtain an Understanding with the Client

A clear understanding of the terms of the engagement should exist between the client and the CPA firm. SAS 83 (AU 310) requires that auditors must document their understanding of an engagement in the audit files, including the engagement's objectives, the responsibilities of the auditor and management, and the engagement's limitations. This is typically done with an **engagement letter,** even though one is not required.

The engagement letter is an agreement between the CPA firm and the client for the conduct of the audit and related services. It should specify whether the auditor will perform an audit, a review, or a compilation, plus any other services such as tax returns or management consulting. It should also state any restrictions to be imposed on the auditor's work, deadlines for completing the audit, assistance to be provided by the client's personnel in obtaining records and documents, and schedules to be prepared for the auditor. It often includes an agreement on fees. The engagement letter is also a means of informing the client that the auditor cannot guarantee that all acts of fraud will be discovered.

The engagement letter does not affect the CPA firm's responsibility to external users of audited financial statements, but it can affect legal responsibilities to the client. For example, if the client sued the CPA firm for failing to find a material misstatement, one defense a CPA firm could use would be a signed engagement letter stating that a review service, rather than an audit, was agreed upon.

Engagement letter information is important in planning the audit principally because it affects the timing of the tests and the total amount of time the audit and other services will take. If the deadline for submitting the audit report is soon after the balance sheet date, a significant portion of the audit must be done before the end of the year. When the auditor is preparing tax returns and a management letter, or if client assistance is not available, arrangements must be made to extend the amount of time for the engagement. Client-imposed restrictions on the audit could affect the procedures performed and possibly even the type of audit opinion issued. An example of an engagement letter for the audit of Hillsburg Hardware Co. is given in Figure 7-2 (p. 174).

Select Staff for the Engagement

Assigning the appropriate staff to the engagement is important to meet generally accepted auditing standards and to promote audit efficiency. The first general standard states:

> The audit is to be performed by a person or persons having adequate technical training and proficiency as an auditor.

Staff must therefore be assigned with that standard in mind, and those assigned to the engagement must be knowledgeable about the client's industry. On larger engagements, there are likely to be one or more partners and staff at several experience levels doing the audit. Specialists in such technical areas as statistical sampling and computer risk assessment may also be assigned. On smaller audits, there may be only one or two staff members.

A major consideration affecting staffing is the need for continuity from year to year. An inexperienced staff assistant is likely to become the most experienced nonpartner on the engagement within a few years. Continuity helps the CPA firm maintain familiarity with the technical requirements and closer interpersonal relations with client personnel.

To illustrate the importance of assigning appropriate staff to engagements, consider a computer manufacturing client with extensive inventory of computers and computer parts. Inherent risk for inventory has been assessed as high. It is essential for the staff person doing the inventory portion of the audit to be experienced in auditing inventory. In addition, the auditor should have a good understanding of the computer manufacturing industry.

FIGURE 7-2 Engagement Letter

BERGER AND ANTHONY, CPAs
Gary, Indiana 46405

June 14, 2002

Mr. Rick Chulick, President
Hillsburg Hardware Co.
2146 Willow St.
Gary, Indiana 46405

Dear Mr. Chulick:

This will confirm our understanding of the arrangements for our audit of the financial statements of Hillsburg Hardware Co. for the year ending December 31, 2002.

We will audit the company's financial statements for the year ending December 31, 2002, for the purpose of expressing an opinion on the fairness with which they present, in all material respects, the financial position, results of operations, and cash flows in conformity with generally accepted accounting principles.

We will conduct our audit in accordance with generally accepted auditing standards. Those standards require that we obtain reasonable, rather than absolute, assurance that the financial statements are free of material misstatement, whether caused by error or fraud. Accordingly, a material misstatement may remain undetected. Also, an audit is not designed to detect error or fraud that is immaterial to the financial statements; therefore, the audit will not necessarily detect misstatements less than this materiality level that might exist because of error, fraudulent financial reporting, or misappropriation of assets. If, for any reason, we are unable to complete the audit or are unable to form or have not formed an opinion, we may decline to express an opinion or decline to issue a report as a result of the engagement.

Although an audit includes obtaining an understanding of internal control sufficient to plan the audit and to determine the nature, timing, and extent of audit procedures to be performed, it is not designed to provide assurance on internal control or to identify reportable conditions. However, we are responsible for ensuring that the audit committee is aware of any reportable conditions that come to our attention.

The financial statements are the responsibility of the company's management. Management is also responsible for (1) establishing and maintaining effective internal control over financial reports, (2) identifying and ensuring the company complies with the laws and regulations applicable to its activities, (3) making all financial records and related information available to us, and (4) providing to us at the conclusion of the engagement a representation letter that, among other things, will confirm management's responsibility for the preparation of the financial statements in conformity with generally accepted accounting principles, the availability of financial records and related data, the completeness and availability of all minutes of the board and committee meetings, and to the best of its knowledge and belief, the absence of fraud involving management or those employees who have a significant role in the entity's internal control.

The timing of our audit and the assistance to be supplied by your personnel, including the preparation of schedules and analyses of accounts, are described on a separate attachment. Timely completion of this work will facilitate the completion of our audit.

As part of our engagement for the year ending December 31, 2002, we will also prepare the federal and state income tax returns for Hillsburg Hardware Co.

Our fees will be billed as work progresses and are based on the amount of time required at various levels of responsibility, plus actual out-of-pocket expenses. Invoices are payable upon presentation. We will notify you immediately of any circumstances we encounter that could significantly affect our initial estimate of total fees of $135,000.

If this letter correctly expresses your understanding, please sign the enclosed copy and return it to us. We appreciate the opportunity to serve you.

Yours very truly:

Joe Anthony

Joe Anthony
Partner

Accepted:

By: *Rick Chulick*
Date: 6-21-02

"BIG ACCOUNTING FIRMS WEED OUT RISKY CLIENTS"

In a *Wall Street Journal* article, Lee Berton discussed the impact of extensive lawsuits against CPAs by their clients on the firms' willingness to accept or continue auditing risky clients. Excerpts from the article follow:

> Big accounting firms say they have begun dropping risky audit clients to lower their risk of lawsuits for allegedly faulty audits. New companies, which have a particularly high chance of failure, are affected most, because almost nothing triggers lawsuits against accountants faster than company failures.
>
> But established companies are getting the ax, too. KPMG, [a large] U.S. accounting firm, is currently dropping fifty to one hundred audit clients annually, up from only zero to twenty five years ago, says Robert W. Lambert, the firm's new director of risk management. "When a client we audit goes bust," he says, "it costs us a bundle in court if we're sued by investors, whether we win or lose the case."
>
> Mr. Lambert says that legal costs were "staggering" for a lawsuit filed in a federal court in Texas alleging a faulty review of a bank's books by KPMG. The bank was taken over by the federal government in 1992 after big losses. The jury ruled in KPMG's favor in 1993, but the firm had to spend $7 million to defend itself "even though the fee for the job was only $15,000," Mr. Lambert says. "We just can't afford to take on risky audit clients anymore."
>
> Lawrence Weinbach, managing partner of Andersen, another leading accounting firm, says his organization has either dropped or declined to audit more than 100 companies over the past two years. "When the company has a risky profile and its stock price is volatile, we're just not going to jump in and do the audit and invite a lawsuit," says Mr. Weinbach.
>
> . . . "No risky client can pay us enough money to defend ourselves after the client develops problems," asserts J. Michael Cook, chairman of Deloitte & Touche, [another large] U.S. accounting firm. "We must reduce our legal risks to remain viable."

Source: Excerpted from an article by Lee Berton, "Big Accounting Firms Weed Out Risky Clients," *The Wall Street Journal* (June 26, 1995), p. B1.

Evaluate Need for Outside Specialists

If the audit of a client requires specialized knowledge, it may be necessary to consult a specialist. SAS 73 (AU 336) establishes the requirements for selecting specialists and reviewing their work. Examples include using a diamond expert in evaluating the replacement cost of diamonds and an actuary for determining the appropriateness of the recorded value of insurance loss reserves. Another common use of specialists is consulting with attorneys on the legal interpretation of contracts and titles. In the previously discussed example of a large inventory of computers and computer parts, the CPA firm may decide to engage a specialist if no one within the firm is qualified to evaluate whether the inventory is obsolete.

The auditor should have a sufficient understanding of the client's business to recognize the need for a specialist. The auditor should evaluate the specialist's professional qualifications and understand the objectives and scope of the specialist's work. The auditor should also consider the specialist's relationship to the client, including circumstances that might impair the specialist's objectivity.

ALL THAT GLITTERS ISN'T GOLD

Gold! Just as the discovery of gold at Sutter's Mill started the 1849 gold rush in California, the announcement of a major gold discovery in Indonesia in 1993 sent Bre-X Minerals, Ltd., shares soaring on the Toronto stock exchange. The discovery had been billed as the "gold discovery of the century," and fights emerged over who had the rights to mine the gold.

Plenty of intrigue surrounded the gold find. Fire destroyed all the geologists' records of the find, and the exploration manager mysteriously plunged from a helicopter in an alleged suicide just before the announcement that the gold discovery appeared to be a fraud.

Auditors often must rely on the evaluation of specialists to value gold and other extractive minerals. Allegedly, the gold samples on which the original discovery was based had been "salted" with gold, and the samples had been destroyed, preventing independent verification. However, a separate, independent analysis of the discovery by another company indicated insignificant amounts of gold, resulting in a 90 percent decline in the value of Bre-X shares.

Source: Adapted from William C. Symonds and Michael Shari, "After Bre-X, the Glow is Gone," *Business Week* (April 14, 1997), pp. 38–39.

UNDERSTAND THE CLIENT'S BUSINESS AND INDUSTRY

OBJECTIVE 7-3

Gain an understanding of the client's business and industry.

Industry Information

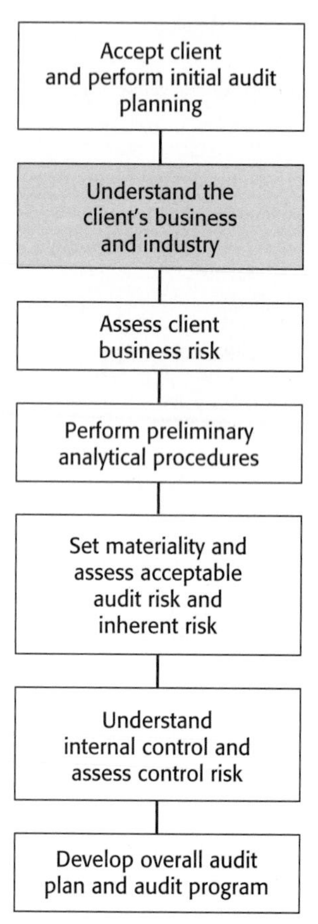

A thorough understanding of the client's business and industry and knowledge about the company's operations are essential for doing an adequate audit. The nature of the client's business and industry affects client business risk and the risk of material misstatements in the financial statements. The auditor uses knowledge of these risks to determine the appropriate extent of audit evidence.

Several factors have increased the importance of understanding the client's business and industry:

- Information technology connects client companies with major customers and suppliers. As a result, auditors need greater knowledge about major customers and suppliers and risks related to those relationships.
- Clients have expanded operations globally, often through joint ventures or strategic alliances.
- Information technology affects internal client processes, improving the quality and timeliness of accounting information.
- The increased importance of human capital and other intangible assets has increased accounting complexity and the importance of management judgments and estimates.
- Auditors need a better understanding of the client's business and industry to provide additional value-added services to clients. For example, audit firms often provide assurance and consulting services related to information technology and risk management services that require an extensive knowledge of the client's industry.

Auditors consider these factors using the strategic systems approach to understanding the client's business that was introduced in Chapter 1. Figure 7-3 provides an overview of the strategic systems approach to understanding the client's business and industry. Important aspects of this understanding are discussed in the following sections.

FIGURE 7-3 Strategic Systems Understanding of the Client's Business and Industry

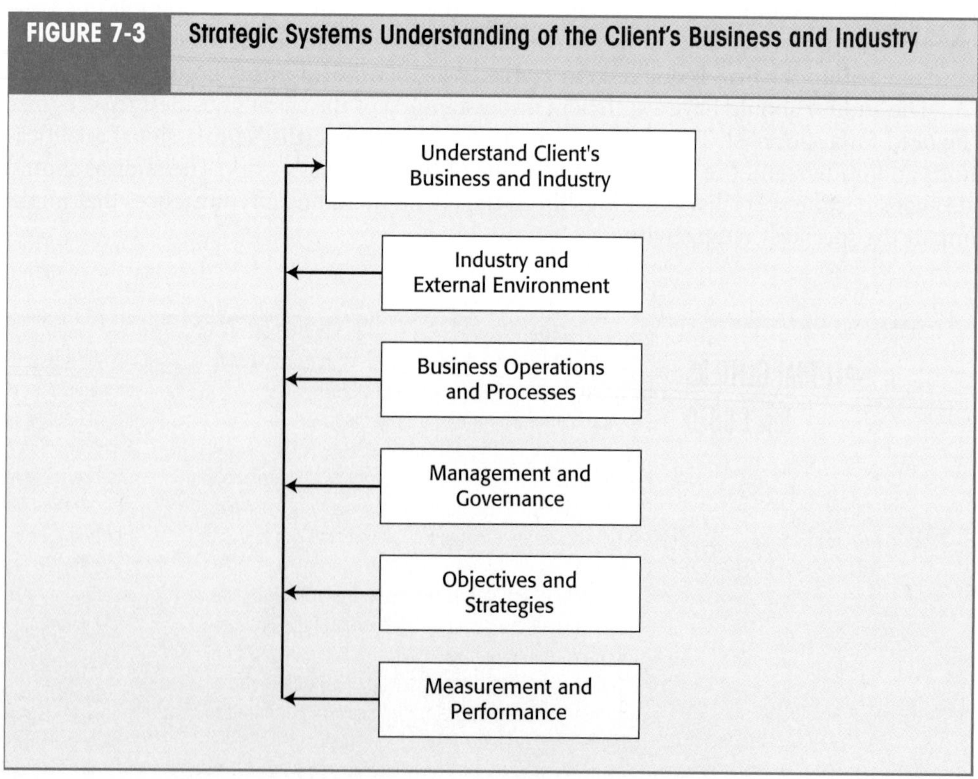

MANY CPA FIRMS REORGANIZE TO FOCUS ON INDUSTRIES

A high level of knowledge of a client's industry and business is so critical to conducting quality audits and providing value-added tax and consulting services that many CPA firms have reorganized to focus on industry lines. For example, KPMG has organized its practice using multidisciplinary teams across industry sectors in the following lines of business: Financial Services; Information, Communications and Entertainment; Industrial Markets; Consumer Markets; and Health Care and Public Sector. Reorganizing along industry lines may help CPA firms such as KPMG better understand their clients' businesses and provide additional value-added services.

Industry and External Environment

There are three primary reasons for obtaining a good understanding of the client's industry and external environment. First, there are risks associated with specific industries. These risks may affect the auditor's assessment of client business risk and acceptable audit risk, or even whether auditing companies in the industry is advisable. As stated earlier, certain industries are more risky than others, such as the savings and loan and health insurance industries.

Second, there are inherent risks that are typically common to all clients in certain industries. Understanding those risks aids the auditor in assessing the client's inherent risks. Examples include potential inventory obsolescence in the fashion clothing industry, accounts receivable collection inherent risk in the consumer loan industry, and reserve for loss inherent risk in the casualty insurance industry.

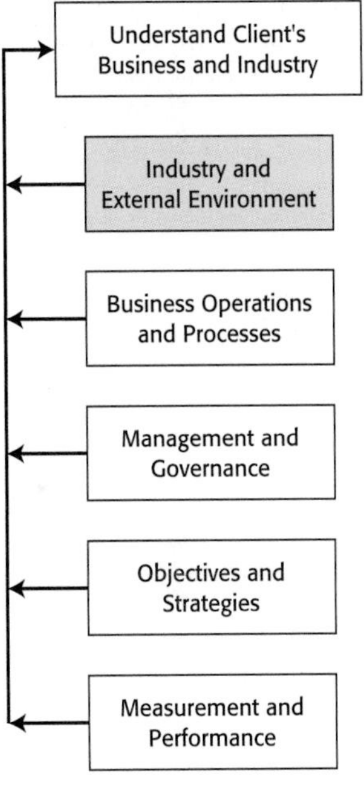

Third, many industries have unique accounting requirements that the auditor must understand to evaluate whether the client's financial statements are in accordance with generally accepted accounting principles. If the auditor is doing an audit of a city, for example, the auditor must understand governmental accounting and auditing requirements. There are also unique accounting requirements for construction companies, railroads, not-for-profit organizations, financial institutions, and many other organizations.

Several auditor litigation cases described in Chapter 4 resulted from the auditor's failure to understand the nature of the client's industry. For example, several major accounting firms paid large settlements to the federal government related to audits of failed savings and loans. In some of these audits, the auditors failed to understand the nature of significant real estate transactions.

The auditor must also understand the client's external environment, including such things as economic conditions, extent of competition, and regulatory requirements. To illustrate, auditors of utility companies need an understanding of the unique regulatory accounting requirements in this industry. In addition, in recent years deregulation in this industry has introduced competition that threatens the survival of less-efficient companies, and utilities are increasingly susceptible to fluctuations in energy prices. Auditors of these companies must assess these risks in developing effective audit plans.

Business Operations and Processes

The auditor should understand factors such as major sources of revenue, key customers and suppliers, sources of financing, and information about related parties that may indicate areas of increased client business risk. Many technology firms are dependent on one or a few products that may become obsolete due to new technologies or stronger competitors. Dependence on a few major customers may result in highly material losses from bad debts or obsolete inventory. For example, many suppliers of Internet and telecommunications equipment provided significant sales financing to customers and suffered losses when the customers were unable to pay for equipment.

The ability to obtain financing is an important factor in determining whether the company is likely to continue as a going concern. This is especially true for Internet and other new companies that are expected to lose money for several years before becoming profitable.

Tour the Plant and Offices A tour of the client's facilities is helpful in obtaining a better understanding of the client's business operations because it provides an opportunity to observe operations firsthand and to meet key personnel. The actual viewing of the physical facilities aids in understanding physical safeguards over assets and in interpreting accounting data by providing a frame of reference in which to visualize such assets as inventory in

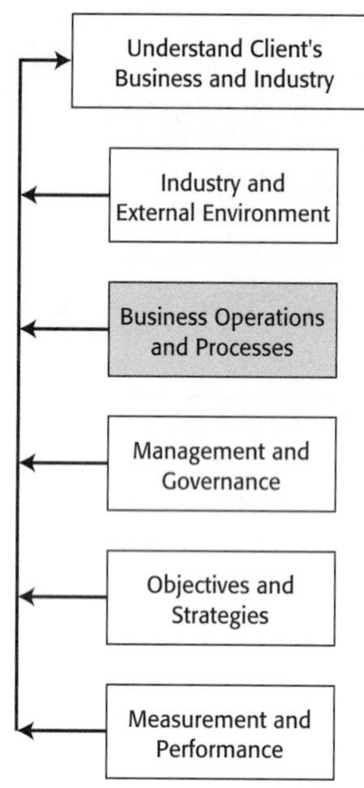

process and factory equipment. Knowledge of the physical layout also facilitates getting answers to questions later in the audit. The tour may also help the auditor identify inherent risks. For example, if the auditor observes unused equipment and potentially unsalable inventory, it will affect the assessment of inherent risks for equipment and inventory. Discussions with nonaccounting employees during the tour and throughout the audit are useful in maintaining a broad perspective.

Identify Related Parties Transactions with related parties are important to auditors because generally accepted accounting principles require that they be *disclosed in the financial statements* if they are material. Transactions with a related party are not arm's-length transactions. Therefore, there is a risk that they were not valued at the same amount as they would have been if the transactions had been with an independent third party. The disclosure requirements include the nature of the related party relationship; a description of transactions, including dollar amounts; and amounts due from and to related parties. Most auditors assess inherent risk as high for related parties and related party transactions, both because of the accounting disclosure requirements and the lack of independence between the parties involved in the transactions.

A **related party** is defined in SAS 45 (AU 334) as an affiliated company, a principal owner of the client company, or any other party with which the client deals where one of the parties can influence the management or operating policies of the other. A **related party transaction** is any transaction between the client and a related party. Common examples include sales or purchase transactions between a parent company and its subsidiary, exchanges of equipment between two companies owned by the same person, and loans to officers. A less common example is the exercise of significant management influence on an audit client by its most important customer.

Because material related party transactions must be disclosed, it is important that all related parties be *identified and included in the permanent files* early in the engagement. Finding undisclosed related party transactions is thereby enhanced. Common ways of identifying related parties include inquiry of management, review of SEC filings, and examination of stockholders' listings to identify principal stockholders.

Management and Governance

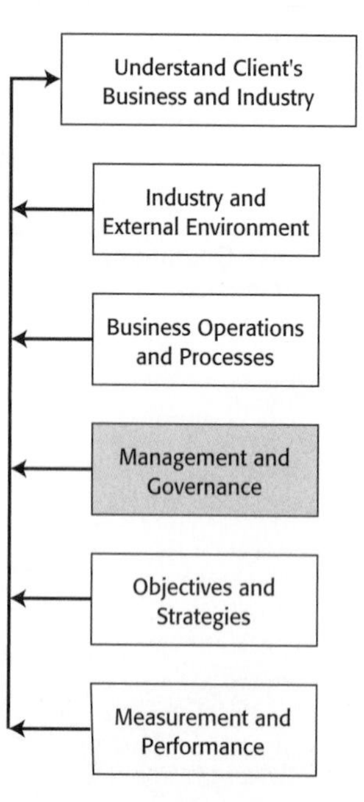

Management establishes the strategies and business processes followed by the client's business. Management's philosophy and operating style, and ability to identify and respond to risk, significantly impact the risk of material misstatements in the financial statements. For example, one of the major financial accounting scandals in the late 1990s involved the aggressive CEO of a consumer products company. The significant annual increase in sales and earnings reported by the company was ultimately determined to be based on various improper accounting techniques encouraged by the CEO.

Governance includes the client's organizational structure, as well as the activities of the board of directors and the audit committee. An effective board of directors helps ensure that the company takes appropriate risks. The audit committee, through oversight of financial reporting, can reduce the likelihood of overly aggressive accounting. As part of understanding the client's governance system, the auditor should gain knowledge of the corporate charter and bylaws and read the corporate minutes.

Corporate Charter and Bylaws The **corporate charter** is granted by the state in which the company is incorporated and is the legal document necessary for recognizing a corporation as a separate entity. It includes the exact name of the corporation, the date of incorporation, the kinds and amounts of capital stock the corporation is authorized to issue, and the types of business activities the corporation is authorized to conduct. In specifying the kinds of capital stock, there is also included such information as the voting rights of each class of stock, par or stated value of the stock, preferences and conditions necessary for dividends, and prior rights in liquidation.

The **bylaws** include the rules and procedures adopted by the stockholders of the corporation. They specify such things as the fiscal year of the corporation, the frequency of stockholder meetings, the method of voting for directors, and the duties and powers of the corporate officers.

Minutes of Meetings The **corporate minutes** are the official record of the meetings of the board of directors and stockholders. They include summaries of the most important topics discussed at these meetings and the decisions made by the directors and stockholders. The auditor should read the minutes to obtain information that is relevant to performing the audit.

Common authorizations in the minutes include compensation of officers, new contracts and agreements, acquisitions of property, loans, and dividend payments. While reading the minutes, the auditor should identify relevant authorizations and include the information in the audit files by making an abstract of the minutes or by obtaining a copy and underlining significant portions. Some time before the audit is completed, there must be a follow-up of this information to be sure that management has complied with actions taken by the stockholders and the board of directors. As an illustration, the authorized compensation of officers should be traced to each individual officer's payroll record as a test of whether the correct total compensation was paid. Similarly, the auditor should compare the authorizations of loans with notes payable to make certain that these liabilities are recorded.

Client Objectives and Strategies

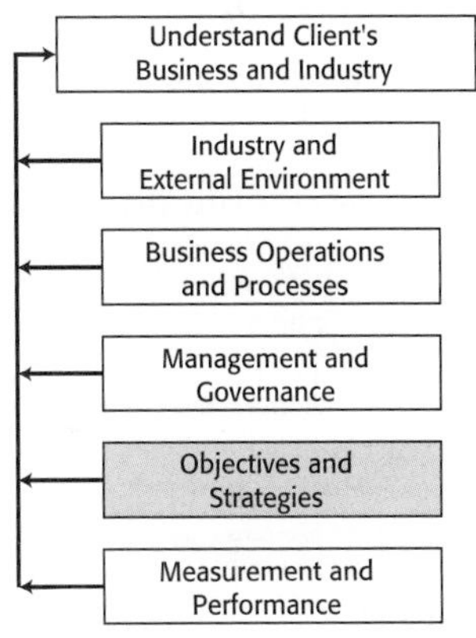

Strategies are approaches followed by the entity to achieve organizational objectives. Auditors should understand client objectives related to (1) reliability of financial reporting, (2) effectiveness and efficiency of operations, and (3) compliance with laws and regulations.

Management is primarily concerned with the effectiveness and efficiency of operations. Auditors need knowledge about operations to assess client business risk and inherent risk in the financial statements. For example, product quality can have a significant impact on the financial statements through lost sales and warranty and product liability claims. One auto manufacturer recently recalled more than $3 billion of tires, which affected the financial statements of the auto company and its tire supplier.

As part of understanding the client's objectives related to compliance with laws and regulations, the auditor should become familiar with the terms of contracts and other legal obligations. These can include such diverse items as long-term notes and bonds payable, stock options, pension plans, contracts with vendors for future delivery of supplies, government contracts for completion and delivery of manufactured products, royalty agreements, union contracts, and leases.

Most contracts are of primary interest in individual parts of the audit and, in practice, receive special attention during the different phases of the detailed tests. For example, the provisions of a pension plan would receive substantial emphasis as a part of the audit of the unfunded liability for pensions. The auditor should review and abstract the documents early in the engagement to gain a better perspective of the organization and to become familiar with potential problem areas. Later, these documents can be examined more carefully as a part of the tests of individual audit areas.

Measurement and Performance

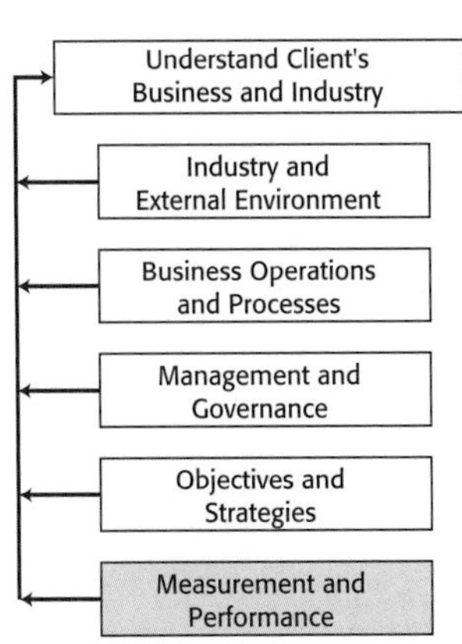

The client's performance measurement system includes the key performance indicators that management uses to measure progress toward objectives. These indicators go beyond financial statement figures such as sales and net income and include measures that are tailored to the client and its objectives. Examples of such key performance indicators include market share and sales per employee, unit sales growth, unique visitors to a Web site, or same-store sales and sales per square foot for a retailer.

The risk of financial misstatements may be increased if the client has set unreasonable objectives or if the performance measurement system encourages aggressive accounting. For example, a company may have as an objective obtaining the leading market share of industry sales. If management and salespeople are compensated based on achieving this sales objective, there is increased incentive to record sales before they have been earned or record sales for nonexistent transactions. In this situation, the auditor is likely to increase assessed inherent risk and the extent of testing for the existence of sales.

Performance measurement includes ratio analysis and benchmarking against key competitors. As part of understanding the client's business, the auditor should perform ratio analysis or review the client's calculations of key performance ratios. Performing preliminary analytical procedures is the fourth step in the planning process and is discussed later in this chapter.

ASSESS CLIENT BUSINESS RISK

OBJECTIVE 7-4

Assess client business risk.

Accept client and perform initial audit planning

Understand the client's business and industry

Assess client business risk

Perform preliminary analytical procedures

Set materiality and assess acceptable audit risk and inherent risk

Understand internal control and assess control risk

Develop overall audit plan and audit program

The auditor uses knowledge gained from the strategic systems understanding of the client's business and industry to assess client business risk. **Client business risk** is the risk that the client will fail to achieve its objectives. Client business risk can arise from any of the factors affecting the client and its environment. For example, a new technology may erode a client's competitive advantage, or the client may fail to execute its strategies as well as competitors.

The auditor's primary concern is the risk of material misstatements in the financial statements due to client business risk. For example, a company that provides Internet networking equipment recently recorded a $3 billion write-down of inventory when actual sales were less than forecast sales due to an economic downturn. For technology companies and clients in other industries with short product cycles, the auditor should be concerned with whether production plans and inventory levels are appropriate for current economic conditions. Similarly, companies often make strategic acquisitions that depend on successfully combining the operations of two or more companies. If the planned synergies do not develop, the fixed assets and goodwill recorded in the acquisition may be impaired, affecting the fair presentation of the financial statements.

Figure 7-4 summarizes the relationship among the client's business and industry, client business risk, and the auditor's assessment of the risk of material financial statement misstatements. The client's industry and other external factors and the client's business strategies, processes, and other internal factors are considered in the auditor's assessment of client business risk. The auditor also considers management controls that may mitigate business risk, such as effective risk assessment practices and corporate governance. Client business risk, after considering the effectiveness of top management controls, is sometimes called residual risk. Client business risk is then evaluated to assess the risk of material misstatement in the financial statements. The risk of material misstatements is used to classify risks using the audit risk model to determine the appropriate extent of audit evidence. Use of the audit risk model is discussed in the next chapter.

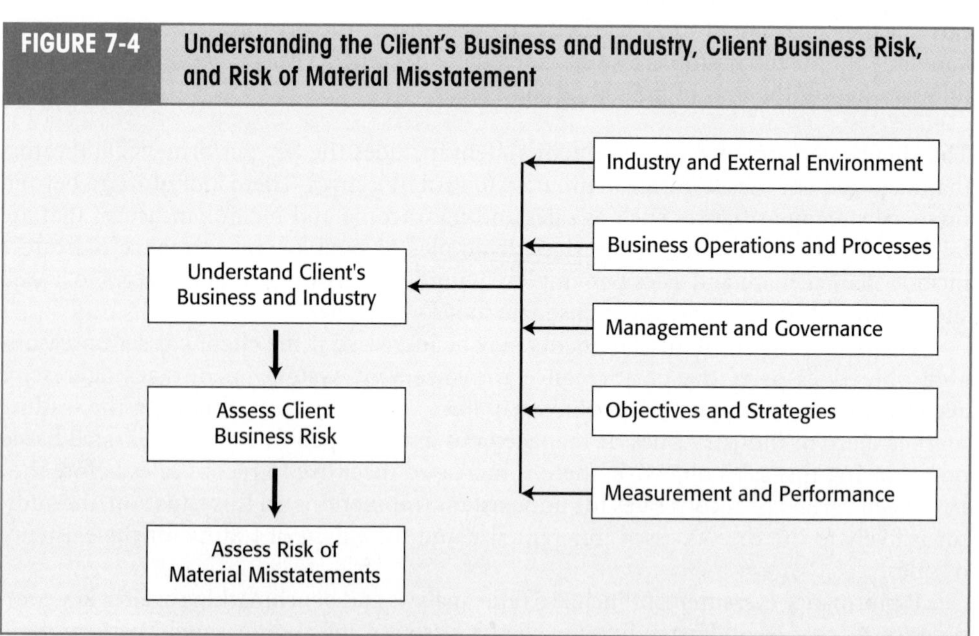

FIGURE 7-4 Understanding the Client's Business and Industry, Client Business Risk, and Risk of Material Misstatement

PERFORM PRELIMINARY ANALYTICAL PROCEDURES

OBJECTIVE 7-5

Perform preliminary analytical procedures.

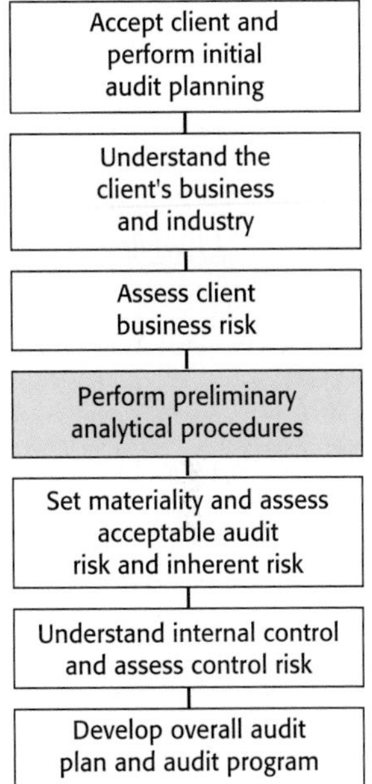

An important part of understanding the client's business and assessing client business risk is performing preliminary analytical procedures. Comparison of client ratios to industry or competitor benchmarks provides an indication of the company's performance. Unusual changes in ratios compared to prior years or to industry averages help identify areas having increased risk of misstatements that require further attention during the audit.

Analytical procedures are also an important part of testing throughout the audit. The use of preliminary analytical procedures as part of audit planning is first illustrated for the Hillsburg Hardware Co. After a summary of the audit planning process, the remainder of the chapter studies the use of analytical procedures throughout the audit.

Table 7-1 presents key financial ratios for Hillsburg Hardware Co. that auditors might consider during audit planning, along with comparative industry information. These ratios are based on the Hillsburg Hardware Co. financial statements in Figure 7-8 on pp. 190–191. Hillsburg is a wholesale distributor of hardware to independent, high-quality hardware stores in the midwestern part of the United States. The company is a niche provider in the overall hardware market, which is recently becoming dominated by huge hardware and building supply national chains. Hillsburg's auditors identified potential increased competition from national chains as a specific client business risk. Hillsburg's market consists of smaller, independent hardware stores. Increased competition could affect the sales and profitability of these customers, which would likely impact Hillsburg's sales and the value of assets such as accounts receivable and inventory. The following discussion indicates how the auditor might use ratio information to further understand Hillsburg's operations and identify areas with increased risk of material misstatements.

The profitability measures indicate that Hillsburg is performing fairly well, despite the increased competition from larger national chains. Although lower than the industry averages, the liquidity measures indicate that the company is in good financial condition and the leverage ratios indicate additional borrowing capacity. Because Hillsburg's market

TABLE 7-1 Examples of Planning Analytical Procedures

SELECTED RATIOS	HILLSBURG 12/31/02	INDUSTRY 12/31/02	HILLSBURG 12/31/01	INDUSTRY 12/31/01
Short-Term Debt-Paying Ability				
Cash ratio	0.06	0.22	0.02	0.20
Quick ratio	1.57	3.10	1.40	3.00
Current ratio	3.86	5.20	4.40	5.10
Liquidity Activity Ratios				
Accounts receivable turnover	7.08	12.15	6.97	12.25
Days to collect accounts receivable	51.55	30.04	52.37	29.80
Inventory turnover	3.46	5.20	3.00	4.90
Days to sell inventory	105.49	70.19	121.67	74.49
Ability to Meet Long-Term Obligations				
Debt to equity	1.73	2.51	1.40	2.53
Times interest earned	3.06	5.50	3.29	5.60
Profitability Ratios				
Gross profit percent	27.85	31.00	27.70	32.00
Profit margin	0.05	0.07	0.05	0.08
Return on assets	0.09	0.09	0.07	0.09
Return on common equity	0.25	0.37	0.20	0.35

consists of smaller, independent hardware stores, the company holds more inventory and takes longer to collect receivables than the industry average.

In identifying areas of specific risk, the auditor would likely focus on the liquidity activity ratios. Inventory and accounts receivable turnover have improved but are still lower than industry averages. The collectibility of accounts receivable and inventory obsolescence will likely warrant attention in the current year's audit. These areas also likely received additional attention during the prior year's audit. The improvement in the turnover ratios suggests that testing in these areas probably will not need to be expanded compared to the prior year.

SUMMARY OF THE PURPOSES OF AUDIT PLANNING

There are several purposes of the planning procedures discussed in this section. A major purpose is to gain an understanding of the client's business and industry. This is used to assess client business risk and the risk of material misstatements in the financial statements.

Keep in mind that there are three additional parts of audit planning, each of which is discussed in subsequent chapters: set materiality and assess acceptable audit risk and inherent risk (Chapter 8), understand internal control and assess control risk (Chapter 9), and develop an overall audit plan and audit program (Chapter 10). Figure 7-5 summarizes the four major parts of audit planning discussed in this section and the key components of each part, with a brief illustration of how a CPA firm applied each component to a continuing client, Hillsburg Hardware Co.

ANALYTICAL PROCEDURES

OBJECTIVE 7-6

State the purposes of analytical procedures and the timing of each purpose.

Analytical procedures are one of the seven types of evidence introduced in Chapter 6. Earlier in this chapter, preliminary analytical procedures were introduced as a part of gaining an understanding of the client's business and industry. Because of the importance of this topic and increased emphasis on analytical procedures in practice, this section expands on the subject. Analytical procedures are defined by SAS 56 (AU 329) as *evaluations of financial information made by a study of plausible relationships among financial and nonfinancial data . . . involving comparisons of recorded amounts to expectations developed by the auditor.* This definition is more formal than the description of analytical procedures used in Chapter 6, but both say essentially the same thing. In both cases, analytical procedures use comparisons and relationships to assess whether account balances or other data appear reasonable. The emphasis in the SAS 56 definition is on expectations developed by the auditor. For example, the auditor might compare current year recorded commissions expense to total recorded sales multiplied by the average commission rate as a test of the overall reasonableness of recorded commissions. For this analytical procedure to be relevant and reliable, the auditor has likely concluded that recorded sales are correctly stated, all sales earn a commission, and there is an average actual commission rate that is readily determinable.

Analytical procedures may be performed at any of three times during an engagement. Some analytical procedures are *required* to be performed in the *planning phase* to assist in determining the nature, extent, and timing of work to be performed. Performance of analytical procedures during planning helps the auditor identify significant matters requiring special consideration later in the engagement. For example, the calculation of inventory turnover before inventory price tests are done may indicate the need for special care during those tests.

Analytical procedures done in the planning phase typically use data aggregated at a high level, and the sophistication, extent, and timing of the procedures vary among clients. For some clients, the comparison of prior year and current year account balances

FIGURE 7-5 Key Parts of Planning: Accept Client and Perform Initial Planning, Understand the Client's Business and Industry, Assess Client Business Risk, and Perform Preliminary Analytical Procedures Applied to Hillsburg Hardware Co.

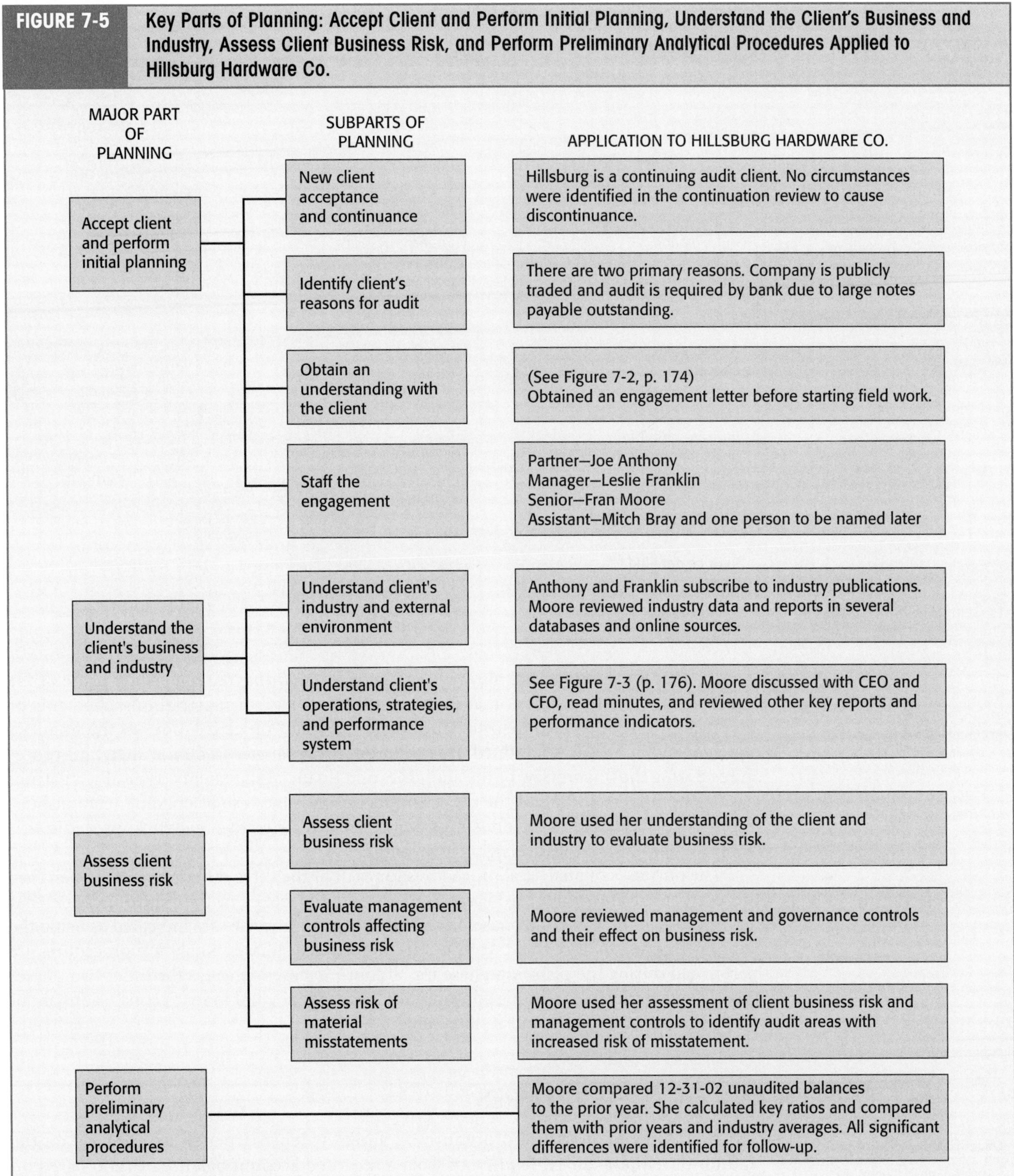

MAJOR PART OF PLANNING
SUBPARTS OF PLANNING
APPLICATION TO HILLSBURG HARDWARE CO.
Accept client and perform initial planning
New client acceptance and continuance
Hillsburg is a continuing audit client. No circumstances were identified in the continuation review to cause discontinuance.
Identify client's reasons for audit
There are two primary reasons. Company is publicly traded and audit is required by bank due to large notes payable outstanding.
Obtain an understanding with the client
(See Figure 7-2, p. 174)
Obtained an engagement letter before starting field work.
Staff the engagement
Partner—Joe Anthony
Manager—Leslie Franklin
Senior—Fran Moore
Assistant—Mitch Bray and one person to be named later
Understand the client's business and industry
Understand client's industry and external environment
Anthony and Franklin subscribe to industry publications. Moore reviewed industry data and reports in several databases and online sources.
Understand client's operations, strategies, and performance system
See Figure 7-3 (p. 176). Moore discussed with CEO and CFO, read minutes, and reviewed other key reports and performance indicators.
Assess client business risk
Assess client business risk
Moore used her understanding of the client and industry to evaluate business risk.
Evaluate management controls affecting business risk
Moore reviewed management and governance controls and their effect on business risk.
Assess risk of material misstatements
Moore used her assessment of client business risk and management controls to identify audit areas with increased risk of misstatement.
Perform preliminary analytical procedures
Moore compared 12-31-02 unaudited balances to the prior year. She calculated key ratios and compared them with prior years and industry averages. All significant differences were identified for follow-up.

using the unaudited trial balance may be sufficient. For other clients, the procedures might involve extensive analysis of quarterly financial statements based on the auditor's judgment.

Analytical procedures are often done *during the testing phase* of the audit in conjunction with other audit procedures. For example, the prepaid portion of each insurance policy might be compared with the same policy for the previous year as a part of doing tests of prepaid insurance.

FIGURE 7-6 Timing and Purposes of Analytical Procedures

Purpose	Phase		
	(Required) Planning Phase	Testing Phase	**(Required)** Completion Phase
Understand client's industry and business	Primary purpose		
Assess going concern	Secondary purpose		Secondary purpose
Indicate possible misstatements (attention directing)	Primary purpose	Secondary purpose	Primary purpose
Reduce detailed tests	Secondary purpose	Primary purpose	

Analytical procedures are also *required* to be done *during the completion phase* of the audit. Such tests are useful at that point as a final review for material misstatements or financial problems and to help the auditor take a final "objective look" at the financial statements that have been audited. It is common for a partner to do the analytical procedures during the final review of the audit files and financial statements. Typically, a partner has a good understanding of the client and its business because of ongoing relationships. Knowledge about the client's business combined with effective analytical procedures is a way to identify possible oversights in an audit.

The purposes of analytical procedures for each of the three different phases when they are performed are shown in Figure 7-6. The shaded boxes in the figure indicate that a purpose is applicable for a phase. In addition, several purposes are indicated as being the primary purpose. Notice that purposes vary for different phases. Analytical procedures are performed during the planning phase for all four purposes, whereas the other two phases are used primarily to determine appropriate audit evidence and to reach conclusions about the fair presentation of financial statements.

FIVE TYPES OF ANALYTICAL PROCEDURES

OBJECTIVE 7-7

Select the most appropriate analytical procedure from among the five major types.

The usefulness of analytical procedures as audit evidence depends significantly on the auditor developing an *expectation* of what a recorded account balance or ratio based on account balances *should be*, regardless of the type of analytical procedures used. Auditors develop an expectation of an account balance or ratio by considering information from prior periods, industry trends, client-prepared budgeted expectations, and nonfinancial information. The auditor typically compares the client's balances and ratios with expected balances and ratios using one or more of the following types of analytical procedures:

- Compare client and industry data
- Compare client data with similar prior period data

- Compare client data with client-determined expected results
- Compare client data with auditor-determined expected results
- Compare client data with expected results, using nonfinancial data

Compare Client and Industry Data

Suppose that you are doing an audit and obtain the following information about the client and the average company in the client's industry:

	Client		Industry	
	2002	2001	2002	2001
Inventory turnover	3.4	3.5	3.9	3.4
Gross margin percent	26.3%	26.4%	27.3%	26.2%

Analytical Procedures—Target and Kmart

If we look only at client information for the two ratios shown, the company appears to be stable with no apparent indication of difficulties. However, if the auditor uses industry data to develop expectations about the two ratios for 2002, the auditor would expect both ratios for the client to increase. Although these two ratios by themselves may not indicate significant problems, the example illustrates how developing expectations using industry data may provide useful information about the client's performance. For example, the company may have lost market share, its pricing may not be competitive, it may have incurred abnormal costs, or it may have obsolete items in inventory.

Dun & Bradstreet, Robert Morris Associates, and other analysts accumulate financial information for thousands of companies and compile the data for different lines of business. Many CPA firms purchase this information for use as a basis for industry comparisons in their audits.

The most important benefits of industry comparisons are as an aid to understanding the client's business and as an indication of the likelihood of financial failure. The ratios in Robert Morris Associates, for example, are primarily of a type that bankers and other credit executives use in evaluating whether a company will be able to repay a loan. That same information is useful to auditors in assessing the relative strength of the client's capital structure, its borrowing capacity, and the likelihood of financial failure.

A major weakness in using industry ratios for auditing is the difference between the nature of the client's financial information and that of the firms making up the industry totals. Because the industry data are broad averages, the comparisons may not be meaningful. Often, the client's line of business is not the same as the industry standards. In addition, different companies follow different accounting methods, and this affects the comparability of data. If most companies in the industry use FIFO inventory valuation and straight-line depreciation and the audit client uses LIFO and double-declining-balance depreciation, comparisons may not be meaningful. This does not mean that industry comparisons should not be made. Rather, it is an indication of the need for care in interpreting the results. One approach to overcome the limitations of industry averages is to compare the client to one or more benchmark firms in the industry.

Compare Client Data with Similar Prior Period Data

Suppose that the gross margin percent for a company has been between 26 and 27 percent for each of the past 4 years but is 23 percent in the current year. This decline in gross margin should be a concern to the auditor if there is no expectation of a decline. The cause of the decline could be a change in economic conditions. However, it could also be caused by misstatements in the financial statements, such as sales or purchase cutoff errors, unrecorded sales, overstated accounts payable, or inventory costing errors. The auditor should determine the cause of the decline in gross margin and consider the effect, if any, on evidence accumulation.

There are a wide variety of analytical procedures in which client data are compared with similar data from one or more prior periods. The following are common examples.

Compare the Current Year's Balance with That for the Preceding Year One of the easiest ways to make this test is to include the preceding year's adjusted trial balance results in a separate

USING ANALYTICAL PROCEDURES EFFECTIVELY

According to an article in the *Journal of Accountancy,* auditors often face potentially serious judgment problems while performing analytical procedures. An auditor can encounter judgment problems when he or she

- Allows unaudited account balances or ratios to unduly influence expectations of what current balances should be.
- Does not fully consider the pattern reflected by several unusual fluctuations when trying to explain what caused them.
- Places reliance on management's explanations about unusual fluctuations without first developing independent explanations.

The authors of the article offer the following recommendations to auditors performing analytical procedures:

- Compare unaudited balances with independent expectations of what those balances should be.
- Examine patterns of discrepancies, rather than analyze each discrepancy on its own.
- Identify reasonable explanations for unexpected fluctuations from knowledge of the client and industry *before* inquiring of the client's management.
- Evaluate management's explanations carefully, including considering how each explanation affects all account balances in question.

Source: Adapted from Timothy B. Bell and Arnold M. Wright, "When Judgment Counts," *Journal of Accountancy* (November 1997), pp. 73–77.

column of the current year's trial balance spreadsheet. The auditor can easily compare the current year's and previous year's balance to decide early in the audit whether an account should receive more than the normal amount of attention because of a significant change in the balance. For example, if the auditor observes a substantial increase in supplies expense, the auditor should determine whether the cause was an increased use of supplies, an error in the account due to a misclassification, or a misstatement of supplies inventory.

Compare the Detail of a Total Balance with Similar Detail for the Preceding Year If there have been no significant changes in the client's operations in the current year, much of the detail making up the totals in the financial statements should also remain unchanged. By briefly comparing the detail of the current period with similar detail of the preceding period, it is often possible to isolate information that needs further examination. Comparison of details may take the form of details over time or details at a point in time. A common example of the former is comparing the monthly totals for the current and preceding year for sales, repairs, and other accounts. An example of the latter is comparing the details of loans payable at the end of the current year with those at the end of the preceding year. In each of these examples, the auditor should first develop an expectation of a change or lack thereof before making the comparison.

Compute Ratios and Percentage Relationships for Comparison with Previous Years The comparison of totals or details with previous years as described in the two preceding paragraphs has two shortcomings. First, it fails to consider growth or decline in business activity. Second, relationships of data to other data, such as sales to cost of goods sold, are ignored. Ratio and percentage relationships overcome both shortcomings. The example discussed earlier about the decline in gross margin is a common percentage relationship used by auditors.

A few types of ratios and internal comparisons are included in Table 7-2 to show the widespread use of ratio analysis. In all cases, the comparisons should be with calculations made in previous years for the same client. There are many potential ratios and comparisons available for use by an auditor. Subsequent chapters dealing with specific audit areas describe other examples.

Many of the ratios and percentages used for comparison with previous years are the same ones used for comparison with industry data. For example, it is useful to compare current year gross margin with industry averages and previous years. The same can be said for most of the ratios described in the following section.

There are also numerous potential comparisons of current- and prior-period data beyond those normally available from industry data. For example, the percentage of each expense category to total sales can be compared with that of previous years. Similarly, in

TABLE 7-2 Internal Comparisons and Relationships

Ratio or Comparison	Possible Misstatement
Raw material turnover for a manufacturing company	Misstatement of inventory or cost of goods sold or obsolescence of raw material inventory
Sales commissions divided by net sales	Misstatement of sales commissions
Sales returns and allowances divided by gross sales	Misclassified sales returns and allowances or unrecorded returns or allowances subsequent to year-end
Cash surrender value of life insurance (current year) divided by cash surrender value of life insurance (preceding year)	Failure to record the change in cash surrender value or an error in recording the change
Each of the individual manufacturing expenses as a percentage of total manufacturing expense	Significant misstatement of individual expenses within a total

a multiunit operation (for example, a retail chain), internal comparisons for each unit can be made with previous periods.

Auditors often prepare common-size financial statements for one or more years to compare changes in account balances and their relation to a common base, such as sales. Common-size income statement data for the last three years for Hillsburg Hardware are included in Figure 7-7 (p. 188). Calculating income statement account balances as a percentage of sales is especially important when the level of sales has changed from the prior year, which is likely in many businesses. Hillsburg's sales have increased significantly compared to the prior year. Note that accounts such as cost of goods sold and sales salaries and commissions have also increased significantly but are fairly consistent as a percentage of sales, which would be expected for these accounts.

The auditor would likely require further explanation and corroborating evidence for the changes in advertising, bad debt expense, and office repairs and maintenance. Advertising expense has increased as a percentage of sales. One possible explanation is the development of a new advertising campaign. The dollar amount of bad debt expense has not changed significantly, but has decreased as a percentage of sales. The auditor would need to gather additional evidence to determine whether bad debt expense and the allowance for doubtful accounts are understated. Repairs and maintenance expense has also increased. Fluctuations in this account are not unusual if the client has incurred unexpected repairs. The auditor would likely investigate major expenditures in this account to determine whether they include any amounts that should be capitalized as a fixed asset.

Compare Client Data with Client-Determined Expected Results

Most companies prepare **budgets** for various aspects of their operations and financial results. Because budgets represent the client's expectations for the period, an investigation of the most significant areas in which differences exist between budgeted and actual results may indicate potential misstatements. The absence of differences may also indicate that misstatements are unlikely. It is common, for example, in the audit of local, state, and federal governmental units to use this type of analytical procedure.

When client data are compared with budgets, there are two special concerns. First, the auditor must evaluate whether the budgets were realistic plans. In some organizations, budgets are prepared with little thought or care and therefore are not realistic expectations. Such information has little value as audit evidence. The second concern is the possibility that current financial information was changed by client personnel to conform to the budget. If that has occurred, the auditor will find no differences in comparing actual data with budgeted data even if there are misstatements in the financial statements. A discussion of budget procedures with client personnel is used to satisfy the first concern. Assessment

FIGURE 7-7 Hillsburg Hardware Common-Size Income Statement

HILLSBURG HARDWARE CO.
COMMON-SIZE INCOME STATEMENT
Three Years Ending December 31, 2002

	2002		2001		2000	
	(000) Preliminary	% of Net Sales	(000) Audited	% of Net Sales	(000) Audited	% of Net Sales
Sales	$144,328	100.87	$132,421	100.91	$123,737	100.86
Less: Returns and allowances	1,242	0.87	1,195	0.91	1,052	0.86
Net sales	143,086	100.00	131,226	100.00	122,685	100.00
Cost of goods sold	103,241	72.15	94,876	72.30	88,724	72.32
Gross profit	39,845	27.85	36,350	27.70	33,961	27.68
Selling expense						
Salaries and commissions	7,739	5.41	7,044	5.37	6,598	5.38
Sales payroll taxes	1,422	0.99	1,298	0.99	1,198	0.98
Travel and entertainment	1,110	0.78	925	0.70	797	0.65
Advertising	2,611	1.82	1,920	1.46	1,790	1.46
Sales and promotional literature	322	0.22	425	0.32	488	0.40
Sales meetings and training	925	0.65	781	0.60	767	0.62
Miscellaneous sales expense	681	0.48	506	0.39	456	0.37
Total selling expense	14,810	10.35	12,899	9.83	12,094	9.86
Administration expense						
Executive and office salaries	5,524	3.86	5,221	3.98	5,103	4.16
Administrative payroll taxes	682	0.48	655	0.50	633	0.52
Travel and entertainment	562	0.39	595	0.45	542	0.44
Computer maintenance and supplies	860	0.60	832	0.63	799	0.65
Stationery and supplies	763	0.53	658	0.50	695	0.57
Postage	244	0.17	251	0.19	236	0.19
Telephone and fax	722	0.51	626	0.48	637	0.52
Rent	312	0.22	312	0.24	312	0.25
Legal fees and retainers	383	0.27	321	0.25	283	0.23
Auditing and related services	303	0.21	288	0.22	265	0.22
Depreciation	1,452	1.01	1,443	1.10	1,505	1.23
Bad debt expense	3,323	2.32	3,394	2.59	3,162	2.58
Insurance	723	0.51	760	0.58	785	0.64
Office repairs and maintenance	844	0.59	538	0.41	458	0.37
Miscellaneous office expense	644	0.45	621	0.47	653	0.53
Miscellaneous general expense	324	0.23	242	0.18	275	0.22
Total administrative expenses	17,665	12.35	16,757	12.77	16,343	13.32
Total selling and administrative expenses	32,475	22.70	29,656	22.60	28,437	23.18
Earnings from operations	7,370	5.15	6,694	5.10	5,524	4.50
Other income and expense						
Interest expense	2,409	1.68	2,035	1.55	2,173	1.77
Gain on sale of assets	(720)	(0.50)	0	0.00	0	0.00
Earnings before income taxes	5,681	3.97	4,659	3.55	3,351	2.73
Income taxes	1,747	1.22	1,465	1.12	1,072	0.87
Net income	$ 3,934	2.75	$ 3,194	2.43	$ 2,279	1.86

of control risk and detailed audit tests of actual data are usually done to minimize the likelihood of the latter concern.

Compare Client Data with Auditor-Determined Expected Results

A second common type of comparison of client data with expected results occurs when the *auditor calculates the expected balance for comparison with the actual balance.* In this type of analytical procedure, the auditor makes an estimate of what an account balance should be by relating it to some other balance sheet or income statement account or accounts or by making a projection based on some historical trend. An example of calculating an expected value based on relationships of accounts is the independent calculation of interest expense on long-term notes payable by multiplying the ending monthly balance in notes payable by the average monthly interest rate. An example of using a historical trend would be when the moving average of the allowance for uncollectible accounts receivable as a percentage of gross accounts receivable is applied to the balance of gross accounts receivable at the end of the audit year to determine an expected value for the current allowance.

Compare Client Data with Expected Results Using Nonfinancial Data

Suppose that in auditing a hotel, you can determine the number of rooms, room rate for each room, and occupancy rate. Using those data, it is relatively easy to estimate total revenue from rooms to compare with recorded revenue. The same approach can sometimes be used to estimate such accounts as tuition revenue at universities (average tuition times enrollment), factory payroll (total hours worked times wage rate), and cost of materials sold (units sold times materials cost per unit).

The major concern in using nonfinancial data is the accuracy of the data. In the previous illustration, it is not appropriate to use an estimated calculation of hotel revenue as audit evidence unless the auditor is satisfied with the reasonableness of the count of the number of rooms, room rate, and occupancy rate. It would be more difficult for the auditor to evaluate the accuracy of the occupancy rate than the other two items.

COMMON FINANCIAL RATIOS

OBJECTIVE 7-8

Compute common financial ratios.

Auditors' analytical procedures often include the use of general financial ratios during planning and final review of the audited financial statements. These are useful for understanding recent events and the financial status of the business and for viewing the statements from the perspective of a user. The general financial analysis may be effective for identifying possible problem areas for additional analysis and audit testing as well as business problem areas for which the auditor can provide other assistance. In using these ratios, it is important to make appropriate comparisons. The most important comparisons are to those of previous years for the company and to industry averages or similar companies for the same year.

Ratios and other analytical procedures are normally calculated using spreadsheets and other types of audit software. These ratios are linked to the trial balance so that the calculations are automatically updated when adjusting entries are made to the client's statements. For example, a change in inventory and cost of goods sold affects a large number of ratios. Several years of client and industry data can be maintained in the computer files for comparative purposes.

The following sections present a number of widely used financial ratios. Computation of the various ratios is illustrated using the 2002 financial statements of Hillsburg Hardware Co. The financial statements appear in Figure 7-8 (pp. 190–191) and were prepared from the trial balance in Figure 5-4 on page 123. The following simplifying assumptions were made for the ratio computations:

- Average receivables and inventories for the year are not significantly different from the year-end balances.
- There is no preferred stock.
- There are 5 million common shares outstanding.

Short-term Debt-Paying Ability

$$\text{Cash ratio} = \frac{\text{cash + marketable securities}}{\text{current liabilities}} \qquad \frac{828}{13{,}216} = 0.06$$

$$\text{Quick ratio} = \frac{\text{cash + marketable securities + net accounts receivable}}{\text{current liabilities}} \qquad \frac{828 + 18{,}957 + 945}{13{,}216} = 1.57$$

$$\text{Current ratio} = \frac{\text{current assets}}{\text{current liabilities}} \qquad \frac{51{,}027}{13{,}216} = 3.86$$

FIGURE 7-8 **Hillsburg Hardware Co. Financial Statements**

HILLSBURG HARDWARE CO.
BALANCE SHEET
December 31, 2002
(in thousands)

Assets			
Current assets			
Cash	$ 828		
Trade accounts receivable (net of allowance of $1,240)	18,957		
Other accounts receivable	945		
Inventories	29,865		
Prepaid expenses	432		
Total current assets		51,027	
Property, plant, and equipment			
Land	3,456		
Buildings	32,500		
Computer and other equipment	3,758		
Furniture and fixtures	2,546		
Less: Accumulated depreciation	(31,920)		
Total property, plant, and equipment		10,340	
Total assets			$61,367
Liabilities and Stockholders' Equity			
Current liabilities			
Trade accounts payable	4,720		
Notes payable	4,180		
Accrued payroll	1,350		
Accrued payroll tax	120		
Accrued interest and dividends payable	2,050		
Accrued income tax	796		
Total current liabilities		13,216	
Long-term liabilities			
Notes payable	24,120		
Deferred tax	738		
Other accrued payables	830		
Total long-term liabilities		25,688	
Stockholders' equity			
Capital stock ($1 par value)	5,000		
Capital in excess of par value	3,500		
Retained earnings	13,963		
Total stockholders' equity		22,463	
Total liabilities and stockholders' equity			$61,367

FIGURE 7-8 **Hillsburg Hardware Co. Financial Statements (Cont.)**

HILLSBURG HARDWARE CO.
COMBINED STATEMENT OF
INCOME AND RETAINED EARNINGS
for Year Ending December 31, 2002
(in thousands)

Sales		$144,328	
Less: Returns and allowances		1,242	
Net sales			143,086
Cost of goods sold			103,241
Gross profit			39,845
Selling expense			
Salaries and commissions	7,739		
Sales payroll taxes	1,422		
Travel and entertainment	1,110		
Advertising	2,611		
Sales and promotional literature	322		
Sales meetings and training	925		
Miscellaneous sales expense	681		
Total selling expense		14,810	
Administrative expense			
Executive and office salaries	5,524		
Administrative payroll taxes	682		
Travel and entertainment	562		
Computer maintenance and supplies	860		
Stationery and supplies	763		
Postage	244		
Telephone and fax	722		
Rent	312		
Legal fees and retainers	383		
Auditing and related services	303		
Depreciation	1,452		
Bad debt expense	3,323		
Insurance	723		
Office repairs and maintenance	844		
Miscellaneous office expense	644		
Miscellaneous general expense	324		
Total administrative expenses		17,665	
Total selling and administrative expenses			32,475
Earnings from operations			7,370
Other income and expense			
Interest expense		2,409	
Gain on sale of assets		(720)	1,689
Earnings before income taxes			5,681
Income taxes			1,747
Net income			3,934
Retained earnings at January 1, 2002			11,929
Dividends			(1,900)
Retained earnings at December 31, 2002			$13,963

Companies need a reasonable level of liquidity to pay their debts as they come due. These three ratios are measures of liquidity. It is apparent by examining the three ratios that the cash ratio may be useful to evaluate the ability to pay debts immediately, whereas the current ratio requires the conversion of assets such as inventory and accounts receivable to cash before debts can be paid. The most important difference between the quick and current ratios is the inclusion of inventory in current assets for the current ratio.

Liquidity Activity Ratios

Accounts receivable turnover	=	$\frac{\text{net sales}}{\text{average gross receivables}}$	$\frac{143{,}086}{18{,}957 + 1{,}240}$	=	7.08
Days to collect receivables	=	$\frac{\text{365 days}}{\text{accounts receivable turnover}}$	$\frac{\text{365 days}}{7.08}$	=	51.55 days
Inventory turnover	=	$\frac{\text{cost of goods sold}}{\text{average inventory}}$	$\frac{103{,}241}{29{,}865}$	=	3.46
Days to sell inventory	=	$\frac{\text{365 days}}{\text{inventory turnover}}$	$\frac{\text{365 days}}{3.46}$	=	105.49 days

If a company does not have sufficient cash and cashlike items to meet its obligations, the key to its debt-paying ability is the time it takes the company to convert less liquid current assets into cash. This is measured by the liquidity activity ratios.

The activity ratios for accounts receivable and inventory are especially useful to auditors. Trends in the accounts receivable turnover ratio are often used in assessing the reasonableness of the allowance for uncollectible accounts. Trends in the inventory turnover ratio are used in identifying potential inventory obsolescence. Average days to collect is a different way of looking at the average accounts receivable turnover data. The same is true of average days to sell compared to average inventory turnover.

Ability to Meet Long-term Debt Obligations

Debt to equity	=	$\frac{\text{total liabilities}}{\text{total equity}}$	$\frac{13{,}216 + 25{,}688}{22{,}463}$	=	1.73
Times interest earned	=	$\frac{\text{operating income}}{\text{interest expense}}$	$\frac{7{,}370}{2{,}409}$	=	3.06

A company's long-run solvency depends on the success of its operations and on its ability to raise capital for expansion, as well as its ability to make principal and interest payments. These two ratios are key measures used by creditors and investors to assess a company's ability to pay its debts.

The debt-to-equity ratio shows the extent of the use of debt in financing a company. If the debt-to-equity ratio is too high, it may indicate that the company has used up its borrowing capacity and has no cushion for additional debt. If it is too low, it may mean that available leverage is not being used to the owners' benefit.

The ability to make interest payments is dependent on the company's ability to generate positive cash flows from operations. Thus, times interest earned shows how comfortably the company should be able to make interest payments, assuming that earnings trends are stable.

Profitability Ratios

A company's ability to generate cash for payment of obligations, expansion, and dividends is heavily dependent on profitability. The most widely used profitability ratio is earnings per share. Additional ratios can be calculated that provide further insights into operations.

Gross profit percent shows the portion of sales available to cover all expenses and profit after deducting the cost of the product. It is especially useful to auditors in assessing misstatements in sales, cost of goods sold, accounts receivable, and inventory.

Profit margin is similar to gross profit margin but subtracts both cost of goods sold and operating expenses in making the calculations. This ratio is especially useful to auditors in assessing potential misstatements in operating expenses and related balance sheet accounts.

$$\text{Earnings per share} = \frac{\text{net income}}{\text{average common shares outstanding}} \quad \frac{3{,}934}{5{,}000} = 0.79$$

$$\text{Gross profit percent} = \frac{\text{net sales} - \text{cost of goods sold}}{\text{net sales}} \quad \frac{143{,}086 - 103{,}241}{143{,}086} = 27.85\%$$

$$\text{Profit margin} = \frac{\text{operating income}}{\text{net sales}} \quad \frac{7{,}370}{143{,}086} = 0.05$$

$$\text{Return on assets} = \frac{\text{income before taxes}}{\text{average total assets}} \quad \frac{5{,}681}{61{,}367} = 0.09$$

$$\text{Return on common equity} = \frac{\text{income} - \text{preferred dividends}}{\text{average stockholders' equity}} \quad \frac{5{,}681 - 0}{22{,}463} = 0.25$$

Two measures of overall profitability of a company are return on assets and return on equity. These ratios show a company's ability to generate profit for each dollar of assets and equity.

SUMMARY OF ANALYTICAL PROCEDURES

Analytical procedures involve the computation of ratios and other comparisons of recorded amounts to auditor expectations. Analytical procedures are used in planning to understand the client's business and industry and throughout the audit to identify possible misstatements, reduce detailed tests, and to assess going-concern issues. The use of analytical procedures has increased because of their effectiveness at identifying possible misstatements at a low cost, and they are required in the planning and completion phases of the audit.

ESSENTIAL TERMS

Acceptable audit risk—a measure of how willing the auditor is to accept that the financial statements may be materially misstated after the audit is completed and an unqualified opinion has been issued

Budgets—written records of the client's expectations for the period; a comparison of budgets with actual results may indicate whether or not misstatements are likely

Bylaws—the rules and procedures adopted by a corporation's stockholders, including the corporation's fiscal year and the duties and powers of its officers

Client business risk—the risk that the client will fail to achieve its objectives related to (1) reliability of financial reporting, (2) effectiveness and efficiency of operations, and (3) compliance with laws and regulations

Corporate charter—a legal document granted by the state in which a company is incorporated that recognizes a corporation as a separate entity; it includes the name of the corporation, the date of incorporation, capital stock the corporation is authorized to issue, and the types of business activities the corporation is authorized to conduct

Corporate minutes—the official record of the meetings of a corporation's board of directors and stockholders, in which corporate issues such as the declaration of dividends and the approval of contracts are documented

Engagement letter—an agreement between the CPA firm and the client as to the terms of the engagement for the conduct of the audit and related services

Inherent risk—a measure of the auditor's assessment of the likelihood that there are material misstatements in a segment before considering the effectiveness of internal control

Initial audit planning—involves deciding whether to accept or continue doing the audit for the client, identifying the client's reasons for the audit, obtaining an engagement letter, and selecting staff for the engagement

Related party—affiliated company, principal owner of the client company, or any other party with which the client deals where one of the parties can influence the management or operating policies of the other

Related party transaction—any transaction between the client and a related party

REVIEW QUESTIONS

7-1 (Objective 7-1) What benefits does the auditor derive from planning audits?

7-2 (Objective 7-1) Identify the seven major steps in planning audits.

7-3 (Objective 7-2) What are the responsibilities of the successor and predecessor auditors when a company is changing auditors?

7-4 (Objective 7-2) What factors should an auditor consider prior to accepting an engagement? Explain.

7-5 (Objective 7-2) What is the purpose of an engagement letter? What subjects should be covered in such a letter?

7-6 (Objective 7-3) Explain why auditors need an understanding of the client's industry. What sources are commonly used by auditors to learn about the client's industry?

7-7 (Objective 7-3) When a CPA has accepted an engagement from a new client who is a manufacturer, it is customary for the CPA to tour the client's plant facilities. Discuss the ways in which the CPA's observations made during the course of the plant tour will be of help in planning and conducting the audit.

7-8 (Objective 7-3) An auditor often tries to acquire background knowledge of the client's industry as an aid to audit work. How does the acquisition of this knowledge aid the auditor in distinguishing between obsolete and current inventory?

7-9 (Objective 7-3) Define what is meant by a related party. What are the auditor's responsibilities for related parties and related party transactions?

7-10 (Objective 7-3) Your firm has performed the audit of the Rogers Company for several years and you have been assigned the audit responsibility for the current audit. How would your review of the corporate charter and bylaws for this audit differ from that of the audit of a client who was audited by a different CPA firm in the preceding year?

7-11 (Objective 7-3) For the audit of Radline Manufacturing Company, the audit partner asks you to carefully read the new mortgage contract with the First National Bank and abstract all pertinent information. List the information in a mortgage that is likely to be relevant to the auditor.

7-12 (Objective 7-3) Identify two types of information in the client's minutes of the board of directors meetings that are likely to be relevant to the auditor. Explain why it is important to read the minutes early in the engagement.

7-13 (Objective 7-3) Identify the three categories of client objectives. Indicate how each objective may affect the auditor's assessment of inherent risk and evidence accumulation.

7-14 (Objective 7-3) What is the purpose of the client's performance measurement system? Give examples of key performance indicators for the following businesses: (1) a chain of retail clothing stores; (2) an Internet portal; (3) a hotel chain.

7-15 (Objective 7-4) Define client business risk and describe several sources of client business risk. What is the auditor's primary concern when evaluating client business risk?

7-16 (Objective 7-4) Describe top management controls and their relation to client business risk. Give examples of effective management and governance controls.

7-17 (Objectives 7-5, 7-6) What are the purposes of preliminary analytical procedures? What types of comparisons are useful when performing preliminary analytical procedures?

7-18 (Objective 7-6) When are analytical procedures required to be performed during the audit? What is the primary purpose of analytical procedures performed during the completion phase of the audit?

7-19 (Objective 7-7) Gale Gordon, CPA, has found ratio and trend analysis relatively useless as a tool in conducting audits. For several engagements, he computed the industry ratios included in publications by Robert Morris Associates and compared them with industry standards. For most engagements, the client's business was significantly different from the industry data in the publication and the client would automatically explain away any discrepancies by attributing them to the unique nature of its operations. In cases in which the client had more than one branch in different industries, Gordon found the ratio analysis no help at all. How could Gordon improve the quality of his analytical procedures?

7-20 **(Objective 7-7)** At the completion of every audit, Roger Morris, CPA, calculates a large number of ratios and trends for comparison with industry averages and prior-year calculations. He believes the calculations are worth the relatively small cost of doing them because they provide him with an excellent overview of the client's operations. If the ratios are out of line, Morris discusses the reasons with the client and often makes suggestions on how to bring the ratio back in line in the future. In some cases, these discussions with management have been the basis for management consulting engagements. Discuss the major strengths and shortcomings in Morris's use of ratio and trend analysis.

7-21 **(Objective 7-8)** Name the four categories of financial ratios and give an example of a ratio in each category. What is the primary information provided by each financial ratio category?

MULTIPLE CHOICE QUESTIONS FROM CPA EXAMINATIONS

7-22 **(Objectives 7-1, 7-3)** The following questions concern the planning of the engagement. Select the best response.

a. Which of the following is an effective audit planning procedure that helps prevent misunderstandings and inefficient use of audit personnel?
   (1) Arrange to make copies, for inclusion in the audit files, of those client supporting documents examined by the auditor.
   (2) Arrange to provide the client with copies of the audit programs to be used during the audit.
   (3) Arrange a preliminary conference with the client to discuss audit objectives, fees, timing, and other information.
   (4) Arrange to have the auditor prepare and post any necessary adjusting or reclassification entries prior to final closing.

b. An auditor is planning an audit engagement for a new client in a business with which he is unfamiliar. Which of the following would be the most useful source of information during the preliminary planning stage, when the auditor is trying to obtain a general understanding of audit problems that might be encountered?
   (1) Client manuals of accounts and charts of accounts.
   (2) AICPA Industry Audit Guides.
   (3) Prior-year audit files of the predecessor auditor.
   (4) Latest annual and interim financial statements issued by the client.

c. An auditor obtains knowledge about a new client's business and industry to
   (1) make constructive suggestions concerning improvements in the client's internal control.
   (2) develop an attitude of professional skepticism concerning management's financial statement assertions.
   (3) evaluate whether the sum of known misstatements causes the financial statements as a whole to be materially misstated.
   (4) understand the events and transactions that may have an effect on the client's financial statements.

7-23 **(Objective 7-2)** The following questions pertain to client acceptance. Choose the best response.

a. In assessing whether to accept a client for an audit engagement, a CPA should consider

	Client Business Risk	Acceptable Audit Risk
(1)	Yes	Yes
(2)	Yes	No
(3)	No	Yes
(4)	No	No

b. When approached to perform an audit for the first time, the CPA should make inquiries of the predecessor auditor. This is a necessary procedure because the predecessor may be able to provide the successor with information that will assist the successor in determining whether
   (1) the predecessor's work should be used.
   (2) the company follows the policy of rotating its auditors.
   (3) in the predecessor's opinion internal control of the company has been satisfactory.
   (4) the engagement should be accepted.

c. What is the responsibility of a successor auditor with respect to communicating with the predecessor auditor in connection with a prospective new audit client?
   (1) The successor auditor has *no* responsibility to contact the predecessor auditor.
   (2) The successor auditor should obtain permission from the prospective client to contact the predecessor auditor.
   (3) The successor auditor should contact the predecessor regardless of whether the prospective client authorizes contact.
   (4) The successor auditor need *not* contact the predecessor if the successor is aware of all available relevant facts.

7-24 **(Objectives 7-5, 7-6, 7-7, 7-8)** The following questions concern the use of analytical procedures during the planning phase of an audit. Select the best response.

a. Analytical procedures used in planning an audit should focus on identifying
   (1) material weaknesses of internal control.
   (2) the predictability of financial data from individual transactions.
   (3) the various assertions that are embodied in the financial statements.
   (4) areas that may represent specific risks relevant to the audit.

b. For all audits of financial statements made in accordance with generally accepted auditing standards, the use of analytical procedures is required to some extent

	In the Planning Stage	As a Sustantive Test	In the Completion Stage
(1)	Yes	No	Yes
(2)	No	Yes	No
(3)	No	Yes	Yes
(4)	Yes	No	No

c. Which of the following would be *least* likely to be comparable between similar corporations in the same industry line of business?
   (1) Accounts receivable turnover.
   (2) Earnings per share.
   (3) Gross profit percent.
   (4) Return on assets before interest and taxes.

d. Which of the following situations has the best chance of being detected when a CPA compares 2002 revenues and expenses with the prior year and investigates all changes exceeding a fixed percentage?
   (1) An increase in property tax rates has not been recognized in the company's 2002 accrual.
   (2) The cashier began lapping accounts receivable in 2002.
   (3) Because of worsening economic conditions, the 2002 provision for uncollectible accounts was inadequate.
   (4) The company changed its capitalization policy for small tools in 2002.

DISCUSSION QUESTIONS AND PROBLEMS

7-25 **(Objectives 7-2, 7-3, 7-4, 7-5)** In late spring, you are advised of a new assignment as in-charge accountant of your CPA firm's recurring annual audit of a major client, the Lancer Company. You are given the engagement letter for the audit covering the current calendar year and a list of personnel assigned to this engagement. It is your responsibility to plan and supervise the field work for the engagement.

Required

Discuss the necessary preparation and planning for the Lancer Company annual audit before beginning field work at the client's office. In your discussion, include the sources you should consult, the type of information you should seek, the preliminary plans and preparation you should make for the field work, and any actions you should take relative to the staff assigned to the engagement.*

7-26 **(Objective 7-3)** Generally accepted accounting principles set certain requirements for disclosure of related parties and related party transactions. Similarly, the SASs set requirements for the audit of related parties and related party transactions. For this problem, you are expected to research appropriate SFASs and SASs.

*AICPA adapted.

Required

a. Define *related party* as used for generally accepted accounting principles and explain the disclosure requirements for related parties and related party transactions.
b. Explain why disclosure of related party transactions is relevant information for decision makers.
c. List the most important related parties who are likely to be involved in related party transactions.
d. List several different types of related party transactions that could take place in a company.
e. Discuss ways the auditor can determine the existence of related parties and related party transactions.
f. For each type of related party transaction, discuss different ways the auditor can evaluate whether it is recorded on an arm's-length basis, assuming that the auditor knows the transactions exist.
g. Assume that you know the material related party transactions occurred and were transacted at significantly less favorable terms than ordinarily occur when business is done with independent parties. The client refuses to disclose these facts in the financial statements. What are your responsibilities?

7-27 **(Objective 7-3)** The minutes of the board of directors of the Marygold Catalog Company for the year ended December 31, 2002, were provided to you.

MEETING OF FEBRUARY 15, 2002

Ruth Jackson, chairman of the board, called the meeting to order at 4:00 PM. The following directors were in attendance:

John Aronson	Licorine Phillips
Fred Brick	Lucille Renolds
Oron Carlson	J. T. Smith
Homer Jackson	Raymond Werd
Ruth Jackson	Ronald Wilder

The minutes of the meeting of October 11, 2001, were read and approved.

Homer Jackson, president, discussed the new marketing plan for wider distribution of catalogs in the southwestern U.S. market. He made a motion for approval of increased expenditures of approximately $500,000 for distribution costs that was seconded by Wilder and unanimously passed.

The unresolved dispute with the Internal Revenue Service over the tax treatment of leased office buildings was discussed with Cecil Makay, attorney. In Mr. Makay's opinion, the matter would not be resolved for several months and may result in an unfavorable settlement.

J. T. Smith moved that the computer equipment that was no longer being used in the Kingston office, because of new equipment acquired in 2001, be donated to the Kingston vocational school for use in their repair and training program. John Aronson seconded the motion and it unanimously passed.

Annual cash dividends were unanimously approved as being payable April 30, 2002, for stockholders of record April 15, 2002, as follows:

Class A common—$10 per share
Class B common—$5 per share

Officers' bonuses for the year ended December 31, 2001, were approved for payment March 1, 2002, as follows:

Homer Jackson—President	$130,000
Lucille Renolds—Vice president	60,000
Ronald Wilder—Controller	60,000
Fred Brick—Secretary-treasurer	45,000

Meeting adjourned 6:30 PM.

Fred Brick, Secretary

MEETING OF SEPTEMBER 16, 2002

Ruth Jackson, chairman of the board, called the meeting to order at 4:00 PM. The following directors were in attendance:

John Aronson	Licorine Phillips
Fred Brick	Lucille Renolds
Oron Carlson	J. T. Smith
Homer Jackson	Raymond Werd
Ruth Jackson	Ronald Wilder

The minutes of the meeting of February 15, 2002, were read and approved.

Homer Jackson, president, discussed the improved sales and financial condition for 2002. He was pleased with the results of the catalog distribution and cost control for the company. No action was taken.

The nominations for officers were made as follows:

President	—Homer Jackson
Vice president	—Lucille Renolds
Controller	—Ronald Wilder
Secretary-treasurer	—Fred Brick

The nominees were elected by unanimous voice vote.

Salary increases of 5%, exclusive of bonuses, were recommended for all officers for the year 2003. Homer Jackson moved that such salary increases be approved, seconded by J. T. Smith, and unanimously approved.

	Salary	
	2002	**2003**
Homer Jackson, President	$240,000	$252,000
Lucille Renolds, Vice president	160,000	168,000
Ronald Wilder, Controller	160,000	168,000
Fred Brick, Secretary-treasurer	120,000	126,000

Ronald Wilder moved that the company consider adopting a pension/profit-sharing plan for all employees as a way to provide greater incentive for employees to stay with the company. Considerable discussion ensued. It was agreed without adoption that Wilder should discuss the legal and tax implications with attorney Cecil Makay and a CPA firm reputed to be knowledgeable about pension and profit-sharing plans, Able and Better, CPAs.

Ronald Wilder discussed expenditure of $58,000 for acquisition of a new computer system for the Kingston office to replace equipment that was purchased in 2001 and has proven ineffective. A settlement has been tentatively reached to return the equipment for a refund of $21,000. Wilder moved that both transactions be approved, seconded by Jackson, and unanimously adopted.

Fred Brick moved that a loan of $360,000, from the Kingston Federal Bank and Trust, be approved. The interest is floating at 2% above prime. The loan is collateralized by accounts receivable, with the loan balance not to exceed 75% of current accounts receivable. Seconded by Phillips and unanimously approved.

Lucille Renolds, chair of the audit committee, moved that the CPA firm of Moss and Lawson be selected again for the company's annual audit and related tax work for the year ended December 31, 2002. Seconded by Aronson and unanimously approved.

Meeting adjourned 6:40 PM.

Fred Brick, Secretary

Required

a. How do you, as the auditor, know that all minutes have been made available to you?

b. Read the minutes of the meetings of February 15 and September 16. Use the following format to list and explain information that is relevant for the 2002 audit:

Information Relevant to 2002 Audit	Audit Action Required
1.	
2.	

c. Read the minutes of the meeting of February 15, 2002. Did any of that information pertain to the December 31, 2001, audit? Explain what the auditor should have done during the December 31, 2001, audit with respect to 2002 minutes.

7-28 **(Objectives 7-3, 7-4, 7-5)** You are engaged in the annual audit of the financial statements of Maulack Company, a medium-sized wholesale company that manufactures light fixtures. The company has 25 stockholders. During your review of the minutes, you observe that the president's salary has been increased substantially over the preceding year by action of the board of directors. His present salary is much greater than salaries paid to presidents of companies of comparable size and is clearly excessive. You determine that the method of computing the president's salary was changed for the year under audit. In previous years, the president's salary was consistently based on sales. In the latest year, however, his salary was based on net income before income taxes. The Maulack Company is in a cyclical industry and would have had an extremely profitable year except that the increase in the president's salary siphoned off much of the income that would have accrued to the stockholders. The president is a substantial stockholder.

Required

a. What is the implication of this condition on the fair presentation of the financial statements?

b. Discuss your responsibility for disclosing this situation.

c. Discuss the effect, if any, that the situation has on your auditor's opinion as to
   (1) the fairness of the presentation of the financial statements.
   (2) the consistency of the application of accounting principles.*

7-29 **(Objectives 7-5, 7-6, 7-7, 7-8)** In auditing the financial statements of a manufacturing company that were prepared using information technology, the CPA has found that the traditional audit trail has been obscured. As a result, the CPA may place increased emphasis on analytical procedures of the data under audit. These tests, which are also applied in auditing visibly posted accounting records, include the computation of ratios that are compared with prior-year ratios or with industrywide norms. Examples of analytical procedures are the computation of the rate of inventory turnover and the computation of the number of days in receivables.

Required

a. Discuss the advantages to the CPA of the use of analytical procedures in an audit.

b. In addition to the computations described, list ratios that an auditor may compute during an audit on balance sheet accounts and related income accounts. For each ratio listed, name the two (or more) accounts used in its computation.

c. When there has been a significant change in a ratio when compared with the preceding year's, the auditor considers the possible reasons for the change. Give the possible reasons for the following significant changes in ratios:
   (1) The rate of inventory turnover (ratio of cost of sales and average inventory) has decreased from the preceding year's rate.
   (2) The number of days' sales in receivables (ratio of average daily accounts receivable and sales) has increased over the prior year.*

7-30 **(Objectives 7-3, 7-7, 7-8)** Your comparison of the gross margin percentage for Jones Drugs for the years 1999 through 2002 indicates a significant decline. This is shown by the following information:

	2002	2001	2000	1999
Sales (thousands)	$14,211	$12,916	$11,462	$10,351
CGS (thousands)	9,223	8,266	7,313	6,573
Gross margin	$4,988	$4,650	$4,149	$3,778
Percent	35.1	36.0	36.2	36.5

A discussion with Marilyn Adams, the controller, brings to light two possible explanations. She informs you that the industry gross profit percentage in the retail drug industry declined fairly steadily for 3 years, which accounts for part of the decline. A second factor was the declining percentage of the total volume resulting from the pharmacy part of the business. The pharmacy sales represent the most profitable portion of the business, yet the competition from discount drugstores prevents it from expanding as fast as the nondrug items such as magazines, candy, and many other items sold. Adams feels strongly that these two factors are the cause of the decline.

The following additional information is obtained from independent sources and the client's records as a means of investigating the controller's explanations:

	Jones Drugs ($ in thousands)				Industry Gross Profit Percent for Retailers of Drugs and Related Products
	Drug Sales	Nondrug Sales	Drug Cost of Goods Sold	Nondrug Cost of Goods Sold	
2002	$5,126	$9,085	$3,045	$6,178	32.7
2001	5,051	7,865	2,919	5,347	32.9
2000	4,821	6,641	2,791	4,522	33.0
1999	4,619	5,732	2,665	3,908	33.2

*AICPA adapted.

Required

a. Evaluate the explanation provided by Adams. Show calculations to support your conclusions.

b. Which specific aspects of the client's financial statements require intensive investigation in this audit?

7-31 **(Objectives 7-7, 7-8)** In the audit of the Worldwide Wholesale Company, you performed extensive ratio and trend analysis. No material exceptions were discovered except for the following:

1. Commission expense as a percentage of sales has stayed constant for several years but has increased significantly in the current year. Commission rates have not changed.
2. The rate of inventory turnover has steadily decreased for 4 years.
3. Inventory as a percentage of current assets has steadily increased for 4 years.
4. The number of days' sales in accounts receivable has steadily increased for 3 years.
5. Allowance for uncollectible accounts as a percentage of accounts receivable has steadily decreased for 3 years.
6. The absolute amounts of depreciation expense and depreciation expense as a percentage of gross fixed assets are significantly smaller than in the preceding year.

Required

a. Evaluate the potential significance of each of the exceptions just listed for the fair presentation of financial statements.

b. State the follow-up procedures you would use to determine the possibility of material misstatements.

7-32 **(Objectives 7-3, 7-5)** As part of the analytical procedures of Mahogany Products, Inc., you perform calculations of the following ratios:

	Industry Averages		Mahogany Products	
Ratio	**2002**	**2001**	**2002**	**2001**
1. Current ratio	3.30	3.80	2.20	2.60
2. Days to collect receivables	87.00	93.00	67.00	60.00
3. Days to sell inventory	126.00	121.00	93.00	89.00
4. Purchases divided by accounts payable	11.70	11.60	8.50	8.60
5. Inventory divided by current assets	.56	.51	.49	.48
6. Operating income divided by tangible assets	.08	.06	.14	.12
7. Operating income divided by net sales	.06	.06	.04	.04
8. Gross profit percentage	.21	.27	.21	.19
9. Earnings per share	$14.27	$13.91	$2.09	$1.93

Required

For each of the preceding ratios:

a. State whether there is a need to investigate the results further and, if so, the reason for further investigation.

b. State the approach you would use in the investigation.

c. Explain how the operations of Mahogany Products appear to differ from those of the industry.

7-33 **(Objectives 7-3, 7-5, 7-7)** Following are the auditor's calculations of several key ratios for Cragston Star Products. The primary purpose of this information is to understand the client's business and assess the risk of financial failure, but any other relevant conclusions are also desirable.

Ratio	2002	2001	2000	1999	1998
Current ratio	2.08	2.26	2.51	2.43	2.50
Quick ratio	.97	1.34	1.82	1.76	1.64
Times interest earned	3.50	3.20	4.10	5.30	7.10
Accounts receivable turnover	4.20	5.50	4.10	5.40	5.60
Days to collect receivables	86.90	66.36	89.02	67.59	65.18
Inventory turnover	2.03	1.84	2.68	3.34	3.36
Days to sell inventory	179.80	198.37	136.19	109.28	108.63
Net sales divided by tangible assets	.68	.64	.73	.69	.67
Profit margin	.13	.14	.16	.15	.14
Return on assets	.09	.09	.12	.10	.09
Return on equity	.05	.06	.10	.10	.11
Earnings per share	$4.30	$4.26	$4.49	$4.26	$4.14

a. What major conclusions can be drawn from this information about the company's future?

b. What additional information would be helpful in your assessment of this company's financial condition?

Required

c. Based on the preceding ratios, which aspects of the company do you believe should receive special emphasis in the audit?

7-34 **(Objectives 7-3, 7-4)** The Internet has dramatically increased global e-commerce activities. Both traditional "brick and mortar" businessess and new dot-com businesses use the Internet to meet business objectives. For example, traditional retailer Toys "R" Us, Inc., also sells toys and other products through its Web site, which is operated in partnership with Amazon.com.

Required

a. Identify three specific business strategies that are likely reasons why Toys "R" Us is offering products for sale online.

b. Describe three business risks related to Toys "R" Us offering online sales.

c. Discuss possible reasons why Toys "R" Us decided to partner with Amazon.com to handle online sales.

d. Identify possible risks that could lead to material misstatements in the Toys "R" Us financial statements if its business risks related to online sales are not effectively managed.

CASES

7-35 **(Objectives 7-2, 7-3, 7-4)** Winston Black was an audit partner in the firm of Henson, Davis & Company. He was in the process of reviewing the audit files for the audit of a new client, McMullan Resources. McMullan was in the business of heavy construction. Black was conducting his first review after the field work was substantially complete. Normally, he would have done an initial review during the planning phase as required by his firm's policies; however, he had been overwhelmed by an emergency with his largest and most important client. He rationalized not reviewing audit planning information because (1) the audit was being overseen by Sarah Beale, a manager in whom he had confidence, and (2) he could "recover" from any problems during his end-of-audit review.

Now, Black found that he was confronted with a couple of problems. First, he found that the firm may have accepted McMullan without complying with its new-client acceptance procedures. McMullan came to Henson, Davis on a recommendation from a friend of Black's. Black got "credit" for the new business, which was important to him because it would affect his compensation from the firm. Because Black was busy, he told Beale to conduct a new-client acceptance review and let him know if there were any problems. He never heard from Beale and assumed everything was okay. In reviewing Beale's preaudit planning documentation, he saw a check mark in the box "Contact prior auditors" but found no details indicating what was done. When he asked Beale about this, she responded with the following:

> I called Gardner Smith [the responsible partner with McMullan's prior audit firm] and left a phone mail message for him. He never returned my call. I talked to Ted McMullan about the change, and he told me that he informed Gardner about the change and that Gardner said, "Fine, I'll help in any way I can." Ted said Gardner sent over copies of analyses of fixed assets and equity accounts, which Ted gave to me. I asked Ted why they replaced Gardner's firm, and he told me it was over the tax contingency issue and the size of their fee. Other than that, Ted said the relationship was fine.

The tax contingency issue that Beale referred to was a situation in which McMullan had entered into litigation with a bank from which it had received a loan. The result of the litigation was that the bank forgave several hundred thousand dollars in debt. This was a windfall to McMullan, and they recorded it as a gain, taking the position that it was nontaxable. The prior auditors disputed this position and insisted that a contingent tax liability existed that required disclosure. This upset McMullan, but the company agreed in order to receive an unqualified opinion. Before hiring Henson, Davis as their new auditors, McMullan requested that Henson, Davis review the situation. Henson, Davis believed the contingency was remote and agreed to the elimination of the disclosure.

The second problem involved a long-term contract with a customer in Montreal. Under GAAP, McMullan was required to recognize income on this contract using the percentage-of-completion method. The contract was partially completed as of year-end and had a material effect on the financial statements. When Black went to review the copy of the contract in the audit files, he found three things. First, there was a contract summary that set out its major features. Second, there was a copy of the contract written in French. Third, there was a signed confirmation confirming the terms and status of the contract. The space requesting information about any contract disputes was left blank, indicating no such problems.

Black's concern about the contract was that to recognize income in accordance with GAAP, the contract had to be enforceable. Often, contracts contain a cancellation clause that might mitigate enforceability. Because he was not able to read French, Black couldn't tell whether the contract contained such a clause. When he asked Beale about this, she responded that she had asked the company's vice president for the Canadian division about the contract and he told her that it was their standard contract. The company's standard contract did have a cancellation clause in it, but it required mutual agreement and could not be cancelled unilaterally by the buyer.

Required

a. Evaluate and discuss whether Henson, Davis & Company complied with generally accepted auditing standards in their acceptance of McMullan Resources as a new client. What can they do at this point in the engagement to resolve deficiencies if they exist?

b. Evaluate and discuss whether sufficient audit work has been done with regard to McMullan's Montreal contract. If not, what more should be done?

c. Evaluate and discuss whether Black and Beale conducted themselves in accordance with generally accepted auditing standards.

7-36 **(Objectives 7-3, 7-4, 7-7)** Solomon is a highly successful, closely held Boston, Massachusetts, company that manufactures and assembles automobile specialty parts that are sold in auto parts stores in the East. Sales and profits have expanded rapidly in the past few years, and the prospects for future years are every bit as encouraging. In fact, the Solomon brothers are currently considering either selling out to a large company or going public to obtain additional capital.

The company originated in 1967 when Frank Solomon decided to manufacture tooled parts. In 1982, the company changed over to the auto parts business. Fortunately, it has never been necessary to expand the facilities, but space problems have recently become severe and expanded facilities will be necessary. Land and building costs in Boston are currently extremely inflated.

Management has always relied on you for help in its problems because the treasurer is sales-oriented and has little background in the controllership function. Salaries of all officers have been fairly modest in order to reinvest earnings in future growth. In fact, the company is oriented toward long-run wealth of the brothers more than toward short-run profit. The brothers have all of their personal wealth invested in the firm.

A major reason for the success of Solomon has been the small but excellent sales force. The sales policy is to sell to small auto shops at high prices. This policy is responsible for fairly high credit losses, but the profit margin is high and the results have been highly successful. The firm has every intention of continuing this policy in the future.

Your firm has been auditing Solomon since 1977, and you have been on the job for the past 3 years. The client has excellent internal controls and has always been cooperative. In recent years, the client has attempted to keep net income at a high level because of borrowing needs and future sellout possibilities. Overall, the client has always been pleasant to deal with and willing to help in any way possible. There have never been any major audit adjustments, and an unqualified opinion has always been issued.

In the current year, you have completed the tests of the sales and collection area. The tests of controls and substantive tests of transactions for sales and sales returns and allowances were excellent, and an extensive confirmation yielded no material misstatements. You have carefully reviewed the cutoff for sales and for sales returns and allowances and find these to be excellent. All recorded bad debts appear reasonable, and a review of the aged trial balance indicates that conditions seem about the same as in past years.

Required

a. Evaluate the information in the case (see p. 203) to provide assistance to management for improved operation of its business. Prepare the supporting analysis using an electronic spreadsheet program (instructor option).

b. Do you agree that sales, accounts receivable, and allowance for doubtful accounts are probably correctly stated? Show calculations to support your conclusion.

INTERNET PROBLEM 7-1: INDUSTRY RESEARCH AND CLIENT ACCEPTANCE

Reference the CW site. The vignette at the beginning of Chapter 5 in the text contains a brief description of the ZZZZ Best fraud. One area in which the auditors were criticized in that audit was the auditors' lack of industry knowledge. With hindsight, it appeared that the fraud should have been easily detected because ZZZZ Best's large restoration contracts were in excess of $7 million, whereas the largest restoration jobs on record in the insurance restoration industry were less than $3 million. This problem requires students to use the Internet to research industry data to determine the reasonableness of reported unit sales.

	12-31-02 (Current Year)	12-31-01	12-31-00	12-31-99
Balance Sheet				
Cash	$ 49,615	$ 39,453	$ 51,811	$ 48,291
Accounts receivable	2,366,938	2,094,052	1,756,321	1,351,470
Allowance for doubtful accounts	(250,000)	(240,000)	(220,000)	(200,000)
Inventory	2,771,833	2,585,820	2,146,389	1,650,959
Current assets	4,938,386	4,479,325	3,734,521	2,850,720
Fixed assets	3,760,531	3,744,590	3,498,930	3,132,133
Total assets	$8,698,917	$8,223,915	$7,233,451	$5,982,853
Current liabilities	$2,253,422	$2,286,433	$1,951,830	$1,625,811
Long-term liabilities	4,711,073	4,525,310	4,191,699	3,550,481
Owners' equity	1,734,422	1,412,172	1,089,922	806,561
Total liabilities and owners' equity	$8,698,917	$8,223,915	$7,233,451	$5,982,853
Income Statement Information				
Sales	$6,740,652	$6,165,411	$5,313,752	$4,251,837
Sales returns and allowances	(207,831)	(186,354)	(158,367)	(121,821)
Sales discounts allowed	(74,147)	(63,655)	(52,183)	(42,451)
Bad debts	(248,839)	(245,625)	(216,151)	(196,521)
Net sales	$6,209,835	$5,669,777	$4,887,051	$3,891,044
Gross margin	$1,415,926	$1,360,911	$1,230,640	$1,062,543
Net income after taxes	$335,166	$322,250	$283,361	$257,829
Aged Accounts Receivable				
0–30 days	$ 942,086	$ 881,232	$ 808,569	$ 674,014
31–60 days	792,742	697,308	561,429	407,271
61–120 days	452,258	368,929	280,962	202,634
>120 days	179,852	146,583	105,361	67,551
Total	$2,366,938	$2,094,052	$1,756,321	$1,351,470

INTERNET PROBLEM 7-2: OBTAIN CLIENT BACKGROUND INFORMATION

Planning is one of the most demanding and important aspects of an audit. A carefully planned audit increases auditor efficiency and provides greater assurance that the audit team addresses the critical issues. Auditors prepare audit planning documents that summarize client and industry background information and discuss important accounting and auditing issues related to the client's financial statements.

Your assignment is to find and document information for inclusion in the audit planning memorandum. Obtain the necessary information by downloading a public company's most recent annual report from its Web site (the company will be selected by you or your instructor). You may also use other sources of information such as recent 10-K filings to find additional information. You should address the following matters in four brief bulleted responses:

- Brief company history.
- Description of the company's business (for example, related companies, competitors).
- Key accounting issues identified from a review of the company's most recent annual report. (Note: Do not concentrate solely on the company's basic financial statements. Careful attention should be given to Management's Discussion and Analysis as well as the Footnotes.)
- Necessary experience levels (that is, years of experience, industry experience) required of the auditors to be involved in the audit.

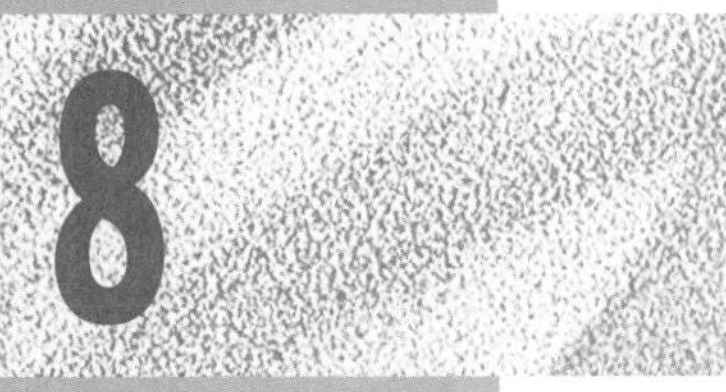

CHAPTER 8

MATERIALITY AND RISK

EXPLAIN TO ME ONE MORE TIME THAT YOU DID A GOOD JOB, BUT THE COMPANY WENT BROKE

Maxwell Spencer is a senior partner in his firm, and one of his regular duties is to attend the firm's annual training session for newly hired auditors. He loves doing this because it gives him a chance to share his many years of experience with inexperienced people who have bright and receptive minds. He covers several topics formally during the day and then sits around and "shoots the breeze" with participants during the evening hours. Here we listen to what he is saying.

> Suppose you are a retired 72-year-old man. You and your wife, Minnie, live on your retirement fund which you elected to manage yourself, rather than receive income from an annuity. You decide that your years in business prepared you with the ability to earn a better return than the annuity would provide.
>
> So when you retired and got your bundle, you called your broker and discussed with him what you should do with it. He tells you the most important thing is to protect your principal and recommends that you buy bonds. You settle on three issues that your broker and his firm believe are good ones, with solid balance sheets: (1) a utility company, (2) a fast-growing alternative energy company, and (3) a major county in Southern California. Now all you have to do is sit back and clip your coupons.
>
> Ah, but the best laid plans of mice and men. . . . First, the utility company goes broke, and you can look forward to recovering only a few cents on the dollar over several years. Then, the alternative energy company fails, and you might get something back—eventually. Finally, the county has a scandal and has to default on all of its outstanding bonds. A recovery plan is initiated, but don't hold your breath. Your best strategy is to apply for a job at McDonald's. They hire older people, don't they?
>
> Now what could the auditors of these three entities ever say to you about how they planned and conducted their audits and decided to issue an unqualified opinion that would justify that opinion in your mind? You don't care about business failure versus audit failure, or risk assessment and reliability of audit evidence, or any of that technical mumbo jumbo. The auditors were supposed to be there for you when you needed them, and they weren't. And materiality? Anything that would have indicated a problem is material to you.
>
> The message is, folks, that it's a lot easier to sweat over doing a tough audit right than it is to justify your judgments and decisions after it's too late. And good luck if you think that a harmed investor will ever see things from your point of view.

LEARNING OBJECTIVES

After studying this chapter, you should be able to

- 8-1 Apply the concept of materiality to the audit.
- 8-2 Make a preliminary judgment about what amounts to consider material.
- 8-3 Allocate preliminary materiality to segments of the audit during planning.
- 8-4 Use materiality to evaluate audit findings.
- 8-5 Define risk in auditing.
- 8-6 Describe the audit risk model and its components.
- 8-7 Consider the impact of engagement risk on acceptable audit risk.
- 8-8 Consider the impact of several factors on the assessment of inherent risk.
- 8-9 Consider information gathered to assess the likelihood of fraud.
- 8-10 Discuss the relationship of risks to audit evidence.
- 8-11 Discuss how materiality and risk are related and integrated into the audit process.

The scope paragraph in auditors' reports includes two important phrases that are directly related to materiality and risk. These phrases are emphasized in italic print in the following two sentences of a standard scope paragraph.

- We conducted our audits in accordance with auditing standards generally accepted in the United States of America. Those standards require that we plan and perform the audit to *obtain reasonable assurance* about whether the financial statements are *free of material misstatement.*

The phrase *obtain reasonable assurance* is intended to inform users that auditors do not guarantee or ensure the fair presentation of the financial statements. The phrase communicates that there is some *risk* that the financial statements are not fairly stated even when the opinion is unqualified.

The phrase *free of material misstatement* is intended to inform users that the auditor's responsibility is limited to *material* financial information. Materiality is important because it is impractical for auditors to provide assurances on immaterial amounts.

Thus, materiality and risk are fundamental concepts that are important to planning the audit and designing the audit approach. This chapter shows how these concepts fit into the planning phase of the audit.

There is a close relationship between this chapter and Chapters 5 and 7. Chapter 5 discussed the auditor's responsibilities, transaction cycles, and audit objectives. In this chapter, both materiality and risk are applied to the concepts studied in these topics. The first part of Chapter 7 dealt with planning the audit, primarily the first four parts, which are shown in the margin below. This chapter deals with the fifth part, which is shaded in the margin. A considerable amount of the information that auditors acquire and document during the first four parts of planning is used when the auditor decides materiality and assesses risks.

MATERIALITY

OBJECTIVE 8-1

Apply the concept of materiality to the audit.

- Accept client and perform initial planning
- Understand the client's business and industry
- Assess client business risk
- Perform preliminary analytical procedures
- **Set materiality and assess acceptable audit risk and inherent risk**
- Understand internal control and assess control risk
- Develop overall audit plan and audit program

As was shown in Chapter 2, materiality is a major consideration in determining the appropriate audit report to issue. The concepts of materiality discussed in this chapter are directly related to those in Chapter 2.

FASB 2 has defined **materiality** as

- The magnitude of an omission or misstatement of accounting information that, in the light of surrounding circumstances, makes it *probable* that the judgment of a reasonable person relying on the information would have been changed or influenced by the omission or misstatement. [italics added]

The auditor's responsibility is to determine whether financial statements are materially misstated. If the auditor determines that there is a material misstatement, he or she will bring it to the client's attention so that a correction can be made. If the client refuses to correct the statements, a qualified or an adverse opinion must be issued, depending on how material the misstatement is. Therefore, auditors must have a thorough knowledge of the application of materiality.

A careful reading of the FASB definition reveals the difficulty that auditors have in applying materiality in practice. The definition emphasizes reasonable users who rely on the statements to make decisions. Therefore, auditors must have knowledge of the likely users of their clients' statements and the decisions that are being made. For example, if an auditor knows that financial statements will be relied on in a buy–sell agreement for the entire business, the amount that the auditor considers material may be smaller than for an otherwise similar audit. In practice, auditors may not know who all users are or what decisions will be made.

There are five closely related steps in applying materiality. They are shown in Figure 8-1 and discussed in the next few sections of this chapter. The steps start with setting a preliminary judgment about materiality and allocating this estimate to the segments of the audit. As shown in the first bracket in Figure 8-1, these two steps are done as part of planning and

FIGURE 8-1 Steps in Applying Materiality

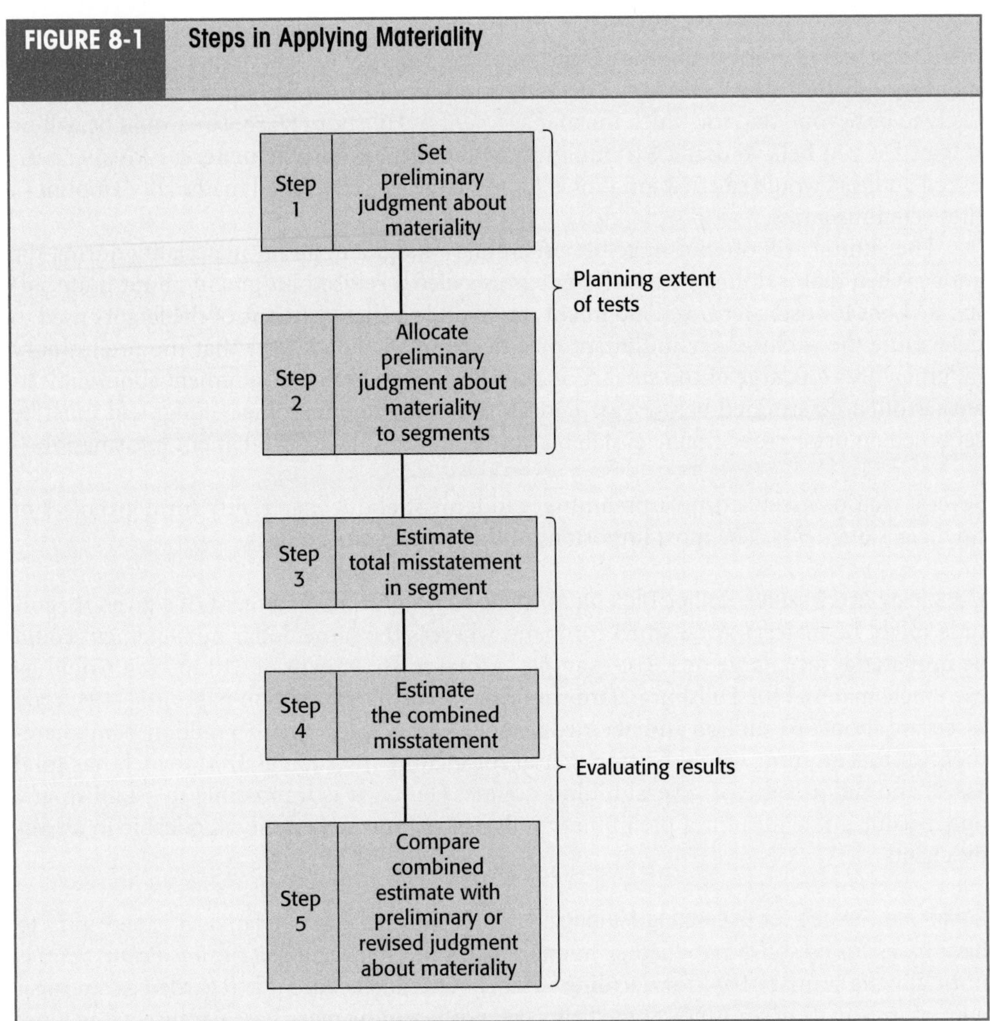

are the primary topics of the discussion of materiality in this chapter. Estimation of the amount of misstatements in each segment takes place throughout the audit. The final two steps are done near the end of the audit during the engagement completion phase. These three steps are shown in the second bracket in Figure 8-1 and are done as part of evaluating the results of audit tests.

SET PRELIMINARY JUDGMENT ABOUT MATERIALITY

OBJECTIVE 8-2

Make a preliminary judgment about what amounts to consider material.

Ideally, an auditor decides early in the audit the combined amount of misstatements in the financial statements that would be considered material. SAS 47 (AU 312) defines the amount as the **preliminary judgment about materiality.** This judgment need not be quantified but often is. It is called a preliminary judgment about materiality because it is a professional judgment and may change during the engagement if circumstances change.

The preliminary judgment about materiality (step 1 in Figure 8-1) is thus the maximum amount by which the auditor believes the statements could be misstated and still *not* affect the decisions of reasonable users. (Conceptually, this would be an amount that is $1 less than materiality as defined by the FASB. Preliminary materiality is defined in this manner as a convenience in application.) This judgment is one of the most important decisions the auditor makes. It requires considerable professional judgment.

The reason for setting a preliminary judgment about materiality is to help the auditor plan the appropriate evidence to accumulate. If the auditor sets a low dollar amount, more evidence is required than for a high amount. Examine the financial statements of Hillsburg

Hardware Co. on pages 190–191. What do you think is the combined amount of misstatements that would affect decisions of reasonable users? Do you believe that a $100 misstatement would affect users' decisions? If so, the amount of evidence required for the audit is likely to be beyond that for which the management of Hillsburg Hardware would be willing to pay. Do you believe that a $10 million misstatement would be material? Most experienced auditors would say that amount is far too large as a combined materiality amount in these circumstances.

The auditor will often change the preliminary judgment about materiality during the audit. When that is done, the new judgment is called a **revised judgment about materiality.** Reasons for using a revised judgment can include a change in one of the factors used to determine the preliminary judgment or a decision by the auditor that the preliminary judgment was too large or too small. For example, the preliminary judgment about materiality is often determined before year-end. In this case, the preliminary judgment must be set based on prior years' financial statements or interim financial statement information.

Factors Affecting Judgment

Several factors affect setting a preliminary judgment about materiality for a given set of financial statements. The most important of these are discussed next.

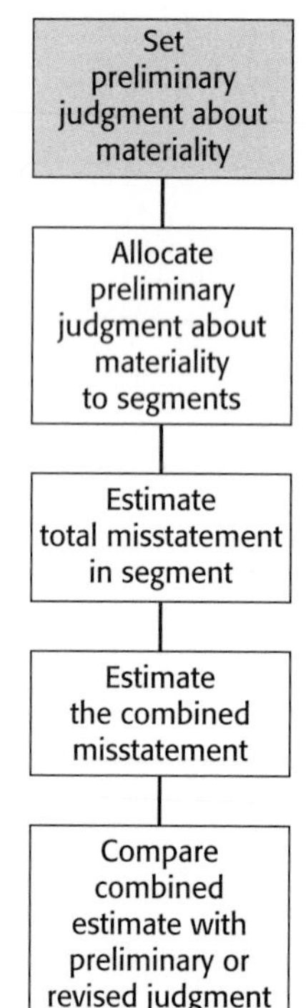

Materiality Is a Relative Rather Than an Absolute Concept A misstatement of a given magnitude might be material for a small company, whereas the same dollar misstatement could be immaterial for a large one. For example, a total misstatement of $10 million would be extremely material for Hillsburg Hardware Co. because, as shown on pages 190–191, total assets are about $61 million and net income before taxes is less than $6 million. A misstatement of this amount would be immaterial for a company such as IBM, which has total assets and net income of several billion dollars. Hence, it is impossible to establish any dollar-value guidelines for a preliminary judgment about materiality applicable to all audit clients.

Bases Are Needed for Evaluating Materiality Because materiality is relative, it is necessary to have bases for establishing whether misstatements are material. *Net income before taxes* is normally the primary base for deciding what is material because it is regarded as a critical item of information for users. Some firms use a different primary base because net income often fluctuates considerably from year to year and therefore does not provide a stable base. Examples of other primary bases used by firms are net sales, gross profit, and total assets. In addition to establishing a primary base, it also is important to decide whether the misstatements could materially affect the reasonableness of other possible bases such as current assets, total assets, current liabilities, and owners' equity.

Assume that for a given company, an auditor decided that a misstatement of income before taxes of $100,000 or more would be material, but a misstatement of $250,000 or more would be material for current assets. It would be inappropriate for the auditor to use a preliminary judgment about materiality of $250,000 for both income before taxes and current assets. The auditor must therefore plan to find all misstatements affecting income before taxes that exceed the preliminary judgment about materiality of $100,000. Because most misstatements affect both the income statement and balance sheet, the auditor will not be greatly concerned about the possibility of misstatement of current assets exceeding $250,000 and will use a materiality level of $100,000 for most tests. However, some misstatements, such as misclassifying a long-term asset as a current one, affect only the balance sheet. The auditor will therefore also need to plan the audit with the $250,000 preliminary judgment about materiality for certain tests of current assets.

Qualitative Factors Also Affect Materiality Certain types of misstatements are likely to be more important to users than others, even if the dollar amounts are the same. For example:

- Amounts involving fraud are usually considered more important than unintentional errors of equal dollar amounts because fraud reflects on the honesty and reliability of the management or other personnel involved. To illustrate, most users would consider an intentional misstatement of inventory as being more important than clerical errors in inventory of the same dollar amount.

- Misstatements that are otherwise minor may be material if there are possible consequences arising from contractual obligations. An example is when net working capital included in the financial statements is only a few hundred dollars more than the required minimum in a loan agreement. If the correct net working capital were less than the required minimum, putting the loan in default, the current and noncurrent liability classifications would be materially affected.
- Misstatements that are otherwise immaterial may be material if they affect a trend in earnings. For example, if reported income has increased 3 percent annually for the past 5 years but income for the current year has declined 1 percent, that change of trend may be material. Similarly, a misstatement that would cause a loss to be reported as a profit would be of concern.

Big Five Materiality Guidelines

Illustrative Guidelines

The FASB and AICPA are currently unwilling to provide specific materiality guidelines to practitioners. The concern is that such guidelines might be applied without considering all the complexities that should affect the auditor's final decision. Therefore, this chapter provides illustrative guidelines to show the application of materiality. They are intended only to help you better understand the concept of applying materiality in practice. The guidelines are stated in Figure 8-2 in the form of a policy guideline for a CPA firm. Notice that the guidelines are formulas using one or more bases and a range of percentages. Guidelines such as the ones presented require considerable professional judgment.

FIGURE 8-2 Illustrative Materiality Guidelines

BERGER AND ANTHONY, CPAs
Gary, Indiana 46405

POLICY STATEMENT
No. 32IC
Title: Materiality Guidelines

Charles G. Berger
Joe Anthony

Professional judgment is to be used at all times in setting and applying materiality guidelines. As a general guideline, the following policies are to be applied:

1. The combined total of misstatements in the financial statements exceeding 10 percent is normally considered material. A combined total of less than 5 percent is presumed to be immaterial in the absence of qualitative factors. Combined misstatements between 5 percent and 10 percent require the greatest amount of professional judgment to determine their materiality.
2. The 5 percent to 10 percent must be measured in relation to the appropriate base. Many times there is more than one base to which misstatements should be compared. The following guides are recommended in selecting the appropriate base:
   a. *Income statement.* Combined misstatements in the income statement should ordinarily be measured at 5 percent to 10 percent of operating income before taxes. A guideline of 5 percent to 10 percent may be inappropriate in a year in which income is unusually large or small. When operating income in a given year is not considered representative, it is desirable to substitute as a base a more representative income measure. For example, average operating income for a 3-year period may be used as the base.
   b. *Balance sheet.* Combined misstatements in the balance sheet should originally be evaluated for current assets, current liabilities, and total assets. For current assets and current liabilities, the guidelines should be between 5 percent and 10 percent, applied in the same way as for the income statement. For total assets, the guidelines should be between 3 percent and 6 percent, applied in the same way as for the income statement.
3. Qualitative factors should be carefully evaluated on all audits. In many instances, they are more important than the guidelines applied to the income statement and balance sheet. The intended uses of the financial statements and the nature of the information in the statements, including footnotes, must be carefully evaluated.

Application to Hillsburg Hardware

Using the illustrative guidelines in Figure 8-2, we will now present a preliminary judgment about materiality for Hillsburg Hardware Co. The guidelines are as follows:

Preliminary Judgment About Materiality (Rounded, in Thousands)

	Minimum		Maximum	
	Percentage	Dollar Amount	Percentage	Dollar Amount
Earnings from operations	5	$ 368	10	$ 737
Current assets	5	2,551	10	5,103
Total assets	3	1,841	6	3,682
Current liabilities	5	661	10	1,322

If the auditor for Hillsburg Hardware decides that the general guidelines are reasonable, the first step is to evaluate whether any qualitative factors significantly affect the materiality judgment. If not, the auditor must decide that if combined misstatements of operating income before taxes were less than $368,000, the statements would be considered fairly stated. If the combined misstatements exceeded $737,000, the statements would not be considered fairly stated. If the misstatements were between $368,000 and $737,000, a more careful consideration of all facts would be required. The auditor then applies the same process to the other three bases.

ALLOCATE PRELIMINARY JUDGMENT ABOUT MATERIALITY TO SEGMENTS (TOLERABLE MISSTATEMENT)

OBJECTIVE 8-3

Allocate preliminary materiality to segments of the audit during planning.

The **allocation of the preliminary judgment about materiality** to segments (step 2 in Figure 8-1) is necessary because evidence is accumulated by segments rather than for the financial statements as a whole. If auditors have a preliminary judgment about materiality for each segment, it helps them decide the appropriate audit evidence to accumulate. For example, an auditor is likely to accumulate more evidence for an accounts receivable balance of $1,000,000 when a misstatement of $50,000 in accounts receivable is considered material than if $300,000 were material.

Most practitioners allocate materiality to balance sheet rather than income statement accounts. Most income statement misstatements have an equal effect on the balance sheet because of the double-entry bookkeeping system. Therefore, the auditor can allocate materiality to either income statement or balance sheet accounts. Because there are fewer balance sheet than income statement accounts in most audits and most audit procedures focus on balance sheet accounts, allocating materiality to balance sheet accounts is the most appropriate alternative.

When auditors allocate the preliminary judgment about materiality to account balances, the materiality allocated to any given account balance is referred to in SAS 39 (AU 350) as **tolerable misstatement.** For example, if an auditor decides to allocate $100,000 of a total preliminary judgment about materiality of $200,000 to accounts receivable, tolerable misstatement for accounts receivable is $100,000. This means that the auditor is willing to consider accounts receivable fairly stated if it is misstated by $100,000 or less.

There are three major difficulties in allocating materiality to balance sheet accounts (segments): Auditors expect certain accounts to have more misstatements than others, both overstatements and understatements must be considered, and relative audit costs affect the allocation. All three of these difficulties are considered in the allocation in Figure 8-3.

Allocation Illustrated

Figure 8-3 illustrates the allocation approach followed by the senior, Fran Moore, for the audit of Hillsburg Hardware Co. It summarizes the balance sheet from page 190, combining certain accounts, and shows the allocation of total materiality of $737,000 (10 percent of earnings from operations). The allocation approach followed by Moore for Hillsburg Hardware Co. is to use judgment in the allocation, subject to two arbitrary requirements established by Berger and Anthony, CPAs: Tolerable misstatement for any account cannot

FIGURE 8-3 **Tolerable Misstatement Allocated to Hillsburg Hardware Co.**

	Balance 12-31-02 (in Thousands)	Tolerable Misstatement (in Thousands)	
Cash	$ 828	$ 10 (a)	
Trade accounts receivable (net)	18,957	442 (b)	
Inventories	29,865	442 (b)	
Other current assets	1,377	100 (c)	
Property, plant, and equipment	10,340	80 (d)	
Total assets	$61,367		
Trade accounts payable	$ 4,720	180 (e)	
Notes payable—total	28,300	0 (a)	
Accrued payroll and payroll tax	1,470	100 (c)	
Accrued interest and dividends payable	2,050	0 (a)	
Other liabilities	2,364	120 (c)	
Capital stock and capital in excess of par	8,500	0 (a)	
Retained earnings	13,963	NA (f)	
Total liabilities and equity	$61,367	$1,474	(2 × $737)

NA = Not applicable

(a) Zero or small tolerable misstatement because account can be completely audited at low cost and no misstatements are expected.

(b) Large tolerable misstatement because account is large and requires extensive sampling to audit the account.

(c) Large tolerable misstatement as a percent of account because account can be verified at extremely low cost, probably with analytical procedures, if tolerable misstatement is large.

(d) Small tolerable misstatement as a percent of account balance because most of the balance is in land and buildings, which is unchanged from the prior year and need not be audited.

(e) Moderately large tolerable misstatement because a relatively large number of misstatements are expected.

(f) Not applicable—retained earnings is a residual account that is affected by the net amount of the misstatements in the other accounts.

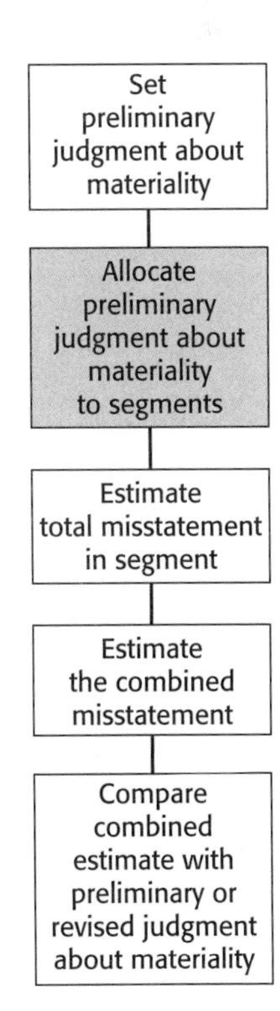

exceed 60 percent of the preliminary judgment (60 percent of $737,000 = $442,000, rounded), and the sum of all tolerable misstatements cannot exceed twice the preliminary judgment about materiality (2 × $737,000 = $1,474,000).

The reason for the first requirement is to keep the auditor from allocating all of total materiality to one account. If, for example, all of the preliminary judgment of $737,000 is allocated to trade accounts receivable, a $737,000 misstatement in that account would be acceptable. However, it may not be acceptable to have such a large misstatement in one account, and even if it is acceptable, it would not allow for any misstatements in other accounts.

There are two reasons for permitting the sum of the tolerable misstatement to exceed overall materiality. First, it is unlikely that all accounts will be misstated by the full amount of tolerable misstatement. If, for example, other current assets have a tolerable misstatement of $100,000 but no misstatements are found in auditing those accounts, it means that the auditor, after the fact, could have allocated zero or a small tolerable misstatement to other current assets. It is common for auditors to find fewer misstatements than tolerable misstatement. Second, some accounts are likely to be overstated, whereas others are likely to be understated, resulting in a net amount that is likely to be less than overall materiality.

Notice in the allocation that the auditor is concerned about the combined effect on operating income of the misstatement of each balance sheet account. An overstatement of an asset account will therefore have the same effect on the income statement as an understatement of a liability account. In contrast, a misclassification in the balance sheet, such as a classification of a note payable as an account payable, will have no effect on operating income. The materiality of items not affecting the income statement must be considered separately.

Figure 8-3 also includes the rationale that Fran Moore followed in deciding tolerable misstatement for each account. For example, she concluded that it was unnecessary to assign any tolerable misstatement to notes payable, even though it is as large as inventories. If she had assigned $221,000 to each of those two accounts, more evidence would have been required in inventories, but the confirmation of the balance in notes payable would still have been required. It was therefore more efficient to allocate $442,000 to inventories and none to notes payable. Similarly, she allocated $100,000 to other current assets and accrued payroll and payroll tax, both of which are large compared with the recorded account balance. Moore did so because she believes that these accounts can be verified within $100,000 by using only analytical procedures, which are low cost. If tolerable misstatement were set lower, she would have to use more costly audit procedures such as documentation and confirmation.

In practice, it is often difficult to predict in advance which accounts are most likely to be misstated and whether misstatements are likely to be overstatements or understatements. Similarly, the relative costs of auditing different account balances often cannot be determined. It is therefore a difficult professional judgment to allocate the preliminary judgment about materiality to accounts. Accordingly, many accounting firms have developed rigorous guidelines and sophisticated statistical methods for doing so.

To summarize, the purpose of allocating the preliminary judgment about materiality to balance sheet accounts is to help the auditor decide the appropriate evidence to accumulate for each account. An aim of the allocation should be to minimize audit costs. Regardless of how the allocation is done, when the audit is completed, the auditor must be confident that the combined misstatements in all accounts are less than or equal to the preliminary (or revised) judgment about materiality.

ESTIMATE MISSTATEMENT AND COMPARE WITH PRELIMINARY JUDGMENT

OBJECTIVE 8-4

Use materiality to evaluate audit findings.

The first two steps in applying materiality involve planning, whereas the last three (steps 3, 4, and 5 in Figure 8-1) result from performing audit tests. The last three steps are discussed in greater detail in later chapters. This section only shows their relationship to the first two.

When the auditor performs audit procedures for each segment of the audit, a worksheet is kept of all misstatements found. For example, assume that the auditor finds six client misstatements in a sample of 200 in testing inventory costs. These misstatements are used to estimate the *total* misstatements in inventory (step 3). The total is called an estimate or often a "projection" because only a sample, rather than the entire population, was audited. Estimation of projected misstatement is required by SAS 39 (AU 350). The projected misstatement amounts for each account are combined on the worksheet (step 4), and then the combined misstatement is compared with materiality (step 5).

Table 8-1 is used to illustrate the last three steps in applying materiality. For simplicity, only three accounts are included. The estimated misstatements are calculated based on actual audit tests. Assume, for example, that in auditing inventory, the auditor found $3,500 of net overstatement amounts in a sample of $50,000 of the total population

TABLE 8-1 Illustration of Comparison of Estimated Total Misstatement to Preliminary Judgment about Materiality

		Estimated Misstatement Amount		
Account	**Tolerable Misstatement**	**Direct Projection**	**Sampling Error**	**Total**
Cash	$ 4,000	$ 0	$ NA	$ 0
Accounts receivable	20,000	12,000	6,000	18,000
Inventory	36,000	31,500	15,750	47,250
Total estimated misstatement amount		$43,500	$16,800	$60,300
Preliminary judgment about materiality	$50,000			

NA = Not applicable.
Cash audited 100 percent.

of $450,000. One way to calculate the estimate of the misstatements is to make a direct projection from the sample to the population and add an estimate for sampling error. The calculation of the **direct projection estimate of misstatement** is

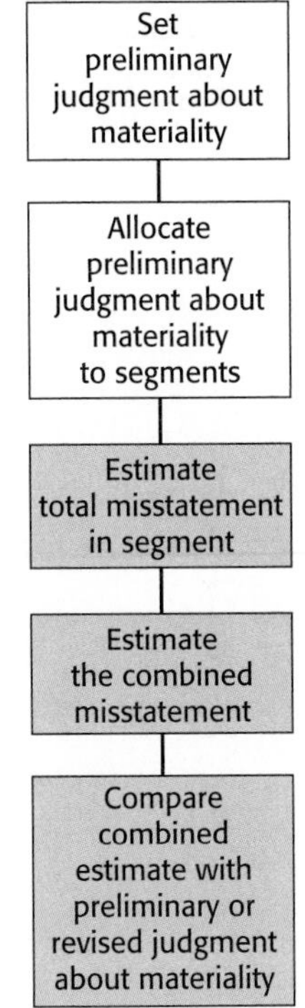

Set preliminary judgment about materiality
Allocate preliminary judgment about materiality to segments
Estimate total misstatement in segment
Estimate the combined misstatement
Compare combined estimate with preliminary or revised judgment about materiality

$$\frac{\text{Net misstatements in the sample (\$3,500)}}{\text{Total sampled (\$50,000)}} \times \begin{array}{c}\text{Total recorded}\\ \text{population value}\\ \text{(\$450,000)}\end{array} = \begin{array}{c}\text{Direct projection}\\ \text{estimate of}\\ \text{misstatement}\\ \text{(\$31,500)}\end{array}$$

The direct projection for accounts receivable of $12,000 is not illustrated.

The estimate for **sampling error** results because the auditor has sampled only a portion of the population (this is discussed in detail in Chapter 13). In this simplified example, the estimate for sampling error is assumed to be 50 percent of the direct projection of the misstatement amounts for the accounts where sampling was used (accounts receivable and inventory).

In combining the misstatements in Table 8-1, observe that the direct projection misstatements for the three accounts add to $43,500. However, the total sampling error is less than the sum of the individual sampling errors. This is because sampling error represents the maximum misstatement in account details not audited. It is unlikely that this maximum misstatement amount would exist in all accounts subjected to sampling. Thus, sampling methodology provides for determining a combined sampling error that takes this into consideration. Again, this is discussed in detail in Chapter 13.

Table 8-1 shows that total estimated misstatement of $60,300 exceeds the preliminary judgment about materiality of $50,000. Furthermore, the major area of difficulty is inventory, where estimated misstatement of $47,250 is significantly greater than tolerable misstatement of $36,000. Because the estimated combined misstatement exceeds the preliminary judgment, the financial statements are not acceptable. The auditor can either determine whether the estimated misstatement actually exceeds $50,000 by performing additional audit procedures or require the client to make an adjustment for estimated misstatements. If additional audit procedures are performed, they would be concentrated in the inventory area.

If the estimated net overstatement amount for inventory had been $28,000 ($18,000 plus $10,000 sampling error), the auditor probably would not need to expand audit tests because it would have met both the tests of tolerable misstatement ($36,000) and the preliminary judgment about materiality ($18,000 + $28,000 = $46,000 < $50,000). In fact, there would be some leeway with that amount because the results of cash and accounts receivable procedures indicate that those accounts are well within their tolerable misstatement limits. If the auditor were to approach the audit of the accounts in a sequential manner, the findings of the audit of the earlier accounts can be used to revise the tolerable misstatement established for other accounts. For example, in the illustration, if the auditor had audited cash and accounts receivable before inventories, tolerable misstatement for inventories could be increased.

RISK

OBJECTIVE 8-5

Define risk in auditing.

There is a close relationship between materiality and risk. In the example in Table 8-1, the auditor estimated a $6,000 sampling error for accounts receivable, which was used to calculate the total estimated misstatement of $18,000 for comparison to tolerable misstatement of $20,000. The $6,000 sampling error *includes a risk* resulting from sampling. This is only one of several kinds of risks auditors must address.

As we saw in Chapter 7, auditors accept some level of **risk** or uncertainty in performing the audit function. The auditor recognizes, for example, that there is uncertainty about the competence of evidence, uncertainty about the effectiveness of a client's internal controls, and uncertainty about whether the financial statements are fairly stated when the audit is completed. An effective auditor recognizes that risks exist and deals with those risks in an appropriate manner. Most risks auditors encounter are difficult to measure and require careful thought to respond to appropriately. Responding to these risks properly is critical to achieving a high-quality audit.

Illustration Concerning Risks and Evidence

As discussed in Chapter 7, the auditor gains an understanding of the client's business and industry and assesses client business risk to assess the likelihood of material misstatements in the client's financial statements. Auditors use the audit risk model to further identify the potential for misstatements and where they are most likely to occur. Before discussing the audit risk model, an illustration for a hypothetical company is provided in Table 8-2 as a frame of reference for the discussion. The table first shows that there are differences among cycles in the frequency and size of expected misstatements (A). For example, there are almost no misstatements expected in payroll and personnel but many in inventory and warehousing. The reason may be that the payroll transactions are highly routine, whereas there may be considerable complexities in recording inventory. Similarly, internal control is believed to differ in effectiveness among the five cycles (B). For example, internal controls in payroll and personnel are considered highly effective, whereas those in inventory and warehousing are considered ineffective. Finally, the auditor has decided on a low willingness that material misstatements exist after the audit is complete for all five cycles (C). It is common for auditors to want an equally low likelihood of misstatements for each cycle after the audit is finished to permit the issuance of an unqualified opinion.

The previous considerations (A, B, C) affect the auditor's decision about the appropriate extent of evidence to accumulate (D). For example, because the auditor expects few misstatements in payroll and personnel (A) and internal controls are effective (B), the auditor plans for less evidence (D) than for inventory and warehousing. Notice that the auditor has the same

TABLE 8-2 Illustration of Differing Evidence Among Cycles

		Sales and Collection Cycle	Acquisition and Payment Cycle	Payroll and Personnel Cycle	Inventory and Warehousing Cycle	Capital Acquisition and Repayment Cycle
A	Auditor's assessment of expectation of material misstatement before considering internal control (inherent risk)	Expect some misstatements (medium)	Expect many misstatements (high)	Expect few misstatements (low)	Expect many misstatements (high)	Expect few misstatements (low)
B	Auditor's assessment of effectiveness of internal controls to prevent or detect material misstatements (control risk)	Medium effectiveness (medium)	High effectiveness (low)	High effectiveness (low)	Low effectiveness (high)	Medium effectiveness (medium)
C	Auditor's willingness to permit material misstatements to exist after completing the audit (acceptable audit risk)	Low willingness (low)	Low willingness (low)	Low willingness (low)	Low willingness (low)	Low willingness (low)
D	Extent of evidence the auditor plans to accumulate (planned detection risk)	Medium level (medium)	Medium level (medium)	Low level (high)	High level (low)	Medium level (medium)

level of willingness to accept material misstatements after the audit is finished for all five cycles, but a different extent of evidence is needed for various cycles. The difference is caused by differences in the auditor's expectations of misstatements and assessment of internal control.

Audit Risk Model for Planning

OBJECTIVE 8-6

Describe the audit risk model and its components.

The primary way that auditors deal with risk in planning audit evidence is through the application of the **audit risk model.** The source of the audit risk model is the professional literature in SAS 39 (AU 350) on audit sampling and SAS 47 (AU 312) on materiality and risk. A thorough understanding of the model is essential to effective audit planning and to the study of the remaining chapters of this book.

The audit risk model is used primarily for planning purposes in deciding how much evidence to accumulate in each cycle. It is usually stated as follows:

$$PDR = \frac{AAR}{IR \times CR}$$

where:

PDR = planned detection risk

AAR = acceptable audit risk

IR = inherent risk

CR = control risk

A numerical example is provided for discussion, even though it is not practical to measure as precisely as these numbers imply. The numbers used are for the inventory and warehousing cycle in Table 8-2.

$$IR = 100\%$$

$$CR = 100\%$$

$$AAR = 5\%$$

$$PDR = \frac{.05}{1.0 \times 1.0} = .05 \text{ or } 5\%$$

TYPES OF RISKS

The four risks in the audit risk model are sufficiently important to merit detailed discussion. All four risks are discussed briefly in this section to provide an overview of the risks. Acceptable audit risk and inherent risk are then discussed in greater detail later in this chapter. Control risk is studied in detail in Chapter 9.

Planned Detection Risk

Planned detection risk is a measure of the risk that audit evidence for a segment will fail to detect misstatements exceeding a tolerable amount, should such misstatements exist. There are two key points about planned detection risk. First, it is dependent on the other three factors in the model. Planned detection risk will change only if the auditor changes one of the other factors. Second, it determines the amount of substantive evidence that the auditor plans to accumulate, inversely with the size of planned detection risk. If planned detection risk is reduced, the auditor needs to accumulate more evidence to achieve the reduced planned risk. For example, in Table 8-2 (D), planned detection risk is low for inventory and warehousing, which causes planned evidence to be high. The opposite is true for payroll and personnel.

The planned detection risk of .05 in the previous numerical example means the auditor plans to accumulate evidence until the risk of misstatements exceeding tolerable misstatement is reduced to 5 percent. If control risk had been .50 instead of 1.0, planned detection risk would be .10 and planned evidence could therefore be reduced.

Inherent Risk

Inherent risk is a measure of the auditor's assessment of the likelihood that there are material misstatements (errors or fraud) in a segment before considering the effectiveness of internal control. Inherent risk is the susceptibility of the financial statements to material misstatement, assuming no internal controls. If the auditor concludes that there is a high likelihood of misstatement, ignoring internal controls, the auditor would conclude that inherent risk is high. Internal controls are ignored in setting inherent risk because they are considered separately in the audit risk model as control risk. In Table 8-2 inherent risk (A) has been assessed high for inventory and warehousing and lower for payroll and personnel and capital acquisition and repayment. The assessment was likely based on discussions with management, knowledge of the company, and results in audits of previous years.

The relationship of inherent risk to planned detection risk and planned evidence is that inherent risk is inversely related to planned detection risk and directly related to evidence. Inherent risk for inventory and warehousing in Table 8-2 is high, and in the numerical example 1.0, which will result in a lower planned detection risk and more planned evidence than would be necessary had inherent risk been lower. Inherent risk is examined in greater detail later in the chapter.

In addition to increasing audit evidence for a higher inherent risk in a given audit area, it is also common to assign more experienced staff to that area and review the completed audit tests more thoroughly. For example, if inherent risk for inventory obsolescence is extremely high, it makes sense for the CPA firm to have an experienced staff person perform more extensive tests for inventory obsolescence and to have the audit results more carefully reviewed.

Control Risk

Control risk is a measure of the auditor's assessment of the likelihood that misstatements exceeding a tolerable amount in a segment will not be prevented or detected by the client's internal controls. Control risk represents (1) an assessment of whether a client's internal controls are effective for preventing or detecting misstatements, and (2) the auditor's intention to make that assessment at a level below the maximum (100 percent) as part of the audit plan. For example, assume that the auditor concludes that internal controls are completely ineffective to prevent or detect misstatements. That is the likely conclusion for inventory and warehousing in Table 8-2 (B). The auditor would therefore assign a high, perhaps 100 percent, risk factor to control risk. The more effective the internal controls, the lower the risk factor that *could* be assigned to control risk.

The audit risk model shows the close relationship between inherent and control risks. For example, an inherent risk of 40 percent and a control risk of 60 percent affect planned detection risk and planned evidence the same as an inherent risk of 60 percent and a control risk of 40 percent. In both cases, multiplying *IR* by *CR* results in a denominator in the audit risk model of 24 percent. The combination of inherent risk and control risk can be thought of as the *expectation of misstatements after considering the effect of internal control.* Inherent risk is the expectation of misstatements before considering the effect of internal control.

As with inherent risk, the relationship between control risk and planned detection risk is inverse, whereas the relationship between control risk and substantive evidence is direct. For example, if the auditor concludes that internal controls are effective, planned detection risk can be increased and evidence therefore decreased. The auditor can increase planned detection risk when controls are effective because effective internal controls reduce the likelihood of misstatements in the financial statements.

Before auditors can set control risk less than 100 percent, they must obtain an understanding of internal control, evaluate how well it should function based on the understanding, and test the internal controls for effectiveness. The first of these is the *understanding* requirement that relates to all audits. The latter two are the *assessment of control risk* steps that are required when the auditor *chooses* to assess control risk below maximum.

Understanding internal control, assessing control risk, and evaluating their impact on evidence requirements are so important that the entire next chapter is devoted to that topic. However, it should be noted here that if the auditor elects not to assess control risk below maximum, control risk must be set at 100 percent regardless of the actual effectiveness of the underlying controls. Use of the audit risk model in this circumstance then causes the auditor to control acceptable audit risk entirely through a low level of planned detection risk (assuming that inherent risk is high).

Acceptable Audit Risk

Acceptable audit risk is a measure of how willing the auditor is to accept that the financial statements may be materially misstated after the audit is completed and an unqualified opinion has been issued. When the auditor decides on a lower acceptable audit risk, it means the auditor wants to be more certain that the financial statements are *not* materially misstated. Zero risk would be certainty, and a 100 percent risk would be complete uncertainty. Complete assurance (zero risk) of the accuracy of the financial statements is not economically practical. It has already been established in Chapter 5 that the auditor cannot guarantee the complete absence of material misstatements.

Often, auditors refer to the terms **audit assurance, overall assurance,** or **level of assurance** instead of acceptable audit risk. Audit assurance or any of the equivalent terms is the complement of acceptable audit risk, that is, one minus acceptable audit risk. For example, acceptable audit risk of 2 percent is the same as audit assurance of 98 percent.

The concept of acceptable audit risk can be more easily understood by thinking in terms of a large number of audits, say, 10,000. What portion of these audits could include material misstatements without having an adverse effect on society? Certainly, the portion would be below 10 percent. It is probably much closer to 1 or one-half of 1 percent or perhaps even one-tenth of 1 percent. If an auditor believes that the appropriate percentage is 1 percent, then acceptable audit risk should be set at 1 percent, or perhaps lower, based on the specific circumstances.

Using the audit risk model, there is a direct relationship between acceptable audit risk and planned detection risk, and an inverse relationship between acceptable audit risk and planned evidence. For example, if the auditor decides to reduce acceptable audit risk, planned detection risk is thereby reduced and planned evidence must be increased. As stated in Chapter 7, auditors also often assign more experienced staff or review the audit files more extensively for a client with lower acceptable audit risk.

ASSESSING ACCEPTABLE AUDIT RISK

Auditors must decide the appropriate acceptable audit risk for an audit, preferably during audit planning. First, auditors decide engagement risk and use engagement risk to modify acceptable audit risk.

Impact of Engagement Risk on Acceptable Audit Risk

OBJECTIVE **8-7**

Consider the impact of engagement risk on acceptable audit risk.

Engagement risk is the risk that the auditor or audit firm will suffer harm because of a client relationship, even though the audit report rendered for the client was correct. Engagement risk is closely related to client business risk. For example, if a client declares bankruptcy after an audit is completed, the likelihood of a lawsuit against the CPA firm is reasonably high even if the quality of the audit was good.

Auditors disagree about whether engagement risk should be considered in planning the audit. Opponents of modifying evidence for engagement risk contend that auditors do not provide audit opinions for different levels of assurance and therefore should not provide more or less assurance because of engagement risk. Proponents contend that it is appropriate for auditors to accumulate additional evidence, assign more experienced personnel, and review the audit more thoroughly on audits where legal exposure is high, as long as the assurance level is not decreased below a reasonably high level when there is low engagement risk.

Factors Affecting Acceptable Audit Risk

When auditors modify evidence for engagement risk, it is done by control of acceptable audit risk. The authors believe that a reasonably low acceptable audit risk is always desirable, but in some circumstances an even lower risk is needed because of engagement risk factors. Research has indicated that several factors affect engagement risk and therefore acceptable audit risk. Only three of those are discussed here: the degree to which external users rely on the statements, the likelihood that a client will have financial difficulties after the audit report is issued, and the integrity of management.

The Degree to Which External Users Rely on the Statements When external users place heavy reliance on the financial statements, it is appropriate that acceptable audit risk be decreased. When the statements are heavily relied on, a great social harm could result if a significant misstatement were to remain undetected in the financial statements. The cost of additional evidence can be more easily justified when the loss to users from material misstatements is substantial. Several factors are good indicators of the degree to which statements are relied on by external users:

- *Client's size.* Generally speaking, the larger a client's operations, the more widely the statements will be used. The client's size, measured by total assets or total revenues, will have an effect on the acceptable audit risk.
- *Distribution of ownership.* The statements of publicly held corporations are normally relied on by many more users than those of closely held corporations. For these companies, the interested parties include the SEC, financial analysts, and the general public.
- *Nature and amount of liabilities.* When statements include a large amount of liabilities, they are more likely to be used extensively by actual and potential creditors than when there are few liabilities.

The Likelihood That a Client Will Have Financial Difficulties After the Audit Report Is Issued If a client is forced to file for bankruptcy or suffers a significant loss after completion of the audit, there is a greater chance of the auditor being required to defend the quality of the audit than if the client were under no financial strain. There is a natural tendency for those who lose money in a bankruptcy or because of a stock price reversal to file suit against the auditor. This can result from the honest belief that the auditor failed to conduct an adequate audit or from the users' desire to recover part of their loss regardless of the adequacy of the audit work.

In situations in which the auditor believes the chance of financial failure or loss is high and there is a corresponding increase in engagement risk, acceptable audit risk should be reduced. If a subsequent challenge does occur, the auditor will then be in a better position to defend the audit results successfully. The total audit evidence and costs will increase, but this is justifiable because of the additional risk of lawsuits that the auditor faces.

It is difficult for an auditor to predict financial failure before it occurs, but certain factors are good indicators of its increased probability:

- *Liquidity position.* If a client is constantly short of cash and working capital, it indicates a future problem in paying bills. The auditor must assess the likelihood and significance of a steadily declining liquidity position.
- *Profits (losses) in previous years.* When a company has rapidly declining profits or increasing losses for several years, the auditor should recognize the future solvency problems that the client is likely to encounter. It is also important to consider the changing profits relative to the balance remaining in retained earnings.
- *Method of financing growth.* The more a client relies on debt as a means of financing, the greater the risk of financial difficulty if the client's operations become less successful. It is also important to evaluate whether fixed assets are being financed with short- or long-term loans. Large amounts of required cash outflows during a short time can force a company into bankruptcy.
- *Nature of the client's operations.* Certain types of businesses are inherently riskier than others. For example, other things being equal, a start-up technology company dependent on one product is much more likely to go bankrupt than a diversified food manufacturer.
- *Competence of management.* Competent management is constantly alert for potential financial difficulties and modifies its operating methods to minimize the effects of short-run problems. The ability of management must be assessed as a part of the evaluation of the likelihood of bankruptcy.

ASSESSING ACCEPTABLE AUDIT RISK IN PRACTICE

Henry Rinsk, of Links, Rinsk, and Rodman, CPAs, is the partner responsible for the audit of Hungry Food Restaurants, a chain of nine Midwestern family restaurants. The firm has audited Hungry Food for 10 years and has always found management competent, cooperative, and easy to deal with. Hungry Food is family-owned with a business succession plan in place; it is profitable, is liquid, and has little debt. Management has a reputation in the community for high integrity and good relationships with employees, customers, and suppliers.

After meeting with the other partners as part of the firm's annual client continuation meeting, Henry recommends that acceptable audit risk for Hungry Food be assessed at high. For Links, Rinsk, and Rodman, this means no expansion of evidence, a "standard" review of audit documentation, and a "standard" assignment of personnel to the engagement.

TABLE 8-3 Methods Practitioners Use to Assess Acceptable Audit Risk

Factors	Methods Used to Assess Acceptable Audit Risk
External users' reliance on financial statements	• Examine the financial statements, including footnotes. • Read minutes of board of directors meetings to determine future plans. • Examine Form 10K for a publicly held company. • Discuss financing plans with management.
Likelihood of financial difficulties	• Analyze the financial statements for financial difficulties using ratios and other analytical procedures. • Examine historical and projected cash flow statements for the nature of cash inflows and outflows.
Management integrity	Follow the procedures discussed in Chapter 7 for client acceptance and continuance.

The Auditor's Evaluation of Management's Integrity As discussed in Chapter 7 as a part of new client investigation and continuing client evaluation, if a client has questionable integrity, the auditor is likely to assess acceptable audit risk lower. Companies with low integrity often conduct their business affairs in a manner that results in conflicts with their stockholders, regulators, and customers. In turn, these conflicts often reflect on the users' perceived quality of the audit and can result in lawsuits and other disagreements. An obvious example of a situation in which management's integrity is questionable is prior criminal convictions of key management personnel. Other examples of questionable integrity might include frequent disagreements with previous auditors, the Internal Revenue Service, and the SEC. Frequent turnover of key financial and internal audit personnel and ongoing conflicts with labor unions and employees may also indicate integrity problems.

Making the Acceptable Audit Risk Decision

To assess acceptable audit risk, the auditor must first assess each of the factors affecting acceptable audit risk. Table 8-3 illustrates the methods used by auditors to assess each of the three factors already discussed. It is easy to see after examining Table 8-3 that the assessment of each of the factors is highly subjective, which means that the overall assessment is also highly subjective. A typical evaluation of acceptable audit risk is high, medium, or low, where a low acceptable audit risk assessment means a "risky" client requiring more extensive evidence, assignment of more experienced personnel, and/or a more extensive review of audit documentation. As the audit progresses, additional information about the client is obtained and acceptable audit risk may be modified.

ASSESSING INHERENT RISK

OBJECTIVE **8-8**

Consider the impact of several factors on the assessment of inherent risk.

The inclusion of inherent risk in the audit risk model is one of the most important concepts in auditing. It implies that auditors should attempt to predict where misstatements are most and least likely in the financial statement segments. This information affects the total amount of evidence that the auditor is required to accumulate and influences how the auditor's efforts to gather the evidence are allocated among the segments of the audit.

Factors Affecting Inherent Risk

At the start of the audit, there is not much that can be done about changing inherent risk. Instead, the auditor must *assess the factors* that make up the risk and *modify audit evidence* to take them into consideration. The auditor should consider several major factors when assessing inherent risk:

- Nature of the client's business
- Results of previous audits
- Initial versus repeat engagement
- Related parties
- Nonroutine transactions
- Judgment required to correctly record account balances and transactions
- Makeup of the population

AICPA *INDUSTRY AUDIT RISK ALERTS* FOR SPECIALIZED INDUSTRIES

Many companies operate in specialized industries that have unique economic, regulatory, and accounting issues. In an effort to provide auditors with current guidance on assessing inherent risks for clients in specialized industries, the AICPA has developed a series of *Industry Audit Risk Alerts*. Some of the industries covered by the publications are banks and savings institutions, construction contractors, healthcare providers, not-for-profit organizations, public utilities, and real estate. The AICPA issues new or revised risk alerts whenever they conclude that auditors should be aware of recent economic, regulatory, or technical developments for companies in specific industries.

Nature of the Client's Business Inherent risk for certain accounts is affected by the nature of the client's business. For example, there is a greater likelihood of obsolete inventory for an electronics manufacturer than for a steel fabricator. Inherent risk is most likely to vary from business to business for accounts such as inventory, accounts and loans receivable, and property, plant, and equipment. The nature of the client's business should have little or no effect on inherent risk for accounts such as cash, notes, and mortgages payable. Information gained while obtaining knowledge about the client's business and industry and assessing client business risk, as discussed in Chapter 7, is useful for assessing this factor.

Results of Previous Audits Misstatements found in the previous year's audit have a high likelihood of occurring again in the current year's audit. This is because many types of misstatements are systemic in nature, and organizations are often slow in making changes to eliminate them. Therefore, an auditor would be negligent if the results of the preceding year's audit were ignored during the development of the current year's audit program. For example, if the auditor found a significant number of misstatements in pricing inventory, inherent risk would likely be high, and extensive testing would have to be done in the current audit as a means of determining whether the deficiency in the client's system had been corrected. If, however, the auditor has found no misstatements for the past several years in conducting tests of an audit area, the auditor is justified in reducing inherent risk, provided that changes in relevant circumstances have not occurred.

Initial Versus Repeat Engagement Auditors gain experience and knowledge about the likelihood of misstatements after auditing a client for several years. The lack of previous years' audit results would cause most auditors to use a larger inherent risk for initial audits than for repeat engagements in which no material misstatements had been found. Most auditors set a high inherent risk in the first year of an audit and reduce it in subsequent years as they gain experience.

Related Parties Transactions between parent and subsidiary companies and those between management and the corporate entity are examples of related-party transactions as defined by SFAS 57. Because these transactions do not occur between two independent parties dealing at "arm's length," a greater likelihood exists that they might be misstated, causing an increase in inherent risk. Determining the existence of related parties was discussed in Chapter 7.

Nonroutine Transactions Transactions that are unusual for the client are more likely to be incorrectly recorded by the client than routine transactions because the client lacks experience in recording them. Examples include fire losses, major property acquisitions, and lease agreements. Knowledge of the client's business and review of minutes of meetings, as discussed in Chapter 7, are useful to learn about nonroutine transactions.

Judgment Required to Correctly Record Account Balances and Transactions Many account balances require estimates and a great deal of management judgment. Examples are allowance for uncollectible accounts receivable, obsolete inventory, liability for warranty payments, and bank loan loss reserves. Similarly, transactions for major repairs or partial replacement of assets are examples where considerable judgment is needed to correctly record the information.

Makeup of the Population Often, the individual items making up the total population also affect the auditor's expectation of material misstatement. For example, most auditors would use a higher inherent risk for accounts receivable where most accounts are significantly overdue than where most accounts are current. Transactions with affiliated companies, amounts due from officers, cash disbursements made payable to cash, and accounts receivable outstanding for several months are examples of situations requiring a higher inherent risk and therefore greater investigation because there is usually a greater likelihood of misstatement than for more typical transactions.

Making the Inherent Risk Decision

The auditor must evaluate the information affecting inherent risk and decide on an appropriate inherent risk factor for each cycle, account, and many times for each audit objective. Some factors, such as the integrity of management, will affect many or perhaps all cycles, whereas others, such as nonroutine transactions, will affect only specific accounts or audit objectives. Although the profession has not established standards or guidelines for setting inherent risk, the authors believe that auditors are generally conservative in making such assessments. For example, assume that in the audit of inventory the auditor notes that (1) a large number of misstatements were found in the previous year and (2) inventory turnover has slowed in the current year. Many auditors would probably set inherent risk at a relatively high level (some would use 100 percent) for each audit objective for inventory in this situation.

Obtain Information to Assess Inherent Risk

Auditors begin their assessments of inherent risk during the planning phase and update the assessments throughout the audit. A considerable portion of Chapter 7 dealt with information that is relevant to inherent risk assessment during the planning phase. For example, the discussion of obtaining knowledge about the client's business and industry, touring the client's plant and offices, and identifying related parties all pertain directly to inherent risk assessment. As the auditor performs the wide variety of tests on an audit, additional information is obtained that often affects the original assessment.

ASSESSING RISKS OF FRAUD

OBJECTIVE 8-9

Consider information gathered to assess the likelihood of fraud.

There was a discussion in Chapter 5 of the auditor's responsibilities to assess the risk of fraud arising from fraudulent financial reporting and misappropriation of assets. It is difficult in concept and practice to separate fraud risk factors into acceptable audit risk, inherent risk, or control risk. For example, management that lacks integrity and is motivated to misstate financial statements is one of the factors in acceptable audit risk, but it may also affect control risk. Similarly, it will be shown in Chapter 9 that several of the other risk factors influencing management characteristics are a part of the control environment. An example is the attitude, actions, and policies that reflect the overall attitudes of top management about integrity, ethical values, and commitment to competence.

To satisfy the requirements of auditing standards, it is more important for the auditor to assess the risks and to respond to them than it is to identify them as acceptable audit risk, inherent risk, or control risk. For this reason, many audit firms assess fraud risk separately from the assessment of the risk model components.

To assess the risks of fraud, the auditor gathers information to determine the extent that fraud conditions exist. Three conditions are generally present when material misstatements due to fraud occur.

1. *Incentives/Pressures.* Management or other employees have incentives or pressures to commit fraud.
2. *Opportunities.* Circumstances provide opportunities for management or employees to commit fraud.

3. *Attitudes/Rationalization.* An attitude, character, or set of ethical values exists that allows management or employees to intentionally commit a dishonest act, or they are in an environment that imposes sufficient pressure that causes them to rationalize committing a dishonest act.

Information Affecting Risk of Fraud

To assess the extent that these three fraud conditions are present, the auditor should consider the following:

- Specific risk factors related to fraudulent financial reporting and misappropriation of assets.
- Information obtained from experienced audit team members about their knowledge of the company and its industry, including how and where the company might be susceptible to material misstatements due to fraud.
- Responses to auditor inquiries of management about their views about the risks of fraud and about existing programs and controls to address specific identified fraud risks.
- Analytical procedures results obtained during planning that indicate possible implausible or unexpected analytical relationships.
- Knowledge obtained through such things as client acceptance and retention decisions, interim reviews of financial statements, and the consideration of inherent risks.

To help the auditor evaluate risk factors related to the three conditions of fraud, Table 8-4 presents examples of risk factors to be considered by the auditor for each of the three conditions for fraudulent financial reporting. Table 8-5 presents examples of risk factors organized in these same three categories for misappropriation of assets.

Making the Risk of Fraud Decision

Similar to what is done for inherent risk, the auditor uses all of the information obtained to identify risks of material misstatements because of fraud. The auditor may identify risks that are pervasive to the financial statements as a whole, such as management manipulating

TABLE 8-4 Examples of Risk Factors for Fraudulent Financial Reporting

THREE CONDITIONS OF FRAUD		
Incentives/Pressures	**Opportunities**	**Attitudes/Rationalization**
Management or other employees have incentives or pressures to materially misstate financial statements.	*Circumstances provide an opportunity for management or employees to misstate financial statements.*	*An attitude, character, or set of ethical values exists that allows management or employees to intentionally commit a dishonest act, or they are in an environment that imposes sufficient pressure that causes them to rationalize committing a dishonest act.*
Examples of Risk Factors	**Examples of Risk Factors**	**Examples of Risk Factors**
Financial stability or profitability is threatened by economic, industry, or entity operating conditions. Examples include significant declines in customer demand and increasing business failures in either the industry or overall economy.	Significant accounting estimates involve subjective judgments or uncertainties that are difficult to verify.	Inappropriate or ineffective communication and support of the entity's values.
Excessive pressure for management to meet debt repayment or other debt covenant requirements.	Ineffective board of director or audit committee oversight over financial reporting.	Known history of violations of securities laws or other laws and regulations.
Management or the board of directors' personal net worth is materially threatened by the entity's financial performance.	High turnover or ineffective accounting, internal audit, or information technology staff.	Management's practice of making overly aggressive or unrealistic forecasts to analysts, creditors, and other third parties.

TABLE 8-5 Examples of Risk Factors for Misappropriations of Assets

THREE CONDITIONS OF FRAUD		
Incentives/Pressures	**Opportunities**	**Attitudes/Rationalization**
Management or other employees have incentives or pressures to misappropriate material assets.	*Circumstances provide an opportunity for management or employees to misappropriate assets.*	*An attitude, character, or set of ethical values exists that allows management or employees to intentionally commit a dishonest act, or they are in an environment that imposes sufficient pressure that causes them to rationalize committing a dishonest act.*
Examples of Risk Factors	**Examples of Risk Factors**	**Examples of Risk Factors**
Personal financial obligations create pressure for those with access to cash or other assets susceptible to theft to misappropriate those assets. Adverse relationships between management and employees with access to assets susceptible to theft motivate employees to misappropriate those assets. Examples include: • Known or expected employee layoffs. • Promotions, compensation, or other rewards inconsistent with expectations.	Presence of large amounts of cash on hand or inventory items that are small, of high value, or in high demand. Inadequate internal control over assets due to lack of: • Appropriate segregation of duties or independent checks. • Job applicant screening for employees with access to assets. • Mandatory vacations for employees with access to assets.	Disregard for the need to monitor or reduce risks of misappropriating assets. Disregard for internal controls by overriding existing controls or failing to correct known internal control deficiencies.

earnings to meet certain debt covenants. The auditor may also identify risks for specific accounts or classes of transactions, such as the risk of employee theft of inventory.

Responding to the Risk of Fraud

When risks of material misstatements due to fraud are identified, the auditor should first discuss these findings with management to obtain management's views of the potential fraud and the existing programs and controls designed to prevent or detect misstatements. The auditor should respond to these risks in three ways:

1. *Design and perform audit procedures to address identified fraud risks.* For example, the auditor may visit inventory locations on a surprise basis because of risks of inventory fraud.
2. *Change the overall conduct of the audit to respond to identified fraud risks.* For example, the auditor may change the staffing on the engagement, place even greater emphasis on the importance of professional skepticism, and do more extensive independent review of the completed audit.

INTERNET FRAUD ON THE RISE

E-fraud Survey

The growth of business on the Internet has been accompanied by an increase in fraud. "Internet fraud runs the gamut from work-at-home scams to bogus travel and vacation schemes . . . for many consumers the Internet can be a virtual nightmare when it comes to fraud," according to New York Consumer Affairs commissioner Jane Hoffman. The top five types of Internet fraud are Web auctions, travel and vacation scams, theft of identity such as ID numbers, "pump and dump" investment schemes, and pyramid schemes that use mass e-mailings promising windfall profits. Hoffman recommends being wary of investment advice in chat rooms, avoid businesses that lack a physical address and phone number, and never give out a Social Security number on a Web site. "If you have a gut feeling that something is not legitimate, you are probably right," says Hoffman.

Source: Dow Jones Newswires, July 15, 2001. interactive.wsj.com/archive/retrieve.cgi?id = DI-CO-20010715-000695.djm

3. *Perform procedures to address the risk of management override of controls.* For example, the auditor may examine nonstandard adjusting or consolidation journal entries for large and unusual transactions.

At the completion of the audit, the auditor should evaluate whether the accumulated results of audit procedures affect the assessment of the risks of material misstatements due to fraud made earlier in the audit. Based on the auditor's judgment, there may be a need to perform additional or different audit procedures.

RELATIONSHIP OF RISKS TO EVIDENCE AND FACTORS INFLUENCING RISKS

OBJECTIVE 8-10

Discuss the relationship of risks to audit evidence.

Figure 8-4 summarizes the factors that determine each of the risks, the effect of the three component risks on the determination of planned detection risk, and the relationship of all four risks to planned audit evidence. "D" in the figure indicates a direct relationship between a component risk and planned detection risk or planned evidence. "I" indicates an inverse relationship. For example, an increase in acceptable audit risk results in an increase in planned detection risk (D) and a decrease in planned audit evidence (I). Compare Figure 8-4 to Table 8-2 on page 214 and observe that these two illustrations include the same concepts.

In addition to modifying audit evidence, there are two other ways that auditors can change the audit to respond to risks. For example:

1. *The engagement may require more experienced staff.* CPA firms should staff all engagements with qualified staff, but for low acceptable audit risk clients, special care is appropriate in staffing. Similarly, if an audit area such as inventory has a high inherent risk, it is important to assign that area to someone with experience in auditing inventory.

FIGURE 8-4 **Relationship of Factors Influencing Risks to Risks and Risks to Planned Evidence**

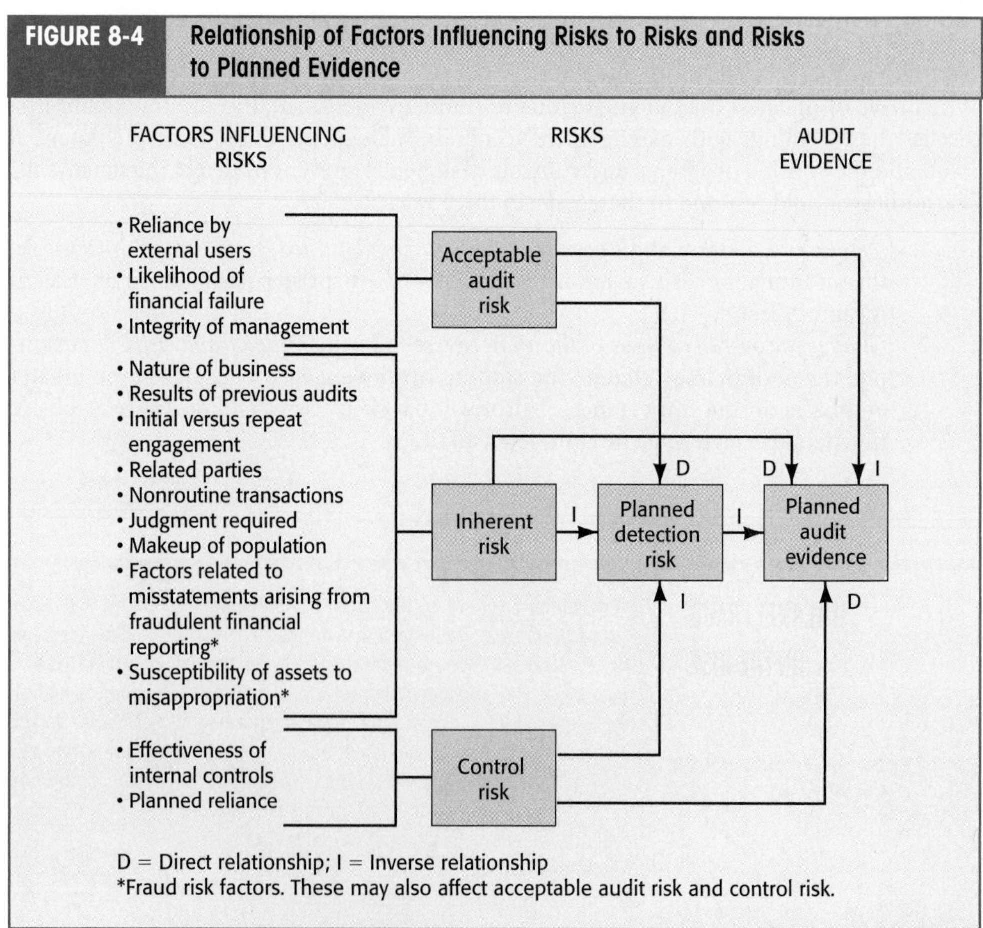

2. *The engagement will be reviewed more carefully than usual.* CPA firms need to be sure that the audit files that document the auditor's planning, evidence accumulation and conclusions, and other matters in the audit are adequately reviewed. When acceptable audit risk is low, there is often more extensive review, including a review by personnel who were not assigned to the engagement. If inherent risk or control risk is high for certain accounts, the reviewer will likely spend more time making sure the evidence was appropriate and correctly evaluated.

Audit Risk for Segments

Both control risk and inherent risk are typically set for each cycle, each account, and often even each audit objective, not for the overall audit, and are likely to vary from cycle to cycle, account to account, and objective to objective on the same audit. Internal controls may be more effective for inventory-related accounts than for those related to fixed assets. Control risk would therefore also be different for different accounts depending on the effectiveness of the controls. Factors affecting inherent risk, such as susceptibility to defalcation and routineness of the transactions, are also likely to differ from account to account. For that reason, it is normal to have inherent risk vary for different accounts in the same audit unless there is some strong overriding factor of concern, such as management integrity.

Acceptable audit risk is ordinarily set by the auditor during planning and held constant for each major cycle and account. Auditors normally use the same acceptable audit risk for each segment because the factors affecting acceptable audit risk are related to the entire audit, not individual accounts. For example, the extent to which financial statements are relied on for external users' decisions is usually related to the overall financial statements, not just one or two accounts.

In some cases, however, a *lower* acceptable audit risk may be more appropriate for one account than for others. In the previous example, even though the auditor decided to use a medium acceptable audit risk for the audit as a whole, the auditor might decide to reduce acceptable audit risk to low for inventory if inventory is used as collateral for a short-term loan.

Some auditors use the same acceptable audit risk for each segment as overall acceptable audit risk, whereas others use a higher acceptable audit risk for each segment. The argument for using a higher acceptable audit risk for each segment is the effect of the interactions of the various accounts and transactions making up the financial statements and the synergy of multiple tests. Stated differently, if all individual segments of the audit are completed at an acceptable audit risk of a given level, the auditor can be assured that the audit risk for the financial statements as a whole will be lower. Other auditors use the same acceptable audit risk for segments as overall acceptable audit risk because of the difficulties of measurement. The latter approach is followed in the illustrations in this and subsequent chapters, but either approach is acceptable.

Because control risk and inherent risk vary from cycle to cycle, account to account, or objective to objective, planned detection risk and required audit evidence will also vary. This conclusion should not be surprising. The circumstances of each engagement are different, and the extent of evidence needed will depend on the unique circumstances. For example, inventory might require extensive testing on an engagement because of weak internal controls and concern about obsolescence resulting from technological changes in the industry. On the same engagement, accounts receivable may require little testing because of effective internal controls, fast collection of receivables, excellent relationships between the client and customers, and good audit results in previous years. Similarly, for a given audit of inventory, an auditor may assess that there is a higher inherent risk of a realizable value misstatement because of the higher potential for obsolescence, but a low inherent risk of a classification misstatement because there is only purchased inventory.

Relating Risk of Fraud to Risk Model Components

The risk of fraud can be assessed for the entire audit or by cycle, account and objective. For example, a strong incentive for management to meet unduly aggressive earnings expectations may affect the entire audit while the susceptibility of inventory to theft may affect the inventory account. For both the risk of fraudulent financial reporting and the risk of misappropriation of assets, the focus is on specific areas of increased fraud risk and designing audit procedures or changing the overall conduct of the audit to respond to those risks. The specific response to an identified risk of fraud could include revising assessments of acceptable audit risk, inherent risk, and control risk. Figure 8-4 shows how risks related to fraud may influence each of the audit risk model components.

Relating Tolerable Misstatement and Risks to Balance-Related Audit Objectives

Although it is common in practice to assess inherent and control risks for each balance-related audit objective, it is not common to allocate materiality to objectives. Auditors are able to effectively associate most risks with different objectives. It is reasonably easy to determine the relationship between a risk and one or two objectives. For example, obsolescence in inventory would be unlikely to affect any objective other than realizable value. It is more difficult to decide how much of the materiality allocated to a given account should in turn be allocated to one or two objectives. Most auditors do not attempt to do so.

Measurement Limitations

Activity-Based Risk Evaluation Model

One major limitation in the application of the audit risk model is the difficulty of measuring the components of the model. Despite the auditor's best efforts in planning, the assessments of acceptable audit risk, inherent risk, and control risk and therefore planned detection risk are highly subjective and are approximations of reality at best. Imagine, for example, attempting to precisely assess inherent risk by determining the impact of factors such as the misstatements discovered in prior years' audits and technology changes in the client's industry.

To offset this measurement problem, many auditors use broad and subjective measurement terms, such as *low, medium,* and *high.* Table 8-6 shows how auditors can use the information to decide on the appropriate amount of evidence to accumulate. For example, in situation 1, the auditor has decided to accept a high audit risk for an account or objective. The auditor has concluded that there is a low risk of misstatement in the financial statements and that internal controls are effective. Therefore, a high planned detection risk is appropriate. As a result, a low level of evidence is needed. Situation 3 is at the opposite extreme. If both inherent and control risks are high and the auditor wants a low audit risk, considerable evidence is required. The other three situations fall between the two extremes.

It is equally difficult to measure the amount of evidence implied by a given planned detection risk. A typical audit program that is intended to reduce detection risk to the planned level is a combination of several audit procedures, each using a different type of evidence that is applied to different audit objectives. Auditors' measurement methods are too imprecise to permit an accurate quantitative measure of the combined evidence. Instead, auditors subjectively evaluate whether sufficient evidence has been planned to satisfy a planned detection risk of low, medium, or high. Presumably, measurement methods are sufficient to permit an auditor to know that more evidence is needed to satisfy a low

TABLE 8-6 Relationships of Risk to Evidence

Situation	Acceptable Audit Risk	Inherent Risk	Control Risk	Planned Detection Risk	Amount of Evidence Required
1	High	Low	Low	High	Low
2	Low	Low	Low	Medium	Medium
3	Low	High	High	Low	High
4	Medium	Medium	Medium	Medium	Medium
5	High	Low	Medium	Medium	Medium

planned detection risk than for medium or high. Considerable professional judgment is needed to decide how much more.

In applying the audit risk model, auditors are concerned about both overauditing and underauditing, but most auditors are more concerned about the latter. Underauditing exposes the CPA firm to legal liability and loss of professional reputation.

Because of the concern to avoid underauditing, auditors typically assess risks conservatively. For example, an auditor might not assess either control risk or inherent risk below .5 even when the likelihood of misstatement is low. In these audits, a low risk might be .5, medium .8, and high 1.0, if the risks are quantified.

Tests of Details of Balances Evidence Planning Worksheet

Practicing auditors develop various types of worksheets to aid in relating the considerations affecting audit evidence to the appropriate evidence to accumulate. One such worksheet is included in Figure 8-5 for the audit of accounts receivable for Hillsburg Hardware Co. The nine balance-related audit objectives introduced in Chapter 5 are included in the columns at the top of the worksheet. Rows one and two are acceptable audit risk and inherent risk, which were studied in this chapter. Tolerable

FIGURE 8-5 Evidence-Planning Worksheet to Decide Tests of Details of Balances for Hillsburg Hardware Co.—Accounts Receivable

	Detail tie-in	Existence	Completeness	Accuracy	Classification	Cutoff	Realizable value	Rights	Presentation and disclosure
Acceptable audit risk	High	High	High	High	High	High	High	High	High
Inherent risk	Low	Low	Low	Low	Low	Low	Medium	Low	Low
Control risk—Sales									
Control risk—Cash receipts									
Control risk—Additional controls									
Substantive tests of transactions—Sales									
Substantive tests of transactions—Cash receipts									
Analytical procedures									
Planned detection risk for tests of details of balances									
Planned audit evidence for tests of details of balances									

Tolerable misstatement $442,000

misstatement is included at the bottom of the worksheet. The engagement in-charge, Fran Moore, made the following decisions in the audit of Hillsburg Hardware Co.:

- *Tolerable misstatement.* The preliminary judgment about materiality was set at \$737,000 (approximately 10 percent of earnings from operations of \$7,370,000). She allocated \$442,000 to the audit of accounts receivable (see p. 237).
- *Acceptable audit risk.* Fran assessed acceptable audit risk as high because of the good financial condition of the company, high management integrity, and the relatively few users of the financial statements. Although Hillsburg is a publicly traded company, its stock is not widely held or extensively followed by financial analysts.
- *Inherent risk.* Fran assessed inherent risk as low for all balance-related audit objectives except realizable value. In past years, there have been audit adjustments to the allowance for uncollectible accounts because it was found to be understated.

Planned detection risk would be approximately the same for each balance-related audit objective in the audit of accounts receivable for Hillsburg Hardware Co. if the only three factors the auditor needs to consider are acceptable audit risk, inherent risk, and tolerable misstatement. The evidence planning worksheet shows that other factors must be considered before making the final evidence decisions. These are studied in subsequent chapters and will be integrated into the evidence planning worksheet at that time.

Relationship of Risk and Materiality to Audit Evidence

OBJECTIVE 8-11

Discuss how materiality and risk are related and integrated into the audit process.

The concepts of materiality and risk in auditing are closely related and inseparable. Risk is a measure of uncertainty, whereas materiality is a measure of magnitude or size. Taken together, they measure the uncertainty of amounts of a given magnitude. For example, the statement that the auditor plans to accumulate evidence such that there is only a 5 percent risk (acceptable audit risk) of failing to uncover misstatements exceeding tolerable misstatements of \$442,000 (materiality) is a precise and meaningful statement. If the statement eliminates either the risk or materiality portion, it would be meaningless. A 5 percent risk without a specific materiality measure could imply that a \$100 or \$1 million misstatement is acceptable. A \$442,000 overstatement without a specific risk could imply that a 1 percent or 80 percent risk is acceptable.

The relationships among tolerable misstatement and the four risks to planned audit evidence are shown in Figure 8-6. This figure expands Figure 8-4 to include tolerable misstatement. Observe that tolerable misstatement does not affect any of the four risks and the risks have no effect on tolerable misstatement, but together they determine the planned evidence.

EVALUATING RESULTS

After the auditor plans the engagement and accumulates audit evidence, results can also be stated in terms of the evaluation version of the audit risk model. The audit risk model for evaluating audit results is stated in SAS 47 as

$$AcAR = IR \times CR \times AcDR$$

where:

AcAR* = *Achieved audit risk. A measure of the risk the auditor has taken that an account in the financial statements is materially misstated after the auditor has accumulated audit evidence.

IR* = *Inherent risk. It is the same inherent risk factor discussed in planning unless it has been revised as a result of new information.

CR* = *Control risk. It is also the same control risk discussed previously unless it has been revised during the audit.

AcDR* = *Achieved detection risk. A measure of the risk that audit evidence for a segment did not detect misstatements exceeding a tolerable amount, if such misstatements existed. The auditor can reduce achieved detection risk only by accumulating substantive evidence.

Research subsequent to the issuance of SAS 47 has shown that it is *not appropriate to use this evaluation formula* in the way it is stated in SAS 47. The research indicates that

FIGURE 8-6 Relationship of Tolerable Misstatement and Risks to Planned Evidence

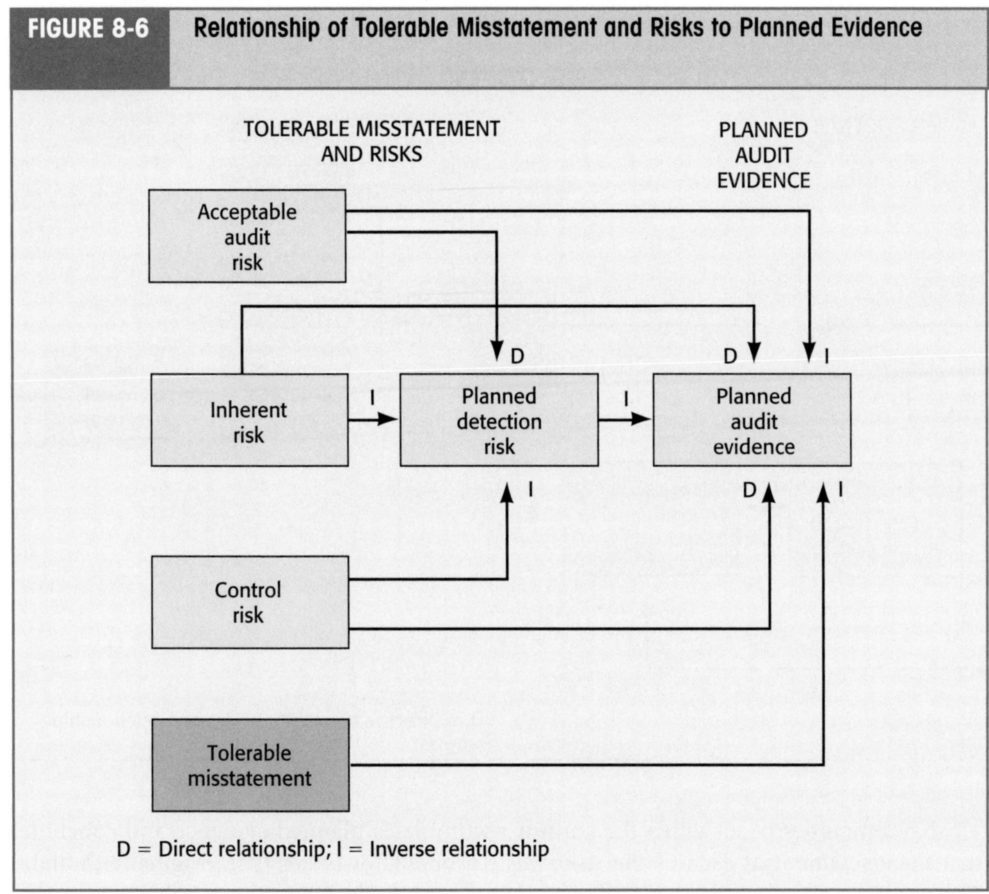

using the formula can result in an understatement of achieved audit risk. Even though it is not appropriate to use the formula to calculate achieved audit risk, the relationships in the formula are valid and should be used in practice. The formula shows that there are three ways to reduce achieved audit risk to an acceptable level:

1. *Reduce inherent risk.* Because inherent risk is assessed by the auditor based on the client's circumstances, this assessment is done during planning and is typically not changed unless new facts are uncovered as the audit progresses.
2. *Reduce control risk.* Assessed control risk is affected by the client's internal controls and the auditor's tests of those controls. Auditors can reduce control risk by more extensive tests of controls if the client has effective controls.
3. *Reduce achieved detection risk by increasing substantive audit tests.* Auditors reduce achieved detection risk by accumulating evidence using analytical procedures, substantive tests of transactions, and tests of details of balances. Additional audit procedures, assuming that they are effective, and larger sample sizes both reduce achieved detection risk.

Subjectively combining these three factors to achieve an acceptably low audit risk requires considerable professional judgment. Some firms develop sophisticated approaches to help their auditors make those judgments, whereas other firms leave those decisions to each audit team.

Figure 8-7 (page 230) graphically shows both the planning and evaluating results versions of the audit risk model. The right side of the figure shows that accumulating more substantive evidence reduces achieved detection risk. A lower achieved detection risk along with lower inherent and control risk reduce achieved audit risk.

Revising Risks and Evidence

As already stated, the audit risk model is primarily a *planning* model and is therefore of limited use in evaluating results. Great care must be used in revising the risk factors when the actual results are not as favorable as planned.

FIGURE 8-7 Audit Risk Models for Planning Evidence and Evaluating Results

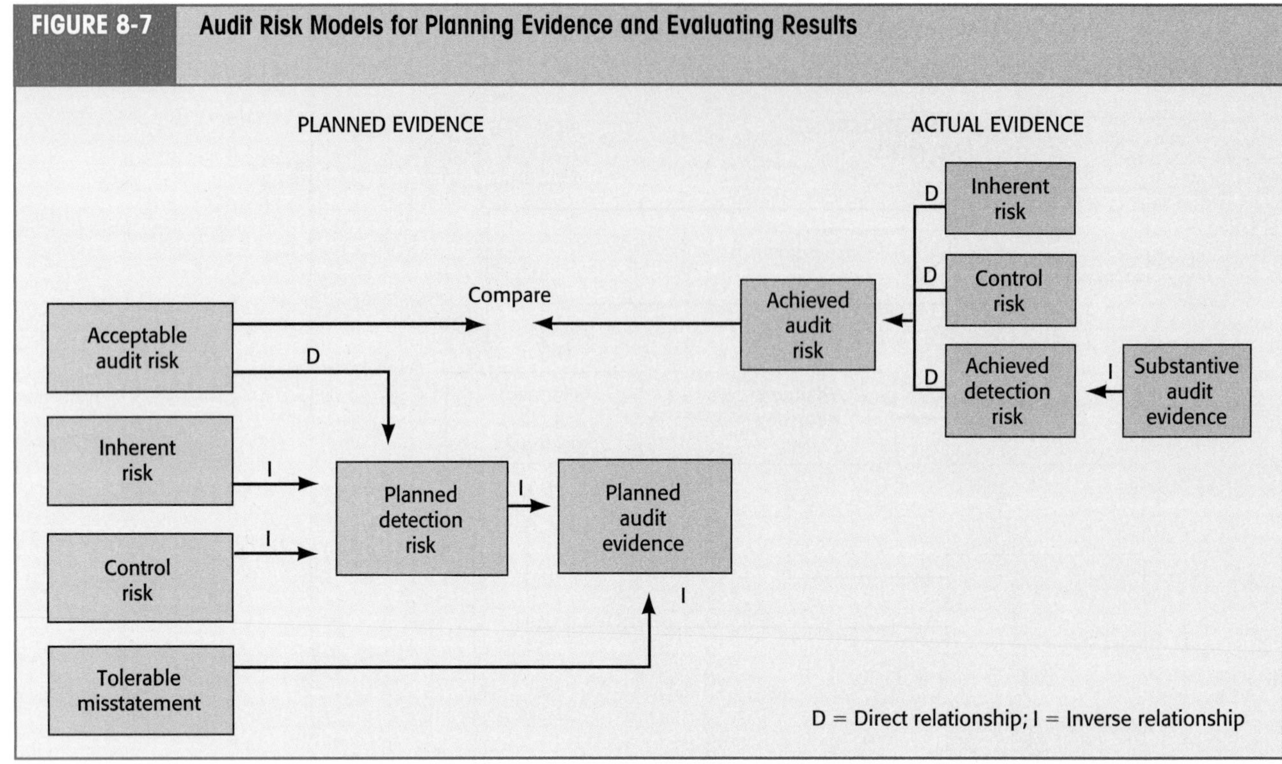

No difficulties occur when the auditor accumulates planned evidence and concludes that the assessment of each of the risks was reasonable or better than originally thought. The auditor will conclude that sufficient competent evidence has been collected for that account or cycle.

Special care must be exercised when the auditor decides, on the basis of accumulated evidence, that the original assessment of control risk or inherent risk was understated or acceptable audit risk was overstated. In such a circumstance, the auditor should follow a two-step approach. First, the auditor must revise the original assessment of the appropriate risk. It would violate due care to leave the original assessment unchanged if the auditor knows it is inappropriate. Second, the auditor should consider the effect of the revision on evidence requirements, *without use of the audit risk model.* Research in auditing has shown that if a revised risk is used in the audit risk model to determine a revised planned detection risk, there is a danger of not increasing the evidence sufficiently. Instead, the auditor should carefully evaluate the implications of the revision of the risk and modify evidence appropriately, outside of the audit risk model. An example is used to illustrate revision of a factor in the audit risk model. Assume that the auditor confirms accounts receivable and, based on the misstatements found, concludes that the original control risk assessment as low was inappropriate. The auditor should revise the estimate of control risk upward and carefully consider the effect of the revision on the additional evidence needed in the sales and collection cycle. That should be done without recalculating planned detection risk.

ESSENTIAL TERMS

Acceptable audit risk—a measure of how willing the auditor is to accept that the financial statements may be materially misstated after the audit is completed and an unqualified audit opinion has been issued; see also *audit assurance*

Allocation of the preliminary judgment about materiality—the process of assigning to each balance sheet account the misstatement amount to be considered material for that account based on the auditor's preliminary judgment

Audit assurance—a complement to acceptable audit risk; an acceptable audit risk of 2 percent is the same as audit assurance of 98 percent; also called *overall assurance* and *level of assurance*

Audit risk model—a formal model reflecting the relationships between acceptable audit risk (AAR), inherent risk (IR), control risk (CR), and planned detection risk (PDR); $PDR = AAR/(IR \times CR)$

Control risk—a measure of the auditor's assessment of the likelihood that misstatements exceeding a tolerable amount in a segment will not be prevented or detected by the client's internal controls

Direct projection estimate of misstatement—estimate of likely misstatement in a population based on a sample, excluding sampling risk, and calculated as net misstatements in the sample, divided by the total sampled, multiplied by the total recorded population value

Engagement risk—the risk that the auditor or audit firm will suffer harm because of a client relationship, even though the audit report rendered for the client was correct

Inherent risk—a measure of the auditor's assessment of the likelihood that there are material misstatements in a segment before considering the effectiveness of internal control

Materiality—the magnitude of an omission or misstatement of accounting information that, in the light of surrounding circumstances, makes it *probable* that the judgment of a reasonable person relying on the information would have been changed or influenced by the omission or misstatement

Planned detection risk—a measure of the risk that audit evidence for a segment will fail to detect misstatements exceeding a tolerable amount, should such misstatements exist; $PDR = AAR/(IR \times CR)$

Preliminary judgment about materiality—the maximum amount by which the auditor believes that the statements could be misstated and still *not* affect the decisions of reasonable users; used in audit planning

Revised judgment about materiality—a change in the auditor's preliminary judgment made when the auditor determines that the preliminary judgment was too large or too small

Risk—the acceptance by auditors that there is some level of uncertainty in performing the audit function

Sampling error—results because the auditor has sampled only a portion of the population

Tolerable misstatement—the materiality allocated to any given account balance; used in audit planning

REVIEW QUESTIONS

8-1 **(Objective 8-1)** Chapter 7 introduced the seven parts of the planning phase of an audit. Which part is the evaluation of materiality and risk?

8-2 **(Objective 8-1)** Define the meaning of the term *materiality* as it is used in accounting and auditing. What is the relationship between materiality and the phrase *obtain reasonable assurance* used in the auditor's report?

8-3 **(Objectives 8-1, 8-2)** Explain why materiality is important but difficult to apply in practice.

8-4 **(Objective 8-2)** What is meant by setting a preliminary judgment about materiality? Identify the most important factors affecting the preliminary judgment.

8-5 **(Objective 8-2)** What is meant by using bases for setting a preliminary judgment about materiality? How would those bases differ for the audit of a manufacturing company and a government unit such as a school district?

8-6 **(Objective 8-2)** Assume that Rosanne Madden, CPA, is using 5% of net income before taxes, current assets, or current liabilities as her major guidelines for evaluating materiality. What qualitative factors should she also consider in deciding whether misstatements may be material?

8-7 **(Objectives 8-2, 8-3)** Distinguish between the terms *tolerable misstatement* and *preliminary judgment about materiality*. How are they related to each other?

8-8 **(Objective 8-3)** Assume a company with the following balance sheet accounts:

Account	Amount
Cash	$10,000
Fixed assets	60,000
	$70,000
Long-term loans	$30,000
M. Johnson, proprietor	40,000
	$70,000

You are concerned only about overstatements of owner's equity. Set tolerable misstatement for the three relevant accounts such that the preliminary judgment about materiality does not exceed $5,000. Justify your answer.

8-9 (Objective 8-4) Explain what is meant by making an estimate of the total misstatement in a segment and in the overall financial statements. Why is it important to make these estimates? What is done with them?

8-10 (Objective 8-2) How would the conduct of an audit of a medium-sized company be affected by the company's being a small part of a large conglomerate as compared with it being a separate entity?

8-11 (Objective 8-6) Define the audit risk model and explain each term in the model.

8-12 (Objective 8-6) What is meant by planned detection risk? What is the effect on the amount of evidence the auditor must accumulate when planned detection risk is increased from medium to high?

8-13 (Objective 8-6) Explain the causes of an increased or decreased planned detection risk.

8-14 (Objectives 8-6, 8-8) Define what is meant by inherent risk. Identify four factors that make for *high* inherent risk in audits.

8-15 (Objective 8-8) Explain why inherent risk is set for segments rather than for the overall audit. What is the effect on the amount of evidence the auditor must accumulate when inherent risk is increased from medium to high for a segment? Compare your answer with the one for question 8-12.

8-16 (Objective 8-8) Explain the effect of extensive misstatements found in the prior year's audit on inherent risk, planned detection risk, and planned audit evidence.

8-17 (Objectives 8-6, 8-7) Explain what is meant by the term *acceptable audit risk.* What is its relevance to evidence accumulation?

8-18 (Objective 8-7) Explain the relationship between acceptable audit risk and the legal liability of auditors.

8-19 (Objective 8-7) State the three categories of factors that affect acceptable audit risk and list the factors that the auditor can use to indicate the degree to which each category exists.

8-20 (Objective 8-9) Describe the three conditions that are generally present when material misstatements due to fraud occur and give one example of each condition.

8-21 (Objective 8-10) Auditors have not been successful in measuring the components of the audit risk model. How is it possible to use the model in a meaningful way without a precise way of measuring the risk?

8-22 (Objective 8-11) Explain the circumstances when the auditor should revise the components of the audit risk model and the effect of the revisions on planned detection risk and planned evidence.

MULTIPLE CHOICE QUESTIONS FROM CPA EXAMINATIONS

8-23 (Objectives 8-1, 8-6, 8-8) The following questions concern materiality and risk. Choose the best response.

a. Edison Corporation has a few large accounts receivable that total $1,400,000. Victor Corporation has a great number of small accounts receivable that also total $1,400,000. The importance of a misstatement in any one account is therefore greater for Edison than for Victor. This is an example of the auditor's concept of
   (1) materiality.
   (2) comparative analysis.
   (3) reasonable assurance.
   (4) relative risk.

b. Which of the following elements ultimately determines the specific auditing procedures that are necessary in the circumstances to afford a reasonable basis for an opinion?
   (1) Auditor judgment
   (2) Materiality
   (3) Inherent risk
   (4) Reasonable assurance

c. Which of the following *best* describes the element of inherent risk that underlies the application of generally accepted auditing standards, specifically the standards of field work and reporting?
   (1) Cash audit work may have to be carried out in a more conclusive manner than inventory audit work.
   (2) Intercompany transactions are usually subject to less detailed scrutiny than arm's-length transactions with outside parties.

(3) Inventories may require more attention by the auditor on an engagement for a merchandising enterprise than on an engagement for a public utility.
(4) The scope of the audit need *not* be expanded if misstatements that arouse suspicion of fraud are of relatively insignificant amounts.

8-24 (Objectives 8-1, 8-2, 8-5, 8-6, 8-8) The following questions deal with materiality and risk. Choose the best response.

a. Which of the following statements is *not* correct about materiality?
   (1) The concept of materiality recognizes that some matters are important for fair presentation of financial statements in conformity with GAAP, whereas other matters are *not* important.
   (2) An auditor considers materiality for planning purposes in terms of the largest aggregate level of misstatements that could be material to any one of the financial statements.
   (3) Materiality judgments are made in light of surrounding circumstances and necessarily involve both quantitative and qualitative judgments.
   (4) An auditor's consideration of materiality is influenced by the auditor's perception of the needs of a reasonable person who will rely on the financial statements.

b. Inherent risk and control risk differ from planned detection risk in that they
   (1) arise from the misapplication of auditing procedures.
   (2) may be assessed in either quantitative or nonquantitative terms.
   (3) exist independently of the financial statement audit.
   (4) can be changed at the auditor's discretion.

c. In considering materiality for planning purposes, an auditor believes that misstatements aggregating $10,000 would have a material effect on an entity's income statement but that misstatements would have to aggregate $20,000 to materially affect the balance sheet. Ordinarily, it would be appropriate to design auditing procedures that would be expected to detect misstatements that aggregate
   (1) $10,000
   (2) $15,000
   (3) $20,000
   (4) $30,000

DISCUSSION QUESTIONS AND PROBLEMS

8-25 (Objectives 8-2, 8-3, 8-4) You are evaluating audit results for current assets in the audit of Quicky Plumbing Co. You set the preliminary judgment about materiality for current assets at $12,500 for overstatements and at $20,000 for understatements. The preliminary and actual estimates are shown below.

	Tolerable Misstatement		Estimate of Total Misstatement	
Account	**Overstatements**	**Understatements**	**Overstatements**	**Understatements**
Cash	$ 2,000	$ 3,000	$ 2,000	$ 0
Accounts receivable	12,000	18,000	4,000	19,000
Inventory	8,000	14,000	3,000	10,000
Prepaid expenses	3,000	5,000	2,000	1,000
Total	$25,000	$40,000	$11,000	$30,000

Required

a. Justify a lower preliminary judgment about materiality for overstatements than understatements in this situation.

b. Explain why the totals of the tolerable misstatements exceed the preliminary judgments about materiality for both understatements and overstatements.

c. Explain how it is possible that three of the estimates of total misstatement have both an overstatement and an understatement.

d. Assume that you are not concerned whether the estimate of misstatement exceeds tolerable misstatement for individual accounts if the total estimate is less than the preliminary judgment.
   (1) Given the audit results, should you be more concerned about the existence of material overstatements or understatements at this point in the audit of Quicky Plumbing Co.?
   (2) Which account or accounts would you be most concerned about in (1)? Explain.

e. Assume that the estimate of total overstatement amount for each account is less than tolerable misstatement but that the total overstatement estimate exceeds the preliminary judgment of materiality.
   (1) Explain why this would occur.
   (2) Explain what the auditor should do.

8-26 (Objectives 8-2, 8-3, 8-4) Below and on page 235 are statements of earnings and financial position for Wexler Industries.

Required

a. Use professional judgment in deciding on the preliminary judgment about materiality for earnings, current assets, current liabilities, and total assets. Your conclusions should be stated in terms of percents and dollars.

b. Assume that you define materiality for this audit as a combined misstatement of earnings from continuing operations before income taxes of 5%. Also assume that you believe there is an equal likelihood of a misstatement of every account in the financial statements and each misstatement is likely to result in an overstatement of earnings. Allocate materiality to these financial statements as you consider appropriate.

c. As discussed in part b, net earnings from continuing operations *before* income taxes was used as a base for calculating materiality for the Wexler Industries audit. Discuss why most auditors use *before*-tax net earnings instead of *after*-tax net earnings when calculating materiality based on the income statement.

d. Now, assume that you have decided to allocate 75% of your preliminary judgment to accounts receivable, inventories, and accounts payable because you believe all other accounts have a low inherent and control risk. How does this affect evidence accumulation on the audit?

e. Assume that you complete the audit and conclude that your preliminary judgment about materiality for current assets, current liabilities, and total assets has been met. The actual estimate of misstatements in *earnings* exceeds your preliminary judgment. What should you do?

Consolidated Statements of Earnings
Wexler Industries (in Thousands)

	For the 53 Weeks Ended March 30, 2002	For the 52 Weeks Ended March 31, 2001	April 1, 2000
Revenue			
Net sales	$8,351,149	$6,601,255	$5,959,587
Other income	59,675	43,186	52,418
	8,410,824	**6,644,441**	**6,012,005**
Costs and expenses			
Cost of sales	5,197,375	4,005,548	3,675,369
Marketing, general, and administrative expenses	2,590,080	2,119,590	1,828,169
Provision for loss on restructured operations	64,100	—	—
Interest expense	141,662	46,737	38,546
	7,993,217	**6,171,875**	**5,542,084**
Earnings from continuing operations before income taxes	**417,607**	**472,566**	**469,921**
Income taxes	**(196,700)**	**(217,200)**	**(214,100)**
Earnings from continuing operations	**220,907**	**255,366**	**255,821**
Provision for loss on discontinued operations, net of income taxes	**(20,700)**	—	—
Net earnings	**$ 200,207**	**$ 255,366**	**$ 255,821**

Consolidated Statements of Financial Position
Wexler Industries (in Thousands)

Assets	March 30, 2002	March 31, 2001
Current assets		
Cash	$ 39,683	$ 37,566
Temporary investments, including time deposits of $65,361 in 2002 and $181,589 in 2001 (at cost, which approximates market)	123,421	271,639
Receivables, less allowances of $16,808 in 2002 and $17,616 in 2001	899,752	759,001
Inventories		
Finished product	680,974	550,407
Raw materials and supplies	443,175	353,795
	1,124,149	904,202
Deferred income tax benefits	9,633	10,468
Prepaid expenses	57,468	35,911
Current assets	**2,254,106**	**2,018,787**
Land, buildings, and equipment, at cost, less accumulated depreciation	**1,393,902**	**1,004,455**
Investments in affiliated companies and sundry assets	**112,938**	**83,455**
Goodwill and other intangible assets	**99,791**	**23,145**
Total	**$3,860,737**	**$3,129,842**

Liabilities and Stockholders' Equity	March 30, 2002	March 31, 2001
Current liabilities		
Notes payable	$ 280,238	$ 113,411
Current portion of long-term debt	64,594	12,336
Accounts and drafts payable	359,511	380,395
Accrued salaries, wages, and vacations	112,200	63,557
Accrued income taxes	76,479	89,151
Other accrued liabilities	321,871	269,672
Current liabilities	**1,214,893**	**928,522**
Long-term debt	**730,987**	**390,687**
Other noncurrent liabilities	**146,687**	**80,586**
Deferred income taxes	**142,344**	**119,715**
Stockholders' equity		
Common stock issued, 51,017,755 shares in 2002 and 50,992,410 in 2001	51,018	50,992
Additional paid-in capital	149,177	148,584
Cumulative foreign currency translation adjustment	(76,572)	—
Retained earnings	1,554,170	1,462,723
Common stock held in treasury, at cost, 1,566,598 shares	(51,967)	(51,967)
Stockholders' equity	**1,625,826**	**1,610,332**
Total	**$3,860,737**	**$3,129,842**

8-27 **(Objectives 8-6, 8-7)** Describe what is meant by acceptable audit risk. Explain why each of the following statements is true:

a. A CPA firm should attempt to achieve the same audit risk for all audit clients when circumstances are similar.

b. A CPA firm should decrease acceptable audit risk for audit clients when external users rely heavily on the statements.

c. A CPA firm should decrease acceptable audit risk for audit clients when there is a reasonably high likelihood of a client's filing bankruptcy.

d. Different CPA firms should attempt to achieve reasonably similar audit risks for clients with similar circumstances.

8-28 **(Objectives 8-5, 8-6, 8-7, 8-8)** State whether each of the following statements is true or false, and give your reasons:

a. The audit evidence accumulated for every client should be approximately the same, regardless of the circumstances.

b. If acceptable audit risk is the same for two different clients, the audit evidence for the two clients should be approximately the same.

c. If acceptable audit risk, inherent risk, and control risk are approximately the same for two different clients, the audit evidence for the two clients should be approximately the same.

8-29 **(Objectives 8-6, 8-7, 8-8)** The following questions deal with the use of the audit risk model.

a. Assume that the auditor is doing a first-year municipal audit of Redwood City, Missouri, and concludes that the internal controls are not likely to be effective.
   (1) Explain why the auditor is likely to set both inherent and control risks at 100% for most segments.
   (2) Assuming (1), explain the relationship of acceptable audit risk to planned detection risk.
   (3) Assuming (1), explain the effect of planned detection risk on evidence accumulation compared with its effect if planned detection risk were larger.

b. Assume that the auditor is doing the third-year municipal audit of Redwood City, Missouri, and concludes that internal controls are effective and inherent risk is low.
   (1) Explain why the auditor is likely to set inherent and control risks for material segments at a higher level than, say, 40%, even when the two risks are low.
   (2) For the audit of fixed asset accounts, assume inherent and control risks of 50% each, and an acceptable audit risk of 5%. Calculate planned detection risk.
   (3) For (2), explain the effect of planned detection risk on evidence accumulation compared with its effect if planned detection risk were smaller.

c. Assume that the auditor is doing the fifth-year municipal audit of Redwood City, Missouri, and concludes that acceptable audit risk can be set high and inherent and control risks should be set low.
   (1) What circumstances would result in these conclusions?
   (2) For the audit of repairs and maintenance, inherent and control risk are set at 20% each. Acceptable audit risk is 5%. Calculate planned detection risk.
   (3) How much evidence should be accumulated in this situation?

8-30 **(Objective 8-6)** Following are six situations that involve the audit risk model as it is used for planning audit evidence requirements. Numbers are used only to help you understand the relationships among factors in the risk model.

	Situation					
Risk	**1**	**2**	**3**	**4**	**5**	**6**
Acceptable audit risk	5%	5%	5%	5%	1%	1%
Inherent risk	100%	40%	60%	20%	100%	40%
Control risk	100%	60%	40%	30%	100%	60%
Planned detection risk	—	—	—	—	—	—

Required

a. Explain what each of the four risks means.

b. Calculate planned detection risk for each situation.

c. Using your knowledge of the relationships among the foregoing factors, state the effect on planned detection risk (increase or decrease) of changing each of the following factors while the other two remain constant:
   (1) A decrease in acceptable audit risk
   (2) A decrease in control risk
   (3) A decrease in inherent risk
   (4) An increase in control risk and a decrease in inherent risk of the same amount

d. Which situation requires the greatest amount of evidence and which requires the least?

8-31 (Objectives 8-6, 8-10) Following are six situations that involve the audit risk model as it is used for planning audit evidence requirements in the audit of inventory.

	Situation					
Risk	**1**	**2**	**3**	**4**	**5**	**6**
Acceptable audit risk	High	High	Low	Low	High	Medium
Inherent risk	Low	High	High	Low	Medium	Medium
Control risk	Low	Low	High	High	Medium	Medium
Planned detection risk	—	—	—	—	—	—
Planned evidence	—	—	—	—	—	—

Required

a. Explain what low, medium, and high mean for each of the four risks and planned evidence.

b. Fill in the blanks for planned detection risk and planned evidence using the terms *low, medium,* or *high.*

c. Using your knowledge of the relationships among the foregoing factors, state the effect on planned evidence (increase or decrease) of changing each of the following five factors, while the other three remain constant:
   (1) An increase in acceptable audit risk
   (2) An increase in control risk
   (3) An increase in planned detection risk
   (4) An increase in inherent risk
   (5) An increase in inherent risk and a decrease in control risk of the same amount

8-32 (Objectives 8-6, 8-11) Using the audit risk model, state the effect on control risk, inherent risk, acceptable audit risk, and planned evidence for each of the following independent events. In each of the events a to j, circle one letter for each of the three independent variables and planned evidence: I = increase, D = decrease, N = no effect, and C = cannot determine from the information provided.

a. The client's management materially increased long-term contractual debt:

Control risk	I D N C	Acceptable audit risk	I D N C
Inherent risk	I D N C	Planned evidence	I D N C

b. The company changed from a privately held company to a publicly held company:

Control risk	I D N C	Acceptable audit risk	I D N C
Inherent risk	I D N C	Planned evidence	I D N C

c. The auditor decided to set assessed control risk below maximum (it was previously assessed at maximum):

Control risk	I D N C	Acceptable audit risk	I D N C
Inherent risk	I D N C	Planned evidence	I D N C

d. The account balance increased materially from the preceding year without apparent reason:

Control risk	I D N C	Acceptable audit risk	I D N C
Inherent risk	I D N C	Planned evidence	I D N C

e. You determined through the planning phase that working capital, debt-to-equity ratio, and other indicators of financial condition had improved during the past year:

Control risk	I D N C	Acceptable audit risk	I D N C
Inherent risk	I D N C	Planned evidence	I D N C

f. This is the second year of the engagement, and there were few misstatements found in the previous year's audit. The auditor also decided to increase reliance on internal control:

Control risk	I D N C	Acceptable audit risk	I D N C
Inherent risk	I D N C	Planned evidence	I D N C

g. The client began selling products online to customers through its Web page during the year under audit. The online customer ordering process is not integrated with the company's accounting system. Client sales staff print out customer order information and enter that data into the sales accounting system.

Control risk	I D N C	Acceptable audit risk	I D N C
Inherent risk	I D N C	Planned evidence	I D N C

h. In discussions with management, you conclude that management is planning to sell the business in the next few months. Because of the planned changes, several key accounting personnel quit several months ago for alternative employment. You also observe that the gross margin percent has significantly increased compared with that of the preceding year:

Control risk	I D N C	Acceptable audit risk	I D N C
Inherent risk	I D N C	Planned evidence	I D N C

i. There has been a change in several key management personnel. You believe that management is somewhat lacking in personal integrity compared with the previous management. You believe it is still appropriate to do the audit:

Control risk	I D N C	Acceptable audit risk	I D N C
Inherent risk	I D N C	Planned evidence	I D N C

j. In auditing inventory, you obtain an understanding of internal control and perform tests of controls. You find it significantly improved compared with that of the preceding year. You also observe that because of technology changes in the industry, the client's inventory may be somewhat obsolete:

Control risk	I D N C	Acceptable audit risk	I D N C
Inherent risk	I D N C	Planned evidence	I D N C

CASE

8-33 (Objectives 8-6, 8-7, 8-8) In the audit of Whirland Chemical Company, a large publicly traded company, you have been assigned the responsibility for obtaining background information for the audit. Your firm is auditing the client for the first time in the current year as a result of a dispute between Whirland and the previous auditor over the proper valuation of work-in-process inventory and the inclusion in sales of inventory that has not been delivered but has for practical purposes been completed and sold.

Whirland Chemical has been highly successful in its field in the past two decades, primarily because of many successful mergers negotiated by Bert Randolph, the president and chairman of the board. Even though the industry as a whole has suffered dramatic setbacks in recent years, Whirland continues to prosper, as evidenced by its constantly increasing earnings and growth. Only in the last 2 years have the company's profits turned downward. Randolph has a reputation for having been able to hire an aggressive group of young executives by the use of relatively low salaries combined with an unusually generous profit-sharing plan.

A major difficulty you face in the new audit is the lack of highly sophisticated accounting records for a company the size of Whirland. Randolph believes that profits come primarily from intelligent and aggressive action based on forecasts, not by relying on historical data that come after the fact. Most of the forecast data are generated by the sales and production department rather than by the accounting department. The personnel in the accounting department do seem competent but somewhat overworked and underpaid relative to other employees. One of the recent changes that will potentially improve the record keeping is the installation of sophisticated computer equipment. All the accounting records are not computerized yet, but such major areas as inventory and sales are included in the new system. Most of the computer time is being reserved for production and marketing because these areas are more essential to operations than the record-keeping function.

The first 6 months' financial statements for the current year include a profit of approximately only 10% less than the first 6 months of the preceding year, which is somewhat surprising, considering the reduced volume and the disposal of a segment of the business, Mercury Supply Co. The disposal of this segment was considered necessary because it had become increasingly unprofitable over the past 4 years. At the time of its acquisition from Roger Randolph, who is a brother of Bert Randolph, the company was highly profitable and it was considered a highly desirable purchase. The major customer of Mercury Supply Co. was the Mercury Corporation, which is owned by Roger Randolph. Gradually, the market for its products declined as the Mercury Corporation began diversifying and phasing out its primary products in favor of more profitable business. Even though Mercury Corporation is no longer buying from Mercury Supply Co., it compensates for it by buying a large volume of other products from Whirland Chemical.

The only major difficulty Whirland faces right now, according to financial analysts, is underfinancing. There is an excessive amount of current debt and long-term debt because of the depressed capital markets. Management is reluctant to obtain equity capital at this point because the increased number of shares would decrease the earnings per share even more than 10%. At the present time, Randolph is negotiating with several cash-rich companies in the hope of being able to merge with them as a means of overcoming the capital problems.

Required

a. List the major concerns you should have in the audit of Whirland Company and explain why they are potential problems.

b. State the appropriate approach to investigating the significance of each item you listed in a.

INTERNET PROBLEM 8-1: MATERIALITY AND TOLERABLE MISSTATEMENT

Reference the CW site. This problem requires students to apply specific materiality and tolerable misstatement guidelines to actual financial statements obtained from the Internet. This problem also asks students to research the recommendations of the Big Five's Audit Materiality Task Force.

CHAPTER 9

INTERNAL CONTROL AND CONTROL RISK

LEARNING OBJECTIVES

After studying this chapter, you should be able to

9-1 Contrast management's need for internal control with the auditor's need to consider internal control when designing an audit.

9-2 Describe how information technology affects internal control.

9-3 Explain the five components of internal control.

9-4 Explain methods used to obtain an understanding of internal control.

9-5 Assess control risk by linking strengths and weaknesses of internal control to transaction-related audit objectives.

9-6 Describe the process of designing and performing tests of controls.

GOOD INTERNAL CONTROL PREVENTS MORE DEFALCATIONS THAN GOOD AUDITORS FIND

Shortly after its tenth consecutive audit of the Foundation for Youth Bible Studies (FYBS), Able & Co. was informed that FYBS's head accountant was found to have embezzled $2 million during the past 4 years. FYBS wanted to know how this could have occurred without Able discovering it. Able responded that he would have to know how the fraud was carried out to answer the question.

The FYBS's camp facility was in a different state than its home office. Funds were collected from campers and sent in the form of a cashier's check to the head accountant, who was supposed to forward the check to the home office cash receipts clerk. The head accountant recorded the revenue using the information on the cashier's check. No record of the source or amount of the cash receipts was maintained at the FYBS camp, which allowed her to occasionally pocket some of the checks. Obviously, she did not record the revenue for these defalcations.

When the auditors gained an understanding of internal control at FYBS, they regularly interviewed employees about how the system functioned. During the course of those discussions, they were never told about the procedure for transmitting funds from the camp. It was not clear that anyone in the home office, other than the embezzler, was aware of it. Fortunately, Able & Co.'s audit report contained a qualification that they could verify only those revenues that were actually recorded. Given the qualification in the audit report and the conduct of their audit, Able & Co. was not held responsible for the loss. They helped FYBS implement new controls to prevent a similar occurrence, but nevertheless, FYBS changed auditors.

As the third chapter dealing with planning the audit, Chapter 9 shows why and how effective internal controls can reduce planned audit evidence. To support the assessment of the control risk component of the audit risk model studied in Chapter 8, auditors must obtain an understanding of internal control and gather related evidence to support that assessment. The shaded part of the chart included in the margin shows where obtaining an understanding of internal control and assessing control risk fit into planning the audit. As the example in the opening vignette involving FYBS demonstrates, weaknesses in internal control can result in material misstatements or fraud.

To effectively assess internal controls for the purpose of reducing planned audit evidence, auditors need to understand key internal control and control risk concepts. Accordingly, this chapter focuses on the objectives of internal control, the components of internal control, and the auditor's methodology for fulfilling the requirements of the second standard of field work. We start by examining both the auditor's and the client's objectives for internal control.

CLIENT AND AUDITOR CONCERNS

OBJECTIVE 9-1

Contrast management's need for internal control with the auditor's need to consider internal control when designing an audit.

A system of internal control consists of policies and procedures designed to provide management with reasonable assurance that the company achieves its objectives and goals. These policies and procedures are often called controls, and collectively they comprise the entity's **internal control.** An understanding of internal control, especially those controls related to the reliability of financial reporting, is important to the auditor's purposes. We will first look at an overview of several key concepts related to internal control before examining both client and auditor concerns about internal control.

Key Concepts

Three key concepts underlie the study of internal control and assessment of control risk.

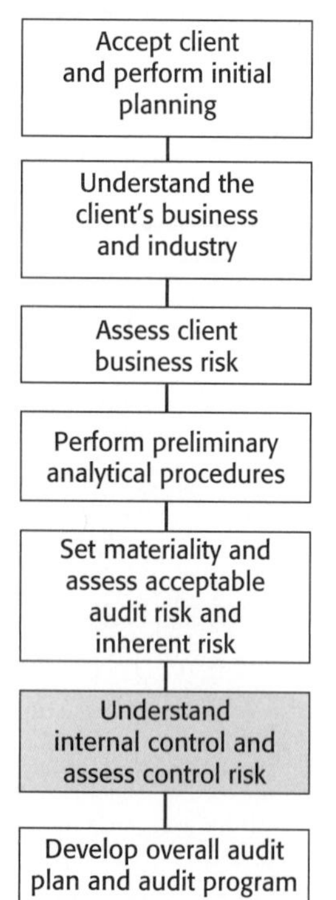

Accept client and perform initial planning
Understand the client's business and industry
Assess client business risk
Perform preliminary analytical procedures
Set materiality and assess acceptable audit risk and inherent risk
Understand internal control and assess control risk
Develop overall audit plan and audit program

Management's Responsibility Management, not the auditor, must establish and maintain the entity's controls. This concept is consistent with the requirement that management, not the auditor, is responsible for the preparation of financial statements in accordance with GAAP.

Reasonable Assurance A company should develop internal controls that provide reasonable, but not absolute, assurance that the financial statements are fairly stated. Internal controls are developed by management after considering both the costs and benefits of the controls. Management is often unwilling to implement an ideal system because the costs may be too high. For example, it is unreasonable to expect management of a small company to hire several additional accounting personnel to make small improvements in the reliability of accounting data. It is often less expensive to have auditors do more extensive auditing than to incur higher internal control costs.*

Inherent Limitations Internal controls can never be regarded as completely effective, regardless of the care followed in their design and implementation. Even if systems personnel could design an ideal system, its effectiveness depends on the competency and dependability of the people using it. For example, assume that a procedure for counting inventory is carefully developed and requires two employees to count independently. If neither of the employees understands the instructions or if both are careless in doing the counts, the inventory count is likely to be wrong. Even if the count is right, management might override the procedure and instruct an employee to increase the count of quantities to improve reported earnings. Similarly, the employees might decide to overstate the counts intentionally to cover up a theft of inventory by one or

*Because the Foreign Corrupt Practices Act requires public companies to have an effective accounting system, public companies must evaluate whether their records meet legal requirements even if it is less expensive to have auditors uncover misstatements.

both of them. An act of two or more employees to steal assets or misstate records is called **collusion.**

Client Concerns

The 1992 study on internal control titled *Internal Control—Integrated Framework* by the Committee of Sponsoring Organizations of the Treadway Commission (COSO) and SAS 94 provide an extensive description of internal control. The client concerns discussed in this section are taken primarily from SAS 94 and the *COSO Report.*

WWW

COSO Report

Management typically has the following three concerns, or broad objectives, in designing an effective control system.

Reliability of Financial Reporting As discussed in Chapter 5, management is responsible for preparing financial statements for investors, creditors, and other users. Management has both a legal and professional responsibility to be sure that the information is fairly prepared in accordance with reporting requirements such as GAAP.

Efficiency and Effectiveness of Operations Controls within an organization are meant to encourage efficient and effective use of its resources, including personnel, to optimize the company's goals. An important part of these controls is accurate information for internal decision making. A variety of information is used for making critical business decisions. For example, the price to charge for products is based in part on information about the cost of making the products.

Another important part of effectiveness and efficiency is safeguarding assets and records. The physical assets of a company can be stolen, misused, or accidentally destroyed unless they are protected by adequate controls. The same is true of nonphysical assets such as accounts receivable, important documents (confidential government contracts), and records (general ledger and journals). Safeguarding certain assets and records has become increasingly important since the advent of computer systems. Large amounts of information stored on computer media can be destroyed if care is not taken to protect them. Safeguarding of accounting records also affects the reliability of financial reporting.

Compliance with Applicable Laws and Regulations Organizations are required to follow many laws and regulations. Some are only indirectly related to accounting. Examples include environmental protection and civil rights laws. Others are closely related to accounting, such as income tax regulations and fraud.

One important law affecting all companies subject to the Securities and Exchange Act of 1934 is the Foreign Corrupt Practices Act of 1977. This law, which amended the securities acts, requires that a company maintain "proper record-keeping systems." A proper record-keeping system is one that allows the preparation of reliable external financial statements and prevents off-the-books slush funds and payment of bribes.

Auditor Concerns

Knowledge about a client's internal control is sufficiently important to the audit process to merit a separate generally accepted auditing standard. Recall that the second GAAS field work standard states, "A sufficient understanding of internal control is to be obtained to plan the audit and to determine the nature, timing, and extent of tests to be performed." Auditors are primarily concerned about controls related to the reliability of financial reporting and controls over classes of transactions.

Controls Related to the Reliability of Financial Reporting To comply with the second standard of field work, the auditor is interested primarily in controls that relate to the first of management's internal control concerns: reliability of financial reporting. This is the area that directly affects the financial statements and their related assertions and therefore affects the auditor's objective of determining that the financial statements are fairly stated. The financial statements are not likely to correctly reflect GAAP if the controls affecting the reliability of financial reporting are inadequate. On the other hand, the statements can be fairly stated even if the company's controls do not promote efficiency and effectiveness in its operations.

As stated in Chapter 5, auditors have significant responsibility for the discovery of material fraudulent financial reporting and misappropriation of assets (fraud) and direct-effects illegal acts. Auditors are therefore also concerned with a client's internal control over the safeguarding of assets and compliance with applicable laws and regulations if they affect the fairness of the financial statements. Internal controls, if properly designed and implemented, can be effective in preventing or detecting fraud. The results of a recent fraud survey by KPMG (see p. 245) indicate that about half of the typical frauds are detected by internal controls.

It has already been stated that auditors should emphasize controls concerned with the reliability of data for *external reporting purposes,* but controls affecting internal management information, such as budgets and internal performance reports, should not be completely ignored. These types of information are often important sources of evidence in helping the auditor decide whether the financial statements are fairly presented. If the controls over these internal reports are considered inadequate, the value of the reports as evidence diminishes.

Controls over Classes of Transactions The primary emphasis by auditors is on internal control over classes of transactions rather than account balances. The reason is that the accuracy of the output of the accounting system (account balances) is heavily dependent on the accuracy of the inputs and processing (transactions). For example, if products sold, units shipped, or unit selling prices are wrong in billing customers for sales, both sales and accounts receivable will be misstated. If controls are adequate to make sure billings, cash receipts, sales returns and allowances, and charge-offs are correct, the ending balance in accounts receivable is likely to be correct.

When gaining an understanding of internal control and assessing control risk, auditors are primarily concerned with the transaction-related audit objectives discussed in Chapter 5. These objectives were discussed in detail on pages 128–129. Table 9-1 illustrates the development of transaction-related audit objectives for sales transactions.

While gaining an understanding of internal control and assessing control risk, the auditor does not, however, ignore internal control over account balances. For example, transaction-related audit objectives typically have no effect on three balance-related audit objectives: realizable value, rights and obligations, and presentation and disclosure. The auditor is likely to evaluate separately whether management has implemented internal controls for each of these three balance-related audit objectives.

Because of the inherent limitations of internal controls and because auditors cannot obtain more than reasonable assurance of their effectiveness, there is almost always some

TABLE 9-1 Sales Transaction-Related Audit Objectives

Transaction-Related Audit Objective—General Form	Sales Transaction-Related Audit Objectives
Recorded transactions exist (existence).	Recorded sales are for shipments made to existing customers.
Existing transactions are recorded (completeness).	Existing sales transactions are recorded.
Recorded transactions are stated at the correct amounts (accuracy).	Recorded sales are for the amount of goods shipped and are correctly billed and recorded.
Transactions are properly classified (classification).	Sales transactions are properly classified.
Transactions are recorded on the correct dates (timing).	Sales are recorded on the correct dates.
Recorded transactions are properly included in the master files and correctly summarized (posting and summarization).	Sales transactions are properly included in the master files and are correctly summarized.

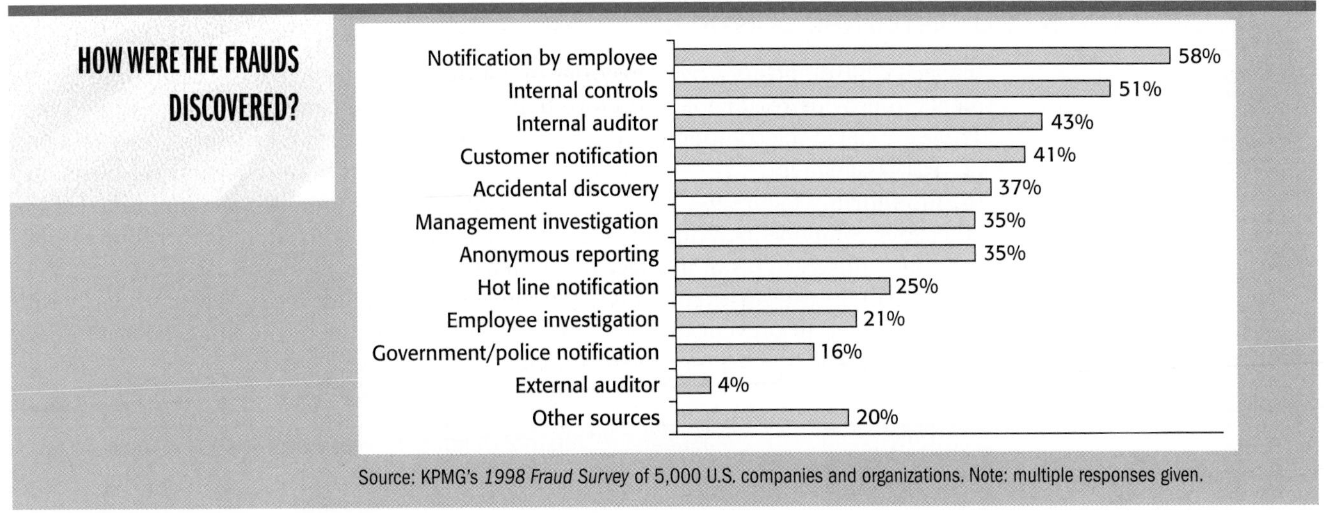

Source: KPMG's *1998 Fraud Survey* of 5,000 U.S. companies and organizations. Note: multiple responses given.

level of control risk greater than zero. Therefore, even with the most effectively designed internal controls, the auditor must obtain audit evidence beyond testing the controls for every material financial statement account.

EFFECT OF INFORMATION TECHNOLOGY ON INTERNAL CONTROL

OBJECTIVE 9-2

Describe how information technology affects internal control.

The use of computers to process and manage information is called **information technology (IT).** An entity's use of IT can improve the effectiveness and efficiency of internal control by consistently processing large volumes of transactions and data. IT also enhances the timeliness and accuracy of information. However, there are also numerous risks associated with the use of IT. For example, management may rely on systems that contain programmed errors that result in inaccurately processed data or allow the processing of data that is incorrect. There is also risk of unauthorized access to data and software programs that could result in unauthorized changes to master files and programs. The extent and nature of these risks vary depending on the nature and characteristics of the information system. As a result, when auditors gain an understanding of internal control, they must consider how IT risks could result in misstatements.

The use of IT affects the way in which transactions are initiated, recorded, processed, and reported. In less sophisticated systems, records exist in paper form and are subject to manual controls such as authorizations and approval. For example, the purchase of goods may be initiated by departments using written purchase requisitions. In contrast, in an organization with more advanced use of IT, goods may be ordered by the computer system based on predetermined rules and payments processed automatically based on information recorded in the system when goods are received. In such situations, electronic data replaces paper documents and controls consist of a combination of automated controls embedded in computer programs and manual controls.

A client's use of IT may also affect internal controls over financial reporting, operations, or compliance objectives. The impact of IT may be limited to specific business units or operating functions, or it may affect all aspects of an entity's internal control. For example, a client may use IT to support accounts receivable for a business unit, or it may have complex, highly integrated systems that share data for all aspects of the business. As the client's systems become more complex, it is likely that auditors will need to increase their understanding of system controls to design effective tests of controls and substantive tests. An auditor or outside professional with IT skills may also be needed to understand or test IT controls.

COMPONENTS OF INTERNAL CONTROL

OBJECTIVE **9-3**

Explain the five components of internal control.

Internal control includes five categories of controls that management designs and implements to provide reasonable assurance that management's control objectives will be met. These are called the components of internal control and are (1) the control environment, (2) risk assessment, (3) control activities, (4) information and communication, and (5) monitoring. Figure 9-1 shows that the control environment is the umbrella for the other four components. Without an effective control environment, the other four components are unlikely to result in effective internal control, regardless of their quality.

Each of the categories contains many controls. The auditor is concerned primarily with those designed to prevent or detect material misstatements in the financial statements. Those aspects are the focus of the remainder of this chapter.

FIGURE 9-1 **Five Components of Internal Control**

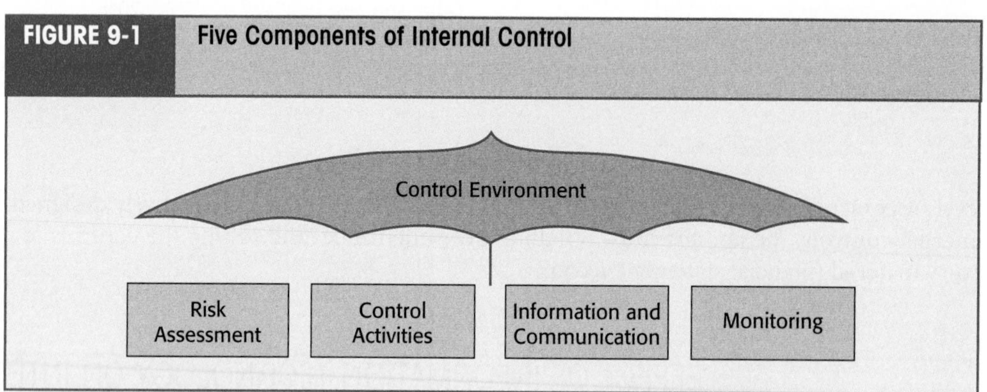

The Control Environment

The essence of an effectively controlled organization lies in the attitude of its management. If top management believes that control is important, others in the organization will sense that and respond by conscientiously observing the controls established. On the other hand, if it is clear to members of the organization that control is not an important concern to top management and it is given lip service rather than meaningful support, it is almost certain that management's control objectives will not be effectively achieved.

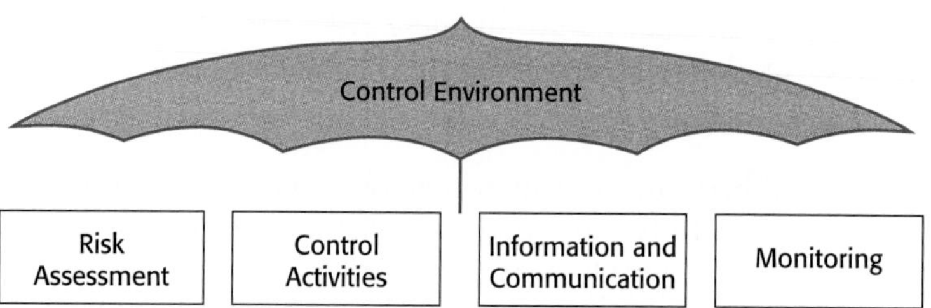

The **control environment** consists of the actions, policies, and procedures that reflect the overall attitudes of top management, directors, and owners of an entity about internal control and its importance to the entity. For the purpose of understanding and assessing the control environment, the following are the most important subcomponents the auditor should consider.

Integrity and Ethical Values Integrity and ethical values are the product of the entity's ethical and behavioral standards and how they are communicated and reinforced in practice. They include management's actions to remove or reduce incentives and temptations that might prompt personnel to engage in dishonest, illegal, or unethical acts. They also include the communication of entity values and behavioral standards to personnel through policy statements and codes of conduct and by example.

Commitment to Competence Competence is the knowledge and skills necessary to accomplish tasks that define the individual's job. Commitment to competence includes

AUDIT COMMITTEE EFFECTIVENESS

An abundance of accounting scandals, such as the alleged recording of millions of dollars in bogus revenues at Cendant Corporation, suggest that audit committees are not always effectively doing their jobs. Investor activists attack such committees for lacking independence or financial expertise to uncover most financial reporting failures. They note that audit committees sometimes fall short because a chief executive picks members who are willing to go with the flow. Audit committees need independent directors with sophisticated financial backgrounds. In response to these concerns, the Securities and Exchange Commission created a blue ribbon committee to study the effectiveness of audit committees. That committee issued a report in 1999 titled *Report and Recommendations of the Blue Ribbon Committee on Improving the Effectiveness of Corporate Audit Committees.* The report contains 10 recommendations designed to (1) strengthen the independence of the audit committee, (2) make the audit committee more effective, and (3) address mechanisms for accountability among the audit committee, the outside auditors, and management.

Sources: "Scandals Signal Laxity of Audit Panels," *The Wall Street Journal* (July 17, 1998), B1. *Report and Recommendations of the Blue Ribbon Committee on Improving the Effectiveness of Corporate Audit Committees,* New York Stock Exchange and the National Association of Securities Dealers, 1999.

management's consideration of the competence levels for specific jobs and how those levels translate into requisite skills and knowledge.

Board of Directors or Audit Committee Participation An effective board of directors is independent of management, and its members are involved in and scrutinize management's activities. The board delegates responsibility for internal control to management and is charged with providing regular independent assessments of management-established internal control. In addition, an active and objective board can often effectively reduce the likelihood that management overrides existing controls. To assist the board in its oversight, the board creates an audit committee that is charged with oversight responsibility for the financial reporting process. The audit committee is also responsible for maintaining ongoing communication with both external and internal auditors. This allows the auditors and directors to discuss matters that might relate to such things as the integrity or actions of management. The audit committee's independence from management and knowledge of financial reporting issues are important determinants of their ability to effectively evaluate internal controls and financial statements prepared by management. The major exchanges (NYSE, AMEX, and NASDAQ) require that listed companies have an audit committee composed entirely of independent directors who are financially literate. Many privately held companies also create effective audit committees, recognizing the importance of effective financial reporting and internal control oversight.

WWW

Blue Ribbon Report on Audit Committees

Management's Philosophy and Operating Style Management, through its activities, provides clear signals to employees about the importance of internal control. For example, does management take significant risks, or is it risk averse? Are sales and earnings targets unrealistic, and are employees encouraged to take aggressive actions to meet those targets? Can management be described as "fat and bureaucratic," "lean and mean," dominated by one or a few individuals, or is it "just right"? Understanding these and similar aspects of management's philosophy and operating style gives the auditor a sense of management's attitude about internal control.

Organizational Structure The entity's organizational structure defines the existing lines of responsibility and authority. By understanding the client's organizational structure, the auditor can learn the management and functional elements of the business and perceive how controls are implemented.

Assignment of Authority and Responsibility In addition to the informal aspects of communication already mentioned, formal methods of communication about authority and responsibility and similar control-related matters are equally important. These might include such methods as memoranda from top management about the importance of control and control-related matters, formal organizational and operating plans, and employee job descriptions and related policies.

Human Resource Policies and Practices The most important aspect of internal control is personnel. If employees are competent and trustworthy, other controls can be absent and reliable financial statements will still result. Honest, efficient people are able to perform at a high level even when there are few other controls to support them. Even if there are numerous other controls, incompetent or dishonest people can reduce the system to a shambles. Even though personnel may be competent and trustworthy, people have certain innate shortcomings. For example, they can become bored or dissatisfied, personal problems can disrupt their performance, or their goals may change.

Because of the importance of competent, trustworthy personnel in providing effective control, the methods by which persons are hired, evaluated, trained, promoted, and compensated are an important part of internal control.

The auditor obtains information about each of the subcomponents of the control environment. The auditor then uses this understanding as a basis for assessing management's and the directors' attitude and awareness about the importance of control. For example, the auditor might determine the nature of a client's budgeting system as a part of understanding the design of the control environment. The operation of the budgeting system might then be evaluated in part by inquiry of budgeting personnel to determine budgeting procedures and follow-up of differences between budget and actual. The auditor might also examine client schedules comparing actual results to budgeted amounts.

Risk Assessment

Risk assessment for financial reporting is *management's* identification and analysis of risks relevant to the preparation of financial statements in conformity with GAAP. For example, if a company frequently sells products at a price below inventory cost because of rapid technology changes, it is essential for the company to incorporate adequate controls to overcome the risk of overstating inventory.

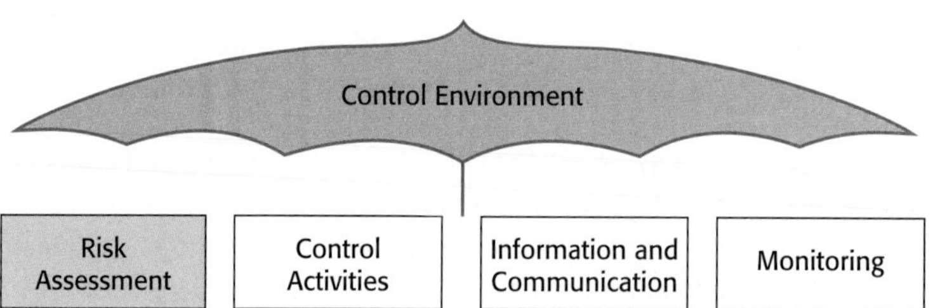

Risk Advisory Services

All entities, regardless of size, structure, nature, or industry, face a variety of risks from external and internal sources that must be managed. Because economic, industry, regulatory, and operating conditions constantly change, management is challenged with developing mechanisms to identify and deal with risks associated with change. Internal control under one set of conditions will not necessarily be effective under another.

Identifying and analyzing risk is an ongoing process and a critical component of effective internal control. Management must focus on risks at all levels of the organization and take necessary actions to manage them. An important first step is for management to identify factors that may increase risk. Failure to meet prior objectives, quality of personnel, geographic dispersion of company operations, significance and complexity of core business processes, introduction of new information technologies, and entrance of new competitors all represent examples of factors that may lead to increased risk. Once a risk is identified, management estimates the significance of that risk, assesses the likelihood of the risk occurring, and develops specific actions that need to be taken to reduce the risk to an acceptable level. Of course, there is no cost-beneficial way to eliminate risk. However, management must assess how much risk is prudently acceptable and strive to maintain risk within this level.

HELPING CLIENTS MANAGE RISK

Many CPAs assist clients in developing processes to identify and manage enterprisewide risks. The AICPA and the Canadian Institute of Chartered Accountants recently issued a report, *Managing Risk in the New Economy,* for CPAs who provide risk management services to their clients or employers. The report highlights how successful organizations take calculated risks to achieve objectives. They weigh opportunities against threats and act decisively. The traditional, negative definitions of risk—harm, loss, danger, and hazard—are only part of the story. The other and equally important part is opportunity.

Although each organization has its own unique approach to risk management, the report highlights a number of consistent steps that represent current best practice. Risk management steps include:

- Establishing the context
- Identifying risks
- Analyzing and assessing risks
- Designing strategies for managing risk
- Implementing and integrating risk management
- Measuring, monitoring, and reporting

These steps can be applied to an entire enterprise, to a part of the organization, or to a specific project. Although an enterprisewide program is the most effective, it is often desirable to initially focus on a few critical areas.

Source: Adapted from *Managing Risk in the New Economy,* American Institute of Certified Public Accountants and The Canadian Institute of Chartered Accountants, 2000.

Management's risk assessment differs from but is closely related to the auditor's risk assessment discussed in Chapter 8. Management assesses risks as a part of designing and operating internal controls to minimize errors and fraud. Auditors assess risks to decide the evidence needed in the audit. If management effectively assesses and responds to risks, the auditor will typically accumulate less evidence than when management fails to identify or respond to significant risks.

The auditor obtains knowledge about management's risk assessment process by determining how management identifies risks relevant to financial reporting, evaluating their significance and likelihood of occurrence, and deciding the actions needed to address the risks. Questionnaires and discussions with management are the most common ways to obtain this understanding.

Control Activities

Control activities are the policies and procedures, in addition to those included in the other four components, that help ensure that necessary actions are taken to address risks in the achievement of the entity's objectives. There are potentially many such control activities in any entity, including both manual and automated controls. SAS 94 and the *COSO Report* note that control activities generally relate to policies and procedures that pertain to (1) segregation of duties, (2) information processing, (3) physical controls, and (4) performance reviews. The development of control activities related to these types of policies and procedures generally falls into the following five types of specific control activities, which are discussed next:

1. Adequate separation of duties
2. Proper authorization of transactions and activities
3. Adequate documents and records
4. Physical control over assets and records
5. Independent checks on performance

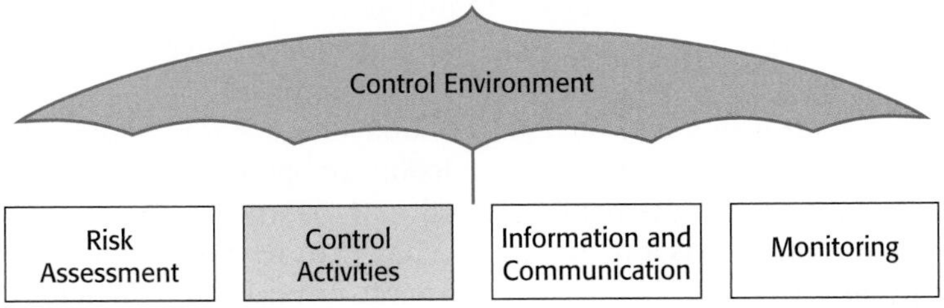

Adequate Separation of Duties Four general guidelines for adequate **separation of duties** to prevent both fraud and errors are of special significance to auditors.

Separation of the Custody of Assets from Accounting The reason for not permitting a person who has temporary or permanent custody of an asset to account for that asset is to protect the company against defalcation. When one person performs both functions, there is an increased risk of that person disposing of the asset for personal gain and adjusting the records to relieve himself or herself of responsibility. If the cashier, for example, receives cash and is responsible for data entry for cash receipts and sales, it is possible for the cashier to take the cash received from a customer and adjust the customer's account by failing to record a sale or by recording a fictitious credit to the account.

Separation of the Authorization of Transactions from the Custody of Related Assets If possible, it is desirable to prevent persons who authorize transactions from having control over the related asset. For example, the same person should not authorize the payment of a vendor's invoice and also sign the check in payment of the bill. The authorization of a transaction and the handling of the related asset by the same person increase the possibility of defalcation within the organization.

Separation of Operational Responsibility from Record-Keeping Responsibility If each department or division in an organization were responsible for preparing its own records and reports, there would be a tendency to bias the results to improve its reported performance. To ensure unbiased information, record keeping is typically included in a separate department under the controller.

Separation of IT Duties from User Departments As the level of complexity of IT systems increases, often the segregation of authorization, record keeping, and custody is blurred. For example, sales agents may enter customer orders online. The computer authorizes those sales based on its comparison of customer credit limits to the master file and posts all approved sales in the sales cycle journals. Therefore, the computer plays a significant role in the authorization and record keeping of sales transactions. To compensate for these potential overlaps of duties, it is important for companies to separate major IT-related functions from key user department functions. In this example, responsibility for designing and controlling accounting software programs that contain the sales authorization and posting controls should be under the authority of IT, whereas the ability to update information in the master file of customer credit limits should reside in the company's credit department outside the IT function.

Naturally, the extent of separation of duties depends heavily on the size of the organization. In many small companies, it is not practical to segregate the duties to the extent suggested. In these cases, audit evidence may require modification.

Proper Authorization of Transactions and Activities Every transaction must be properly authorized if controls are to be satisfactory. If any person in an organization could acquire or expend assets at will, complete chaos would result. Authorization can be either *general* or *specific.* **General authorization** means that management establishes policies for the organization to follow. Subordinates are instructed to implement these general authorizations by approving all transactions within the limits set by the policy. Examples of general authorization are the issuance of fixed price lists for the sale of products, credit limits for customers, and fixed reorder points for making acquisitions.

Specific authorization applies to individual transactions. Management is often unwilling to establish a general policy of authorization for some transactions. Instead, it prefers to make authorizations on a case-by-case basis. An example is the authorization of a sales transaction by the sales manager for a used-car company.

There is also a distinction between authorization and approval. Authorization is a policy decision for either a general class of transactions or specific transactions. Approval is the implementation of management's general authorization decisions. For example, assume that management sets a policy authorizing the ordering of inventory when less than a 3-week supply is on hand. That is a general authorization. When a department orders inventory, the clerk responsible for maintaining the perpetual record approves the order to indicate that the authorization policy has been met. In other cases, the computer performs the general approval of transactions. The comparison of quantities of inventory on hand to a master file of reorder points may be performed by the computer, and the computer may use that comparison to decide whether to submit purchase orders to authorized suppliers in the vendor master file. In that case, the computer is performing the general approval function using preauthorized information contained in the master files. The authorization in this case is performed by purchasing department personnel when they authorize changes to reorder points and vendors in the inventory and vendor master files, respectively.

Adequate Documents and Records Documents and records are the physical objects upon which transactions are entered and summarized. They include such diverse items as sales invoices, purchase orders, subsidiary records, sales journals, and employee time cards. Many of these documents and records are maintained in the form of computer files until they are printed out for specific purposes. Both documents of original entry and records upon which transactions are entered are important, but the inadequacy of documents typically causes greater control problems.

Documents perform the function of transmitting information throughout the client's organization and between different organizations. The documents must be adequate to provide reasonable assurance that all assets are properly controlled and all transactions are correctly recorded. For example, if the receiving department fills out a receiving report when material is obtained, the accounts payable department can verify the quantity and description on the vendor's invoice by comparing it with the information on the receiving report.

A control closely related to documents and records is the **chart of accounts,** which classifies transactions into individual balance sheet and income statement accounts. The chart of accounts is an important control because it provides the framework for determining the information presented to management and other financial statement users. The chart of accounts is helpful in preventing classification errors if it accurately and precisely describes which type of transactions should be in each account.

The procedures for proper record keeping should be spelled out in systems manuals to encourage consistent application. The manuals should provide sufficient information to facilitate adequate record keeping and maintain proper control over assets. Many software applications contain Help screens, which assist in the proper use of accounting software.

Physical Control Over Assets and Records To maintain adequate internal control, it is essential to protect assets and records. If assets are left unprotected, they can be stolen. If records are not adequately protected, they can be stolen, damaged, or lost. In the event of such an occurrence, the accounting process and normal operations could be seriously disrupted. When a company is highly computerized, it is especially important to protect its computer equipment, programs, and data files. The equipment and programs are expensive and essential to operations. The data files are the records of the company and, if damaged, could be costly or even impossible to reconstruct.

The most important type of protective measure for safeguarding assets and records is the use of physical precautions. An example is the use of storerooms for inventory to guard against theft. When the storeroom is under the control of a competent employee, there is further assurance that obsolescence is minimized. Fireproof safes and safety deposit vaults for the protection of assets such as currency and securities are other important physical safeguards.

There are three categories of controls related to safeguarding IT equipment, programs, and data files. As with other types of assets, physical controls are used to protect the computer facilities. Examples are locks on doors to the computer room and terminals, proper control of environmental conditions such as temperature and humidity in the computer room, adequate storage space for software and data files to protect them from loss, and proper fire-extinguishing systems. Access controls deal with ensuring that only authorized people can use the equipment and have access to software and data files. An example is an online access password system. Backup and recovery procedures are steps an organization can take in the event of a loss of equipment, programs, or data. For example, a backup copy of programs and critical data files stored in a safe remote location is a common backup control.

Independent Checks on Performance The last category of control activities is the careful and continuous review of the other four, often called **independent checks** or internal verification. The need for independent checks arises because internal control tends to change over time unless there is a mechanism for frequent review. Personnel are likely to forget or intentionally fail to follow procedures, or they may become careless unless someone observes and evaluates their performance. In addition, both fraudulent and unintentional misstatements are possible, regardless of the quality of the controls.

An essential characteristic of the persons performing internal verification procedures is independence from the individuals originally responsible for preparing the data. The least expensive means of internal verification is the separation of duties in the manner previously discussed. For example, when the bank reconciliation is performed by a person independent of the accounting records and handling of cash, there is an opportunity for verification without incurring significant additional costs.

Computerized accounting systems can be designed so that many internal verification procedures can be automated as part of the system. For example, the computer will prevent the processing of payment on a vendor invoice if there is no matching purchase order number or receiving report number for that invoice recorded in the system.

Auditors obtain an understanding of the control environment and risk assessment in a similar manner for most audits, but obtaining an understanding of control activities varies considerably. For smaller clients, it is common to identify few or even no control activities because controls are often ineffective because of limited personnel. In that case, the auditor sets a high assessed control risk. For clients with extensive controls that the auditor believes to be excellent, it is often appropriate to identify many controls during the understanding phase. In other audits, the auditor may identify a limited number of controls during this phase and then identify additional controls later in the process. The extent to which controls are identified is a matter of audit judgment. A methodology for identifying controls is studied later in the chapter.

Information and Communication

The purpose of an entity's accounting **information and communication** system is to initiate, record, process, and report the entity's transactions and to maintain accountability for the related assets. An accounting information and communication system has several subcomponents, typically made up of classes of transactions such as sales, sales returns, cash receipts, acquisitions, and so on. For each class of transactions, the accounting system must satisfy all of the six transaction-related audit objectives identified earlier in Table 9-1 (p. 244). For example, the sales accounting system should be designed to ensure that all shipments of goods by a company are correctly recorded as sales (completeness and accuracy objectives) and reflected in the financial statements in the proper period (timing objective). The system must also avoid duplicate recording of sales and recording a sale if a shipment did not occur (existence objective).

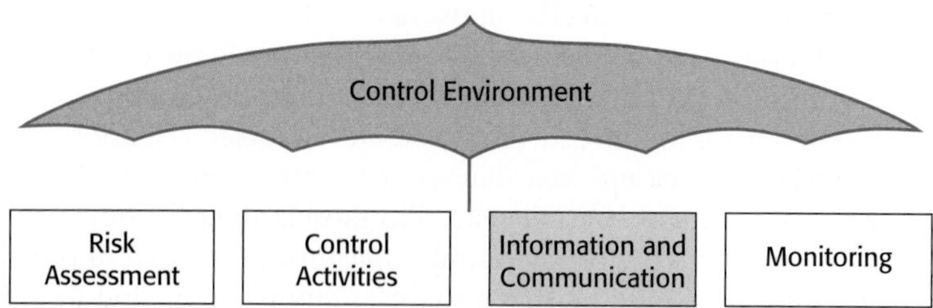

For a small company with active involvement by the owner, a simple computerized accounting system that involves primarily one honest, competent accountant may provide an adequate accounting information system. A larger company requires a more complex system that includes carefully defined responsibilities and written procedures.

To understand the design of the accounting information system, the auditor determines (1) the major classes of transactions of the entity; (2) how those transactions are initiated and recorded; (3) what accounting records exist and their nature; (4) how the system captures other events that are significant to the financial statements, such as declines in asset values; and (5) the nature and details of the financial reporting process followed, including procedures to enter transactions and adjustments in the general ledger. Typically, this is accomplished and documented by a narrative description of the system or by a flowchart. (These are described later in the chapter.) The operation of the accounting information system is often determined by tracing one or a few transactions through the system (called a **transaction walk-through**).

Monitoring

Monitoring activities deal with ongoing or periodic assessment of the quality of internal control performance by management to determine that controls are operating as intended and that they are modified as appropriate for changes in conditions. Information for assessment and modification comes from a variety of sources, including studies of existing internal controls, internal auditor reports, exception reporting on control activities, reports by regulators such as bank regulatory agencies, feedback from operating personnel, and complaints from customers about billing charges.

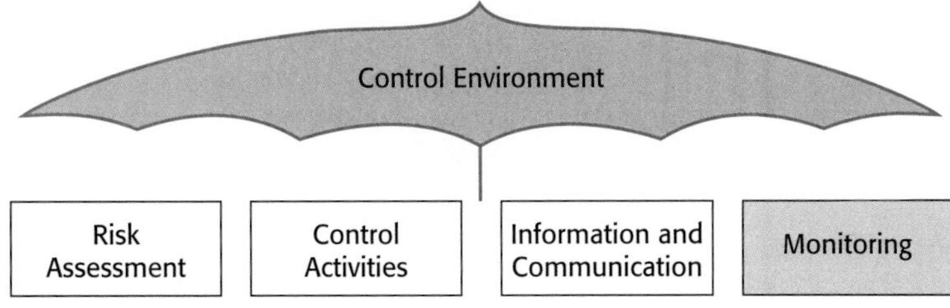

The most important things the auditor needs to know about monitoring are the major types of monitoring activities a company uses and how these activities are used to modify internal controls when necessary. Discussion with management is the most common way to obtain this understanding.

For many companies, especially larger ones, an internal audit department is essential for effective monitoring. For an internal audit function to be effective, it is essential that the internal audit staff be independent of both the operating and accounting departments and that it report directly to a high level of authority within the organization, either top management or the audit committee of the board of directors.

In addition to its role in monitoring an entity's internal control, an adequate internal audit staff can reduce external audit costs by providing direct assistance to the external auditor. SAS 65 (AU 322) defines the way internal auditors affect the external auditor's evidence accumulation. If the external auditor obtains evidence that supports the competence, integrity, and objectivity of internal auditors, the external auditor can rely on the internal auditor's work in a number of ways.

How the Size of the Business Affects the Components of Internal Control

A company's size has a significant effect on the nature of internal control and the specific controls that are placed in operation. Obviously, it is more difficult to establish adequate separation of duties in a small company. It would also be unreasonable to expect a small firm to have internal auditors. However, if the various subcomponents of internal control are examined, it becomes apparent that most are applicable to both large and small companies. Even though it may not be common to formalize policies in manuals, it is certainly possible for a small company to have (1) competent, trustworthy personnel with clear lines of authority; (2) proper procedures for authorization, execution, and recording of transactions; (3) adequate documents, records, and reports; (4) physical controls over assets and records; and, to a limited degree, (5) independent checks on performance.

A major control available in a small company is the knowledge and concern of the top operating person, who is often an owner-manager. A personal interest in the organization and a close relationship with personnel make careful evaluation of the competence of the employees and the effectiveness of the overall system possible. For example, internal control can be significantly strengthened if the owner conscientiously performs such duties as

TABLE 9-2 Components of Internal Control

INTERNAL CONTROL		
Components	**Description of Component**	**Further Subdivision (if applicable)**
Control environment	Actions, policies, and procedures that reflect the overall attitude of top management, directors, and owners of an entity about internal control and its importance	Subcomponents of the control environment: • Integrity and ethical values • Commitment to competence • Board of directors or audit committee participation • Management's philosophy and operating style • Organizational structure • Assignment of authority and responsibility • Human resource policies and practices
Risk assessment	Management's identification and analysis of risks relevant to the preparation of financial statements in accordance with GAAP	Risk assessment processes: • Identify factors affecting risks. • Assess significance of risks and likelihood of occurrence. • Determine actions necessary to manage risks. Management assertions that must be satisfied: • Existence or occurrence • Completeness • Valuation or allocation • Rights and obligations • Presentation and disclosure
Control activities	Policies and procedures that management has established to meet its objectives for financial reporting	Types of specific control activities: • Adequate separation of duties • Proper authorization of transactions and activities • Adequate documents and records • Physical control over assets and records • Independent checks on performance
Information and communication	Methods used to initiate, record, process, and report an entity's transactions and to maintain accountability for related assets	Transaction-related audit objectives that must be satisfied: • Existence • Completeness • Accuracy • Classification • Timing • Posting and summarization
Monitoring	Management's ongoing and periodic assessment of the quality of internal control performance to determine whether controls are operating as intended and modified when needed	Not applicable

signing all checks after carefully reviewing supporting documents, reviewing bank reconciliations, examining accounts receivable statements sent to customers, approving credit, examining all correspondence from customers and vendors, and approving bad debts.

The five components of internal control discussed in the preceding sections are summarized in Table 9-2.

PROCEDURES TO OBTAIN AN UNDERSTANDING OF INTERNAL CONTROL

OBJECTIVE **9-4**

Explain methods used to obtain an understanding of internal control.

Now that the various components of internal control have been discussed, we turn our attention to considering these components when obtaining an understanding of internal control and assessing control risk. The procedures used to gather evidence about design and placement in operation during the understanding phase are called **procedures to obtain an understanding.** Auditors obtain information about internal control and use that

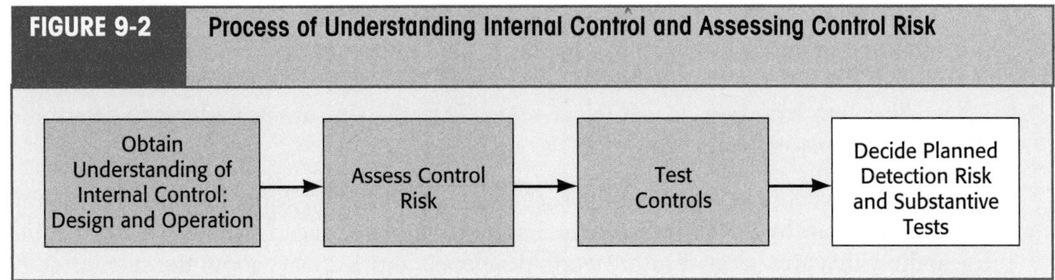
Obtain Understanding of Internal Control: Design and Operation
Assess Control Risk
Test Controls
Decide Planned Detection Risk and Substantive Tests
FIGURE 9-2 Process of Understanding Internal Control and Assessing Control Risk

information as a basis for audit planning. Figure 9-2 shows how the auditor's consideration of internal control affects substantive testing of account balances. The auditor considers internal control by first obtaining an understanding of internal control, which is then used to initially assess control risk. When the auditor's control risk assessment is below maximum, the auditor performs tests of controls. Once the results of the tests of controls are known, the auditor considers how those results affect planned detection risk and substantive testing. The remainder of this chapter deals with ways that practitioners implement the first three parts of Figure 9-2.

In practice, the procedures used to gain an understanding of internal control and assess control risk vary considerably from client to client. For smaller clients, many auditors obtain a level of understanding sufficient only to assess whether the statements are auditable, evaluate the control environment for management's attitude toward internal control and financial reporting, and determine the adequacy of the client's accounting system. Often, for efficiency, internal controls are ignored, control risk is assumed to be maximum, and detection risk is therefore low. For many larger clients, especially for repeat engagements, the auditor sets a low assessed control risk for most parts of the audit before the audit starts.

Reasons for Understanding Internal Control Sufficiently to Plan the Audit

SAS 55 (as amended by SAS 78 and SAS 94, AU 319) *requires the auditor to obtain an understanding of internal control for every audit.* The extent of that understanding must, at a minimum, be sufficient to adequately plan the audit, in terms of four specific planning matters.

Auditability The auditor must obtain information about the integrity of management and the nature and extent of the accounting records to be satisfied that sufficient, competent evidence is available to support the financial statement balances.

Potential Material Misstatements The understanding should allow the auditor to identify the types of potential errors and fraud that might affect the financial statements and to assess the risk that such misstatements might occur in amounts that are material to the financial statements.

Detection Risk Control risk in the planning form of the audit risk model directly affects planned detection risk for each audit objective [$PDR = AAR \div (IR \times CR)$]. Information about internal control is used to assess control risk for each objective, which affects planned detection risk and planned audit evidence.

Design of Tests The information obtained should allow the auditor to design effective tests of the financial statement balances. Such tests include tests for monetary correctness of both transactions and balances, and analytical procedures.

A common approach used by auditors is to (1) obtain an understanding of the control environment, risk assessment procedures, accounting information and communication system, and monitoring methods at a fairly detailed level; (2) identify specific controls that will reduce control risk and make an assessment of control risk; and (3) test the controls for effectiveness. The auditor can conclude that control risk is low only after all three steps are completed. The three steps just discussed are now explained in more detail to illustrate further how gaining an understanding of a client's internal controls and assessing control risk are done.

Procedures to Determine Design and Placement in Operation

The auditor's task in obtaining an understanding of internal control is to find out about each of the five components of internal control. In obtaining that understanding, the auditor should consider two aspects: (1) the *design* of the various controls within each component and (2) whether they have been *placed in operation.* The following are procedures to determine the design and placement in operation.

Update and Evaluate Auditor's Previous Experience with the Entity Most audits of a company are done annually by the same CPA firm. Except for initial engagements, the auditor begins the audit with a great deal of information developed in prior years about the client's internal control. Because systems and controls usually do not change frequently, this information can be updated and carried forward to the current year's audit.

Make Inquiries of Client Personnel A logical starting place for updating information carried forward from the previous audit, or for obtaining information initially, is with appropriate client personnel. Inquiries of client personnel at the management, supervisory, and staff level will usually be conducted as part of obtaining an understanding of internal control.

Read Client's Policy and Systems Manuals To design, implement, and maintain internal controls, an entity must have extensive documentation of its own. This includes policy manuals and documents (such as a corporate code of conduct) and systems manuals and documents (such as an accounting manual and an organization chart). This information is read by the auditor and discussed with company personnel to ensure that it is properly interpreted and understood.

Examine Documents and Records The five components of internal control all involve the creation of many documents and records. These will have been presented to some degree in the policy and systems manuals. By examining completed documents, records, and computer files, the auditor can bring the contents of the manuals to life and better understand them. Examination of the documents and records also provides evidence that the control policies and procedures have been placed in operation.

Observe Entity Activities and Operations In addition to examining completed documents and records, the auditor can observe client personnel in the process of preparing them and carrying out their normal accounting and control activities. This further enhances understanding and knowledge that controls have been placed in operation.

Observation, documentation, and inquiry can be conveniently and effectively combined in the form of the transaction walk-through mentioned earlier (p. 253). With that procedure, the auditor selects one or a few documents for the initiation of a transaction type and traces it (them) through the entire accounting process. At each stage of processing, the auditor makes inquiries and observes current activities, in addition to examining completed documentation for the transaction or transactions selected.

Documentation of the Understanding

Three commonly used methods of documenting the understanding of internal control are narratives, flowcharts, and internal control questionnaires. These may be used separately or in combination, as discussed in the following sections.

Narrative A **narrative** is a written description of a client's internal controls. A proper narrative of an accounting system and related controls includes four characteristics:

1. *The origin of every document and record in the system.* For example, the description should state where customer orders come from and how sales invoices are generated.
2. *All processing that takes place.* For example, if sales amounts are determined by a computer program that multiplies quantities shipped by standard prices contained in price master files, that should be described.
3. *The disposition of every document and record in the system.* The filing of documents, sending them to customers, or destroying them should be shown.
4. *An indication of the controls relevant to the assessment of control risk.* These typically include separation of duties (such as separating recording cash from handling

cash), authorizations and approvals (such as credit approvals), and internal verification (such as comparison of unit selling price to sales contracts).

Flowchart An internal control **flowchart** is a symbolic, diagrammatic representation of the client's documents and their sequential flow in the organization. An adequate flowchart includes the same four characteristics identified for narratives.

Flowchart Software

Flowcharting is advantageous primarily because it can provide a concise overview of the client's system, which is useful to the auditor as an analytical tool in evaluation. A well-prepared flowchart aids in identifying inadequacies by facilitating a clear understanding of how the system operates. For most uses, it is superior to narratives as a method of communicating the characteristics of a system, especially to show adequate separation of duties. It is easier to follow a diagram than to read a description. It is also usually easier to update a flowchart than a narrative.

It would be unusual to use both a narrative and a flowchart to describe the same system because both are intended to describe the flow of documents and records in an accounting system. Sometimes, a combination of a narrative and flowchart is used. The decision to use one or the other or a combination of the two is dependent on two factors: (1) the relative ease of understanding by current- and subsequent-year auditors and (2) the relative cost of preparation. Several flowcharting software packages can be downloaded at no charge from the Internet.

Internal Control Questionnaire An **internal control questionnaire** asks a series of questions about the controls in each audit area as a means of indicating to the auditor aspects of internal control that may be inadequate. In most instances, it is designed to require a "yes" or a "no" response, with "no" responses indicating potential internal control deficiencies.

The primary advantage of using a questionnaire is the ability to thoroughly cover each audit area reasonably quickly at the beginning of the audit. The primary disadvantage is that individual parts of the client's systems are examined without providing an overall view. In addition, a standard questionnaire is often inapplicable to some audit clients, especially smaller ones.

Figure 9-3 (p. 258) illustrates part of an internal control questionnaire for the sales and collection cycle of Hillsburg Hardware Co. The questionnaire is also designed for use with the six transaction-related audit objectives. Notice that each objective (A through F) is a transaction-related audit objective as it applies to sales transactions (see shaded portions). The same is true for all other audit areas.

The use of both questionnaires and flowcharts is highly desirable for understanding the client's internal control. Flowcharts provide an overview of the system, and questionnaires are useful checklists to remind the auditor of many different types of internal controls that should exist. When properly used, a combination of these two approaches should provide the auditor with an excellent description of the system.

It is often desirable to use the client's narratives or flowcharts and have the client fill out the internal control questionnaire. When understandable and reliable narratives, flowcharts, and questionnaires are not available from a client, which is often the case, the auditor must prepare them. Many auditors rely on electronic auditing tools, including industry-specific checklists and industry-specific flowcharting templates that can be completed and viewed electronically, to assist them in the audit.

ASSESS CONTROL RISK

OBJECTIVE 9-5

Assess control risk by linking strengths and weaknesses of internal control to transaction-related audit objectives.

Now that the auditor's procedures for gaining an understanding of internal control have been discussed, the chapter focuses on how the auditor uses that information to assess control risk. Once the auditor obtains an understanding of internal control sufficient for audit planning, an initial assessment of control risk must be made. Four specific assessments must be made to arrive at the initial assessment.

Assess Whether the Financial Statements Are Auditable The first assessment is whether the entity is auditable. Two primary factors determine auditability: the integrity of management and the adequacy of accounting records. Many audit procedures rely to some

FIGURE 9-3 Partial Internal Control Questionnaire for Sales

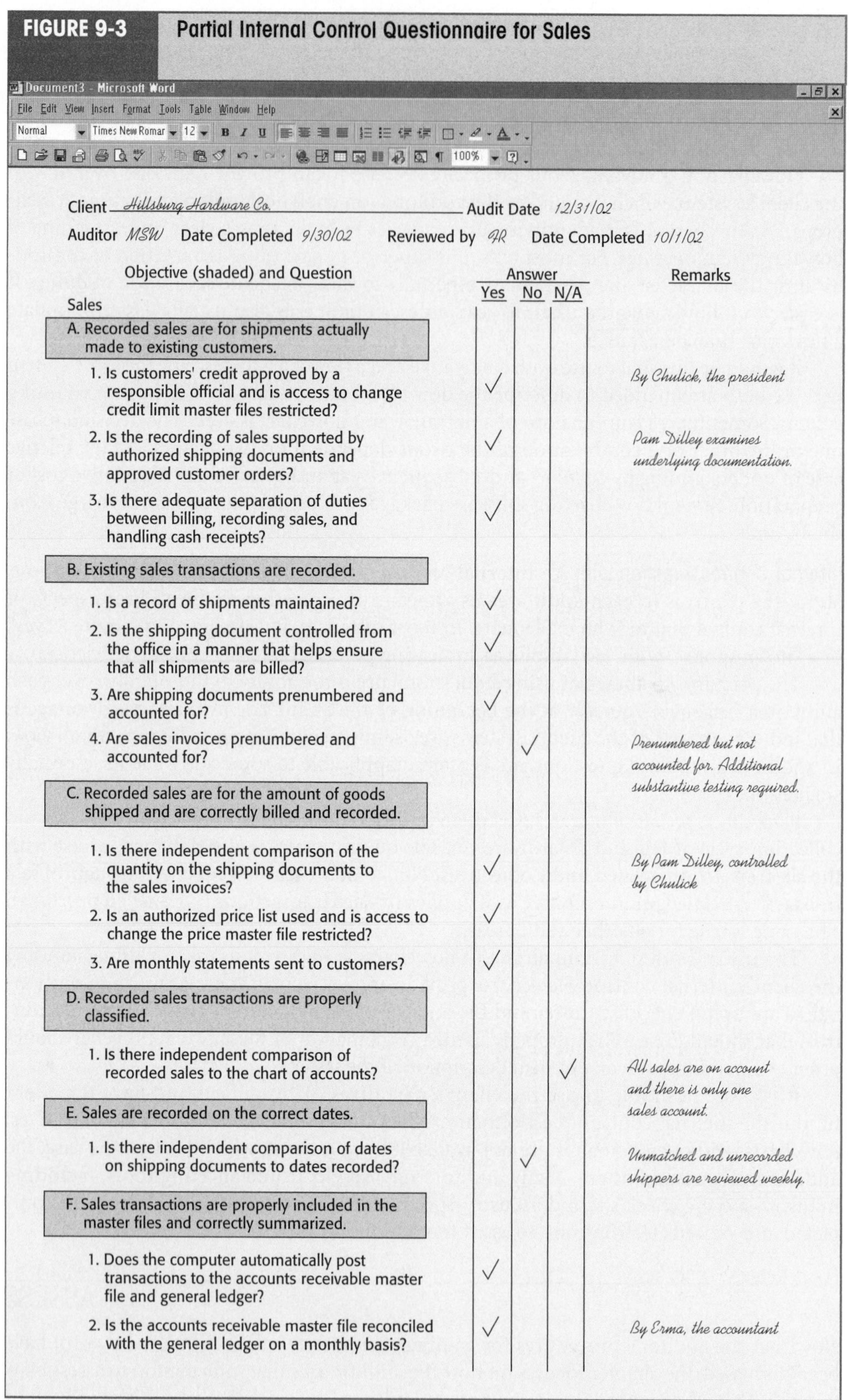

Client *Hillsburg Hardware Co.* Audit Date *12/31/02*

Auditor *MSW* Date Completed *9/30/02* Reviewed by *JR* Date Completed *10/1/02*

Objective (shaded) and Question	Yes	No	N/A	Remarks
Sales				
A. Recorded sales are for shipments actually made to existing customers.				
1. Is customers' credit approved by a responsible official and is access to change credit limit master files restricted?	✓			*By Chulick, the president*
2. Is the recording of sales supported by authorized shipping documents and approved customer orders?	✓			*Pam Dilley examines underlying documentation.*
3. Is there adequate separation of duties between billing, recording sales, and handling cash receipts?	✓			
B. Existing sales transactions are recorded.				
1. Is a record of shipments maintained?	✓			
2. Is the shipping document controlled from the office in a manner that helps ensure that all shipments are billed?	✓			
3. Are shipping documents prenumbered and accounted for?	✓			
4. Are sales invoices prenumbered and accounted for?		✓		*Prenumbered but not accounted for. Additional substantive testing required.*
C. Recorded sales are for the amount of goods shipped and are correctly billed and recorded.				
1. Is there independent comparison of the quantity on the shipping documents to the sales invoices?	✓			*By Pam Dilley, controlled by Chulick*
2. Is an authorized price list used and is access to change the price master file restricted?	✓			
3. Are monthly statements sent to customers?	✓			
D. Recorded sales transactions are properly classified.				
1. Is there independent comparison of recorded sales to the chart of accounts?			✓	*All sales are on account and there is only one sales account.*
E. Sales are recorded on the correct dates.				
1. Is there independent comparison of dates on shipping documents to dates recorded?		✓		*Unmatched and unrecorded shippers are reviewed weekly.*
F. Sales transactions are properly included in the master files and correctly summarized.				
1. Does the computer automatically post transactions to the accounts receivable master file and general ledger?	✓			
2. Is the accounts receivable master file reconciled with the general ledger on a monthly basis?	✓			*By Erma, the accountant*

extent on the representations of management. For example, it is difficult for the auditor to evaluate whether inventory is obsolete without an honest assessment by management. If management lacks integrity, management may provide false representations, causing the auditor to rely on unreliable evidence.

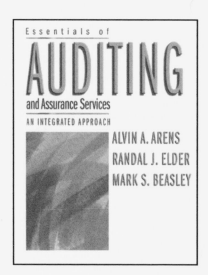

The accounting records serve as a direct source of audit evidence for most audit objectives. If the accounting records are deficient, necessary audit evidence may not be available. For example, if the client has not kept duplicate sales invoices and vendors' invoices, it would usually be impractical to do an audit. Unless the auditor can identify an alternative source of reliable evidence or appropriate records can be constructed for the auditor's use, the only recourse may be to consider the entity unauditable.

In complex IT environments, much of the transaction information is available only in electronic form without generating a visible audit trail of documents and records. In that case, the company is generally still auditable; however, auditors must assess whether they have the necessary skills to gather evidence that is in electronic form and can assign personnel with adequate IT training and experience.

When the auditor concludes that the entity is not auditable, the circumstances are discussed with the client (usually at the highest level) and the auditor either withdraws from the engagement or issues a disclaimer form of audit report.

Determine Assessed Control Risk Supported by the Understanding Obtained After obtaining an understanding of internal control, the auditor makes an initial **assessment of control risk.** This assessment is a measure of the auditor's expectation that internal controls *will neither prevent material misstatements* from occurring *nor detect and correct them* if they have occurred.

The initial assessment is generally made for each transaction-related audit objective for each major type of transaction. For example, the auditor makes an assessment of the existence objective for sales and a separate assessment of the completeness objective. There are different ways to express this expectation. Some auditors use a subjective expression such as high, moderate, or low. Others use numerical probabilities such as 1.0, 0.6, or 0.2.

The initial assessment usually starts with consideration of the control environment. If the attitude of management is that control is unimportant, it is doubtful that detailed control activities will be reliable. The best course of action in that case is to assume that control risk for all transaction-related audit objectives is at the maximum (such as high or 1.0). On the other hand, if management's attitude is positive, the auditor then considers the specific policies and procedures within the subcomponents of the control environment and those of the four other components of internal control. The controls within all five components are used as a basis for an assessment below the maximum.

There are three important considerations about the initial assessment: First, the auditor does not have to make the initial assessment in a formal, detailed manner. In many audits, such as audits of smaller companies, the auditor assumes that the control risk is at the maximum whether or not it actually is. The reason for taking this approach is that the auditor has concluded that it is more economical to more extensively audit the financial statement balances than to test related internal controls.

Second, in some circumstances where significant information supporting transactions is available only in electronic form, it may be necessary for the auditor to assess control risk below the maximum and perform more extensive tests of controls. In such cases, it may not be possible to rely only on substantive tests to support financial statement assertions. For example, an Internet service provider may use IT to log services provided to users, initiate bills for the services, process billing transactions, and automatically record amounts in electronic accounting records that are used to produce the financial statements. The auditor would likely have to test controls related to these electronic processes to obtain sufficient audit evidence for some or all of the financial statement assertions.

Third, even though the auditor believes control risk is low, assessed control risk is limited to that level supported by the evidence obtained. For example, suppose that the auditor believes that control risk for unrecorded sales is low but has gathered little evidence in support of controls for the completeness transaction-related audit objective. The auditor's assessment of control risk for unrecorded sales must be either moderate or high. It could be low only if additional evidence was obtained in support of the pertinent controls.

Assess Whether It Is Likely That a Lower Assessed Control Risk Could Be Supported When the auditor believes that actual control risk may be significantly lower than the initial assessment, the auditor may decide to support a lower assessed control risk. The most likely case in which this occurs is when the auditor has identified a limited number of controls during the understanding phase. Based on the results of the initial assessment, the auditor now believes that additional controls can be identified and tested to further reduce assessed control risk.

Determine the Appropriate Assessed Control Risk After the initial assessment is completed and the likelihood of a lower assessed control risk is considered, the auditor is in a position to decide which assessed control risk should be used: either a level already supported in the initial assessment or a lower level. The decision about which level to use is essentially an economic one, recognizing the trade-off between the costs of testing relevant controls and the costs of substantive tests that would be avoided by reducing assessed control risk. Assume, for example, that for the existence and accuracy transaction-related audit objectives for sales, the auditor believes that the cost of confirming accounts receivable could be reduced by $5,000 by incurring $2,000 to support a lower assessed control risk. It would be cost-effective to incur the $2,000 additional cost.

Identify Transaction-Related Audit Objectives

The auditor typically assesses control risk for transaction-related audit objectives for each major type of transaction in each transaction cycle. For example, in the sales and collection cycle, the types of transactions usually involve sales, sales returns and allowances, cash receipts, and the provision for and write-off of uncollectible accounts. The first step in the assessment is to identify the transaction-related audit objectives to which the assessment applies. This is done by applying the transaction-related audit objectives introduced earlier, which are stated in general form, to each major type of transaction for the entity.

Identify Specific Controls

The next step is to identify the specific controls that contribute to accomplishing each transaction-related audit objective. The auditor identifies pertinent controls by proceeding through the descriptive information about the client's system. Those policies, procedures, and activities that in the auditor's judgment provide control over the transactions involved are identified. In doing this, it is often helpful to refer back to the types of controls that might exist, and ask whether they do exist. For example: Is there adequate separation of duties and how is it achieved? Are the documents used well designed? Are prenumbered documents properly accounted for? Are key master files properly restricted from unauthorized access?

In making this analysis, it is not necessary to consider every control. The auditor should identify and include controls that are expected to have the greatest effect on meeting the transaction-related audit objectives. These are often called key controls. The reason for including only key controls is that they will be sufficient to achieve the transaction-related audit objectives and should provide audit efficiency.

Identify and Evaluate Weaknesses

An **internal control weakness** is the *absence of adequate controls,* which increases the risk of misstatements existing in the financial statements. If, in the auditor's judgment, controls are inadequate to satisfy one of the transaction-related audit objectives, expectation of such a misstatement occurring increases. For example, if payroll accounting personnel have the ability to modify items in the payroll master file, the auditor may conclude that there is a weakness in internal control.

A four-step approach can be used for identifying significant weaknesses.

Identify Existing Controls Because weaknesses are the absence of adequate controls, the auditor must first know which controls exist. The methods for identifying existing controls have already been discussed.

Identify the Absence of Key Controls Internal control questionnaires, narratives, and flowcharts are useful to identify areas in which key controls are lacking and in which the likelihood of misstatements is thereby increased. When control risk is assessed as moderate or high, there is usually an absence of controls.

Determine Potential Material Misstatements That Could Result This step is intended to identify specific misstatements that are likely to result because of the absence of controls. The importance of a weakness is proportionate to the magnitude of the misstatements that are likely to result from it.

FIGURE 9-4 Weaknesses in Internal Control

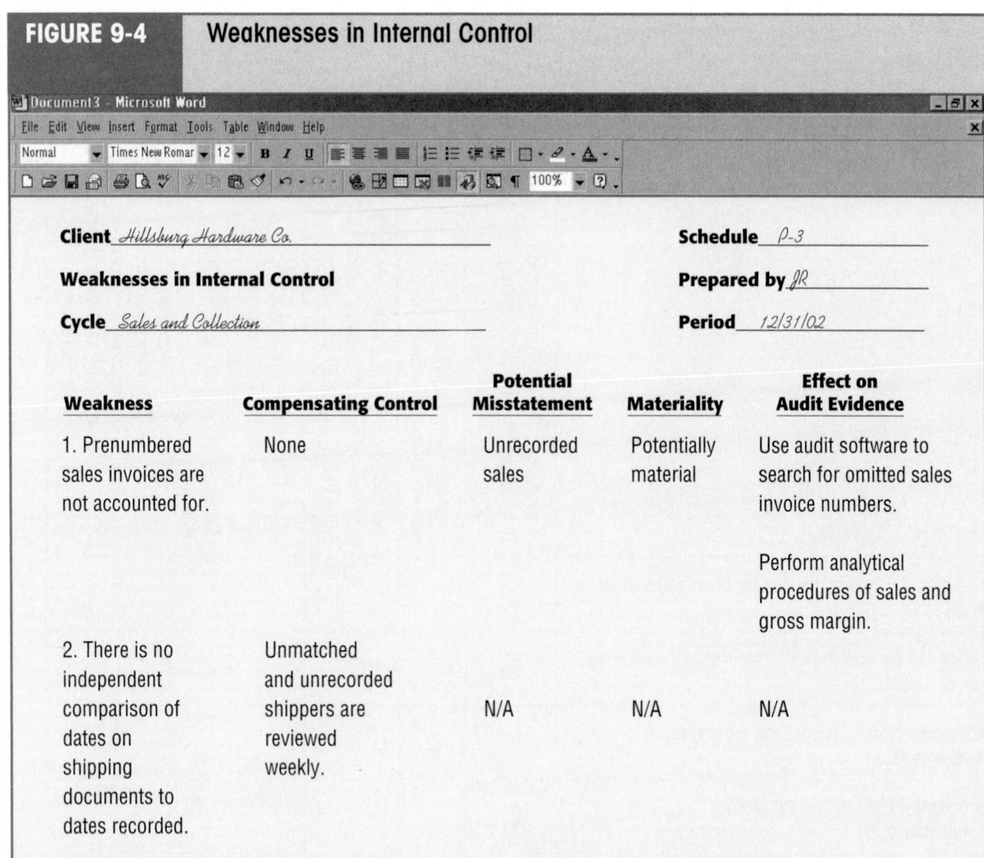

Client Hillsburg Hardware Co. — Schedule P-3

Weaknesses in Internal Control — Prepared by JR

Cycle Sales and Collection — Period 12/31/02

Weakness	Compensating Control	Potential Misstatement	Materiality	Effect on Audit Evidence
1. Prenumbered sales invoices are not accounted for.	None	Unrecorded sales	Potentially material	Use audit software to search for omitted sales invoice numbers. Perform analytical procedures of sales and gross margin.
2. There is no independent comparison of dates on shipping documents to dates recorded.	Unmatched and unrecorded shippers are reviewed weekly.	N/A	N/A	N/A

Consider the Possibility of Compensating Controls A compensating control is one elsewhere in the system that offsets a weakness. A common example in a smaller company is active involvement of the owner. When a compensating control exists, the weakness is no longer a concern because the potential for misstatement has been sufficiently reduced.

Figure 9-4 shows the documentation of weaknesses for the sales and collection cycle of Hillsburg Hardware Co. The fifth column shows the effect of the weakness on the auditor's planned audit program.

The Control Risk Matrix

Many auditors use a **control risk matrix** to assist in the control risk–assessment process. Most controls affect more than one transaction-related audit objective, and often several different controls affect a given transaction-related audit objective. These complexities make a control risk matrix a useful way to help assess control risk. The auditor uses the control risk matrix to identify both controls and weaknesses and to assess control risk.

Figure 9-5 (p. 262) illustrates the use of a control risk matrix for sales transactions of Hillsburg Hardware Co. In constructing the matrix, the transaction-related audit objectives for sales were listed as column headings and pertinent controls that were identified were listed as headings for the rows. In addition, where significant weaknesses were identified, they were also entered as row headings below the listing of key controls. The body of the matrix was then used to show how the controls contribute to the accomplishment of the transaction-related audit objectives and how weaknesses affect the objectives. In this illustration, a C was entered in each cell where a control partially or fully satisfied an objective and a W was entered to show the effect of the weaknesses.

Assess Control Risk

Once controls and weaknesses are identified and related to transaction-related audit objectives, the auditor can assess control risk. Again, the control risk matrix is a useful tool for that purpose. Referring to Figure 9-5, the auditor assessed control risk for Hillsburg's sales by reviewing each column for pertinent controls and weaknesses and asking, "What is the likelihood that a material misstatement of the type to be controlled would not be prevented

FIGURE 9-5 Control Risk Matrix for Hillsburg Hardware Co.—Sales

	INTERNAL CONTROL	SALES TRANSACTION-RELATED AUDIT OBJECTIVES: Recorded sales are for shipments actually made to nonfictitious customers (existence).	Existing sales transactions are recorded (completeness).	Recorded sales are for the amount of goods shipped and are correctly billed and recorded (accuracy).	Sales transactions are properly classified (classification).	Sales are recorded on the correct dates (timing).	Sales transactions are properly included in the accounts receivable master file and correctly summarized (posting and summarization).
CONTROLS	Credit is approved automatically by computer by comparison to authorized credit limits (C1).	C					
	Recorded sales are supported by authorized shipping documents and approved customer orders (C2).	C		C			
	Separation of duties between billing, recording of sales, and handling of cash receipts (C3).	C	C				C
	Shipping documents are forwarded to billing daily and billed the subsequent day (C4).	C				C	
	Shipping documents are prenumbered and accounted for weekly (C5).		C			C	
	Batch totals of quantities shipped are compared with quantities billed (C6).	C	C	C			
	Unit selling prices are obtained from the price list master file of approved prices (C7).			C			
	Sales transactions are internally verified (C8).				C		
	Statements are mailed to customers each month (C9).	C		C			C
	Computer automatically posts transactions to the accounts receivable subsidiary records and to the general ledger (C10).						C
	Accounts receivable master file is reconciled to the general ledger on a monthly basis (C11).						C
WEAKNESSES	There is a lack of internal verification for the possibility of sales invoices being recorded more than once (W1).	W					
	There is a lack of control to test for timely recording (W2).					W	
	Assessed control risk	Medium	Low	Low	Low*	High	Low

*Because there are no cash sales, classification is not a problem.
C = Control; W = Weakness.
Note: This matrix was developed using an internal control questionnaire, part of which is included in Figure 9-3 (p. 258), as well as flowcharts and other documentation of the auditor's understanding of internal control.

or detected and corrected by these controls, and what is the effect of the weaknesses?" If the likelihood is high, then control risk is high, and so forth.

Once a preliminary assessment of control risk is made for sales and cash receipts, the auditor can complete the three control risk rows of the evidence planning worksheet that was introduced in Chapter 8 on page 227. If tests of controls results do not support the preliminary assessment of control risk, the auditor must modify the worksheet accordingly. Alternatively, the auditor can wait until tests of controls are done to complete the three control risk rows of the worksheet. An evidence planning worksheet for Hillsburg Hardware with the three rows for control risk completed is illustrated in Figure 13-6 on page 394.

Communicate Reportable Conditions and Related Matters

During the course of obtaining an understanding of internal control and assessing control risk, auditors obtain information that is of interest to the audit committee in fulfilling its responsibilities. Generally, such information concerns significant deficiencies in the design or operation of internal control. Such matters are called **reportable conditions** in SAS 60 (AU 325).

Audit Committee Communications Reportable conditions should be communicated to the audit committee as a part of every audit. If the client does not have an audit committee, the communication should go to the person or persons in the organization who have overall responsibility for internal control, such as the board of directors or the owner-manager.

The form of communication would typically be a letter, although oral communication, documented in the working papers, is also allowable under professional standards. An illustrative reportable conditions letter is shown in Figure 9-6.

POB Panel on Audit Effectiveness

FIGURE 9-6 Reportable Conditions Letter

JOHNSON AND SEYGROVES
Certified Public Accountants
2016 Village Boulevard
Troy, Michigan 48801

February 12, 2003

Board of Directors
Airtight Machine Company
1729 Athens Street
Troy, MI 48801

In planning and performing our audit of the financial statements of Airtight Machine Company for the year ended December 31, 2002, we considered its internal control in order to determine our auditing procedures for the purpose of expressing our opinion on the financial statements and not to provide assurance on internal control. However, we noted certain matters involving internal control and its operation that we consider to be a reportable condition under standards established by the American Institute of Certified Public Accountants. Reportable conditions involve matters coming to our attention relating to significant deficiencies in the design or operation of internal control that, in our judgment, could adversely affect the organization's ability to record, process, summarize, and report financial data consistent with the assertions of management in the financial statements.

The matter noted is that there is a lack of independent verification of the key entry of the customer's name, product number, quantity shipped, prices used, and the related mathematical extensions on sales invoices and credit memos. As a consequence, errors in these activities could occur and remain uncorrected, adversely affecting both recorded net sales and accounts receivable. This deficiency is significant because of the large size of the average sale of Airtight Machine Company.

This report is intended solely for the information and use of the board of directors, management, and others in Airtight Machine Company.

Very truly yours,
Johnson and Seygroves

Johnson and Seygroves, CPAs

Management Letters In addition to reportable conditions, auditors often observe less significant internal control-related matters, as well as opportunities for the client to make operational improvements. These types of matters should also be communicated to the client. The form of communication is often a separate letter for that purpose, called a **management letter.** Although management letters are not required by auditing standards, auditors generally prepare them as a value-added service of the audit.

TESTS OF CONTROLS

OBJECTIVE **9-6**

Describe the process of designing and performing tests of controls.

This chapter has examined how auditors link the strengths and weaknesses of internal control to transaction-related audit objectives to assess control risk for each objective. This section of the chapter now discusses how auditors test those controls that are used to support a control risk assessment below maximum. For example, each key control in Figure 9-5 (p. 262) that the auditor intends to rely on to support a control risk of moderate or low must be supported by sufficient tests of controls.

Assessing control risk requires the auditor to consider the design of controls to evaluate whether they should be effective in meeting transaction-related audit objectives. Some evidence will have been gathered in support of the design of the controls, as well as evidence that they have been placed in operation, during the understanding phase. To use specific controls as a basis for reducing assessed control risk, however, specific evidence must be obtained about their *operating effectiveness* throughout all, or at least most, of the period under audit. The procedures to test effectiveness of controls in support of a reduced assessed control risk are called **tests of controls.**

When the results of tests of controls support the design of controls as expected, the auditor proceeds to use the same assessed control risk. If, however, the tests of controls indicate that the controls did not operate effectively, the assessed control risk must be reconsidered. For example, the tests may indicate that the application of a control was curtailed midway through the year or that the person applying it made frequent misstatements. In such situations, the auditor uses a higher assessed control risk, unless additional controls for the same transaction-related audit objectives are identified and found to be effective.

Procedures for Tests of Controls

Four types of procedures are used to support the operation of internal controls. They are as follows.

Make Inquiries of Appropriate Client Personnel Although inquiry is not generally a strong source of evidence about the effective operation of controls, it is an appropriate form of evidence. For example, the auditor may determine that unauthorized personnel are not allowed access to computer files by making inquiries of the person who controls the computer library and of the person who controls online access security password assignments.

Examine Documents, Records, and Reports Many controls leave a clear trail of documentary evidence. Suppose, for example, that when a customer order is received, it is used to create a customer sales order, which is approved for credit. (See the first and second key controls in Figure 9-5.) The customer order is attached to the sales order as authorization for further processing. The auditor examines the documents to make sure that they are complete and properly matched and that required signatures or initials are present.

Observe Control-Related Activities Other types of control-related activities do not leave an evidential trail. For example, separation of duties relies on specific persons performing specific tasks, and there is typically no documentation of the separate performance. (See the third key control in Figure 9-5.) For controls that leave no documentary evidence, the auditor generally observes them being applied at various points during the year.

Reperform Client Procedures There are also control-related activities for which there are related documents and records, but their content is insufficient for the auditor's purpose of assessing whether controls are operating effectively. For example, assume that prices on sales invoices are to be verified with a standard price list by client personnel as an internal verification procedure, but no indication of performance is entered on the sales invoices.

(See the seventh key control in Figure 9-5.) In these cases, it is common for the auditor to actually reperform the control activity to see whether the proper results were obtained. For this example, the auditor can reperform the procedure by tracing the sales prices to the authorized price list in effect at the date of the transaction. If no misstatements are found, the auditor can conclude that the procedure is operating as intended.

Extent of Procedures

The extent to which tests of controls are applied depends on the desired assessed level of control risk. If the auditor wants a lower assessed control risk, more extensive tests of controls are applied, both in terms of the number of controls tested and the extent of the tests for each control. For example, if the auditor wants to use a low assessed control risk, a larger sample size for documentation, observation, and reperformance procedures should be applied.

Reliance on Evidence from Prior Year's Audit If evidence was obtained in the prior year's audit that indicates that a key control was operating effectively and the auditor determines that it is still in place, the extent of the tests of that control may be reduced somewhat in the current year. For example, in such circumstances, the auditor might use a reduced sample size in testing a control that leaves documentary evidence.

Testing Less Than the Entire Audit Period Ideally, tests of controls should be applied to transactions and controls for the entire period under audit. However, it is not always practical to do so. When less than the entire period is tested, the auditor should determine whether changes in controls occurred in the period not tested and obtain evidence about the nature and extent of any changes.

Rotating Tests of Controls An important characteristic of computerized systems that permits auditors to test them less frequently is their consistency in processing information. If the auditor is satisfied that internal controls are properly designed and operating effectively at a point of time, the auditor should also be satisfied the controls will continue to operate effectively until changes are made in the software. Auditors can therefore focus on evaluating and testing changes in the system instead of retesting stable systems. When software has only infrequent changes, it is common for auditors to rotate testing among areas across 2 years or more.

Relationship of Tests of Controls to Procedures to Obtain an Understanding

There is a significant overlap between tests of controls and procedures to obtain an understanding. Both include inquiry, documentation, and observation. There are two primary differences in the application of these common procedures between phases. First, in obtaining an understanding, the procedures are applied to all the controls identified as part of the understanding of internal control. Tests of controls, on the other hand, are applied only when the assessed control risk is below the maximum, and then only to the key controls.

Second, procedures to obtain an understanding are performed only on one or a few transactions or, in the case of observations, at a single point in time. Tests of controls are performed on larger samples of transactions (perhaps 20 to 100), and often observations are made at more than one point in time.

For key controls, tests of controls other than reperformance are essentially an *extension* of related procedures to obtain an understanding. Therefore, when auditors plan from the beginning of the audit to obtain a low assessed control risk, they will combine both types of procedures and perform them simultaneously.

Table 9-3 (p. 266) illustrates this concept in more detail. When only the required minimum understanding of internal control is planned, the auditor will conduct a transaction walk-through. In so doing, the auditor determines that the audit documentation is complete and accurate and observes that the control-related activities described are in operation.

When control risk is assessed below maximum, not only is a transaction walk-through performed but a larger sample of documents is examined for indications of the effectiveness of the operation of controls. (The determination of appropriate sample size is discussed in Chapter 13) Similarly, when observations are made, they will be more extensive and often at several points in time. Also, the auditors will do reperformance for some controls.

TABLE 9-3 Relationship of Assessed Control Risk and Extent of Procedures

	Assessed Control Risk	
Type of Procedure	**High Level: Obtaining an Understanding Only**	**Lower Level: Tests of Controls**
Inquiry	Yes—extensive	Yes—some
Documentation	Yes—with transaction walk-through	Yes—using sampling
Observation	Yes—with transaction walk-through	Yes—at multiple times
Reperformance	No	Yes—using sampling

DECIDE PLANNED DETECTION RISK AND DESIGN SUBSTANTIVE TESTS

We've focused on how auditors assess control risk for each transaction-related audit objective and support control risk assessments that are below the maximum with specific tests of controls. The auditor uses the results of the control risk assessment process and tests of controls to determine the planned detection risk and related substantive tests. The auditor does this by linking the control risk assessments to the balance-related audit objectives for the accounts affected by the major transaction types. The appropriate level of detection risk for each balance-related audit objective is then determined using the audit risk model. The relationship of transaction-related audit objectives to balance-related audit objectives and the selection and design of audit procedures for substantive tests of financial statement balances are discussed and illustrated in Chapter 10.

SUMMARY

This chapter highlighted how effective internal controls can reduce planned audit evidence. To use the strengths of a client's internal control to reduce planned audit evidence, the auditor must first obtain an understanding of each of the five components of internal control. Knowledge about the design of the client's control environment, risk assessment, control activities, information and communication, and monitoring activities and information about whether internal control components have been placed in operation assist the auditor in assessing the level of control risk for each transaction-related audit objective. When internal control components support a control risk assessment below the maximum level, the auditor must perform tests of controls to assess the operating effectiveness of those controls. When the results of tests of controls support the control risk assessment below maximum, the auditor is able to reduce planned substantive testing for related accounts. This entire process is summarized in Figure 9-7.

ESSENTIAL TERMS

Assessment of control risk—a measure of the auditor's expectation that internal controls will neither prevent material misstatements from occurring nor detect and correct them if they have occurred; control risk is assessed for each transaction-related audit objective in a cycle or class of transactions

Chart of accounts—a listing of all the entity's accounts, which classifies transactions into individual balance sheet and income statement accounts

Collusion—a cooperative effort among employees to defraud a business of cash, inventory, or other assets

Control activities—policies and procedures, in addition to those included in the other four components of internal control, that help ensure that necessary actions are taken to address risks in the achievement of the entity's objectives; they typically include the following five specific control activities: (1) adequate separation of duties, (2) proper authorization of transactions and activities, (3) adequate documents and records, (4) physical control over assets and records, and (5) independent checks on performance

Control environment—the actions, policies, and procedures that reflect the overall attitudes of top management, directors, and owners of an entity about internal control and its importance to the entity

Control risk matrix—a methodology used to help the auditor assess control risk by match-

FIGURE 9-7 Summary of Understanding Internal Control and Assessing Control Risk

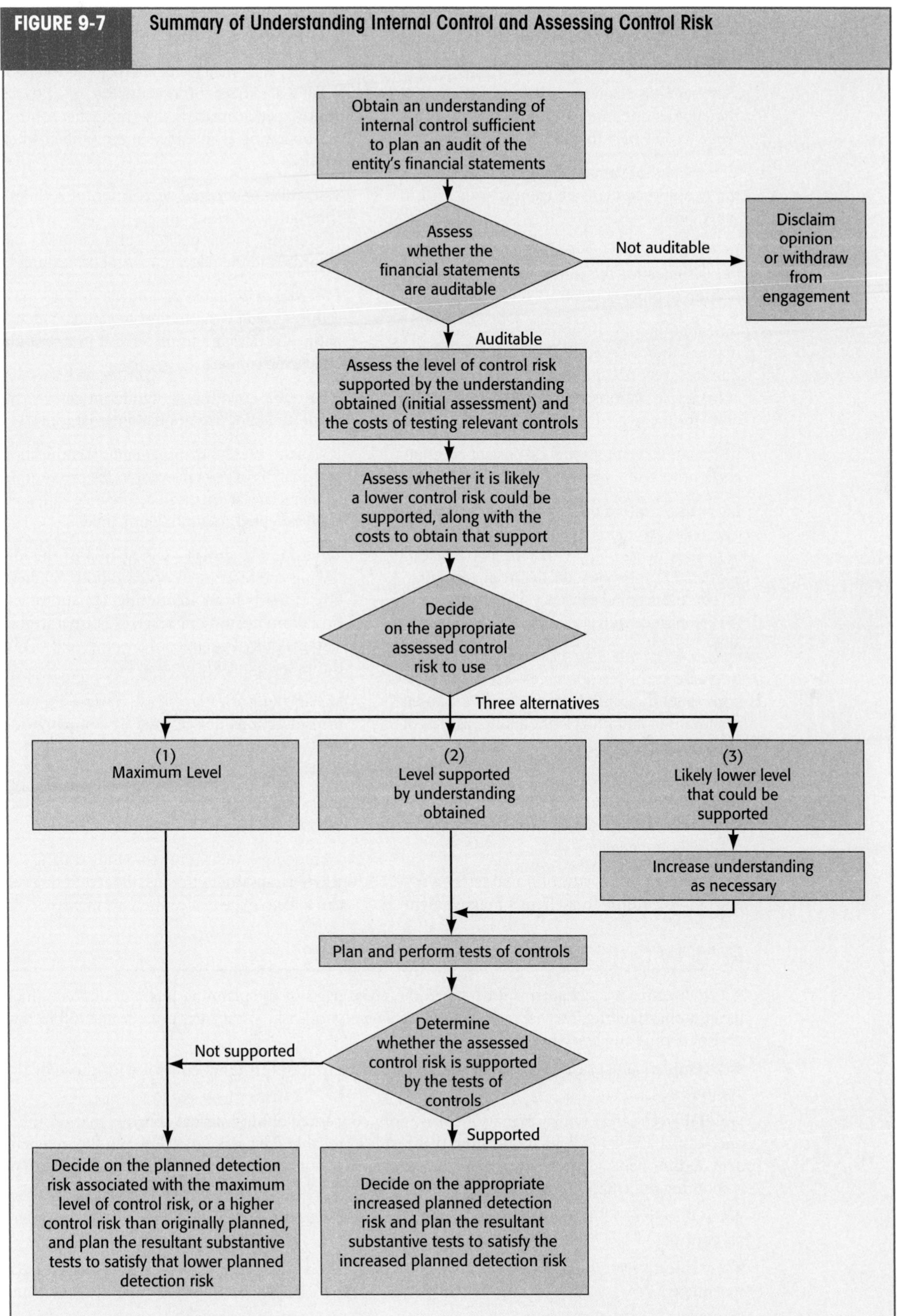

ing key internal controls and internal control weaknesses with transaction-related audit objectives

Flowchart—a diagrammatic representation of the client's documents and records and the sequence in which they are processed

General authorization—companywide policies for the approval of all transactions within stated limits

Independent checks—internal control activities designed for the continuous internal verification of other controls

Information and communication—the set of manual and/or computerized procedures that initiates, records, processes, and reports an entity's transactions and maintains accountability for the related assets

Information technology (IT)—use of computers to process and manage information

Internal control—a process designed to provide reasonable assurance regarding the achievement of management's objectives in the following categories: (1) reliability of financial reporting, (2) effectiveness and efficiency of operations, and (3) compliance with applicable laws and regulations

Internal control questionnaire—a series of questions about the controls in each audit area used as a means of indicating to the auditor aspects of internal control that may be inadequate

Internal control weakness—the absence of adequate controls; an internal control weakness increases the risk of misstatements in the financial statements

Management letter—an optional letter written by the auditor to a client's management containing the auditor's recommendations for improving any aspect of the client's business

Monitoring—management's ongoing and periodic assessment of the quality of internal control performance to determine that controls are operating as intended and modified when needed

Narrative—a written description of a client's internal controls, including the origin, processing, and disposition of documents and records, and the relevant control procedures

Procedures to obtain an understanding—procedures used by the auditor to gather evidence about the design and placement in operation of specific controls

Reportable conditions—significant deficiencies in the design or operation of internal control

Risk assessment—management's identification and analysis of risks relevant to the preparation of financial statements in accordance with generally accepted accounting principles

Separation of duties—segregation of the following activities in an organization: (1) custody of assets from accounting, (2) authorization from custody of assets, (3) operational responsibility from record keeping, and (4) IT duties from outside users of IT

Specific authorization—case-by-case approval of transactions not covered by companywide policies

Tests of controls—audit procedures to test the operating effectiveness of controls in support of reduced assessed control risk

Transaction walk-through—the tracing of selected transactions through the accounting system to determine that controls are in place

REVIEW QUESTIONS

9-1 (Objective 9-1) Chapter 7 introduced the seven parts of the planning phase of audits. Which part is understanding internal control and assessing control risk? What parts precede and follow that understanding and assessing?

9-2 (Objective 9-1) Compare management's concerns about internal control with those of the auditor.

9-3 (Objective 9-1) Often, management is more concerned about internal controls that promote operational efficiency than about those that result in reliable financial data. How can the independent auditor persuade management to devote more attention to controls affecting the reliability of accounting information when management has this attitude?

9-4 (Objective 9-2) Describe how the use of IT may increase the effectiveness and efficiency of internal control.

9-5 (Objective 9-2) Identify ways in which IT may increase the risk of misstatements in financial statements.

9-6 (Objectives 9-1, 9-5) State the six transaction-related audit objectives.

9-7 (Objective 9-3) What is meant by the control environment? What are the factors the auditor must evaluate to understand it?

9-8 **(Objective 9-3)** What is the relationship among the five components of internal control?

9-9 **(Objective 9-3)** List the types of specific control activities and provide one specific illustration of a control in the sales area for each control activity.

9-10 **(Objective 9-3)** The separation of operational responsibility from record keeping is meant to prevent different types of misstatements than the separation of the custody of assets from accounting. Explain the difference in the purposes of these two types of separation of duties.

9-11 **(Objective 9-3)** Distinguish between general and specific authorization of transactions and give one example of each type.

9-12 **(Objective 9-3)** For each of the following, give an example of a physical control the client can use to protect the asset or record:

1. Petty cash
2. Cash received by retail clerks
3. Accounts receivable records
4. Raw material inventory
5. Perishable tools
6. Manufacturing equipment
7. Marketable securities

9-13 **(Objective 9-3)** Explain what is meant by independent checks on performance and give five specific examples.

9-14 **(Objectives 9-4, 9-5)** Distinguish between obtaining an understanding of internal control and assessing control risk. Also explain the methodology the auditor uses for each of them.

9-15 **(Objective 9-5)** Define what is meant by a control and a weakness in internal control. Give two examples of each in the sales and collection cycle.

9-16 **(Objectives 9-3, 9-5)** Frank James, a highly competent employee of Brinkwater Sales Corporation, had been responsible for accounting-related matters for two decades. His devotion to the firm and his duties had always been exceptional, and over the years, he had been given increased responsibility. Both the president of Brinkwater and the partner of an independent CPA firm in charge of the audit were shocked and dismayed to discover that James had embezzled more than $500,000 over a 10-year period by not recording billings in the sales journal and subsequently diverting the cash receipts. What major factors permitted the defalcation to take place?

9-17 **(Objective 9-5)** Jeanne Maier, CPA, believes that it is appropriate to obtain an understanding of internal control about halfway through the audit, after she is familiar with the client's operations and the way the system actually works. She has found through experience that filling out internal control questionnaires and flowcharts early in the engagement is not beneficial because the system rarely functions the way it is supposed to. Later in the engagement, the auditor can prepare flowcharts and questionnaires with relative ease because of the knowledge already obtained on the audit. Evaluate her approach.

9-18 **(Objective 9-4)** Distinguish between the objectives of an internal control questionnaire and the objectives of a flowchart for documenting information about a client's internal control. State the advantages and disadvantages of each of these two methods.

9-19 **(Objective 9-5)** Explain what is meant by reportable conditions as they relate to internal control. What should the auditor do with reportable conditions?

9-20 **(Objective 9-5)** Examine the control risk matrix in Figure 9-5 (p. 262). Explain the purpose of the matrix. Also explain the meaning and effect of an assessment of control risk of low compared with one of medium.

9-21 **(Objectives 9-5, 9-6)** Explain what is meant by tests of controls. Write one examination of documents test of control and one reperformance test of control for the following internal control: hours on time cards are re-added by an independent payroll clerk and initialed to indicate performance.

MULTIPLE CHOICE QUESTIONS FROM CPA EXAMINATIONS

9-22 **(Objectives 9-1, 9-4)** The following are general questions about internal control. Choose the best response.

a. When considering internal control, an auditor must be aware of the concept of reasonable assurance, which recognizes that the
   (1) employment of competent personnel provides assurance that management's control objectives will be achieved.
   (2) establishment and maintenance of internal control is an important responsibility of the management and not of the auditor.

(3) cost of internal control should not exceed the benefits expected to be derived therefrom.
(4) separation of incompatible functions is necessary to ascertain that the internal control is effective.

b. When an auditor issues an unqualified opinion, it is implied that the
(1) entity has not violated provisions of the Foreign Corrupt Practices Act.
(2) likelihood of fraud is minimal.
(3) financial records are sufficiently reliable to permit the preparation of financial statements.
(4) entity's internal control conforms with criteria established by its audit committee.

c. Which of the following statements about the auditor's responsibility for internal control is correct?
(1) The auditor must gain an understanding of internal controls in every audit given that the auditor's opinion on the financial statements addresses assurance obtained about internal controls.
(2) The nature and extent of procedures performed to gain an understanding of internal controls and to test controls are essentially the same.
(3) Even when controls are adequately designed and placed in operation, the auditor can assess control at maximum and not perform tests of controls when substantive tests are less costly to perform.
(4) The second standard of field work requires that the auditor obtain evidence in every audit that internal controls are operating effectively on a consistent basis throughout the year.

d. What is the independent auditor's principal purpose for obtaining an understanding of internal control and assessing control risk?
(1) To comply with generally accepted accounting principles.
(2) To obtain a measure of assurance of management's efficiency.
(3) To maintain a state of independence in mental attitude during the audit.
(4) To determine the nature, timing, and extent of subsequent audit work.

9-23 **(Objective 9-5)** The following questions deal with assessing control risk. Choose the best response.

a. The ultimate purpose of assessing control risk is to contribute to the auditor's evaluation of the
(1) factors that raise doubts about the auditability of the financial statements.
(2) operating effectiveness of internal controls.
(3) risk that material misstatements exist in the financial statements.
(4) possibility that the nature and extent of substantive tests may be reduced.

b. An auditor uses assessed control risk to
(1) evaluate the effectiveness of the entity's internal controls.
(2) identify transactions and account balances where inherent risk is at the maximum.
(3) indicate whether materiality thresholds for planning and evaluation purposes are sufficiently high.
(4) determine the acceptable level of detection risk for financial statement assertions.

c. On the basis of audit evidence gathered and evaluated, an auditor decides to increase assessed control risk from that originally planned. To achieve an audit risk level (*AcAR*) that is substantially the same as the planned audit risk level (*AAR*), the auditor would
(1) increase inherent risk.
(2) increase materiality levels.
(3) decrease substantive testing.
(4) decrease planned detection risk.

DISCUSSION QUESTIONS AND PROBLEMS

9-24 **(Objectives 9-2, 9-3, 9-4, 9-5, 9-6)** Each of the following internal controls has been taken from a standard internal control questionnaire used by a CPA firm for assessing control risk in the payroll and personnel cycle.

1. Approval of department head or foreman on time cards is required before preparing payroll.
2. All prenumbered time cards are accounted for before beginning data entry for preparation of checks.
3. The payroll accounting software application will not accept data input for an employee number not contained in the employee master file.
4. Persons preparing the payroll do not perform other payroll duties (timekeeping, distribution of checks) or have access to payroll data master files or cash.

5. The computer calculates gross and net pay based on hours inputted and information in employee master files, and payroll accounting personnel double-check the mathematical accuracy on a test basis.
6. All voided and spoiled payroll checks are properly mutilated and retained.
7. Personnel requires an investigation of an employment application from new employees. Investigation includes checking the employee's background, former employers, and references.
8. Written termination notices, with properly documented reasons for termination, and approval of an appropriate official are required.
9. All checks not distributed to employees are returned to the treasurer for safekeeping.
10. Online ability to add employees or change pay rates to the payroll master file is restricted via passwords to authorized human resource personnel.

Required

a. For each internal control, identify the type(s) of specific control activity (activities) to which it applies (such as adequate documents and records or physical control over assets and records).

b. For each internal control, identify the transaction-related audit objective(s) to which it applies.

c. For each internal control, identify a specific misstatement that is likely to be prevented if the control exists and is effective.

d. For each control, list a specific misstatement that could result from the absence of the control.

e. For each control, identify one audit test that the auditor could use to uncover misstatements resulting from the absence of the control.

9-25 **(Objectives 9-2, 9-3, 9-5)** The following are misstatements that have occurred in Fresh Foods Grocery Store, a retail and wholesale grocery company:

1. The incorrect price was used on sales invoices for billing shipments to customers because the wrong price was entered into the computer master file of prices.
2. A vendor's invoice was paid twice for the same shipment. The second payment arose because the vendor sent a duplicate copy of the original 2 weeks after the payment was due.
3. Employees in the receiving department took sides of beef for their personal use. When a shipment of meat was received, the receiving department filled out a receiving report and forwarded it to the accounting department for the amount of goods actually received. At that time, two sides of beef were put in an employee's pickup truck rather than in the storage freezer.
4. During the physical count of inventory of the retail grocery, one counter wrote down the wrong description of several products and miscounted the quantity.
5. A salesperson sold an entire carload of lamb at a price below cost because she did not know the cost of lamb had increased in the past week.
6. On the last day of the year, a truckload of beef was set aside for shipment but was not shipped. Because it was still on hand the inventory was counted. The shipping document was dated the last day of the year, so it was also included as a current-year sale.
7. A vendor invoice was paid even though no merchandise was ever received. The accounts payable software application does not require the input of a valid receiving report number before payment can be made.
8. An accounts payable clerk processed payments to himself by adding a fictitious vendor address to the approved vendor master file.

Required

a. For each misstatement, identify one or more types of controls that were absent.

b. For each misstatement, identify the transaction-related audit objectives that have not been met.

c. For each misstatement, suggest a control to correct the deficiency.

9-26 **(Objectives 9-1, 9-3, 9-5)** Recently, while eating lunch with your family at a local cafeteria, you observe a practice that is somewhat unusual. As you reach the end of the cafeteria line, an employee asks how many persons are in your party. He then totals the food purchases on the trays for all of your family and enters the number of persons included in the group. He hands you the receipt and asks you to pay when you finish eating. Near the end of the meal, you decide you want a piece of pie and coffee so you return to the line, select your food, and again go through the line. The employee goes through the same procedures, but this time he staples the second receipt to the original and returns it to you.

When you leave the cafeteria, you hand the stapled receipts to the cash register operator, who totals the two receipts, takes your money, and puts the receipts on a spindle.

Required

a. What internal controls has the cafeteria instituted for its operations?

b. How can the manager of the cafeteria evaluate the effectiveness of the controls?

c. How do these controls differ from those used by most cafeterias?

d. What are the costs and benefits of the cafeteria's system?

9-27 **(Objectives 9-1, 9-4)** Lew Pherson and Vera Collier are friends who are employed by different CPA firms. One day during lunch they are discussing the importance of internal control in determining the amount of audit evidence required for an engagement. Pherson expresses the view that internal control must be evaluated carefully in all companies, regardless of their size, in a similar manner. His CPA firm requires a standard internal control questionnaire on every audit as well as a flowchart of every transaction area. In addition, he says the firm requires a careful evaluation of the system and a modification in the evidence accumulated based on the controls and weaknesses in the system.

Collier responds by saying she believes that internal control cannot be adequate in many of the small companies she audits; therefore, she simply ignores internal control and acts under the assumption of inadequate controls. She goes on to say, "Why should I spend a lot of time obtaining an understanding of internal control and assessing control risk when I know it has all kinds of weaknesses before I start? I would rather spend the time it takes to fill out all those forms in testing whether the statements are correct."

Required

a. Express in general terms the most important difference between the nature of the potential controls available for large and small companies.

b. Criticize the positions taken by Pherson and Collier, and express your own opinion about the similarities and differences that should exist in understanding internal control and assessing control risk for different-sized companies.

9-28 **(Objectives 9-2, 9-5)** The following are partial descriptions of internal controls for companies engaged in the manufacturing business:

1. When Mr. Clark orders materials for his machine-rebuilding plant, he sends a duplicate purchase order to the receiving department. During the delivery of materials, Mr. Smith, the receiving clerk, records the receipt of shipment on this purchase order. After recording, Mr. Smith sends the purchase order to the accounting department, where it is used to record materials purchased and accounts payable. The materials are transported to the storage area by forklifts. The additional purchased quantities are recorded on storage records.
2. Every day, hundreds of employees clock in using time cards at Generous Motors Corporation. The timekeepers collect these cards once a week and deliver them to the computer department. There, the data on these time cards are entered into the computer. The information entered into the computer is used in the preparation of the labor cost distribution records, the payroll journal, and the payroll checks. The treasurer, Mrs. Webber, compares the payroll journal with the payroll checks, signs the checks, and returns them to Mr. Strode, the supervisor of the computer department. The payroll checks are distributed to the employees by Mr. Strode.
3. The smallest branch of Connor Cosmetics in South Bend employs Mary Cooper, the branch manager, and her sales assistant, Janet Hendrix. The branch uses a bank account in South Bend to pay expenses. The account is kept in the name of "Connor Cosmetics—Special Account." To pay expenses, checks must be signed by Mary Cooper or by the treasurer of Connor Cosmetics, John Winters. Cooper receives the cancelled checks and bank statements. She reconciles the branch account herself and files cancelled checks and bank statements in her records. She also periodically prepares reports of cash disbursements and sends them to the home office.

Required

a. List the weaknesses in internal control for each of these situations. To identify the weaknesses, use the methodology that was discussed in this chapter.

b. For each weakness, state the type(s) of misstatement(s) that is (are) likely to result. Be as specific as possible.

c. How would you improve internal controls for each of the three companies?*

9-29 **(Objective 9-5)** The Art Appreciation Society operates a museum for the benefit and enjoyment of the community.

When the museum is open to the public, two clerks who are positioned at the entrance collect a \$5.00 admission fee from each nonmember patron. Members of the Art Appreciation Society are permitted to enter free of charge upon presentation of their membership cards.

*AICPA adapted.

At the end of each day, one of the clerks delivers the proceeds to the treasurer. The treasurer counts the cash in the presence of the clerk and places it in a safe. Each Friday afternoon, the treasurer and one of the clerks deliver all cash held in the safe to the bank and receive an authenticated deposit slip that provides the basis for the weekly entry in the accounting records.

The Art Appreciation Society board of directors has identified a need to improve its internal controls over cash admission fees. The board has determined that the cost of installing turnstiles, sales booths, or otherwise altering the physical layout of the museum will greatly exceed any benefits. However, the board has agreed that the sale of admission tickets must be an integral part of its improvement efforts.

Smith has been asked by the board of directors of the Art Appreciation Society to review the internal control over cash admission fees and provide suggestions for improvements.

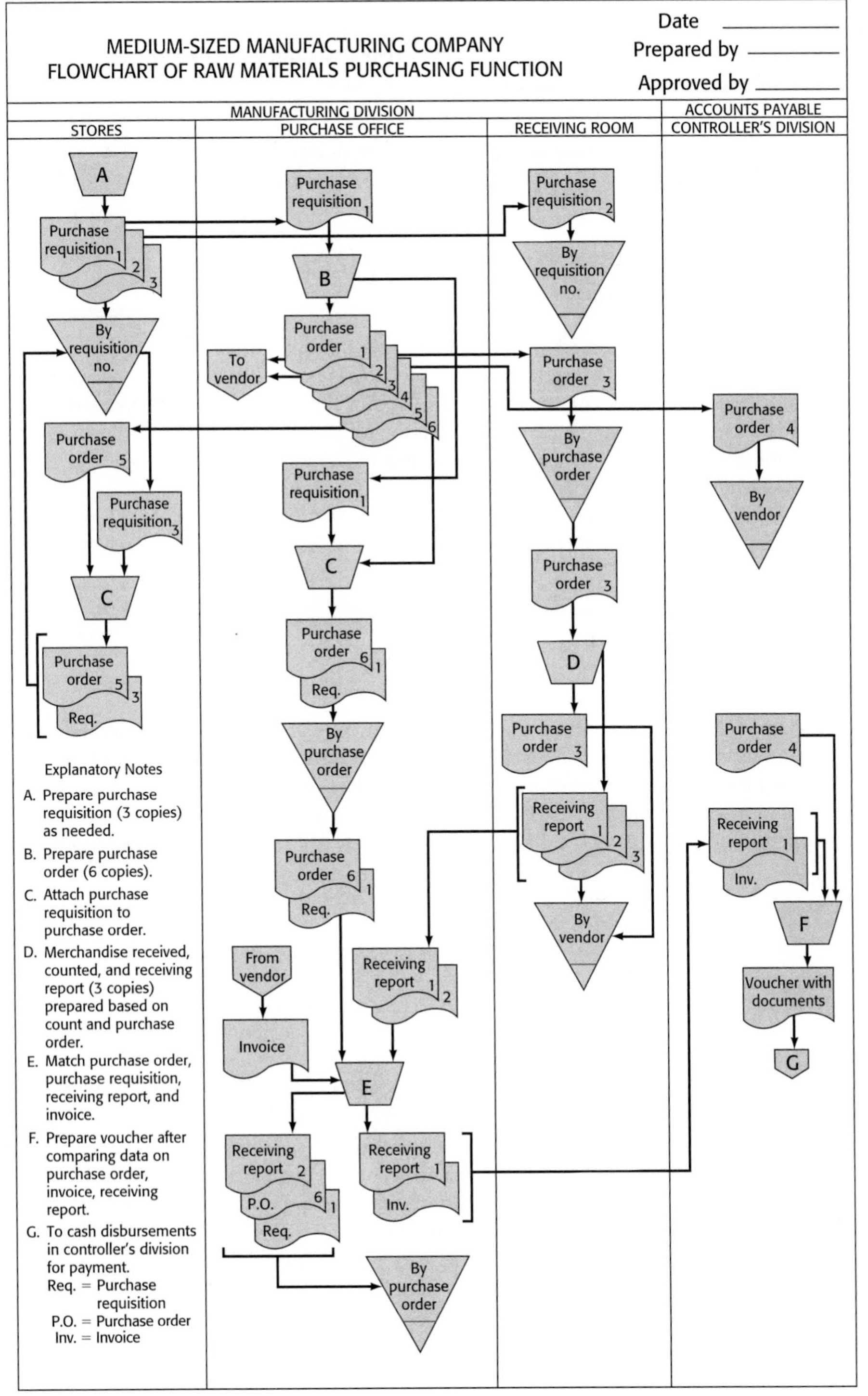

Required Indicate weaknesses in the existing internal controls over cash admission fees that Smith should identify, and recommend one improvement for each of the weaknesses identified. To identify the weaknesses, use the methodology that was discussed in this chapter. Organize the answer as indicated in the following illustrative example.*

Weakness	Recommendation
1. There is no basis for establishing the documentation of the number of paying patrons.	1. Prenumbered admission tickets should be issued upon payment of the admission fee.

CASE

9-30 (Objective 9-5) Anthony, CPA, prepared the flowchart on page 273, which portrays the raw materials purchasing function of one of Anthony's clients, Medium-Sized Manufacturing Company, from the preparation of initial documents through the vouching of invoices for payment in accounts payable. Assume that all documents are prenumbered.

Required Identify the weaknesses of internal control that can be determined from the flowchart. Use the methodology discussed in this chapter. Include internal control weaknesses resulting from activities performed or not performed.*

INTEGRATED CASE APPLICATION—PINNACLE MANUFACTURING: PART I

9-31 (Objective 9-5) This case study is presented in four parts. Each part deals with the material in the chapter in which that part appears. However, the parts are connected in such a way that in completing all four, you will gain a better understanding of how the parts of the audit are interrelated and integrated by the audit process. The parts appear in the following locations:

Part I—Understand internal control and assess control risk for the acquisition and payment cycle, Chapter 9, pages 274–276.

Part II—Design tests of controls and substantive tests of transactions, Chapter 11, page 336.

Part III—Design, perform, and evaluate results for tests of details of balances, Chapter 12, pages 365–370.

Part IV—Determine sample sizes using audit sampling and evaluate results, Chapter 13, pages 412–413.

Background Information

Pinnacle Manufacturing is a medium-sized manufacturing company with a December 31, 2002, year-end. You have been assigned the responsibility of auditing the acquisition and payment cycle and one related balance sheet account, accounts payable. The general approach to be taken will be to reduce assessed control risk to a low level, if possible, for the two main types of transactions affecting accounts payable: acquisitions and cash disbursements. The following are furnished as background information:

Figure 9-8 (p. 275)—A summary of key information from the audit of the acquisition and payment cycle and accounts payable in the prior year's audit.

Figure 9-9 (p. 276)—A flowchart description of the accounting system and internal controls for the acquisition and payment cycle.

Part I

The purpose of Part I is to obtain an understanding of internal control and assess control risk for Pinnacle Manufacturing's acquisition and cash disbursement transactions.

Required Study Figures 9-8 and 9-9 to gain an understanding of Pinnacle's internal control for the acquisition and payment cycle. Assess control risk as high, medium, or low on an objective-by-objective basis for the acquisition and payment cycle's internal controls, considering both internal controls and weaknesses. You should use a matrix similar to the one in Figure 9-5 (p. 262) for the assessment. There should be one matrix for acquisitions and a separate one for cash disbursements. The source of the internal controls and weaknesses is the information in Figure 9-9.

*AICPA adapted.

FIGURE 9-8 Information for Audit of Accounts Payable—Previous Year

Accounts payable, 12-31-01	
Number of accounts	52
Total accounts payable	$163,892.27
Range of individual balances	$27.83–$14,819.62
Tolerable misstatement for accounts payable	$6,500
Transactions, 2001	
Acquisitions:	
Number of acquisitions	3,800
Total acquisitions	$2,933,812
Cash disbursements:	
Number of disbursements	2,600
Total cash disbursements	$3,017,112
Results of audit procedures–tests of controls and substantive tests of transactions for acquisitions (sample size of 100):	
Purchase order not approved	2
Purchase quantities, prices, and/or extensions not correct	1
Transactions charged to wrong general ledger account	1
Transactions recorded in wrong period	1
No other exceptions	
Results of audit procedures–cash disbursements (sample size of 100):	
Cash disbursement recorded in wrong period	1
No other exceptions	
Results of audit procedures–accounts payable	
50% of vendors' balances were verified; combined net understatement amounts were projected to the population as follows:	
Three cutoff misstatements	$4,873.28
One difference in amounts due to disputes and discounts	$1,103.12
No adjustment was necessary because the total projected misstatement was not material.	

FIGURE 9-9 **Pinnacle Manufacturing—Acquisition and Payment Cycle**

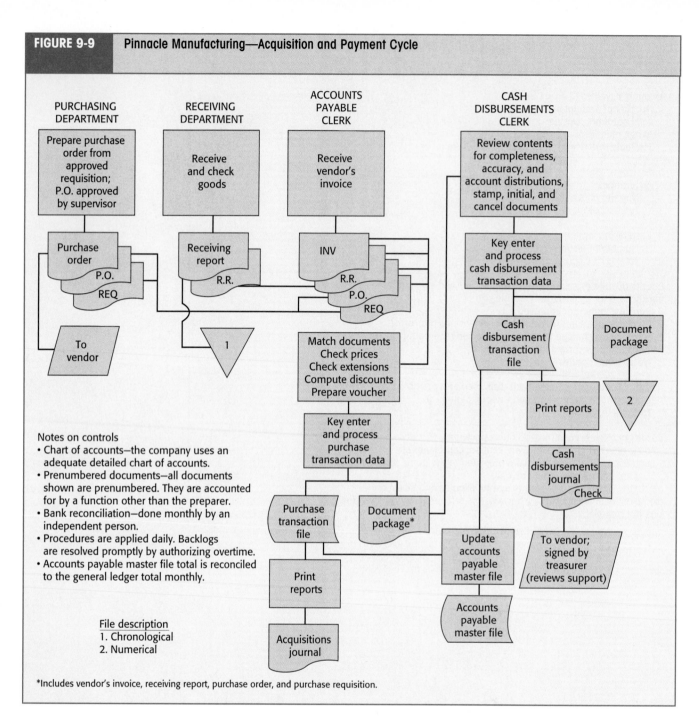

PURCHASING DEPARTMENT

Prepare purchase order from approved requisition; P.O. approved by supervisor

Purchase order

P.O.

REQ

To vendor

RECEIVING DEPARTMENT

Receive and check goods

Receiving report

R.R.

1

ACCOUNTS PAYABLE CLERK

Receive vendor's invoice

INV

R.R.

P.O.

REQ

Match documents
Check prices
Check extensions
Compute discounts
Prepare voucher

Key enter and process purchase transaction data

Purchase transaction file

Document package*

Print reports

Acquisitions journal

CASH DISBURSEMENTS CLERK

Review contents for completeness, accuracy, and account distributions, stamp, initial, and cancel documents

Key enter and process cash disbursement transaction data

Cash disbursement transaction file

Document package

2

Print reports

Cash disbursements journal

Check

To vendor; signed by treasurer (reviews support)

Update accounts payable master file

Accounts payable master file

Notes on controls

- Chart of accounts–the company uses an adequate detailed chart of accounts.
- Prenumbered documents–all documents shown are prenumbered. They are accounted for by a function other than the preparer.
- Bank reconciliation–done monthly by an independent person.
- Procedures are applied daily. Backlogs are resolved promptly by authorizing overtime.
- Accounts payable master file total is reconciled to the general ledger total monthly.

File description
1. Chronological
2. Numerical

*Includes vendor's invoice, receiving report, purchase order, and purchase requisition.

INTERNET PROBLEM 9-1: CORPORATE GOVERNANCE

Reference the CW site. The problem requires students to use the Internet to research (1) the purpose of the Business Roundtable (BR), and (2) specific issues within the BR's Statement on Corporate Governance (for example, board of directors' function with respect to risk management, controls, and compliance).

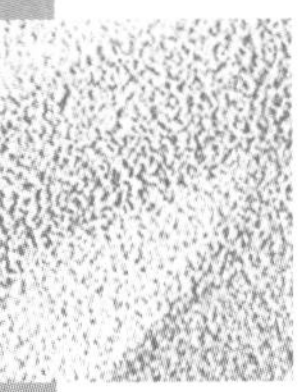

CHAPTER 10

OVERALL AUDIT PLAN AND AUDIT PROGRAM

LEARNING OBJECTIVES

After studying this chapter, you should be able to

- 10-1 Use the five types of audit tests to determine whether financial statements are fairly stated.
- 10-2 Select the appropriate types of audit tests.
- 10-3 Understand how information technology affects audit testing.
- 10-4 Understand the concept of evidence mix and how it should be varied in different circumstances.
- 10-5 Design an audit program.
- 10-6 Compare and contrast transaction-related audit objectives and balance-related audit objectives.
- 10-7 Integrate the four phases of the audit process.

HOW MUCH AND WHAT KIND OF TESTING WILL GET THE JOB DONE?

Terry Holland and Al Baker have known each other for years, and it seems like the debate they are having has been going on that long as well. Terry is a partner in the Southern California office of a national accounting firm. Al is an auditing professor at a nearby university. They get together once a month faithfully for lunch, and the conversation always gets around to auditing theory versus practice. Following is their most recent conversation:

PROFESSOR AL: A shortcoming of GAAS is that it offers too many choices of approaches. An auditor can do an audit with virtually no testing of detailed transactions by relying on observation, inquiry, analytical procedures, and tests of details of balances involving only large items. In a highly competitive market like we have now, I am concerned that firms will take the lowest-cost approach instead of being concerned enough about quality. There is already evidence that this is happening by CPA firms shifting away from large sample sizes.

PARTNER TERRY: Auditors must understand internal control on all audits, and where control risk is reduced below the maximum, some tests of controls and substantive tests of transactions are always done to support that reduction. Detailed audit tests are always performed and it is appropriate to concentrate on larger items in tests of details of balances. We only take this efficient approach on the clients that don't present any real risks. Where risks are high, we pull out all the stops and do a lot of detailed testing.

PROFESSOR AL: That sounds fine, but there are certain things that only detailed testing will find. I'm thinking specifically about misappropriation of assets. I'm sure your clients expect you to find it, but analytical procedures and tests of large items at year-end won't get that job done. What about that?

PARTNER TERRY: Well, Al, our clients also tell us they want our opinion on their financial statements at as low a cost as possible. If we went looking for misappropriation of assets in every audit, our costs would go through the roof. And I'll tell you, the best way for the client to deal with fraud is to have good controls. We focus our attention on giving them good recommendations for improving their controls. It's "value-added" and they appreciate that.

PROFESSOR AL: I'm not convinced. I'm sure your clients would appreciate it a lot more if you actually found that John Bookkeeper was dipping his fingers into the till, but I'm also concerned about the reduction in testing to search for errors as well as fraud. It seems to me you guys are taking the requirements of GAAS and figuring out how to audit so efficiently that you're not allowing any slack in the process. I think you're creeping more and more toward being an insurer rather than an assurer of the financial statements.

PARTNER TERRY: What do you mean, Al? I don't understand your theory at all.

PROFESSOR AL: Well, you guys are counting on most of your clients not having misstated financial statements, doing minimal audit work at relatively high fees, and then banking on the fact that you'll be able to absorb the cost of any damages you suffer from bad audit opinions.

PARTNER TERRY: Oh come on, Al, sitting in this ivory tower of yours has turned you into a cynic. I hope you don't talk to your students this way. Auditors do a terrific job, and there are lots of incentives for high quality. We want people to come into the profession with a positive attitude. Let's talk about something else. Say, I believe it's your turn to pay.

This chapter deals with the seventh and last step in the planning phase of an audit. It is a critical step because it results in the entire audit program the auditor plans to follow in the audit, including all audit procedures, sample sizes, items to select, and timing. This chapter's opening vignette deals with the importance of making the correct decisions in forming the overall audit plan and developing the detailed audit program, considering both the effectiveness of evidence and the efficiency of the audit process.

The first part of this chapter discusses the overall audit plan, which means selecting a mix of five types of tests that will result in an effective and efficient audit. This topic includes discussion of the trade-offs among the types of tests and consideration of the cost of each type of test. After the auditor decides the most cost-effective mix of the types of tests, a detailed audit program can be designed. This topic is covered later in the chapter. Because the material in this chapter is the final step in phase I, the planning phase, the relationship of phase I to the other three phases of the audit is discussed at the end of this chapter.

TYPES OF TESTS

OBJECTIVE 10-1

Use the five types of audit tests to determine whether financial statements are fairly stated.

In developing an overall audit plan, auditors have five **types of tests** they can use to determine whether financial statements are fairly stated. These tests are included in Figure 10-1, which shows the relationship of each type of test to the audit risk model. All five of these tests were introduced in earlier chapters and are now discussed in more detail, including the relationships among them. All audit procedures fall into one, and sometimes more than one, of these five categories.

As shown in Figure 10-1, procedures to gain an understanding and tests of controls reduce control risk, whereas analytical procedures and tests of details of balances are used to satisfy planned detection risk. Substantive tests of transactions affect both control risk and planned detection risk because they are used to test the effectiveness of internal controls and the dollar amounts of transactions.

Procedures to Obtain an Understanding of Internal Control

Procedures to obtain an understanding of internal control were studied in Chapter 9. During this part of an audit, the auditor must focus attention on both the *design* and the *operation* of aspects of internal control to the extent necessary to effectively plan the rest of the audit. After appropriately documenting internal controls, it is critical that a system walk-through be completed to ensure that the described controls have actually been put into place. The five types of audit procedures that relate to the auditor's understanding of internal control were identified in Chapter 9.

Tests of Controls

A major use of the auditor's understanding of internal control is to assess control risk for each transaction-related audit objective. Examples are assessing the accuracy objective for sales transactions as low and the existence objective as moderate. When control policies

FIGURE 10-1 Types of Audit Tests and the Audit Risk Model

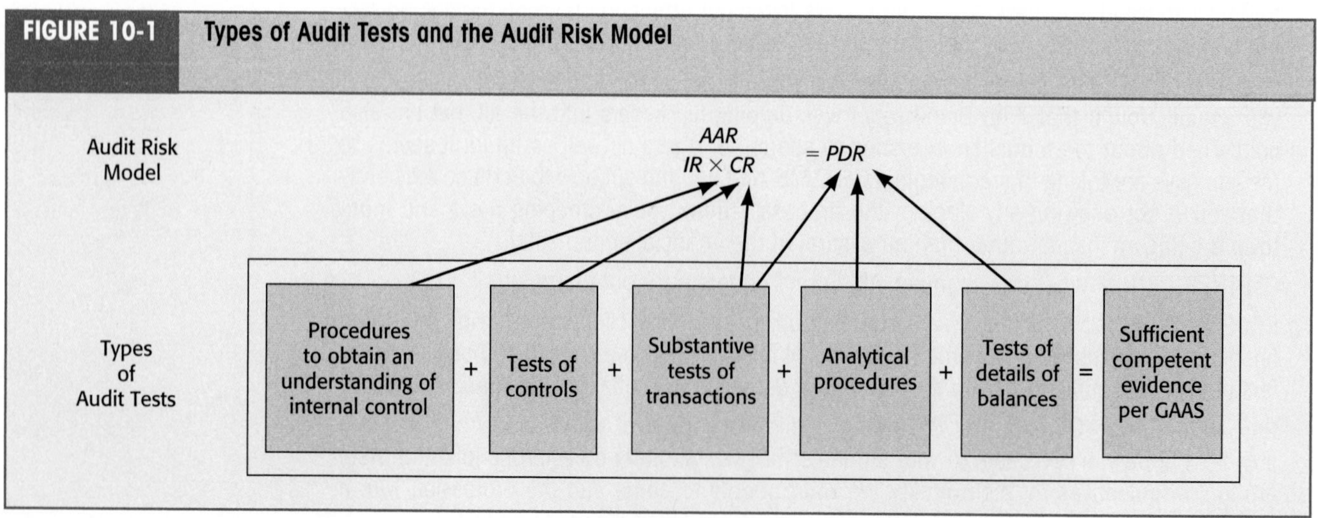

and procedures are believed to be effectively designed and when it is efficient to do so, the auditor will elect to assess control risk at a level that reflects that evaluation. In making this risk assessment, however, assessed control risk must be limited to the level supported by evidence. The procedures used to obtain such evidence are called **tests of controls.**

Tests of controls are performed to determine the appropriateness of the design and operating effectiveness of specific internal controls. The controls may be manual or automated.

A system walk-through performed as part of procedures to gain an understanding is used to determine whether controls are in place and is normally applied to one or a few transactions. Tests of controls are used to determine whether those controls are effective and usually involve testing a sample of transactions. For example, the auditor may select one sales transaction for a system walk-through of the credit approval process. As part of the walk-through, the auditor would follow the credit approval process from initiation of the sales transaction through the granting of credit. In tests of controls, the auditor might examine a sample of sales transactions from throughout the year to determine whether credit was granted before the shipment of goods as a test of the operating effectiveness of the credit approval process. For some objectives, procedures to gain an understanding may provide sufficient evidential matter to support a reduced level of control risk. The amount of additional evidence required for tests of controls depends on the extent of evidence obtained in gaining the understanding and on the planned reduction in control risk.

The role of tests of controls in the audit of the sales and collection cycle is shown in Figure 10-2 by the circles with no shading and the words "Audited by TOC." Procedures to gain an understanding of internal control and tests of controls are combined in Figure 10-2 because they are essentially the same. For simplicity, two assumptions are made. First, only sales and cash receipts transactions and three general ledger balances make up the sales and collection cycle. Second, the beginning balances in cash and accounts receivable were audited in the previous year and are considered correct. If the auditor verifies that sales and cash receipts transactions are correctly recorded in the accounting records and posted to the general ledger, then the conclusion can be made that the ending balances in

FIGURE 10-2 Role of All Audit Tests in the Audit of the Sales and Collection Cycle

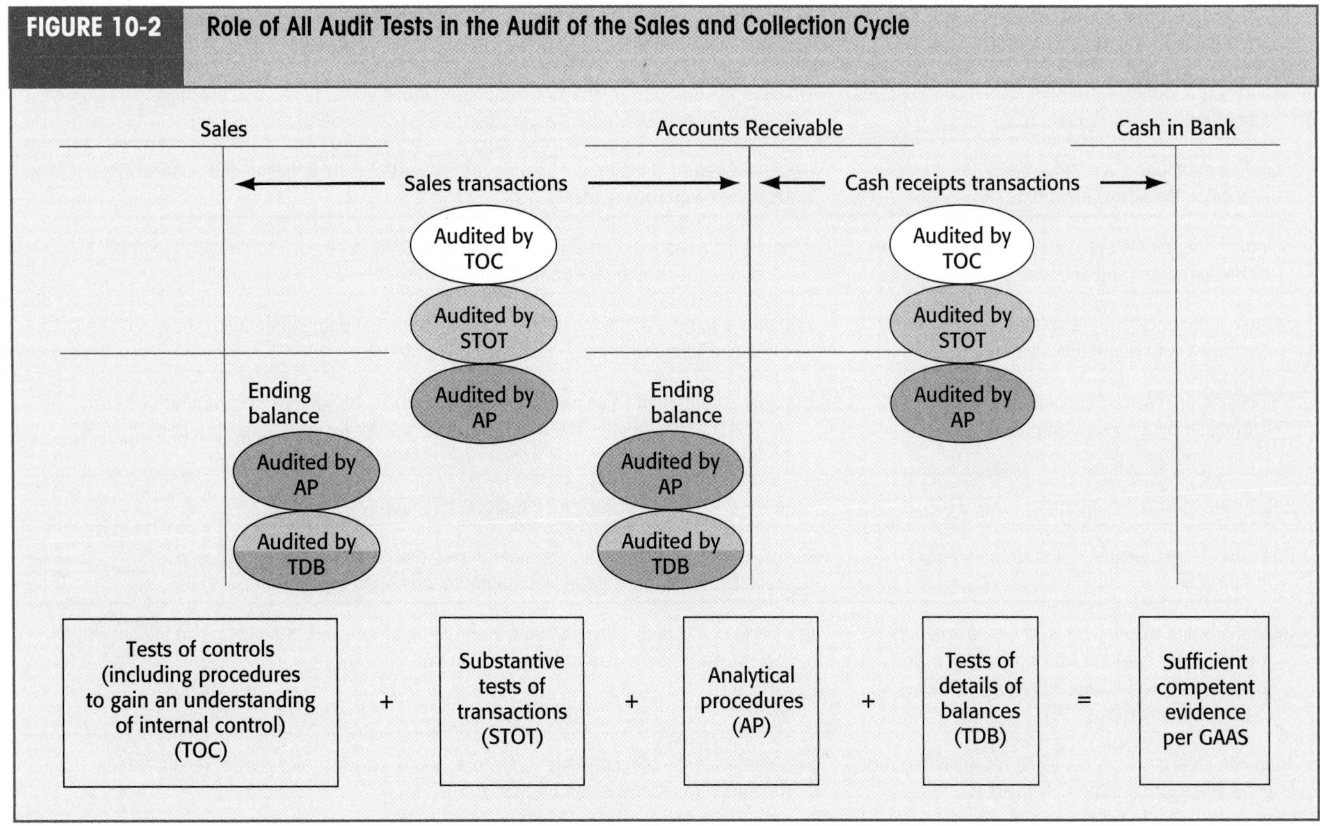

accounts receivable and sales are correct. (Cash disbursements transactions will have to be audited before the auditor can reach a conclusion about the ending balance in the cash account.) One way the auditor can verify this is to perform tests of controls. If controls are in place over sales and cash receipts transactions, the auditor can perform tests of controls to determine whether the six transaction-related audit objectives are being met for the cycle. Substantive tests of transactions, which are studied in the next section, also affect audit assurance for sales and cash receipts transactions.

To illustrate typical tests of controls, it is useful to return to the control risk matrix for Hillsburg Hardware Co. in Figure 9-5 (p. 262). For each of the 11 controls included in Figure 9-5, Table 10-1 identifies a test of control that might be performed to test its effectiveness.

Substantive Tests of Transactions

Substantive tests are procedures designed to test for dollar misstatements directly affecting the correctness of financial statement balances. Such misstatements (often termed *monetary misstatements*) are a clear indication of the misstatement of the accounts. There are three types of substantive tests: substantive tests of transactions, analytical procedures, and tests of details of balances.

The purpose of **substantive tests of transactions** is to determine whether all six transaction-related audit objectives have been satisfied for each class of transactions. For example, the auditor performs substantive tests of transactions to test whether recorded transactions exist and existing transactions are recorded. The auditor also performs these

TABLE 10-1 Illustration of Tests of Controls

Illustrative Key Controls	Typical Tests of Controls
Credit is approved automatically by the computer by comparison to authorized credit limits (C1).	Examine a sample of sales invoices and compare customer order to authorized credit limit (reperformance).
Recorded sales are supported by authorized shipping documents and approved customer orders, which are attached to the duplicate sales invoice (C2).	Examine a sample of duplicate sales invoices to determine that each one is supported by an attached authorized shipping document and approved customer order (documentation).
Separation of duties between billing, recording sales, and handling cash receipts (C3).	Observe whether personnel responsible for handling cash have no accounting responsibilities and inquire as to their duties (observation and inquiry).
Shipping documents are forwarded to billing daily and billed the subsequent day (C4).	Observe whether shipping documents are forwarded daily to billing and observe when they are billed (observation).
Shipping documents are issued in numerical order by the computer and accounted for weekly (C5).	Account for a sequence of shipping documents and trace each to the sales journal (documentation and reperformance).
Shipping documents are batched daily and compared with quantities billed (C6).	Examine a sample of daily batches, recalculate the shipping quantities, and trace totals to reconciliation with input reports (reperformance).
Unit selling prices are obtained from the price list master file of approved prices (C7).	Examine a sample of sales invoices and agree prices to authorized computer price list. Review changes to price file throughout the year for proper approval (reperformance and documentation).
Sales transactions are internally verified (C8).	Examine document package for internal verification (classification).
Statements are mailed to all customers each month (C9).	Observe whether statements are mailed for 1 month and inquire about who is responsible for mailing the statements (observation and inquiry).
Once the batch of sales transactions is entered, the computer automatically posts transactions to the accounts receivable subsidiary records and to the general ledger (C10).	Use audit software to trace postings from the batch of sales transactions to the subsidiary records and general ledger (reperformance).
Accounts receivable master file is reconciled to the general ledger on a monthly basis (C11).	Examine evidence of reconciliation for test month, and test accuracy of reconciliation (documentation and reperformance).

tests to determine whether recorded sales transactions are accurately recorded, recorded in the appropriate time period, correctly classified, and accurately summarized and posted to the general ledger and master files. If the auditor is confident that transactions were correctly recorded in the journals and correctly posted, the auditor can be confident that general ledger totals are correct.

The role of substantive tests of transactions in the audit of the sales and collection cycle is illustrated in Figure 10-2 (p. 279) by the circles with partial shading and the words "Audited by STOT." Observe that both tests of controls and substantive tests of transactions are performed for transactions in the cycle, not on the ending account balances. The auditor verifies the recording and summarizing of sales and cash receipts transactions by performing substantive tests of transactions. In this example, there is one set of tests for sales and another for cash receipts.

Tests of controls can be performed separately from all other tests, but for efficiency they are often done at the same time as substantive tests of transactions. For example, tests of controls involving documentation and reperformance usually are applied to the same transactions tested for monetary misstatements. In fact, reperformance always simultaneously provides evidence about both controls and monetary correctness. In the remainder of this book, it is assumed that tests of controls and substantive tests of transactions are done at the same time.

Analytical Procedures

As first discussed in Chapter 6, **analytical procedures** involve comparisons of recorded amounts to expectations developed by the auditor. They often involve the calculation of ratios by the auditor for comparison with previous years' ratios and other related data.

The two most important purposes of analytical procedures in the audit of account balances are to (1) indicate the presence of possible misstatements in the financial statements and (2) reduce tests of details of balances. There is typically a difference in the analytical procedures done during planning and those done in the testing phase. Even if, for example, the gross margin is calculated during planning, it is probably done using interim data. Later, during the tests of the ending balances, the auditor will recalculate the ratio using full-year data. If the auditor believes that analytical procedures indicate a reasonable possibility of misstatement, additional analytical procedures may be performed or the auditor may decide to modify tests of details of balances.

When the auditor develops expectations using analytical procedures and concludes that the client's ending balances in certain accounts appear reasonable, certain tests of details of balances may be eliminated or sample sizes may be reduced. The SASs state that analytical procedures can be used as substantive tests.

The role of analytical procedures in the audit of the sales and collection cycle is illustrated in Figure 10-2 by the circles with dark shading and the words "Audited by AP." Observe that the auditor performs analytical procedures on sales and cash receipts transactions, as well as on the ending balances of the accounts in the cycle.

Tests of Details of Balances

Tests of details of balances focus on the ending general ledger balances for both balance sheet and income statement accounts, but the primary emphasis in most tests of details of balances is on the balance sheet. Examples include confirmation of customer balances for accounts receivable, physical examination of inventory, and examination of vendors' statements for accounts payable. These tests of ending balances are essential because the evidence is usually obtained from a source independent of the client and thus is considered highly reliable.

The role of tests of details of balances is illustrated in Figure 10-2 by the circles with half dark and half light shading and the words "Audited by TDB." Detailed tests of the ending balances are performed for sales and accounts receivable. These include audit procedures such as confirmation of account receivable balances and sales cutoff tests. The extent of these tests depends on the results of tests of controls, substantive tests of transactions, and analytical procedures for these accounts.

Tests of details of balances have the objective of establishing the monetary correctness of the accounts they relate to and therefore are substantive tests. For example, confirmations test for monetary misstatements and are therefore substantive. Similarly, counts of inventory and cash on hand are also substantive tests.

Summary of Types of Tests

Examining Figure 10-2 overall summarizes how the five types of audit tests are used to obtain audit assurance in the audit of the sales and collection cycle. Procedures to gain an understanding of internal control and tests of controls evaluate whether controls over transactions in the cycle are sufficiently effective to reduce control risk and thereby reduce substantive testing. Substantive tests of transactions emphasize the verification of transactions recorded in the journals and then posted in the general ledger. Analytical procedures emphasize the overall reasonableness of transactions and the general ledger balances. Tests of details of balances emphasize the ending balances in the general ledger. By combining the types of audit tests shown in Figure 10-2, the auditor obtains a higher overall assurance for transactions and accounts in the sales and collection cycle than the assurance obtained from any one test. To increase overall assurance for the cycle, the auditor can increase the assurance obtained from any one of the tests.

SELECTING WHICH TYPES OF TESTS TO PERFORM

OBJECTIVE 10-2

Select the appropriate types of audit tests.

Typically, auditors use all five types of tests when performing an audit, but certain types are emphasized, depending on the circumstances. Factors such as the availability of the seven types of evidence, the cost of each type of test, the effectiveness of internal controls, and the existence of inherent risks all affect the mix of the types of tests the auditor selects.

Types of Evidence

Each of the five types of tests involves only certain types of evidence (confirmation, documentation, and so forth). Table 10-2 summarizes the relationship between types of tests and types of evidence. Several observations about Table 10-2 follow:

- Procedures to obtain an understanding of internal control and tests of controls involve only observation, documentation, inquiry, and reperformance. Substantive tests of transactions involve only the last three of these types of evidence.
- More types of evidence are obtained by using tests of details of balances than by using any other type of test. Only tests of details of balances involve confirmation and physical examination.
- Inquiries of clients are made with every type of test.
- Documentation and reperformance are used for every type of test except analytical procedures.

TABLE 10-2 Relationship Between Types of Tests and Evidence

	Type of Evidence						
Type of Test	Physical Examination	Confirmation	Documentation	Observation	Inquiries of the Client	Reperformance	Analytical Procedures
Procedures to obtain an understanding of internal control			√	√	√	√	
Tests of controls			√	√	√	√	
Substantive tests of transactions			√		√	√	
Analytical procedures					√		√
Tests of details of balances	√	√	√		√	√	

Relative Costs

In deciding which type of test to select for obtaining sufficient competent evidence, the cost of the evidence is one important consideration. The types of tests are listed in order of increasing cost as follows:

- Analytical procedures
- Procedures to obtain an understanding of internal control and tests of controls
- Substantive tests of transactions
- Tests of details of balances

The reason analytical procedures are least costly is the relative ease of making calculations and comparisons. Often, considerable information about potential misstatements can be obtained by simply comparing two or three numbers. Auditors often calculate these ratios using computer software at almost no cost.

Tests of controls are also low in cost because the auditor is making inquiries and observations and examining such things as approvals on documents or in computer files and outward indications of other controls. Often, tests of controls can be done on a large number of items in a few minutes. Auditors often take advantage of audit software to test controls included in clients' computerized accounting systems. For example, many computerized accounts receivable systems automatically authorize sales to existing customers by comparing the proposed sales amount and existing accounts receivable balance with the customer's credit limit. The auditor can test this control using audit software.

Substantive tests of transactions are more expensive than tests of controls that do not include reperformance because recalculations and tracings are often required. In a computerized environment, however, the auditor can often perform substantive tests of transactions quickly for a large number of transactions.

Tests of details of balances are almost always considerably more costly than any of the other types of procedures. It is costly to send confirmations and to count assets. Because of the high cost of tests of details of balances, auditors usually try to plan the audit to minimize their use.

Naturally, the cost of each type of evidence varies in different situations. For example, the cost of an auditor's test-counting inventory (a substantive test of the details of the inventory balance) often depends on the nature and dollar value of the inventory, its location, and the number of different items.

Relationship Between Tests of Controls and Substantive Tests

To better understand the nature of tests of controls and substantive tests, an examination of how they differ is useful. An exception in a test of control is only an *indication* of the likelihood of misstatements affecting the dollar value of the financial statements, whereas an exception in a substantive test of transactions or a test of details of balances *is* a financial statement misstatement. Exceptions in tests of controls are often called *control test deviations.* Thus, control test deviations are significant only if they occur with sufficient frequency to cause the auditor to believe there may be material dollar misstatements in the statements. Substantive tests of transactions or tests of details of balances should then be performed to determine whether dollar misstatements have actually occurred.

As an illustration, assume that the client's controls require an independent clerk to verify the quantity, price, and extension of each sales invoice, after which the clerk must initial the duplicate invoice to indicate performance. A test of control audit procedure would be to examine a sample of duplicate sales invoices for the initials of the person who verified the quantitative data. If a significant number of documents do not have initials, the auditor should follow up with substantive tests. This can be done by extending the tests of the duplicate sales invoices to include verifying prices, extensions, and footings (substantive tests of transactions) or by increasing the sample size for the confirmation of accounts receivable (substantive test of details of balances). Of course, even though the control is not operating effectively, the invoices may still be correct. This will be the case if the person originally preparing the sales invoices did a conscientious and competent job.

On the other hand, if no or only a few documents have missing initials, the control would be considered effective and the auditor could therefore reduce substantive tests of transactions and tests of details of balances. Some substantive tests are still necessary to provide the auditor assurance that the initials were not written without the clerk performing the control procedures or performing them carelessly. Because of the need to complete some reperformance tests, many auditors prefer to perform them as a part of the original tests of controls. Others prefer to reperform, in the form of a substantive test, only when there is indication of the need to do so.

Relationship Between Analytical Procedures and Substantive Tests

Similar to the relationships discussed in the previous section, analytical procedures also provide only an indication of the likelihood of misstatements affecting the dollar value of the financial statements. Unusual fluctuations in the relationships of an account to other accounts or to nonfinancial information provide an indication of an increased likelihood that material misstatements exist without necessarily providing direct evidence of a material misstatement. When unusual analytical procedure fluctuations are identified, substantive tests of transactions or tests of details of balances should be performed to determine whether dollar misstatements have actually occurred. If the auditor performs analytical procedures and believes that the likelihood of material misstatement is small, other substantive tests can be reduced.

Trade-Off Between Tests of Controls and Substantive Tests

As explained in Chapter 9, there is a trade-off between tests of controls and substantive tests. The auditor makes a decision during planning whether to assess control risk below the maximum. Tests of controls must be performed to determine whether the assessed control risk is supported. If it is, planned detection risk in the audit risk model is increased, and planned substantive tests can therefore be reduced. Figure 10-3 shows the relationship between substantive tests and control risk assessment (including tests of controls) at differing levels of internal control effectiveness.

The shaded area in Figure 10-3 is the maximum assurance obtainable from control risk assessment and tests of controls. For example, at any point to the left of point *A*, assessed control risk is 1.0 because the auditor evaluates internal controls as ineffective. Any point to the right of point *B* results in no further reduction of control risk because the CPA firm has established a minimum assessed control risk it will permit. Notice in Figure 10-3 that regardless of the level of audit assurance obtained from control risk assessment and tests of controls, some substantive procedures are always required.

FIGURE 10-3 **Audit Assurance from Substantive Tests and Tests of Controls at Different Levels of Internal Control Effectiveness**

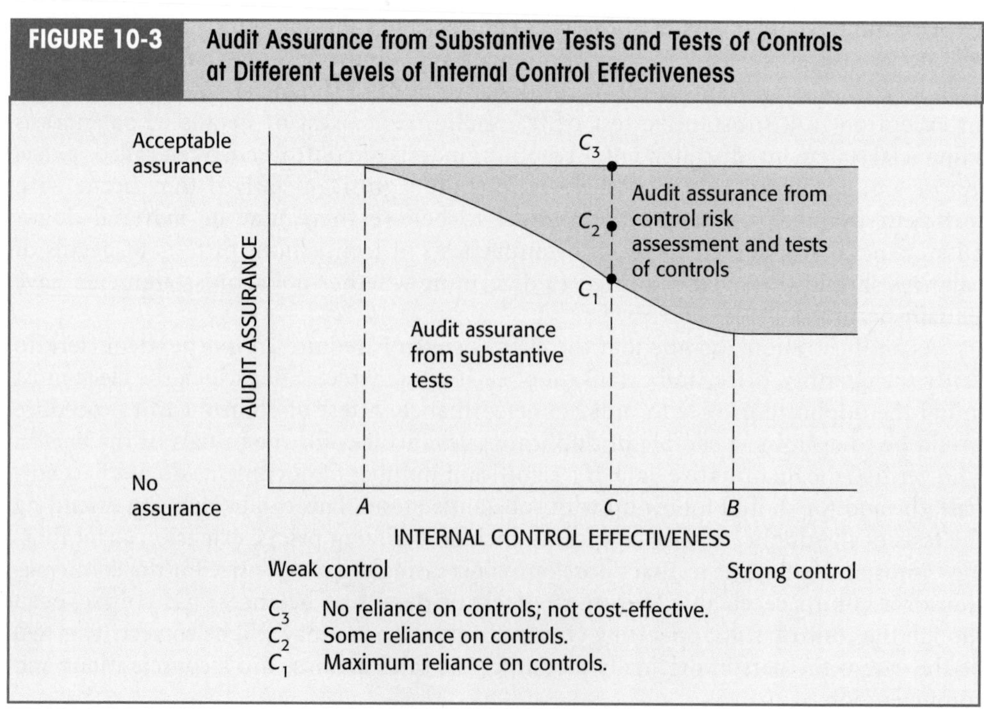

After the auditor decides the effectiveness of the client's internal controls, it is appropriate to select any point within the shaded area of Figure 10-3 consistent with the assessed control risk the auditor decides to support. To illustrate, assume that the auditor contends that internal control effectiveness is at point C. Tests of controls at the C_1 level would provide the minimum control risk, given the internal controls. The auditor could choose to perform no tests of controls (point C_3), which would support a control risk of 1.0. Any point between the two, such as C_2, would also be appropriate. If C_2 is selected, the audit assurance from tests of controls is $C_3 - C_2$ and from substantive tests is $C - C_2$. The auditor will likely select C_1, C_2, or C_3 based on the relative cost of tests of controls and substantive tests.

IMPACT OF INFORMATION TECHNOLOGY ON AUDIT TESTING

OBJECTIVE 10-3

Understand how information technology affects audit testing.

ITAudit.org

SAS 80 (AU 326) and SAS 94 (AU 319) provide guidance for auditors of entities that transmit, process, maintain, or access significant information electronically. Examples of electronic evidence include records of electronic fund transfers and purchase orders transmitted through electronic data interchange (EDI). The standards recognize that in instances in which a significant amount of audit evidence is in electronic form, it may not be practical or possible to reduce detection risk to an acceptable level by performing only substantive tests. For example, the potential for improper initiation or alteration of information may be greater if information is maintained only in electronic form. In these circumstances, the auditor should perform tests of controls to gather evidence to support an assessed level of control risk below maximum for the affected financial statement assertions. Although some substantive tests are still required, the auditor can significantly reduce substantive tests if the tests of controls results support the effectiveness of computer controls.

Because of the inherent consistency of IT processing, the auditor may be able to reduce the extent of testing of an automated control. For example, a software-based control is almost certain to function consistently unless the program is changed. Once it is determined that an automated control is functioning properly, the auditor can focus subsequent tests on assessing whether any changes have occurred that would limit the effectiveness of the control. Such tests might include determining whether any changes have occurred to the program and whether these changes were properly authorized and tested prior to implementation. This approach leads to significant audit efficiencies when the auditor determines that automated controls tested in the prior year's audit have not been changed and continue to be subject to effective general controls.

To test automated controls, the auditor may need to use techniques that are different from those used to test manual controls. For example, computer-assisted audit techniques may be used to test automated controls or data, and the auditor may use reports produced by IT to test the operating effectiveness of IT general controls, such as program change controls and access controls.

When auditors test manual controls that rely on IT-generated reports, they must consider both the effectiveness of management's review and the controls related to the accuracy of the information in the report.

EVIDENCE MIX

OBJECTIVE 10-4

Understand the concept of evidence mix and how it should be varied in different circumstances.

The choice of which types of tests to use and how extensively they need to be performed can vary widely among audits for differing levels of internal control effectiveness and inherent risks. There can also be variations from cycle to cycle within a given audit. The combination of the five types of tests used for any given cycle is often called the **evidence mix.** Table 10-3 (p. 286) shows the evidence mix for four different audits. In each case, assume that sufficient competent evidence was accumulated. An analysis of each audit follows.

Analysis of Audit 1 This client is a large company with sophisticated internal controls and low inherent risk. Therefore, the auditor performs extensive tests of controls and relies heavily on the client's internal controls to reduce substantive tests. Extensive analytical

TABLE 10-3 Variations in Evidence Mix

	Procedures to Obtain an Understanding of Internal Control	Tests of Controls	Substantive Tests of Transactions	Analytical Procedures	Tests of Details of Balances
Audit 1	E	E	S	E	S
Audit 2	M	M	M	E	M
Audit 3	M	N	E	M	E
Audit 4	M	M	E	E	E

E = Extensive amount of testing; M = Medium amount of testing; S = Small amount of testing; N = No testing.

procedures are also performed to reduce other substantive tests. Substantive tests of transactions and tests of details of balances are therefore minimized. Because of the emphasis on tests of controls and analytical procedures, this audit can be done relatively inexpensively.

Analysis of Audit 2 This company is medium sized, with some controls and a few inherent risks. Therefore, the auditor has decided to do a medium amount of testing for all types of tests except analytical procedures, which will be done extensively. There will be more extensive testing done where there are specific inherent risks.

Analysis of Audit 3 This company is medium sized but has few effective controls and significant inherent risks. Management has decided that it is not cost effective to have better internal controls. No tests of controls are done because reliance on internal controls is inappropriate when controls are insufficient. The emphasis is on tests of details of balances and substantive tests of transactions, but some analytical procedures are also done. Analytical procedures are usually performed to reduce other substantive tests because they provide evidence about the likelihood of material misstatements. The auditor already expects to find material misstatements in the account balances, so additional analytical procedures are not cost effective. The cost of the audit is likely to be relatively high because of the amount of detailed substantive testing.

Analysis of Audit 4 The original plan on this audit was to follow the approach used in Audit 2. However, the auditor found extensive control test deviations and significant misstatements while performing substantive tests of transactions and analytical procedures. Therefore, the auditor concluded that the internal controls were not effective. Extensive tests of details of balances are performed to offset the unacceptable results of the other tests. The cost of this audit is higher because tests of controls and substantive tests of transactions were performed but could not be used to reduce tests of details of balances.

DESIGN OF THE AUDIT PROGRAM

OBJECTIVE 10-5
Design an audit program.

After the auditor determines the appropriate emphasis on each of the five types of tests, the specific audit program for each type must be designed. The audit procedures, when combined, form the audit program. In most audits, the engagement in-charge auditor recommends the evidence mix to the engagement manager. After the evidence mix is approved, the in-charge prepares the audit program or modifies an existing program to satisfy all audit objectives, considering such things as evidence mix, inherent risk, and control risk. The in-charge is also likely to get approval from the manager before performing the audit procedures or delegating their performance to an assistant. This part of the chapter focuses on designing audit programs to satisfy transaction-related and balance-related audit objectives.

The audit program for most audits is designed in three parts: tests of controls and substantive tests of transactions, analytical procedures, and tests of details of balances. There will likely be a separate set of subaudit programs for each transaction cycle. An example in the sales and collection cycle might be tests of controls and substantive tests of transactions audit programs for sales and cash receipts; an analytical procedures audit program for the entire cycle; and tests of details of balances audit programs for cash, accounts receivable, bad debt expense, allowance for uncollectible accounts, and miscellaneous accounts receivable.

WWW

Audit Programs Resource

Tests of Controls and Substantive Tests of Transactions

The tests of controls and substantive tests of transactions audit program normally includes a descriptive section documenting the understanding obtained about internal control. It is also likely to include a description of the procedures performed to obtain an understanding of internal control and assessed control risk. Both of these affect the tests of controls and substantive tests of transactions audit program. The methodology to design these tests is shown in Figure 10-4. The first three steps in the figure were described in Chapter 9. The audit procedures include both tests of controls and substantive tests of transactions and vary depending on assessed control risk. When controls are effective and assessed control risk is low, there will be heavy emphasis on tests of controls. Some substantive tests of transactions will also be included. If control risk is assessed at 1.0, only substantive tests of transactions will be used. The procedures already performed in obtaining an understanding of internal control will affect both tests of controls and substantive tests of transactions.

Audit Procedures The approach to designing tests of controls and substantive tests of transactions emphasizes satisfying the transaction-related audit objectives developed in Chapter 5. A four-step approach is followed when the auditor plans to reduce assessed control risk.

1. Apply the transaction-related audit objectives to the class of transactions being tested, such as sales.
2. Identify key controls that should reduce control risk for each transaction-related audit objective.

FIGURE 10-4 Methodology for Designing Tests of Controls and Substantive Tests of Transactions

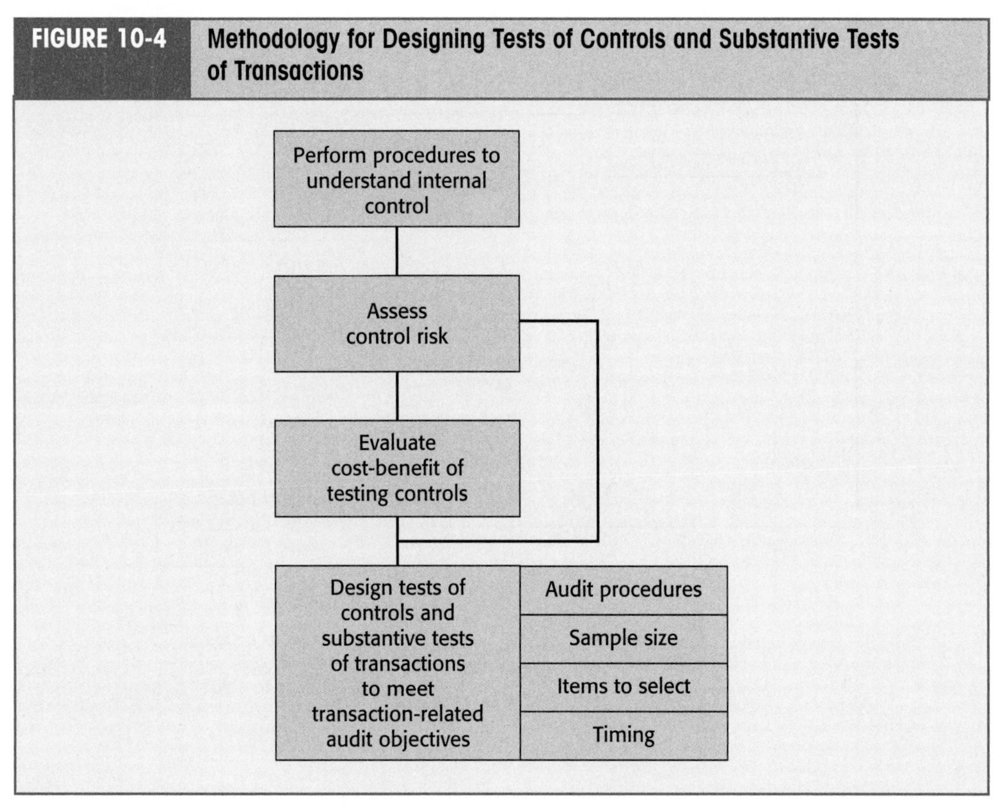
Perform procedures to understand internal control
Assess control risk
Evaluate cost-benefit of testing controls
Design tests of controls and substantive tests of transactions to meet transaction-related audit objectives
Audit procedures
Sample size
Items to select
Timing

3. For all internal controls used to reduce the initial assessment of control risk below maximum (key controls), develop appropriate tests of controls.
4. For the potential types of misstatements related to each transaction-related audit objective, design appropriate substantive tests of transactions, considering weaknesses in internal control and expected results of the tests of controls in step 3.

This four-step approach to designing tests of controls and substantive tests of transactions is summarized in Figure 10-5. The approach in Figure 10-5 is illustrated in several chapters in the text. For example, see Table 11-2 on pages 315–316 for an application of the four-step procedure for the audit of sales transactions. Each of the steps corresponds to a column in Table 11-2.

Analytical Procedures

Because they are relatively inexpensive, many auditors perform extensive analytical procedures on all audits. Analytical procedures performed during substantive testing, such as for the audit of accounts receivable, are typically more focused and extensive than those done as part of planning. For example, during planning, the auditor might calculate the gross margin percentage for total sales. During substantive testing of accounts receivable, the auditor might calculate gross margin percentage by month or by line of business, or possibly both. Analytical procedures calculated using monthly amounts will typically be more effective in detecting misstatements than those calculated using annual amounts, and comparisons by line of business will usually be more effective than companywide comparisons. If sales and accounts receivable are based on predictable relationships with nonfinancial data, the auditor often uses that information for analytical procedures. For

FIGURE 10-5 Four-Step Approach to Designing Tests of Controls and Substantive Tests of Transactions

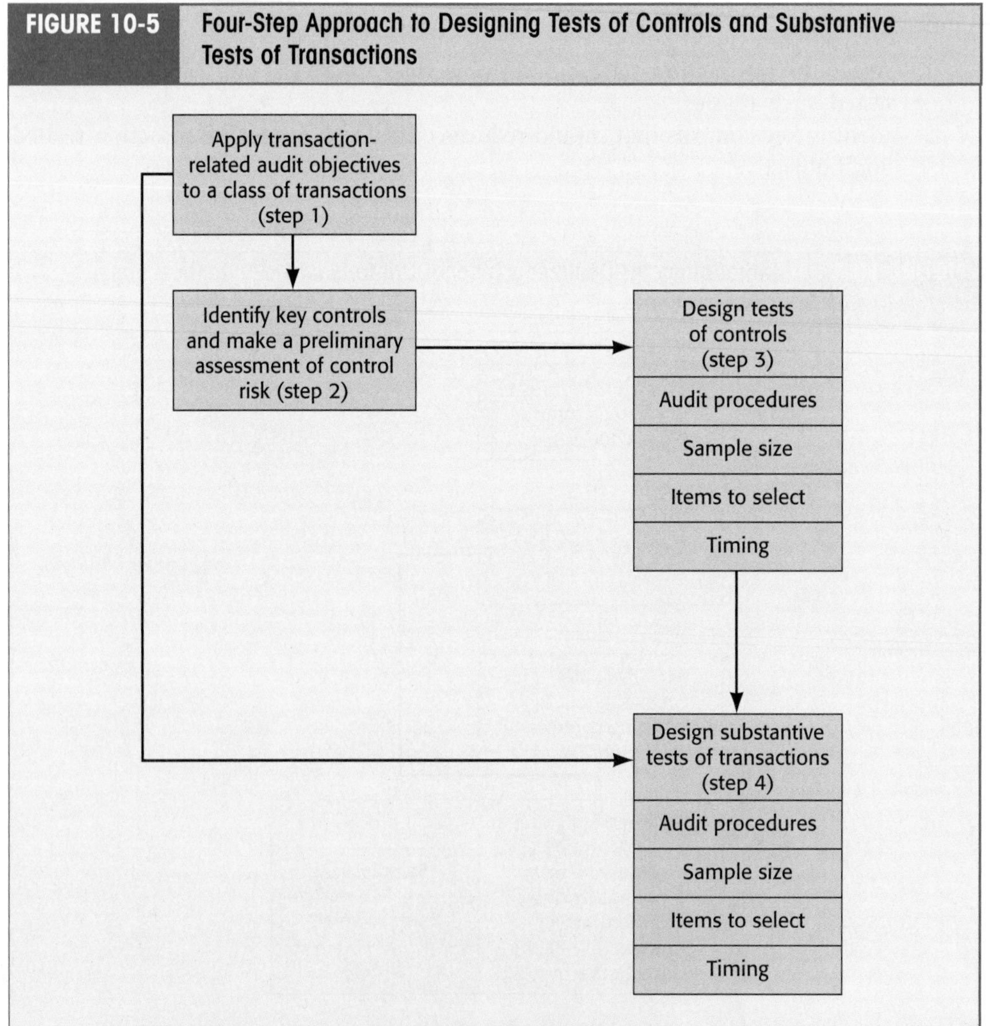

example, if revenue billings are based on the number of hours professionals charge to clients, such as in law firms and other organizations that provide services, the auditor can estimate total revenue by multiplying hours billed by average billing rate.

When the auditor plans to use analytical procedures as a part of the assurance gained through substantive testing, it is important that the data used in the calculations be considered sufficiently reliable. This is important for all data, especially nonfinancial data. For example, if hours billed and the average billing rate are used to estimate total revenue, the auditor must be confident that both of these are reasonably reliable numbers.

Tests of Details of Balances

The methodology for designing tests of details of balances audit procedures is oriented to the balance-related audit objectives developed in Chapter 5 (pp. 130–132). For example, if the auditor is verifying accounts receivable, the planned audit procedures must be sufficient to satisfy each of the balance-related audit objectives. In planning tests of details of balances audit procedures to satisfy these objectives, many auditors follow a methodology such as the one shown in Figure 10-6 for accounts receivable. The design of these procedures is normally the most difficult part of the entire planning process. Designing such procedures is subjective and requires considerable professional judgment. A discussion of the key decisions in designing tests of details of balances audit procedures as shown in Figure 10-6 follows.

Identify Client Business Risks Affecting Accounts Receivable As discussed in Chapter 7, as part of gaining an understanding of the client's business and industry, the auditor identifies significant client business risks. These risks are then evaluated to determine whether they

FIGURE 10-6 Methodology for Designing Tests of Details of Balances—Accounts Receivable

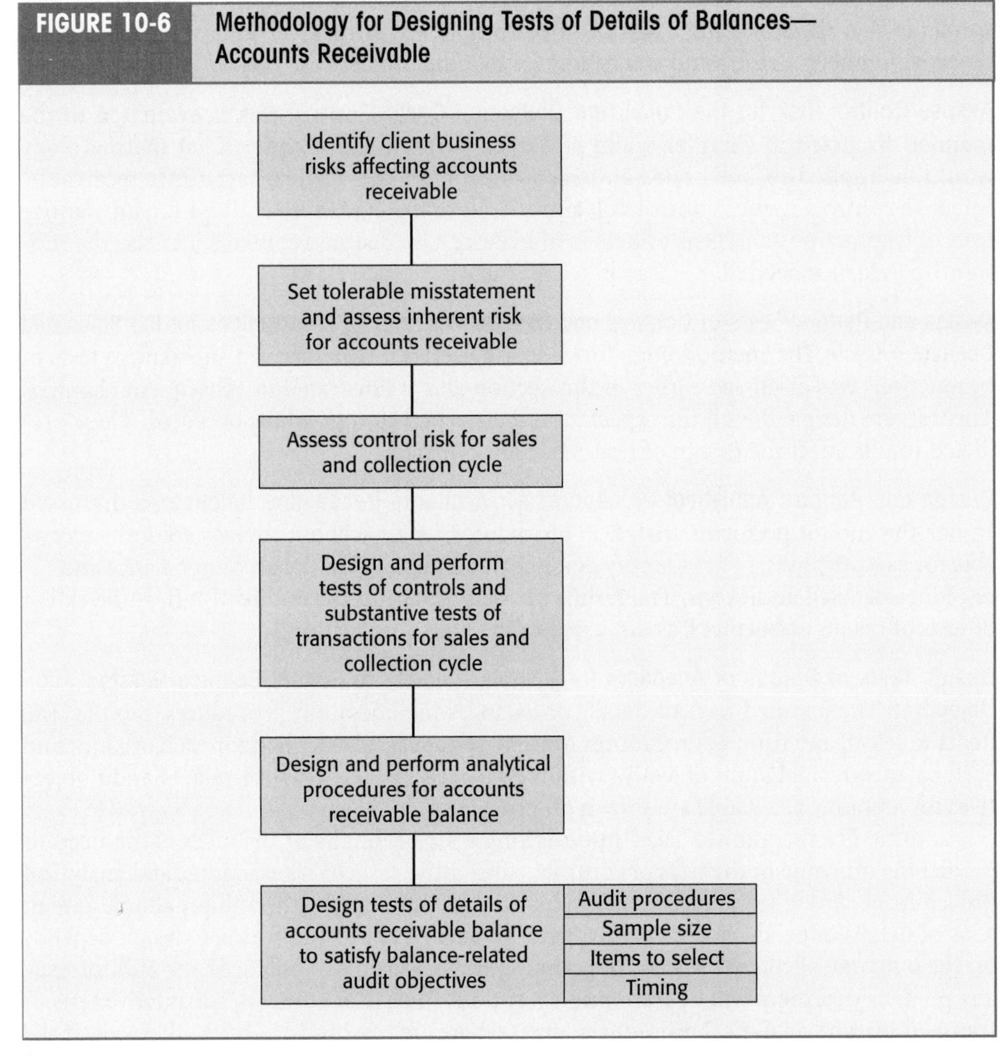

Identify client business risks affecting accounts receivable
Set tolerable misstatement and assess inherent risk for accounts receivable
Assess control risk for sales and collection cycle
Design and perform tests of controls and substantive tests of transactions for sales and collection cycle
Design and perform analytical procedures for accounts receivable balance
Design tests of details of accounts receivable balance to satisfy balance-related audit objectives
Audit procedures
Sample size
Items to select
Timing

result in increased risk of material misstatements in the financial statements. If any of the identified client business risks affect accounts receivable, they should be incorporated in the auditor's evaluation of inherent risk or control risk and the appropriate extent of evidence. For example, the auditor may identify competitive factors or industry conditions that may have a negative impact on sales. If the performance measurement system encourages attainment of overly optimistic sales goals for the current economic environment, the auditor may decide to increase inherent risk and the extent of evidence for the existence and cutoff objectives for sales and accounts receivable.

Set Tolerable Misstatement and Assess Inherent Risk for Accounts Receivable Setting the preliminary judgment about materiality for the audit as a whole and allocating the total to account balances (tolerable misstatement) are auditor decisions that were discussed in Chapter 8. After the preliminary judgment about materiality is made, tolerable misstatement is set for each significant balance. A lower tolerable misstatement would result in more testing of details than a higher amount. Some auditors may allocate tolerable misstatement to individual balance-related audit objectives, but most do not.

Inherent risk is assessed by identifying any aspect of the client's history, environment, or operations that indicates a high likelihood of misstatement in the current year's financial statements. Considerations affecting inherent risk that were discussed in Chapter 8 applied to accounts receivable include makeup of accounts receivable, nature of the client's business, initial engagement, and so on. An account balance for which inherent risk has been assessed as high would result in more evidence accumulation than for an account with low inherent risk.

Inherent risk also can be extended to individual balance-related audit objectives. For example, because of adverse economic conditions in the client's industry, the auditor may conclude that there is a high risk of uncollectible accounts receivable (realizable value objective). Inherent risk could still be low for all other objectives.

Assess Control Risk for the Sales and Collection Cycle Control risk is evaluated in the manner discussed in Chapter 9 and in earlier parts of this chapter. That methodology would be applied to both sales and cash receipts in the audit of accounts receivable. Effective controls reduce control risk and therefore the evidence required for substantive tests of transactions and tests of details of balances; inadequate controls increase the substantive evidence needed.

Design and Perform Tests of Controls and Substantive Tests of Transactions for the Sales and Collection Cycle The methodology for designing tests of controls and substantive tests of transactions was discussed earlier in this section and is illustrated in subsequent chapters. The tests are designed with the expectation that certain results will be obtained. These predicted results affect the design of tests of details of balances.

Design and Perform Analytical Procedures for Accounts Receivable Balance As discussed earlier, the auditor performs analytical procedures for an account such as accounts receivable for two purposes: (1) to identify possible misstatements in the account balance and (2) to reduce detailed audit tests. The results of analytical procedures directly affect the extent of tests of details of balances, as discussed in the following section.

Design Tests of Details of Accounts Receivable Balance to Satisfy Balance-Related Audit Objectives The planned tests of details of balances include audit procedures, sample size, items to select, and timing. Procedures must be selected and designed for each account and each balance-related audit objective within each account. The balance-related audit objectives for accounts receivable are shown on page 338.

A difficulty the auditor faces in designing tests of details of balances is the need to predict the outcome of the tests of controls, substantive tests of transactions, and analytical procedures before they are performed. This is necessary because the auditor should design tests of details of balances during the planning phase, but the appropriate design depends on the outcome of the other tests. In planning tests of details of balances, the auditor usually predicts that there will be few or no exceptions in tests of controls, substantive tests of transactions, and analytical procedures, unless there are reasons to believe otherwise. If the

FIGURE 10-7 Approach to Designing Tests of Details of Balances

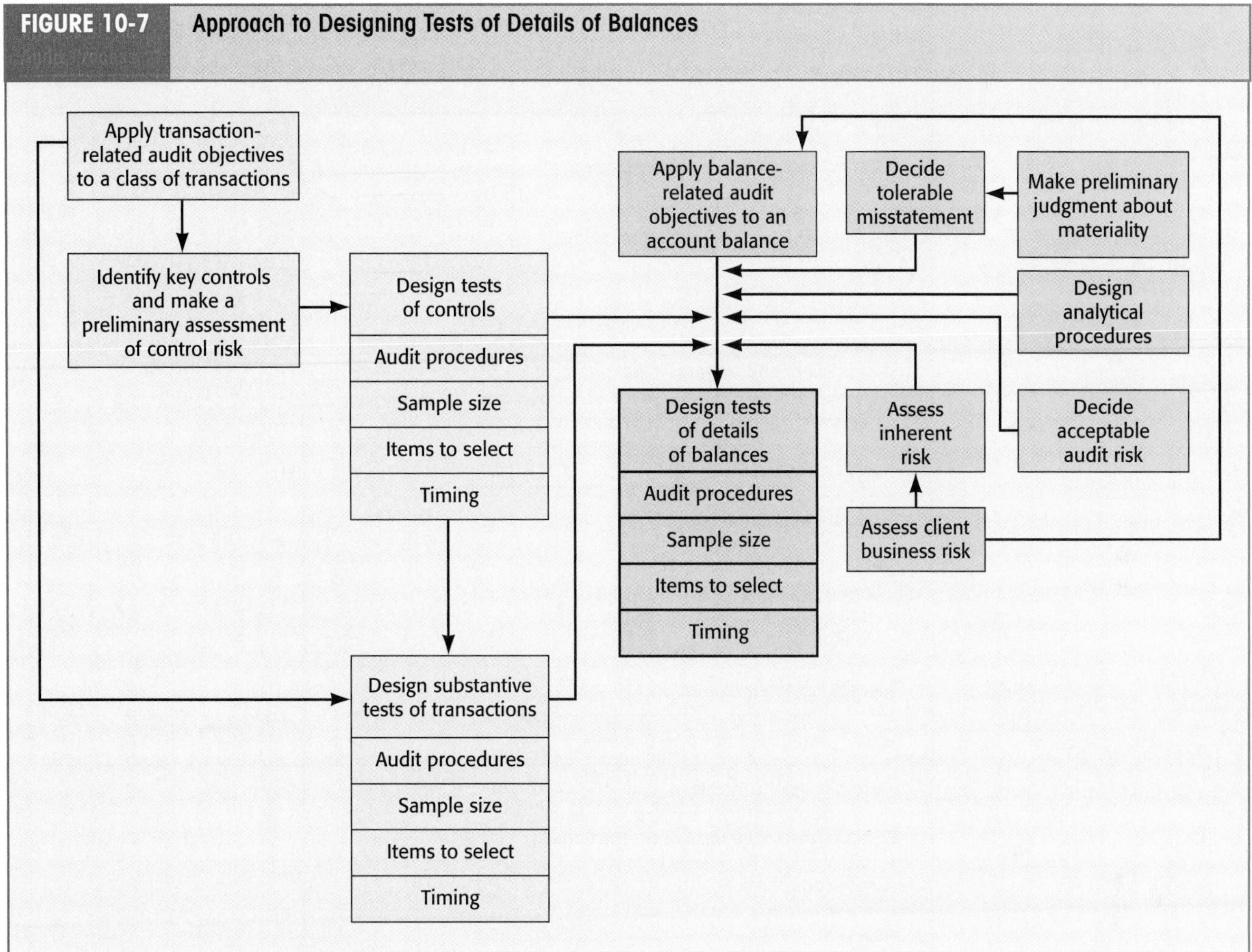

Apply transaction-related audit objectives to a class of transactions
Identify key controls and make a preliminary assessment of control risk
Design tests of controls
Audit procedures
Sample size
Items to select
Timing
Design substantive tests of transactions
Audit procedures
Sample size
Items to select
Timing
Apply balance-related audit objectives to an account balance
Decide tolerable misstatement
Make preliminary judgment about materiality
Design analytical procedures
Design tests of details of balances
Audit procedures
Sample size
Items to select
Timing
Assess inherent risk
Decide acceptable audit risk
Assess client business risk

results of the tests of controls, substantive tests of transactions, and analytical procedures are *not* consistent with the predictions, the tests of details of balances will need to be changed as the audit progresses.

The discussion about the approach to designing tests of details of balances applied to accounts receivable is summarized in Figure 10-7. The light shading on the left side of the figure is the design of tests of controls and substantive tests of transactions as presented in Figure 10-5. The figure shows that the tests of controls and substantive tests of transactions affect the design of the tests of details of balances. The darker shading on the right side of the figure shows the design of tests of details of balances and the factors affecting that decision.

One of the most difficult parts of auditing is properly applying the factors that affect tests of details of balances. Each of the factors is subjective, requiring considerable professional judgment. The impact of each factor on tests of details of balances is equally subjective. For example, if inherent risk is reduced from medium to low, there is agreement that tests of details of balances can be reduced. Deciding the specific effect on audit procedures, sample size, timing, and items to select is a difficult decision.

Level of Disaggregation of Planning Activities

The various planning activities discussed in Chapters 5 through 10 are applied at different levels of disaggregation, depending on the nature of the activity. Figure 10-8 (p. 292) shows the primary planning activities and the levels of disaggregation normally applied. These levels of disaggregation range from the overall audit to the balance-related audit objective for each account. For example, when the auditor obtains background information about the client's business and industry, it pertains to the overall audit. As the audit progresses, the information will first be used in assessing

FIGURE 10-8 **Disaggregation Level to Which Planning Activities Are Applied**

PLANNING ACTIVITY	LEVEL OF DISAGGREGATION				
	Overall Audit	Cycle	Account	Transaction-Related Audit Objective	Balance-Related Audit Objective
Accept client and perform initial planning.	P				
Understand client's business and industry.	P				
Assess client business risk.	P				
Understand internal control.					
Control environment	P				
Risk assessment		P			
Control activities		P			
Information and communication		P			
Monitoring		P			
Identify key internal controls.				P	
Identify internal control weaknesses.				P	
Design tests of controls.				P	
Design substantive tests of transactions.				P	
Assess control risk.				P	
Assess inherent risk.			P		P
Assess acceptable audit risk.	P				
Set preliminary judgment about materiality.	P				
Set tolerable misstatement.			P		
Design analytical procedures.			P		P
Design tests of details of balances.					P

P = Primary level to which planning activity is applied.

acceptable audit risk and assessing inherent risk and later is likely to affect tests of details of balances.

Illustrative Audit Program

SAS 77 (AU 311) requires the auditor to use a written audit program. Table 10-4 shows the tests of details of balances segment of an audit program for accounts receivable. The format used relates the audit procedures to the balance-related audit objectives. Notice that most procedures satisfy more than one objective. Also, more than one audit procedure is used for each objective. Audit procedures can be added or deleted as the auditor considers necessary. Sample size, items to select, and timing can also be changed for most procedures.

City of Tampa Internal Audit Programs

The audit program in Table 10-4 was developed after consideration of all the factors affecting tests of details of balances and is based on several assumptions about inherent risk, control risk, and the results of tests of controls, substantive tests of transactions, and analytical procedures. As indicated, if those assumptions are materially incorrect, the

TABLE 10-4 Tests of Details of Balances Audit Program for Accounts Receivable

Tests of Details of Balances Audit Procedures	Sample Size for Each Audit Procedure	Items to Select from the Population	Timing of the Test	Detail tie-in	Existence	Completeness	Accuracy	Classification	Cutoff	Realizable value	Rights	Presentation and disclosure
				Accounts Receivable Balance-Related Audit Objectives								
1. Obtain an aged list of receivables: trace accounts to the master file, foot schedule, and trace to general ledger.	Trace 20 items; foot 2 pages and all subtotals	Random	I	X								
2. Obtain an analysis of the allowance for doubtful accounts and bad debt expense: test accuracy, examine authorization for write-offs, and trace to general ledger.	All	All	Y	X	X	X	X			X		
3. Obtain direct confirmation of accounts receivable and perform alternative procedures for nonresponses.	50	10 largest 40 random	I		X		X	X	X		X	
4. Review accounts receivable control account for the period. Investigate the nature of and review support for any large or unusual entries or any entries not arising from normal journal sources. Also investigate any significant increases or decreases in sales toward year-end.	NA	NA	Y		X		X	X	X		X	X
5. Review receivables for any that have been assigned or discounted.	All	All	Y								X	X
6. Investigate collectibility of account balances.	NA	NA	Y							X		
7. Review lists of balances for amounts due from related parties or employees, credit balances, and unusual items, as well as notes receivable due after 1 year.	All	All	Y		X			X				X
8. Determine that proper cutoff procedures were applied at the balance sheet date to ensure that sales, cash receipts, and credit memos have been recorded in the correct period.	20 transactions for sales and cash receipts; 10 for credit memos	50% before and 50% after year-end	Y						X			

I = Interim; Y = Year-end; NA = Not applicable.

planned audit program will require revision. For example, analytical procedures could indicate potential misstatements for several balance-related audit objectives, tests of controls results could indicate weak internal controls, or new facts could cause the auditor to change inherent risk.

Audit programs are often computerized. The simplest form of this application is to type the audit program on a word processor and save it from one year to the next to facilitate changes and updating. A more sophisticated use is to have a special-use program that helps the auditor think through the planning considerations of the audit and select appropriate procedures from an audit procedures database. These are then formulated into an audit program.

Relationship of Transaction-Related Audit Objectives to Balance-Related Audit Objectives

OBJECTIVE 10-6

Compare and contrast transaction-related audit objectives and balance-related audit objectives.

It has already been shown that tests of details of balances must be designed to satisfy balance-related audit objectives for each account and the extent of these tests can be reduced when transaction-related audit objectives have been satisfied by tests of controls or substantive tests of transactions. Therefore, it is important to understand how each transaction-related audit objective relates to each balance-related audit objective. A general presentation of these relationships is shown in Table 10-5. The major implication of Table 10-5 is that even when all transaction-related audit objectives are met, the auditor will still rely primarily on substantive tests of balances to meet the following balance-related audit objectives: realizable value, rights and obligations, and presentation and disclosure. Some substantive tests of balances are also likely for the other balance-related audit objectives, depending on the results of the tests of controls and substantive tests of transactions.

TABLE 10-5 Relationship of Transaction-Related Audit Objectives to Balance-Related Audit Objectives

Transaction-Related Audit Objective	Balance-Related Audit Objective	Nature of Relationship	Explanation
Existence	Existence or completeness	Direct	There is a direct relationship of the existence transaction-related audit objective to the existence balance-related audit objective if a class of transactions increases the related account balance (e.g., sales transactions increase accounts receivable). There is a direct relationship of the existence transaction-related audit objective to the completeness balance-related audit objective if a class of transactions decreases the related account balance (e.g., cash receipts transactions decrease accounts receivable).
Completeness	Completeness or existence	Direct	See comments above for existence objective.
Accuracy	Accuracy	Direct	–
Classification	Classification	Direct	–
Timing	Cutoff	Direct	–
Posting and summarization	Detail tie-in	Direct	–
	Realizable value	None	Few internal controls over realizable value are related to classes of transactions, but the credit approval process affects the extent of tests.
	Rights and obligations	None	Few internal controls over rights and obligations are related to classes of transactions.
	Presentation and disclosure	None	Internal controls provide little assurance that proper presentations and disclosures will be made and there are no relevant substantive tests of transactions.

REVISING AUDIT PROGRAMS FOR GREATER EFFICIENCY

The audit program should be carefully reviewed during audit planning to determine whether any audit procedures should be increased or eliminated. Deborah Lambert, CPA, advises that risk assessments should affect audit procedures. Risk assessments should result in a reduction of testing in low-risk areas and greater focus on trouble spots.

Another CPA, Tony Lynn, finds that firms often overaudit and don't know why. Many times, he asks the purpose of an audit schedule. The auditor often responds, "I don't know, we've always done it that way." Lynn suggests, "If you can't say why you're doing something, you should get rid of it." Careful planning and review of the audit program can result in significant time savings.

Source: Adapted from an article by Anita Dennis, "Best Practices for Audit Efficiency," *Journal of Accountancy* (September 2000), pp. 65-68.

SUMMARY OF KEY EVIDENCE-RELATED TERMS

Several descriptions of evidence-related terms have been used in the past several chapters. It is essential to distinguish among these terms and understand the meaning of each. The following summarizes the terms. Table 10-6 shows the relationship among the terms.

Phases of the Audit Process The four aspects of a complete audit: (1) plan and design an audit approach, (2) perform tests of controls and substantive tests of transactions, (3) perform analytical procedures and tests of details of balances, and (4) complete the audit and issue an audit report.

TABLE 10-6 Relationship Among Five Key Evidence-Related Terms

Phases of the Audit Process	Audit Objectives	Types of Tests	Evidence Decisions	Types of Evidence
Plan and Design an Audit Approach		Analytical procedures	• Audit procedures • Timing	Documentation Inquiries of client Analytical procedures
Perform Tests of Controls and Substantive Tests of Transactions	Transaction-related audit objectives • Existence • Completeness • Accuracy • Classification • Timing • Posting and summarization	Procedures to obtain an understanding and tests of controls Substantive tests of transactions	• Audit procedures • Sample size • Items to select • Timing • Audit procedures • Sample size • Items to select • Timing	Documentation Observation Inquiries of client Reperformance
Perform Analytical Procedures and Tests of Details of Balances	Balance-related audit objectives • Existence • Completeness • Accuracy • Classification • Cutoff • Detail tie-in • Realizable value • Rights and obligations • Presentation and disclosure	Analytical procedures Tests of details of balances	• Audit procedures • Timing • Audit procedures • Sample size • Items to select • Timing	Physical examination Confirmation Documentation Inquiries of client Reperformance Analytical procedures
Complete the Audit and Issue an Audit Report		Analytical procedures Tests of details of balances	• Audit procedures • Timing • Audit procedures • Sample size • Items to select • Timing	Analytical procedures Documentation Inquiries of client

Audit Objectives The objectives on an audit that must be met before the auditor can conclude that any given class of transactions or account balance is fairly stated. There are six transaction-related and nine balance-related audit objectives.

Types of Tests The five categories of audit tests auditors use to determine whether financial statements are fairly stated: procedures to obtain an understanding of internal control, tests of controls, substantive tests of transactions, analytical procedures, and tests of details of balances.

Evidence Decisions The four subcategories of decisions the auditor makes in accumulating audit evidence: audit procedures, sample size, items to select, and timing of performance.

Types of Evidence The seven broad categories of evidence auditors use: physical examination, confirmation, documentation, analytical procedures, observation, inquiry of the client, and reperformance.

SUMMARY OF THE AUDIT PROCESS

OBJECTIVE 10-7

Integrate the four phases of the audit process.

The four **phases of the audit process** were introduced at the end of Chapter 5. Considerable portions of Chapters 6 through 10 have discussed the seven steps in phase I. Figure 10-9 shows the four phases for the entire audit process. Table 10-7 (p. 298) shows the timing of the tests in each phase for an audit with a December 31 balance sheet date.

Phase I: Plan and Design an Audit Approach

Chapters 6 through 10 have emphasized various aspects of planning the audit. At the end of phase I, the auditor should have a well-defined audit plan and a specific audit program for the entire audit.

Information obtained during client acceptance and initial planning, understanding the client's business and industry, assessing the client's business risks, and performing preliminary analytical procedures (first four boxes in Figure 10-9) is used primarily to assess inherent risk and acceptable audit risk. Assessments of materiality, acceptable audit risk, inherent risk, and control risk are used to develop an overall audit plan and audit program.

Phase II: Perform Tests of Controls and Substantive Tests of Transactions

Performance of the tests of controls and substantive tests of transactions occurs during this phase. The objectives of phase II are to (1) obtain evidence in support of the specific controls that contribute to the auditor's assessed control risk (that is, where it is reduced below the maximum) and (2) obtain evidence in support of the monetary correctness of transactions. The former objective is met by performing tests of controls, and the latter by performing substantive tests of transactions. Many of both types of tests are conducted simultaneously on the same transactions. When controls are not considered effective or when control deviations are discovered, substantive tests can be expanded in this phase or in phase III.

Because the results of tests of controls and substantive tests of transactions are a major determinant of the extent of tests of details of balances, the tests are often performed 2 or 3 months before the balance sheet date. This helps the auditor plan for contingencies, revise the audit program for unexpected results, and complete the audit as soon as possible after the balance sheet date.

For computerized accounting systems, auditors often perform tests of controls and substantive tests of transactions throughout the year to identify significant or unusual transactions and determine whether any changes have been made to the computer programs. This approach is often called continuous auditing.

Phase III: Perform Analytical Procedures and Tests of Details of Balances

The objective of phase III is to obtain sufficient additional evidence to determine whether the ending balances and footnotes in financial statements are fairly stated. The nature and extent of the work will depend heavily on the findings of the two previous phases.

There are two general categories of phase III procedures: analytical procedures and tests of details of balances. Analytical procedures are those that assess the overall reasonableness of transactions and balances. Tests of details of balances are specific procedures intended to test for monetary misstatements in the balances in the financial statements. Certain key transactions and amounts are so important that each one must be audited. Other items can be sampled.

FIGURE 10-9 Summary of the Audit Process

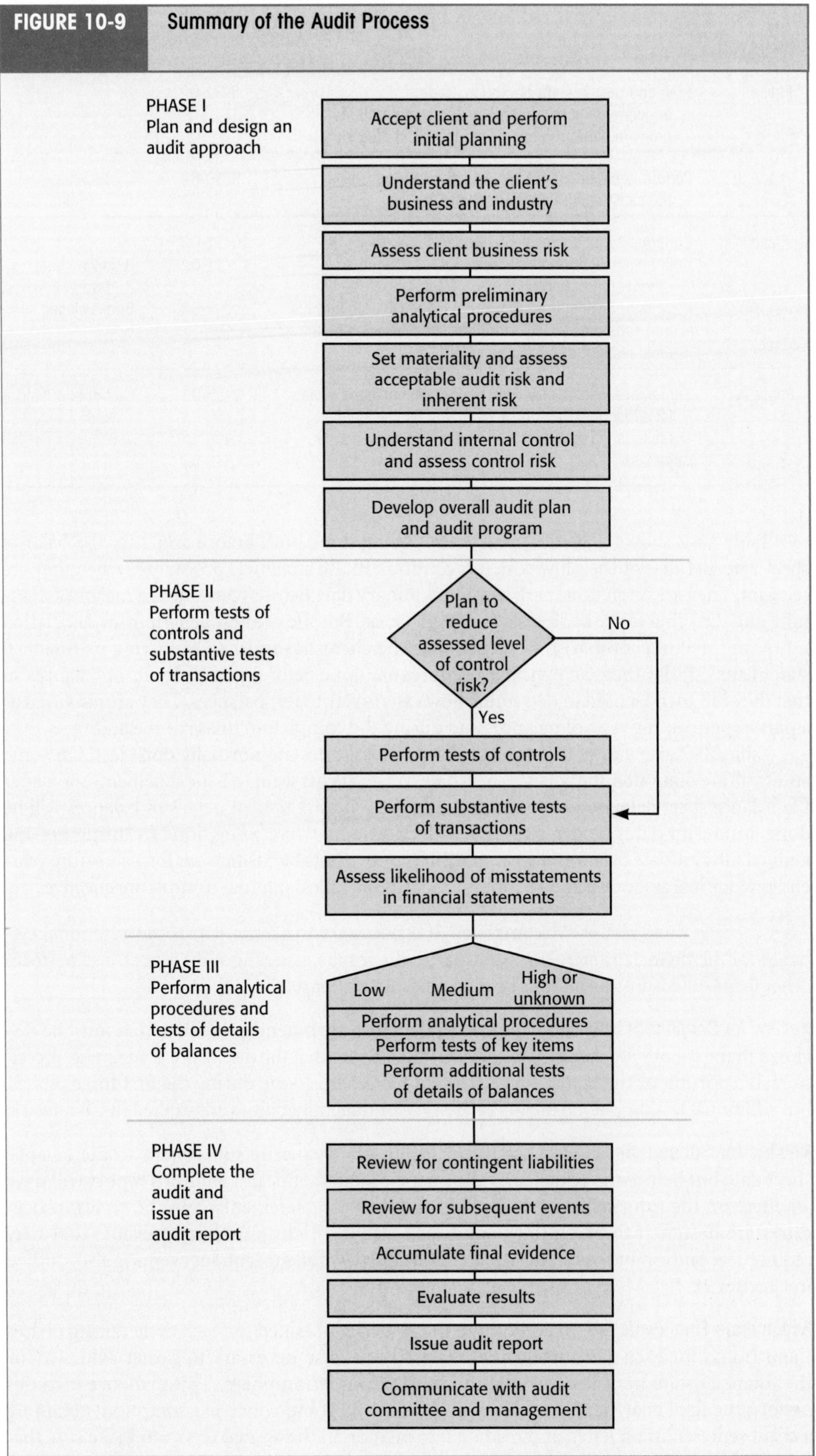
PHASE I
Plan and design an audit approach
Accept client and perform initial planning
Understand the client's business and industry
Assess client business risk
Perform preliminary analytical procedures
Set materiality and assess acceptable audit risk and inherent risk
Understand internal control and assess control risk
Develop overall audit plan and audit program
PHASE II
Perform tests of controls and substantive tests of transactions
Plan to reduce assessed level of control risk?
No
Yes
Perform tests of controls
Perform substantive tests of transactions
Assess likelihood of misstatements in financial statements
PHASE III
Perform analytical procedures and tests of details of balances
Low
Medium
High or unknown
Perform analytical procedures
Perform tests of key items
Perform additional tests of details of balances
PHASE IV
Complete the audit and issue an audit report
Review for contingent liabilities
Review for subsequent events
Accumulate final evidence
Evaluate results
Issue audit report
Communicate with audit committee and management

TABLE 10-7 Timing of Tests

Phase I	Plan and design audit approach. Update understanding of internal control. Update audit program. Perform preliminary analytical procedures.	8-31-02	
Phase II	Perform tests of controls and substantive tests of transactions for first 9 months of the year.	9-30-02	
Phase III	Confirm accounts receivable. Observe inventory.	10-31-02	
	Count cash. Perform cutoff tests. Request various other confirmations.	12-31-02	Balance sheet date
	Perform analytical procedures, complete tests of controls and substantive tests of transactions, and complete most tests of details of balances.	1-7-03	Books closed
Phase IV	Summarize results, review for contingent liabilities, review for subsequent events, accumulate final evidence (including analytical procedures), and finalize audit.	2-15-03	Last date of field work
	Issue audit report.	3-1-03	

Table 10-7 shows analytical procedures being done both before and after the balance sheet date. Because of their low cost, it is common to use analytical procedures when they are relevant. They are often done early with preliminary data before year-end as a means of planning and directing other audit tests to specific areas. But the greatest benefit from calculating ratios and making comparisons occurs after the client has finished preparing its financial statements. Ideally, these analytical procedures are done before tests of details of balances so that they can then be used to determine how extensively to test balances. They are also used as a part of performing tests of balances and during the completion phase of the audit.

Table 10-7 also shows that tests of details of balances are normally done last. On some audits, all are done after the balance sheet date. When clients want to issue statements soon after the balance sheet date, however, the more time-consuming tests of details of balances will be done at interim dates before year-end with additional work being done to "bring up" the audited interim-date balances to year-end. Substantive tests of balances performed before year-end provide less assurance and are not normally done unless internal controls are effective.

Phase IV: Complete the Audit and Issue an Audit Report

After the first three phases are completed, it is necessary to accumulate some additional evidence for the financial statements, summarize the results, issue the audit report, and perform other forms of communication. This phase has several parts.

Review for Contingent Liabilities Contingent liabilities are potential liabilities that must be disclosed in the client's footnotes. Auditors must make sure that the disclosure is adequate. A considerable portion of the search for contingent liabilities is done during the first three phases, but additional testing is done during phase IV. Contingent liabilities are studied in Chapter 18.

Review for Subsequent Events Occasionally, events occurring subsequent to the balance sheet date but before the issuance of the financial statements and auditor's report will have an effect on the information presented in the financial statements. Specific review procedures are designed to bring to the auditor's attention any subsequent events that may require recognition in the financial statements. Review for subsequent events is also studied in Chapter 18.

Accumulate Final Evidence In addition to the evidence obtained for each cycle during phases I and II and for each account during phase III, it is also necessary to gather evidence for the financial statements as a whole during the completion phase. This evidence includes performing final analytical procedures, evaluating the going-concern assumption, obtaining a client representation letter, and reading information in the annual report to make sure that it is consistent with the financial statements.

Issue Audit Report The type of audit report issued depends on the evidence accumulated and the audit findings. The appropriate reports for differing circumstances were studied in Chapter 2.

Communicate with Audit Committee and Management The auditor is required to communicate reportable conditions to the audit committee or senior management. The SASs also require the auditor to communicate certain other matters to the audit committee or a similarly designated body upon completion of the audit or sooner. Although not required, auditors often also make suggestions to management to improve business performance.

ESSENTIAL TERMS

Analytical procedures—use of comparisons and relationships to assess whether account balances or other data appear reasonable

Evidence mix—the combination of the five types of tests to obtain sufficient competent evidence for a cycle; there are likely to be variations in the mix from cycle to cycle depending on the circumstances of the audit

Phases of the audit process—the four aspects of a complete audit: (1) plan and design an audit approach, (2) perform tests of controls and substantive tests of transactions, (3) perform analytical procedures and tests of details of balances, and (4) complete the audit and issue the audit report

Procedures to obtain an understanding of internal control—procedures used by the auditor to gather evidence about the design and placement in operation of specific controls

Substantive tests—audit procedures designed to test for dollar (monetary) misstatements of financial statement balances

Substantive tests of transactions—audit procedures testing for monetary misstatements to determine whether the six transaction-related audit objectives have been satisfied for each class of transactions

Tests of controls—audit procedures to test the effectiveness of controls in support of a reduced assessed control risk

Tests of details of balances—audit procedures testing for monetary misstatements to determine whether the nine balance-related audit objectives have been satisfied for each significant account balance

Types of tests—the five categories of audit tests auditors use to determine whether financial statements are fairly stated: procedures to obtain an understanding of internal control, tests of controls, substantive tests of transactions, analytical procedures, and tests of details of balances

REVIEW QUESTIONS

10-1 (Objective 10-1) What are the five types of tests auditors use to determine whether financial statements are fairly stated? Identify which tests are performed to reduce control risk and which tests are performed to reduce planned detection risk.

10-2 (Objective 10-1) What is the purpose of tests of controls? Identify specific accounts on the financial statements that are affected by performing tests of controls for the acquisition and payment cycle.

10-3 (Objective 10-1) Distinguish between a test of control and a substantive test of transactions. Give two examples of each.

10-4 (Objectives 10-1, 10-4) State a test of control audit procedure to test the effectiveness of the following control: Approved wage rates are used in calculating employees' earnings. State a substantive test of transactions audit procedure to determine whether approved wage rates are actually used in calculating employees' earnings.

10-5 (Objective 10-1) A considerable portion of the tests of controls and substantive tests of transactions are performed simultaneously as a matter of audit convenience. But the substantive tests of transactions procedures and sample size, in part, depend on the results of the tests of controls. How can the auditor resolve this apparent inconsistency?

10-6 (Objectives 10-2, 10-4) Evaluate the following statement: "Tests of sales and cash receipts transactions are such an essential part of every audit that I like to perform them as near the end of the audit as possible. By that time I have a fairly good understanding of the client's business and its internal controls because confirmations, cutoff tests, and other procedures have already been completed."

10-7 (Objectives 10-1, 10-2) Explain how the calculation and comparison to previous years of the gross margin percentage and the ratio of accounts receivable to sales are related to the confirmation of accounts receivable and other tests of the accuracy of accounts receivable.

10-8 (Objective 10-1) Distinguish between substantive tests of transactions and tests of details of balances. Give one example of each for the acquisition and payment cycle.

10-9 (Objective 10-3) The auditor of Ferguson's Inc. identified two internal controls in the sales and collection receipts cycle for testing. In the first control, the computer verifies that a planned sale on account will not exceed the customer's credit limit entered in the accounts receivable master file. In the second control, the accounts receivable clerk matches bills of lading, sales invoices, and customer orders before recording in the sales journal. Describe how the presence of general controls over software programs and master file changes affects the extent of audit testing of each of these two internal controls.

10-10 (Objective 10-4) Assume that the client's internal controls over the recording and classifying of fixed asset additions are considered weak because the individual responsible for recording new acquisitions has inadequate technical training and limited experience in accounting. How would this situation affect the evidence you should accumulate in auditing fixed assets as compared with another audit in which the controls are excellent? Be as specific as possible.

10-11 (Objective 10-2) For each of the seven types of evidence discussed in Chapter 6, identify whether it is applicable for procedures to obtain an understanding of internal control, tests of controls, substantive tests of transactions, analytical procedures, and tests of details of balances.

10-12 (Objective 10-2) Rank the following types of tests from most costly to least costly: analytical procedures, tests of details of balances, procedures to obtain an understanding of internal control and tests of controls, and substantive tests of transactions.

10-13 (Objective 10-2) In Figure 10-3, explain the difference among C_1, C_2, and C_3. Explain the circumstances under which it would be a good decision to obtain audit assurance from substantive tests at point C_1. Do the same for points C_2 and C_3.

10-14 (Objective 10-2) The following are three decision factors related to assessed control risk: effectiveness of internal controls, cost-effectiveness of a reduced assessed control risk, and results of tests of controls. Identify the combination of conditions for these three factors that is required before reduced substantive testing is permitted.

10-15 (Objective 10-4) Table 10-3 illustrates variations in the emphasis on different types of audit tests. What are the benefits to the auditor of identifying the best mix of tests?

10-16 (Objective 10-5) State the four-step approach to designing tests of controls and substantive tests of transactions.

10-17 (Objective 10-5) Explain the relationship between the methodology for designing tests of controls and substantive tests of transactions in Figure 10-4 to the methodology for designing tests of details of balances in Figure 10-6.

10-18 (Objective 10-5) Why is it desirable to design tests of details of balances before performing tests of controls and substantive tests of transactions? State the assumptions that the auditor must make in doing that. What does the auditor do if the assumptions are wrong?

10-19 (Objective 10-5) Explain the relationship of tolerable misstatement, inherent risk, and control risk to planned tests of details of balances.

10-20 (Objective 10-5) List the nine balance-related audit objectives in the verification of the ending balance in inventory and provide one useful audit procedure for each of the objectives.

10-21 (Objective 10-7) Why do auditors often consider it desirable to perform audit tests throughout the year rather than wait until year-end? List several examples of evidence that can be accumulated before year-end.

MULTIPLE CHOICE QUESTIONS FROM CPA EXAMINATIONS

10-22 (Objective 10-1) The following questions concern types of audit tests. Choose the best response.

a. The auditor looks for an indication on duplicate sales invoices to see whether the invoices have been verified. This is an example of
   (1) a test of details of balances.
   (2) a test of control.
   (3) a substantive test of transactions.
   (4) both a test of control and a substantive test of transactions.

b. Analytical procedures may be classified as being primarily
   (1) tests of controls.
   (2) substantive tests.
   (3) tests of ratios.
   (4) tests of details of balances.

c. To support the auditor's initial assessment of control risk below maximum, the auditor performs procedures to determine that internal controls are operating effectively. Which of the following audit procedures is the auditor performing?
   (1) Tests of details of balances
   (2) Substantive tests of transactions
   (3) Tests of controls
   (4) Tests of trends and ratios

d. The auditor faces a risk that the audit will not detect material misstatements that occur in the accounting process. To minimize this risk, the auditor relies primarily on
   (1) substantive tests.
   (2) tests of controls.
   (3) internal control.
   (4) statistical analysis.

10-23 (Objectives 10-5, 10-7) The following questions concern the sequence and timing of audit tests. Choose the best response.

a. A conceptually logical approach to the auditor's evaluation of internal control consists of the following four steps:
   I. Determining the internal controls that should prevent or detect errors and fraud
   II. Identifying weaknesses to determine their effect on the nature, timing, or extent of auditing procedures to be applied and suggestions to be made to the client
   III. Determining whether the necessary procedures are prescribed and are being followed satisfactorily
   IV. Considering the types of errors and fraud that could occur

   What should be the order in which these four steps are performed?
   (1) I, II, III, and IV
   (2) I, III, IV, and II
   (3) III, IV, I, and II
   (4) IV, I, III, and II

b. The sequence of steps in gathering evidence as the basis of the auditor's opinion is
   (1) substantive tests, initial assessment of control risk, and tests of controls.
   (2) initial assessment of control risk, substantive tests, and tests of controls.
   (3) initial assessment of control risk, tests of controls, and substantive tests.
   (4) tests of controls, initial assessment of control risk, and substantive tests.

DISCUSSION QUESTIONS AND PROBLEMS

10-24 (Objectives 10-1, 10-2) The following are 11 audit procedures taken from an audit program:

1. Foot the accounts payable trial balance and compare the total with the general ledger.
2. Examine vendors' invoices to verify the ending balance in accounts payable.
3. Compare the balance in payroll tax expense with previous years. The comparison takes the increase in payroll tax rates into account.
4. Discuss the duties of the cash disbursements clerk with him and observe whether he has responsibility for handling cash or preparing the bank reconciliation.
5. Confirm accounts payable balances directly with vendors.
6. Account for a sequence of checks in the cash disbursements journal to determine whether any have been omitted.
7. Examine the internal auditor's initials on monthly bank reconciliations as an indication of whether they have been reviewed.
8. Examine vendors' invoices and other documentation in support of recorded transactions in the acquisitions journal.
9. Multiply the commission rate by total sales and compare the result with commission expense.
10. Examine vendors' invoices and other supporting documents to determine whether large amounts in the repair and maintenance account should be capitalized.

11. Inquire about the accounts payable supervisor's monthly review of a computer-generated exception report of receiving reports and purchase orders that have not been matched with a vendor invoice.

Required

a. Indicate whether each procedure is a test of control, substantive test of transactions, analytical procedure, or a test of details of balances.

b. Identify the type of evidence for each procedure.

10-25 (Objectives 10-1, 10-2, 10-3, 10-6) The following are audit procedures from different transaction cycles:

1. Use audit software to foot and cross-foot the cash disbursements journal and trace the balance to the general ledger.
2. Select a sample of entries in the acquisitions journal and trace each one to a related vendor's invoice to determine whether one exists.
3. Compute inventory turnover for each major product and compare with previous years.
4. Confirm a sample of notes payable balances, interest rates, and collateral with lenders.
5. Use audit software to foot the accounts payable trial balance and compare the balance with the general ledger.
6. Examine documentation for acquisition transactions before and after the balance sheet date to determine whether they are recorded in the proper period.
7. Inquire of the credit manager whether each account receivable on the aged trial balance is collectible.

Required

a. For each audit procedure, identify the transaction cycle being audited.

b. For each audit procedure, identify the type of evidence.

c. For each audit procedure, identify whether it is a test of control or a substantive test.

d. For each substantive audit procedure, identify whether it is a substantive test of transactions, a test of details of balances, or an analytical procedure.

e. For each test of control or substantive test of transactions procedure, identify the transaction-related audit objective or objectives being satisfied.

f. For each analytical procedure or test of details of balances procedure, identify the balance-related audit objective or objectives being satisfied.

10-26 (Objective 10-1) For each of the following controls, identify whether the control leaves a paper audit trail. Also identify a test of control audit procedure the auditor can use to test the effectiveness of the control.

a. An accounting clerk accounts for all shipping documents on a monthly basis and initials the monthly shipping log.

b. Bank reconciliations are prepared by the controller, who does not have access to cash receipts.

c. As employees check in daily by using time clocks, a supervisor observes to make certain that no individual "punches in" more than one time card.

d. Vendors' invoices are approved by the controller after she examines the purchase order and receiving report attached to each invoice.

e. The cashier, who has no access to accounting records, prepares the deposit slip and delivers the deposit directly to the bank daily.

f. An accounting clerk verifies the price, extensions, and footings of all sales invoices in excess of $300 and initials the duplicate sales invoice when he has completed the procedure.

g. All mail is opened and cash is prelisted daily by the president's secretary, who has no other responsibility for handling assets or recording accounting data.

10-27 (Objectives 10-1, 10-5, 10-6) The following are independent internal controls commonly found in the acquisition and payment cycle. Each control is to be considered independently.

1. At the end of each month, an accounting clerk accounts for all prenumbered receiving reports (documents evidencing the receipt of goods) issued during the month, and he traces each one to the related vendor's invoice and acquisitions journal entry. The clerk's tests do not include testing quantity or description of the merchandise received.
2. The cash disbursements clerk is prohibited from handling cash. The bank account is reconciled by another person even though the clerk has sufficient expertise and time to do it.
3. Before a check is prepared to pay for acquisitions by the accounts payable department, the related purchase order and receiving report are attached to the vendor's invoice being paid. A clerk compares the quantity on the invoice with the receiving report and purchase order, compares the price with the purchase order, recomputes the extensions, re-adds the total, and exam-

ines the account number indicated on the invoice to determine whether it is properly classified. He indicates his performance of these procedures by initialing the invoice.

4. Before a check is signed by the controller, she examines the supporting documentation accompanying the check. At that time, she initials each vendor's invoice to indicate her approval.
5. After the controller signs the checks, her secretary writes the check number and the date the check was issued on each of the supporting documents to prevent their reuse.

Required

a. For each of the internal controls, state the transaction-related audit objective(s) the control is meant to fulfill.

b. For each control, list one test of control the auditor could perform to test the effectiveness of the control.

c. For each control, list one substantive test the auditor could perform to determine whether financial misstatements are actually taking place.

10-28 (Objectives 10-1, 10-5, 10-6) The following internal controls for the acquisition and payment cycle were selected from a standard internal control questionnaire.

1. Vendors' invoices are recalculated before payment.
2. Approved price lists are used for acquisitions.
3. Prenumbered receiving reports are prepared as support for acquisitions and numerically accounted for.
4. Dates on receiving reports are compared with vendors' invoices before entry into the acquisitions journal.
5. The accounts payable master file is updated, balanced, and reconciled to the general ledger monthly.
6. Account classifications are reviewed by someone other than the preparer.
7. All checks are signed by the owner or manager.
8. The check signer compares data on supporting documents with checks.
9. All supporting documents are cancelled after the checks are signed.
10. Checks are mailed by the owner or manager or a person under her supervision after signing.

Required

a. For each control, identify which element of the five categories of control activities is applicable (separation of duties, proper authorization, adequate documents or records, physical control over assets and records, or independent checks on performance).

b. For each control, state which transaction-related audit objective(s) is (are) applicable.

c. For each control, write an audit procedure that could be used to test the control for effectiveness.

d. For each control, identify a likely misstatement, assuming that the control does not exist or is not functioning.

e. For each likely misstatement, identify a substantive audit procedure to determine whether the misstatement exists.

10-29 (Objective 10-3) Beds and Spreads, Inc. specializes in bed and bath furnishings. Its inventory system is linked through the Internet to key suppliers. The auditor identified the following internal controls in the inventory cycle:

1. The computer initiates an order only when perpetual inventory levels fall below prespecified inventory levels in the inventory master file.
2. The sales and purchasing department managers review inventory reorder points on a monthly basis for reasonableness. Approved changes to reorder points are entered into the master file by the purchasing department manager and an updated printout is generated for final review. Both managers verify that all changes were entered correctly and initial the final printout indicating final approval. These printouts are maintained in the purchasing department.
3. The computer will initiate a purchase order only for inventory product numbers maintained in the inventory master file.
4. The purchasing department manager reviews a computer-generated exception report that highlights weekly purchases that exceed $10,000 per vendor.
5. Salesclerks send damaged merchandise on the store shelves to the back storage room. The sales department manager examines the damaged merchandise each month and prepares a listing showing the estimated salvage value by product number. The accounting department uses the listing to prepare a monthly adjustment to recorded inventory values.

Required

a. Consider each of the preceding controls separately. Identify whether the control is a(n)
   (1) automated control embedded in computer software.
   (2) manual control whose effectiveness is based significantly on IT-generated information.
   (3) manual control whose effectiveness is not significantly reliant on IT-generated information.

b. Describe how the extent of testing of each control would be affected in subsequent years if general controls are effective, particularly controls over program and master file changes.

10-30 (Objectives 10-5, 10-7) Jennifer Schaefer, CPA, follows the philosophy of performing interim tests of controls and substantive tests of transactions on every December 31 audit as a means of keeping overtime to a minimum. Typically, the interim tests are performed some time between August and November.

Required

a. Evaluate her decision to perform interim tests of controls and substantive tests of transactions.

b. Under what circumstances is it acceptable for her to perform no additional tests of controls and substantive tests of transactions work as a part of the year-end audit tests?

c. If she decides to perform no additional testing, what is the effect on other tests she performs during the remainder of the engagement?

10-31 (Objectives 10-4, 10-5) Following are several decisions that the auditor must make in an audit. Letters indicate alternative conclusions that could be made.

Decisions	Alternative Conclusions
1. Determine whether it is cost effective to perform tests of controls.	A. It is cost effective B. It is not cost effective
2. Perform substantive tests of details of balances.	C. Perform reduced tests D. Perform expanded tests
3. Complete initial assessment of control risk.	E. Controls are effective F. Controls are ineffective
4. Perform tests of controls.	G. Controls are effective H. Controls are ineffective

Required

a. Identify the sequence in which the auditor should make decisions 1 to 4.

b. For the audit of the sales and collection cycle and accounts receivable, an auditor reached the following conclusions: A, D, E, H. Put the letters in the appropriate sequence and evaluate whether the auditor's logic was reasonable. Explain your answer.

c. For the audit of inventory and related inventory cost records, an auditor reached the following conclusions: B, C, E, G. Put the letters in the appropriate sequence and evaluate whether the auditor used good professional judgment. Explain your answer.

d. For the audit of property, plant, and equipment and related acquisition records, an auditor reached the following conclusions; A, C, F, G. Put the letters in the appropriate sequence and evaluate whether the auditor used good professional judgment. Explain your answer.

e. For the audit of payroll expenses and related liabilities, an auditor recorded the following conclusions: D, F. Put the letters in the appropriate sequence and evaluate whether the auditor used good professional judgment. Explain your answer.

10-32 (Objective 10-4) The following are three situations in which the auditor is required to develop an audit strategy:

1. The client has inventory at approximately 50 locations in a three-state region. The inventory is difficult to count and can be observed only by traveling by automobile. The internal controls over acquisitions, cash disbursements, and perpetual records are considered effective. This is the fifth year that you have done the audit, and audit results in past years have always been excellent. The client is in excellent financial condition and is privately held.
2. This is the first year of an audit of a medium-sized company that is considering selling its business because of severe underfinancing. A review of the acquisition and payment cycle indicates that controls over cash disbursements are excellent but controls over acquisitions cannot be considered effective. The client lacks receiving reports and a policy as to the proper timing to record acquisitions. When you review the general ledger, you observe that there are many large adjusting entries to correct accounts payable.
3. You are doing the audit of a small loan company with extensive receivables from customers. Controls over granting loans, collections, and loans outstanding are considered effective, and there is extensive follow-up of all outstanding loans weekly. You have recommended a computer system for the past 2 years, but management believes the cost is too great, given their low profitability. Collections are an ongoing problem because many of the customers have severe financial problems. Because of adverse economic conditions, loans receivable have significantly increased and collections are less than normal. In previous years, you have had relatively few adjusting entries.

a. For audit 1, recommend an evidence mix for the five types of tests for the audit of inventory and cost of goods sold. Justify your answer. Include in your recommendations both tests of controls and substantive tests. **Required**

b. For audit 2, recommend an evidence mix for the audit of the acquisition and payment cycle, including accounts payable. Justify your answer.

c. For audit 3, recommend an evidence mix for the audit of outstanding loans. Justify your answer.

10-33 (Objectives 10-1, 10-5) Brad Jackson was assigned to the audit of a client that had not been audited by any CPA firm in the preceding year. In conducting the audit, he did no testing of the beginning balance of accounts receivable, inventory, or accounts payable on the grounds that the audit report is being limited to the ending balance sheet, the income statement, and the statement of cash flows. No comparative financial statements are to be issued.

a. Explain the error in Jackson's reasoning. **Required**

b. Suggest an approach that Jackson can follow in verifying the beginning balance in accounts receivable.

c. Why does the same problem not exist in the verification of beginning balances on continuing audit engagements?

10-34 (Objective 10-4) Kim Bryan, a new staff auditor, is confused by the inconsistency of the three audit partners she has been assigned to on her first three audit engagements. On the first engagement, she spent a considerable amount of time in the audit of cash disbursements by examining cancelled checks and supporting documentation, but almost no testing was spent in the verification of fixed assets. On the second engagement, a different partner had her do less intensive tests in the cash disbursements area and take smaller sample sizes than in the first audit, even though the company was much larger. On her most recent engagement under a third audit partner, there was a thorough test of cash disbursement transactions, far beyond that of the other two audits, and an extensive verification of fixed assets. In fact, this partner insisted on a complete physical examination of all fixed assets recorded on the books. The total audit time on the most recent audit was longer than that of either of the first two audits despite the smaller size of the company. Bryan's conclusion is that the amount of evidence to accumulate depends on the audit partner in charge of the engagement.

a. State several factors that could explain the difference in the amount of evidence accumulated in each of the three audit engagements as well as the total time spent. **Required**

b. What could the audit partners have done to help Bryan understand the difference in the audit emphasis on the three audits?

c. Explain how these three audits are useful in developing Bryan's professional judgment. How could the quality of her judgment have been improved on the audits?

10-35 (Objectives 10-5, 10-7) The following are parts of a typical audit for a company with a fiscal year-end of July 31.

1. Confirm accounts payable.
2. Do tests of controls and substantive tests of transactions for the acquisition and payment and payroll and personnel cycles.
3. Do other tests of details of balances for accounts payable.
4. Do tests for review of subsequent events.
5. Accept the client.
6. Issue the audit report.
7. Understand internal control and assess control risk.
8. Do analytical procedures for accounts payable.
9. Set acceptable audit risk and decide preliminary judgment about materiality and tolerable misstatement.

a. Put parts 1 through 9 of the audit in the sequential order in which you would expect them to be performed in a typical audit. **Required**

b. Identify those parts that would frequently be done before July 31.

INTERNET PROBLEM 10-1: ASSESSING EFFECTS OF EVIDENCE MIX

Reference the CW site. Auditors develop overall audit plans to ensure that they obtain "sufficient competent evidential matter." This problem requires students to visit company Web sites and assess how the date of the completion of field work and company characteristics might affect the timing and mix of evidence procedures.

PART 3 CHAPTERS 11-13

APPLICATION OF THE AUDIT PROCESS TO THE SALES AND COLLECTION CYCLE

To understand how auditing is done in practice, it is important to understand how auditing concepts are applied to specific auditing areas. The sales and collection cycle is the first area we look at for a detailed application of auditing concepts because this cycle is an important part of every audit and because it is reasonably straightforward. These three chapters apply the concepts you learned in Part 2 to the audit of sales, cash receipts, and the related income statement and balance sheet accounts in the cycle.

The objective of Chapter 11 is to help you learn the methodology for designing tests of controls and substantive tests of transactions audit procedures for sales, cash receipts, and the other classes of transactions in the sales and collection cycle. Chapter 12 presents the methodology for designing audit procedures for the audit of account balances in the sales and collection cycle. Chapter 13 deals with nonstatistical sampling methods for tests of controls, substantive tests of transactions, and tests of details of balances.

CHAPTER 11

AUDIT OF THE SALES AND COLLECTION CYCLE: TESTS OF CONTROLS AND SUBSTANTIVE TESTS OF TRANSACTIONS

LEARNING OBJECTIVES

After studying this chapter, you should be able to

- 11-1 Identify the accounts and the classes of transactions in the sales and collection cycle.
- 11-2 Identify the business functions and the related documents and records in the sales and collection cycle.
- 11-3 Understand how e-commerce activities affect the sales and collection cycle.
- 11-4 Understand internal control, and design and perform tests of controls and substantive tests of transactions for sales.
- 11-5 Apply the methodology for controls over sales transactions to controls over sales returns and allowances.
- 11-6 Understand internal control, and design and perform tests of controls and substantive tests of transactions for cash receipts.
- 11-7 Apply the methodology for controls over the sales and collection cycle to write-offs of uncollectible accounts receivable.

THE CHOICE IS SIMPLE—RELY ON INTERNAL CONTROL OR RESIGN

City Finance is the largest client managed out of the Pittsburgh office of a Big Five firm. It is a financial services conglomerate with almost 1,000 offices in the United States and Canada, as well as correspondent offices overseas. The company's records contain more than a million accounts receivable and it processes millions of sales and other transactions annually.

The company's computer center is in a large, environmentally controlled room that contains several large mainframe computers and a great deal of ancillary equipment. There are two complete online systems, one serving as a backup for the other, as systems failure would preclude operations in all of the company's branches.

The company has an unusual system of checks and balances in which branch office transaction records are reconciled to data processing controls daily, which, in turn, are reconciled to outside bank account records monthly. Whenever this reconciliation process indicates a significant out-of-balance condition, procedures are initiated to resolve the problem as quickly as possible. A large internal audit staff oversees any special investigative efforts that are required.

Because City Finance is a public company, it must file its report on Form 10-K with the Securities and Exchange Commission within 90 days after its fiscal year-end. In addition, the company likes to announce annual earnings and issue its annual report as soon after year-end as reasonably feasible. Under these circumstances, there is always a great deal of pressure on the CPA firm to complete the audit quickly.

A standard audit planning question is: "How much shall we rely on internal control?" In the case of the City Finance audit, there is only one possible answer: as much as we can. Otherwise, how could the audit possibly be completed to meet the reporting deadlines, let alone control audit cost to a reasonable level? Accordingly, the CPA firm conducts the audit with significant reliance on IT controls, reconciliation processes, and internal audit procedures. They test these controls extensively and perform many of their substantive procedures before year-end. In all honesty, if City Finance did not have excellent internal controls, the CPA firm would admit that an audit of the company just could not be done.

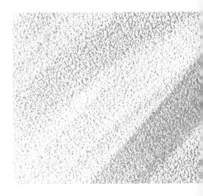

The circumstances of City Finance Company in the opening vignette illustrate an audit in which extensive reliance on internal controls in the sales and collection cycle will likely require the auditor to expand tests of controls and substantive tests of transactions. In other situations, the auditor is likely to rely far less on internal controls but, as was shown in Chapter 9, will still need to understand the internal controls over sales and cash receipts. It is important for auditors to know when they should rely extensively on internal controls and when they should not. This chapter studies assessing control risk and designing tests of controls and substantive tests of transactions for each of the classes of transactions in the sales and collection cycle.

Before studying the process of assessing control risk and designing tests of controls and substantive tests of transaction for each class of transactions in detail, two related topics are covered. First, it is important to know the sales and collection cycle classes of transactions and account balances in a typical company. These were discussed earlier but are reviewed here. Second, because a considerable portion of the audit of transactions in the sales and collection cycle involves documents and records, it is essential to understand the typical documents and records used in the cycle.

ACCOUNTS AND CLASSES OF TRANSACTIONS IN THE SALES AND COLLECTION CYCLE

OBJECTIVE 11-1

Identify the accounts and the classes of transactions in the sales and collection cycle.

The overall objective in the audit of the sales and collection cycle is to evaluate whether the account balances affected by the cycle are fairly presented in accordance with generally accepted accounting principles. Typical accounts included in the sales and collection cycle are shown in Figure 11-1 with the use of T accounts. The nature of the accounts may vary, of course, depending on the industry and client involved. There are differences in account titles for a service industry, a retail company, and an insurance company, but the key concepts are the same. To provide a frame of reference for understanding the material in this chapter, a wholesale merchandising company is assumed.

FIGURE 11-1 Accounts in the Sales and Collection Cycle

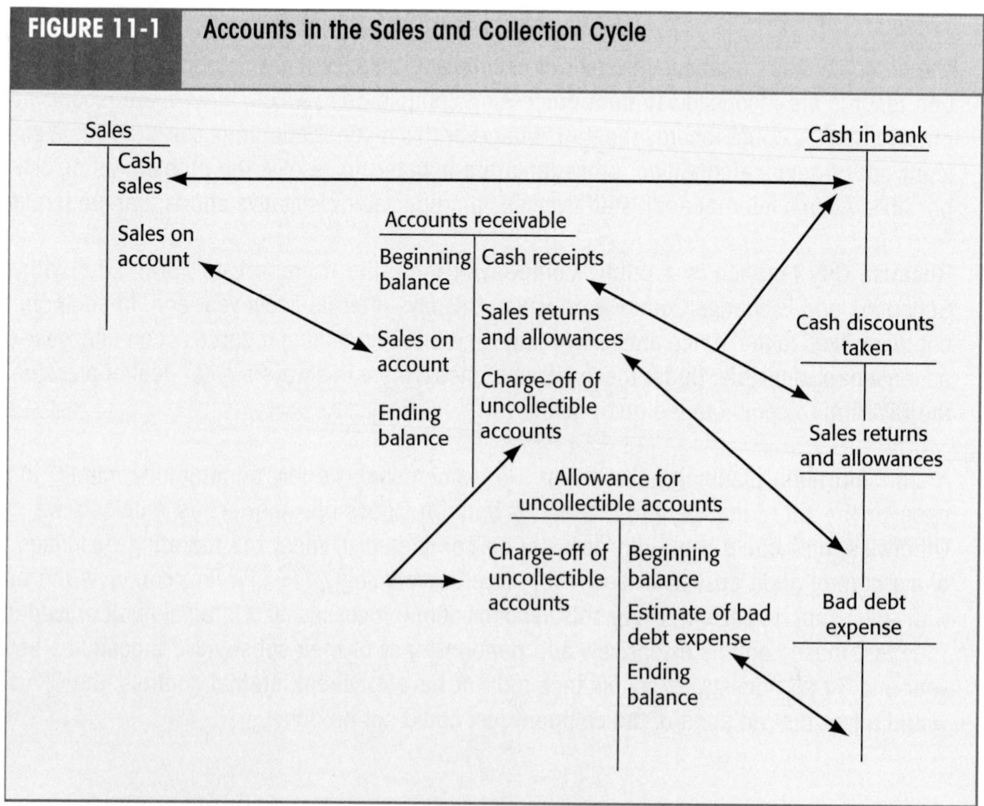

Figure 11-1 shows the way accounting information flows through the various accounts in the sales and collection cycle. This figure shows that there are five **classes of transactions in the sales and collection cycle:**

1. Sales (cash and sales on account)
2. Cash receipts
3. Sales returns and allowances
4. Charge-off of uncollectible accounts
5. Estimate of bad debt expense

Figure 11-1 also shows that with the exception of cash sales, every transaction and amount ultimately is included in one of two balance sheet accounts, accounts receivable or allowance for uncollectible accounts. For simplicity, assume that the same internal controls exist for both cash and credit sales.

BUSINESS FUNCTIONS IN THE CYCLE AND RELATED DOCUMENTS AND RECORDS

OBJECTIVE 11-2

Identify the business functions and the related documents and records in the sales and collection cycle.

The **sales and collection cycle** involves the decisions and processes necessary for the transfer of the ownership of goods and services to customers after they are made available for sale. It begins with a request by a customer and ends with the conversion of material or service into an account receivable, and ultimately into cash.

There are eight **business functions for the sales and collection cycle** shown in the third column of Table 11-1. They occur in every business in the recording of the five classes of transactions in the sales and collection cycle. Observe in Table 11-1 that the first four processes are for recording sales, whereas every other class of transactions includes only one business function.

TABLE 11-1 Classes of Transactions, Accounts, Business Functions, and Related Documents and Records for the Sales and Collection Cycle

Classes of Transactions	Accounts	Business Functions	Documents and Records
Sales	Sales Accounts receivable	Processing customer orders	Customer order Sales order
		Granting credit	Customer order or sales order
		Shipping goods	Shipping document
		Billing customers and recording sales	Sales invoice Sales transaction file Sales journal or listing Accounts receivable master file Accounts receivable trial balance Monthly statements
Cash receipts	Cash in bank (debits from cash receipts) Accounts receivable	Processing and recording cash receipts	Remittance advice Prelisting of cash receipts Cash receipts transaction file Cash receipts journal or listing
Sales returns and allowances	Sales returns and allowances Accounts receivable	Processing and recording sales returns and allowances	Credit memo Sales returns and allowances journal
Charge-off of uncollectible accounts	Accounts receivable Allowance for uncollectible accounts	Charging off uncollectible accounts receivable	Uncollectible account authorization form General journal
Bad debt expense	Bad debt expense Allowance for uncollectible accounts	Providing for bad debts	General journal

There are also common documents and records for each business function. These documents and records are shown in the fourth column of Table 11-1. It is essential to understand the business functions and documents and records in a business before assessing control risk and designing tests of controls and substantive tests of transactions. It is assumed that you have learned about these in other accounting courses. An illustrative flowchart that includes the business functions and typical related documents and records for sales and cash receipts is included in Figure 11-4, page 312. That flowchart also includes key internal controls.

Effect of E-commerce on the Sales and Collection Cycle

OBJECTIVE 11-3

Understand how e-commerce activities affect the sales and collection cycle.

The Internet and other developing technologies allow companies to develop new business models to generate sales through electronic markets. Both existing companies and start-ups use the Internet to engage in business-to-business (B2B) and business-to-consumer (B2C) e-commerce. These Internet-based markets allow companies to expand sales of their products and services by interacting with customers around the world on a 24-hour, seven-day-per-week basis. These new models often allow companies to charge lower prices by eliminating traditional distributors and other middlemen from the sales distribution process. The Internet also provides additional sources of revenue, such as banner ads and sponsorships on company Web sites. These ad agreements are often complex, with fees based on the number of hits to the ad links. Other companies engage in barterlike transactions as payment for the exchange of goods and services.

Management's assertions for sales and collection activities remain the same whether sales are generated through traditional or electronic markets. Management also continues to be responsible for adopting sound accounting policies and internal controls when engaging in e-commerce activities. In some companies, the online sales system is effectively integrated with the traditional sales system, while other companies create separate accounting systems and internal controls for online sales.

Auditors should obtain an understanding of the design and operation of key internal controls over e-commerce revenues as part of gaining an understanding of internal controls in the sales and collection cycle. Evidence for e-commerce activities is likely to be in electronic form. The auditor's tests of controls and substantive tests of transactions may therefore need to be modified to ensure that this electronic evidence is available for audit testing.

METHODOLOGY FOR DESIGNING TESTS OF CONTROLS AND SUBSTANTIVE TESTS OF TRANSACTIONS FOR SALES

OBJECTIVE 11-4

Understand internal control, and design and perform tests of controls and substantive tests of transactions for sales.

The account balances, classes of transactions, business functions, and related documents and records for the sales and collection cycle were identified in earlier sections of this chapter. It is now appropriate to study the design of tests of controls and substantive tests of transactions for each of the five classes of transactions in the cycle. This is the topic for the remainder of this chapter.

The methodology for obtaining an understanding of internal control and designing tests of controls and substantive tests of transactions for sales is shown in Figure 11-2. That methodology was studied in general terms in Chapters 9 and 10. It is applied specifically to sales in this section. The bottom box in Figure 11-2 shows the four evidence decisions the auditor must make. This section deals with deciding the appropriate audit procedures. The following sections deal with each of the parts in Figure 11-2, starting with gaining an understanding of internal control for sales.

Understand Internal Control—Sales

Chapter 9 discussed how auditors obtain an understanding of internal control. A typical approach for sales is to study the client's flowcharts, prepare an internal control questionnaire, and perform walk-through tests of sales. Figures 11-3 (p. 311) and 11-4 (p. 312) include an organization chart and a flowchart for the Hillsburg Hardware Co. that are used to demonstrate the design of tests of controls and substantive tests of transactions audit procedures. The company's general ledger trial balance and financial statements were shown in Chapters 5 and 7. Additional information was included in other chapters.

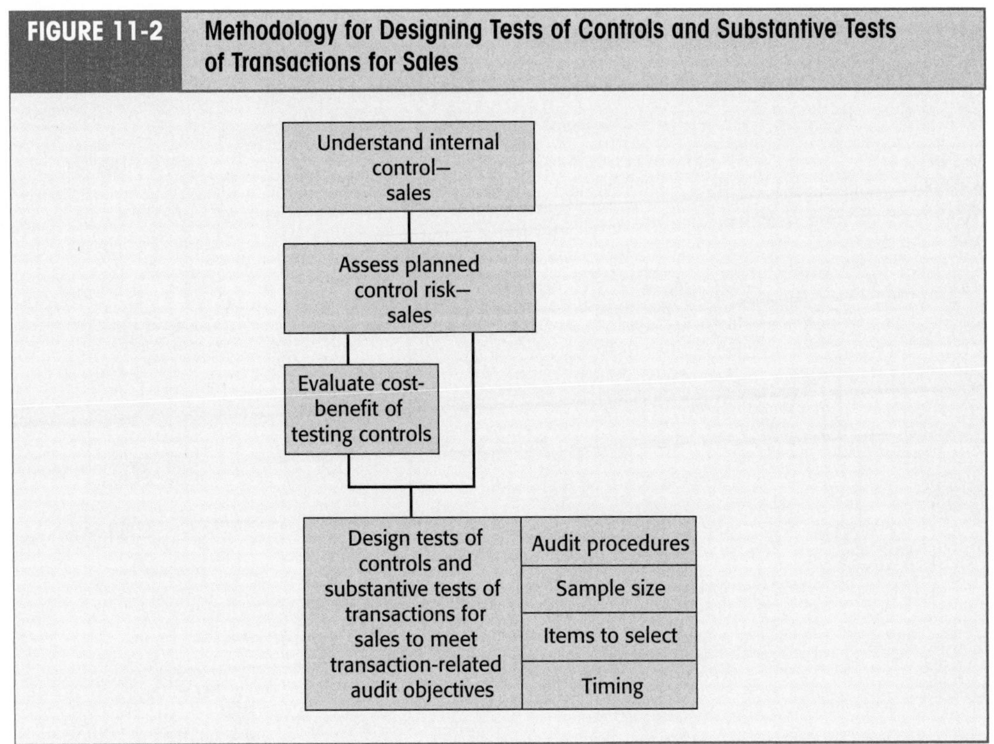

Hillsburg Hardware Co. is a small wholesale distributor of hardware to independent, high-quality hardware stores in the southeastern part of the United States. This is the fourth year of the audit of this client, and there have never been any significant misstatements discovered in the tests. During the current year, a major change has occurred. The controller left the firm and has been replaced by Erma Swanson. There has also been some turnover of other accounting personnel.

The overall assessment by management is that the accounting personnel are reasonably competent and highly trustworthy. The president, Rick Chulick, has been the chief operating officer for approximately 10 years. He is regarded as a highly competent, honest individual who does a conscientious job.

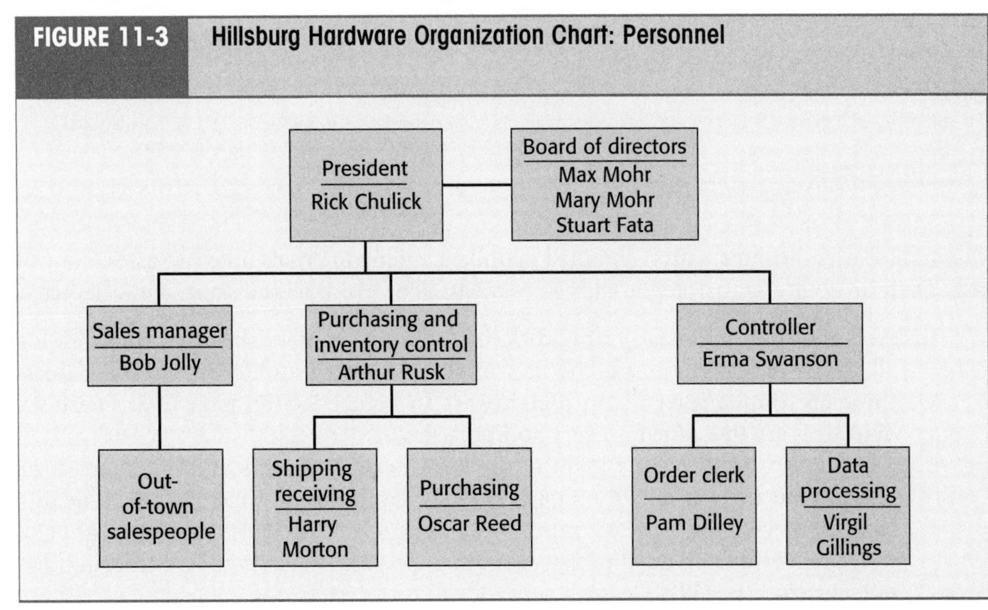

FIGURE 11-4 Hillsburg Hardware—Flowchart of Sales and Cash Receipts

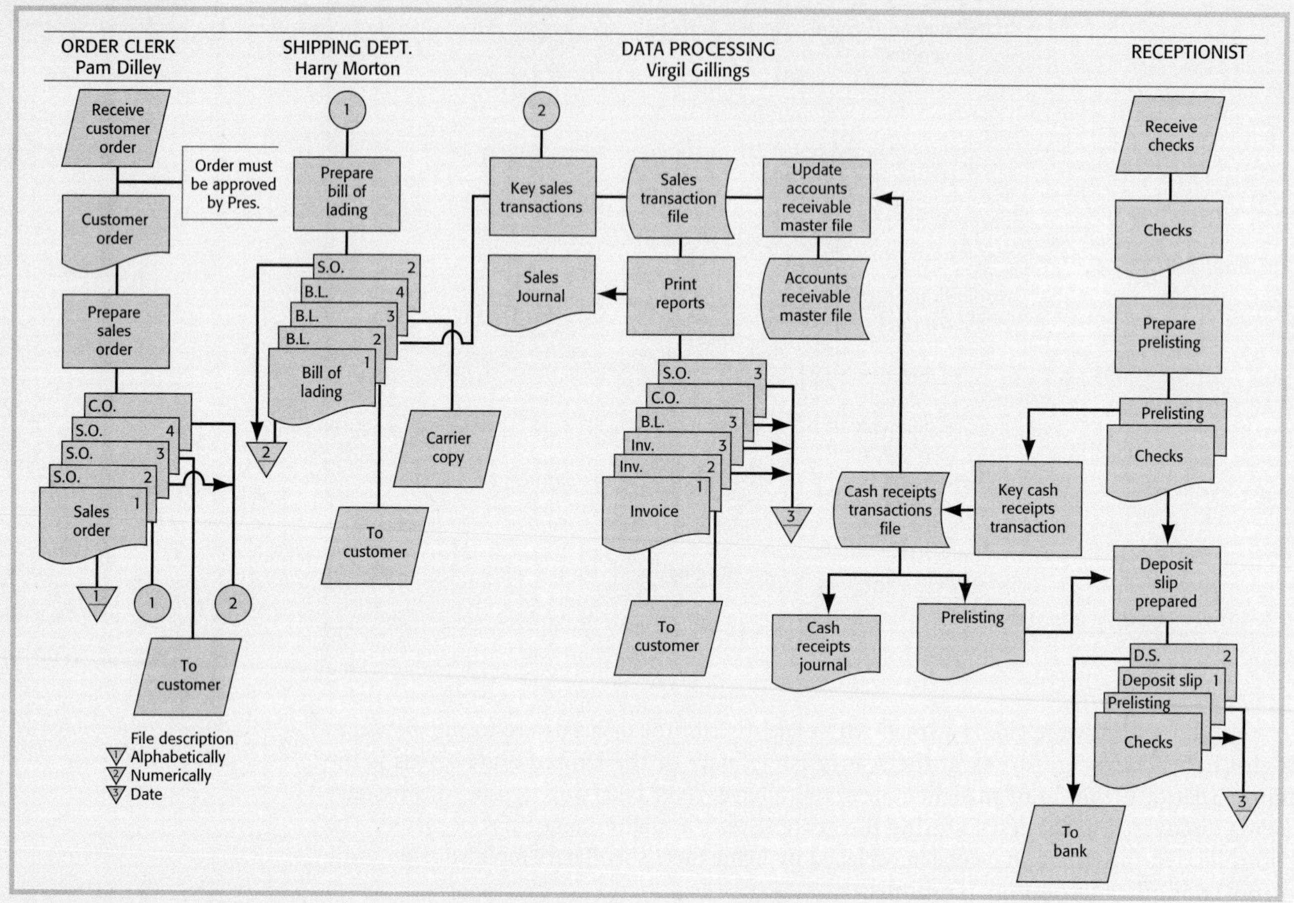

NOTES

1. All correspondence is sent to the president.
2. All sales order numbers are accounted for weekly by the controller.
3. All bills of lading numbers are accounted for weekly by the controller.
4. Sales amount recorded on sales invoice is based on standard price list. It is stored in the inventory master file and can be changed only with authorization of the controller.
5. Duplicate sales invoice is compared with bill of lading daily by Pam Dilley for descriptions and quantities and the sales invoice is reviewed for reasonableness of the extensions and footing. She initials a copy of the invoice before the original is mailed to the customer.
6. Sales are batched daily by Pam Dilley. The batch totals are compared with the sales journal weekly.
7. Statements are sent to customers monthly.
8. Accounts receivable master file total is compared with general ledger by the controller on a monthly basis.
9. Unpaid invoices are filed separately from paid invoices.
10. The receptionist stamps incoming checks with a restrictive endorsement immediately upon receipt.
11. There are no cash sales.
12. Deposits are made daily.
13. Cash receipts are batched daily by the receptionist. The batch totals are compared with the cash receipts journal weekly.
14. The bank account is reconciled by the controller on a monthly basis.
15. All bad debt expense and charge-off of bad debts are approved by the president after being initiated by the controller.
16. Financial statements are printed monthly by the controller and reviewed by the president.
17. All errors are reviewed daily by the controller immediately after the updating run. Corrections are made the same day.

Assess Planned Control Risk—Sales

The auditor uses the information obtained in understanding internal control to assess control risk. There are four essential steps to this assessment, all of which were discussed in Chapter 9.

1. First, the auditor needs a framework for assessing control risk. The framework for all classes of transactions is the six transaction-related audit objectives. For sales, these are shown for Hillsburg Hardware in Figure 9-5 on page 262. These six objectives are the same for every audit of sales.
2. Second, the auditor must identify the key internal controls and weaknesses for sales. These are also shown on page 262. The controls and weaknesses will be different for every audit. The controls and weaknesses for Hillsburg Hardware Co. were identified from the flowchart in Figure 11-4 and the internal control checklist in Figure 9-3 (p. 258).

3. After identifying the controls and weaknesses, the auditor associates them with the objectives. This is also shown on page 262 with W's and C's in appropriate columns.
4. Finally, the auditor assesses control risk for each objective by evaluating the controls and weaknesses for each objective. This step is critical because it affects the auditor's decisions about both tests of controls and substantive tests. It is a highly subjective decision. The bottom of page 262 shows the auditor's conclusions for Hillsburg Hardware.

We will now examine key control activities (see pp. 249–252) for sales. A knowledge of these control activities is important for identifying the key controls and weaknesses for sales, which was first discussed in Chapter 9.

Adequate Separation of Duties Proper separation of duties is useful to prevent various types of misstatements, both intentional and unintentional. To prevent fraud, it is important that anyone responsible for inputting sales and cash receipts transaction information into the computer be denied access to cash. It is also desirable to separate the credit-granting function from the sales function because credit checks are intended to offset the natural tendency of sales personnel to optimize volume even at the expense of high bad debt write-offs. It is equally desirable that personnel responsible for doing internal comparisons are independent of those entering the original data. For example, comparison of batch control totals with summary reports and comparison of accounts receivable master file totals with the general ledger balance should be done by someone independent of those who input sales and cash receipt transactions.

Proper Authorization The auditor is concerned about authorization at *three key points:* credit must be properly authorized before a sale takes place; goods should be shipped only after proper authorization; and prices, including basic terms, freight, and discounts, must be authorized. The first two controls are meant to prevent the loss of company assets by shipping to fictitious customers or those who will fail to pay for the goods. Price authorization is meant to ensure that the sale is billed at the price set by company policy. As discussed in Chapter 9 (pp. 250–251), authorization may be done for each individual transaction or general authorization may be given for specific classes of transactions. General authorizations are often done automatically by computer.

Adequate Documents and Records Because each company has a unique system of originating, processing, and recording transactions, it may be difficult to evaluate whether its procedures are designed for maximum control; nevertheless, adequate record-keeping procedures must exist before most of the transaction-related audit objectives can be met. Some companies, for example, automatically prepare a multicopy prenumbered sales invoice at the time a customer order is received. Copies of this document are used to approve credit, authorize shipment, record the number of units shipped, and bill customers. Under this system, there is almost no chance of the failure to bill a customer if all invoices are accounted for periodically. Under a different system, in which the sales invoice is prepared only after a shipment has been made, the likelihood of failure to bill a customer is high unless some compensating control exists.

Prenumbered Documents An important characteristic of documents for sales is the use of prenumbering, which is meant to prevent both the *failure* to bill or record sales and the occurrence of *duplicate* billings and recordings. Of course, it does not do much good to have prenumbered documents unless they are properly accounted for. An example of the use of this control is the filing, by a billing clerk, of a copy of all shipping documents in sequential order after each shipment is billed, with someone else periodically accounting for all numbers and investigating the reason for any missing documents. Another example is to program the computer to prepare a listing of unused numbers at month's end with follow-up by appropriate personnel.

Monthly Statements Sending monthly statements automatically by computer or by someone who has no responsibility for handling cash or preparing the sales and accounts receivable records is a useful control because it encourages a response from customers if the balance is improperly stated. For maximum effectiveness, all disagreements about the balance in the account should be directed to a designated official who has no responsibility for handling cash or recording sales or accounts receivable.

Internal Verification Procedures The use of computer programs or independent persons for checking the processing and recording of sales transactions is essential for fulfilling each of the six transaction-related audit objectives. Examples of these procedures include accounting for the numerical sequence of prenumbered documents, checking the accuracy of document preparation, and reviewing reports for unusual or incorrect items.

Evaluate Cost-Benefit of Testing Controls

After the auditor has identified the key internal controls and weaknesses and assessed control risk, it is appropriate to decide whether substantive tests will be reduced sufficiently to justify the cost of performing tests of controls. When practical, auditors make this decision before completing a matrix such as the one illustrated in Figure 9-5 on page 262. It makes little sense to incur the cost of identifying controls and assessing control risk below the maximum if there will be no reduction of substantive tests.

Design Tests of Controls for Sales

For each control the auditor plans to rely on to reduce assessed control risk, one or more tests of controls must be designed to verify its effectiveness. In most audits, it is relatively easy to determine the nature of the test of the control from the nature of the control. For example, if the internal control is to initial customer orders after they have been approved for credit, the test of control is to examine the customer order for a proper initial.

The first three columns of Table 11-2 (pp. 315–316) illustrate the design of tests of controls for sales for Hillsburg Hardware Co. Column three in Table 11-2 shows one test of control for each key internal control in column two. Observe that Table 11-2 is organized by transaction-related audit objective. For example, the second key internal control for the existence objective is "sales are supported by authorized shipping documents and approved customer orders." The test of control is to "examine sales invoice for supporting bill of lading and customer order." For this test, the auditor should start with sales invoices and examine documents in support of the sales invoices rather than going in the opposite direction. If the auditor traced from shipping documents to sales invoices, it would be a test of completeness. Direction of tests is discussed further on pages 317–318.

As shown in the third column of Table 11-2 for the completeness objective, a common test of control for sales is to account for a sequence of various types of documents. For example, accounting for a sequence of shipping documents and tracing each one to the duplicate sales invoice and recording in the sales journal provides evidence of completeness.

Accounting for the sequence of sales invoices selected from the sales journal and watching for omitted and duplicate numbers or invoices outside the normal sequence is a test that simultaneously provides evidence of both the existence and completeness objectives. As an illustration, assume that the auditor selects sales invoices #18100 to #18199. The completeness objective will be partially satisfied if all 100 sales invoices are recorded. The existence objective will be satisfied if there is no duplicate recording of any of the invoice numbers. As indicated in Table 11-2, the lack of verification to prevent the possibility of duplicate recording of sales invoices is a weakness at the Hillsburg Hardware Co.

The appropriate tests of controls for separation of duties are ordinarily restricted to the auditor's observations of activities and discussions with personnel. For example, it is possible to observe whether the billing clerk has access to cash when incoming mail is opened or cash is deposited. It is usually also necessary to ask personnel what their responsibilities are and if there are any circumstances where their responsibilities are different from the normal policy. For example, the employee responsible for billing customers may state that he or she does not have access to cash. Further discussion may bring out that when the cashier is on vacation, that person takes over the cashier's duties.

Several of the tests of controls in Table 11-2 can be performed using the computer. For example, the auditor can test whether credit is properly authorized by the computer by attempting to initiate transactions that exceed a customer's credit limit. If the control is working effectively, the proposed sales order should be rejected. The existence of sales can

TABLE 11-2 Transaction-Related Audit Objectives, Key Existing Controls, Tests of Controls, Weaknesses, and Substantive Tests of Transaction for Sales—Hillsburg Hardware Co.

Transaction-Related Audit Objective	Key Existing Control*	Test of Control†	Weaknesses*	Substantive Tests of Transactions†
Recorded sales are for shipments actually made to customers (existence).	Credit is approved automatically by computer by comparison to authorized credit limits (C1). Sales are supported by authorized shipping documents and approved customer orders (C2). Batch totals of quantities shipped are compared with quantities billed (C6). Statements are sent to customers each month (C9).	Examine customer order for evidence of customer approval (13e). Examine sales invoice for supporting bill of lading and customer order (13b). Account for a sequence of sales invoices (12). Examine file of batch totals for initials of data control clerk (8). Observe whether monthly statements are sent (6).	There is a lack of internal verification for the possibility of sales invoices being recorded more than once (W1).	Review sales journal and master file for unusual transactions and amounts (1). Trace sales journal entries to supporting documents, including duplicate sales invoice, bill of lading, sales order, and customer order (14).
Existing sales transactions are recorded (completeness).	Shipping documents are prenumbered and accounted for weekly (C5). Batch totals of quantities shipped are compared with quantities billed (C6).	Account for a sequence of shipping documents (10). Examine file of batch totals for initials of data control clerk (8).		Trace selected shipping documents to the sales journal to be sure that each one is included (11).
Recorded sales are for the amount of goods shipped and are correctly billed and recorded (accuracy).	Sales are supported by authorized shipping documents and approved customer orders (C2). Batch totals of quantities shipped are compared with quantities billed (C6). Unit selling prices are obtained from the price list master file of approved prices (C7). Statements are sent to customers each month (C9).	Examine sales invoice for supporting documents (13b). Examine file of batch totals for initials of data control clerk (8). Examine the approved price list for accuracy and proper authorization (9). Observe whether monthly statements are sent (6).		Trace entries in sales journal to sales invoices (13). Recompute prices and extensions on sales invoices (13b). Trace details on sales invoices to · shipping documents (13c) · sales order (13d) · customer order (13e)
Sales transactions are properly classified (classification).	Sales transactions are internally verified (C8).	Examine document package for internal verification (13b).		Examine duplicate sales invoice for proper account classification (13b).
Sales are recorded on the correct dates (timing).	Shipping documents are prenumbered and accounted for weekly by the accountant (C5).	Account for a sequence of shipping documents (10).	There is a lack of control to test for timely recording (W2).	Compare date of recording of sale in sales journal with duplicate sales invoice and bill of lading (13b and 13c).

(cont. on p. 316)

TABLE 11-2 (Cont.)

Transaction-Related Audit Objective	Key Existing Control*	Test of Control†	Weaknesses*	Substantive Tests of Transactions†
Sales transactions are properly included in the accounts receivable master file and are correctly summarized (posting and summarization).	Computer automatically posts transactions to the accounts receivable master file and general ledger (C10). Accounts receivable master file is reconciled to the general ledger on a monthly basis (C11). Statements are sent to customers each month (C9).	Examine evidence that accounts receivable master file is reconciled to the general ledger (7). Examine evidence that accounts receivable master file is reconciled to the general ledger (7). Observe whether monthly statements are sent (6).		Trace selected sales invoices from the sales journal to the accounts receivable master file and test for amount, date, and invoice number (13a). Use audit software to foot and cross-foot the sales journal and trace totals to the general ledger (2).

*Controls (C) and Weaknesses (W) are from the control matrix for sales in Figure 9-5 (p. 262). Controls C4 and C5 from the control matrix are not included here.
†The number in parentheses after each test of control and substantive test of transaction refers to an audit procedure in the performance format audit program in Figure 11-7 (p. 325).

be similarly tested by attempting to input nonexistent customer numbers, which should be rejected by the computer. This latter control is a key control for preventing fictitious sales.

Design Substantive Tests of Transactions for Sales

In deciding on substantive tests of transactions, some procedures are commonly used on every audit regardless of the circumstances, whereas others are dependent on the adequacy of the controls and the results of the tests of controls. In Table 11-2, the substantive tests of transactions in column five are related to the transaction-related audit objectives in the first column and are designed to determine whether any monetary misstatements for that objective exist in the transaction. The audit procedures used are affected by the internal controls and tests of controls for that objective. Materiality, results of the prior year, and the other factors discussed in Chapter 8 also affect the procedures used. Some of the audit procedures used when internal controls are inadequate are discussed in a later section.

Determining the proper substantive tests of transactions procedures for sales is relatively difficult because they vary considerably depending on the circumstances. In subsequent paragraphs, the procedures often *not* performed are emphasized because they are the ones requiring an audit decision. The substantive tests of transactions procedures are discussed in the order of the sales transaction-related audit objectives in Table 11-2. It should be noted that some procedures fulfill more than one objective.

Recorded Sales Exist For this objective, the auditor is concerned with the possibility of *three types of misstatements:* sales being included in the journals for which no shipment was made, sales recorded more than once, and shipments being made to nonexistent customers and recorded as sales. The first two types of misstatements can be intentional or unintentional. The last type is always intentional. The potential consequences are significant because they lead to an overstatement of assets and income.

There is an important difference between finding intentional and unintentional overstatements of sales. An unintentional overstatement normally also results in a clear overstatement of accounts receivable, which can often be easily found through confirmation procedures. For fraud, the perpetrator will attempt to conceal the overstatement, making it more difficult for auditors to find. Substantive tests of transactions may be necessary to discover overstated sales in these circumstances.

The appropriate substantive tests of transactions for testing the existence objective depend on where the auditor believes the misstatements are likely to take place. Many auditors do substantive tests of transactions for the existence objective only if they believe that a control weakness exists; therefore, the nature of the tests depends on the nature of the potential misstatement as follows:

Recorded Sale for Which There Was No Shipment The auditor can trace from selected entries in the sales journal to make sure that related copies of the shipping and other supporting documents exist. If the auditor is concerned about the possibility of a fictitious duplicate copy of a shipping document, it may be necessary to trace the amounts to the perpetual inventory records as a test of whether inventory was reduced.

Sale Recorded More Than Once Duplicate sales can be determined by reviewing a numerically sorted list of recorded sales transactions for duplicate numbers. The auditor can also test for the proper cancellation of shipping documents. Proper cancellation decreases the likelihood that a shipping document will be used to record another sale.

Shipment Made to Nonexistent Customers This type of fraud normally occurs only when the person recording sales is also in a position to authorize shipments. When internal controls are weak, it is difficult to detect fictitious shipments.

Another effective approach to detecting the three types of misstatements of sales transactions discussed previously is to trace the *credit* in the accounts receivable master file to its source. If the receivable was actually collected in cash or the goods were returned, there must originally have been a sale. If the credit was for a bad debt charge-off or a credit memo or if the account was still unpaid at the time of the audit, intensive follow-up by examining shipping and customer order documents is required because each of these could indicate an inappropriate sales transaction.

It should be kept in mind that *the ordinary audit is not primarily intended to detect fraud* unless the effect on the financial statements is material. The preceding substantive tests of transactions should be necessary only if the auditor is concerned about the occurrence of fraud because of inadequate controls.

Existing Sales Transactions Are Recorded In many audits, no substantive tests of transactions are made for the completeness objective on the grounds that overstatements of assets and income are a greater concern in the audit of sales transactions than their understatement. If controls are inadequate, which is likely if the client does no independent internal tracing from shipping documents to the sales journal, substantive tests are necessary.

An effective procedure to test for unbilled shipments is to trace selected shipping documents from a file in the shipping department to related duplicate sales invoices and the sales journal. To conduct a meaningful test using this procedure, the auditor must be confident that all shipping documents are included in the file. This can be done by accounting for a numerical sequence of the documents.

Direction of Tests It is important that auditors understand the difference between tracing from source documents to the journals and tracing from the journals back to source documents. The former is a test for *omitted transactions* (completeness objective), whereas the latter is a test for *nonexistent transactions* (existence objective).

In testing for the existence objective, the starting point is the journal. A sample of invoice numbers is selected *from* the journal and traced *to* duplicate sales invoices, shipping documents, and customer orders. In testing for the completeness objective, the likely starting point is the shipping document. A sample of shipping documents is selected and traced *to* duplicate sales invoices and the sales journal as a test of omissions.

When designing audit procedures for the existence and completeness objectives, the starting point for tracing the document is essential. This is called the direction of tests. For example, if the auditor is concerned about the existence objective but traces in the wrong direction (from shipping documents to the journals), a serious audit deficiency exists. The direction of tests is illustrated in Figure 11-5 (p. 318).

In testing for the other four transaction-related audit objectives, the direction of tests is usually not relevant. For example, the accuracy of sales transactions can be tested by tracing from a duplicate sales invoice to a shipping document or vice versa.

FIGURE 11-5 Direction of Tests for Sales

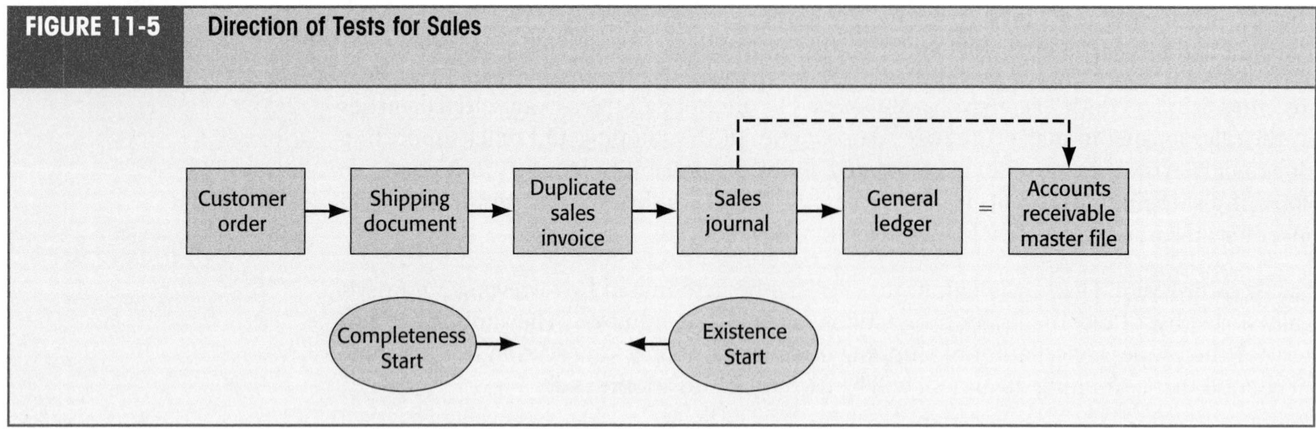

Sales Are Accurately Recorded The accurate recording of sales transactions concerns shipping the amount of goods ordered, accurately billing for the amount of goods shipped, and accurately recording the amount billed in the accounting records. Substantive tests to ensure that each of these aspects of accuracy is correct are ordinarily conducted in every audit.

Typical substantive tests of transactions include recomputing information in the accounting records to verify whether it is proper. A common approach is to start with entries in the sales journal and compare the total of selected transactions with accounts receivable master file entries and duplicate sales invoices. Prices on the duplicate sales invoices are normally compared with an approved price list, extensions and footings are recomputed, and the details listed on the invoices are compared with shipping records for description, quantity, and customer identification. Often, customer orders and sales orders are also examined for the same information.

The comparison of tests of controls and substantive tests of transactions for the accuracy objective is a good example of how audit time can be saved when effective internal controls exist. It is obvious that the test of control for this objective takes almost no time because it involves examining only an initial or other evidence of internal verification. Because the sample size for substantive tests of transactions can be reduced if this control is effective, a significant savings will result from performing the test of control because of its lower cost.

When sales invoices are automatically calculated and posted by a computer, the auditor may be able to reduce substantive tests of transactions for the accuracy objective. If the auditor determines that the computer is programmed accurately and the price list master file is authorized and correct, detailed invoice computations can be reduced or eliminated. In this case, the auditor focuses on determining that effective computer controls exist to ensure that the computer is properly programmed and has not been altered since it was last tested by the auditor.

Recorded Sales Are Properly Classified Charging the correct general ledger account is less of a problem in sales than in some other transaction cycles, but it is still of some concern. When there are cash and credit sales, it is important not to debit accounts receivable for a cash sale or to credit sales for collection of a receivable. It is also important not to classify sales of operating assets, such as buildings, as sales. For those companies using more than one sales classification, such as companies issuing segmented earnings statements, proper classification is essential.

It is common to test sales for proper classification as part of testing for accuracy. The auditor examines supporting documents to determine the proper classification of a given transaction and compares this with the actual account to which it is charged.

Sales Are Recorded on the Correct Dates Sales should be billed and recorded as soon after shipment takes place as possible to prevent the unintentional omission of transactions from the records and to make sure that sales are recorded in the proper period. Timely recorded transactions are also less likely to contain misstatements. At the same time that substantive tests of transactions procedures for accuracy are being performed, it is common to compare the date on selected bills of lading or other shipping documents with the date on related duplicate sales invoices, the sales journal, and the accounts receivable master file. Significant differences indicate a potential cutoff problem.

Sales Transactions Are Properly Included in the Master File and Correctly Summarized The proper inclusion of all sales transactions in the accounts receivable master file is essential because the accuracy of these records affects the client's ability to collect outstanding receivables. Similarly, the sales journal must be correctly totaled and posted to the general ledger if the financial statements are to be correct. In most audits, it is common to perform some clerical accuracy tests such as footing the journals and tracing the totals and details to the general ledger and the master file to check whether there are intentional or unintentional misstatements in the processing of sales transactions. The extent of such tests is affected by the quality of the internal controls and can often be performed using spreadsheet or generalized audit software. Tracing from the sales journal to the master file is typically done as a part of fulfilling other transaction-related audit objectives, but footing the sales journal and tracing the totals to the general ledger is done as a separate procedure.

The distinction between posting and summarization and other transaction-related audit objectives is that posting and summarization includes footing journals, master file records, and ledgers and tracing from one to the other among these three. When footing and comparisons are restricted to these three records, the process is posting and summarization. In contrast, accuracy involves determining the monetary correctness of transactions and comparing amounts between documents or with journals and master file records. To illustrate, comparing a duplicate sales invoice with either the sales journal or master file entry is an accuracy objective procedure. Tracing an entry from the sales journal to the master file is a posting and summarization procedure.

Summary of Methodology for Sales

Figure 11-2 and Table 11-2 provide summaries of the previous discussion. Figure 11-2 (p. 311) shows the methodology for designing tests of controls and substantive tests of transactions for sales. Table 11-2 (pp. 315–316) combines the four parts of the previous discussion.

Transaction-Related Audit Objectives (Column 1) The transaction-related audit objectives included in the table are derived from the framework developed in Chapters 5 and 9. Although certain internal controls satisfy more than one objective, it is desirable to consider each objective separately to facilitate a better assessment of control risk.

Key Internal Controls (Column 2) The internal controls for sales are designed to achieve the six transaction-related audit objectives discussed in Chapters 5 and 9. If the controls necessary to satisfy any one of the objectives are inadequate, the likelihood of misstatements related to that objective is increased, regardless of the controls for the other objectives. The methodology for determining existing controls was studied in Chapter 9.

The source of the controls in column 2 is the controls from a control risk matrix such as the one illustrated in Figure 9-5 (p. 262). A control will be included in more than one row in Table 11-2 if there is more than one C for that control on the control risk matrix.

Tests of Controls (Column 3) For each internal control in column 2, the auditor designs a test of control to verify its effectiveness. Observe that the tests of controls in Table 11-2 relate directly to the internal controls. For each control, there should be at least one test of control.

Weaknesses (Column 4) Weaknesses identified by the auditor indicate the absence of effective controls. As discussed in Chapter 9, the auditor should evaluate weaknesses by considering potential misstatements that could occur and any compensating controls. One response to a weakness in internal control is to expand substantive tests of transactions to determine whether the weakness resulted in a significant number of misstatements.

Substantive Tests of Transactions (Column 5) The purpose of these tests is to determine whether there are monetary misstatements in sales transactions. In Table 11-2, the substantive tests of transactions are related to the objectives in the first column.

It is essential to understand the relationships among the columns in Table 11-2. The first column includes the six transaction-related audit objectives. The general objectives are the same for any class of transactions, but the specific objectives vary for sales, cash receipts, or any other classes of transactions. Column 2 lists one or more illustrative internal controls *for each transaction-related audit objective.* It is essential that any given control be related to one or more specific objective(s). Next, each common test of control in column 3 relates *to a given internal control.* A test of control has no meaning unless it tests a specific control. The table contains at least one test of control in column 3 for each internal control in column 2. Finally, the common substantive tests of transactions in the table's last column are evidence to support *a specific transaction-related audit objective* in column 1. The substantive tests of transactions are not directly related to the key control or test of control columns, but the extent of substantive tests of transactions depends, in part, on which key controls exist and on results of the tests of controls.

Design and Performance Format Audit Procedures

The information presented in Table 11-2 is intended to help auditors design audit programs that satisfy the transaction-related audit objectives in a given set of circumstances. If certain objectives are important in a given audit or when the controls are different for different clients, the methodology helps the auditor design an effective and efficient audit program.

After the appropriate audit procedures for a given set of circumstances have been designed, they must be performed. It is likely to be inefficient to do the audit procedures as they are stated in the design format of Table 11-2. In converting from a **design format audit program** to a **performance format audit program,** procedures are combined. This will do the following:

- Eliminate duplicate procedures.
- Make sure that when a given document is examined, all procedures to be performed on that document are done at that time.
- Enable the auditor to do the procedures in the most effective order. For example, by footing the journal and reviewing the journal for unusual items first, the auditor gains a better perspective in doing the detailed tests.

The process of converting from a design to a performance format is illustrated in Figure 11-7 (page 325) for Hillsburg Hardware.

SALES RETURNS AND ALLOWANCES

OBJECTIVE 11-5

Apply the methodology for controls over sales transactions to controls over sales returns and allowances.

The transaction-related audit objectives and the client's methods of controlling misstatements are essentially the same for processing credit memos as those described for sales, with two important differences. The first relates to *materiality*. In many instances, sales returns and allowances are so immaterial that they can be ignored in the audit altogether. The second major difference relates to *emphasis on objectives*. For sales returns and allowances, the primary emphasis is normally on testing the existence of recorded transactions as a means of uncovering any diversion of cash from the collection of accounts receivable that has been covered up by a fictitious sales return or allowance.

Although the emphasis for the audit of sales returns and allowances is often on testing the existence of recorded transactions, the *completeness* objective is especially important at year-end. Unrecorded sales returns and allowances can be material and can be used by

SALES CAN BE RETURNED (AND COME BACK TO HAUNT YOU)

Late in 1993, Bausch & Lomb, Inc., informed its independent distributors that they would have to purchase up to 2 years' inventory of contact lenses. The lenses had to be purchased before December 24, when Bausch & Lomb closed its books. The distributors claimed that they had oral agreements with Bausch & Lomb that they would not have to pay for the lenses until they were sold. If these agreements existed, the shipments of lenses should not have been recognized as sales.

Ten months after the December sales, most of the lenses had not been sold and Bausch & Lomb had collected less than 15 percent of the accounts receivable from the sales. In October 1994, Bausch & Lomb agreed to take back three-quarters of the inventory that had been shipped the previous December, resulting in an unexpected charge to quarterly earnings.

Source: Adapted from Mark Maremont, "Numbers Game at Bausch & Lomb?" *Business Week* (December 19, 1994), pp. 108–110.

a company's management to overstate net income. The extent of sales returns and potential liability at year-end varies greatly by industry. Sales returns for mail-order and Web-site sales are typically higher than for in-store sales because the purchaser is not able to physically examine the merchandise prior to purchasing.

Naturally, the other objectives should not be ignored. But because the objectives and methodology for auditing sales returns and allowances are essentially the same as for sales, we will not include a detailed study of the area. The reader should be able to apply the same logic to arrive at suitable controls, tests of controls, and substantive tests of transactions to verify the amounts.

METHODOLOGY FOR DESIGNING TESTS OF CONTROLS AND SUBSTANTIVE TESTS OF TRANSACTIONS FOR CASH RECEIPTS

OBJECTIVE 11-6

Understand internal control, and design and perform tests of controls and substantive tests of transactions for cash receipts.

The same methodology used for designing tests of controls and substantive tests of transactions for sales is used for cash receipts. Similarly, cash receipts tests of controls and substantive tests of transactions audit procedures are developed around the same framework used for sales; that is, given the transaction-related audit objectives, key internal controls for each objective are determined, tests of control are developed for each control, and substantive tests of transactions for the monetary misstatements related to each objective are developed. As in all other audit areas, the tests of controls depend on the controls the auditor has identified and the extent they will be relied on to reduce assessed control risk. Figure 11-6 (p. 322) is the control risk matrix for cash receipts for Hillsburg Hardware. It is based on the information in the sales and cash receipt flowchart in Figure 11-4 (p. 312).

Key internal controls, common tests of controls, and common substantive tests of transactions to satisfy each of the transaction-related audit objectives for cash receipts are listed in Table 11-3 (pp. 323–324) for Hillsburg Hardware Co. Because this summary follows the same format as the previous one for sales, no further explanation of its meaning is necessary. The tests of controls and substantive tests of transactions for cash receipts are combined with those for sales in the performance format audit program in Figure 11-7 (p. 325).

The detailed discussion of the internal controls, tests of controls, and substantive tests of transactions that was included for the audit of sales is not included for cash receipts. Instead, the audit procedures that are most likely to be misunderstood are explained in more detail.

An essential part of the auditor's responsibility in auditing cash receipts is identification of weaknesses in internal control that increase the likelihood of fraud. In expanding on Table 11-3, the emphasis will be on those audit procedures that are designed primarily for the discovery of fraud. Those procedures that are not discussed are omitted only because their purpose and the methodology for applying them should be apparent from their description.

FIGURE 11-6 Control Risk Matrix for Hillsburg Hardware Co.—Cash Receipts

	INTERNAL CONTROL	Recorded cash receipts are for funds actually received by the company (existence).	Cash received is recorded in the cash receipts journal (completeness).	Cash receipts are deposited at the amount received (accuracy).	Cash receipts transactions are properly classified (classification).	Cash receipts are recorded on the correct dates (timing).	Cash receipts are properly included in the accounts receivable master file and are correctly summarized (posting and summarization).
CONTROLS	Accountant independently reconciles bank account (C1).	C		C			
	Prelisting of cash receipts is prepared (C2).		C				
	Checks are restrictively endorsed (C3).		C				
	Batch totals of cash receipts are compared with computer summary reports (C4).	C	C	C			
	Statements are sent to customers each month (C5).		C	C			C
	Cash receipts transactions are internally verified (C6).				C		
	Procedures require recording of cash on a daily basis (C7).					C	
	Computer automatically posts transactions to the accounts receivable subsidiary records and to the general ledger (C8).						C
	Accounts receivable master file is reconciled to the general ledger on a monthly basis (C9).						C
WEAKNESS	Prelisting of cash is not used to verify recorded cash receipts (W1).		W				
	Assessed control risk	Low	Medium	Low	Low	Low	Low

(Column group heading: CASH RECEIPTS TRANSACTION-RELATED AUDIT OBJECTIVES)

C = Control; W = Weakness.

Determine Whether Cash Received Was Recorded

The most difficult type of cash defalcation for the auditor to detect is that which occurs *before the cash is recorded* in the cash receipts journal or other cash listing, especially if the sale and cash receipt are recorded simultaneously. For example, if a grocery store clerk takes cash and intentionally fails to process the receipt of cash on the cash register, it is extremely difficult to discover the theft. To prevent this type of fraud, internal controls such as those included in the second objective in Table 11-3 are implemented by many companies. The type of control will, of course, depend on the type of business. For example, the controls for a retail store in which the cash is received by the same person who sells the merchandise and rings up the cash receipts should be different from the controls for a company in which all receipts are received through the mail several weeks after the sales have taken place.

NACHA Electronic Payments

It is normal practice to trace from prenumbered remittance advices or prelists of cash receipts to the cash receipts journal and subsidiary accounts receivable records as a substantive test of the recording of actual cash received. This test will be effective only if a cash register tape or some other prelisting was prepared at the time cash was received.

Prepare Proof of Cash Receipts

A useful audit procedure to test whether all recorded cash receipts have been deposited in the bank account is a **proof of cash receipts.** In this test, the total cash receipts recorded in the cash receipts journal for a given period, such as a month, are reconciled with the actual deposits made to the bank during the same period. There may be a difference in the two as a result of deposits in transit and other items, but the amounts can be reconciled and compared. The procedure is not useful in discovering cash receipts that have not been

TABLE 11-3 Transaction-Related Audit Objectives, Key Existing Controls, Tests of Controls, Weaknesses, and Substantive Tests of Transactions for Cash Receipts —Hillsburg Hardware Co.

Transaction-Related Audit Objective	Key Existing Control*	Test of Control†	Weaknesses*	Substantive Tests of Transactions†
Recorded cash receipts are for funds actually received by the company (existence).	Accountant independently reconciles bank account (C1). Batch totals of cash receipts are compared with computer summary reports (C4).	Observe whether accountant reconciles bank account (3). Examine file of batch totals for initials of data control clerk (8).		Review cash receipts journal and master file for unusual transactions and amounts (1). Trace cash receipts entries from the cash receipts journal entries to the bank statement (19). Prepare a proof of cash receipts (18).
Cash received is recorded in the cash receipts journal (completeness).	Prelisting of cash receipts is prepared (C2). Checks are restrictively endorsed (C3). Batch totals of cash receipts are compared with computer summary reports (C4). Statements are sent to customers each month (C5).	Observe prelisting of cash receipts (4). Observe endorsement of incoming checks (5). Examine file of batch totals for initials of data control clerk (8). Observe whether monthly statements are sent (6).	Prelisting of cash is not used to verify recorded cash receipts (W1).	Obtain prelisting of cash receipts and trace amounts to the cash receipts journal, testing for names, amounts, and dates (15). Compare the prelisting with the duplicate deposit slip (16).
Cash receipts are deposited and recorded at the amounts received (accuracy).	Accountant independently reconciles bank account (C1). Batch totals of cash receipts are compared with computer summary reports (C4). Statements are sent to customers each month (C5).	Observe whether accountant reconciles bank account (3). Examine file of batch totals for initials of data control clerk (8). Observe whether monthly statements are sent (6).		Obtain prelisting of cash receipts and trace amounts to the cash receipts journal, testing for names, amounts, and dates (15). Prepare proof of cash receipts (18).

(cont. on p. 324)

TABLE 11-3 (Cont.)

Transaction-Related Audit Objective	Key Existing Control*	Test of Control†	Weaknesses*	Substantive Tests of Transactions†
Cash receipts transactions are properly classified (classification).	Cash receipts transactions are internally verified (C6).	Examine evidence of internal verification (15).		Examine prelisting for proper account classification (17).
Cash receipts are recorded on the correct dates (timing).	Procedures require recording of cash on a daily basis (C7).	Observe unrecorded cash at a point in time (4).		Compare date of deposit per bank statement to the dates in the cash receipts journal and prelisting of cash receipts (16).
Cash receipts are properly included in the accounts receivable master file and are correctly summarized (posting and summarization).	Statements are sent to customers each month (C5). Computer automatically posts transactions to the accounts receivable master file and general ledger (C8). Accounts receivable master file is reconciled to the general ledger on a monthly basis (C9).	Observe whether monthly statements are sent (6). Examine evidence that accounts receivable master file is reconciled to general ledger (7). Examine evidence that accounts receivable master file is reconciled to general ledger (7).		Trace selected entries from the cash receipts journal to the accounts receivable master file and test for dates and amount (20). Trace selected credits from the accounts receivable master file to the cash receipts journal and test for dates and amounts (21). Use audit software to foot and cross-foot the sales journal and trace totals to the general ledger (2).

*Controls (C) and Weaknesses (W) are from control matrix for cash receipts in Figure 11-6 (p. 322).

†The number in parentheses after each test of control and substantive test of transaction refers to an audit procedure in the performance format audit program in Figure 11-7 (p. 325).

recorded in the journals or time lags in making deposits, but it can help uncover recorded cash receipts that have not been deposited, unrecorded deposits, unrecorded loans, bank loans deposited directly into the bank account, and similar misstatements. This somewhat time-consuming procedure is ordinarily used only when the controls are weak. In rare instances in which controls are extremely weak, the period covered by the proof of cash receipts may be the entire year.

Test to Discover Lapping of Accounts Receivable

Lapping of accounts receivable is the postponement of entries for the collection of receivables to *conceal an existing cash shortage.* The defalcation is perpetrated by a person who handles cash receipts and then enters them into the computer system. He or she defers recording the cash receipts from one customer and covers the shortages with receipts of another. These in turn are covered from the receipts of a third customer a few days later. The employee must continue to cover the shortage through repeated lapping, replace the stolen money, or find another way to conceal the shortage.

This defalcation can be easily prevented by separation of duties and a mandatory vacation policy for employees who both handle cash and enter cash receipts into the system. It can be detected by comparing the name, amount, and dates shown on remittance advices with cash receipts journal entries and related duplicate deposit slips. Because the procedure is relatively time-consuming, it is ordinarily performed only when there is specific concern with defalcation because of a weakness in internal control.

FIGURE 11-7 Audit Program for Tests of Controls and Substantive Tests of Transactions for Sales and Cash Receipts for Hillsburg Hardware Co. (Performance Format)

HILLSBURG HARDWARE CO.
Tests of Controls and Substantive Tests of Transactions Audit Procedures for Sales and Cash Receipts
(Sample size and the items in the sample are not included.)

General

1. Review journals and master file for unusual transactions and amounts.
2. Use audit software to foot and cross-foot the sales and cash receipts journals and trace the totals to the general ledger.
3. Observe whether accountant reconciles the bank account.
4. Observe whether cash is prelisted and the existence of any unrecorded cash.
5. Observe whether restrictive endorsement is used on cash receipts.
6. Observe whether monthly statements are sent.
7. Observe whether accountant compares master file total with general ledger account.
8. Examine file of batch totals for initials of data control clerk.
9. Examine the approved price list in the inventory master file for accuracy and proper authorization.

Shipment of Goods

10. Account for a sequence of shipping documents.
11. Trace selected shipping documents to the sales journal to be sure that each one has been included.

Billing of Customers and Recording the Sales in the Records

12. Account for a sequence of sales invoices in the sales journal.
13. Trace selected sales invoice numbers from the sales journal to
    a. accounts receivable master file and test for amount, date, and invoice number.
    b. duplicate sales invoice and check for the total amount recorded in the journal, date, customer name, and account classification. Check the pricing, extensions, and footings. Examine underlying documents for indication of internal verification.
    c. bill of lading and test for customer name, product description, quantity, and date.
    d. duplicate sales order and test for customer name, product description, quantity, date, and indication of internal verification.
    e. customer order and test for customer name, product description, quantity, date, and credit approval.
14. Trace recorded sales from the sales journal to the file of supporting documents, which includes a duplicate sales invoice, bill of lading, sales order, and customer order.

Processing Cash Receipts and Recording the Amounts in the Records

15. Obtain the prelisting of cash receipts and trace amounts to the cash receipts journal, testing for names, amounts, dates, and internal verification.
16. Compare the prelisting of cash receipts with the duplicate deposit slip, testing for names, amounts, and dates. Trace the total from the cash receipts journal to the bank statement, testing for a delay in deposit.
17. Examine prelisting for proper account classification.
18. Prepare a proof of cash receipts.
19. Trace cash receipt entries from the cash receipts journal to the bank statement, testing for dates and amounts of deposits.
20. Trace selected entries from the cash receipts journal to entries in the accounts receivable master file and test for dates and amounts.
21. Trace selected credits from the accounts receivable master file to the cash receipts journal and test for dates and amounts.

AUDIT TESTS FOR UNCOLLECTIBLE ACCOUNTS

OBJECTIVE 11-7

Apply the methodology for controls over the sales and collection cycle to write-offs of uncollectible accounts receivable.

Existence of recorded write-offs is the most important transaction-related audit objective that the auditor should keep in mind in the verification of the write-off of individual uncollectible accounts. A major concern in testing accounts charged off as uncollectible is the possibility of the client covering up a defalcation by charging off accounts receivable that have already been collected. The major control for preventing this type of misstatement is proper authorization of the write-off of uncollectible accounts by a designated level of management only after a thorough investigation of the reason the customer has not paid.

Normally, verification of the accounts charged off takes relatively little time. A typical procedure is the examination of approvals by the appropriate persons. For a sample of accounts charged off, it is also usually necessary for the auditor to examine correspondence in the client's files establishing their uncollectibility. In some cases, the auditor will also examine credit reports such as those provided by Dun & Bradstreet. After the auditor has concluded that the accounts charged off by general journal entries are proper, selected items should be traced to the accounts receivable master file as a test of the records.

ADDITIONAL INTERNAL CONTROLS OVER ACCOUNT BALANCES

The preceding discussion emphasized internal controls, tests of controls, and substantive tests of transactions for the five classes of transactions that affect account balances in the sales and collection cycle. If the internal controls for these classes of transactions are determined to be effective and the related substantive tests of transactions support the conclusions, the likelihood of misstatements in the financial statements is reduced.

In addition, there may be internal controls directly related to account balances that have not been identified or tested as a part of tests of controls or substantive tests of transactions. For the sales and collection cycle, these are most likely to affect three balance-related audit objectives: realizable value, rights and obligations, and presentation and disclosure.

Realizable value is an essential balance-related audit objective for accounts receivable because collectibility of receivables is often a major financial statement item and has been an issue in a number of accountants' liability cases. Therefore, it is common for inherent risk to be high for the realizable value objective. Several controls are common for the realizable value objective. One that has already been discussed is credit approval by an appropriate person. A second is the preparation of a periodic aged accounts receivable trial balance for review and follow-up by appropriate management personnel. A third control is a policy of charging off uncollectible accounts when they are no longer likely to be collected.

Rights and obligations and presentation and disclosure are rarely a significant problem for accounts receivable. Therefore, competent accounting personnel are typically sufficient controls for these two balance-related audit objectives.

UPDATE THE EVIDENCE PLANNING WORKSHEET

After the auditor has completed the control risk matrix for sales and cash receipts and identified any additional controls over account balances, the auditor can complete rows three through five of the evidence planning worksheet. This worksheet is illustrated for Hillsburg Hardware in Figure 11-8. These control risk assessments may be revised, depending on the results of tests of controls and substantive tests of transactions. As a result, some auditors prefer to wait until these tests have been performed to complete the control risk assessments in the evidence planning worksheet.

EFFECT OF RESULTS OF TESTS OF CONTROLS AND SUBSTANTIVE TESTS OF TRANSACTIONS

The results of the tests of controls and substantive tests of transactions will have a significant effect on the remainder of the audit, especially on the substantive tests of details of balances. The parts of the audit most affected by the tests of controls and substantive tests of transactions for the sales and collection cycle are the balances in *accounts receivable, cash, bad debt expense,* and *allowance for doubtful accounts.* Furthermore, if the test results are unsatisfactory, it is necessary to do additional substantive testing for the propriety of sales, sales returns and allowances, charge-off of uncollectible accounts, and processing of cash receipts.

FIGURE 11-8 **Evidence-Planning Worksheet to Decide Tests of Details of Balances for Hillsburg Hardware Co.—Accounts Receivable**

	Detail tie-in	Existence	Completeness	Accuracy	Classification	Cutoff	Realizable value	Rights	Presentation and disclosure
Acceptable audit risk	High	High	High	High	High	High	High	High	High
Inherent risk	Low	Low	Low	Low	Low	Low	Medium	Low	Low
Control risk–Sales	Low	Medium	Low	Low	Low	High	Low	Not applicable	Not applicable
Control risk–Cash receipts	Low	Medium	Low	Low	Low	Low	Not applicable	Not applicable	Not applicable
Control risk–Additional controls	None	None	None	None	None	None	None	Low	Low
Substantive tests of transactions–Sales									
Substantive tests of transactions–Cash receipts									
Analytical procedures									
Planned detection risk for tests of details of balances									
Planned audit evidence for tests of details of balances									

Tolerable misstatement $442,000

At the completion of the tests of controls and substantive tests of transactions, it is essential to *analyze each exception* to determine its cause and the implication of the exception on assessed control risk, which may affect the supported detection risk and thereby the remaining substantive tests. The methodology and implications of exceptions analysis are explained more fully in a later chapter.

The most significant effect of the results of the tests of controls and substantive tests of transactions in the sales and collection cycle is on the confirmation of accounts receivable. The type of confirmation, the size of the sample, and the timing of the test are all affected. The effect of the tests on accounts receivable, bad debt expense, and allowance for uncollectible accounts is considered in Chapter 12.

Figure 11-9 (p. 328) illustrates the major accounts in the sales and collection cycle and the types of audit tests used to audit these accounts. This figure was introduced in the last chapter (p. 279) and is presented here for further review.

FIGURE 11-9 Types of Audit Tests for the Sales and Collection Cycle (see Figure 11-1 on page 308 for accounts)

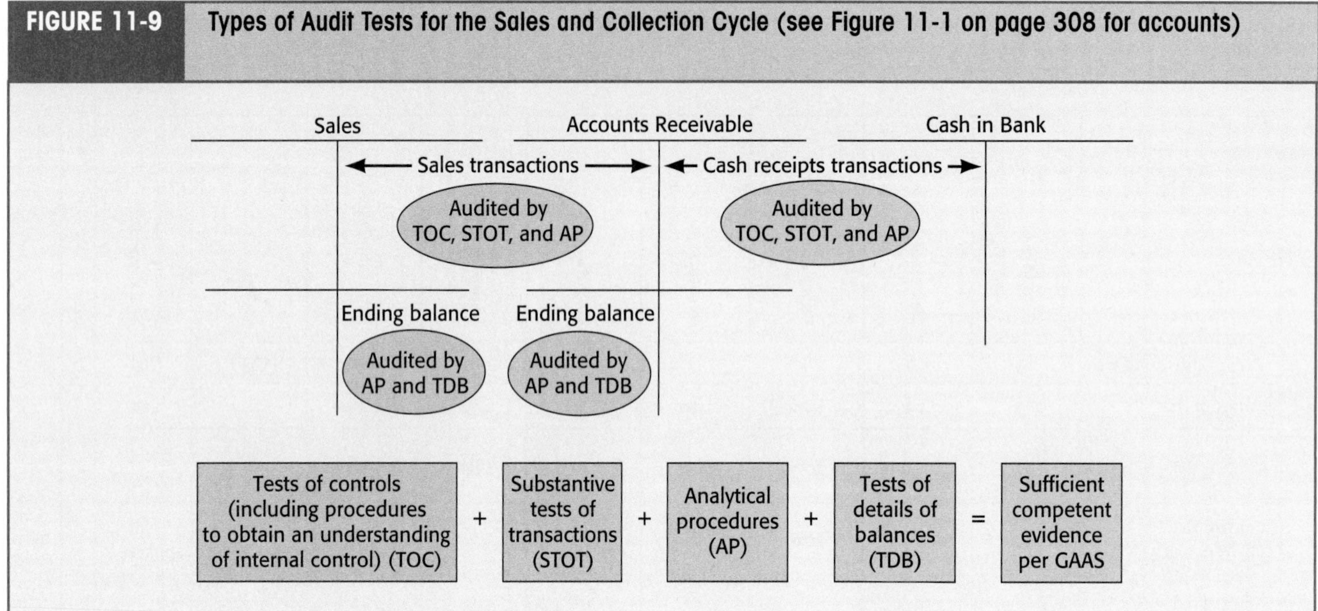

SUMMARY

This chapter deals with designing tests of controls and substantive tests of transactions for each of the five classes of transactions in the sales and collection cycle. The classes of transactions in the cycle are sales, cash receipts, sales returns and allowances, charge-off of uncollectible accounts receivable, and bad debt expense.

The methodology for designing tests of controls and substantive tests of transactions is, in concept, the same for each of the five classes of transactions and includes the following steps:

- Understand internal control
- Assess planned control risk
- Evaluate the cost-benefit of testing the controls
- Design tests of controls and substantive tests of transactions to meet transaction-related audit objectives

In designing tests of controls, the emphasis for each class of transactions is on testing internal controls that the auditor intends to rely on to reduce control risk. First, the auditor identifies internal controls, if any exist, for each transaction-related audit objective. After assessing control risk for each objective, the auditor then evaluates the cost-benefit of testing the controls. If it is cost effective, the auditor designs tests of controls to determine the effectiveness of the existing controls.

The auditor also designs substantive tests of transactions for each class of transactions to determine whether the monetary amounts of transactions are correctly recorded. Like tests of controls, substantive tests of transactions are designed for each transaction-related audit objective.

After the design of tests of controls and substantive tests of transactions for each audit objective and each class of transactions is completed, the auditor organizes the audit procedures into a performance format audit program. The purpose of this audit program is to help the auditor complete the audit tests efficiently.

ESSENTIAL TERMS

Business functions for the sales and collection cycle—the key activities that an organization must complete to execute and record business transactions for sales, cash receipts, sales returns and allowances, charge-off of uncollectible accounts, and bad debt expense

Classes of transactions in the sales and collection cycle—the categories of transactions for the sales and collection cycle in a typical company: sales, cash receipts, sales returns and allowances, charge-off of uncollectible accounts, and bad debt expense

Design format audit program—the audit procedures resulting from the auditor's decisions about the appropriate audit procedures for each audit objective; this audit program is used to prepare a performance format audit program

Lapping of accounts receivable—the postponement of entries for the collection of receivables to *conceal an existing cash shortage*; a common type of defalcation

Performance format audit program—the audit procedures for a class of transactions organized in the format in which they will be performed; this audit program is prepared from a design format audit program

Proof of cash receipts—an audit procedure to test whether all recorded cash receipts have been deposited in the bank account by reconciling the total cash receipts recorded in the cash receipts journal for a given period with the actual deposits made to the bank

Sales and collection cycle—involves the decisions and processes necessary for the transfer of the ownership of goods and services to customers after they are made available for sale; it begins with a request by a customer and ends with the conversion of material or service into an account receivable, and ultimately into cash

REVIEW QUESTIONS

11-1 **(Objective 11-2)** Explain the importance of proper credit approval for sales. What effect do adequate controls in the credit function have on the auditor's evidence accumulation?

11-2 **(Objective 11-2)** Distinguish between bad debt expense and the charge-off of uncollectible accounts for a company using the allowance method for recording uncollectible accounts receivable. Explain why they are audited in completely different ways.

11-3 **(Objective 11-3)** BestSellers.com sells fiction and nonfiction books to customers through the company's Web site. Customers place orders for books via the Web site by providing their name, address, credit card number, and expiration date. What internal controls could BestSellers.com implement to ensure that shipments of books occur only for customers who have the ability to pay for those books? At what point would BestSellers.com be able to record the sale as revenue?

11-4 **(Objective 11-4)** List the transaction-related audit objectives for the verification of sales transactions. For each objective, state one internal control that the client can use to reduce the likelihood of misstatements.

11-5 **(Objective 11-4)** State one test of control and one substantive test of transactions that the auditor can use to verify the following sales transaction-related audit objective: Recorded sales are stated at the proper amount.

11-6 **(Objective 11-4)** List the most important duties that should be segregated in the sales and collection cycle. Explain why it is desirable that each duty be segregated.

11-7 **(Objective 11-4)** Explain how prenumbered shipping documents and sales invoices can be useful controls for preventing misstatements in sales.

11-8 **(Objective 11-4)** What three types of authorizations are commonly used as internal controls for sales? For each authorization, state a substantive test that the auditor could use to verify whether the control was effective in preventing misstatements.

11-9 **(Objective 11-4)** Explain the purpose of footing and cross-footing the sales journal and tracing the totals to the general ledger.

11-10 **(Objective 11-5)** What is the difference between the auditor's approach in verifying sales returns and allowances and that for sales? Explain the reasons for the difference.

11-11 **(Objective 11-6)** Explain why auditors usually emphasize the detection of fraud in the audit of cash. Is this consistent or inconsistent with the auditor's responsibility in the audit? Explain.

11-12 **(Objective 11-6)** List the transaction-related audit objectives for the verification of cash receipts. For each objective, state one internal control that the client can use to reduce the likelihood of misstatements.

11-13 **(Objective 11-6)** List several audit procedures that the auditor can use to determine whether all cash received was recorded.

11-14 **(Objective 11-6)** Explain what is meant by a proof of cash receipts and state its purpose.

11-15 **(Objective 11-6)** Explain what is meant by lapping and discuss how the auditor can uncover it. Under what circumstances should the auditor make a special effort to uncover lapping?

11-16 **(Objective 11-7)** What audit procedures are most likely to be used to verify accounts receivable charged off as uncollectible? State the purpose of each of these procedures.

11-17 **(Objectives 11-4, 11-6)** State the relationship between the confirmation of accounts receivable and the results of the tests of controls and substantive tests of transactions.

11-18 **(Objectives 11-4, 11-6)** Under what circumstances is it acceptable to perform tests of controls and substantive tests of transactions for sales and cash receipts at an interim date?

11-19 **(Objective 11-4)** Diane Smith, CPA, performed tests of controls and substantive tests of transactions for sales for the month of March in an audit of the financial statements for the year ended December 31, 2002. Based on the excellent results of both the tests of controls and the substantive tests of transactions, she decided to significantly reduce her substantive tests of details of balances at year-end. Evaluate this decision.

MULTIPLE CHOICE QUESTIONS FROM CPA EXAMINATIONS

11-20 **(Objectives 11-4, 11-5, 11-6, 11-7)** The following questions deal with internal controls in the sales and collection cycle. Choose the best response.

a. When a customer fails to include a remittance advice with a payment, it is common for the person opening the mail to prepare one. Consequently, mail should be opened by which of the following four company employees?
   (1) Credit manager.
   (2) Sales manager.
   (3) Accounts receivable clerk.
   (4) Receptionist.

b. A key internal control in the sales and collection cycle is the separation of duties between cash handling and record keeping. The objective most directly associated with this control is to verify that
   (1) cash receipts recorded in the cash receipts journal are reasonable.
   (2) cash receipts are properly classified.
   (3) recorded cash receipts result from legitimate transactions.
   (4) existing cash receipts are recorded.

c. An auditor tests a company's policy of obtaining credit approval before shipping goods to customers in support of management's financial statement assertion of
   (1) valuation or allocation.
   (2) completeness.
   (3) existence or occurrence.
   (4) rights and obligations.

11-21 **(Objectives 11-4, 11-5)** For each of the following types of misstatements (parts a through d), select the control that should have prevented the misstatement:

a. A manufacturing company received a substantial sales return in the last month of the year, but the credit memorandum for the return was not prepared until after the auditors had completed their field work. The returned merchandise was included in the physical inventory.
   (1) Aged trial balance of accounts receivable is prepared.
   (2) Credit memoranda are prenumbered and all numbers are accounted for.
   (3) A reconciliation of the trial balance of customers' accounts with the general ledger control is prepared periodically.
   (4) Receiving reports are prepared for all materials received and such reports are accounted for on a regular basis.

b. The sales manager credited a salesman, Jack Smith, with sales that were actually "house account" sales. Later, Smith divided his excess sales commissions with the sales manager.
   (1) The summary sales entries are checked periodically by persons independent of sales functions.
   (2) Sales orders are reviewed and approved by persons independent of the sales department.
   (3) The internal auditor compares the sales commission statements with the cash disbursements record.
   (4) Sales orders are prenumbered, and all numbers are accounted for.

c. A sales invoice for $5,200 was computed correctly but, by mistake, was key-entered as $2,500 to the sales journal and to the accounts receivable master file. The customer remitted only $2,500, the amount on his monthly statement.
   (1) Prelistings and predetermined totals are used to control postings.
   (2) Sales invoice serial numbers, prices, discounts, extensions, and footings are independently checked.

(3) The customers' monthly statements are verified and mailed by a responsible person other than the bookkeeper who prepared them.
(4) Unauthorized remittance deductions made by customers or other matters in dispute are investigated promptly by a person independent of the accounts receivable function.

11-22 **(Objectives 11-1, 11-4)** The following questions deal with audit evidence for the sales and collection cycle. Choose the best response.

a. Auditors sometimes use comparison of ratios as audit evidence. For example, an unexplained decrease in the ratio of gross profit to sales may suggest which of the following possibilities?
   (1) Unrecorded acquisitions.
   (2) Unrecorded sales.
   (3) Merchandise acquisitions being charged to selling and general expense.
   (4) Fictitious sales.
b. An auditor is performing substantive tests of transactions for sales. One step is to trace a sample of debit entries from the accounts receivable master file back to the supporting duplicate sales invoices. What would the auditor intend to establish by this step?
   (1) Sales invoices represent existing sales.
   (2) All sales have been recorded.
   (3) All sales invoices have been properly posted to customer accounts.
   (4) Debit entries in the accounts receivable master file are properly supported by sales invoices.
c. To verify that all sales transactions have been recorded, a substantive test of transactions should be completed on a representative sample drawn from
   (1) entries in the sales journal.
   (2) the billing clerk's file of sales orders.
   (3) a file of duplicate copies of sales invoices for which all prenumbered forms in the series have been accounted.
   (4) the shipping clerk's file of duplicate copies of bills of lading.

DISCUSSION QUESTIONS AND PROBLEMS

11-23 **(Objectives 11-3, 11-4, 11-5, 11-6)** Items 1 through 9 are selected questions of the type generally found in internal control questionnaires used by auditors to obtain an understanding of internal control in the sales and collection cycle. In using the questionnaire for a client, a "yes" response to a question indicates a possible internal control, whereas a "no" indicates a potential weakness.

1. Are sales invoices independently compared with customers' orders for prices, quantities, extensions, and footings?
2. Are sales orders, invoices, and credit memoranda issued and filed in numerical sequence and are the sequences accounted for periodically?
3. Are the selling and cash register functions independent of the cash receipts, shipping, delivery, and billing functions?
4. Are all C.O.D., scrap, equipment, and cash sales accounted for in the same manner as charge sales and is the record keeping independent of the collection procedure?
5. Is the collection function independent of and does it constitute a check on billing and recording sales?
6. Are accounts receivable master files balanced regularly to control accounts by an employee independent of billing functions?
7. Are cash receipts recorded by persons independent of the mail-opening and receipts-listing functions?
8. Are receipts deposited intact daily on a timely basis?
9. Are sales generated through the company's Web site automatically recorded in the sales system?

Required

a. For each of the preceding questions, state the transaction-related audit objectives being fulfilled if the control is in effect.
b. For each control, list a test of control to test its effectiveness.
c. For each of the preceding questions, identify the nature of the potential financial misstatements.
d. For each of the potential misstatements in part c, list a substantive audit procedure to determine whether a material misstatement exists.

11-24 **(Objectives 11-3, 11-4, 11-6)** The following misstatements are included in the accounting records of the Joyce Manufacturing Company:

1. A sales invoice was misadded by $1,000 as a result of a key-entry mistake.
2. A material sale was unintentionally recorded for the second time on the last day of the year. The sale had originally been recorded 2 days earlier.

3. Cash paid on accounts receivable was stolen by the mail clerk when the mail was opened.
4. Cash paid on accounts receivable that had been prelisted by a secretary was stolen by the bookkeeper who records cash receipts and accounts receivable. He failed to record the transactions.
5. A shipment to a customer was not billed because of the loss of the bill of lading.
6. Merchandise was shipped to a customer, but no bill of lading was prepared. Because billings are prepared from bills of lading, the customer was not billed.
7. A sale to a residential customer was unintentionally classified as a commercial sale.
8. Sales generated through the company's Web site are recorded at the point the customers submit the orders online.

Required

a. Identify whether each misstatement is an error or a fraud.

b. For each misstatement, state a control that should have prevented it from occurring on a continuing basis.

c. For each misstatement, state a substantive audit procedure that could uncover it.

11-25 **(Objectives 11-4, 11-5, 11-6)** The following are commonly performed tests of controls and substantive tests of transactions audit procedures in the sales and collection cycle:

1. Examine sales returns for approval by an authorized official.
2. Account for a sequence of shipping documents and examine each one to make sure that a duplicate sales invoice is attached.
3. Account for a sequence of sales invoices and examine each one to make sure that a duplicate copy of the shipping document is attached.
4. Compare the quantity and description of items on shipping documents with the related duplicate sales invoices.
5. Trace recorded sales in the sales journal to the related accounts receivable master file and compare the customer name, date, and amount for each one.
6. Review the prelisting in the cash receipts book to determine whether cash is prelisted daily.
7. Reconcile the recorded cash receipts on the prelisting with the cash receipts journal and the bank statement for a 1-month period.

Required

a. Identify whether each audit procedure is a test of control or a substantive test of transactions.

b. State which of the six transaction-related audit objectives each of the audit procedures fulfills.

c. Identify the type of evidence used for each audit procedure, such as confirmation and observation.

11-26 **(Objective 11-4)** The following are selected transaction-related audit objectives and audit procedures for sales transactions:

Transaction-Related Audit Objectives

1. Recorded sales exist.
2. Existing sales are recorded.
3. Sales transactions are properly included in the accounts receivable master file and are correctly summarized.

Procedures

1. Trace a sample of shipping documents to related duplicate sales invoices and the sales journal to make sure that the shipment was billed.
2. Examine a sample of duplicate sales invoices to determine whether each one has a shipping document attached.
3. Examine the sales journal for a sample of sales transactions to determine whether each one has a tick mark in the margin indicating that it has been compared with the accounts receivable master file for customer name, date, and amount.
4. Examine a sample of shipping documents to determine whether each one has a duplicate sales invoice number written on the bottom left corner.
5. Trace a sample of debit entries in the accounts receivable master file to the sales journal to determine whether the date, customer name, and amount are the same.
6. Trace a sample of duplicate sales invoices to related shipping documents filed in the shipping department to make sure that a shipment was made.

Required

a. For each objective, identify at least one specific misstatement that could occur.

b. Describe the differences between the purposes of the first and second objectives.

c. For each audit procedure, identify it as a test of control or substantive test of transactions. (There are three of each.)

d. For each objective, identify one test of control and one substantive test of transactions.

e. For each test of control, state the internal control that is being tested. Also, identify or describe a misstatement that the client is trying to prevent by use of the control.

11-27 (Objectives 11-2, 11-4) The following sales procedures were encountered during the annual audit of Marvel Wholesale Distributing Company:

Customer orders are received by the sales order department. A clerk computes the approximate dollar amount of the order and sends it to the credit department for approval. Credit approval is stamped on the order and sent to the accounting department. A computer is then used to generate two copies of a sales invoice. The order is filed in the customer order file.

The customer copy of the sales invoice is held in a pending file awaiting notification that the order was shipped. The shipping copy of the sales invoice is routed through the warehouse, and the shipping department has authority for the respective departments to release and ship the merchandise. Shipping department personnel pack the order and manually prepare a three-copy bill of lading: The original copy is mailed to the customer, the second copy is sent with the shipment, and the other is filed in sequence in the bill of lading file. The sales invoice shipping copy is sent to the accounting department with any changes resulting from lack of available merchandise.

A clerk in accounting matches the received sales invoice shipping copy with the sales invoice customer copy from the pending file. Quantities on the two invoices are compared and prices are compared on an approved price list. The customer copy is then mailed to the customer, and the shipping copy is sent to the data processing department.

The data processing clerk in accounting enters the sales invoice data into the computer, which is used to prepare the sales journal and update the accounts receivable master file. She files the shipping copy in the sales invoice file in numerical sequence.

a. To determine whether the internal controls operated effectively to minimize instances of failure to post invoices to customers' accounts receivable master file, the auditor would select a sample of transactions from the population represented by the
   (1) customer order file.
   (2) bill of lading file.
   (3) customers' accounts receivable master file.
   (4) sales invoice file.

b. To determine whether the internal controls operated effectively to minimize instances of failure to invoice a shipment, the auditor would select a sample of transactions from the population represented by the
   (1) customer order file.
   (2) bill of lading file.
   (3) customers' accounts receivable master file.
   (4) sales invoice file.

c. To gather audit evidence that uncollected items in customers' accounts represented existing trade receivables, the auditor would select a sample of items from the population represented by the
   (1) customer order file.
   (2) bill of lading file.
   (3) customers' accounts receivable master file.
   (4) sales invoice file.*

11-28 (Objectives 11-4, 11-6) The following are common audit procedures for tests of sales and cash receipts:

1. Compare the quantity and description of items on duplicate sales invoices with related shipping documents.
2. Trace recorded cash receipts in the accounts receivable master file to the cash receipts journal and compare the customer name, date, and amount of each one.
3. Examine duplicate sales invoices for an indication that unit selling prices were compared to the approved price list.
4. Examine duplicate sales invoices to determine whether the account classification for sales has been included on the document.
5. Examine the sales journal for related-party transactions, notes receivable, and other unusual items.
6. Select a sample of customer orders and trace the document to related shipping documents, sales invoices, and the accounts receivable master file for comparison of name, date, and amount.

*AICPA adapted.

7. Perform a proof of cash receipts.
8. Examine a sample of remittance advices for approval of cash discounts.
9. Account for a numerical sequence of remittance advices and determine whether there is a cross-reference mark for each one, indicating that it has been recorded in the cash receipts journal.

Required

a. Identify whether each audit procedure is a test of control or substantive test of transactions.

b. State which transaction-related audit objective(s) each of the audit procedures fulfills.

c. For each test of control in part a, state a substantive test that could be used to determine whether there was a monetary misstatement.

11-29 **(Objective 11-6)** Appliances Repair and Service Company bills all customers rather than collecting in cash when services are provided. All mail is opened by Tom Gyders, treasurer. Gyders, a CPA, is the most qualified person in the company who is in the office daily. Therefore, he can solve problems and respond to customers' needs quickly. Upon receipt of cash, he immediately prepares a listing of the cash and a duplicate deposit slip. Cash is deposited daily. Gyders uses the listing to enter the financial transactions in the computerized accounting records. He also contacts customers about uncollected accounts receivable. Because he is so knowledgeable about the business and each customer, he grants credit, authorizes all sales allowances, and charges off uncollectible accounts. The owner is extremely pleased with the efficiency of the company. He can run the business without spending much time there because of Gyders' effectiveness.

Imagine the owner's surprise when he discovers that Gyders has committed a major theft of the company's cash receipts. He did so by not recording sales, recording improper credits to recorded accounts receivable, and overstating receivables.

Required

a. Given that cash was prelisted, went only to the treasurer, and was deposited daily, what internal control deficiency permitted the fraud?

b. What are the benefits of a prelisting of cash? Who should prepare the prelisting and what duties should that person not perform?

c. Assume that an appropriate person, as discussed in part b, prepares a prelisting of cash. What is to prevent that person from taking the cash after it is prelisted but before it is deposited?

d. Who should deposit the cash, given your answer to part b?

11-30 **(Objective 11-6)** You have been asked by the board of trustees of a local church to review its accounting procedures. As part of this review you have prepared the following comments about the collections made at weekly services and record keeping for members' pledges and contributions:

1. The church's board of trustees has delegated responsibility for financial management and audit of the financial records to the finance committee. This group prepares the annual budget and approves major cash disbursements but is not involved in collections or record keeping. No audit has been considered necessary in recent years because the same trusted employee has kept church records and served as financial secretary for 15 years.

2. The collection at the weekly service is taken by a team of ushers. The head usher counts the collection in the church office after each service. He then places the collection and a notation of the amount in the church safe. The next morning, the financial secretary opens the safe and recounts the collection. He withholds about $100 to meet cash expenditures during the coming week and deposits the remainder intact. To facilitate the deposit, members who contribute by check are asked to draw their checks to cash.

3. At their request, a few members are furnished prenumbered predated envelopes in which to insert their weekly contributions. The head usher removes the cash from the envelopes to be counted with the loose cash included in the collection and discards the envelopes. No record is maintained of issuance or return of the envelopes, and the envelope system is not encouraged.

4. Each member is asked to prepare a contribution pledge card annually. The pledge is regarded as a moral commitment by the member to contribute a stated weekly amount. Based on the amounts shown on the pledge cards, the financial secretary furnishes a letter to members, upon request, to support the tax deductibility of their contributions.

Required

Identify the weaknesses and recommend improvements in procedures for collection made at weekly services and record keeping for members' pledges and contributions. Use the methodology for identifying weaknesses that was discussed in Chapter 9. Organize your answer sheets as follows:*

Weakness	Recommended Improvement

11-31 **(Objectives 11-3, 11-4)** YourTeam.com is an online retailer of college and professional sports team memorabilia, such as hats, shirts, pennants and other sports logo products. Consumers select

*AICPA adapted.

the college or professional team from a pull-down menu on the company's Web site. For each listed team, the Web site provides a product description, picture, and price for all products sold online. Customers click on the product number of the items they wish to purchase. The following are internal controls YourTeam.com has established for its online sales:

1. Only products shown on the Web site can be purchased online. Other company products not shown on the Web site listing are unavailable for online sale.
2. The online sales system is linked to the perpetual inventory system that verifies quantities on hand before processing the sale.
3. Before the sale is authorized, YourTeam.com obtains credit card authorization codes electronically from the credit card agency.
4. Online sales are rejected if the customer's shipping address does not match the credit card's billing address.
5. Before the sale is finalized, the online screen shows the product name, description, unit price, and total sales price for the online transaction. Customers must click on the Accept or Reject sales buttons to indicate approval or rejection of the online sale.
6. Once customers approve the online sale, the online sales system generates a Pending Sales file, which is an online data file that is used by warehouse personnel to process shipments. Online sales are not recorded in the sales journal until warehouse personnel enter the bill of lading number and date of shipment into the Pending Sales data file.

Required

a. For each control, identify the transaction-related audit objective(s) being fulfilled if each control is in effect.

b. For each control, describe potential financial misstatements that could occur if the control was not present.

CASE

11-32 (Objectives 11-4, 11-6) The customer billing and cash receipts functions of the Robinson Company, a small paint manufacturer, are attended to by a receptionist, an accounts receivable clerk, and a cashier who also serves as a secretary. The company's paint products are sold to wholesalers and retail stores. The following describes all the procedures performed by the employees of the Robinson Company pertaining to customer billings and cash receipts:

1. The mail is opened by the receptionist, who gives the customers' purchase orders to the accounts receivable clerk. Fifteen to twenty orders are received each day. Under instructions to expedite the shipment of orders, the accounts receivable clerk at once prepares a five-copy sales invoice form that is distributed as follows:

(a) Copy 1 is the customer billing copy and is held by the accounts receivable clerk until notice of shipment is received.
(b) Copy 2 is the accounts receivable department copy and is held for the ultimate updating of the accounting records.
(c) Copies 3 and 4 are sent to the shipping department.
(d) Copy 5 is sent to the storeroom as authority for the release of goods to the shipping department.

2. After the paint order has been moved from the storeroom to the shipping department, the shipping department prepares the bills of lading and labels the cartons. Sales invoice copy 4 is inserted in a carton as a packing slip. After the trucker has picked up the shipment, the customer's copy of the bill of lading and copy 3, on which are noted any undershipments, are returned to the accounts receivable clerk. The company does not "back order" in the event of undershipments; customers are expected to reorder the merchandise. The Robinson Company's copy of the bill of lading is filed by the shipping department.

3. When copy 3 and the customer's copy of the bill of lading are received by the accounts receivable clerk, copies 1 and 2 are completed by numbering them and inserting quantities shipped, unit prices, extensions, discounts, and totals. Copies 2 and 3 are stapled together.

4. The accounts receivable clerk then enters the sales transactions into the computerized accounting records from copy 2. Only the quantities, prices, discounts, and accounts are entered because the computer computes extensions and totals. These extensions and totals are then compared with copy 1. The accounts receivable clerk then mails copy 1 and the copy of the bill of lading to the customer. Copy 2 is then filed, along with staple-attached copy 3, in numerical order.

5. Because the Robinson Company is short of cash, the deposit of cash receipts is also expedited. The receptionist turns over all mail receipts and related correspondence to the accounts receivable clerk, who examines the checks and determines that the accompanying vouchers or correspondence contain enough detail to permit the entering of the transactions into the computer. The accounts receivable clerk then endorses the checks and gives them to the cashier, who prepares the daily deposit. No currency is received in the mail, and no paint is sold over the counter at the factory.

6. The accounts receivable clerk uses the vouchers or correspondence that accompanied the checks to enter the transactions into the computerized accounting records. The accounts receivable clerk is the one who corresponds with customers about unauthorized deductions for discounts, freight or advertising allowances, returns, and so forth, and prepares the appropriate credit memos. Disputed items of large amounts are turned over to the sales manager for settlement. Each month, the accounts receivable clerk prints out a trial balance of accounts receivable and compares the total with the general ledger control accounts for accounts receivable.

Required

a. Identify the internal control weaknesses in the Robinson Company's procedures related to customer billings and cash receipts and the accounting for these transactions. Use the methodology for identifying weaknesses that was discussed in Chapter 9.

b. For each weakness, identify the error or fraud that could result.

c. For each weakness, list one substantive audit procedure for testing the significance of the potential misstatement.*

INTEGRATED CASE APPLICATION—PINNACLE MANUFACTURING: PART II

11-33 (Objectives 11-4, 11-6) In Part I of this case study (pp. 274–276), you obtained an understanding of internal control and made an initial assessment of control risk for each transaction-related audit objective for acquisition and cash disbursement transactions. The purpose of Part II is to continue the assessment of control risk by determining the appropriate tests of controls and substantive tests of transactions.

Assume that in Part I it was determined that the key internal controls are the following:

1. Segregation of the purchasing, receiving, and cash disbursement functions
2. Review of supportive documents and signing of checks by an independent, authorized person
3. Use of prenumbered checks, properly accounted for
4. Use of prenumbered purchase orders, properly accounted for
5. Use of prenumbered document package, properly accounted for
6. Internal verification of document package before check preparation
7. Independent monthly reconciliation of bank statement

For requirements a and b, you should follow a format similar to the one illustrated for sales in Table 11-2 (pp. 315–316). You should prepare one matrix for acquisitions and a separate one for cash disbursements. Observe that the first column in each matrix should include the transaction-related audit objectives from the top row in the worksheet you prepared for Problem 9-31. Also, the key internal controls include only those seven just listed, and the tests of controls include only those you developed in requirement a. The substantive tests of transactions procedures should be designed based on an assumption that the results of the tests of controls will be favorable.

Required

a. Design tests of controls audit procedures that will provide appropriate evidence for each of these controls. Do not include more than two tests of control for each internal control.

b. Although controls appear to be well designed and test of control deviations are not expected, last year's results indicate that misstatements may still exist. Therefore, you decide to perform substantive tests of transactions for acquisitions and cash disbursements. Design substantive tests of transactions for each transaction-related audit objective. Do not includse more than two substantive tests of transactions for any objective. Use Tables 11-2 on pages 315–316 and 11-3 on pages 323–324 as frames of reference.

c. Combine the tests of controls and substantive tests of transactions designed in requirements a and b into a performance format. Include both tests of acquisitions and cash disbursements in the same audit program. Use Figure 11-7 on page 325 as a frame of reference for preparing the performance format audit program.

INTERNET PROBLEM 11-1: ELECTRONIC SIGNATURES

Reference the CW site. When conducting traditional forms of business, handwritten signatures entered onto contracts and other documents establish a legal basis to enforce the terms of the transaction. However, when companies engage in e-commerce to transact business, the ability to obtain handwritten signatures is absent, requiring companies to rely on electronically generated digital signatures. This problem requires students to learn about recent legislation, summarized on the Office of Management and Budget's Web site, designed to establish the legal enforceability of certain electronic signatures and documents.

*AICPA adapted.

CHAPTER 12

COMPLETING THE TESTS IN THE SALES AND COLLECTION CYCLE: ACCOUNTS RECEIVABLE

LEARNING OBJECTIVES

After studying this chapter, you should be able to

12-1 Describe the methodology for designing tests of details of balances using the audit risk model.

12-2 Design and perform analytical procedures for accounts in the sales and collection cycle.

12-3 Design and perform tests of details of balances for accounts receivable for each balance-related audit objective.

12-4 Obtain and evaluate accounts receivable confirmations.

12-5 Design audit procedures for the audit of accounts receivable, using an evidence planning worksheet as a guide.

WHEN MORE ISN'T BETTER

On Susan Jackson's first audit assignment, she is asked to handle the confirmation of accounts receivable. She is excited because it was one of the areas in her auditing class that she was confident that she understood. The audit client is a retailer with a large number of customer accounts. In previous years, Susan's firm confirmed these accounts using negative confirmations. Last year, 200 negative confirmations were sent. Confirmations were sent 1 month before year-end. Those that were returned showed only timing differences; none represented a misstatement in the client's books.

The tentative audit plan for the current year is to do about the same as the prior year. Before the current year's planned confirmation date, Susan obtains an understanding of internal controls over sales and cash receipts transactions. She discovers that a new system for sales transactions that includes Internet-based sales has been implemented, but the client is having considerable problems getting the system to work properly. There are a significant number of misstatements in recording sales during the past few months. Susan's tests of controls and substantive tests of sales transactions also identify similar misstatements.

When Susan takes her findings to her supervisor and asks him what to do, he responds, "No problem, Susan. Just send 300 confirmation requests instead of the usual 200. And be sure you get a good random sample so we can get a good projection of the results." Susan is seriously bothered by this instruction. She recalls from her auditing class that negative confirmation requests aren't considered to be good evidence when there are weak controls. Because customers are asked to respond only when there are differences, the auditor cannot be confident of the correct value for each misstatement in the sample. If this is so, then the results of using negative confirmations will be misleading even if a request is sent to *every* account. Susan concludes that expanding the sample size is the wrong solution. When Susan talks with her supervisor about her point of view, this time he responds, "You are absolutely right. I spoke too quickly. We need to sit down and think about a better strategy to find out if accounts receivable is materially misstated."

In the last chapter we examined tests of controls and substantive tests of transactions for the sales and collection cycle. Both types of tests are a part of phase II of the audit process. We now move on to phase III and turn our attention to analytical procedures and tests of details of balances for the sales and collection cycle.

As was shown in the vignette introducing this chapter, it is essential for the auditor to select the appropriate evidence, given the conclusions that are reached in evaluating initial controls and performing tests of controls and substantive tests of transactions. Because reliable evidence is available, auditors do extensive analytical procedures and tests of details of balances in almost all audits to reduce detection risk for account balances to a reasonable level. To obtain reasonable assurance that account balances are fairly stated at a reasonable cost, the auditor must carefully design the most appropriate and cost-effective analytical procedures and tests of details of balances. This chapter examines designing analytical procedures and tests of details of balances for accounts receivable.

METHODOLOGY FOR DESIGNING TESTS OF DETAILS OF BALANCES

OBJECTIVE 12-1

Describe the methodology for designing tests of details of balances using the audit risk model.

Figure 12-1 shows the methodology that auditors follow in designing the appropriate tests of details of balances for accounts receivable. Notice that the second to the last step includes designing and performing analytical procedures. The methodology was introduced in Chapter 10 and is now applied to the audit of accounts receivable. The methodology shown in Figure 12-1 relates directly to the evidence planning worksheet first introduced in Chapter 8. The worksheet was partially completed in Chapter 8 for materiality and risk considerations (part of phase I) and was further completed as a part of the study of controls in the last chapter (phase II). The results of tests of controls and substantive tests of transactions (also part of phase II) must also be incorporated in the evidence planning worksheet. We will continue to complete the worksheet as we proceed through phase III in this chapter.

Deciding the appropriate tests of details of balances evidence is complicated because it must be decided on an objective-by-objective basis, and there are several interactions that affect the evidence decision. For example, the auditor must consider inherent risk, which may differ by objective, and results of substantive tests of sales and cash receipts, which also may vary by objective. The auditor must also consider the results of tests of controls and the related control risk assessment.

In designing tests of details of balances for accounts receivable, it is essential to satisfy each of the nine balance-related audit objectives first discussed in Chapter 5. It was shown in Chapter 5 that these nine general objectives are the same for all accounts. Specifically applied to accounts receivable, they are called **accounts receivable balance-related audit objectives** and are as follows:[1]

1. Accounts receivable in the aged trial balance agree with related master file amounts, and the total is correctly added and agrees with the general ledger. (Detail tie-in)
2. Recorded accounts receivable exist. (Existence)
3. Existing accounts receivable are included. (Completeness)
4. Accounts receivable are accurate. (Accuracy)
5. Accounts receivable are properly classified. (Classification)
6. Cutoff for accounts receivable is correct. (Cutoff)
7. Accounts receivable is stated at realizable value. (Realizable value)
8. The client has rights to accounts receivable. (Rights)
9. Accounts receivable presentation and disclosures are proper. (Presentation and disclosure)

The columns in the evidence planning worksheet in Figure 12-7 (p. 356) include the balance-related audit objectives. The auditor uses the factors in the rows to aid in assessing planned detection risk for accounts receivable, by objective. These factors were studied in earlier chapters.

[1]Detail tie-in is included as the first objective here, compared with being objective 6 in Chapter 5, because tests for detail tie-in are normally done first.

FIGURE 12-1 Methodology for Designing Tests of Details of Balances for Accounts Receivable

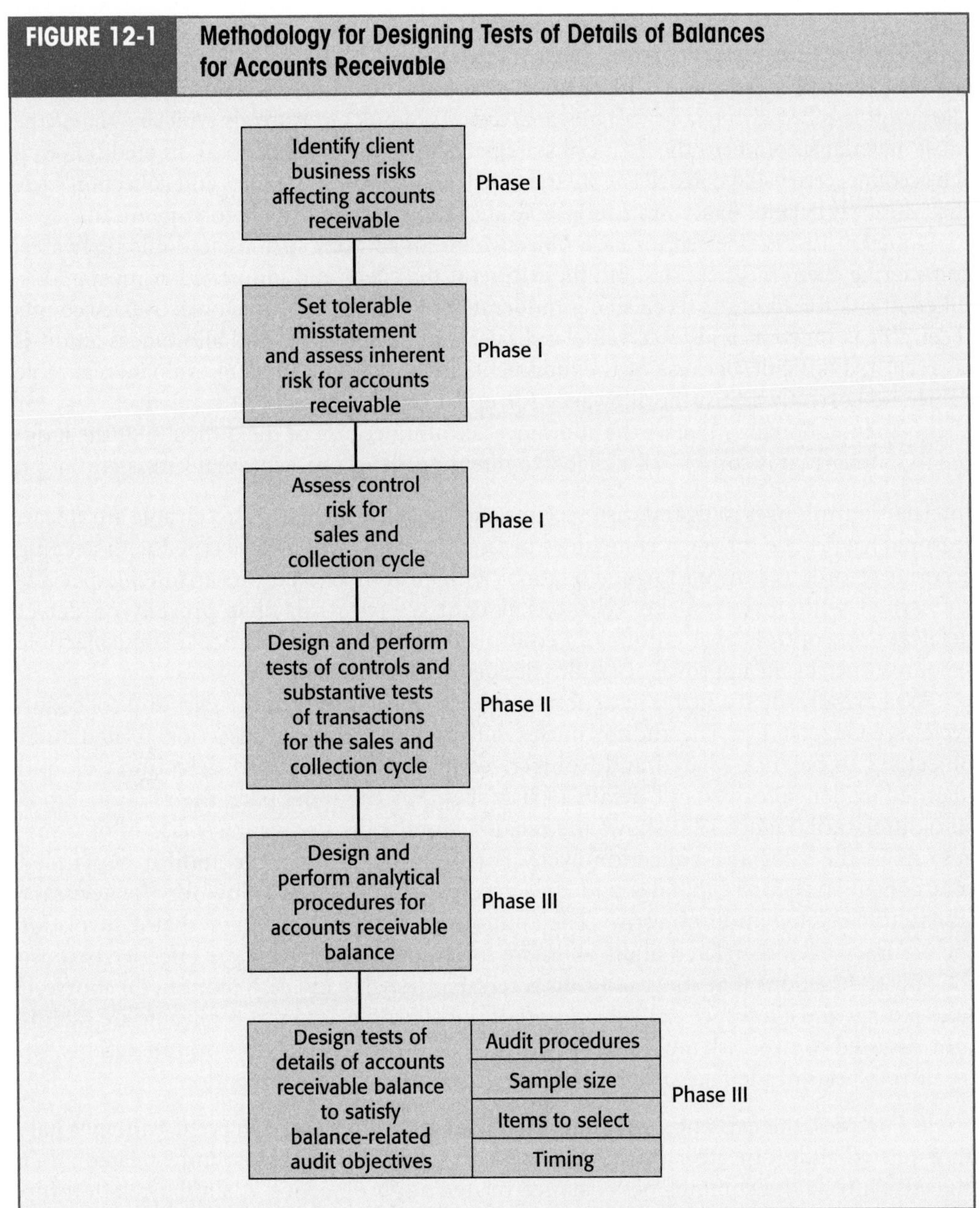

Identify client business risks affecting accounts receivable
Phase I
Set tolerable misstatement and assess inherent risk for accounts receivable
Phase I
Assess control risk for sales and collection cycle
Phase I
Design and perform tests of controls and substantive tests of transactions for the sales and collection cycle
Phase II
Design and perform analytical procedures for accounts receivable balance
Phase III
Design tests of details of accounts receivable balance to satisfy balance-related audit objectives
Audit procedures
Sample size
Items to select
Timing
Phase III

It is important for students of auditing to understand the entire methodology for designing tests of details of balances for accounts receivable and all other accounts. The following discussion explains the methodology. Portions of the discussion are a review of information studied in earlier chapters, but they are intended to aid in understanding the relationship of each part of Figure 12-1 to designing tests of details of balances.

Identify Client Business Risks Affecting Accounts Receivable (Phase I)

Tests of accounts receivable are based on the auditor's understanding of the client's business and industry, discussed in Chapter 7. As part of this understanding, the auditor studies the client's industry and external environment and evaluates management objectives and business processes to identify significant client business risks that could affect the financial statements, including accounts receivable. As part of gaining this understanding, the auditor also performs preliminary analytical procedures that may indicate increased risk of misstatements in accounts receivable.

Client business risks affecting accounts receivable are considered in the auditor's evaluation of inherent risk and planned evidence for accounts receivable. For example, as a result of adverse changes in the industry's economic environment, the auditor may increase inherent risk for net realizable value of accounts receivable.

Set Tolerable Misstatement and Assess Inherent Risk (Phase I)

As studied in Chapter 8, the auditor first decides the preliminary judgment about materiality for the entire financial statements. Next, the auditor allocates the preliminary judgment amount to each significant balance sheet account, including accounts receivable. This allocation is called *setting tolerable misstatement.* Accounts receivable is typically one of the most material accounts in the financial statements for companies that sell on credit. Even if the accounts receivable balance is not large, the transactions in the sales and collection cycle that affect the balance in accounts receivable are almost certain to be highly significant.

Inherent risk is assessed for each objective for an account such as accounts receivable, considering client business risk and the nature of the client and industry. For most audits, inherent risk for accounts receivable is moderate or low except for two objectives: Accounts receivable is stated at realizable value and sales and sales returns and allowances cutoff is correct. It is difficult, because of the judgments involved, for clients to evaluate realizable value and correctly adjust the allowance for uncollectible accounts. It is relatively easy for clients to intentionally misstate the allowance account because of the difficulty of the judgments. Similarly, it is common for clients to intentionally or unintentionally misstate cutoff.

Assess Control Risk for the Sales and Collection Cycle (Phase I)

Internal controls over sales and cash receipts and the related accounts receivable are at least reasonably effective for most companies because management is concerned with keeping accurate records as a means to good relations with customers. Auditors are often especially concerned with three aspects of internal controls: controls that prevent or detect defalcations, controls over cutoff, and controls related to the allowance for uncollectible accounts, such as the approval of credit sales before shipment.

We have already studied transaction-related audit objectives in the sales and collection cycle (see Chapter 11). The auditor must relate control risk for transaction-related audit objectives to balance-related audit objectives in deciding planned detection risk and planned evidence for tests of details of balances. For the most part, the relationship is straightforward. Figure 12-2 shows the relationship for the two primary classes of transactions in the sales and collection cycle. For example, assume the auditor concluded that control risk for both sales and cash receipts transactions is low for the accuracy transaction-related audit objective. The auditor can therefore conclude that controls for the accuracy balance-related audit objective for accounts receivable are effective because the only transactions that affect accounts receivable are sales and cash receipts. Of course, if sales returns and allowances and charge-off of uncollectible accounts receivable are significant, assessed control risk must also be considered for these two classes of transactions.

Two aspects of the relationships in Figure 12-2 deserve special mention:

Retail Revenue Management

1. For sales, the existence transaction-related audit objective affects the existence balance-related audit objective, but for cash receipts the existence transaction-related audit objective affects the completeness balance-related audit objective. A similar relationship exists for the completeness transaction-related audit objective. The reason for this somewhat surprising conclusion is that an increase of sales increases accounts receivable, but an increase of cash receipts decreases accounts receivable. For example, recording a sale that did not occur violates the existence transaction-related audit objective and existence balance-related audit objective (both overstatements). Recording a cash receipt that did not occur violates the existence transaction-related audit objective, but it violates the completeness balance-related audit objective for accounts receivable because a receivable that is still outstanding is no longer included in the records.

2. Three accounts receivable balance-related audit objectives are not affected by assessed control risk for classes of transactions. These are realizable value, rights, and presentation and disclosure. When the auditor wants to reduce assessed control risk below the maximum for these three objectives, separate controls are identified and tested.

Figure 12-7 on page 356 includes three rows for assessed control risk: one for sales, one for cash receipts, and one for additional controls related to the accounts receivable balance. The source of each control risk for sales and cash receipts is the control risk matrix, assuming that the tests of controls results supported the original assessment. The auditor makes a separate assessment of control risk for objectives related only to the accounts receivable balance.

FIGURE 12-2 **Relationship Between Transaction-Related Audit Objectives for the Sales and Collection Cycle and Balance-Related Audit Objectives for Accounts Receivable**

CLASS OF TRANSACTIONS	TRANSACTION-RELATED AUDIT OBJECTIVES	ACCOUNTS RECEIVABLE BALANCE-RELATED AUDIT OBJECTIVES								
		Detail tie-in	Existence	Completeness	Accuracy	Classification	Cutoff	Realizable value	Rights	Presentation and disclosure
Sales	Existence		X							
	Completeness			X						
	Accuracy				X					
	Classification					X				
	Timing						X			
	Posting and summarization	X								
Cash receipts	Existence			X						
	Completeness		X							
	Accuracy				X					
	Classification					X				
	Timing						X			
	Posting and summarization	X								

Design and Perform Tests of Controls and Substantive Tests of Transactions (Phase III)

Designing audit procedures for tests of controls and substantive tests of transactions were covered in the last chapter. The results of the tests of controls determine whether assessed control risk for sales and cash receipts needs to be revised. The results of the substantive tests of transactions are used to determine the extent to which planned detection risk is satisfied for each accounts receivable balance-related audit objective. Chapter 13, which deals with audit sampling, includes deciding sample sizes, performing tests of controls and substantive tests of transactions, and projecting sample results to the population. The evidence planning worksheet in Figure 12-7 shows three rows for control risk and two for substantive tests of transactions, one for sales, and the other for cash receipts. These results assume that audit sampling for tests of sales and cash receipts has been completed and evaluated. Figure 12-7 shows the conclusions reached after the tests were completed.

Design and Perform Analytical Procedures (Phase III)

OBJECTIVE 12-2

Design and perform analytical procedures for accounts in the sales and collection cycle.

As discussed in Chapter 7, analytical procedures are often done during three phases of the audit: during planning, when performing detailed tests, and as a part of completing the audit. This chapter covers those done during planning and when performing detailed tests for accounts in the sales and collection cycle.

Most analytical procedures performed during the detailed testing phase are done after the balance sheet date but before tests of details of balances. It makes little sense to perform extensive analytical procedures before the client has recorded all transactions for the year and finalized the financial statements.

Analytical procedures are done for the entire sales and collection cycle, not only for accounts receivable. This is because of the close relationship between income statement

TABLE 12-1 Analytical Procedures for the Sales and Collection Cycle

Analytical Procedure	Possible Misstatement
Compare gross margin percentage with previous years (by product line).	Overstatement or understatement of sales and accounts receivable.
Compare sales by month (by product line) over time.	Overstatement or understatement of sales and accounts receivable.
Compare sales returns and allowances as a percentage of gross sales with previous years (by product line).	Overstatement or understatement of sales returns and allowances and accounts receivable.
Compare individual customer balances over a stated amount with previous years.	Misstatements in accounts receivable and related income statement accounts.
Compare bad debt expense as a percentage of gross sales with previous years.	Uncollectible accounts receivable that have not been provided for.
Compare number of days that accounts receivable are outstanding with previous years and related turnover of accounts receivable.	Overstatement or understatement of allowance for uncollectible accounts and bad debt expense; also may indicate fictitious accounts receivable.
Compare aging categories as a percentage of accounts receivable with previous years.	Overstatement or understatement of allowance for uncollectible accounts and bad debt expense.
Compare allowance for uncollectible accounts as a percentage of accounts receivable with previous years.	Overstatement or understatement of allowance for uncollectible accounts and bad debt expense.
Compare charge-off of uncollectible accounts as a percentage of total accounts receivable with previous years.	Overstatement or understatement of allowance for uncollectible accounts and bad debt expense.

and balance sheet accounts. If the auditor determines possible misstatement in sales or sales returns and allowances through analytical procedures, accounts receivable will likely be the offsetting misstatement.

Table 12-1 presents examples of the major types of ratios and comparisons for the sales and collection cycle and potential misstatements that may be indicated by the analytical procedures. Although Table 12-1 focuses on the comparison of current year results with previous years, the auditor also considers current year results compared to budgets and industry trends. It is important to observe in the "possible misstatement" column that both balance sheet and income statement accounts are affected. For example, when the auditor performs analytical procedures for sales, evidence is being obtained about both sales and accounts receivable.

In addition to the analytical procedures in Table 12-1, there should also be a review of accounts receivable for large and unusual amounts. Individual receivables that deserve special attention are large balances, accounts that have been outstanding for a long time, receivables from affiliated companies, officers, directors, and other related parties, and credit balances. The auditor should review the listing of accounts (aged trial balance) at the balance sheet date to determine which accounts should be investigated further.

Information about the sales and collection cycle at Hillsburg Hardware Co. is provided as an illustration of the use of analytical procedures during the detailed testing phase. Table 12-2 includes comparative trial balance information for the sales and collection cycle for Hillsburg. Some of that information is used to illustrate several analytical procedures in Table 12-3. None of the analytical procedures indicate potential misstatements except for the ratio of the allowance of uncollectible accounts to accounts receivable. The explanation at the bottom of Table 12-3 describes the potential misstatement.

The auditor's conclusion about analytical procedures for the sales and collection cycle is incorporated into the third row from the bottom on the evidence planning worksheet in

TABLE 12-2 **Comparative Information for Hillsburg Hardware Co.—Sales and Collection Cycle**

	Amount				
	12-31-02 (in Thousands)	Percent Change 2001–2002	12-31-01 (in Thousands)	Percent Change 2000–2001	12-31-00 (in Thousands)
Sales	$144,328	9.0%	$132,421	7.0%	$123,737
Sales returns and allowances	1,242	3.9	1,195	13.6	1,052
Gross margin	39,845	9.6	36,350	7.0	33,961
Accounts receivable	20,197	7.3	18,827	14.1	16,505
Allowance for uncollectible accounts	1,240	(19.5)	1,540	11.6	1,380
Bad debt expense	3,323	(2.1)	3,394	7.3	3,162
Total current assets	51,027	14.0	44,779	6.6	41,989
Total assets	61,367	(7.0)	66,021	8.0	61,147
Net earnings before taxes	5,681	21.9	4,659	39.0	3,351
Number of accounts receivable	258	16.7	221	5.7	209
Number of accounts receivable with balances over $100,000	37	15.6	32	6.7	30

Figure 12-7. Analytical procedures are substantive tests and therefore reduce the extent to which the auditor needs to test details of balances, if the analytical procedures' results are favorable.

When analytical procedures in the sales and collection cycle uncover unusual fluctuations, the auditor should make additional inquiries of management. Management's responses should be critically evaluated to determine whether they adequately explain the unusual fluctuations and whether they are supported by other corroborative evidence.

TABLE 12-3 **Analytical Procedures for Hillsburg Hardware Co.—Sales and Collection Cycle**

	12-31-02	12-31-01	12-31-00
Gross margin/net sales	27.85%	27.70%	27.68%
Sales returns and allowances/gross sales	.9%	.9%	.9%
Bad debt expense/net sales	2.3%	2.6%	2.6%
Allowance for uncollectible accounts/accounts receivable	6.1%	8.2%	8.4%
Number of days receivables outstanding*	51.55	52.37	49.13
Net accounts receivable/total current assets	37.2%	38.6%	36.0%

*Based on year-end accounts receivable only.

Comment: Allowance as a percentage of accounts receivable has declined from 8.4% to 6.1%. Number of days receivables outstanding and economic conditions do not justify this change. Potential misstatement is approximately $465,000 ($20,197,000 × .084 – .061), which is greater than tolerable misstatement.

Design and Perform Tests of Details of Accounts Receivable Balance (Phase III)

The appropriate tests of details of balances depend on the factors incorporated into the evidence planning worksheet in Figure 12-7. The second row from the bottom shows planned detection risk for each accounts receivable balance-related audit objective. Planned detection risk for each objective is an auditor decision, decided by subjectively combining the conclusions reached about each of the factors listed above that row.

Combining the factors that determine planned detection risk is complex because the measurement for each factor is imprecise and the appropriate weight to be given each factor is highly judgmental. Conversely, the relationship between each factor and planned detection risk is well established. For example, the auditor knows that a high inherent risk or control risk decreases planned detection risk and increases planned substantive tests, whereas good results of substantive tests of transactions increase planned detection risk and decrease other planned substantive tests.

The bottom row in Figure 12-7 shows the planned audit evidence for tests of details of balances for accounts receivable, by objective. As discussed in previous chapters, planned audit evidence is the complement of planned detection risk.

The conclusion that planned audit evidence for a given objective is high, medium, or low is implemented by the auditor deciding the appropriate audit procedures, sample size, items to select, and timing. The remainder of this chapter discusses deciding the specific audit procedures and timing decisions for auditing accounts receivable. Chapter 13 deals with sample size and selecting items from the population for testing.

PRACTICE APPLICATION OF ANALYTICAL PROCEDURES FOR GROSS MARGIN

Ron Stopps, CPA, is the auditor for Great Western Lumber Company, a wholesale wood milling company. Ron calculates the gross margin by three product lines and obtains industry information from published data in the table below.

In discussing the results, the controller states that Great Western has always had a higher gross margin on hardwood products than the industry because they focus on the markets where they are able to sell at higher prices instead of emphasizing volume. The opposite is true of plywood, for which they have a reasonably small number of customers, each of whom demands lower prices because of high volume. The controller states that competitive forces have caused reductions in plywood gross margin for both the industry and Great Western in 2001 and 2002. Great Western has traditionally had a somewhat lower gross margin for softwood than the industry until 2002, when gross margin went up significantly due to aggressive selling.

Stopps observed that most of what the controller said was reasonable given the facts. Hardwood gross margin for the industry was stable and approximately 3.5 percent to 4 percent lower than Great Western's every year. Industry gross margin for plywood has declined annually but is about 10 percent higher than Great Western's. Industry gross margin for softwood has been stable for the three years, but Great Western's has increased by a fairly large amount.

The change in Great Western's softwood gross margin from 20.3 percent to 23.9 percent is a concern to Stopps, so he goes through a three-step procedure:

1. Calculate the potential misstatement and evaluate the materiality of that amount. He calculates 23.9% – 20.3% × softwood sales and concludes the amount is potentially material.
2. Identify potential causes of the change.
   - Overstatement of sales
   - Overstatement of inventory (understatement of cost of goods sold)
   - Understatement of purchases (understatement of cost of goods sold)
   - Good results of aggressive selling
3. Indicate in the audit files a concern for the potential overstatement of sales and inventory and understatement of purchases of softwood. This may require an expansion of other substantive audit tests.

	2002 Gross Margin Percent		2001 Gross Margin Percent		2000 Gross Margin Percent	
	Great Western	Industry	Great Western	Industry	Great Western	Industry
Hardwood	36.3	32.4	36.4	32.5	36.0	32.3
Softwood	23.9	22.0	20.3	22.1	20.5	22.3
Plywood	40.3	50.1	44.2	54.3	45.4	55.6

OBJECTIVE 12-3

Design and perform tests of details of balances for accounts receivable for each balance-related audit objective.

Tests of details of balances for all cycles are directed to balance sheet accounts, but income statement accounts are not ignored because they are verified as a by-product of the balance sheet tests. For example, if the auditor confirms accounts receivable balances and finds overstatements because of mistakes in billing customers, there are overstatements of both accounts receivable and sales.

Confirmation of accounts receivable is the most important test of details of accounts receivable. Confirmation is discussed briefly in studying the appropriate tests for each of the balance-related audit objectives, then separately in more detail later in this chapter.

The discussion of tests of details of balances for accounts receivable that follows assumes that the auditor has completed an evidence planning worksheet similar to the one in Figure 12-7 and has decided planned detection risk for tests of details for each balance-related audit objective. The audit procedures selected and their sample size will depend heavily on whether planned evidence for a given objective is low, medium, or high. The discussion focuses on accounts receivable balance-related audit objectives.

Accounts Receivable Are Correctly Added and Agree with the Master File and the General Ledger

Most tests of accounts receivable and the allowance for uncollectible accounts are based on the aged trial balance. An **aged trial balance** is a listing of the balances in the accounts receivable master file at the balance sheet date. It includes the individual customer balances outstanding and a breakdown of each balance by the time passed between the date of sale and the balance sheet date. An illustration of a typical aged trial balance is given in Figure 12-3 for Hillsburg Hardware. Notice that the total is the same as accounts receivable on the general ledger trial balance on page 123.

Testing the information on the aged trial balance for detail tie-in is a necessary audit procedure. It is ordinarily done before any other tests to assure the auditor that the population being tested agrees with the general ledger and accounts receivable master file. The total column and the columns depicting the aging must be test footed, and the total on the trial balance compared with the general ledger. In addition, a sample of individual balances should be traced to supporting documents such as duplicate sales invoices to verify the customer's name, balance, and proper aging. The extent of the testing for detail tie-in depends

FIGURE 12-3 Aged Trial Balance for Hillsburg Hardware Co.

PBC

Hillsburg Hardware Co.
Accounts Receivable
Aged Trial Balance
12/31/02

Schedule
Prepared by Client
Approved by

Date
1/5/03

Account Number	Customer	Balance 12/31/02	Aging, Based on Invoice Date: 0–30 days	31–60 days	61–90 days	91–120 days	over 120
01011	Adams Supply	146,589	90,220	56,369			
01044	Argonaut, Inc.	30,842	30,842				
01100	Atwater Brothers	210,389	210,389				
01191	Beekman Bearings	83,526	73,526		10,000		
01270	Brown and Phillips	60,000				60,000	
01301	Christopher Plumbing	15,789					15,789
09733	Travelers Equipment	59,576	59,576				
09742	Underhill Parts and Maintenance	179,263	179,263				
09810	UJW Co.	102,211	34,911	34,700	32,600		
09907	Zephyr Plastics	286,300	186,000	100,300			
		$20,196,800	$14,217,156	$2,869,366	$1,408,642	$1,038,926	$662,710

on the number of accounts involved, the degree to which the master file has been tested as a part of tests of controls and substantive tests of transactions, and the extent to which the schedule has been verified by an internal auditor or other independent person before it is given to the auditor. Audit software can be used to perform footing and cross-footing of the aged trial balance, as well as to recalculate the aging.

Recorded Accounts Receivable Exist

The most important test of details of balances for determining the existence of recorded accounts receivable is the confirmation of customers' balances. Confirmations were defined and discussed in detail in Chapter 6. When customers do not respond to confirmations, auditors also examine supporting documents to verify the shipment of goods and evidence of subsequent cash receipts to determine whether the accounts were collected. Normally, auditors do not examine shipping documents or evidence of subsequent cash receipts for any account in the sample that is confirmed, but these documents are used extensively as alternative evidence for nonresponses.

Existing Accounts Receivable Are Included

It is difficult to test for account balances omitted from the aged trial balance except by relying on the self-balancing nature of the accounts receivable master file. For example, if the client accidentally excluded an account receivable from the trial balance, the only likely way it would be discovered is by footing the accounts receivable trial balance and reconciling the balance with the control account in the general ledger.

If all sales to a customer are omitted from the sales journal, the understatement of accounts receivable is almost impossible to uncover by tests of details of balances. For example, auditors rarely send accounts receivable confirmations to customers with zero balances, in part because research shows that customers are unlikely to respond to requests that indicate their balances are understated. In addition, unrecorded sales to a new customer are difficult to identify for confirmation because that customer is not included in the accounts receivable master file. The understatement of sales and accounts receivable is best uncovered by substantive tests of transactions for shipments made but not recorded (completeness objective for tests of sales transactions) and by analytical procedures.

Accounts Receivable Are Accurate

Confirmation of accounts selected from the trial balance is the most common test of details of balances for the accuracy of accounts receivable. When customers do not respond to confirmation requests, auditors examine supporting documents, in the same way as described for the existence objective. Tests of the debits and credits to individual customers' balances are done by examining supporting documentation for shipments and cash receipts.

Accounts Receivable Are Properly Classified

It is normally relatively easy to evaluate the classification of accounts receivable by reviewing the aged trial balance for material receivables from affiliates, officers, directors, or other related parties. When client Web sites include banner advertisements for external parties, auditors should be alert for the presence of nontrade receivables due from advertisers. If notes receivable or accounts that should not be classified as a current asset are included with the regular accounts, these should also be segregated. Finally, if credit balances in accounts receivable are significant, it is appropriate to reclassify them as accounts payable.

There is a close relationship between the classification objective as discussed here and the presentation and disclosure objective. Classification concerns determining whether the client has correctly separated different classifications of accounts receivable. Presentation and disclosure concerns making sure that the classifications are properly presented. For example, under the classification objective, the auditor determines whether receivables from related parties have been separated on the aged trial balance. Under the presentation and disclosure objective, the auditor determines whether related party transactions are correctly shown in the financial statements.

Cutoff for Accounts Receivable Is Correct

Cutoff misstatements exist when current period transactions are recorded in the subsequent period or subsequent period transactions are recorded in the current period. The objective of cutoff tests, regardless of the type of transaction, is to verify whether transactions near the end of the accounting period are recorded in the proper period. The cutoff objective is one of the most important in the cycle because misstatements in cutoff can significantly affect current period income. For example, the intentional or unintentional inclusion of several large, subsequent period sales in the current period or the exclusion of several current period sales returns and allowances can materially overstate net earnings.

In determining the reasonableness of cutoff, a threefold approach is needed: (1) decide on the appropriate *criteria for cutoff,* (2) evaluate whether the client has established *adequate procedures* to ensure a reasonable cutoff, and (3) *test* whether a reasonable cutoff was obtained. Cutoff misstatements can occur for *sales, sales returns and allowances,* and *cash receipts.*

Sales Cutoff The criterion used by most merchandising and manufacturing clients for determining when a sale takes place is the *shipment of goods,* but some companies record invoices at the time title passes. The passage of title can take place before shipment (as in the case of custom-manufactured goods), at the time of shipment, or subsequent to shipment. For the correct measurement of current period income, the method must be in accordance with generally accepted accounting principles (GAAP) and consistently applied.

Revenue Recognition

The most important part of evaluating the client's method of obtaining a reliable cutoff is to determine the procedures in use. When a client issues prenumbered shipping documents sequentially, it is usually a simple matter to evaluate and test cutoff. Moreover, the segregation of duties between the shipping and the billing function also enhances the likelihood of recording transactions in the proper period. However, if shipments are made by company truck, if the shipping records are unnumbered, and if shipping and billing department personnel are not independent of each other, it may be difficult, if not impossible, to be assured of an accurate cutoff.

When the client's internal controls are adequate, the cutoff can usually be verified by obtaining the shipping document number for the last shipment made at the end of the period and comparing this number with current and subsequent period recorded sales. As an illustration, assume that the shipping document number for the last shipment in the current period is 1489. All recorded sales before the end of the period should bear a shipping document number preceding number 1490. There should also be no sales recorded in the subsequent period for a shipment with a bill of lading numbered 1489 or lower. This can easily be tested by comparing recorded sales with the related shipping documents for the last few days of the current period and the first few days of the subsequent period.

Sales Returns and Allowances Cutoff GAAP requires that sales returns and allowances be *matched with related sales* if the amounts are material. For example, if current period shipments are returned in the subsequent period, the proper treatment is to include the sales return in the current period. (The returned goods would be treated as current period inventory.) For most companies, however, sales returns and allowances are recorded in the *accounting period in which they occur,* under the assumption of approximately equal, offsetting amounts at the beginning and end of each accounting period. This is acceptable as long as the amounts are not significant.

When the auditor is confident that the client records all sales returns and allowances promptly, the cutoff tests are simple and straightforward. The auditor can examine supporting documentation for a sample of sales returns and allowances recorded during several weeks subsequent to the closing date to determine the date of the original sale. If the amounts recorded in the subsequent period are significantly different from unrecorded returns and allowances at the beginning of the period under audit, an adjustment must be considered. If the internal controls for recording sales returns and allowances are evaluated as ineffective, a larger sample is needed to verify cutoff.

Companies may experience higher returns for Internet sales. Because customers who purchase online are unable to view the actual products before purchase, they may be more likely to return goods after they have received and inspected them. As a result, auditors of companies that have e-commerce sales applications may need to evaluate sales returns from e-commerce-based sales separately from sales returns generated through traditional sales systems.

Cash Receipts Cutoff For most audits, a proper cash receipts cutoff is *less important* than either the sales or the sales returns and allowances cutoff because the improper cutoff of cash affects only the cash and the accounts receivable balances, not earnings. Nevertheless, if the misstatement is material, it could affect the fair presentation of these accounts, especially when cash is a small or negative balance.

It is easy to test for a cash receipts cutoff misstatement (often called *holding the cash receipts book open*) by tracing recorded cash receipts to subsequent period bank deposits on the bank statement. If there is a delay of several days, this could indicate a cutoff misstatement.

The confirmation of accounts receivable may also be relied on to some degree to uncover cutoff misstatements for sales, sales returns and allowances, and cash receipts, especially when there is a long interval between the date the transaction took place and the recording date. However, when the interval is only a few days, mail delivery delays may cause confusion of a cutoff misstatement with a normal **timing difference.** For example, if a customer mails and records a check to a client for payment of an unpaid account on December 30 and the client receives and records the amount on January 2, the records of the two organizations will be different on December 31. This is not a cutoff misstatement, but a timing difference due to the delivery time. It may be difficult for the auditor to evaluate whether a cutoff misstatement or a timing difference occurred when a confirmation reply is the source of information. This type of situation requires additional investigation, such as inspection of underlying documents.

Accounts Receivable Is Stated at Realizable Value

Tests of the **realizable value of accounts receivable** objective are for the purpose of evaluating the account, *allowance for uncollectible accounts.* GAAP requires that accounts receivable be stated at the amount that will ultimately be collected, which is gross accounts receivable less the allowance. The client's estimate of the total amount that is uncollectible is represented by the allowance for uncollectible accounts. Although it is not possible to predict the future precisely, it is necessary for the auditor to evaluate whether the allowance is reasonable, considering all available facts. To assist with this evaluation, the auditor often prepares an audit schedule that analyzes the allowance for uncollectible accounts. An illustration of this schedule for Hillsburg Hardware is shown in Figure 12-4. In the example, the analysis indicates that the allowance is understated. This could be the result of the client failing to adjust the allowance or economic factors. Note that the potential understatement of the reserve was signaled by the analytical procedures in Table 12-3 (p. 343).

FIGURE 12-4 Analysis of Allowance for Uncollectible Accounts for Hillsburg Hardware Co.

Hillsburg Hardware Co.
Analysis of Allowance for Uncollectible Accounts
12/31/02

		Date
Schedule	B-4	
Prepared by	TW	1/8/03
Approved by	SB	1/10/03

A/R Category	A/R Balance 12/31/02	Estimated Allowance Percentage	Estimated Required Allowance
0–30 days	$14,217,156 ✓	3% ×	$ 426,515
31–60 days	2,869,366 ✓	6% ×	172,162
61–90 days	1,408,642 ✓	20% ×	281,728
91–120 days	1,038,926 ✓	35% ×	363,624
Over 120	662,710 ✓	60% ×	397,626
Total	$20,196,800		$1,641,655
Recorded Allowance			$1,240,000 TB

✓ – Traced to aged accounts receivable trial balance.
× – Allowance percentages are consistent with prior year, and appear reasonable based on historical loss percentages documented in permanent file.
TB – Agreed to trial balance.

Conclusion: Recorded allowance appears understated based on aging analysis. Propose adjustment to allowance of $400,000.

The starting point for the evaluation of the allowance for uncollectible accounts is to review the results of the tests of controls that are concerned with the client's credit policy. If the client's credit policy has remained unchanged and the results of the tests of credit policy and credit approval are consistent with those of the preceding year, the change in the balance in the allowance for uncollectible accounts should reflect only changes in economic conditions and sales volume. However, if the client's credit policy or the degree to which it correctly functions has significantly changed, great care must be taken to consider the effects of these changes as well.

A common way to evaluate the adequacy of the allowance is to carefully examine the noncurrent accounts on the aged trial balance to determine which ones have not been paid subsequent to the balance sheet date. The size and age of unpaid balances can then be compared with similar information from previous years to evaluate whether the amount of noncurrent receivables is increasing or decreasing over time. The examination of credit files, discussions with the credit manager, and review of the client's correspondence file may also provide insights into the collectibility of the accounts. These procedures are especially important if a few large balances are noncurrent and are not being paid on a regular basis.

There are two pitfalls in evaluating the allowance by reviewing individual noncurrent balances on the aged trial balance. First, the current accounts are ignored in establishing the adequacy of the allowance, even though some of these amounts will undoubtedly become uncollectible. Second, it is difficult to compare the results of the current year with those of previous years on such an unstructured basis. If the accounts are becoming progressively uncollectible over several years, this fact could be overlooked. A way to avoid these difficulties is to establish the history of bad debt charge-offs over a period of time as a frame of reference for evaluating the current year's allowance. As an example, if historically a certain percentage of the total of each age category becomes uncollectible, it is relatively easy to compute whether the allowance is properly stated. If 2 percent of current accounts, 10 percent of 30- to 90-day accounts, and 35 percent of all balances over 90 days ultimately become uncollectible, these percentages can easily be applied to the current year's aged trial balance totals, and the result can be compared with the balance in the allowance account. Of course, the auditor has to be careful to modify the calculations for changed conditions.

Bad Debt Expense After the auditor is satisfied with the allowance for uncollectible accounts, it is easy to verify bad debt expense. Assume that (1) the beginning balance in the allowance account was verified as a part of the previous audit, (2) the uncollectible accounts charged off were verified as a part of the substantive tests of transactions, and (3) the ending balance in the allowance account has been verified by various means. Then bad debt expense is simply a residual balance that can be verified by a reperformance test.

The Client Has Rights to Accounts Receivable

The client's rights to accounts receivable ordinarily cause no audit problems because the receivables usually belong to the client, but in some cases, a portion of the receivables may have been pledged as collateral, assigned to someone else, factored, or sold at discount. Normally, the client's customers are not aware of the existence of such matters; therefore, the confirmation of receivables will not bring them to light. A review of the minutes, discussions with the client, confirmation with banks, the examination of debt contracts for evidence of accounts receivable pledged as collateral, and the examination of correspondence files are usually sufficient to uncover instances in which the client has limited rights to receivables.

Accounts Receivable Presentation and Disclosures Are Proper

In addition to testing for the proper statement of the dollar amount in the general ledger, the auditor must also determine that information about the account balance resulting from the sales and collection cycle is properly presented and disclosed in the financial statements. The auditor must decide whether the client has properly combined amounts and disclosed related party information in the statements. To evaluate the adequacy of the presentation and disclosure, the auditor must have a thorough understanding of generally accepted accounting principles and presentation and disclosure requirements.

THE SOFTER SIDE OF SEARS?

Sears, Roebuck & Co. was enjoying a remarkable turnaround in earnings in 1996. However, most of the increase in profits was attributable to interest on Sears credit card balances. In the early 1990s, Sears had added more than 17 million new credit card customers. However, many of these new customers were not good credit risks, and they tended to carry high balances. As a result, in 1997, Sears had to increase its allowance for credit card delinquencies to $393 million, a 44 percent increase.

Unfortunately, the delinquencies were only part of the problem. Many of these delinquent customers also filed for bankruptcy. In fact, by 1997 Sears was a creditor in more than one-third of all bankruptcies filed in the United States. Sears aggressively sought reaffirmation agreements with these customers, in which they pledged to continue making payments on their accounts. However, many of these agreements were not filed in the bankruptcy cases, which meant the company was collecting on unenforceable agreements for debt that no longer legally existed. As a result of a federal investigation, Sears was forced to pay a $60 million fine and set aside $475 million in reserves to cover complaints over its debt collection practices.

Sources: Adapted from 1. De'Ann Weimer, "Put the Comeback on My Card," *Business Week* (November 10, 1997), pp. 118–119. 2. John McCormick, "The Sorry Side of Sears," *Newsweek* (February 22, 1999), pp. 36–39.

An important part of the evaluation involves deciding whether material amounts requiring separate disclosure have actually been separated in the statements. For example, receivables from officers and affiliated companies must be segregated from accounts receivable from customers if the amounts are material. Similarly, under SEC requirements, it is necessary to disclose sales and assets for different business segments separately. The proper aggregation of general ledger balances in the financial statements also requires combining account balances that are not relevant for external users of the statements. If all accounts included in the general ledger were disclosed separately on the statements, most statement users would be more confused than enlightened.

As a part of proper presentation and disclosure, the auditor is also required to evaluate the adequacy of the *footnotes.* One of the major lawsuits in the history of the profession, the Continental Vending case, revolved primarily around the inadequacy of the footnote disclosure of a major receivable from an affiliated company. The required footnote disclosure for accounts receivable includes information about the pledging, discounting, factoring, assignment of accounts receivable, and amounts due from related parties. Of course, to evaluate the adequacy of these disclosures, it is first necessary to know of their existence and to have complete information about their nature. As discussed in the previous section, this is generally obtained in other parts of the audit.

CONFIRMATION OF ACCOUNTS RECEIVABLE

OBJECTIVE 12-4

Obtain and evaluate accounts receivable confirmations.

In the preceding discussion of designing the tests of details of balances, you should have noticed the recurrence of confirmation issues. Confirmation is extremely important because, as discussed in Chapter 6, confirmations are highly reliable evidence. The primary purpose of accounts receivable confirmation is to satisfy the *existence, accuracy,* and *cutoff* objectives.

AICPA Requirements

Auditing standards require the confirmation of accounts receivable in normal circumstances, but SAS 67 (AU 330) permits an unqualified report even when accounts receivable are not confirmed in any of three circumstances:

1. *Accounts receivable are immaterial.* This is common for certain companies such as discount stores with primarily cash or credit card sales.
2. *The auditor considers confirmations ineffective evidence because response rates will likely be inadequate or unreliable.* In certain industries, such as hospitals, response rates to confirmations are very low.
3. *The combined level of inherent risk and control risk is low and other substantive evidence can be accumulated to provide sufficient evidence.* If a client has effective internal controls and low inherent risk for the sales and collection cycle, the auditor should often be able to satisfy the evidence requirements by tests of controls, substantive tests of transactions, and analytical procedures.

If the auditor decides not to confirm accounts receivable, the justification for doing so must be documented in the audit files.

Although the remaining sections in this chapter refer specifically to the confirmation of accounts receivable from customers, the concepts apply equally to other receivables, such as notes receivable, amounts due from officers, and employee advances. Confirmations are not required by auditing standards for any other accounts.

Confirmation Decisions

In performing confirmation procedures, the auditor must decide the type of confirmation to use, timing of the procedures, sample size, and individual items to select.

Type of Confirmation Two common types of confirmations are used for confirming accounts receivable: positive and negative. A **positive confirmation** is a communication addressed to the debtor requesting the recipient to confirm directly whether the balance as stated on the confirmation request is correct or incorrect. Figure 12-5 illustrates a positive confirmation in the audit of Hillsburg Hardware Co. Notice that this confirmation is for one of the largest

FIGURE 12-5 Positive Confirmation

HILLSBURG HARDWARE CO.
Gary, Indiana

January 5, 2003

Atwater Brothers
19 South Main Street
Middleton, Ohio 36947

To Whom It May Concern:

In connection with an audit of our financial statements, please confirm directly to our auditors

BERGER & ANTHONY, CPAs
Gary, Indiana

the correctness of the balance of your account with us as of December 31, 2002, as shown below.

This is not a request for payment; please do not send your remittance to our auditors. Your prompt attention to this request will be appreciated. An envelope is enclosed for your reply.

Erma Swanson

Erma Swanson, Controller

BERGER & ANTHONY, CPAs
Gary, Indiana

The balance receivable from us of $210,389 as of December 31, 2002, is correct except as noted below:

____
____
____
____
____
____

Date __________ By __________

FIGURE 12-6 **Negative Confirmation**

AUDITOR'S ACCOUNT CONFIRMATION

Please examine this statement carefully. If it does NOT agree with your records, please report any exceptions directly to our auditors

BERGER & ANTHONY, CPAs
Gary, Indiana

who are conducting an audit of our financial statements as of December 31, 2002. An addressed envelope is enclosed for your convenience in replying.

Do not send your remittance to our auditors.

accounts on the aged trial balance in Figure 12-3 on page 345. A second type of positive confirmation, often called a **blank confirmation form,** does not state the amount on the confirmation but requests the recipient to fill in the balance or furnish other information. Because blank forms require the recipient to determine the information requested, they are considered more reliable than confirmations that include balance information. Blank forms are rarely used in practice because they often result in lower response rates.

An **invoice confirmation** is another type of positive confirmation in which an individual invoice is confirmed, rather than the customer's entire accounts receivable balance. Many customers use voucher systems that allow them to confirm individual invoices but not balance information. As a result, invoice confirmations may improve confirmation response rates. Invoice confirmations also result in fewer timing differences and other reconciling items than balance confirmations. However, invoice confirmations have the disadvantage of not directly confirming ending balances.

A **negative confirmation** is also addressed to the debtor but requests a response only when the debtor disagrees with the stated amount. Figure 12-6 illustrates a negative confirmation in the audit of Hillsburg Hardware Co. that has been attached to a customer's monthly statement with a gummed label.

A positive confirmation is *more reliable* evidence because the auditor can perform follow-up procedures if a response is not received from the debtor. With a negative confirmation, failure to reply must be regarded as a correct response, even though the debtor may have ignored the confirmation request.

Offsetting the reliability disadvantage, negative confirmations are *less expensive* to send than positive confirmations, and thus more can be distributed for the same total cost. Negative confirmations cost less because there are no second requests and no follow-up of nonresponses.

The determination of which type of confirmation to use is an auditor's decision, and it should be based on the facts in the audit. SAS 67 states that it is acceptable to use negative confirmations only when *all* of the following circumstances are present:

- Accounts receivable is made up of a large number of small accounts.
- Combined assessed control risk and inherent risk is low. The combined risk is unlikely to be low if either internal controls are ineffective or there is a high expectation of misstatements. For example, if prior years' audits indicate that there are often disputed or inaccurate accounts receivable, negative confirmations would be inappropriate.
- There is no reason to believe that the recipients of the confirmations are unlikely to give them consideration. For example, if the response rate to positive confirmations in prior years was extremely high or if there are high response rates on audits of similar clients, it is likely that recipients will give confirmations reasonable consideration.

Typically, when negative confirmations are used, the auditor puts considerable emphasis on the effectiveness of internal controls, substantive tests of transactions, and analytical procedures as evidence of the fairness of accounts receivable and assumes that the large majority of the recipients will provide a conscientious reading and response to the confirmation request. Negative confirmations are often used for audits of hospitals, retail stores, banks, and other industries in which the receivables are due from the general public.

It is also common to use a combination of negative and positive confirmations by sending the latter to accounts with large balances and the former to those with small balances.

The discussion of confirmations to this point shows that there is a continuum for the type of confirmation decision, starting with using no confirmations in some circumstances, to using only negatives, to using both negatives and positives, to using only positives. The primary factors affecting the decision are the materiality of total accounts receivable, the number and size of individual accounts, control risk, inherent risk, the effectiveness of confirmations as audit evidence, and the availability of other audit evidence.

Timing The most reliable evidence from confirmations is obtained when they are sent as close to the balance sheet date as possible, as opposed to confirming the accounts several months before year-end. This permits the auditor to directly test the accounts receivable balance on the financial statements without making any inferences about the transactions taking place between the confirmation date and the balance sheet date. However, as a means of completing the audit on a timely basis, it is often necessary to confirm the accounts at an interim date. This is permissible if internal controls are adequate and can provide reasonable assurance that sales, cash receipts, and other credits are properly recorded between the date of the confirmation and the end of the accounting period. Other factors the auditor is likely to consider in making the decision are the materiality of accounts receivable and the auditor's exposure to lawsuits because of the possibility of client bankruptcy and similar risks.

If the decision is made to confirm accounts receivable before year-end, it may be necessary to test the transactions occurring between the confirmation date and the balance sheet date by examining such internal documents as duplicate sales invoices, shipping documents, and evidence of cash receipts, in addition to performing analytical procedures of the intervening period.

Sample Size The major factors affecting sample size for confirming accounts receivable fall into several categories and include the following:

- Tolerable misstatement
- Inherent risk (relative size of total accounts receivable, number of accounts, prior year results, and expected misstatements)
- Control risk
- Achieved detection risk from other substantive tests (extent and results of substantive tests of transactions, analytical procedures, and other tests of details)
- Type of confirmation (negatives normally require a larger sample size)

Selection of the Items for Testing Some type of *stratification* is desirable with most confirmations. A typical approach to stratification is to consider both the dollar size of individual accounts and the length of time an account has been outstanding as a basis for selecting the balances for confirmation. In most audits, the emphasis should be on confirming larger and older balances because these are most likely to include a significant misstatement. But it is also important to sample some items from every material segment of the population. In many cases, the auditor selects all accounts above a certain dollar amount and selects a random sample from the remainder.

When selecting a sample of accounts receivable for confirmation, the auditor should be careful to avoid being influenced by the client. If a client tries to discourage the auditor from sending confirmations to certain customers, the auditor should consider the possibility that the client is attempting to conceal fictitious or known misstatements of accounts receivable.

Maintaining Control

After the items for confirmation have been selected, the auditor must maintain control of the confirmations until they are returned from the customer. When the client assists by preparing the confirmations, enclosing them in envelopes, or putting stamps on the envelopes, close supervision by the auditor is required. A return address must be included on all envelopes to make sure that undelivered mail is received by the CPA firm. Similarly, self-addressed return envelopes accompanying the confirmations must be addressed for delivery to the CPA firm's office. It is even important to mail the confirmations *outside* the client's office. All of these steps are necessary to ensure independent communication between the auditor and the customer.

Follow-Up on Nonresponses

It is inappropriate to regard confirmations mailed but not returned by customers as significant audit evidence. For example, nonresponses to positive confirmations do not provide audit evidence. Similarly, for negative confirmations, the auditor should not conclude that the recipient received the confirmation request and verified the information requested. Negative confirmations do, however, provide some evidence of the existence assertion.

When positive confirmations are used, SAS 67 requires follow-up procedures for confirmations not returned by the customer. It is common to send second and sometimes even third requests for confirmations. Even with these efforts, some customers do not return the confirmation, so it is necessary to follow up with **alternative procedures.** The objective of alternative procedures is to determine by a means other than confirmation whether the nonconfirmed account existed and was properly stated at the confirmation date. For any positive confirmation not returned, the following documentation can be examined to verify the existence and accuracy of individual sales transactions making up the ending balance in accounts receivable.

Sales Fraud

Subsequent Cash Receipts Evidence of the receipt of cash subsequent to the confirmation date includes examining remittance advices, entries in the cash receipts records, or perhaps even subsequent credits in the accounts receivable master file. On the one hand, the examination of evidence of subsequent cash receipts is a highly useful alternative procedure because it is reasonable to assume that a customer would not make a payment unless it was an existing receivable. On the other hand, the fact of payment does not establish whether there was an obligation on the date of the confirmation. In addition, care should be taken to match each unpaid sales transaction with evidence of its subsequent payment as a test for disputes or disagreements over individual outstanding invoices.

Duplicate Sales Invoices These are useful in verifying the actual issuance of a sales invoice and the actual date of the billing.

Shipping Documents These are important in establishing whether the shipment was actually made and as a test of cutoff.

Correspondence with the Client Usually, the auditor does not need to review correspondence as a part of alternative procedures, but correspondence can be used to disclose disputed and questionable receivables not uncovered by other means.

The extent and nature of the alternative procedures depend primarily on the materiality of the nonresponses, the types of misstatements discovered in the confirmed responses, the subsequent cash receipts from the nonresponses, and the auditor's conclusions about internal control. It is normally desirable to account for all unconfirmed balances with alternative procedures even if the amounts are small, as a means of properly generalizing from the sample to the population. Another acceptable approach is to assume that nonresponses are 100 percent overstatement amounts.

Analysis of Differences

When the confirmation requests are returned by the customer, it is necessary to determine the reason for any reported differences. In many cases, they are caused by timing differences between the client's and the customer's records. It is important to distinguish between these and *exceptions,* which represent misstatements of the accounts receivable balance. The most commonly reported types of differences in confirmations follow.

Payment Has Already Been Made Reported differences typically arise when the customer has made a payment before the confirmation date, but the client has not received the payment in time for recording before the confirmation date. Such instances should be carefully investigated to determine the possibility of a cash receipts cutoff misstatement, lapping, or a theft of cash.

Goods Have Not Been Received These differences typically result because the client records the sale at the date of shipment and the customer records the acquisition when the goods are received. The time that the goods are in transit is often the cause of differences reported on confirmations. These should be investigated to determine the possibility of the customer not receiving the goods at all or the existence of a cutoff misstatement on the client's records.

The Goods Have Been Returned The client's failure to record a credit memo could result from timing differences or the improper recording of sales returns and allowances. Like other differences, these must be investigated.

Clerical Errors and Disputed Amounts The most likely types of reported differences in a client's records are when the customer states that there is an error in the price charged for the goods, the goods are damaged, the proper quantity of goods was not received, and so forth. These differences must be investigated to determine whether the client is in error and what the amount of the error is.

In most instances, the auditor will ask the client to reconcile the difference and, if necessary, will communicate with the customer to resolve any disagreements. Naturally, the auditor must carefully verify the client's conclusions on each significant difference.

Drawing Conclusions

When all differences have been resolved, including those discovered in performing alternative procedures, it is important to *reevaluate internal control.* Each client misstatement must be analyzed to determine whether it was consistent or inconsistent with the original assessed level of control risk. If a significant number of misstatements take place that are inconsistent with the assessment of control risk, it is necessary to revise the assessment and consider the effect of the revision on the audit.

It is also necessary to generalize from the sample to the entire population of accounts receivable. Even though the sum of the misstatements in the sample may not significantly affect the financial statements, the auditor must consider whether the population is likely to be materially misstated. This conclusion can be arrived at by using statistical sampling techniques or on a nonstatistical basis. Projection of misstatements was discussed in Chapter 8 and is further explained in Chapter 13.

The auditor should always evaluate the *qualitative* nature of the misstatements found in the sample, regardless of the dollar amount of the projected misstatement. Even if the projected misstatement is less than tolerable misstatement for accounts receivable, the misstatements found in a sample can be symptomatic of a more serious problem.

The final decision about accounts receivable and sales is whether sufficient evidence has been obtained through tests of controls and substantive tests of transactions, analytical procedures, cutoff procedures, confirmation, and other substantive tests to justify drawing conclusions about the correctness of the stated balance.

DEVELOPING TESTS OF DETAILS AUDIT PROGRAM

OBJECTIVE 12-5

Design audit procedures for the audit of accounts receivable, using an evidence planning worksheet as a guide.

Hillsburg Hardware Co. is used to illustrate the development of audit program procedures for tests of details in the sales and collection cycle. The determination of these procedures is based on the results of the analytical procedures described in this chapter and the results of the tests of controls and substantive tests of transactions described in Chapter 11. The results of the performance of these tests are included in Chapter 13.

Fran Moore prepared the evidence planning worksheet in Figure 12-7 on page 356 as an aid to help her decide the extent of planned tests of details of balances. The source of each of the rows is as follows:

- *Tolerable misstatement.* The preliminary judgment of materiality was set at $737,000 (approximately 10 percent of earnings from operations of $7,370,000). She allocated $442,000 to the audit of accounts receivable (see p. 211).
- *Acceptable audit risk.* Fran assessed acceptable audit risk as high because of the good financial condition of the company, its financial stability, and the relatively few users of the financial statements.

FIGURE 12-7 **Evidence Planning Worksheet to Decide Tests of Details of Balances for Hillsburg Hardware Co.—Accounts Receivable**

	Detail tie-in	Existence	Completeness	Accuracy	Classification	Cutoff	Realizable value	Rights	Presentation and disclosure
Acceptable audit risk	High	High	High	High	High	High	High	High	High
Inherent risk	Low	Low	Low	Low	Low	Low	Medium	Low	Low
Control risk–Sales	Low	Medium	Low	High	Low	High	High	Not applicable	Not applicable
Control risk–Cash receipts	Low	Medium	Low	Low	Low	Low	Not applicable	Not applicable	Not applicable
Control risk–Additional controls	None	None	None	None	None	None	None	Low	Low
Substantive tests of transactions–Sales	Good results	Good results	Good results	Fair results	Good results	Unacceptable results	Not applicable	Not applicable	Not applicable
Substantive tests of transactions–Cash receipts	Good results	Good results	Good results	Good results	Good results	Good results	Not applicable	Not applicable	Not applicable
Analytical procedures	Good results	Good results	Good results	Good results	Good results	Good results	Unacceptable results	Not applicable	Not applicable
Planned detection risk for tests of details of balances	High	Medium	High	Medium	High	Low	Low	High	High
Planned audit evidence for tests of details of balances	Low	Medium	Low	Medium	Low	High	High	Low	Low

Tolerable misstatement $442,000

- *Inherent risk.* Fran assessed inherent risk as low for all objectives except realizable value. In past years, there have been audit adjustments to the allowance for uncollectible accounts because it was found to be understated.
- *Control risk.* Control risk assessments are based on the results of tests of controls and substantive tests of transactions. These results are consistent with the initial control risk assessments in Figure 11-8, except for the accuracy and realizable value objective for sales, which were increased based on the unfavorable results of tests of transactions. Determining sample sizes and evaluating sample results are studied in the next chapter.
- *Substantive tests of transactions results.* The results for substantive tests of transactions were favorable for all objectives except for the accuracy and cutoff objectives for sales. As for tests of controls, determining sample sizes and evaluating sample results are studied in the next chapter.
- *Analytical procedures.* See Tables 12-2 and 12-3 (p. 343).
- *Planned detection risk and planned audit evidence.* These two rows are decided for each objective based on the conclusions in the other rows.

TABLE 12-4 Balance-Related Audit Objectives and Audit Program for Hillsburg Hardware Co.— Sales and Collection Cycle (Design Format)

Balance-Related Audit Objective	Audit Procedure
Accounts receivable in the aged trial balance agree with related master file amounts, and the total is correctly added and agrees with the general ledger (detail tie-in).	Trace 10 accounts from the trial balance to accounts on master file (6). Foot two pages of the trial balance, and total all pages (7). Trace the balance to the general ledger (8).
The accounts receivable on the aged trial balance exist (existence).	Confirm accounts receivable, using positive confirmations. Confirm all amounts over $100,000 and a nonstatistical sample of the remainder (10). Perform alternative procedures for all confirmations not returned on the first or second request (11). Review accounts receivable trial balance for large and unusual receivables (1).
Existing accounts receivable are included in the aged trial balance (completeness).	Trace 5 accounts from the accounts receivable master file to the aged trial balance (9).
Accounts receivable in the trial balance are accurate (accuracy).	Confirm accounts receivable, using positive confirmations. Confirm all amounts over $100,000 and a nonstatistical sample of the remainder (10). Perform alternative procedures for all confirmations not returned on the first or second request (11). Review accounts receivable trial balance for large and unusual receivables (1).
Accounts receivable on the aged trial balance are properly classified (classification).	Review the receivables listed on the aged trial balance for notes and related party receivables (3). Inquire of management whether there are any related party notes or long-term receivables included in the trial balance (4).
Transactions in the sales and collection cycle are recorded in the proper period (cutoff).	Select the last 20 sales transactions from the current year's sales journal and the first 20 from the subsequent year's and trace each to the related shipping documents, checking for the date of actual shipment and the correct recording (14). Review large sales returns and allowances before and after the balance sheet date to determine whether they are recorded in the correct period (15).
Accounts receivable is stated at realizable value (realizable value).	Trace 10 accounts from the aging schedule to the accounts receivable master file to test for the correct aging on the trial balance (6). Foot the aging columns on the trial balance and total the pages (7). Cross-foot the aging columns (7). Discuss with the credit manager the likelihood of collecting older accounts. Examine subsequent cash receipts and the credit file on all accounts over 90 days and evaluate whether the receivables are collectible (12). Evaluate whether the allowance is adequate after performing other audit procedures for collectibility of receivables (13).
The client has rights to accounts receivable on the trial balance (rights).	Review the minutes of the board of directors meetings for any indication of pledged or factored accounts receivable (5). Inquire of management whether any receivables are pledged or factored (5).
Accounts in the sales and collection cycle and related information are properly presented and disclosed (presentation and disclosure).	Review the minutes of the board of directors meetings for any indication of pledged or factored accounts receivable (5). Inquire of management whether any receivables are pledged or factored (5).

Note: The procedures are summarized into a performance format in Table 12-5 on page 358. The numbers in parentheses after the procedures refer to Table 12-5.

Table 12-4 shows the tests of details audit program for accounts receivable, by objective, and for the allowance for uncollectible accounts. The audit program reflects the conclusions for planned audit evidence on the evidence planning worksheet in Figure 12-7. Table 12-5 (p. 358) shows the audit program in a performance format. The audit procedures are identical to those in Table 12-4 except for procedure 2, which is an analytical procedure. The numbers in parentheses are a cross reference between the two tables.

TABLE 12-5 Test of Details of Balances Audit Program for Hillsburg Hardware Co.—Sales and Collection Cycle (Performance Format)

1. Review accounts receivable trial balance for large and unusual receivables.
2. Calculate analytical procedures indicated in carry-forward audit schedules (not included) and follow up on any significant changes from prior years.
3. Review the receivables listed on the aged trial balance for notes and related party receivables.
4. Inquire of management whether there are any related party, notes, or long-term receivables included in the trial balance.
5. Review the minutes of the board of directors meetings and inquire of management to determine whether any receivables are pledged or factored.
6. Trace 10 accounts from the trial balance to the accounts receivable master file for aging and the balance.
7. Foot 2 pages of the trial balance for aging columns and balance and total all pages and cross-foot the aging.
8. Trace the balance to the general ledger.
9. Trace 5 accounts from the accounts receivable master file to the aged trial balance.
10. Confirm accounts receivable, using positive confirmations. Confirm all amounts over $100,000 and a nonstatistical sample of the remainder.
11. Perform alternative procedures for all confirmations not returned on the first or second request.
12. Discuss with the credit manager the likelihood of collecting older accounts. Examine subsequent cash receipts and the credit file on all larger accounts over 90 days and evaluate whether the receivables are collectible.
13. Evaluate whether the allowance is adequate after performing other audit procedures for collectibility of receivables.
14. Select the last 20 sales transactions from the current year's sales journal and the first 20 from the subsequent year's and trace each to the related shipping documents, checking for the date of actual shipment and the correct recording.
15. Review large sales returns and allowances before and after the balance sheet date to determine whether they are recorded in the correct period.

ESSENTIAL TERMS

Accounts receivable balance-related audit objectives—the nine specific audit objectives used by the auditor to decide the appropriate audit evidence for accounts receivable

Aged trial balance—a listing of the balances in the accounts receivable master file at the balance sheet date broken down according to the amount of time passed between the date of sale and the balance sheet date

Alternative procedures—the follow-up of a positive confirmation not returned by the debtor with the use of documentation evidence to determine whether the recorded receivable exists and is collectible

Blank confirmation form—a letter, addressed to the debtor, requesting the recipient to fill in the amount of the accounts receivable balance; it is considered a positive confirmation

Cutoff misstatements—misstatements that take place as a result of current period transactions being recorded in a subsequent period, or subsequent period transactions being recorded in the current period

Invoice confirmation—a type of positive confirmation in which an individual invoice is confirmed, rather than the customer's entire accounts receivable balance

Negative confirmation—a letter, addressed to the debtor, requesting a response only if the recipient disagrees with the amount of the stated account balance

Positive confirmation—a letter, addressed to the debtor, requesting that the recipient indicate directly on the letter whether the stated account balance is correct or incorrect and, if incorrect, by what amount

Realizable value of accounts receivable—the amount of the outstanding balances in accounts receivable that will ultimately be collected

Timing difference—a reported difference in a confirmation from a debtor that is determined to be a timing difference between the client's and debtor's records and therefore not a misstatement

REVIEW QUESTIONS

12-1 **(Objective 12-1)** Distinguish among tests of details of balances, tests of controls, and substantive tests of transactions for the sales and collection cycle. Explain how the tests of controls and substantive tests of transactions affect the tests of details of balances.

12-2 **(Objective 12-1)** Cynthia Roberts, CPA, expresses the following viewpoint: "I do not believe in performing tests of controls and substantive tests of transactions for the sales and collection cycle. As an alternative, I send a lot of negative confirmations on every audit at an interim date. If I find a lot of misstatements, I analyze them to determine their cause. If internal controls are inadequate, I send positive confirmations at year-end to evaluate the amount of misstatements. If the negative confirmations result in minimal misstatements, which is often the case, I have found that the internal controls are effective without bothering to perform tests of controls and substantive tests of transactions, and the AICPA's confirmation requirement has been satisfied at the same time. In my opinion, the best test of internal controls is to go directly to third parties." Evaluate her point of view.

12-3 **(Objective 12-2)** List five analytical procedures for the sales and collection cycle. For each test, describe a misstatement that could be identified.

12-4 **(Objective 12-3)** Identify the nine accounts receivable balance-related audit objectives. For each objective, list one audit procedure.

12-5 **(Objective 12-3)** Which of the nine accounts receivable balance-related audit objectives can be partially satisfied by confirmations with customers?

12-6 **(Objective 12-3)** State the purpose of footing the total column in the client's trial balance, tracing individual customer names and amounts to the accounts receivable master file, and tracing the total to the general ledger. Is it necessary to trace each amount to the master file? Why?

12-7 **(Objective 12-3)** Distinguish between accuracy tests of gross accounts receivable and tests of the realizable value of receivables.

12-8 **(Objective 12-3)** Explain why you agree or disagree with the following statement: "In most audits, it is more important to test carefully the cutoff for sales than for cash receipts." Describe how you perform each type of test, assuming the existence of prenumbered documents.

12-9 **(Objective 12-4)** Evaluate the following statement: "In many audits in which accounts receivable is material, the requirement of confirming customer balances is a waste of time and would not be performed by competent auditors if it were not required by the AICPA. When internal controls are excellent and there are a large number of small receivables from customers who do not recognize the function of confirmation, it is a meaningless procedure. Examples include well-run utilities and department stores. In these situations, tests of controls and substantive tests of transactions are far more effective than confirmations."

12-10 **(Objective 12-4)** Distinguish between a positive and a negative confirmation and state the circumstances in which each should be used. Why do CPA firms often use a combination of positive and negative confirmations on the same audit?

12-11 **(Objective 12-4)** Under what circumstances is it acceptable to confirm accounts receivable before the balance sheet date?

12-12 **(Objective 12-4)** State the most important factors affecting the sample size in confirmations of accounts receivable.

12-13 **(Objective 12-4)** In Chapter 13, one of the points to be emphasized is the need to obtain a representative sample of the population. How can this concept be reconciled with the statement in this chapter that the emphasis should be on confirming larger and older balances because these are most likely to contain misstatements?

12-14 **(Objective 12-4)** Define what is meant by alternative procedures in the confirmation of accounts receivable and explain their purpose. Which alternative procedures are the most reliable? Why?

12-15 **(Objective 12-4)** Explain why the analysis of differences is important in the confirmation of accounts receivable, even if the misstatements in the sample are not material.

12-16 **(Objective 12-4)** State three types of differences that might be observed in the confirmation of accounts receivable that do not constitute misstatements. For each, state an audit procedure that would verify the difference.

12-17 **(Objective 12-1)** What is the relationship of each of the following to the sales and collection cycle: flowcharts, assessing control risk, tests of controls, and tests of details of balances?

12-18 **(Objective 12-3)** Describe GAAP requirements for proper recording of sales returns and allowances.

12-19 **(Objective 12-3)** Customers purchasing products through a company's Internet Web site generally pay for those goods by providing their personal credit card information. Describe how a company's sale of products through its Web site affects the auditor's tests of accounts receivable in the financial statement audit.

MULTIPLE CHOICE QUESTIONS FROM CPA EXAMINATIONS

12-20 **(Objective 12-2)** The following questions concern analytical procedures in the sales and collection cycle. Choose the best response.

a. As a result of analytical procedures, the independent auditor determines that the gross profit percentage has declined from 30% in the preceding year to 20% in the current year. The auditor should
   (1) express a qualified opinion due to inability of the client company to continue as a going concern.
   (2) evaluate management's performance in causing this decline.
   (3) require footnote disclosure.
   (4) consider the possibility of a misstatement in the financial statements.

b. Once a CPA has determined that accounts receivable have increased as a result of slow collections in a "tight money" environment, the CPA would be likely to
   (1) increase the balance in the allowance for bad debt account.
   (2) review the going concern ramifications.
   (3) review the credit and collection policy.
   (4) expand tests of collectibility.

c. In connection with his review of key ratios, the CPA notes that Pyzi had accounts receivable equal to 30 days' sales at December 31, 2001, and to 45 days' sales at December 31, 2002. Assuming that there had been no changes in economic conditions, clientele, or sales mix, this change most likely would indicate
   (1) a steady increase in sales in 2002.
   (2) an easing of credit policies in 2002.
   (3) a decrease in accounts receivable relative to sales in 2002.
   (4) a steady decrease in sales in 2002.

12-21 **(Objective 12-4)** The following questions deal with confirmation of accounts receivable. Choose the best response.

a. In connection with his audit of the Beke Supply Company for the year ended August 31, 2002, Derek Lowe, CPA, has mailed accounts receivable confirmations to three groups as follows:

Group Number	Type of Customer	Type of Confirmation
1	Wholesale	Positive
2	Current retail	Negative
3	Past-due retail	Positive

   The confirmation responses from each group vary from 10 percent to 90 percent. The most likely response percents are
   (1) Group 1—90 percent, group 2—50 percent, group 3—10 percent
   (2) Group 1—90 percent, group 2—10 percent, group 3—50 percent
   (3) Group 1—50 percent, group 2—90 percent, group 3—10 percent
   (4) Group 1—10 percent, group 2—50 percent, group 3—90 percent

b. The negative form of accounts receivable confirmation request is useful *except* when
   (1) internal control surrounding accounts receivable is considered to be effective.
   (2) a large number of small balances are involved.
   (3) the auditor has reason to believe the persons receiving the requests are likely to give them consideration.
   (4) individual account balances are relatively large.

c. The return of a positive confirmation of accounts receivable without an exception attests to the
   (1) collectibility of the receivable balance.
   (2) accuracy of the receivable balance.
   (3) accuracy of the aging of accounts receivable.
   (4) accuracy of the allowance for uncollectible accounts.

d. In confirming a client's accounts receivable in prior years, an auditor found that there were many differences between the recorded account balances and the confirmation responses. These differences, which were not misstatements, required substantial time to resolve. In defining the sampling unit for the current year's audit, the auditor would most likely choose
   (1) individual overdue balances.
   (2) individual invoices.
   (3) small account balances.
   (4) large account balances.

12-22 (Objective 12-3) The following questions concern audit objectives and management assertions for accounts receivable. Choose the best response.

a. When evaluating the adequacy of the allowance for uncollectible accounts, an auditor reviews the entity's aging of receivables to support management's financial assertion of
   (1) existence or occurrence.
   (2) valuation or allocation.
   (3) completeness.
   (4) rights and obligations.

b. Which of the following audit procedures would best uncover an understatement of sales and accounts receivable?
   (1) Test a sample of sales transactions, selecting the sample from prenumbered shipping documents.
   (2) Test a sample of sales transactions, selecting the sample from sales invoices recorded in the sales journal.
   (3) Confirm accounts receivable.
   (4) Review the aged accounts receivable trial balance.

DISCUSSION QUESTIONS AND PROBLEMS

12-23 (Objective 12-3) The following are common tests of details of balances for the audit of accounts receivable:

1. Obtain a list of aged accounts receivable, foot the list, and trace the total to the general ledger.
2. Trace 35 accounts to the accounts receivable master file for name, amount, and age categories.
3. Examine and document cash receipts on accounts receivable for 20 days after the engagement date.
4. Request 25 positive and 65 negative confirmations of accounts receivable.
5. Perform alternative procedures on accounts not responding to second requests by examining subsequent cash receipts documentation and shipping reports or sales invoices.
6. Test the sales cutoff by tracing entries in the sales journal for 15 days before and after the balance sheet date to shipping documents, if available, and/or sales invoices.
7. Determine and disclose accounts pledged, discounted, sold, assigned, or guaranteed by others.
8. Evaluate the materiality of credit balances in the aged trial balance.

Required

For each audit procedure, identify the balance-related audit objective or objectives it partially or fully satisfies.

12-24 (Objective 12-3) The following misstatements are sometimes found in the sales and collection cycle's account balances:

1. Cash received from collections of accounts receivable in the subsequent period is recorded as current period receipts.
2. The allowance for uncollectible accounts is inadequate because of the client's failure to reflect depressed economic conditions in the allowance.
3. Several accounts receivable are in dispute as a result of claims of defective merchandise.
4. The pledging of accounts receivable to the bank for a loan is not disclosed in the financial statements.
5. Goods shipped and included in the current period sales were returned in the subsequent period.
6. Several accounts receivable in the accounts receivable master file are not included in the aged trial balance.

7. One account receivable in the accounts receivable master file is included on the aged trial balance twice.
8. Long-term interest-bearing notes receivable from affiliated companies are included in accounts receivable.
9. The trial balance total does not equal the amount in the general ledger.

Required

a. For each misstatement, identify the balance-related audit objective to which it pertains.

b. For each misstatement, list an internal control that should prevent it.

c. For each misstatement, list one test of details of balances audit procedure that the auditor can use to detect it.

12-25 (Objective 12-3) The following are audit procedures in the sales and collection cycle:

1. Examine a sample of shipping documents to determine whether each has a sales invoice number included on it.
2. Discuss with the sales manager whether any sales allowances have been granted after the balance sheet date that may apply to the current period.
3. Add the columns on the aged trial balance and compare the total with the general ledger.
4. Observe whether the controller makes an independent comparison of the total in the general ledger with the trial balance of accounts receivable.
5. Compare the date on a sample of shipping documents throughout the year with related duplicate sales invoices and the accounts receivable master file.
6. Examine a sample of customer orders and see if each has a credit authorization.
7. Compare the date on a sample of shipping documents a few days before and after the balance sheet date with related sales journal transactions.
8. Compute the ratio of allowance for uncollectible accounts divided by accounts receivable and compare with previous years.
9. Examine a sample of noncash credits in the accounts receivable master file to determine if the internal auditor has initialed each, indicating internal verification.

Required

a. For each procedure, identify the applicable type of audit evidence.

b. For each procedure, identify which of the following it is:
   (1) Test of control
   (2) Substantive test of transactions
   (3) Analytical procedure
   (4) Test of details of balances

c. For those procedures you identified as a test of control or substantive test of transactions, what transaction-related audit objective or objectives are being satisfied?

d. For those procedures you identified as a test of details of balances, what balance-related audit objective or objectives are being satisfied?

12-26 (Objective 12-3) The following are the nine balance-related audit objectives, seven tests of details of balances for accounts receivable, and seven tests of controls or substantive tests of transactions for the sales and collection cycle:

Balance-Related Audit Objective

Detail tie-in
Existence
Completeness
Accuracy
Classification
Cutoff
Realizable value
Rights
Presentation and disclosure

Test of Details of Balances, Test of Control, or Substantive Test of Transactions Audit Procedure

1. Confirm accounts receivable.
2. Review sales returns after the balance sheet date to determine whether any are applicable to the current year.
3. Compare dates on shipping documents and the sales journal throughout the year.
4. Perform alternative procedures for nonresponses to confirmation.
5. Examine sales transactions for related party or employee sales recorded as regular sales.

6. Examine duplicate sales invoices for consignment sales and other shipments for which title has not passed.
7. Trace a sample of accounts from the accounts receivable master file to the aged trial balance.
8. Trace recorded sales transactions to shipping documents to determine whether a document exists.
9. Examine the financial statements to determine whether all related parties, notes, and pledged receivables are properly presented.
10. Examine duplicate sales invoices for initials that indicate internal verification of extensions and footings.
11. Trace a sample of shipping documents to related sales invoice entries in the sales journal.
12. Compare amounts and dates on the aged trial balance and accounts receivable master file.
13. Trace from the sales journal to the accounts receivable master file to make sure the information is the same.
14. Inquire of management whether there are notes from related parties included with trade receivables.

Required

a. Identify which procedures are tests of details of balances, which are tests of controls, and which are substantive tests of transactions.

b. Identify one test of details and one test of control or substantive test of transactions that will partially satisfy each balance-related audit objective. (Tests of controls and substantive tests of transactions are not used for presentation and disclosure.) Each procedure must be used at least once.

12-27 **(Objective 12-3)** Niosoki Auto Parts sells new parts for foreign automobiles to auto dealers. Company policy requires that a prenumbered shipping document be issued for each sale. At the time of pickup or shipment, the shipping clerk writes the date on the shipping document. The last shipment made in the fiscal year ended August 31, 2002, was recorded on document 2167. Shipments are billed in the order that the billing clerk receives the shipping documents.

For late August and early September, shipping documents are billed on sales invoices as follows:

Shipping Document No.	Sales Invoice No.
2163	4332
2164	4326
2165	4327
2166	4330
2167	4331
2168	4328
2169	4329
2170	4333
2171	4335
2172	4334

The August and September sales journals have the following information included:

SALES JOURNAL—AUGUST 2002

Day of Month	Sales Invoice No.	Amount of Sale
30	4326	$ 726.11
30	4329	1,914.30
31	4327	419.83
31	4328	620.22
31	4330	47.74

SALES JOURNAL—SEPTEMBER 2002

Day of Month	Sales Invoice No.	Amount of Sale
1	4332	$4,641.31
1	4331	106.39
1	4333	852.06
2	4335	1,250.50
2	4334	646.58

Required

a. What are the GAAP requirements for a correct sales cutoff?

b. Which sales invoices, if any, are recorded in the wrong accounting period? Prepare an adjusting entry to correct the financial statement for the year ended August 31, 2002. Assume that the company uses a periodic inventory system (inventory and cost of sales do not need to be adjusted).

c. Assume that the shipping clerk accidentally wrote August 31 on shipping documents 2168 through 2172. Explain how that would affect the correctness of the financial statements. How would you, as an auditor, discover that error?

d. Describe, in general terms, the audit procedures you would follow in making sure that cutoff for sales is accurate at the balance sheet date.

e. Identify internal controls that would reduce the likelihood of cutoff misstatements. How would you test each control?

12-28 **(Objective 12-4)** Dodge, CPA, is auditing the financial statements of a manufacturing company with a significant amount of trade accounts receivable. Dodge is satisfied that the accounts are properly summarized and classified and that allocations, reclassifications, and valuations are made in accordance with GAAP. Dodge is planning to use accounts receivable confirmation requests to satisfy the third standard of field work as to trade accounts receivable.

Required

a. Identify and describe the two forms of accounts receivable confirmation requests and indicate what factors Dodge will consider in determining when to use each.

b. Assume that Dodge has received a satisfactory response to the confirmation requests. Describe how Dodge could evaluate collectibility of the trade accounts receivable.

c. What are the implications to a CPA if during an audit of accounts receivable some of a client's trade customers do not respond to a request for positive confirmation of their accounts?

d. What auditing steps should a CPA perform if there is no response to a second request for a positive confirmation?*

12-29 **(Objective 12-2)** Johnson Clock Company sells specialty clocks, watches, and other timekeeping devices. Since its inception, the company has sold items through its home office store and at industry and collector trade shows around the country. To meet the demand from collectors around the world, the company began selling items through its Internet Web site three years ago. Recent financial information about Johnson's sales is summarized in the accompanying table.

	Year Ended 12/31/02	Year Ended 12/31/01	Year Ended 12/31/00
Sales:			
Home office	$1,279,480	$1,218,552	$1,163,851
Trade show	773,265	739,259	704,391
Internet-based	147,772	122,462	52,884
Sales Returns:			
Home office	$ 25,589	$ 23,152	$ 25,605
Trade show	13,946	13,676	12,679
Internet-based	13,254	11,022	4,760
Cost of Goods Sold:			
Home office	$ 831,662	$ 816,429	$ 768,142
Trade show	491,023	480,518	454,332
Internet-based	81,275	66,129	28,822
Receivables Related to Sales from:			
Home office	$ 126,195	$ 123,524	$ 127,545
Trade show	74,149	68,862	67,544
Internet-based	3,239	3,020	1,159

Tolerable misstatement for sales and receivables is $12,000.

*AICPA adapted.

Using the information given, design and perform analytical procedures for the sales and collection cycle at Johnson Clock Company. Based on the results of your analytical procedures, describe how the results related to the Internet-based sales differ from the home office and trade show sales.

Required

12-30 (Objective 12-4) You have been assigned to the first audit of the Chicago Company for the year ending March 31, 2002. Accounts receivable were confirmed on December 31, 2001, and at that date the receivables consisted of approximately 200 accounts with balances totaling $956,750. Seventy-five of these accounts with balances totaling $650,725 were selected for confirmation. All but 20 of the confirmation requests have been returned; 30 were signed without comments, 14 had minor differences that have been cleared satisfactorily, and 11 confirmations had the following comments:

1. We are sorry, but we cannot answer your request for confirmation of our account as the PDQ Company uses an accounts payable voucher system.
2. The balance of $1,050 was paid on December 23, 2001.
3. The balance of $7,750 was paid on January 5, 2002.
4. The balance noted above has been paid.
5. We do not owe you anything at December 31, 2001, as the goods, represented by your invoice dated December 30, 2001, number 25050, in the amount of $11,550, were received on January 5, 2002, on FOB destination terms.
6. An advance payment of $2,500 made by us in November 2001 should cover the two invoices totaling $1,350 shown on the statement attached.
7. We never received these goods.
8. We are contesting the propriety of this $12,525 charge. We think the charge is excessive.
9. Amount okay. As the goods have been shipped to us on consignment, we will remit payment upon selling the goods.
10. The $10,000, representing a deposit under a lease, will be applied against the rent due to us during 2003, the last year of the lease.
11. Your credit memo dated December 5, 2001, in the amount of $440 cancels the balance above.

What steps would you take to satisfactorily clear each of the preceding 11 comments.*

Required

INTEGRATED CASE APPLICATION—PINNACLE MANUFACTURING: PART III

12-31 (Objectives 12-2, 12-3, 12-4) Parts I (pp. 274–276) and II (p. 336) of this case study dealt with obtaining an understanding of internal control and assessing control risk for transactions affecting accounts payable of Pinnacle Manufacturing. In Part III, we design analytical procedures and design and perform tests of details of balances for accounts payable.

Assume that your understanding of internal controls over acquisitions and cash disbursements and the related tests of controls and substantive tests of transactions support an assessment of a low control risk. Also assume that analytical procedures support the overall reasonableness of the balance. Accounts payable at December 31, 2002, are included in Figure 12-8 (p. 366).

Required

a. List those relationships, ratios, and trends that you believe will provide useful information about the overall reasonableness of accounts payable.

b. Prepare an audit program in a design format for tests of details of balances for accounts payable. Before preparing the audit program, you should review the Hillsburg Hardware Co. design format audit program in Table 12-4 (p. 357) and performance format audit program in Table 12-5 (p. 358). You should prepare a matrix similar to the one in Figure 12-7 on page 356 for accounts payable. Assume that acceptable audit risk was assessed as high. Use your judgment to assess inherent risk for each objective. Assume that assessed control risk is low for all transaction-related audit objectives and analytical procedures results were satisfactory for those balance-related audit objectives where analytical procedures are relevant. The design format audit program should include audit procedures and sample sizes for procedures that involve sampling. Use your judgment and the evidence planning worksheet in determining sample sizes.

c. Prepare an audit program for accounts payable in a performance format, using the audit procedures and sample sizes from part b.

*AICPA adapted.

FIGURE 12-8 **Pinnacle Manufacturing Trial Balance of Trade Accounts Payable—December 31, 2002**

Advent Sign Mfg. Co.	$ 2,500.00	M & A Milling	$ 4,662.00
Alder Insurance Co.	660.00	Midwest Electric Utility	3,698.15
American Computing Service	1,211.00	Midwest Gas Co.	2,442.10
Bauer and Adamson	86.00	Mobil Oil Co.	11,480.00
Bleyl & Sons	1,500.00	Monsanto Chemical	14,622.15
Central Steel Inc.	8,753.00	Nielsen Enterprises	437.56
Chelsea Development Co.	1,800.00	Norris Industries	9,120.00
Commercial Supply	3,250.00	Pacific Title Co.	320.00
Country Electric	980.00	Permaloy Manufacturing	3,290.00
Diamond Janitorial Service	750.00	Polein Drill and Bit	2,870.16
Dictaphone Corp.	675.00	Propec Inc.	510.00
Douglas Equipment	6,425.00	Rayno Sales and Service	1,917.80
Ellison, Robt. & Assoc.	346.10	Reames Construction	4,500.00
FMC Corp.	15,819.00	Remington Supply Co.	9,842.10
Fiberchem Inc.	6,315.80	Ritter Engineering Corp.	1,200.00
Fuller Travel	943.00	Roberts Bros. Service	189.73
GAFCO	5,750.00	S & S Truck Painting	819.00
Glade Specialties	1,000.00	Sanders, Geo. A. & Co.	346.00
Granger Supply Co.	4,250.00	Semco, Inc.	50.20
Hesco Services	719.62	Standard Oil Co.	12,816.27
Innes, Brush & Co. CPAs	1,500.00	Stationery Supply	619.12
J & L Plastics Corp.	1,412.00	Thermal Tape Co.	123.00
Judkins Co.	2,500.00	Todd Machinery, Inc.	6,888.12
Kazco. Mfg. Co.	1,627.30	Valco Sales	1,429.00
Kedman Company	19.27	Vermax Corp.	284.00
Koch Plumbing Contractors	2,750.00	Waco Electronics, Inc.	126.33
Kohler Products	10,483.23	Western Telephone Co.	2,369.62
Lakeshore Inc.	1,850.00	Williams Controls, Inc.	1,915.00
Landscape Services	420.00	Xerox Corp.	3,250.00
Lundberg Coatings, Inc.	2,733.10	Yates Supply Co.	919.70
		Total	$192,085.53

Other related information:

- The vendors with the greatest volume of transactions during the year are as follows:

Central Steel Inc.	Mobil Oil Co.
Commercial Supply	Monsanto Chemical
FMC Corp.	Norris Industries
Fiberchem Inc.	Remington Supply Co.
GAFCO	Standard Oil Co.

- Tolerable misstatement for accounts payable is $7,500.00.

d. Assume for requirement b that (1) assessed control risk had been high rather than low for each transaction-related audit objective, (2) inherent risk was high for each balance-related audit objective, and (3) analytical procedures indicated a high potential for misstatement. What would the effect have been on the audit procedures and sample sizes for part b?

e. Confirmation requests were sent to the 20 vendors listed in Figure 12-9. Fourteen confirmation responses were returned indicating no difference between the vendor's and the company's records. Figure 12-10 (pp. 368–369) presents the six replies that indicate a difference between the vendor's balance and the company's records. The auditor's follow-up findings are indicated on each reply. Prepare an audit schedule similar to the one illustrated in Figure 12-11 on page 370 to determine the misstatements, if any, for each difference. The exception for Fiberchem is analyzed as an illustration. Assume that Pinnacle Manufacturing took a complete physical inventory at December 31, 2002, and the auditor concluded that recorded inventory reflects all inventory on hand at the balance sheet date. Include the 14 balances confirmed without exception as one amount on the schedule, and total the schedule columns.

Use a computer with appropriate software to prepare this audit schedule and analysis (instructor option).

f. Estimate the total misstatement in accounts payable based on the sample misstatements you identified in requirement e. What is your conclusion about the fairness of the recorded balance in accounts payable for Pinnacle Manufacturing and your assessment of control risk as low for all transaction-related audit objectives?

FIGURE 12-9 Pinnacle Manufacturing Sample of Accounts Payable Selected for Confirmation—December 31, 2002

High-Volume Items	
1. Central Steel	$ 8,753.00
2. Commercial Supply	3,250.00
3. FMC	15,819.00
4. Fiberchem	6,315.80
5. GAFCO	5,750.00
6. Mobil Oil	11,480.00
7. Monsanto	14,622.15
8. Norris Industries	9,120.00
9. Remington Supply	9,842.10
10. Standard Oil	12,816.27
Other Material Items	
11. Kohler Products	10,483.23
Random Sample of Additional Items	
12. Advent Sign Mfg. Co.	2,500.00
13. Country Electric	980.00
14. Fuller Travel	943.00
15. J & L Plastics	1,412.00
16. M & A Milling	4,662.00
17. Permaloy Manufacturing	3,290.00
18. S & S Truck Painting	819.00
19. Todd Machinery	6,888.12
20. Western Telephone Co.	2,369.62
TOTAL TESTED	$132,115.29

FIGURE 12-10 Replies to Requests for Information

STATEMENT FROM FIBERCHEM

Pinnacle Manufacturing
Midvale, IL

Amounts due as of December 31, 2002:

Invoice No.	Date	Amount	Balance Due
8312	11-22-02	$2,217.92	$2,217.92
8469	12-02-02	2,540.11	4,758.03
8819	12-18-02	1,557.77	6,315.80(1)
9002	12-30-02	2,403.42(2)	8,719.22

Auditor's notes:
(1) Agrees with accounts payable listing.
(2) Goods received December 31, 2002. As a result of the New Year's Eve shutdown, recorded on January 2, 2003.

STATEMENT FROM MOBIL OIL

Pinnacle Manufacturing
Midvale, IL

Amounts due as of December 31, 2002:

Invoice No.	Date	Amount	Balance Due
DX10037	12-02-02	$2,870.00	$2,870.00
DX11926	12-09-02	2,870.00	5,740.00
DX12619	12-16-02	2,870.00	8,610.00
DX14777	12-23-02	2,870.00	11,480.00(1)
DX16908	12-30-02	2,870.00(2)	14,350.00

Auditor's notes:
(1) Agrees with accounts payable listing.
(2) Goods shipped FOB Pinnacle Manufacturing. Arrived on January 3, 2003.

STATEMENT FROM NORRIS INDUSTRIES

Pinnacle Manufacturing
Midvale, IL

Amounts due as of December 31, 2002:

Invoice No.	Date	Amount	Balance Due
14896	12-27-02	$9,120.00	$ 9,120.00(1)
15111	12-27-02	4,300.00(2)	13,420.00

Auditor's notes:
(1) Agrees with accounts payable listing.
(2) Goods shipped FOB Norris Industries' plant on December 21, 2002, arrived at Pinnacle Manufacturing on January 4, 2003.

FIGURE 12-10 Replies to Requests for Information (Cont.)

STATEMENT FROM REMINGTON SUPPLY

Pinnacle Manufacturing
Midvale, IL

Amounts due as of December 31, 2002:

Invoice No.	Date	Amount	Balance Due
141702	11-11-02	$3,712.09(2)	$ 3,712.09
142619	11-19-02	1,984.80(1)	5,696.89
142811	12-04-02	2,320.00(2)	8,016.89
143600	12-21-02	3,810.01(2)	11,826.90
143918	12-26-02	3,707.00(3)	15,533.90

Auditor's notes:
(1) Paid by Pinnacle Manufacturing on December 28, 2002. Payment in transit at year-end.
(2) The total of these items of $9,842.10 agrees with accounts payable listing.
(3) Goods shipped FOB Remington Supply on December 26, 2002, arrived at Pinnacle Manufacturing on January 3, 2003.

STATEMENT FROM ADVENT SIGN MFG. CO.

Pinnacle Manufacturing
Midvale, IL

Amounts due as of December 31, 2002:

First progress billing per contract	$2,500.00(1)
Second progress billing per contract	1,500.00(2)
Total due	$4,000.00

Auditor's notes:
(1) Agrees with accounts payable listing.
(2) Progress payment due as of December 31, 2002, per contract for construction of new custom electric sign. Sign installation completed on January 15, 2003.

STATEMENT FROM FULLER TRAVEL

Pinnacle Manufacturing
Midvale, IL

Amounts due as of December 31, 2002:

Ticket No.	Date	Amount	Balance Due
843 601 102	12-04-02	$280.00(2)	$ 280.00
843 601 819	12-12-02	280.00(2)	560.00
843 602 222	12-21-02	383.00(1)	943.00
843 602 919	12-26-02	383.00(2)	1,326.00

Auditor's notes:
(1) Ticket not used and returned for credit. Credit given on January 2003 statement.
(2) The total of these items of $943.00 agrees with accounts payable listing.

FIGURE 12-11 Pinnacle Manufacturing Analysis of Trade Accounts Payable—December 31, 2002

Vendor	Balance per Books	Amount Confirmed by Vendor	Difference: Books Over (Under) Amount Confirmed	Timing Difference: No Misstatement	Misstatement in Accounts Payable DR (CR)	Misstatement in Related Accounts: Balance Sheet Misstatement DR (CR)	Misstatement in Related Accounts: Income Statement Misstatement DR (CR)	Brief Explanation
Fiberchem	6,315.80	8,719.22	(2,403.42)		(2,403.42)		2,403.42	Unrecorded A/P: Dr Purchases Cr A/P

INTERNET PROBLEM 12-1: REVENUE RECOGNITION

WWW

Reference the CW site. In recent years, several high-profile incidents of improper revenue recognition attracted the attention of the business media. The SEC has also expressed concerns about the number of instances of improper revenue recognition identified by SEC staff. In response to the concerns about audit issues associated with revenue recognition, the AICPA put together a "tool kit" summarizing audit guidance in this area. This problem requires students to use the Internet to (1) identify deterrents to improper revenue recognition, (2) define a "bill and hold" sale, and (3) evaluate bill and hold transactions.

CHAPTER 13

AUDIT SAMPLING

IF YOU ARE NOT GOING TO BELIEVE IT, DON'T USE IT

Brooks & Company, CPAs, uses random samples in performing audit tests whenever possible. They believe that this gives them the best chance of getting representative samples of their clients' accounting information. In the audit of Sensational Products, a random sample of 30 inventory items was taken from a population of 1,800 items in doing a test of unit and total costs. Only 1 of the 30 items was in error, but it was large. In investigating the error, Harold Davis, the audit staff person doing the test, was told by Sensational's controller that the error occurred while the regular inventory clerk was on vacation and was really only an "isolated error."

Harold knew that generally accepted auditing standards require that errors in random samples be projected to the entire population. In this case, such a projection would involve multiplying the error found by a factor of 60 (1,800 divided by 30). This would result in an audit adjustment or additional audit work. Harold knew that the client would not be happy about this because the adjustment would reduce an already "strained" net income figure and additional auditing would increase the audit fee. If the error was, in fact, an isolated one, it would not be significant enough to require an audit adjustment.

Harold decided to look at the situation in terms of the probability of the error being an isolated example. He calculated the chance to be about only 1 in 60 of including an isolated error in a sample of 30 from a population of 1,800. He then looked at accepting the client's representation about the uniqueness of the error as a bet. If he accepted the representation and didn't do the projection and act on it, he was in effect betting his career in a situation where the odds were 60 to 1 against him. It didn't take Harold long to recognize the wisdom of the professional standards and conclude that the projection should be done.

LEARNING OBJECTIVES

After studying this chapter, you should be able to

13-1 Explain the concept of representative sampling.

13-2 Distinguish between statistical and nonstatistical sampling and between probabilistic and nonprobabilistic sample selection.

13-3 Select representative samples.

13-4 Define and describe audit sampling for tests of controls and substantive tests of transactions.

13-5 Use audit sampling in tests of controls and substantive tests of transactions.

13-6 Differentiate between audit sampling for tests of details of balances and for tests of controls and substantive tests of transactions.

13-7 Apply audit sampling to tests of details of balances.

In the last two chapters, we learned about designing tests of controls, substantive tests of transactions, and tests of details of balances needed to perform an audit of the sales and collection cycle. Before these tests can be performed, the auditor needs to decide for each audit procedure the sample size and sample items to select from the population. When the auditor decides to select less than 100 percent of the population for testing for the purpose of making inferences about the population, it is called **audit sampling.** As demonstrated by Harold Davis of Brooks & Company in the chapter vignette, evaluating audit samples is an essential, and often challenging, part of the audit process. When is a sample size sufficiently large to evaluate a population? Does a given sample accurately represent the accounting information? This chapter discusses sampling issues for tests of controls, substantive tests of transactions, and tests of details of balances. These sampling concepts are illustrated for the sales and collection cycle, but they are equally applicable to all other cycles.

It is useful to think of the chapter as being divided into three closely related parts. The first part is about general sampling concepts. The second part deals with sampling for exceptions, which is about audit sampling for tests of controls and substantive tests of transactions. The last part concerns audit sampling for tests of details of balances.

REPRESENTATIVE SAMPLES

OBJECTIVE 13-1

Explain the concept of representative sampling.

When an auditor selects a sample from a population, the objective is to obtain a representative one. A **representative sample** is one in which the characteristics in the sample of audit interest are approximately the same as those of the population. This means that the sampled items are similar to the items not sampled. For example, assume that a client's internal controls require a clerk to attach a shipping document to every duplicate sales invoice, but the procedure is not followed exactly 3 percent of the time. If the auditor selects a sample of 100 duplicate sales invoices and finds three missing, the sample is highly representative. If two or four such items are found in the sample, the sample is reasonably representative. If no or many missing items are found, the sample is nonrepresentative.

In practice, auditors do not know whether a sample is representative, even after all testing is complete. However, auditors can increase the likelihood of a sample being representative by using care in its design, selection, and evaluation. Two things can cause a sample result to be nonrepresentative: nonsampling error and sampling error. The risk of these occurring is termed nonsampling risk and sampling risk. Both of these can be controlled.

Nonsampling risk is the risk that audit tests do not uncover existing exceptions in the sample. The two causes of nonsampling risk are the auditor's failure to recognize exceptions and inappropriate or ineffective audit procedures. An auditor might fail to recognize an exception because of exhaustion, boredom, or lack of understanding of what to look for. In the previous example in which three shipping documents were not attached to duplicate sales invoices, if the auditor concluded that no exceptions existed, there is a nonsampling error. An ineffective audit procedure for the exceptions in question would be to examine a sample of shipping documents and determine whether each is attached to a set of duplicate sales invoices, rather than to examine a sample of duplicate sales invoices. In this case, the auditor has done the test in the wrong direction by starting with the shipping document instead of the duplicate sales invoice. Careful design of audit procedures, proper instruction, supervision, and review are ways to control nonsampling risk.

Sampling risk is the risk that an auditor reaches an incorrect conclusion because the sample is not representative of the population. Sampling risk is an inherent part of sampling that results from testing less than the entire population. For example, assume that an auditor accepts a population based on a sample of 100 items that contains two exceptions. However, the population actually has an 8 percent exception rate, which the auditor would reject as unacceptable. The auditor has incorrectly accepted the population because the sample was not sufficiently representative of the population.

There are two ways to control sampling risk: by adjusting sample size and by using an appropriate method of selecting sample items from the population. Increasing sample size will reduce sampling risk, and vice versa. At the extreme, a sample of all the items of a population will have a zero sampling risk. Using an appropriate sampling method will reasonably ensure representativeness. This does not eliminate or even reduce sampling risk, but it does allow the auditor to measure the risk associated with a given sample size in a reliable manner. Determining the appropriate sample size to reduce sampling risk to an appropriate level is a major topic of this chapter.

STATISTICAL VERSUS NONSTATISTICAL SAMPLING AND PROBABILISTIC VERSUS NONPROBABILISTIC SAMPLE SELECTION

Before discussing the methods of sample selection to obtain representative samples, it is useful to make two distinctions and discuss the terms involved: statistical versus nonstatistical sampling and probabilistic versus nonprobabilistic sample selection.

Statistical Versus Nonstatistical Sampling

OBJECTIVE 13-2

Distinguish between statistical and nonstatistical sampling and between probabilistic and nonprobabilistic sample selection.

Audit sampling methods can be divided into two broad categories: statistical sampling and nonstatistical sampling. These categories have important similarities and differences. They are similar in that they both involve three steps: (1) plan the sample, (2) select the sample and perform the tests, and (3) evaluate the results. The purpose of planning the sample is to make sure that the audit tests are performed in a manner that provides the desired sampling risk and minimizes the likelihood of nonsampling error. Selecting the sample involves deciding how to select sample items from the population. Performing the tests is the examination of documents and doing other audit procedures. Evaluating the results involves drawing conclusions based on the audit tests. To illustrate, assume that an auditor selects a sample of 100 duplicate sales invoices from a population, tests each to determine whether a shipping document is attached, and determines that there are three exceptions. Deciding that a sample size of 100 is needed is a part of planning the sample. Deciding which 100 items to select from the population is a sample selection problem. Doing the audit procedure for each of the 100 items and determining that there were three exceptions constitute performing the tests. Reaching conclusions about the likely exception rate in the total population when there is a sample exception rate of 3 percent is evaluating the results.

Statistical sampling differs from nonstatistical sampling in that, through the application of mathematical rules, it allows the quantification (measurement) of sampling risk in planning the sample (step 1) and evaluating the results (step 3). (You may remember calculating a statistical result at a 95 percent confidence level in a statistics course. The 95 percent confidence level provides a 5 percent sampling risk.)

Statistical sampling was used extensively by CPA firms in the 1980s and the early 1990s but for a variety of reasons, including legal liability and cost issues, statistical sampling is now seldom used in practice. For this reason, the study of audit sampling in this chapter focuses on nonstatistical sampling, which is used extensively by almost all practitioners, in both large and small CPA firms.

In **nonstatistical sampling,** the auditor does not quantify sampling risk. Instead, those sample items that the auditor believes will provide the most useful information in the circumstances are selected. Conclusions are reached about populations on a judgmental basis. For that reason, the selection of nonprobabilistic samples is often termed **judgmental sampling.**

Probabilistic Versus Nonprobabilistic Sample Selection

Both probabilistic and nonprobabilistic sample selection are a part of step 2 in using auditing sampling, selecting sample items from the population. **Probabilistic sample selection** is a method of selecting a sample such that each population item has a known probability of being included in the sample and the sample is selected by a random process. To satisfy this definition, the auditor must use great care in selecting samples using one of several methods to be discussed shortly. **Nonprobabilistic sample selection** is a method of selecting a sample in which the auditor uses professional judgment rather than probabilistic methods to select sample items. There are also several nonprobabilistic sample selection methods.

Applying Statistical and Nonstatistical Sampling in Practice and Sample Selection Methods

It is equally acceptable under professional standards for auditors to use either statistical or nonstatistical sampling methods. However, it is essential that either method be applied with due care. All steps of the process must be followed carefully. When statistical sampling is used, the sample *must be a probabilistic one* and appropriate statistical evaluation methods must be used with the sample results to make the sampling risk computations.

It is also acceptable to make nonstatistical evaluations by using probabilistic selection. It is *never* acceptable, however, to evaluate a nonprobabilistic sample as if it were a statistical sample.

Three types of sample selection methods are commonly associated with nonstatistical audit sampling. All three methods are nonprobabilistic. Four types of sample selection methods are commonly associated with either nonstatistical or statistical audit sampling. All four methods are probabilistic.

Nonprobabilistic (judgmental) sample selection methods include the following:

1. Directed sample selection
2. Block sample selection
3. Haphazard sample selection

Probabilistic sample selection methods include the following:

1. Simple random sample selection
2. Systematic sample selection
3. Probability proportional to size sample selection
4. Stratified sample selection

We will now discuss each of these seven sample selection methods, starting with nonprobabilistic methods.

NONPROBABILISTIC SAMPLE SELECTION METHODS

Nonprobabilistic sample selection methods are those that do not meet the technical requirements for probabilistic sample selection. Because these methods are not based on strict mathematical probabilities, the representativeness of the sample may be difficult to determine. The information content of the sample, including its representativeness, will be based on the knowledge and skill of the auditor in applying judgment in the circumstances.

Directed Sample Selection

Directed sample selection is the selection of each item in the sample based on some judgmental criteria established by the auditor. The auditor does not rely on equal chances of selection, but instead deliberately selects items according to the criteria. These criteria may relate to representativeness, or they may not. Commonly used criteria are the following:

Items Most Likely to Contain Misstatements Often, auditors are able to identify which population items are most likely to be misstated. Examples are receivables outstanding for a long time, purchases from and sales to officers and affiliated companies, and unusually large or complex transactions. These kinds of items can be efficiently investigated by the auditor, and the results can be applied to the population on a judgmental basis. The reasoning underlying the evaluation of such samples is often that, if none of the items selected contains misstatements, it is highly unlikely that a material misstatement exists in the population.

Items Containing Selected Population Characteristics The auditor may be able to describe the various types and sources of items that make up the population and design the sample to be representative by selecting one or more items of each type. For example, a sample of cash disbursements might include some from each month, each bank account or location, and each major type of acquisition.

Large Dollar Coverage A sample can often be selected to cover such a large portion of total population dollars that the risk of drawing an improper conclusion by not examining small items is not a concern. This is a practical approach on many audits, especially smaller ones.

Block Sample Selection

Block sample selection is the selection of several items in sequence. Once the first item in the block is selected, the remainder of the block is chosen automatically. One example of a block sample is the selection of a sequence of 100 sales transactions from the sales journal for the third week of March. A total sample of 100 could also be selected by taking 5 blocks of 20 items each, 10 blocks of 10, or 50 blocks of 2.

It is ordinarily acceptable to use block samples only if a reasonable number of blocks is used. If few blocks are used, the probability of obtaining a nonrepresentative sample is too great, considering the possibility of such things as employee turnover, changes in the accounting system, and the seasonal nature of many businesses. An auditor using block sampling should exercise special care to control sampling risk in designing that sample.

Block sampling can also be used to supplement other samples when there is a high likelihood of misstatement for a known period. For example, selecting all 100 cash receipts from the third week of March may be appropriate if that is when the accounting clerk was on vacation and an inexperienced temporary employee processed the cash receipt transactions.

Haphazard Sample Selection

Haphazard sample selection is the selection of items without any conscious bias on the part of the auditor. In such cases, the auditor selects population items without regard to their size, source, or other distinguishing characteristics.

The most serious shortcoming of haphazard sample selection is the difficulty of remaining completely unbiased in the selection. Because of the auditor's training and "cultural bias," certain population items are more likely than others to be included in the sample.

Although haphazard and block sample selection appear to be less logical than directed sample selection, they are often useful as audit tools and should not be ignored. In some situations, the cost of more complex sample selection methods outweighs the benefits obtained from using them. For example, assume that the auditor wants to trace credits from the accounts receivable master files to the cash receipts journal and other authorized sources as a test for fictitious credits in the master files. A haphazard or block approach is simpler and much less costly than other selection methods in this situation and would be used by many auditors. However, for most sampling applications involving tests of controls and substantive tests of transactions, auditors often prefer to use a probabilistic sample selection method to increase the likelihood of selecting a representative sample.

PROBABILISTIC SAMPLE SELECTION METHODS

OBJECTIVE 13-3

Select representative samples.

For probabilistic samples, the auditor uses no judgment about which sample items are selected, except to select which of the four selection methods to use. The four probabilistic methods are discussed next.

Simple Random Sample Selection

A simple **random sample** is one in which every possible combination of elements in the population has an equal chance of constituting the sample. Simple random sampling is used to sample populations that are not segmented for audit purposes. For example, the auditor may wish to sample the client's cash disbursements for the year. A simple random sample of 60 items contained in the cash disbursements journal might be selected for that purpose. Appropriate auditing procedures would be applied to the 60 items selected, and conclusions would be drawn and applied to all cash disbursement transactions recorded for the year.

Random Number Tables When a simple random sample is obtained, a method must be used that ensures that all items in the population have an equal chance of selection. Suppose that in the preceding example, there were a total of 12,000 cash disbursement transactions for the year. A simple random sample of one transaction would be such that each of the 12,000 transactions would have an equal chance of being selected. This would be done by obtaining a random number between 1 and 12,000. If the number was 3,895, the auditor would select and test the 3,895th cash disbursement transaction recorded in the cash disbursements journal.

Random numbers are a series of digits that have equal probabilities of occurring over long runs and which have no discernible pattern. A **random number table** is a presentation of these random digits in table form with numbered rows and columns. The auditor chooses a random sample by first establishing a correspondence between the client's document numbers to be tested and the digits in the random number table. After selecting a random starting point, the auditor reads down the table and finds the first random number that falls within the sequence of the document numbers being tested. The process continues until the final sample item is selected.

Computer Generation of Random Numbers It is useful to understand the use of random number tables as a means of understanding the concept of selecting simple random samples. However, most random samples obtained by auditors are obtained by using computers. There are three main types: electronic spreadsheet programs, random number generators, and generalized audit software programs.

The advantages of using computer programs in selecting random samples are time savings, reduced likelihood of auditor error in selecting the numbers, and automatic documentation. Because most auditors have access to a computer and to electronic spreadsheets or random number generator programs, auditors often prefer to use computer generation of random numbers over other probabilistic selection methods.

To illustrate computer generation of random numbers, Figure 13-1 shows the random selection of sales invoices for the audit of Hillsburg Hardware Co. using an electronic spreadsheet program. In the application illustrated, the auditor wishes to sample 50 items from a population of sales invoices numbered from 3689 to 9452. The program requires only input parameters by the auditor for a sample to be selected. It possesses great flexibility in the formatting of the numbers. For example, the program can generate random dates

FIGURE 13-1 Computer Generation of Random Numbers—Hillsburg Hardware Co.

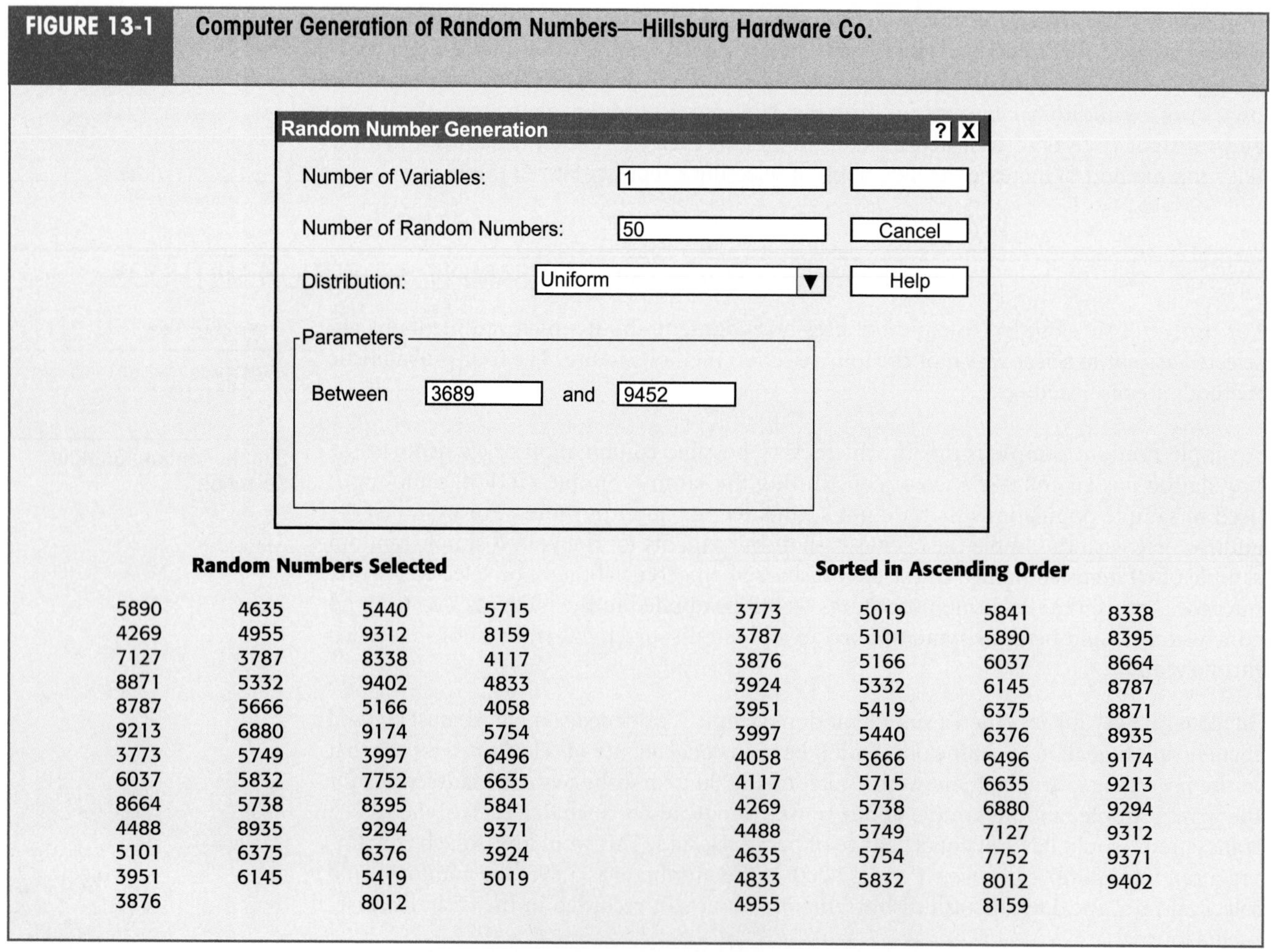

Random Numbers Selected

5890	4635	5440	5715
4269	4955	9312	8159
7127	3787	8338	4117
8871	5332	9402	4833
8787	5666	5166	4058
9213	6880	9174	5754
3773	5749	3997	6496
6037	5832	7752	6635
8664	5738	8395	5841
4488	8935	9294	9371
5101	6375	6376	3924
3951	6145	5419	5019
3876		8012	

Sorted in Ascending Order

3773	5019	5841	8338
3787	5101	5890	8395
3876	5166	6037	8664
3924	5332	6145	8787
3951	5419	6375	8871
3997	5440	6376	8935
4058	5666	6496	9174
4117	5715	6635	9213
4269	5738	6880	9294
4488	5749	7127	9312
4635	5754	7752	9371
4833	5832	8012	9402
4955		8159	

or ranges of sets of numbers (such as page and line numbers). It also provides output in both sorted and selection orders.

Random numbers may be obtained with replacement or without replacement. In replacement sampling, an element in the population can be included in the sample more than once, whereas in nonreplacement sampling, an element can be included only once. If the random number corresponding to an element is selected more than once in nonreplacement sampling, it is not included in the sample a second time. Although both selection approaches are consistent with sound statistical theory, auditors rarely use replacement sampling.

Systematic Sample Selection

In **systematic sample selection** (also called systematic sampling), the auditor calculates an interval and then methodically selects the items for the sample based on the size of the interval. The interval is determined by dividing the population size by the number of sample items desired. For example, if a population of sales invoices ranges from 652 to 3,151 and the desired sample size is 125, the interval is 20 [(3,151 – 651)/125]. The auditor must now select a random number between 0 and 19 to determine the starting point for the sample. If the randomly selected number is 9, the first item in the sample is invoice number 661 (652 + 9). The remaining 124 items are 681 (661 + 20), 701 (681 + 20), and so on through item 3,141.

The advantage of systematic selection is its ease of use. In most populations, a systematic sample can be drawn quickly, the approach automatically puts the numbers in sequence, and it is easy to develop the appropriate documentation.

A major problem with systematic selection is the possibility of bias. Because of the way systematic selection works, once the first item in the sample is selected, all other items are chosen automatically. This causes no problem if the characteristic of interest, such as a possible control deviation, is distributed randomly throughout the population; however, in some cases, characteristics of interest may not be randomly distributed. For example, if a control deviation occurred at a certain time of the month or with certain types of documents, a systematic sample could have a higher likelihood of failing to be representative than a simple random sample. Therefore, when systematic selection is used, possible patterns in the population data that could cause sample bias must be considered.

Probability Proportional to Size and Stratified Sample Selection

There are many situations in auditing when it is advantageous to select samples that emphasize population items that have larger recorded amounts. There are two ways to obtain such samples. The first is to take a sample where the probability of selecting any individual population item is proportional to its recorded amount. This method is called sampling with **probability proportional to size sample selection (PPS).**

In PPS sampling, the auditor selects a sample of the individual dollars in the population and then associates the dollar with the related physical unit. A simple example is where the auditor wants to select a sample of one from a population of two physical units, the first of which is $10,000 and the second $5,000. The auditor now takes a random sample of one from a population between 1 and 15,000. If the sample item is between 1 and 10,000, the physical unit selected is item 1. If it is between 10,001 and 15,000, the physical unit is item 2. Observe that the effect is to give the first item twice the likelihood of being included in the sample, which is the objective of PPS sampling.

The second way of emphasizing larger items in the population is to divide the population into subpopulations by size and take larger samples of the larger subpopulations. This is called stratified sampling. Sample selection methods and their related evaluation for tests of details of balances are discussed later in the chapter.

AUDIT SAMPLING FOR TESTS OF CONTROLS AND SUBSTANTIVE TESTS OF TRANSACTIONS

OBJECTIVE 13-4

Define and describe audit sampling for tests of controls and substantive tests of transactions.

Audit sampling for tests of controls and substantive tests of transactions is used to estimate the proportion of items in a population containing a characteristic or **attribute** of interest. This proportion is called the **occurrence rate** or **exception rate** and is the ratio of the items containing the specific attribute to the total number of population items. The occurrence rate is usually expressed as a percentage. For example, an auditor might conclude that the exception rate for the internal verification of sales invoices is approximately 3 percent, meaning that invoices are not properly verified 3 percent of the time.

Auditors are interested in the occurrence of the following types of exceptions in populations of accounting data: (1) deviations from client's established controls, (2) monetary misstatements in populations of transaction data, and (3) monetary misstatements in populations of account balance details. Knowing the occurrence rate of such exceptions is particularly helpful for the first two types of exceptions, which relate to transactions. Therefore, auditors make extensive use of audit sampling that measures the occurrence or exception rate in performing tests of controls and substantive tests of transactions. With the third type of exception, the auditor usually needs to estimate the total dollar amount of the exceptions because a judgment must be made about whether the exceptions are material. When the auditor wants to know the total amount of a misstatement, then methods that measure dollars, not the exception or occurrence rate, will be used. This topic is studied later in the chapter.

The exception rate in a sample is intended to be an estimate of the exception rate in the entire population. It means that for a given sample, the sample exception rate is the auditor's "best estimate" of the population exception rate. The term *exception* should be understood to refer to both deviations from prescribed controls and situations when amounts are not monetarily correct, whether because of an unintentional accounting error or any other cause. The term *deviation* refers to the specific type of exception of a departure from prescribed controls.

Assume, for example, that the auditor wants to determine the percentage of duplicate sales invoices that do not have shipping documents attached. There is an actual, but unknown, percentage of missing shipping documents. The auditor will obtain a sample of duplicate sales invoices and determine what percentage of the invoices do not have shipping documents attached. The auditor will conclude that the sample exception rate is the best estimate of the population exception rate.

Because it is based on a sample, however, there is a significant likelihood that the sample exception rate and the actual population exception rate differ. This difference is called *sampling error,* a term that was first introduced in Chapter 8. The auditor is concerned with the estimate of the sampling error and the reliability of that estimate, called *sampling risk,* a term that was introduced earlier in this chapter. Assume that the auditor determines that there is a 3 percent sample exception rate and a sampling error of 1 percent with a sampling risk of 10 percent. The auditor can now state an interval estimate of the population exception rate as between 2 percent and 4 percent (3 percent ± 1) at a 10 percent risk of being wrong (and a 90 percent chance of being right).

APPLICATION OF AUDIT SAMPLING IN TESTS OF CONTROLS AND SUBSTANTIVE TESTS OF TRANSACTIONS

OBJECTIVE 13-5

Use audit sampling in tests of controls and substantive tests of transactions.

We will now examine the application of nonstatistical audit sampling in testing transactions for control deviations and monetary misstatements. Before doing so, the terminology from SAS 39 (AU 350) and other terminology are defined. These are summarized in Table 13-1.

Audit sampling is applied to tests of controls and substantive tests of transactions through a set of 14 well-defined steps. The steps are divided into three sections: plan the sample, select the sample and perform the audit procedures, and evaluate the results. It is important to follow these steps carefully as a means of ensuring that both the auditing and the sampling aspects of the process are properly applied. The steps provide an outline of the discussion that follows and are illustrated for the audit of Hillsburg Hardware Co.

Plan the Sample

1. State the objectives of the audit test.
2. Decide whether audit sampling applies.
3. Define attributes and exception conditions.

TABLE 13-1 Terms Used in Audit Sampling

TERM	DEFINITION
Terms Related to Planning	
Characteristics or attribute	The characteristic being tested in the application
Acceptable risk of assessing control risk too low (ARACR)	The risk that the auditor is willing to take of accepting a control as effective or a rate of monetary misstatements as tolerable, when the true population exception rate is greater than the tolerable exception rate
Tolerable exception rate (TER)	Exception rate that the auditor will permit in the population and still be willing to use the assessed control risk and/or the amount of monetary misstatements in the transactions established during planning
Estimated population exception rate (EPER)	Exception rate that the auditor expects to find in the population before testing begins
Initial sample size	Sample size decided after considering the above factors in planning
Terms Related to Evaluating Results	
Exception	Exception from the attribute in a sample item
Sample exception rate (SER)	Number of exceptions in the sample divided by the sample size
Computed upper exception rate (CUER)	The highest estimated exception rate in the population at a given ARACR

4. Define the population.
5. Define the sampling unit.
6. Specify the tolerable exception rate.
7. Specify acceptable risk of assessing control risk too low.
8. Estimate the population exception rate.
9. Determine the initial sample size.

Select the Sample and Perform the Audit Procedures

10. Select the sample.
11. Perform the audit procedures.

Evaluate the Results

12. Generalize from the sample to the population.
13. Analyze exceptions.
14. Decide the acceptability of the population.

State the Objectives of the Audit Test

The overall objectives of the test must be stated in terms of the transaction cycle being tested. Typically, the overall objectives of tests of controls and substantive tests of transactions are to test the application of controls and to determine whether the transactions contain monetary misstatements.

In the tests of the sales and collection cycle, the overall objectives are usually to test the effectiveness of internal controls over sales and cash receipts and to determine whether sales and cash receipts transactions contain monetary misstatements. The objectives of the audit test are normally decided as a part of designing the audit program, which was discussed for the sales and collection cycle in Chapter 11. The audit program for the sales and collection cycle for Hillsburg Hardware is included in Figure 11-7 (p. 325).

Decide Whether Audit Sampling Applies

Audit sampling applies whenever the auditor plans to reach conclusions about a population based on a sample. The auditor should examine the audit program and decide those audit procedures for which audit sampling applies. Assume the following partial audit program:

1. Review sales transactions for large and unusual amounts (analytical procedure).
2. Observe whether the duties of the accounts receivable clerk are separate from handling cash (test of control).

3. Examine a sample of duplicate sales invoices for
   a. credit approval by the credit manager (test of control).
   b. existence of an attached shipping document (test of control).
   c. inclusion of a chart of accounts number (test of control).
4. Select a sample of shipping documents and trace each to related duplicate sales invoices (test of control).
5. Compare the quantity on each duplicate sales invoice with the quantity on related shipping documents (substantive test of transactions).

Audit sampling is inappropriate for the first two procedures in this audit program. The first is an analytical procedure for which sampling is inappropriate. The second is an observation procedure for which no documentation exists to perform audit sampling. Audit sampling can be used for the remaining three procedures. Table 13-2 indicates the audit procedures for the sales cycle for Hillsburg Hardware Co. for which audit sampling is appropriate.

TABLE 13-2 Audit Procedures—Hillsburg Hardware Co.

PROCEDURE	COMMENT
Shipment of Goods	
10. Account for a sequence of shipping documents.	It is possible to do this by selecting a random sample and accounting for all shipping documents selected. This requires a separate set of random numbers because the sampling unit is different from that used for the other tests.
11. Trace selected shipping documents to the sales journal to be sure that each one has been included.	No exceptions are expected, and a 6 percent TER is considered acceptable at an ARACR of 10 percent. A sample size of 40 is selected. The shipping documents are traced to the sales journal. This is done for all 40 items. There are no exceptions for either test. The results are considered acceptable. There is no further information about this portion of the tests in this illustration.
Billing of Customers and Recording the Sales in the Records	
12. Account for a sequence of sales invoices in the sales journal.	The audit procedures for billing and recording sales (procedures 12 to 14) are the only ones included for illustration throughout this chapter.
13. Trace selected sales invoice numbers from the sales journal to a. accounts receivable master file and test for amount, date, and invoice number. b. duplicate sales invoice and check for the total amount recorded in the journal, date, customer name, and account classification. Check the pricing, extensions, and footings. Examine underlying documents for indication of internal verification. c. bill of lading and test for customer name, product description, quantity, and date. d. duplicate sales order and test for customer name, product description, quantity, date, and indication of internal verification by Pam Dilley. e. customer order and test for customer name, product description, quantity, date, and credit approval.	
14. Trace recorded sales from the sales journal to the file of supporting documents, which includes a duplicate sales invoice, bill of lading, sales order, and customer order.	

Note: Random selection and audit sampling are not applicable for the nine general audit procedures in Figure 11-7. Random selection could be used for procedure 2.

Define Attributes and Exception Conditions

When audit sampling is used, the auditor must carefully define the characteristics (attributes) being tested and the exception conditions. Unless a precise statement of what constitutes an attribute is made in advance, the staff person who performs the audit procedure will have no guidelines for identifying exceptions.

Attributes of interest and exception conditions come directly from the audit procedures for which the auditor has decided to use audit sampling. Table 13-3 shows nine attributes of interest and exception conditions taken directly from audit procedures 12 through 14 in the audit of Hillsburg's billing function. Samples of sales invoices will be used to verify these attributes. The absence of the attribute for any sample item will be an exception for that attribute. It is important to note that both missing documents and immaterial misstatements result in exceptions unless the auditor specifically states otherwise in the exception conditions.

Define the Population

The population represents the body of data about which the auditor wishes to generalize. The auditor can define the population to include whatever data are desired but must sample from the entire population as it has been defined. The auditor may generalize *only* about that population that has been sampled. For example, in performing tests of controls and substantive tests of sales transactions, the auditor generally defines the population as all recorded sales for the year. If the auditor samples from only 1 month's transactions, it is invalid to draw conclusions about the invoices for the entire year.

The auditor must carefully define the population in advance, consistent with the objectives of the audit tests. Furthermore, in some cases, it may be necessary to define more than one population for a given set of audit procedures. For example, in the audit of the sales and collection cycle at Hillsburg Hardware Co., the direction of testing in audit procedures 12 through 14 in Table 13-2 is from sales invoices in the sales journal to source documentation. In contrast, the direction of testing for audit procedures 10 and 11 is from

TABLE 13-3 Attributes Defined—Tests of Hillsburg Hardware Co.'s Billing Function

Attribute	Exception Condition
1. Existence of the sales invoice number in the sales journal (procedure 12).	No record of sales invoice number in the sales journal.
2. Amount and other data in the master file agree with sales journal entry (procedure 13a).	The amount recorded in the master file differs from the amount recorded in the sales journal.
3. Amount and other data on the duplicate sales invoice agree with the sales journal entry (procedure 13b).	Customer name and account number on the invoice differ from the information recorded in the sales journal.
4. Evidence that pricing, extensions, and footings are checked (initials and correct amount) (procedure 13b).	Lack of initials indicating verification of pricing, extensions, and footings.
5. Quantity and other data on the bill of lading agree with the duplicate sales invoice and sales journal (procedure 13c).	Quantity of goods shipped differs from quantity on the duplicate sales invoice.
6. Quantity and other data on the sales order agree with the duplicate sales invoice (procedure 13d).	Quantity on the sales order differs from the quantity on the duplicate sales invoice.
7. Quantity and other data on the customer order agree with the duplicate sales invoice (procedure 13e).	Product number and description on the customer order differ from information on the duplicate sales invoice.
8. Credit is approved (procedure 13e).	Lack of initials indicating credit approval.
9. For recorded sales in the sales journal, the file of supporting documents includes a duplicate sales invoice, bill of lading, sales order, and customer order (procedure 14).	Bill of lading is not attached to the duplicate sales invoice and the customer order.

the shipping documents to the sales journal. Thus, there are two populations (one population of sales invoices in the sales journal and another of shipping documents). It is also important to test the population for completeness and detail tie-in before a sample is selected to ensure that all population items will be properly subjected to sample selection.

Define the Sampling Unit

The major consideration in defining the sampling unit is to make it consistent with the objectives of the audit tests. Thus, the definition of the population and the planned audit procedures usually dictate the appropriate sampling unit. For example, if the auditor wants to determine how often the client fails to fill a customer's order, the sampling unit must be defined as the customer's order. If, however, the objective is to determine whether the proper quantity of the goods described on the customer's order is correctly shipped and billed, it is possible to define the sampling unit as the customer's order, the shipping document, or the duplicate sales invoice.

Audit procedure 14 in Table 13-2 is a test for the existence of recorded sales. Therefore, the appropriate sampling unit is the duplicate sales invoice. However, it is impossible to test the attribute related to audit procedure 14 if the sampling unit is the shipping document. The appropriate sampling unit for audit procedure 11 is the shipping document because this tests that existing sales are recorded (completeness). The attribute related to audit procedure 11 cannot be tested if the sampling unit is the duplicate sales invoice. Either the duplicate sales invoice or the shipping document is appropriate for audit procedures 13a through 13e because these are all nondirectional tests.

The auditor could define the sampling unit as the duplicate sales invoice to perform audit procedures 12 through 14. Audit procedures 10 and 11 would still have to be tested separately using a sample of shipping documents.

Specify the Tolerable Exception Rate

Establishing the **tolerable exception rate (TER)** requires professional judgment on the part of the auditor. TER represents the exception rate that the auditor will permit in the population and still be willing to use the assessed control risk and/or the amount of monetary misstatements in the transactions established during planning. For example, assume that the auditor decides that TER for attribute 8 in Table 13-3 is 8 percent. That means that the auditor has decided that even if 8 percent of the duplicate sales invoices are not approved for credit, the credit approval control is still effective in terms of the assessed control risk included in the audit plan.

TER is the result of an auditor's judgment. The suitable TER is a question of materiality and is therefore affected by both the definition and the importance of the attribute in the audit plan. For example, if only one internal control is used to support a low control risk assessment for an objective, TER will be lower for this attribute than if there are multiple controls used to support a low control risk assessment for the objective.

TER has a significant impact on sample size. A larger sample size is needed for a low TER than for a high TER. For example, a larger sample is required for a TER of 3 percent for attribute 8 than for a TER of 8 percent in the previous example.

Most auditors use some type of preprinted form to document each sampling application. An example of a commonly used form is given in Figure 13-2. The top part of the form includes a definition of the objective, the population, and the sampling unit.

The TER for each attribute being tested in audit procedures 12 through 14 in Table 13-3 is decided on the basis of the auditor's judgment of what exception rate is material. The failure to record a sales invoice would be highly significant, especially considering the system; therefore, as indicated in Figure 13-2, the lowest TER (3 percent) is chosen for attribute 1. The incorrect billing of the customer represents potentially significant misstatements, but no misstatement is likely to be for the full amount of the invoice. As a result, a 4 percent TER is chosen for each of the attributes directly related to the billing of shipments and recording the amounts in the records. The last four attributes have higher TERs because they are of less importance for the audit.

Specify Acceptable Risk of Assessing Control Risk Too Low

When a sample is taken, there is a risk that the quantitative conclusions about the population will be incorrect. This is always true unless 100 percent of the population is tested. As has already been stated, this is the case with both nonstatistical and statistical sampling.

FIGURE 13-2 Sampling Data Sheet: Tests of Hillsburg Hardware Co.'s Billing Function

Client: Hillsburg Hardware **Year-end:** 12/31/02
Audit Area: Tests of Controls and Substantive Tests of Transactions—Billing Function **Pop. size:** 5,764

Define the objective(s): Examine duplicate sales invoices and related documents to determine whether the system has functioned as intended and as described in the audit program.

Define the population precisely (including stratification, if any): Sales invoices for the period 1/1/02 to 12/31/02. First invoice number = 3689. Last invoice number = 9452.

Define the sampling unit, organization of population items, and random selection procedures: Sales invoice number, recorded in the sales journal sequentially; computer generation of random numbers.

Description of Attributes	Planned Audit				Actual Results			
	EPER	TER	ARACR	Initial sample size	Sample size	Number of exceptions	Sample exception rate	Calculated Sampling Error (TER – SER)
1. Existence of the sales invoice number in the sales journal (procedure 12).	0	3	Medium	75				
2. Amount and other data in the master file agree with sales journal entry (procedure 13a).	1	4	Medium	100				
3. Amount and other data on the duplicate sales invoice agree with the sales journal entry (procedure 13b).	1	4	Medium	100				
4. Evidence that pricing, extensions, and footings are checked (initials and correct amount) (procedure 13b).	1	4	Medium	100				
5. Quantity and other data on the bill of lading agree with the duplicate sales invoice and sales journal (procedure 13c).	1	4	Medium	100				
6. Quantity and other data on the sales order agree with the duplicate sales invoice (procedure 13d).	1	6	Medium	65				
7. Quantity and other data on the customer order agree with the duplicate sales invoice (procedure 13e).	2	8	Medium	50				
8. Credit is approved by Rick Chulick (procedure 13e).	2	8	Medium	50				
9. For recorded sales in the sales journal, the file of supporting documents includes a duplicate sales invoice, bill of lading, sales order, and customer order (procedure 14).	1	6	Medium	65				

Intended use of sampling results:

1. Effect on Audit Plan:

2. Recommendations to Management:

For audit sampling in tests of controls and substantive tests of transactions, that risk is called the **acceptable risk of assessing control risk too low (ARACR).** ARACR is the risk that the auditor is willing to take of accepting a control as effective (or a rate of monetary misstatements as tolerable) when the true population exception rate is greater than TER. ARACR is the auditor's measure of sampling risk. To illustrate, assume that TER is 6 percent, ARACR is 10 percent, and the true population exception rate is 8 percent. The control in this case is not acceptable because the true exception rate of 8 percent exceeds TER. The auditor, of course, does not know the true population exception rate. The ARACR of 10 percent means that the auditor is willing to take a 10 percent risk of concluding that the control is

TABLE 13-4 Guidelines for ARACR and TER for Nonstatistical Sampling: Tests of Controls

Factor	Judgment	Guideline
Assessed control risk. Consider: Nature, extent, and timing of substantive tests (extensive planned substantive tests relate to higher assessed control risk and vice versa) Quality of evidence available for tests of controls (a lower quality of evidence available results in a higher assessed control risk and vice versa).	• Lowest assessed control risk • Moderate assessed control risk • Higher assessed control risk • 100% assessed control risk	• ARACR of low • ARACR of medium • ARACR of high • ARACR is not applicable
Significance of the transactions and related account balances that the internal controls are intended to affect.	• Highly significant balances • Significant balances • Less significant balances	• TER of 4% • TER of 5% • TER of 6%

Note: The guidelines should recognize that there may be variations in ARACRs based on audit considerations. The guidelines above are the most conservative that should be followed.

effective after all testing is completed, even when it is ineffective. If the control is found effective in this illustration, the auditor will have overrelied on the system of internal control (used a lower assessed control risk than justified).

In choosing the appropriate ARACR in a situation, auditors must use their best judgment. Because ARACR is a measure of the risk that the auditor is willing to take, the main consideration is the extent to which the auditor plans to reduce assessed control risk as a basis for the extent of tests of details of balances. The lower the assessed control risk, the lower will be the ARACR chosen and the planned extent of tests of details of balances. Referring to Figure 9-7 (p. 267), the most common situation in which audit sampling would be used for tests of controls and substantive tests of transactions is when the auditor decides to assess control risk at a lower level than can be supported by understanding internal control (alternative 3). If the auditor decides to assess control risk at maximum (alternative 1), tests of controls are not performed. If control risk is assessed below maximum, tests of controls must be performed. In some cases, this testing may have already been done as part of procedures to obtain an understanding of internal control.

It is common for auditors to use ARACR of high, medium, or low instead of a percentage. A low ARACR implies that the tests of controls are important and would correspond to a low assessed control risk and reduced substantive tests of details of balances. As summarized in Figure 13-2, ARACR for the audit of the billing function at Hillsburg Hardware Co. is assessed as medium for all attributes. A lower ARACR is not appropriate due to the internal control weaknesses identified.

The auditor can establish different TER and ARACR levels for different attributes of an audit test. For example, it is common for auditors to use higher TER and ARACR levels for tests of credit approval than for tests of the existence of duplicate sales invoices and bills of lading. This is because the exceptions for the latter are likely to have a more direct impact on the correctness of the financial statements than the former.

Tables 13-4 and 13-5 present illustrative guidelines for establishing TER and ARACR. The guidelines should not be interpreted as representing broad professional standards; however, they are typical of the types of guidelines CPA firms issue to their staff.

Estimate the Population Exception Rate

An advance estimate of the population exception rate should be made to plan the appropriate sample size. If the **estimated population exception rate (EPER)** is low, a relatively small sample size will satisfy the auditor's tolerable exception rate. This is because a less precise estimate is required. In other words, to be more precise, an estimate of the population exception rate must be based on more data, that is, a larger sample. As the EPER approaches the auditor's tolerable exception rate, the need for more precision arises.

It is common to use the results of the preceding year's audit to make this estimate. If prior-year results are not available or if they are considered unreliable, the auditor can take a small preliminary sample of the current year's population for this purpose. It is not critical that the estimate be precise because the current year's sample exception rate is ultimately used to estimate the population characteristics. Note that if a preliminary sample

TABLE 13-5 Guidelines for ARACR and TER for Nonstatistical Sampling: Substantive Tests of Transactions

Planned Reduction in Substantive Tests of Details of Balances	Results of Understanding Internal Control and Tests of Controls	ARACR for Substantive Tests of Transactions	TER for Substantive Tests of Transactions
Large	Excellent[1] Good Not good	High Medium Low	Percent or amount based on materiality considerations for related accounts
Moderate	Excellent[1] Good Not good	High Medium Medium-low	Percent or amount based on materiality considerations for related accounts
Small[2]	Excellent[1] Good Not good	High Medium-high Medium	Percent or amount based on materiality considerations for related accounts

Note: The guidelines should also recognize that there may be variations in ARACRs based on audit considerations. The guidelines above are the most conservative that should be followed.

[1]In this situation, both internal control and evidence about it are good. Substantive tests of transactions are least likely to be performed in this situation.

[2]In this situation, little emphasis is being placed on internal controls. Neither tests of controls nor substantive tests of transactions are likely in this situation.

is used, it can be included in the ultimate sample, as long as appropriate sample selection procedures are followed. For example, assume that an auditor takes a preliminary sample of 30 items to estimate the EPER that considers the entire population. Later, if the auditor decides that a total sample size of 100 is needed, only 70 additional items will need to be properly selected and tested. In the Hillsburg Hardware Co. audit, the estimated population exception rates for the attributes in Figure 13-2 are based on previous years' results, modified slightly upward to account for the change in personnel.

Determine the Initial Sample Size

Four factors determine the **initial sample size** for audit sampling: population size, TER, ARACR, and EPER. Population size is not nearly as significant a factor as the others and typically can be ignored, especially for large populations. An important characteristic of nonstatistical sampling compared with statistical methods is the need to decide the sample size using professional judgment for nonstatistical methods rather than by calculation using a statistical formula. Once the three major factors affecting sample size have been determined, the auditor can decide an initial sample size. The initial sample size is called that because the exceptions in the actual sample must be evaluated before it is possible to know whether the sample is sufficiently large to achieve the objectives of the tests.

Sensitivity of Sample Size to a Change in the Factors To properly understand the concepts underlying sampling in auditing, it is helpful to understand the effect of changing any of the four factors that determine sample size while the other factors are held constant. Table 13-6 illustrates the effect of increasing each of the four factors; a decrease will have the opposite effect.

TABLE 13-6 Effect on Sample Size of Changing Factors

Type of Change	Effect on Initial Sample Size
Increase acceptable risk of assessing control risk too low	Decrease
Increase tolerable exception rate	Decrease
Increase estimated population exception rate	Increase
Increase population size	Increase (minor effect)

A combination of two factors has the greatest effect on sample size: TER minus EPER. The difference is the *precision* of the planned sample estimate. A smaller precision, which is called a more precise estimate, requires a larger sample.

Figure 13-2 (p. 385) summarizes the different sample sizes selected for testing attributes 1 through 9 for the Hillsburg audit. The largest sample (a size of 100) is selected for tests of attributes 2 through 5, given the degree of precision required for those attributes. For those attributes, the difference between TER and EPER is smallest, thus requiring a larger sample size than attributes 6 through 9. Although the difference between TER and EPER for attribute 1 is similar to that between attributes 2 through 5, the estimated population exception rate of zero justifies a smaller sample of 75 items. The degree of precision is smallest for attributes 7 and 8. Thus, a sample size of only 50 items is selected.

Select the Sample

After the initial sample size for the audit sampling application has been computed, the auditor must choose the items in the population to be included in the sample. The sample can be chosen by using any of the probabilistic or nonprobabilistic methods discussed earlier in this chapter. To minimize the possibility of the client altering the sample items, the auditor should not inform the client too far in advance of the sample items selected. The auditor should also control the sample after the client provides the documents. Several additional sample items may be selected as extras to replace any voided items that may be included in the original sample.

The random selection for the Hillsburg audit procedures is straightforward except for different sample sizes for different attributes. This problem can be overcome by selecting a random sample of 50 for use on all nine attributes followed by another sample of 15 for all attributes except attributes 7 and 8, an additional 10 for attributes 1 through 5, and 25 more for attributes 2 through 5. Figure 13-1 on page 378 illustrates the selection of the first 50 sample items for Hillsburg Hardware using computer generation of random numbers.

Perform the Audit Procedures

The auditor performs the audit procedures by examining each item in the sample to determine whether it is consistent with the definition of the attribute and maintains a record of all the exceptions found. When audit procedures have been completed for a sampling application, there will be a sample size and number of exceptions for each attribute.

As means of documenting the tests and providing information for review, it is common to include a schedule of the results. Some auditors prefer to include a schedule containing a listing of all items in the sample; others prefer to limit the documentation to identifying the exceptions. This latter approach is followed in Figure 13-3.

Generalize from the Sample to the Population

The **sample exception rate (SER)** can be easily calculated from the actual sample results. SER equals the actual number of exceptions divided by the actual sample size. Figure 13-3 summarizes the exceptions found for tests of attributes 1 through 9. The auditor uses this information to calculate the SER for each attribute. For example, the auditor found zero exceptions for attribute 1 and 2 exceptions for attribute 2. Thus, the SER is 0 percent (0 ÷ 75) for attribute 1, while the SER is 2 percent for attribute 2 (2 ÷ 100).

It is improper for the auditor to conclude that the population exception rate is exactly the same as the sample exception rate; the chance that they are exactly the same is too small. For nonstatistical methods, there are two ways to generalize from the sample to the population.

1. Add an estimate of sampling error to SER to arrive at a **computed upper exception rate (CUER)** for a given acceptable risk of assessing control risk too low. CUER is the highest exception rate likely in the population with a given sample size, exception

FIGURE 13-3 Inspection of Sample Items for Attributes

CLIENT: Hillsburg Hardware
INSPECTION OF SAMPLE ITEMS
FOR ATTRIBUTES
YEAR-END: DECEMBER 31, 2002

Prepared by MSW
Date 2/3/03

Identity of Item Selected	Attributes										X = Exception
Invoice no.	1	2	3	4	5	6	7	8	9	10	11
3787					X						
3924				X				X			
3990				X							
4058		X		X							
4117								X			
4222					X						
4488								X			
4635				X	X						
4955						X		X			
4969				X							
5101								X			
5166								X			
5419								X			
5832								X			
5890								X			
6157		X		X							
6229				X							
6376								X			
6635					X						
7127				X							
8338								X			
8871				X							
9174								X			
9371				X							
No. Exceptions	0	2	0	10	4	1	0	12	0		
Sample Size	75	100	100	100	100	65	50	50	65		

rate, and acceptable risk of accepting control risk too low. It is extremely difficult for auditors to make sampling error estimates using nonstatistical sampling because of the judgment required to do so; therefore, this approach is generally not used.

2. Subtract the sample exception rate from the tolerable exception rate, which is calculated sampling error (TER – SER = calculated sampling error), and evaluate whether calculated sampling error is sufficiently large to indicate the true population exception rate is acceptable. Under this approach, the auditor does not make an estimate of the computed upper exception rate. Most auditors using nonstatistical sampling follow this approach. For example, if an auditor takes a sample of 100 items for an attribute and finds no exceptions (SER = 0) and TER is 5 percent, calculated sampling error is 5 percent

(TER of 5 percent – SER of 0 = 5 percent). On the other hand, if there had been four exceptions, calculated sampling error would have been 1 percent (TER of 5 percent – SER of 4 percent). It is much more likely that the true population exception rate is less than or equal to the tolerable exception rate in the first case than in the second one. Therefore, most auditors would probably find the population acceptable based on the first sample result and not acceptable based on the second. Furthermore, if the SER exceeds the EPER used in designing the sample, it is generally appropriate for the auditor to assume that the sample results do not support the planned assessed level of control risk. In that case, there is likely to be an unacceptably high risk that the true deviation rate in the population exceeds TER.

In addition, the auditor's consideration of whether sampling error is sufficiently large will depend on sample size. For example, if the sample size in the previous example had been only 20 items, the auditor would have been much less confident that finding no exceptions was an indication that the true population exception rate does not exceed TER.

The SER and the calculated sampling error (TER minus SER) for Hillsburg Hardware is summarized in Figure 13-4.

Analyze Exceptions

In addition to determining the SER for each attribute and evaluating whether the true but unknown exception rate is likely to exceed the tolerable exception rate, it is necessary to analyze individual exceptions to determine the breakdown in the internal controls that caused them. Exceptions could be caused by carelessness of employees, misunderstood instructions, intentional failure to perform procedures, or many other factors. The nature of an exception and its cause have a significant effect on the qualitative evaluation of the system. For example, if all the exceptions in the tests of internal verification of sales invoices occurred while the person normally responsible for performing the tests was on vacation, this would affect the auditor's evaluation of the internal controls and the subsequent investigation.

Decide the Acceptability of the Population

It was shown under generalizing from the sample to the population that most auditors subtract SER from TER when they use nonstatistical sampling and evaluate whether the difference, which is calculated sampling error, is sufficiently large. If the auditor concludes that the difference is sufficiently large, the control being tested can be used to reduce assessed control risk as planned, provided a careful analysis of the cause of exceptions does not indicate the possibility of other significant problems with internal controls.

As shown in Figure 13-4, SER exceeds TER for attributes 4 and 8, while SER equals TER for attribute 5. For all other attributes SER is less than TER. It is important to analyze the exceptions to determine their cause and to draw conclusions about each attribute tested. The exception analysis is illustrated for Hillsburg in Figure 13-5 on page 392.

When the auditor concludes that TER – SER is too small to conclude that the population is acceptable, or when SER exceeds TER, the auditor must take specific action. Four courses of action can be followed.

Revise TER or ARACR This alternative should be followed only when the auditor has concluded that the original specifications were too conservative. Relaxing either TER or ARACR may be difficult to defend if the auditor is ever subject to review by a court or a commission. If these requirements are changed, it should be done on the basis of careful thought.

Sampling Software

Expand the Sample Size An increase in the sample size has the effect of decreasing the sampling error if the actual sample exception rate does not increase. Of course, SER may also increase or decrease if additional items are selected.

Revise Assessed Control Risk If the results of the tests of controls and substantive tests of transactions do not support the planned assessed control risk, the auditor should revise

FIGURE 13-4 Sampling Data Sheet: Tests of Hillsburg Hardware Co.'s Billing Function

Client: Hillsburg Hardware **Year-end:** 12/31/02
Audit Area: Tests of Controls and Substantive Tests of Transactions—Billing Function **Pop. size:** 5,764

Define the objective(s): Examine duplicate sales invoices and related documents to determine whether the system has functioned as intended and as described in the audit program.

Define the population precisely (including stratification, if any): Sales invoices for the period 1/1/02 to 12/31/02. First invoice number = 3689. Last invoice number = 9452.

Define the sampling unit, organization of population items, and random selection procedures: Sales invoice number, recorded in the sales journal sequentially; computer generation of random numbers.

Description of Attributes	Planned Audit				Actual Results			
	EPER	TER	ARACR	Initial sample size	Sample size	Number of exceptions	Sample exception rate	Calculated Sampling Error (TER – SER)
1. Existence of the sales invoice number in the sales journal (procedure 12).	0	3	Medium	75	75	0	0	3.0
2. Amount and other data in the master file agree with sales journal entry (procedure 13a).	1	4	Medium	100	100	2	2	2.0
3. Amount and other data on the duplicate sales invoice agree with the sales journal entry (procedure 13b).	1	4	Medium	100	100	0	0	4.0
4. Evidence that pricing, extensions, and footings are checked (initials and correct amount) (procedure 13b).	1	4	Medium	100	100	10	10	SER exceeds TER
5. Quantity and other data on the bill of lading agree with the duplicate sales invoice and sales journal (procedure 13c).	1	4	Medium	100	100	4	4	0
6. Quantity and other data on the sales order agree with the duplicate sales invoice (procedure 13d).	1	6	Medium	65	65	1	1.5	4.5
7. Quantity and other data on the customer order agree with the duplicate sales invoice (procedure 13e).	2	8	Medium	50	50	0	0	8.0
8. Credit is approved by Rick Chulick (procedure 13e).	2	8	Medium	50	50	12	24	SER exceeds TER
9. For recorded sales in the sales journal, the file of supporting documents includes a duplicate sales invoice, bill of lading, sales order, and customer order (procedure 14).	1	6	Medium	65	65	0	0	6.0

Intended use of sampling results:

1. Effect on Audit Plan: Controls tested through attributes 1, 3, 6, 7, and 9 can be viewed as operating effectively. Additional emphasis is needed in confirmation, allowance for uncollectible accounts, cutoff tests, and price tests due to results of tests for attributes 2, 4, 5, and 8.

2. Recommendations to Management: Each of the exceptions should be discussed with management. Specific recommendations are needed to correct the internal verification of sales invoices and to improve the approach to credit approvals.

assessed control risk upward. The effect of the revision is likely to increase substantive tests of transactions and tests of details of balances. For example, if tests of controls of internal verification procedures for verifying prices, extensions, and quantities on sales invoices indicate that those procedures are not being followed, the auditor should increase substantive tests of transactions for the accuracy of sales. If the substantive tests of transactions

FIGURE 13-5 Analysis of Exceptions

		CLIENT: Hillsburg Hardware **ANALYSIS OF EXCEPTIONS** **YEAR-END:** December 31, 2002	**Prepared by:** MSW **Date:** 2/3/03
Attribute	**Number of exceptions**	**Nature of exceptions**	**Effect on the audit and other comments**
2	2	Both errors were posted to the wrong account and were still outstanding after several months. The amounts were for $2,500 and $7,900.	Perform expanded confirmation procedures and review older uncollected balances thoroughly.
4	10	In 6 cases there were no initials for internal verification. In 2 cases the wrong price was used but the errors were under $200 in each case. In 1 case there was a pricing error of $5,000. In 1 case freight was not charged. (Three of the last 4 exceptions had initials for internal verification.)	As a result, have independent client personnel recheck a random sample of 500 duplicate sales invoices under our control. Also, expand the confirmation of accounts receivable.
5	4	In each case the date on the duplicate sales invoice was several days later than the shipping date.	Do extensive tests of the sales cutoff by comparing recorded sales with the shipping documents.
6	1	Just 106 items were shipped and billed though the sales order was for 112 items. The reason for the difference was an error in the perpetual inventory master file. The perpetuals indicated that 112 items were on hand, when there were actually 106. The system does not backorder for undershipments smaller than 25%.	No expansion of tests of controls or substantive tests. The system appears to be working effectively.
8	12	Credit was not approved. Four of these were for new customers. Discussed with Chulick, who stated his busy schedule did not permit approving all sales.	Expand the year-end procedures extensively in evaluating allowance for uncollectible accounts. This includes scheduling of cash receipts subsequent to year-end and for all outstanding accounts receivable to determine collectibility at year-end.

results are unacceptable, the auditor must increase tests of details of balances for accounts receivable.

The decision whether to increase sample size until sampling error is sufficiently small or to revise assessed control risk must be made on the basis of cost versus benefit. If the sample is not expanded, it is necessary to revise assessed control risk upward and therefore perform additional substantive tests. The cost of additional tests of controls must be compared with that of additional substantive tests. If an expanded sample still continues to produce unacceptable results, additional substantive tests will still be necessary.

If the original test performed is to test transactions for monetary misstatements and an exception rate higher than that assumed is indicated, the response would generally be the same as for tests of controls.

Communicate with the Audit Committee or Management This action is desirable, in combination with one of the other three just described, regardless of the nature of the exceptions. When the auditor determines that the internal controls are not operating effectively, management should be informed. If there is a significant deficiency in the design or operation of internal control, SAS 60 (AU 325) requires the auditor to communicate this reportable condition to the audit committee.

In some instances, it may be acceptable to limit the action to writing a letter to management when TER minus SER is too small. This occurs if the auditor has no intention of reducing the assessed control risk or has already carried out sufficient procedures to his or her own satisfaction as a part of substantive tests of transactions.

For the Hillsburg audit, there were two attributes (4 and 8) where the SER exceeded TER, requiring some conclusion concerning additional follow-up actions. The last column in Figure 13-5 summarizes the follow-up actions identified. Because the difference between SER and TER was zero for attribute 5 and small for attribute 2, Figure 13-5 contains follow-up actions for those attributes. No follow-up actions are required to address the exception noted for attribute 6, given the large difference between SER and TER. The conclusions reached about each attribute are also documented at the bottom of Figure 13-4.

Adequate Documentation

It is important that the auditor retain adequate records of the procedures performed, the methods used to select the sample and perform the tests, the results found in the tests, and the conclusions drawn. This is necessary as a means of evaluating the combined results of all tests and as a basis for defending the audit if the need arises. Figures 13-2 through 13-5 illustrate the type of documentation commonly found in practice.

After completing tests of controls and substantive tests of transactions, the auditor should complete rows three through seven of the evidence planning worksheet. This worksheet is illustrated for Hillsburg Hardware in Figure 12-7 on page 356.

Recall that rows one and two were completed in Chapter 8. Rows three through five document control risk for sales, cash receipts, and additional controls. The control risk assessments in Figure 12-7 are the same as the planned assessments in the control risk matrices for Hillsburg Hardware on pages 262 and 322, with the following modifications:

- Control risk is high for the accuracy objective for sales because of the unsatisfactory results for attribute 4 (procedure 13b).
- Control risk is high for the realizable value objective for sales based on the results for attribute 8 (procedure 13e).
- Recall that the existence (completeness) objective for cash receipts relates to the completeness (existence) objective for accounts receivable.

Finally, note in Figure 12-7 that all substantive tests of transactions results were satisfactory except for the accuracy and cutoff objectives for sales. The substantive tests of transactions results for the accuracy objective were only fair because of exceptions found for attribute 2 (procedure 13a). Results were unacceptable for the cutoff objective because of unsatisfactory results for attribute 5 (procedure 13c).

Summary of Audit Sampling for Tests of Controls and Substantive Tests of Transactions

The steps involved in nonstatistical sampling for tests of controls and substantive tests of transactions are summarized in Figure 13-6 (p. 394). The summary assumes that the auditor is not calculating a computed upper exception rate.

FIGURE 13-6 Summary of Audit Sampling Steps for Tests of Controls and Substantive Tests of Transactions

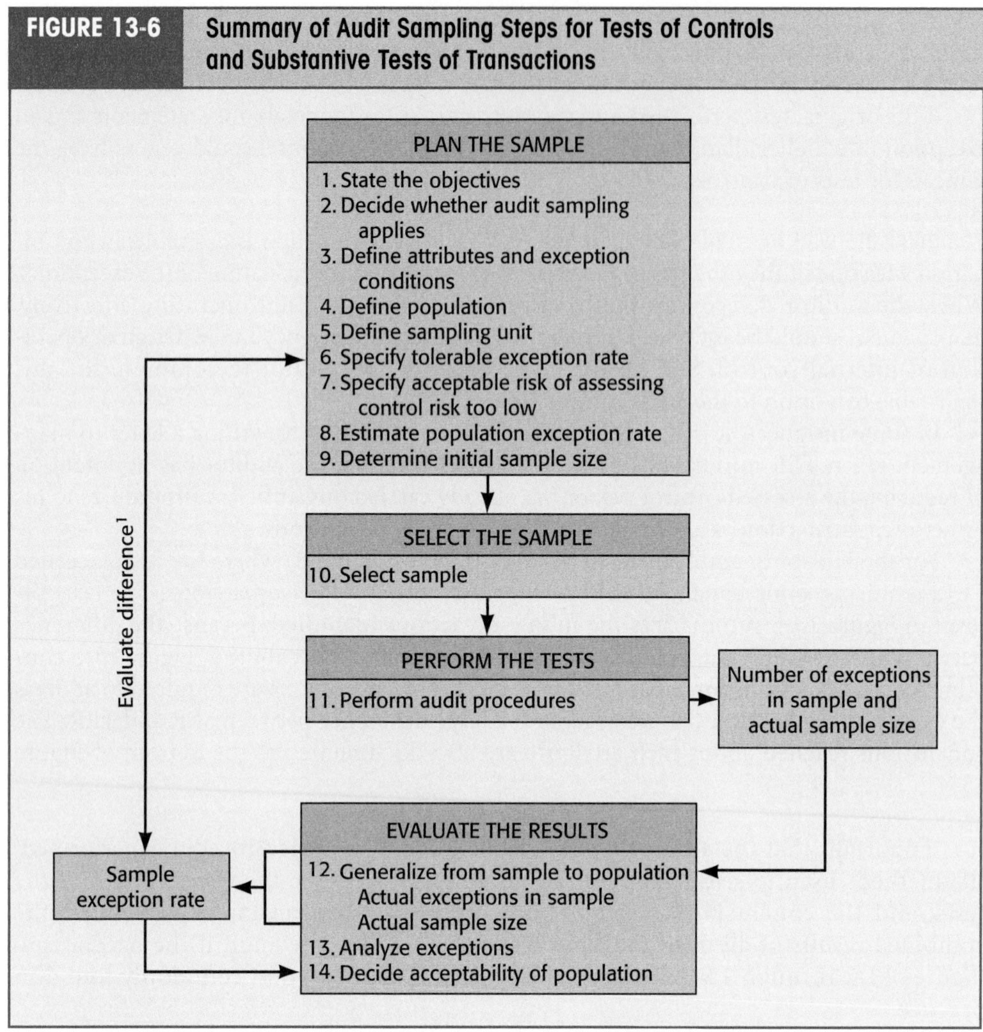

PLAN THE SAMPLE
1. State the objectives
2. Decide whether audit sampling applies
3. Define attributes and exception conditions
4. Define population
5. Define sampling unit
6. Specify tolerable exception rate
7. Specify acceptable risk of assessing control risk too low
8. Estimate population exception rate
9. Determine initial sample size
SELECT THE SAMPLE
10. Select sample
PERFORM THE TESTS
11. Perform audit procedures
Number of exceptions in sample and actual sample size
EVALUATE THE RESULTS
12. Generalize from sample to population
Actual exceptions in sample
Actual sample size
13. Analyze exceptions
14. Decide acceptability of population
Sample exception rate
Evaluate difference[1]

[1]For each attribute, consider the size of the difference, sample size, and acceptable risk of assessing control risk too low.

AUDIT SAMPLING FOR TESTS OF DETAILS OF BALANCES

We now turn our attention to audit sampling for tests of details of balances. Like for tests of controls and substantive tests of transactions, almost all auditors use nonstatistical methods, which is the reason for including that approach in the text.

Comparisons of Audit Sampling for Tests of Details of Balances and for Tests of Controls and Substantive Tests of Transactions

OBJECTIVE 13-6

Differentiate between audit sampling for tests of details of balances and for tests of controls and substantive tests of transactions.

Most of the sampling concepts discussed about audit sampling for tests of controls and substantive tests of transactions in the previous section apply equally to sampling for tests of details of balances. In both cases, the auditor wants to make inferences about the entire population based on a sample. Both sampling and nonsampling risks are therefore important for tests of controls, substantive tests of transactions, and tests of details of balances. In dealing with sampling risk, it is acceptable to use either nonstatistical or statistical methods for all three types of tests.

The most important differences among tests of controls, substantive tests of transactions, and tests of details of balances are in what the auditor wants to measure. In tests of controls, the concern is testing the effectiveness of internal controls using tests of controls. When an auditor performs tests of controls, the purpose is to determine whether the exception rate in the population is sufficiently low to justify reducing assessed control risk to reduce substantive tests. In substantive tests of transactions, the auditor is concerned about both the effectiveness of controls and the monetary correctness of transactions in the accounting system. In tests of details of balances, the concern is determining whether the dollar amount of an account balance is materially misstated. Tests for the rate of occurrence, therefore, are seldom useful for tests of details of balances. Instead, auditors use sampling methods that provide results in *dollar* terms.

ISACA Audit Sampling

APPLICATION OF AUDIT SAMPLING FOR TESTS OF DETAILS OF BALANCES

OBJECTIVE 13-7

Apply audit sampling to tests of details of balances.

There are 14 steps required in audit sampling for tests of details of balances. These steps parallel the 14 steps used for sampling for tests of controls and substantive tests of transactions, although there are a few differences because of the different objectives of the tests. Understanding the similarities and differences in the application of audit sampling for tests of details of balances compared to those for tests of controls and substantive tests of transactions is essential. The following are the 14 steps, with the steps for tests of controls and substantive tests of transactions included in the right column for comparison:

Steps—Audit Sampling for Tests of Details of Balances	Steps—Audit Sampling for Tests of Controls and Substantive Tests of Transactions (see p. 380–381)
Plan the Sample	*Plan the Sample*
1. State the objectives of the audit test.	1. State the objectives of the audit test.
2. Decide whether audit sampling applies.	2. Decide whether audit sampling applies.
3. Define misstatement conditions.	3. Define attributes and exception conditions.
4. Define the population.	4. Define the population.
5. Define the sampling unit.	5. Define the sampling unit.
6. Specify tolerable misstatement.	6. Specify the tolerable exception rate.
7. Specify acceptable risk of incorrect acceptance.	7. Specify acceptable risk of assessing control risk too low.
8. Estimate misstatements in the population.	8. Estimate the population exception rate.
9. Determine the initial sample size.	9. Determine the initial sample size.
Select the Sample and Perform the Audit Procedures	*Select the Sample and Perform the Audit Procedures*
10. Select the sample.	10. Select the sample.
11. Perform the audit procedures.	11. Perform the audit procedures.
Evaluate the Results	*Evaluate the Results*
12. Generalize from the sample to the population.	12. Generalize from the sample to the population.
13. Analyze the misstatements.	13. Analyze the exceptions.
14. Decide the acceptability of the population.	14. Decide the acceptability of the population.

State the Objectives of the Audit Test

When auditors sample for tests of details of balances, the objective is to determine whether the account balance being audited is fairly stated. The population of 40 accounts receivable in Table 13-7 (p. 396), totaling $207,295, is used as an illustration in applying nonstatistical sampling. The objective of the audit test will be to determine whether the total of $207,295 is materially misstated. Typically, materially misstated is defined in terms of tolerable misstatement.

TABLE 13-7 Illustrative Accounts Receivable Population

Population Item	Recorded Amount	Population Item (cont.)	Recorded Amount (cont.)
1	$ 1,410	21	$ 4,865
2	9,130	22	770
3	660	23	2,305
4	3,355	24	2,665
5	5,725	25	1,000
6	8,210	26	6,225
7	580	27	3,675
8	44,110	28	6,250
9	825	29	1,890
10	1,155	30	27,705
11	2,270	31	935
12	50	32	5,595
13	5,785	33	930
14	940	34	4,045
15	1,820	35	9,480
16	3,380	36	360
17	530	37	1,145
18	955	38	6,400
19	4,490	39	100
20	17,140	40	8,435
			$207,295

Decide Whether Audit Sampling Applies

As stated earlier in the chapter, "Audit sampling applies whenever the auditor plans to reach conclusions about a population based on a sample." Although it is common to sample in many accounts, there are situations when sampling does not apply. For the population in Table 13-7, the auditor may decide to audit only items over $5,000 and ignore all others because the total of the smaller ones is immaterial. In this case, the auditor has not sampled. Similarly, if the auditor is verifying fixed asset additions and there are many small additions and one extremely large purchase of a building, the auditor may decide to ignore the small items entirely. Again, the auditor has not sampled.

Define Misstatement Conditions

Audit sampling for tests of details of balances measures monetary misstatements in the population. Thus, the misstatement conditions are any conditions that represent a monetary misstatement in a sample item. In auditing accounts receivable, any client misstatement in a sample item is a misstatement.

Define the Population

The population is defined as the *recorded dollar population*. The auditor then evaluates whether the recorded population is overstated or understated. The recorded population is appropriate for testing for the existence objective. If the completeness objective is a concern, the sample should be selected from a different source, such as customers with zero balances. The population of accounts receivable in Table 13-7 consists of 40 accounts totaling $207,295. Most accounting populations subject to audit would, of course, contain far more items totaling a much larger dollar amount.

Stratified Sampling For many populations, auditors subdivide the population into two or more subpopulations before applying audit sampling. Subdividing populations is called **stratified sampling,** where each subpopulation is a stratum. The purpose of stratification is to permit the auditor to emphasize certain population items and deemphasize others. In most audit sampling situations, including confirming accounts receivable, auditors want to emphasize the larger recorded dollar values; therefore, stratification is typically done on the basis of the size of recorded dollar values.

Examining the population in Table 13-7, there are different ways to stratify the population. Assume that the auditor decided to stratify as follows:

Stratum	Stratum Criteria	No. in Population	Dollars in Population
1	>$10,000	3	$ 88,955
2	$5,000–$10,000	10	71,235
3	<$5,000	27	47,105
		40	$207,295

Define the Sampling Unit

The sampling unit for nonstatistical audit sampling in tests of details of balances is almost always the item making up the account balance. For accounts receivable, it is usually the customer account balance, which is represented by the customer account name or number on the accounts receivable list. The sampling unit can also be an individual invoice that is part of an account balance.

Specify Tolerable Misstatement

Tolerable misstatement as it was discussed in Chapter 8 is used for determining sample size and evaluating results. The auditor starts with a preliminary judgment about materiality and uses that total in deciding tolerable misstatement for each account. The required sample size increases as the auditor's tolerable misstatement for the account balance or class of transactions decreases.

Specify Acceptable Risk of Incorrect Acceptance

For all sampling applications, there is a risk that the quantitative conclusions about the population will be incorrect. This is always true unless 100 percent of the population is tested.

Acceptable risk of incorrect acceptance (ARIA) is the risk that the auditor is willing to take of accepting a balance as correct when the true misstatement in the balance is greater than tolerable misstatement. It is a measure of the auditor's desired assurance for an account balance. If the auditor wants more assurance in auditing a balance, ARIA is set lower. ARIA is the equivalent term to ARACR (acceptable risk of assessing control risk too low) for tests of controls and substantive tests of transactions.

There is an inverse relationship between ARIA and required sample size. If, for example, the auditor decides to reduce ARIA from 10 percent to 5 percent, the required sample size would increase.

The primary factor affecting the auditor's decision about ARIA is assessed control risk in the audit risk model. When internal controls are effective, control risk can be reduced, permitting the auditor to increase ARIA. This, in turn, reduces the sample size required for the test of details of the related account balance.

Understanding how ARACR and ARIA affect evidence accumulation can be difficult. Earlier it was shown that tests of details of balances for monetary misstatements can be reduced if internal controls are found to be effective through assessing control risk and performing tests of controls. The effects of ARACR and ARIA are consistent with that conclusion. If the auditor concludes that internal controls may be effective, control risk can be reduced. A lower control risk requires a lower ARACR in testing the controls, which requires a larger sample size. If controls are found to be effective, control risk can remain low, which permits the auditor to increase ARIA (through use of the audit risk model), thereby requiring a smaller sample size in the related substantive tests of details of balances. The effect of ARACR and ARIA on substantive testing in the two different circumstances is shown in Figure 13-7 (p. 398).

Besides control risk, ARIA is also directly affected by acceptable audit risk and inversely by other substantive tests already performed or planned for the account balance. For example, if acceptable audit risk is reduced, ARIA should also be reduced. If analytical procedures were performed and indicate that the account balance is fairly stated, ARIA should be increased. Stated differently, the analytical procedures are evidence in support of the account balance; therefore, less evidence from the detailed test using sampling is required to achieve acceptable audit risk. The same conclusion is appropriate for the relationship among substantive tests of transactions, ARIA, and

FIGURE 13-7 Effect of ARACR and ARIA on Substantive Testing

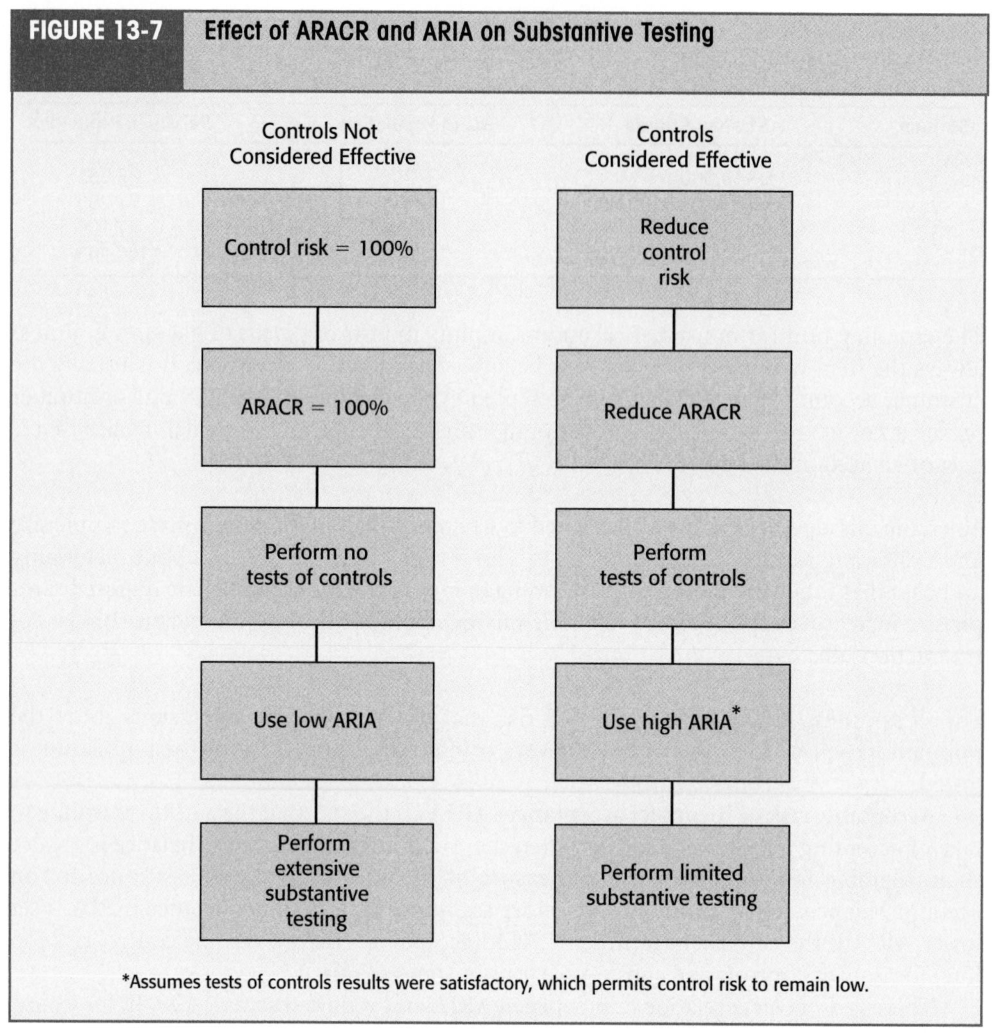

*Assumes tests of controls results were satisfactory, which permits control risk to remain low.

sample size for tests of details of balances. The various relationships affecting ARIA are summarized in Table 13-8.

Estimate Misstatements in the Population

The auditor typically makes this estimate based on prior experience with the client and by assessing inherent risk, considering the results of tests of controls, substantive tests of transactions, and analytical procedures already performed. The planned sample size

TABLE 13-8 Relationship Among Factors Affecting ARIA, Effect on ARIA, and Required Sample Size for Audit Sampling

Factor Affecting ARIA	Example	Effect on ARIA	Effect on Sample Size
Effectiveness of internal controls (control risk)	Internal controls are effective (reduced control risk).	Increase	Decrease
Substantive tests of transactions	No exceptions were found in substantive tests of transactions.	Increase	Decrease
Acceptable audit risk	Likelihood of bankruptcy is low (increased acceptable audit risk).	Increase	Decrease
Analytical procedures	Analytical procedures are performed with no indications of likely misstatements.	Increase	Decrease

increases as the amount of misstatements expected in the population approaches tolerable misstatement.

Determine the Initial Sample Size

Auditors using nonstatistical sampling determine the initial sample size judgmentally considering the factors discussed so far. Table 13-9 summarizes the primary factors that influence sample size for nonstatistical sampling and how sample size is affected.

When the auditor uses stratified sampling, the sample size must be allocated among the strata. Typically, auditors allocate a higher portion of the sample items to larger population items. For example, in the example from Table 13-7 on page 396, allocating a sample size of 15, the auditor might decide to select all three accounts from stratum 1, and six each from strata 2 and 3. Observe that audit sampling does not apply to stratum 1 because all population items are being audited.

As Table 13-9 illustrates, determining a nonstatistical sample size is based on several factors and requires considerable judgment. A table for combining these factors and a formula for computing sample size based on the *AICPA Audit Sampling Auditing Guide* is presented in Figure 13-8 (p. 400).

For example, assume that the auditor applied this formula to the population in Table 13-7 and that tolerable misstatement is \$20,000. The auditor first eliminates population items 8 and 30 from the recorded population because they exceed tolerable misstatement. These two individually material accounts will be tested separately. The remaining population to be sampled is \$135,480 (\$207,295 − \$44,110 − \$27,705). Further, assume that the combined assessed inherent and control risk is moderate and that there is a moderate risk that substantive tests of transactions and analytical procedures will not detect a material misstatement. The required assurance factor is 1.6 based on the table. The computed sample size is 11 [(\$135,480/\$20,000) × 1.6 = 10.8].

Select the Sample

For nonstatistical sampling, auditing standards permit the auditor to use any of the selection methods discussed earlier in the chapter. It is important for the auditor to use a method that will permit meaningful conclusions about the sample results.

TABLE 13-9 Factors Influencing Sample Sizes for Tests of Details of Balances

Factor	Conditions Leading to Smaller Sample Size	Conditions Leading to Larger Sample Size
Control risk (ARACR)—Affects acceptable risk of incorrect acceptance	Low control risk	High control risk
Results of other substantive tests related to the same assertion (including analytical procedures and other relevant substantive tests)—Affect acceptable risk of incorrect acceptance	Satisfactory results in other related substantive tests	Unsatisfactory results in other related substantive tests
Acceptable audit risk—Affects acceptable risk of incorrect acceptance	High acceptable audit risk	Low acceptable audit risk
Tolerable misstatement for a specific account	Larger tolerable misstatement	Smaller tolerable misstatement
Inherent risk—Affects estimated misstatements in the population	Low inherent risk	High inherent risk
Expected size and frequency of misstatements—Affect estimated misstatements in the population	Smaller misstatements or lower frequency	Larger misstatements or higher frequency
Dollar amount of population	Smaller account balance	Larger account balance
Number of items in the population	Almost no effect on sample size unless population is very small	Almost no effect on sample size unless population is very small

FIGURE 13-8 **Formula for Computing Nonstatistical Tests of Details of Balances Sample Size Based on AICPA Audit Sampling Formula**

$$\frac{\text{Population's recorded amount*}}{\text{Tolerable misstatement}} \times \text{Assurance factor} = \text{Sample size}$$

Select the appropriate assurance factor as follows:

Assessed Inherent and Control Risk	Risk That Other Substantive Procedures Will Fail to Detect a Material Misstatement		
	Maximum	**Moderate**	**Low**
Maximum	3.0	2.3	2.0
Slightly below maximum	2.7	2.0	1.6
Moderate	2.3	1.6	1.2
Low	2.0	1.2	1.0

*Individual items exceeding tolerable misstatement are tested individually and subtracted from the population for this calculation.

For stratified sampling, the auditor selects samples independently from each stratum. For example, in stratum 3 in the previous example, the auditor will select 6 sample items from the 27 population items in that stratum.

Perform the Audit Procedures

To perform the audit procedures, the auditor applies the appropriate audit procedures to each item in the sample to determine whether it is correct or contains a misstatement. For example, in the confirmation of accounts receivable, the auditor will mail the sample of positive confirmations in the manner described in Chapter 12 and determine the amount of misstatement in each account confirmed. For nonresponses, alternative procedures will be used to determine the misstatements. The auditor cannot expect meaningful results from using audit sampling unless the audit procedures are applied carefully.

Assume that the auditor sends first and second requests for confirmations and performs alternative procedures in the previous example. Assume also that the following conclusions are reached about the sample after reconciling all timing differences:

Stratum	Sample Size	Dollars Audited: Recorded Value	Dollars Audited: Audited Value	Client Misstatement
1	3	$ 88,955	$ 91,695	$(2,740)
2	6	43,995	43,024	971
3	6	13,105	10,947	2,158
	15	$146,055	$145,666	$ 389

Generalize from the Sample to the Population and Decide the Acceptability of the Population

The auditor must generalize from the sample to the population by (1) projecting misstatements from the sample results to the population and (2) considering sampling error and sampling risk (ARIA). For example, in the previous example does the auditor conclude that accounts receivable is overstated by $389? No, the auditor is interested in the *population* results, not those for the sample. It is therefore necessary to project from the sample to the population to estimate the population misstatement. The first step is to make a **point estimate,** which was first shown on page 213 in Chapter 8. There are different ways to calculate the point estimate, but a common way is to assume that misstatements in the unaudited population are proportional to the misstatements in the sample. That calculation must be done for each stratum and then totaled, rather than from the total misstatements in the sample. Thus, the point estimate of the misstatement from the preceding example is determined by using a weighted-average method, as shown next.

Stratum	Client Misstatement ÷ Recorded Value of the Sample	×	Recorded Book Value for the Stratum	=	Point Estimate of Misstatement
1	$(2,740)/$88,955		$88,955		$ (2,740)
2	$ 971 /$43,995		71,235		1,572
3	$ 2,158 /$13,105		47,105		7,757
Total					$ 6,589

The point estimate of the misstatement in the population is $6,589, indicating an overstatement. The point estimate, by itself, is not an adequate measure of the population misstatement, however, because of sampling error. In other words, because the estimate is based on a sample, it will be close to the true population misstatement, but it is unlikely that it is exactly the same. The auditor must consider the possibility that the true population misstatement is greater than the amount of misstatement that is tolerable in the circumstances whenever the point estimate is less than the tolerable misstatement amount. This must be done for both statistical and nonstatistical samples.

An auditor using nonstatistical sampling cannot formally measure sampling error and therefore must subjectively consider the possibility that the true population misstatement exceeds a tolerable amount. This is done by considering (1) the difference between the point estimate and tolerable misstatement, (2) the extent to which items in the population have been audited 100 percent, (3) whether misstatements tend to be offsetting or in only one direction, (4) the amounts of individual misstatements, and (5) the sample size. To continue the example, suppose that tolerable misstatement is $40,000. In that case, the auditor may conclude that there is little chance, given the point estimate of $6,589, that the true population misstatement exceeds the tolerable amount.

Suppose that tolerable misstatement is $12,000, only $5,411 greater than the point estimate. In that case, other factors would be considered. For example, if the larger items in the population were audited 100 percent (as was done here), any unidentified misstatements would be restricted to smaller items. If the misstatements tend to be offsetting and are relatively small in size, the auditor may conclude that the true population misstatement is likely to be less than the tolerable amount. Also, the larger the sample size, the more confident the auditor can be that the point estimate is close to the true population value. Therefore, the auditor would be more willing to accept that the true population misstatement is less than tolerable misstatement in this example where the sample size is considered large, than where it is considered moderate or small. However, if one or more of these other conditions is different, the chance of a misstatement in excess of the tolerable amount may be judged to be high and the recorded population unacceptable.

Even if the amount of likely misstatement is not considered material, the auditor must wait to make a final evaluation until the entire audit is completed. For example, the estimated total misstatement and estimated sampling error in accounts receivable must be combined with estimates of misstatements in all other parts of the audit to evaluate the effect of all misstatements on the financial statements as a whole.

Analyze the Misstatements

As for sampling for tests of controls and substantive tests of transactions, an evaluation of the nature and cause of each misstatement found is essential. For example, in confirming accounts receivable, suppose that all misstatements resulted from the client's failure to record returned goods. The auditor would determine why that type of misstatement occurred so often, the implications of the misstatements on other audit areas, the potential impact on the financial statements, and its effect on company operations.

An important part of misstatement analysis is deciding whether any modification of the audit risk model is needed. If the auditor concluded that the failure to record the returns discussed in the previous paragraph resulted from a breakdown of internal controls, it might be necessary to reassess control risk. That in turn would probably cause the auditor to reduce ARIA, which would increase planned sample size. As discussed in Chapter 8, revisions of the audit risk model must be done with extreme care because the model is intended primarily for planning, not evaluating results.

Action When a Population Is Rejected

When the auditor concludes that the misstatement in a population may be larger than tolerable misstatement after considering sampling error, the population is not considered acceptable. There are several possible courses of action.

Take No Action Until Tests of Other Audit Areas Are Completed Ultimately, the auditor must evaluate whether the financial statements taken as a whole are materially misstated. If offsetting misstatements are found in other parts of the audit, such as in inventory, the auditor may conclude that the estimated misstatements in accounts receivable are acceptable. Of course, before the audit is finalized, the auditor must evaluate whether a misstatement in one account may make the financial statements misleading even if there are offsetting misstatements.

Perform Expanded Audit Tests in Specific Areas If an analysis of the misstatements indicates that most of the misstatements are of a specific type, it may be desirable to restrict the additional audit effort to the problem area. For example, if an analysis of the misstatements in confirmations indicates that most of the misstatements result from failure to record sales returns, an extended search could be made of returned goods to make sure that they have been recorded. However, great care must be taken to evaluate the cause of all misstatements in the sample before a conclusion is reached about the proper emphasis in the expanded tests. There may be more than one problem area.

When a problem area is analyzed and corrected by adjusting the client's records, the sample items that led to isolating the problem area can then be shown as "correct." The point estimate can now be recalculated without the misstatements that have been "corrected." Sampling error and the acceptability of the population will also have to be reconsidered with the new facts.

Increase the Sample Size When the auditor increases the sample size, sampling error is reduced if the rate of misstatements in the expanded sample, their dollar amount, and their direction are similar to those in the original sample. Therefore, increasing the sample size may satisfy the auditor's tolerable misstatement requirements.

Increasing the sample size enough to satisfy the auditor's tolerable misstatement standards is often costly, especially when the difference between tolerable misstatement and projected misstatement is small. Even if the sample size is increased, there is no assurance of a satisfactory result. If the number, amount, and direction of the misstatements in the extended sample are proportionately greater or more variable than in the original sample, the results are still likely to be unacceptable.

For tests such as accounts receivable confirmation and inventory observation, it is often difficult to increase the sample size because of the practical problem of "reopening" those procedures once the initial work is done. By the time the auditor discovers that the sample was not large enough, several weeks have usually passed.

Despite these difficulties, sometimes the auditor must increase the sample size after the original testing is completed. It is much more common to increase sample size in audit areas other than confirmations and inventory observation, but it is occasionally necessary to do so even for these two areas. When stratified sampling is used, increased samples usually focus on the strata containing larger amounts, unless misstatements appear to be concentrated in some other strata.

Adjust the Account Balance When the auditor concludes that an account balance is materially misstated, the client may be willing to adjust the book value based on the sample results. In the previous example, assume the client is willing to reduce book value by the amount of the point estimate ($6,589) to adjust for the estimate of the misstatement. The auditor's estimate of the misstatement is now zero, but it is still necessary to consider sampling error. Again, assuming a tolerable misstatement of $12,000, the auditor must now assess whether sampling error exceeds $12,000, not the $5,411 originally considered. If the auditor believes sampling error is $12,000 or less, accounts receivable is acceptable after the adjustment. If the auditor believes it is more than $12,000, adjusting the account balance is not a practical option.

Request the Client to Correct the Population In some cases, the client's records are so inadequate that a correction of the entire population is required before the audit can be completed. For example, in accounts receivable, the client may be asked to prepare the aging schedule again if the auditor concludes that it has significant misstatements. When the client changes the valuation of some items in the population, the results must be audited again.

Refuse to Give an Unqualified Opinion If the auditor believes that the recorded amount in an account is not fairly stated, it is necessary to follow at least one of the preceding alternatives or to qualify the audit report in an appropriate manner. If the auditor believes that there is a reasonable chance that the financial statements are materially misstated, it would be a serious breach of auditing standards to issue an unqualified opinion.

Summary of Audit Sampling for Tests of Details of Balances

The steps involved in nonstatistical sampling for tests of details of balances are summarized in Figure 13-9.

FIGURE 13-9 Summary of Audit Sampling Steps for Tests of Details of Balances

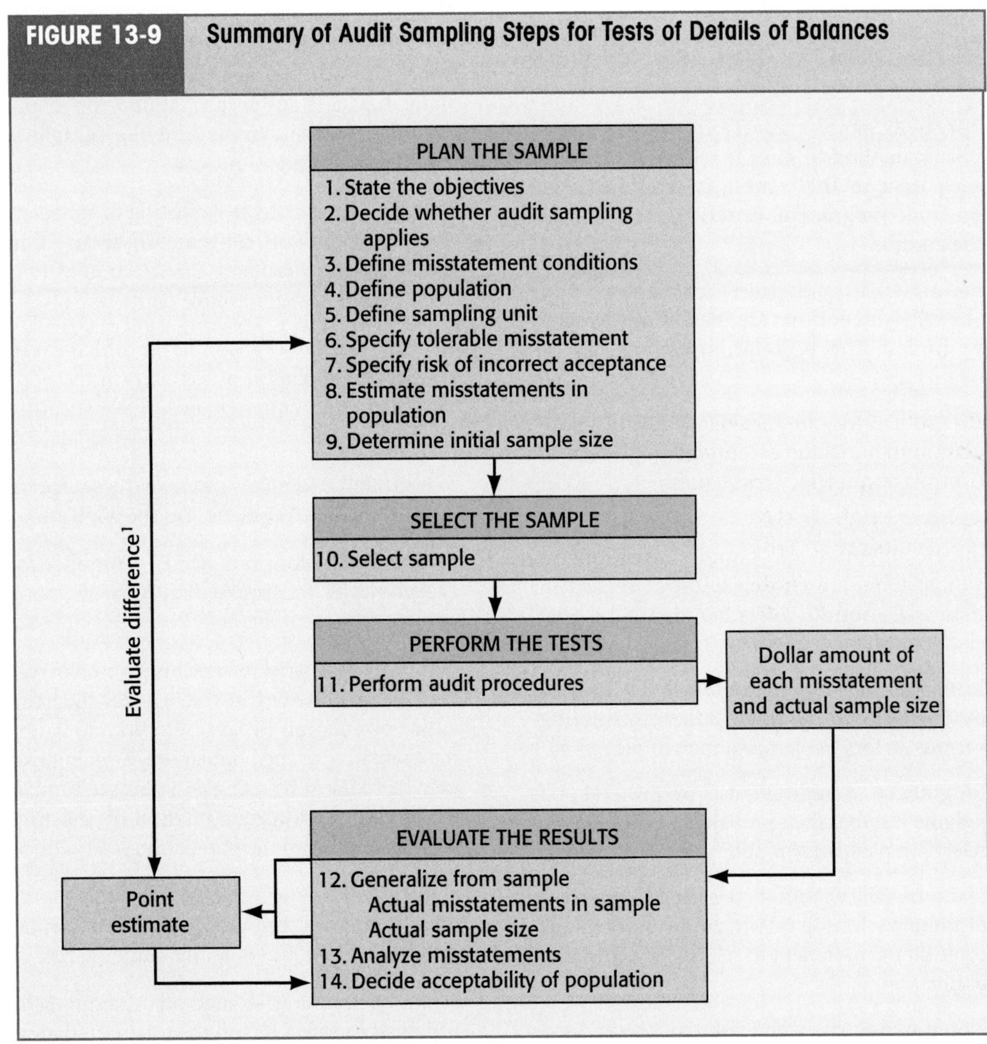

[1]Consider the size of the difference, extent to which items in the population have been audited 100%, extent of offsetting misstatements, amounts of individual misstatements, acceptable risk of incorrect acceptance, and sample size.

ESSENTIAL TERMS

Acceptable risk of assessing control risk too low (ARACR)—the risk that the auditor is willing to take of accepting a control as effective or a rate of monetary misstatements as tolerable, when the true population exception rate is greater than the tolerable exception rate

Acceptable risk of incorrect acceptance (ARIA)—the risk that the auditor is willing to take of accepting a balance as correct when the true misstatement in the balance is equal to or greater than tolerable misstatement

Attribute—the characteristic being tested for in the population

Audit sampling—testing less than 100 percent of a population for the purpose of making inferences about that population

Block sample selection—a nonprobabilistic method of sample selection in which items are selected in measured sequences

Computed upper exception rate (CUER)—the highest estimated exception rate in the population at a given ARACR

Directed sample selection—a nonprobabilistic method of sample selection in which each item in the sample is selected based on some judgmental criteria established by the auditor

Estimated population exception rate (EPER)—exception rate the auditor expects to find in the population before testing begins

Exception rate—the percent of items in a population that include exceptions in prescribed controls or monetary correctness

Haphazard sample selection—a nonprobabilistic method of sample selection in which items are chosen without regard to their size, source, or other distinguishing characteristics

Initial sample size—sample size determined by professional judgment after considering various factors in planning the sample

Judgmental sampling—use of professional judgment rather than probabilistic methods to select sample items for audit tests

Nonprobabilistic sample selection—a method of sample selection in which the auditor uses professional judgment to select items from the population

Nonsampling risk—the risk that the auditor fails to identify existing exceptions in the sample; nonsampling risk (nonsampling error) is caused by failure to recognize exceptions and by inappropriate or ineffective audit procedures

Nonstatistical sampling—the auditor's use of professional judgment to select sample items, estimate the population values, and estimate sampling risk

Occurrence rate—the ratio of items in a population that contain a specific attribute to the total number of population items

Point estimate—a method of projecting from the sample to the population to estimate the population misstatement, commonly by assuming that misstatements in the unaudited population are proportional to the misstatements found in the sample

Probability proportion to size sample selection (PPS)—sample selection of individual dollars in a population by the use of random or systematic sample selection

Probabilistic sample selection—a method of selecting a sample such that each population item has a known probability of being included in the sample and the sample is selected by a random process

Random number table—a listing of independent random digits conveniently arranged in tabular form to facilitate the selection of random numbers with multiple digits

Random sample—a sample in which every possible combination of elements in the population has an equal chance of constituting the sample

Representative sample—a sample whose characteristics are the same as those of the population

Sample exception rate (SER)—number of exceptions in the sample divided by the sample size

Sampling risk—risk of reaching an incorrect conclusion inherent in tests of less than the entire population because the sample is not representative of the population; sampling risk may be reduced by using an increased sample size and an appropriate method of selecting sample items from the population

Statistical sampling—the use of mathematical measurement techniques to calculate formal statistical results and quantify sampling risk

Stratified sampling—a method of sampling in which all the elements in the total population are divided into two or more subpopulations that are independently tested and evaluated

Systematic sample selection—a probabilistic method of sampling in which the auditor calculates an interval (the population size divided by the number of sample items desired) and selects the items for the sample based on the size of the interval and a randomly selected starting point between zero and the length of the interval

Tolerable exception rate (TER)—the exception rate that the auditor will permit in the population and still be willing to use the assessed control risk and/or the amount of monetary misstatements in the transactions established during planning

REVIEW QUESTIONS

13-1 (Objective 13-1) State what is meant by a representative sample and explain its importance in sampling audit populations.

13-2 (Objective 13-2) Explain the major difference between statistical and nonstatistical sampling. What are the three main parts of statistical and nonstatistical methods?

13-3 (Objective 13-3) What are the two types of simple random sample selection methods? Which of the two methods is used most often by auditors and why?

13-4 (Objective 13-4) What is the purpose of using nonstatistical sampling for tests of controls and substantive tests of transactions?

13-5 (Objective 13-5) Define each of the following terms:

a. Acceptable risk of assessing control risk too low (ARACR)

b. Computed upper exception rate (CUER)

c. Estimated population exception rate (EPER)

d. Sample exception rate (SER)

e. Tolerable exception rate (TER)

13-6 (Objective 13-5) Describe what is meant by a sampling unit. Explain why the sampling unit for verifying the existence of recorded sales differs from the sampling unit for testing for the possibility of omitted sales.

13-7 (Objective 13-5) Distinguish between the TER and the CUER. How is each determined?

13-8 (Objective 13-1) Distinguish between a sampling error and a nonsampling error. How can each be reduced?

13-9 (Objective 13-4) What is meant by an attribute in sampling for tests of controls and substantive tests of transactions? What is the source of the attributes that the auditor selects?

13-10 (Objective 13-4) Explain the difference between an attribute and an exception condition. State the exception condition for the audit procedure: The duplicate sales invoice has been initialed indicating the performance of internal verification.

13-11 (Objective 13-5) Identify the factors an auditor uses to decide the appropriate TER. Compare the sample size for a TER of 6% with that of 3%, all other factors being equal.

13-12 (Objective 13-5) State the relationship between the following:

a. ARACR and sample size

b. Population size and sample size

c. TER and sample size

d. EPER and sample size

13-13 (Objective 13-5) Explain what is meant by analysis of exceptions and discuss its importance.

13-14 (Objective 13-5) When the CUER exceeds the TER, what courses of action are available to the auditor? Under what circumstances should each of these be followed?

13-15 (Objectives 13-6, 13-7) What are the major differences in the 14 steps used to do nonstatistical sampling for tests of details of balances versus for tests of controls and substantive tests of transactions?

13-16 (Objective 13-7) Define stratified sampling and explain its importance in auditing. How could an auditor obtain a stratified sample of 30 items from each of three strata in the confirmation of accounts receivable?

13-17 (Objective 13-7) Distinguish between the point estimate of the total misstatements and the true value of the misstatements in the population. How can each be determined?

13-18 (Objective 13-7) Evaluate the following statement made by an auditor: "On every aspect of the audit where it is possible, I calculate the point estimate of the misstatements and evaluate whether the amount is material. If it is, I investigate the cause and continue to test the population until I determine whether there is a serious problem. The use of statistical sampling in this manner is a valuable audit tool."

13-19 (Objective 13-7) Explain what is meant by acceptable risk of incorrect acceptance. What are the major audit factors affecting ARIA?

13-20 (Objective 13-7) What is the relationship between ARIA and ARACR?

13-21 (Objective 13-7) What alternative courses of action are appropriate when a population is rejected using nonstatistical sampling for tests of details of balances? When should each option be followed?

MULTIPLE CHOICE QUESTIONS FROM CPA EXAMINATIONS

13-22 (Objective 13-5) The following items apply to determining sample sizes using random sampling from large populations in sampling for tests of controls and substantive tests of transactions. Select the most appropriate response for each question.

a. If all other factors specified in a sampling plan remain constant, changing the ARACR from 10% to 5% would cause the required sample size to
   (1) increase.
   (2) remain the same.
   (3) decrease.
   (4) become indeterminate.

b. If all other factors specified in a sampling plan remain constant, changing the TER from 8% to 12% would cause the required sample size to
   (1) increase.
   (2) remain the same.
   (3) decrease.
   (4) become indeterminate.

c. If an auditor wishes to select a random sample that must have a 10% ARACR and a TER of 10%, the size of the sample selected will decrease as the estimate of the
   (1) population exception rate increases.
   (2) population exception rate decreases.
   (3) population size increases.
   (4) ARACR increases.

d. In planning a sample for tests of controls, an auditor increases the expected population exception rate from the prior year's rate because of the results of the prior year's tests of controls. As a result, the auditor would most likely increase the planned
   (1) tolerable exception rate.
   (2) allowance for sampling risk.
   (3) acceptable risk of assessing control risk too low.
   (4) sample size.

13-23 (Objectives 13-1, 13-2) The following questions concern sampling risk. Choose the best response.

a. Which of the following is an element of sampling risk?
   (1) Choosing an audit procedure that is inconsistent with the audit objective.
   (2) Choosing a sample size that is too small to achieve the sampling objective.
   (3) The auditor failing to detect an error on a document in the sample.
   (4) Failing to perform audit procedures.

b. Which of the following best illustrates the concept of sampling risk?
   (1) The documents related to the chosen sample may not be available to the auditor for inspection.
   (2) An auditor may fail to recognize errors in the documents from the sample.
   (3) A randomly chosen sample may not be representative of the population as a whole for the characteristic of interest.
   (4) An auditor may select audit procedures that are not appropriate to achieve the specific objective.

13-24 (Objectives 13-6, 13-7) The following apply to audit sampling. For each one, select the best response.

a. The auditor's failure to recognize a misstatement in an amount or a control deviation is described as a
   (1) statistical error.
   (2) sampling error.
   (3) standard error of the mean.
   (4) nonsampling error.
b. An auditor uses audit sampling to perform tests of controls in the acquisition and payment cycle. Those tests indicate that the related controls are operating effectively. The auditor plans to use audit sampling to perform tests of details of balances for accounts payable. The auditor's acceptable risk of incorrect acceptance (ARIA) for the tests of details of balances for accounts payable would most likely be
   (1) the same as the ARACR for tests of controls.
   (2) greater than the ARACR for tests of controls.
   (3) less than the ARACR for tests of controls.
   (4) totally independent from the ARACR used for tests of controls.
c. Which of the following sample planning factors would influence the sample size for a test of details of balances for a specific account?

	Expected Amount of Misstatements	Measure of Tolerable Misstatements
(1)	No	No
(2)	Yes	Yes
(3)	No	Yes
(4)	Yes	No

DISCUSSION QUESTIONS AND PROBLEMS

13-25 (Objective 13-3)

a. In each of the following independent problems, design an unbiased random sampling plan, using an electronic spreadsheet or a random number generator program. The plan should include defining the sampling unit and establishing a numbering system for the population. After the plan has been designed, select the sample using the computer. Assume that the sample size is 50 for each of (1) through (4).
   (1) Prenumbered sales invoices in a sales journal where the lowest invoice number is 1 and the highest is 6211.
   (2) Prenumbered bills of lading where the lowest document number is 21926 and the highest is 28511.
   (3) Accounts receivable on 10 pages with 60 lines per page except the last page, which has only 36 full lines. Each line has a customer name and an amount receivable.
   (4) Prenumbered invoices in a sales journal where each month starts over with number 1. (Invoices for each month are designated by the month and document number.) There is a maximum of 20 pages per month with a total of 185 pages for the year. All pages have 75 invoices except for the last page for each month.
b. Using systematic sampling, select the first five sample items for populations (1) through (3) from part a, using the random starting points shown. Recall that the sample size is 50 in each case.
   (1) Invoice #67
   (2) Bill of lading #22011
   (3) Page 1, line #8

13-26 (Objectives 13-3, 13-5) Lenter Supply Company is a medium-sized distributor of wholesale hardware supplies in the central Ohio area. It has been a client of yours for several years and has instituted excellent internal controls for sales at your recommendation.

In providing control over shipments, the client has prenumbered "warehouse removal slips" that are used for every sale. It is company policy never to remove goods from the warehouse without an authorized warehouse removal slip. After shipment, two copies of the warehouse removal slip are sent to billing for the computerized preparation of a sales invoice. One copy is stapled to the duplicate copy of a prenumbered sales invoice, and the other copy is filed numerically. In some cases, more than one warehouse removal slip is used for billing one sales invoice. The smallest warehouse removal slip number for the year is 14682 and the largest is 37521. The smallest sales invoice number is 47821 and the largest is 68507.

In the audit of sales, one of the major concerns is the effectiveness of the controls in ensuring that all shipments are billed. You have decided to use audit sampling in testing internal controls.

Required

a. State an effective audit procedure for testing whether shipments have been billed. What is the sampling unit for the audit procedure?

b. Assuming that you expect no exceptions in the sample but are willing to accept a TER of 3%, at a 10% ARACR, what is a reasonable sample size for the audit test?

c. Design a random selection plan for selecting the sample from the population, using either systematic sampling or computer generation of random numbers. Use the sample size determined in part b. If you use systematic sampling, use a random starting point of 14825.

d. Your supervisor suggests the possibility of performing other sales tests with the same sample as a means of efficiently using your audit time. List two other audit procedures that could conveniently be performed using the same sample and state the purpose of each of the procedures.

e. Is it desirable to test the existence of sales with the random sample you have designed in part c? Why?

13-27 (Objective 13-5) The following is a partial audit program for the audit of cash receipts.

1. Review the cash receipts journal for large and unusual transactions.
2. Trace entries from the prelisting of cash receipts to the cash receipts journal to determine whether each is recorded.
3. Compare customer name, date, and amount on the prelisting with the cash receipts journal.
4. Examine the related remittance advice for entries selected from the prelisting to determine whether cash discounts were approved.
5. Trace entries from the prelisting to the deposit slip to determine whether each has been deposited.

Required

a. Identify which audit procedures could be tested using audit sampling.

b. What is the appropriate sampling unit for the tests in part a?

c. List the attributes for testing in part a.

d. Assume an ARACR of 5% and a TER of 8% for tests of controls and 6% for substantive tests of transactions. The EPER for tests of controls is 2%, and for substantive tests of transactions it is 1%. What is an appropriate initial sample size for each attribute?

13-28 (Objective 13-5) The following questions concern the determination of the proper sample size in audit sampling using the following table:

	1	2	3	4	5	6	7
ARACR (in percent)	10	5	5	5	10	10	5
TER	6	6	5	6	20	20	2
EPER (in percent)	2	2	2	2	8	2	0
Population size	1,000	100,000	6,000	1,000	500	500	1,000,000

Required

a. Assume that the initial sample size for column 1 was determined to be 90 items, using nonstatistical sampling. For each of columns 2 through 7, use your judgment to decide the appropriate nonstatistical sample size. In deciding each sample size, consider the effects of changes in each of the four factors (ARACR, TER, EPER, and population size) compared with column 1.

b. Using your understanding of the relationship between the following factors and sample size, state the effect on the initial sample size (increase or decrease) of changing each of the following factors while the other three are held constant:
(1) An increase in ARACR
(2) An increase in the TER
(3) An increase in the EPER
(4) An increase in the population size

c. Explain why there is such a large difference in the sample sizes for columns 3 and 6.

d. Compare your answers in part b with the results you determined in part a. Which of the four factors appears to have the greatest effect on the initial sample size? Which one appears to have the least effect?

e. Why is the sample size called the initial sample size?

13-29 **(Objective 13-5)** The questions below relate to determining the CUER in audit sampling for tests of controls, using the following table:

	1	2	3	4	5	6	7	8
ARACR (in percent)	10	5	5	5	5	5	5	5
Population size	5,000	5,000	5,000	50,000	500	900	5,000	500
Sample size	200	200	50	200	100	100	100	25
Number of exceptions	4	4	1	4	2	10	0	0

Required

a. Using nonstatistical sampling, calculate TER – SER for each of columns 1 through 8 and evaluate whether or not sampling error is large enough to accept the population. Assume that TER is 5% for each column.

b. Using your understanding of the relationship between the four preceding factors and the CUER, state the effect on the CUER (increase or decrease) of changing each of the following factors while the other three are held constant:
(1) A decrease in the ARACR
(2) A decrease in the population size
(3) A decrease in the sample size
(4) A decrease in the number of exceptions in the sample

c. Compare your answers in part b with the results you determined in part a. Which of the factors appears to have the greatest effect on the CUER? Which one appears to have the least effect?

d. Why is it necessary to evaluate the difference between TER and SER?

13-30 **(Objective 13-5)** For the audit of the financial statements of Mercury Fifo Company, Stella Mason, CPA, has decided to apply nonstatistical audit sampling in the tests of controls and substantive tests of transactions for sales transactions. Based on her knowledge of Mercury's operations in the area of sales, she decides that the EPER is likely to be 3% and that she is willing to accept a 5% risk that the true population exception rate is not greater than 6%. Given this information, Mason selects a random sample of 150 sales invoices from the 5,000 generated during the year and examines them for exceptions. She notes the following exceptions in her audit schedules. There is no other documentation.

Invoice No.	Comment
5028	Sales invoice was originally footed incorrectly but was corrected by client before the bill was sent out.
6791	Voided sales invoice examined by auditor.
6810	Shipping document for a sale of merchandise could not be located.
7364	Sales invoice for $2,875 has not been collected and is 6 months past due.
7625	Client unable to locate the duplicate sales invoice.
8431	Invoice was dated 3 days later than the date entered in the sales journal.
8528	Customer order is not attached to the duplicate sales invoice.
8566	Billing is for $100 less than it should be due to an unintentional pricing error. No indication of internal verification is included on the invoice.
8780	Client unable to locate the duplicate sales invoice.
9169	Credit not authorized, but the sale was for only $7.65.
9974	Lack of indication of internal verification of price extensions and postings of sales invoice.

Required

a. Which of the preceding should be defined as an exception?

b. Explain why it is inappropriate to set a single acceptable TER and EPER for the combined exceptions.

c. For each attribute in the population that is tested, calculate SER for each attribute. (You must decide which attributes should be combined, which should be kept separate, and which exceptions are actual exceptions before you can calculate SER.)

d. Calculate TER – SER for each attribute and evaluate whether sampling error is sufficiently large given the 5% ARACR. Assume TER is 6% for each attribute.

e. State the appropriate analysis of exceptions for each of the exceptions in the sample, including additional procedures to be performed.

13-31 (Objective 13-7) You are planning to use nonstatistical sampling to evaluate the results of accounts receivable confirmation for the Meridian Company. You have already performed tests of controls for sales, sales returns and allowances, and cash receipts, and they are considered excellent. Because of the quality of the controls, you decide to use an acceptable risk of incorrect acceptance of 10%. There are 3,000 accounts receivable with a gross value of $6,900,000. The accounts are similar in size and will be treated as a single stratum. An overstatement or understatement of more than $150,000 would be considered material.

Required

a. Calculate the required sample size. Assume your firm uses the following nonstatistical formula to determine sample size:

Sample size = (Book value of population / Tolerable misstatement) × Assurancefactor

Assurance factor:

5% ARIA = 3
10% ARIA = 2
20% ARIA = 1

b. Assume that instead of good results, poor results were obtained for tests of controls and substantive tests of transactions for sales, sales returns and allowances, and cash receipts. How would this affect your required sample size? How would you use this information in your sample size determination?

c. Regardless of your answer to part a, assume you decide to select a sample of 100 accounts for testing. Indicate how you would select the accounts for testing using systematic selection.

d. Assume a total book value of $230,000 for the 100 accounts selected for testing. You uncover three overstatements totaling $1,500 in the sample. Evaluate whether the population is fairly stated.

13-32 (Objective 13-7) The accounts receivable population for Jake's Bookbinding Company follows. This table is the same as Table 13-7 on page 396, except that cumulative amounts are included to assist you in completing the problem. The population is smaller than would ordinarily be the case for audit sampling, but an entire population is useful to show how to select PPS samples.

Required

a. Select a random PPS sample of 10 items, using computer software.

b. Select a sample of 10 items using systematic PPS sampling using the same concepts discussed for systematic sampling. Use a starting point of 1857. Identify the physical units associated with the sample dollars. (*Hint:* The interval is 207,295 ÷ 10.)

c. Which sample items will always be included in the systematic PPS sample regardless of the starting point? Will that also be true of random PPS sampling?

d. Which method is preferable in terms of ease of selection in this case?

Population Item	Recorded Amount	Cumulative Amount	Population Item (cont.)	Recorded Amount (cont.)	Cumulative Amount (cont.)
1	$ 1,410	$ 1,410	21	$ 4,865	$117,385
2	9,130	10,540	22	770	118,155
3	660	11,200	23	2,305	120,460
4	3,355	14,555	24	2,665	123,125
5	5,725	20,280	25	1,000	124,125
6	8,210	28,490	26	6,225	130,350
7	580	29,070	27	3,675	134,025
8	44,110	73,180	28	6,250	140,275
9	825	74,005	29	1,890	142,165
10	1,155	75,160	30	27,705	169,870
11	2,270	77,430	31	935	170,805
12	50	77,480	32	5,595	176,400
13	5,785	83,265	33	930	177,330
14	940	84,205	34	4,045	181,375
15	1,820	86,025	35	9,480	190,855
16	3,380	89,405	36	360	191,215
17	530	89,935	37	1,145	192,360
18	955	90,890	38	6,400	198,760
19	4,490	95,380	39	100	198,860
20	17,140	112,520	40	8,435	207,295

13-33 (Objective 13-7) In the audit of Price Seed Company for the year ended September 30, the auditor set a tolerable misstatement of $50,000 at an ARIA of 10%. A random sample of 50 was selected from an accounts receivable population that had a recorded balance of $1,975,000. The table below shows the differences uncovered in the confirmation process. The 43 sample items without exceptions had a recorded value of $106,000.

Accounts Receivable per Records	Accounts Receivable per Confirmation	Follow-up Comments by Auditor
1. $2,728.00	$2,498.00	Pricing error on two invoices.
2. $5,125.00	-0-	Customer mailed check 9/26; company received check 10/3.
3. $3,890.00	$1,190.00	Merchandise returned 9/30 and counted in inventory; credit was issued 10/6.
4. $ 791.00	$ 815.00	Footing error on an invoice.
5. $ 548.00	$1,037.00	Goods were shipped 9/28; sale was recorded on 10/6.
6. $3,115.00	$3,190.00	Pricing error on a credit memorandum.
7. $1,540.00	-0-	Goods were shipped on 9/29; customer received goods 10/3; sale was recorded on 9/30.

Required

a. Calculate the point estimate of the client misstatements in the sample.

b. Is the population acceptable as stated? Explain why or why not. If not, what options are available to the auditor at this point? Which option should the auditor select? Explain.

13-34 (Objective 13-7) An audit partner is developing an office training program to familiarize her professional staff with audit sampling decision models applicable to the audit of dollar-value balances. She wishes to demonstrate the relationship of sample sizes to population size and estimated population exception rate and the auditor's specifications as to tolerable misstatement and ARIA. The partner prepared the following table to show comparative population characteristics and audit specifications of the two populations:

	Characteristics of Population 1 Relative to Population 2		Audit Specifications as to a Sample from Population 1 Relative to a Sample from Population 2	
	Size	Estimated Population Exception Rate	Tolerable Misstatement	ARIA
Case 1	Equal	Equal	Equal	Lower
Case 2	Smaller	Smaller	Equal	Higher
Case 3	Larger	Equal	Equal	Lower
Case 4	Equal	Larger	Larger	Equal
Case 5	Larger	Equal	Smaller	Higher

Required

In items (1) through (5) you are to indicate for the specific case from the table the required sample size to be selected from population 1 relative to the sample from population 2.

(1) In case 1, the required sample size from population 1 is _____.
(2) In case 2, the required sample size from population 1 is _____.
(3) In case 3, the required sample size from population 1 is _____.
(4) In case 4, the required sample size from population 1 is _____.
(5) In case 5, the required sample size from population 1 is _____.

Your answer choice should be selected from the following responses:

a. Larger than the required sample size from population 2.
b. Equal to the required sample size from population 2.
c. Smaller than the required sample size from population 2.
d. Indeterminate relative to the required sample size from population 2.*

*AICPA adapted.

13-35 **(Objective 13-7)** In auditing the valuation of inventory, the auditor, Claire Butler, decided to use audit sampling. She decided to select an unrestricted random sample of 80 inventory items from a population of 1,840 that had a book value of $175,820. Butler decided in advance that she was willing to accept a maximum misstatement in the population of $6,000 at an ARIA of 5 percent. The book value of the 80 items sampled was $7,825. There were eight misstatements in the sample, which were as follows:

	Audit Value	Book Value	Sample Misstatements
	$ 812.50	$ 740.50	$(72.00)
	12.50	78.20	65.70
	10.00	51.10	41.10
	25.40	61.50	36.10
	600.10	651.90	51.80
	.12	0	(.12)
	51.06	81.06	30.00
	83.11	104.22	21.11
Total	$1,594.79	$1,768.48	$173.69

Required

a. Calculate the point estimate for the population.

b. Should Butler accept the book value of the population? Explain.

c. What should Butler do at this point?

d. Now assume she had found two additional errors, one a $500 overstatement and the other a $500 understatement. How would this affect the answers to parts a, b, and c?

CASE

13-36 **(Objective 13-5)** For the audit of Carbald Supply Company, Carole Wever, CPA, is conducting a test of sales for 9 months of the year ended December 31, 2002. Included among her audit procedures are the following:

1. Foot and cross-foot the sales journal and trace the balance to the general ledger.
2. Review all sales transactions for reasonableness.
3. Select a sample of recorded sales from the sales journal and trace the customer name and amounts to duplicate sales invoices and the related shipping document.
4. Select a sample of shipping document numbers and perform the following tests:
   a. Trace the shipping document to the related duplicate sales invoice.
   b. Examine the duplicate sales invoice to determine whether copies of the shipping document, shipping order, and customer order are attached.
   c. Examine the shipping order for an authorized credit approval.
   d. Examine the duplicate sales invoice for an indication of internal verification of quantity, price, extensions, footings, and tracing the balance to the accounts receivable master file.
   e. Compare the price on the duplicate sales invoice with the approved price list and the quantity with the shipping document.
   f. Trace the balance in the duplicate sales invoice to the sales journal and accounts receivable master file for customer name, amount, and date.

Required

a. For which of these procedures could audit sampling for exceptions be conveniently used?

b. Considering the audit procedures Wever developed, what is the most appropriate sampling unit for conducting most of the audit sampling tests?

c. Set up a sampling data sheet using nonstatistical sampling. For all tests of controls, assume a TER rate of 5% and an EPER of 1%. For all substantive tests of transactions, use a 10% TER and a 0% EPER. Use a 10% ARACR for all tests.

INTEGRATED CASE APPLICATION—PINNACLE MANUFACTURING: PART IV

13-37 **(Objectives 13-3, 13-5)** In Parts II and III of the Pinnacle Manufacturing integrated case application, the audit programs for tests of controls, substantive tests of transactions, and tests of details of balances were designed for acquisitions, cash disbursements, and accounts payable. In Part IV, sample sizes will be determined by using nonstatistical sampling, and the results will be evaluated.

Required

a. Use the performance format audit program you prepared for acquisitions and cash disbursements from Problem 11-33 to prepare a sampling data sheet. Use Figure 13-2 on page 385 as a frame of reference for preparing the data sheet. Complete all parts of the data sheet except those parts that are blank in Figure 13-2. Use the following additional information to complete this requirement:
   (1) Prepare only one sampling data sheet.
   (2) Decide the appropriate sampling unit and select all audit procedures that are appropriate for that sampling unit from the performance format audit program you prepared in Problem 11-33. The following information is available to define the population on the sampling data sheet for the sampling unit selected:

Acquisitions Journal		**Cash Disbursements Journal**	
First voucher number	8672	First check number	6240
Last voucher number	13652	Last check number	9875

   (3) Decide EPER, TER, and ARACR for each attribute. Base EPER on the prior year's results of tests of controls and substantive tests of transactions in Figure 9-8 on page 275. Use your judgment in deciding TER, considering the nature and importance of each attribute. Assume that assessed control risk is low for each procedure.

b. Design a random sampling plan using an electronic spreadsheet or systematic selection for the attribute with the largest sample size in requirement a. Document the design and the first 10 numbers selected under the sampling plan.

c. Assume that you performed all audit procedures included in Problem 11-33 using the sample sizes in requirement a. The only exceptions found when you performed the tests were one missing indication of internal verification on a vendor's invoice, one acquisition of inventory transaction recorded for $200 more than the amount stated in the vendor's invoice (the vendor was also overpaid by $200), and one vendor invoice recorded as an acquisition 18 days after the receipt of the goods. Complete the sampling data sheet prepared in part a. Use Figure 13-4 on page 391 as a frame of reference for completing the data sheet.

d. (Instructor Option) Develop the sampling data sheet, using an electronic spreadsheet.

INTERNET PROBLEM 13-1: SAMPLING FOR U.S. CENSUS

Reference the CW site. Sampling concepts are used in a variety of contexts. This problem highlights the use of sampling by the U.S. Census Bureau and emphasizes how key judgments affect the sampling process. Students use the Internet to learn how the U.S. Census Bureau uses sampling techniques to make estimates of the U.S. population.

PART 4 CHAPTERS 14–17

APPLICATION OF THE AUDIT PROCESS TO OTHER CYCLES

The chapters in Part 4 apply auditing concepts first presented in Chapters 5 through 10 and then expanded in Chapters 11 through 13 to the other cycles in an audit. Although there are considerable similarities in auditing each cycle, there are also important differences that auditors need to understand.

Each of these chapters deals with a specific transaction cycle or part of a transaction cycle in much the same manner as Chapters 11 through 13 cover the sales and collection cycle. Each chapter in Part 4 demonstrates the relationship of internal controls, tests of controls, substantive tests of transactions, and analytical procedures to the related balance sheet and income statement accounts in the cycle and to tests of details of balances.

The chapters in Part 4 apply auditing concepts first presented in Chapters 5 through 10 and then expanded in Chapters 11 through 13 to the acquisition and payment and inventory and warehousing cycles. Although there are considerable similarities in auditing each cycle, there are also important differences that auditors need to understand. The two other cycles in an audit, the payroll and personnel cycle and the capital acquisition and repayment cycle, are not presented. The audit of these two cycles is generally straightforward and involves the same concepts and approaches used in other cycles.

CHAPTER 14

AUDIT OF THE ACQUISITION AND PAYMENT CYCLE: TESTS OF CONTROLS, SUBSTANTIVE TESTS OF TRANSACTIONS, AND ACCOUNTS PAYABLE

FALSE PURCHASES CAMOUFLAGE OVERSTATED PROFITS

On November 25, 1992, Comptronix Corporation announced that members of its senior management team had overstated profits and that there would be material adjustments to the prior years' audited financial statements. In its subsequent investigation, the SEC determined that Comptronix's chief executive officer (CEO), chief operating officer (COO), and the controller/treasurer colluded to overstate assets and profits by recording fictitious sales, accounts receivable, and purchases of equipment on account.

To camouflage the fraud, the executives made it appear that collections from customers were received on the nonexistent receivables and that payments were made to fictitious accounts payable vendors. They even prepared cash disbursement checks to the phony vendors but retained the unendorsed checks and redeposited them into the company's disbursement account on which they had been drawn. These fraudulent disbursements were recorded in the accounting records as payments against the nonexistent accounts payable, which eliminated the phony liabilities.

The senior executives circumvented Comptronix's existing internal controls by bypassing the purchasing and receiving departments so that no one at Comptronix could discover the scheme. Comptronix employees usually created a fairly extensive paper trail for equipment purchases. Company internal controls over acquisition and cash disbursement transactions typically required a purchase order, receiving report, and vendor invoice before payment could be authorized by the COO or the controller/treasurer, who were both participants in the fraud. As a result, the executives were able to bypass controls related to cash disbursements and authorize payment for nonexistent purchases without creating any documents for the fictitious transactions.

The fraud scheme grossly exaggerated the company's performance by reporting profits when the company was actually incurring losses. On the day that the public announcement of the fraud was made, Comptronix's common stock price declined abruptly by 72 percent! The SEC ultimately charged all three executives with violating the antifraud provisions of the Securities Act of 1933 and the Securities Exchange Act of 1934. The SEC permanently barred the executives from serving as officers or directors of any public company, ordered them to repay bonuses and trading losses avoided, and imposed civil monetary penalties against them.

Source: *Accounting and Auditing Enforcement Release No. 543,* Commerce Clearing House, Inc., Chicago.

LEARNING OBJECTIVES

After studying this chapter, you should be able to

14-1 Identify the accounts and the classes of transactions in the acquisition and payment cycle.

14-2 Identify the business functions and the related documents and records in the acquisition and payment cycle.

14-3 Describe how e-commerce affects the acquisition of goods and services.

14-4 Understand internal control, and design and perform tests of controls and substantive tests of transactions for the acquisition and payment cycle.

14-5 Describe the methodology for designing tests of details of balances for accounts payable using the audit risk model.

14-6 Design and perform analytical procedures for accounts payable.

14-7 Design and perform tests of details of balances for accounts payable, including out-of-period liability tests.

14-8 Distinguish the reliability of vendors' invoices, vendors' statements, and confirmations of accounts payable as audit evidence.

The second major transaction cycle discussed is the **acquisition and payment cycle.** The acquisition of goods and services includes such items as the acquisition of raw materials, equipment, supplies, utilities, repairs and maintenance, and research and development. This chapter first discusses assessing control risk and designing tests of controls and substantive tests of transactions for the classes of transactions in the acquisition and payment cycle. It also covers performing tests of details of balances for accounts payable.

ACCOUNTS AND CLASSES OF TRANSACTIONS IN THE ACQUISITION AND PAYMENT CYCLE

OBJECTIVE 14-1

Identify the accounts and the classes of transactions in the acquisition and payment cycle.

The overall objective in the audit of the acquisition and payment cycle is to evaluate whether the accounts affected by the acquisitions of goods and services and the cash disbursements for those acquisitions are fairly presented in accordance with generally accepted accounting principles. Figure 14-1 shows the way accounting information flows through the various accounts in the acquisition and payment cycle. This figure shows that there are three classes of transactions included in the cycle:

1. Acquisitions of goods and services
2. Cash disbursements
3. Purchase returns and allowances and purchase discounts

Typical accounts included in the acquisition and payment cycle are shown by T accounts in Figure 14-1. Note the large number of accounts affected by this cycle. To keep the illustration manageable, only the control accounts are shown for the three major

FIGURE 14-1 Accounts in the Acquisition and Payment Cycle

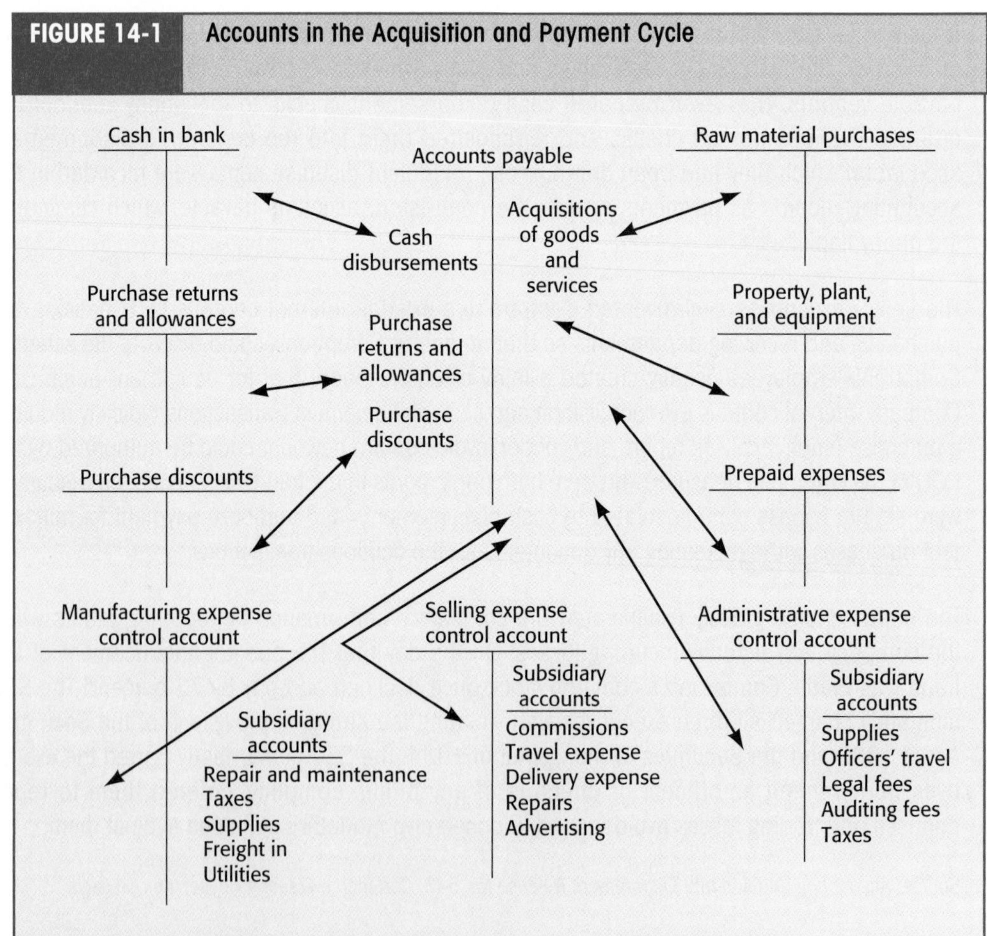

categories of expenses used by most companies. For each control account, examples of the subsidiary expense accounts are also given. Because of the large number of accounts in the cycle, it is not surprising that it often takes more time to audit the acquisition and payment cycle than any other.

Figure 14-1 shows that every transaction is either debited or credited to accounts payable. Because many companies make acquisitions directly by check or through petty cash, the figure is an oversimplification. We assume that cash disbursement transactions are processed in the same manner as all others.

BUSINESS FUNCTIONS IN THE CYCLE AND RELATED DOCUMENTS AND RECORDS

OBJECTIVE 14-2

Identify the business functions and the related documents and records in the acquisition and payment cycle.

The acquisition and payment cycle involves the decisions and processes necessary for obtaining the goods and services for operating a business. The cycle typically begins with the initiation of a purchase requisition by an authorized employee who needs the goods or services and ends with payment for the benefits received.

There are four business functions shown in the third column of Table 14-1. These functions occur in every business in the recording of the three classes of transactions in the acquisition and payment cycle. Observe that the first three business functions are for recording the acquisition of goods and services on account and the last process is for recording the cash disbursements for payments to vendors. Processing purchase returns and allowances and purchase discounts are also business functions in the cycle, but these are not separately shown in Table 14-1 because the amounts are not significant for most companies.

Typical documents and records for each function are shown in the fourth column of Table 14-1. It is important to understand the business functions and documents and records in a company before assessing control risk and designing tests of controls and substantive tests of transactions.

TABLE 14-1 Classes of Transactions, Accounts, Business Functions, and Related Documents and Records for the Acquisition and Payment Cycle

Classes of Transactions	Accounts	Business Functions	Documents and Records
Acquisitions	Inventory Property, plant, and equipment Prepaid expenses Leasehold improvements Accounts payable Manufacturing expenses Selling expenses Administrative expenses	Processing purchase orders	Purchase requisition Purchase order
		Receiving goods and services	Receiving report
		Recognizing the liability	Acquisitions transaction file Acquisitions journal or listing Vendor's invoice Debit memo Voucher Accounts payable master file Accounts payable trial balance Vendor's statement
Cash disbursements	Cash in bank (from cash disbursements) Accounts payable Purchase discounts	Processing and recording cash disbursements	Check Cash disbursements transaction file Cash disbursements journal or listing

HOW E-COMMERCE AFFECTS THE ACQUISITION AND PAYMENT CYCLE

OBJECTIVE 14-3

Describe how e-commerce affects the acquisition of goods and services.

Companies use the Internet and other e-commerce options to streamline processes surrounding the acquisition of goods and services, fostering a revolution in processes surrounding supply-chain management. While the use of electronic data interchange (EDI) has been around for years for larger suppliers and customers, technologies enabled by the Internet have now been extended to smaller suppliers and customers, allowing them to link relatively inexpensively.

E-procurement

Information about product descriptions, pricing, delivery schedules, and other terms are readily available over the Internet through supplier Web sites and other easily accessible databases. Purchasing agents access information about products needed from a host of providers before making acquisition decisions. Often, the actual purchase decision can be initiated through company Web site portals hosted by the supplier or independent providers, bypassing the traditional paper-based procurement process.

Some companies use extranets, which are private networks built on Internet technology, allowing business suppliers and customers to communicate and conduct business directly in a secure setting. Companies needing to purchase goods access the extranet to link to preapproved suppliers to order products or services and to obtain information useful to future purchasing decisions. The use of an extranet often increases the ability to conduct business with remote business partners who once were not feasible business partners. Even companies who compete with one another for the sale of goods and services are actually partnering to build online marketplaces that integrate common suppliers.

Other companies use business-to-business auctions hosted on the Internet to negotiate the purchase of needed supplies and services in open auctions. These Internet-based auctions often bring in a larger pool of suppliers and customers, who negotiate through the auction portal for the purchase and sale of products and services. There are a variety of auction styles, with some of the auctions being hosted by independent third-party specialists while others are hosted privately by company suppliers.

Many argue that the use of the Internet to acquire goods and services leads to market efficiencies and cheaper prices because the online markets enable a greater number of suppliers and customers to negotiate for the purchase and sale of products and services. In addition, the use of the Internet for the acquisition of goods and services often enables a faster delivery of products and services because of the time-savings associated with placing the order online. The online availability of product and other supply-chain information, such as order status, helps reduce payroll-related costs once associated with staffing customer service and other sales functions.

METHODOLOGY FOR DESIGNING TESTS OF CONTROLS AND SUBSTANTIVE TESTS OF TRANSACTIONS

OBJECTIVE 14-4

Understand internal control, and design and perform tests of controls and substantive tests of transactions for the acquisition and payment cycle.

In a typical audit, the most time-consuming accounts to verify by substantive tests of details of balances are accounts receivable, inventory, fixed assets, accounts payable, and expense accounts. Of these five, four are directly related to the acquisition and payment cycle. The net time saved can be dramatic if the auditor can reduce the tests of details of the account balances by using tests of controls and substantive tests of transactions to verify the effectiveness of internal controls for acquisitions and cash disbursements. Therefore, it should not be surprising that tests of controls and substantive tests of transactions for the acquisition and payment cycle receive a considerable amount of attention in well-conducted audits, especially when the client has effective internal controls.

The same methodology is used for designing tests of controls and substantive tests of transactions for the acquisition and payment cycle that was used in Chapter 11 for the sales and collection cycle. Tests of controls and substantive tests of transactions for the acquisition and payment cycle are divided into two broad areas: tests of acquisitions and tests of payments. Acquisition tests concern three of the four business functions shown in

Table 14-1: processing purchase orders, receiving goods and services, and recognizing the liability. Tests of payments concern the fourth function, processing and recording cash disbursements.

Understand Internal Control

The auditor gains an understanding of internal control for the acquisition and payment cycle by studying the client's flowcharts, preparing internal control questionnaires, and performing walk-through tests for acquisitions and cash disbursements. The procedures for understanding internal control in the acquisition and payment cycle are similar to the procedures performed in other transaction cycles.

Assess Planned Control Risk

There are key internal controls for each of the business functions identified earlier in this chapter. Key internal controls are for the authorization of purchases, the separation of the custody of the received goods from other functions, the timely recording and independent review of transactions, and the authorization of payments to vendors. We now examine each of these key controls.

Authorization of Purchases Proper authorization for acquisitions is essential because it ensures that the goods and services acquired are for authorized company purposes and it avoids the acquisition of excessive or unnecessary items. Most companies permit general authorization for the acquisition of regular operating needs, such as inventory, at one level and acquisitions of capital assets or similar items at another. For example, acquisitions of fixed assets in excess of a specified dollar limit may require approval from the board of directors; items acquired relatively infrequently, such as insurance policies and long-term service contracts, are approved by certain officers; supplies and services costing less than a designated amount are approved by supervisors and department heads; and some types of raw materials and supplies are reordered automatically when they fall to a predetermined level, often by direct communication with vendors' computers.

After the purchase requisition for an acquisition has been approved, a purchase order to acquire the goods or services must be initiated. A purchase order is issued to a vendor for a specified item at a certain price to be delivered at or by a designated time. The purchase order is usually in writing and is a legal document that is an offer to buy.

It is common for companies to establish purchasing departments to ensure an adequate quality of goods and services at a minimum price. For good internal control, the purchasing department should not be responsible for authorizing the acquisition or receiving the goods. All purchase orders should be prenumbered and should include sufficient columns and spaces to minimize the likelihood of unintentional omissions on the form when goods are ordered.

Separation of Asset Custody from Other Functions Most companies have the receiving department initiate a receiving report as evidence of the receipt and examination of goods. One copy is normally sent to the raw materials storeroom and another to the accounts payable department for their information needs. To prevent theft and misuse, it is important that the goods be *physically controlled* from the time of their receipt until their use or disposal. The personnel in the receiving department should be independent of the storeroom personnel and the accounting department. Finally, the accounting records should transfer responsibility for the goods as they are transferred from receiving to storage and from storage to manufacturing.

Timely Recording and Independent Review of Transactions In some companies, the recording of the liability for acquisitions is made on the basis of the receipt of goods and services, and in other companies, it is deferred until the vendor's invoice is received. In either case, the accounts payable department typically has responsibility for verifying the propriety of acquisitions. This is done by comparing the details on the purchase order, the receiving report, and the vendor's invoice to determine that the descriptions, prices, quantities, terms, and freight on the vendor's invoice are correct. Typically, extensions, footings, and account distributions are also verified. In some cases, the matching of documents and verification of invoice accuracy are done automatically by computer.

An important control in the accounts payable and information technology departments is to require that those personnel who record acquisitions do not have access to cash, marketable securities, and other assets. Adequate documents and records, proper procedures for record keeping, and independent checks on performance are also necessary controls in the accounts payable function.

Authorization of Payments The most important controls over cash disbursements include the signing of checks by an individual with proper authority, separation of responsibilities for signing the checks and performing the accounts payable function, and careful examination of the supporting documents by the check signer at the time the check is signed.

The checks should be prenumbered and printed on special paper that makes it difficult to alter the payee or amount. Care should be taken to provide physical control over blank, voided, and signed checks. It is also important to have a method of cancelling the supporting documents to prevent their reuse as support for another check at a later time. A common method is to write the check number on the supporting documents.

Evaluate Cost-Benefit of Testing Controls

After the auditor has identified the key internal controls and weaknesses and assessed control risk, it is appropriate to decide whether substantive tests will be reduced sufficiently to justify the cost of performing tests of controls. It makes little sense to incur the cost of identifying controls and assessing control risk below the maximum if there will be no reduction of substantive tests.

Design Tests of Controls and Substantive Tests of Transactions for Acquisitions

Key internal controls, common tests of controls, and common substantive tests of transactions for each transaction-related audit objective are summarized in Table 14-2. An assumption underlying the internal controls and audit procedures is the existence of a separate acquisitions journal or listing for recording all acquisitions.

In studying Table 14-2, it is important to relate internal controls to transaction-related audit objectives, tests of controls to internal controls, and substantive tests of transactions to monetary misstatements that would be absent or present due to controls and weaknesses in the system. The audit evidence for an audit engagement will vary with the internal controls and other circumstances. Significant audit efficiencies may be realized when controls are operating effectively.

Four of the six transaction-related audit objectives for acquisitions deserve special attention. A discussion of each of these objectives follows.

Recorded Acquisitions Are for Goods and Services Received, Consistent with the Best Interests of the Client (Existence) If the auditor is satisfied that the controls are adequate for this objective, tests for improper and nonexistent transactions can be greatly reduced. Adequate controls are likely to prevent the client from including as a business expense or asset those transactions that primarily benefit management or other employees rather than the entity being audited. In some instances, improper transactions are obvious, such as the acquisition of unauthorized personal items by employees or the actual embezzlement of cash by recording a fraudulent acquisition in the acquisitions journal. In other instances, the propriety of a transaction is more difficult to evaluate, such as the payment of officers' memberships to country clubs, expense-paid vacations to foreign countries for members of management and their families, and management-approved illegal payments to officials of foreign countries. If the controls over improper or nonexistent transactions are inadequate, more extensive examination of supporting documentation is necessary.

Existing Acquisitions Are Recorded (Completeness) Failure to record the acquisition of goods and services received directly affects the balance in accounts payable and may result in an overstatement of net income and owners' equity. Therefore, auditors are usually very concerned with the completeness objective. In some instances, it may be difficult to perform tests of details to determine whether there are unrecorded transactions, and the auditor must rely on controls for this purpose. In addition, because the audit of accounts payable generally takes a considerable amount of audit time, effective internal controls, properly tested, can significantly reduce audit costs.

Acquisitions Are Accurately Recorded (Accuracy) Because the accuracy of many asset, liability, and expense accounts depends on the correct recording of transactions in the acquisitions journal, the extent of tests of details of many balance sheet and expense accounts depends on the auditor's evaluation of the effectiveness of the internal controls over the accuracy of recorded acquisitions transactions. For example, if the auditor believes that the

TABLE 14-2 Summary of Transaction-Related Audit Objectives, Key Controls, Tests of Controls, and Substantive Tests of Transactions for Acquisitions

Transaction-Related Audit Objective	Key Internal Control	Common Test of Control	Common Substantive Tests of Transactions
Recorded acquisitions are for goods and services received, consistent with the best interests of the client (existence).	Purchase requisition, purchase order, receiving report, and vendor's invoice are attached to the voucher.* Acquisitions are approved at the proper level. Computer accepts entry of purchases only from authorized vendors in the vendor master file. Documents are cancelled to prevent their reuse. Vendors' invoices, receiving reports, purchase orders, and purchase requisitions are internally verified.*	Examine documents in voucher package for existence. Examine indication of approval. Attempt to input transactions with valid and invalid vendors. Examine indication of cancellation. Examine indication of internal verification.	Review the acquisitions journal, general ledger, and accounts payable master file for large or unusual amounts.† Examine underlying documents for reasonableness and authenticity (vendors' invoices, receiving reports, purchase orders, and purchase requisitions).* Examine vendor master file for unusual vendors. Trace inventory acquisitions to inventory master file. Examine fixed assets acquired.
Existing acquisition transactions are recorded (completeness).	Purchase orders are prenumbered and accounted for. Receiving reports are prenumbered and accounted for.* Vouchers are prenumbered and accounted for.	Account for a sequence of purchase orders. Account for a sequence of receiving reports. Account for a sequence of vouchers.	Trace from a file of receiving reports to the acquisitions journal.* Trace from a file of vendors' invoices to the acquisitions journal.
Recorded acquisition transactions are accurate (accuracy).	Calculations and amounts are internally verified. Batch totals are compared with computer summary reports. Acquisitions are approved for prices and discounts.	Examine indication of internal verification. Examine file of batch totals for initials of data control clerk; compare totals to summary reports. Examine indication of approval.	Compare recorded transactions in the acquisitions journal with the vendor's invoice, receiving report, and other supporting documentation.* Recompute the clerical accuracy on the vendor's invoice, including discounts and freight.
Acquisition transactions are properly classified (classification).	An adequate chart of accounts is used. Account classifications are internally verified.	Examine procedures manual and chart of accounts. Examine indication of internal verification.	Compare classification with chart of accounts by reference to vendors' invoices.
Acquisition transactions are recorded on the correct dates (timing).	Procedures require recording transactions as soon as possible after the goods and services have been received. Dates are internally verified.	Examine procedures manual and observe whether unrecorded vendors' invoices exist. Examine indication of internal verification.	Compare dates of receiving reports and vendors' invoices with dates in the acquisitions journal.*
Acquisition transactions are properly included in the accounts payable and inventory master files and are properly summarized (posting and summarization).	Accounts payable master file contents are internally verified. Accounts payable master file or trial balance totals are compared with general ledger balances.	Examine indication of internal verification. Examine initials on general ledger accounts indicating comparison.	Test clerical accuracy by footing the journals and tracing postings to general ledger and accounts payable and inventory master files.

*Receiving reports are used only for tangible goods and are therefore not used for services, such as utilities and repairs and maintenance. Often, vendors' invoices are the only documentation available.

†This analytical procedure can also apply to other objectives, including completeness, accuracy, and timing.

fixed assets are correctly recorded in the books of original entry, it is acceptable to vouch fewer current period acquisitions than if the controls are inadequate.

When a client uses perpetual inventory records, the tests of details of inventory can also be significantly reduced if the auditor believes the perpetual records are accurate. The controls over the acquisitions included in the perpetual records are normally tested as a part of the tests of controls and substantive tests of transactions for acquisitions. The inclusion of both quantity and unit costs in the inventory perpetual records permits a reduction in the tests of the physical count and the unit costs of inventory if the controls are operating effectively.

Acquisitions Are Correctly Classified (Classification) The tests of details of certain individual accounts can be reduced if the auditor believes that internal controls are adequate to provide reasonable assurance of correct classification in the acquisitions journal. Although all accounts are affected to some degree by effective controls over classification, the two areas most affected are current period acquisitions of fixed assets and all expense accounts, such as repairs and maintenance, utilities, and advertising. Because performing documentation tests of current period fixed asset acquisitions and expense accounts for accuracy and classification are relatively time-consuming audit procedures, the time-savings can be significant when controls are effective.

Design Tests of Controls and Substantive Tests of Transactions for Cash Disbursements

The same format used in Table 14-2 for acquisitions is also used in Table 14-3 for cash disbursements. The assumption underlying these controls and audit procedures is separate cash disbursements and acquisitions journals. The comments about the methodology and process for developing audit procedures for acquisitions apply equally to cash disbursements.

Once the auditor has decided on procedures, the acquisitions and cash disbursements tests are typically performed concurrently. For example, for a transaction selected for examination from the acquisitions journal, the vendor's invoice and the receiving report are examined at the same time as the related cancelled check. Thus, the verification is done efficiently without reducing the effectiveness of the tests.

Audit Sampling for Tests of Controls and Substantive Tests of Transactions

Because of the importance of tests of controls and substantive tests of transactions for acquisitions and cash disbursements, the use of audit sampling is common in this audit area. The approach is similar to that used for the tests of controls and substantive tests of transactions for sales discussed in Chapter 13. With reference to the most essential transaction-related audit objectives presented earlier, however, it should be noted that most of the important attributes in the acquisition and payment cycle have a direct monetary effect on the accounts. Furthermore, many of the types of errors and fraud that may be found represent a misstatement of earnings and are of significant concern to the auditor. For example, there may be inventory cutoff misstatements or an incorrect recording of an expense amount. Because of this, the tolerable exception rate selected by the auditor in tests of many of the attributes in this cycle is relatively low. Because the dollar amounts of individual transactions in the cycle cover a wide range, it is also common to segregate large and unusual items and to test them on a 100 percent basis.

METHODOLOGY FOR DESIGNING TESTS OF DETAILS OF BALANCES FOR ACCOUNTS PAYABLE

OBJECTIVE 14-5

Describe the methodology for designing tests of details of balances for accounts payable using the audit risk model.

Because all acquisition and payment cycle transactions typically flow through accounts payable, this account is critical to any audit of the acquisition and payment cycle. If tests of controls and related substantive tests of transactions show that controls are operating effectively, the auditor may be able to reduce analytical procedures and tests of details of balances for accounts payable. However, because accounts payable tend to be material for many companies, auditors almost always perform extensive analytical procedures and some tests of details of balances of that account.

Accounts payable are *unpaid obligations* for goods and services received in the ordinary course of business. It is sometimes difficult to distinguish between accounts payable and accrued liabilities, but it is useful to define a liability as an account payable if the total amount of the obligation is *known and owed at the balance sheet date.* The accounts payable account therefore includes obligations for the acquisition of raw materials, equipment, utilities, repairs, and many other types of goods and services that were received before the end of the year. Most accounts payable can also be identified by the existence of vendors' invoices for the obligation. Accounts payable should also be distinguished from

A/P Recap

TABLE 14-3 Summary of Transaction-Related Audit Objectives, Key Controls, Tests of Controls, and Substantive Tests of Transactions for Cash Disbursements

Transaction-Related Audit Objective	Key Internal Control	Common Test of Control	Common Substantive Tests of Transactions
Recorded cash disbursements are for goods and services actually received (existence).	There is adequate segregation of duties between accounts payable and custody of signed checks. Supporting documentation is examined before signing of checks by an authorized person. Approval of payment on supporting documents at the time checks are signed.	Discuss with personnel and observe activities. Discuss with personnel and observe activities. Examine indication of approval.	Review the cash disbursements journal, general ledger, and accounts payable master file for large or unusual amounts.* Trace the cancelled check to the related acquisitions journal entry and examine for payee name and amount. Examine cancelled check for authorized signature, proper endorsement, and cancellation by the bank. Examine supporting documents as a part of the tests of acquisitions.
Existing cash disbursement transactions are recorded (completeness).	Checks are prenumbered and accounted for. The bank reconciliation is prepared monthly by an employee independent of recording cash disbursements or custody of assets.	Account for a sequence of checks. Examine bank reconciliations and observe their preparation.	Reconcile recorded cash disbursements with the cash disbursements on the bank statement.
Recorded cash disbursement transactions are accurate (accuracy).	Calculations and amounts are internally verified. The bank reconciliation is prepared monthly by an independent person.	Examine indication of internal verification. Examine bank reconciliations and observe their preparation.	Compare cancelled checks with the related acquisitions journal and cash disbursements journal entries. Recompute cash discounts.
Cash disbursement transactions are properly classified (classification).	An adequate chart of accounts is used. Account classifications are internally verified.	Examine procedures manual and chart of accounts. Examine indication of internal verification.	Compare classification with chart of accounts by reference to vendors' invoices and acquisitions journal.
Cash disbursement transactions are recorded on the correct dates (timing).	Procedures require recording of transactions as soon as possible after the check has been signed. Dates are internally verified.	Examine procedures manual and observe whether unrecorded checks exist. Examine indication of internal verification.	Compare dates on cancelled checks with the cash disbursements journal. Compare dates on cancelled checks with the bank cancellation date.
Cash disbursement transactions are properly included in the accounts payable master file and are properly summarized (posting and summarization).	Accounts payable master file contents are internally verified. Accounts payable master file or trial balance totals are compared with general ledger balances.	Examine indication of internal verification. Examine initials on general ledger accounts indicating comparison.	Test clerical accuracy by footing journals and tracing postings to general ledger and accounts payable master file.

*This analytical procedure can also apply to other objectives, including completeness, accuracy, and timing.

interest-bearing obligations. If an obligation includes the payment of interest, it should be recorded as a note payable, contract payable, mortgage payable, or bond payable.

The methodology for designing tests of details for accounts payable is the same as that used for accounts receivable in Chapter 12.

Identify Client Business Risks Affecting Accounts Payable

The recent focus by many companies on improving their supply-chain management activities has led to numerous changes in the design of systems used to initiate and record acquisition and payment activities. Efforts to streamline the purchasing of goods and services, including greater emphasis on just-in-time inventory purchasing, increased sharing of information with suppliers, and the use of technology and e-commerce to transact business, are changing all aspects of the acquisition and payment cycle for many companies. These arrangements and systems can be complex.

Significant client business risks are likely to arise from these changes. For example, suppliers may have greater access to accounts payable records, allowing them to continually monitor the status of payable balances and to perform detailed reconciliations of transactions. Also, increased focus on improving the logistics of physically moving inventory throughout a company's distribution chain may increase the difficulty of establishing effective cutoff of accounts payable balances at period end. The auditor should understand the nature of changes to these systems to identify whether client business risks and related management controls affect the likelihood of material misstatements in accounts payable.

Set Tolerable Misstatement and Assess Inherent Risk

Like accounts receivable, there are typically a large number of transactions affecting accounts payable, the balance is often made up of a large number of accounts, the balance is large, and it is relatively expensive to audit the account. For these reasons, auditors typically set tolerable misstatement for accounts payable relatively high. For the same reasons, the auditor also often assesses inherent risk as medium or high. Auditors are usually especially concerned about the completeness and the cutoff balance-related audit objectives for accounts payable because of the potential for understatements in the account balance.

Assess Control Risk and Design and Perform Tests of Controls and Substantive Tests of Transactions

Once the auditor sets tolerable misstatement and inherent risk for accounts payable, the auditor uses his or her understanding of internal control to assess control risk. The auditor's ultimate substantive tests depend on the relative effectiveness of internal controls related to accounts payable. Therefore, it is important to have an understanding of how these controls relate to accounts payable.

The effects of the client's internal controls on accounts payable tests can be illustrated by two examples. In the first, assume that the client has highly effective internal controls over recording and paying for acquisitions. The receipt of goods is promptly documented by prenumbered receiving reports; prenumbered vouchers are promptly and efficiently prepared and recorded in the acquisition transactions file and the accounts payable master file. Cash disbursements are also made promptly when due and immediately recorded in the cash disbursements transactions file and the accounts payable master file. Individual accounts payable balances in the master file are reconciled monthly with vendors' statements, and the computer automatically reconciles the master file total to the general ledger. Under these circumstances, the verification of accounts payable should require little audit effort once the auditor concludes that internal controls are operating effectively.

In the second example, assume that receiving reports are not used, the client defers recording acquisitions until cash disbursements are made, and because of a weak cash position, bills are often paid several months after their due date. When an auditor faces such a situation, there is a high likelihood of an understatement of accounts payable; therefore, extensive tests of details of accounts payable are necessary to determine whether accounts payable is properly stated on the balance sheet date.

The most important controls over accounts payable and the related tests of controls and substantive tests of transactions were discussed earlier in this chapter. In addition to those controls, it is important to have a monthly reconciliation of vendors' statements with recorded liabilities and the accounts payable master file with the general ledger. This should be done by an independent person or by the computer.

After assessing control risk, the auditor designs and performs tests of controls and substantive tests of transactions for the acquisitions and cash disbursements. These procedures were discussed in detail earlier in this chapter and are not repeated here.

Design and Perform Analytical Procedures

OBJECTIVE 14-6

Design and perform analytical procedures for accounts payable.

The use of analytical procedures is as important in the acquisition and payment cycle as it is in every other cycle, especially for uncovering misstatements in accounts payable. Table 14-4 illustrates analytical procedures for the balance sheet and income statement accounts in the acquisition and payment cycle that are useful for uncovering areas in which additional investigation is desirable.

One of the most important analytical procedures for uncovering misstatements of accounts payable is comparing current year expense totals with prior years. For example, by comparing utilities expense with the prior year, the auditor may determine that the last utilities bill for the year was not recorded. Comparing expenses with prior years is an effective analytical procedure for accounts payable when expenses from year to year are expected to be relatively stable. Typical examples include rent, utilities, and other expenses billed on a regular basis.

Design and Perform Tests of Details of Accounts Payable Balance

OBJECTIVE 14-7

Design and perform tests of details of balances for accounts payable, including out-of-period liability tests.

The overall objective in the audit of accounts payable is to determine whether the accounts payable balance is fairly stated and properly disclosed. Eight of the nine balance-related audit objectives discussed in Chapter 5 are applicable to accounts payable. Realizable value is not applicable to liabilities.

The auditor should recognize the difference in emphasis between the audit of liabilities and the audit of assets. When assets are being verified, attention is focused on making certain that the balance in the account is not overstated. The existence of recorded assets is constantly questioned and verified by confirmation, physical examination, and examination of supporting documents. The auditor should certainly not ignore the possibility of assets being understated, but the auditor is more concerned about the possibility of overstatement than understatement. The opposite approach is taken in verifying liability balances; that is, the main focus is on understated or omitted liabilities.

The difference in emphasis in auditing assets and liabilities results directly from the *legal liability of CPAs.* If equity investors, creditors, and other users determine subsequent to the issuance of the audited financial statements that owners' equity was materially overstated, a lawsuit against the CPA firm is fairly likely. Because an overstatement of owners' equity can arise either from an overstatement of assets or from an understatement of liabilities, it is natural for CPAs to emphasize those two types of misstatements. The probability of a successful lawsuit against a CPA for failing to discover an understatement of owners' equity is far less likely.

TABLE 14-4 Analytical Procedures for the Acquisition and Payment Cycle

Analytical Procedure	Possible Misstatement
Compare acquisition-related expense account balances with prior years.	Misstatement of accounts payable and expenses.
Review list of accounts payable for unusual, nonvendor, and interest-bearing payables.	Classification misstatement for nontrade liabilities.
Compare individual accounts payable with previous years.	Unrecorded or nonexistent accounts, or misstatements.
Calculate ratios such as purchases divided by accounts payable, and accounts payable divided by current liabilities.	Unrecorded or nonexistent accounts, or misstatements.

Nevertheless, the auditing profession must avoid too much emphasis on protecting users from overstatements of owners' equity at the expense of ignoring understatements. If assets are consistently understated and liabilities are consistently overstated for large numbers of audited companies, the decision-making value of financial statement information is likely to decline. Therefore, even though it is natural for auditors to emphasize the possibility of overstating assets and understating liabilities, uncovering the opposite types of misstatements is also a significant responsibility.

The same balance-related audit objectives that were used as a frame of reference for verifying accounts receivable in Chapter 12 are also applicable to liabilities, with three minor modifications. The most obvious difference in verifying liabilities is the nonapplicability of the realizable value objective. The second difference is in the rights and obligations objective. For assets, the auditor is concerned with the client's rights to the use and disposal of the assets. For liabilities, the auditor is concerned with the client's obligations for the payment of the liability. If the client has no obligation to pay a liability, it should not be included as a liability. The third difference was discussed earlier: In auditing liabilities, the emphasis is on the search for understatements rather than for overstatements.

Table 14-5 includes the balance-related audit objectives and common tests of details of balances procedures for accounts payable. The actual audit procedures will vary considerably depending on the nature of the entity, the materiality of accounts payable, the nature and effectiveness of internal controls, and inherent risk.

TABLE 14-5 Balance-Related Audit Objectives and Tests of Details of Balances for Accounts Payable

Balance-Related Audit Objective	Common Tests of Details of Balances Procedures	Comments
Accounts payable in the accounts payable list agree with related master file, and the total is correctly added and agrees with the general ledger (detail tie-in).	Re-add or use the computer to total the accounts payable list. Trace the total to the general ledger. Trace individual vendors' invoices to master file for names and amounts.	All pages need not ordinarily be footed if footing manually. Unless controls are weak, tracing to master file should be limited.
Accounts payable in the accounts payable list exist (existence).	Trace from accounts payable list to vendors' invoices and statements. Confirm accounts payable, emphasizing large and unusual amounts.	Ordinarily receives little attention because the primary concern is with understatements.
Existing accounts payable are included in the accounts payable list (completeness).	Perform out-of-period liability tests (see discussion).	These are essential audit tests for accounts payable.
Accounts payable in the accounts payable list are accurate (accuracy).	Perform same procedures as those used for existence objective and out-of-period liability tests.	Ordinarily, the emphasis in these procedures for accuracy is understatement rather than omission.
Accounts payable in the accounts payable list are properly classified (classification).	Review the list and master file for related parties, notes or other interest-bearing liabilities, long-term payables, and debit balances.	Knowledge of the client's business is essential for these tests.
Transactions in the acquisition and payment cycle are recorded in the proper period (cutoff).	Perform out-of-period liability tests (see discussion). Perform detailed tests as a part of physical observation of inventory (see discussion). Test for inventory in transit (see discussion).	These are essential audit tests for accounts payable. These are called *cutoff* tests.
The company has an obligation to pay the liabilities included in accounts payable (obligations).	Examine vendors' statements and confirm accounts payable.	Normally, not a concern in the audit of accounts payable because all accounts payable are obligations.
Accounts in the acquisition and payment cycle are properly presented and disclosed (presentation and disclosure).	Review statements to make sure material related parties, long-term, and interest-bearing liabilities are segregated.	Ordinarily not a problem.

Out-of-Period Liability Tests Because of the emphasis on understatements in liability accounts, *out-of-period liability tests* are important for accounts payable. The extent of tests to uncover unrecorded accounts payable, often called the *search for unrecorded accounts payable,* depends heavily on assessed control risk and the materiality of the potential balance in the account. The same audit procedures used to uncover unrecorded payables are applicable to the accuracy objective. The audit procedures that follow are typical tests.

Examine Underlying Documentation for Subsequent Cash Disbursements The purpose of this audit procedure is to uncover cash disbursements made in the subsequent accounting period that represent liabilities at the balance sheet date. Supporting documentation is examined to determine whether a cash disbursement was for a current period obligation. The receiving report indicates the date inventory was received and is therefore an especially useful document. Similarly, the vendor's invoice often indicates the date services were provided. Often, documentation for cash disbursements made in the subsequent period is examined for several weeks, especially when the client does not pay bills on a timely basis. Any cash disbursement that is for a current period obligation should be traced to the accounts payable trial balance to make sure that it has been included as a liability.

Examine Underlying Documentation for Bills Not Paid Several Weeks After the Year-End This procedure is carried out in the same manner as the preceding one and serves the same purpose. The only difference is that it is done for unpaid obligations near the end of the audit field work rather than for obligations that have already been paid. For example, in an audit with a March 31 year-end, if the auditor examines the supporting documentation for checks paid until June 28, bills that are still unpaid at that date should be examined to determine whether they are obligations at March 31.

Trace Receiving Reports Issued Before Year-End to Related Vendors' Invoices All merchandise received before the year-end of the accounting period, indicated by the issuance of a receiving report, should be included as accounts payable. By tracing receiving reports issued at and before year-end to vendors' invoices and making sure that they are included in accounts payable, the auditor is testing for unrecorded obligations.

Trace Vendors' Statements That Show a Balance Due to the Accounts Payable Trial Balance If the client maintains a file of vendors' statements, any statement indicating a balance due at the balance sheet date can be traced to the listing to make sure that it is included as an account payable.

Send Confirmations to Vendors with Which the Client Does Business Although the use of confirmations for accounts payable is less common than for accounts receivable, it is often used to test for vendors omitted from the accounts payable list, omitted transactions, and misstated account balances. Sending confirmations to active vendors for which a balance has not been included in the accounts payable list is a useful means of searching for omitted amounts. This type of confirmation is commonly called zero balance confirmation. Additional discussion of confirmation of accounts payable is deferred until the end of this chapter.

Cutoff Tests **Cutoff tests** for accounts payable are intended to determine whether transactions recorded a few days before and after the balance sheet date are included in the correct period. The five out-of-period liability audit tests just discussed are directly related to cutoff for acquisitions, but they emphasize understatements. For the first three procedures, it is also appropriate to examine supporting documentation as a test of overstatement of accounts payable. For example, the third procedure is to trace receiving reports issued before year-end to related vendors' invoices in order to test for unrecorded accounts payable. To test for overstatement cutoff amounts, the auditor should trace receiving reports issued *after* year-end to related invoices to make sure that they are not recorded as accounts payable (unless they are inventory in transit, which is discussed shortly).

Because most cutoff tests have already been discussed, only two aspects are expanded on here: the relationship of cutoff to physical observation of inventory and the determination of the amount of inventory in transit.

Relationship of Cutoff to Physical Observation of Inventory In determining that the accounts payable cutoff is correct, *it is essential that the cutoff tests be coordinated with the physical observation of inventory.* For example, assume that an inventory acquisition for $400,000 is received late in the afternoon of December 31, after the physical inventory is completed. If the acquisition is included in accounts payable and purchases but excluded from inventory, the result is an understatement of net earnings of $400,000. Conversely, if the acquisition is excluded from both inventory and accounts payable, there is a misstatement in the balance sheet but the income statement is correct. The only way the auditor will know which type of misstatement has occurred is to coordinate cutoff tests with the observation of inventory.

The cutoff information for acquisitions should be obtained *during the physical observation* of the inventory. At this time, the auditor should review the procedures in the receiving department to determine that all inventory received was counted, and the auditor should record in the audit documentation the last receiving report number of inventory included in the physical count. During the year-end field work, the auditor should then test the accounting records for cutoff. The auditor should trace receiving report numbers to the accounts payable records to verify that they are correctly included or excluded.

For example, assume that the last receiving report number representing inventory included in the physical count was 3167. The auditor should record this document number and subsequently trace it and several preceding numbers to their related vendors' invoices and to the accounts payable list or the accounts payable master file to determine that they are all included. Similarly, accounts payable for acquisitions recorded on receiving reports with numbers larger than 3167 should be excluded from accounts payable.

When the client's physical inventory takes place before the last day of the year, it is still necessary to perform an accounts payable cutoff at the time of the physical count in the manner described in the preceding paragraph. In addition, the auditor must verify whether all acquisitions taking place between the physical count and the end of the year were added to the physical inventory and accounts payable. For example, if the client takes the physical count on December 27 for a December 31 year-end, the cutoff information is taken as of December 27. During the year-end field work, the auditor must first test to determine whether the cutoff was accurate as of December 27. After determining that the December 27 cutoff is accurate, the auditor must test whether all inventory received subsequent to the physical count, but on or before the balance sheet date, was added to inventory and accounts payable by the client.

Inventory in Transit A distinction in accounts payable must be made between acquisitions of inventory that are on an **FOB destination** basis and those that are made **FOB origin.** With the former, title passes to the buyer when it is received for inventory. Therefore, only inventory received on or before the balance sheet date should be included in inventory and accounts payable at year-end. When an acquisition is on an FOB origin basis, the inventory and related accounts payable must be recorded in the current period if shipment occurred on or before the balance sheet date.

Determining whether inventory has been acquired on an FOB destination or origin basis is done by examining vendors' invoices. The auditor should examine invoices for merchandise received shortly after year-end to determine whether they were on an FOB origin basis. For those that were, and when the shipment dates were on or before the balance sheet date, the inventory and related accounts payable must be recorded in the current period if the amounts are material.

Reliability of Evidence

OBJECTIVE 14-8

Distinguish the reliability of vendors' invoices, vendors' statements, and confirmations of accounts payable as audit evidence.

In deciding the appropriate evidence for verifying accounts payable, it is essential that the auditor understand the relative reliability of the three primary types of evidence ordinarily used: vendors' invoices, vendors' statements, and confirmations.

Distinction Between Vendors' Invoices and Vendors' Statements In verifying the amount due to a vendor, the auditor should make a distinction between vendors' invoices and vendors' statements. In examining vendors' invoices and related supporting documents, such as receiving reports and purchase orders, the auditor gets highly reliable *evidence about individual transactions.* A vendor's statement is not as desirable as invoices for verifying individual transactions because a statement includes only the total amount of the transaction. The units acquired, price, freight, and other data are not included. However, a statement has the advantage of including the ending balance according to the vendor's records. Which of these two documents is better for verifying the correct balance in accounts payable? *The vendor's statement is superior for verifying accounts payable* because it includes the ending balance. The auditor could compare existing vendors' invoices with the client's list and still not uncover missing ones, which is the primary concern in accounts payable. Which of these two documents is better for testing acquisitions in tests of controls and substantive tests of transactions? *The vendor's invoice is superior for verifying transactions* because the auditor is verifying individual transactions and the invoice shows the details of the acquisitions.

Difference Between Vendors' Statements and Confirmations The most important distinction between a vendor's statement and a confirmation of accounts payable is the source of the information. A vendor's statement has been prepared by an independent third party but is in the hands of the client at the time the auditor examines it. This provides the client with an opportunity to alter a vendor's statement or to not make certain statements available to the auditor. A confirmation of accounts payable, which normally is a request for an itemized statement sent directly to the CPA's office, provides the same information but can be regarded as more reliable. In addition, confirmations of accounts payable often include a request for information about notes and acceptances payable as well as consigned inventory owned by the vendor but stored on the client's premises. An illustration of a typical accounts payable confirmation request is given in Figure 14-2.

Because of the availability of vendors' statements and vendors' invoices, which are both relatively reliable evidence because they originate from a third party, the confirmation of accounts payable is less common than confirmation of accounts receivable. If the client has adequate internal controls and vendors' statements are available for examination, confirmations are normally not sent. However, when the client's internal controls are weak, when statements are not available, or when the auditor questions the client's

FIGURE 14-2 Accounts Payable Confirmation Request

ROGER MEAD, INC. January 15, 2003
Jones Sales, Inc.
2116 Stewart Street
Wayneville, Kentucky 36021

Gentlemen:

Our auditors, Murray and Rogers, CPAs, are conducting an audit of our financial statements. For this purpose, please furnish them with the following information as of December 31, 2002.

(1) Itemized statements of our accounts payable to you showing all unpaid items;
(2) A complete list of any notes and acceptances payable to you (including any which have been discounted) showing the original date, dates due, original amount, unpaid balance, collateral, and endorsers; and
(3) An itemized list of your merchandise consigned to us.

Your prompt attention to this request will be appreciated. An envelope is enclosed for your reply.

Yours truly,

Phil Geriovini

Phil Geriovini, President

integrity, it is desirable to send confirmation requests to vendors. Because of the emphasis on understatements of liability accounts, the accounts confirmed should include large, active, zero balance accounts and a representative sample of all others.

In most instances in which accounts payable are confirmed, it is done shortly after the balance sheet date. However, if assessed control risk is low, it may be possible to confirm accounts payable at an interim date as a test of the effectiveness of internal controls. Then if the confirmations indicate that the internal controls are ineffective, it is possible to design other audit procedures to test accounts payable at year-end.

When vendors' statements are examined or confirmations received, there must be a *reconciliation* of the statement or confirmation with the accounts payable list. Differences are often caused by inventory in transit, checks mailed by the client but not received by the vendor at the statement date, and delays in processing the accounting records. The reconciliation is of the same general nature as that discussed in Chapter 12 for accounts receivable. The documents typically used to reconcile the balances on the accounts payable list with the confirmations or vendors' statements include receiving reports, vendors' invoices, and cancelled checks.

Sample Size

The discussion of tests of details of the accounts payable balance has focused heavily on the typical audit procedures performed, the documents and records examined, and the timing of the tests. The auditor must also consider sample sizes in the audit of accounts payable.

Sample sizes for accounts payable tests vary considerably, depending on such factors as the materiality of accounts payable, number of accounts outstanding, assessed control risk, and results of the prior year. When a client's internal controls are weak, which is not uncommon for accounts payable, almost all population items must be verified. In other situations, minimal testing is needed.

SUMMARY

The five types of audit tests discussed in earlier chapters are used to obtain audit assurance for transactions and accounts in the acquisition and payment cycle. Procedures to gain an understanding of internal control and tests of controls evaluate whether controls over transactions in the cycle are operating effectively to reduce control risk and thereby reduce substantive testing of ending balances in the related accounts. By combining all types of audit tests, the auditor obtains a higher overall assurance for transactions and accounts in the acquisition and payment cycle than the assurance obtained from any one test. To increase overall assurance for the cycle, the auditor can increase the assurance obtained from any one of the tests.

ESSENTIAL TERMS

Acquisition and payment cycle—the transaction cycle that includes the acquisition of and payment for goods and services from suppliers outside the organization

Cutoff tests—tests to determine whether transactions recorded a few days before and after the balance sheet date are included in the correct period

FOB destination—shipping contract in which title to the goods passes to the buyer when the goods are received

FOB origin—shipping contract in which title to the goods passes to the buyer at the time that the goods are shipped

REVIEW QUESTIONS

14-1 **(Objective 14-1)** List five asset accounts, three liability accounts, and five expense accounts included in the acquisition and payment cycle for a typical manufacturing company.

14-2 **(Objective 14-4)** List one possible internal control for each of the six transaction-related audit objectives for cash disbursements. For each control, list a test of control to test its effectiveness.

14-3 **(Objective 14-4)** List one possible control for each of the six transaction-related audit objectives for acquisitions. For each control, list a test of control to test its effectiveness.

14-4 **(Objective 14-4)** Evaluate the following statement by an auditor concerning tests of acquisitions and cash disbursements: "In selecting the acquisitions and cash disbursements sample for testing, the best approach is to select a random month and test every transaction for the period. Using this approach enables me to thoroughly understand internal control because I have examined everything that happened during the period. As a part of the monthly test, I also test the beginning and ending bank reconciliations. At the completion of these tests I feel I can evaluate the effectiveness of internal control."

14-5 **(Objective 14-4)** What is the importance of cash discounts to the client and how can the auditor verify whether they are being taken in accordance with company policy?

14-6 **(Objective 14-4)** What are the similarities and differences in the objectives of the following two procedures? (1) Select a random sample of receiving reports and trace them to related vendors' invoices and acquisitions journal entries, comparing the vendor's name, type of material and quantity acquired, and total amount of the acquisition. (2) Select a random sample of acquisitions journal entries and trace them to related vendors' invoices and receiving reports, comparing the vendor's name, type of material and quantity acquired, and total amount of the acquisition.

14-7 **(Objectives 14-2, 14-4)** If an audit client does not have prenumbered checks, what type of misstatement has a greater chance of occurring? Under the circumstances, what audit procedure can the auditor use to compensate for the weakness?

14-8 **(Objective 14-2)** What is meant by a voucher? Explain how its use can improve an organization's internal controls.

14-9 **(Objective 14-2)** Explain why most auditors consider the receipt of goods and services the most important point in the acquisition and payment cycle.

14-10 **(Objectives 14-4, 14-7)** Explain the relationship between tests of the acquisition and payment cycle and tests of inventory. Give specific examples of how these two types of tests affect each other.

14-11 **(Objectives 14-4, 14-5)** Explain the relationship between tests of the acquisition and payment cycle and tests of accounts payable. Give specific examples of how these two types of tests affect each other.

14-12 **(Objective 14-7)** The CPA examines all unrecorded invoices on hand as of February 29, 2003, the last day of field work. Which of the following misstatements is most likely to be uncovered by this procedure? Explain.

a. Accounts payable are overstated at December 31, 2002.
b. Accounts payable are understated at December 31, 2002.
c. Operating expenses are overstated for the 12 months ended December 31, 2002.
d. Operating expenses are overstated for the two months ended February 29, 2003.*

14-13 **(Objective 14-8)** Explain why it is common for auditors to send confirmation requests to vendors with "zero balances" on the client's accounts payable listing but uncommon to follow the same approach in verifying accounts receivable.

14-14 **(Objectives 14-2, 14-8)** Distinguish between a vendor's invoice and a vendor's statement. Which document should ideally be used as evidence in auditing acquisition transactions and which for verifying accounts payable balances? Why?

14-15 **(Objective 14-8)** It is less common to confirm accounts payable at an interim date than accounts receivable. Explain why.

14-16 **(Objective 14-7)** In testing the cutoff of accounts payable at the balance sheet date, explain why it is important that auditors coordinate their tests with the physical observation of inventory. What can the auditor do during the physical inventory to enhance the likelihood of an accurate cutoff?

14-17 **(Objective 14-7)** Distinguish between FOB destination and FOB origin. What procedures should the auditor follow concerning acquisitions of inventory on an FOB origin basis near year-end?

MULTIPLE CHOICE QUESTIONS FROM CPA EXAMINATIONS

14-18 **(Objective 14-4)** The following questions concern internal controls in the acquisition and payment cycle. Choose the best response.

a. Effective internal control over the purchasing of raw materials should usually include all of the following procedures except
   (1) systematic reporting of product changes that will affect raw materials.
   (2) determining the need for the raw materials prior to preparing the purchase order.

*AICPA adapted.

(3) obtaining third-party, written quality and quantity reports prior to payment for the raw materials.
(4) obtaining financial approval prior to making a commitment.

b. Budd, the purchasing agent of Lake Hardware Wholesalers, has a relative who owns a retail hardware store. Budd arranged for hardware to be delivered by manufacturers to the retail store on a COD basis, thereby enabling his relative to buy at Lake's wholesale prices. Budd was probably able to accomplish this because of Lake's poor internal control over
(1) purchase requisitions.
(2) cash receipts.
(3) perpetual inventory records.
(4) purchase orders.

c. Which of the following is an internal control that would prevent paid cash disbursement documents from being presented for payment a second time?
(1) Unsigned checks should be prepared by individuals who are responsible for signing checks.
(2) Cash disbursement documents should be approved by at least two responsible management officials.
(3) The date on cash disbursement documents should be within a few days of the date that the document is presented for payment.
(4) The official signing the check should compare the check with the documents and should deface the documents.

14-19 (Objectives 14-7, 14-8) The following questions concern accumulating evidence in the acquisition and payment cycle. Choose the best response.

a. In comparing the confirmation of accounts payable with suppliers and confirmation of accounts receivable with debtors, the true statement is that
(1) confirmation of accounts payable with suppliers is a more widely accepted auditing procedure than is confirmation of accounts receivable with debtors.
(2) sampling techniques are more widely accepted in the confirmation of accounts payable than in the confirmation of accounts receivable.
(3) as compared with the confirmation of accounts payable, the confirmation of accounts receivable will tend to emphasize accounts with zero balances at the balance sheet date.
(4) it is less likely that the confirmation request sent to the supplier will show the amount owed than that the request sent to the debtor will show the amount due.

b. Which of the following audit procedures is best for identifying unrecorded trade accounts payable?
(1) Examining unusual relationships between monthly accounts payable balances and recorded cash payments.
(2) Reconciling vendors' statements to the file of receiving reports to identify items received just prior to the balance sheet date.
(3) Reviewing cash disbursements recorded subsequent to the balance sheet date to determine whether the related payables apply to the prior period.
(4) Investigating payables recorded just prior to and just subsequent to the balance sheet date to determine whether they are supported by receiving reports.

c. In auditing accounts payable, an auditor's procedures most likely would focus primarily on management's assertion of
(1) existence or occurrence.
(2) presentation and disclosure.
(3) completeness.
(4) valuation or allocation.

DISCUSSION QUESTIONS AND PROBLEMS

14-20 (Objective 14-4) Questions 1 through 8 are typically found in questionnaires used by auditors to obtain an understanding of internal control in the acquisition and payment cycle. In using the questionnaire for a client, a "yes" response to a question indicates a possible internal control, whereas a "no" indicates a potential weakness.

1. Is the purchasing function performed by personnel who are independent of the receiving and shipping functions and the payables and disbursing functions?
2. Are all vendors' invoices routed directly to accounting from the mailroom?
3. Are all receiving reports prenumbered and the numerical sequence checked by a person independent of check preparation?

4. Are all extensions, footings, discounts, and freight terms on vendors' invoices checked for accuracy?
5. Does a responsible employee review and approve the invoice account distribution before the transaction is entered in the computer?
6. Are checks automatically posted in the cash disbursements journal as they are prepared?
7. Are all supporting documents properly cancelled at the time the checks are signed?
8. Is the custody of checks after signature and before mailing handled by an employee independent of all payable, disbursing, cash, and general ledger functions?

Required

a. For each of the preceding questions, state the transaction-related audit objective(s) being fulfilled if the control is in effect.

b. For each internal control, list a test of control to test its effectiveness.

c. For each of the preceding questions, identify the nature of the potential financial misstatement(s) if the control is not in effect.

d. For each of the potential misstatements in part c, list a substantive audit procedure that can be used to determine whether a material misstatement exists.

14-21 **(Objective 14-4)** Following are some of the tests of controls and substantive tests of transactions procedures commonly performed in the acquisition and payment cycle. Each is to be done on a sample basis.

1. Trace transactions recorded in the acquisitions journal to supporting documentation, comparing the vendor's name, total dollar amounts, and authorization for acquisition.
2. Account for a sequence of receiving reports and trace selected ones to related vendors' invoices and acquisitions journal entries.
3. Review supporting documents for clerical accuracy, propriety of account distribution, and reasonableness of expenditure in relation to the nature of the client's operations.
4. Examine documents in support of acquisition transactions to make sure that each transaction has an approved vendor's invoice, receiving report, and purchase order included.
5. Foot the cash disbursements journal, trace postings of the total to the general ledger, and trace postings of individual cash disbursements to the accounts payable master file.
6. Account for a numerical sequence of checks in the cash disbursements journal and examine all voided or spoiled checks for proper cancellation.
7. Compare dates on cancelled checks with dates on the cash disbursements journal and the bank cancellation date.

Required

a. State whether each procedure above is primarily a test of control or substantive test of transactions.

b. State the purpose(s) of each procedure.

14-22 **(Objective 14-3)** Donnen Designs, Inc. is a small manufacturer of women's casual-wear jewelry, including bracelets, necklaces, earrings, and other moderately priced accessory items. Most of their products are made from silver, various low-cost stones, beads, and other decorative jewelry pieces. Donnen Designs is not involved in the manufacturing of high-end jewelry items, such as those made of gold and semiprecious or precious stones.

Personnel responsible for purchasing raw material jewelry items for Donnen Designs would like to place orders directly with suppliers who offer their products for sale through Internet Web sites. Most suppliers provide pictures of all jewelry components on their Web sites, along with pricing and other sales-term information. Customers who have valid business licenses are able to purchase the products at wholesale, rather than retail prices. Customers can place orders online and pay for those goods immediately by using a valid credit card. Purchases made by credit card are shipped by the suppliers once the credit approval is received from the credit card agency, which usually occurs the same day. Customers can also place orders online with payment being later made by check. However, in that event, purchases are not shipped until the check is received and cashed by the supplier. Some of the suppliers allow a 30-day full-payment refund policy, whereas other suppliers accept returns but only grant credit toward future purchases from that supplier.

Required

a. Identify advantages for Donnen Designs if management allows purchasing personnel to order goods online through supplier Web sites.

b. Identify potential risks associated with Donnen Designs' purchase of jewelry pieces through supplier Internet Web sites.

c. Describe advantages of allowing purchasing agents to purchase products online using a Donnen Designs credit card.

d. Describe advantages of allowing purchasing agents to purchase products online with payment made only by check.

e. What internal controls could be implemented to ensure that
   (1) purchasing agents do not use Donnen credit cards to purchase nonjewelry items for their own purposes, if Donnen allows purchasing agents to purchase jewelry using Donnen credit cards?
   (2) purchasing agents do not order jewelry items from the suppliers and ship those items to addresses other than Donnen addresses?
   (3) Donnen does not end up with unused credits with jewelry suppliers as a result of returning unacceptable jewelry items to suppliers who only grant credit toward future purchases?

14-23 (Objectives 14-4, 14-7) The following misstatements are included in the accounting records of Westgate Manufacturing Company.

1. Telephone expense (account 2112) was unintentionally charged to repairs and maintenance (account 2121).
2. Acquisitions of raw materials are often not recorded until several weeks after the goods are received because receiving personnel fail to forward receiving reports to accounting. When pressure from a vendor's credit department is put on Westgate's accounting department, it searches for the receiving report, records the transactions in the acquisitions journal, and pays the bill.
3. The accounts payable clerk prepares a monthly check to Story Supply Company for the amount of an invoice owed and submits the unsigned check to the treasurer for payment along with related supporting documents that have already been approved. When she receives the signed check from the treasurer, she records it as a debit to accounts payable and deposits the check in a personal bank account for a company named Story Company. A few days later, she records the invoice in the acquisitions journal again, resubmits the documents and a new check to the treasurer, and sends the check to the vendor after it has been signed.
4. The amount of a check in the cash disbursements journal is recorded as $4,612.87 instead of $6,412.87.
5. The accounts payable clerk intentionally excluded from the cash disbursements journal seven larger checks written and mailed on December 26 to prevent cash in the bank from having a negative balance on the general ledger. They were recorded on January 2 of the subsequent year.
6. Each month, a fraudulent receiving report is submitted to accounting by an employee in the receiving department. A few days later, he sends Westgate an invoice for the quantity of goods ordered from a small company he owns and operates in the evening. A check is prepared, and the amount is paid when the receiving report and the vendor's invoice are matched by the accounts payable clerk.

Required

a. For each misstatement, identify the transaction-related audit objective that was not met.
b. For each misstatement, state a control that should have prevented it from occurring on a continuing basis.
c. For each misstatement, state a substantive audit procedure that could uncover it.

14-24 (Objectives 14-6, 14-7, 14-8) The following auditing procedures were performed in the audit of accounts payable:

1. Examine supporting documents for cash disbursements several days before and after year-end.
2. Examine the acquisitions and cash disbursements journals for the last few days of the current period and first few days of the succeeding period, looking for large or unusual transactions.
3. Trace from the general ledger trial balance and supporting documentation to determine whether accounts payable, related parties, and other related assets and liabilities are properly included on the financial statements.
4. For liabilities that are payable in a foreign currency, determine the exchange rate and check calculations.
5. Discuss with the bookkeeper whether any amounts included on the accounts payable list are due to related parties, debit balances, or notes payable.
6. Obtain vendors' statements from the controller and reconcile to the listing of accounts payable.
7. Obtain vendors' statements directly from vendors and reconcile to the listing of accounts payable.
8. Obtain a list of accounts payable. Re-add and compare with the general ledger.

Required

a. For each procedure, identify the type of audit evidence used.
b. For each procedure, use the following matrix to identify which balance-related audit objective(s) were satisfied. (Procedure 1 is completed as an illustration.)
c. Evaluate the need to have certain objectives satisfied by more than one audit procedure.

AUDIT PROCEDURE	BALANCE-RELATED AUDIT OBJECTIVE							
	Detail tie-in	Existence	Completeness	Accuracy	Classification	Cutoff	Obligations	Presentation and disclosure
1			X			X		
2								
3								
4								
5								
6								
7								
8								

14-25 (Objectives 14-4, 14-5) In testing cash disbursements for the Jay Klein Company, you have obtained an understanding of internal control. The controls are reasonably good, and no unusual audit problems have arisen in previous years.

Although there are not many individuals in the accounting department, there is a reasonable separation of duties in the organization. There is a separate purchasing agent who has responsibility for ordering goods and a separate receiving department for counting the goods when they are received and for preparing receiving reports. There is a separation of duties between recording acquisitions and cash disbursements, and all information is recorded in the two journals independently. The controller reviews all supporting documents before signing the checks, and he immediately mails the check to the vendor. Check copies are used for subsequent recording.

All aspects of internal control seem satisfactory to you, and you perform minimum tests of 25 transactions as a means of assessing control risk. In your tests, you discover the following exceptions:

1. Two items in the acquisitions journal have been misclassified.
2. Three invoices had not been initialed by the controller, but there were no dollar misstatements evident in the transactions.
3. Five receiving reports were recorded in the acquisitions journal at least 2 weeks later than their date on the receiving report.
4. One invoice has been paid twice. The second payment was supported by a duplicate copy of the invoice. Both copies of the invoice had been marked "paid."
5. One check amount in the cash disbursements journal was for $100 less than the amount stated on the vendor's invoice.
6. One voided check was missing.
7. Two receiving reports for vendors' invoices were missing from the transaction packets. One vendor's invoice had an extension error, and the invoice had been initialed that the amount had been checked.

Required

a. Identify whether each of 1 through 7 was a control test deviation, a monetary misstatement, or both.

b. For each exception, identify which transaction-related audit objective was not met.

c. What is the audit importance of each of these exceptions?

d. What follow-up procedures would you use to determine more about the nature of each exception?

e. How would each of these exceptions affect the balance of your audit? Be specific.

f. Identify internal controls that should have prevented each misstatement.

14-26 (Objective 14-4) Each year near the balance sheet date, when the president of Bargon Construction, Inc. takes a 3-week vacation to Hawaii, she signs several checks to pay major bills during the period she is absent. Jack Morgan, head bookkeeper for the company, uses this practice to his advantage. Morgan makes out a check to himself for the amount of a large vendor's invoice, and because there is no acquisitions journal, he records the amount in the cash disbursements journal as an acquisition from the supplier listed on the invoice. He holds the check until several weeks into the subsequent period to make sure that the auditors do not get an opportunity to examine the cancelled check. Shortly after the first of the year when the president returns, Morgan resubmits the invoice for payment and again records the check in the cash disbursements journal. At that point, he marks the invoice "paid" and files it with all other paid invoices. Morgan has been following this practice successfully for several years and feels confident that he has developed a foolproof method.

Required

a. What is the auditor's responsibility for discovering this type of embezzlement?

b. What weaknesses exist in the client's internal control?

c. What audit procedures are likely to uncover the fraud?

14-27 (Objective 14-7) You were in the final stages of your audit of the financial statements of Ozine Corporation for the year ended December 31, 2002, when you were consulted by the corporation's president, who believes there is no point to your examining the year 2003 acquisitions journal and testing data in support of year 2003 entries. He stated that (a) bills pertaining to 2002 that were received too late to be included in the December acquisitions journal were recorded as of the year-end by the corporation by journal entry, (b) the internal auditor made tests after the year-end, and (c) he would furnish you with a letter certifying that there were no unrecorded liabilities.

Required

a. Should a CPA's test for unrecorded liabilities be affected by the fact that the client made a journal entry to record 2002 bills that were received late? Explain.

b. Should a CPA's test for unrecorded liabilities be affected by the fact that a letter is obtained in which a responsible management official certifies that to the best of his or her knowledge all liabilities have been recorded? Explain.

c. Should a CPA's test for unrecorded liabilities be eliminated or reduced because of the internal audit tests? Explain.

d. Assume that the corporation, which handled some government contracts, had no internal auditor but that an auditor for a federal agency spent 3 weeks auditing the records and was just completing his work at this time. How would the CPA's unrecorded liability test be affected by the work of the auditor for a federal agency?

e. What sources in addition to the year 2003 acquisitions journal should the CPA consider to locate possible unrecorded liabilities?*

14-28 (Objectives 14-2, 14-4, 14-5, 14-7) Because of the small size of the company and the limited number of accounting personnel, the Dry Goods Wholesale Company initially records all acquisitions of goods and services at the time cash disbursements are made. At the end of each quarter, when financial statements for internal purposes are prepared, accounts payable are recorded by adjusting journal entries. The entries are reversed at the beginning of the subsequent period. Except for the lack of an acquisitions journal, the controls over acquisitions are excellent for a small company. (There are adequate prenumbered documents for all acquisitions, proper approvals, and adequate internal verification wherever possible.)

Before the auditor arrives for the year-end audit, the bookkeeper prepares adjusting entries to record the accounts payable as of the balance sheet date. A list of all outstanding balances is prepared, by vendor, on an accounts payable listing and is given to the auditor. All vendors' invoices supporting the list are retained in a separate file for the auditor's use.

In the current year, the accounts payable balance has increased dramatically because of a severe cash shortage. (The cash shortage apparently arose from expansion of inventory and facilities rather than lack of sales.) Many accounts have remained unpaid for several months and the client is getting pressure from several vendors to pay the bills. Because the company had a relatively profitable year, management is anxious to complete the audit as early as possible so that the audited statements can be used to obtain a large bank loan.

Required

a. Explain how the lack of an acquisitions journal will affect the auditor's tests of controls and substantive tests of transactions for acquisitions and cash disbursements.

b. What should the auditor use as a sampling unit in performing tests of acquisitions?

c. Assuming no misstatements are discovered in the auditor's tests of controls and substantive tests of transactions for acquisitions and cash disbursements, how will that result affect the verification of accounts payable?

d. Discuss the reasonableness of the client's request for an early completion of the audit and the implications of the request from the auditor's point of view.

*AICPA adapted.

e. List the audit procedures that should be performed in the year-end audit of accounts payable to meet the cutoff objective.

f. State your opinion as to whether it is possible to conduct an adequate audit in these circumstances.

14-29 (Objectives 14-7, 14-8) Mincin, CPA, is the auditor of the Raleigh Corporation. Mincin is considering the audit work to be performed in the accounts payable area for the current year's engagement.

The prior year's audit schedules show that confirmation requests were mailed to 100 of Raleigh's 1,000 suppliers. The selected suppliers were based on Mincin's sample, which was designed to select accounts with large dollar balances. A substantial number of hours were spent by Raleigh and Mincin resolving relatively minor differences between the confirmation replies and Raleigh's accounting records. Alternative audit procedures were used for those suppliers who did not respond to the confirmation requests.

Required

a. Identify the accounts payable balance-related audit objectives that Mincin must consider in determining the audit procedures to be followed.

b. Identify situations in which Mincin should use accounts payable confirmations and discuss whether Mincin is required to use them.

c. Discuss why the use of large dollar balances as the basis for selecting accounts payable for confirmation might not be the most effective approach and indicate what more effective procedures could be followed when selecting accounts payable for confirmation.*

14-30 (Objective 14-7) The physical inventory for Ajak Manufacturing was taken on December 30, 2002, rather than December 31, because the client had to operate the plant for a special order the last day of the year. At the time of the client's physical count, you observed that acquisitions represented by receiving report number 2631 and all preceding ones were included in the physical count, whereas inventory represented by succeeding numbers was excluded. On the evening of December 31, you stopped by the plant and noted that inventory represented by receiving report numbers 2632 through 2634 was received subsequent to the physical count but before the end of the year. You later noted that the final inventory on the financial statements contained only those items included in the physical count. In testing accounts payable at December 31, 2002, you obtain a schedule from the client to aid you in testing the adequacy of the cutoff. The following schedule includes the information that you have not yet resolved:

Receiving Report Number	Amount of Vendor's Invoice	Amount Presently Included in or Excluded from Accounts Payable*	INFORMATION ON THE VENDOR'S INVOICE: Invoice Date	Shipping Date	FOB Origin or Destination
2631	$2,619.26	Included	12-30-02	12-30-02	Origin
2632	3,709.16	Excluded	12-26-02	12-15-02	Destination
2633	5,182.31	Included	12-31-02	12-26-02	Origin
2634	6,403.00	Excluded	12-16-02	12-27-02	Destination
2635	8,484.91	Included	12-28-02	12-31-02	Origin
2636	5,916.20	Excluded	01-03-03	12-31-02	Destination
2637	7,515.50	Excluded	01-05-03	12-26-02	Origin
2638	2,407.87	Excluded	12-31-02	01-03-03	Origin

*All entries to record inventory acquisitions are recorded by the client as a debit to purchases and a credit to accounts payable.

Required

a. Explain the relationship between inventory and accounts payable cutoff.

b. For each of the receiving reports, state the misstatement in inventory or accounts payable, if any exists, and prepare an adjusting entry to correct the financial statements, if a misstatement exists.

c. Which of the misstatements in part b are most important? Explain.

INTERNET PROBLEM 14-1: MANAGING THE ACCOUNTS PAYABLE FUNCTION

Reference the CW site. Many companies have hundreds, if not thousands, of vendors who supply products and services. This problem uses the Internet to expose students to important issues associated with evaluating how well a company manages its vendor information as part of the acquisition and payment cycle.

*AICPA adapted.

CHAPTER 15

COMPLETING THE TESTS IN THE ACQUISITION AND PAYMENT CYCLE: VERIFICATION OF SELECTED ACCOUNTS

LEARNING OBJECTIVES

After studying this chapter, you should be able to

15-1 Recognize the many accounts in the acquisition and payment cycle.

15-2 Design and perform audit tests of property, plant, and equipment and related accounts.

15-3 Design and perform audit tests of prepaid expenses.

15-4 Design and perform audit tests of accrued liabilities.

15-5 Design and perform audit tests of income and expense accounts.

IMPROPER CLASSIFICATIONS HIDE A GREATER NET LOSS

TV Communications Network (TVCN), a Denver-based wireless cable television company, materially understated losses in its 1992 financial statements by improperly recording $2.5 million of expenses as a direct decrease in stockholders' equity. The misstatement took the company from an actual 1992 net loss of $4.7 million to a reported loss of only $2.2 million.

According to the investigation by the SEC, the expenses charged to equity were from disbursements for the development and distribution of brochures promoting the company's business prospects. The payments should have been expensed and reflected in the income statement as advertising expenses.

The internal controls associated with the advertising expenses were clearly inadequate. TVCN typically did not have invoices or other documentation available when payments were made by the company's president, who controlled the bank account. Because of the lack of adequate documentation, when the financial statements were prepared, TVCN employees responsible for recording the expenses did not have sufficient information to properly classify the disbursements. The SEC found that even when documentation was available, the accounts where the transactions were recorded conflicted with the supporting documentation.

Unfortunately, TVCN's auditor relied on inquiry of the company president as the primary evidence about the nature of the advertising payments. In his substantive testing of transactions exceeding $10,000, the auditor relied on the company controller to identify all transactions meeting the criteria for review. Needless to say, the controller didn't present all transactions meeting the $10,000 scope. As you might expect, the SEC brought charges against the auditor for failing to comply with generally accepted auditing standards.

Source: *Accounting and Auditing Enforcement Release No. 534*, Commerce Clearing House, Inc., Chicago.

The last chapter noted that transactions in the acquisition and payment cycle affect several accounts. Acquisitions of assets affect supplies, property, plant and equipment, and prepaid expenses accounts, to name a few. In addition, payments made for services incurred affect many expense accounts. This chapter continues the discussion of the acquisition and payment cycle by highlighting unique audit issues related to other accounts commonly found in the acquisition and payment cycles of most businesses.

The opening vignette about TVCN highlights the importance of understanding the nature of acquisition and payment cycle transactions. Because transactions in this cycle affect numerous accounts in both the balance sheet and the income statement, improperly classified transactions may significantly affect reported results, as they did for TVCN. Therefore, auditors must understand the nature of transactions flowing through the acquisition and payment cycle so that they can effectively evaluate the accounts in the cycle.

TYPES OF OTHER ACCOUNTS IN THE ACQUISITION AND PAYMENT CYCLE

OBJECTIVE 15-1

Recognize the many accounts in the acquisition and payment cycle.

Table 15-1 highlights many of the typical accounts associated with transactions in the acquisition and payment cycle. These accounts are common in many types of businesses. As the nature of the industry or the client's business becomes more specialized, however, the types of assets, expenses, and liabilities change. The methodology associated with auditing these accounts is similar to the audits of other accounts discussed in earlier chapters.

Federal Acquisitions Regulations

The last chapter presented an overview of typical tests of controls and substantive tests of transactions for acquisition and payment cycle transactions, as well as commonly used analytical procedures and tests of details of balances for accounts payable. Later chapters highlight audit issues unique to cash, inventory, and costs of goods sold, which are accounts commonly associated with acquisition and payment cycle transactions. This chapter discusses unique issues for some of the other key accounts in this cycle. In this chapter, we take a closer look at the audit of property, plant, and equipment; prepaid expenses; other liabilities; and income and expense accounts.

AUDIT OF PROPERTY, PLANT, AND EQUIPMENT

OBJECTIVE 15-2

Design and perform audit tests of property, plant, and equipment and related accounts.

We focus first on issues associated with auditing property, plant, and equipment accounts because many transactions in the acquisition and payment cycle are likely to affect these accounts. Property, plant, and equipment are assets that have expected lives of more than 1 year, are used in the business, and are not acquired for resale. The intent to use the assets as part of the operation of the client's business and their expected lives of more than 1 year are the significant characteristics that distinguish these assets from inventory, prepaid expenses, and investments.

Because the audits of these property, plant, and equipment accounts are similar, this section focuses on auditing manufacturing equipment to illustrate an approach to auditing all types of property, plant, and equipment accounts. When there are significant differences

TABLE 15-1 Accounts Typically Associated with Acquisition and Payment Cycle Transactions

Assets	Expenses	Liabilities
Cash	Cost of goods sold	Accounts payable
Inventory	Rent expense	Rent payable
Supplies	Property taxes	Accrued professional fees
Property, plant, and equipment	Income tax expense	Accrued property taxes
Patents, trademarks, and copyrights	Insurance expense	Other accrued expenses
Prepaid rent	Professional fees	Income taxes payable
Prepaid taxes	Retirement benefits	
Prepaid insurance	Utilities	

in the verification of other types of property, plant, and equipment accounts, the differences are briefly discussed.

Overview of Equipment-Related Accounts

In addition to manufacturing equipment, other accounts audited concurrently include depreciation expense, accumulated depreciation, and gain or loss on the disposal of the assets. Because equipment additions are recorded in the acquisitions journal, the accounting system has already been tested for recording current period additions to manufacturing equipment as part of the tests of the acquisition and payment cycle studied in the last chapter. Because equipment additions are infrequent and may be subject to special controls, such as board of directors approval, the auditor may decide not to rely heavily on these tests.

The primary accounting record for manufacturing equipment and other property, plant, and equipment accounts is generally a **fixed asset master file.** The contents of the fixed asset master file must be understood for a meaningful study of the audit of manufacturing equipment. The master file is composed of a set of records, one for each piece of equipment and other types of property owned. In turn, each record includes descriptive information, date of acquisition, original cost, current year depreciation, and accumulated depreciation for the property. The totals for all records in the master file equal the general ledger balances for the related accounts. The master file will also contain information about property acquired and disposed of during the year. For disposals, proceeds, gains, and losses will be included.

Fixed Asset Management

Manufacturing equipment is normally audited differently from current asset accounts for three reasons: (1) There are usually fewer current period acquisitions of manufacturing equipment, (2) the amount of any given acquisition is often material, and (3) the equipment is likely to be kept and maintained in the accounting records for several years. Because of these differences, the emphasis in auditing manufacturing equipment is on the verification of current period acquisitions rather than on the balance in the account carried forward from the preceding year. In addition, the expected life of assets over 1 year requires depreciation and accumulated depreciation accounts, which are verified as a part of the audit of the assets. Finally, equipment may be sold or disposed of, triggering a gain or loss entry that the auditor may need to verify.

Although the approach to verifying manufacturing equipment is dissimilar from that used for current assets, several other asset accounts are verified in much the same manner. These include patents, copyrights, catalog costs, and all property, plant, and equipment accounts.

In the audit of manufacturing equipment and related accounts, it is helpful to separate the tests into the following categories:

- Analytical procedures
- Verifying current year acquisitions
- Verifying current year disposals
- Verifying the ending balance in the asset account
- Verifying depreciation expense
- Verifying the ending balance in accumulated depreciation

The next several sections highlight the use of these categories of tests in the audit of manufacturing equipment, depreciation expense, accumulated depreciation, and gain or loss on disposal accounts.

Analytical Procedures

As in all audit areas, the nature of the analytical procedures depends on the nature of the client's operations. Table 15-2 (p. 442) illustrates the type of ratio and trend analysis often performed for manufacturing equipment.

As you can see, most of the typical analytical procedures performed relate to assessing the likelihood of material misstatements in the depreciation expense and accumulated depreciation accounts. In a later section, we focus on other substantive tests that are often performed for these accounts.

TABLE 15-2	Analytical Procedures for Manufacturing Equipment
Analytical Procedure	**Possible Misstatement**
Compare depreciation expense divided by gross manufacturing equipment cost with previous years.	Misstatement in depreciation expense and accumulated depreciation.
Compare accumulated depreciation divided by gross manufacturing equipment cost with previous years.	Misstatement in accumulated depreciation.
Compare monthly or annual repairs and maintenance, supplies expense, small tools expense, and similar accounts with previous years.	Expensing amounts that should be capitalized.
Compare gross manufacturing cost divided by some measure of production with previous years.	Idle equipment or equipment that has been disposed of but not written off.

TABLE 15-3	Balance-Related Audit Objectives and Tests of Details of Balances for Manufacturing Equipment Additions	
Balance-Related Audit Objective	**Common Tests of Details of Balances Procedures**	**Comments**
Current year acquisitions in the acquisitions schedule agree with related master file amounts, and the total agrees with the general ledger (detail tie-in).	Foot the acquisitions schedule. Trace the total to the general ledger. Trace the individual acquisitions to the master file for amounts and descriptions.	These tests should be limited unless controls are weak. All increases in the general ledger balance for the year should reconcile to the schedule.
Current year acquisitions as listed exist (existence).	Examine vendors' invoices and receiving reports. Physically examine assets.	It is uncommon to physically examine acquisitions unless controls are weak or amounts are material.
Existing acquisitions are recorded (completeness).	Examine vendors' invoices of closely related accounts such as repairs and maintenance to uncover items that should be manufacturing equipment. Review lease and rental agreements.	This objective is one of the most important ones for manufacturing equipment.
Current year acquisitions as listed are accurate (accuracy).	Examine vendors' invoices.	Extent depends on inherent risk and effectiveness of internal controls.
Current year acquisitions as listed are properly classified (classification).	Examine vendors' invoices in manufacturing equipment account to uncover items that should be classified as office equipment, part of the buildings, or repairs. Examine vendors' invoices of closely related accounts such as repairs to uncover items that should be manufacturing equipment. Examine rent and lease expense for capitalizable leases.	The objective is closely related to tests for completeness. It is done in conjunction with that objective and tests for accuracy.
Current year acquisitions are recorded in the proper period (cutoff).	Review transactions near the balance sheet date for proper period.	Usually done as a part of accounts payable cutoff tests.
The client has rights to current year acquisitions (rights).	Examine vendors' invoices.	Ordinarily no problem for equipment. Property deeds, abstracts, and tax bills are frequently examined for land or major buildings.

Verifying Current Year Acquisitions

The proper recording of current year additions is important because of the long-term effect the assets have on the financial statements. The failure to capitalize a fixed asset, or the recording of an acquisition at the improper amount, affects the balance sheet until the company disposes of the asset. The income statement is affected until the asset is fully depreciated.

Because of the importance of current period acquisitions in the audit of manufacturing equipment, seven of the nine balance-related audit objectives for tests of details of balances are used as a frame of reference. (Realizable value and presentation and disclosure are discussed in connection with verifying ending balances.)

The balance-related audit objectives and common audit tests are shown in Table 15-3. As in all other audit areas, the actual audit tests and sample size depend heavily on tolerable misstatement, inherent risk, and assessed control risk. Tolerable misstatement is of special importance for verifying current year additions. These transactions vary from immaterial amounts in some years to a large number of significant acquisitions in others. Completeness, accuracy, and classification are usually the major objectives for this part of the audit.

In testing acquisitions, the auditor must know the client's capitalization policies to determine whether acquisitions are recorded in accordance with generally accepted accounting principles (GAAP) and are treated consistently with those of the preceding year. For example, many clients automatically expense items that are less than a certain amount, such as $1,000. The auditor should be alert for the possibility of material transportation and installation costs, as well as the trade-in of existing equipment.

The inclusion of transactions that should properly be recorded as assets in repairs and maintenance expense, lease expense, supplies, small tools, and similar accounts is a common client error. The error results from lack of understanding GAAP and some clients' desire to avoid income taxes. If the auditor concludes that this type of material misstatement is likely, it may be necessary to vouch the larger amounts debited to the expense accounts. It is a common practice to do so as a part of the audit of the property, plant, and equipment accounts.

Verifying Current Year Disposals

Transactions involving the disposal of manufacturing equipment are often misstated when company internal controls lack a formal method to inform management of the sale, trade-in, abandonment, or theft of recorded machinery and equipment. If the client fails to

AUDIT THAT WHICH IS UNCOMFORTABLE!

"Although this landscaping plan is expensive, the project is long overdue. I heartily approve!" wrote the president of a West Coast company in an internal memo.

One year later, the internal audit department conducted a routine review of expenditures for the relandscaping of the company's corporate headquarters. When the auditors went to the facilities department to get the contract, design blueprint, bidding records, and other supporting documents, the manager informed them that the relandscaping had not been administered by his department, but by the department's vice president and the recently retired former president.

The auditors decided to probe further because the landscaping cost of $1 million seemed excessive, there was no competitive bidding, and the contract was administered by high-level executives rather than those usually administering such contracts.

The contractor initially defended his pricing as reasonable, because of adverse soil and site condition. However, after several intense meetings and discussion of possible legal action, the contractor reluctantly disclosed the true circumstances of the transaction. He was instructed by the vice president and former president to price the project so that it would also cover extensive landscaping and building renovation at each of their homes. The internal auditors' review of the contractor's records confirmed that excess charges of almost $600,000 covered the cost of a pool, hot tub, deck, marble patio, sprinkler system, fountain, dock, landscaping, and extensive building renovation at the homes of both executives. The contractor also said that the former president had contacted him during the audit to discourage cooperation.

The company went public with the audit findings, and the investigative file was turned over to the prosecutor. As a result of their no contest pleas, the two executives were convicted of obtaining money under false pretenses. Virtually all losses were recovered through successful bonding claims. This situation highlights the importance of auditors following up on matters that make them feel uncomfortable.

Source: Courtenay Thompson, "Fraud in the Executive Suite." This article was adapted from pp. 68-69 of the October 1993 issue of *Internal Auditor*, published by The Institute of Internal Auditors, Inc.

record disposals, the original cost of the manufacturing equipment account will be overstated indefinitely, and net book value will be overstated until the asset is fully depreciated. Formal methods of tracking disposals and provisions for proper authorization of the sale or other disposal of manufacturing equipment help reduce the risk of misstatement. There should also be adequate internal verification of recorded disposals to make sure that assets are correctly removed from the accounting records.

The auditor's main objectives in the verification of the sale, trade-in, or abandonment of manufacturing equipment are to gather sufficient evidence that (1) existing disposals are recorded and (2) disposals are accurately recorded. Because the failure to record disposals of manufacturing equipment no longer used in the business can significantly affect the financial statements, *the search for unrecorded disposals is essential.* The nature and adequacy of the controls over disposals affect the extent of the search. The following procedures are often used for verifying disposals:

- Review whether newly acquired assets replace existing assets.
- Analyze gains and losses on the disposal of assets and miscellaneous income for receipts from the disposal of assets.
- Review plant modifications and changes in product line, property taxes, or insurance coverage for indications of deletions of equipment.
- Make inquiries of management and production personnel about the possibility of the disposal of assets.

Verifying Ending Balance of Asset Account

Two of the auditor's objectives when auditing manufacturing equipment include determining that (1) all equipment owned is recorded and (2) all recorded equipment physically exists on the balance sheet date. In designing audit tests to meet these objectives, the auditor first considers the nature of internal controls over manufacturing equipment. Ideally, the auditor is able to conclude that controls are sufficiently strong to allow the auditor to rely on balances carried forward from the prior year. Important controls include the use of a master file for individual fixed assets, adequate physical controls over assets that are easily movable (such as computers, tools, and vehicles), assignment of identification numbers to each plant asset, and periodic physical count of fixed assets and their reconciliation by accounting personnel. A formal method of informing the accounting department of all disposals of fixed assets is also an important control over the balance of assets carried forward into the current year.

Usually, the auditor does not obtain a list from the client of all assets included in the ending balance of manufacturing equipment. Instead, audit tests are determined on the basis of the master file.

Typically, the first audit step concerns the detail tie-in objective: Manufacturing equipment as listed in the master file agrees with the general ledger. Examining a printout of the master file that totals to the general ledger balance is ordinarily sufficient. The auditor may choose to use audit software to foot an electronic version of the master file or manually test-foot a few pages.

After assessing control risk for the existence objective, the auditor must decide whether it is necessary to verify the existence of individual items of manufacturing equipment included in the master file. If the auditor believes there is a high likelihood of significant missing fixed assets that are still recorded on the accounting records, an appropriate procedure is to select a sample from the master file and examine the actual assets. In rare cases, the auditor may believe it is necessary for the client to take a complete physical inventory of fixed assets to make sure they exist. If a physical inventory is taken, the auditor normally observes the count.

Ordinarily, it is unnecessary to test the accuracy or classification of fixed assets recorded in prior periods because presumably they were verified in previous audits at the time they were acquired. But the auditor should be aware that companies may occasionally have manufacturing equipment on hand that is no longer used in operations. If the amounts are material, the auditor should evaluate whether they should be written down to net realizable value (realizable value objective) or at least disclosed separately as "nonoperating equipment."

A major consideration in verifying the ending balance in fixed assets is the possibility of *legal encumbrances* (presentation and disclosure objective). Methods to determine whether manufacturing equipment is encumbered include reading the terms of loan and credit agreements, mailing loan confirmation requests to banks and other lending institutions, and discussions with the client or letters to legal counsel.

The *proper presentation and disclosure* of manufacturing equipment in the financial statements must be evaluated carefully to make sure that GAAP is followed. Manufacturing equipment should include the gross cost and should ordinarily be separated from other fixed assets. Leased property should also be disclosed separately, and all liens on property must be included in the footnotes.

Verifying Depreciation Expense

Depreciation expense is one of the few expense accounts that is not verified as a part of tests of controls and substantive tests of transactions. The recorded amounts are determined by *internal allocations* rather than by exchange transactions with outside parties. When depreciation expense is material, more tests of details of depreciation expense are required than for an account that has already been verified through tests of controls and substantive tests of transactions.

The most important objective for depreciation expense is accuracy. Two major concerns are involved in the accuracy objective: determining whether the client is following *a consistent depreciation policy* from period to period and whether the client's *calculations are correct*. In determining the former, there are four considerations: the useful life of current period acquisitions, the method of depreciation, the estimated salvage value, and the policy of depreciating assets in the year of acquisition and disposition. The client's policies can be determined by discussions with appropriate personnel and comparing the responses with the information in the auditor's permanent files.

A useful method of auditing depreciation is an overall reasonableness test made by multiplying the undepreciated fixed assets by the depreciation rate for the year. In making these calculations, the auditor must make adjustments for current year additions and disposals, assets with different lengths of life, and assets with different methods of depreciation. Many CPA firms include an electronic spreadsheet in their permanent file that includes a breakdown of the fixed assets by method of depreciation and length of life. If the calculations using the software are reasonably close to the client's totals and if assessed control risk for depreciation expense is low, tests of details for depreciation can be eliminated.

When an overall reasonableness test cannot be accomplished, more detailed tests are usually needed. This is done by recomputing depreciation expense for selected assets to determine whether the client is following a proper and consistent depreciation policy. To be relevant, the detailed calculations should be tied in to the total depreciation calculations by footing the depreciation expense on the property master file and reconciling the total with the general ledger. If the client maintains computerized depreciation and amortization records, it may be desirable to consider using the computer in testing the calculations.

Verifying Ending Balance in Accumulated Depreciation

The debits to accumulated depreciation are normally tested as a part of the audit of disposals of assets, whereas the credits are verified as a part of depreciation expense. If the auditor traces selected transactions to the accumulated depreciation records in the property master file as a part of these tests, little additional testing should be required for the ending balance in accumulated depreciation.

Two objectives are usually emphasized in the audit of the ending balance in accumulated depreciation:

1. Accumulated depreciation as stated in the property master file agrees with the general ledger. This objective can be satisfied by test-footing the accumulated depreciation or the property master file and tracing the total to the general ledger.
2. Accumulated depreciation in the master file is accurate.

In some cases, the life of manufacturing equipment may be significantly reduced because of such changes as reductions in customer demands for products, unexpected physical deterioration, or a modification in operations. Because of these possibilities, it is necessary to evaluate the adequacy of the allowances for accumulated depreciation each year to make sure that the net book value does not exceed the realizable value of the assets.

AUDIT OF PREPAID EXPENSES

OBJECTIVE 15-3

Design and perform audit tests of prepaid expenses.

Prepaid expenses, deferred charges, and intangibles are assets that vary in life from several months to several years. Their inclusion as assets results more from the concept of matching expenses with revenues than from their resale or liquidation value. The following are examples:

- Prepaid rent
- Organization costs
- Prepaid taxes
- Patents
- Prepaid insurance
- Trademarks
- Deferred charges
- Copyrights

One typical difference between these assets and others, such as accounts receivable and inventory, is their immateriality in many audits. Analytical procedures are often sufficient for prepaid expenses, deferred charges, and intangibles. However, in certain audits, some of these assets can be significant. We therefore discuss some of the typical internal controls and related audit tests commonly associated with prepaid expenses.

In this section, the audit of prepaid insurance is discussed as an account representative of this group because (1) it is found in most audits—virtually every company has some type of insurance, (2) it is typical of the problems commonly encountered in the audit of this class of accounts, and (3) the auditor's responsibility for the review of insurance coverage is an additional consideration not encountered in the other accounts in this category.

Overview of Prepaid Insurance

The accounts typically used for prepaid insurance include prepaid insurance and insurance expense. Because insurance premiums are recorded in the acquisitions journal, the payments of insurance premiums have already been partially tested by means of the tests of controls and substantive tests of acquisition and cash disbursement transactions.

Internal Controls

The internal controls for prepaid insurance and insurance expense can be conveniently divided into three categories: controls over the acquisition and recording of insurance, controls over the insurance register, and controls over the charge-off of insurance expense.

Controls over the acquisition and recording of insurance are a part of the acquisition and payment cycle. These include proper authorization for new insurance policies and payment of insurance premiums consistent with the procedures discussed in that cycle.

An **insurance register** is a record of insurance policies in force and the expiration date of each policy. Use of an insurance register is an essential control to ensure that the company has adequate insurance. The control should include a provision for periodic review of the adequacy of the insurance coverage by an independent qualified person.

After the detailed records of the information in the prepaid insurance register have been completed, they should be verified by someone independent of the person preparing them. A closely related control is the use of monthly standard journal entries for insurance expense. If a significant entry is required to adjust the balance in prepaid insurance at the end of the year, it indicates a potential misstatement in the recording of the acquisition of insurance throughout the year or in the calculation of the year-end balance in prepaid insurance.

Audit Tests

Throughout the audit of prepaid insurance and insurance expense, the auditor should keep in mind that the amount in insurance expense is a residual based on the beginning balance in prepaid insurance, the payment of premiums during the year, and the ending balance. The only verification of the balance in the expense account that is ordinarily necessary are analytical procedures and a brief test to be sure that the charges to insurance expense arose from credits to prepaid insurance. Because the payments of premiums are tested as part of the tests of controls and substantive tests of transactions and analytical procedures, the emphasis in the tests of details of balances is on prepaid insurance.

In the audit of prepaid insurance, a schedule is obtained from the client or prepared by the auditor that includes each insurance policy in force, policy number, insurance coverage for each policy, premium amount, premium period, insurance expense for the year, and prepaid insurance at the end of the year.

A major consideration in the audit of prepaid insurance is the frequent *immateriality* of the beginning and ending balances. Furthermore, few transactions are debited and credited to the balance during the year, most of which are small and simple to understand. Therefore, the auditor can generally spend little time verifying the balance. When the auditor plans not to verify the balance in detail, analytical procedures become increasingly important as a means of identifying potentially significant misstatements. The following are commonly performed analytical procedures of prepaid insurance and insurance expense:

- Compare total prepaid insurance and insurance expense with previous years as a test of reasonableness.
- Compute the ratio of prepaid insurance to insurance expense and compare it with previous years.
- Compare the individual insurance policy coverage on the schedule of insurance obtained from the client with the preceding year's schedule as a test of the elimination of certain policies or a change in insurance coverage.
- Compare the computed prepaid insurance balance for the current year on a policy-by-policy basis with that of the preceding year as a test of an error in calculation.
- Review the *insurance coverage* listed on the prepaid insurance schedule with an appropriate client official or insurance broker for adequacy of coverage. The auditor cannot be an expert on insurance matters, but the auditor's understanding of accounting and the valuation of assets is important in making certain that a company is not underinsured.

For many audits, no additional tests need be performed beyond the review for overall reasonableness unless the tests indicate a high likelihood of a significant misstatement or assessed control risk is high. The remaining audit procedures should be performed only when there is a special reason for doing so. The discussion of these tests is organized around the balance-related audit objectives for performing tests of details of asset balances. Realizable value is not applicable.

Insurance Policies in the Prepaid Insurance Schedule Exist and Existing Policies Are Listed (Existence and Completeness) The verification of existence and tests for omissions of the insurance policies in force can be performed in one of two ways: by referring to supporting documentation or by obtaining a confirmation of insurance information from the company's insurance agent. The first approach entails examining insurance invoices and policies in force. If these tests are performed, they should be done on a limited test basis. Sending a confirmation to the client's insurance agent is preferable because it is usually less time-consuming than vouching tests and it provides 100 percent verification.

The Client Has Rights to All Insurance Policies in the Prepaid Insurance Schedule (Rights) The party who will receive the benefit if an insurance claim is filed has the rights. Ordinarily, the recipient named in the policy is the client, but when there are mortgages or other liens, the insurance claim may be payable to a creditor. The review of insurance policies for claimants other than the client is an excellent test of unrecorded liabilities and pledged assets.

Prepaid Amounts on the Schedule Are Accurate and the Total Is Correctly Added and Agrees with the General Ledger (Accuracy and Detail Tie-in) The accuracy of prepaid insurance involves verifying the total amount of the insurance premium, the length of the policy period, and the allocation of the premium to unexpired insurance. The amount of the premium for a given policy and its time period can be verified simultaneously by examining the premium invoice or the confirmation from an insurance agent. Once these two have been verified, the client's calculations of unexpired insurance can be tested by recalculation. The schedule of prepaid insurance can then be footed and the totals traced to the general ledger to complete the detail tie-in tests.

The Insurance Expense Related to Prepaid Insurance Is Properly Classified (Classification) The proper classification of debits to different insurance expense accounts should be reviewed as a test of the income statement. In some cases, the appropriate expense account is obvious because of the type of insurance (such as insurance on a piece of equipment), but in other cases, allocations are necessary. For example, fire insurance on the building may require allocation to several accounts, including manufacturing overhead. Consistency with previous years is the major consideration in evaluating classification.

Insurance Transactions Are Recorded in the Proper Period (Cutoff) Cutoff for insurance expense is normally not a significant problem because of the small number of policies and the immateriality of the amount. If the cutoff is checked at all, it is reviewed as a part of accounts payable cutoff tests.

Prepaid Insurance Is Properly Presented and Disclosed (Presentation and Disclosure) In most audits, prepaid insurance is combined with other prepaid expenses and included as a current asset. The amount is usually small and not a significant consideration to statement users.

AUDIT OF ACCRUED LIABILITIES

OBJECTIVE 15-4

Design and perform audit tests of accrued liabilities.

A third major category of accounts in the acquisition and payment cycle is accrued liabilities. **Accrued liabilities** are estimated unpaid obligations for services or benefits that have been received before the balance sheet date. Many accrued liabilities represent future obligations for unpaid services resulting from the passage of time but are not payable at the balance sheet date. For example, the benefits of property rental accrue throughout the year; therefore, at the balance sheet date, a certain portion of the total rent cost that has not been paid should be accrued. If the balance sheet date and the date of the termination of the rent agreement are the same, any unpaid rent is more appropriately called rent payable than an accrued liability.

A second type of accrual is one in which the amount of the obligation must be estimated due to the uncertainty of the amount due. An illustration is the obligation for federal income taxes when there is a reasonable likelihood that the amount reported on the tax return will be changed after an audit has been conducted by the Internal Revenue Service. Other examples include accrued payroll, accrued payroll taxes, accrued officers' bonuses, and accrued commissions. The following are other common accrued liabilities:

- Accrued income taxes
- Accrued interest
- Accrued pension costs
- Accrued professional fees
- Accrued rent
- Accrued warranty costs

The verification of accrued expenses varies depending on the nature of the accrual and the circumstances of the client. For most audits, accruals take little audit time, but in some instances, accounts such as accrued income taxes, warranty costs, and pension costs are material and require considerable audit effort. To illustrate, the audit of accrued property taxes is discussed in this section.

Auditing Accrued Property Taxes

The accounts typically used by companies for accrued property taxes include property tax expense and the accrued account. The relationship between accrued property taxes and the acquisition and payment cycle is the same as for prepaid insurance. Because property tax payments are recorded in the cash disbursements journal, the payments of property taxes have already been partially tested by means of the tests of the acquisition and payment cycle transactions.

As for insurance expense, the balance in property tax expense is a residual amount that results from the beginning and ending balances in accrued property taxes and the payments of property taxes. Therefore, the emphasis in the tests should be on the ending property tax liability and payments. In verifying accrued property taxes, all nine balance-related audit objectives except realizable value are relevant. But two are of special significance:

1. Existing properties for which accrual of taxes is appropriate are on the accrual schedule. The failure to include properties for which taxes should be accrued would understate the liability (completeness). A material misstatement could occur, for example, if taxes on property were not paid before the balance sheet date and not included as accrued property taxes.
2. Accrued property taxes are accurately recorded. The greatest concern in accuracy is the consistent treatment of the accrual from year to year (accuracy).

The primary methods of testing for the inclusion of all accruals are (1) to perform the accrual tests in conjunction with the audit of current year property tax payments and (2) to compare the accruals with those of previous years. In most audits, there are few property tax payments, but each payment is often material, and therefore it is common to verify each one.

First, the auditor should obtain a schedule of property tax payments from the client and compare each payment with the preceding year's schedule to determine whether all payments have been included in the client-prepared schedule. The fixed asset audit schedules also must be examined for major additions and disposals of assets that may affect the property taxes accrual. If the client is expanding its operations, all property affected by local property tax regulations should be included in the schedule even if the first tax payment has not yet been made.

After the auditor is satisfied that all taxable property has been included in the client-prepared schedule, it is necessary to evaluate the reasonableness of the total amount of property taxes on each property being used as a basis to estimate the accrual. In some instances, the total amount has already been set by the taxing authority, and it is possible to verify the total by comparing the amount on the schedule with the tax bill in the client's possession. In other instances, the preceding year's total payments must be adjusted for the expected increase in property tax rates.

The auditor can verify the accrued property tax by recomputing the portion of the total tax applicable to the current year for each piece of property. The most important consideration in making this calculation is to use the same portion of each tax payment as the accrual that was used in the preceding year unless justifiable conditions exist for a change. After the accrual and property tax expense for each piece of property have been recomputed, the totals should be added and compared with the general ledger. In many cases, property taxes are charged to more than one expense account. When this happens, the auditor should test for proper classification by evaluating whether the proper amount was charged to each account.

AUDIT OF INCOME AND EXPENSE ACCOUNTS

OBJECTIVE 15-5

Design and perform audit tests of income and expense accounts.

The final look at key accounts in the acquisition and payment cycle includes an overview of procedures auditors typically use to determine whether the income and expense accounts in the financial statements are fairly presented in accordance with GAAP. The auditor must be satisfied that each of the income and expense totals included in the income statement as well as net earnings are not materially misstated.

In conducting audit tests of the financial statements, the auditor must be aware of the importance of the income statement to users of the statements. Many users rely more heavily on the income statement than on the balance sheet for making decisions. Equity investors, long-term creditors, union representatives, and often even short-term creditors are more interested in the ability of a firm to generate profit than in the historical cost or book value of the individual assets.

Considering the purposes of the income statement, the following are two essential concepts in the audit of income and expense accounts:

1. The matching of periodic income and expense is necessary for a proper determination of operating results.
2. The consistent application of accounting principles for different periods is necessary for comparability.

These concepts must be applied to the recording of individual transactions and to the combining of accounts in the general ledger for statement presentation.

Approach to Auditing Income and Expense Accounts

The audit of income and expense accounts is directly related to the balance sheet and is not a separate part of the audit process. A misstatement of an income statement account almost always equally affects a balance sheet account, and vice versa. The audit of income and expense accounts is so intertwined with the other parts of the audit that it is necessary to interrelate different aspects of testing these accounts with the different types of tests previously discussed. A brief description of these tests serves as a review of material covered in other chapters; more important, it shows the interrelationship of different parts of the audit with income and expense account testing. The parts of the audit directly affecting these accounts are as follows:

- Analytical procedures
- Tests of controls and substantive tests of transactions
- Tests of details of account balances

The emphasis in this section is on income and expense accounts directly related to the acquisition and payment cycle, but the same concepts apply to the income statement accounts in all other cycles.

Analytical Procedures

Analytical procedures were first discussed in Chapter 7 as a general concept and have been referred to in subsequent chapters as a part of specific audit areas. Analytical procedures should be thought of as a part of the test of the fairness of the presentation of both balance sheet and income statement accounts. A few analytical procedures and the possible misstatements they may uncover in the audit of income and expense accounts are shown in Table 15-4.

Tests of Controls and Substantive Tests of Transactions

Tests of controls and substantive tests of transactions both have the effect of simultaneously verifying balance sheet and income statement accounts. For example, when an auditor concludes that internal controls are adequate to provide reasonable assurance that

TABLE 15-4 Analytical Procedures for Income and Expense Accounts

Analytical Procedure	Possible Misstatement
Compare individual expenses with previous years.	Overstatement or understatement of a balance in an expense account.
Compare individual asset and liability balances with previous years.	Overstatement or understatement of a balance sheet account that would also affect an income statement account (for example, a misstatement of inventory affects cost of goods sold).
Compare individual expenses with budgets.	Misstatement of expenses and related balance sheet accounts.
Compare gross margin percentage with previous years.	Misstatement of cost of goods sold and inventory.
Compare inventory turnover ratio with previous years.	Misstatement of cost of goods sold and inventory.
Compare prepaid insurance expense with previous years.	Misstatement of insurance expense and prepaid insurance.
Compare commission expense divided by sales with previous years.	Misstatement of commission expense and accrued commissions.
Compare individual manufacturing expenses divided by total manufacturing expenses with previous years.	Misstatement of individual manufacturing expenses and related balance sheet accounts.

transactions in the acquisitions journal exist, are accurately recorded, correctly classified, and recorded in a timely manner, evidence exists as to the correctness of individual balance sheet accounts such as accounts payable and fixed assets and income statement accounts such as advertising and repairs. Conversely, inadequate controls and misstatements discovered through tests of controls and substantive tests of transactions are an indication of the likelihood of misstatements in both the income statement and the balance sheet.

Understanding internal control and the related tests of controls and substantive tests of transactions to determine the appropriate assessed control risk are the most important means of verifying many of the income statement accounts in each of the transaction cycles. For example, if the auditor concludes after adequate tests that assessed control risk can be reduced to low, the only additional verification of income statement accounts such as utilities, advertising, and purchases should be analytical procedures and cutoff tests. However, certain income and expense accounts are not verified at all by tests of controls and substantive tests of transactions, and others must be tested more extensively by other means. These are discussed next.

Tests of Details of Account Balances—Expense Analysis

The amounts included in certain income statement accounts must be analyzed even though the previously mentioned tests have been performed. The meaning and methodology of analysis of accounts are described first, followed by a discussion of when expense account analysis is appropriate.

Expense account analysis is the examination of underlying documentation of the individual transactions and amounts making up the detail of the total of an expense account. The underlying documents are of the same nature as those used for examining transactions as a part of tests of acquisition transactions and include invoices, receiving reports, purchase orders, and contracts.

Expense account analysis concentrates on transactions that make up the details of an individual expense account. Although the focus of expense account analysis is on transactions, these tests differ from tests of controls and substantive tests of transactions. Because the tests of controls and substantive tests of transactions are meant to assess the appropriate control risk, they are tests of classes of transactions, such as acquisitions, that include many different accounts. In the analysis of expense and other income statement accounts, the auditor verifies the transactions in specific accounts to determine the propriety, classification, accuracy, and other specific information of each account analyzed.

Assuming satisfactory classification results are found in tests of controls and substantive tests of transactions, auditors normally restrict expense analysis to those accounts with a relatively high likelihood of material misstatement. For example, auditors often analyze repairs and maintenance expense accounts to determine whether they erroneously include property, plant, and equipment transactions; rent and lease expenses are analyzed to determine the need to capitalize leases; and legal expense is analyzed to determine whether there are potential contingent liabilities, disputes, illegal acts, or other legal issues that may affect the financial statements. Accounts such as utilities, travel expense, and advertising are rarely analyzed unless analytical procedures indicate high potential for material misstatement.

Expense account analysis is often done as a part of the verification of the related asset. For example, it is common to analyze repairs and maintenance as a part of verifying fixed assets, rent expense as a part of verifying prepaid or accrued rent, and insurance expense as a part of testing prepaid insurance.

Tests of Details of Account Balances—Allocation

Several expense accounts result from the **allocation** of accounting data rather than discrete transactions. These include expenses such as depreciation, depletion, and the amortization of copyrights and catalog costs. The allocation of manufacturing overhead between inventory and cost of goods sold is an example of a different type of allocation that affects expenses.

Allocations are important because they determine whether an expenditure is an asset or a current period expense. If the client fails to follow GAAP or fails to calculate the allocation properly, the financial statements can be materially misstated. The allocation of many expenses such as the depreciation of fixed assets and the amortization of copyrights is required because the life of the asset is greater than 1 year. The original cost of the asset is verified at the time of acquisition, but the charge-off takes place over several years. Other types of allocations directly affecting the financial statements arise because the life of a short-lived asset does not expire on the balance sheet date. Examples include prepaid rent and insurance. Finally, the allocation of costs between current period manufacturing expenses and inventory is required by GAAP as a means of reflecting all costs of making a product.

In auditing the allocation of expenditures such as prepaid insurance and manufacturing overhead, the two most important considerations are adherence to GAAP and consistency with the preceding period. The two most important audit procedures for allocations are tests for overall reasonableness using analytical procedures and recalculation of the client's results. It is common to perform these tests as a part of the audit of the related asset or liability accounts. For example, depreciation expense is usually verified as part of the audit of property, plant, and equipment; amortization of patents is tested as part of verifying new patents or the disposal of existing ones; and allocations between inventory and cost of goods sold are verified as part of the audit of inventory.

SUMMARY

This chapter concludes the discussion of accounts and transactions in the acquisition and payment cycle. Auditors need an understanding of key accounts, classes of transactions, business functions, documents, and records related to acquisition and payment cycle transactions to adequately audit the numerous accounts associated with this cycle. Many of these accounts, such as accounts payable, property, plant, and equipment, depreciation expense, and prepaid expenses, have unique characteristics that affect how the auditor gathers sufficient competent evidence about related account balances. The analysis of the audit tests associated with accounts in this cycle has provided an overview of how audit tests in different cycles interrelate to provide a basis for the auditor's verification of many financial statement accounts.

ESSENTIAL TERMS

Accrued liabilities—estimated unpaid obligations for services or benefits that have been received prior to the balance sheet date; common accrued liabilities include accrued commissions, accrued income taxes, accrued payroll, and accrued rent

Allocation—the division of certain expenses, such as depreciation and manufacturing overhead, among several expense accounts

Expense account analysis—the examination of underlying documentation of individual transactions and amounts making up the total of an expense account

Fixed asset master file—a computer file containing records for each piece of equipment and other types of property owned; the primary accounting record for manufacturing equipment and other property, plant, and equipment accounts

Insurance register—a record of insurance policies in force and the expiration date of each policy

REVIEW QUESTIONS

15-1 **(Objective 15-2)** Explain the relationship between substantive tests of transactions for the acquisition and payment cycle and tests of details of balances for the verification of property, plant, and equipment. Which aspects of property, plant, and equipment are directly affected by the tests of controls and substantive tests of transactions and which are not?

15-2 **(Objective 15-2)** Explain why the emphasis in auditing property, plant, and equipment is on the current period acquisitions and disposals rather than on the balances in the account carried forward from the preceding year. Under what circumstances will the emphasis be on the balances carried forward?

15-3 **(Objective 15-2)** What is the relationship between the audit of property, plant, and equipment accounts and the audit of repair and maintenance accounts? Explain how the auditor organizes the audit to take this relationship into consideration.

15-4 **(Objective 15-2)** List and briefly state the purpose of all audit procedures that might reasonably be applied by an auditor to determine that all property, plant, and equipment retirements have been recorded in the accounting system.

15-5 **(Objective 15-2)** In auditing depreciation expense, what major considerations should the auditor keep in mind? Explain how each can be verified.

15-6 **(Objective 15-3)** Explain the relationship between substantive tests of transactions for the acquisition and payment cycle and tests of details of balances for the verification of prepaid insurance.

15-7 **(Objective 15-3)** Explain why the audit of prepaid insurance should ordinarily take a relatively small amount of audit time if the client's assessed control risk for acquisitions is low.

15-8 **(Objective 15-3)** Distinguish between the evaluation of the adequacy of insurance coverage and the verification of prepaid insurance. Explain which is more important in a typical audit.

15-9 **(Objective 15-3)** What are the major differences between the audit of prepaid expenses and other asset accounts such as accounts receivable or property, plant, and equipment?

15-10 **(Objective 15-4)** Explain the relationship between accrued rent and substantive tests of transactions for the acquisition and payment cycle. Which aspects of accrued rent are not verified as a part of the substantive tests of transactions?

15-11 **(Objective 15-4)** In verifying accounts payable, it is common to restrict the audit sample to a small portion of the population items, whereas in auditing accrued property taxes, it is common to verify all transactions for the year. Explain the reason for the difference.

15-12 **(Objective 15-4)** Which documents will be used to verify accrued property taxes and the related expense accounts?

15-13 **(Objective 15-5)** List three expense accounts that are tested as part of the acquisition and payment cycle. List three expense accounts that are not directly verified as a part of this cycle.

15-14 **(Objective 15-5)** What is meant by the analysis of expense accounts? Explain how expense account analysis relates to the tests of controls and substantive tests of transactions that the auditor has already completed for the acquisition and payment cycle.

15-15 **(Objectives 15-2, 15-5)** How would the approach for verifying repair expense differ from that used to audit depreciation expense? Why would the approach be different?

15-16 **(Objective 15-5)** List the factors that should affect the auditor's decision whether to analyze an account balance. Considering these factors, list four expense accounts that are commonly analyzed in audit engagements.

MULTIPLE CHOICE QUESTIONS FROM CPA EXAMINATIONS

15-17 **(Objectives 15-2, 15-5)** The following questions concern analytical procedures in the acquisition and payment cycle. Choose the best response.

a. Which of the following comparisons would be most useful to an auditor in auditing an entity's income and expense accounts?
   (1) Prior year accounts payable to current year accounts payable.
   (2) Prior year payroll expense to budgeted current year payroll expense.
   (3) Current year revenue to budgeted current year revenue.
   (4) Current year warranty expense to current year contingent liabilities.

b. The controller of Excello Manufacturing, Inc., wants to use analytical procedures to identify the possible existence of idle equipment or the possibility that equipment has been disposed of without having been written off. Which of the following ratios would best accomplish this objective?
   (1) Depreciation expense/book value of manufacturing equipment.
   (2) Accumulated depreciation/book value of manufacturing equipment.
   (3) Repairs and maintenance cost/direct labor costs.
   (4) Gross manufacturing equipment cost/units produced.

c. Which of the following analytical procedures should be applied to the income statement?
   (1) Select sales and expense items and trace amounts to related supporting documents.
   (2) Ascertain that the net income amount in the statement of cash flows agrees with the net income amount in the income statement.
   (3) Obtain from the proper client representatives the beginning and ending inventory amounts that were used to determine costs of sales.
   (4) Compare the actual revenues and expenses with the corresponding figures of the previous year and investigate significant differences.

15-18 (Objective 15-2) The following questions concern the audit of asset accounts in the acquisition and payment cycle. Choose the best response.

a. In testing for unrecorded retirements of equipment, an auditor most likely would
   (1) select items of equipment from the accounting records and then locate them during the plant tour.
   (2) compare depreciation journal entries with similar prior-year entries in search of fully depreciated equipment.
   (3) inspect items of equipment observed during the plant tour and then trace them to the equipment master file.
   (4) scan the general journal for unusual equipment additions and excessive debits to repairs and maintenance expense.

b. Which of the following is the *best* evidence of real estate ownership at the balance sheet date?
   (1) Title insurance policy.
   (2) Original deed held in the client's safe.
   (3) Paid real estate tax bills.
   (4) Closing statement.

15-19 (Objectives 15-2, 15-4, 15-5) The following questions concern the audit of liabilities or income and expense accounts. Choose the best response.

a. Which of the following audit procedures is *least* likely to detect an unrecorded liability?
   (1) Analysis and recomputation of interest expense.
   (2) Analysis and recomputation of depreciation expense.
   (3) Mailing of standard bank confirmation forms.
   (4) Reading of the minutes of meetings of the board of directors.

b. Which of the following *best* describes the independent auditor's approach to obtaining satisfaction concerning depreciation expense in the income statement?
   (1) Verify the mathematical accuracy of the amounts charged to income as a result of depreciation expense.
   (2) Determine the method for computing depreciation expense and ascertain that it is in accordance with GAAP.
   (3) Reconcile the amount of depreciation expense to those amounts credited to accumulated depreciation accounts.
   (4) Establish the basis for depreciable assets and verify the depreciation expense.

c. Before expressing an opinion concerning the audit of income and expenses, the auditor would *best* proceed with the audit of the income statement by
   (1) applying a rigid measurement standard designed to test for understatement of net income.
   (2) analyzing the beginning and ending balance sheet inventory amounts.
   (3) making net income comparisons to published industry trends and ratios.
   (4) auditing income statement accounts concurrently with the related balance sheet accounts.

DISCUSSION QUESTIONS AND PROBLEMS

15-20 (Objective 15-2) For each of the following misstatements in property, plant, and equipment accounts, state an internal control that the client could install to prevent the misstatement from occurring and a substantive audit procedure that the auditor could use to discover the misstatement:

1. The asset lives used to depreciate equipment are less than reasonable, expected useful lives.
2. Capitalizable assets are routinely expensed as repairs and maintenance, perishable tools, or supplies expense.
3. Computer equipment that is abandoned or traded for replacement equipment is not removed from the accounting records.
4. Depreciation expense for manufacturing operations is charged to administrative expenses.
5. Tools necessary for the maintenance of equipment are stolen by company employees for their personal use.
6. Acquisitions of property are recorded at an improper amount.
7. A loan against existing equipment is not recorded in the accounting records. The cash receipts from the loan never reached the company because they were used for the down payment on a piece of equipment now being used as an operating asset. The equipment is also not recorded in the records.

15-21 (Objective 15-2) The following types of internal controls are commonly used by organizations for property, plant, and equipment:

1. A fixed asset master file is maintained with a separate record for each fixed asset.
2. Written policies exist and are known by accounting personnel to differentiate between capitalizable additions, freight, installation costs, replacements, and maintenance expenditures.

3. Acquisitions of fixed assets in excess of $20,000 are approved by the board of directors.
4. When practical, equipment is labeled with metal tags and is inventoried on a systematic basis.
5. Depreciation charges for individual assets are calculated for each asset; recorded in a fixed asset master file that includes cost, depreciation, and accumulated depreciation for each asset; and verified periodically by an independent clerk.

Required

a. State the purpose of each of the internal controls just listed. Your answer should be in the form of the type of misstatement that is likely to be reduced because of the control.

b. For each internal control, list one test of control the auditor can use to test for its existence.

c. List one substantive procedure for testing whether the control is actually preventing misstatements in property, plant, and equipment.

15-22 **(Objectives 15-1, 15-2, 15-3, 15-5)** The following audit procedures were planned by Linda King, CPA, in the audit of the acquisition and payment cycle for Cooley Products, Inc.:

1. Review the acquisitions journal for large and unusual transactions.
2. Send letters to several vendors, including a few for which the recorded accounts payable balance is zero, requesting them to inform us of their balance due from Cooley. Ask the controller to sign the letter.
3. Examine a sample of receiving report numbers and determine whether each one has an initial indicating that it was recorded as an account payable.
4. Select a sample of equipment listed on fixed asset master files and inspect the asset to determine that it exists and to determine its condition.
5. Refoot the acquisitions journal for 1 month and trace all totals to the general ledger.
6. Calculate the ratio of equipment repairs and maintenance to total equipment and compare with previous years.
7. Obtain from the client a written statement that all mortgages payable have been included in the current period financial statements and have been accurately recorded and that the collateral for each is included in the footnotes.
8. Select a sample of cancelled checks and trace each one to the cash disbursements journal, comparing the name, date, and amount.
9. For 20 nontangible acquisitions, select a sample of line items from the acquisitions journal and trace each to related vendors' invoices. Examine whether each transaction appears to be a legitimate expenditure for the client and that each was approved and recorded at the correct amount and date in the journal and charged to the correct account per the chart of accounts.
10. Examine invoices and related shipping documents included in the client's unpaid invoice file at the audit report date to determine whether they were recorded in the appropriate accounting period and at the correct amounts.
11. Recalculate the portion of insurance premiums on the client's prepaid insurance schedule that is applicable to future periods.
12. When the check signer's assistant writes "paid" on supporting documents, watch whether she does it after the documents are reviewed and the checks are signed.

Required

a. For each procedure, identify the type of evidence being used.

b. For each procedure, identify whether it is an analytical procedure, a test of control, a substantive test of transactions, or a test of details of balances.

c. For each test of control or substantive test of transactions, identify the transaction-related audit objective(s) being met.

d. For each test of details of balances, identify the balance-related audit objective(s) being met.

15-23 **(Objective 15-3)** As part of the audit of different audit areas, it is important to be alert for the possibility of unrecorded liabilities. For each of the following audit areas or accounts, describe a liability that could be uncovered and the audit procedures that could uncover it:

a. Minutes of the board of directors' meetings

b. Land and buildings

c. Rent expense

d. Interest expense

e. Cash surrender value of life insurance

f. Cash in the bank

g. Officers' travel and entertainment expense

15-24 (Objective 15-5) While you are having lunch with a banker friend, you become involved in explaining to him how your firm conducts an audit in a typical engagement. Much to your surprise, your friend is interested and is able to converse intelligently in discussing your philosophy of emphasizing the study of internal control, analytical procedures, tests of controls, substantive tests of transactions, and tests of details of balance sheet accounts. At the completion of your discussion, he says, "That all sounds great except for a couple of things. The point of view we take these days at our bank is the importance of a continuous earnings stream. You seem to be emphasizing fraud detection and a fairly stated balance sheet. We would rather see you put more emphasis than you apparently do on the income statement."

Required How would you respond to your friend's comments?

CASE

15-25 (Objective 15-2) You are doing the audit of the Ute Corporation, for the year ended December 31, 2002. The following schedule for the property, plant, and equipment and related allowance for depreciation accounts has been prepared by the client. You have compared the opening balances with your prior year's audit working papers.

UTE Corporation Analysis of Property, Plant, and Equipment and Related Allowance for Depreciation Accounts
Year Ended December 31, 2002

Description	Final 12/31/01	Additions	Retirements	Per Books 12/31/02
Assets				
Land	$ 225,000	$ 50,000		$ 275,000
Buildings	1,200,000	175,000		1,375,000
Machinery and equipment	3,850,000	404,000	260,000	3,994,000
	$5,275,000	$629,000	$260,000	$5,644,000
Allowance for Depreciation				
Building	$ 600,000	$ 51,500		$ 651,500
Machinery and equipment	1,732,500	392,200		2,124,700
	$2,332,500	$443,700		$2,776,200

The following information is found during your audit:

1. All equipment is depreciated on the straight-line basis (no salvage value taken into consideration) based on the following estimated lives: buildings, 25 years; all other items, 10 years. The corporation's policy is to take one-half year's depreciation on all asset acquisitions and disposals during the year.
2. On April 1, the corporation entered into a 10-year lease contract for a die-casting machine with annual rentals of $50,000, payable in advance every April 1. The lease is cancelable by either party (60 days' written notice is required), and there is no option to renew the lease or buy the equipment at the end of the lease. The estimated useful life of the machine is 10 years with no salvage value. The corporation recorded the die-casting machine in the machinery and equipment account at $404,000, the present value at the date of the lease, and $20,200, applicable to the machine, has been included in depreciation expense for the year.
3. The corporation completed the construction of a wing on the plant building on June 30. The useful life of the building was not extended by this addition. The lowest construction bid received was $175,000, the amount recorded in the buildings account. Company personnel were used to construct the addition at a cost of $160,000 (materials, $75,000; labor, $55,000; and overhead, $30,000).
4. On August 18, $50,000 was paid for paving and fencing a portion of land owned by the corporation and used as a parking lot for employees. The expenditure was charged to the land account.
5. The amount shown in the machinery and equipment asset retirement column represents cash received on September 5, upon disposal of a machine acquired in July 1998 for $480,000. The bookkeeper recorded depreciation expense of $35,000 on this machine in 2002.
6. Crux City donated land and building appraised at $100,000 and $400,000, respectively, to the Ute Corporation for a plant. On September 1, the corporation began operating the plant. Because no costs were involved, the bookkeeper made no entry for the foregoing transaction.

a. In addition to inquiry of the client, explain how you would have found each of these six items during the audit.

b. Prepare the adjusting journal entries with supporting computations that you would suggest at December 31, 2002, to adjust the accounts for the preceding transactions. Disregard income tax implications.*

Required

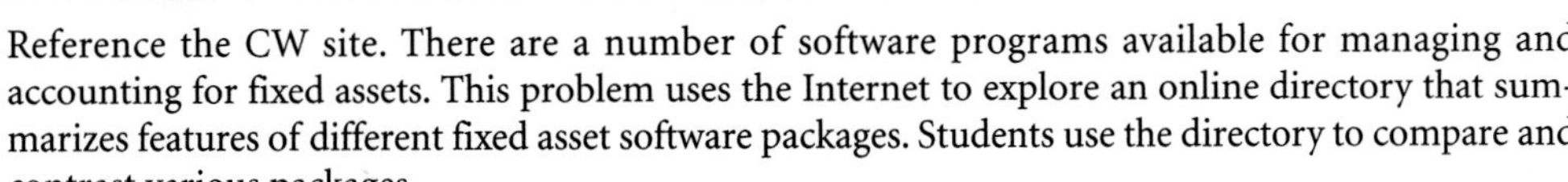

INTERNET PROBLEM 15-1: MANAGING FIXED ASSETS

Reference the CW site. There are a number of software programs available for managing and accounting for fixed assets. This problem uses the Internet to explore an online directory that summarizes features of different fixed asset software packages. Students use the directory to compare and contrast various packages.

*AICPA adapted.

CHAPTER 16

AUDIT OF THE INVENTORY AND WAREHOUSING CYCLE

DON'T IGNORE RED FLAGS

Packard, Packard & Dodge (PP&D) had audited Farago, a commercial finance company owned by a large heavy equipment dealer, for the past 7 years. When equipment was sold on credit by the dealer, the transaction was financed through Farago. If customers defaulted on their loan payments, Farago would repossess the equipment inventory.

In assessing inherent risk for repossessed inventory, the engagement senior, Rich Haney, noted that the commercial finance industry was experiencing problems and that Farago's management was aggressive in its choice of accounting policies and seemed quite concerned about earnings. Rich believed that inherent risk should probably be increased at least to a medium level, leading to increased testing of the repossessed inventory. However, the engagement manager, Jerry Bliss, thought differently. Jerry told Rich, "Nothing has changed on this audit. Just state that risk is low and do the same amount of testing."

In determining the existence of repossessed equipment inventory, PP&D had always relied on internal reports from the branch managers who held the equipment. Based on the prior year's work, Rich concluded that physical inspection was not necessary. In determining the value of equipment inventory, Rich relied on discussions with management, the same as in the prior year. As in the past, management did not get appraisals of the equipment, stating that their familiarity with the industry allowed them to make reasonable estimates. The auditors accepted this without further challenge. Based on finding no significant exceptions, PP&D issued an unqualified report.

When PP&D conducted their audit of Farago the next year, Jerry Bliss had left the firm and a new manager was assigned. Conditions in the commercial finance industry had deteriorated even more during the year, and the amount of repossessed inventory had increased significantly. The listing of repossessed equipment included many large items that had been included in the previous year. The new audit manager insisted on physical inspection of larger repossessed items. The result of this procedure was the discovery that the items did not exist. Investigation revealed that they had been sold and the proceeds recorded against the allowance for uncollectible loans, which was also understated. It was also clear that these practices had existed for at least the past 2 or 3 years.

LEARNING OBJECTIVES

After studying this chapter, you should be able to

16-1 Identify the business functions and the related documents and records in the inventory and warehousing cycle.

16-2 Describe how e-commerce affects inventory management.

16-3 Explain the five parts of the audit of the inventory and warehousing cycle.

16-4 Design and perform audit tests of cost accounting.

16-5 Apply analytical procedures to the accounts in the inventory and warehousing cycle.

16-6 Design and perform physical observation audit tests for inventory.

16-7 Design and perform audit tests of pricing and compilation for inventory.

16-8 Integrate the various parts of the audit of the inventory and warehousing cycle.

The **inventory and warehousing cycle** is unique because of its close relationships to other transaction cycles. Raw material and direct labor enter the inventory and warehousing cycle from the acquisition and payment cycle and the payroll and personnel cycle, respectively. The inventory and warehousing cycle ends with the sale of goods in the sales and collection cycle.

The audit of inventory, especially tests of the year-end inventory balance, is often the most complex and time-consuming part of the audit. As the example involving the audit of Farago in the opening vignette demonstrates, it is often difficult to establish the existence and appropriate valuation of inventories. Factors affecting the complexity of the audit of inventory include the following:

Inventory Fraud

- Inventory is generally a major item on the balance sheet, and it is often the largest item making up the accounts included in working capital.
- The inventory is in different locations, which makes physical control and counting difficult. Companies must have their inventory accessible for the efficient manufacture and sale of the product, but this dispersal creates significant auditing problems.
- The diversity of the items in inventories creates difficulties for the auditor. Such items as jewels, chemicals, and electronic parts present problems of observation and valuation.
- The valuation of inventory is also difficult because of such factors as obsolescence and the need to allocate manufacturing costs to inventory.
- There are several acceptable inventory valuation methods, but any given client must apply a method consistently from year to year. Moreover, an organization may prefer to use different valuation methods for different parts of the inventory, which is acceptable under GAAP.

This chapter begins the discussion of the audit of the inventory and warehousing cycle by identifying the business functions in the cycle and the related documents and records.

BUSINESS FUNCTIONS IN THE CYCLE AND RELATED DOCUMENTS AND RECORDS

OBJECTIVE **16-1**

Identify the business functions and the related documents and records in the inventory and warehousing cycle.

Inventory takes many different forms, depending on the nature of the business. For retail or wholesale businesses, the most important inventory is merchandise on hand, available for sale. For hospitals, it includes food, drugs, and medical supplies. A manufacturing company has raw materials, purchased parts and supplies for use in production, goods in the process of being manufactured, and finished goods available for sale. We have selected manufacturing company inventories for presentation in this text. However, most of the principles discussed apply to other types of businesses as well.

The inventory and warehousing cycle can be thought of as comprising two separate but closely related systems, one involving the actual *physical flow of goods* and the other the *related costs.* As inventories move through the company, there must be adequate controls over both their physical movement and their related costs. The physical flow, the six functions and the related documents that make up the inventory and warehousing cycle are shown in Figure 16-1.

Observe that most of the documents and records were included in previous chapters in the study of the sales and collection cycle and acquisition and payment cycle. Acquisitions are related to inventory and warehousing because raw materials and manufacturing costs included in manufacturing overhead are initially accounted for in the acquisition and payment cycle. Similarly, all sales of inventory are initially recorded in the sales and collection cycle. Although not covered in the text, manufacturing payroll is initially accounted for in the payroll and personnel cycle.

In the initial recording of inventory-related transactions in other cycles, inventory records are typically recorded simultaneously. For example, when acquisitions of inventory are recorded most accounting systems automatically record the purchase in perpetual inventory records.

In any company involved in manufacturing, an adequate cost accounting system is important. The system is necessary to indicate the relative profitability of the various

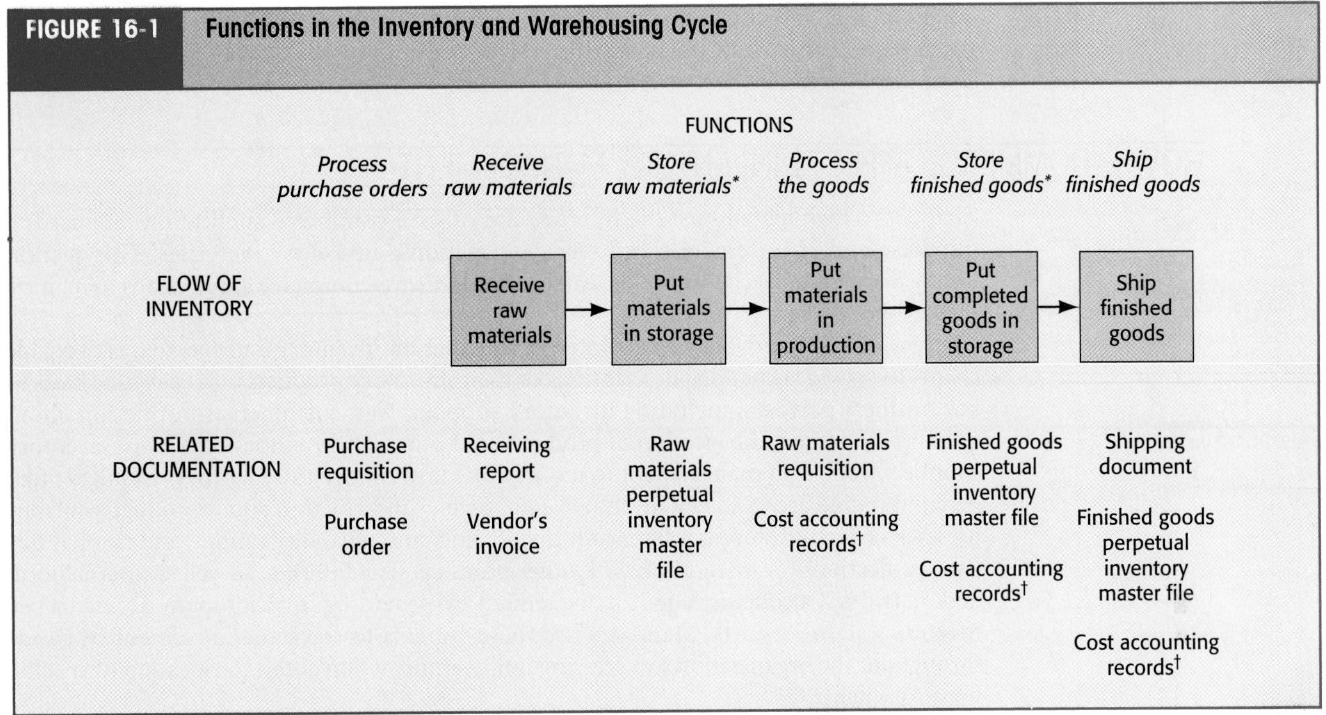

*Inventory counts are taken and compared with perpetual and book amounts at any stage of the cycle. The auditor must determine that cutoff for recording documents corresponds to the physical location of the items. A count must ordinarily be taken once a year. If the perpetual inventory system is operating well, this can be done on a cycle basis throughout the year.
†Includes cost information for materials, direct labor, and overhead.

products for management planning and control and to value inventories for financial statement purposes. Two types of cost systems exist, although many variations and combinations of these systems are used: **job cost systems** and **process cost systems.** The main difference is whether costs are accumulated by individual jobs when material is issued and labor costs incurred (job cost) or whether they are accumulated by processes, with unit costs for each process assigned to the products passing through the process (process cost).

Cost accounting records consist of master files, worksheets, and reports that accumulate material, labor, and overhead costs by job or process as the costs are incurred. When jobs or products are completed, the related costs are transferred from work-in-process to finished goods on the basis of production department reports.

A record used for inventory that has not been previously discussed is a **perpetual inventory master file.** Separate perpetual records are normally kept for raw materials and finished goods. Most companies do not use perpetuals for work-in-process.

Perpetual inventory master files can include only information about the units of inventory acquired, sold, and on hand, or they can also include information about unit costs. The latter is more typical of well-designed computerized systems.

For acquisitions of raw materials, the perpetual inventory master file is updated automatically when acquisitions of inventory are processed as a part of recording acquisitions. For example, when the computer system enters the number of units and unit cost for each raw material acquisition, this information is used to update perpetual inventory master files along with the acquisitions journal and accounts payable master file.

Transfers of raw material from the storeroom must be separately entered into the computer to update the perpetual records. Typically, only the units transferred need to be entered because the computer can determine the unit costs from the master file. Raw material perpetual inventory master files that have unit costs include, for each raw material, beginning and ending units on hand and unit costs, units and unit cost of each acquisition, and units and unit cost of each transfer into production.

Finished goods perpetual inventory master files include the same type of information as raw materials perpetuals but are considerably more complex if costs are included along with units. Finished goods costs include raw materials, direct labor, and manufacturing overhead, which often requires allocations and detailed record keeping. When finished goods perpetuals include unit costs, the cost accounting records must be integrated into the computer system.

HOW E-COMMERCE AFFECTS INVENTORY MANAGEMENT

OBJECTIVE 16-2

Describe how e-commerce affects inventory management.

Chapter 14 highlighted how the Internet and other e-commerce applications are used to purchase and acquire goods and services, including inventory materials. This section briefly discusses how clients use the Internet and other e-commerce applications to manage inventories.

One of the key advantages the Internet provides for inventory management is to enable clients to provide expanded descriptions of their inventory products on a real-time basis to key business partners, including inventory suppliers and customers. Information about quantities on hand, the location of products, and other key inventory data helps inventory suppliers work with management to monitor the flow of inventory items. Customers often demand online access to key inventory data, such as information about product availability, back order and shipping status, product quality and reliability ratings, and compatibility specifications for integration with other products. The Internet, as well as internal local area networks, also assist client management by providing intracompany access to key inventory status reports. Managers use these systems to track the movement of goods throughout the organization by accessing online information about the location of specific inventory items.

Expanded access to information may increase business risks, such as the risk that sensitive proprietary information may unintentionally be made available to unauthorized users. The use of the Internet and other e-commerce applications may lead to financial reporting risks if access to inventory databases and systems is not adequately controlled. The use of security access restrictions such as passwords, firewalls, and other IT management controls are critical to reducing the risk of external parties manipulating a company's inventory records that are used to prepare financial statement information.

PARTS OF THE AUDIT OF INVENTORY

OBJECTIVE 16-3

Explain the five parts of the audit of the inventory and warehousing cycle.

Now that you are familiar with the business functions and the related documents and records in the inventory and warehousing cycle, we are ready to turn our attention to the audit of the cycle. The overall objective in the audit of the inventory and warehousing cycle is to determine that raw materials, work-in-process, finished goods inventory, and cost of goods sold are fairly stated on the financial statements. The audit of the inventory and warehousing cycle can be divided into five distinct parts.

Acquire and Record Raw Materials, Labor, and Overhead

This part of the audit of the inventory and warehousing cycle includes the first three functions in Figure 16-1: process purchase orders, receive raw materials, and store raw materials. The internal controls over these three functions are first understood then tested as a part of performing tests of controls and substantive tests of transactions in the acquisition and payment cycle and the payroll and personnel cycle. At the completion of the acquisition and payment cycle, the auditor is likely to be satisfied that acquisitions of raw materials and manufacturing costs are correctly stated and samples should be designed to ensure that these systems are adequately tested. Similarly, when labor is a significant part of inventory, the payroll and personnel cycle tests should verify the proper accounting for these costs.

Transfer Assets and Costs

Internal transfers include the fourth and fifth functions in Figure 16-1: process the goods and store finished goods. These activities are accounted for in the cost accounting records. These records are independent of other cycles and are tested as part of the audit of the inventory and warehousing cycle.

Ship Goods and Record Revenue and Costs

Recording of shipments and related costs, the last function in Figure 16-1, is part of the sales and collection cycle. Therefore, internal controls over the function are understood and tested as a part of auditing the sales and collection cycle. Tests of controls and substantive tests of transactions should include procedures to verify the accuracy of the perpetual inventory master files.

Physically Observe Inventory

Observing the client taking a physical inventory count is necessary to determine whether recorded inventory actually exists at the balance sheet date and is properly counted by the client. Inventory is the first audit area for which physical examination is an essential type of evidence used to verify the balance in an account. The example at the beginning of the chapter involving the audit of Farago demonstrates the importance of physically observing inventories that are material to the financial statements.

Price and Compile Inventory

Costs used to value the physical inventory must be tested to determine whether the client has correctly followed an inventory method that is in accordance with GAAP and is consistent with previous years. Audit procedures used to verify these costs are called price tests. In addition, the auditor must verify whether the physical counts were correctly summarized, the inventory quantities and prices were correctly extended, and the extended inventory was correctly footed. These tests are called compilation tests.

Figure 16-2 summarizes the five parts of the audit of the inventory and warehousing cycle. Because of the interrelationships of the inventory and warehousing cycle with other cycles, some parts of the audit of inventory are most efficiently tested with the audit tests of other cycles. As noted in Figure 16-2, the acquisition and recording of raw materials, labor, and overhead is tested as part of the audit of the acquisition and payment and payroll and personnel cycles. The shipment of goods and recording of revenue and related costs are addressed in the audit of the sales and collection cycle. Because most of these activities involving the audit of other cycles have previously been discussed, they are not addressed in this chapter. However, the results of these tests of other cycles are important to the overall evaluation of the audit of inventory.

The following section discusses the audit of cost accounting. We begin by discussing the internal transfer of assets and costs, which are accounted for in the cost accounting records. The internal transfer of assets and costs is one of the three parts of the audit of the inventory and warehousing cycle that is not tested in other cycles.

FIGURE 16-2 Audit of Inventory

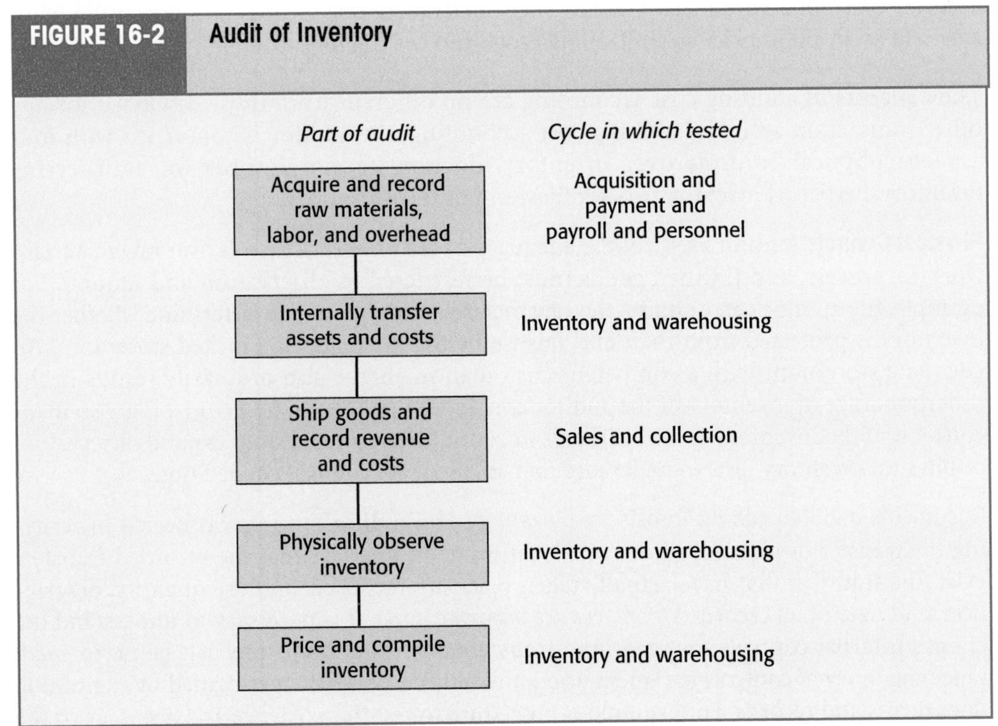

AUDIT OF COST ACCOUNTING

OBJECTIVE 16-4

Design and perform audit tests of cost accounting.

Cost accounting systems and controls of different companies vary more than most other areas because of the wide variety of items of inventory and the level of sophistication desired by management. For example, a company that manufactures an entire line of farm machines will have a completely different kind of cost records and internal controls than a steel fabricating shop that makes and installs custom-made metal cabinets. It should also not be surprising that small companies whose owners are actively involved in the manufacturing process will need less sophisticated records than will large, multiproduct companies.

Cost Accounting Controls

Cost accounting controls are those related to the physical inventory and the related costs from the point at which raw materials are requisitioned to the point at which the manufactured product is completed and transferred to storage. It is convenient to divide these controls into two broad categories: (1) physical controls over raw materials, work-in-process, and finished goods inventory, and (2) controls over the related costs.

Almost all companies need physical controls over their assets to prevent loss from misuse and theft. The use of physically segregated, limited-access storage areas for raw material, work-in-process, and finished goods is one major control to protect assets. In some instances, the assignment of custody of inventory to specific responsible individuals may be necessary to protect the assets. Approved prenumbered documents for authorizing movement of inventory also protect the assets from improper use. Copies of these documents should be sent directly to accounting by the persons issuing them, bypassing people with custodial responsibilities. An example of an effective document of this type is an approved materials requisition for obtaining raw materials from the storeroom.

Acquire and record raw materials, labor, and overhead

Internally transfer assets and costs

Ship goods and record revenue and costs

Physically observe inventory

Price and compile inventory

Perpetual inventory master files maintained by persons who do not have custody of or access to assets are another useful cost accounting control. Perpetual inventory master files are important for a number of reasons: They provide a record of items on hand, which is used to initiate production or acquisition of additional materials or goods; they provide a record of the use of raw materials and the sale of finished goods, which can be reviewed for obsolete or slow-moving items; and they provide a record that can be used to pinpoint responsibility for custody as a part of the investigation of differences between physical counts and the amount shown on the records.

Another important consideration in cost accounting is the existence of adequate internal controls that integrate production and accounting records for the purpose of obtaining accurate costs for all products. The existence of adequate cost records is important to management as an aid in pricing, controlling costs, and costing inventory.

Tests of Cost Accounting

The concepts in auditing cost accounting are no different from those discussed for any other transaction cycle. In auditing cost accounting, the auditor is concerned with four aspects: physical controls over inventory, documents and records for transferring inventory, perpetual inventory master files, and unit cost records.

Physical Controls Auditor's tests of the adequacy of the physical controls over raw materials, work-in-process, and finished goods must be restricted to observation and inquiry. For example, the auditor can examine the raw materials storage area to determine whether the inventory is protected from theft and misuse by the existence of a locked storeroom. An adequate storeroom with a competent custodian in charge also ordinarily results in the orderly storage of inventory. If the auditor concludes that the physical controls are so inadequate that the inventory will be difficult to count, the auditor should expand observation of physical inventory tests to make sure that an adequate count is carried out.

Documents and Records for Transferring Inventory The auditor's primary concerns in verifying the transfer of inventory from one location to another are that the recorded transfers exist, the transfers that have actually taken place are recorded, and the quantity, description, and date of all recorded transfers are accurate. First, it is necessary to understand the client's internal controls for recording transfers before relevant tests can be performed. Once the internal controls are understood, the tests can easily be performed by examining documents and records. For example, a procedure to test the existence and accuracy of the transfer of goods from the raw material storeroom to the manufacturing assembly line is to account for a sequence of raw material requisitions, examine the requisitions for proper approval, and compare the quantity, description, and date with the information on the raw material perpetual inventory master files. Similarly, completed production records can be compared with perpetual inventory master files to be sure that all manufactured goods were physically delivered to the finished goods storeroom.

Technology has improved the ability to track the movement of goods throughout production. For example, products are labeled with standardized bar codes that can be scanned by laser to track the movement of inventory items.

Perpetual Inventory Master Files Adequate perpetual inventory master files have a major effect on the *timing* and *extent* of the auditor's physical examination of inventory. When there are accurate perpetual inventory master files, it is often possible to test the physical inventory before the balance sheet date. An interim physical inventory can result in significant cost savings for both the client and the auditor, and it enables the client to get the audited statements earlier. Perpetual inventory master files also enable the auditor to reduce the extent of the tests of physical inventory when the assessed control risk related to physical observation of inventory is low.

Tests of the perpetual inventory master files for the purpose of reducing tests of physical inventory or changing their timing are done through the use of documentation. Documents to verify the acquisition of raw materials can be examined when the auditor is verifying acquisitions as part of the tests of the acquisition and payment cycle. Documents supporting the reduction of raw material inventory for use in production and the increase in the quantity of finished goods inventory when goods have been manufactured are examined as part of the tests of the cost accounting records in the manner discussed in the preceding section. Support for the reduction in the finished goods inventory through the sale of goods to customers is ordinarily tested as part of the sales and collection cycle. Usually, it is relatively easy to test the accuracy of the perpetuals after the auditor determines how the internal controls are designed and decides to what degree assessed control risk should be reduced.

For many companies, traditional documents exist only in electronic form. Also, the perpetual inventory system is often integrated with other accounting cycles and is automatically updated with activity in those cycles. As a result, there may be opportunities to test computer-performed controls to support a reduction in control risk, which reduces the extent of substantive testing. This in turn may lead to audit efficiencies in the testing of the inventory and warehousing cycle.

Unit Cost Records Obtaining accurate cost data for raw materials, direct labor, and manufacturing overhead is an essential part of cost accounting. Adequate cost accounting records must be integrated with production and other accounting records to produce accurate costs of all products. Cost accounting records are pertinent to the auditor in that the valuation of ending inventory depends on the proper design and use of these records.

In testing the inventory cost records, the auditor must first develop an understanding of internal control. This is often somewhat time-consuming because the flow of costs is usually integrated with other accounting records, and it may not be obvious how the internal controls provide for the internal transfers of raw materials and for direct labor and manufacturing overhead as production is carried out.

Once the auditor understands internal control, the approach to internal verification involves the same concepts that were discussed in the verification of sales and acquisition transactions. When possible, it is desirable to test cost accounting records as a part of the acquisition, payroll, and sales tests to avoid testing the records more than once. For example, when the auditor is testing acquisition transactions as a part of the acquisition and payment cycle, it is desirable to trace the units and unit costs of raw materials to the perpetual inventory master files and the total cost to cost accounting records. Similarly, when payroll costs data are maintained for different jobs, it is desirable to trace from the payroll summary directly to job cost records as a part of testing the payroll and personnel cycle.

A major difficulty in the verification of inventory cost records is determining the reasonableness of cost allocations. For example, the assignment of manufacturing overhead costs to individual products entails certain assumptions that can significantly affect the unit costs of inventory and therefore the fairness of the inventory valuation. In evaluating these allocations, the auditor must consider the reasonableness of both the numerator and the denominator that result in the unit costs. For example, in testing overhead applied to inventory on the basis of direct labor dollars, the overhead rate should approximate total actual manufacturing overhead divided by total actual direct labor dollars. Because total manufacturing overhead is tested as part of the tests of the acquisition and payment cycle and direct labor is tested as part of the payroll and personnel cycle, determining the reasonableness of the rate is not difficult. However, if manufacturing overhead is applied on the basis of machine hours, the auditor must verify the reasonableness of the machine hours by separate tests of the client's machine records. The major considerations in evaluating the reasonableness of all cost allocations, including manufacturing overhead, are compliance with generally accepted accounting principles and consistency with previous years.

Because the internal controls over cost accounting records vary significantly among organizations, specific tests of controls are not presented here. The auditor should design appropriate tests based on the understanding of the nature of the cost accounting records and the extent to which they will be relied on to reduce substantive tests. The quality of the cost accounting records also affects the use of analytical procedures, which is discussed in the next section.

ANALYTICAL PROCEDURES

OBJECTIVE 16-5

Apply analytical procedures to the accounts in the inventory and warehousing cycle.

Analytical procedures are as important in auditing inventory and warehousing as in any other cycle. Table 16-1 includes several common analytical procedures and possible misstatements that may be indicated when fluctuations exist. Several of those analytical procedures have also been included in other cycles. An example is the gross margin percentage.

In addition to performing analytical procedures that examine the relationship of inventory account balances with other financial statement accounts, auditors often use nonfinancial information to assess the reasonableness of inventory-related balances. For example, knowledge about the size and weight of inventory products, their methods of

TABLE 16-1 Analytical Procedures for the Inventory and Warehousing Cycle

Analytical Procedure	Possible Misstatement
Compare gross margin percentage with that of previous years.	Overstatement or understatement of inventory and cost of goods sold.
Compare inventory turnover (cost of goods sold divided by average inventory) with that of previous years.	Obsolete inventory, which affects inventory and cost of goods sold. Overstatement or understatement of inventory.
Compare unit costs of inventory with those of previous years.	Overstatement or understatement of unit costs, which affect inventory and cost of goods sold.
Compare extended inventory value with that of previous years.	Misstatements in compilation, unit costs, or extensions, which affect inventory and cost of goods sold.
Compare current year manufacturing costs with those of previous years (variable costs should be adjusted for changes in volume).	Misstatements of unit costs of inventory, especially direct labor and manufacturing overhead, which affect inventory and cost of goods sold.

storage (stacks, tanks, etc.), and the capacity of storage facilities (such as available square footage) can be used to determine whether recorded inventory is consistent with available inventory storage.

After performing the appropriate tests of the cost accounting records and analytical procedures, the auditor is prepared to design and perform tests of details of the ending inventory balance.

METHODOLOGY FOR DESIGNING TESTS OF DETAILS OF BALANCES

The methodology for deciding which tests of details of balances to perform for inventory and warehousing is essentially the same as that discussed for accounts receivable, accounts payable, and all other balance sheet accounts.

Obtaining an understanding of the client's business is even more important for inventory than for most aspects of the audit because inventory varies so significantly for different companies. A proper understanding of the client's business and its industry enables the auditor to ask about and discuss such problems as inventory valuation, potential obsolescence, and the existence of consignment inventory intermingled with owned inventory. A useful starting point for becoming familiar with the client's inventory is for the auditor to tour the client's facilities, including receiving, storage, production, planning, and record-keeping areas. The tour should be led by a supervisor who can answer questions about production, especially about any changes in the past year.

As part of gaining an understanding of the effect of the client's business and industry on inventory in the planning phase of the audit, the auditor assesses client business risk. There may be significant sources of business risk related to inventory because of such factors as short product cycles and the risk of obsolescence, use of just-in-time inventory and other supply-chain management techniques, reliance on a few key suppliers, and use of sophisticated inventory management technology.

After assessing client business risk, the auditor then sets tolerable misstatement and assesses inherent risk for inventory. Inventory is typically one of the most material items in the financial statements for manufacturing, wholesale, and retail companies. Inherent risk is often assessed at a relatively high level for companies with significant inventory. Inventory may be stored in multiple locations, increasing concerns about the existence of inventory, including the potential for theft. The pricing of inventory is often complex, increasing the risk of misstatement for the accuracy objective. There may also be concerns about inventory obsolescence, which relates to the net realizable value objective.

In assessing control risk, the auditor is primarily concerned about internal controls over perpetual records, physical controls, inventory counts, and inventory pricing. The nature and extent of controls vary widely from company to company. Note that the test results from several cycles other than inventory and warehousing also affect tests of details of balances for inventory.

Because of the complexity of auditing inventory, two aspects of tests of details of balances are discussed separately: (1) physical observation and (2) pricing and compilation. These topics are studied in the next two sections.

PHYSICAL OBSERVATION OF INVENTORY

OBJECTIVE 16-6

Design and perform physical observation audit tests for inventory.

Auditors have been required to perform physical observation tests of inventory since a major fraud was uncovered in 1938 at the McKesson & Robbins Company. The company recorded significant amounts of nonexistent inventory. This was possible because the auditors did not physically observe the inventory. SAS 1 (AU 331) states that the following requirement exists for inventory observation:

- . . . it is ordinarily necessary for the independent auditor to be present at the time of count and, by suitable observation, tests, and inquiries, satisfy himself respecting the effectiveness of the methods of inventory-taking and the measure of reliance which

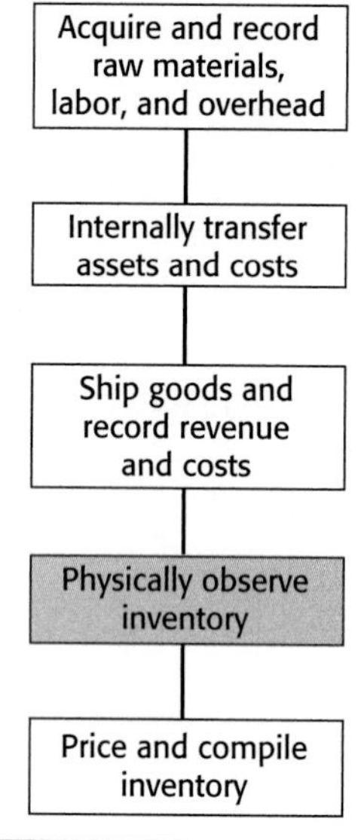

may be placed upon the client's representations about the quantities and physical condition of the inventories.

An essential point in the SAS 1 requirement is the distinction between the observation of the physical inventory count and the responsibility for taking the count. The client has responsibility for setting up the procedures for taking an accurate physical inventory and actually making and recording the counts. The auditor's responsibility is to evaluate and observe the client's physical procedures and draw conclusions about the adequacy of the physical inventory.

The requirement of physical examination of inventory is not applicable in the case of inventory in a public warehouse. Inventory in a public warehouse or with other outside custodians is normally verified by confirmation with the custodian. However, if the inventory amounts involved are a significant portion of current assets or total assets, the auditor should apply additional procedures. These may include investigating the custodian's performance, receiving an independent accountant's report on the custodian's control procedures over the custody of goods, and observing the physical count of the goods held by the custodian, if practical.

Controls

Regardless of the client's inventory record-keeping method, there must be a periodic physical count of the inventory items on hand. The client can take the physical count at or near the balance sheet date, at a preliminary date, or on a cycle basis throughout the year. The last two approaches are appropriate only if there are adequate controls over the preparation and maintenance of perpetual inventory master files.

In connection with the client's physical count of inventory, adequate controls include proper instructions for the physical count, supervision by responsible personnel, independent internal verification of the counts, independent reconciliations of the physical counts with perpetual inventory master files, and adequate control over count sheets or tags.

An important aspect of the auditor's understanding of the client's physical inventory controls is complete familiarity with them before the inventory begins. This is obviously necessary to evaluate the effectiveness of the client's procedures, but it also enables the auditor to make constructive suggestions beforehand. If the inventory instructions do not provide adequate controls, the auditor must spend more time making sure that the physical count is accurate.

Audit Decisions

The auditor's decisions in the physical observation of inventory are similar to those made for other audit areas and include selecting audit procedures, deciding the timing of the procedures, determining sample size, and selecting items for testing. The last three decisions are discussed next, followed by a discussion of selecting the appropriate audit procedures.

Timing The auditor decides whether the physical count can be taken before year-end primarily on the basis of the accuracy of the perpetual inventory master files. When an interim physical count is permitted, the auditor observes it at that time and also tests the perpetuals for transactions from the date of the count to year-end. When the perpetuals are accurate, it may be unnecessary for the client to count the inventory every year. Instead, the auditor can compare the perpetuals with the actual inventory on a sample basis at a convenient time. When there are no perpetuals and the inventory is material, a complete physical inventory must be taken by the client near the end of the accounting period and tested by the auditor at the same time.

Sample Size Sample size in physical observation is usually impossible to specify in terms of the number of items because the emphasis during the tests is on observing the client's procedures rather than on selecting items for testing. A convenient way to think of sample size in physical observation is in terms of the total number of hours spent rather than the number of inventory items counted. The most important determinants of the amount of time needed to test inventory are the adequacy of the internal controls over the physical counts, accuracy of the perpetual inventory master files, total dollar amount and type of inventory, number of different significant inventory locations, nature and extent of misstatements discovered in previous years, and other inherent risks. In some situations, inventory is such a significant item that dozens of auditors are necessary to observe the physical count, whereas in other situations one person can complete the observation in a short time. Special care is warranted in the observation of inventory because of the difficulty of expanding sample sizes or reperforming tests after the physical inventory has been taken.

Selection of Items The selection of items for testing is an important part of the audit decision in inventory observation. Care should be taken to observe the counting of the most significant items and a representative sample of typical inventory items, to inquire about items that are likely to be obsolete or damaged, and to discuss with management the reasons for excluding any material items.

Physical Observation Tests

The same balance-related audit objectives that have been used in previous sections for tests of details of balances provide the frame of reference for discussing the physical observation tests. However, before the objectives are discussed, some comments that apply to all the objectives are appropriate.

The most important part of the observation of inventory is determining whether the physical count is being taken in accordance with the client's instructions. To do this effectively, *it is essential that the auditor be present* while the physical count is taking place. When the client's employees are not following the inventory instructions, the auditor must either contact the supervisor to correct the problem or modify the physical observation procedures. For example, if the procedures require one team to count the inventory and a second team to recount it as a test of accuracy, the auditor should inform management if both teams are observed counting together.

Common tests of details of balances audit procedures for physical inventory observation are shown in Table 16-2 (p. 470). Detail tie-in and presentation and disclosure are the only balance-related audit objectives not included in the table. These objectives are discussed under compilation of inventory. The assumption throughout is that the client records inventory on prenumbered tags on the balance sheet date.

In addition to the detailed procedures included in Table 16-2, the auditor should walk through all areas where inventory is warehoused to make sure that all inventory has been counted and properly tagged. When inventory is in boxes or other containers, these should be opened during test counts. It is desirable to compare high-dollar-value inventory to counts in the previous year and inventory master files as a test of reasonableness. These two procedures should not be done until the client has completed the physical counts.

THE CRAZY EDDIE, INC., FRAUD

By 1970, Crazy Eddie, Inc., a consumer electronics retail company, had 43 consumer sales outlets, sales of $350 million, reported net income before taxes of $21 million, and a market value of more than $500 million. Consumer electronics is a highly cyclical and competitive industry, with significant client business risk. Crazy Eddie seemed to be bucking industry trends by growing as other electronics retailers were struggling, but it was an illusion. By the end of 1989, the company had filed for bankruptcy, closed all stores, and liquidated all assets at a huge loss to investors.

Investigation by regulatory authorities found extensive financial fraud, the most important being a $65 million overstatement of inventory. There were extensive lawsuits against many parties, including the CEO, who was found guilty of fraud and sent to prison.

Naturally, the question arose as to why the auditors failed to uncover the fraud in their annual audit. The defense used by the auditor was the difficulty of uncovering the well-conceived fraud. The parties involved in or who knew of the fraud included the acting controller, the director of internal auditing, and the director of accounts payable. One example of fraud was the shipment of inventory from store to store immediately before the auditor arrived to count the inventory. Another was the destruction of documentation to conceal inventory shortages at various locations. The auditor argued that it is almost impossible to uncover fraud when there is extensive collusion. The suit against the CPA firm and other defendants was settled out of court in 1993.

Sources: Adapted from 1. Michael C. Knapp, *Contemporary Auditing: Issues and Cases*, 4th edition. West Publishing, 2001, pp. 71–81. 2. Joseph T. Wells, "Crazy Eddie and the $120 Million Ripoff," *Journal of Accountancy* (October 2000), pp. 93–95.

TABLE 16-2 Balance-Related Audit Objectives and Tests of Details of Balances for Physical Inventory Observation

Balance-Related Audit Objective	Common Inventory Observation Procedures	Comments
Inventory as recorded on tags exists (existence).	Select a random sample of tag numbers and identify the tag with that number attached to the actual inventory. Observe whether movement of inventory takes place during the count.	The purpose is to uncover the inclusion of nonexistent items as inventory.
Existing inventory is counted and tagged and tags are accounted for to make sure none are missing (completeness).	Examine inventory to make sure it is tagged. Observe whether movement of inventory takes place during the count. Inquire as to inventory in other locations. Account for all used and unused tags to make sure none are lost or intentionally omitted. Record the tag numbers for those used and unused for subsequent follow-up.	Special concern should be directed to omission of large sections of inventory. This test should be done at the completion of the physical count. This test should be done at the completion of the physical count.
Inventory is counted accurately (accuracy).	Recount client's counts to make sure the recorded counts are accurate on the tags (also check descriptions and unit of count, such as dozen or gross). Compare physical counts with perpetual inventory master file. Record client's counts for subsequent testing.	Recording client counts in the audit files on *inventory count sheets* is done for two reasons: to obtain documentation that an adequate physical examination was made, and to test for the possibility that the client might change the recorded counts after the auditor leaves the premises.
Inventory is classified correctly on the tags (classification).	Examine inventory descriptions on the tags and compare with the actual inventory for raw material, work-in-process, and finished goods. Evaluate whether the percent of completion recorded on the tags for work-in-process is reasonable.	These tests would be done as a part of the first procedure in the accuracy objective.
Information is obtained to make sure sales and inventory purchases are recorded in the proper period (cutoff).	Record in the audit files for subsequent follow-up the last shipping document number used at year-end. Make sure the inventory for the above item was excluded from the physical count. Review shipping area for inventory set aside for shipment but not counted. Record in the audit files for subsequent follow-up the last receiving report number used at year-end. Make sure the inventory for the above item was included in the physical count. Review receiving area for inventory that should be included in the physical count.	Obtaining proper cutoff information for sales and acquisitions is an essential part of inventory observation. The appropriate tests during the field work were discussed for sales in Chapter 11 and acquisitions in Chapter 14.
Obsolete and unusable inventory items are excluded or noted (realizable value).	Test for obsolete inventory by inquiry of factory employees and management and alertness for items that are damaged, rust- or dust-covered, or located in inappropriate places.	
The client has rights to inventory recorded on tags (rights).	Inquire about consignment or customer inventory included on client's premises. Be alert for inventory that is set aside or specially marked as indications of nonownership.	

AUDIT OF PRICING AND COMPILATION

OBJECTIVE 16-7

Design and perform audit tests of pricing and compilation for inventory.

An important part of the audit of inventory is to perform all the procedures necessary to make certain that the physical counts or perpetual record quantities were properly priced and compiled. **Inventory price tests** include all the tests of the client's unit prices to determine whether they are correct. **Inventory compilation tests** include all the tests of the summarization of the physical quantities, the extension of price times quantity, footing the inventory summary, and tracing the totals to the general ledger.

Pricing and Compilation Controls

The existence of adequate internal controls for unit costs that are integrated with production and other accounting records is important to ensure that reasonable costs are used for valuing ending inventory. One important internal control is the use of **standard cost records** that indicate variances in material, labor, and overhead costs and can be used to evaluate production. When standard costs are used, procedures must be designed to keep the standards updated for changes in production processes and costs. The review of unit costs for reasonableness by someone independent of the department responsible for developing the costs is also a useful control over valuation.

An internal control designed to prevent the overstatement of inventory through the inclusion of obsolete inventory is a formal review and reporting of obsolete, slow-moving, damaged, and overstated inventory items. The review should be done by a competent employee by reviewing perpetual inventory master files for inventory turnover and holding discussions with engineering or production personnel.

Compilation internal controls are needed to provide a means of ensuring that the physical counts are properly summarized, priced at the same amount as the unit records, correctly extended and totaled, and included in the general ledger at the proper amount. Important compilation internal controls are adequate documents and records for taking the physical count and proper internal verification. If the physical inventory is taken on prenumbered tags and carefully reviewed before the personnel are released from the physical examination of inventory, there should be little risk of misstatement in summarizing the tags. The most important internal control over accurate determination of prices, extensions, and footings is internal verification by a competent, independent person.

Acquire and record raw materials, labor, and overhead

Internally transfer assets and costs

Ship goods and record revenue and costs

Physically observe inventory

Price and compile inventory

Pricing and Compilation Procedures

Balance-related audit objectives for tests of details of balances are also useful in discussing pricing and compilation procedures. The objectives and related tests are shown in Table 16-3 (p. 472), except for the cutoff objective. Physical observation, which was previously discussed, is a major source of cutoff information for sales and purchases. Tests of the accounting records for cutoff are done as a part of sales (sales and collection cycle) and acquisitions (acquisition and payment cycle).

The frame of reference for applying the objectives is a listing of inventory obtained from the client that includes each inventory item's description, quantity, unit price, and extended value. The inventory listing is in inventory item description order, with raw material, work-in-process, and finished goods separated. The totals equal the general ledger balance.

Valuation of Inventory

The proper valuation (pricing) of inventory is often one of the most important and time-consuming parts of the audit. In performing pricing tests, three things about the client's method of pricing are extremely important: The method must be in accordance with GAAP, the application of the method must be consistent from year to year, and cost versus market value (replacement cost or net realizable value) must be considered. Because the method of verifying the pricing of inventory depends on whether items are acquired or manufactured, these two categories are discussed separately.

Pricing Purchased Inventory The primary types of inventory included in this category are raw materials, purchased parts, and supplies. As a first step in verifying the valuation of purchased inventory, it is necessary to establish clearly whether LIFO, FIFO, weighted average, or some other valuation method is being used. It is also necessary to determine which costs should be included in the valuation of an item of inventory. For example, the auditor must find out whether freight, storage, discounts, and other costs are included and compare the findings with the preceding year's audit documentation to make sure that the methods are consistent.

In selecting specific inventory items for pricing, emphasis should be put on the larger dollar amounts and on products that are known to have wide fluctuations in price, but a representative sample of all types of inventory and departments should be included as well. Stratified variables or monetary unit sampling is commonly used in these tests.

TABLE 16-3 Balance-Related Audit Objectives and Tests of Details of Balances for Inventory Pricing and Compilation

Balance-Related Audit Objective	Common Inventory Pricing and Compilation Procedures	Comments
Inventory in the inventory listing schedule agrees with the physical inventory counts, the extensions are correct, and the total is correctly added and agrees with the general ledger (detail tie-in).	Perform compilation tests (see existence, completeness, and accuracy objectives). Foot the inventory listing schedules for raw materials, work-in-process, and finished goods. Trace the totals to the general ledger. Extend the quantity times the price on selected items.	Unless controls are weak, extending and footing tests should be limited.
Inventory items in the inventory listing schedule exist (existence).	Trace inventory listed in the schedule to inventory tags and auditor's recorded counts for existence and description.	The next six objectives are affected by the results of the physical inventory observation. The tag numbers and counts verified as a part of physical inventory observation are traced to the inventory listing schedule as a part of these tests.
Existing inventory items are included in the inventory listing schedule (completeness).	Account for unused tag numbers shown in the auditor's documentation to make sure no tags have been added. Trace from inventory tags to the inventory listing schedules and make sure inventory on tags is included. Account for tag numbers to make sure none have been deleted.	
Inventory items in the inventory listing schedule are accurate (accuracy).	Trace inventory listed in the schedule to inventory tags and auditor's recorded counts for quantity and description. Perform price tests of inventory. For a discussion of price tests, see text material on pages 470–473.	
Inventory items in the inventory listing schedule are properly classified (classification).	Verify the classification into raw materials, work-in-process, and finished goods by comparing the descriptions on inventory tags and auditor's recorded test counts with the inventory listing schedule.	
Inventory items in the inventory listing are stated at realizable value (realizable value).	Perform tests of lower of cost or market, selling price, and obsolescence.	
The client has rights to inventory items in the inventory listing schedule (rights).	Trace inventory tags identified as nonowned during the physical observation to the inventory listing schedule to make sure these have not been included. Review contracts with suppliers and customers and inquire of management for the possibility of the inclusion of consigned or other nonowned inventory, or the exclusion of owned inventory.	
Inventory and related accounts in the inventory and warehousing cycle are properly presented and disclosed (presentation and disclosure).	Examine financial statements for proper presentation and disclosure, including: Separate disclosure of raw materials, work-in-process, and finished goods. Proper description of the inventory costing method. Description of pledged inventory. Inclusion of significant sales and purchase commitments.	Pledging of inventory and sales and purchase commitments are usually uncovered as a part of other audit tests.

The auditor should list the inventory items intended to be verified for pricing and request the client to locate the appropriate vendors' invoices. It is important that sufficient invoices be examined to account for the entire quantity of inventory for the item being tested, especially for the FIFO valuation method. Examining sufficient invoices is useful to uncover situations in which clients value their inventory on the basis of the most recent invoice only and, in some cases, to discover obsolete inventory. As an illustration, assume that the client's valuation of an inventory item is $12.00 per unit for 1,000 units, using FIFO. The auditor should examine the most recent invoices for acquisitions of that inventory item made in the year under audit until the valuation of all of the 1,000 units is accounted for. If the most recent acquisition of the inventory item was for 700 units at $12.00 per unit and the immediately preceding acquisition was for 600 units at $11.30 per unit, the inventory item in question is overstated by $210.00 (300 × $.70).

When the client has perpetual inventory master files that include unit costs of acquisitions, it is usually desirable to test the pricing by tracing the unit costs to the perpetuals rather than to vendors' invoices. In most cases, the effect is to reduce the cost of verifying inventory valuation significantly. Naturally, when the perpetuals are used to verify unit costs, it is essential to test the unit costs on the perpetuals to vendors' invoices as a part of the tests of the acquisition and payment cycle.

Pricing Manufactured Inventory The auditor must consider the cost of raw materials, direct labor, and manufacturing overhead in pricing work-in-process and finished goods. The need to verify each of these has the effect of making the audit of work-in-process and finished goods inventory more complex than the audit of purchased inventory. Nevertheless, such considerations as selecting the items to be tested, testing for whether cost or market value is lower, and evaluating the possibility of obsolescence also apply.

In pricing raw materials in manufactured products, it is necessary to consider both the unit cost of the raw materials and the number of units required to manufacture a unit of output. The unit cost can be verified in the same manner as that used for other purchased inventory—by examining vendors' invoices or perpetual inventory master files. Then it is necessary to examine engineering specifications, inspect the finished product, or find a similar method to determine the number of units it takes to manufacture a product.

Similarly, the hourly costs of direct labor and the number of hours it takes to manufacture a unit of output must be verified while testing direct labor. Hourly labor costs can be verified by comparison with labor payroll or union contracts. The number of hours needed to manufacture the product can be determined from engineering specifications or similar sources.

The proper manufacturing overhead in work-in-process and finished goods is dependent on the approach being used by the client. It is necessary to evaluate the method being used for consistency and reasonableness and to recompute the costs to determine whether the overhead is correct. For example, if the rate is based on direct labor dollars, the auditor can divide the total manufacturing overhead by the total direct labor dollars to determine the actual overhead rate. This rate can then be compared with the overhead rate used by the client to determine unit costs. Testing of pricing for work-in-process and finished goods is often done in conjunction with tests of standard costs. When standard costs have been tested with satisfactory results, testing of unit costs for ending inventory can be limited to tracing the price used to value ending inventory to the standard cost records.

When the client has standard costs records, an efficient and useful method of determining valuation is by the review and analysis of variances. If the variances in material, labor, and manufacturing overhead are small, it is evidence of reliable cost records.

Cost or Market In pricing inventory, it is necessary to consider whether replacement cost or net realizable value is lower than historical cost. For purchased finished goods and raw materials, the most recent cost of an inventory item as indicated on a vendor's invoice of the subsequent period is a useful way to test for replacement cost. All manufacturing costs must be considered for work-in-process and finished goods for manufactured inventory. It is also necessary to consider the sales value of inventory items and the possible effect of rapid fluctuation of prices to determine net realizable value. Finally, it is necessary to consider the possibility of obsolescence in the valuation process.

INTEGRATION OF THE TESTS

OBJECTIVE 16-8

Integrate the various parts of the audit of the inventory and warehousing cycle.

The most difficult part of understanding the audit of the inventory and warehousing cycle is grasping the interrelationships of the many different tests the auditor makes to evaluate whether inventory and cost of goods sold are fairly stated. Figure 16-3 (p. 474) and the discussions that follow are designed to aid the reader in perceiving the audit of the inventory and warehousing cycle as a series of integrated tests.

FIGURE 16-3 Interrelationship of Various Audit Tests

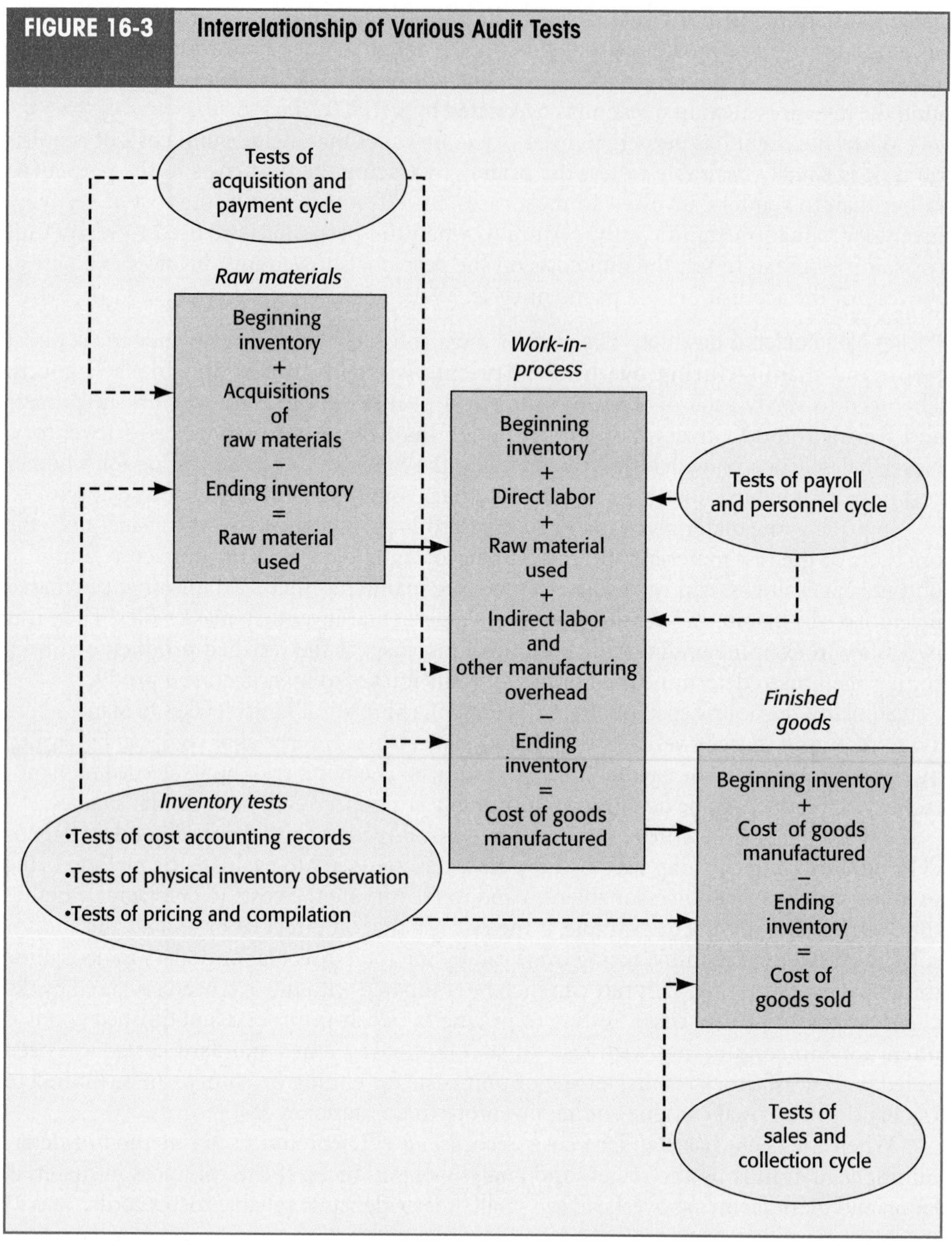

Tests of the Acquisition and Payment Cycle When the auditor verifies acquisitions as part of the tests of the acquisition and payment cycle, evidence is being obtained about the accuracy of raw materials acquired and all manufacturing overhead costs except labor. These acquisition costs either flow directly into cost of goods sold or become the most significant part of the ending inventory of raw material, work-in-process, and finished goods. In audits involving perpetual inventory master files, it is common to test these as a part of tests of controls and substantive tests of transactions procedures in the acquisition and payment cycle. Similarly, if manufacturing costs are assigned to individual jobs or processes, they are usually tested as a part of the same cycle.

Tests of the Payroll and Personnel Cycle When the auditor verifies labor costs, the same comments apply as for acquisitions. In most cases, the cost accounting records for direct and indirect labor costs can be tested as part of the audit of the payroll and personnel cycle if there is adequate advance planning.

Tests of the Sales and Collection Cycle Although the relationship is less close between the sales and collection cycle and the inventory and warehousing cycle than between the two previously discussed, it is still important. Most of the audit testing in the storage of finished goods as well as the shipment and recording of sales takes place when the sales and collection cycle is tested. In addition, if standard cost records are used, it may be possible to test the standard cost of goods sold at the same time that sales tests are performed.

Tests of Cost Accounting Tests of cost accounting are meant to verify the controls affecting inventory that were not verified as part of the three previously discussed cycles. Tests are made of the physical controls, transfers of raw material costs to work-in-process, transfers of costs of completed goods to finished goods, perpetual inventory master files, and unit cost records.

Physical Inventory, Pricing, and Compilation In most audits, the underlying assumption in testing the inventory and warehousing cycle is that cost of goods sold is a residual of beginning inventory plus acquisitions of raw materials, direct labor, and other manufacturing costs minus ending inventory. When the audit of inventory and cost of goods sold is approached with this idea in mind, the importance of ending inventory becomes obvious. Physical inventory, pricing, and compilation are each equally important in the audit because a misstatement in any one results in misstated inventory and cost of goods sold.

In testing the physical inventory, it is possible to rely heavily on the perpetual inventory master files if they have been tested as a part of one or more of the previously discussed tests. In fact, if the perpetual inventory master files are considered reliable, the auditor can observe and test the physical count at some time during the year and rely on the perpetuals to keep adequate records of the quantities.

When testing the unit costs, it is also possible to rely, to some degree, on the tests of the cost records made during the substantive tests of transactions. The existence of standard cost records is also useful for the purpose of comparison with the actual unit costs. If the standard costs are used to represent historical cost, they must be tested for reliability.

SUMMARY

This chapter discussed the audit of the inventory and warehousing cycle. Because of the difficulties associated with establishing the existence and valuation of inventories, the cycle is often the most time-consuming and complex part of the audit. The cycle is also unique because many of the tests of the inputs to the cycle are tested as part of the audit of other cycles. Tests performed as part of the inventory and warehousing cycle focus on the cost accounting records, physical observation, and tests of the pricing and compilation of the ending inventory balance.

ESSENTIAL TERMS

Cost accounting controls—controls over physical inventory and the related costs from the point at which raw materials are requisitioned to the point at which the manufactured product is completed and transferred to storage

Cost accounting records—the accounting records concerned with the manufacture and processing of the goods and storing finished goods

Inventory and warehousing cycle—the transaction cycle that involves the physical flow of goods through the organization, as well as related costs

Inventory compilation tests—audit procedures used to verify whether physical counts of inventory are correctly summarized, inventory quantities and prices are correctly extended, and extended inventory is correctly footed

Inventory price tests—audit procedures used to verify the costs used to value physical inventory

Job cost systems—systems of cost accounting in which costs are accumulated by individual jobs when material is used and labor costs are incurred

Perpetual inventory master file—a continuously updated computerized record of inventory items purchased, used, sold, and on hand for merchandise, raw materials, and finished goods

Process cost systems—systems of cost accounting in which costs are accumulated for a process, with unit costs for each process assigned to the products passing through the process

Standard cost records—records that indicate variances between projected material, labor, and overhead costs and the actual costs

REVIEW QUESTIONS

16-1 (Objective 16-1) Give the reasons why inventory is often the most difficult and time-consuming part of many audit engagements.

16-2 (Objectives 16-1, 16-2, 16-8) Explain the relationship between the acquisition and payment cycle and the inventory and warehousing cycle in the audit of a manufacturing company. List several audit procedures in the acquisition and payment cycle that support your explanation.

16-3 (Objective 16-2) Give reasons why companies provide online access to descriptions of inventory products and on-hand quantity levels to key inventory suppliers. Discuss risks associated with making that information available on an online basis.

16-4 (Objectives 16-1, 16-4) State what is meant by cost accounting records and explain their importance in the conduct of an audit.

16-5 (Objectives 16-3, 16-4) Many auditors assert that certain audit tests can be significantly reduced for clients with adequate perpetual records that include both unit and cost data. What are the most important tests of the perpetual records that the auditor must make before reducing assessed control risk? Assuming the perpetuals are determined to be accurate, which tests can be reduced?

16-6 (Objective 16-6) Before the physical examination, the auditor obtains a copy of the client's inventory instructions and reviews them with the controller. In obtaining an understanding of inventory procedures for a small manufacturing company, these deficiencies are identified: Shipping operations will not be completely halted during the physical examination, and there will be no independent verification of the original inventory count by a second counting team. Evaluate the importance of each of these deficiencies and state its effect on the auditor's observation of inventory.

16-7 (Objective 16-6) At the completion of an inventory observation, the controller requested the auditor to give him a copy of all recorded test counts to facilitate the correction of all discrepancies between the client's and the auditor's counts. Should the auditor comply with the request? Why?

16-8 (Objective 16-6) What major audit procedures are involved in testing for the ownership of inventory during the observation of the physical counts and as a part of subsequent valuation tests?

16-9 (Objectives 16-5, 16-6, 16-7) In the verification of the amount of the inventory, one of the auditor's concerns is that slow-moving and obsolete items be identified. List the auditing procedures that could be used to determine whether slow-moving or obsolete items have been included in inventory.

16-10 (Objective 16-6) During the taking of physical inventory, the controller intentionally withheld several inventory tags from the employees responsible for the physical count. After the auditor left the client's premises at the completion of the inventory observation, the controller recorded nonexistent inventory on the tags and thereby significantly overstated earnings. How could the auditor have uncovered the misstatement, assuming that there are no perpetual records?

16-11 (Objective 16-6) Explain why a proper cutoff of purchases and sales is heavily dependent on the physical inventory observation. What information should be obtained during the physical count to make sure that cutoff is accurate?

16-12 (Objective 16-7) Define what is meant by compilation tests. List several examples of audit procedures to verify compilation.

16-13 (Objective 16-5) List the major analytical procedures for testing the overall reasonableness of inventory. For each test, explain the type of misstatement that could be identified.

16-14 (Objective 16-7) Included in the December 31, 2002, inventory of the Wholeridge Supply Company are 2,600 deluxe ring binders in the amount of $5,902. An examination of the most recent acquisitions of binders showed the following costs: January 26, 2003, 2,300 at $2.42 each; December 6, 2002, 1,900 at $2.28 each; November 26, 2002, 2,400 at $2.07 each. What is the misstatement in valuation of the December 31, 2002, inventory for deluxe ring binders, assuming FIFO inventory valuation? What would your answer be if the January 26, 2003, acquisition was for 2,300 binders at $2.12 each?

16-15 (Objectives 16-7, 16-8) The Ruswell Manufacturing Company applied manufacturing overhead to inventory at December 31, 2002, on the basis of $3.47 per direct labor hour. Explain how you would evaluate the reasonableness of total direct labor hours and manufacturing overhead in the ending inventory of finished goods.

16-16 (Objective 16-8) Each employee for the Gedding Manufacturing Co., a firm using a job-cost inventory costing method, must reconcile his or her total hours worked with the hours worked on individual jobs using a job time sheet at the time weekly payroll time cards are prepared. The job time sheet is then stapled to the time card. Explain how you could test the direct labor dollars included in inventory.

16-17 (Objective 16-6) Assuming that the auditor properly documents receiving report numbers as a part of the physical inventory observation procedures, explain how the proper cutoff of purchases, including tests for the possibility of raw materials in transit, should be verified later in the audit.

MULTIPLE CHOICE QUESTIONS FROM CPA EXAMINATIONS

16-18 (Objective 16-1) The following questions concern internal controls in the inventory and warehousing cycle. Choose the best response.

a. In a company whose materials and supplies include a great number of items, a fundamental deficiency in control requirements would be indicated if
   (1) a perpetual inventory master file is not maintained for items of small value.
   (2) the storekeeping function were to be combined with production and record keeping.
   (3) the cycle basis for physical inventory taking was to be used.
   (4) minor supply items were to be expensed when acquired.

b. For control purposes, the quantities of materials ordered may be omitted from the copy of the purchase order that is
   (1) forwarded to the accounting department.
   (2) retained in the purchasing department's files.
   (3) returned to the requisitioner.
   (4) forwarded to the receiving department.

c. Which of the following procedures would *best* detect the theft of valuable items from an inventory that consists of hundreds of different items selling for $1 to $10 and a few items selling for hundreds of dollars?
   (1) Maintain a perpetual inventory master file of only the more valuable items with frequent periodic verification of the validity of the perpetuals.
   (2) Have an independent CPA firm prepare an internal control report on the effectiveness of the administrative and accounting controls over inventory.
   (3) Have separate warehouse space for the more valuable items with sequentially numbered tags.
   (4) Require an authorized officer's signature on all requisitions for the more valuable items.

16-19 (Objectives 16-1, 16-4) The following questions concern testing the client's internal controls for inventory and warehousing. Choose the best response.

a. When an auditor tests a client's cost accounting records, the auditor's tests are *primarily* designed to determine that
   (1) quantities on hand have been computed based on acceptable cost accounting techniques that reasonably approximate actual quantities on hand.
   (2) physical inventories are in substantial agreement with book inventories.
   (3) the internal controls are in accordance with generally accepted accounting principles and are functioning as planned.
   (4) costs have been properly assigned to finished goods, work-in-process, and cost of goods sold.

b. The accuracy of perpetual inventory master files may be established, in part, by comparing perpetual inventory records with
   (1) purchase requisitions.
   (2) receiving reports.
   (3) purchase orders.
   (4) vendor payments.

c. When evaluating inventory controls with respect to segregation of duties, a CPA would be *least* likely to
   (1) inspect documents.
   (2) make inquiries.
   (3) observe procedures.
   (4) consider policy and procedure manuals.

16-20 (Objectives 16-1, 16-5, 16-6, 16-7) The following questions deal with tests of details of balances and analytical procedures for inventory. Choose the best response.

a. An auditor would be *most* likely to learn of slow-moving inventory through
   (1) inquiry of sales personnel.
   (2) inquiry of store personnel.
   (3) physical observation of inventory.
   (4) review of perpetual inventory master files.

b. An inventory turnover analysis is useful to the auditor because it may detect
   (1) inadequacies in inventory pricing.
   (2) methods of avoiding cyclical holding costs.
   (3) the optimum automatic reorder points.
   (4) the existence of obsolete merchandise.

c. A CPA auditing inventory may appropriately apply attributes sampling to estimate the
   (1) average price of inventory items.
   (2) percentage of slow-moving inventory items.
   (3) dollar value of inventory.
   (4) physical quantity of inventory items.

DISCUSSION QUESTIONS AND PROBLEMS

16-21 (Objectives 16-1, 16-4, 16-6, 16-7) Following are audit procedures commonly performed in the inventory and warehousing cycle for a manufacturing company:

1. Compare the client's count of physical inventory at an interim date with the perpetual inventory master file.
2. Trace the auditor's test counts recorded in the audit files to the final inventory compilation and compare the tag number, description, and quantity.
3. Compare the unit price on the final inventory summary with vendors' invoices.
4. Read the client's physical inventory instructions and observe whether they are being followed by those responsible for counting the inventory.
5. Account for a sequence of raw material requisitions and examine each requisition for an authorized approval.
6. Trace the recorded additions on the finished goods perpetual inventory master file to the records for completed production.
7. Account for a sequence of inventory tags and trace each tag to the physical inventory to make sure it actually exists.

Required

a. Identify whether each of the procedures is primarily a test of control or a substantive test.

b. State the purpose(s) of each of the procedures.

16-22 (Objectives 16-1, 16-6, 16-7) The following misstatements are included in the inventory and related records of Westbox Manufacturing Company:

1. An inventory item was priced at $12 each instead of at the correct cost of $12 per dozen.
2. In taking the physical inventory, the last shipments for the day were excluded from inventory and were not included as a sale until the subsequent year.
3. The clerk in charge of the perpetual inventory master file altered the quantity on an inventory tag to cover up the shortage of inventory caused by its theft during the year.
4. After the auditor left the premises, several inventory tags were lost and were not included in the final inventory summary.
5. When raw material acquisitions were recorded, the improper unit price was included in the perpetual inventory master file. Therefore, the inventory valuation was misstated because the physical inventory was priced by referring to the perpetual records.
6. During the physical count, several obsolete inventory items were included.
7. Because of a significant increase in volume during the current year and excellent control over manufacturing overhead costs, the manufacturing overhead rate applied to inventory was far greater than actual cost.

Required

a. For each misstatement, state an internal control that should have prevented it from occurring.

b. For each misstatement, state a substantive audit procedure that could be used to uncover it.

16-23 (Objective 16-2) Technology Parts, Inc., is a retailer of computer hardware components. The company purchases inventory items in bulk directly from parts manufacturers and sells the parts to computer and other technology equipment manufacturers that use them as components in their products. Technology Parts, Inc., grants suppliers access to its inventory management system through its Internet Web site. Suppliers have real-time access to information about the parts inventory, including information about quantities held, storage locations, and forecasted product demand. In addition, customers have online access through the Web site to information containing product descriptions, price, delivery estimates, availability status, and quality and reliability ratings. Customers can also access information to assess the compatibility of selected parts with other components used in their production processes.

a. Identify business objectives that Technology Parts' management may be able to achieve by providing this information online to key suppliers and customers. **Required**

b. How might the availability of the information to suppliers and customers increase Technology Parts' business risk?

c. What processes should Technology Parts' management implement to minimize business risks?

d. How might the availability of the information increase the risk of material misstatements in the financial statements?

16-24 (**Objectives 16-6, 16-7**) Often, an important aspect of a CPA's audit of financial statements is observation of the taking of physical inventory.

a. What are the general objectives or purposes of the CPA's observation of the taking of the physical inventory? (Do not discuss the procedures or techniques involved in making the observation.) **Required**

b. For what purposes does the CPA make and record test counts of inventory quantities during observation of the taking of the physical inventory? Discuss.

c. A number of companies employ outside service companies that specialize in counting, pricing, extending, and footing inventories. These service companies usually furnish a certificate attesting to the value of the inventory.

Assuming that the service company took the inventory on the balance sheet date:

(1) How much reliance, if any, can the CPA place on the inventory certificate of outside specialists? Discuss.

(2) What effect, if any, would the inventory certificate of outside specialists have upon the type of report the CPA would render? Discuss.

(3) What reference, if any, would the CPA make to the certificate of outside specialists in the short-form report?*

16-25 (**Objective 16-6**) You encountered the following situations during the December 31, 2002, physical inventory of Latner Shoe Distributor Company:

a. Latner maintains a large portion of the shoe merchandise in 10 warehouses throughout the eastern United States. This ensures swift delivery service for its chain of stores. You are assigned alone to the Boston warehouse to observe the physical inventory process. During the inventory count, several express trucks pulled in for loading. Although infrequent, express shipments must be attended to immediately. As a result, the employees who were counting the inventory stopped to assist in loading the express trucks. What should you do? **Required**

b. (1) In one storeroom of 10,000 items, you have test-counted about 200 items of high value and a few items of low value. You found no misstatements. You also note that the employees are diligently following the inventory instructions. Do you think you have tested enough items? Explain.

(2) What would you do if you test-counted 150 items and found a substantial number of counting errors?

c. In observing an inventory of liquid shoe polish, you note that one lot is 5 years old. From inspection of some bottles in an open box, you find that the liquid has solidified in most of the bottles. What action should you take?

d. During your observation of the inventory count in the main warehouse, you found that most of the prenumbered tags that had been incorrectly filled out are being destroyed and thrown away. What is the significance of this procedure and what action should you take?

16-26 (**Objective 16-6**) In connection with his audit of the financial statements of Knutson Products Co., an assembler of home appliances, for the year ended May 31, 2002, Ray Abel, CPA, is reviewing with Knutson's controller the plans for a physical inventory at the company warehouse on May 31, 2002.

Finished appliances, unassembled parts, and supplies are stored in the warehouse, which is attached to Knutson's assembly plant. The plant will operate during the count. On May 30, the warehouse will deliver to the plant the estimated quantities of unassembled parts and supplies required for May 31 production, but there may be emergency requisitions on May 31. During the count, the warehouse will continue to receive parts and supplies and to ship finished appliances. However, appliances completed on May 31 will be held in the plant until after the physical inventory.

What procedures should the company establish to ensure that the inventory count includes all items that should be included and that nothing is counted twice?* **Required**

*AICPA adapted.

16-27 (Objective 16-5) The following are sales, cost of sales, and inventory data for Aladdin Products Supply Company, a wholesale distributor of cleaning supplies. Dollar amounts are in millions.

	2002	2001	2000	1999
Sales	$23.2	$21.7	$19.6	$17.4
Cost of sales	17.1	16.8	15.2	13.5
Beginning inventory	2.3	2.1	1.9	1.5
Ending inventory	2.9	2.3	2.1	1.9

Required

a. Calculate the following ratios, using an electronic spreadsheet program (instructor's option):
   (1) Gross margin as a percentage of sales
   (2) Inventory turnover

b. List several logical causes of the changes in the two ratios.

c. Assume that $500,000 is considered material for audit planning purposes for 2002. Could any of the fluctuations in the computed ratios indicate a possible material misstatement? Demonstrate this by using the spreadsheet program to perform a sensitivity analysis.

d. What should the auditor do to determine the actual cause of the changes?

16-28 (Objective 16-6) In an annual audit at December 31, 2002, you find the following transactions near the closing date:

1. Merchandise costing $1,822 was received on January 3, 2003, and the related acquisition invoice recorded January 5. The invoice showed the shipment was made on December 29, 2002, FOB destination.
2. Merchandise costing $625 was received on December 28, 2002, and the invoice was not recorded. You located it in the hands of the purchasing agent; it was marked "on consignment."
3. A packing case containing products costing $816 was standing in the shipping room when the physical inventory was taken. It was not included in the inventory because it was marked "Hold for shipping instructions." Your investigation revealed that the customer's order was dated December 18, 2002, but that the case was shipped and the customer billed on January 10, 2003. The product was a stock item of your client.
4. Merchandise received on January 6, 2003, costing $720 was entered in the acquisitions journal on January 7, 2003. The invoice showed shipment was made FOB supplier's warehouse on December 31, 2002. Because it was not on hand at December 31, it was not included in inventory.
5. A special machine, fabricated to order for a customer, was finished and in the shipping room on December 31, 2002. The customer was billed on that date and the machine excluded from inventory, although it was shipped on January 4, 2003.

Assume that each of the amounts is material.

Required

a. State whether the merchandise should be included in the client's inventory.

b. Give your reason for your decision on each item.*

16-29 (Objective 16-7) As a part of your clerical tests of inventory for Martin Manufacturing, you have tested about 20% of the dollar items and have found the following exceptions:

1. Extension errors:

Description	Quantity	Price	Extension as Recorded
Wood	465 board feet	$ .12/board foot	$ 5.58
Metal-cutting tools	29 units	30.00 each	670.00
Cutting fluid	16 barrels	40.00/barrel	529.00
Sandpaper	300 sheets	.95/hundred	258.00

2. Differences located in comparing last year's costs with the current year's costs on the client's inventory lists:

*AICPA adapted.

Description	Quantity	This Year's Cost	Preceding Year's Cost
TA-114 precision-cutting torches	12 units	$500.00 each	Unable to locate
Aluminum scrap	4,500 pounds	5.00/ton	$65.00/ton
Lubricating oil	400 gallons	6.00/gallon	4.50/barrel

3. Test counts that you were unable to find when tracing from the test counts to the final inventory compilation:

Tag No.	Quantity	Current Year Cost	Description
2958	15 tons	$75.00/ton	Cold-rolled bars
0026	2,000 feet	2.25/foot	4-inch aluminum stripping

4. Page total, footing errors:

Page No.	Client Total	Correct Total
14	$1,375.12	$1,375.08
82	8,721.18	8,521.18

Required

a. State the amount of the actual misstatement in each of the four tests. For any item for which the amount of the misstatement cannot be determined from the information given, state the considerations that would affect your estimate of the misstatement.

b. As a result of your findings, what would you do about clerical accuracy tests of the inventory in the current year?

c. What changes, if any, would you suggest in internal controls and procedures for Martin Manufacturing during the compilation of next year's inventory to prevent each type of misstatement?

16-30 (Objective 16-6) You have been engaged for the audit of the Y Company for the year ended December 31, 2002. The Y Company is in the wholesale chemical business and makes all sales at 25% over cost.

Following are portions of the client's sales and purchases accounts for the calendar year 2002.

SALES

Date	Reference	Amount	Date	Reference	Amount
				Balance Forward	
12-31	Closing entry	$699,860			$658,320
			12-27	*SI#965	5,195
			12-28	SI#966	19,270
			12-28	SI#967	1,302
			12-31	SI#969	5,841
			12-31	SI#970	7,922
			12-31	SI#971	2,010
		$699,860			$699,860

PURCHASES

Date	Reference	Amount	Date	Reference	Amount
	Balance Forward				
		$360,300	12-31	Closing entry	$385,346
12-28	†RR#1059	3,100			
12-30	RR#1061	8,965			
12-31	RR#1062	4,861			
12-31	RR#1063	8,120			
		$385,346			$385,346

*SI = Sales invoice.
†RR = Receiving report.

You observed the physical inventory of goods in the warehouse on December 31, 2002, and were satisfied that it was properly taken.

When performing a sales and purchases cutoff test, you found that at December 31, 2002, the last receiving report that had been used was no. 1063 and that no shipments have been made on any sales invoices with numbers larger than no. 968. You also obtained the following additional information:

1. Included in the warehouse physical inventory at December 31, 2002, were chemicals that had been acquired and received on receiving report no. 1060 but for which an invoice was not received until the year 2003. Cost was $2,183.
2. In the warehouse at December 31, 2002, were goods that had been sold and paid for by the customer but which were not shipped out until the year 2003. They were all sold on sales invoice no. 965 and were not inventoried.
3. On the evening of December 31, 2002, there were two cars on the Y company siding:
   (a) Car AR38162 was unloaded on January 2, 2003, and received on receiving report no. 1063. The freight was paid by the vendor.
   (b) Car BAE74123 was loaded and sealed on December 31, 2002, and was switched off the company's siding on January 2, 2003. The sales price was $12,700 and the freight was paid by the customer. This order was sold on sales invoice no. 968.
4. Temporarily stranded at December 31, 2002 on a railroad siding were two cars of chemicals en route to the Z Pulp and Paper Co. They were sold on sales invoice no. 966, and the terms were FOB destination.
5. En route to the Y Company on December 31, 2002, was a truckload of material that was received on receiving report no. 1064. The material was shipped FOB destination, and freight of $75 was paid by the Y Company. However, the freight was deducted from the purchase price of $975.
6. Included in the physical inventory were chemicals exposed to rain in transit and deemed unsalable. Their invoice cost was $1,250, and freight charges of $350 had been paid on the chemicals.

Required

a. Compute the adjustments that should be made to the client's physical inventory at December 31, 2002.

b. Prepare a worksheet of adjusting entries that are required as of December 31, 2002.*

CASE

16-31 **(Objective 16-7)** You are assigned to the December 31, 2002, audit of Sea Gull Airframes, Inc. The company designs and manufactures aircraft superstructures and airframe components. You observed the physical inventory at December 31 and are satisfied that it was properly taken. The inventory at December 31, 2002, has been priced, extended, and totaled by the client and is made up of about 5,000 inventory items with a total valuation of $8,275,000. In performing inventory price tests, you have decided to stratify your tests and conclude that you should have two strata: items with a value over $5,000 and those with a value of less than $5,000. The book values are as follows:

	No. of Items	Total Value
More than $5,000	500	$4,150,000
Less than $5,000	4,500	4,125,000
	5,000	$8,275,000

In performing your pricing and extension tests, you have decided to test about 50 inventory items in detail. You selected 40 of the over $5,000 items and 10 of those under $5,000 at random from the population. You find all items to be correct except for items A through G at the top of page 624, which you believe may be misstated. You have tested the following items, to this point, exclusive of A through G:

	No. of Items	Total Value
More than $5,000	36	$360,000
Less than $5,000	7	2,600

Sea Gull Airframes uses a periodic inventory system and values its inventory at the lower of FIFO cost or market. You were able to locate all invoices needed for your examination. The seven inventory items in the sample you believe may be misstated, along with the relevant data for determining the proper valuation, are shown next.

*AICPA adapted.

INVENTORY ITEMS POSSIBLY MISSTATED

Description	Quantity	Price	Total*
A. L37 spars	3,000 meters	$ 8.00/meter	$24,000
B. B68 metal formers	10,000 inches	1.20/foot	12,000
C. R01 metal ribs	1,500 yards	10.00/yard	15,000
D. St26 struts	1,000 feet	8.00/foot	8,000
E. Industrial hand drills	45 units	20.00 each	900
F. L803 steel leaf springs	40 pairs	69.00 each spring	276
G. V16 fasteners	5.50 dozen	10.00/dozen	55

*Amounts are as stated on client's inventory.

INFORMATION FOR PRICING FROM INVOICES (SEA GULL AIRFRAMES)

Voucher Number	Voucher Date	Date Paid	Terms	Receiving Report Date	Invoice Description
7-68	8-01-97	8-21-97	Net FOB destination	8-01-97	77 V16 fasteners at $10 per dozen
11-81	10-16-02	11-15-02	Net FOB destination	10-18-02	1,100 yards R01 metal ribs at $9.50 per yard; 2,000 feet St26 struts at $8.20 per foot
12-06	12-08-02	12-30-02	2/10, n/30 FOB S.P.	12-10-02	180 L803 steel leaf springs at $69 each
12-09	12-10-02	12-18-02	Net FOB destination	12-11-02	45 industrial hand drills at $20 each; guaranteed for 4 years
12-18	12-27-02	12-27-02	2/10, n/30 FOB S.P.	12-21-02	4,200 meters L37 spars at $8 per meter
12-23	12-24-02	1-03-03	2/10, n/30 FOB dest.	12-26-02	12,800 inches B68 metal formers at $1.20 per foot
12-61	12-29-02	1-08-03	Net FOB destination	12-29-02	1,000 yards R01 metal ribs at $10 per yard; 800 feet St26 struts at $8 per foot
12-81	12-31-02	1-20-03	Net FOB destination	1-06-03	2,000 meters L37 spars at $7.50 per meter; 2,000 yards R01 metal ribs at $10 per yard

In addition, you noted a freight bill for voucher 12-23 in the amount of $200. This bill was entered in the freight-in account. Virtually all freight was for the metal formers.

This is the first time Sea Gull Airframes has been audited by your firm.

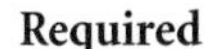

Required

a. Review all information and determine the inventory misstatements of the seven items in question. State any assumptions you consider necessary to determine the amount of the misstatements.

b. Prepare an audit schedule to summarize your findings. Use the computer to prepare the schedule (instructor's option).

INTERNET PROBLEM 16-1: USING INVENTORY COUNT SPECIALISTS

Reference the CW site. Many organizations hire outside inventory count specialists to conduct physical counts of their inventory balances. This problem uses the Internet to expose students to inventory count specialists' organizations. Based on this exposure, students address issues related to a company's use of these specialists to count inventory.

CHAPTER 17

AUDIT OF CASH BALANCES

SOCIETY EXPECTS A LOT FROM AUDITORS

Bert Sampson was the controller of Pardoe Manufacturing Company. From 1997 through 2001, Bert paid himself an extra $2 million in "bonuses." He did this by transferring funds from the general account, writing checks to himself from the payroll account, destroying the checks when received from the bank, and making entries directly into the company's computer files to disguise the theft. Bert was able to do this because he had almost complete control of the company's accounting process.

Jack Baker of Tramenier and Baker, CPAs, was the partner on the Pardoe audit. Although Baker found a strong control environment at Pardoe and a good budgeting and reporting system, he assessed control risk at maximum because there was limited segregation of duties. Accordingly, Baker used a "substantive" approach to the audit. Baker applied tests of details of balances and analytical procedures to the year-end financial statements. He did no tests of controls or substantive tests of transactions.

Because Sampson had lost all of the $2 million and Pardoe had no fidelity bond insurance, the company sued Tramenier and Baker, CPAs, for the loss, claiming breach of contract. Baker's defense was that he had done the audit in accordance with generally accepted auditing standards.

The trial revolved around the testimony of two expert witnesses. The witness for the company argued that even though the auditors took a substantive approach to the audit, they should have seen that Sampson had the opportunity to commit the theft, extended their audit, and found it.

The expert for the defense argued that a substantive audit approach is allowed by generally accepted auditing standards. Sampson manipulated the records so carefully that the substantive procedures of the various payroll accounts did not indicate that the theft had occurred. Because no "red flags" were evident that would have caused the auditors to extend their tests, the audit was clearly satisfactory.

The jury found against the auditors, and Tramenier and Baker, CPAs, was required to pay approximately $2.3 million in damages. When jury members were interviewed about their decision, they indicated that they didn't really understand the technical nature of the arguments made by the expert witnesses, but it was apparent to them that the people who did the audit were extremely bright and competent. Accordingly, the jury members believed that *the auditors certainly had the ability to find the theft* and the fact that they didn't meant that they failed to perform up to their potential.

LEARNING OBJECTIVES

After studying this chapter, you should be able to

17-1 Show the relationship of cash in the bank to the various transaction cycles.

17-2 Identify the major types of cash accounts maintained by business entities.

17-3 Design and perform audit tests of the general cash account.

17-4 Recognize when to extend audit tests of the general cash account to test further for material fraud.

17-5 Design and perform audit tests of the imprest payroll bank account.

17-6 Design and perform audit tests of imprest petty cash.

Cash is the only account that is included in several cycles. It is a part of every cycle except inventory and warehousing. The audit of cash balances is the last audit area studied because the evidence accumulated for cash balances depends heavily on the results of the tests in other cycles. For example, if the understanding of internal control and tests of controls and substantive tests of transactions in the acquisition and payment cycle lead the auditor to believe that it is appropriate to reduce assessed control risk to low, the auditor can reduce detailed tests of the ending balance in cash. If, however, the auditor concludes that assessed control risk should be higher, extensive year-end testing may be necessary.

Cash is important primarily because of the potential for fraud but also because there may be errors. The opening vignette provides one example of what can happen if an auditor is not careful in assessing risks in auditing the cash account.

CASH IN THE BANK AND TRANSACTION CYCLES

OBJECTIVE 17-1

Show the relationship of cash in the bank to the various transaction cycles.

A brief discussion of the relationship between cash in the bank and the other transaction cycles serves a dual function: It clearly shows the importance of the tests of various transaction cycles to the audit of cash, and it aids in further understanding the integration of the different transaction cycles.

The general cash account is considered significant in almost all audits even when the ending balance is immaterial. The amount of cash *flowing* into and out of the cash account is often larger than that for any other account in the financial statements. Furthermore, the susceptibility of cash to defalcation is greater than for other types of assets because most other assets must be converted to cash to make them usable.

In the audit of cash, an important distinction should be made between verifying the client's reconciliation of the balance on the bank statement to the balance in the general ledger and verifying whether recorded cash in the general ledger correctly reflects all cash transactions that took place during the year. It is relatively easy to verify the client's reconciliation of the balance in the bank account to the general ledger, but a significant part of the total audit of a company involves verifying whether cash transactions are properly recorded. For example, each of the following misstatements ultimately results in the improper payment of or the failure to receive cash, but none will normally be discovered as a part of the audit of the bank reconciliation:

- Failure to bill a customer
- Billing a customer at a lower price than called for by company policy
- A defalcation of cash by interception of cash receipts from customers before they are recorded, with the account charged off as a bad debt
- Duplicate payment of a vendor's invoice
- Improper payments of officers' personal expenditures
- Payment for raw materials that were not received
- Payment to an employee for more hours than he or she worked
- Payment of interest to a related party for an amount in excess of the going rate

If these misstatements are to be uncovered in the audit, their discovery must come about through the tests of controls and substantive tests of transactions that were discussed in the preceding chapters. The first three misstatements could be discovered as part of the audit of the sales and collection cycle and the next three in the audit of the acquisition and payment cycle. Although not discussed in the text, the last two misstatements could be discovered in tests of the payroll and personnel cycle and the capital acquisition and repayment cycle, respectively.

Entirely different types of misstatements are normally discovered as a part of the tests of a bank reconciliation. For example,

- Failure to include a check that has not cleared the bank on the outstanding check list, even though it has been recorded in the cash disbursements journal
- Cash received by the client subsequent to the balance sheet date but recorded as cash receipts in the current year

- Deposits recorded as cash receipts near the end of the year, deposited in the bank in the same month, and included in the bank reconciliation as a deposit in transit
- Payments on notes payable debited directly to the bank balance by the bank but not entered in the client's records
- Deposits received by the bank on behalf of the company from credit card agencies and other vendors making payments electronically, but not recorded in the client's records

Before we focus on audit tests related to the client's bank reconciliation, it is helpful to discuss the types of cash accounts commonly used by most companies. This is the subject of the next section.

TYPES OF CASH ACCOUNTS

OBJECTIVE 17-2

Identify the major types of cash accounts maintained by business entities.

It is important to understand the different types of cash accounts because the auditing approach to each varies. When obtaining an understanding of the client's business, the auditor is likely to learn about the various types of cash balances that may exist. For example, when learning about operations at various company locations, the auditor may obtain information about cash accounts maintained at the local and corporate office levels. The following are the major types of cash accounts.

General Cash Account

The **general cash account** is the focal point of cash for most organizations because virtually all cash receipts and disbursements flow through this account. The disbursements for the acquisition and payment cycle are normally paid from this account, and the receipts of cash in the sales and collection cycle are deposited in the account. In addition, the deposits and disbursements for all other cash accounts are normally made through the general account.

Imprest Payroll Account

As a means of improving internal control, many companies establish a separate imprest bank account for such things as making payroll payments to employees or separate cash receipts and disbursements accounts for branch banking. In an **imprest payroll account,** a fixed balance, such as $5,000, is maintained in a separate bank account. Immediately before each pay period, one check or electronic transfer is drawn on the general cash account to deposit the total amount of the net payroll into the payroll account. After all payroll checks have cleared the imprest payroll account, the bank account should have a $5,000 balance. The only deposits into the account are for the weekly and semimonthly payroll, and the only disbursements are paychecks to employees. For companies with many employees, the use of an imprest payroll account can improve internal control and reduce the time needed to reconcile bank accounts.

WWW

Electronic Funds Transfer

A somewhat different type of imprest account consists of one bank account for receipts and a separate one for disbursements. There may be several of these in a company for different divisions. All receipts are deposited in the imprest account, and the total is transferred to the general account periodically. The disbursement account is set up on an *imprest basis*, but in a different manner than an imprest payroll account. A fixed balance is maintained in the imprest account, and the authorized personnel use these funds for disbursements at their own discretion as long as the payments are consistent with company policy. When the cash balance has been depleted, a reimbursement is made to the imprest disbursement account from the general account *after* the expenditures have been approved. The use of such an imprest bank account improves controls over receipts and disbursements. Many companies using imprest bank accounts have online access with their banks that management uses to monitor daily cash balances. When funds need to be transferred into the general account to cover expenditures, approved company personnel can initiate the transfer electronically through the online system.

Branch Bank Account

For a company operating in multiple locations, it is often desirable to have a separate bank balance at each location. **Branch bank accounts** are useful for building public relations in local communities and permitting the centralization of operations at the branch level.

In some companies, the deposits and disbursements for each branch are made to a separate bank account, and the excess cash is periodically electronically transferred to the main office general bank account. The branch account in this instance is much like a general account, but at the branch level.

FIGURE 17-1 Relationship of General Cash to Other Cash Accounts

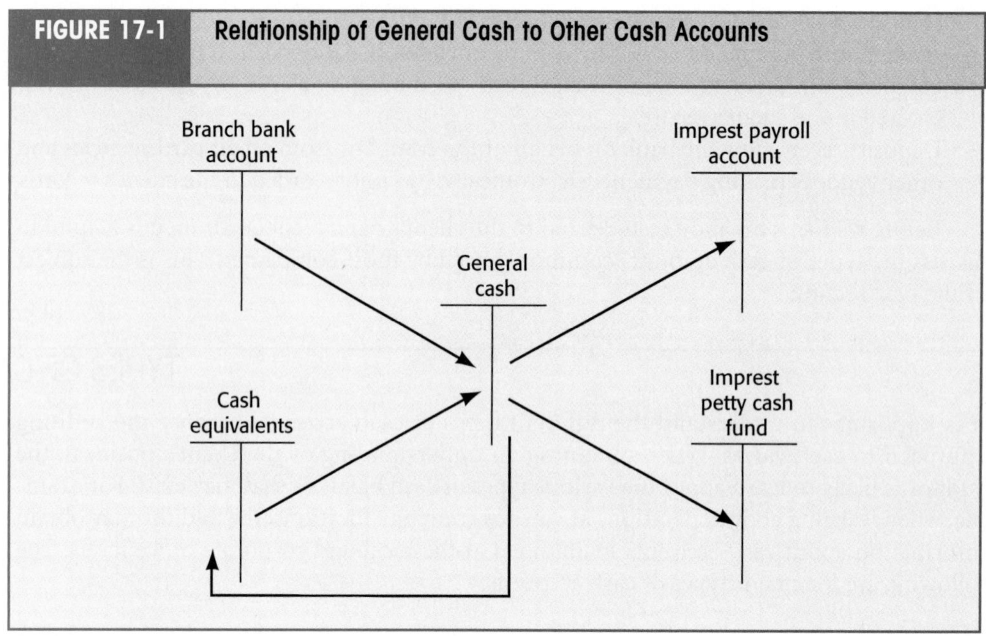

Imprest Petty Cash Fund

An **imprest petty cash fund** is actually not a bank account, but it is sufficiently similar to cash on deposit to merit inclusion. A petty cash account is often something as simple as a preset amount of cash set aside in a strong box for incidental expenses. It is used for small cash acquisitions that can be paid more conveniently and quickly by cash than by check, or for the convenience of employees in cashing personal or payroll checks. An imprest cash account is set up on the same basis as an imprest branch bank account, but the expenditures are normally for a much smaller amount. Typical expenses include minor office supplies, stamps, and small contributions to local charities. A petty cash account usually does not exceed a few hundred dollars and may not be reimbursed more than once or twice each month.

Cash Equivalents

Excess cash accumulated during certain parts of the operating cycle that will be needed in the reasonably near future is often invested in short-term, highly liquid **cash equivalents.** Examples include time deposits, certificates of deposit, and money market funds. Cash equivalents, which can be highly material, are included in the financial statements as a part of the cash account only if they are short-term investments that are readily convertible to known amounts of cash within a short time and there is insignificant risk of a change of value from interest rate changes. Marketable securities and longer-term interest-bearing investments are not cash equivalents.

Figure 17-1 shows the relationship of general cash to the other cash accounts. All cash either originates from or is deposited in general cash. The remainder of this chapter focuses on auditing three types of accounts: the general cash account, imprest payroll bank account, and imprest petty cash. The others are similar to these and need not be discussed.

AUDIT OF THE GENERAL CASH ACCOUNT

OBJECTIVE 17-3

Design and perform audit tests of the general cash account.

On the trial balance of Hillsburg Hardware Co. on page 123, there is only one cash account. Notice, however, that all cycles, except inventory and warehousing, affect cash in the bank.

In testing the year-end balance in the general cash account, the auditor must accumulate sufficient evidence to evaluate whether cash, as stated on the balance sheet, is fairly stated and properly disclosed in accordance with six of the nine balance-related audit objectives used for all tests of details of balances. Rights to general cash, its classification on the balance sheet, and the realizable value of cash are not a problem.

The methodology for auditing year-end cash is essentially the same as that for all other balance sheet accounts. The methodology is now discussed in detail.

Identify Client Business Risks Affecting Cash

Most companies are unlikely to have significant client business risks affecting cash balances. However, client business risk may arise from inappropriate cash management policies or handling of funds held in trust for others. For example, one financial services firm was recently found to have engaged in fraud by intentionally overdrawing cash balances by significant amounts.

Client business risk is more likely to arise from cash equivalents and other types of investments. Many governmental units and other entities suffered losses from repurchases of government securities in the ESM Government Securities case described in Chapter 4. Several financial services firms have suffered large trading losses from the activities of individual traders that were hidden by misstating investment and cash balances. The auditor should understand the risks from the client's investment policies and strategies, as well as management controls that mitigate these risks.

Set Tolerable Misstatement and Assess Inherent Risk

The cash balance is immaterial in most audits, but cash transactions affecting the balance are almost always extremely material. Therefore, there is often potential for material misstatement of cash.

Because cash is more susceptible to theft than other assets, there is high inherent risk for the existence, completeness, and accuracy objectives. These objectives are usually the focus in auditing cash balances. Typically, inherent risk is low for all other objectives.

Assess Control Risk

Internal controls over year-end cash balances in the general account can be divided into two categories: *controls over the transaction cycles* affecting the recording of cash receipts and disbursements and *independent bank reconciliations.*

Controls affecting the recording of cash transactions have been discussed in preceding chapters, but they are essential in deciding control risk for cash. For example, in the acquisition and payment cycle, major controls include adequate segregation of duties between the check signing and accounts payable functions, signing of checks only by a properly authorized person, use of prenumbered checks printed on special paper, adequate control of blank and voided checks, careful review of supporting documentation by the check signer before checks are signed, adequate control over the initiation and approval of wire transfer funds, and adequate internal verification. If controls affecting cash-related transactions are adequate, it is possible to reduce control risk and therefore the audit tests for the year-end bank reconciliation.

A monthly **bank reconciliation** of the general bank account on a timely basis by someone independent of the handling or recording of cash receipts and disbursements is an essential control over the cash balance. If a business defers preparing bank reconciliations for long periods, the value of the control is reduced and may affect the auditor's assessment of control risk for cash. The reconciliation is important to ensure that the books reflect the same cash balance as the actual amount of cash in the bank after considering reconciling items, but even more important, the *independent* reconciliation provides a unique opportunity for an internal verification of cash receipts and disbursements transactions. If the bank statements are received unopened by the reconciler and physical control is maintained over the statements until the reconciliations are complete, the cancelled checks, duplicate deposit slips, and other documents included in the statement can be examined without concern for the possibility of alteration, deletions, or additions. A careful bank reconciliation by competent client personnel includes the following:

- Compare cancelled checks with the cash disbursements records for date, payee, and amount.
- Examine cancelled checks for signature, endorsement, and cancellation.
- Compare deposits in the bank with recorded cash receipts for date, customer, and amount.
- Account for the numerical sequence of checks, and investigate missing ones.
- Reconcile all items causing a difference between the book and bank balance and verify their propriety.
- Reconcile total debits on the bank statement with the totals in the cash disbursements records.

Cash Handling Procedures

- Reconcile total credits on the bank statement with the totals in the cash receipts records.
- Review month-end interbank transfers for propriety and proper recording.
- Follow up on outstanding checks and stop-payment notices.

Most accounting software packages incorporate a bank reconciliation as a part of end-of-month procedures. Even though the software reduces the clerical efforts in performing the bank reconciliations, it does not eliminate the need for the preparer to do most of the procedures just identified.

Because of the importance of monthly reconciliation of bank accounts, another common control for many companies is to have a responsible employee review the monthly reconciliation as soon as possible after its completion.

Design and Perform Tests of Controls and Substantive Tests of Transactions

Because the cash balance is affected by all other cycles except inventory and warehousing, an extremely large number of transactions affect cash. The appropriate tests of controls and substantive tests of transactions have been discussed in detail in several earlier chapters as the audit of each cycle was studied.

Design and Perform Analytical Procedures

In many audits, the year-end bank reconciliation is extensively audited. Using analytical procedures to test the reasonableness of the cash balance is therefore less important than it is for most other audit areas.

It is common for auditors to compare the ending balance on the bank reconciliation, deposits in transit, outstanding checks, and other reconciling items with the prior-year reconciliation. Similarly, auditors normally compare the ending balance in cash with previous months' balances. These analytical procedures may uncover misstatements in cash.

Design Tests of Details of Cash Balance

The starting point for the verification of the balance in the general bank account is to obtain a bank reconciliation from the client for inclusion in the auditor's documentation. Figure 17-2 shows a bank reconciliation after adjustments. Notice that the bottom figure in the audit schedule is the adjusted balance in the general ledger, which is the balance that should appear on the financial statements. The auditor must determine that the client has made adjustments such as those at the bottom of Figure 17-2 if they are material.

The frame of reference for the audit tests is the bank reconciliation. The balance-related audit objectives and common tests of details of balances are shown in Table 17-1 on page 492. As in all other audit areas, the actual audit procedures depend on the materiality and the risks the auditor has identified in other parts of the audit that are related to cash. Also, because of their close relationship in the audit of year-end cash, the existence of recorded cash in the bank, accuracy, and inclusion of existing cash (completeness) are combined. These three objectives are the most important ones for cash and therefore receive the greatest attention.

The following three procedures merit additional discussion because of their importance and complexity.

Receipt of a Bank Confirmation The direct receipt of a confirmation from every bank or other financial institution with which the client does business is typically done but not required by auditing standards for every audit except when there is an unusually large number of inactive accounts. If the bank does not respond to a confirmation request, the auditor should send a second request or ask the client to telephone the bank. As a convenience to auditors as well as to bankers who are requested to fill out bank confirmations, the AICPA has approved the use of a **standard bank confirmation form.** Figure 17-3 on page 493 is an illustration of a completed standard confirmation. As shown in Figure 17-3, it is called a standard form to confirm account balance information with financial institutions. This standard form has been agreed upon by the AICPA and the American Bankers Association.

The importance of bank confirmations in the audit extends beyond the verification of the actual cash balance. It is typical for the bank to confirm loan information and bank balances on the same form. The confirmation in Figure 17-3 includes three outstanding loans. Information on liabilities to the bank for notes, mortgages, or other debt typically includes the amount of the loan, the date of the loan, its due date, interest rate, and the existence of collateral.

Banks are *not responsible* for searching their records for bank balances or loans beyond those included on the form by the CPA firm's client. A sentence near the bottom of the

FIGURE 17-2 Audit Schedule for a Bank Reconciliation

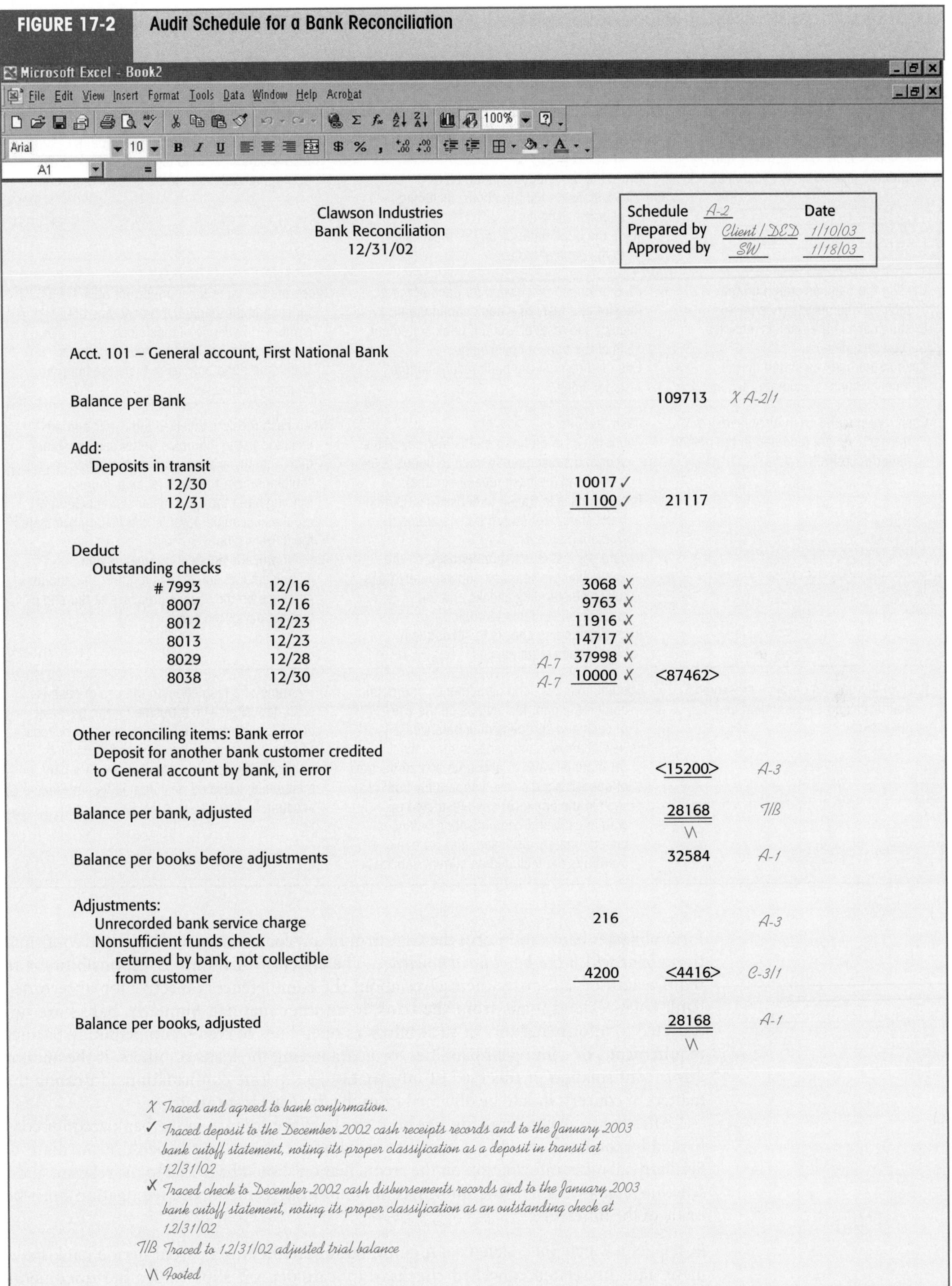

Microsoft Excel - Book2

File Edit View Insert Format Tools Data Window Help Acrobat

Clawson Industries
Bank Reconciliation
12/31/02

		Date
Schedule	A-2	
Prepared by	Client / DED	1/10/03
Approved by	SW	1/18/03

Acct. 101 – General account, First National Bank

Balance per Bank			109713	X A-2/1
Add:				
Deposits in transit				
12/30		10017 ✓		
12/31		11100 ✓	21117	
Deduct				
Outstanding checks				
# 7993	12/16	3068 ✗		
8007	12/16	9763 ✗		
8012	12/23	11916 ✗		
8013	12/23	14717 ✗		
8029	12/28	A-7 37998 ✗		
8038	12/30	A-7 10000 ✗	<87462>	
Other reconciling items: Bank error Deposit for another bank customer credited to General account by bank, in error			<15200>	A-3
Balance per bank, adjusted			28168 Λ	T/B
Balance per books before adjustments			32584	A-1
Adjustments:				
Unrecorded bank service charge		216		A-3
Nonsufficient funds check returned by bank, not collectible from customer		4200	<4416>	C-3/1
Balance per books, adjusted			28168 Λ	A-1

X Traced and agreed to bank confirmation.

✓ Traced deposit to the December 2002 cash receipts records and to the January 2003 bank cutoff statement, noting its proper classification as a deposit in transit at 12/31/02

✗ Traced check to December 2002 cash disbursements records and to the January 2003 bank cutoff statement, noting its proper classification as an outstanding check at 12/31/02

T/B Traced to 12/31/02 adjusted trial balance

Λ Footed

TABLE 17-1 Balance-Related Audit Objectives and Tests of Details of Balances for General Cash in the Bank

Balance-Related Audit Objective	Common Tests of Details of Balances Procedures	Comments
Cash in the bank as stated on the reconciliation foots correctly and agrees with the general ledger (detail tie-in).	Foot the outstanding check list and deposits in transit. Prove the bank reconciliation as to additions and subtractions, including all reconciling items. Trace the book balance on the reconciliation to the general ledger.	These tests are done entirely on the bank reconciliation, with no reference to documents or other records except the general ledger.
Cash in the bank as stated on the reconciliation exists (existence). Existing cash in the bank is recorded (completeness). Cash in the bank as stated on the reconciliation is accurate (accuracy).	*(See extended discussion for each of these.)* Receipt and tests of a bank confirmation. Receipt and tests of a cutoff bank statement. Tests of the bank reconciliation. Extended tests of the bank reconciliation. Tests for kiting.	These are the three most important objectives for cash in the bank. The procedures are combined because of their close interdependence. The last two procedures should be done only when there are internal control weaknesses.
Cash receipts and cash disbursements transactions are recorded in the proper period (cutoff).	*Cash receipts:* Count the cash on hand on the last day of the year and subsequently trace to deposits in transit and the cash receipts journal. Trace deposits in transit to subsequent period bank statement (cutoff bank statement). *Cash disbursements:* Record the last check number used on the last day of the year and subsequently trace to the outstanding checks and the cash disbursements journal. Trace outstanding checks to subsequent period bank statement.	When cash receipts received after year-end are included in the journal, a better cash position than actually exists is shown. It is called "holding open" the cash receipts journal. Holding open the cash disbursements journal reduces accounts payable and usually overstates the current ratio. The first procedure listed for receipts and disbursements cutoff tests requires the auditor's presence on the client's premises at the end of the last day of the year.
Cash in the bank is properly presented and disclosed (presentation and disclosure).	Examine minutes, loan agreements, and obtain confirmation for restrictions on the use of cash and compensating balances. Review financial statements to make sure (a) material savings accounts and certificates of deposit are disclosed separately from cash in the bank, (b) cash restricted to certain uses and compensating balances are adequately disclosed, and (c) bank overdrafts are included as current liabilities.	An example of a restriction on the use of cash is cash deposited with a trustee for the payment of mortgage interest and taxes on the proceeds of a construction mortgage. A compensating balance is the client's agreement with a bank to maintain a specified minimum in its checking account.

form obligates banks to inform the CPA firm of any loans not included on the confirmation *about which the bank has knowledge*. The effect of this limited responsibility is to require auditors to satisfy themselves about the completeness objective for unrecorded bank balances and loans from the bank in another manner. Similarly, banks are not expected to inform auditors of such things as open lines of credit, compensating balance requirements, or contingent liabilities for guaranteeing the loans of others. If the auditor wants confirmation of this type of information, a separate confirmation addressing the matters of concern should be obtained from the financial institution.

After the bank confirmation has been received, the balance in the bank account confirmed by the bank should be traced to the amount stated on the bank reconciliation. Similarly, all other information on the reconciliation should be traced to the relevant audit schedules. In any case, if the information is not in agreement, an investigation must be made of the difference.

Receipt of a Cutoff Bank Statement A **cutoff bank statement** is a partial-period bank statement and the related cancelled checks, duplicate deposit slips, and other documents included in bank statements, mailed by the bank directly to the CPA firm's office. The

FIGURE 17-3 Standard Confirmation of Financial Institution Account Balance Information

Clawson Industries
Bank Confirmation
12/31/02

Schedule A-2/1	Date
Prepared by DCD	1/10/03
Approved by SW	1/18/03

STANDARD FORM TO CONFIRM ACCOUNT BALANCE INFORMATION WITH FINANCIAL INSTITUTIONS

Clawson Industries
CUSTOMER NAME

Financial Institution's Name and Address

[*First National Bank*
200 Oak Street
Midvale, Illinois 40093]

We have provided to our accountants the following information as of the close of business on **December 31, 2002,** regarding our deposit and loan balances. Please confirm the accuracy of the information, noting any exceptions to the information provided. If the balances have been left blank, please complete this form by furnishing the balance in the appropriate space below.* Although we do not request nor expect you to conduct a comprehensive, detailed search of your records, if during the process of completing this confirmation additional information about other deposit and loan accounts we may have with you comes to your attention, please include such information below. Please use the enclosed envelope to return the form directly to our accountants.

1. At the close of business on the date listed above, our records indicated the following deposit balance(s):

ACCOUNT NAME	ACCOUNT NUMBER	INTEREST RATE	BALANCE*
General account	*19751-974*	*None*	*109,713.11* A-2

2. We were directly liable to the financial institution for loans at the close of business on the date listed above as follows:

ACCOUNT NO./ DESCRIPTION	BALANCE*	DATE DUE	INTEREST RATE	DATE THROUGH WHICH INTEREST IS PAID	DESCRIPTION OF COLLATERAL
N/A	*50,000.00*	*1/9/03*	*10%*	*N/A*	*General*
N/A	*90,000.00*	*1/9/03*	*10%*	*N/A*	*Security*
N/A	*60,000.00*	*1/23/03*	*11%*	*N/A*	*Agreement*

A L Moore — January 3, 2003
(Customer's Authorized Signature) (Date)

The information presented above by the customer is in agreement with our records. Although we have not conducted a comprehensive, detailed search of our records, no other deposit or loan accounts have come to our attention except as noted below.

Margaret Davis — January 10, 2003
(Financial Institution Authorized Signature) (Date)

Vice President
(Title)

EXCEPTIONS AND/OR COMMENTS

None

Please return this form directly to our accountants:

Jones and Smith CPAs
2111 First Street
Detroit, Michigan 48711

Approved 1990 by American Bankers Association, American Institute of Certified Public Accountants, and Bank Administration Institute. Additional forms available from: AICPA-Order Department, P.O. Box 1003, NY, NY 10108-1003

*Ordinarily, balances are intentionally left blank if they are not available at the time the form is prepared.

purpose of the cutoff bank statement is to verify the reconciling items on the client's year-end bank reconciliation with evidence that is inaccessible to the client. To fulfill this purpose, the auditor requests the client to have the bank send directly to the auditor the statement for 7 to 10 days subsequent to the balance sheet date.

Many auditors verify the subsequent period bank statement if a cutoff statement is not received directly from the bank. The purpose of this verification is to test whether the client's employees have omitted, added, or altered any of the documents accompanying the statement. It is obviously a test for intentional misstatements. The auditor performs the verification in the month subsequent to the balance sheet date by (1) footing all the cancelled checks, debit memos, deposits, and credit memos; (2) checking to see that the bank statement balances when the footed totals are used; and (3) reviewing the items included in the footings to make sure that they were cancelled by the bank in the proper period and do not include any erasures or alterations.

Tests of the Bank Reconciliation As stated earlier, a well-prepared independent bank reconciliation is an essential internal control over cash. The reasons for testing the bank reconciliation are to determine whether client personnel have carefully prepared the bank reconciliation and to verify whether the client's recorded bank balance is the same amount as the actual cash in the bank except for deposits in transit, outstanding checks, and other reconciling items. In testing the reconciliation, the auditor can obtain the information for conducting the tests from the cutoff bank statement. Several major procedures are involved:

- Verify that the client's bank reconciliation is mathematically accurate.
- Trace the balance on the bank confirmation and/or the beginning balance on the cutoff statement to the balance per bank on the bank reconciliation; a reconciliation cannot take place until these balances are the same.
- Trace checks written before year-end and included with the cutoff bank statement to the list of outstanding checks on the bank reconciliation and to the cash disbursements journal in the period or periods prior to the balance sheet date. All checks that cleared the bank after the balance sheet date and were included in the cash disbursements journal should also be included on the outstanding check list. If a check was included in the cash disbursements journal, it should be included as an outstanding check if it did not clear before the balance sheet date. Similarly, if a check cleared the bank before the balance sheet date, it should not be on the bank reconciliation.
- Investigate all significant checks included on the outstanding check list that have not cleared the bank on the cutoff statement. The first step in the investigation should be to trace the amount of any items not clearing to the cash disbursements journal. The reason for the check not being cashed should be discussed with the client, and if the auditor is concerned about the possibility of fraud, the vendor's accounts payable balance should be confirmed to determine whether the vendor has recognized the receipt of the cash in its records. In addition, the cancelled check should be examined before the last day of the audit if it becomes available.
- Trace deposits in transit to the cutoff bank statement. All cash receipts not deposited in the bank at the end of the year should be traced to the cutoff bank statement to make sure that they were deposited shortly after the beginning of the new year.
- Account for other reconciling items on the bank statement and bank reconciliation. These include such items as bank service charges, bank errors and corrections, and unrecorded transactions debited or credited directly to the bank account by the bank. These reconciling items should be investigated carefully to be sure that they have been treated properly by the client.

FRAUD-ORIENTED PROCEDURES

OBJECTIVE 17-4

Recognize when to extend audit tests of the general cash account to test further for material fraud.

A major consideration in the audit of the general cash balance is the possibility of fraud. The auditor must extend the procedures in the audit of year-end cash to determine the possibility of a material fraud when there are inadequate internal controls, especially the improper segregation of duties between the handling of cash and the recording of cash transactions in the accounting records.

In designing audit procedures for uncovering fraud, careful consideration should be given to the nature of the weaknesses in internal control, the type of fraud that is likely to result from the weaknesses, the potential materiality of the fraud, and the audit procedures that are most effective in uncovering the fraud. When auditors are specifically testing for fraud, they should keep in mind that audit procedures other than tests of details of cash balances can also be useful. Examples of procedures that may uncover fraud in the cash receipts area include the confirmation of accounts receivable, tests for lapping, reviewing the general ledger entries in the cash account for unusual items, tracing from customer orders to sales and subsequent cash receipts, and examining approvals and supporting documentation for bad debts and sales returns and allowances. Similar tests can be used for testing for the possibility of fraudulent cash disbursements.

Even with reasonably elaborate fraud-oriented procedures, it is extremely difficult to detect fraud, especially omitted transactions and account balances. If, for example, a company has illegal offshore cash accounts and makes deposits to those accounts from unrecorded sales, it is unlikely that an auditor will uncover the fraud. Nevertheless, auditors are responsible for making a reasonable effort to detect fraud when they have reason to believe it may exist. The following procedures for uncovering fraud that are directly related to year-end cash balances are discussed in this section: extended tests of the bank reconciliation and tests of interbank transfers.

Extended Tests of the Bank Reconciliation

When the auditor believes that the year-end bank reconciliation may be intentionally misstated, it is appropriate to perform extended tests of the year-end bank reconciliation. The purpose of the extended procedures is to verify whether all transactions included in the journals for the last month of the year were correctly included in or excluded from the bank reconciliation and to verify whether all items in the bank reconciliation were correctly included. Let us assume that there are material internal control weaknesses and the client's year-end is December 31. A common approach is to start with the bank reconciliation for November and compare all reconciling items with cancelled checks and other documents in the December bank statement. In addition, all remaining cancelled checks and deposit slips in the December bank statement should be compared with the December cash disbursements and receipts journals. All uncleared items in the November bank reconciliation and the December cash disbursements and receipts journals should be included in the client's December 31 bank reconciliation. Similarly, all reconciling items in the December 31 bank reconciliation should be items from the November bank reconciliation and December's journals that have not yet cleared the bank.

In addition to the tests just described, the auditor must also carry out procedures subsequent to the end of the year with the use of the bank cutoff statement. These tests would be performed in the same manner as previously discussed.

Tests of Interbank Transfers

Embezzlers occasionally cover a defalcation of cash by a practice known as **kiting:** transferring money from one bank to another and improperly recording the transaction. Near the balance sheet date, a check is drawn on one bank account and immediately deposited in a second account for credit before the end of the accounting period. In making this transfer, the embezzler is careful to make sure that the check is deposited at a late enough date so that it does not clear the first bank until after the end of the period. If the interbank transfer is not recorded until after the balance sheet date, the amount of the transfer is recorded as an asset in both banks. Although there are other ways of perpetrating this fraud, each involves the device of increasing the bank balance to cover a shortage by the use of interbank transfers.

A useful approach to test for kiting, as well as for unintentional errors in recording interbank transfers, is to list all interbank transfers made a few days before and after the balance sheet date and to trace each to the accounting records for proper recording. An example of an interbank transfer schedule is included in Figure 17-4 (p. 496). The schedule shows that four interbank transfers were made shortly before and after the balance sheet date.

There are several things that should be audited on the interbank transfer schedule.

- *The accuracy of the information on the interbank transfer schedule should be verified.* The auditor should compare the disbursement and receipt information on the schedule to the cash disbursements and cash receipts records to make sure that it is accurate. Similarly, the dates on the schedule for transfers that were received and disbursed

FIGURE 17-4 Interbank Transfer Schedule

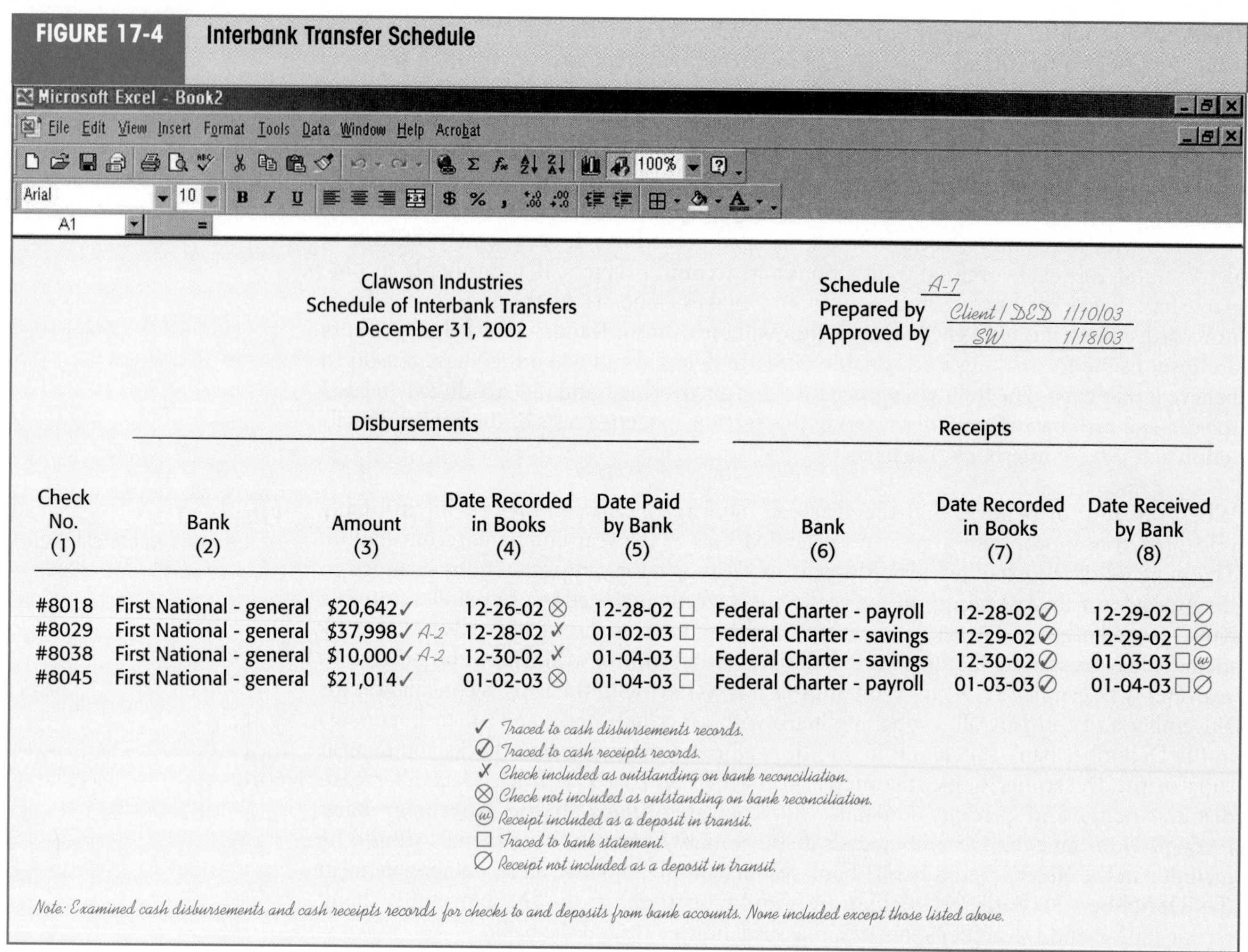

Clawson Industries
Schedule of Interbank Transfers
December 31, 2002

Schedule *A-7*
Prepared by *Client / DED 1/10/03*
Approved by *SW 1/18/03*

		Disbursements				Receipts	
Check No. (1)	Bank (2)	Amount (3)	Date Recorded in Books (4)	Date Paid by Bank (5)	Bank (6)	Date Recorded in Books (7)	Date Received by Bank (8)
#8018	First National - general	$20,642✓	12-26-02 ⊗	12-28-02 □	Federal Charter - payroll	12-28-02 ⊘	12-29-02 □∅
#8029	First National - general	$37,998✓ *A-2*	12-28-02 ✗	01-02-03 □	Federal Charter - savings	12-29-02 ⊘	12-29-02 □∅
#8038	First National - general	$10,000✓ *A-2*	12-30-02 ✗	01-04-03 □	Federal Charter - savings	12-30-02 ⊘	01-03-03 □ⓦ
#8045	First National - general	$21,014✓	01-02-03 ⊗	01-04-03 □	Federal Charter - payroll	01-03-03 ⊘	01-04-03 □∅

✓ Traced to cash disbursements records.
⊘ Traced to cash receipts records.
✗ Check included as outstanding on bank reconciliation.
⊗ Check not included as outstanding on bank reconciliation.
ⓦ Receipt included as a deposit in transit.
□ Traced to bank statement.
∅ Receipt not included as a deposit in transit.

Note: Examined cash disbursements and cash receipts records for checks to and deposits from bank accounts. None included except those listed above.

should be compared with the bank statement. Finally, cash disbursements and receipts records should be examined to make sure that all transfers a few days before and after the balance sheet date have been included on the schedule. The tick mark explanations on the schedule in Figure 17-4 indicate that these steps have been taken.

- *The interbank transfers must be recorded in both the receiving and disbursing banks.* If, for example, there was a $10,000 transfer from Bank A to Bank B but only the disbursement was recorded, this is evidence of an attempt to conceal a cash theft.
- *The date of the recording of the disbursements and receipts for each transfer must be in the same fiscal year.* In Figure 17-4, the dates in the two "date recorded in books" columns [columns (4) and (7)] are in the same period for each transfer; therefore, they are correct. If a cash receipt was recorded in the current fiscal year and the disbursement in the subsequent fiscal year, it may be an attempt to cover a cash shortage.
- *Disbursements on the interbank transfer schedule should be correctly included in or excluded from year-end bank reconciliations as outstanding checks.* In Figure 17-4, the 12-31-02 bank reconciliation for the general cash account should include outstanding checks for the second and third transfers but not the other two. [Compare the dates in columns (4) and (5).] Understating outstanding checks on the bank reconciliation indicates the possibility of kiting.
- *Receipts on the interbank transfer schedule should be correctly included in or excluded from year-end bank reconciliations as deposits in transit.* In Figure 17-4, the 12-31-02 bank reconciliations for the savings and payroll accounts should indicate a deposit in transit for the third transfer but not for the other three. (Compare the dates for each transfer in the last two columns.) Overstating deposits in transit on the bank reconciliation indicates the possibility of kiting.

ELECTRONIC TRANSFER OF CASH

Many organizations use electronic transfer when they are transferring cash among banks, collecting from customers, and paying vendors. Companies engaging in e-commerce sales activities may receive electronic funds from credit card agencies submitting payments on behalf of customers. Under these systems, cash is transferred instantly. For example, when Company A collects from Credit Card Agency X, the cash is instantly transferred from Credit Card Agency X's bank account to Company A's. There is no check.

Electronic transfers have the potential to improve internal controls in that no cash is handled by employees. However, there is also potential risk of cash thefts through inappropriate cash transfers. It is essential that excellent internal controls be in place for electronic transfers.

Even though audit tests of interbank transfers are usually fraud oriented, they are often performed on audits in which there are numerous bank transfers, regardless of internal controls. When there are numerous interbank transfers, it is difficult to be sure that each is correctly handled unless a schedule of transfers near the end of the year is prepared and each transfer is traced to the accounting records and bank statements. In addition to the possibility of kiting, inaccurate handling of transfers could result in a misclassification between cash and accounts payable. The materiality of transfers and the relative ease of performing the tests make many auditors believe they should always be performed.

AUDIT OF THE IMPREST PAYROLL BANK ACCOUNT

OBJECTIVE 17-5

Design and perform audit tests of the imprest payroll bank account.

Tests of the payroll bank reconciliation should take only a few minutes if there is an imprest payroll account and an independent reconciliation of the bank account such as that described for the general account. Typically, the only reconciling items are outstanding checks, and for most audits, the great majority clear shortly after the checks are issued. In testing the payroll bank account balances, it is necessary to obtain a bank reconciliation, a bank confirmation, and a cutoff bank statement. The reconciliation procedures are performed in the same manner as those described for general cash except that tests of the outstanding checks are normally limited to a reasonableness test. Naturally, extended procedures are necessary if the controls are inadequate or if the bank account does not reconcile with the general ledger imprest cash balance. Keep in mind that these procedures pertain only to the imprest bank account, not to the overall payroll cycle.

AUDIT OF IMPREST PETTY CASH

OBJECTIVE 17-6

Design and perform audit tests of imprest petty cash.

Petty cash is a unique account because it is often immaterial in amount, yet it is verified on many audits. The account is verified primarily because of the potential for defalcation and the client's expectation of auditor consideration even when the amount is immaterial.

Internal Controls Over Petty Cash

The most important internal control for petty cash is the use of an imprest fund that is the responsibility of *one individual.* In addition, petty cash funds should not be mingled with other receipts, and the fund should be kept separate from all other activities. There should also be limits on the amount of any expenditure from petty cash, as well as on the total amount of the fund. The type of expenditure that can be made from petty cash transactions should be well defined by company policy.

When a disbursement is made from petty cash, adequate internal controls require a responsible official's approval on a prenumbered petty cash form. The total of the actual cash and checks in the fund plus the total unreimbursed petty cash forms that represent actual expenditures should equal the total amount of the petty cash fund stated in the general ledger. Periodically, surprise counts and a reconciliation of the petty cash fund should be made by the internal auditor or other responsible official.

When the petty cash balance runs low, a check payable to the petty cash custodian should be written on the general cash account for the reimbursement of petty cash. The check should be for the exact amount of the prenumbered vouchers that are submitted as evidence of actual expenditures. These vouchers should be verified by the accounts payable clerk and cancelled to prevent their reuse.

Audit Tests for Petty Cash

The emphasis in verifying petty cash should be on testing controls over petty cash transactions rather than the ending balance in the account. Even if the amount of the petty cash fund is small, there is potential for numerous improper transactions if the fund is frequently reimbursed.

An important part of testing petty cash is first to determine the client's procedures for handling the fund by discussing internal controls with the custodian and examining the documentation of a few transactions. As a part of obtaining an understanding of internal control, it is necessary to identify internal controls and weaknesses. Even though most petty cash systems are not complex, it is often desirable to use a flowchart and an internal control questionnaire, primarily for documentation in subsequent audits.

Tests of controls and substantive tests of transactions depend on the number and size of the petty cash reimbursements and the auditor's assessed control risk. When control risk is assessed as low and there are few reimbursement payments during the year, it is common for auditors not to test any further, for reasons of immateriality. When the auditor decides to test petty cash, the two most common procedures are to count the petty cash balance and to carry out detailed tests of one or two reimbursement transactions. In such a case, the primary procedures should include footing the petty cash vouchers supporting the amount of the reimbursement, accounting for a sequence of petty cash vouchers, examining the petty cash vouchers for authorization and cancellation, and examining the attached documentation for reasonableness. Typical supporting documentation includes cash register tapes, invoices, and receipts.

Petty cash tests can ordinarily be performed at any time during the year, but as a matter of convenience, they are typically done on an interim date. If the balance in the petty cash fund is considered material, which is rarely the case, it should be counted at the end of the year. Unreimbursed expenditures should be examined as a part of the count to determine whether the amount of unrecorded expenses is material.

SUMMARY

We have seen in this chapter that transactions in most cycles affect the cash account. Because of the relationship between transactions in several cycles and the ending cash account balance, the auditor typically waits to audit the ending cash balance until the results of tests of controls and substantive tests of transactions for all cycles are completed and analyzed. As shown in this chapter, tests of the cash balance normally include tests of the bank reconciliations of key cash accounts, such as the general cash account, imprest payroll account, and imprest petty cash fund. If the auditor assesses a high likelihood of fraud in cash, additional tests may also be performed, such as extended bank reconciliation procedures or tests of interbank transfers.

ESSENTIAL TERMS

Bank reconciliation—the monthly reconciliation, usually prepared by client personnel, of the differences between the cash balance recorded in the general ledger and the amount in the bank account

Branch bank accounts—separate bank accounts maintained at local banks by branches of a company

Cash equivalents—excess cash invested in short-term, highly liquid investments such as time deposits, certificates of deposit, and money market funds

Cutoff bank statement—a partial-period bank statement and the related cancelled checks, duplicate deposit slips, and other documents included in bank statements, mailed by the bank directly to the auditor; the auditor uses it to verify reconciling items on the client's year-end bank reconciliation

General cash account—the primary bank account for most organizations; virtually all cash receipts and disbursements flow through this account at some time

Imprest payroll account—a bank account to which the exact amount of payroll for the pay period is transferred by check or electronic transfer from the employer's general cash account

Imprest petty cash fund—a fund of cash maintained within the company for small cash acquisitions or to cash employees' checks; the fund's fixed balance is comparatively small and is periodically reimbursed

Kiting—the transfer of money from one bank to another and improperly recording the transfer so that the amount is recorded as an asset in both accounts; this practice is used by embezzlers to cover a defalcation of cash

Standard bank confirmation form—a form approved by the AICPA and American Bankers Association through which the bank responds to the auditor about bank balance and loan information provided on the confirmation

REVIEW QUESTIONS

17-1 (Objectives 17-1, 17-2) Explain the relationships among the initial assessed control risk, tests of controls and substantive tests of transactions for cash receipts, and the tests of details of cash balances.

17-2 (Objectives 17-1, 17-2) Explain the relationships among the initial assessed control risk, tests of controls and substantive tests of transactions for cash disbursements, and the tests of details of cash balances. Give one example in which the conclusions reached about internal controls in cash disbursements would affect the tests of cash balances.

17-3 (Objective 17-3) Why is the monthly reconciliation of bank accounts by an independent person an important internal control over cash balances? Which individuals would generally not be considered independent for this responsibility?

17-4 (Objective 17-3) Evaluate the effectiveness and state the shortcomings of the preparation of a bank reconciliation by the controller in the manner described in the following statement: "When I reconcile the bank account, the first thing I do is to sort the checks in numerical order and find which numbers are missing. Next I determine the amount of the uncleared checks by referring to the cash disbursements journal. If the bank account reconciles at that point, I am all finished with the reconciliation. If it does not, I search for deposits in transit, checks from the beginning outstanding check list that still have not cleared, other reconciling items, and bank errors until it reconciles. In most instances, I can do the reconciliation in 20 minutes."

17-5 (Objective 17-3) How do bank confirmations differ from positive confirmations of accounts receivable? Distinguish between them in terms of the nature of the information confirmed, the sample size, and the appropriate action when the confirmation is not returned after the second request. Explain the rationale for the differences between these two types of confirmations.

17-6 (Objective 17-3) Evaluate the necessity of following the practice described by an auditor: "In confirming bank accounts I insist upon a response from every bank the client has done business with in the past 2 years, even though the account may be closed at the balance sheet date."

17-7 (Objective 17-3) Describe what is meant by a cutoff bank statement and state its purpose.

17-8 (Objective 17-3) Why are auditors usually less concerned about the client's cash receipts cutoff than the cutoff for sales? Explain the procedure involved in testing for the cutoff for cash receipts.

17-9 (Objective 17-2) What is meant by an imprest bank account for a branch operation? Explain the purpose of using this type of bank account.

17-10 (Objective 17-3) When the auditor fails to obtain a cutoff bank statement, it is common to verify the entire statement for the month subsequent to the balance sheet date. How is this done and what is its purpose?

17-11 (Objective 17-4) Distinguish between lapping and kiting. Describe audit procedures that can be used to uncover each.

17-12 (Objective 17-5) Assume that a client with excellent internal controls uses an imprest payroll bank account. Explain why the verification of the payroll bank reconciliation ordinarily takes less time than the tests of the general bank account, even if the number of checks exceeds those written on the general account.

17-13 (Objective 17-6) Distinguish between the verification of petty cash reimbursements and the verification of the balance in the fund. Explain how each is done. Which is more important?

17-14 (Objectives 17-3, 17-4) Why is there a greater emphasis on the detection of fraud in tests of details of cash balances than for other balance sheet accounts? Give two specific examples that demonstrate how this emphasis affects the auditor's evidence accumulation in auditing year-end cash.

17-15 (Objective 17-3) Explain why, in verifying bank reconciliations, most auditors emphasize the possibility of a nonexistent deposit in transit being included in the reconciliation and an outstanding check being omitted rather than the omission of a deposit in transit and the inclusion of a nonexistent outstanding check.

17-16 **(Objective 17-3)** How would a company's bank reconciliation reflect an electronic deposit of cash received by the bank from credit card agencies making payments on behalf of customers purchasing products from the company's online Web site, but not recorded in the company's records?

MULTIPLE CHOICE QUESTIONS FROM CPA EXAMINATIONS

17-17 **(Objectives 17-3, 17-4)** The following questions deal with auditing year-end cash. Choose the best response.

a. A CPA obtains a January 10 cutoff bank statement for his client directly from the bank. Few of the outstanding checks listed on his client's December 31 bank reconciliation cleared during the cutoff period. A probable cause for this is that the client
   (1) is engaged in kiting.
   (2) is engaged in lapping.
   (3) transmitted the checks to the payees after year-end.
   (4) has overstated its year-end bank balance.

b. The auditor should ordinarily mail confirmation requests to all banks with which the client has conducted any business during the year, regardless of the year-end balance, because
   (1) the confirmation form also seeks information about indebtedness to the bank.
   (2) this procedure will detect kiting activities that would otherwise not be detected.
   (3) the mailing of confirmation forms to all such banks is required by generally accepted auditing standards.
   (4) this procedure relieves the auditor of any responsibility with respect to nondetection of forged checks.

c. The usefulness of the standard bank confirmation request may be limited because the bank employee who completes the form may
   (1) not believe the bank is obligated to verify confidential information to a third party.
   (2) sign and return the form without inspecting the accuracy of the client's bank reconciliation.
   (3) not have access to the client's bank statement.
   (4) be unaware of all the financial relationships that the bank has with the client.

17-18 **(Objective 17-4)** The following questions deal with discovering fraud in auditing year-end cash. Choose the best response.

a. Which of the following is one of the better auditing techniques to detect kiting?
   (1) Review composition of authenticated deposit slips.
   (2) Review subsequent bank statements and cancelled checks received directly from the banks.
   (3) Prepare a schedule of bank transfers from the client's books.
   (4) Prepare year-end bank reconciliations.

b. The cashier of Baker Company covered a shortage in his cash working fund with cash obtained on December 31 from a local bank by cashing an unrecorded check drawn on the company's New York bank. The auditor would discover this manipulation by
   (1) preparing independent bank reconciliations as of December 31.
   (2) counting the cash working fund at the close of business on December 31.
   (3) investigating items returned with the bank cutoff statements.
   (4) confirming the December 31 bank balances.

c. A cash shortage may be concealed by transporting funds from one location to another or by converting negotiable assets to cash. Because of this, which of the following is vital?
   (1) Simultaneous bank confirmations.
   (2) Simultaneous bank reconciliations.
   (3) Simultaneous four-column proofs of cash.
   (4) Simultaneous surprise cash counts.

DISCUSSION QUESTIONS AND PROBLEMS

17-19 **(Objectives 17-3, 17-4)** The following are misstatements that might be found in the client's year-end cash balance (assume that the balance sheet date is June 30):

1. A check was omitted from the outstanding check list on the June 30 bank reconciliation. It cleared the bank July 7.
2. A check was omitted from the outstanding check list on the bank reconciliation. It cleared the bank September 6.

3. Cash receipts collected on accounts receivable from July 1 to July 5 were included as June 29 and 30 cash receipts.
4. A loan from the bank on June 26 was credited directly to the client's bank account. The loan was not entered as of June 30.
5. A check that was dated June 26 and disbursed in June was not recorded in the cash disbursements journal, but it was included as an outstanding check on June 30.
6. A bank transfer recorded in the accounting records on July 1 was included as a deposit in transit on June 30.
7. The outstanding checks on the June 30 bank reconciliation were underfooted by $2,000.

Required

a. Assuming that each of these misstatements was intentional (fraud), state the most likely motivation of the person responsible.

b. What control could be instituted for each fraud to reduce the likelihood of occurrence?

c. List an audit procedure that could be used to discover each fraud.

17-20 (Objectives 17-3, 17-4) The following are misstatements that an auditor might find through substantive tests of transactions or by tests of details of cash balances:

1. The bookkeeper failed to record checks in the cash disbursements journal that were written and mailed during the first month of the year.
2. The bookkeeper failed to record or deposit a material amount of cash receipts during the last month of the year. Cash is prelisted by the president's secretary.
3. The cash disbursements journal was held open for 2 days after the end of the year.
4. A check was paid to a vendor for a carload of raw materials that was never received by the client.
5. A discount on an acquisition was not taken, even though the check was mailed before the discount period had expired.
6. Cash receipts for the last 2 days of the year were recorded in the cash receipts journal for the subsequent period and listed as deposits in transit on the bank reconciliation.
7. A check written to a vendor during the last month of the year was recorded in the cash disbursements journal twice to cover an existing fraud. The check cleared the bank and did not appear on the bank reconciliation.

Required

a. List a substantive audit procedure to uncover each of the preceding misstatements.

b. For each procedure in part a, state whether it is a test of details of cash balances or a substantive test of transactions.

17-21 (Objectives 17-3, 17-4) The following audit procedures are concerned with tests of details of general cash balances:

1. Compare the bank cancellation date with the date on the cancelled check for checks dated on or shortly before the balance sheet date.
2. Trace deposits in transit on the bank reconciliation to the cutoff bank statement and the current year cash receipts journal.
3. Obtain a standard bank confirmation from each bank with which the client does business.
4. Compare the balance on the bank reconciliation obtained from the client with the bank confirmation.
5. Compare the checks returned along with the cutoff bank statement with the list of outstanding checks on the bank reconciliation.
6. List the check number, payee, and amount of all material checks not returned with the cutoff bank statement.
7. Review minutes of the board of directors meetings, loan agreements, and bank confirmation for interest-bearing deposits, restrictions on the withdrawal of cash, and compensating balance agreements.

Required

Explain the objective of each.

17-22 (Objective 17-3) You are auditing general cash for the Pittsburg Supply Company for the fiscal year ended July 31, 2002. The client has not prepared the July 31 bank reconciliation. After a brief discussion with the owner, you agree to prepare the reconciliation, with assistance from one of Pittsburg Supply's clerks. You obtain the following information:

	General Ledger	Bank Statement
Beginning balance 7/1/02	$ 4,611	$ 5,753
Deposits		25,056
Cash receipts journal	25,456	
Checks cleared		(23,615)
Cash disbursements journal	(21,811)	
July bank service charge		(87)
Note paid directly		(6,100)
NSF check		(311)
Ending balance 7/31/02	$ 8,256	$ 696

June 30 Bank Reconciliation

Information in General Ledger and Bank Statement	
Balance per bank	$5,753
Deposits in transit	600
Outstanding checks	1,742
Balance per books	4,611

Additional information obtained is as follows:

1. Checks clearing that were outstanding on June 30 totaled $1,692.
2. Checks clearing that were recorded in the July disbursements journal totaled $20,467.
3. A check for $1,060 cleared the bank but had not been recorded in the cash disbursements journal. It was for an acquisition of inventory. Pittsburg Supply uses the periodic-inventory method.
4. A check for $396 was charged to Pittsburg Supply but had been written on a different company's bank account.
5. Deposits included $600 from June and $24,456 for July.
6. The bank charged Pittsburg Supply's account for a nonsufficient check totaling $311. The credit manager concluded that the customer intentionally closed its account and the owner left the city. The check was turned over to a collection agency.
7. A note for $5,800, plus interest, was paid directly to the bank under an agreement signed 4 months ago. The note payable was recorded at $5,800 on Pittsburg Supply's books.

Required

a. Prepare a bank reconciliation that shows both the unadjusted and adjusted balance per books.

b. Prepare all adjusting entries.

c. What audit procedures would you use to verify each item in the bank reconciliation?

d. What is the cash balance that should appear on the July 31, 2002, financial statements?

17-23 (Objectives 17-3, 17-4) In the audit of the Regional Transport Company, a large branch that maintains its own bank account, cash is periodically transferred to the central account in Cedar Rapids. On the branch account's records, bank transfers are recorded as a debit to the home office clearing account and a credit to the branch bank account. Similarly, the home office account is recorded as a debit to the central bank account and a credit to the branch office clearing account. Gordon Light is the head bookkeeper for both the home office and the branch bank accounts. Because he also reconciles the bank account, the senior auditor, Cindy Marintette, is concerned about the internal control weakness.

As a part of the year-end audit of bank transfers, Marintette asks you to schedule the transfers for the last few days in 2002 and the first few days of 2003. You prepare the following list:

Amount of Transfer	Date Recorded in the Home Office Cash Receipts Journal	Date Recorded in the Branch Office Cash Disbursements Journal	Date Deposited in the Home Office Bank Account	Date Cleared the Branch Bank Account
$12,000	12-27-02	12-29-02	12-26-02	12-27-02
26,000	12-28-02	01-02-03	12-28-02	12-29-02
14,000	01-02-03	12-30-02	12-28-02	12-29-02
11,000	12-26-02	12-26-02	12-28-02	01-03-03
15,000	01-02-03	01-02-03	12-28-02	12-31-02
28,000	01-07-03	01-05-03	12-28-02	01-03-03
37,000	01-04-03	01-06-03	01-03-03	01-05-03

Required

a. In verifying each bank transfer, state the appropriate audit procedures you should perform.

b. Prepare any adjusting entries required in the home office records.

c. Prepare any adjusting entries required in the branch bank records.

d. State how each bank transfer sshould be included in the December 31, 2002, bank reconciliation for the home office account after your adjustments in part b.

e. State how each bank transfer should be included in the December 31, 2002, bank reconciliation of the branch bank account after your adjustments in part c.

17-24 (Objective 17-3) In connection with an audit you are given the following worksheet:

Bank Reconciliation, December 31, 2002

Balance per ledger December 31, 2002		$17,174.86
Add:		
Cash receipts received on the last day of December and charged to "cash in bank" on books but not deposited		2,662.25
Debit memo for customer's check returned unpaid (check is on hand but no entry has been made on the books)		200.00
Debit memo for bank service charge for December		5.50
		$20,142.61
Deduct:		
Checks drawn but not paid by bank (see detailed list below)	$2,267.75	
Credit memo for proceeds of a note receivable that had been left at the bank for collection but which has not been recorded as collected	400.00	
Checks for an account payable entered on books as $240.90 but drawn and paid by bank as $419.00	178.10	(2,945.85)
Computed balance		17,196.76
Unlocated difference		(200.00)
Balance per bank (checked to confirmation)		$16,996.76

Checks Drawn but Not Paid by Bank

No.	Amount
573	$ 67.27
724	9.90
903	456.67
907	305.50
911	482.75
913	550.00
914	366.76
916	10.00
917	218.90
	$2,267.75

Required

a. Prepare a corrected reconciliation.

b. Prepare journal entries for items that should be adjusted prior to closing the books.*

INTERNET PROBLEM 17-1: ELECTRONIC MONEY

Reference the CW site. To address consumer concerns about providing credit card information when engaging in transactions over the Internet, a number of new electronic payment methods have been developed. This problem requires students to access the U.S. Department of Treasury's Web site to learn about the various types of eMoney that are currently available.

*AICPA adapted.

PART 5 CHAPTER 18

COMPLETING THE AUDIT

The last of the four phases of an audit is completing the audit, which is covered in Chapter 18, the only chapter in Part 5. Even when the other phases of the audit are done well, if the completion phase is done poorly, the quality of the audit will be low. If the planning phase (phase I) and the two testing phases (phases II and III) are done well, the completion phase is typically relatively easy.

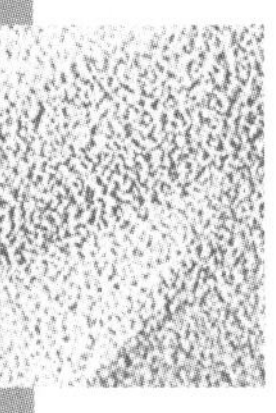

CHAPTER 18

COMPLETING THE AUDIT

GOOD REVIEW REQUIRES MORE THAN LOOKING AT AUDIT FILES

Larry Lenape, an audit senior of Santro, Best & Harmon, assigned staff assistant Clawson Little the audit of accounts payable for Westside Industries, a large equipment manufacturer. Accounts payable is a major liability account for a manufacturing company, and testing accounts payable cutoff is an important audit area. Testing primarily involves reviewing the liability recorded by the client by examining subsequent payments to suppliers and other creditors to ensure that they were properly recorded.

Lenape observed that Little was spending a lot of time on the phone, apparently on personal matters. Shortly before the audit was completed, Little announced that he was leaving the firm. Despite Little's distractions due to his personal affairs, he completed the audit work he was assigned within the budgeted time.

Because of Lenape's concern about Little's work habits, he decided to review the audit files with extreme care. Every schedule he reviewed was properly prepared, with tick marks entered and explained by Little, indicating that he had made an extensive examination of underlying data and documents and had found the client's balance to be adequate as stated. Specifically, there were no payments subsequent to year-end for inventory purchases received during the audit period that had not been accrued by the company.

When Lenape finished the audit, he notified Kelsey Mayburn, an audit manager on the engagement, that the files were ready for her review. She had considerable knowledge about equipment manufacturers and also about Westside Industries. Mayburn reviewed all of the audit files, including analytical procedures performed during the audit. After calculating additional analytical procedures during her review, she contacted Lenape and told him accounts payable didn't seem reasonable to her. She asked him to do some additional checking. Lenape went back and looked at all the documents that Little had indicated in the audit files that he had inspected. It was quickly apparent that Little had either not looked at the documents or did not know what he was doing when he inspected them. There were almost $1 million of documents applicable to the December 31, 2002, audit period that had not been included as liabilities. Mayburn's review probably saved Santro, Best & Harmon significant embarrassment or worse.

LEARNING OBJECTIVES

After studying this chapter, you should be able to

- 18-1 Conduct a review for contingent liabilities and commitments.
- 18-2 Obtain and evaluate letters from the client's attorneys.
- 18-3 Conduct a post-balance-sheet review for subsequent events.
- 18-4 Design and perform the final steps in the evidence-accumulation segment of the audit.
- 18-5 Integrate the audit evidence gathered, and evaluate the overall audit results.
- 18-6 Communicate effectively with the audit committee and management.
- 18-7 Identify the auditor's responsibilities when facts affecting the audit report are discovered after its issuance.

The entire textbook starting with Chapter 5 has dealt with the first three phases of the audit process shown in the margin below. The last of the four phases of an audit, which is shaded in the figure, is completing the audit. Although completing the audit is covered in only one chapter, the topic is extremely important to auditors. The opening vignette illustrates the importance of careful and thoughtful review of the audit by an experienced and knowledgeable person. There are several other aspects of completing the audit besides reviewing the results that are critical to the success of an audit. The figure in the margin on page 507 shows the six parts of the completing the audit phase that are discussed in this chapter.

REVIEW FOR CONTINGENT LIABILITIES AND COMMITMENTS

OBJECTIVE 18-1

Conduct a review for contingent liabilities and commitments.

Summary of the Audit Process

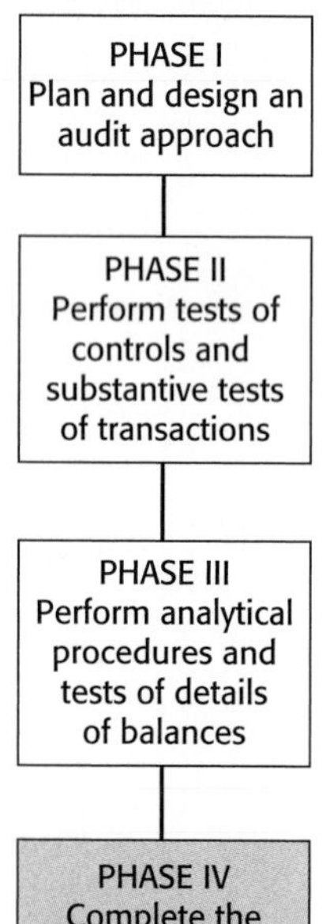

A **contingent liability** is a potential future obligation to an outside party for an unknown amount resulting from activities that have already taken place. Three conditions are required for a contingent liability to exist: (1) There is a potential future payment to an outside party or the impairment of some other asset that would result from an existing condition, (2) there is uncertainty about the amount of the future payment or impairment, and (3) the outcome will be resolved by some future event or events. For example, a lawsuit that has been filed but not yet resolved meets all three of these conditions.

This uncertainty of the future payment can vary from extremely likely to highly unlikely. SFAS 5 describes three levels of likelihood of occurrence and the appropriate financial statement treatment for each likelihood. These requirements are summarized in Table 18-1. The decision as to the appropriate treatment requires considerable professional judgment.

When the proper disclosure in the financial statements of a material contingency is through a footnote, the footnote should describe the nature of the contingency to the extent it is known and the opinion of legal counsel or management as to the expected outcome. Figure 18-1 is an illustration of a footnote for pending litigation and company guarantees of debt.

Certain contingent liabilities are of considerable concern to the auditor:

- Pending litigation for patent infringement, product liability, or other actions
- Income tax disputes
- Product warranties
- Notes receivable discounted
- Guarantees of obligations of others
- Unused balances of outstanding letters of credit

Auditing standards make it clear that management, not the auditor, is responsible for identifying and deciding the appropriate accounting treatment for contingent liabilities. In many audits, it is impractical for auditors to uncover contingencies without management's cooperation.

TABLE 18-1 Likelihood of Occurrence and Financial Statement Treatment

Likelihood of Occurrence of Event	Financial Statement Treatment
Remote (slight chance)	No disclosure is necessary.
Reasonably possible (more than remote, but less than probable)	Footnote disclosure is necessary.
Probable (likely to occur)	• If the amount can be reasonably estimated, financial statement accounts are adjusted. • If the amount cannot be reasonably estimated, note disclosure is necessary.

FIGURE 18-1 **Contingent Liability Footnote**

There are various suits and claims pending against the company and its consolidated subsidiaries. It is the opinion of the company's management, based on current available information, that the ultimate liability, if any, resulting from such suits and claims will not materially affect the consolidated financial position or results of operations of the company and its consolidated subsidiaries.

The company has agreed to guarantee the repayment of approximately $14,000,000 loaned by a bank to several affiliated corporations in which the company owns a minority interest.

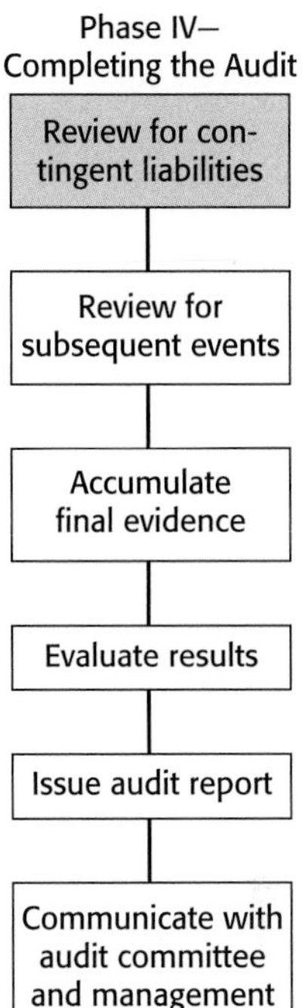

The auditor's objectives in verifying contingent liabilities are to evaluate the accounting treatment of known contingent liabilities and to identify, to the extent practical, any contingencies not already identified by management.

Closely related to contingent liabilities are **commitments** to purchase raw materials or to lease facilities at a certain price, agreements to sell merchandise at a fixed price, bonus plans, profit-sharing and pension plans, royalty agreements, and similar items. In a commitment, the most important characteristic is the *agreement to commit the firm to a set of fixed conditions* in the future regardless of what happens to profits or the economy as a whole. In a free economy, presumably the entity agrees to commitments as a means of bettering its own interests, but they may turn out to be less or more advantageous than originally anticipated. All commitments are ordinarily either described together in a separate footnote or combined in a footnote related to contingencies.

Audit Procedures for Finding Contingencies

Many of these potential obligations are ordinarily verified as an integral part of various segments of the engagement rather than as a separate activity near the end of the audit. For example, unused balances in outstanding letters of credit may be tested as a part of confirming bank balances and loans from banks. Similarly, income tax disputes can be checked as a part of analyzing income tax expense, reviewing the general correspondence file, and examining revenue agent reports. Even if contingencies are verified separately, it is common to perform the tests well before the last few days of completing the engagement to ensure their proper verification. Tests of contingent liabilities near the end of the engagement are more a review than an initial search.

The appropriate audit procedures for testing contingencies are less well defined than those already discussed in other audit areas because the primary objective at the initial stage of the tests is to determine the *existence* of contingencies. As you know from the study of other audit areas, it is more difficult to discover unrecorded transactions or events than to verify recorded information. Once the auditor is aware that contingencies exist, evaluation of their materiality and disclosure requirements can ordinarily be satisfactorily resolved.

The following are some audit procedures commonly used to search for contingent liabilities. The list is not all-inclusive, and each procedure is not necessarily performed on every audit.

- Inquire of management (orally and in writing) about the possibility of unrecorded contingencies. In these inquiries, the auditor must be specific in describing the different kinds of contingencies that may require disclosure. Naturally, inquiries of management are not useful in uncovering the intentional failure to disclose existing contingencies, but if management has overlooked a certain type of contingency or does not fully comprehend accounting disclosure requirements, the inquiry can be fruitful. At the completion of the audit, management is typically asked to make a written statement as a part of the letter of representation, which is discussed later in this chapter, that it is aware of no undisclosed contingent liabilities.
- Review current and previous years' internal revenue agent reports for income tax settlements. The reports may indicate areas or years in which there are unsettled disagreements. If a review has been in progress for a long time, there is an increased likelihood of a tax dispute.
- Review the minutes of directors' and stockholders' meetings for indications of lawsuits or other contingencies.

- Analyze legal expense for the period under audit and review invoices and statements from legal counsel for indications of contingent liabilities, especially lawsuits and pending tax assessments.
- Obtain a letter from each major attorney performing legal services for the client as to the status of pending litigation or other contingent liabilities. This procedure is discussed in more depth shortly.
- Review audit documentation for any information that may indicate a potential contingency. For example, bank confirmations may indicate notes receivable discounted or guarantees of loans.
- Examine letters of credit in force as of the balance sheet date and obtain a confirmation of the used and unused balance.

Evaluation of Known Contingent Liabilities

Litigation and Claims Disclosure

If the auditor concludes that there are contingent liabilities, the significance of the potential liability and the nature of the disclosure needed in the financial statements must be evaluated. The potential liability is sufficiently well known in some instances to be included in the statements as an actual liability. In other instances, disclosure may be unnecessary if the contingency is highly remote or immaterial. The CPA firm may obtain a separate evaluation of the potential liability from its own legal counsel rather than relying on management or management's attorneys. The client's attorney is an advocate for the client and often loses perspective in evaluating the likelihood of losing the case and the amount of the potential judgment.

Audit Procedures for Finding Commitments

The search for unknown commitments is usually performed as a part of the audit of each audit area. For example, in verifying sales transactions, the auditor should be alert for sales commitments. Similarly, commitments for the purchase of raw materials or equipment can be identified as a part of the audit of each of these accounts. The auditor should also be aware of the possibility of commitments when reading contracts and correspondence files.

Inquiry of Client's Attorneys

OBJECTIVE 18-2

Obtain and evaluate letters from the client's attorneys.

A major procedure that auditors rely on for evaluating known litigation or other claims against the client and identifying additional ones is the **inquiry of the client's attorneys.** The auditor relies on the attorney's expertise and knowledge of the client's legal affairs to provide a professional opinion about the expected outcome of existing lawsuits and the likely amount of the liability, including court costs. The attorney is also likely to know of pending litigation and claims that management may have overlooked.

As a matter of general practice, many CPA firms analyze legal expense for the entire year and have the client send a standard inquiry letter to every attorney the client has been involved with in the current or preceding year, plus any attorney the firm occasionally engages. In some cases, this involves a large number of attorneys, including some who deal in aspects of law that are far removed from potential lawsuits.

The standard inquiry to the client's attorney, which should be prepared on the client's letterhead and signed by one of the company's officials, should include the following:

- *A list including (1) pending threatened litigation and (2) asserted or unasserted claims or assessments with which the attorney has had significant involvement.* This list is typically prepared by management, but management may request that the attorney prepare the list.
- *A request that the attorney furnish information or comment about the progress of each item listed.* The desired information includes the legal action the client intends to take, the likelihood of an unfavorable outcome, and an estimate of the amount or range of the potential loss.
- *A request for the identification of any unlisted pending or threatened legal actions or a statement that the client's list is complete.*
- *A statement informing the attorney of the attorney's responsibility to inform management of legal matters requiring disclosure in the financial statements and to respond directly to the auditor.* If the attorney chooses to limit a response, reasons for doing so are to be included in the letter.

An example of a typical standard letter sent to the attorney for return directly to the CPA's office is shown in Figure 18-2. Notice in the first paragraph that the attorney is requested to communicate about contingencies up to approximately *the date of the auditor's report.*

FIGURE 18-2 Typical Inquiry of Attorney

Microsoft Word

File Edit View Insert Format Tools Table Window Help Acrobat

HILLSBURG HARDWARE CO.
2146 Willow St.
Gary, Indiana 46405

January 26, 2003

Bailwick & Bettle, Attorneys
11216 Michigan Avenue
Chicago, IL 60606

Gentlemen:

Our auditors, Berger and Anthony, CPAs (P.O. Box 8175, Gary, Indiana 46405), are conducting an audit of our financial statements for the fiscal year ended December 31, 2002. In connection with their audit, we have prepared and furnished to them a description and evaluation of certain contingencies, including those attached, involving matters with respect to which you have been engaged and to which you have devoted substantive attention on behalf of the company in the form of legal consultation or representation. For the purpose of your response to this letter, we believe that as to each contingency an amount in excess of $100,000 would be material, and in total, $700,000. However, determination of materiality with respect to the overall financial statements cannot be made until our auditors complete their audit. Your response should include matters that existed at December 31, 2002, and during the period from that date to the date of the completion of their audit, which is anticipated to be on or about February 13, 2003.

Please provide to our auditors the following information:

(1) Such explanation, if any, that you consider necessary to supplement the listed judgments rendered or settlements made involving the company from the beginning of this fiscal year through the date of your reply.
(2) Such explanation, if any, that you consider necessary to supplement the listing of pending or threatened litigation, including an explanation of those matters as to which your views may differ from those stated and an identification of the omission of any pending or threatened litigation, claim, and assessment or a statement that the list of such matters is complete.
(3) Such explanation, if any, that you consider necessary to supplement the attached information concerning unasserted claims and assessments, including an explanation of those matters as to which your views may differ from those stated.

We understand that whenever, in the course of performing legal services for us with respect to a matter recognized to involve an unasserted possible claim or assessment that may call for financial statement disclosure, you have formed a professional conclusion that we should disclose or consider disclosure concerning such possible claim or assessment, as a matter of professional responsibility to us, you will so advise us and will consult with us concerning the question of such disclosure and the applicable requirements of Statement of Financial Accounting Standards No. 5. Please specifically confirm to our auditors that our understanding is correct.

Please specifically identify the nature of and reasons for any limitations in your response.

Yours very truly,
Hillsburg Hardware Co.

Rick Chulick

Rick Chulick, Pres.

Attorneys in recent years have become reluctant to provide certain information to auditors because of their own exposure to legal liability for providing incorrect or confidential information. The nature of the refusal of attorneys to provide auditors with complete information about contingent liabilities falls into two categories: the refusal to respond due to a lack of knowledge about matters involving contingent liabilities and the refusal to disclose information that the attorney considers confidential. As an example of the latter, the attorney might be aware of a violation of a patent agreement that could result in a significant loss to the client if it were known **(unasserted claim).** The inclusion of the information in a footnote could actually cause the lawsuit and therefore be damaging to the client. Review the attorney concerns described in the box "The Legal View."

If an attorney refuses to provide the auditor with information about material existing lawsuits (asserted claims) or unasserted claims, *the auditor must modify the audit report to reflect the lack of available evidence.* This requirement in SAS 12 (AU 337) has the effect of requiring management to give its attorneys permission to provide contingent liability information to auditors and to encourage attorneys to cooperate with auditors in obtaining information about contingencies.

THE LEGAL VIEW

The lawyer is the expert on litigation, yet differences in lawyers' and CPAs' responsibilities with respect to common clients have resulted in contentious difficulties. Although CPAs are responsible for determining there is "adequate disclosure" under Statement no. 5 [SFAS 5] . . . lawyers are responsible for "winning the case." Because information provided by lawyers may affect a case adversely, these responsibilities may conflict.

Many lawyers believe that, despite a client's request they provide the auditor with information, they should be less than candid in letters to CPAs because of concern their replies may

- Impair the client–lawyer confidentiality privilege.
- Disclose a client confidence or secret.
- Prejudice the client's defense of a claim.
- Constitute an admission by the client.

The authoritative guidance for lawyers . . . warns lawyers they must be careful in communications with auditors. Indeed, the first sentence of the ABA statement says, "The public interest in protecting the confidentiality of lawyer-client communications is fundamental."

The ABA statement also says lawyers normally should refrain from expressing judgments on outcome—either likelihood or amount of loss. The net effect is CPAs generally can obtain relatively complete responses on the existence of litigation and the dates when the underlying cause occurred . . . but less complete responses on the likelihood of an unfavorable outcome and the amount of potential loss.

In addition to an implicit hesitancy to provide evidential matter on likelihood and amount of loss, the ABA statement gives lawyers definitions of *probable* and *remote* that are different from those in Statement no. 5:

- ***Remote.*** The ABA says an unfavorable outcome is remote if the prospects for the client not succeeding in its defense are judged to be extremely doubtful and the prospects of success by the claimant are judged to be slight.
- ***Probable.*** The ABA says an unfavorable outcome for the client is probable if the claimant's prospects of not succeeding are judged to be extremely doubtful and the client's prospects for success in its defense are judged to be slight.

Source: Excerpted from an article by Bruce K. Behn and Kurt Pany, "Limitations of Lawyers' Letters", *Journal of Accountancy* (February 1995), pp. 62–63.

REVIEW FOR SUBSEQUENT EVENTS

OBJECTIVE 18-3

Conduct a post-balance-sheet review for subsequent events.

The second part of completing the audit is the review for subsequent events. The auditor must review transactions and events occurring after the balance sheet date to determine whether anything occurred that might affect the fair presentation or disclosure of the current period statements. The auditing procedures required by SAS 1 (AU 560) to verify these transactions and events are commonly called the **review for subsequent events** or **post–balance-sheet review.**

WWW

Auditor Knowledge

The auditor's responsibility for reviewing for subsequent events is normally limited to the period beginning with the balance sheet date and ending with the date of the auditor's report. Because the date of the auditor's report corresponds to the completion of the important auditing procedures in the client's office, the subsequent events review should be

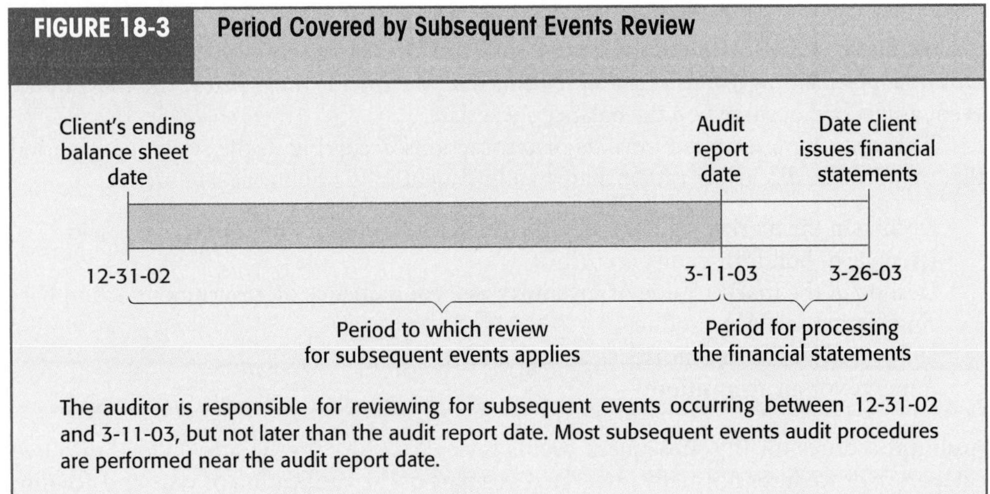

completed near the end of the engagement.[1] Figure 18-3 shows the period covered by a subsequent events review and the timing of that review.

Types of Subsequent Events

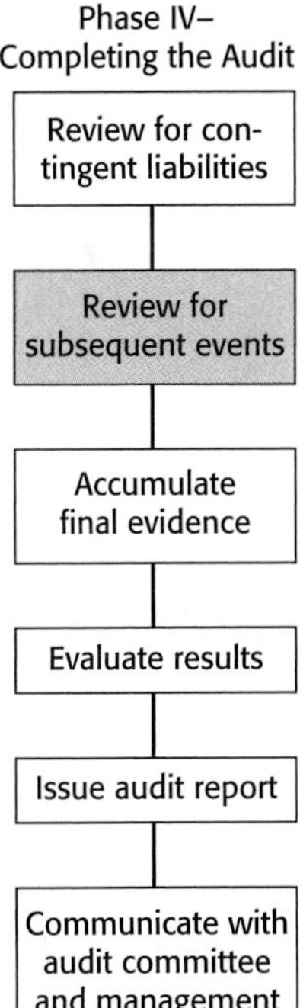

Two types of **subsequent events** require consideration by management and evaluation by the auditor: those that have a direct effect on the financial statements and require adjustment and those that have no direct effect on the financial statements but for which disclosure is advisable.

Those That Have a Direct Effect on the Financial Statements and Require Adjustment These events or transactions provide additional information to management in determining the fair presentation of account balances as of the balance sheet date and to auditors in verifying the balances. For example, if the auditor is having difficulty determining the correct valuation of inventory because of obsolescence, the sale of raw material inventory as scrap in the subsequent period would indicate the correct value of the inventory as of the balance sheet date.

Such subsequent period events as the following require an adjustment of account balances in the current year's financial statements if the amounts are material:

- Declaration of bankruptcy by a customer with an outstanding accounts receivable balance because of deteriorating financial condition
- Settlement of a litigation at an amount different from the amount recorded on the books
- Disposal of equipment not being used in operations at a price below the current book value
- Sale of investments at a price below recorded cost

When subsequent events are used to evaluate the amounts included in the statements, care must be taken to distinguish between conditions that existed at the balance sheet date and those that came into being after the end of the year. The subsequent information should not be incorporated directly into the statements if the conditions causing the change in valuation did not take place until after year-end. For example, assume one type of a client's inventory suddenly becomes obsolete because of a technology change after the balance sheet date. The sale of the inventory at a loss in the subsequent period would not be relevant in the valuation of inventory for obsolescence in this case.

Those That Have No Direct Effect on the Financial Statements but for Which Disclosure Is Advisable Subsequent events of this type provide evidence of conditions that did not exist at the date of the balance sheet being reported on but are so significant that they require

[1]When the auditor's name is associated with a registration statement under the Securities Act of 1933, the auditor's responsibility for reviewing subsequent events extends beyond the date of the auditor's report to the date the registration becomes effective.

disclosure even though they do not require adjustment. Ordinarily, these events can be adequately disclosed by the use of footnotes, but occasionally, one may be so significant as to require *supplementing the historical statements* with statements that include the effect of the event as if it had occurred on the balance sheet date.

Following are examples of events or transactions occurring in the subsequent period that may require disclosure rather than an adjustment in the financial statements:

- Decline in the market value of securities held for temporary investment or resale
- Issuance of bonds or equity securities
- Decline in the market value of inventory as a consequence of government action barring further sale of a product
- Uninsured loss of inventories as a result of fire
- A merger or an acquisition

Audit Tests

Audit procedures for the subsequent events review can be conveniently divided into two categories: procedures normally integrated as a part of the verification of year-end account balances and those performed specifically for the purpose of discovering events or transactions that must be recognized as subsequent events.

The first category includes cutoff and valuation tests done as a part of the tests of details of balances. For example, subsequent period sales and acquisition transactions are examined to determine whether the cutoff is accurate. Similarly, many valuation tests involving subsequent events are also performed as a part of the verification of account balances. As an example, it is common to test the collectibility of accounts receivable by reviewing subsequent period cash receipts. It is also a normal audit procedure to compare the subsequent period purchase price of inventory with the recorded cost as a test of lower of cost or market valuation. The procedures for cutoff and valuation have been discussed sufficiently in preceding chapters and are not repeated here.

The second category of tests is performed specifically to obtain information to incorporate into the current year's account balances or footnotes. These tests include the following.

Inquire of Management Inquiries vary from client to client but normally are about potential contingent liabilities or commitments, significant changes in the assets or capital structure of the company, the current status of items that were not completely resolved at the balance sheet date, and unusual adjustments made subsequent to the balance sheet date.

Inquiries of management about subsequent events must be held with the proper client personnel to obtain meaningful answers. For example, discussing tax or union matters with the accounts receivable supervisor would not be appropriate. Most inquiries should be held with the controller, the vice presidents, and the president, depending on the information desired.

Correspond with Attorneys Correspondence with attorneys, which was previously discussed, takes place as a part of the search for contingent liabilities. In obtaining letters from attorneys, the auditor must remember the responsibility for testing for subsequent events up to the date of the audit report. A common approach is to request the attorney to date and mail the letter as of the expected completion date for field work.

Review Internal Statements Prepared Subsequent to the Balance Sheet Date The emphasis in the review should be on (1) changes in the business relative to results for the same period in the year under audit and (2) changes after year-end. The auditor should pay careful attention to major changes in the business or environment in which the client is operating. The statements should be discussed with management to determine whether they are prepared on the same basis as the current period statements, and there should be inquiries about significant changes in the operating results.

Review Records Prepared Subsequent to the Balance Sheet Date Journals and ledgers should be reviewed to determine the existence and nature of significant transactions related to the current year. If the journals are not kept up-to-date, documents relating to the journals should be reviewed.

Examine Minutes Issued Subsequent to the Balance Sheet Date The minutes of stockholders and directors meetings subsequent to the balance sheet date must be examined for important subsequent events affecting the current period financial statements.

Obtain a Letter of Representation The letter of representation written by the client's management to the auditor formalizes statements that management has made about different matters throughout the audit, including discussions about subsequent events. This letter is mandatory and includes other relevant matters too. This letter is discussed in detail during the discussion of evidence accumulation, which is the next part discussed in completing the audit.

Dual Dating

Occasionally, the auditor determines that an important subsequent event occurred after the field work was completed but *before the audit report was issued.* The source of such information is typically management or the media. An example using the dates in Figure 18-3 on page 511 is the acquisition of another company by an audit client on March 23, when the last day of field work was March 11. In such a situation, SAS 1 (AU 530) requires the auditor to extend audit tests for the newly discovered subsequent event to make sure that it is correctly disclosed. The auditor has two equally acceptable options for expanding subsequent events tests: expand all subsequent events tests to the new date or restrict the subsequent events review to matters related to the new subsequent event. For the first option, the audit report date is changed to the new date. For the second option, the auditor issues a **dual-dated audit report,** which means that the audit report includes two dates. The first date is the date for the completion of field work except for a specific exception. The second date, which is always later, deals with the exception. In the example of the acquisition, assume that the auditor returned to the client's premises and completed audit tests on March 31 pertaining only to the acquisition. The audit report is dual-dated as follows: March 11, 2003, except for note 17, as to which the date is March 31, 2003.

FINAL EVIDENCE ACCUMULATION

OBJECTIVE 18-4

Design and perform the final steps in the evidence-accumulation segment of the audit.

In addition to the review for subsequent events, the auditor has several final accumulation responsibilities that apply to all cycles. Five types of final evidence accumulation that are discussed in this section are (1) perform final analytical procedures, (2) evaluate the going-concern assumption, (3) obtain a management representation letter, (4) consider information accompanying the basic financial statements, and (5) read other information in the annual report. Each of these is done late in the engagement.

Perform Final Analytical Procedures

Analytical procedures done during the completion of the audit are useful as a final review for material misstatements or financial problems not noted during other testing and to help the auditor take a final objective look at the financial statements. It is common for a partner to do the analytical procedures during the final review of audit documentation and financial statements. Typically, a partner has a good understanding of the client and its business because of ongoing relationships. Knowledge of the client's business combined with effective analytical procedures help identify possible oversights in an audit.

When performing analytical procedures during the final review stage, the partner would generally read the financial statements, including footnotes, and consider (1) the adequacy of evidence gathered about unusual or unexpected account balances or relationships identified during planning or while conducting the audit and (2) unusual or unexpected account balances or relationships that were not previously identified. Results from final analytical procedures may indicate that additional audit evidence is necessary.

Evaluate Going-Concern Assumption

SAS 59 (AU 341) requires the auditor to evaluate whether there is a substantial doubt about a client's ability to continue as a going concern for at least 1 year beyond the balance sheet date. That assessment is initially made as a part of planning but is revised when significant new information is obtained. For example, if the auditor discovered during the audit that the company had defaulted on a loan, lost its primary customer, or decided to dispose of substantial assets to pay off loans, the initial assessment of going concern may need revision. A final assessment is desirable after all evidence has been accumulated and proposed audit adjustments have been incorporated into the financial statements.

Analytical procedures are one of the most important types of evidence to assess going concern. Discussions with management and a review of future plans are important considerations in evaluating analytical procedures. Knowledge of the client's business gained throughout the audit is important information used to assess the likelihood of financial failure within the next year.

When the auditor has reservations about the going-concern assumption, it is necessary to evaluate management's plans to avoid bankruptcy and the feasibility of achieving these plans. Making the final decision whether to issue a report with a going-concern explanatory paragraph is typically time-consuming and difficult. Going-concern explanatory paragraphs were discussed in Chapter 2.

Obtain Management Representation Letter

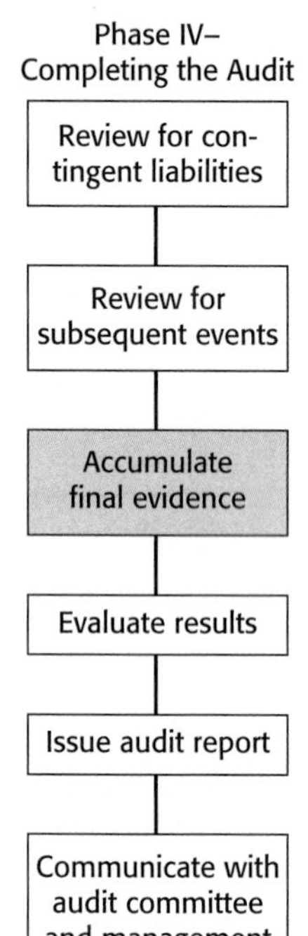

SAS 85 (AU 333) requires the auditor to obtain a **letter of representation** documenting management's most important oral representations during the audit. The client representation letter is prepared on the client's letterhead, addressed to the CPA firm, and signed by high-level corporate officials, usually the president and chief financial officer.

There are two purposes of the client letter of representation:

1. *To impress upon management its responsibility for the assertions in the financial statements.* For example, if the letter of representation includes a reference to pledged assets and contingent liabilities, honest management may be reminded of its unintentional failure to disclose the information adequately. To fulfill this objective, the letter of representation should be sufficiently detailed to act as a reminder to management.

2. *To document the responses from management to inquiries about various aspects of the audit.* This provides written documentation of client representations in the event of disagreement or a lawsuit between the auditor and client. Because it is more formal than oral communication, a letter of representation also helps reduce misunderstandings between management and the auditor.

The letter should be dated no earlier than the date of the auditor's report to make sure that there are representations related to the subsequent events review. The letter implies that it has originated with the client, but it is common practice for the auditor to prepare the letter and request the client to type it on the company's letterhead and sign it. Refusal by a client to prepare and sign the letter would require a qualified opinion or disclaimer of opinion.

SAS 85 suggests four categories of specific matters that should be included. The four categories are as follows, with examples in each category.

1. *Financial statements*
   - Management's acknowledgment of its responsibility for the fair presentation in the financial statements of financial position, results of operations, and cash flows in conformity with generally accepted accounting principles
   - Management's belief that the financial statements are fairly presented in conformity with generally accepted accounting principles
2. *Completeness of information*
   - Availability of all financial records and related data
   - Completeness and availability of all minutes of meetings of stockholders, directors, and committees of directors
   - Absence of unrecorded transactions
3. *Recognition, measurement, and disclosure*
   - Management's belief that the effects of any uncorrected financial statement misstatements are immaterial to the financial statements
   - Information concerning fraud involving (1) management, (2) employees who have significant roles in internal control, or (3) others where the fraud could have a material effect on the financial statements
   - Information concerning related party transactions and amounts receivable from or payable to related parties
   - Unasserted claims or assessments that the entity's lawyer has advised are probable of assertion and must be disclosed in accordance with Financial Accounting Standards Board (FASB) Statement No. 5, *Accounting for Contingencies*

- Satisfactory title to assets, liens or encumbrances on assets, and assets pledged as collateral
- Compliance with aspects of contractual agreements that may affect the financial statements

4. *Subsequent events*
   - Bankruptcy of a major customer with an outstanding account receivable at the balance sheet date
   - A merger or acquisition after the balance sheet date

A client representation letter is a written statement from a nonindependent source and therefore *cannot be regarded as reliable evidence.* The letter does provide documentation that management has been asked certain questions to make sure that management understands its responsibilities and to protect the auditor if there are claims against the auditor by management.

In some audits, the auditor may find other evidence that contradicts statements in the letter of representation. In such cases, the auditor should investigate the circumstances and consider whether representations in the letter are reliable.

Consider Information Accompanying the Basic Financial Statements

Clients often request auditors to include additional information beyond the basic financial statements in the set of materials prepared for management or outside users. SAS 29 (AU 551) refers to this additional information as *information accompanying the basic financial statements in auditor-submitted documents.* In the past, the same information was called a *long-form report.* Figure 18-4 illustrates the basic financial statements and additional information.

The profession has intentionally refrained from defining or restricting the appropriate supplementary information included to enable auditors to individualize the information to meet the needs of statement users. However, several types of information are commonly included in the additional information section:

- Detailed comparative statements supporting the control totals on the primary financial statements for accounts such as cost of goods sold, operating expenses, and miscellaneous assets
- Supplementary information required by the Financial Accounting Standards Board or the SEC
- Statistical data for past years in the form of ratios and trends
- A schedule of insurance coverage
- Specific comments on the changes that have taken place in the statements

FIGURE 18-4 Information Accompanying Basic Financial Statements

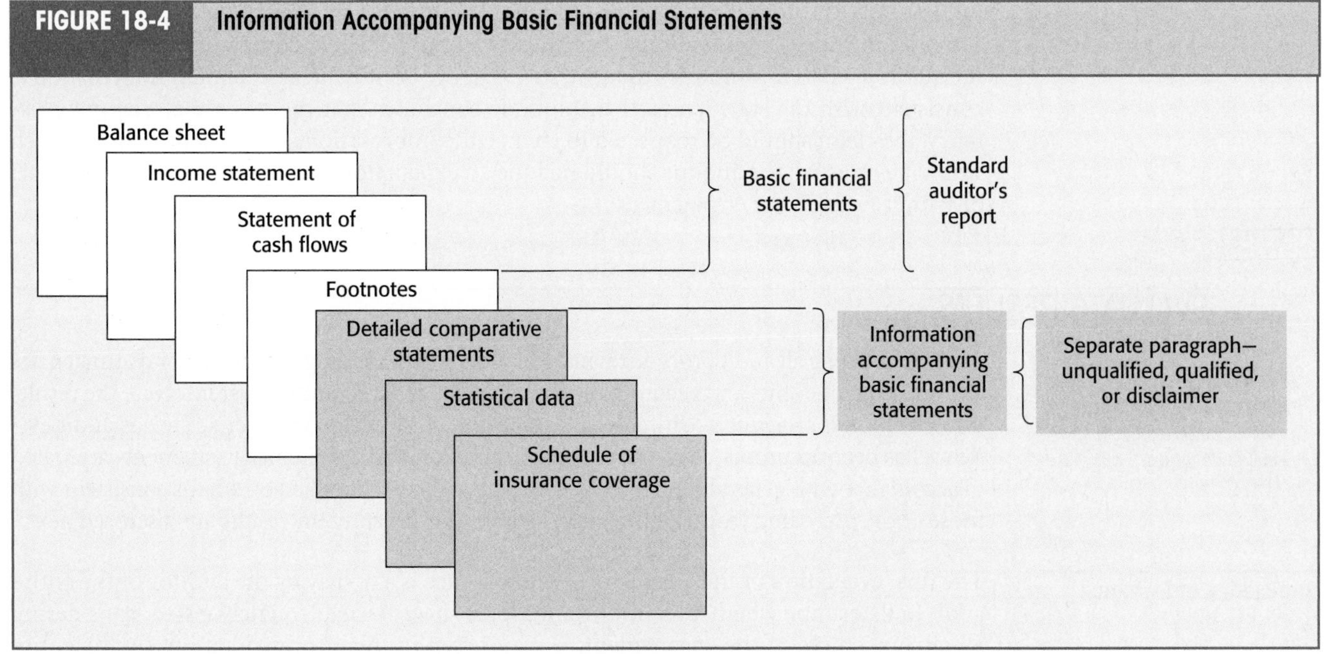

It is important that the auditor clearly distinguish between responsibility for the primary financial statements and for additional information. Usually, the auditor has not performed a sufficiently detailed audit to justify an opinion on the additional information, but in some instances, the auditor may be confident that the information is fairly presented. The profession's reporting standards require the auditor to make a clear statement about the degree of responsibility taken for the additional information. Two types of opinions are allowed: a positive opinion indicating a high level of assurance or a disclaimer indicating no assurance. When the auditor issues an opinion on additional information accompanying the financial statements, materiality is the same as that used in forming an opinion on the basic financial statements. As a result, the additional procedures required are less extensive than if the auditor were issuing an opinion on the information taken by itself, such as in a report on specified elements or accounts. The following is an example of the additional wording to be added to the auditor's standard report when expressing an opinion on the additional information:

- Our audit was conducted for the purpose of forming an opinion on the basic financial statements taken as a whole. The accompanying information on pages x through y is presented for purposes of additional analysis and is not a required part of the basic financial statements. Such information has been subjected to the auditing procedures applied in the audit of the basic financial statements and, in our opinion, is fairly stated in all material respects in relation to the basic financial statements taken as a whole.

If the auditor decided that sufficient evidence had *not* been accumulated for the additional data to justify an unqualified opinion, SAS 29 requires that a disclaimer paragraph such as the following be added to the standard audit report:

- Our audit was made for the purpose of forming an opinion on the basic financial statements taken as a whole. The accompanying information on pages x through y is presented for purposes of additional analysis and is not a required part of the basic financial statements. Such information has not been subjected to the auditing procedures applied in the audit of the basic financial statements, and, accordingly, we express no opinion on it.

Read Other Information in the Annual Report

SAS 8 (AU 550) requires the auditor to read **other information included in annual reports** pertaining directly to the financial statements. For example, assume that the president's letter in the annual report refers to an increase in earnings per share from $2.60 to $2.93. The auditor is required to compare that information with the financial statements to make sure it corresponds.

SAS 8 pertains only to information that is not a part of the financial statements but is published with them. Examples are the president's letter and explanations of company activities included in annual reports of nearly all publicly held companies. It usually takes the auditor only a few minutes to make sure that the nonfinancial statement information is consistent with the statements. If the auditor concludes that there is a material inconsistency, the client should be requested to change the information. If the client refuses, which would be unusual, the auditor should include an explanatory paragraph in the audit report or withdraw from the engagement.

EVALUATE RESULTS

OBJECTIVE 18-5

Integrate the audit evidence gathered, and evaluate the overall audit results.

After performing all audit procedures in each audit area, including the review for contingencies and subsequent events and accumulating final evidence, the auditor must integrate the results into *one overall conclusion*. Ultimately, the auditor must decide whether sufficient audit evidence has been accumulated to warrant the conclusion that the financial statements are stated in accordance with generally accepted accounting principles, applied on a basis consistent with those of the preceding year. The five main aspects of evaluating the results are discussed next.

Sufficiency of Evidence

The final evaluation of the adequacy of the evidence is a review by the auditor of the entire audit to determine whether all important aspects have been adequately tested, considering all circumstances of the engagement. A major step in this process is to review the entire audit program to make sure that all parts have been accurately completed and documented and that all audit objectives have been met. This review includes deciding whether the audit program is adequate, considering problem areas identified as the audit progressed. For example, if misstatements were discovered during tests of sales, the initial plans for tests of details of accounts receivable may have been insufficient. The final review should evaluate whether the revised audit program is adequate.

As an aid in drawing final conclusions about the adequacy of the audit evidence, auditors often use a **completing the engagement checklist.** Such a checklist is a reminder of aspects of the audit that must not be overlooked. An illustration of part of a completing the engagement checklist is given in Figure 18-5.

If the auditor concludes that sufficient evidence has *not* been obtained to draw a conclusion about the fairness of the client's representations, there are two choices: Additional evidence must be obtained or either a qualified opinion or a disclaimer of opinion must be issued.

Evidence Supports Auditor's Opinion

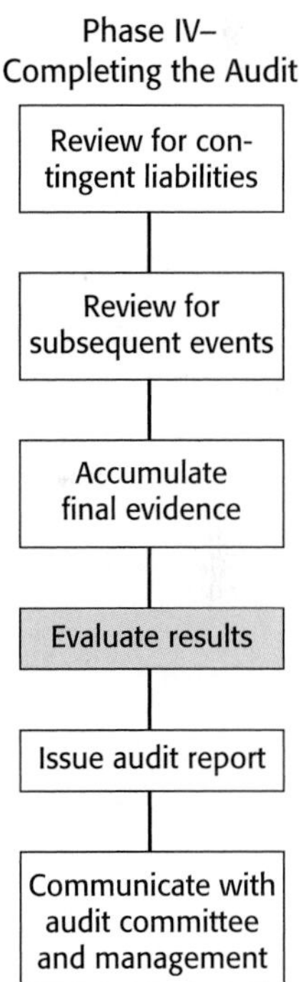

An important part of evaluating whether the financial statements are fairly stated is summarizing the misstatements uncovered in the audit. When the auditor uncovers misstatements that are in themselves material, entries should be proposed to the client to correct the statements. It may be difficult to determine the appropriate amount of adjustment because the true value of a misstatement may be unknown; nevertheless, it is the auditor's responsibility to decide on the required adjustment. In addition to the material misstatements, there are often a large number of immaterial misstatements discovered that are not adjusted at the time they are found. It is necessary to combine individually immaterial misstatements to evaluate whether the combined amount is material. The auditor can keep track of these misstatements and combine them in several different ways, but many auditors use a convenient method called an **unadjusted misstatement audit schedule** or **summary of possible misstatements.** It is relatively easy to evaluate the overall significance of several immaterial misstatements with this type of audit schedule. An example of an unadjusted misstatement worksheet is given in Figure 18-6 (p. 518).

The schedule in Figure 18-6 includes both known misstatements that the client has decided not to adjust and projected misstatements, including sampling error. Observe that in the bottom left portion of the audit schedule there is a comparison of possible adjustments to materiality. A summary of this audit schedule is often included with management's representation that the uncorrected misstatements are immaterial.

FIGURE 18-5 Completing the Engagement Checklist

	YES	NO
1. Examination of prior year's audit documentation		
a. Were last year's audit files examined for areas of emphasis in the current year audit?	___	___
b. Was the permanent file reviewed for items that affect the current year?	___	___
2. Internal control		
a. Has internal control been adequately understood?	___	___
b. Is the scope of the audit adequate in light of the assessed control risk?	___	___
c. Have all major weaknesses been included as reportable conditions in a letter to the audit committee or to senior management?	___	___
3. General documents		
a. Were all current year minutes and resolutions reviewed, abstracted, and followed up?	___	___
b. Has the permanent file been updated?	___	___
c. Have all major contracts and agreements been reviewed and abstracted, copied, or downloaded to ascertain that the client complies with all existing legal requirements?	___	___

FIGURE 18-6 Unadjusted Misstatement Audit Schedule

Microsoft Excel

File Edit View Insert Format Tools Data Window Help Acrobat

Hillsburg Hardware Co.
Summary of Possible Misstatements
12/31/02

Schedule A-3 Date
Prepared by LF 1/28/03
Approved by JA 1/31/03

Audit File Source		Type of Misstatement	Total Amount	POSSIBLE MISSTATEMENT—OVERSTATEMENT (UNDERSTATEMENT) Current Assets	Noncurrent Assets	Current Liabilities	Income Before Tax
C-8	Accounts receivable/Sales cutoff misstatements	[P]	60,000	(60,000)			(60,000)
D-2	Difference between physical inventory and book figures	[A]	120,000	(120,000)			(120,000)
H-7/2	Unrecorded liabilities	[P]	285,000	(100,000)	(85,000)	(285,000)	100,000
V-10	Repairs expense items that should have been capitalized	[A]	90,000		(90,000)		(90,000)
Totals				(280,000)	(175,000)	(285,000)	(170,000)

[A] Actual population misstatements.
[P] Estimated population misstatements based on the sample, including sampling error.

Conclusions

The net effects of the above items are as follows:

	Possible Overstatements (Understatements)	Materiality
Current assets	(280,000)	2,550,000
Total assets	(455,000)	300,000
Income before taxes	(170,000)	737,000

None of these aggregate effects or the individual items has a material effect on the financial statements in total or with respect to the components they pertain to. On this basis, adjustment of any or all of the items is passed.

Leslie Franklin
1/28/03

If the auditor believes that there *is* sufficient evidence but it does not warrant a conclusion of fairly presented financial statements, the auditor again has two choices: The statements must be revised to the auditor's satisfaction or either a qualified or an adverse opinion must be issued. Notice that the options here are different from those in the case of insufficient evidence obtained.

Financial Statement Disclosures

A major consideration in completing the audit is to determine whether the disclosures in the financial statements are adequate. Throughout the audit, the emphasis is most often on verifying the accuracy of the balances in the general ledger by testing the most important accounts on the auditor's trial balance. Another important task is to make sure that the account balances on the trial balance are correctly aggregated and disclosed on the financial statements. Naturally, adequate disclosure includes consideration of all of the statements, including related footnotes.

The auditor actually prepares the financial statements from the trial balance in many small audits and submits them to the client for approval. Performing this function may seem to imply that the client has been relieved of responsibility for the fair representation in the statements, but that is not the case. The auditor acts in the role of advisor when preparing financial statements, but *management retains the final responsibility for approving the issuance of the statements.*

Review for adequate disclosure in the financial statements at the completion of the audit is not the only time the auditor is interested in proper disclosure. Unless the auditor is constantly alert for disclosure problems, it is impossible to perform the final disclosure review adequately. For example, as part of the audit of accounts receivable, the auditor must be aware of the need to separate notes receivable and amounts due from affiliates and trade accounts due from customers. Similarly, there must be a segregation of current from noncurrent receivables and a disclosure of the factoring or discounting of notes receivable if such is the case. An important part of verifying all account balances is determining whether generally accepted accounting principles were properly applied on a basis consistent with that of the preceding year. The auditor must carefully document this information in the audit files to facilitate the final review.

As part of the final review for financial statement disclosure, many CPA firms require the completion of a **financial statement disclosure checklist** for every engagement. These questionnaires are designed to remind the auditor of common disclosure problems encountered in audits and also to facilitate the final review of the entire audit by an independent partner. An illustration of a partial financial statement disclosure checklist is given in Figure 18-7. Naturally, it is not sufficient to rely on a checklist to replace the auditor's own knowledge of generally accepted accounting principles. In any given audit, some aspects of the engagement require much greater expertise in accounting than can be obtained from such a checklist.

Audit Documentation Review

There are three main reasons why it is essential that audit documentation be thoroughly reviewed by another member of the audit firm at the completion of the audit:

1. *To evaluate the performance of inexperienced personnel.* A considerable portion of most audits is performed by audit personnel with less than 4 or 5 years of experience. These people may have sufficient technical training to conduct an adequate audit, but their lack of experience affects their ability to make sound professional judgments in complex situations.
2. *To make sure that the audit meets the CPA firm's standard of performance.* Within any organization the performance quality of individuals varies considerably, but careful review by top-level personnel in the firm assists in maintaining a uniform quality of auditing.
3. *To counteract the bias that often enters into the auditor's judgment.* Auditors must attempt to remain objective throughout the audit, but it is easy to lose proper perspective on a long audit when there are complex problems to solve.

Except for a final independent review, which is discussed shortly, the **review of audit documentation** should be conducted by someone who is knowledgeable about the client and the unique circumstances in the audit. Therefore, the initial review of the audit files prepared by any given auditor is normally done by the auditor's immediate supervisor. For

FIGURE 18-7 Financial Statement Disclosure Checklist: Property, Plant, and Equipment

1. Are the following disclosures included in the financial statements or notes (APB 12, para. 5):
   a. Balances of major classes of depreciable assets (land, building, equipment, and so forth) at the balance sheet date?
   b. Allowances for depreciation, by class or in total, at the balance sheet date?
   c. General description of depreciation methods for major classes of PP&E (APB 22, para. 13)?
   d. Total amount of depreciation charged to expense for each income statement presented?
   e. Basis of evaluation (SAS 32, AU 431.02)?

2. Are carrying amounts of property mortgaged and encumbered by indebtedness disclosed (FASB 5, para. 18)?

3. Are details of sale and leaseback transactions during the period disclosed (FASB 13, para. 32–34)?

4. Is the carrying amount of property not a part of operating plant—for example, idle or held for investment or sale—segregated?

5. Has consideration been given to disclosure of fully depreciated capital assets still in use and capital assets not presently in use?

Note: Information in parentheses refers to authoritative professional literature.

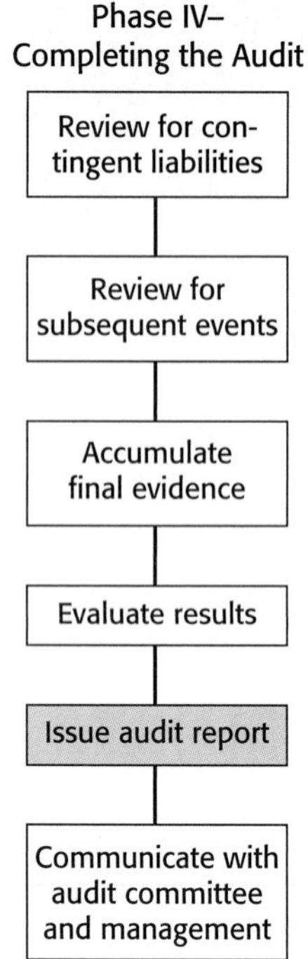

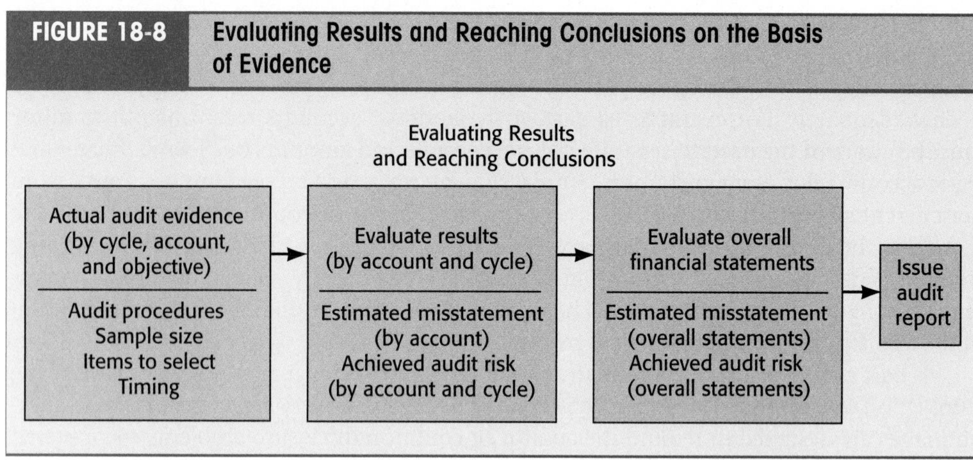

FIGURE 18-8 Evaluating Results and Reaching Conclusions on the Basis of Evidence

example, the least experienced auditor's work is ordinarily reviewed by the audit senior. The senior's immediate superior, who is normally a supervisor or manager, reviews the senior's work and also reviews less thoroughly the schedules of the inexperienced auditor. Finally, the partner assigned to the audit must ultimately review all audit documentation, but the partner reviews those prepared by the supervisor or manager more thoroughly than the others. While performing the review, the reviewer will frequently interview the auditor responsible for preparing the audit documentation to learn how significant audit issues were resolved. Except for the final independent review, most of the audit documentation review is done as each segment of the audit is completed.

Independent Review

At the completion of larger audits, it is common to have the financial statements and the entire set of audit files reviewed by a completely independent reviewer who has not participated in the engagement. An **independent review** is required for SEC engagements. This reviewer often takes an adversary position to make sure that the conduct of the audit was adequate. The audit team must be able to justify the evidence it has accumulated and the conclusions it reached on the basis of the unique circumstances of the engagement.

Summary of Evidence Evaluation

Figure 18-8 summarizes the evaluation of the sufficiency of the evidence and deciding whether the evidence supports the opinion. It shows that the auditor evaluates the sufficiency of actual evidence by first evaluating achieved audit risk, by account and by cycle, and then making the same evaluation for the overall financial statements. The auditor also evaluates whether the evidence supports the audit opinion by first estimating misstatements in each account and then for the overall financial statements. In practice, the evaluation of achieved audit risk and estimated misstatement are made at the same time. On the basis of these evaluations, the audit report is issued for the financial statements.

ISSUE THE AUDIT REPORT

The auditor should not decide the appropriate audit report to issue until all evidence has been accumulated and evaluated, including all parts of completing the audit discussed so far. Because the audit report is the only thing that most users see in the audit process and the consequences of issuing an inappropriate report can be severe, it is critical that the report be correct.

In most audits, the auditor issues an unqualified report with standard wording. Almost all firms have this report included in a word processing file and need to change only the name of the client, title of the financial statements, and date.

When a CPA firm decides that a standard unqualified report is inappropriate, there will almost certainly be extensive discussions among technical partners in the CPA firm and often with client personnel. Most CPA firms have comprehensive audit reporting manuals to assist them in selecting the appropriate wording of the report they decide to issue.

COMMUNICATE WITH THE AUDIT COMMITTEE AND MANAGEMENT

OBJECTIVE 18-6

Communicate effectively with the audit committee and management.

After the audit is completed, there are several potential communications from the auditor to client personnel. The first three of these communications discussed in this section are required by auditing standards to make certain that the audit committee and senior management are informed of audit findings and auditor recommendations. The fourth item discussed in this section, management letters, is often communicated to operating management.

Communicate Fraud and Illegal Acts

SAS 82 (AU 316) and SAS 54 (AU 317) require the auditor to communicate all fraud and illegal acts to the audit committee or similarly designated group, regardless of materiality. The purpose is to assist the audit committee in performing its supervisory role for reliable financial statements. This requirement indicates the increased concern of the profession over the auditor's responsibility for the detection and prevention of fraud.

Communicate Reportable Conditions

As discussed in Chapter 9, the auditor must also communicate significant deficiencies in the design or operation of internal control. In larger companies, this communication is made to the audit committee and in smaller companies, to the owners or senior management. The nature and form of that communication were discussed in Chapter 9.

Other Communication with Audit Committee

SAS 61 (AU 380) and amendments require the auditor to communicate certain additional information obtained during the audit for all SEC engagements and other audits where there is an audit committee or similarly designated body. This communication is not required for most small, nonpublic companies. As with all communications to the audit committee, the purpose is to keep the committee informed of auditing issues and findings that will assist it in performing its supervisory role for financial statements.

Audit Committees

The following are major items that must be communicated to the audit committee or similarly designated body under SAS 61:

- Auditor's responsibilities under generally accepted auditing standards, including responsibility for evaluating internal control and the concept of reasonable rather than absolute assurance.
- Significant accounting policies selected and applied to the financial statements, including management's judgments and estimates of accounting-related issues.
- Significant financial statement adjustments found during the audit and the implications of both those that management has chosen to record and those proposed but not recorded, as well as uncorrected misstatements determined by management to be immaterial both individually and in the aggregate.
- Auditor's judgment about the quality, not just the acceptability, of the client's accounting principles.
- Disagreements with management about the scope of the audit, applicability of accounting principles, or wording of the audit report.
- Difficulties encountered in performing the audit, such as lack of availability of client personnel and failure to provide necessary information.
- Significant issues discussed with management prior to the retention of the auditor, especially those related to the application of accounting principles and auditing standards.
- Auditor's responsibilities for other information included in documents containing audited financial statements, if applicable.

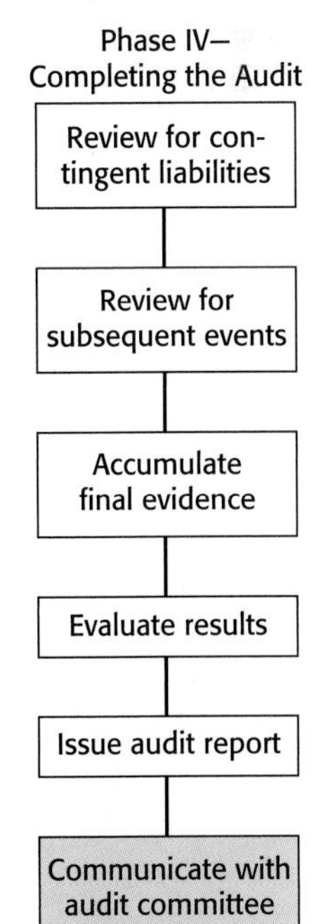

Communication with the audit committee normally takes place more than once during each audit and can be oral, written, or both. For example, issues dealing with the auditor's responsibilities and significant accounting policies are usually discussed early in the audit, preferably during the planning phase. Disagreements with management and difficulties encountered in performing the audit are communicated after the audit is completed, or earlier if the problems hinder the auditor's ability to complete the audit. The most important matters are communicated in writing to minimize misunderstanding and to provide documentation in the event of subsequent disagreement.

Management Letters

A **management letter** is intended to inform client personnel of the CPA's recommendations for improving any aspect of the client's business. The recommendations focus on suggestions for more efficient operations. The combination of the auditor's experience in various businesses and a thorough understanding gained in conducting the audit places the auditor in a unique position to provide management with assistance.

Many CPA firms write a management letter for every audit to demonstrate to management that the firm adds value to the business beyond the audit service provided. The intent is to encourage a better relationship between the CPA firm and management and to suggest additional tax and management services that the CPA firm can provide. Some CPA firms generate considerable additional revenue from the additional services.

A management letter is different from a reportable conditions letter, which was discussed in Chapter 9. The latter is required by SAS 60 (AU 325) when there are reportable conditions. It must follow a prescribed format and be sent in accordance with SAS requirements. A management letter is optional and is intended to help the client operate its business more effectively.

There is no standard format or approach for writing management letters. Each letter should be developed to meet the style of the auditor and the needs of the client, consistent with the CPA firm's concept of management letters. It should be noted that many auditors combine the management letter with the reportable conditions letter. On smaller audits, it is common for the auditor to communicate operational suggestions orally rather than by a management letter.

SUBSEQUENT DISCOVERY OF FACTS

OBJECTIVE 18-7

Identify the auditor's responsibilities when facts affecting the audit report are discovered after its issuance.

After the auditor issues the audit report and completes all communications with management and the audit committee, the audit is finished. The next major contact the auditor has with the client is when the planning process for next year's audit begins. Although it rarely happens, if the auditor becomes aware *after the audited financial statements have been issued* that some information included in the statements is materially misleading, the auditor has an obligation to make certain that users who are relying on the financial statements are informed about the misstatements. If the auditor had known about the misstatements before the audit report was issued, the auditor would have insisted that management correct the misstatements or, alternatively, a different audit report would have been issued. When this occurs, it is referred to as subsequent discovery of facts. Although subsequent discovery of facts is not a part of completing the audit, it is included in this chapter because it is easier to understand when compared and contrasted with subsequent events.

The most likely case in which the auditor is faced with this problem occurs when the financial statements are determined to include a material misstatement subsequent to the issuance of an unqualified report. Some possible causes of misstatements are the inclusion of material nonexistent sales, the failure to write off obsolete inventory, or the omission of an essential footnote. Regardless of whether the failure to discover the misstatement was the fault of the auditor or the client, the auditor's responsibility remains the same.

The most desirable approach to follow if the auditor discovers that the statements are misleading after they have been issued is to request that the client issue an immediate revision of the financial statements containing an explanation of the reasons for the revision. If a subsequent period's financial statements are completed before the revised statements would be issued, it is acceptable to disclose the misstatements in the subsequent period's statements. When pertinent, the client should inform the SEC and other regulatory agencies of the misleading financial statements. The auditor has the responsibility for making certain that the client has taken the appropriate steps in informing users of the misleading statements.

If the client refuses to cooperate in disclosing the misstated information, the auditor must inform the board of directors of this fact. The auditor must also notify regulatory agencies having jurisdiction over the client and, when practical, each person who relies on

FIGURE 18-9 Review for Subsequent Events and Subsequent Discovery of Facts

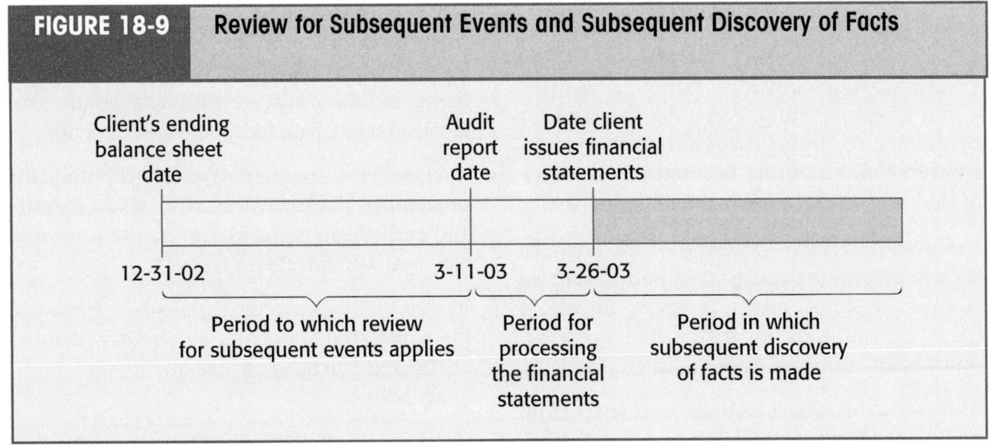

the financial statements that the statements are no longer trustworthy. If the stock is publicly held, it is acceptable to request the SEC and the stock exchange to notify the stockholders.

It is important to understand that the subsequent discovery of facts requiring the recall or reissuance of financial statements *does not arise from business events occurring after the date of the auditor's report.* For example, if an account receivable is believed to be collectible after an adequate review of the facts at the date of the audit report but the customer subsequently files bankruptcy, a revision of the financial statements is not required. The statements must be recalled or reissued only when information that would indicate that the statements were not fairly presented *already existed at the audit report date.* If, in the previous example, the customer had filed for bankruptcy before the audit report date, there is a subsequent discovery of facts.

In an earlier section, it was shown that the auditor's responsibility for subsequent events review begins as of the balance sheet date and ends on the date of the completion of the field work. Any pertinent information discovered as a part of the review can be incorporated in the financial statements before they are issued. Note that the auditor has no responsibility to search for subsequent facts of the nature discussed in this section, but if the auditor discovers that issued financial statements are improperly stated, the auditor must take action to correct them. The auditor's responsibility for reporting on improperly issued financial statements does not start until the date of the audit report. Typically, an existing material misstatement is found as a part of the subsequent year's audit, or it may be reported to the auditor by the client.

Figure 18-9, which includes the same dates as Figure 18-3 on page 511, shows the difference in the period covered by the review for subsequent events and that for the discovery of facts after the audit report date. If the auditor discovers subsequent facts after the audit report date but before the financial statements are issued, the auditor will require that the financial statements be revised before they are issued.

The auditor's responsibility for the period from 3-11-03 to 3-26-03 is the same as that for the period after 3-26-03. If a subsequent event is discovered in this period, one of the two options discussed under the Dual Dating heading on page 513 should be followed.

ESSENTIAL TERMS

Commitments—agreements that the entity will hold to a fixed set of conditions, such as the purchase or sale of merchandise at a stated price, at a future date, regardless of what happens to profits or to the economy as a whole

Completing the engagement checklist—a reminder to the auditor of aspects of the audit that may have been overlooked

Contingent liability—a potential future obligation to an outside party for an unknown amount resulting from activities that have already taken place

Dual-dated audit report—the use of one audit report date for normal subsequent events and a later date for one or more subsequent events that come to the auditor's attention after the field work has been completed

Financial statement disclosure checklist—a questionnaire that reminds the auditor of disclosure problems commonly encountered in audits and that facilitates final review of the entire audit by an independent partner

Independent review—a review of the financial statements and the entire set of audit files by a completely independent reviewer to whom the audit team must justify the evidence accumulated and the conclusions reached

Inquiry of the client's attorneys—a letter from the client's legal counsel informing the auditor of pending litigation or any other information involving legal counsel that is relevant to financial statement disclosure

Letter of representation—a written communication from the client to the auditor formalizing statements that the client has made about matters pertinent to the audit

Management letter—an optional letter written by the auditor to a client's management containing the auditor's recommendations for improving any aspect of the client's business

Other information included in annual reports—information that is not a part of published financial statements but is published with them; auditors must read this information for inconsistencies with the financial statements

Review for subsequent events—the auditing procedures performed by auditors to identify and evaluate subsequent events; also known as a *post-balance-sheet review*

Review of audit documentation—a review of the completed audit files by another member of the audit firm to ensure quality and counteract bias

Subsequent events—transactions and other pertinent events that occurred after the balance sheet date that affect the fair presentation or disclosure of the statements being audited

Unadjusted misstatement audit schedule—a summary of immaterial misstatements not adjusted at the time they were found, used to help the auditor assess whether the combined amount is material; also known as a *summary of possible misstatements*

Unasserted claim—a potential legal claim against a client where the condition for a claim exists but no claim has been filed

REVIEW QUESTIONS

18-1 **(Objective 18-1)** Distinguish between a contingent liability and an actual liability and give three examples of each.

18-2 **(Objective 18-1)** In the audit of the James Mobley Company, you are concerned about the possibility of contingent liabilities resulting in income tax disputes. Discuss the procedures you could use for an extensive investigation in this area.

18-3 **(Objective 18-1)** Explain why an auditor would be interested in a client's future commitments to purchase raw materials at a fixed price.

18-4 **(Objective 18-2)** Explain why the analysis of legal expense is an essential part of every audit engagement.

18-5 **(Objectives 18-1, 18-2)** During the audit of the Merrill Manufacturing Company, Ralph Pyson, CPA, has become aware of four lawsuits against the client through discussions with the client, reading corporate minutes, and reviewing correspondence files. How should Pyson determine the materiality of the lawsuits and the proper disclosure in the financial statements?

18-6 **(Objective 18-2)** Distinguish between an asserted and an unasserted claim. Explain why a client's attorney may not reveal an unasserted claim.

18-7 **(Objective 18-2)** Describe the action that an auditor should take if an attorney refuses to provide information that is within the attorney's jurisdiction and may directly affect the fair presentation of the financial statements.

18-8 **(Objective 18-3)** Distinguish between the two general types of subsequent events and explain how they differ. Give two examples of each type.

18-9 (Objectives 18-2, 18-3) In obtaining letters from attorneys, Bill Malano's aim is to receive the letters as early as possible after the balance sheet date. This provides him with a signed letter from every attorney in time to properly investigate any exceptions. It also eliminates the problem of a lot of unresolved loose ends near the end of the audit. Evaluate Malano's approach.

18-10 (Objective 18-3) What major considerations should the auditor take into account in determining how extensive the review of subsequent events should be?

18-11 (Objective 18-3) Identify five audit procedures normally done as a part of the review for subsequent events.

18-12 (Objectives 18-3, 18-7) Distinguish between subsequent events occurring between the balance sheet date and the date of the auditor's report, and subsequent discovery of facts existing at the date of the auditor's report. Give two examples of each and explain the appropriate action by the auditor in each instance.

18-13 (Objective 18-4) Miles Lawson, CPA, believes that the final summarization is the easiest part of the audit if careful planning is followed throughout the engagement. He makes sure that each segment of the audit is completed before he goes on to the next. When the last segment of the engagement is completed, he is finished with the audit. He believes this may cause each part of the audit to take a little longer, but he makes up for it by not having to do the final summarization. Evaluate Lawson's approach.

18-14 (Objectives 18-4, 18-5) Compare and contrast the accumulation of audit evidence and the evaluation of the adequacy of the disclosures in the financial statements. Give two examples in which adequate disclosure could depend heavily on the accumulation of evidence and two others in which audit evidence does not normally significantly affect the adequacy of the disclosure.

18-15 (Objectives 18-4, 18-6) Distinguish between a client letter of representation and a management letter and state the primary purpose of each. List some items that might be included in each letter.

18-16 (Objective 18-4) Explain what is meant by information accompanying basic financial statements. Provide two examples of such information. What levels of assurance may the CPA offer for this information?

18-17 (Objective 18-4) What is meant by reading other financial information in annual reports? Give an example of the type of information the auditor is examining.

18-18 (Objective 18-5) Distinguish between regular audit documentation review and independent review and state the purpose of each. Give two examples of important potential findings in each of these two types of review.

MULTIPLE CHOICE QUESTIONS FROM CPA EXAMINATIONS

18-19 (Objective 18-1) The following questions deal with contingent liabilities. Choose the best response.

a. The audit step most likely to reveal the existence of contingent liabilities is
   (1) a review of vouchers paid during the month following the year-end.
   (2) accounts payable confirmations.
   (3) an inquiry directed to legal counsel.
   (4) mortgage-note confirmation.

b. When obtaining evidence regarding litigation against a client, the CPA would be *least* interested in determining
   (1) an estimate of when the matter will be resolved.
   (2) the period in which the underlying cause of the litigation occurred.
   (3) the probability of an unfavorable outcome.
   (4) an estimate of the potential loss.

c. When a contingency is resolved subsequent to the issuance of audited financial statements, which correctly contained disclosure of the contingency in the footnotes based on information available at the date of issuance, the auditor should

(1) insist that the client issue revised financial statements.
(2) inform the audit committee that the report cannot be relied on.
(3) take no action regarding the event.
(4) inform the appropriate authorities that the report cannot be relied on.

18-20 (Objective 18-4) The following questions concern letters of representation. Choose the best response.

a. A principal purpose of a letter of representation from management is to
   (1) serve as an introduction to company personnel and an authorization to examine the records.
   (2) discharge the auditor from legal liability for the audit.
   (3) confirm in writing management's approval of limitations on the scope of the audit.
   (4) remind management of its primary responsibility for financial statements.

b. The date of the management representation letter should coincide with the
   (1) date of the auditor's report.
   (2) balance sheet date.
   (3) date of the latest subsequent event referred to in the notes to the financial statements.
   (4) date of the engagement agreement.

c. Management's refusal to furnish a written representation on a matter that the auditor considers essential constitutes
   (1) prima facie evidence that the financial statements are not presented fairly.
   (2) a violation of the Foreign Corrupt Practices Act.
   (3) an uncertainty sufficient to preclude an unqualified opinion.
   (4) a scope limitation sufficient to preclude an unqualified opinion.

18-21 (Objective 18-3) The following questions deal with review of subsequent events. Choose the best response.

a. Subsequent events for reporting purposes are defined as events that occur subsequent to the
   (1) balance sheet date.
   (2) date of the auditor's report.
   (3) balance sheet date but before the date of the auditor's report.
   (4) date of the auditor's report and concern contingencies that are not reflected in the financial statements.

b. An example of an event occurring in the period of the auditor's field work subsequent to the end of the year being audited that normally would not require disclosure in the financial statements or auditor's report would be
   (1) decreased sales volume resulting from a general business recession.
   (2) serious damage to the company's plant from a widespread flood.
   (3) issuance of a widely advertised capital stock issue with restrictive covenants.
   (4) settlement of a large liability for considerably less than the amount recorded.

c. Karr has audited the financial statements of Lurch Corporation for the year ended December 31, 2002. Karr's field work was completed on February 27, 2003; Karr's auditor's report was dated February 28, 2003, and was received by the management of Lurch on March 5, 2003. On April 4, 2003, the management of Lurch asked that Karr approve inclusion of this report in their annual report to stockholders, which will include unaudited financial statements for the first quarter ended March 31, 2003. Karr approved the inclusion of this auditor's report in the annual report to stockholders. Under the circumstances, Karr is responsible for inquiring as to subsequent events occurring through
   (1) February 27, 2003.
   (2) February 28, 2003.
   (3) March 31, 2003.
   (4) April 4, 2003.

18-22 (Objective 18-4) The following questions concern information accompanying basic financial statements. Choose the best response.

a. Which of the following best describes the auditor's reporting responsibility concerning information accompanying the basic financial statements in an auditor-submitted document?
   (1) The auditor has no reporting responsibility concerning information accompanying the basic financial statements.

(2) The auditor should report on the information accompanying the basic financial statements only if the auditor participated in its preparation.
(3) The auditor should report on the information accompanying the basic financial statements only if the auditor did not participate in its preparation.
(4) The auditor should report on all the information included in the document.

b. Ansman, CPA, has been requested by a client, Rainco Corp., to prepare information in addition to the basic financial statements for this year's audit engagement. Which of the following is the best reason for Rainco's requesting the additional information?
(1) To provide an opinion about the supplemental information when certain items are not in accordance with GAAP.
(2) To provide Rainco's creditors a greater degree of assurance as to the financial soundness of the company.
(3) To provide Rainco's management with information to supplement and analyze the basic financial statements.
(4) To provide the documentation required by the SEC in anticipation of a public offering of Rainco's stock.

c. Ansman, CPA, has been requested by a client, Rainco Corp., to prepare additional information accompanying the basic financial statements for this year's audit engagement. In issuing the additional information, Ansman must be certain to
(1) issue a standard short-form report on the same engagement.
(2) include a description of the scope of the audit in more detail than the description in the usual short-form report.
(3) state the source of any statistical data and that such data have not been subjected to the same auditing procedures as the basic financial statements.
(4) maintain a clear-cut distinction between management's representations and the auditor's representations.

DISCUSSION QUESTIONS AND PROBLEMS

18-23 (Objective 18-1) Elizabeth Johnson, CPA, has completed the audit of notes payable and other liabilities for Valley River Electrical Services and now plans to audit contingent liabilities and commitments.

Required

a. Distinguish between contingent liabilities and commitments and explain why both are important in an audit.
b. Identify three useful audit procedures for uncovering contingent liabilities that Johnson would likely perform in the normal conduct of the audit, even if she had no responsibility for uncovering contingencies.
c. Identify three other procedures Johnson is likely to perform specifically for the purpose of identifying undisclosed contingencies.

18-24 (Objective 18-1) In an audit of the Marco Corporation as of December 31, 2002, the following situations exist. No entries have been made in the accounting records in relation to these items.

1. The Marco Corporation has guaranteed the payment of interest on the 10-year, first mortgage bonds of the Newart Company, an affiliate. Outstanding bonds of the Newart Company amount to $150,000 with interest payable at 5% per annum, due June 1 and December 1 of each year. The bonds were issued by the Newart Company on December 1, 2000, and all interest payments have been met by that company with the exception of the payment due December 1, 2002. The Marco Corporation states that it will pay the defaulted interest to the bondholders on January 15, 2003.
2. During the year 2002, the Marco Corporation was named as a defendant in a suit for damages by the Dalton Company for breach of contract. An adverse decision to the Marco Corporation was rendered and the Dalton Company was awarded $40,000 damages. At the time of the audit, the case was under appeal to a higher court.
3. On December 23, 2002, the Marco Corporation declared a common stock dividend of 1,000 shares with a par value of $100,000 of its common stock, payable February 2, 2003, to the common stockholders of record December 30, 2002.

Required

a. Define contingent liability.

b. Describe the audit procedures you would use to learn about each of the situations listed.

c. Describe the nature of the adjusting entries or disclosure, if any, you would make for each of these situations.*

18-25 (Objectives 18-3, 18-7) The field work for the June 30, 2002, audit of Tracy Brewing Company was finished August 19, 2002, and the completed financial statements, accompanied by the signed audit reports, were mailed September 6, 2002. In each of the highly material independent events (a through i), state the appropriate action (1 through 4) for the situation and justify your response. The alternative actions are as follows:

1. Adjust the June 30, 2002, financial statements.
2. Disclose the information in a footnote in the June 30, 2002, financial statements.
3. Request the client to recall the June 30, 2002, statements for revision.
4. No action is required.

The events are as follows:

a. On December 14, 2002, the auditor discovered that a debtor of Tracy Brewing went bankrupt on October 2, 2002. The sale had taken place April 15, 2002, but the amount appeared collectible at June 30, 2002, and August 19, 2002.

b. On August 15, 2002, the auditor discovered that a debtor of Tracy Brewing went bankrupt on August 1, 2002. The most recent sale had taken place April 2, 2001, and no cash receipts had been received since that date.

c. On December 14, 2002, the auditor discovered that a debtor of Tracy Brewing went bankrupt on July 15, 2002, due to declining financial health. The sale had taken place January 15, 2002.

d. On August 6, 2002, the auditor discovered that a debtor of Tracy Brewing went bankrupt on July 30, 2002. The cause of the bankruptcy was an unexpected loss of a major lawsuit on July 15, 2002, resulting from a product deficiency suit by a different customer.

e. On August 6, 2002, the auditor discovered that a debtor of Tracy Brewing went bankrupt on July 30, 2002, for a sale that took place July 3, 2002. The cause of the bankruptcy was a major uninsured fire on July 20, 2002.

f. On May 31, 2002, the auditor discovered an uninsured lawsuit against Tracy Brewing that had originated on February 28, 2002.

g. On July 20, 2002, Tracy Brewing settled a lawsuit out of court that had originated in 1999 and is currently listed as a contingent liability.

h. On September 14, 2002, Tracy Brewing lost a court case that had originated in 2001 for an amount equal to the lawsuit. The June 30, 2002, footnotes state that in the opinion of legal counsel there will be a favorable settlement.

i. On July 20, 2002, a lawsuit was filed against Tracy Brewing for a patent infringement action that allegedly took place in early 2002. In the opinion of legal counsel, there is a danger of a significant loss to the client.

18-26 (Objective 18-5) Mel Adams, CPA, is a partner in a medium-sized CPA firm and takes an active part in the conduct of every audit he supervises. He follows the practice of reviewing all audit files of subordinates as soon as it is convenient, rather than waiting until the end of the audit. When the audit is nearly finished, Adams reviews the audit files again to make sure that he has not missed anything significant. Because he makes most of the major decisions on the audit, there is rarely anything that requires further investigation. When he completes the review, he prepares a draft of the financial statements, gets them approved by management, and has them assembled in his firm's office. No other partner reviews the audit documentation because Adams is responsible for signing the audit reports.

Required

a. Evaluate the practice of reviewing the audit files of subordinates on a continuing basis rather than when the audit is completed.

b. Is it acceptable for Adams to prepare the financial statements rather than make the client assume the responsibility?

c. Evaluate the practice of not having a review of the audit documentation by another partner in the firm.

*AICPA adapted.

18-27 (Objective 18-4) Leslie Morgan, CPA, has prepared a letter of representation for the president and controller to sign. It contains references to the following items:

1. Inventory is fairly stated at the lower of cost or market and includes no obsolete items.
2. All actual and contingent liabilities are properly included in the financial statements.
3. All subsequent events of relevance to the financial statements have been disclosed.

Required

a. Why is it desirable to have a letter of representation from the client concerning these matters when the audit evidence accumulated during the course of the engagement is meant to verify the same information?

b. To what extent is the letter of representation useful as audit evidence? Explain.

c. List several other types of information commonly included in a letter of representation.

18-28 (Objective 18-6) In a letter to the audit committee of the Cline Wholesale Company, Jerry Schwartz, CPA, informed them of weaknesses in the control of inventory. In a separate letter to senior management, he elaborated on how the weaknesses could result in a significant misstatement of inventory by the failure to recognize the existence of obsolete items. In addition, Schwartz made specific recommendations in the management letter on how to improve internal control and save clerical time by installing a computer system for the company's perpetual records. Management accepted the recommendations and installed the system under Schwartz's direction. For several months, the system worked beautifully, but unforeseen problems developed when a master file was erased. The cost of reproducing and processing the inventory records to correct the error was significant, and management decided to scrap the entire project. The company sued Schwartz for failure to use adequate professional judgment in making the recommendations.

Required

a. What is Schwartz's legal and professional responsibility in the issuance of management letters?

b. Discuss the major considerations that will determine whether he is liable in this situation.

18-29 (Objective 18-3) The following unrelated events occurred after the balance sheet date but before the audit report was prepared:

1. The granting of a retroactive pay increase
2. Determination by the federal government of additional income tax due for a prior year
3. Filing of an antitrust suit by the federal government
4. Declaration of a stock dividend
5. Sale of a fixed asset at a substantial profit

Required

a. Explain how each of the items might have come to the auditor's attention.

b. Discuss the auditor's responsibility to recognize each of these in connection with the report.*

18-30 (Objective 18-3) The philosophy of Irene Hatton, CPA, is to intensively audit transactions taking place during the current audit period but to ignore subsequent transactions. She believes that each year should stand on its own and be audited in the year in which the transactions take place. According to Hatton, "If a transaction recorded in the subsequent period is audited in the current period, it is verified twice—once this year and again in next year's audit. That is a duplication of effort and a waste of time."

Required

a. Explain the fallacy in Hatton's argument.

b. Give six specific examples of information obtained by examining subsequent events that are essential to the current period audit.

18-31 (Objective 18-2) In analyzing legal expense for the Boastman Bottle Company, Mary Little, CPA, observes that the company has paid legal fees to three different law firms during the current year. In accordance with her CPA firm's normal operating practice, Little requests standard attorney letters as of the balance sheet date from each of the three law firms.

On the last day of field work, Little notes that one of the attorney letters has not yet been received. The second letter contains a statement to the effect that the law firm deals exclusively in registering patents and refuses to comment on any lawsuits or other legal affairs of the client. The third attorney's letter states that there is an outstanding unpaid bill due from the client and recognizes the existence of a potentially material lawsuit against the client but refuses to comment further to protect the legal rights of the client.

Required

a. Evaluate Little's approach to sending the attorney letters and her follow-up on the responses.

b. What should Little do about each of the letters?

*AICPA adapted.

18-32 **(Objective 18-4)** As a part of the audit of Ren Gold Manufacturing Company, management requests basic financial statements and separately, the same basic financial statements accompanied by additional information. Management informs you that the intent is to use the basic financial statements for bankers, other creditors, and the two owners who are not involved in management. The basic financial statements accompanied by the additional information are to be used only by management. Management requests the inclusion of specific information but asks that no audit work be done beyond what is needed for the basic financial statements. The following is requested:

1. A schedule of insurance in force.
2. The auditor's feelings about the adequacy of the insurance coverage.
3. A 5-year summary of the most important company ratios, the appropriate ratios to be determined at the auditor's discretion.
4. A schedule of notes payable accompanied by interest rates, collateral, and a payment schedule.
5. An aged trial balance of accounts receivable and evaluation of the adequacy of the allowance for uncollectible accounts.
6. A summary of fixed asset additions.
7. Material weaknesses in internal control and recommendations to improve internal control.

Required

a. What is the difference between basic financial statements and additional information?

b. What are the purposes of additional information accompanying basic financial statements?

c. For the previously listed items (1 through 7), state which ones could appropriately be included as additional information. Give reasons for your answer.

d. Identify three other items that may appropriately be included as additional information.

e. Assume that an unqualified opinion is proper for the basic financial statements report, that no testing was done beyond that required for the basic financial statements report, and that only appropriate information is included in the additional information. Write the proper auditor's report.

CASE

18-33 **(Objective 18-5)** In your audit of Aviary Industries for calendar year 2002, you found a number of matters that you believe represent possible adjustments to the company's books. These matters are described below. Management's attitude is that "once the books are closed, they're closed," and management does not want to make any adjustments. Planning materiality for the engagement was $100,000, determined by computing 5% of expected income before taxes. Actual income before taxes on the financial statements prior to any adjustments is $1,652,867.

Possible adjustments:

1. Several credit memos that were processed and recorded after year-end relate to sales and accounts receivable for 2002. These total $23,529.
2. Inventory cutoff tests indicate that $22,357 of inventory received on December 30, 2002, was recorded as purchases and accounts payable in 2003. These items were included in the inventory count at year-end and therefore were included in ending inventory.
3. Inventory cutoff tests also indicate several sales invoices recorded in 2002 for goods that were shipped in early 2003. The goods were not included in inventory but were set aside in a separate shipping area. The total amount of these shipments was $36,022. (Ignore cost of sales for this item.)
4. The company wrote several checks at the end of 2002 for accounts payable that were held and not mailed until January 15, 2003. These totaled $48,336. Recorded cash and accounts payable at December 31, 2002, are $2,356,553 and $2,666,290, respectively.
5. The company has not established a reserve for obsolescence of inventories. Your tests indicate that such a reserve is appropriate in an amount somewhere between $20,000 and $40,000.
6. Your review of the allowance for uncollectible accounts indicates that it may be understated by between $25,000 and $50,000.

Required

a. Determine the adjustments that you believe must be made for Aviary's financial statements to be fairly presented. Include the amounts and accounts affected by each adjustment.

b. Why may Aviary Industries' management resist making these adjustments?

c. Explain what you consider the most positive way of approaching management personnel to convince them to make your proposed changes.

d. Describe your responsibilities related to unadjusted misstatements that management has determined are immaterial individually and in the aggregate.

INTERNET PROBLEM 18-1: SUBSEQUENT EVENTS

Reference the CW site. This problem requires students to use the Internet to research and classify actual subsequent event disclosures reported in SEC filings.

INDEX

Note: Essential terms in bold face.

B

C

D

E

U

V

W